BRIEF CONTENTS

CONTENTS

COLIN DRURY

10TH EDITION

MANAGEMENT AND COST ACCOUNTING

CENGAGE

Australia • Brazil • Mexico • Singapore • United Kingdom • United States

Management and Cost Accounting,
10th Edition
Colin Drury

Publisher: Annabel Ainscow

List Manager: Jenny Grene

Development Editor: Hannah Close

Content Project Manager: Sue Povey

Manufacturing Buyer: Elaine Bevan

Marketing Manager: Sophie Clarke

Typesetter: MPS Limited

Cover design: Simon Levy Associates

Text design: Design Deluxe Ltd

Cover Image: © Kalisson/Thinkstock Photos

For product information and technology assistance, contact us at **emea.info@cengage.com.**

For permission to use material from this text or product and for permission queries, email **emea.permissions@cengage.com.**

British Library Cataloguing-in-Publication Data
A catalogue record for this book is available from the British Library

ISBN: 978-1-4737-4887-3

Cengage Learning EMEA
Cheriton House, North Way,
Andover, Hampshire SP10 5BE
United Kingdom

Cengage Learning is a leading provider of customized learning solutions with employees residing in nearly 40 different countries and sales in more than 125 countries around the world. Find your local representative at: **www.cengage.co.uk**

Cengage Learning products are represented in Canada by Nelson Education, Ltd.

For your course and learning solutions, visit **www.cengage.co.uk**

Purchase any of our products at your local college store or at our preferred online store **www.cengagebrain.com.**

Printed in China by RR Donnelley
Print Number: 02   Print Year: 2018

PREFACE

The aim of the tenth edition of this book is to explain the principles involved in designing and evaluating management and cost accounting information systems. Management accounting systems accumulate, classify, summarize and report information that will assist employees within an organization in their decision-making, planning, control and performance measurement activities. A cost accounting system is concerned with accumulating costs for inventory valuation to meet external financial accounting and internal monthly or quarterly profit measurement requirements. As the title suggests, this book is concerned with both management and cost accounting, but with emphasis placed on the former.

A large number of cost and management accounting textbooks have been published. Many of these books contain a detailed description of accounting techniques without any discussion of the principles involved in evaluating management and cost accounting systems. Such books often lack a conceptual framework and ignore the considerable amount of research conducted in management accounting in the past three decades. At the other extreme, some books focus entirely on a conceptual framework of management accounting with an emphasis on developing normative models of what ought to be. These books pay little attention to accounting techniques. My objective has been to produce a book that falls within these two extremes.

This book is intended primarily for undergraduate students who are pursuing a one-year or two-year management accounting course, and for students who are preparing for the cost and management accounting examinations of the professional accountancy bodies at an intermediate or advanced professional level. It should also be of use to postgraduate and higher national diploma students who are studying cost and management accounting for the first time. An introductory course in financial accounting is not a pre-requisite, although many students will have undertaken such a course.

STRUCTURE AND PLAN OF THE BOOK

A major theme of this book is that different financial information is required for different purposes, but my experience indicates that this approach can confuse students. In one chapter of a typical book, students are told that costs should be allocated to products including a fair share of overhead costs; in another chapter, they are told that some of the allocated costs are irrelevant and should be disregarded. In yet another chapter, they are told that costs should be related to people (responsibility centres) and not products, whereas elsewhere no mention is made of responsibility centres.

In writing this book, I have devised a framework that is intended to overcome these difficulties. The framework is based on the principle that there are three ways of constructing accounting information. The first is cost accounting with its emphasis on producing product (or service) costs for allocating costs between cost of goods sold and inventories to meet external and internal financial accounting inventory valuation and profit measurement requirements. The second is the notion of decision-relevant costs with the emphasis on providing information to help managers to make good decisions. The third is responsibility accounting and performance measurement that focuses on both financial and non-financial information; in particular, the assignment of costs and revenues to responsibility centres.

This book is divided into six parts. Part One consists of two chapters and provides an introduction to management and cost accounting and a framework for studying the remaining chapters. The following three parts reflect the three different ways of constructing accounting information. Part Two consists of five chapters and is entitled 'Cost Accumulation for Inventory Valuation and Profit Measurement'. This section focuses mainly on assigning costs to products to separate the costs incurred during a period between costs of goods sold and the closing inventory valuation for internal and external profit measurement. The extent to which product costs accumulated for inventory valuation and profit measurement should be adjusted for meeting decision-making, cost control and performance measurement requirements is also briefly considered. Part Three consists of seven chapters and is entitled 'Information for Decision-Making'. Here the focus is on measuring and identifying those costs that are relevant for different types of decision.

The title of Part Four is 'Information for Planning, Control and Performance Measurement'. It consists of six chapters and concentrates on the process of translating goals and objectives into specific activities and the resources that are required, via the short-term (budgeting) and long-term planning processes, to achieve the goals and objectives. In addition, the management control systems that organizations use are described and the role that management accounting control systems play within the overall control process is examined. The emphasis here is on the accounting process as a means of providing information to help managers control the activities for which they are responsible. Performance measurement and evaluation within different segments of the organization is also examined.

Part Five consists of three chapters and is entitled 'Strategic Performance and Cost Management and Challenges for the Future'. The first chapter focuses on strategic performance management, the second on strategic cost management and value creation. The third chapter concentrates on the emerging issues that are likely to have an impact on management accounting and considers some potential future developments in management accounting. Part Six consists of three chapters and is entitled 'The Application of Quantitative Methods to Management Accounting'.

In devising a framework around the three methods of constructing financial information, there is a risk that the student will not appreciate that the three categories use many common elements, that they overlap, and that they constitute a single overall management accounting system, rather than three independent systems. I have taken steps to minimize this risk in each section by emphasizing why financial information for one purpose should or should not be adjusted for another purpose. In short, each section of the book is not presented in isolation and an integrative approach has been taken.

When I wrote this book, one important consideration was the extent to which the application of quantitative techniques should be integrated with the appropriate topics or considered separately. I have chosen to integrate quantitative techniques whenever they are an essential part of a chapter. For example, the use of probability statistics are essential to Chapter 12 (Decision-making under conditions of risk and uncertainty) but my objective has been to confine them, where possible, to Part Six.

This approach allows for maximum flexibility. Lecturers wishing to integrate quantitative techniques with earlier chapters may do so but those who wish to concentrate on other matters will not be hampered by having to exclude the relevant quantitative portions of chapters.

MAJOR CHANGES IN THE CONTENT OF THE TENTH EDITION

The feedback relating to the structure and content of the previous editions has been extremely favourable and therefore no major changes have been made to the existing structure. The major objective in writing the tenth edition has been to produce a less complex and more accessible text and incorporate appropriate recent developments in the management accounting literature. This objective created the need to thoroughly review the entire content of the ninth edition and to rewrite, simplify and improve the presentation of much of the existing material. Many of the chapters have been rewritten and some new material has been added (e.g. time-driven activity-based costing, environmental and sustainability issues, ethical considerations and the impact of the emergence of the knowledge base economy). In addition, a new chapter ('Challenges for the future') has been added that focuses on the emerging issues that are likely to have an impact on management accounting and considers some potential future developments in management accounting. The end result has been an extensive rewrite of the text.

Substantial changes have been made to the end-of-chapter assessment material that contains the solutions in a separate section at the end of the book. Finally, most of the 'Real world views' that provide examples of the practical application of management accounting have been replaced by more recent examples that provide better illustrations of the practical applications. Suggested outline solutions to the answers to the questions accompanying the 'Real world views' have been added to the Instructor's Manual accompanying this book.

LEARNING NOTES

Feedback from previous editions indicated that a significant majority of the respondents identified specific topics contained in the text that were not included in their teaching programmes, whereas a minority of respondents indicated that the same topics *were* included in their teaching programmes. In order to meet the different requirements of lecturers and different course curriculum, various topics are included as learning notes that can be accessed by students and lecturers in the digital support resources accompanying this book. Examples of topics that are incorporated as learning notes include: determining the cost driver denominator level for use with ABC systems, the contingency approach to management accounting and statistical variance investigation models. The learning notes tend to include the more complex issues that often do not feature as part of the content of other management accounting textbooks. All learning notes are appropriately referenced within the text. For example, at appropriate points within specific chapters the reader's attention is drawn to the fact that, for a particular topic, more complex issues exist and that a discussion of these issues can be found by referring to a specific learning note in the digital support resources accompanying this book.

CASE STUDIES

Over 30 case studies are available in the digital support resources for this book. Both lecturers and students can download these case studies from the book's companion website. Teaching notes for the case studies are only available for lecturers to download. The cases generally cover the content of several chapters and contain questions to which there is no ideal answer. They are intended to encourage independent thought and initiative and to relate and apply your understanding of the content of this book in more uncertain situations. They are also intended to develop your critical thinking and analytical skills.

HIGHLIGHTING OF ADVANCED READING SECTIONS

Feedback relating to previous editions has indicated that one of the major advantages of this book has been the comprehensive treatment of management accounting. Some readers, however, will not require a comprehensive treatment of all of the topics that are contained in the book. To meet the different requirements of the readers, the more advanced material that is not essential for those readers not requiring an in-depth knowledge of a particular topic, has been highlighted using a vertical coloured line. If you do require an in-depth knowledge of a topic, you may find it helpful to initially omit the advanced reading sections, or skim them, on your first reading. You should read them in detail only when you fully understand the content of the remaining parts of the chapter. The advanced reading sections are more appropriate for an advanced course and may normally be omitted if you are pursuing an introductory course. For some chapters, all of the content represents advanced reading. Where this situation occurs, readers are informed at the beginning of the relevant chapters and the highlighting mechanism is not used.

INTERNATIONAL FOCUS

The book has now become an established text in many different countries throughout the world. Because of this, a more international focus has been adopted. A major feature is the presentation of boxed exhibits of surveys and practical applications of management accounting in companies in many different countries, particularly on the European mainland. Most of the assessment material has incorporated questions set by the UK professional accountancy bodies. These questions are appropriate for worldwide use and users who are not familiar with the requirements of the UK professional accountancy bodies should note that many of the advanced-level questions also contain the beneficial features described above for case study assignments.

RECOMMENDED READING

A separate section is included at the end of most chapters providing advice on key articles or books which you are recommended to read if you wish to pursue topics and issues in more depth. Many of the references are the original work of writers who have played a major role in the development of management accounting. The contribution of such writers is often reflected in this book but there is frequently no substitute for original work of the authors. The detailed references are presented in the Bibliography towards the end of the book.

ASSESSMENT MATERIAL

Throughout this book, I have kept the illustrations simple. You can check your understanding of each chapter by answering the review questions. Each question is followed by page numbers within parentheses that indicate where in the text the answers to specific questions can be found. More complex review problems are also set at the end of each chapter to enable students to pursue certain topics in more depth. Each question is graded according to the level of difficulty. Questions graded 'Basic' are appropriate for a first-year course and normally take less than 20 minutes to complete. Questions graded 'Intermediate' are also normally appropriate for a first-year course but take about 30–45 minutes to complete, whereas questions graded 'Advanced' are normally appropriate for a second-year course or the final stages of the professional accountancy examinations. Fully worked solutions to the review problems not prefixed by the term 'IM' (Instructor's Manual) are provided in a separate section at the end of the book.

This book is part of an integrated educational package. A *Student Manual* has been extensively rewritten and provides additional review problems with fully worked solutions. Students are strongly recommended to purchase the *Student Manual*, which complements this book. In addition, the Instructor's Manual provides suggested solutions to the questions at the end of each chapter that are prefixed by the term 'IM'. The solutions to these questions are not available to students. The Instructor's Manual can be downloaded free by lecturers.

Also available to lecturers is a Cognero testbank offering 1800 + questions and answers tailored to the content of the book, for use in classroom assessment.

ALTERNATIVE COURSE SEQUENCES

Although conceived and developed as a unified whole, the book can be tailored to the individual requirements of a course and so the preferences of the individual reader. For a discussion of the alternative sequencing of the chapters see 'Guidelines to using the book' in Chapter 1.

SUPPLEMENTARY MATERIAL

The tenth edition of the print *Student Manual* helps you work through the text and is available from all good bookshops (ISBN 9781473748880).

The tenth edition of Colin Drury's *Management* and *Cost Accounting* text is accompanied by the following dedicated digital support resources:

- **Dedicated instructor resources** only available to lecturers, who can register for access either at login.cengage.com or by speaking to their local Cengage representative.

- Cengage **MindTap**, an online learning solution that allows lecturers to easily customize and combine learning tools such as readings, interactive content and assessment activities to create a personalized learning path for students. Lecturers can add or remove existing content within the learning path or add their own content in order to deliver a seamless student experience that aligns exactly with the way they teach their course.

- Cengage **Aplia**, an online homework solution dedicated to improving learning by increasing student effort and engagement. A demo is available at www.aplia.com. Instructors can find out more about accessing Aplia by speaking to their local Cengage representative, and on the advice of their instructor, students can purchase access to Aplia at www.cengagebrain.com.

DEDICATED INSTRUCTOR RESOURCES

This includes the following resources for lecturers:

- **Instructor's Manual** which includes answers to 'IM Review Problems' in the text
- **Online Testbank** provides over 1800 questions and answers
- **PowerPoint** slides to use in your teaching
- **Teaching notes** to accompany the case studies
- **Downloadable figures and tables** from the book to use in your teaching

APLIA

Cengage Aplia is a fully tailored online homework solution, dedicated to improving learning by increasing student effort and engagement. Aplia has been used by more than 1 million students at over 1300 institutions worldwide, and offers automatically graded assignments and detailed explanations for every question, to help students stay focussed, alert and thinking critically. A demo is available at www.aplia.com.

Aplia accounting features include:

- **Embedded ebook**
- **An easy-to-use course management system**
- **Personalized customer support**
- **Automatically graded chapter assignments with instant detailed feedback**

ABOUT THE AUTHOR

Colin Drury was employed at Huddersfield University from 1970 until his retirement in 2004. He was awarded the title of professor in 1988 and emeritus professor in 2004. Colin is the author of three books published by Cengage: *Management and Cost Accounting*, which is Europe's best selling management accounting textbook, *Management Accounting for Business* and *Cost and Management Accounting*. Colin has also been an active researcher and has published approximately 100 articles in professional and academic journals. In recognition for his contribution to accounting education and research, Colin was given a lifetime achievement award by the British Accounting Association in 2009.

ACKNOWLEDGEMENTS

I am indebted to many individuals for their ideas and assistance in preparing this and previous editions of the book. In particular, I would like to thank the following who have provided material for inclusion in the text and the dedicated digital support resources or who have commented on this and earlier editions of the book:

Anthony Atkinson, University of Waterloo, Canada

F.J.C. Benade, UNISA, South Africa

Keith Best, University of Huddersfield, UK

Gordian Bowa, Polytechnic of Namibia, Africa

Stan Brignall, Aston Business School, UK

Jose Manuel de Matos Carvalho, ISCA de Coimbra, Portugal

Peter Clarke, University College Dublin, Ireland

Christopher Coles, Glasgow University, UK

Paul Collier, University of Exeter, UK

John Currie, National University of Ireland, Galway, Ireland

Jayne Ducker, Sheffield Hallam University, UK

Steve Dungworth, De Montford University, Leicester, UK

Wayne Fiddler, University of Huddersfield, UK

Ian G. Fisher, John Moores University, UK

Lin Fitzgerald, Loughborough University, UK

John Fletcher, Middlesex University, UK

Alicia Gazely, Nottingham Trent University, UK

Lewis Gordon, Liverpool John Moores University, UK

Richard Grey, University of Strathclyde, UK

Clare Guthrie, Manchester Metropolitan University, UK

Antony Head, Sheffield Hallam University, UK

Ian Herbert, Loughborough University, UK

Sophie Hoozee, IESEG School of Management, Lille Catholic University, France

Khaled Hussainey, Stirling University, UK

John Innes, University of Dundee, UK

Mike Johnson, University of Dundee, UK

Finland Joset Jordaan-Marais, University of Johannesburg, South Africa

Bjarni Frimann Karlsson, University of Iceland, Iceland

Cathy Knowles, Oxford Brookes University, UK

Michel Lebas, HEC Paris, France

Hugh McBride, GMIT, Ireland

Melissa McGill, University of Johannesburg, South Africa

David MacKerrell, Bromley College, UK

Falconer Mitchell, University of Edinburgh, UK

Jodie Moll, University of Manchester, UK

Peter Nordgaard, Copenhagen Business School, Denmark

Deryl Northcott, Auckland University of Technology, New Zealand

Fanus Nortje, UNISA, South Africa

Rona O'Brien, Sheffield Hallam University, UK

Dermot O'Leary, Athlone Institute of Technology, Ireland

Ruth O'Leary, National College of Ireland, Ireland

Dan Otzen, Copenhagen Business School, Denmark

Gary Owen, University of Greenwich, UK

Graham Parker, Kingston University, UK

Ronnie Patton, University of Ulster, Ireland

Jukka Pellinen, University of Jyväskylä, Finland

John Perrin, University of Exeter, UK

Martin Quinn, Dublin City University, Ireland

Tony Rayman, University of Bradford, UK

James S. Reece, University of Michigan, USA

Carsten Rohde, Copenhagen Business School, Denmark

Jonathan Rooks, London South Bank University, UK

Robin Roslender, Heriot-Watt University, UK

David Russell, De Montfort University, UK

Corinna Schwarze, University of Stellenbosch, South Africa

John Shank, The Amos Tuck School of Business, Dartmouth College, UK

Julia Smith, University of Wales Cardiff, UK

Francois Steyn, University of Stellenbosch, South Africa

Jim Stockton, University of Chester, UK

Mike Tayles, University of Hull, UK

Ben Ukaegbu, London Metropolitan University, UK

Annie van der Merwe, University of Johannesburg, South Africa

Richard M.S. Wilson, Loughborough University Business School, UK

Obert Matarirano, University of Forth Hare, South Africa

Dinah-Ann Rogers, Manchester Metropolitan University, UK

I am also indebted to Martin Quinn for providing the new Real world views and outline solutions that have been added to the tenth edition and Hannah Close, Annabel Ainscow and Sue Povey at Cengage for their valuable publishing advice, support and assistance. My appreciation goes also to the Chartered Institute of Management Accountants, the Association of Chartered Certified Accountants, the Institute of Chartered Accountants in England and Wales and the Association of Accounting Technicians for permission to reproduce past examination questions. Questions from the Chartered Institute of Management Accountants' examinations are designated CIMA; questions from the Association of Chartered Certified Accountants are designated ACCA; questions from the Institute of Chartered Accountants in England and Wales are designated ICAEW; and questions from the Association of Accounting Technicians are designated AAT. On the supporting digital support resources, I acknowledge and thank: Alicia Gazely of Nottingham Trent University for the spreadsheet exercises; and Steve Rickaby for his Guide to Excel. I also thank Wayne Fiddler of York University for his work on the ExamView testbank for lecturers. The answers in the text and accompanying Student and Instructor's Manuals to this book are my own and are in no way the approved solutions of the above professional bodies. Finally, and most importantly, I would like to thank my wife, Bronwen, for converting the original manuscript of the earlier editions into final typewritten form and for her continued help and support throughout the ten editions of this book.

Thanks are also given to the many contributors who have provided case studies for the online support resource, as well as those who have contributed to the MindTap resources:

Manjit Biant, University of Wales Trinity Saint David, UK

Liz Crookes, University of Derby, UK

Maria Gee, Royal Holloway, University of London, UK

Alexander Himme, Kühne Logistics University, Germany

Tessa de Jongh, North-West University, South Africa

Rosemarie Kelly, Waterford Institute of Technology, Ireland

Chris Kelsall, University of Central Lancashire, UK

Alastair Marais, University of KwaZulu-Natal, South Africa

Lorenzo Neri, University of Greenwich, UK

Yolande Reyneke, UNISA, South Africa

Mohamed Saeudy, University of Bedfordshire, UK

Carla Serfontein, University of the Free State, South Africa

Ed Tew, University of Winchester, UK

Henry Ababio, National University of Lesotho, Lesotho

Zani-Andrea Labuschagne, University of Pretoria, South Africa

CENGAGE

Teaching & Learning Support Resources

Cengage's peer reviewed content for higher and further education courses is accompanied by a range of digital teaching and learning support resources. The resources are carefully tailored to the specific needs of the instructor, student and the course. Examples of the kind of resources provided include:

- A password protected area for instructors with, for example, a testbank, PowerPoint slides and an instructor's manual.

- An open-access area for students including, for example, useful weblinks and glossary terms.

Lecturers: to discover the dedicated lecturer digital support resources accompanying this textbook please register here for access: login.cengage.com.

Students: to discover the dedicated student digital support resources accompanying this textbook, please search for **MANAGEMENT AND COST ACCOUNTING** on: cengagebrain.co.uk.

BE UNSTOPPABLE

Learn more at cengage.co.uk/education

PART ONE

INTRODUCTION TO MANAGEMENT AND COST ACCOUNTING

The objective of this section is to provide an introduction to management and cost accounting. In Chapter 1, we define accounting and distinguish between financial, management and cost accounting. This is followed by an examination of the role of management accounting in providing information to managers for decision-making, planning, control and performance measurement. We also consider the important changes that are taking place in the business environment. As you progress through the book you will learn how these changes are influencing management accounting systems. In Chapter 2, the basic cost terms and concepts that are used in the cost and management accounting literature are described.

1
INTRODUCTION TO MANAGEMENT ACCOUNTING

LEARNING OBJECTIVES After studying this chapter, you should be able to:

- distinguish between management accounting and financial accounting;
- identify and describe the elements involved in the decision-making, planning and control process;
- justify the view that a major objective of commercial organizations is to broadly seek to maximize future profits;
- explain the important changes that have taken place in the business environment that have influenced management accounting practice;
- outline and describe the key success factors that directly affect customer satisfaction;
- identify and describe the functions of a cost and management accounting system.

There are many definitions of accounting, but the one that captures the theme of this book is the definition formulated by the American Accounting Association. It describes accounting as:

> the process of identifying, measuring and communicating economic information to permit informed judgements and decisions by users of the information.

In other words, accounting is concerned with providing both financial and non-financial information that will help decision-makers to make good decisions. In order to understand accounting, you need to know something about the decision-making process, and also to be aware of the various users of accounting information.

During the past two decades many organizations in both the manufacturing and service sectors have faced dramatic changes in their business environment. Deregulation and extensive competition from overseas companies in domestic markets have resulted in a situation in which most companies now operate in a highly competitive global market. At the same time there has been a significant reduction in product life cycles arising from technological innovations and the need to meet increasingly discriminating customer demands. To succeed in today's highly competitive environment, companies have made customer satisfaction an overriding priority. They have also adopted new management approaches and manufacturing companies have changed their manufacturing systems and invested in new technologies. These changes have had a significant influence on management accounting systems.

The aim of this first chapter is to give you the background knowledge that will enable you to achieve a more meaningful insight into the issues and problems of cost and management accounting that are discussed in the book. We begin by looking at the users of accounting information and identifying their requirements. This is followed by a description of the decision-making, planning and control process and the changing business environment. Finally, the different functions of management accounting are described.

THE USERS OF ACCOUNTING INFORMATION

Accounting is a language that communicates economic information to various parties (known as stakeholders) who have an interest in the organization. Stakeholders fall into several groups (e.g. managers, shareholders and potential investors, employees, creditors and the government) and each of these groups has its own requirements for information:

- Managers require information that will assist them in their decision-making and control activities; for example, information is needed on the estimated selling prices, costs, demand, competitive position and profitability of various products/services that are provided by the organization.

- Shareholders require information on the value of their investment and the income that is derived from their shareholding.

- Employees require information on the ability of the firm to meet wage demands and avoid redundancies.

- Creditors and the providers of loan capital require information on a firm's ability to meet its financial obligations.

- Government agencies such as the Central Statistical Office collect accounting information and require such information as the details of sales activity, profits, investments, stocks (i.e. inventories), dividends paid, the proportion of profits absorbed by taxation and so on. In addition, government taxation authorities require information on the amount of profits that are subject to taxation. All this information is important for determining policies to manage the economy.

The need to provide accounting information is not confined to business organizations. Individuals sometimes have to provide information about their own financial situation; for example, if you want to obtain a mortgage or a personal loan, you may be asked for details of your private financial affairs. Non-profit-making organizations such as churches, charitable organizations, clubs and government units such as local authorities, also require accounting information for decision-making, and for reporting the results of their activities. For example, a tennis club will require information on the cost of undertaking its various activities so that a decision can be made as to the amount of the annual subscription that it will charge to its members. Similarly, municipal authorities, such as local government and public sector organizations, need information on the costs of undertaking specific activities so that decisions can be made as to which activities will be undertaken and the resources that must be raised to finance them.

As you can see, there are many different users of accounting information who require information for decision-making. The objective of accounting is to provide sufficient information to meet the needs of the various users at the lowest possible cost. Obviously, the benefit derived from using an information system for decision-making must be greater than the cost of operating the system.

The users of accounting information can be divided into two categories:

1 internal users within the organization;

2 external users such as shareholders, creditors and regulatory agencies, outside the organization.

It is possible to distinguish between two branches of accounting, which reflect the internal and external users of accounting information. Management accounting is concerned with the provision of information to people within the organization to help them make better decisions and improve the efficiency and effectiveness of existing operations, whereas financial accounting is concerned with the provision of information to external parties outside the organization. Thus, management accounting could be called internal reporting and financial accounting could be called external reporting. This book concentrates on management accounting.

DIFFERENCES BETWEEN MANAGEMENT ACCOUNTING AND FINANCIAL ACCOUNTING

The major differences between these two branches of accounting are:

- *Legal requirements.* There is a statutory requirement for public limited companies to produce annual financial accounts, regardless of whether or not management regards this information as useful. Management accounting, by contrast, is entirely optional and information should be produced only if it is considered that the benefits it offers management exceed the cost of collecting it.

- *Focus on individual parts or segments of the business.* Financial accounting reports describe the whole of the business, whereas management accounting focuses on small parts of the organization; for example, the cost and profitability of products, services, departments, customers and activities.

- *Generally accepted accounting principles.* Financial accounting statements must be prepared to conform with the legal requirements and the generally accepted accounting principles established by the regulatory bodies such as the Financial Accounting Standards Board (FASB) in the USA, the Financial Reporting Council (FRC) in the UK and the International Accounting Standards Board (IASB). These requirements are essential to ensure uniformity and consistency, which make intercompany and historical comparisons possible. Financial accounting data should be verifiable and objective. In contrast, management accountants are not required to adhere to generally accepted accounting principles when providing managerial information for internal purposes. Instead, the focus is on the serving management's needs and providing information that is useful to managers when they are carrying out their decision-making, planning and control functions.

- *Time dimension.* Financial accounting reports what has happened in the past in an organization, whereas management accounting is concerned with *future* information as well as past information. Decisions are concerned with *future* events and management, therefore, requires details of expected *future* costs and revenues.

- *Report frequency and less emphasis on precision.* A detailed set of financial accounts is published annually and less detailed accounts are published semi-annually. Management usually requires information more quickly than this if it is to act on it. Managers are often more concerned with timeliness rather than precision. They prefer a good estimate now rather than a precise answer much later. Consequently, management accounting reports on various activities may be prepared at daily, weekly or monthly intervals.

THE DECISION-MAKING, PLANNING AND CONTROL PROCESS

Information produced by management accountants must be judged in the light of its ultimate effect on the outcome of decisions. It is therefore important to have an understanding of the *decision-making, planning and control process.* Figure 1.1 presents a diagram of the decision-making, planning and control process. The first four stages represent the decision-making or planning process. The final two stages represent the control process, which is the process of measuring and correcting actual performance to ensure the alternatives that are chosen and the plans for implementing them are carried out. We will now examine the stages in more detail.

**REAL WORLD
VIEWS 1.1**

*Chartered Institute of Management
Accountants (CIMA) – activities and skills*

What is management accounting?
Management accounting combines accounting,
finance and management with the leading edge
techniques needed to drive successful businesses.
Chartered management accountants:

- Advise managers about the financial
  implications of projects.
- Explain the financial consequences of business
  decisions.
- Formulate business strategy.
- Monitor spending and financial control.
- Conduct internal business audits.
- Explain the impact of the competitive landscape.
- Bring a high level of professionalism and
  integrity to business.

Management accounting skillset
Our members are qualified to work across an organization, not just in finance. In addition to strong

accounting fundamentals, CIMA teaches strategic
business and management skills:

- Analysis – they analyse information and using
  it to make business decisions.
- Strategy – they formulate business strategy to
  create wealth and shareholder value.
- Risk – they identify and manage risk.
- Planning – they apply accounting techniques to
  plan and budget.
- Communication – they determine what
  information management needs and explain
  the numbers to non-financial managers.

Question

1 Provide more detailed illustrations for each of
  the first four items in the first category of the
  above list of how the management accountant
  can be of assistance in an organization with
  which you are familiar.

Reference
Extracted from the website of Chartered Institute
  of Management Accountants (www.cimaglobal
  .com/About-us/What-is-management
  -accounting/)

Identifying objectives

Before good decisions can be made there must be some guiding aim or direction that will enable the
decision-makers to assess the desirability of choosing one course of action over another. Hence, the
first stage in the decision-making process should be to specify the company's goals or organizational
objectives.

FIGURE 1.1
The decision-
making, planning
and control
process

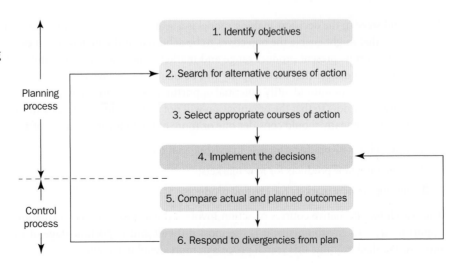

This is an area in which there is considerable controversy. Economic theory normally assumes that firms seek to maximize profits for the owners of the firm or, more precisely, the maximization of shareholders' wealth, which, we as shall see in Chapter 13, is equivalent to the maximization of the present value of future cash flows. Various arguments have been used to support the profit maximization objective. There is the legal argument that the ordinary shareholders are the owners of the firm, which therefore should be run for their benefit by trustee managers. Another argument supporting the profit objective is that profit maximization leads to the maximization of overall economic welfare. That is, by doing the best for yourself, you are unconsciously doing the best for society. Moreover, it seems a reasonable belief that the interests of firms will be better served by a larger profit than by a smaller profit, so that maximization is at least a useful approximation. Some writers (e.g. Simon, 1959) believe that many managers are content to find a plan that provides satisfactory profits rather than to maximize profits.

Cyert and March (1969) have argued that the firm is a coalition of various different groups – shareholders, employees, customers, suppliers and the government – each of whom must be paid a minimum to participate in the coalition. Any excess benefits after meeting these minimum constraints are seen as being the object of bargaining between the various groups. In addition, a firm is subject to constraints of a societal nature. Maintaining a clean environment, employing disabled workers and providing social and recreation facilities are all examples of social goals that a firm may pursue.

Clearly it is too simplistic to say that the only objective of a business firm is to maximize profits. Some managers seek to establish a power base and build an empire. Another common goal is security, and the removal of uncertainty regarding the future may override the pure profit motive. Organizations may also pursue more specific objectives, such as producing high-quality products or being the market leader within a particular market segment. Nevertheless, the view adopted in this book is that, *broadly,* firms seek to maximize future profits. There are three reasons for us to concentrate on this objective:

1 It is unlikely that any other objective is as widely applicable in measuring the ability of the organization to survive in the future.

2 It is unlikely that maximizing future profits can be realized in practice, but by establishing the principles necessary to achieve this objective you will learn how to increase profits.

3 It enables shareholders as a group in the bargaining coalition to know how much the pursuit of other goals is costing them by indicating the amount of cash distributed among the members of the coalition.

The search for alternative courses of action

The second stage in the decision-making model is a search for a range of possible courses of action (or strategies) that might enable the objectives to be achieved. If the management of a company concentrates entirely on its present product range and markets, and market shares and profits are allowed to decline, there is a danger that the company will be unable to survive in the future. If the business is to survive, management must identify potential opportunities and threats in the current environment and take specific steps now so that the organization will not be taken by surprise by future developments. In particular, the company should consider one or more of the following courses of action:

1 developing *new* products for sale in *existing* markets;

2 developing *new* products for *new* markets;

3 developing *new* markets for *existing* products.

The search for alternative courses of action involves the acquisition of information concerning future opportunities and environments; it is the most difficult and important stage of the decision-making process. We shall examine this search process in more detail in Chapter 15.

Select appropriate alternative courses of action

In order for managers to make an informed choice of action, data about the different alternatives must be gathered. For example, managers might ask to see projected figures on:

● the potential growth rates of the alternative activities under consideration;

● the market share the company is likely to achieve;

● projected profits for each alternative activity.

The alternatives should be evaluated to identify which course of action best satisfies the objectives of an organization. The selection of the most advantageous alternative is central to the whole decision-making process and the provision of information that facilitates this choice is one of the major functions of management accounting. These aspects of management accounting are examined in Chapters 8 to 14.

Implementation of the decisions

Once the course of action has been selected, it should be implemented as part of the budgeting and long-term planning process. The **budget** is a financial plan for implementing the decisions that management has made. The budgets for all of the various decisions a company takes are expressed in terms of cash inflows and outflows, and sales revenues and expenses. These budgets are initially prepared at the departmental/responsibility centre level (i.e. a unit or department within an organization where a manager is held responsible for performance) and merged together into a single unifying statement for the organization as a whole that specifies the organization's expectations for future periods. This statement is known as a **master budget** and consists of budgeted profit and cash flow statements. The budgeting process communicates to everyone in the organization the part that they are expected to play in implementing management's decisions. We shall examine the budgeting process in Chapter 15.

Comparing actual and planned outcomes and responding to divergencies from plan

The final stages in the process outlined in Figure 1.1 involve comparing actual and planned outcomes and responding to divergencies from plan. The managerial function of **control** consists of the measurement, reporting and subsequent correction of performance in an attempt to ensure that the firm's objectives and plans are achieved.

To monitor performance, the accountant produces **performance reports** and presents them to the managers who are responsible for implementing the various decisions. These reports compare actual outcomes (actual costs and revenues) with planned outcomes (budgeted costs and revenues) and should be issued at regular intervals. Performance reports provide feedback information and should highlight those activities that do not conform to plans, so that managers can devote their limited time to focusing mainly on these items. This process represents the application of **management by exception**. Effective control requires that corrective action is taken so that actual outcomes conform to planned outcomes. Alternatively, the plans may require modification if the comparisons indicate that the plans are no longer attainable.

The process of taking corrective action or modifying the plans if the comparisons indicate that actual outcomes do not conform to planned outcomes is indicated by the arrowed lines in Figure 1.1 linking stages 6 and 4 and 6 and 2. These arrowed lines represent 'feedback loops'. They signify that the process is dynamic and stress the interdependencies between the various stages in the process. The feedback loop between stages 6 and 2 indicates that the plans should be regularly reviewed, and if they are no longer attainable then alternative courses of action must be considered for achieving the organization's objectives. The second loop stresses the corrective action taken so that actual outcomes conform to planned outcomes. Chapters 15 to 18 focus on the planning and control process.

THE IMPACT OF THE CHANGING BUSINESS ENVIRONMENT ON MANAGEMENT ACCOUNTING

During the last few decades, global competition, deregulation, declines in product life cycles, advances in manufacturing and information technologies, environmental issues and a competitive environment requiring companies to become more customer driven, have changed the nature of the business environment. These changes have significantly altered the ways in which firms operate, which in turn, have resulted in changes in management accounting practices.

Global competition

During the last few decades reductions in tariffs and duties on imports and exports, and dramatic improvements in transportation and communication systems, have resulted in many firms operating in a global market. Prior to this, many organizations operated in a protected competitive environment. Barriers of communication and geographical distance, and sometimes protected markets, limited the ability of overseas companies to compete in domestic markets. There was little incentive for firms to maximize efficiency and improve management practices, or to minimize costs, as cost increases could often be passed on to customers. During the 1990s, however, organizations began to encounter severe competition from overseas competitors who offered high-quality products at low prices. Manufacturing companies can now establish global networks for acquiring raw materials and distributing goods overseas, and service organizations can communicate with overseas offices instantaneously using internet and digital technologies. These changes have enabled competitors to gain access to domestic markets throughout the world. Nowadays, organizations have to compete against the best companies in the world. This new competitive environment has increased the demand for information relating to quality and customer satisfaction and cost information relating to cost management and profitability analysis by product/service lines and geographical locations.

Changing product life cycles

A product's life cycle is the period of time from initial expenditure on research and development to the time at which support to customers is withdrawn. Intensive global competition and technological

---

REAL WORLD VIEWS 1.2

The internet of things – new products and services

The internet of things (IoT) refers to an ever-growing network of physical objects which are connected to the internet. This includes household devices and many business and industrial applications. The IoT has given way to a vast array of new products and services. Take for example fill-level sensors developed by smartbin™. These products can be placed inside industrial bins and send data on the fill level and bin location back to the waste collection firm via an internet connection.

The sensors also allow the waste collection firm to optimize the waste collection routes.

Question

1 Can you think of any barriers to entry for a business entering the market for IoT sensors or similar?

Reference
www.smartbin.com/solutions/iot-level-sensors/

innovation, combined with increasingly discriminating and sophisticated customer demands, have resulted in a dramatic decline in product life cycles. To be successful companies must now speed up the rate at which they introduce new products to the market and constantly develop new products and services. Being later to the market than the competitors can have a dramatic effect on product profitability.

In many industries a large fraction of a product's life cycle costs are determined by decisions made early in its life cycle. This has created a need for management accounting to place greater emphasis on providing information at the design stage because many of the costs are committed or locked in at this time. Therefore, to compete successfully, companies must be able to manage their costs effectively at the design stage, have the capability to adapt to new, different and changing customer requirements and reduce the time to market of new and modified products.

Advances in manufacturing technologies

Excellence in manufacturing can provide a competitive weapon to compete in sophisticated worldwide markets. In order to compete effectively, companies must be capable of manufacturing innovative products of high quality at a low cost, and also provide a first-class customer service. At the same time, they must have the flexibility to cope with short product life cycles, demands for greater product variety from more discriminating customers and increasing international competition. World-class manufacturing companies have responded to these competitive demands by replacing traditional production systems with lean manufacturing systems that seek to reduce waste by implementing just-in-time (JIT) production systems, focusing on quality, simplifying processes and investing in advanced manufacturing technologies (AMTs). The major features of these new systems and their implications for management accounting will be described throughout the book.

The impact of information technology

During the past two decades the use of information technology (IT) to support business activities has increased dramatically and the development of electronic business communication technologies known as e-business, e-commerce or internet commerce have had a major impact. For example, consumers are more discerning in their purchases because they can access the internet to compare the relative merits of different products and services. Internet trading also allows buyers and sellers to undertake transactions from diverse locations in different parts of the world. E-commerce (such as bar coding) has allowed considerable cost savings to be made by streamlining business processes and has generated extra revenues from the adept use of online sales facilities (such as ticketless airline bookings and internet banking). The proficient use of e-commerce has given many companies a competitive advantage.

The developments in IT have had a significant impact on the work of management accountants. They have substantially reduced information gathering and the processing of information. Instead of managers asking management accountants for information, they can access the system on their personal computers to derive the information they require directly and do their own analyses. This has freed accountants to adopt the role of advisers and internal consultants to the business. Management accountants have now become more involved in interpreting the information generated from the accounting system and providing business support for managers.

Environmental and sustainability issues

Increasing attention is now being given to making companies accountable for ethical, social and environmental issues and the need for organizations to be managed in a sustainable way. There is now a general recognition that environmental resources are limited and should be preserved for future generations.

Customers are no longer satisfied if companies simply comply with the legal requirements of undertaking their activities. They expect company managers to be more proactive in terms of their social responsibility, safety and environmental issues. Environmental management accounting is becoming increasingly

REAL WORLD VIEWS 1.3

Changing product life cycles – consumer medical sciences

Medical devices are normally associated with use by hospitals and medical practices. Some devices are used by normal consumers and, according to an article on the Medical Device and Diagnostic Industry website (www.mddionline.com), are proliferating. The market for devices such as insulin pumps and blood pressure monitors has become more consumer-driven and is putting pressure on manufacturers to design better products and get them to the market faster.

According to the article, 'patients want their medical devices to have the same kind of design and appeals as iPods'. This convergence of medical and mass consumer electronics is creating many challenges for medical device manufacturers. These challenges include widely divergent product life cycles, varying scenarios of use and safety, and efficacy concerns. The typical life cycle of a consumer device is likely to be measured more in months than years. Compare this to the long approval cycles of drug and medical device regulatory authorities – which, according to the article, can be anything from 27 to 36 months in the USA depending on the type of medical device. During this timeframe, an iPod/iPad has probably gone through at least two generations, and smart devices are now the norm. It may be that medical devices will never get as savvy as a consumer iPad due to regulatory concerns and device efficacy. However, increasing consumer-driven requirements are likely to shorten the product life cycle over coming years as devices move further towards personal smart devices. As of April 2016, for example, a *Financial Times* article notes there are more than 165 000 health and fitness apps available at the Apple App Store. While Apple's devices are not medical devices they do pose a competitive threat.

Questions

1 Do you think the costs of the electronic components in a smart device such as an iPod/iPad are more or less than those in a medical device like a blood pressure monitor?

2 Would decreasing the product life cycle of medical devices, or medical devices being more like consumer electronics, pose any risks for manufacturers?

References

mddiadmin (2009) Developing medical devices in a consumer-driven market, MDDI, 1 February. Available at www.mddionline.com/article /developing-medical-devices-consumer-driven -market
Financial Times (2016) Healthcare apps battle to be taken seriously. Available at www.ft.com /content/ed3268f2-e620-11e5-a09b -1f8b0d268c39

important in many organizations. There are several reasons for this. First, environmental costs can be large for some industrial sectors. Second, regulatory requirements involving huge fines for non-compliance have increased significantly over the past decade. Therefore, selecting the least costly method of compliance has become a major objective. Third, society is demanding that companies focus on being more environmentally friendly. Companies are finding that becoming a good social citizen and being environmentally responsible improves their image and enhances their ability to sell their products and services.

These developments have created the need for companies to develop systems of measuring and reporting environmental costs, the consumption of scarce environmental resources and details of hazardous materials used or pollutants emitted to the environment. Knowledge of environmental costs and their causes provides the information that managers need to redesign processes to minimize the usage of scarce environmental resources and the emission pollutants and to also make more sensitive environmental decisions.

Pressures to adopt higher standards of ethical behaviour

Earlier in this chapter it was suggested that management accounting practices were developed to provide information that assist managers to maximize future profits. It was, however, pointed out that it is too simplistic to assume that the only objective of a business firm is to maximize profits. The profit maximization objective should be constrained by the need for firms to also give high priority to their social responsibilities and ensure that their employees adopt high standards of ethical behaviour. A code of ethics has now become an essential part of corporate culture.

Identification of what is acceptable ethical behaviour has attracted much attention in recent years with numerous examples of companies attracting negative coverage for ethical failings and their impact on reported profits. For example, Volkswagen (VW), Europe's biggest car maker has suffered a dramatic decline in its reputation after the revelation that it fitted software designed to cheat emission tests to 11 million cars worldwide. Volkswagen has set aside €18.4 billion to cover the costs of legal action, compensation and refits. Public distrust and protests against corporate misdemeanours have resulted in calls for increased regulation and the need to focus on improving ethical behaviour.

Management accountants have a critical part to play in the management of ethical performance and an obligation to uphold ethical standards. Professional accounting organizations play an important role in promoting a high standard of ethical behaviour by their members. Both of the professional bodies representing management accountants, in the UK (Chartered Institute of Management Accountants), and in the USA (The American Institute of Certified Public Accountants), have issued codes of ethical guidelines for their members and established mechanisms for monitoring and enforcing professional ethics. You can view each organization's ethical standards at www.cimaglobal.com/ethics and www .aicpa.org/research/standards/codesofconduct/pages/default.aspx

Deregulation and privatization

Before the 1990s many organizations, such as those operating in the airline, utility and financial service industries, were either government-owned monopolies or operated in a highly regulated, protected and non-competitive environment. These organizations were not subject to any great pressure to improve the quality and efficiency of their operations or to improve profitability by eliminating services or products that were making losses. Prices were set to cover operating costs and provide a predetermined return on capital. Hence, cost increases could often be absorbed by increasing the prices of the products or services. Little attention was therefore given to developing management accounting systems that accurately measured the costs and profitability of individual products or services.

Privatization of government-controlled companies and deregulation has resulted in the elimination of pricing and competitive restrictions. Deregulation, intensive competition and an expanding product range create the need for these organizations to focus on cost management and develop management accounting information systems that enable them to understand their cost base and determine the sources of profitability for their products, customers and markets.

Focus on value creation

There is now an increasing recognition that management accounting needs to place greater emphasis on creating value rather than an overemphasis on managing and recording costs. Reducing cost is still important because it enables a company to remain competitive by reducing or maintaining selling prices and thus increasing customer value. You will see in Chapter 22 that recent developments have resulted in management accounting distinguishing between value-added and non-value-added activities with the former representing those activities that the customers perceive as adding value to the product or service and the latter adding costs but no value. Cost management seeks to eliminate or reduce non-value-added activities and to identify ways of performing the value-added activities in such a way that they enhance the value to the product or service.

Recently, increasing attention has been given to the importance of intellectual capital (also known as intangible assets) arising from the observed dramatic differences between the book and market values of many companies, particularly the dotcom companies in the late 1990s. Examples of items that represent intellectual capital include resources such as the organization's reputation, the morale of its staff, customer satisfaction, knowledge and skills of employees, established relationships with suppliers, etc. It is important that intangible assets are taken into account in order to assess the value of future business opportunities. This presents a challenge to management accountants as to how to identify, measure and report on the value of intellectual capital.

Customer orientation

In order to survive in today's competitive environment companies have had to become more customer driven and to recognize that customers are crucial to their future success. This has resulted in companies making customer satisfaction an overriding priority and to focus on identifying and achieving the key success factors that are necessary to be successful in today's competitive environment. These key success factors are discussed in the next section.

FOCUS ON CUSTOMER SATISFACTION AND NEW MANAGEMENT APPROACHES

The key success factors that organizations must concentrate on to provide customer satisfaction are cost, quality, reliability, delivery and the choice of innovative new products. In addition, firms are attempting to increase customer satisfaction by adopting a philosophy of continuous improvement to reduce costs and improve quality, reliability and delivery.

Cost efficiency

Keeping costs low and being cost efficient provides an organization with a strong competitive advantage. Increased competition has also made decision errors, due to poor cost information, more potentially hazardous to an organization. Many companies have become aware of the need to improve their cost systems so that they can produce more accurate cost information to determine the cost of their products and services, monitor trends in costs over time, pinpoint loss-making activities and analyse profits by products, sales outlets, customers and markets.

Quality

In addition to demanding low costs, customers are demanding high-quality products and services. Most companies are responding to this by focusing on total quality management (TQM). TQM is a term used to describe a situation in which *all* business functions are involved in a process of continuous quality improvement that focuses on delivering products or services of consistently high quality in a timely fashion. The emphasis on TQM has created fresh demands on the management accounting function to measure and evaluate the quality of products and services and the activities that produce them.

Time as a competitive weapon

Organizations are also seeking to increase customer satisfaction by providing a speedier response to customer requests, ensuring 100 per cent on-time delivery and reducing the time taken to develop and bring new products to market. For these reasons management accounting systems now place more emphasis on time-based measures, such as cycle time. This is the length of time from start to completion of a product or service. It consists of the sum of processing time, move time, wait time and inspection time. Only processing time adds value to the product, and the remaining activities are non-value-added activities in the sense that they can be reduced or eliminated without altering the product's service potential to the customer. Organizations are therefore focusing on minimizing cycle time by reducing the time spent on such activities. The management accounting system has an important role to play in this process by identifying and reporting on the time devoted to value-added and non-value-added activities. Cycle time measures have also become important for service organizations. For example, the time taken to process mortgage loan applications by financial organizations can be considerable, involving substantial non-value-added waiting time. Reducing the time to process applications enhances customer satisfaction and creates the potential for increasing sales revenue.

Innovation and continuous improvement

To be successful, companies must develop a steady stream of innovative new products and services and have the capability to adapt to changing customer requirements. Management accounting information systems have begun to report performance measures relating to innovation. Examples include:

● the total launch time for new products/services;

● an assessment of the key characteristics of new products relative to those of competitors;

● feedback on customer satisfaction with the new features and characteristics of newly introduced products and the number of new products launched.

Organizations are also attempting to enhance customer satisfaction by adopting a philosophy of continuous improvement. Traditionally, organizations have sought to study activities and establish standard operating procedures. Management accountants developed systems and measurements that compared actual results with predetermined standards. This process created a climate in which the predetermined standards represented a target to be achieved and maintained. In today's competitive environment, companies must adopt a philosophy of continuous improvement, an ongoing process that involves a continuous search to reduce costs, eliminate waste and improve the quality and performance of activities that increase customer value or satisfaction. Management accounting supports continuous improvement by identifying opportunities for change and then reporting on the progress of the methods that have been implemented.

Benchmarking is a technique that is increasingly being adopted as a mechanism for achieving continuous improvement. It is a continuous process of measuring a firm's products, services or activities against the other best performing organizations, either internal or external, to the firm. The objective is to ascertain how the processes and activities can be improved. Ideally, benchmarking should involve an external focus on the latest developments, best practice and model examples that can be incorporated within various operations of business organizations. It therefore represents the ideal way of moving forward and achieving high competitive standards.

In their quest for the continuous improvement of organizational activities, managers have found that they need to rely more on the people closest to the operating processes and customers, to develop new approaches to performing activities. This has led to employees being provided with relevant information to enable them to make continuous improvements to the output of processes. Allowing employees to take such actions without the authorization by superiors has come to be known as employee empowerment. It is argued that by empowering employees and giving them relevant information they will be able to respond faster to customers, increase process flexibility, reduce cycle time and improve morale. Management accounting is therefore moving from its traditional emphasis on providing information to managers to monitor the activities of employees, to providing information to employees to empower them to focus on the continuous improvement of activities.

FUNCTIONS OF MANAGEMENT ACCOUNTING

A cost and management accounting system should generate information to meet the following requirements. It should:

1 allocate costs between cost of goods sold and inventories for internal and external profit reporting;

2 provide relevant information to help managers make better decisions;

3 provide information for planning, control, performance measurement and continuous improvement.

Financial accounting rules require that we match costs with revenues to calculate profit. Consequently, any unsold finished goods inventories (or partly completed work in progress) will *not* be included in the cost of goods sold, which is matched against sales revenue during a given period. In an organization that produces a wide range of different products it will be necessary, for inventory valuation purposes, to trace the costs to each individual product. The total value of the inventories of completed products and work in progress, plus any unused raw materials, forms the basis for determining the inventory valuation to be deducted from the current period's costs when calculating profit. This total is also the basis for determining the inventory valuation for inclusion in the balance sheet. Costs are therefore traced to each individual job or product for financial accounting requirements, in order to allocate the costs incurred during a period between cost of goods sold and inventories. (Note that the terms 'stocks' and 'inventories' are used synonymously throughout this book.) This information is required for meeting *external* financial accounting requirements, but most organizations also produce *internal* profit reports at monthly intervals. Thus, product costs are also required for periodic internal profit reporting. Many service organizations, however, do not carry any inventories and product costs are therefore not required by these organizations for valuing inventories.

The second requirement of a cost and management accounting system is to provide relevant financial information to managers to help them make better decisions. Information is required relating to the profitability of various segments of the business such as products, services, customers and distribution channels, in order to ensure that only profitable activities are undertaken. Information is also required for making resource allocation and product/service mix and discontinuation decisions.

In some situations, information extracted from the costing system also plays a crucial role in determining selling prices, particularly in markets in which customized products and services that do not have readily available market prices are provided.

Management accounting systems should also provide information for planning, control, performance measurement and continuous improvement. Planning involves translating goals and objectives into the specific activities and resources that are required to achieve them. Companies develop both long-term and short-term plans and the management accounting function plays a critical role in this process. Short-term plans, in the form of the budgeting process, are prepared in more detail than the longer term plans and are one of the mechanisms used by managers as a basis for control and performance evaluation. The control process involves the setting of targets or standards (often derived from the budgeting process) against which actual results are measured. The management accountant's role is to provide managers with feedback information in the form of periodic reports, suitably analysed, to enable them to determine if operations for which they are responsible are proceeding according to plan, and to identify those activities where corrective action is necessary. In particular, the management accounting function should provide economic feedback to managers to assist them in controlling costs and improving the efficiency and effectiveness of operations.

It is appropriate at this point to distinguish between cost accounting and management accounting. Cost accounting is concerned with cost accumulation for inventory valuation to meet the requirements of external reporting and internal profit measurement, whereas management accounting relates to the provision of appropriate information for decision-making, planning, control and performance evaluation. However, a study of the literature reveals that the distinction between cost accounting and management accounting is not clear cut and the two terms are often used synonymously. In this book, no further attempt will be made to distinguish between them.

You should now be aware that a management accounting system serves multiple purposes. The emphasis throughout this book is that costs must be assembled in different ways for different purposes. Most organizations record cost information in a single database, with costs appropriately coded and classified, so that relevant information can be extracted to meet the requirements of different users. We shall examine this topic in the next chapter.

SUMMARY OF THE CONTENTS OF THIS BOOK

This book is divided into six parts. Part One contains two chapters and provides an introduction to management and cost accounting and a framework for studying the remaining chapters. Part Two consists of five chapters and is entitled 'Cost Accumulation for Inventory Valuation and Profit Measurement'. This section focuses mainly on cost accounting. It is concerned with assigning costs to products to separate costs incurred during a period between costs of goods sold and the closing inventory valuation. The extent to which product costs accumulated for inventory valuation and profit measurement should be adjusted for meeting decision-making, cost control and performance measurement requirements, is also briefly considered. Part Three is made up of seven chapters and is entitled 'Information for Decision-making'. Here the focus is on measuring and identifying those costs that are relevant for different types of decision.

The title of Part Four is 'Information for Planning, Control and Performance Measurement'. It consists of six chapters and concentrates on the process of translating goals and objectives into specific activities and the resources that are required, via the short-term (budgeting) and long-term planning processes, to achieve the goals and objectives. In addition, the management control systems that organizations use are described and the role that management accounting control systems play within the overall control process is examined. The emphasis here is on the accounting process as a means of providing information to help managers control the activities for which they are responsible. Performance measurement and evaluation within different segments of the organization is also examined.

Part Five contains three chapters and is entitled 'Strategic Performance and Cost Management and Challenges for the Future.' The first chapter focuses on strategic performance management, the second on strategic cost management and the third chapter discusses the challenges for the future facing management accounting. Part Six consists of three chapters and is entitled 'The Application of Quantitative Methods to Management Accounting'.

GUIDELINES FOR USING THIS BOOK

If you are pursuing a course of management accounting, without cost accumulation for inventory valuation and profit measurement, Chapters 4 to 7 in Part Two can be omitted, since the rest of this book does not rely heavily on these chapters. Alternatively, you could delay your reading of Chapters 4 to 7 in Part Two until you have studied Parts Three and Four. If you wish to gain an insight into cost accumulation for inventory valuation and profit measurement but do not wish to study it in depth, you may prefer to read only Chapters 3 and 7 of Part Two. It is important that you read Chapter 3, which focuses on traditional methods of tracing overheads to cost objects, prior to reading Chapter 11 on activity-based costing.

The chapters on the application of quantitative techniques to management accounting have been delayed until Part Six. An alternative approach would be to read Chapter 24 immediately after reading Chapter 8 on cost–volume–profit analysis. Chapter 25 is self-contained and may be assigned to follow any of the chapters in Part Four. Chapter 26 should be read only after you have studied Chapter 9.

A comprehensive treatment of all of the topics that are contained in this book will not be essential for all readers. To meet different requirements, the more advanced material that is not essential for those readers not requiring an in-depth knowledge of a particular topic has been highlighted. The start of each advanced reading section has a clearly identifiable heading and a vertical green line is used to highlight the full section. The advanced reading sections are more appropriate for an advanced course and may normally be omitted if you are pursuing an introductory course.

SUMMARY

The following items relate to the learning objectives listed at the beginning of the chapter.

- **Distinguish between management accounting and financial accounting.**

Management accounting differs from financial accounting in several ways. Management accounting is concerned with the provision of information to internal users to help them make better decisions and improve the efficiency and effectiveness of operations. Financial accounting is concerned with the provision of information to external parties outside the organization. Unlike financial accounting there is no statutory requirement for management accounting to produce financial statements or to follow externally imposed rules. Furthermore, management accounting provides information relating to different parts of the business whereas financial accounting reports focus on the whole business. Management accounting also tends to be more future oriented and reports are often published on a daily basis whereas financial accounting reports are published semi-annually.

- **Identify and describe the elements involved in the decision-making, planning and control process.**

The following elements are involved in the decision-making, planning and control process: (a) identify the objectives that will guide the business; (b) search for a range of possible courses of action that might enable the objectives to be achieved; (c) select appropriate alternative courses of action that will enable the objectives to be achieved; (d) implement the decisions as part of the planning and budgeting process; (e) compare actual and planned outcomes; and (f) respond to divergencies from plan by taking corrective action so that actual outcomes conform to planned outcomes, or modify the plans if the comparisons indicate that the plans are no longer attainable.

● **Justify the view that a major objective of commercial organizations is to broadly seek to maximize future profits.**

The reasons for identifying maximizing future profits as a major objective are: (a) it is unlikely that any other objective is as widely applicable in measuring the ability of the organization to survive in the future; (b) although it is unlikely that maximizing future profits can be realized in practice, it is still important to establish the principles necessary to achieve this objective; and (c) it enables shareholders as a group in the bargaining coalition to know how much the pursuit of other goals is costing them by indicating the amount of cash distributed among the members of the coalition.

● **Explain the important changes that have taken place in the business environment that have influenced management accounting practice.**

The important changes are: (a) globalization of world trade; (b) deregulation in various industries; (c) changing product life cycles; (d) advances in manufacturing and information technologies; (e) focus on environmental and ethical issues; (f) a greater emphasis on value creation; (g) the need to become more customer driven.

● **Outline and describe the key success factors that directly affect customer satisfaction.**

The key success factors are: cost efficiency, quality, time, and innovation and continuous improvement. Keeping costs low and being cost efficient provides an organization with a strong competitive advantage. Customers also demand high-quality products and services and this has resulted in companies making quality a key competitive variable. Organizations are also seeking to increase customer satisfaction by providing a speedier response to customer requests, ensuring 100 per cent on-time delivery and reducing the time taken to bring new products to the market. To be successful, companies must be innovative and develop a steady stream of new products and services and have the capability to rapidly adapt to changing customer requirements.

● **Identify and describe the functions of a cost and management accounting system.**

A cost and management accounting system should generate information to meet the following requirements: (a) allocate costs between cost of goods sold and inventories for internal and external profit reporting and inventory valuation; (b) provide relevant information to help managers make better decisions; and (c) provide information for planning, control and performance measurement.

KEY TERMS AND CONCEPTS

Each chapter includes a section like this. You should make sure that you understand each of the terms listed below before you proceed to the next chapter.

Benchmarking A mechanism for achieving continuous improvement by measuring products, services or activities against those of other best performing organizations.

Budget A financial plan for implementing management decisions.

Continuous improvement An ongoing search to reduce costs, eliminate waste and improve the quality and performance of activities that increase customer value or satisfaction.

Control A managerial function that consists of the measurement, reporting and subsequent correction of performance in order to achieve the organization's objectives.

Control process The process of setting targets or standards against which actual results are measured.

Cost accounting Accounting concerned with cost accumulation for inventory valuation to meet the requirements of external reporting and internal profit measurement.

Cycle time The length of time from start to completion of a product or service and is the sum of processing time, move time, wait time and inspection time.

E-business The use of information and communication technologies to support any business activities, including buying and selling.

E-commerce The use of information and communication technologies to support the purchase, sale and exchange of goods.

Employee empowerment Providing employees with relevant information to allow them to make continuous improvements to the output of processes without the authorization of superiors.

Ethical behaviour Behaviour that is consistent with the standards of honesty, fairness and social responsibility that have been adopted by the organization.

Financial accounting Accounting concerned with the provision of information to parties that are external to the organization.

Intellectual capital The intangible benefits accessible by a firm from its workforce, and more broadly, from its established relationships with groups such as customers, suppliers and competitors. It is often used interchangeably with other terms such as 'knowledge capital', 'knowledge economy' and 'intangible assets'.

Internet commerce The buying and selling of goods and services over the internet.

Lean manufacturing systems Systems that seek to reduce waste in manufacturing by implementing just-in-time production systems, focusing on quality, simplifying processes and investing in advanced technologies.

Management accounting Accounting concerned with the provision of information to people within the organization to aid decision-making and improve the efficiency and effectiveness of existing operations.

Management by exception A situation in which management attention is focused on areas where outcomes do not meet targets.

Master budget A single unifying statement of an organization's expectations for future periods comprising budgeted profit and cash flow statements.

Non-value-added activities Activities that can be reduced or eliminated without altering the product's service potential to the customer.

Performance reports Regular reports to management that compare actual outcomes with planned outcomes.

Product's life cycle The period of time from initial expenditure on research and development to the withdrawal of support to customers.

Stakeholders Various parties that have an interest in an organization. Examples include managers, shareholders and potential investors, employees, creditors and the government.

Strategies Courses of action designed to ensure that objectives are achieved.

Total quality management (TQM) A customer-oriented process of continuous improvement that focuses on delivering products or services of consistent high quality in a timely fashion.

KEY EXAMINATION POINTS

Chapter 1 has provided an introduction to the scope of management accounting. It is unlikely that examination questions will be set that refer to the content of an introductory chapter. However, questions are sometimes set requiring you to outline how a costing system can assist the management of an organization. Note that the examiner may not distinguish between cost accounting and management accounting. Cost accounting is often used to also embrace management accounting. Your discussion of a cost accounting system should therefore include a description (with illustrations) of how the system provides information for decision-making, planning and control. Make sure that you draw off your experience from the whole of a first-year course and not just this introductory chapter.

ASSESSMENT MATERIAL

The review questions are short questions that enable you to assess your understanding of the main topics included in the chapter. The numbers in parentheses provide you with the page numbers to refer to if you cannot answer a specific question.

The remaining chapters also contain review problems. These are more complex and require you to relate and apply the chapter content to various business problems. Fully worked solutions to the review problems are provided in a separate section at the end of the book.

REVIEW QUESTIONS

1.1 Identify and describe the different users of accounting information. (pp. 5–6)

1.2 Describe the differences between management accounting and financial accounting. (p. 6)

1.3 Explain each of the elements of the decision-making, planning and control process. (pp. 7–9)

1.4 Describe what is meant by management by exception. (p. 9)

1.5 Explain how the business environment that businesses face has changed over the past decades and discuss how this has had an impact on management accounting. (pp. 10–14)

1.6 Describe each of the key success factors that companies should concentrate on to achieve customer satisfaction. (pp. 14–15)

1.7 Explain why firms are beginning to concentrate on social responsibility and corporate ethics. (pp. 12–13)

1.8 Describe the different functions of management accounting. (pp. 16–17)

2
AN INTRODUCTION TO COST TERMS AND CONCEPTS

LEARNING OBJECTIVES After studying this chapter, you should be able to:

- explain why it is necessary to understand the meaning of different cost terms;

- define and illustrate a cost object;

- explain the meaning of each of the key terms or concepts highlighted in bold text in this chapter;

- explain why in the short term some costs and revenues are not relevant for decision-making;

- describe the three purposes for which cost information is required.

In Chapter 1 it was pointed out that accounting systems measure costs which are used for profit measurement and inventory (i.e. stock) valuation, decision-making, performance measurement and control. The term cost is a frequently used word that reflects a monetary measure of the resources sacrificed or forgone to achieve a specific objective, such as acquiring a good or service. However, the term must be defined more precisely before the 'cost' can be determined. You will find that the word *cost* is rarely used without a preceding adjective to specify the type of cost being considered.

To understand how accounting systems calculate costs and to communicate accounting information effectively to others requires a thorough understanding of what the term cost means. Unfortunately, the term has multiple meanings and different types of cost are used in different situations. Therefore, a preceding term must be added to clarify the assumptions that underlie a cost measurement. A large terminology has emerged to indicate more clearly which cost meaning is being conveyed. Examples include variable cost, fixed cost, opportunity cost and sunk cost. The aim of this chapter is to provide you with an understanding of the basic cost terms and concepts that are used in the management accounting literature.

COST OBJECTS

A cost object is any activity for which a separate measurement of costs is desired. In other words, if the users of accounting information want to know the cost of something, this something is called a cost object. Examples of cost objects include the cost of a product, the cost of rendering a service to a bank customer or hospital patient, the cost of operating a particular department or sales territory, or indeed anything for which one wants to measure the cost of resources used.

We shall see that the cost collection system typically accounts for costs in two broad stages:

1 It accumulates costs by classifying them into certain categories such as by type of expense (e.g. direct labour, direct materials and indirect costs) or by cost behaviour (such as fixed and variable costs).

2 It then assigns these costs to cost objects.

In this chapter, we shall focus on the following cost terms and concepts:

- direct and indirect costs;
- period and product costs;
- cost behaviour in relation to volume of activity;
- relevant and irrelevant costs;
- avoidable and unavoidable costs;
- sunk costs;
- opportunity costs;
- incremental and marginal costs.

MANUFACTURING, MERCHANDISING AND SERVICE ORGANIZATIONS

To provide a better understanding of how different cost terms are used in organizations, it is appropriate to describe the major features of activities undertaken in the manufacturing, merchandising and service organizations. Manufacturing organizations purchase raw materials from suppliers and convert these materials into tangible products through the use of labour and capital inputs (e.g. plant and machinery). This process results in manufacturing organizations having the following types of inventory:

- Raw material inventories consisting of purchased raw materials in stock awaiting use in the manufacturing process.
- Work in progress inventory (also called work in process) consisting of partially complete products awaiting completion.
- Finished goods inventory consisting of fully completed products that have not yet been sold.

Merchandising companies such as supermarkets, retail departmental stores and wholesalers sell tangible products that they have previously purchased in the same basic form from suppliers. Therefore they have only finished goods inventories. Service organizations such as accounting firms, insurance companies, advertising agencies and hospitals provide tasks or activities for customers. A major feature of service organizations is that they provide perishable services that cannot be stored for future use. Therefore service organizations do not have finished goods inventory but some service organizations do have work in process. For example, a firm of lawyers may have clients whose work is partially complete at the end of the accounting period.

DIRECT AND INDIRECT COSTS

Costs that are assigned to cost objects can be divided into two broad categories – direct and indirect costs. Both categories can be further divided into direct and indirect materials and direct and indirect labour costs.

Direct materials

Direct material costs represent those material costs that can be specifically and exclusively identified with a particular cost object. In manufacturing organizations where the cost object is a product, physical observation can be used to measure the quantity consumed by each individual product and the cost of direct materials can be directly charged to them. In other words, direct materials become part of a physical product. For example, wood used in the manufacture of different types of furniture can be directly identified with each specific type of furniture such as chairs, tables and bookcases.

The term direct materials is normally not applicable to merchandising and service organizations. The equivalent term in a merchandising organization is the purchase cost of the items that are for resale. For example, with a departmental store where the cost object is a department (e.g. televisions and DVD players, computers, clothing and furniture departments) the purchase cost of the goods from the suppliers will be directly charged to the appropriate department that resells the goods. Some service organizations do purchase materials or parts to provide a service. For example, a garage may purchase parts for vehicle repairs. These parts can be identified with the repair of each customer's vehicle (i.e. the cost object) and thus are equivalent to direct materials.

Direct labour

Direct labour costs are those labour costs that can be specifically and exclusively identified with a particular cost object. Physical observation can be used to measure the quantity of labour used to produce a specific product or provide a service. The direct labour cost in producing a product includes the cost of converting the raw materials into a product, such as the costs of the machine operatives engaged in the production process in the manufacture of televisions. The direct labour cost used to provide a service includes the labour costs in providing a service that can be specifically identified with an individual client or with a specific instance of service. The direct labour costs for a departmental store are the labour costs of the staff that can be attributed specifically to a department.

Indirect costs

Indirect costs cannot be identified specifically and exclusively with a given cost object. They consist of indirect labour, materials and expenses. In a manufacturing organization where products are the cost object, the wages of all employees whose time cannot be identified with a specific product, represent indirect labour costs. Examples include the labour cost of staff employed in the maintenance and repair of production equipment and staff employed in the stores department. The cost of materials used to repair machinery cannot be identified with a specific product and can therefore be classified as indirect material costs. Examples of indirect expenses in manufacturing, service or a departmental store where products, the provision of a service or departments are the cost objectives, include lighting and heating expenses and property taxes. These costs cannot be specifically identified with a particular product, service or department.

The term **overheads** is widely used instead of indirect costs. In a manufacturing organization, overhead costs are categorized as manufacturing, administration or marketing (or selling) overheads. Manufacturing overheads include all the costs of manufacturing apart from direct labour and material costs. Administrative overheads consist of all costs associated with the general administration of the organization that cannot be assigned to manufacturing, marketing and distribution overheads. Examples of administrative overheads include top executive salaries, general accounting, secretarial, and research and development costs. Those costs that are necessary to market and distribute a product or service are categorized as marketing (selling) costs, also known as order-getting and order-filling costs. Examples of marketing costs include advertising, sales personnel salaries/commissions, warehousing and delivery transportation costs.

FIGURE 2.1
Manufacturing and non-manufacturing costs

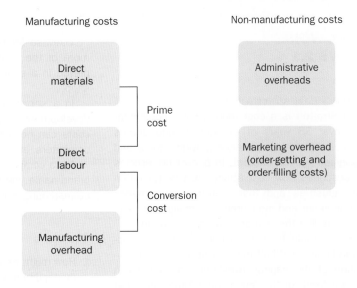

Figure 2.1 illustrates the various classifications of manufacturing and non-manufacturing costs. You will see from this figure that two further classifications of manufacturing costs are sometimes used. Prime cost consists of all direct manufacturing costs (i.e. it is the sum of direct material and direct labour costs). Conversion cost is the sum of direct labour and manufacturing overhead costs. It represents the cost of converting raw materials into finished products.

Distinguishing between direct and indirect costs

Sometimes, direct costs are treated as indirect because it is not cost effective to trace costs directly to the cost object. For example, the nails used to manufacture a particular desk can be identified specifically with the desk, but, because the cost is likely to be insignificant, the expense of tracing such items does not justify the possible benefits from calculating more accurate product costs.

The distinction between direct and indirect costs also depends on the cost object. A cost can be treated as direct for one cost object but indirect in respect of another. For example, if the cost object is the cost of using different distribution channels, then the rental of warehouses and the salaries of storekeepers will be regarded as direct for each distribution channel. If, by the same token, the cost object is the product, both the warehouse rental and the salaries of the storekeepers will be an indirect cost because these costs cannot be specifically identified with the product.

Assigning direct and indirect costs to cost objects

Direct costs can be traced easily and accurately to a cost object. For example, where products are the cost object, direct materials and labour used can be physically identified with the different products that an organization produces. It is a relatively simple process to establish an information technology system that records the quantity and cost of direct labour and material resources used to produce specific products.

In contrast, indirect costs cannot be traced to cost objects. Instead, an estimate must be made of the resources consumed by cost objects using cost allocations. A cost allocation is the process of assigning costs when a direct measure does not exist for the quantity of resources consumed by a particular cost object. Cost allocations involve the use of surrogate rather than direct measures. For example, consider an activity such as receiving incoming materials. Assuming that the cost of receiving materials is strongly influenced by the number of receipts, then costs can be allocated to products (i.e. the cost object) based on the number of material receipts each product requires. If 20 per cent of the total number of receipts for a period were required for a particular product then 20 per cent of the total costs of

REAL WORLD VIEWS 2.1

Industry cost structures

Allan Stratton is a cost management consultant with over 35 years of experience, who shares the benefit of his experience providing tools and resources via the internet. In one of his articles he describes how cost structures vary for different industries and that therefore performance management and measurement should differ and should reflect the cost structures being used.

For example, the semiconductor industry is capital intensive and half the cost structure is depreciation of the capital investment, a cost which is then fixed for the foreseeable future once the investment has been made.

The main expenditures in the oil and gas industry are likely to be incurred by drilling exploratory wells looking for new reserves of oil and natural gas, many of which will turn out to be dry or not commercially viable, or investing in activities related to collecting seismic data and evaluating underground formations.

In a manufacturing organization around half of the costs might be incurred by purchasing component parts or raw materials from suppliers.

Regardless of the industry, in distribution most of the costs will be incurred when purchasing products from manufacturers.

Likewise for retail operations, 70 per cent or more of the costs are likely to be on food displayed in a supermarket or clothes in a clothing shop.

In a service organization such as a software development firm, however, up to 70 per cent of the costs can be people and people-related (offices, computers, etc.).

For a company like Nike, with a hugely valuable brand name, the largest expenditures are likely to be marketing, advertising and promotion.

Questions

1 How might performance measurement and management vary between different industries?

2 Provide examples of direct labour, direct materials and indirect costs for the different industries mentioned above.

Reference

Stratton, A. (2012) Industry Cost Structures. Available at www.costmatters.com/180 -perspective/industry-cost-structures (accessed 30 March, 2017).

receiving incoming materials would be allocated to that product. If that product were discontinued, and not replaced, we would expect action to be taken to reduce the resources required for receiving materials by 20 per cent.

In this example, the surrogate allocation measure is assumed to be a significant determinant of the cost of receiving incoming materials. The process of assigning indirect costs (overheads) and the accuracy of such assignments will be discussed in Chapter 3, but, at this stage, you should note that only direct costs can be accurately assigned to cost objects. Therefore, the more direct costs that can be traced to a cost object, the more accurate is the cost assignment.

PERIOD AND PRODUCT COSTS

For profit measurement and inventory/stock valuation (i.e. the valuation of completed unsold products and partly completed products or services) purposes it is necessary to classify costs as either product costs or period costs. Product costs are those costs that are identified with goods purchased or produced for resale. In a manufacturing organization, they are costs that are attached to the product and that are included in the inventory valuation for finished goods or for partly completed goods (work in progress), until they are sold; they are then recorded as expenses and matched against sales for calculating profit. Period costs are those costs that are not specifically related to manufacturing or purchasing a product

FIGURE 2.2
Treatment of
period and
product costs

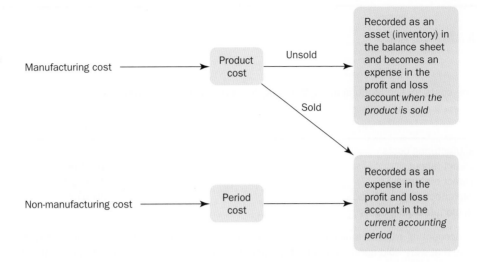

or providing a service that generates revenues. Therefore they are not included in the inventory valuation and as a result are treated as expenses in the period in which they are incurred. *Hence no attempt is made to attach period costs to products for inventory valuation purposes.*

In a manufacturing organization, all manufacturing costs are regarded as product costs and non-manufacturing costs are regarded as period costs. The treatment of period and product costs for a manufacturing organization is illustrated in Figure 2.2. You will see that both product and period costs are eventually classified as expenses. The major difference is the point in time at which they are so classified.

There are two reasons why non-manufacturing costs are treated as period costs and not included in the inventory valuation. First, inventories are assets (unsold production) and assets represent resources that have been acquired and that are expected to contribute to future revenue. Manufacturing costs incurred in making a product can be expected to generate future revenues to cover the cost of production. There is no guarantee, however, that non-manufacturing costs will generate future revenue, because they do not represent value added to any specific product. Therefore, they are not included in the inventory valuation. Second, many non-manufacturing costs (e.g. distribution costs) are not incurred when the product is being stored. Hence it is inappropriate to include such costs within the inventory valuation.

You should now refer to Example 2.1, which provides an illustration of the accounting treatment of period and product costs for income (profit) measurement purposes for a manufacturing organization. Do merchandising and service organizations need to distinguish between product and period costs? The answer is yes. Companies operating in the merchandising sector purchase goods for resale without changing their basic form. The cost of the goods purchased is regarded as a product cost and all other costs, such as administration and selling and distribution expenses, are considered to be period costs. Therefore, the cost of goods sold for a merchandising company would consist of the beginning merchandise inventory, plus the purchase of merchandise during the period, less the closing merchandise inventory. Note that the opening and closing inventories would be valued at the purchase cost of acquiring the inventories. Service organizations do not have beginning and closing finished goods inventories since it is not possible to store services but they may have work in progress (WIP). The cost of direct materials (if applicable) plus direct labour and overheads that are assigned to cost objects (typically clients/customers) represent the product costs. All other costs represent the period costs. The beginning WIP, plus the cost assigned to the clients during the period, less the closing WIP represents the cost of the services sold for the period. This is equivalent to the cost of goods sold in a manufacturing organization.

EXAMPLE 2.1

The costs for Lee Manufacturing Company for period 1 are as follows:

	(£)	(£)
Manufacturing costs:		
Direct labour	400 000	
Direct materials	200 000	
Manufacturing overheads	200 000	800 000
Non-manufacturing costs		300 000

The accounting records indicate that 70 per cent of the above costs were assigned to the cost of the goods that were sold during the period, 10 per cent to work in progress and 20 per cent to finished goods inventory. Sales were £910 000 for the period. The opening and closing inventory of raw materials were identical and there were no opening WIP and finished goods inventories at the start of the period. The profit statement for period 1 will be as follows:

	(£)	(£)
Sales (50 000)		910 000
Manufacturing costs (*product costs*):		
Direct labour	400 000	
Direct materials	200 000	
Manufacturing overheads	200 000	
	800 000	
Less closing inventory: WIP (10%)	80 000	
Finished good inventory (20%)	160 000	240 000
Cost of goods sold (70%)		560 000
Gross profit		350 000
Less non-manufacturing costs (*period costs*)		300 000
Net profit		50 000

During the period 70 per cent of the production was sold and the remaining 30 per cent was produced for WIP and finished goods inventories. Seventy per cent of the product costs are therefore identified as an expense for the period and the remainder are included in the closing inventory valuations. If we assume that the closing inventory is sold in the next accounting period, the remaining 30 per cent of the product costs will become expenses in the next accounting period. However, all the period costs became an expense in this accounting period, because this is the period to which they relate. Note that only product costs form the basis for the calculation of cost of goods sold and that period costs do not form part of this calculation.

COST BEHAVIOUR

A knowledge of how costs and revenues will vary with different levels of activity (or volume) is essential for decision-making. Managers might require information in order to answer questions such as these:

1 How will costs and revenues change if activity is increased (or decreased) by 15 per cent?

2 What will be the impact on profits if we reduce selling price by 10 per cent based on the estimate that this will increase sales volume by 15 per cent?

3 How do the cost and revenues change for a university if the number of students is increased by 5 per cent?

FIGURE 2.3
Variable costs:
(a) total; (b) unit

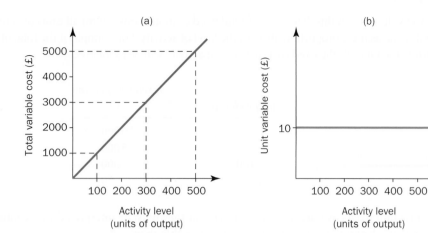

4 How do costs and revenues of a hotel change if a room and meals are provided for two guests for a three-day stay?

5 How many tickets must be sold for a concert in order to break even?

Activity or volume may be measured in terms of units of production or sales, hours worked, miles travelled, patients seen, students enrolled or any other appropriate measure of the activity of an organization.

The terms 'variable', 'fixed', 'semi-variable' and 'semi-fixed' have been traditionally used in the management accounting literature to describe how a cost reacts to changes in activity. **Variable costs** vary in direct proportion to the volume of activity; that is, doubling the level of activity will double the *total* variable cost. Consequently, *total* variable costs are linear and *unit* variable cost is constant. Examples of variable costs in a manufacturing organization include direct materials, energy to operate the machines and sales commissions. Examples of variable costs in a merchandising company, such as a supermarket, include the purchase costs of all items that are sold. In a hospital, variable costs include the cost of drugs and meals which may be assumed to fluctuate with the number of patient days.

Consider the example of a bicycle manufacturer who purchases component parts. Assume that the cost of purchasing two wheels for a particular bicycle is £10 per bicycle. Figure 2.3(a) illustrates the concept of variable costs in graphic form. You can see that as the number of units of output of bicycles increases or decreases, the *total* variable cost of wheels increases and decreases proportionately. Look at Figure 2.3(b). This diagram shows that variable cost per *unit* of output is constant even though total variable cost increases/decreases proportionately with changes in activity.

Fixed costs remain constant over wide ranges of activity for a specified time period. They are not affected by changes in activity. Examples of fixed costs include depreciation of equipment, property taxes, insurance costs, supervisory salaries and leasing charges for cars used by the sales force. Figure 2.4 illustrates how *total* fixed costs and fixed cost per unit of activity react with changes in the level of activity.

FIGURE 2.4
Fixed costs:
(a) total; (b) unit

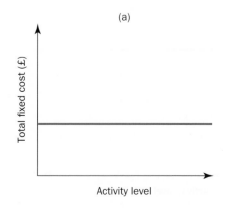
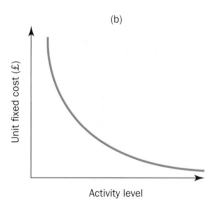

You will see from this diagram that *total* fixed costs are constant for all units of activity whereas *unit* fixed costs decrease proportionally with the level of activity. For example, if the total of the fixed costs is £50 000 for a month the fixed costs per *unit* of activity will be as follows:

Units produced	Fixed cost per unit (£)
1	50 000
10	5 000
100	500
1 000	50

Because unit fixed costs are not constant per unit they must be interpreted with caution. For decision-making, it is better to work with total fixed costs rather than unit costs.

The distinction between fixed and variable costs must be made relative to the time period under consideration. Over a period of several years, virtually all costs are variable. During such a long period of time, contraction in demand will be accompanied by reductions in virtually all categories of cost. For example, senior managers can be released, machinery need not be replaced and even buildings and land can be sold. Similarly, large expansions in activity will eventually cause all categories of cost to increase. Within shorter time periods, costs will be fixed or variable in relation to changes in activity.

Spending on some fixed costs, such as direct labour and supervisory salaries, can be adjusted in the short term to reflect changes in activity. For example, if production activity declines significantly, then direct workers and supervisors might continue to be employed in the hope that the decline in demand will be temporary; but if there is no upsurge in demand then staff might eventually be made redundant. If, by way of contrast, production capacity expands to some critical level, additional workers might be employed, but the process of recruiting such workers may take several months. Thus, within a short-term period, such as one year, labour costs can change in response to changes in demand in a manner similar to that depicted in Figure 2.5. Costs that behave in this manner are described as semi-fixed or step-fixed costs. The distinguishing feature of step-fixed costs is that within a given time period they are fixed within specified activity levels, but they are eventually subject to step increases or decreases by a constant amount at various critical activity levels.

Our discussion so far has assumed a one-year time period. If we consider a shorter time period, such as one month, the step-fixed costs described in the previous paragraph will not occur, because it takes several months to respond to changes in activity and alter spending levels. Over very short-term periods such as one month, spending on direct labour and supervisory salaries will be fixed in relation to changes in activity.

Even though fixed costs are normally assumed to remain unchanged in response to changes in the level of activity in the short term, they may change in response to other factors. For example, if price levels increase then some fixed costs such as management salaries will increase.

Before concluding our discussion of cost behaviour in relation to volume of activity, we must consider semi-variable costs (also known as mixed costs). These include both a fixed and a variable component.

FIGURE 2.5
Step-fixed costs

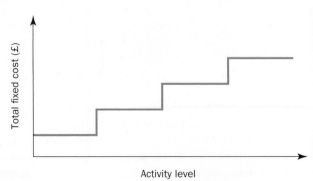

REAL WORLD VIEWS 2.2

Cost structures in the airline sector

Many low-cost carriers such as easyJet and Ryanair regularly offer flights to customers at low prices. They continue to do this even during depressed economic times. Both continued to make good profits in 2015 with easyJet posting pre-tax profits of £686m and Ryanair €867m. More traditional carriers like Air France-KLM and British Airways reported actual and forecasted profits of €118m and £601m respectively. Why do low-cost carriers continue to do well even though they offer much lower fares? One reason is their cost structures.

You might be thinking, surely there is a cost of providing a seat to a passenger, so how can low-cost carriers sell some so cheaply? To answer this, we need to consider the nature of costs at low-cost carriers. Most costs are fixed in nature. First, the aircraft cost (of about US$75m–$90m for a Boeing 737) is fixed. Second, the salaries of the pilot, first officer and cabin crew are also fixed. Third, maintenance costs would also be considered as a fixed cost. And what about the fuel cost? This is also treated as a fixed cost, since it is incurred once the aircraft flies. Thus, if one additional passenger flies with a low-cost carrier, the variable cost associated with this passenger is zero and hence tickets can be sold cheaply.

Traditional carriers like Air France-KLM and British Airways have similar costs to the low-cost carriers – fuel, fleet purchase, maintenance and salaries, etc. These costs too are likely to be fixed.

The difference is that these costs are probably at a higher level than low cost carriers. For example, low cost carriers typically use one model of aircraft which reduces maintenance costs and adds buying leverage. Salaries are also likely to be higher. Traditional airlines may have some variable costs, e.g. passenger meals. Thus, with overall higher costs, it is more difficult to reduce ticket prices. Low-cost carriers do, however, have sophisticated yield management systems to maximize the revenues from flights. This might mean that some customers pay a high price while others travel free. Overall, they try to ensure all fixed costs are covered on every flight.

Questions

1 Do you agree that the variable cost associated with a passenger can be zero? Can this be said for both low-cost and traditional carriers?

2 What options do more traditional carriers have to improve their fixed cost base?

References

Air France-KLM 2015 Annual Report, available at: http://www.airfranceklm.com/sites/default/files/publications/annual_report_2015-en.pdf

EasyJet 2015 Annual Report, available at: www.corporate.easyjet.com/~/media/Files/E/Easyjet-Plc-V2/pdf/investors/result-center-investor/annual-report-2015.pdf

Ryanair 2015 Annual Report, available at: www.investor.ryanair.com/wp-content/uploads/2015/07/Annual-Report-2015.pdf

2014 737 Range price list, available at www.boeing.com/boeing/commercial/prices/

If you refer to your telephone account for your land line you will probably find that it consists of a fixed component (the line rental) plus a variable component (the number of telephone calls made multiplied by the cost per call). Similarly, the office photocopying costs may consist of a fixed rental charge for the photocopiers plus a variable cost (the cost of the paper multiplied by the number of photocopies). The approaches that are used to separate semi-variable costs into their fixed and variable elements are explained in Chapter 24.

RELEVANT AND IRRELEVANT COSTS AND REVENUES

For decision-making, costs and revenues can be classified according to whether they are relevant to a particular decision. Relevant costs and revenues are those *future* costs and revenues that will be changed by a decision, whereas irrelevant costs and revenues are those that will not be affected by the decision. For example, if you are faced with a choice of making a journey using your own car or by public transport, the car tax and insurance costs are irrelevant, since they will remain the same whether or not you use your car for this journey. However, fuel costs for the car will differ depending on which alternative is chosen and this cost will be relevant for decision-making.

Let us now consider a further illustration of the classification of relevant and irrelevant costs. A company purchased raw materials for £1000 per unit and then found that it was impossible to use them in future production or to sell them in their current state. A former customer is prepared to purchase a product that will require the use of all these materials, but is not prepared to pay more than £2500 for this product. The additional costs of converting these materials into the required product are £2000. Should the company accept the order for £2500? It might appear that the cost of the order is £3000, consisting of £1000 material cost and £2000 conversion cost, but this is incorrect because the £1000 material cost will remain the same whether the order is accepted or rejected. The material cost is therefore irrelevant for the decision. If the order is accepted the conversion costs will change by £2000, and this conversion cost is a relevant cost. If we compare the revenue of £2500 with the relevant cost for the order of £2000, it means that the order should be accepted, assuming of course that no higher priced orders can be obtained elsewhere. The following calculation shows that this is the correct decision:

	Do not accept order (£)	Accept order (£)
Materials	1 000	1 000
Conversion costs	—	2 000
Revenue	—	(2 500)
Net costs	1 000	500

The net costs of the company are £500 less; in other words, the company is £500 better off as a result of accepting the order. This agrees with the £500 advantage which was suggested by the relevant cost method.

In this illustration, the sales revenue was relevant to the decision because future revenue changed depending on which alternative was selected. However, in some circumstances, sales revenue may also be irrelevant for decision-making. Consider a situation where a company can meet its sales demand by purchasing either machine A or machine B. The output of both machines is identical, but the operating costs and purchase costs of the machines are different. In this situation, the sales revenue will remain unchanged irrespective of which machine is purchased (assuming, of course, that the quality of output is identical for both machines). Consequently, sales revenue is irrelevant for this decision; the relevant items are the operating costs and the cost of the machines. We have now established an important principle regarding the classification of cost and revenues for decision-making; namely, that in the short term not all costs and revenues are relevant for decision-making.

AVOIDABLE AND UNAVOIDABLE COSTS

Sometimes the terms avoidable and unavoidable costs are used instead of relevant and irrelevant cost. Avoidable costs are those costs that may be saved by not adopting a given alternative, whereas unavoidable costs cannot be saved. Only avoidable costs are relevant for decision-making purposes. In the example that we used to illustrate relevant and irrelevant costs, the material costs of £1000 are unavoidable and irrelevant, but the conversion costs of £2000 are avoidable and hence relevant. The decision rule is to accept those alternatives that generate revenues in excess of the avoidable costs.

SUNK COSTS

These costs are the cost of resources already acquired where the total will be unaffected by the choice between various alternatives. They are costs that have been created by a decision made in the past and that cannot be changed by any decision that will be made now or in the future.

The expenditure of £1000 on materials that were no longer required, referred to in the preceding section, is an example of a sunk cost. Similarly, the written down values of assets previously purchased are sunk costs. For example, if equipment was purchased four years ago for £100 000 with an expected life of five years and nil scrap value, then the written down value will be £20 000 if straight line depreciation is used. This written down value will have to be written off, no matter what possible alternative future action might be chosen. If the equipment was scrapped, the £20 000 would be written off; if the equipment was used for productive purposes, the £20 000 would still have to be written off. This cost cannot be changed by any future decision and is therefore classified as a sunk cost.

Sunk costs are irrelevant for decision-making, but not all irrelevant costs are sunk costs. For example, two alternative production methods may involve identical direct material expenditure. The direct material cost is irrelevant because it will remain the same whichever alternative is chosen, but the material cost is not a sunk cost since it will be incurred in the future.

OPPORTUNITY COSTS

An opportunity cost is a cost that measures the opportunity that is lost or sacrificed when the choice of one course of action requires that an alternative course of action is given up. Consider the situation where a student is contemplating taking a gap year overseas after completing his or her studies. Assume

REAL WORLD VIEWS 2.3

We must stop falling into the 'sunk costs' fallacy

An article written by Ben Chu published in *The Independent* newspaper in 2016 demonstrated why the classical economic view of humans as rational decision-makers is often very wide of the mark. When individuals evaluate a financial decision, when a business leader decides whether or not to continue with an investment project, when a politician decides on a policy, they are all supposed to weigh up the costs and benefits dispassionately. And those decisions are supposed to be made on the basis of future potential costs and benefits, not costs from the past. Anything spent to get to that point of decision should be irrelevant. They are sunk costs which cannot make a project a better or worse proposition.

Nevertheless, we find it very hard to avoid looking back. Business leaders will often plough on with dubious investments because they are so emotionally invested in the project. Fund managers have a tendency to hold on to bad company investments that they spent a great deal of time and effort researching. Football managers will play the hugely expensive striker they bought, even when the player is obviously misfiring.

Managers are often unable to make the decisions to scrap projects that are already up and running in order to cut their losses. For example, the sunk costs fallacy draws attention to how Sadiq Khan, the Mayor of London, originally opposed the construction of a new £175m Garden Bridge across the Thames but later changed his mind because the money [spent on the design] is spent. Cancelling would mean we lose that money and have nothing.

This kind of behaviour is hard-wired into our psyches but nevertheless we should recognize when the sunk costs fallacy is leading us seriously astray.

Questions

1 What are the relevant costs and benefits relating to the Garden Bridge?

2 Why might managers be reluctant to abandon loss-making projects?

Reference

Chu, B. (2016) *We must stop falling into the 'sunk costs' fallacy*, Independent Print Ltd, London (UK). www.search.proquest.com/docview/178145 8259?accountid=11526

EXAMPLE 2.2

A company has an opportunity to obtain a contract for the production of a special component. This component will require 100 hours of processing on machine X. Machine X is working at full capacity on the production of product A, and the only way in which the contract can be fulfilled is by reducing the output of product A. This will result in a lost profit contribution of £200. The contract will also result in *additional* variable costs of £1000.

If the company takes on the contract, it will sacrifice a profit contribution of £200 from the lost output of product A. This represents an opportunity cost, and should be included as part of the cost when negotiating for the contract. The contract price should at least cover the additional costs of £1000 plus the £200 opportunity cost to ensure that the company will be better off in the short term by accepting the contract.

that the student has an offer of a job on completion of his/her studies. The lost salary is an opportunity cost of choosing the gap year that must be taken into account when considering the financial implications of the decision. For a further illustration of an opportunity cost you should now look at Example 2.2.

Opportunity costs cannot normally be recorded in the accounting system since they do not involve cash outlays. They also only apply to the use of scarce resources. Where resources are not scarce, no sacrifice exists from using these resources. In Example 2.2, if machine X were operating at 80 per cent of its potential capacity and the decision to accept the contract would not have resulted in reduced production of product A, there would have been no loss of revenue, and the opportunity cost would be zero.

Opportunity costs are of vital importance for decision-making. If no alternative use of resources exists then the opportunity cost is zero, but if resources have an alternative use, and are scarce, then an opportunity cost does exist.

INCREMENTAL AND MARGINAL COSTS

Incremental costs, which are also called **differential costs**, are the difference between the costs of each alternative action that is being considered. For example, a university is evaluating the financial implications of increasing student numbers by 20 per cent. The two alternatives are:

1 No increase in the number of students.

2 A 20 per cent increase in the number of students.

If alternative 2 is chosen, the university will have to increase its budget for full-time lecturers on permanent contracts by £150000 per annum. It will also need to employ additional part-time lecturers at a cost of £15000 (300 hours at £50 per hour) per annum. The incremental/differential cost between the two alternatives is £165000.

Incremental costs can include both fixed and variable costs. In the example above, the full-time staff represent a fixed cost and the part-time staff represent a variable cost. You will also meet the concept of incremental, or differential, revenues. These are the difference in revenues resulting from each alternative.

If you have studied economics, you may have noticed that incremental costs and revenues are similar in principle to the concept of **marginal cost** and **marginal revenue**. The main difference is that marginal cost/revenue represents the additional cost/revenue of one extra unit of output, whereas

REAL WORLD VIEWS 2.4

Opportunity costs and auto bail-outs

According to Andrew Coyne, the author of an article published in the *National Post* (Canada), the $14 billion in public funds handed out to General Motors and Chrysler by the governments of Canada and Ontario was one of the largest corporate bail-outs in the history of the country. The author claims that the question of opportunity costs (what else might have been done with the same money, what other investments might have been made or jobs created with the $14 billion governments taken out of the capital markets to lend to GM and Chrysler) never came up and that it never does. Instead, the focus tends to be only on the benefits, and that opportunity costs are neither counted nor understood.

Questions

1 Why might opportunity costs not be considered when making decisions?

2 Provide examples of opportunity costs that you might incur.

References

Wired (2011) Homeland Security Junks billion dollar 'virtual fence'. Available at www.wired.com /danger room/2011/01/homeland-security-junks -its-sensorladen-border-fence/

RTÉ News (2009) Electronic voting system to be scrapped, 23 April. Available at www.rte.ie /news/2009/0423/evoting.html

---

incremental cost/revenue represents the additional cost/revenue resulting from a group of additional units of output. Business decisions normally entail identifying the change in costs and revenues arising from comparing two alternative courses of action and where this involves a change in activity, it is likely that this will involve multiple, rather than single, units of activity.

REAL WORLD VIEWS 2.5

Marginal costs of downloadable products

A distinguishing feature of today's digital technology is that it is characterized by zero (or near-zero) marginal costs. Once you've made the investment needed to create a digital good, it costs next to nothing to roll out and distribute millions of copies. Software, e-books and music are increasingly available as downloadable products. Each software, book or music download has no marginal cost. As download purchases are typically fully automated, there are no labour costs. Also, as the software development, publishing or music production costs are all in the past (i.e. sunk costs), there are no material or component type costs. There are, of course, fixed costs incurred with running servers and other components of the technology behind downloadable software and other media. Compare this with a purchase of an item of clothing from a leading high street retail outlet such as Zara. The purchase in this case is processed by a member of staff at the store. Going back along the supply chain, there may be logistical or delivery costs and, of course, the labour and material cost of the item of clothing itself.

Questions

1 Do you agree the marginal cost of downloaded software or music is nil?

2 What marginal costs, if any, might be incurred by the provider of the servers where software/music is downloaded from?

References

Prodham, B. 'The marginal cost of software', Enterprise Irregulars Blog, available at www.enterpriseirregulars .com/31274/the-marginal-cost-of-software Naughton, J. (2015), 'How Amazon took control of the cloud', *The Observer*, 4 November 2015 Guardian News & Media Limited, London (UK). search.proquest.com /docview/1729584646?accountid=11526

THE COST AND MANAGEMENT ACCOUNTING INFORMATION SYSTEM

In the previous chapter, we noted that a cost and management accounting information system should generate information to meet the following requirements:

1 to allocate costs between cost of goods sold and inventories for internal and external profit measurement and inventory valuation;

2 to provide relevant information to help managers make better decisions;

3 to provide information for planning, control and performance measurement.

Modern information technology uses bar coding to gather cost information at source that is appropriately coded and classified to establish a database that enables data to be stored in a coherent way. Database software is now available from companies such as Oracle, Microsoft and IBM that enables relevant cost information to be extracted in different ways to meet each of the above requirements according to the specific needs of the different users of cost information. A suitable coding system enables costs to be accumulated by the required *cost objects* (such as products or services, departments, responsibility centres, distribution channels, etc.) and also to be classified by appropriate *categories of expense* (e.g. direct materials, direct labour and overheads) and also by *cost behaviour* (i.e. fixed and variable costs). In practice, direct material costs will be accumulated by each individual type of material, direct labour costs by different grades of labour and overhead costs by different categories of indirect expenses (e.g. rent, depreciation, supervision, etc.).

For *inventory valuation* in a manufacturing organization, the costs of all partly completed products (i.e. work in progress) and unsold finished products can be extracted from the database to ascertain the total cost assigned to inventories. The cost of goods sold that is deducted from sales revenues to compute the profit for the period can also be extracted by summing the manufacturing costs of all those products that have been sold during the period. We shall consider this process in more detail in Chapters 3 and 4.

Future costs, rather than past costs, are required for *decision-making*. Therefore, costs extracted from the database should be adjusted for anticipated price changes. Where a company sells many products or services their profitability should be monitored at regular intervals so that potentially unprofitable products can be highlighted for a more detailed study of their future viability. This information is extracted from the database with costs reported by categories of expenses and divided into their fixed and variable elements. In Chapter 10, we shall focus in more detail on product/segmented profitability analysis.

For *cost control and performance measurement*, costs and revenues must be traced to the individuals who are responsible for incurring them. This system is known as responsibility accounting. Responsibility accounting involves the creation of responsibility centres. A responsibility centre is an organization unit or part of a business for whose performance a manager is held accountable. At this stage, it may be easier for you to consider responsibility centres as being equivalent to separate departments within an organization. Responsibility accounting enables accountability for financial results and outcomes to be allocated to individuals (typically, heads of departments) throughout the organization. Performance reports are produced at regular intervals for each responsibility centre. The reports are generated by extracting costs from the database analysed by responsibility centres and cost category divided into controllable costs that can be influenced by the manager of the responsibility centre and those uncontrollable costs that cannot be influenced by the manager. Actual costs for each cost item listed on the performance report should be compared with budgeted costs so that those costs that do not conform to plan can be pinpointed and investigated. We examine responsibility accounting in more detail in Chapter 16.

SUMMARY

The following items relate to the learning objectives listed at the beginning of the chapter.

- **Explain why it is necessary to understand the meaning of different cost terms.**

The term 'cost' has multiple meanings and different types of cost are used in different situations. Therefore, a preceding term must be added to clarify the assumptions that underlie the measurement. A knowledge of cost and management accounting depends on a clear understanding of the terminology it uses.

- **Define and illustrate a cost object.**

A cost object is any activity for which a separate measurement of cost is required. In other words, managers often want to know the cost of something and the 'thing' that they want to know the cost of is a cost object. Examples of cost objects include the cost of a new product, the cost of operating a sales outlet, the cost of operating a specific machine and the cost of providing a service for a client.

- **Explain the meaning of each of the key terms highlighted in bold type in this chapter.**

You should check your understanding of each of the terms or concepts highlighted in bold by referring to the Key terms and concepts section.

- **Explain why in the short term some costs and revenues are not relevant for decision-making.**

In the short term, some costs and revenues may remain unchanged for all alternatives under consideration. For example, if you wish to determine the costs of driving to work in your own car or using public transport, the cost of the road fund taxation licence and insurance will remain the same for both alternatives, assuming that you intend to keep your car for leisure purposes. Therefore, the costs of these items are not relevant for assisting you in your decision to travel to work by public transport or in your own car. Costs that remain unchanged for all alternatives under consideration are not relevant for decision-making.

- **Describe the three purposes for which cost information is required.**

A cost and management accounting system should generate information to meet the following requirements:

(a) to allocate costs between cost of goods sold and inventories for internal and external profit reporting and inventory valuation;

(b) to provide relevant information to help managers make better decisions;

(c) to provide information for planning, control and performance measurement.

A database should be maintained with costs appropriately coded or classified, so that relevant information can be extracted for meeting each of the above requirements.

KEY TERMS AND CONCEPTS

Avoidable costs Costs that may be saved by not adopting a given alternative.

Conversion cost The sum of direct labour and manufacturing overhead costs; it is the cost of converting raw materials into finished products.

Cost allocation The process of assigning costs to cost objects where a direct measure of the resources consumed by these cost objects does not exist.

Cost object Any activity for which a separate measurement of costs is desired.

Differential costs The difference between the costs of each alternative action under consideration, also known as incremental costs.

Direct labour costs Labour costs that can be specifically and exclusively identified with a particular cost object.

Direct material costs Material costs that can be specifically and exclusively identified with a particular cost object.

Fixed costs Costs that remain constant for a specified time period and which are not affected by the volume of activity.

Incremental costs The difference between the costs of each alternative action under consideration, also known as differential costs.

Indirect costs Costs that cannot be identified specifically and exclusively with a given cost object, also known as overheads.

Irrelevant costs and revenues Future costs and revenues that will not be affected by a decision.

Marginal cost The additional cost of one extra unit of output.

Marginal revenue The additional revenue from one extra unit of output.

Mixed costs Costs that contain both a fixed and a variable component, also known as semi-variable costs.

Opportunity costs Costs that measure the opportunity that is sacrificed when the choice of one course of action requires that an alternative is given up.

Overheads Costs that cannot be identified specifically and exclusively with a given cost object, also known as indirect costs.

Period costs Costs that are not included in the inventory valuation of goods and which are treated as expenses for the period in which they are incurred.

Prime cost The sum of all direct manufacturing costs.

Product costs Costs that are identified with goods purchased or produced for resale and which are attached to products and included in the inventory valuation of goods.

Relevant costs and revenues Future costs and revenues that will be changed by a decision.

Responsibility accounting Accounting that involves tracing costs and revenues to responsibility centres.

Responsibility centre A unit or department within an organization for whose performance a manager is held responsible.

Semi-fixed costs Costs that remain fixed within specified activity levels for a given amount of time but which eventually increase or decrease by a constant amount at critical activity levels; also known as step-fixed costs.

Semi-variable costs Costs that contain both a fixed and a variable component, also known as mixed costs.

Step-fixed costs Costs that remain fixed within specified activity levels for a given amount of time but which eventually increase or decrease by a constant amount at critical activity levels; also known as semi-fixed costs.

Sunk costs Costs that have been incurred by a decision made in the past and that cannot be changed by any decision that will be made in the future.

Unavoidable costs Costs that cannot be saved, whether or not an alternative is adopted.

Variable costs Costs that vary in direct proportion to the volume of activity.

RECOMMENDED READING

This chapter has explained the meaning of important terms that you will encounter when reading this book. For a more comprehensive description and detailed explanation of various cost terms, you should refer to the Chartered Institute of Management Accountants' Official Terminology (2005).

KEY EXAMINATION POINTS

First year management accounting course examinations frequently involve short essay questions requiring you to describe various cost terms or to discuss the concept that different costs are required for different purposes (see Review problems 2.20–2.26 for examples). It is therefore important that you understand all of the cost terms that have been described in this chapter. In particular, you should be able to explain the context within which a cost term is normally used. For example, a cost such as wages paid to casual labourers will be classified as indirect for inventory valuation purposes, but as a direct charge to a responsibility centre or department for cost control purposes. A common error is for students to produce a very short answer, but you must be prepared to expand your answer and to include various situations within which the use of a cost term is appropriate. Always make sure your answer includes illustrations of cost terms. Multiple choice questions are also often set on topics included in this chapter. Review problems 2.15–2.19 are typical examples of such questions. You should now attempt these and compare your answers with the solutions.

ASSESSMENT MATERIAL

The review questions are short questions that enable you to assess your understanding of the main topics included in the chapter. The numbers in parentheses provide you with the page numbers to refer to if you cannot answer a specific question.

The review problems are more complex and require you to relate and apply the content to various business problems. The problems are graded by their level of difficulty. Solutions to review problems that are not preceded by the term 'IM' are provided in a separate section at the end of the book. Solutions to problems preceded by the term 'IM' are provided in the Instructor's Manual accompanying this book that can be downloaded from the lecturer's digital support resources. Additional review problems with fully worked solutions are provided in the *Student Manual* that accompanies this book.

REVIEW QUESTIONS

2.1 Define the meaning of the term 'cost object' and provide three examples of cost objects. (pp. 22–23)

2.2 Distinguish between a direct and indirect cost. (pp. 23–24)

2.3 Describe how a given direct cost item can be both a direct and indirect cost. (p. 25)

2.4 Provide examples of each of the following: (a) direct labour, (b) indirect labour, (c) direct materials, (d) indirect materials and (e) indirect expenses. (p. 24)

2.5 Explain the meaning of the terms: (a) prime cost, (b) overheads and (c) cost allocations. (pp. 25–26)

2.6 Distinguish between product costs and period costs. (pp. 26–28)

2.7 Provide examples of decisions that require knowledge of how costs and revenues vary with different levels of activity. (pp. 28–29)

2.8 Explain the meaning of each of the following terms: (a) variable costs, (b) fixed costs, (c) semi-fixed costs and (d) semi-variable costs. Provide examples of costs for each of the four categories. (pp. 29–31)

2.9 Distinguish between relevant (avoidable) and irrelevant (unavoidable) costs and provide examples of each type of cost. (pp. 31–32)

2.10 Explain the meaning of the term 'sunk cost'. (p. 33)

2.11 Distinguish between incremental and marginal costs. (pp. 34–35)

2.12 What is an opportunity cost? Give some examples. (pp. 33–34)

2.13 Explain responsibility accounting. (p. 36)

REVIEW PROBLEMS

2.14 **Basic.** Classify each of the following as being usually fixed (F), variable (V), semi-fixed (SF) or semi-variable (SV):

(i)   direct labour;
(ii) depreciation of machinery;
(iii) factory rental;
(iv) supplies and other indirect materials;
(v)   advertising;
(vi) maintenance of machinery;
(vii) factory manager's salary;
(viii) supervisory personnel;
(ix) royalty payments.

2.15 **Basic.** The audit fee paid by a manufacturing company would be classified by that company as:

(a) A production overhead cost;
(b) A selling and distribution cost;
(c) A research and development cost;
(d) An administration cost.

CIMA Fundamentals of Management Accounting

2.16 **Basic.** Which ONE of the following costs would NOT be classified as a production overhead cost in a food processing company?

(a) The cost of renting the factory building;
(b) The salary of the factory manager;
(c) The depreciation of equipment located in the materials store;
(d) The cost of ingredients.

CIMA Fundamentals of Management Accounting

2.17 **Basic.** Which one of the following would be classified as indirect labour?

(a) assembly workers on a car production line;
(b) bricklayers in a house building company;

(c) machinists in a factory producing clothes;
(d) forklift truck drivers in the stores of an engineering company.

ACCA 1.2: Financial Information for Management

2.18 **Basic.** Fixed costs are conventionally deemed to be:

(a) constant per unit of output;
(b) constant in total when production volume changes;
(c) outside the control of management;
(d) those unaffected by inflation.

CIMA Stage 1 Cost Accounting

2.19 **Intermediate.** A manufacturing company has four types of cost (identified as T1, T2, T3 and T4). The total cost for each type at two different production levels is:

Cost type	Total cost for 125 units (£)	Total cost for 180 units (£)
T1	1 000	1 440
T2	1 750	2 520
T3	2 475	2 826
T4	3 225	4 644

Which cost types would be classified as being semi-variable?

(a) T1
(b) T2
(c) T3
(d) T4

ACCA Financial Information for Management

2.20 Intermediate. Prepare a report for the managing director of your company explaining how costs may be classified by their behaviour, with particular reference to the effects both on total and on unit costs. Your report should:

   (i) say why it is necessary to classify costs by their behaviour; and

   (ii) be illustrated by sketch graphs within the body of the report.   *(15 marks)*

CIMA Stage 1 Accounting

2.21 Intermediate. Cost classifications used in costing include:

   (i) period costs;
   (ii) product costs;
   (iii) variable costs;
   (iv) opportunity costs.

Required:
Explain each of these classifications, with examples of the types of cost that may be included.   *(17 marks)*

ACCA Level 1 Costing

2.22 Intermediate.

  (a) Describe the role of the cost accountant in a manufacturing organization.   *(8 marks)*

  (b) Explain whether you agree with each of the following statements:

   (i) 'All direct costs are variable.'
   (ii) 'Variable costs are controllable and fixed costs are not.'
   (iii) 'Sunk costs are irrelevant when providing decision making information.'   *(9 marks)*

ACCA Level 1 Costing

2.23 Intermediate. 'Costs may be classified in a variety of ways according to their nature and the information needs of management.' Explain and discuss this statement, illustrating with examples of the classifications required for different purposes.   *(22 marks)*

ICSA Management Accounting

2.24 Intermediate. It is commonly suggested that a management accounting system should be capable of supplying different measures of cost for different purposes. You are required to set out the main types of purpose for which cost information may be required in a business organization and to discuss the alternative measures of cost that might be appropriate for each purpose.

ICAEW Management Accounting

2.25 Intermediate. *Opportunity* cost and *sunk* cost are among the concepts of cost commonly discussed. You are required:

   (i) to define these terms precisely;   *(4 marks)*
   (ii) to suggest for each of them situations in which the concept might be applied;   *(4 marks)*
   (iii) to assess briefly the significance of each of the concepts.   *(4 marks)*

ICAEW P2 Management Accounting

2.26 Intermediate. Distinguish between, and provide an illustration of:

   (i) 'avoidable' and 'unavoidable' costs;
   (ii) 'cost centres' and 'cost units'.   *(8 marks)*

ACCA Foundation Paper 3

2.27 Intermediate: Cost behaviour.

Data	(£)
Cost of motor car	5500
Trade-in price after two years or 60000 miles is expected to be	1500
Maintenance – six-monthly service costing	60

Data	(£)
Spares/replacement parts, per 1000 miles	20
Vehicle licence, per annum	80
Insurance, per annum	150
Tyre replacements after 25000 miles, four at £37.50 each	
Petrol, per gallon	1.90

Average mileage from one gallon is 25 miles.

  (a) From the above data, you are required:

   (i) To prepare a schedule to be presented to management showing for the mileages of 5000, 10000, 15000 and 30000 miles per annum:

    1 total variable cost;
    2 total fixed cost;
    3 total cost;
    4 variable cost per mile (in pence to nearest penny);
    5 fixed cost per mile (in pence to nearest penny);
    6 total cost per mile (in pence to nearest penny).

If, in classifying the costs, you consider that some can be treated as either variable or fixed, state the assumption(s) on which your answer is based together with brief supporting reason(s).

   (ii) On graph paper, plot the information given in your answer to (i) above for the costs listed against (1), (2), (3) and (6).
   (iii) To read off from your graph(s) in (ii) and state the approximate total costs applicable to 18000 miles and 25000 miles and the total cost per mile at these two mileages.

  (b) 'The more miles you travel, the cheaper it becomes.' Comment briefly on this statement.   *(25 marks)*

CIMA Cost Accounting 1

2.28 Intermediate: Sunk and opportunity costs for decision-making. Mrs Johnston has taken out a lease on a shop for a down payment of £5000. Additionally, the rent under the lease amounts to £5000 per annum. If the lease is cancelled, the initial payment of £5000 is forfeit. Mrs Johnston plans to use the shop for the sale of clothing, and has estimated operations for the next 12 months as follows:

	(£)	(£)
Sales	115000	
Less Value-added tax (VAT)	15000	
Sales less VAT		100000
Cost of goods sold	50000	
Wages and wage related costs	12000	
Rent including down payment	10000	
Rates, heating, lighting and insurance	13000	
Audit, legal and general expenses	2000	
		87000
Net profit before tax		13000

In the figures, no provision has been made for the cost of Mrs Johnston but it is estimated that one half of her time will be devoted to the business. She is undecided whether to continue with her plans, because she knows that she can sublet the shop to a friend for a monthly rent of £550 if she does not use the shop herself.

You are required to:

  (a) (i) explain and identify the 'sunk' and 'opportunity' costs in the situation depicted above;
    (ii) state what decision Mrs Johnston should make according to the information given, supporting your conclusion with a financial statement;   *(11 marks)*

(b) explain the meaning and use of 'notional' (or 'imputed') costs and quote two supporting examples.   *(4 marks)*

CIMA Foundation Cost Accounting 1

IM2.1 **Basic: Cost classification.** For the relevant cost data in items (1)–(7), indicate which of the following is the best classification.

(a) sunk cost;
(b) incremental cost;
(c) variable cost;
(d) fixed cost;
(e) semi-variable cost;
(f) semi-fixed cost;
(g) controllable cost;
(h) non-controllable cost;
(i) opportunity cost.

1 A company is considering selling an old machine. The machine has a book value of £20 000. In evaluating the decision to sell the machine, the £20 000 is a _____.

2 As an alternative to the old machine, the company can rent a new one. It will cost £3000 a year. In analysing the cost-volume behaviour the rental is a _____.

3 To run the firm's machines, there are two alternative courses of action. One is to pay the operators a base salary plus a small amount per unit produced. This makes the total cost of the operators a _____.

4 As an alternative, the firm can pay the operators a flat salary. It would then use one machine when volume is low, two when it expands, and three during peak periods. This means that the total operator cost would now be a _____.

5 The machine mentioned in (1) could be sold for £8000. If the firm considers retaining and using it, the £8000 is a _____.

6 If the firm wishes to use the machine any longer, it must be repaired. For the decision to retain the machine, the repair cost is a _____.

7 The machine is charged to the foreman of each department at a rate of £3000 a year. In evaluating the foreman, the charge is a _____.

IM2.2 **Basic: Cost classification.** A company manufactures and retails clothing. You are required to group the costs that are listed below and numbered (1)–(20) into the following classifications (each cost is intended to belong to only one classification):

(i)   direct materials;
(ii) direct labour;
(iii) direct expenses;
(iv) indirect production overhead;
(v)   research and development costs;
(vi) selling and distribution costs;
(vii) administration costs;
(viii) finance costs.

1 lubricant for sewing machines;
2 floppy disks for general office computer;
3 maintenance contract for general office photocopying machine;
4 telephone rental plus metered calls;
5 interest on bank overdraft;
6 Performing Rights Society charge for music broadcast throughout the factory;
7 market research undertaken prior to a new product launch;
8 wages of security guards for factory;
9 carriage on purchase of basic raw material;
10 royalty payable on number of units of product XY produced;
11 road fund licences for delivery vehicles;
12 parcels sent to customers;
13 cost of advertising products on television;
14 audit fees;
15 chief accountant's salary;
16 wages of operatives in the cutting department;
17 cost of painting advertising slogans on delivery vans;
18 wages of storekeepers in materials store;
19 wages of forklift truck drivers who handle raw materials;
20 developing a new product in the laboratory.   *(10 marks)*

CIMA Cost Accounting 1

IM2.3 **Intermediate: Analysis of costs by behaviour for decision-making.** The Northshire Hospital Trust operates two types of specialist X-ray scanning machine, XR1 and XR50. Details for the next period are estimated as follows:

Machine	XR1	XR50
Running hours	1 100	2 000
	(£)	(£)
Variable running costs (excluding plates)	27 500	64 000
Fixed costs	20 000	97 500

A brain scan is normally carried out on machine type XR1: this task uses special X-ray plates costing £40 each and takes four hours of machine time. Because of the nature of the process, around 10 per cent of the scans produce blurred and therefore useless results.

Required:

(a) Calculate the cost of a satisfactory brain scan on machine type XR1.   *(7 marks)*

(b) Brain scans can also be done on machine type XR50 and would take only 1.8 hours per scan with a reduced reject rate of 6 per cent. However, the cost of the X-ray plates would be £55 per scan.

Required:
Advise which type should be used, assuming sufficient capacity is available on both types of machine.   *(8 marks)*

CIMA Stage 1 Cost Accounting

IM2.4 **Intermediate: Product cost calculation.** From the information given below you are required to:

(a) Prepare a standard cost sheet for one unit and enter on the standard cost sheet the costs to show sub-totals for:

(i)   prime cost;
(ii) variable production cost;
(iii) total production cost;
(iv) total cost.

(b) Calculate the selling price per unit allowing for a profit of 15 per cent of the selling price.
The following data are given:
Budgeted output for the year 9800 units
Standard details for one unit:
Direct materials 40 square metres at £5.30 per square metre
Direct wages:
Bonding department 48 hours at £12.50 per hour
Finishing department 30 hours at £7.60 per hour
Budgeted costs and hours per annum:
Variable overhead:

	(£)	(hours)
Bonding department	375 000	500 000
Finishing department	150 000	300 000

Fixed overhead:

	(£)	(hours)
Production	392 000	
Selling and distribution	196 000	
Administration	98 000	

(15 marks)

CIMA Cost Accounting 1

PART TWO

COST ACCUMULATION FOR INVENTORY VALUATION AND PROFIT MEASUREMENT

This section focuses mainly on assigning costs to products to divide costs incurred during a period between costs of goods sold and the closing inventory valuation. The extent to which product costs accumulated for inventory valuation and profit measurement should be adjusted for meeting decision-making, cost control and performance measurement requirements is also briefly considered. Inventory valuation is a topic that is mainly applicable to manufacturing organizations but some service organizations do have work in progress inventories. Because inventory valuation is a major issue in manufacturing organizations, most of the content in this section is related to the manufacturing environment.

Chapter 3 aims to provide you with an understanding of how costs are assigned to cost objects. In particular, the chapter focuses on the assignment of indirect costs using traditional and activity-based systems. In Chapter 4, the emphasis is on the accounting entries necessary to record transactions within a job-order costing system. The issues relating to a cost accumulation procedure for a process costing system are described in Chapter 5. This is a system that is applicable to industries that produce many units of the same product during a particular period. In Chapter 6, the problems associated with calculating product costs in those industries that produce joint and by-products are discussed. Chapter 7 is concerned with the alternative accounting methods of assigning fixed manufacturing overheads to products and their implications for profit measurement and inventory valuation.

The topics covered in the chapters in Section 2 focus mainly on technical aspects relating to how costs are accumulated for inventory valuation and profit measurement. Apart from Chapter 3 the content relates mainly to readers who are pursuing specialist accounting courses. If you are not pursuing a specialist accounting course, your syllabus is unlikely to require an understanding of the content covered in Chapters 4–7 and it is likely that only Chapter 3 will be relevant to you. It is therefore important that you check your course syllabus prior to determining which chapters within this section are relevant to you.

3

COST ASSIGNMENT

LEARNING OBJECTIVES After studying this chapter, you should be able to:

- distinguish between cause-and-effect and arbitrary cost allocations;

- explain why different cost information is required for different purposes;

- describe how cost systems differ in terms of their level of sophistication;

- understand the factors influencing the choice of an optimal cost system;

- explain why departmental overhead rates should be used in preference to a single blanket overhead rate;

- construct an overhead analysis sheet and calculate cost centre allocation rates;

- distinguish between traditional and activity-based costing (ABC) systems and calculate product costs derived from an ABC system;

- justify why budgeted overhead rates should be used in preference to actual overhead rates;

- calculate and explain the accounting treatment of the under-/over-recovery of overheads;

- explain how the cost assignment approach described for manufacturing organizations can be extended to non-manufacturing organizations.

In the previous chapter, it was pointed out that companies need cost and management accounting systems to perform a number of different functions. In this chapter, we are going to concentrate on two of these functions – they are (i) allocating costs between cost of goods sold and inventories for internal and external profit reporting and (ii) providing relevant decision-making information for distinguishing between profitable and unprofitable activities.

In order to perform the above functions, a cost accumulation system is required that assigns costs to cost objects. The aim of this chapter is to provide you with an understanding of how costs are accumulated and assigned to cost objects. You should have remembered from the previous chapter that a cost object is anything for which a separate measurement of cost is desired. Typical cost objects include products, services, customers and locations. In this chapter, we shall initially assume that products are the cost object. In particular, we shall concentrate on how costs are assigned to products in manufacturing firms that produce unique individual products or unique batches of products and where the products or batches of products incur different costs resulting in the need to keep track of the cost of each product or batch. This cost assignment system is referred to as a job-order costing system. Our initial focus is also cost assignment for allocating costs between cost of goods sold and inventories for profit reporting. Later in the chapter we shall look at how the approaches that have been described for inventory (stock) valuations in manufacturing organizations can be applied to non-manufacturing organizations. We shall also consider how they can be adapted to providing decision-making information for distinguishing between profitable and unprofitable activities.

We begin by explaining how the cost assignment process differs for direct and indirect costs.

ASSIGNMENT OF DIRECT AND INDIRECT COSTS

Costs that are assigned to cost objects can be divided into two categories – direct costs and indirect costs. Sometimes the term overheads is used instead of indirect costs. Direct costs can be accurately traced to cost objects because they can be specifically and exclusively traced to a particular cost object whereas indirect costs cannot. Where a cost can be directly assigned to a cost object the term direct cost tracing is used. In contrast, direct cost tracing cannot be applied to indirect costs because they are usually common to several cost objects. Indirect costs are therefore assigned to cost objects using cost allocations.

A cost allocation is the process of assigning costs when the quantity of resources consumed by a particular cost object cannot be directly measured. Cost allocations involve the use of surrogate rather than direct measures. For example, consider an activity such as receiving incoming materials. Assuming that the cost of receiving materials is strongly influenced by the number of receipts, then costs can be allocated to products (i.e. the cost object) based on the number of material receipts each product requires. The basis that is used to allocate costs to cost objects (i.e. the number of material receipts in our example) is called an allocation base or cost driver. If 20 per cent of the total number of receipts for a period were required for a particular product then 20 per cent of the total costs of receiving incoming materials would be allocated to that product. Assuming that the product were discontinued, and not replaced, we would expect action to be taken to reduce the resources required for receiving materials by 20 per cent.

In the above illustration, the allocation base is assumed to be a significant determinant of the cost of receiving incoming materials. Where allocation bases are significant determinants of costs the terms cause-and-effect allocations or driver tracing are used. Where a cost allocation base is used that is not a significant determinant of its cost, the term arbitrary allocation is used. An example of an arbitrary allocation would be if direct labour hours were used as the allocation base to allocate the costs of materials receiving. If a labour intensive product required a large proportion of direct labour hours (say 30 per cent) but few material receipts, it would be allocated with a large proportion of the costs of material receiving. The allocation would be an inaccurate assignment of the resources consumed by the product. Furthermore, if the product were discontinued, and not replaced, the cost of the material receiving activity would not decline by 30 per cent because the allocation base is not a significant determinant of the costs of the materials receiving activity. Arbitrary allocations are therefore likely to result in inaccurate allocations of indirect costs to cost objects.

Figure 3.1 provides a summary of the three methods of assigning costs to cost objects. You can see that direct costs are assigned to cost objects using direct cost tracing whereas indirect costs are assigned using either cause-and-effect or arbitrary cost allocations. For accurate assignment of indirect costs to cost objects, cause-and-effect allocations should be used. Two types of system can be used to assign costs to cost objects. They are direct and absorption costing systems. A direct costing system (also known as a marginal or variable costing system) assigns only direct costs to cost objects whereas an absorption costing system assigns both direct and indirect costs to cost objectives. Absorption costing systems can be sub-divided into traditional costing systems and activity-based costing (ABC) systems. Traditional costing systems were developed in the early 1900s and are still widely used today. They tend to use arbitrary cost allocations. ABC systems began to be implemented only in the 1990s.

FIGURE 3.1

FIGURE 3.1

Cost assignment methods

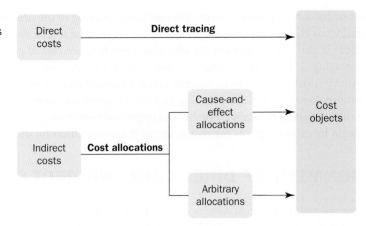

Absorption costing used in practice

A questionnaire survey based on the responses of 272 practising UK management accountants who were members of the Chartered Institute of Management Accountants (CIMA) revealed that approximately 81 per cent of the respondent firms used absorption costing techniques to allocate overheads to products. The survey also revealed that absorption costing was used to a greater degree in larger companies. Only 58 per cent of the smaller companies (defined as having less than 50 employees) used absorption costing with the remaining 42 per cent using direct/variable costing.

Questions

1 Why do you think absorption costing is more likely to be used by larger business?

2 What difficulties might be faced by smaller firms who may want to utilize absorption costing?

Reference

Brierley, J.A. (2011) 'A comparison of the product costing practices of large and small-to medium-sized enterprises: A survey of British manufacturing firms', *International Journal of Management* 28(4): 184–195.

One of the major aims of ABC systems is to use mainly cause-and-effect cost allocations and avoid arbitrary allocations. Both cost systems adopt identical approaches to assigning direct costs to cost objects. We shall look at traditional and ABC systems in more detail later in the chapter.

DIFFERENT COSTS FOR DIFFERENT PURPOSES

Manufacturing organizations assign costs to products for two purposes: first, for internal profit measurement and external financial accounting requirements in order to allocate the manufacturing costs incurred during a period between cost of goods sold and inventories; second, to provide useful information for managerial decision-making requirements. In order to meet financial accounting requirements, it may not be necessary to accurately trace costs to *individual* products. Consider a situation where a firm produces 1000 different products and the costs incurred during a period are £10 million. A well-designed product costing system should accurately analyse the £10 million costs incurred between cost of sales and inventories. Let us assume the true figures are £7 million and £3 million. Approximate but inaccurate *individual* product costs may provide a reasonable approximation of how much of the £10 million should be attributed to cost of sales and inventories. Some product costs may be overstated and others may be understated, but this would not matter for financial accounting purposes as long as the *total* of the individual product costs assigned to cost of sales and inventories was approximately £7 million and £3 million.

For decision-making purposes, however, more accurate *individual* product costs are required so that we can distinguish between profitable and unprofitable products. By more accurately measuring the resources consumed by products, or other cost objects, a firm can identify its sources of profits and losses. If the cost system does not capture sufficiently accurately the consumption of resources by products, the reported product costs will be distorted, and there is a danger that managers may drop profitable products or continue production of unprofitable products.

Besides different levels of accuracy, different cost information is required for different purposes. For meeting external financial accounting requirements, financial accounting regulations and legal requirements in most countries require that inventories should be valued at manufacturing cost. Therefore, only manufacturing costs are assigned to products for meeting external financial accounting requirements. For decision-making, non-manufacturing costs must be taken into account and assigned to products. Not all costs, however, may be relevant for decision-making. For example, depreciation of plant and machinery will not be affected by a decision to discontinue a product. Such costs were described in the previous chapter as irrelevant and sunk for decision-making. Thus, depreciation of plant must be assigned to products for inventory valuation but it should not be assigned for discontinuation decisions.

COST–BENEFIT ISSUES AND COST SYSTEMS DESIGN

Until the 1990s most organizations relied on traditional costing systems that had been designed primarily for meeting external financial accounting requirements. These systems were designed decades ago when information processing costs were high and precluded the use of more sophisticated methods of assigning indirect costs to products. Such systems are still widely used today. They rely extensively on arbitrary cost allocations which may not be sufficiently accurate for meeting decision-making requirements.

In the 1990s ABC systems were promoted as a mechanism for more accurately assigning indirect costs to cost objects. Surveys in many countries suggest that between 20 and 30 per cent of the surveyed organizations currently use ABC systems. The majority of organizations, therefore, continue to operate traditional systems. Both traditional and ABC systems vary in their level of sophistication but, as a general rule, traditional systems tend to be simplistic whereas ABC systems tend to be more sophisticated. What determines the chosen level of sophistication of a costing system? The answer is that the choice should be made on costs versus benefits criteria. Simplistic systems are inexpensive to operate, but they are likely to result in inaccurate cost assignments and the reporting of inaccurate costs, which can cause managers to make dangerous mistakes. The end result may be a high cost of errors. Conversely, sophisticated systems are more expensive to operate but they minimize the cost of errors.

Figure 3.2 illustrates the above points with costing systems ranging from simplistic to sophisticated. In practice, cost systems in most organizations are not located at either of these extreme points but are positioned somewhere within the range shown in Figure 3.2. The aim should not be to have the most accurate cost system. Improvements should be made in the level of sophistication of the costing system

FIGURE 3.2
Cost systems – varying levels of sophistication for cost assignment

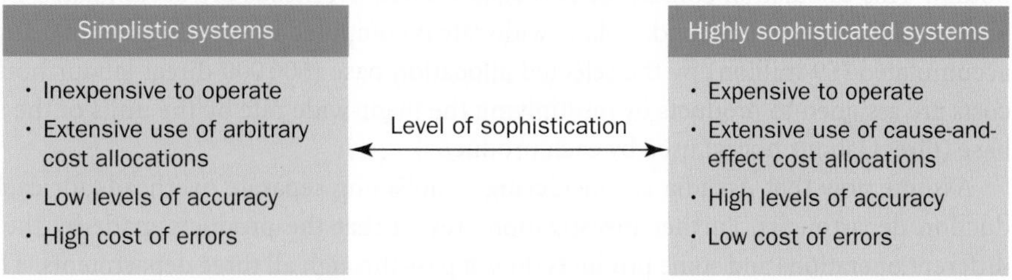

Simplistic systems	Level of sophistication	Highly sophisticated systems
· Inexpensive to operate · Extensive use of arbitrary cost allocations · Low levels of accuracy · High cost of errors	⟵⟶	· Expensive to operate · Extensive use of cause-and-effect cost allocations · High levels of accuracy · Low cost of errors

up to the point where the marginal/incremental cost of improvement equals the marginal/incremental benefit from the improvement.

The optimal cost system for an organization can be influenced by several factors. For example, the optimal costing system will be located towards the extreme left for an organization whose indirect costs are a low percentage of total costs and which also has a fairly standardized product range, all consuming organizational resources in similar proportions. In these circumstances, simplistic systems may not result in the reporting of inaccurate costs. In contrast, the optimal costing system for organizations with a high proportion of indirect costs, whose products consume organizational resources in different proportions, will be located towards the extreme right. More sophisticated costing systems are required to capture the diversity of consumption of organizational resources and accurately assign the high level of indirect costs to different cost objects.

ASSIGNING DIRECT COSTS TO COST OBJECTS

Both simplistic and sophisticated systems accurately assign direct costs to cost objects. Cost assignment merely involves the implementation of suitable data processing procedures to identify and record the resources consumed by cost objects. Consider direct labour. The time spent on providing a service to a specific customer, or manufacturing a specific product, is recorded on source documents, such as time sheets or job cards. Details of the customer's account number, job number or the product's code are also entered on these documents. The employee's hourly rate of pay is then entered so that the direct labour cost for the employee can be assigned to the appropriate cost object.

For direct materials, the source document is a materials requisition. Details of the materials issued for manufacturing a product, or providing a specific service, are recorded on the materials requisition. The customer's account number, job number or product code is also entered and the items listed on the requisition are priced at their cost of acquisition. The details on the material requisition thus represent the source information for assigning the cost of the materials to the appropriate cost object. A more detailed explanation of this procedure is provided in the next chapter.

In many organizations, the recording procedure for direct costs is computerized using bar coding and other forms of online information recording. The source documents exist only in the form of computer records. Because the assignment of direct costs to cost objects is a straightforward process, whereas the assignment of indirect costs is a more complex process, the remainder of this chapter will focus on indirect cost assignment.

PLANT-WIDE (BLANKET) OVERHEAD RATES

The most simplistic traditional costing system assigns indirect costs (overheads) to cost objects using a single overhead rate for the organization as a whole, known as blanket overhead rate or plant-wide rate. Such a costing system would be located at the extreme left of the level of sophistication shown in Figure 3.2. Let us assume that the total manufacturing overheads for the manufacturing plant of Arcadia are £9 million and that the company has selected direct labour hours as the allocation base for assigning overheads to products. Assuming that the total number of direct labour hours are 600 000 for the period, the plant-wide overhead rate for Arcadia is £15 per direct labour hour (£9 million/600 000 direct labour hours). This calculation consists of two stages. First, overheads are accumulated in one single plant-wide pool for a period. Second, a plant-wide rate is computed by dividing the total amount of overheads accumulated (£9 million) by the selected allocation base (600 000 direct labour hours). The overhead costs are assigned to products by multiplying the plant-wide rate by the units of the selected allocation base (direct labour hours) used by each product.

Assume now that Arcadia is considering establishing separate overheads for each of its three production departments. Further investigations reveal that the products made by the company require different operations and some products do not pass through all three departments. These investigations also indicate that the £9 million total manufacturing overheads and 600 000 direct labour hours can be analysed as follows:

	Department A	Department B	Department C	Total
Overheads	£2 000 000	£6 000 000	£1 000 000	£9 000 000
Direct labour hours	200 000	200 000	200 000	600 000
Overhead rate per direct labour hour	£10	£30	£5	£15

Now consider a situation where product Z requires 20 direct labour hours in department C but does not pass through departments A and B. If a plant-wide overhead rate is used then overheads of £300 (20 hours at £15 per hour) will be allocated to product Z. Contrariwise, if a departmental overhead rate is used, only £100 (20 hours at £5 per hour) would be allocated to product Z. Which method should be used? The logical answer must be to establish separate departmental overhead rates, since product Z only consumes overheads in department C. If the plant-wide overhead rate were applied, all the factory overhead rates would be averaged out and product Z would be indirectly allocated with some of the overheads of department B. This would not be satisfactory, since product Z does not consume any of the resources and this department incurs a large amount of the overhead expenditure.

Where some departments are more 'overhead intensive' than others, products spending more time in these departments should be assigned more overhead costs than those spending less time. Departmental rates capture these possible effects but plant-wide rates do not, because of the averaging process. We can conclude that a plant-wide rate will generally result in the reporting of inaccurate product costs and can only be justified when all products consume departmental overheads in approximately the same proportions (i.e. low product diversity applies). In the above illustration, each department accounts for one-third of the total direct labour hours. If all products spend approximately one-third of their time in each department, a plant-wide overhead rate can safely be used. Consider a situation in which product X spends one hour in each department and product Y spends five hours in each department. Overheads of £45 and £225 respectively would be allocated to products X and Y using either a plant-wide rate (three hours at £15 and 15 hours at £15) or separate departmental overhead rates. However, if a diverse product range is produced with products spending different proportions of time in each department, separate departmental overhead rates should be established.

Surveys indicate that less than 5 per cent of the surveyed organizations use a single plant-wide overhead rate. In Scandinavia, only 5 per cent of the Finnish companies (Lukka and Granlund, 1996), one Norwegian company (Bjornenak, 1997b) and none of the Swedish companies sampled (Ask, Ax and Jonsson, 1996) used a single plant-wide rate. Zero usage of plant-wide rates was also reported from a survey of Greek companies (Ballas and Venieris, 1996). In a more recent study of UK organizations, Al-Omiri and Drury (2007) reported that a plant-wide rate was used by 4 per cent of the surveyed organizations.

THE TWO-STAGE ALLOCATION PROCESS

It is apparent from the previous section that separate departmental overhead rates should normally be established. To establish departmental overhead rates, an approach known as the two-stage allocation process is used. This process applies to assigning costs to other cost objects, besides products, and is applicable to all organizations that assign indirect costs to cost objects. The approach applies to both traditional and ABC systems.

The two-stage allocation process for traditional and ABC systems is illustrated in Figure 3.3. You can see in the upper section for a traditional costing system that in the *first stage,* overheads are assigned to cost centres (also called cost pools). The terms cost centres or cost pools are used to describe a location to which overhead costs are initially assigned. Normally cost centres consist of departments, but in some cases they consist of smaller segments such as separate work centres within a department.

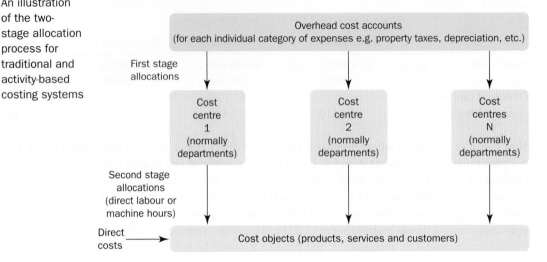

(a) Traditional costing systems

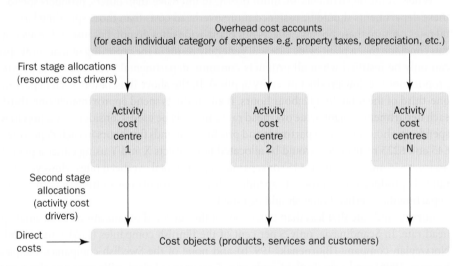

(b) Activity-based costing systems

In the *second stage,* the costs accumulated in the cost centres are allocated to cost objects using selected allocation bases (you should remember from our discussion earlier that allocation bases are also called cost drivers). Traditional costing systems tend to use a small number of second stage allocation bases, typically direct labour hours or machine hours. In other words, traditional systems assume that direct labour or machine hours have a significant influence in the long term on the level of overhead expenditure. Other allocation bases used to a lesser extent by traditional systems are direct labour cost, direct materials cost and units of output. These methods are described and illustrated in Learning Note 3.1 on the dedicated digital support resources (see Preface for details).

Within the two-stage allocation process, ABC systems (see the lower section of Figure 3.3) differ from traditional systems by having a greater number of cost centres in the first stage and a greater number, and variety, of cost drivers or allocation bases in the second stage. Both systems will be described in more detail later in the chapter.

How many cost centres should a firm establish? If only a small number of cost centres are established it is likely that activities within a cost centre will not be homogeneous and, if the consumption of the activities by products/services within the cost centres varies, activity resource consumption will not be accurately measured. Therefore, in most situations, increasing the number of cost centres increases the accuracy of measuring the indirect costs consumed by cost objects. The choice of the number of cost centres should be based on cost–benefit criteria using the principles described on pages 47–48. A survey by Drury and Tayles (2007) of 170 UK organizations reported that 35 per cent of the organizations used fewer than 11 cost centres whereas 36 per cent used more than 20 cost centres. In terms of the number of different types of second stage cost drivers/allocation bases, 59 per cent of the responding organizations used fewer than three.

AN ILLUSTRATION OF THE TWO-STAGE PROCESS FOR A TRADITIONAL COSTING SYSTEM

We shall now use Example 3.1 to provide a more detailed illustration of the two-stage allocation process for a traditional costing system. Note that a manufacturing company is used to illustrate the process. We shall also assume that the aim is to calculate product costs that are required for inventory valuation and profit measurement purposes. To keep the illustration manageable it is assumed that the company has only five cost centres – machine departments X and Y, an assembly department and materials handling and general factory support cost centres. The illustration focuses on manufacturing costs but we shall look at non-manufacturing costs later in the chapter. Applying the two-stage allocation process requires the following four steps:

1 assigning all manufacturing overheads to production and service cost centres;

2 reallocating the costs assigned to service cost centres to production cost centres;

3 computing separate overhead rates for each production cost centre;

4 assigning cost centre overheads to products or other chosen cost objects.

Steps 1 and 2 comprise stage one and steps 3 and 4 relate to the second stage of the two-stage allocation process. Let us now consider each of these steps in detail.

Step 1 – Assigning all manufacturing overheads to production and service cost centres

Using the information given in Example 3.1, our initial objective is to assign all manufacturing overheads to production and service cost centres. To do this requires the preparation of an **overhead analysis sheet**, which is shown in Exhibit 3.1. In most organizations, it will consist only in computer form.

If you look at Example 3.1, you will see that the indirect labour and indirect material costs have been directly traced to cost centres. Although these items cannot be directly assigned to products they can be directly assigned to the cost centres. In other words, they are indirect costs when products are the cost objects, and direct costs when cost centres are the cost object. Therefore they are traced directly to the cost centres shown in the overhead analysis sheet in Exhibit 3.1. The remaining costs shown in Example 3.1 cannot be traced directly to the cost centres and must be allocated to the cost centre using appropriate allocation bases.

The term **first-stage allocation bases** is used to describe allocations at this point. The following list summarizes commonly used first-stage allocation bases:

Cost	Basis of allocation
Property taxes, lighting and heating	Area
Employee-related expenditure:	
works management, works canteen, payroll office	Number of employees
Depreciation and insurance of plant and machinery	Value of items of plant and machinery

EXAMPLE 3.1

The annual overhead costs for the Enterprise Company which has three production centres (two machine centres and one assembly centre) and two service centres (materials procurement and general factory support) are as follows:

	(£)	(£)
Indirect wages and supervision		
Machine centres: X	1 000 000	
Y	1 000 000	
Assembly	1 500 000	
Materials procurement	1 100 000	
General factory support	1 480 000	6 080 000
Indirect materials		
Machine centres: X	500 000	
Y	805 000	
Assembly	105 000	
Materials procurement	0	
General factory support	10 000	1 420 000
Lighting and heating	500 000	
Property taxes	1 000 000	
Insurance of machinery	150 000	
Depreciation of machinery	1 500 000	
Insurance of buildings	250 000	
Salaries of works management	800 000	4 200 000
		11 700 000

The following information is also available:

	Book value of Machinery (£)	Area occupied (sq. metres)	Number of employees	Direct labour hours	Machine hours
Machine shop: X	8 000 000	10 000	300	1 000 000	2 000 000
Y	5 000 000	5 000	200	1 000 000	1 000 000
Assembly	1 000 000	15 000	300	2 000 000	
Stores	500 000	15 000	100		
Maintenance	500 000	5 000	100		
	15 000 000	50 000	1000		

Details of total materials issues (i.e. direct and indirect materials) to the production centres are as follows:

	£
Machine shop X	4 00 0000
Machine shop Y	3 000 000
Assembly	1 000 000
	8 000 000

To allocate the overheads listed above to the production and service centres, we must prepare an overhead analysis sheet, as shown in Exhibit 3.1.

EXHIBIT 3.1 Overhead analysis sheet

| Item of expenditure | Basis of allocation | Total (£) | Production centres | | | Service centres | |
			Machine centre X (£)	Machine centre Y (£)	Assembly (£)	Materials procurement (£)	General factory support (£)
Indirect wage and supervision	Direct	6080000	1000000	1000000	1500000	1100000	1480000
Indirect materials	Direct	1420000	500000	805000	105000		10000
Lighting and heating	Area	500000	100000	50000	150000	150000	50000
Property taxes	Area	1000000	200000	100000	300000	300000	100000
Insurance of machinery	Book value of machinery	150000	80000	50000	10000	5000	5000
Depreciation of machinery	Book value of machinery	1500000	800000	500000	100000	50000	50000
Insurance of buildings	Area	250000	50000	25000	75000	75000	25000
Salaries of works management	Number of employees	800000	240000	160000	240000	80000	80000
Step 1 of stage 1		11700000	2970000	2690000	2480000	1760000	1800000
Reallocation of service centre costs							
Materials procurement	Value of materials issued	—	880000	660000	220000	(1760000)	
General factory support	Direct labour hours	—	450000	450000	900000		(1800000)
Step 2 of stage 1		11700000	4300000	3800000	3600000	—	—
Machine hours and direct labour hours			2000000	1000000	2000000		
Machine hour overhead rate	Step 3		£2.15	£3.80			
Direct labour hour overhead rate	Step 3				£1.80		

Where utility consumption, such as lighting and heating, can be measured by separate meters located in each department, departmental consumption can be measured and the costs directly traced to the user departments.

Applying the allocation bases to the data given in respect of the Enterprise Company in Example 3.1, it is assumed that property taxes, lighting and heating, and insurance of buildings are related to the total floor area of the buildings, and the benefit obtained by each cost centre can therefore be ascertained according to the proportion of floor area which it occupies. The total floor area of the factory shown in Example 3.1 is 50000 square metres; machine centre X occupies 20 per cent of this and machine centre Y a further 10 per cent. Therefore, if you refer to the overhead analysis sheet in

Exhibit 3.1, you will see that 20 per cent of property taxes, lighting and heating and insurance of buildings are allocated to machine centre X, and 10 per cent are allocated to machine centre Y.

The insurance premium paid and depreciation of machinery are generally regarded as being related to the book value of the machinery. Because the book value of machinery for machine centre X is 8/15 of the total book value, and machine centre Y is 5/15 of the total book value, then 8/15 and 5/15 of the insurance and depreciation of machinery is allocated to machine centres X and Y.

It is assumed that the amount of time that works management devotes to each cost centre is related to the number of employees in each centre; since 30 per cent of the total employees are employed in machine centre X, 30 per cent of the salaries of works management will be allocated to this centre.

If you now look at the overhead analysis sheet shown in Exhibit 3.1, you will see in the row labelled 'step 1 of stage 1' that all manufacturing overheads for the Enterprise Company have been assigned to the three production and two service cost centres.

Step 2 – Reallocating the costs assigned to service cost centres to production cost centres

The next step is to reallocate the costs that have been assigned to service cost centres to production cost centres. Service departments (i.e. service cost centres) are those departments that exist to provide services of various kinds to other units within the organization. They are sometimes called support departments. The Enterprise Company has two service centres. They are materials procurement and general factory support which includes activities such as production scheduling and machine maintenance. These service centres render essential services that support the production process, but they do not deal directly with the products. Therefore service centre costs are not allocated to products because products do not pass through these centres. Nevertheless, the costs of providing support services are part of the total product costs and therefore should be assigned to products. To assign costs to products traditional costing systems reallocate service centre costs to production centres that actually work on the product. The method that is chosen to allocate service centre costs to production centre should be related to the benefits that the production centres derive from the service rendered.

We shall assume that the value of materials issued (shown in Example 3.1) provides a suitable approximation of the benefit that each of the production centres receives from materials procurement. Therefore 50 per cent of the value of materials is issued to machine centre X, resulting in 50 per cent of the total costs of materials procurement being allocated to this centre. If you refer to Exhibit 3.1, you will see that £880 000 (50 per cent of material procurement costs of £1 760 000) has been reallocated to machine centre X. It is also assumed that direct labour hours provides an approximation of the benefits received by the production centres from general factory support resulting in the total costs for this centre being reallocated to the production centres proportionate to direct labour hours. Therefore, since machine centre X consumes 25 per cent of the direct labour hours, £450 000 (25 per cent of the total costs of £1 800 000 assigned to general factory support) has been reallocated to machine centre X. You will see in the row labelled 'step 2 of stage 1' in Exhibit 3.1 that all manufacturing costs have now been assigned to the three production centres. This completes the first stage of the two-stage allocation process.

Step 3 – Computing separate overhead rates for each production cost centre

The second stage of the two-stage process is to allocate overheads of each production centre to products passing through that centre by establishing departmental overhead rates. It is necessary to establish departmental overhead rates because multiple products are worked on by each producing department.

If each department worked only on one product all of the costs allocated to that department would be assigned to the product and step 3 would not be required. The allocation bases most frequently used by traditional costing systems for computing production cost centre rates, are based on the amount of time products spend in each production centre – for example direct labour hours, machine hours and direct wages. In respect of non-machine centres, direct labour hours is the most frequently used allocation base. This implies that the overheads incurred by a production centre are closely related to direct labour hours worked. In the case of machine centres, a machine hour overhead rate is preferable since most of the overheads (e.g. depreciation) are likely to be more closely related to machine hours. We shall assume that the Enterprise Company uses a *machine hour rate* for the machine production centres and a *direct labour hour rate* for the assembly centre. The overhead rates are calculated by applying the following formula:

$$\frac{\text{cost centre overheads}}{\text{cost centre direct labour hours or machine hours}}$$

The calculations (i.e. step 3 of the four steps of the two-stage allocation process) using the information given in Exhibit 3.1 are as follows:

$$\text{Machine centre X} = \frac{£4\,300\,000}{2\,000\,000 \text{ machine hours}} = £2.15 \text{ per machine hour}$$

$$\text{Machine centre Y} = \frac{£3\,800\,000}{1\,000\,000 \text{ machine hours}} = £3.80 \text{ per machine hour}$$

$$\text{Assembly department} = \frac{£3\,600\,000}{2\,000\,000 \text{ direct labour hours}} = £1.80 \text{ per direct labour hour}$$

Step 4 – Assigning cost centre overheads to products or other chosen cost objects

The final step is to allocate the overheads to products passing through the production centres. Therefore, if a product spends ten hours in machine cost centre A, overheads of £21.50 (10 × £2.15) will be allocated to the product. We shall compute the manufacturing costs of two products. Product A is a low sales volume product with direct costs of £100. It is manufactured in batches of 100 units and each unit requires five hours in machine centre A, ten hours in machine centre B and ten hours in the assembly centre. Product B is a high sales volume product thus enabling it to be manufactured in larger batches. It is manufactured in batches of 200 units and each unit requires ten hours in machine centre A, 20 hours in machine centre B and 20 hours in the assembly centre. Direct costs of £200 have been assigned to product B. The calculations of the manufacturing costs assigned to the products are as follows:

Product A	£
Direct costs (100 units × £100)	10 000
Overhead allocations	
Machine centre A (100 units × 5 machine hours × £2.15)	1 075
Machine centre B (100 units × 10 machine hours × £3.80)	3 800
Assembly (100 units × 10 direct labour hours × £1.80)	1 800
Total cost	16 675
Cost per unit (£16 675/100 units) = £166.75	

Product B	£
Direct costs (200 units × £200)	40 000
Overhead allocations	
Machine centre A (200 units × 10 machine hours × £2.15)	4 300
Machine centre B (200 units × 20 machine hours × £3.80)	15 200
Assembly (200 units × 20 direct labour hours × £1.80)	7 200
Total cost	66 700
Cost per unit (£66 700/200 units) = £333.50	

The overhead allocation procedure is more complicated where service cost centres serve each other. In Example 3.1, it was assumed that materials procurement does not provide any services for general factory support and that general factory support does not provide any services for materials procurement. An understanding of situations where service cost centres do serve each other is not, however, necessary for a general understanding of the overhead procedure, and the problem of service centre reciprocal cost allocations is therefore dealt with in Appendix 3.1.

AN ILLUSTRATION OF THE TWO-STAGE PROCESS FOR AN ABC SYSTEM

Earlier in this chapter, Figure 3.3 was used to contrast the general features of ABC systems with traditional costing systems. It was pointed out that ABC systems differ from traditional systems by having a greater number of cost centres in the first stage, and a greater number, and variety, of cost drivers/allocation bases in the second stage of the two-stage allocation process. We shall now look at ABC systems in more detail.

You will see from Figure 3.3 that another major distinguishing feature of ABC is that overheads are assigned to each major activity, rather than departments, which normally represent cost centres with traditional systems. Activities consist of the aggregation of many different tasks, events or units of work that cause the consumption of resources. They tend to consists of verbs associated with objects. Typical production support activities include schedule production, set-up machines, move materials, purchase materials, inspect items and process supplier records. When costs are accumulated by activities they are known as activity cost centres. Production process activities include machine products and assemble products. Thus, within the production process, activity cost centres are sometimes identical to the cost centres used by traditional cost systems. Generally with ABC systems cost centres are often decomposed into many different activity centres.

We shall now use Example 3.1 for the Enterprise Company to compute the product costs for an ABC system. The computations are shown in Exhibit 3.2. ABC systems normally decompose production cost centres into many different activity centres but to keep things simple we shall assume that the three production centres (i.e. the two machine centres and the assembly centre) established for the traditional costing system have also been identified as activity centres with the ABC system. Therefore, the production activity cost centres shown in Exhibit 3.2 are identical to the cost centres used by the traditional cost system shown in Exhibit 3.1. However, we shall assume that three activity centres have been established for each of the two support functions. For materials procurement the following activity centres have been established:

Activity	£	Activity cost driver
Purchasing materials	960 000	Number of purchase orders
Receiving materials	600 000	Number of material receipts
Disburse materials	200 000	Number of production runs
	1 760 000	

EXHIBIT 3.2 Overheads assigned to the production of 1 000 units of products A and B (ABC system)

	Machine centre X	Machine centre Y	Assembly	Purchasing components	Receiving components	Disburse materials	Production scheduling	Set-up machines	Quality inspection
1 Stage 1 assignment (£)	2970000	2690000	2480000	960000	600000	200000	1000000	600000	200000
2 Activity cost driver	Machine hours	Machine hours	Direct labour hours	Number of purchase orders	Number of material receipts	Number of production runs	Number of production runs	Number of set-up hours	Number of first item inspections
3 Quantity of activity cost driver	2000000	1000000	2000000	10000	5000	2000	2000	12000	1000
4 Activity cost driver rate (£)	£1.485	£2.69	£1.24	£96	£120	£100	£500	£50	£200
5 Quantity of activity cost driver for 100 units of product A	500 hours	1 000 hours	1000 hours	1 purchased component	1 component received	5 production runs	5 production runs	50 set-up hours	1 inspection
6 Quantity of activity cost driver for 200 units of product B	2000 hours	4000 hours	4000 hours	1 purchased component	1 purchased component	1 production run	1 production run	10 set-up hours	1 inspection
7 Overheads assigned to Product A (£)	742.50	2690.00	1240.00	96.00	120.00	500.00	2500.00	2500.00	200.00
8 Overheads assigned to Product B (£)	2970.00	10760.00	4960.00	96.00	120.00	100.00	500.00	500.00	200.00

9 Product A total overhead cost = £10588.50 (sum of row 7)
10 Product B total overhead cost = £20206.00 (sum of row 8)

Therefore the assignment of £1 760 000 to the materials procurement department in Exhibit 3.1 is replaced by the assignments to the above three activities totalling £1 760 000 that are shown in row 1 of Exhibit 3.2. For the second support department (i.e. general factory support) used as a cost centre with the traditional costing system we shall assume that the following three activity cost centres have been identified:

Activity	£	Activity cost driver
Production scheduling	1 000 000	Number of production runs
Set-up machines	600 000	Number of set-up hours
Quality inspection	200 000	Number of first item inspection
	1 800 000	

You can see that the total costs assigned to the production scheduling, machines set up and quality inspection activities shown in row 1 in Exhibit 3.2 total £1 800 000, the same as the total allocated to the general factory support cost centre with the traditional costing system in the row labelled 'step 1 of stage 1' in Exhibit 3.1. The process of allocating the costs of £11 700 000 to the activity cost centres is the same as that used to allocate these costs with the traditional costing system. To simplify the presentation in Exhibit 3.2 the stage 1 cost assignments for the ABC system are not shown. Row 1 of Exhibit 3.2 therefore shows the completion of the first stage of the two-stage allocation process for both the traditional and ABC systems. The row labelled 'step 2 of stage 1' in Exhibit 3.1 indicates that overhead costs are assigned to *three* cost centres with the traditional system whereas row 1 of Exhibit 3.2 indicates that overheads are assigned to *nine* activity cost centres. Thus a major distinguishing feature between the two exhibits is that the ABC system uses a greater number of cost centres than traditional systems in the first stage of the two-stage allocation process.

We shall now compare the second stage of the two-stage allocation process for the traditional and ABC systems. You will see by referring back to Exhibit 3.1 that in the two final rows labelled 'step 3', separate machine hour overhead rates have been established for the two machine production centres and a direct labour hour rate has been established for the assembly department. Overheads are assigned to products A and B by multiplying the overhead rates by the quantity of the selected allocation base used by each product (see 'step 4' shown on page 55).

The same approach is used in Exhibit 3.2 with the ABC system. You will see from row 2 that seven different types of second stage cost drivers have been established for the ABC system. Cost driver rates are computed in row 4 by dividing the costs assigned to the activity cost centres in row 1 by the estimated quantity of the cost drivers for the period shown in row 3. Activity centre costs are assigned to products by multiplying the cost driver rate by the quantity of the cost driver used by products. These calculations are shown in rows 5–8 of Exhibit 3.2. For example, £960 000 has been assigned to the purchasing activity for processing 10 000 purchasing orders resulting in a cost driver rate of £96 per purchasing order. Rows 5 and 6 indicate that a batch of 100 units of product A, and 200 units of product B, each require one purchased component and thus one purchase order. Therefore purchase order costs of £96 are allocated to each batch in rows 7 and 8. Now look at the production scheduling column in Exhibit 3.2. You will see that £1m has been assigned to this activity for 2000 production runs resulting in a cost driver rate of £500 per production run. Rows 5 and 6 show that a batch of 100 units of product A requires five production runs whereas a batch of 200 units of product B requires one production run. Therefore production scheduling activity costs of £2500 (5 × £500) are allocated to a batch of product A and £500 to a batch of product B in rows 7 and 8. The same approach is used to allocate the costs of the remaining activities shown in Exhibit 3.2. You should now work through Exhibit 3.2 and study the product cost calculations.

By comparing Exhibits 3.1 and 3.2 the major differences between traditional and ABC systems can be identified. They are:

1 ABC systems have a greater number of cost centres than traditional costing systems. Exhibit 3.1 indicates that three cost centres are used with the traditional costing system to determine cost centre overhead rates whereas Exhibit 3.2 indicates that nine cost centres are used with the ABC system.

2 ABC systems use a greater number and variety of second stage cost drivers (Exhibit 3.2 shows that nine cost drivers consisting of seven different types are used with the ABC system whereas three cost drivers consisting of two different types are used by the traditional system shown in Exhibit 3.1).

3 The traditional costing system reallocates service/support department costs to production cost centres and allocates these costs within the production cost centre overhead rates (see 'Reallocation of service department costs' in Exhibit 3.1) whereas the ABC system does not reallocate these costs. Instead, the ABC system establishes separate cost driver rates for the support activities (see row 4 relating to the final six columns in Exhibit 3.2).

Step 4 of the traditional system (see page 55) and rows 9 and 10 of Exhibit 3.2 indicate that the overhead costs assigned to products A and B are as follows:

	Traditional costing system	*ABC system*
	£	£
Batch of 100 units of product A	6675	10 588.50
Batch of 200 units of product B	26 700	20 206.00
Product A cost per unit	66.75 (£6 675/100 units)	105.88 (£10 588.50/100 units)
Product B cost per unit	133.50 (£26 700/200 units)	101.03 (£20 206/200 units)

Compared with the ABC system the traditional system under-costs product A and over-costs product B. By reallocating the service centre costs to the production centres, and allocating the costs to products on the basis of either machine hours or direct labour hours, the traditional system incorrectly assumes that these allocation bases are the cause of the costs of the support activities. Compared with product A, product B consumes twice as many machine and direct labour hours per unit of output. Therefore, relative to product A, the traditional costing system allocates twice the amount of support costs to product B.

In contrast, ABC systems create separate cost centres for each major support activity and allocate costs to products using cost drivers that are the significant determinants of the cost of the activities. The ABC system recognizes that a batch of both products consume the same quantity of purchasing, receiving and inspection activities and, for these activities, allocates the same costs to both products. Because product B is manufactured in batches of 200 units, and product A in batches of 100 units, the cost per unit of output for product B is half the amount of product A for these activities. Product A also has five unique machined components, whereas product B has only one, resulting in a batch of product A requiring five production runs whereas a batch of product B only requires one. Therefore, relative to product B, the ABC system assigns five times more costs to product A for the production scheduling and disbursement of materials activities (see rows 5–8 for these activities in Exhibit 3.2). Because product A is a more complex product it requires relatively more support activity resources and the cost of this complexity is captured by the ABC system.

It should be apparent from the computation of the product costs that traditional and ABC systems use the same basic approach. It is unfortunate that the terms traditional and ABC systems have emerged. They have now have become the conventional terms used in the literature but using these terms gives the impression that they are two very different type of cost systems, when in reality they represent the same type of cost assignment system. If you re-examine the workings it will become apparent that one approach (ABC systems) merely uses more cost centres and different types of cost drivers. Rather than viewing the approaches as two separate systems it is preferable to view ABC systems as sophisticated or complex cost assignment systems and traditional systems as simple or unsophisticated cost assignment systems.

EXTRACTING RELEVANT COSTS FOR DECISION-MAKING

The cost computations relating to the Enterprise Company for products A and B represent the costs that should be generated for meeting inventory valuation and profit measurement requirements. For decision-making, non-manufacturing costs should also be taken into account. In addition, some of the costs that have been assigned to the products may not be relevant for certain decisions. For example, if you look at the overhead analysis sheet in Exhibit 3.1, you will see that property taxes, depreciation of machinery and insurance of buildings and machinery have been assigned to cost centres, and thus included in the costs assigned to products for both traditional and ABC systems. If these costs are unaffected by a decision to discontinue a product they should not be assigned to products when undertaking product discontinuation reviews. However, if cost information is used to determine selling prices, such costs may need to be assigned to products to ensure that the selling price of a customer's order covers a fair share of all organizational costs. It is therefore necessary to ensure that the costs incorporated in the overhead analysis are suitably coded so that different overhead rates can be extracted for different combinations of cost. This will enable relevant cost information to be extracted from the database for meeting different requirements. For an illustration of this approach you should refer to the answer to Review problem 3.23.

Our objective in this chapter has not been to focus on the cost information that should be extracted from the costing system for meeting decision-making requirements. Instead, it is to provide you with an understanding of how cost systems assign costs to cost objects. In Chapter 9, we shall concentrate on the cost information that should be extracted for decision-making. Also, only the basic principles of ABC have been introduced. A more theoretical approach to ABC will be presented in Chapter 10 with an emphasis being given to how cost information generated from an ABC system can be used for decision-making.

REAL WORLD VIEWS 3.2

Three cost allocation myths

Allan Stratton is a cost management consultant with over 35 years of experience who shares the benefit of his experience providing tools and resources via the internet. In one of his articles he debunks three myths on cost allocation.

All sorts of businesses and government organizations use cost allocation. It is a way of dividing and assigning the money that an entity spends. Sometimes this means spreading costs incurred by one department amongst others who also benefitted from the expense, sometimes it means distributing a cost across all products. Over time, several dangerous myths about cost allocation have developed.

First, that allocating costs improves decision-making; this is the intent but the outcome depends on the way it is done. Attention must be paid to cause and effect and/or the actual operating relationships, otherwise those using the data to make decisions may be misled.

Second, that all costs must be allocated. There is no reason to allocate a cost that will not influence a decision.

Third, that idle capacity cost must be allocated to actual products and services. A dangerous downward spiral could be started if idle capacity cost is allocated to products because this would result in higher product costs. If higher product costs are reported then the company may raise their prices in order to continue making the same profit margin.

Questions

1 Explain how applying each of the above three myths can lead to bad decisions.

2 What changes should be made to cost allocations to avoid the bad decisions?

Reference

Stratton, A. (2012) *Three Cost Allocation Myths*. Available at www.costmatters.com/2012/06 /three-cost-allocation-myths/#more-415 (accessed 30 March, 2017).

BUDGETED OVERHEAD RATES

Our discussion in this chapter has assumed that the *actual* overheads for an accounting period have been allocated to the products. However, the use of actual figures can be problematic. This is because the product cost calculations have to be delayed until the end of the accounting period, since the overhead rate calculations cannot be obtained before this date. However, information on product costs is required more quickly if it is to be used for monthly profit calculations and inventory valuations or as a basis for setting selling prices. One may argue that the timing problem can be resolved by calculating actual overhead rates at more frequent intervals, say on a monthly basis, but the difficulty here is that a large amount of overhead expenditure is fixed in the short term whereas activity will vary from month to month, giving large fluctuations in the overhead rates.

REAL WORLD VIEWS 3.3

Product diversity and costing system design choice

Two Australian firms, one with three divisions (HC1, HC2 and HC3), and the second with two divisions (FT1 and FT2) were studied. HC1 and FT1 had the simplest costing systems with all of the overheads accumulated into a single cost pool. In other words, a plant-wide overhead rate was used. HC2 and HC3 established separate 'work centre cost pools' that reflect manufacturing processes (e.g. HC2 had three cost pools and HC3 two cost pools). Overheads such as power were directly traced to the work centres. The remaining overheads were allocated to the work centres based on their levels of direct labour hours (DLHs) usage. The work centre overhead was then determined by dividing the work centre cost pool by the number of DLHs and allocating the costs to the product according to the consumption of DLHs in each of the work centres.

FT2 was the only research site that had a highly sophisticated costing system consisting of many different cost pools. The overheads for each cost pool were allocated to products on the basis of two cost drivers, namely direct labour hours and machine hours. The overheads allocated based on DLHs included indirect labour associated with materials handling, packers and factory foremen. Overheads allocated on the basis of machine hours include costs that vary with machine hours (e.g. power and electricity) as well as fixed costs such as factory management and depreciation.

HC1, HC2 and FT1 all had low product diversity (i.e. products consumed organizational resources in similar proportions) and users were satisfied with the information provided by the costing system. Both HC3 and FT2 had high levels of product diversity. FT2 had a relatively sophisticated costing system while HC3 maintained a simplistic system. The users of the costing system at FT2 were very satisfied with the system whereas there was much dissatisfaction with HC3's system. Costing information at HC3 was particularly important for determining product costs. However, management believed that the costs were highly inaccurate and were inadequate for setting prices. Overheads were large and product diversity was high, creating the need for a relatively sophisticated costing system. However, a simplistic costing system was implemented. This absence of 'fit' was a major dissatisfaction with the existing costing system. In contrast, there was a 'fit' between the costing systems and the level of product diversity in the four other business units and a general satisfaction with the costing systems.

Questions

1 Why might increasing the number of cost centres (pools) result in the reporting of more accurate product costs?

2 What other factors, besides product diversity, might enable a simplistic product costing system to report reasonably accurate product costs?

Reference

Adapted from Abernethy, M.A. et al. (2001), 'Product diversity and costing system design: Field study evidence', *Management Accounting Research* 12(3): 261–280.

EXAMPLE 3.2

The fixed overheads for Euro are £24 million per annum, and monthly production varies from 400 000 to one million hours. The monthly overhead rate for fixed overhead will therefore fluctuate as follows:

Monthly overhead	£2 000 000	£2 000 000
Monthly production	400 000 hours	1 000 000 hours
Monthly overhead rate	£5 per hour	£2 per hour

Overhead expenditure that is fixed in the short term remains constant each month, but monthly production fluctuates because of holiday periods and seasonal variations in demand. Consequently, the overhead rate varies from £2 to £5 per hour. It would be unreasonable for a product worked on in one month to be allocated overheads at a rate of £5 per hour and an identical product worked on in another month allocated at a rate of only £2 per hour.

Consider Example 3.2. The monthly overhead rates of £2 and £5 per hour are not representative of typical, normal production conditions. Management has committed itself to a specific level of fixed costs in the light of foreseeable needs for beyond one month. Thus, where production fluctuates, monthly overhead rates may be volatile. Furthermore, some costs such as repairs, maintenance and heating are not incurred evenly throughout the year. Therefore, if monthly overhead rates are used, these costs will not be allocated fairly to units of output. For example, heating costs would be charged only to winter production so that products produced in winter would be more expensive than those produced in summer.

An average, annualized rate based on the relationship of total annual overhead to total annual activity is more representative of typical relationships between total costs and volume than a monthly rate. What is required is a normal product cost, based on average long-term production rather than an actual product cost, which is affected by month-to-month fluctuations in production volume. Taking these factors into consideration, it is preferable to establish a budgeted overhead rate based on annual *estimated* overhead expenditure and activity.

Consequently, the procedure outlined in the previous sections for calculating cost centre overhead rates for traditional and ABC systems should be based on *standard* (*estimated*) activity levels and not *actual* activity levels. We shall consider how we might determine standard activity in Chapter 7. Surveys of product costing practices indicate that most organizations use annual budgeted activity as a measure of standard activity.

UNDER- AND OVER-RECOVERY OF OVERHEADS

The effect of calculating overhead rates based on budgeted annual overhead expenditure and activity is that it will be most unlikely that the overhead allocated to products manufactured during the period will be the same as the actual overhead incurred. Consider a situation where the estimated annual fixed overheads are £2 000 000 and the estimated annual activity is 1 000 000 direct labour hours. The estimated fixed overhead rate will be £2 per hour. Assume that actual overheads are £2 000 000 and are therefore identical with the estimate, but that actual activity is 900 000 direct labour hours instead of the estimated 1 000 000 hours. In this situation, only £1 800 000 will be charged to production. This calculation is based on 900 000 direct labour hours at £2 per hour, giving an under-recovery of overheads of £200 000.

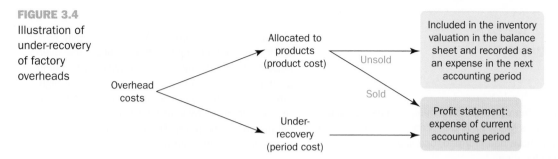

Consider an alternative situation where the actual overheads are £1 950 000 instead of the estimated £2 000 000, and actual activity is 1 000 000 direct labour hours, which is identical to the original estimate. In this situation, 1 000 000 direct labour hours at £2 per hour will be charged to production giving an over-recovery of £50 000. This example illustrates that there will be an under- or over-recovery of overheads whenever actual *activity* or overhead *expenditure* is different from the budgeted overheads and activity used to estimate the budgeted overhead rate. This under- or over-recovery of *fixed* overheads arising from actual activity differing from budgeted activity is also called a volume variance and any under- or over-recovery arising from actual fixed overhead expenditure differing from budget is also called a fixed overhead expenditure variance.

Accounting regulations in most countries recommend that the under- or over-recovery of overheads should be regarded as a period cost adjustment. For example, the UK Financial Reporting Standard 102 (FRS 102) on Stocks and Work in Progress, and the international accounting standard on inventories (IAS2), recommend that the allocation of overheads in the valuation of inventories and work in progress needs to be based on the company's normal level of activity and that any under- or over-recovery should be written off in the current year. This procedure is illustrated in Figure 3.4. Note that any under- or over-recovery of overhead is not allocated to products. Also note that the under-recovery is recorded as an expense in the current accounting period whereas an over-recovery is recorded as a reduction in the expenses for the period. Finally, you should note that our discussion here is concerned with how to treat any under- or over-recovery for the purpose of financial accounting and its impact on inventory valuation and profit measurement.

NON-MANUFACTURING OVERHEADS

For financial accounting purposes, only manufacturing costs are allocated to products. Non-manufacturing overheads are regarded as period costs and are disposed of in exactly the same way as the under- or over-recovery of manufacturing overheads outlined in Figure 3.4. For external reporting, it is therefore unnecessary to allocate non-manufacturing overheads to products. However, for decision-making, it may be necessary to assign non-manufacturing costs to products. For example, in many organizations, it is not uncommon for selling prices to be based on estimates of total cost or even actual cost. Housing contractors and garages often charge for their services by adding a percentage profit margin to actual cost.

Some non-manufacturing costs may be a direct cost of the product. Delivery costs, salesmen's salaries and travelling expenses may be directly identifiable with the product, but it is likely that many non-manufacturing overheads cannot be allocated directly to specific products. On what basis should we allocate non-manufacturing overheads? The answer is that we should select an allocation base/cost driver that corresponds most closely to the causation of non-manufacturing overheads. The problem is that cause-and-effect allocation bases cannot be established for many non-manufacturing overheads. Therefore, an allocation base must be used which, although arbitrary, allocates costs on

REAL WORLD VIEWS 3.4

Overheads in cafés

Bubble tea cafés are becoming increasingly popular across Malaysia and in recent years, many new chains have been formed, opening cafés in mainly urban locations.

Leading bubble tea firms provide some interesting information on the rapid growth of the product in recent years. According to Bryan Loo of Chatime (which is quoted on the Taiwan stock exchange), the rationale for setting up a bubble tea business was that there is a strong demand for tea in Malaysia, but no tea businesses as such – in the coffee business names like Starbucks are already in situ. Bubble tea is also more appealing to health-conscious consumers. Globally, Chatime has more than 800 outlets as of 2016, 116 of which are in Malaysia.

The primary business model for the new cafés is a franchise model. The cost of setting up a café in Malaysia is at least RM200 000 (about £45 000), depending on factors such as location,

size and renovation costs. According to Billy Koh, the franchisor for Gong Cha brand bubble tea, overhead costs of running a café are typically higher in a shopping mall franchise than in a normal high-street type shop. However, the profit margins are reasonable at approximately 30 per cent for a typical franchise operation. The lower margin is attributable to the high materials cost.

Questions

1 Can you think of some examples of overhead costs that might be incurred by cafés such as those described above?

2 How would these overheads affect profit if sales declined?

References

Wei-Shen, W. (2012) Bubble tea craze leads to a flurry of stores opening in Klang Valley, *The Star* (Malaysia), 19 March. Available at www.thestar.com.my/news /community/2012/03/19/bubble-tea-craze-leads -to-a-flurry-of-stores-opening-in-klang-valley/

Chatime (2015) Nothing but bubbling good ... Available at www.chatime.com.my/main/story.php

EXAMPLE 3.3

The estimated non-manufacturing and manufacturing costs of a company for the year ending 31 December are £500 000 and £1 million, respectively. The non-manufacturing overhead absorption rate is calculated as follows:

$$\frac{\text{estimated non-manufacturing overhead}}{\text{estimated manufacturing cost}}$$

In percentage terms, each product will be allocated with non-manufacturing overheads at a rate of 50 per cent of its total manufacturing cost.

as reasonable a basis as possible. A widely used approach is to allocate non-manufacturing overheads on the ability of the products to bear such costs. This approach can be implemented by allocating non-manufacturing costs to products on the basis of their manufacturing costs. This procedure is illustrated in Example 3.3.

COST ASSIGNMENT IN NON-MANUFACTURING ORGANIZATIONS

So far in this chapter we have concentrated on describing a job-order costing system that is used in manufacturing firms where the products incur different costs resulting in the need to keep track of the cost of each product or batch of products. In particular, we have focused on cost assignment for allocating costs between cost of goods sold and inventories for profit reporting. Many service organizations also use a job-order costing system. For example, accounting, law, printing, automotive and appliance repair firms provide unique services to customers resulting in the need to track the costs of the services provided to each customer. The costs assigned to each customer are also often used to determine the prices of the services that have been provided. These firms may also have inventories consisting of work partially completed (i.e. WIP) at the end of the accounting period. The same basic concepts and procedures that are used by manufacturing organizations can therefore be applied where the cost of a service provided to customer differs.

Consider a firm of accountants that provide three different types of service – audit, taxation and financial consultancy. These three services can be viewed as being equivalent to production departments in manufacturing organizations. Direct labour costs consist of chargeable hours that can be specifically identified with individual customers. Separate overhead rates can be established for each of the three service departments. Some costs, such as the cost of non-chargeable hours arising for staff development and training and departmental secretarial salaries, can be directly traced to each of the three service departments. The cost of the support departments such as printing and photocopying, data processing and general administration are reallocated to the three service departments (audit, tax and consultancy departments) using appropriate allocation bases. The choice of specific allocation bases should be based on a detailed study of the benefits received by the three service departments from the support departments.

We shall assume that the identified allocation bases are number of pages printed/photocopied for the printing/photocopying department and the number of chargeable hours for the data processing and general administration departments. The total costs assigned to each of the three service departments (audit, taxation and consultancy) after support department reallocation are divided by the number of chargeable (direct) labour hours to establish an overhead rate for each service department (audit, taxation and consultancy). Therefore, the total cost assigned to each customer is the sum of the direct costs plus the chargeable hours in each department multiplied by the appropriate overhead rate. In other words, it is assumed that the overheads incurred by each service department are closely related to chargeable hours.

However, a job-order costing system as described above is inappropriate for many non-manufacturing organizations for the following reasons:

1 They do not provide unique services for customers. Instead, they provide similar services for a large number of customers. Consider a bank whose principal activities include mortgage lending, personal lending, variable interest and fixed interest savings accounts, insurance, foreign currency, etc. It is not feasible or useful to track the costs of undertaking these activities to individual customers. Instead, costs are assigned to each activity so that the total costs incurred can be deducted from sales revenue to periodically determine the profits/losses of each activity.

2 They do not need to assign costs to individual customers to determine prices of the services provided because prices are determined by market forces rather than cost.

3 They do not convert purchased materials into finished products or have work in progress. Therefore, there is no legal requirement to assign indirect costs to cost objects for inventory valuation.

Instead of using job-order costing systems, the above organizations require costing systems that support profitability analysis. They need to undertake periodic profitability analysis that analyses profits by appropriate activities (e.g. products, services, departments, locations, etc.) so that they can distinguish between profitable and unprofitable activities in order to ensure that only profitable activities are undertaken. Consider a merchandising company such as a departmental store that analyses profits by departments (e.g. televisions and DVD players, computers, clothing, and furniture departments). The company does not have to adhere to legal requirements for assigning indirect costs to goods processed for inventory valuation. It may choose not to assign indirect costs to departments where they are a small proportion of total costs or are common to all departments resulting in arbitrary allocations not having to be relied upon. In other words, only direct costs are assigned to departments so that departmental profits cannot be reported. Instead, departmental profit contributions to indirect costs (i.e. sales revenues less direct costs) are reported. A system that assigns only direct costs to cost objects is called direct costing. This costing system will be examined in detail in Chapter 7.

Alternatively, indirect costs can be assigned to departments using suitable allocation bases. For example, utility and property costs may be allocated based on the floor area occupied by each department. Other indirect costs may initially be assigned to relevant support departments such as payroll, data processing and personnel and then reallocated to the user departments (i.e. television, computing, clothing, etc.) using appropriate allocation bases. This approach enables all costs (direct and indirect) to be assigned to departments so that departmental profits can be reported.

THE INDIRECT COST ASSIGNMENT PROCESS

The following is a summary of the process of assigning indirect costs to cost objects for a job-order traditional costing system:

1 identify the production departments (or their equivalent in service organizations) that are responsible for creating the products of services that are sold;

2 identify the support departments that provide essential support services for the production departments;

3 assign all indirect (overhead) costs in the firm to a producing or support department;

4 reallocate the support department costs to the production departments;

5 calculate predetermined overhead rates for each producing department;

6 allocate the departmental overhead costs to the units of the individual products or services using the predetermined overhead rates.

Where a job-order costing system is not used the process may end at stage 4. For example, in the preceding section, the costs of the merchandising departmental store were assigned to departments and not to the individual products sold within the departments. We also noted that a bank may assign costs to the principal activities that it undertakes for profitability analysis purposes. These activities may be performed by separate departments so that the mortgage lending department is responsible for all mortgage lending activities, the insurance department is responsible for all insurance activities, the foreign currency department is responsible for all foreign currency transactions and so on. Therefore, the costs assigned to the departments are equivalent to the costs of undertaking the activities. Thus for profitability analysis purposes the assignment of costs can end at the fourth stage since the costs assigned to the departments also represents the costs of undertaking the principal activities.

SUMMARY

The following items relate to the learning objectives listed at the beginning of the chapter.

● **Distinguish between cause-and-effect and arbitrary allocations.**

Allocation bases which are significant determinants of costs that are being allocated are described as cause-and-effect allocations whereas arbitrary allocations refer to allocation bases that are not the significant determinants of the costs. To accurately measure the cost of resources used by cost objects, cause-and-effect allocations should be used.

● **Explain why different cost information is required for different purposes.**

Manufacturing organizations assign costs to products for two purposes: first, for external (financial accounting) profit measurement and inventory valuation purposes in order to allocate manufacturing costs incurred during a period to cost of goods sold and inventories; second, to provide useful information for managerial decision-making requirements. Financial accounting regulations specify that only manufacturing costs should be assigned to products for meeting inventory and profit measurement requirements. Both manufacturing and non-manufacturing costs, however, may be relevant for decision-making. In addition, not all costs that are assigned to products for inventory valuation and profit measurement are relevant for decision-making. For example, costs that will not be affected by a decision (e.g. depreciation) are normally not relevant for product/service discontinuing decisions.

● **Describe how cost systems differ in terms of their level of sophistication.**

Cost systems range from simplistic to sophisticated. Simplistic systems are inexpensive to operate, involve extensive use of arbitrary allocations, have a high likelihood of reporting inaccurate product costs and generally result in a high cost of errors. Sophisticated costing systems are more expensive to operate, rely more extensively on cause-and-effect allocations, generally report more accurate product costs and have a low cost of errors. Further distinguishing features are that simplistic costing systems have a small number of first-stage cost centres/pools and use a single second-stage cost driver. In contrast, sophisticated costing systems use many first-stage cost centres/pools and many different types of second-stage driver.

● **Understand the factors influencing the choice of an optimal costing system.**

The optimal costing system is different for different organizations and should be determined on a costs versus benefits basis. Simplistic costing systems are appropriate in organizations whose indirect costs are a low percentage of total costs and which also have a fairly standardized product range, all consuming organizational resources in similar proportions. Under these circumstances, simplistic costing systems may report costs that are sufficiently accurate for decision-making purposes. Conversely, organizations with a high proportion of indirect costs, whose products consume organizational resources in different proportions, are likely to require sophisticated costing systems. Relying on sophisticated costing systems under these circumstances is likely to result in the additional benefits from reporting more accurate costs exceeding the costs of operating more sophisticated systems.

● **Explain why departmental overhead rates should be used in preference to a single blanket overhead rate.**

A blanket (also known as plant-wide) overhead rate establishes a single overhead rate for the organization as a whole, whereas departmental rates involve indirect costs being accumulated by different departments and a separate overhead rate being established for each department. A blanket overhead rate can only be justified when all products or services consume departmental overheads in approximately the same proportions. Such circumstances are unlikely to be applicable to most organizations, resulting in blanket overheads generally reporting inaccurate product/service costs.

● **Construct an overhead analysis sheet and calculate cost centre allocation rates.**

Cost centre overhead allocation rates are established and assigned to cost objects using the two-stage allocation overhead procedure. In the first stage, an overhead analysis sheet is used to (a) allocate overheads to production and service centres or departments; and (b) to reallocate the total service department overheads to production departments. The second stage involves (a) the calculation of appropriate departmental overhead rates and (b) the allocation of overheads to products passing through each department. These steps were illustrated using data presented in Example 3.1.

- **Distinguish between traditional and activity-based costing systems and calculate product costs derived from an ABC system.**

The major distinguishing features of ABC compared with traditional costing systems are that ABC systems assign costs to activity cost centres rather than departments. ABC systems thus tend to use a greater number of cost centres in the first stage of the allocation process. In the second stage, they also use a greater number, and variety, of second-stage allocation bases that mostly rely on cause-and-effect allocation bases. In contrast, traditional systems use second-stage allocation bases that rely on arbitrary allocations. The assignment of costs to products using an ABC system was illustrated in Exhibit 3.2.

- **Justify why budgeted overhead rates should be used in preference to actual overhead rates.**

Because the uses of actual overhead rates causes a delay in the calculation of product or service costs, and the establishment of monthly rates results in fluctuations in the overhead rates throughout the year, it is recommended that annual budgeted overhead rates should be used.

- **Calculate and explain the treatment of the under-/over-recovery of overheads.**

The use of annual budgeted overhead rates gives an under- or over-recovery of overheads whenever actual overhead expenditure or activity is different from budget. Any under- or over-recovery is generally regarded as a period cost adjustment and written off to the profit and loss statement and thus not allocated to products.

- **Explain how the cost assignment approach described for manufacturing organizations can be extended to non-manufacturing organizations.**

The same basic cost assignment procedures that are used by manufacturing organizations can be applied where there is a need to track the cost of the services provided to each individual customer. Where a job-order costing system is inappropriate, cost information is required for profitability analysis by products, services, departments, etc. Organizations may choose to assign only direct costs to cost objects using a direct costing system. Alternatively, they may also use only the first stage of the two-stage overhead allocation procedure to assign indirect costs to departments that are synonymous with the products/services that are sold by the organization.

- **Additional learning objectives presented in Appendix 3.1.**

The appendix to this chapter includes the following additional learning objective: to be able to reallocate service department costs to production departments when service departments provide services for other service departments as well as production departments. This topic tends to be included in the syllabus requirements of the examinations set by professional accountancy bodies but may not be part of the course curriculum for other courses. You may omit Appendix 3.1 if this topic is not part of your course curriculum.

APPENDIX 3.1: INTER-SERVICE DEPARTMENT REALLOCATIONS

Service departments may provide services for other service departments as well as for production departments. For example, a personnel department provides services for other service departments such as the power generating plant, maintenance department and stores. The power generating department also provides heat and light for other service departments, including the personnel department and so on. When such interactions occur, the allocation process can become complicated. Difficulties arise because each service department begins to accumulate charges from other service departments from which it receives services and these must be reallocated back to the user department. Once it has

EXAMPLE 3A.1

A company has three production departments and two service departments. The overhead analysis sheet provides the following totals of the overheads analysed to production and service departments:

		(£)
Production department	X	48 000
	Y	42 000
	Z	30 000
Service department	1	14 040
	2	18 000
		152 040

The expenses of the service departments are apportioned as follows:

	Production departments			Service departments	
	X	Y	Z	1	2
Service department 1	20%	40%	30%	—	10%
Service department 2	40%	20%	20%	20%	—

begun, this allocation and reallocation process can continue for a long time before a solution is found. The problem is illustrated in Example 3A.1. We shall use the example to illustrate four different methods of allocating the service department costs:

1. repeated distribution (reciprocal) method;
2. simultaneous equation method;
3. specified order of closing method;
4. direct allocation method.

When determining which of the above methods to use, companies should consider the extent of service department interaction and the cost and benefits associated with each method. You should also note at this point that the emergence of just-in-time production methods involving manufacturing cells (see Chapter 22) and activity-based costing have reduced or eliminated the need for reallocating support department costs. In manufacturing cells, many support activities such as machine maintenance, materials handling and performing set-ups are performed by cell workers so that these costs can be assigned to products processed within each manufacturing cell. You should also remember from our discussion in the main body of this chapter that ABC systems tend to establish separate cost driver rates for support (service) centres and assign the cost of support activities directly to cost objects without any reallocation to production centres.

1. Repeated distribution (reciprocal) method

Where this method is adopted, the service department costs are repeatedly allocated in the specified percentages until the figures become too small to be significant. You can see from line 2 of Exhibit 3A.1 that the overheads of service department 1 are allocated according to the prescribed percentages. As a result, some of the overheads of service department 1 are transferred to service department 2. In line 3, the overheads of service department 2 are allocated, which means that service department 1 receives

EXHIBIT 3A.1 Repeated distribution method

	Line	Production departments			Service departments		
		X	Y	Z	1	2	Total
1	Allocation as per overhead analysis	48 000	42 000	30 000	14 040	18 000	152 040
2	Allocation of service department 1	2 808 (20%)	5 616 (40%)	4 212 (30%)	(14 040)	1 404 (10%) 19 404	
3	Allocation of service department 2	7 762 (40%)	3 881 (20%)	3 880 (20%)	3 881 (20%)	(19 404)	
4	Allocation of service department 1	776 (20%)	1 552 (40%)	1 165 (30%)	(3 881)	388 (10%)	
5	Allocation of service department 2	154 (40%)	78 (20%)	78 (20%)	78 (20%)	(388)	
6	Allocation of service department 1	16 (20%)	31 (40%)	23 (30%)	(78)	8 (10%)	
7	Allocation of service department 2	4 (40%)	2 (20%)	2 (20%)	—	(8)	
8	Total overheads	59 520	53 160	39 360	—	—	152 040

some further costs. The costs of service department 1 are again allocated and service department 2 receives some further costs. This process continues until line 7, by which time the costs have become so small that any further detailed apportionments are unnecessary. As a result, the total overheads in line 8 of £152 040 are allocated to production departments only.

2. Simultaneous equation method

Instead of using the repeated distribution (reciprocal) method the same allocations can be derived using the simultaneous equation method. When this method is used simultaneous equations are initially established as follows: Let

$$x = \text{total overhead of service department 1}$$
$$y = \text{total overhead of service department 2}$$

The total overhead transferred into service departments 1 and 2 can be expressed as

$$x = 14\,040 + 0.2y$$
$$y = 18\,000 + 0.1x$$

Rearranging the above equations:

$$x - 0.2y = 14\,040 \tag{1}$$
$$-0.1x + y = 18\,000 \tag{2}$$

We can now multiply equation (1) by 5 and equation (2) by 1, giving

$$5x - y = 70\,200$$
$$-0.1x + y = 18\,000$$

Adding the above equations together we have

$$4.9x = 88\,200$$

Therefore
$$x = 18\,000 \,(= 88\,200/4.9)$$

Substituting this value for x in equation (1), we have

$$18\,000 - 0.2y = 14\,040$$

Therefore $\qquad\qquad -0.2y = -3\,960$

Therefore $\qquad\qquad\qquad y = 19\,800$

We now apportion the values for x and y to the production departments in the agreed percentages.

	Line	X	Y	Z	Total
1	Allocation as per overhead analysis	48 000	42 000	30 000	120 000
2	Allocation of service department	3 600 (20%)	7 200 (40%)	5 400 (30%)	16 200
3	Allocation of service department 2	7 920 (40%)	3 960 (20%)	3 960 (20%)	15 840
		59 520	53 160	39 360	152 040

You will see from line 2 that the value for X (service department 1) of £18 000 is allocated in the specified percentages. Similarly, in line 3, the value for Y (service department 2) of £19 800 is apportioned in the specified percentages. As a result the totals in line 4 are in agreement with the totals in line 8 of the repeated distribution method (Exhibit 3A.1).

3. Specified order of closing

If this method (also known as the sequential or step allocation method) is used, the service departments' overheads are allocated to the production departments in a certain order. The service department that does the largest proportion of work for other service departments is closed first; the service department that does the second largest proportion of work for other service departments is closed second; and so on. Return charges are not made to service departments whose costs have previously been allocated. Let us now apply this method to the information contained in Example 3A.1. The results are given in Exhibit 3A.2.

The costs of service department 2 are allocated first (line 2) because 20 per cent of its work is related to service department 1, whereas only 10 per cent of the work of service department 1 is related to service department 2. In line 3, we allocate the costs of service department 1, but the return charges are not made to department 2. This means that the proportions allocated have changed as 10 per cent of the costs of service department 1 have not been allocated to service department 2.

EXHIBIT 3A.2 Specified order of closing method

		Production departments			Service departments		
	Line	X	Y	Z	1	2	Total
1	Allocation as per overhead analysis	48 000	42 000	30 000	14 040	18 000	152 040
2	Allocate service department 2	7 200 (40%)	3 600 (20%)	3 600 (20%)	3 600 (20%)	(18 000)	
3	Allocate service department 1	3 920 (2/9)	7 840 (4/9)	5 880 (3/9)	(17 640)	—	
4		59 120	53 440	39 480	—	—	152 040

Therefore 20 per cent out of a 90 per cent total or 2/9 of the costs of service department 1 are allocated to department X.

You will see that the totals allocated in line 4 do not agree with the totals allocated under the repeated distribution or simultaneous equation methods. This is because the specified order of closing method sacrifices accuracy for clerical convenience. However, if this method provides a close approximation to an alternative accurate calculation then there are strong arguments for its use.

4. Direct allocation method

This method is illustrated in Exhibit 3A.3. It ignores inter-service department service reallocations. Therefore service department costs are reallocated only to production departments. This means that the proportions allocated have changed, as 10 per cent of the costs of service department 1 have not been allocated to service department 2. Therefore, 20 per cent out of a 90 per cent total, or 2/9 of the costs of service department 1, are allocated to department X, 4/9 are allocated to department Y and 3/9 are allocated to department Z. Similarly the proportions allocated for service department 2 have changed with 4/8 (40 per cent out of 80 per cent) of the costs of service department 2 being allocated to department X, 2/8 to department Y and 2/8 to department Z. The only justification for using the direct allocation method is its simplicity. The method is recommended when inter-service reallocations are relatively insignificant.

EXHIBIT 3A.3 Direct allocation method

		Production departments			Service departments		
Line	X	Y	Z	1	2	Total
1 Allocation as per overhead analysis	48 000	42 000	30 000	14 040	18 000	152 040
2 Allocate service department 1	3 120 (2/9)	6 240 (4/9)	4 680 (3/9)	(14 040)		
3 Allocate service department 2	9 000 (4/8)	4 500 (2/8)	4 500 (2/8)	—	(18 000)	
4	60 120	52 740	39 180	—	—	152 040

KEY TERMS AND CONCEPTS

Absorption costing system A costing system that allocates all manufacturing costs, including fixed manufacturing costs, to products and values unsold stocks at their total cost of manufacture.

Activity The aggregation of different tasks, events or units of work that cause the consumption of resources.

Activity cost centre A cost centre in which costs are accumulated by activities.

Activity-based costing (ABC) A system of cost allocation that aims to use mainly cause-and-effect cost allocations by assigning costs to activities.

Allocation base The basis used to allocate costs to cost objects.

Arbitrary allocation The allocation of costs using a cost base that is not a significant determinant of cost.

Blanket overhead rate An overhead rate that assigns indirect costs to cost objects using a single overhead rate for the whole organization, also known as plant-wide rate.

Budgeted overhead rate An overhead rate based on estimated annual expenditure on overheads and levels of activity.

Cause-and-effect allocation The use of an allocation base that is a significant determinant of cost, also known as driver tracing.

Cost allocation The process of assigning costs to cost objects where a direct measure of the resources consumed by these cost objects does not exist.

Cost centre A location to which costs are assigned, also known as a cost pool.

Cost driver The basis used to allocate costs to cost objects in an ABC system.

Cost pool A location to which overhead costs are assigned, also known as a cost centre.

Direct cost tracing The process of assigning a cost directly to a cost object.

Direct costing system A costing system that assigns only direct manufacturing costs, not fixed manufacturing costs, to products or services. Also known as variable costing system or marginal costing system.

Direct labour hour rate An hourly overhead rate calculated by dividing the cost centre overheads by the number of direct labour hours.

Driver tracing The use of an allocation base that is a significant determinant of cost, also known as cause-and-effect allocation.

First-stage allocation bases The various bases, such as area, book value of machinery and number of employees, used to allocate indirect costs to production and service centres.

Fixed overhead expenditure variance The difference between the budgeted fixed overheads and the actual fixed overhead spending.

Job cards A source document that records the amount of time spent on a particular job, together with the employee's hourly rate, so that direct labour costs can be assigned to the appropriate cost object.

Job-order costing system A system of assigning costs to products or services that is used in situations where many different products or services are produced.

Machine hour rate An hourly overhead rate calculated by dividing the cost centre overheads by the number of machine hours.

Materials requisition A source document that records the cost of acquisition of the materials issued for manufacturing a product, or providing a specific service, so that the cost of the materials can be assigned to the appropriate cost object.

Overhead analysis sheet A document used to assign manufacturing overheads to production and service cost centres.

Overheads Another term for indirect costs, which are costs that cannot be specifically traced to a particular cost object.

Plant-wide rate An overhead rate that assigns indirect costs to cost objects using a single overhead rate for the whole organization, also known as a blanket overhead rate.

Sequential allocation method A method of allocating service departments' overheads to production departments in a certain order, also known as the step allocation method.

Service departments Departments that exist to provide services to other units within the organization, also known as support departments.

Step allocation method A method of allocating service departments' overheads to production departments in a certain order, also known as the sequential allocation method.

Support departments Departments that exist to provide services to other units within the organization, also known as service departments.

Time sheets Source documents that record the time spent by an employee on particular jobs which can be used to allocate direct labour costs to the appropriate cost object.

Traditional costing systems Widely used costing systems that tend to use arbitrary allocations to assign indirect costs to cost objects.

Under- or over-recovery of overheads The difference between the overheads that are allocated to products or services during a period and the actual overheads that are incurred.

Volume variance The difference between actual activity or overhead expenditure and the budgeted overheads and activity used to estimate the budgeted overhead rate, also known as under- or over-recovery of overheads.

RECOMMENDED READING

If your course requires a detailed understanding of accounting for direct labour and materials you should refer to Learning Note 3.2 on the digital support resources for this book. For an explanation of how you can access the digital support resources you should refer to the Preface. For a more detailed review of cost allocations for different purposes, see Ahmed and Scapens (2000). You should refer to Brierley, Cowton and Drury (2001) for a review of European product costing practices. See also Drury and Tayles (2005) for a description of overhead absorption procedures in UK organizations.

KEY EXAMINATION POINTS

A typical question (e.g. Review problem 3.22) will require you to analyse overheads by departments and calculate appropriate overhead allocation rates. These questions may require a large number of calculations, and it is possible that you will make calculation errors. Do make sure that your answer is clearly presented, since marks tend to be allocated according to whether you have adopted the correct method. You are recommended to present your answer in a format similar to that in Exhibit 3.1. For a traditional costing system you should normally recommend a direct labour hour rate if a department is non-mechanized and a machine hour rate if machine hours are the dominant activity. You should only recommend the direct wages percentage method when the rates within a non-mechanized department are uniform.

Where a question requires you to present information for decision-making, do not include apportioned fixed overheads in the calculations. Remember the total manufacturing costs should be calculated for inventory valuation, but incremental costs should be calculated for decision-making purposes (see answer to Review problem 3.23).

Finally, ensure that you can calculate under- or over-recoveries of overheads. To check your understanding of this topic, you should refer to the solution to Review problem 3.16.

ASSESSMENT MATERIAL

The review questions are short questions that enable you to assess your understanding of the main topics included in the chapter. The numbers in parentheses provide you with the page numbers to refer to if you cannot answer a specific question.

The review problems are more complex and require you to relate and apply the content to various business problems. The problems are graded by their level of difficulty. Solutions to review problems that are not preceded by the term 'IM' are provided in a separate section at the end of the book. Solutions to problems preceded by the term 'IM' are provided in the Instructor's Manual that can be downloaded from the lecturer's digital support resources. Additional review problems with fully worked solutions are provided in the *Student Manual* that accompanies this book.

REVIEW QUESTIONS

3.1   Why are indirect costs not directly traced to cost objects in the same way as direct costs? (p. 45)

3.2   Define cost tracing, cost allocation, allocation base and cost driver. (p. 45)

3.3   Distinguish between arbitrary and cause-and-effect allocations. (p. 45)

3.4   Explain how cost information differs for profit measurement/inventory valuation requirements compared with decision-making requirements. (pp. 46–47)

3.5   Explain why cost systems should differ in terms of their level of sophistication. (pp. 47–48)

3.6   Describe the process of assigning direct labour and direct materials to cost objects. (p. 48)

3.7   Why are separate departmental or cost centre overhead rates preferred to a plant-wide (blanket) overhead rate? (pp. 48–49)

3.8   Describe the two-stage overhead allocation procedure. (pp. 49–51)

3.9   Define the term 'activities'. (p. 56)

3.10 Describe two important features that distinguish activity-based costing from traditional costing systems. (pp. 58–59)

3.11 Why are some overhead costs sometimes not relevant for decision-making purposes? (p. 60)

3.12 Why are budgeted overhead rates preferred to actual overhead rates? (pp. 61–62)

3.13 Give two reasons for the under-or over-recovery of overheads at the end of the accounting period. (pp. 62–63)

3.14 Explain how the cost assignment approach described for manufacturing organizations can be extended to non-manufacturing organizations. (pp. 64–66)

REVIEW PROBLEMS

3.15 Basic. A company uses a predetermined overhead recovery rate based on machine hours. Budgeted factory overhead for a year amounted to £720 000, but actual factory overhead incurred was £738 000. During the year, the company absorbed £714 000 of factory overhead on 119 000 actual machine hours.

What was the company's budgeted level of machine hours for the year?

(a) 116 098
(b) 119 000
(c) 120 000
(d) 123 000

3.16 Basic. A company uses an overhead absorption rate of $3.50 per machine hour, based on 32 000 budgeted machine hours for the period. During the same period the actual total overhead expenditure amounted to $108 875 and 30 000 machine hours were recorded on actual production.

By how much was the total overhead under- or over-absorbed for the period?

(a) Under-absorbed by $3875
(b) Under-absorbed by $7000
(c) Over-absorbed by $3875
(d) Over-absorbed by $7000

ACCA F2 Management Accounting

3.17 Basic. A company has over-absorbed fixed production overheads for the period by £6000. The fixed production overhead absorption rate was £8 per unit and is based on the normal level of activity of 5000 units. Actual production was 4500 units.

What was the actual fixed production overheads incurred for the period?

(a) £30 000
(b) £36 000
(c) £40 000
(d) £42 000

ACCA Paper 1.2 – Financial Information for Management

3.18 Basic. A company absorbs overheads on machine hours. In a period, actual machine hours were 17 285, actual overheads were £496 500 and there was under-absorption of £12 520.

What was the budgeted level of overheads?

(a) £483 980
(b) £496 500
(c) £509 020
(d) It cannot be calculated from the information provided.

CIMA Stage 1 Cost Accounting

3.19 Basic. Canberra has established the following information regarding fixed overheads for the coming month:
Budgeted information:

Fixed overheads	£180 000
Labour hours	3000
Machine hours	10 000
Units of production	5000

Actual fixed costs for the last month were £160 000.

Canberra produces many different products using highly automated manufacturing processes and absorbs overheads on the most appropriate basis.

What will be the predetermined overhead absorption rate?

(a) £16
(b) £18
(c) £36
(d) £60

ACCA Paper 1.2 – Financial Information for Management

3.20 Basic. An engineering firm operates a job costing system. Production overhead is absorbed at the rate of $8.50 per machine hour. In order to allow for non-production overhead costs and profit, a mark-up of 60 per cent of prime cost is added to the production cost when preparing price estimates.

The estimated requirements of job number 808 are as follows:

Direct materials	$10 650
Direct labour	$3 260
Machine hours	140

The estimated price notified to the customer for job number 808 will be:

(a) $22 256
(b) $22 851

(c) $23 446
(d) $24 160

CIMA – Management Accounting Fundamentals

3.21 Basic. A factory consists of two production cost centres (P and Q) and two service cost centres (X and Y). The total allocated and apportioned overhead for each is as follows:

P	Q	X	Y
$95 000	$82 000	$46 000	$30 000

It has been estimated that each service cost centre does work for other cost centres in the following proportions:

	P	Q	X	Y
Percentage of service cost centre X to	50	50	—	—
Percentage of service cost centre Y to	30	60	10	—

The reapportionment of service cost centre costs to other cost centres fully reflects the above proportions.

After the reapportionment of service cost centre costs has been carried out, what is the total overhead for production cost centre P?

(a) $124 500
(b) $126 100
(c) $127 000
(d) $128 500

ACCA F2 Management Accounting

3.22 Intermediate: Overhead analysis and calculation of product costs. A furniture making business manufactures quality furniture to customers' orders. It has three production departments and two service departments. Budgeted overhead costs for the coming year are as follows:

	Total (£)
Rent and rates	12 800
Machine insurance	6 000
Telephone charges	3 200
Depreciation	18 000
Production supervisor's salaries	24 000
Heating and lighting	6 400
	70 400

The three production departments – A, B and C, and the two service departments – X and Y, are housed in the new premises, the details of which, together with other statistics and information, are given as follows:

	Departments				
	A	B	C	X	Y
Floor area occupied (sq. metres)	3000	1800	600	600	400
Machine value (£000)	24	10	8	4	2
Direct labour hrs budgeted	3200	1800	1000		
Labour rates per hour	£3.80	£3.50	£3.40	£3.00	£3.00
Allocated overheads: Specific to each department (£000)	2.8	1.7	1.2	0.8	0.6
Service department X's costs apportioned	50%	25%	25%		
Service department Y's costs apportioned	20%	30%	50%		

Required:

(a) Prepare a statement showing the overhead cost budgeted for each department, showing the basis of apportionment used. Also calculate suitable overhead absorption rates.

(9 marks)

(b) Two pieces of furniture are to be manufactured for customers. Direct costs are as follows:

	Job 123	Job 124
Direct material	£154	£108
Direct labour	20 hours Dept A	16 hours Dept A
	12 hours Dept B	10 hours Dept B
	10 hours Dept C	14 hours Dept C

Calculate the total costs of each job.   (5 marks)

(c) If the firm quotes prices to customers that reflect a required profit of 25 per cent on selling price, calculate the quoted selling price for each job.   (2 marks)

(d) If material costs are a significant part of total costs in a manufacturing company, describe a system of material control that might be used in order to effectively control costs, paying practical attention to the stock control aspect.   (9 marks)

AAT Stage 3 Cost Accounting and Budgeting

3.23 Intermediate: Make or buy decision. Shown below is next year's budget for the forming and finishing departments of Tooton Ltd. The departments manufacture three different types of component, which are incorporated into the output of the firm's finished products.

	Component		
	A	B	C
Production (units)	14000	10000	6000
Prime cost (£ per unit):			
Direct materials			
Forming dept	8	7	9
Direct labour			
Forming dept	6	9	12
Finishing dept	10	15	8
	24	31	29
Manufacturing times			
(hours per unit):			
Machining			
Forming dept	4	3	2
Direct labour			
Forming dept	2	3	4
Finishing dept	3	10	12

	Forming department (£)	Finishing Department (£)
Variable overheads	200900	115500
Fixed overheads	401800	231000
	£602700	£346500
Machine time required and available	98000 hours	—
Labour hours required and available	82000 hours	154000 hours

The forming department is mechanized and employs only one grade of labour, the finishing department employs several grades of labour with differing hourly rates of pay.

Required:

(a) Calculate suitable overhead absorption rates for the forming and finishing departments for next year and include a brief explanation for your choice of rates.

(6 marks)

(b) Another firm has offered to supply next year's budgeted quantities of the above components at the following prices:

Component A	£30
Component B	£65
Component C	£60

Advise management whether it would be more economical to purchase any of the above components from the outside supplier. You must show your workings and, considering cost criteria only, clearly state any assumptions made or any aspects that may require further investigation.   (8 marks)

(c) Critically consider the purpose of calculating production overheads absorption rates.   (8 marks)

ACCA Foundation Costing

3.24 Intermediate: Calculation of gross profit using ABC. MS manufactures three types of skincare product for sale to retailers. MS currently operates a standard absorption costing system. Budgeted information for next year is given below:

Products	Anti-ageing cream ($000)	Facial masks ($000)	Collagen fillers ($000)	Total ($000)
Sales	60000	38000	22000	120000
Direct material	11800	6200	4000	22000
Direct labour	3700	2400	1900	8000
Fixed production overheads				15400
Gross profit				74600

	Anti-ageing cream	Facial masks	Collagen fillers
Production and sales (units)	1000000	1200000	600000

Fixed production overheads are absorbed using a direct material cost percentage rate.

The management accountant of MS is proposing changing to an activity-based costing system. The main activities and their associated cost drivers and overhead cost have been identified as follows:

Activity	Cost driver	Production overhead cost ($000)
Machine set up	Number of set ups	3600
Quality inspection	Number of quality inspections	1200
Processing	Processing time	6500
Purchasing	Number of purchase orders	1800
Packaging	Number of units of product	2300
		15400

Further details have been ascertained as follows:

	Anti-ageing cream	Facial masks	Collagen fillers
Batch size (units)	1000	2000	1500
Machine set-ups per batch	3	3	4
Purchase orders per batch	2	2	1
Processing time per unit (minutes)	2	3	4
Quality inspections per batch	1	1	1

Required:

Calculate for each product:

(i) the total fixed production overhead costs using the current absorption costing system;   *(2 marks)*

(ii) the total gross profit using the proposed activity-based costing system.   *(13 marks)*

CIMA P1 Performance Operations

3.25 Intermediate: Calculation of ABC product cost and discussion as to whether ABC should be implemented.
Beckley Hill (BH) is a private hospital carrying out two types of procedures on patients. Each type of procedure incurs the following direct costs:

Procedure	A ($)	B ($)
Surgical time and materials	1200	2640
Anaesthesia time and materials	800	1620

BH currently calculates the overhead cost per procedure by taking the total overhead cost and simply dividing it by the number of procedures, then rounding the cost to the nearest twp decimal places. Using this method, the total cost is $2475.85 for Procedure A and $4735.85 for Procedure B.

Recently, another local hospital has implemented activity-based costing (ABC). This has led the finance director at BH to consider whether this alternative costing technique would bring any benefits to BH. He has obtained an analysis of BH's total overheads for the last year and some additional data, all of which is shown below:

Cost	Cost driver	($)
Administrative costs	Administrative time per procedure	1870160
Nursing costs	Length of patient stay	6215616
Catering costs	Number of meals	966976
General facility costs	Length of patient stay	8553600
Total overhead costs		17606352

Procedure	A	B
No. of procedures	14600	22400
Administrative time per procedure (hours)	1	1.5
Length of patient stay per procedure (hours)	24	48
Average no. of meals required per patient	1	4

Required:

(a) Calculate the full cost per procedure using activity-based costing.   *(6 marks)*

(b) Making reference to your findings in part (a), advise the finance director as to whether activity-based costing should be implemented at BH.   *(4 marks)*

ACCA F2 Management Accounting

3.26 Intermediate: Reapportionment of service department costs. A company reapportions the costs incurred by two service cost centres, materials handling and inspection, to the three production cost centres of machining, finishing and assembly.

The following are the overhead costs which have been allocated and apportioned to the five cost centres:

	(£000)
Machining	400
Finishing	200
Assembly	100
Materials handling	100
Inspection	50

Estimates of the benefits received by each cost centre are as follows:

	Machining %	Finishing %	Assembly %	Materials handling %	Inspection %
Materials handling	30	25	35	—	10
Inspection	20	30	45	5	—

You are required to:

(a) Calculate the charge for overhead to *each* of the *three* production cost centres, including the amounts reapportioned from the two service centres, using:

(i) the continuous allotment (or repeated distribution) method

(ii) an algebraic method   *(15 marks)*

(b) Comment on whether reapportioning service cost centre costs is generally worthwhile and suggest an alternative treatment for such costs.   *(4 marks)*

(c) Discuss the following statement: 'Some writers advocate that an under- or over-absorption of overhead should be apportioned between the cost of goods sold in the period to which it relates and to closing stocks. However, the United Kingdom practice is to treat under- or over-absorption of overhead as a period cost'.   *(6 marks)*

CIMA Stage 2 Cost Accounting 3

IM3.1 Intermediate.

(a) Explain why predetermined overhead absorption rates are preferred to overhead absorption rates calculated from factual information after the end of a financial period.

(b) The production overhead absorption rates of factories X and Y are calculated using similar methods. However, the rate used by factory X is lower than that used by factory Y. Both factories produce the same type of product. You are required to discuss whether or not this can be taken to be a sign that factory X is more efficient than factory Y.   *(20 marks)*

CIMA Cost Accounting 1

IM3.2 Intermediate. Critically consider the purpose of calculating production overhead absorption rates.

IM3.3 Intermediate.

(a) Specify and explain the factors to be considered in determining whether to utilize a single factory-wide recovery rate for all production overheads or a separate rate for each cost centre, production or service department.   *(12 marks)*

(b) Describe three methods of determining fixed overhead recovery rates and specify the circumstances under which each method is superior to the other methods mentioned.   *(8 marks)*

ACCA P2 Management Accounting

IM3.4 Intermediate: Overhead analysis, calculation of overhead rate and overhead charged to a unit of output. A company makes a range of products with total budgeted manufacturing overheads of £973560 incurred in three production departments (A, B and C) and one service department.

Department A has ten direct employees, who each work 37 hours per week.

Department B has five machines, each of which is operated for 24 hours per week.

Department C is expected to produce 148000 units of final product in the budget period.

The company will operate for 48 weeks in the budget period.

Budgeted overheads incurred directly by each department are:

Production department A	£261745
Production department B	£226120
Production department C	£93890
Service department	£53305

The balance of budgeted overheads are apportioned to departments as follows:

Production department A	40%
Production department B	35%
Production department C	20%
Service department	5%

Service department overheads are apportioned equally to each production department. You are required to:

(a) Calculate an appropriate predetermined overhead absorption rate in each production department. *(9 marks)*
(b) Calculate the manufacturing overhead cost per unit of finished product in a batch of 100 units which take nine direct labour hours in department A and three machine hours in department B to produce. *(3 marks)*

(Total 12 marks)
ACCA Foundation Paper 3

IM3.5 Intermediate: Overhead analysis sheet and calculation of overhead rates. Dunstan Ltd manufactures tents and sleeping bags in three separate production departments. The principal manufacturing processes consist of cutting material in the pattern cutting room and sewing the material in either the tent or the sleeping bag departments. For the year to 31 July cost centre expenses and other relevant information are budgeted as follows:

	Total (£)	Cutting room (£)	Tents (£)	Sleeping bags (£)	Raw material stores (£)	Canteen (£)	Main-tenance (£)
Indirect wages	147200	6400	19500	20100		41200	15000	45000
Consumable materials	54600	5300	4100	2300	—	18700	24200
Plant depreciation	84200	31200	17500	24600	2500	3400	5000
Power	31700						
Heat and light	13800						
Rent and rates	14400						
Building insurance	13500						
Floor area (sq. ft)	30000	8000	10000	7000	1500	2500	1000
Estimated power usage (%)	100	17	38	32	3	8	2
Direct labour (hours)	112000	7000	48000	57000	—	—	—
Machine usage (hours)	87000	2000	40000	45000	—	—	—
Value of raw material issues (%)	100	62.5	12.5	12.5	—	—	12.5

Requirements:

(a) Prepare in columnar form a statement calculating the overhead absorption rates for each machine hour and each direct labour hour for each of the three production units. You should use bases of apportionment and absorption which you consider most appropriate, and the bases used should be clearly indicated in your statement. *(16 marks)*

(b) 'The use of predetermined overhead absorption rates based on budgets is preferable to the use of absorption rates calculated from historical data available after the end of a financial period.'

Discuss this statement insofar as it relates to the financial management of a business. *(5 marks)*

ICAEW PI AC Techniques

IM3.6 Intermediate: Computation of three different overhead absorption rates and a cost-plus selling price. A manufacturing company has prepared the following budgeted information for the forthcoming year:

	£
Direct material	800000
Direct labour	200000
Direct expenses	40000
Production overhead	600000
Administrative overhead	328000
Budgeted activity levels include:	
Budgeted production units	600000
Machine hours	50000
Labour hours	40000

It has recently spent heavily on advanced technological machinery and reduced its workforce. As a consequence, it is thinking about changing its basis for overhead absorption from a percentage of direct labour cost to either a machine hour or labour hour basis. The administrative overhead is to be absorbed as a percentage of factory cost.

Required:

(a) Prepare predetermined overhead absorption rates for production overheads based on the three different bases for absorption mentioned above. *(6 marks)*
(b) Outline the reasons for calculating a predetermined overhead absorption rate. *(2 marks)*
(c) Select the overhead absorption rate that you think the organization should use giving reasons for your decision. *(3 marks)*
(d) The company has been asked to price job AX, this job requires the following:

Direct material	£3788
Direct labour	£1100
Direct expenses	£422
Machine hours	120
Labour hours	220

Compute the price for this job using the absorption rate selected in (c) above, given that the company profit margin is equal to 10 per cent of the price. *(6 marks)*
(e) The company previously paid its direct labour workers on a time basis but is now contemplating moving over to an incentive scheme.

Required:

Draft a memo to the chief accountant outlining the general characteristics and advantages of employing a successful incentive scheme. *(8 marks)*

AAT Cost Accounting and Budgeting

IM3.7 Intermediate: Calculation of overhead absorption rates and under-/over-recovery of overheads. BEC Limited operates an absorption costing system. Its budget for the year ended 31 December shows that it expects its production overhead expenditure to be as follows:

	Fixed £	Variable £
Machining department	600000	480000
Hand finishing department	360000	400000

During the year it expects to make 200 000 units of its product. This is expected to take 80 000 machine hours in the machining department and 120 000 labour hours in the hand finishing department. The costs and activity are expected to arise evenly throughout the year and the budget has been used as the basis of calculating the company's absorption rates.

During March the monthly profit statement reported:

(i) that the actual hours worked in each department were:
Machining 6000 hours
Hand finishing 9600 hours

(ii) that the actual overhead costs incurred were:

	Fixed £	Variable £
Machining	48 500	36 000
Hand finishing	33 600	33 500

(iii) that the actual production was 15 000 units.

Required:

(a) Calculate appropriate pre-determined absorption rates for the year ended 31 December. *(4 marks)*

(b) (i) Calculate the under/over-absorption of overhead for each department of the company for March. *(4 marks)*

(ii) Comment on the problems of using predetermined absorption rates based on the arbitrary apportionment of overhead costs, with regard to comparisons of actual/target performance. *(4 marks)*

(c) State the reasons why absorption costing is used by companies. *(3 marks)*

CIMA Stage 1 Accounting

IM3.8 Intermediate: Calculation of under-/over-recovery of overheads. A company produces several products which pass through the two production departments in its factory. These two departments are concerned with filling and sealing operations. There are two service departments, maintenance and canteen, in the factory.

Predetermined overhead absorption rates, based on direct labour hours, are established for the two production departments. The budgeted expenditure for these departments for the period just ended, including the apportionment of service department overheads, was £110 040 for filling, and £53 300 for sealing. Budgeted direct labour hours were 13 100 for filling and 10 250 for sealing.

Service department overheads are apportioned as follows:

Maintenance	—	Filling	70%
Maintenance	—	Sealing	27%
Maintenance	—	Canteen	3%
Canteen	—	Filling	60%
	—	Sealing	32%
	—	Maintenance	8%

During the period just ended, actual overhead costs and activity were as follows:

	(£)	Direct labour hours
Filling	74 260	12 820
Sealing	38 115	10 075
Maintenance	25 050	
Canteen	24 375	

Required:

(a) Calculate the overheads absorbed in the period and the extent of the under-/over-absorption in each of the two production departments. *(14 marks)*

(b) State, and critically assess, the objectives of overhead apportionment and absorption. *(11 marks)*

ACCA Level 1 Cost and Management Accounting 1

IM3.9 Intermediate: Under- and over-absorption of overheads and calculation of budgeted expenditure and activity. A large firm of solicitors uses a job costing system to identify costs with individual clients. Hours worked by professional staff are used as the basis for charging overhead costs to client services. A predetermined rate is used, derived from budgets drawn up at the beginning of each year commencing on 1 April.

Actual overheads incurred for the year ending 31 March 2018 were £742 600 and 1360 professional hours over budget were worked. Overheads were absorbed at a rate of £7.50 per hour and were over-absorbed by £4760.

The solicitors' practice has decided to refine its overhead charging system by differentiating between the hours of senior and junior professional staff, respectively. A premium of 40 per cent is to be applied to the hourly overhead rate for senior staff compared with junior staff.

Budgets for the year to 31 March 2019 are as follows:

Senior professional staff hours	21 600
Junior professional staff hours	79 300
Practice overheads	£784 000

Required:

(a) Using the data for the actual results for year ended 31 March 2018 calculate for year ending 2018:

(i) budgeted professional staff hours

(ii) budgeted overhead expenditure *(5 marks)*

(b) Calculate, for the budgeted year ending 31 March 2019, the overhead absorption rates (to three decimal places of a £) to be applied to:

(i) senior professional staff hours

(ii) junior professional staff hours *(4 marks)*

(c) How is the change in method of charging overheads likely to improve the firm's job costing system? *(3 marks)*

(d) Explain briefly why overhead absorbed using predetermined rates may differ from actual overhead incurred for the same period. *(2 marks)*

ACCA Foundation Paper 3

IM3.10 Intermediate: Reapportionment of service department costs. JR Co. Ltd's budgeted overheads for the forthcoming period applicable to its production departments, are as follows:

	(£000)
1	870
2	690

The budgeted total costs for the forthcoming period for the service departments, are as follows:

	(£000)
G	160
H	82

The use made of each of the services has been estimated as follows:

	Production department		Service department	
	1	2	G	H
G (%)	60	30	—	10
H (%)	50	30	20	—

Required:

Apportion the service department costs to production departments:

(i) using the step-wise (elimination) method, starting with G;

(ii) using the reciprocal (simultaneous equation) method;

(iii) commenting briefly on your figures. *(8 marks)*

ACCA Paper 8 Managerial Finance

IM3.11 Advanced: Reapportionment of service department costs and comments on apportionment and absorption calculation. The Isis Engineering Company operates a job-order costing system which includes the use of predetermined overhead absorption rates. The company has two service cost centres and two production cost centres. The production cost centre overheads are charged to jobs via direct labour hour rates which are currently £3.10 per hour in production cost centre A and £11.00 per hour in production cost centre B. The calculations involved in determining these rates have excluded any consideration of the services that are provided by each service cost centre to the other.

The bases used to charge general factory overhead and service cost centre expenses to the production cost centres are as follows:

(i) General factory overhead is apportioned on the basis of the floor area used by each of the production and service cost centres.

(ii) The expenses of service cost centre 1 are charged out on the basis of the number of personnel in each production cost centre.

(iii) The expenses of service cost centre 2 are charged out on the basis of the usage of its services by each production cost centre.

The company's overhead absorption rates are revised annually prior to the beginning of each year, using an analysis of the outcome of the current year and the draft plans and forecasts for the forthcoming year. The revised rates for next year are to be based on the following data:

	General factory overhead	Service cost centres		Product cost centres	
		1	2	A	B
Budgeted overhead for next year (before any reallocation) (£)	210 000	93 800	38 600	182 800	124 800
% of factory floor area	—	5	10	15	70
% of factory personnel		10	18	63	9
Estimated usage of services of service cost centre 2 in forthcoming year (hours)	—	1 000	—	4 000	25 000
Budgeted direct labour hours for next year (to be used to calculate next year's absorption rates)	—	—	—	120 000	20 000
Budgeted direct labour hours for current year (these figures were used in the calculation of this year's absorption rates)	—	—	—	100 000	30 000

(a) Ignoring the question of reciprocal charges between the service cost centres, you are required to calculate the revised overhead absorption rates for the two production cost centres. Use the company's established procedures. *(6 marks)*

(b) Comment on the extent of the differences between the current overhead absorption rates and those you have calculated in your answer to (a). Set out the likely reasons for these differences. *(4 marks)*

(c) Each service cost centre provides services to the other. Recalculate next year's overhead absorption rates, recognizing the existence of such reciprocal services and assuming that they can be measured on the same bases as those used to allocate costs to the production cost centres. *(6 marks)*

(d) Assume that:

(i) General factory overhead is a fixed cost.

(ii) Service cost centre 1 is concerned with inspection and quality control, with its budgeted expenses (before any reallocations) being 10 per cent fixed and 90 per cent variable.

(iii) Service cost centre 2 is the company's plant maintenance section, with its budgeted expenses (before any reallocations) being 90 per cent fixed and 10 per cent variable.

(iv) Production cost centre A is labour intensive, with its budgeted overhead (before any reallocation) being 90 per cent fixed and 10 per cent variable.

(v) Production cost centre B is highly mechanized, with its budgeted overhead (before any reallocations) being 20 per cent fixed and 80 per cent variable.

In the light of these assumptions, comment on the cost apportionment and absorption calculations made in parts (a) and (c) and suggest any improvements that you would consider appropriate. *(6 marks)*

ACCA Level 2 Management Accounting

IM3.12 Advanced: Product cost calculation and costs for decision-making. Kaminsky Ltd manufactures belts and braces. The firm is organized into five departments. These are belt-making, braces-making and three service departments (maintenance, warehousing and administration).

Direct costs are accumulated for each department. Factory-wide indirect costs (which are fixed for all production levels within the present capacity limits) are apportioned to departments on the basis of the percentage of floorspace occupied. Service department costs are apportioned on the basis of estimated usage, measured as the percentage of the labour hours operated in the service department utilized by the user department.

Each service department also services at least one other service department.

	Belts	Braces	Admini-stration dept	Main-tenance dept	Ware-housing	Company total
(1) Output and sales (units):						
Output capacity	150 000	60 000				
Output budgeted	100 000	50 000				
Sales budgeted	100 000	50 000				
(2) Direct variable costs (£000)						
Materials	120	130	—	20	30	300
Labour	80	70	50	80	20	300
Total	200	200	50	100	50	600
(3) Factory-wide fixed indirect costs (£000)						1 000

(Continued)

	Belts	Braces	Administration dept	Maintenance dept	Warehousing	Company total
(4) Floorspace (%)	40	40	5	10	5	100
(5) Usage of service department Labour hours (%)						
Administration	40	40	—	10	10	100
Warehousing	50	25	—	25	—	100
Maintenance	30	30	—	—	40	100

(a) You are required to calculate the total cost per unit of belts and braces, respectively, in accordance with the system operated by Kaminsky Ltd.

(b) In addition to the above data, it has been decided that the selling prices of the products are to be determined on a cost-plus basis, as the unit total cost plus 20 per cent. Two special orders have been received, outside the normal run of business, and not provided for in the budget. They are as follows:

(i) an order for 1000 belts from Camfam, an international relief organization, offering to pay £5000 for them,

(ii) a contract to supply 2000 belts a week for 50 weeks to Mixon Spenders, a chainstore, at a price per belt of 'unit total cost plus 10 per cent'.

You are required to set out the considerations which the management of Kaminsky Ltd should take into account in deciding whether to accept each of these orders, and to advise them as far as you are able on the basis of the information given.

(8 marks)

(c) 'Normalized overhead rates largely eliminate from inventories, from cost of goods sold, and from gross margin any unfavourable impact of having production out of balance with the long-run demand for a company's products.'

You are required to explain and comment on the above statement.

(5 marks)

ICAEW Management Accounting

4
ACCOUNTING ENTRIES FOR A JOB COSTING SYSTEM

LEARNING OBJECTIVES After studying this chapter, you should be able to:

- describe the materials recording procedure;
- distinguish between first in, first out (FIFO), last in, first out (LIFO) and average cost methods of stores pricing;
- record the accounting entries for an integrated and interlocking accounting system;
- distinguish between an integrated and an interlocking accounting system;
- describe backflush costing.

This chapter is concerned with the accounting entries necessary to record transactions within a job-order costing system. This chapter can be omitted if you are pursuing a management accounting course that does not require you to focus on cost accumulation for inventory valuation and profit measurement (see 'Guidelines for Using this Book' in Chapter 1). In Chapter 3, it was pointed out that job-order costing relates to a costing system that is required in organizations where each unit or batch of output of a product or service is unique. This creates the need for the cost of each unit to be calculated separately. The term 'job' thus relates to each unique unit or batch of output. In the next chapter, we shall describe a process costing system that relates to those situations in which masses of identical units are produced and it is unnecessary to assign costs to individual units of output. Instead, the cost of a single unit of output can be obtained by merely dividing the total costs assigned to the cost object for a period by the units of output for that period. In practice, these two costing systems represent extreme ends of a continuum. The output of many organizations requires a combination of the elements of both job costing and process costing. However, the accounting methods described in this chapter can be applied to all types of costing system ranging from purely job to process, or a combination of both. You should also note that the term contract costing is used to describe a job costing system that is applied to relatively large cost units that take a considerable amount of time to complete (e.g. building and civil engineering work). If your course curriculum requires an understanding of contract costing, you will find that this topic is covered in Learning Note 4.1 on the digital support resources (see Preface for details).

The accounting system on which we shall concentrate our attention is one in which the cost and financial accounts are combined in one set of accounts; this is known as an integrated cost accounting system. An alternative system, where the cost and financial accounts are maintained independently,

EXHIBIT 4.1 A Stores ledger account

Stores ledger account												
Material:			Code:					Maximum quantity:				
								Minimum quantity:				
	Receipts				Issues					Stock balance		
Date	GRN no.	Quantity	Unit price (£)	Amount (£)	Stores req. no.	Quantity	Unit price (£)	Amount (£)	Quantity	Unit price (£)	Amount (£)	

is known as an **interlocking cost accounting system**. The integrated cost accounting system is generally considered to be preferable to the interlocking system, since the latter involves a duplication of accounting entries.

A knowledge of the materials recording procedure will enable you to have a better understanding of the accounting entries. Therefore, we shall begin by looking at this procedure.

MATERIALS RECORDING PROCEDURE

When goods are received they are inspected and details of the quantity of each type of goods received are listed on a goods received note. The goods received note is the source document for entering details of the items received in the receipts column of the appropriate **stores ledger account.** An illustration of a stores ledger account is provided in Exhibit 4.1. This document is merely a record of the quantity and value of each individual item of material stored by the organization. In most organizations, this document will only consist in the form of a computer record.

The formal authorization for the issue of materials is a **stores requisition**. The type and quantity of materials issued are listed on the requisition. This document also contains details of the job number, product code or overhead account for which the materials are required. Exhibit 4.2 provides an illustration of a typical stores requisition. Each of the items listed on the materials requisition are priced from the information recorded in the receipts column of the appropriate stores ledger account. The information on the stores requisition is then recorded in the issues column of the appropriate stores ledger account and a balance of the quantity and value for each of the specific items of materials is calculated. The cost of each item of material listed on the stores requisition is assigned to the appropriate job number or overhead account. In practice, this clerical process will be computerized.

EXHIBIT 4.2 A stores requisition

Stores requisition					No.	
Material required for: (job or overhead account)						
Department:					Date:	
[Quantity]	Description	Code no.	Weight	Rate	£	[Notes]
Head of department						

PRICING THE ISSUES OF MATERIALS

One difficulty that arises with material issues is the cost to associate with each issue. This is because the same type of material may have been purchased at several different prices. Actual cost can take on several different values, and some method of pricing material issues must be selected. Consider the situation presented in Example 4.1.

There are three alternative methods that you might consider for calculating the cost of materials issued to job Z which will impact on both the cost of sales and the inventory valuation that is incorporated in the April monthly profit statement and balance sheet. First, you can assume that the first item received was the first item to be issued, that is first in, first out (FIFO). In the example the 5000 units issued to job Z would be priced at £1 and the closing inventory would be valued at £6000 (5000 units at £1.20 per unit).

Second, you could assume that the last item to be received was the first item to be issued, that is, last in, first out (LIFO). Here a material cost of £6000 (5000 units at £1.20 per unit) would be recorded against the cost of job Z and the closing inventory would be valued at £5000 (5000 units at £1 per unit).

Third, there may be a strong case for issuing the items at the average cost of the materials in stock (i.e. £1.10 per unit). With an average cost system, the job cost would be recorded at £5500 and the closing inventory would also be valued at £5500. The following is a summary of the three different materials pricing methods relating to Example 4.1:

	Cost of sales (i.e. charge to job Z) (£)	Closing inventory (£)	Total costs (£)
First in first out (FIFO)	5000 (5000 × £1)	6000 (5000 × £1.20)	11 000
Last in, first out (LIFO)	6000 (5000 × £1.20)	5000 (5000 × £1)	11 000
Average cost	5500 (5000 × £1.10)	5500 (5000 × £1.10)	11 000

FIFO appears to be the most logical method in the sense that it makes the same assumption as the physical flow of materials through an organization; that is, it is assumed that items received first will be issued first.

During periods of inflation, the earliest materials that have the lowest purchase price will be issued first. This assumption leads to a lower cost of sales calculation, and therefore a higher profit than would be obtained by using either of the other methods. Note also that the closing inventory will be at the latest and therefore higher prices. With the LIFO method the latest and higher prices are assigned to the cost of sales and therefore lower profits will be reported compared with using either FIFO or average cost. The value of the closing inventory will be at the earliest and therefore lower prices. Under the average cost method, the cost of sales and the closing inventory will fall somewhere between the values recorded for the FIFO and LIFO methods.

LIFO is not an acceptable method of pricing for taxation purposes in the UK, although this does not preclude its use provided that the accounts are adjusted for taxation purposes. Also, the International Accounting Standard (IAS2) on inventory valuation states that LIFO does not bear a reasonable

EXAMPLE 4.1

On 5 March, Nordic purchased 5000 units of materials at £1 each. A further 5000 units were purchased on 30 March at £1.20 each. During April, 5000 units were issued to job Z. No further issues were made during April and you are now preparing the monthly accounts for April.

relationship to actual costs obtained during the period. FIFO or the average cost method are therefore preferable for external financial accounting purposes.

The above discussion relates to pricing the issue of materials for internal and external profit measurement and inventory valuation. For decision-making, the focus is on future costs, rather than the allocation of past costs and therefore using different methods of pricing materials is not an issue.

CONTROL ACCOUNTS

The cost accumulation recording system is based on a system of control accounts. A control account is a summary account, where entries are made from totals of transactions for a period. For example, the balance in the stores ledger control account will be supported by a voluminous file of stores ledger accounts, which will add up to agree with the total in the stores ledger control account. Assuming 1000 items of materials were received for a period that totalled £200 000, an entry of the total of £200 000 would be recorded on the debit (receipts side) of the stores ledger *control* account. This will be supported by 1000 separate entries in each of the individual stores ledger accounts. The total of all these *individual* entries will add up to £200 000. A system of control accounts enables one to check the accuracy of the various accounting entries, since the total of all the *individual* entries in the various stores ledger accounts should agree with the control account, which will have received the *totals* of the various transactions. The file of all the individual accounts (for example the individual stores ledger accounts) supporting the total control account is called the subsidiary ledger.

We shall now examine the accounting entries necessary to record the transaction outlined in Example 4.2. A manual system is described so that the accounting entries can be followed, but the normal practice now is for these accounts to be maintained on a computer. You will find a summary of the accounting entries set out in Exhibit 4.3, where each transaction is prefixed by the appropriate number to give a clearer understanding of the necessary entries relating to each transaction. In addition, the appropriate journal entry is shown for each transaction, together with a supporting explanation.

REAL WORLD VIEWS 4.1

Commercial Metals changes the method it uses to value inventories

It was decided in the first quarter of fiscal 2016 that Commercial Metals Company Ltd would change the accounting method it used to value its inventories. This change would be for its Americas Mills, Americas Recycling and Americas Fabrication segments. This development would see them using the weighted average cost method instead of the last in, first out method. The company applied this change in accounting principle retrospectively to all prior periods presented.

Furthermore, during this first quarter, the company changed the accounting method it used to value its inventories within its International Marketing and Distribution segment; a specific identification method elected to be used rather than the first in, first out method. As this change in accounting principle was immaterial in all prior periods, it was not applied retrospectively.

Questions

1 Why did the company apply the change in valuation method retrospectively for some of its segments but did not make retrospective changes to its International Marketing and Distribution segment?

2 What do you think is meant by the term 'specific identification method' of tracking inventories?

Reference
www.prnewswire.com/news-releases/commercial -metals-company-reports-

EXAMPLE 4.2

The following are the transactions of AB Ltd for the month of April.

1 Raw materials of £182 000 were purchased on credit.

2 Raw materials of £2000 were returned to the supplier because of defects.

3 The total of stores requisitions for direct materials issued for the period was £165 000.

4 The total issues for indirect materials for the period was £10 000.

5 Gross wages of £185 000 were incurred during the period consisting of wages paid to employees £105 000

   Tax deductions payable to the government (i.e. Inland Revenue) £60 000

   National Insurance contributions due £20 000

6 All the amounts due in transaction 5 were settled in cash during the period.

7 The allocation of the gross wages for the period was as follows:

   Direct wages £145 000

   Indirect wages £40 000

8 The employer's contribution for National Insurance deductions was £25 000.

9 Indirect factory expenses of £41 000 were incurred during the period.

10 Depreciation of factory machinery was £30 000.

11 Overhead expenses allocated to jobs by means of overhead allocation rates was £140 000 for the period.

12 Non-manufacturing overhead incurred during the period was £40 000.

13 The cost of jobs completed and transferred to finished goods inventory was £300 000.

14 The sales value of goods withdrawn from inventory and delivered to customers was £400 000 for the period.

15 The cost of goods withdrawn from inventory and delivered to customers was £240 000 for the period.

RECORDING THE PURCHASE OF RAW MATERIALS

The entry to record the purchase of materials in transaction 1 is

Dr Stores ledger control account	182 000	
Cr Creditors control account		182 000

This accounting entry reflects the fact that the company has incurred a short-term liability to acquire a current asset consisting of raw material inventory. Each purchase is also entered in the receipts column of an individual stores ledger account (a separate record is used for each item of materials purchased) for the quantity received, a unit price and amount. In addition, a separate credit entry is made in each individual creditor's account. Note that the entries in the control accounts form part of the system of double entry, whereas the separate entries in the individual accounts are detailed subsidiary records, which do not form part of the double entry system.

EXHIBIT 4.3 Summary of accounting transactions for AB Ltd

Stores ledger control account

1. Creditors a/c	182 000	2. Creditors a/c	2 000
		3. Work in progress a/c	165 000
		4. Factory overhead a/c	10 000
		Balance c/d	5 000
	182 000		182 000
Balance b/d	5 000		

Factory overhead control account

4. Stores ledger a/c	10 000	11. Work in progress a/c	140 000
7. Wages control a/c	40 000	Balance – under-recovery	6 000
8. National Insurance contributions a/c	25 000	transferred to costing P&L a/c	
9. Expense creditors a/c	41 000		
10. Provision for depreciation a/c	30 000		
	146 000		146 000

Non-manufacturing overhead control account

12. Expense creditor a/c	40 000	Transferred to costing P&L a/c	40 000

Creditors account

2. Stores ledger a/c	2 000	1. Stores ledger a/c	182 000

Wages accrued account

6. Cash/bank	105 000	5. Wages control a/c	105 000

Tax payable account

6. Cash/bank	60 000	5. Wages control a/c	60 000

National Insurance contributions account

6. Cash/bank	20 000	5. Wage control a/c	20 000
8. Cash/bank	25 000	8. Factory overhead a/c	25 000
	45 000		45 000

Expense creditors account

		9. Factory overhead a/c	41 000
		12. Non-manufacturing overhead	40 000

Work in progress control account

3. Stores ledger a/c	165 000	13. Finished goods	
7. Wages control a/c	145 000	inventory a/c	300 000
11. Factory overhead a/c	140 000	Balance c/d	150 000
	450 000		450 000
Balanced b/d	150 000		

Finished goods inventory account

13. Work in progress a/c	300 000	15. Cost of sales a/c	240 000
		Balance c/d	60 000
	300 000		300 000
Balance b/d	60 000		

Cost of sales account				
15. Finished goods inventory a/c	240000	Transferred to costing P&L a/c		240000

Provision for depreciation account			
		10. Factory overhead	30000

Wages control account				
5. Wages accrued a/c	105000	7. Work in progress a/c		145000
5. Tax payable a/c	60000	7. Factory overhead a/c		40000
5. National Insurance a/c	20000			
	185000			185000

Sales account				
Transferred to costing P&L	400000	14. Debtors		400000

Debtors account		
14. Sales a/c	400000	

Costing profit and loss account			
Sales a/c			400000
Less cost of sales a/c			240000
Gross profit			160000
Less under-recovery of factory overhead		6000	
Non-manufacturing overhead		40000	46000
Net profit			114000

The entry for transaction 2 for materials returned to suppliers is:

Dr Creditors control account	2000	
Cr Stores ledger control account		2000

An entry for the returned materials is also made in the appropriate stores ledger records and in the individual creditors' accounts.

RECORDING THE ISSUE OF MATERIALS

The stores department issues materials from store in exchange for a duly authorized stores requisition. For direct materials, the job number will be recorded on the stores requisition, while for indirect materials, the overhead account number will be entered on the requisition. The issue of direct materials involves a transfer of the materials from stores to production. For transaction 3, material requisitions will have been summarized and the resulting totals will be recorded as follows:

Dr Work in progress account	165000	
Cr Stores ledger control account		165000

This accounting entry reflects the fact that raw material inventory is being converted into work in progress (WIP) inventory. In addition to the above entries in the control accounts, the individual jobs will be charged with the cost of the material issued so that job costs can be calculated. Each issue is also entered in the issues column on the appropriate stores ledger record.

The entry for transaction 4 for the issue of indirect materials is:

Dr Factory overhead control account	10000	
Cr Stores ledger control account		10000

In addition to the entry in the factory overhead account, the cost of material issued will be entered in the individual overhead accounts. These separate overhead accounts will normally consist of individual indirect material accounts for each responsibility centre. Periodically, the totals of each responsibility centre account for indirect materials will be entered in performance reports for comparison with the budgeted indirect material cost.

After transactions 1–4 have been recorded, the stores ledger control account would look like this:

Stores ledger control account

1. Creditors a/c	182 000	2. Creditors a/c	2 000
		3. Work in progress a/c	165 000
		4. Factory overhead a/c	10 000
		Balance c/d	5 000
	182 000		182 000
Balance b/d	5 000		

ACCOUNTING PROCEDURE FOR LABOUR COSTS

Accounting for labour costs can be divided into the following two distinct phases:

1 Computations of the gross pay for each employee and calculation of payments to be made to employees, government, pension funds, etc. (payroll accounting).

2 Allocation of labour costs to jobs, overhead account and capital accounts (labour cost accounting).

An entry is then made in the payroll for each employee, showing the gross pay, tax deductions and other authorized deductions. The gross pay less the deductions gives the net pay, and this is the amount of cash paid to each employee. The payroll gives details of the total amount of cash due to employees and the amounts due to the government (i.e. for taxes and national insurance payable by each employee), pension funds and savings funds, etc. To keep the illustration simple at this stage, transaction 5 includes only deductions in respect of taxes and National Insurance. The accounting entries for transaction 5 are:

Dr Wages control account	185 000	
Cr Tax payable account		60 000
Cr National Insurance contributions account		20 000
Cr Wages accrued account		105 000

The credit entries in transaction 5 will be cleared by a payment of cash. The payment of wages will involve an immediate cash payment, but some slight delay may occur with the payment of tax and National Insurance since the final date for payment of these items is normally a few weeks after the payment of wages. The entries for the cash payments for these items (transaction 6) are:

Dr Tax payable account	60 000	
Dr National Insurance contributions account	20 000	
Dr Wages accrued account	105 000	
Cr Cash/bank		185 000

Note that the credit entries for transaction 5 merely represent the recording of amounts due for future payments. The wages control account, however, represents the gross wages for the period, and it is the amount in this account that must be allocated to the job, overhead and capital accounts. Transaction 7 gives details of the allocation of the gross wages. The accounting entries are:

Dr Work in progress control account	145 000	
Dr Factory overhead control account	40 000	
Cr Wages control account		185 000

In addition to the total entry in the work in progress control account, the labour cost will be charged to the individual job accounts. Similarly, the total entry in the factory overhead control account will be supported by an entry in each individual overhead account for the indirect labour cost incurred.

Transaction 8 represents the employer's contribution for National Insurance payments. The National Insurance deductions in transaction 5 represent the employees' contributions where the company acts merely as an agent, paying these contributions on behalf of the employee to the government. The employer is also responsible for making a contribution in respect of each employee. To keep the accounting entries simple here, the employer's contributions will be charged to the factory overhead account. The accounting entry for transaction 8 is therefore:

Dr Factory overhead control account   25000
  Cr National Insurance contributions account   25000

The National Insurance contributions account will be closed with the following entry when the cash payment is made:

Dr National Insurance contributions account   25000
  Cr Cash/bank   25000

After recording these transactions, the wages control account would look like this:

Wages control account

5. Wages accrued a/c	105000	7. Work in progress a/c	145000
5. Tax payable a/c	60000	7. Factory overhead a/c	40000
5. National Insurance a/c	20000		
	185000		185000

ACCOUNTING PROCEDURE FOR MANUFACTURING OVERHEADS

Accounting for manufacturing overheads involves entering details of the actual amount of manufacturing overhead incurred on the debit side of the factory overhead control account. The total amount of overheads charged to production is recorded on the credit side of the factory overhead account. In the previous chapter, we established that manufacturing overheads are charged to production using budgeted overhead rates. It is most unlikely, however, that the actual amount of overhead incurred, which is recorded on the debit side of the account, will be in agreement with the amount of overhead allocated to jobs, which is recorded on the credit side of the account. The difference represents the under- or over-recovery of factory overheads, which is transferred to the profit and loss account, in accordance with the requirements of the UK Financial Reporting Standard 102 (FRS 102) and the International Accounting Standard (IAS2) on inventory valuation.

Transaction 9 represents various indirect expenses that have been incurred and that will eventually have to be paid in cash, for example, property taxes and lighting and heating. Transaction 10 includes other indirect expenses that do not involve a cash commitment. For simplicity, it is assumed that depreciation of factory machinery is the only item that falls into this category. The accounting entries for transactions 9 and 10 are:

Dr Factory overhead control account	71 000	
Cr Expense creditors control account		41 000
Cr Provision of depreciation account		30 000

In addition, subsidiary entries, not forming part of the double entry system, will be made in individual overhead accounts. These accounts will be headed by the title of the cost centre followed by the object of expenditure. For example, it may be possible to assign indirect materials directly to specific cost centres and separate records can then be kept of the indirect materials charge for each centre. It will not, however, be possible to allocate property taxes, lighting and heating directly to cost centres and entries should be made in individual overhead accounts for these items. These expenses should then be apportioned to cost centres (using the procedures described in Chapter 3) to compute product costs for meeting financial accounting inventory valuation requirements.

Transaction 11 refers to the total overheads that have been charged to jobs using the estimated overhead absorption rates. The accounting entry in the control accounts for allocating overheads to jobs is:

Dr Work in progress control account	140 000	
Cr Factory overhead control account		140 000

In addition to this entry, the individual jobs are charged so that job costs can be calculated. When these entries have been made, the factory overhead control account would look like this:

Factory overhead control account

4. Stores ledger control a/c	10 000	11. Work in progress		
7. Wages control a/c	40 000	control a/c	140 000	
8. Employer's National		Balance – under-recovery		
Insurance contributions a/c	25 000	of overhead transferred to		
		costing profit and loss a/c	6 000	
9. Expense creditors a/c	41 000			
10. Provision for				
depreciation a/c	30 000			
	146 000		146 000	

The debit side of this account indicates that £146 000 overhead has been incurred, but examination of the credit side indicates that only £140 000 has been allocated to jobs via overhead allocation rates. The balance of £6000 represents an under-recovery of factory overhead, which is regarded as a period cost to be charged to the costing profit and loss account in the current accounting period. The reasons for this were explained in the previous chapter.

NON-MANUFACTURING OVERHEADS

You will have noted in the previous chapter that non-manufacturing overhead costs are regarded as period costs and not product costs, and non-manufacturing overheads are not therefore charged to the work in progress control account. The accounting entry for transaction 12 is:

Dr Non-manufacturing overheads account	40 000	
Cr Expense creditors account		40 000

At the end of the period the non-manufacturing overheads will be transferred to the profit and loss account as a period cost by means of the following accounting entry:

Dr Profit and loss account	40 000	
Cr Non-manufacturing overheads account		40 000

In practice, separate control accounts are maintained for administrative, marketing and financial overheads, but, to simplify this example, all the non-manufacturing overheads are included in one control account. In addition, subsidiary records will be kept that analyse the total non-manufacturing overheads by individual accounts, for example office stationery account, sales person's travelling expenses account, etc.

ACCOUNTING PROCEDURES FOR JOBS COMPLETED AND PRODUCTS SOLD

When jobs have been completed, they are transferred from the factory floor to the finished goods store. The total of the job accounts for the completed jobs for the period is recorded as a transfer from the work in progress control account to the finished goods inventory account. The accounting entry for transaction 13 is:

Dr Finished goods inventory account	300 000	
Cr Work in progress control account		300 000

When the goods are removed from the finished goods inventory and delivered to the customers, the revenue is recognized. It is a fundamental principle of financial accounting that only costs associated with earning the revenue are included as expenses. The cost of those goods that have been delivered to customers must therefore be matched against the revenue due from delivery of the goods so that the gross profit can be calculated. Any goods that have not been delivered to customers will be included as part of the finished inventory valuation. The accounting entries to reflect these transactions are:

Transaction 14		
Dr Debtors control account	400 000	
Cr Sales account		400 000

Transaction 15		
Dr Cost of sales account	240 000	
Cr Finished goods inventory account		240 000

COSTING PROFIT AND LOSS ACCOUNT

At frequent intervals management may wish to ascertain the profit to date for the particular period. The accounting procedure outlined in this chapter provides a database from which a costing profit and loss account may easily be prepared. The costing profit and loss account for AB Ltd based on the information given in Example 4.2 is set out in Exhibit 4.3 shown on pages 87–88. Alternatively, management may prefer the profit statement to be presented in a format similar to that which is necessary for external reporting. Such information can easily be extracted from the subsidiary records.

JOB-ORDER COSTING IN SERVICE ORGANIZATIONS

In the two previous chapters, it was pointed out that some service organizatons (e.g. accounting, automotive and appliance repair firms) have partially completed work (i.e. work in progress) at the end of the accounting period. Therefore they need to track the flow of costs incurred using accounting procedures similar to those described in this chapter. The major difference is that service organizations do not have finished goods inventory so a finished goods inventory account is not required. The costs incurred will be initially debited to stores ledger, wages and service overhead control accounts. The individual customer accounts will be charged with the labour, material and overhead costs incurred and the total allocated to the work in progress account. When the customers are invoiced for the services provided, the work in progress account is credited and cost of sales account is debited with total of the amounts invoiced for the period. The balance of the work in progress represents the total amount of work in progress at the end of the accounting period.

INTERLOCKING ACCOUNTING

With an **interlocking accounting system** the cost and financial accounts are maintained independently of one another and in the cost accounts no attempt is made to keep a separate record of the financial accounting transactions. Examples of financial accounting transactions include entries in the various creditors, debtors and capital accounts. To maintain the double entry records, an account must be maintained in the cost accounts to record the corresponding entry that, in an integrated accounting system, would normally be made in one of the financial accounts (creditors, debtors accounts, etc.). This account is called a cost control or general ledger adjustment account.

Using an interlocking accounting system to record the transactions listed in Example 4.2, the entries in the creditors, wages accrued, taxation payable, National Insurance contributions, expense creditors, provision for depreciation and debtors accounts would be replaced by the entries shown below in the cost control account. Note that the entries in the remaining accounts will be unchanged.

Cost control account

2. Stores ledger control a/c	2 000	1. Stores ledger control a/c	182 000
14. Sales a/c	400 000	5. Wages control a/c	185 000
Balance c/d	215 000	8. Factory overhead control a/c	25 000
		9. Expense creditors a/c	41 000
		12. Non-manufacturing overhead a/c	40 000
		10. Factory overhead a/c	30 000
		Profit and loss a/c (profit for period)	114 000
	617 000		617 000
		Balance b/d	215 000

ACCOUNTING ENTRIES FOR A JIT MANUFACTURING SYSTEM

Many organizations have adopted a just-in-time (JIT) manufacturing philosophy. The major features of a JIT philosophy will be explained in Chapter 22 but at this point it is appropriate to note that implementing a JIT philosophy is normally accompanied by a cellular production layout whereby each cell produces similar products. Consequently, a form of process costing environment emerges. There is also a high velocity of WIP movement throughout the cell, and so it is extremely difficult to trace actual costs to *individual* products. Adopting a JIT philosophy also results in a substantial reduction in inventories so that inventory valuation becomes less relevant. Therefore, simplified accounting procedures can be adopted for allocating costs between cost of sales and inventories. This simplified procedure is known as backflush costing.

Backflush costing aims to eliminate detailed accounting transactions. Rather than tracking the movement of materials through the production process, a backflush costing system focuses first on the output of the organization and then works backwards when allocating cost between costs of goods sold and inventories, with no separate accounting for WIP. In contrast, conventional product costing systems track costs in synchronization with the movement of the products from direct materials, through WIP to finished goods. We shall now use Example 4.3 to illustrate two variants of backflush costing. Trigger points determine when the entries are made in the accounting system.

Actual conversion costs are recorded as incurred, just the same as conventional recording systems. Conversion costs are then applied to products at various trigger points. It is assumed that any conversion costs not applied to products are carried forward and disposed of at the year end. The accounting entries are as follows.

Method 1

Trigger points

1 – The purchase of raw materials and components

2 – The manufacture of finished goods

EXAMPLE 4.3

The transactions for the month of May for JIT plc are as follows:

Purchase of raw materials	£1515000
Conversion costs incurred during the period	£1010000
Finished goods manufactured during the period	100000 units
Sales for the period	98000 units

There are no opening inventories of raw materials, WIP or finished goods. The standard and actual cost per unit of output is £25 (£15 materials and £10 conversion cost). The company uses an integrated cost accounting system.

	(£)	(£)
1. Dr Raw material inventory account	1515000	
Cr Creditors		1515000
2. Dr Conversion costs	1010000	
Cr Expense creditors		1010000
3. Dr Finished goods inventory	2500000	
(100000 × £25)		
Cr Raw material inventory		1500000
(100000 × £15)		
Cr Conversion costs		1000000
(100000 × £10)		
4. Dr Cost of goods sold	2450000	
(98000 × £25)		
Cr Finished goods inventory		2450000

The ledger accounts in respect of the above transactions are shown in Exhibit 4.4.

Method 2

This is the simplest variant of backflush costing. There is only one trigger point. We shall assume that the trigger point is the manufacture of a finished unit. Conversion costs are debited as the actual costs are incurred. The accounting entries are:

	(£)	(£)
1. Dr Finished goods inventory (100000 × £25)	2500000	
Cr Creditors		1500000
Cr Conversion costs		1000000
2. Dr Cost of goods sold (98000 × £25)	2450000	
Cr Finished goods inventory		2450000

The end of month inventory balance is £50000 finished goods. At the end of the period the £15000 of raw materials purchased but not yet manufactured into finished goods will not have been recorded in the internal product costing system. It is therefore not included in the closing inventory valuation.

EXHIBIT 4.4 Ledger accounts for a backflush costing system (Method 1)

Raw materials inventory

1. Creditors	£1 515 000	3. Finished goods	£1 500 000

Finished goods inventory

3. Raw materials	£1 500 000	4. COGS	£2 450 000
3. Conversion costs	£1 000 000		

Conversion costs

2. Creditors	£1 010 000	3. Finished goods	£1 000 000

Cost of goods sold (COGS)

4. Finished goods	£2 450 000

The end of month inventory balances are

	(£)
Raw materials	15 000
Finished goods	50 000
	65 000

You will see that the WIP account is eliminated with both the variants that are illustrated. If inventories are low, the vast majority of manufacturing costs will form part of cost of goods sold and will not be deferred in inventory. In this situation, the volume of work involved in tracking costs through WIP, cost of goods sold and finished goods is unlikely to be justified. This considerably reduces the volume of transactions recorded in the internal accounting system. Note, however, that it may be necessary to track the progress of units on the production line, but there will be no attempt to trace costs to units progressing through the system.

The second variant is suitable only for JIT systems with minimum raw materials and WIP inventories. Note that both methods allocate identical amounts to the cost of goods sold for the period. The second method may yield significantly different inventory valuations from conventional product costing systems. It is therefore claimed that this method of backflush costing may not be acceptable for external financial reporting. However, if inventories are low or not subject to significant change from one accounting period to the next, operating income and inventory valuations derived from backflush costing will not be materially different from the results reported by the conventional system. In these circumstances, backflush costing is acceptable for external financial reporting.

SUMMARY

The following items relate to the learning objectives listed at the beginning of the chapter.

● **Describe the materials recording procedure.**

When the materials are received the quantities and values are recorded in a separate stores ledger account for each item of material. The issues of materials are recorded on a stores requisition, which contains details of the job number product code or overhead account for which the materials are required. The information on the stores requisition is then recorded in the issues column of the appropriate stores ledger account and after each issue a balance of the quantity and value for each of the specific items of materials is calculated. The cost of each item of material listed on the stores requisition is assigned to the appropriate job number, product or overhead account. In practice, this clerical process will be computerized.

● **Distinguish between first in, first out (FIFO), last in, first out (LIFO) and average cost methods of stores pricing.**

Because the same type of materials may have been purchased at several different prices, actual cost can take on several different values. Therefore an assumption must be made when pricing the materials used. FIFO assumes that the first item that was received in stock was the first item issued so the earlier purchase prices are used. LIFO assumes that the last item to be received is the first item to be issued, resulting in the later purchase prices being used. The average cost method assumes that materials are issued at the average cost of materials in stock.

● **Record the accounting entries for an integrated and interlocking accounting system.**

A summary of the accounting entries for an integrated accounting system, where all purchases and expenses are settled in cash, is shown diagrammatically in Figure 4.1.

● **Distinguish between an integrated and an interlocking accounting system.**

With an integrated cost accounting system, the cost and financial accounts are combined in one set of accounts, whereas the cost and financial accounts are maintained independently with an interlocking accounting system. An integrated accounting system is recommended since it avoids the duplication of accounting entries.

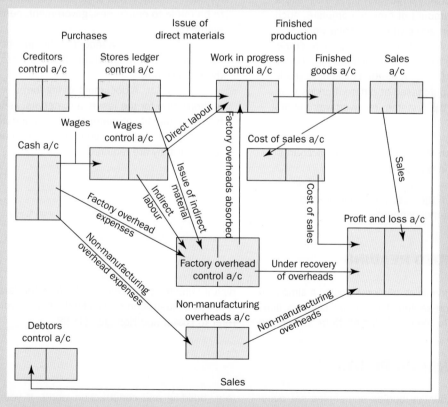

FIGURE 4.1

Flow of accounting entries in an integrated accounting system

● **Describe backflush costing.**

Backflush costing is a simplified costing system that aims to eliminate detailed accounting transactions. It is applied when a just-in-time production philosophy is adopted. Instead of tracking the movement of materials through the production process, a backflush costing system focuses first on the output of the organization and then works backwards when allocating cost between cost of goods sold and inventories, with no separate accounting for work in progress. In contrast, a conventional integrated accounting system tracks costs in synchronization with the movement of the products from direct materials, through work in progress to finished goods.

KEY TERMS AND CONCEPTS

Average cost A method of valuing stock that has been purchased at different prices that values all items at the average cost.

Backflush costing A simplified costing system that is applied when a just-in-time production philosophy is adopted and which focuses first on the output of the organization and then works backwards when allocating cost between cost of goods sold and inventories, with no separate accounting for work in progress.

Contract costing A job costing system that is applied to relatively large cost units that take a considerable amount of time to complete, such as construction and civil engineering work.

Control account A summary account, where entries are made from totals of transactions for a period.

First in, first out (FIFO) A method of valuing stock that has been purchased at different prices that assumes that the first item received was the first to be issued.

Integrated cost accounting system An accounting system in which the cost and financial accounts are combined in one set of accounts.

Interlocking accounting system An accounting system in which the cost and financial accounts are maintained independently.

Interlocking cost accounting system An accounting system in which the cost and financial accounts are maintained independently.

Labour cost accounting The allocation of labour costs to jobs, overhead account and capital accounts.

Last in, first out (LIFO) A method of valuing stock that has been purchased at different prices that assumes that the last item received was the first to be issued.

Payroll accounting The computation of the gross pay for each employee and calculation of payments to be made to employees, government, pension funds, etc.

Stores ledger account A record of the quantity and value of each individual item of material stored by the organization.

Stores requisition A document giving formal authorization for the issue of materials, listing the type and quantity of materials issued and details of the job number, product code or overhead account for which they are required.

RECOMMENDED READING

To illustrate the principles of stores pricing a simplistic illustration was presented. For a more complex illustration you should refer to Learning Note 3.2 on the digital support resources (see Preface for details). For a detailed illustration of backflush costing, you should refer to Foster and Horngren (1988).

KEY EXAMINATION POINTS

Professional accounting bodies sometimes set questions relating to contract costing. Contract costing is a system of job costing that is applied to relatively large cost units, which take a considerable time to complete (e.g. building and construction work). If your course curriculum requires a knowledge of contract costing, you should refer to Learning Note 4.1 on the digital support resources (see Preface for details).

ASSESSMENT MATERIAL

he review questions are short questions that enable you to assess your understanding of the main topics included in the chapter. The numbers in parentheses provide you with the page numbers to refer to if you cannot answer a specific question.

The review problems are more complex and require you to relate and apply the content to various business problems. The problems are graded by their level of difficulty. Solutions to review problems that are not preceded by the term 'IM' are provided in a separate section at the end of the book. Solutions to problems preceded by the term 'IM' are provided in the Instructor's Manual accompanying this book that can be downloaded from the lecturer's digital support resources. Additional review problems with fully worked solutions are provided in the *Student Manual* that accompanies this book.

REVIEW QUESTIONS

4.1 Distinguish between an integrated and interlocking accounting system. (pp. 82–83)

4.2 Describe the first in, first out, last in, first out and average cost methods of stores pricing. (pp. 84–85)

4.3 Explain the purpose of a stores ledger account. (p. 83)

4.4 Explain the purpose of control accounts. (p. 85)

4.5 List the accounting entries for the purchase and issues of direct and indirect materials. (pp. 86–89)

4.6 List the accounting entries for the payment and the allocation of gross wages. (pp. 89–90)

4.7 List the accounting entries for the payment and allocation of overheads. (pp. 91–92)

4.8 Explain the circumstances when backflush costing is used. (p. 94)

4.9 Describe the major aims of backflush costing. (p. 94)

REVIEW PROBLEMS

4.10 Basic. An organization's stock records show the following transactions for a specific item during last month:

Date	Receipts units	Issues units
4th		50
13th	200	
20th		50
27th		50

The stock at the beginning of last month consisted of 100 units valued at £6700.

The receipts last month cost £62 per unit.

The value of the closing stock for last month has been calculated twice – once using a FIFO valuation and once using a LIFO valuation.

Which of the following statements about the valuation of closing stock for last month is correct?

(a) The FIFO valuation is higher than the LIFO valuation by £250.

(b) The LIFO valuation is higher than the FIFO valuation by £250.

(c) The FIFO valuation is higher than the LIFO valuation by £500.

(d) The LIFO valuation is higher than the FIFO valuation by £500.

ACCA Financial Information for Management

4.11 Basic. An organization's records for last month show the following in respect of one store's item:

Date	Receipt units	Issues units	Stock units
1st			200
5th		100	100
7th	400		500
19th		190	310
27th		170	140

Last month's opening stock was valued at a total of £2900 and the receipts during the month were purchased at a cost of £17.50 per unit.

The organization uses the weighted average method of valuation and calculates a new weighted average after each stores receipt.

What was the total value of the issues last month?

(a) £7360
(b) £7534
(c) £7590
(d) £7774

ACCA Financial Information for Management

4.12 Basic. The following data relate to material J for last month:

			£
Opening stock	300kg	valued at	3300
Purchases:			
4th	400kg	for	4800
18th	500kg	for	6500
Issues:			
13th	600kg		
25th	300kg		

Using the LIFO valuation method, what was the value of the closing stock for last month?

(a) £3300
(b) £3500
(c) £3700
(d) £3900

ACCA Financial Information for Management

4.13 Basic. In an integrated bookkeeping system, when the actual production overheads exceed the absorbed production overheads, the accounting entries to close off the production overhead account at the end of the period would be:

(a) Debit the production overhead account and credit the work in progress account.
(b) Debit the work in progress account and credit the production overhead account.
(c) Debit the production overhead account and credit the profit and loss account.
(d) Debit the profit and loss account and credit the production overhead account.

CIMA: Fundamentals of Management Accounting

4.14 Basic. A company uses a blanket overhead absorption rate of $5 per direct labour hour. Actual overhead expenditure in a period was as budgeted.

The under/over-absorbed overhead account for the period have the following entries:

DR ($)		CR ($)
Production overhead	4000 Profit or loss account	4000

Which of the following statements is true?

(a) Actual direct labour hours were 800 less than budgeted
(b) Actual direct labour hours were 800 more than budgeted
(c) Actual direct labour hours were 4000 less than budgeted
(d) Production overhead was over absorbed by $4000

ACCA F2 Management Accounting

4.15 Basic. The following data have been taken from the books of CB plc, which uses a non-integrated accounting system:

	Financial accounts £	Cost accounts £
Opening stock of materials	5000	6400
Closing stock of materials	4000	5200
Opening stock of finished goods	9800	9600
Closing stock of finished goods	7900	7600

The effect of these stock valuation differences on the profit reported by the financial and cost accounting ledgers is that:

(a) the financial accounting profit is £300 greater than the cost accounting profit;
(b) the financial accounting profit is £2100 greater than the cost accounting profit;
(c) the cost accounting profit is £300 greater than the financial accounting profit;
(d) the cost accounting profit is £900 greater than the financial accounting profit;
(e) the cost accounting profit is £2100 greater than the financial accounting profit.

CIMA Stage 2 – Operational Cost Accounting

4.16 Intermediate. MN plc uses a JIT system and backflush accounting. It does not use a raw material stock control account. During April 1000 units were produced and sold. The standard cost per unit is £100: this includes materials of £45. During April £60000 of conversion costs were incurred.

The debit balance on the cost of goods sold account for April was:

(a) £90000
(b) £95000
(c) £105000
(d) £110000
(e) £11500 (2 marks)

CIMA Management Accounting – Decision Making

4.17 Basic: Stores pricing. Z Ltd had the following transactions in one of its raw materials during April:

Opening stock		40 units	@£10 each
April 4	Bought	140 units	@£11 each
10	Used	90 units	
12	Bought	60 units	@£12 each
13	Used	100 units	
16	Bought	200 units	@£10 each
21	Used	70 units	
23	Used	80 units	
26	Bought	50 units	@£12 each
29	Used	60 units	

You are required to:

(a) Write up the stores ledger card using

(i) FIFO and
(ii) LIFO

methods of stock valuation. (8 marks)
(b) State the cost of material used for each system during April. (2 marks)
(c) Describe the weighted average method of valuing stocks and explain how the use of this method would affect the cost of materials used and the balance sheet of Z Ltd compared to FIFO and LIFO in times of consistently rising prices. (Do NOT restate the stores ledger card for the above transactions using this method.) (5 marks)

CIMA Stage 1 Accounting

4.18 Intermediate: Integrated accounts. In the absence of the accountant you have been asked to prepare a month's cost accounts for a company which operates a batch costing system fully integrated with the financial accounts. The cost clerk has provided you with the following information, which he thinks is relevant:

	(£)
Balances at beginning of month:	
Stores ledger control account	24175
Work in progress control account	19210
Finished goods control account	34164
Prepayments of production overheads brought forward from previous month	2100

	(£)
Transactions during the month:	
Materials purchased	76150
Materials issued: to production	26350
for factory maintenance	3280
Materials transferred between batches	1450

	Direct workers (£)	Indirect workers (£)
Total wages paid:		
Net	17646	3342
Employees deductions	4364	890
Direct wages charged to batches from work tickets	15236	
Recorded non-productive time of direct workers	5230	
Direct wages incurred on production of capital equipment, for use in the factory	2670	

(Continued)

	Direct workers (£)	Indirect workers (£)
Selling and distribution overheads incurred	5 240	
Other production overheads incurred	12 200	
Sales	75 400	
Cost of finished goods sold	59 830	
Cost of goods completed and transferred into finished goods store during the month	62 130	
Physical stock value of work in progress at end of month	24 360	

The production overhead absorption rate is 150 per cent of direct wages and it is the policy of the company to include a share of production overheads in the cost of capital equipment constructed in the factory.

Required:

(a) Prepare the following accounts for the month: stores ledger control account wages control account work in progress control account finished goods control account production overhead control account profit/loss account. *(12 marks)*

(b) Identify any aspects of the accounts which you consider should be investigated. *(4 marks)*

(c) Explain why it is necessary to value a company's stocks at the end of each period and also why, in a manufacturing company, expense items such as factory rent, wages of direct operatives, power costs, etc. are included in the value of work in progress and finished goods stocks. *(6 marks)*

ACCA Level 1 Costing

4.19 Intermediate: Backflush costing.

(a) Explain the term 'backflush accounting' and the circumstances in which its use would be appropriate. *(6 marks)*

(b) CSIX Ltd manufactures fuel pumps using a just-in-time manufacturing system which is supported by a backflush accounting system. The backflush accounting system has two trigger points for the creation of journal entries. These trigger points are:

the purchase of raw materials

the manufacture of finished goods

The transactions during the month of November were as follows:

Purchase of raw materials	£5 575 000
Conversion costs incurred:	
Labour	£1 735 000
Overheads	£3 148 000
Finished goods completed (units)	210 000
Sales for the month (units)	206 000

There were no opening inventories of raw materials, work in progress or finished goods at 1 November. The standard cost per unit of output is £48. This is made up of £26 for materials and £22 for conversion costs (of which labour comprises £8.20).

Required:

(i) Prepare ledger accounts to record the above transactions for November. *(6 marks)*

(ii) Briefly explain whether the just-in-time system operated by CSIX Ltd can be regarded as 'perfect'. *(3 marks)*

ACCA Performance Measurement Paper 3.3

IM4.1 Intermediate: Integrated cost accounting. XY Limited commenced trading on 1 February with fully paid issued share capital of £500 000, Fixed Assets of £275 000 and Cash at Bank of £225 000. By the end of April, the following transactions had taken place:

1. Purchases on credit from suppliers amounted to £572 500 of which £525 000 was raw materials and £47 500 was for items classified as production overhead.
2. Wages incurred for all staff were £675 000, represented by cash paid £500 000 and wage deductions of £175 000 in respect of income tax etc.
3. Payments were made by cheque for the following overhead costs:

	£
Production	20 000
Selling	40 000
Administration	25 000

4. Issues of raw materials were £180 000 to Department A, £192 500 to Department B and £65 000 for production overhead items.
5. Wages incurred were analysed to functions as follows:

	£
Work in progress – Department A	300 000
Work in progress – Department B	260 000
Production overhead	42 500
Selling overhead	47 500
Administration overhead	25 000
	675 000

6. Production overhead absorbed in the period by Department A was £110 000 and by Department B £120 000.
7. The production facilities, when not in use, were patrolled by guards from a security firm and £26 000 was owing for this service. £39 000 was also owed to a firm of management consultants which advises on production procedures; invoices for these two services are to be entered into the accounts.
8. The cost of finished goods completed was:

	Department A £	Department B £
Direct labour	290 000	255 000
Direct materials	175 000	185 000
Production overhead	105 000	115 000
	570 000	555 000

9. Sales on credit were £870 000 and the cost of those sales was £700 000.
10. Depreciation of productive plant and equipment was £15 000.
11. Cash received from debtors totalled £520 000.
12. Payments to creditors were £150 000.

You are required:

(a) To open the ledger accounts at the commencement of the trading period.

(b) Using integrated accounting, to record the transactions for the three months ended 30 April.

(c) To prepare, in vertical format, for presentation to management,

(i) a profit statement for the period;

(ii) the balance sheet at 30 April.

CIMA Stage 2 Cost Accounting

IM4.2 Intermediate: Preparation of interlocking accounts from incomplete information.

(a) Describe briefly three major differences between:

(i) financial accounting, and
(ii) cost and management accounting.   *(6 marks)*

(b) Below are incomplete cost accounts for a period:

	Stores ledger control account (£000)
Opening balance	176.0
Financial ledger control a/c	224.2

	Production wages control account (£000)
Financial ledger control a/c	196.0

	Production overhead control account (£000)
Financial ledger control a/c	119.3

	Job ledger control account (£000)
Opening balance	114.9

The balances at the end of the period were:

	(£000)
Stores ledger	169.5
Jobs ledger	153.0

During the period 64500 kilos of direct material were issued from stores at a weighted average price of £3.20 per kilo. The balance of materials issued from stores represented indirect materials.

75 per cent of the production wages are classified as 'direct'. Average gross wages of direct workers was £10.00 per hour. Production overheads are absorbed at a predetermined rate of £13 per direct labour hour.

Required:
Complete the cost accounts for the period.   *(8 marks)*

ACCA Foundation Paper 3

IM4.3 Intermediate: Integrated accounts and stores pricing.
On 30 October the following were among the balances in the cost ledger of a company manufacturing a single product (Product X) in a single process operation:

	Dr	Cr
Raw material control account	£87460	
Manufacturing overhead control account		£5123
Finished goods account	£148352	

The raw material ledger comprised the following balances at 30 October:

Direct materials:		
Material A:	18760kg	£52715
Material B:	4242kg	£29994
Indirect materials:		£4751

12160kg of Product X were in finished goods stock on 30 October. During November the following occurred:

(i) Raw materials purchased on credit:

Material A:	34220kg at £2.85/kg
Material B:	34520kg at £7.10/kg
Indirect:	£7221

(ii) Raw materials issued from stock:

Material A:	35176kg
Material B:	13364kg
Indirect:	£6917

Direct materials are issued at weighted average prices (calculated at the end of each month to three decimal places of £).

(iii) Wages incurred:

Direct:	£186743 (23900 hours)
Indirect:	£74887

(iv) Other manufacturing overhead costs totalled £112194. Manufacturing overheads are absorbed at a predetermined rate of £16.00 per direct labour hour. Any over-/under- absorbed overhead at the end of November should be left as a balance on the manufacturing overhead control account.

(v) 45937kg of Product X were manufactured. There was no work in progress at the beginning or end of the period. A normal loss of 5 per cent of input is expected.

(vi) 43210kg of Product X were sold. A monthly weighted average cost per kg (to three decimal places of £) is used to determine the production cost of sales.

Required:

(a) Prepare the following cost accounts for the month of November:

Raw material control account
Manufacturing overhead control account
Work in progress account
Finished goods account
All entries to the accounts should be rounded to the nearest whole £. Clearly show any workings supporting your answer.   *(16 marks)*

(b) Explain the concept of equivalent units and its relevance in a process costing system.   *(4 marks)*

ACCA Management Information Paper 3

IM4.4 Intermediate: Labour cost accounting and recording of journal entries.

(a) Identify the costs to a business arising from labour turnover.   *(5 marks)*

(b) A company operates a factory which employed 40 direct workers throughout the four-week period just ended. Direct employees were paid at a basic rate of £10.00 per hour for a 38-hour week. Total hours of the direct workers in the four-week period were 6528. Overtime, which is paid at a premium of 35 per cent, is worked in order to meet general production requirements. Employee deductions total 30 per cent of gross wages. 188 hours of direct workers' time were registered as idle.

Required:
Prepare journal entries to account for the labour costs of direct workers for the period.   *(7 marks)*

ACCA Foundation Stage Paper 3

IM4.5 Intermediate: Preparation of the wages control account plus an evaluation of the impact of a proposed piecework system. One of the production departments in A Ltd's factory employs 52 direct operatives and nine indirect operatives. Basic hourly rates of pay are £14.40 and £11.70, respectively. Overtime, which is worked regularly to meet general production requirements, is paid at a premium of 30 per cent over basic rate.

The following further information is provided for the period just ended:

Hours worked:

Direct operatives:

Total hours worked	25 520 hours
Overtime hours worked	2 120 hours

Indirect operatives:

Total hours worked	4 430 hours
Overtime hours worked	380 hours

Production:

Product 1, 36 000 units in 7200 hours
Product 2, 116 000 units in 11 600 hours
Product 3, 52 800 units in 4400 hours

Non-productive time:	2 320 hours

Wages paid (net of tax and employees'
  National Insurance):

Direct operatives	£293 865
Indirect operatives	£41 577

The senior management of A Ltd is considering the introduction of a piecework payment scheme into the factory.

Following work study analysis, expected productivities and proposed piecework rates for the direct operatives, in the production department referred to above, have been determined as follows:

	Productivity (output per hour)	Piecework rate (per unit)
Product 1	66 units	£3.00
Product 2	12 units	£1.50
Product 3	14.4 units	£1.20

Non-productive time is expected to remain at 10 per cent of productive time and would be paid at £10.50 per hour.

Required:

(a) Prepare the production department's wages control account for the period in A Ltd's integrated accounting system. (Ignore employers' National Insurance.)

(9 marks)

(b) Examine the effect of the proposed piecework payment scheme on direct labour and overhead costs.

(11 marks)

ACCA Cost and Management Accounting 1

5
PROCESS COSTING

LEARNING OBJECTIVES After studying this chapter you should be able to:

- explain when process costing systems are appropriate;
- explain the accounting treatment of normal and abnormal losses;
- prepare process, normal loss, abnormal loss and abnormal gain accounts when there is no ending work in progress;
- explain and calculate equivalent units;
- compute the value of closing work in progress and completed production using the weighted average and first in, first out, methods of valuing work in progress.

A process costing system is used in industries where masses of similar products or services are produced. Products are produced in the same manner and consume the same amount of direct costs and overheads. It is therefore unnecessary to assign costs to individual units of output. Instead, the average cost per unit of output is calculated by dividing the total costs assigned to a product or service for a period by the number of units of output for that period. Industries in which process costing is widely used include chemical processing, oil refining, food processing and brewing. For example, one litre of beer that is produced is identical to another litre so the cost of one litre is identical to another.

In this chapter, we will examine the cost accumulation procedure that is required for inventory valuation and profit measurement for a process costing system. This chapter can be omitted if you are pursuing a management accounting course that does not require you to focus on cost accumulation for inventory valuation and profit measurement (see 'Guidelines for using this book' in Chapter 1). We begin with a description of the flow of production and costs in a process costing environment. We shall then look in detail at the cost accumulation system. Three different scenarios will be presented. First, all output is fully complete. Second, ending work in progress exists, but no beginning work in progress, and some of the units started during the period are incomplete at the end of the period. Our third scenario is the existence of both beginning and ending work in progress of uncompleted units. One of the most complex areas in process costing is accounting for losses when units within the process are both fully and partially complete. Because some courses omit this topic, it will be discussed in Appendix 5.1.

FLOW OF PRODUCTION AND COSTS IN A PROCESS COSTING SYSTEM

The flow of production and costs in a process costing system is illustrated in Exhibit 5.1. The major differences between process and job costing are also highlighted. You will see that production moves from one process (or department) to the next until final completion occurs. Each production process performs some part of the total operation and transfers its completed production to the next process, where it becomes the input for further processing. The completed production of the last process is transferred to the finished goods inventory.

The cost accumulation procedure follows this production flow. Control accounts are established for each process (or department) and direct and indirect costs are assigned to each process. A process costing system is easier to operate than a job costing system because the detailed work of allocating costs to many individual cost units is unnecessary. Also, many of the costs that are indirect in a job costing system may be regarded as direct in a process costing system. For example, supervision and depreciation that is confined to one process would be treated as part of the direct costs of that process, since these costs are directly attributable to the cost object (i.e. the department or process). By contrast, such costs are normally regarded as indirect in a job costing system because they are not directly attributable to a specific job.

As production moves from process to process, costs are transferred with it. For example, in Exhibit 5.1, the costs of process A would be transferred to process B; process B costs would then be added to this cost and the resulting total cost transferred to process C; process C costs would then added to this cost. Therefore the cost becomes cumulative as production proceeds. The cost per unit of the completed product thus consists of the total cost accumulated in process C for the period, divided by the output for that period.

In contrast, job costing relates to a costing system where each unit or batch of output is unique. This creates the need for the cost of each unit to be calculated separately. In practice, these two costing

EXHIBIT 5.1 A comparison of job and process costing

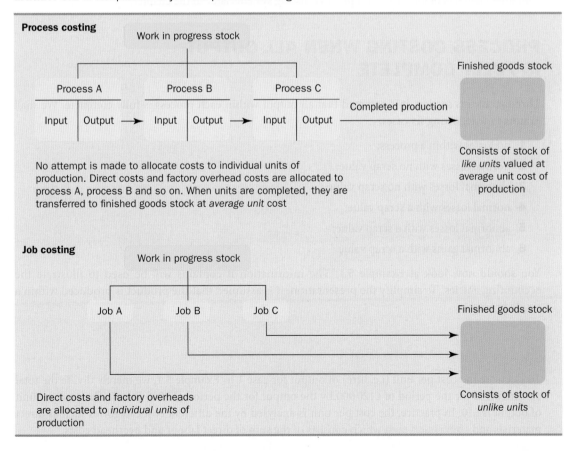

The brewing process at SAB Miller
Almost all beer contains four basic ingredients – a grain (typically barley), water, hops and yeast. While the process of brewing can be complex and some ingredients varied, the basic process is quite consistent. First the barley (or other grain) is soaked in water and allowed to begin development into plants. Enzymes are released that break down the grain into simple sugars. Once this process has begun, the barley is cooked, stopping the growth while the enzymes are at their peak – this is the process of malting. Next is mashing, where the grain is actually transformed into sugar by being crushed into a fine powder, or grist, and then soaked in water. The mash is heated and strained to yield a substance called wort. The wort is then cooled and placed in a fermentation vessel. Yeast is added and then the fermentation process produces alcohol. After about ten days, the beer is separated from the yeast, then stored, filtered, pasteurized and finally packed into bottles, cans or kegs.

Questions

1 When does the 'product' materialize in the brewing process described above?

2 Would you imagine there is any waste in the brewing process?

Reference
'The Brewing of Beer', available at www.sabmiller.in/know-beer_brewing.aspx

---

systems represent extreme ends of a continuum. The output of many organizations requires a combination of the elements of both job costing and process costing. We shall examine a costing system that combines elements of job-order and process costing systems later in the chapter.

PROCESS COSTING WHEN ALL OUTPUT IS FULLY COMPLETE

Throughout this section, it is assumed that all output within each process is fully complete. We shall examine the following six cases:

1 no losses within a process;

2 normal losses with no scrap value;

3 abnormal losses with no scrap value;

4 normal losses with a scrap value;

5 abnormal losses with a scrap value;

6 abnormal gains with a scrap value.

You should now look at Example 5.1. The information it contains will be used to illustrate the accounting entries. To simplify the presentation, it is assumed that the product is produced within a single process.

No losses within the process

To calculate the cost per unit (i.e. litre) of output for case 1 in Example 5.1, we merely divide the total cost incurred for the period of £120 000 by the output for the period (12 000 litres). The cost per unit of output is £10. In practice, the cost per unit is analysed by the different cost categories such as direct materials and conversion cost which consists of the sum of direct labour and overhead costs.

EXAMPLE 5.1

Dartmouth Company produces a liquid fertilizer within a single production process. During the month of May the input into the process was 12000 litres at a cost of £120000. There were no opening or closing inventories and all output was fully complete. We shall prepare the process account and calculate the cost per litre of output for the single process for each of the six cases listed below:

Case	Input (litres)	Output (litres)	Normal loss (litres)	Abnormal loss (litres)	Abnormal gain (litres)	Scrap value of spoilt output (£ per litre)
1	12000	12000	0	0	0	0
2	12000	10000	2000 (1/6)	0	0	0
3	12000	9000	2000 (1/6)	1000	0	0
4	12000	10000	2000 (1/6)	0	0	5
5	12000	9000	2000 (1/6)	1000	0	5
6	12000	11000	2000 (1/6)	0	1000	5

Normal losses in process with no scrap value

Certain losses are inherent to the production process. For example, liquids may evaporate, part of the cloth required to make a suit may be lost and losses occur in cutting wood to make furniture. These losses occur under efficient operating conditions and are unavoidable. They are referred to as normal or uncontrollable losses and are absorbed by the good production. Where normal losses apply the cost per unit of output is calculated by dividing the costs incurred for a period by the *expected* output from the actual input for that period. In case 2 in Example 5.1, the normal loss is one-sixth of the input. Therefore, for an input of 12000 litres the *expected* output is 10000 litres so that the cost per unit of output is £12 (£120000/10000 litres). When actual output is equal to expected output, there is neither an abnormal loss nor gain. Compared with case 1, the unit cost has increased by £2 per unit because the cost of the normal loss has been absorbed by the good production. Our objective is to calculate the cost of normal production under normal efficient operating conditions.

Abnormal losses in process with no scrap value

There may be some losses that are not expected to occur under efficient operating conditions, caused for example by the improper mixing of ingredients, the use of inferior materials and the incorrect cutting of cloth. These losses are not an inherent part of the production process, and are referred to as abnormal or controllable losses. Because they are not an inherent part of the production process and arise from inefficiencies, they are not included in the process costs. Instead, they are removed from the appropriate process account and reported separately as an abnormal loss. The abnormal loss is treated as a period cost and written off in the profit statement at the end of the accounting period. This ensures that abnormal losses are not incorporated in any inventory valuations.

For case 3 in Example 5.1, the expected output is 10000 litres but the actual output was 9000 litres, resulting in an abnormal loss of 1000 litres. Our objective is the same as that for normal losses. We need to calculate the cost per litre of the *expected* output (i.e. normal production), which is:

$$\frac{\text{input cost (£120\,000)}}{\text{expected output (10\,000 litres)}} = £12$$

Note that the unit cost is the same for an output of 10000 or 9000 litres since our objective is to calculate the cost per unit of normal output. The distribution of the input costs is as follows:

	(£)
Completed production transferred to the next process (or finished goods inventory) 9000 litres at £12	108000
Abnormal loss: 1000 litres at £12	12000
	120000

The abnormal loss is valued at the cost per unit of normal production. Abnormal losses can only be controlled in the future by establishing the cause of the abnormal loss and taking appropriate remedial action. The entries in the process account will look like this:

Process account

	Litres	Unit cost (£)	(£)		Litres	Unit cost (£)	(£)
Input cost	12000	10	120000	Normal loss	2000	—	—
				Output to finished goods inventory	9000	12	108000
				Abnormal loss	1000	12	12000
			120000				120000

Process accounts represent work in progress accounts. Input costs are debited to the process account and the output from the process is entered on the credit side. You will see from the process account that no entry is made in the account for the normal loss (except for an entry made in the units column). The transfer to the finished goods inventory (or the next process) is at the cost of normal production. The abnormal loss is removed from the process costs and reported separately as a loss in the abnormal loss account. This draws the attention of management to those losses that may be controllable. At the end of the accounting period the abnormal loss account is written off in the profit statement as a period cost. The inventory valuation will not therefore include any abnormal expenses. The overall effect is that the abnormal losses are correctly allocated to the period in which they arise and are not carried forward as a future expense in the closing inventory valuation.

Normal losses in process with a scrap value

In case 4, actual output is equal to the expected output of 10000 litres so there is neither an abnormal gain nor loss. All of the units lost represent a normal loss in process. However, the units lost now have a scrap value of £5 per litre. The sales value of the spoiled units should be offset against the costs of the appropriate process where the loss occurred. Therefore the sales value of the normal loss is credited to the process account and a corresponding debit entry will be made in the cash or accounts receivable (debtors) account. The calculation of the cost per unit of output is as follows:

$$\frac{\text{Input cost less scrap value of normal loss}}{\text{Expected output}} = \frac{£120\,000 - (2000 \times £5)}{10\,000 \text{ litres}} = £11$$

Compared with cases 2 and 3, the cost per unit has declined from £12 per litre to £11 per litre to reflect the fact that the normal spoilage has a scrap value which has been offset against the process costs.

Producing a world-famous whiskey

Bushmills Irish Whiskey, a world-renowned brand of Diageo plc, is distilled in County Antrim in Northern Ireland. The Old Bushmills distillery has been in operation since 1608 and currently markets five distinct whiskeys under the Bushmills brand. Whiskey production is essentially a five-part process. The basic raw materials are barley and natural water. The first process, malting, allows barley corns to germinate for four days. An enzyme called diastase is formed inside each grain, which converts the starch in the grain to sugar. The corns are then dried in an oven. The second process, mashing, takes the dried barley and grinds it into a flour called 'grist'. Hot water is added to the grist to produce a sugary liquid called 'wort'. The wort is now ready to be transformed into alcohol by fermentation. The third process, fermentation, is a simple natural process which occurs when yeast and sugar are mixed. The wort is pumped into a large vessel, where yeast is added. Fermentation is allowed to proceed for two days. The resultant liquid, called the 'wash' is now ready for transfer to the still house for distillation, the fourth process.

Distillation involves heating the wash gradually in a large copper kettle called the pot still. As alcohol has a lower boiling point than water, the alcohol vapours condense first, run off and cool down to a liquid. Two further distillations are performed to ensure purity. The resulting liquid, called spirit, is a clear liquid with a high alcohol content. The final step, maturation, sees the spirit placed in seasoned oak casks for a number of years – ranging from three to 21 years. The casks tend to be former American bourbon or Spanish sherry casks. The spirit acquires its colour and flavour from the casks. Once matured for the required period, the whiskies are bottled in the bottling plant at Bushmills, typically in 750ml bottles.

Questions

1 Why is job costing not appropriate to a process such as whiskey production?

2 Do you think losses of spirit might occur during the maturation process?

Reference
www.bushmills.com

The entries in the process account will look like this:

Process account

	Litres	Unit cost (£)	(£)		Litres	Unit cost (£)	(£)
Input cost	12 000	10	120 000	Normal loss	2 000	—	10 000
				Output to finished goods inventory	10 000	11	110 000
			120 000				120 000

Note that the scrap value of the normal loss is credited against the normal loss entry in the process account.

Abnormal losses in process with a scrap value

In case 5, expected output is 10 000 litres for an input of 12 000 litres and actual output is 9 000 litres, resulting in a normal loss of 2 000 litres and an abnormal loss of 1 000 litres. The lost units have a scrap value of £5 per litre. Since our objective is to calculate the cost per unit for the expected (normal) output, only the scrap value of the normal loss of 2 000 litres should be deducted in ascertaining the cost per unit. Therefore, the cost per unit calculation is the same as that for case 4 (i.e. £11). The sales value of the additional 1000 litres lost represents revenue of an abnormal nature and should not be used to reduce the process unit cost. This revenue is offset against the cost of the abnormal loss which is of interest to management. The net cost incurred in the process is £105000 (£120000 input cost less 3000 litres lost with a scrap value of £5 per litre), and the distribution of this cost is:

	(£)	(£)
Completed production transferred to the next process (or finished goods inventory) (9000 litres at £11 per litre)		99000
Abnormal loss:		
1000 litres at £11 per litre	11000	
Less scrap value (1000 litres at £5)	5000	6000
		105000

The entries in the process account will be as follows:

Process account

	Litres	Unit cost (£)	(£)		Litres	Unit cost (£)	(£)
Input cost	12000	10	120000	Normal loss	2000	—	10000
				Output to finished goods inventory	9000	11	99000
				Abnormal loss	1000	11	11000
			120000				120000

Abnormal loss account

	(£)		(£)
Process account	11000	Cash sale for units scrapped	5000
		Balance transferred to profit statement	6000
	11000		11000

Abnormal gains with a scrap value

On occasions the actual loss in process may be less than expected, in which case an **abnormal gain** occurs (see case 6 in Example 5.1). As in the previous cases, it is necessary with case 6 to begin by calculating the cost per unit of normal output. For normal output, our assumptions are the same as those for cases 4 and 5 (i.e. a normal loss of 1/6 and a scrap value of £5 per litre) so the cost per unit of output is the same (i.e. £11 per litre). The calculation is as follows:

$$\frac{\text{Input cost less scrap value of normal loss}}{\text{Expected output}} = \frac{£120000 - (2000 \times £5)}{10000 \text{ litres}} = £11$$

The net cost incurred in the process is £115000 (£120000 input cost less 1000 litres spoilt with a sales value of £5 per litre), and the distribution of this cost is as follows:

	(£)	
Transferred to finished goods inventory (11000 litres at £11 per litre)		121000
Less: abnormal gain (1000 litres at £11 per litre)	11000	
lost sales of spoiled units (1000 litres at £5 per litre)	5000	6000
		115000

Note that the cost per unit is based on the normal production cost per unit and is not affected by the fact that an abnormal gain occurred or that sales of the spoiled units with a sales value of £5000 did not materialize. As before, our objective is to produce a cost per unit based on normal operating efficiency.

The accounting entries are as follows:

Process account

	Litres	Unit cost (£)	(£)		Litres	Unit cost (£)	(£)
Input cost	12 000	10	120 000	Normal loss	2 000	—	10 000
Abnormal gain	1 000	11	11 000	Output to finished goods inventory	11 000	11	121 000
			131 000				131 000

Abnormal gain account

	(£)		(£)
Normal loss account	5 000	Process account	11 000
Profit and loss statement (Balance)	6 000		
	11 000		11 000

Income due from normal losses

	(£)		(£)
Process account	10 000	Abnormal gain account	5 000
		Cash from spoiled units (1000 litres at £5)	5 000
	10 000		10 000

You will see that the abnormal gain has been removed from the process account and that it is valued at the cost per unit of normal production (£11). However, as 1000 litres were gained, there was a loss of sales revenue of £5000, and this lost revenue is offset against the abnormal gain. The net gain is therefore £6000, and this is the amount that should be credited to the profit statement.

The process account is credited with the expected sales revenue from the normal loss (2000 litres at £5), since the objective is to record in the process account normal net costs of production. Because the normal loss of 2000 litres does not occur, the company will not obtain the sales value of £10 000 from the expected lost output. This problem is resolved by making a corresponding debit entry in a normal loss account, which represents the amount due from the sale proceeds from the expected normal loss. The amount due (£10 000) is then reduced by £5000 to reflect the fact that only 1000 litres were lost. This is achieved by crediting the normal loss account (income due) and debiting the abnormal gain account with £5000, so that the balance of the normal loss account shows the actual amount of cash received for the income due from the spoiled units (i.e. £5000, which consists of 1000 litres at £5 per litre).

PROCESS COSTING WITH ENDING WORK IN PROGRESS PARTIALLY COMPLETE

So far we have assumed that all output within a process is fully complete. We shall now consider situations where output started during a period is partially complete at the end of the period. In other words, ending work in progress exists within a process. In this situation, unit costs cannot be computed by simply dividing the total costs for a period by the output for that period. For example, if 8000 units were started and completed during a period and another 2000 units were partly completed then these two items cannot be added together to ascertain their unit cost. We must convert the work in progress into finished equivalents (also referred to as equivalent production) so that the unit cost can be obtained.

To do this, we must estimate the percentage degree of completion of the work in progress and multiply this by the number of units in progress at the end of the accounting period. If the 2000 partly completed units were 50 per cent complete, we could express this as an equivalent production of 1000 fully completed units. This would then be added to the completed production of 8000 units to give a total equivalent production of 9000 units. The cost per unit would then be calculated in the normal way. For example, if the costs for the period were £180 000 then the cost per unit completed would be £20 (£180 000/9000 units) and the distribution of this cost would be as follows:

	(£)
Completed units transferred	
to the next process (8000 units at £20)	160 000
Work in progress	20 000
(1000 equivalent units at £20)	
	180 000

Elements of costs with different degrees of completion

One complication that may arise is that, in any given inventory of work in progress, not all of the elements that make up the total cost may have reached the same degree of completion. For example, materials may be added at the start of the process, and are thus fully complete, whereas labour and manufacturing overhead (i.e. the conversion costs) may be added uniformly throughout the process. Hence, the ending work in progress may consist of materials that are 100 per cent complete and conversion costs that are only partially complete. Where this situation arises, separate equivalent production calculations must be made for each element of cost.

The following statement shows the calculation of the cost per unit for process A in Example 5.2:

Calculation of cost per unit for process A

Cost element	Total cost (£)	Completed units	WIP equivalent units	Total equivalent units	Cost per unit (£)
Materials	210 000	10 000	4 000	14 000	15.00
Conversion cost	144 000	10 000	2 000	12 000	12.00
	354 000				27.00

	(£)	(£)
Value of work in progress:		
Materials (4000 units at £15)	60 000	
Conversion cost (2000 units at £12)	24 000	84 000
Completed units (10 000) units at £27)		270 000
		354 000

EXAMPLE 5.2

The Fontenbleau Company manufactures a product that passes through two processes. The following information relates to the two processes:

	Process A	Process B
Opening work in progress	—	—
Units introduced into the process	14 000	10 000
Units completed and transferred to the next process or finished goods inventory	10 000	9 000
Closing work in progress	4 000	1 000
Costs of production transferred from process A[a]		£270 000
Material costs added	£210 000	£108 000
Conversion costs	£144 000	£171 000

Materials are added at the start of process A and at the end of process B and conversion costs are added uniformly throughout both processes. The closing work in progress is estimated to be 50 per cent complete for both processes.

Note

[a]This information is derived from the preparation of process A accounts.

The process account will look like this:

Process A account

Materials	210 000	Completed units transferred to process B	270 000
Conversion cost	144 000	Closing WIP c/fwd	84 000
	354 000		354 000
Opening WIP b/fwd	84 000		

You will see from the above statement that details are collected relating to the equivalent production for completed units and work in progress by materials and conversion costs. This information is required to calculate the cost per unit of equivalent production for each element of cost. As materials are issued at the start of the process, any partly completed units in ending work in progress must be fully complete as far as materials are concerned. Therefore an entry of 4000 units is made in the work in progress equivalent units column. Regarding conversion cost, the 4000 units in progress are only 50 per cent complete and therefore the entry in the work in progress column for this element of cost is 2000 units. To compute the value of work in progress, the unit costs are multiplied separately by the materials and conversion cost work in progress equivalent production figures. Only one calculation is required to ascertain the value of completed production. This is obtained by multiplying the total cost per unit of £27 by the completed production. Note that the cost of the output of £354 000 in the above statement is in agreement with the cost of input of £354 000.

Previous process cost

As production continues, the output of one process becomes the input of the next process. The next process will carry out additional conversion work, and may add further materials. It is important to distinguish between these different cost items and this is achieved by labelling the transferred cost from the previous process as previous process cost. Note that this element of cost will always be fully complete as far as closing work in progress is concerned. Let us now calculate the unit costs and the value of work in progress and completed production for process B in Example 5.2. To do this, we prepare a statement similar to the one we prepared for process A.

Calculation of cost per unit for process B

Cost element	Total cost (£)	Completed units	WIP equivalent units	Total equivalent units	Cost per unit (£)
Previous process cost	270 000	9 000	1 000	10 000	27.00
Materials	108 000	9 000	—	9 000	12.00
Conversion cost	171 000	9 000	500	9 500	18.00
	549 000				57.00

	(£)	(£)
Value of work in progress:		
Previous process cost (1000 units at £27)	27 000	
Materials	—	
Conversion cost (500 units at £18)	9 000	36 000
Completed units (9000 units at £57)		513 000
		549 000

Process B account

Previous process cost	270 000	Completed production transferred to	
Materials	108 000	finished inventory	513 000
Conversions cost	171 000	Closing work in progress c/fwd	36 000
	549 000		549 000
Opening WIP b/fwd	36 000		

You will see that the previous process cost is treated as a separate process cost, and, since this element of cost will not be added to in process B, the closing work in progress must be fully complete as far as previous process cost is concerned. Note that, after the first process, materials may be issued at different stages of production. In process B, materials are not issued until the end of the process, and the closing work in progress will not have reached this point; the equivalent production for the closing work in progress will therefore be zero for materials.

Normally, material costs are introduced at one stage in the process and not uniformly throughout the process. If the work in progress has passed the point at which the materials are added then the materials will be 100 per cent complete. If this point has not been reached then the equivalent production for materials will be zero.

BEGINNING AND ENDING WORK IN PROGRESS OF UNCOMPLETED UNITS

When opening inventories of work in progress exist, an assumption must be made regarding the allocation of this opening inventory to the current accounting period to determine the unit cost for the period. Two alternative assumptions are possible:

- First, one may assume that opening work in progress is inextricably merged with the units introduced in the current period and can no longer be identified separately – the *weighted average method*.

- Second, one may assume that the opening work in progress is the first group of units to be processed and completed during the current month – the *first in, first out method.*

We now compare these methods using the information contained in Example 5.3.

For more complex problems it is always a good idea to start by calculating the number of units completed during the period. The calculations are as follows:

	Process X	Process Y
Opening work in progress	6 000	2 000
Units introduced during period	16 000	18 000
Total input for period	22 000	20 000
Less closing work in progress	4 000	8 000
Balance – completed production	18 000	12 000

Weighted average method

The calculation of the unit cost for process X using the weighted average method is as follows:

Process X – weighted average method

Cost element	Opening WIP (£)	Current cost (£)	Total cost (£)	Completed units	WIP equiv. units	Total equiv. units	Cost per unit (£)
Materials	72 000	192 000	264 000	18 000	4 000	22 000	12.00
Conversion cost	45 900	225 000	270 900	18 000	3 000	21 000	12.90
	117 900		534 900				24.90

		(£)	(£)
Work in progress:			
Materials (4000 units at £12)		48 000	
Conversion (3000 units at £12.90)		38 700	86 700
Completed units (18 000 units at £24.90)			448 200
			534 900

Process X account

Opening work in progress b/fwd	117 900	Completed production	
Materials	192 000	transferred to process Y	448 200
Conversion cost	225 000	Closing work in progress c/fwd	86 700
	534 900		534 900
Opening work in progress b/fwd	86 700		

You can see from the statement of unit cost calculations that the opening work in progress is assumed to be completed in the current period. The current period's costs will include the cost of finishing off the opening work in progress, and the cost of the work in progress will be included in the total cost figure. The completed units will include the 6000 units in progress that will have been completed during the period. The statement therefore includes all the costs of the opening work in progress and the resulting units, fully completed. In other words, we have assumed that the opening work in progress is merged with the production of the current period to form one homogeneous batch of production. The equivalent number of units for this batch of production is divided into the costs of the current period, plus the value of the opening work in progress, to calculate the cost per unit.

EXAMPLE 5.3

The Baltic Company has two processes, X and Y. Material is introduced at the start of process X, and additional material is added to process Y when the process is 70 per cent complete. Conversion costs are applied uniformly throughout both processes. The completed units of process X are immediately transferred to process Y, and the completed production of process Y is transferred to finished goods inventory. Data for the period include the following:

	Process X	Process Y
Opening work in progress	6000 units 60% converted, consisting of materials £72000 and conversion cost £45900	2000 units 80% converted, consisting of previous process cost of £91800, materials £12000 and conversion costs £38400
Units started during the period	16000 units	18000 units
Closing work in progress	4000 units 3/4 complete	8000 units 1/2 complete
Material costs added during the period	£192000	£60000
Conversion costs added during the period	£225000	£259200

Let us now calculate the unit cost for process Y using the weighted average method. From the calculation of the unit costs (shown below), you can see the previous process cost is fully complete as far as the closing work in progress is concerned. Note that materials are added when the process is 70 per cent complete, but the closing work in progress is only 50 per cent complete. At the stage

Process Y – weighted average method

Cost element	Opening WIP value (£)	Current period cost (£)	Total cost (£)	Completed units	WIP equiv. units	Total equiv. units	Cost per unit (£)
Previous process cost	91800	448200	540000	12000	8000	20000	27.00
Materials	12000	60000	72000	12000	—	12000	6.00
Conversion cost	38400	259200	297600	12000	4000	16000	18.60
	142200		909600				51.60

	(£)	(£)
Value of work in progress:		
Previous process cost (8000 units at £27)	216000	
Materials	—	
Conversion cost (4000 units at £18.60)	74400	290400
Completed units (12000 units at £51.60)		619200
		909600

Process Y account

Opening work in progress	142 200	Completed production	
Transferred from process X	448 200	transferred to finished inventory	619 200
Materials	60 000	Closing work in progress c/fwd	290 400
Conversion cost	259 200		
	909 600		909 600
Opening work in progress b/fwd	290 400		

in question, no materials will have been added to the closing work in progress, and the equivalent production will be zero. As with process X, it is necessary to add the opening work in progress cost to the current cost. The equivalent production of opening work in progress is ignored since this is included as being fully complete in the completed units column. Note also that the completed production cost of process X is included in the current cost column for 'the previous process cost' in the unit cost calculation for process Y.

First in, first out (FIFO) method

Many courses focus only on the weighted average method of process costing. You should therefore check your course curriculum to ascertain whether or not you need to read this section relating to the FIFO method. The FIFO method of process costing is based on the assumption that current period unit costs should be reported rather than unit costs that are reported with the weighted average method that include costs incurred in the previous period. Therefore the FIFO method assumes that the opening work in progress is the first group of units to be processed and completed during the current period. The opening work in progress is charged separately to completed production, and the cost per unit for the current period is based only on the *current period* costs and production for the *current period*. The closing work in progress is assumed to come from the new units started during the period.

Let us now use Example 5.3 to illustrate the FIFO method for process X and Y.

Process X – FIFO method

Cost element	Current period cost (£)	Completed units less opening WIP equiv. units	Closing WIP equiv. units	Current total equiv. units	Cost per unit (£)
Materials	192 000	12 000 (18 000 − 6 000)	4 000	16 000	12.000
Conversion cost	225 000	14 400 (18 000 − 3 600)	3 000	17 400	12.931
	417 000				24.931

		(£)	(£)
Completed production:			
Opening WIP		117 900	
Materials (12 000 units at £12)		144 000	
Conversion cost (14 400 units at £12.931)		186 207	448 107
Closing WIP:			
Materials (4000 units at £12)		48 000	
Conversion cost (3000 units at £12.931)		38 793	86 793
			534 900

From this calculation, you can see that the average cost per unit is based on current period costs divided by the current total equivalent units for the period. The latter figure excludes the equivalent production for opening work in progress since this was performed in the previous period. Note that the closing work in progress is multiplied by the current period average cost per unit. The closing work in progress includes only the current costs and does not include any of the opening work in progress, which is carried forward from the previous period. The objective is to ensure that the opening work in progress is kept separate and is identified as part of the cost of the completed production. The opening work in progress of £117 900 is not therefore included in the unit cost calculations, but is added directly to the completed production.

Let us now calculate the unit costs for process Y:

Process Y – FIFO method

Cost element	Current costs (£)	Completed units less opening WIP equiv. units	Closing WIP equiv. units	Current total equiv. units	Cost per unit (£)
Previous					
process cost	448 107	10 000 (12 000 − 2 000)	8 000	18 000	24.8948
Materials	60 000	10 000 (12 000 − 2 000)	—	10 000	6.0
Conversion					
cost	259 200	10 400 (12 000 − 1 600)	4 000	14 400	18.0
	767 307				48.8948

	(£)	(£)
Cost of completed production:		
Opening WIP	142 200	
Previous process cost (10 000 units at £24.8948)	248 948	
Materials (10 000 units at £6)	60 000	
Conversion cost (10 400 units at £18)	187 200	638 348
Cost of closing work in progress:		
Previous process cost (8000 units at £24.8948)	199 159	
Materials	—	
Conversion cost (4000 units at £18)	72 000	271 159
		909 507

Note that in this calculation the *opening* work in progress is 80 per cent completed, and that the materials are added when the process is 70 per cent complete. Hence, materials will be fully complete. Remember also that previous process cost is always 100 per cent complete. Therefore in the third column of the above statement, 2000 units opening work in progress is deducted for these two elements of cost from the 12 000 units of completed production. Conversion cost will be 80 per cent complete so 1600 equivalent units are deducted from the completed production. Our objective in the third column is to extract the equivalent completed units that were derived from the units started during the current period. You should also note that the previous process cost of £448 107 represents the cost of completed production of process X, which has been transferred to process Y.

The closing work in progress valuations and the charges to completed production are fairly similar for both methods. The difference in the calculations between FIFO and the weighted average method is likely to be insignificant where the quantity of inventories and the input prices do not fluctuate significantly from month to month. Both methods are acceptable for product costing.

Losses in processes – reducing process waste in UHT milk production

The term TetraPak® is one which is familiar to most consumers – it is the name you will see on the card cartons in which milk, juice and other liquid products are frequently packaged. The Tetra group offers a broader range of food processing solutions besides the TetraPak®. For example, it offers a processing solution which can reduce the wastage in UHT milk production. UHT milk is processed from normal milk that, once processed, is passed through a sterile filling machine. However, like most food processing equipment, both the milk processing equipment and the filling machine need to be cleaned regularly. If the filling machine requires cleaning, product loss can occur, increasing the overall process waste. Tetra's solution to reducing the process waste is to install an aseptic holding tank between the processing equipment and the filling machine. This tank holds the milk temporarily in a sterile environment. This means that the filling machine or the UHT processing equipment can be cleaned without the process stopping or without any loss or impairment of product.

Questions

1 Do you think waste which is regarded as 'normal' in a process should remain unchallenged?

2 How would you value waste in the UHT milk production described above?

Reference

'For maximum UHT dairy production', available at www.tetrapak.com/us/Documents/processing /Dairy/MaximumUHTDairyProduction.pdf

PARTIALLY COMPLETED OUTPUT AND LOSSES IN PROCESS

Earlier in this chapter we looked at how to deal with losses in process when all of the output in a process was fully complete. We also need to look at the treatment of losses when all of the output is not fully complete. When this situation occurs the computations can become complex. Accounting for losses when all of the output is not fully complete form part of the curriculum for few courses. However, some professional management accounting courses do require you to have a knowledge of this topic. Because of these different requirements, this topic is dealt with in Appendix 5.1. You should therefore check the requirements of your curriculum to ascertain whether you may omit Appendix 5.1.

PROCESS COSTING IN SERVICE ORGANIZATIONS

Process costing is used in service organizations where repetitive services that require similar inputs are provided. For example, the average cost of processing a standard loan application in a bank can be determined by dividing the total costs incurred for the period by the number of loans processed during the period. Many services consist of a single process, but some do require a sequence of processes. The cost per passenger for a flight on a particular route consists of the sum of the costs of the reservation, checking-in, flight and baggage collection processes divided by the number of passengers using the service.

BATCH/OPERATING COSTING

It is not always possible to classify cost accumulation systems into job costing and process costing systems. Where manufactured goods have some common characteristics and also some individual characteristics, the cost accumulation system may be a combination of both the job costing

EXHIBIT 5.2 A batch costing system

	Operations					
Product	1	2	3	4	5	Product cost
A	✓	✓	✓			A = cost of operations 1, 2, 3
B	✓			✓	✓	B = cost of operations 1, 4, 5
C	✓	✓		✓		C = cost of operations 1, 2, 4
D	✓		✓		✓	D = cost of operations 1, 3, 5
E	✓	✓			✓	E = cost of operations 1, 2, 5

and process costing systems. For example, the production of footwear, clothing and furniture often involves the production of batches, which are variations of a single design and require a sequence of standardized operations. Let us consider a company that makes kitchen units. Each unit may have the same basic frame, and require the same operation, but the remaining operations may differ: some frames may require sinks, others may require to be fitted with work tops; different types of door may be fitted to each unit, some may be low-quality doors while others may be of a higher quality. The cost of a kitchen unit will therefore consist of the basic frame plus the conversion costs of the appropriate operations. The principles of the cost accumulation system are illustrated in Exhibit 5.2.

The cost of each product consists of the cost of operation 1 plus a combination of the conversion costs for operations 2 to 5. The cost per unit produced for a particular operation consists of the average unit cost of each batch produced for each operation. It may well be that some products may be subject to a final operation that is unique to the product. The production cost will then consist of the average cost of a combination of operations 1 to 5 plus the specific cost of the final unique operation. The cost of the final operation will be traced specifically to the product using a job costing system. The final product cost therefore consists of a combination of process costing techniques and job costing techniques. This system of costing is referred to as operation costing or batch costing.

SUMMARY

The following items relate to the learning objectives listed at the beginning of the chapter.

● **Explain when process costing systems are appropriate.**

A process costing system is appropriate in those situations where masses of identical units or batches are produced thus making it unnecessary to assign costs to individual or batches of output. Instead, the average cost per unit or batch of output is calculated by dividing the total costs assigned to a product or service for the period by the number of units or batches of output for that period. Industries using process costing systems include chemicals, textiles and oil refining.

● **Explain the accounting treatment of normal and abnormal losses.**

Normal losses are inherent in the production process and cannot be eliminated: their cost should be borne by the good production. This is achieved by dividing the costs incurred for a period by the expected output rather than the actual output. Abnormal losses are avoidable, and the cost of these losses should not be assigned to products but recorded separately as an abnormal loss and written off as a period cost in the profit statement. Scrap sales (if any) that result from the losses should be allocated to the appropriate process account (for normal losses) and the abnormal loss account (for abnormal losses).

● **Prepare process, normal loss, abnormal loss and abnormal gain accounts when there is no ending work in progress.**

The cost accumulation procedure follows the production flow. Control accounts are established for each process (or department) and costs are assigned (debited) to each process. Abnormal losses are credited to the process where they were incurred and debited to an abnormal loss account. Scrap sales arising from normal losses are credited to the process account and any sales of scrap arising from abnormal losses are credited to the abnormal losses account. The accounting entries were illustrated using Example 5.1.

● **Explain and calculate equivalent units.**

Where stocks of work in progress are in existence, it is necessary in order to create homogeneous units of output to convert the work in progress into finished equivalent units of output. To do this we must estimate the percentage degree of completion of the work in progress and multiply this by the number of units in progress at the end of the accounting period. For example, if there are 5000 completed units estimated to be 40 per cent complete, this represents an equivalent production of 2000 completed units.

● **Compute the value of closing work in progress and completed production using the weighted average and first in, first out methods of valuing work in progress.**

There are two alternative methods of allocating opening work in progress costs to production: the weighted average and first in, first out methods. If the weighted average method is used, both the units and the value of opening work in progress are merged with the current period costs and production to calculate the average cost per unit. Using the first in, first out method, the opening work in progress is assumed to be the first group of units to be processed and completed during the current period. The opening work in progress is therefore assigned separately to completed production and the cost per unit is based only on current costs and production for the period. The closing work in progress is assumed to come from the new units that have been started during the period.

● **Additional learning objectives specified in Appendix 5.1.**

The appendix to this chapter includes one additional objective: to compute the value of normal and abnormal losses when there is ending work in progress. Because accounting for losses when all of the output is not fully complete is a complex topic that does not form part of the curriculum for many first level courses, this topic is dealt with in Appendix 5.1. You should check your course curriculum to ascertain if you need to read Appendix 5.1.

APPENDIX 5.1: LOSSES IN PROCESS AND PARTIALLY COMPLETED UNITS

Normal losses

Losses can occur at different stages within a process. Where losses are assumed to occur at the final stage of completion, only units that have reached this stage should be allocated with the cost of the loss. Therefore none of the costs should be allocated to closing work in progress (WIP), since they represent incomplete units. Consider Example 5A.1.

EXAMPLE 5A.1

A department with no opening work in progress introduces 1000 units into the process; 600 are completed, 300 are half-completed and 100 units are lost (all normal). *Losses occur on completion.* Material costs are £5000 (all introduced at the start of the process) and conversion costs are £3400.

The cost per unit is calculated as follows:

Element of cost	Total cost (£)	Completed units	Normal loss	WIP equiv. units	Total equiv. units	Cost per unit (£)
Materials	5000	600	100	300	1000	5.0
Conversion cost	3400	600	100	150	850	4.0
	8400					9.0

	(£)	(£)
Value of work in progress:		
Materials (300 units at £5)	1500	
Conversion cost (150 units at £4)	600	2100
Completed units (600 units at £9)	5400	
Normal loss (100 units at £9)	900	6300
		8400

You can see from the unit cost calculation that an additional column is added for the equivalent units of normal loss. Note also that the cost of the normal loss is added to the cost of completed production, since it is detected at the final stage of completion. The closing WIP has not reached this stage, and therefore does not bear any of the loss. The cost per unit completed after the allocation of the normal loss is £10.50 (£6300/600 units).

Let us now assume for Example 5A.1 that the loss is detected when the process has reached the *50 per cent stage of completion.* In our revised example it is assumed that the WIP has been processed beyond the point where the loss occurs (the 50 per cent stage of completion) so it is now appropriate to allocate a share of the cost of normal loss to WIP. The revised cost per unit is as follows:

Element of cost	Total cost (£)	Completed units	Normal loss	WIP equiv. units	Total equiv. units	Cost per unit (£)
Materials	5000	600	100	300	1000	5.00
Conversion cost	3400	600	50	150	800	4.25
	8400					9.25

The 100 lost units will not be processed any further once the loss is detected at the 50 per cent completion stage. Therefore, 50 units equivalent production (100 units × 50 per cent) is entered in the normal loss column for conversion cost equivalent production. Note that materials are introduced at the start of the process and are fully complete when the loss is detected. The cost of the normal loss is:

	(£)
Materials (100 × £5)	500.00
Conversion cost (50 × £4.25)	212.50
	712.50

How should we allocate the normal loss between completed production and work in progress? Several different approaches are advocated, but the most common approach is to apportion the normal loss in the ratio of completed units and WIP equivalent units as follows:

Completed units	(£)	WIP	(£)
Materials 600/900 × £500	333.33	300/900 × £500	166.67
Conversion cost 600/750 × £212.50	170.00	150/750 × £212.50	42.50
	503.33		209.17

The cost of completed units and WIP is:

	(£)	(£)
Completed units:		
(600 × £9.25)	5 550.00	
Share of normal loss	503.33	6 053.33
WIP:		
Materials (300 × £5)	1 500.00	
Conversion cost (150 × £4.25)	637.50	
Share of normal loss	209.17	2 346.67
		8 400.00

Where the WIP has reached the stage where losses are assumed to have occurred you can adopt a more simplistic method known as the short-cut method. With this method no entry is made in the unit cost statement for normal losses. The calculations adopting the short-cut method are as follows:

	Total cost (£)	Completed units	WIP equiv. units	Total equiv. units	Cost per unit (£)	WIP (£)
Materials	5 000	600	300	900	5.5555	1 666.65
Conversion cost	3 400	600	150	750	4.5333	680.00
					10.0888	2 346.65
			Completed units (600 × £10.0888)			6 053.35
						8 400.00

Here the cost of completed production and the value of WIP using the short-cut approach are identical to the costs computed above when the cost of the normal loss was computed and allocated to WIP and completed production. This is because the short cut method allocates the cost of the normal loss to both closing WIP and completed units based on the ratio of WIP and completed units equivalent production. The short cut method is only theoretically correct where losses occur at an earlier stage in the production process and the WIP has reached or passed this stage. In these circumstances it is appropriate to use the short-cut method and allocate the cost of the normal loss between WIP and completed units. Conversely, if WIP has not reached or passed the point where the loss occurs the short-cut method should not be used.

EXAMPLE 5A.2

A department with no opening work in progress introduced 1000 units into the process; 600 are completed, 250 are 60 per cent complete, and 150 units are lost consisting of 100 units normal loss and 50 units of abnormal loss. Losses are detected *when production is 50 per cent complete*. Material costs are £8000 (all introduced at the start of the process), conversion costs are £2900 and previous process cost is £10 000.

Abnormal losses

Where abnormal losses occur the normal unit cost statement using the short-cut method should be prepared (i.e. without a column for normal losses) but with an additional column for abnormal loss equivalent units. Consider the information presented in Example 5A.2. You can see from this example that losses are detected when production has reached the 50 per cent stage of completion and that WIP has been processed beyond this point. Therefore it is appropriate to use the short-cut method. The unit cost calculations are as follows:

Element of cost	Total cost (£)	Completed units	Abnormal loss	WIP equiv. units	Total equiv. units	Cost per unit (£)
Previous process cost	10 000	600	50	250	900	11.111
Materials	8 000	600	50	250	900	8.888
Conversion cost	2 900	600	25	150	775	3.742
	20 900					23.741

From this calculation you can see that materials and the previous process cost are 100 per cent complete when the loss is discovered. However, spoilt units will not be processed any further once the loss is detected, and the lost units will be 50 per cent complete in respect of conversion costs.

The costs are accounted for as follows:

	(£)	(£)
Value of work in progress		
Previous process cost (250 units at £11.111)	2 777	
Materials (250 units at £8.888)	2 222	
Conversion cost (150 units at £3.742)	561	5 560
Completed units:		
600 units at £23.741		14 246
Abnormal loss:		
Previous process cost (50 units at £11.111)	556	
Materials (50 units at £8.888)	444	
Conversion cost (25 units at £3.742)	94	1 094
		20 900

KEY TERMS AND CONCEPTS

Abnormal gain A gain that occurs when the level of a normal loss is less than expected.

Abnormal losses Losses that are not inherent to the production process and which are not expected

to occur under efficient operating conditions, also known as controllable losses.

Batch costing A method of costing that makes use of a combination of job costing and process

5.17 Basic. The following information is required for sub-questions (a) to (c).

The incomplete process account relating to period 4 for a company which manufactures paper is shown below:

Process account

	Units	$		Units	$
Material	4000	16000	Finished goods	2750	
Labour		8125	Normal loss	400	700
Production overhead		3498	Work in progress	700	

There was no opening work in progress (WIP). Closing WIP, consisting of 700 units, was complete as shown:

Material	100%
Labour	50%
Production overhead	40%

Losses are recognized at the end of the production process and are sold for $1.75 per unit.

(a) Given the outcome of the process, which ONE of the following accounting entries is needed to complete the double entry to the process account?

	Debit	Credit
A	Abnormal loss account	Process account
B	Process account	Abnormal loss account
C	Abnormal gain account	Process account
D	Process account	Abnormal gain account

(b) The value of the closing WIP was:

(A) $3868
(B) $4158
(C) $4678
(D) $5288

(c) The total value of the units transferred to finished goods was:

(A) $21052.50
(B) $21587.50
(C) $22122.50
(D) $22656.50

CIMA Management Accounting Fundamentals

5.18 Basic. A company operates a process costing system using the first in, first out (FIFO) method of valuation. No losses occur in the process. All materials are input at the commencement of the process. Conversion costs are incurred evenly throughout the process.

The following data relate to last period:

	Units	Degree of completion
Opening work in progress	2000	60%
Total number of units completed	14000	
Closing work in progress	3000	30%
Costs arising:		
Materials		51000
Conversion		193170

(a) What was the total number of units input during last period?

(A) 12000
(B) 13000
(C) 15000
(D) 17000

(b) What was the value of the closing work in progress for last period?

(A) £21330
(B) £21690
(C) £22530
(D) £22890

ACCA Financial Information for Management

5.19 Basic. A company operates a process costing system using the first in, first out (FIFO) system of valuation. No losses occur in the process. The following data relate to last month:

	Units
Opening work in progress	200 with a total value of £1530
Input to the process	1000
Completed production	1040

Last month the cost per equivalent unit of production was £20 and the degree of completion of the work in progress was 40 per cent throughout the month.

(a) What was the value (at cost) of last month's closing work in progress?

(A) £1224
(B) £1280
(C) £1836
(D) £1920

(b) What was the cost of the 1040 units completed last month?

(A) £19200
(B) £19930
(C) £20730
(D) £20800

ACCA Financial Information for Management

5.20 Intermediate. CW Ltd makes one product in a single process.

The details of the process for period 2 were as follows:

There were 800 units of opening work in progress valued as follows:

Material	£98000
Labour	£46000
Production overheads	£7600

During the period 1800 units were added to the process and the following costs were incurred:

Material	£387800
Labour	£276320
Production overheads	£149280

There were 500 units of closing work in progress, which were 100 per cent complete for material, 90 per cent complete for labour and 40 per cent complete for production overheads.

A normal loss equal to 10 per cent of new material input during the period was expected. The actual loss amounted to 180 units. Each unit of loss was sold for £10 per unit.

CW Ltd uses weighted average costing.

Calculate the cost of the output for the period.

CIMA P1 Management Accounting: Performance Evaluation

5.21 Intermediate: Preparation of process accounts with all output fully complete. 'No Friction' is an industrial lubricant, which is formed by subjecting certain crude chemicals to two successive processes. The output of process 1 is passed to process 2, where it is blended with other chemicals. The process costs for period 3 were as follows:

Process 1
    Material: 3000kg @ £0.25 per kg
    Labour: £120 Process plant time: 12 hours
      @ £20 per hour

Process 2
    Material: 2000kg @ £0.40 per kg
    Labour: £84
Process plant time: 20 hours @ £13.50 per hour
General overhead for period 3 amounted to £357 and is absorbed into process costs on a process labour basis.

The normal output of process 1 is 80 per cent of input, while that of process 2 is 90 per cent of input.

Waste matter from process 1 is sold for £0.20 per kg, while that from process 2 is sold for £0.30 per kg.

The output for period 3 was as follows:
    Process 1   2300kg
    Process 2   4000kg

There was no stock or work in progress at either the beginning or the end of the period, and it may be assumed that all available waste matter had been sold at the prices indicated.

You are required to show how the foregoing data would be recorded in a system of cost accounts.

5.22 Intermediate: Losses in process (weighted average). Chemical Processors manufacture Wonderchem using two processes, mixing and distillation. The following details relate to the distillation process for a period:

No opening work in progress (WIP)

Input from mixing	36 000kg at a cost of	£166 000
Labour for period		£43 800
Overheads for period		£29 200

Closing WIP of 8000kg, which was 100 per cent complete for materials and 50 per cent complete for labour and overheads.

The normal loss in distillation is 10 per cent of fully complete production. Actual loss in the period was 3600kg, fully complete, which were scrapped.

Required:

(a) Calculate whether there was a normal or abnormal loss or abnormal gain for the period.   (2 marks)
(b) Prepare the distillation process account for the period, showing clearly weights and values.   (10 marks)
(c) Explain what changes would be required in the accounts if the scrapped production had a resale value, and give the accounting entries.   (3 marks)

CIMA Stage 1 Cost Accounting

5.23 Intermediate: Equivalent production with losses (FIFO method). Yeoman Ltd uses process costing and the FIFO method of valuation. The following information for last month relates to Process G, where all the material is added at the beginning of the process:

Opening work in progress:	2000 litres (30 per cent complete in respect of in progress: conversion costs) valued in total at £24 600 (£16 500 for direct materials; £8100 for conversion)
Costs incurred:	Direct materials £99 600 for 12 500 litres of input conversion £155 250

Normal loss:	8 per cent of input in the period. All losses, which are incurred evenly throughout the process, can be sold for £3 per litre
Actual output:	10 000 litres were transferred from Process G to the finished goods warehouse
Closing work in progress:	3000 litres (45 per cent complete in respect of conversion costs)

Required:

(a) Prepare the Process G account for last month in pounds and litres.   (10 marks)
(b) Identify TWO types of organization where it would be appropriate to use service (operation) costing. For each one, suggest a suitable unit cost measure.   (2 marks)

ACCA Financial Information for Management

IM5.1 Intermediate.

(a) Describe the distinguishing characteristics of production systems where:

  (i) job costing techniques would be used, and
  (ii) process costing techniques would be used.   (3 marks)

(b) Job costing produces more accurate product costs than process costing. Critically examine the above statement by contrasting the information requirements, procedures and problems associated with each costing method.   (14 marks)

ACCA Level 1 Costing

IM5.2 Intermediate: Preparation of process accounts with all output fully completed. A product is manufactured by passing through three processes: A, B and C. In process C a by-product is also produced which is then transferred to process D where it is completed. For the first week in October, actual data included:

	Process A	Process B	Process C	Process D
Normal loss of input (%)	5	10	5	10
Scrap value (£ per unit)	1.50	2.00	4.00	2.00
Estimated sales value of by-product (£ per unit)	—	—	8.00	—
Output (units)	5 760	5 100	4 370	—
Output of by-product (units)	—	—	510	450
	(£)	(£)	(£)	(£)
Direct materials (6000 units)	12 000	—	—	—
Direct materials added in process	5 000	9 000	4 000	220
Direct wages	4 000	6 000	2 000	200
Direct expenses	800	1 680	2 260	151

Budgeted production overhead for the week is £30 500. Budgeted direct wages for the week are £12 200. You are required to prepare:

(a) Accounts for process A, B, C and D.   (20 marks)
(b) Abnormal loss account and abnormal gain account.   (5 marks)

CIMA P1 Cost Accounting 2

IM5.3 Intermediate: Discussion question on methods of apportioning joint costs and the preparation of process accounts with all output fully completed.

(a) 'While the ascertainment of product costs could be said to be one of the objectives of cost accounting, where joint products are produced and joint costs incurred, the total cost computed for the product may depend on the method selected for the apportionment of joint costs, thus making it difficult for management to make decisions about the future of products.'

You are required to discuss the above statement and to state *two* different methods of apportioning joint costs to joint products. *(8 marks)*

(b) A company using process costing manufactures a single product which passes through two processes, the output of process 1 becoming the input to process 2. Normal losses and abnormal losses are defective units having a scrap value and cash is received at the end of the period for all such units.

The following information relates to the four-week period of accounting period number 7.

Raw material issued to process 1 was 3000 units at a cost of £5 per unit.

There was no opening or closing work in progress but opening and closing stocks of finished goods were £20 000 and £23 000 respectively.

	Process 1	Process 2
Normal loss as a percentage of input	10%	5%
Output in units	2800	2600
Scrap value per unit	£2	£5
Additional components	£1 000	£780
Direct wages incurred	£4 000	£6 000
Direct expenses incurred	£10 000	£14 000
Production overhead as a percentage of direct wages	75%	125%

You are required to present the accounts for:
Process 1
Process 2
Finished goods
Normal loss
Abnormal loss
Abnormal gain
Profit and loss (so far as it relates to any of the accounts listed above). *(17 marks)*

CIMA Stage 2 Cost Accounting

IM5.4 Intermediate: Equivalent production and losses in process. Industrial Solvents Limited mixes together three chemicals – A, B and C – in the ratio 3:2:1 to produce Allklean, a specialized anti-static fluid. The chemicals cost £8, £6 and £3.90 per litre respectively.

In a period, 12 000 litres in total were input to the mixing process. The normal process loss is 5 per cent of input and in the period there was an abnormal loss of 100 litres while the completed production was 9500 litres.

There was no opening work in progress (WIP) and the closing WIP was 100 per cent complete for materials and 40 per cent complete for labour and overheads. Labour and overheads were £41 280 in total for the period. Materials lost in production are scrapped.

Required:
(a) Calculate the volume of closing WIP. *(3 marks)*
(b) Prepare the mixing process account for the period, showing clearly volumes and values. *(9 marks)*

(c) Briefly explain what changes would be necessary in your account if an abnormal gain were achieved in a period. *(3 marks)*

CIMA Stage 1 Cost Accounting

IM5.5 Intermediate: Losses in process (weighted average).

(a) A company uses a process costing system in which the following terms arise:
conversion costs
work in progress
equivalent units
normal loss
abnormal loss.

Required:
Provide a definition of each of these terms. *(5 marks)*
(b) Explain how you would treat normal and abnormal losses in process costs accounts. *(4 marks)*
(c) One of the products manufactured by the company passes through two separate processes. In each process losses, arising from rejected material, occur. In Process 1, normal losses are 20 per cent of input. In Process 2, normal losses are 10 per cent of input. The losses arise at the end of each of the processes. Reject material can be sold. Process 1 reject material can be sold for £1.20 per kilo and Process 2 reject material for £1.42 per kilo.

Information for a period is as follows:

Process 1:
Material input 9000 kilos, cost £14 964
Direct labour £12 250
Production overhead £2450
Material output 7300 kilos

Process 2:
Material input 7300 kilos
Direct labour £5000
Production overhead £1300
Material output 4700 kilos

At the end of the period 2000 kilos of material were incomplete in Process 2. These were 50 per cent complete as regards direct labour and production overhead. There was no opening work in progress in either process, and no closing work in progress in Process 1.

Required:
Prepare the relevant cost accounts for the period. *(16 marks)*

ACCA Level 1 Costing

IM5.6 Intermediate: Losses in process and weighted averages method. ABC plc operates an integrated cost accounting system and has a financial year which ends on 30 September. It operates in a processing industry in which a single product is produced by passing inputs through two sequential processes. A normal loss of 10 per cent of input is expected in each process.

The following account balances have been extracted from its ledger at 31 August:

	Debit (£)	Credit (£)
Process 1 (Materials £4400; Conversion costs £3744)	8144	
Process 2 (Process 1 £4431; Conversion costs £5250)	9681	
Abnormal loss	1400	
Abnormal gain		300
Overhead control account		250
Sales		585 000
Cost of sales	442 500	
Finished goods stock	65 000	

ABC plc uses the weighted average method of accounting for work in progress.

During September the following transactions occurred:

Process 1

materials input	4 000kg costing	£22 000
labour cost		£12 000
transfer to process 2	2 400kg	

Process 2

transfer from process 1	2 400kg	
labour cost		£15 000
transfer to finished goods	2 500kg	
Overhead costs incurred amounted to	£54 000	
Sales to customers were	£52 000	

Overhead costs are absorbed into process costs on the basis of 150 per cent of labour cost.

The losses which arise in process 1 have no scrap value: those arising in process 2 can be sold for £2 per kg.

Details of opening and closing work in progress for the month of September are as follows:

	Opening	Closing
Process 1	3 000kg	3 400kg
Process 2	2 250kg	2 600kg

In both processes closing work in progress is fully complete as to material cost and 40 per cent complete as to conversion cost. Stocks of finished goods at 30 September were valued at cost of £60 000.

Required:
Prepare the ledger accounts for September and the annual profit and loss account of ABC plc. (Commence with the balances given above, balance off and transfer any balances as appropriate.)   *(25 marks)*

CIMA Stage 2 Operational Cost Accounting

IM5.7 Intermediate: Process accounts involving an abnormal gain and equivalent production. The following information relates to a manufacturing process for a period:

| Materials costs | £16 445 |
| Labour and overhead costs | £28 596 |

10 000 units of output were produced by the process in the period, of which 420 failed testing and were scrapped. Scrapped units normally represent 5 per cent of total production output. Testing takes place when production units are 60 per cent complete in terms of labour and overheads. Materials are input at the beginning of the process. All scrapped units were sold in the period for £0.40 per unit.

Required:
Prepare the process accounts for the period, including those for process scrap and abnormal losses/gains.   *(12 marks)*

ACCA Foundation Stage Paper 3

IM5.8 Intermediate: Losses in process (FIFO and weighted average methods). A company produces a single product from one of its manufacturing processes. The following information of process inputs, outputs and work in progress relates to the most recently completed period:

	kg
Opening work in progress	21 700
Materials input	105 600

	kg
Output completed	92 400
Closing work in progress	28 200

The opening and closing work in progress are respectively 60 per cent and 50 per cent complete as to conversion costs. Losses occur at the beginning of the process and have a scrap value of £0.45 per kg.

The opening work in progress included raw material costs of £56 420 and conversion costs of £30 597. Costs incurred during the period were:

| Materials input | £276 672 |
| Conversion costs | £226 195 |

Required:

(a) Calculate the unit costs of production (£ per kg to four decimal places) using:

(i) the weighted average method of valuation and assuming that all losses are treated as normal;

(ii) the FIFO method of valuation and assuming that normal losses are 5 per cent of materials input.
    (13 marks)

(b) Prepare the process account for situation (a) (ii) above.
    (6 marks)

(c) Distinguish between:

(i) joint products, and

(ii) by-products and contrast their treatment in process accounts.   *(6 marks)*

ACCA Cost and Management Accounting 1

IM5.9 Advanced: FIFO method and losses in process.

(a) You are required to explain and discuss the alternative methods of accounting for normal and abnormal spoilage.   *(8 marks)*

(b) Weston Harvey Ltd assembles and finishes trapfoils from bought-in components which are utilized at the beginning of the assembly process. The other assembly costs are incurred evenly throughout that process. When the assembly process is complete, the finishing process is undertaken. Overhead is absorbed into assembly, but not finishing, at the rate of 100 per cent of direct assembly cost.

It is considered normal for some trapfoils to be spoiled during assembly and finishing. Quality control inspection is applied at the conclusion of the finishing process to determine whether units are spoiled.

It is accepted that the spoilage is normal if spoiled units are no more than one-eighteenth of the completed good units produced. Normal spoilage is treated as a product cost, and incorporated into the cost of good production. Any spoilage in excess of this limit is classed as abnormal, and written off as a loss of the period in which it occurs.

Trapfoils are valuable in relation to their weight and size. Despite vigilant security precautions, it is common that some units are lost, probably by pilferage. The cost of lost units is written off as a loss of the period in which it occurs. This cost is measured as the cost of the bought-in components plus the assembly process, but no finishing cost is charged.

Weston Harvey uses a FIFO system of costing. The following data summarize the firm's activities during November:

Opening work in progress:

Bought-in components	£60 000
Direct assembly cost to 31 October	£25 000
No. of units (on average one-half assembled)	50 000
Direct costs incurred during November	
Bought-in components received	£120 000

(Continued)

Opening work in progress:

Direct assembly cost	£40 000
Direct finishing cost	£30 000
Production data for November:	Trapfoils
Components received into assembly	112 000
Good units completed	90 000
Spoiled units	10 000
Lost units	2 000

None of the opening work in process had at that stage entered the finishing process. Similarly, neither had any of the closing work in progress at the end of the month. The units in the closing work in progress were, on average, one-third complete as to assembly; none had entered the finishing process. You are required:

(i) to calculate the number of units in the closing work in progress; *(3 marks)*

(ii) to calculate the number of equivalent units processed in November, distinguishing between bought-in components, assembly and finishing; *(6 marks)*

(iii) to calculate the number of equivalent units processed in November, subdivided into the amounts for good units produced, spoilage, lost units and closing work in progress. *(8 marks)*

ICAEW Management Accounting

IM5.10 Advanced: Comparison of FIFO and weighted average, stock valuation methods. On 1 October Bland Ltd opened a plant for making verniers. Data for the first two months' operations are shown below:

	October (units)	November (units)
Units started in month	3 900	2 700
Units completed (all sold)	2 400	2 400
Closing work in progress	1 500	1 800
	(£)	(£)
Variable costs:		
Materials	58 500	48 600
Labour	36 000	21 000
Fixed costs	63 000	63 000
Sales revenue	112 800	120 000

At 31 October the units in closing work in progress were 100 per cent complete for materials and 80 per cent complete for labour. At 30 November the units in closing work in progress were 100 per cent complete for materials and 50 per cent complete for labour.

The company's policy for valuation of work in progress is under review. The board of directors decided that two alternative profit and loss statements should be prepared for October and November. One statement would value work in progress on a weighted average cost basis and the other would adopt a first in, first out basis. Fixed costs would be absorbed in proportion to actual labour costs in both cases.

For October both bases gave a closing work in progress valuation of £55 500 and a profit of £10 800. When the statements for November were presented to the board the following suggestions were made:

1 'We wouldn't have a problem over the valuation basis if we used standard costs.'

2 'Standard cost valuation could be misleading for an operation facing volatile costs; all data should be on a current cost basis for management purposes.'

3 'It would be simpler and more informative to go to a direct cost valuation basis for management use.'

4 'All that management needs is a cash flow report; leave the work in progress valuation to the year-end financial accounts.'

Requirements:

(a) Prepare profit and loss statements for November on the two alternative bases decided by the board of directors, showing workings. *(9 marks)*

(b) Explain, with supporting calculations, the differences between the results shown by each statement you have prepared. *(6 marks)*

(c) Assess the main strengths and weaknesses of each of the suggestions made by the directors, confining your assessment to matters relating to the effects of work in progress valuation on performance measurement. *(10 marks)*

ICAEW P2 Management Accounting

6
JOINT AND BY-PRODUCT COSTING

LEARNING OBJECTIVES After studying this chapter, you should be able to:

- distinguish between joint products and by-products;

- explain and identify the split-off point in a joint cost situation;

- explain the alternative methods of allocating joint costs to products;

- discuss the arguments for and against each of the methods of allocating joint costs to products;

- present relevant financial information for a decision as to whether a product should be sold at a particular stage or further processed;

- describe the accounting treatment of by-products.

A distinguishing feature of the production of joint and by-products is that the products are not identifiable as different products until a specific point in the production process is reached. Before this point, joint costs are incurred on the production of all products emerging from the joint production process. It is therefore not possible to trace joint costs to individual products. A classic example of joint products is the meat packing industry, where various cuts of meat (e.g. pork chops, bacon and ham) are joint products that are processed from one original carcass. The cost of obtaining the carcass is a joint cost that must be allocated to the various cuts of meat. Another example of joint products is the production of gasoline, where the derivation of gasoline inevitably results in the production of various joint products such as gasoline, fuel oil, kerosene and paraffin.

To meet internal and external profit measurement and inventory valuation requirements, it is necessary to assign all product-related costs (including joint costs) to products so that costs can be allocated to inventories and cost of goods sold. The assignment of joint costs to products, however, is of little use for decision-making. We shall begin by distinguishing between joint and by-products. This will be followed by an examination of the different methods that can be used to allocate joint costs to products for inventory valuation. We shall then go on to discuss which costs are relevant for decision-making. As with the previous two chapters, this chapter can be omitted if you are pursuing a management accounting course that does not require you to focus on cost accumulation for inventory valuation and profit measurement (see 'Guidelines for using this book' in Chapter 1).

JOINT PRODUCTS AND BY-PRODUCTS

Joint products and by-products arise in situations where the production of one product makes inevitable the production of other products. For example, the extraction of gasoline from crude oil also produces kerosene and paraffin. We can distinguish between joint products and by-products by looking at their relative sales value. When a group of individual products is produced simultaneously and each product has a significant relative sales value, the outputs are usually called joint products. Products that only have a minor sales value when compared with the joint products are called by-products.

As their name implies, by-products are those products that result incidentally from the main joint products. By-products may have a considerable absolute value, but the crucial classification test is that the sales value is small when compared with the values of the joint products. Joint products are crucial to the commercial viability of an organization, whereas by-products are incidental. In other words, by-products do not usually influence the decision as to whether or not to produce the main product, and they normally have little effect on the prices set for the main (joint) products. Examples of industries that produce both joint and by-products include chemicals, oil refining, mining, flour milling and gas manufacturing.

A distinguishing feature of the production of joint and by-products is that the products are not identifiable as different individual products until a specific point in the production process is reached, known as the split-off point. All products may separate at one time, or different products may emerge at intervals. Before the split-off point, costs cannot be traced to particular products. For example, it is not possible to determine what part of the cost of processing a barrel of crude oil should be allocated to petrol, kerosene or paraffin. After the split-off point, joint products may be sold or subjected to further processing. In the latter case, any further processing costs can be traced to the specific products involved.

Figure 6.1 illustrates a simplified production process for joint and by-products. In this example, joint products A and B and by-product C all emerge at the same split-off point. Before this point, they share the same raw materials, labour and overhead costs. After the split-off point, further processing costs

REAL WORLD VIEWS 6.1

Accounting for by-products – by-products of gold mining

South Africa is one of the top gold producers in the world, holding about 6000 metric tons of reserves in mines as of 2015. Most mining operations have waste and by-products, some of which are disposable, reusable or even saleable, others are not. A by-product of gold mining is the heavy metal uranium. In fact, as both gold and uranium are heavy metals, they are often present together in the same mine. The nuclear industry is the number one customer for uranium, and it is also mined for separately. When gold mining is the main objective, the uranium by-product is separated using acid that drains the mines. A report in the *Mail & Guardian* in November 2010 estimated that 100 000 tonnes of the uranium by-product were in mine dumps in one western region of South Africa alone. The reasons were that gold prices were at high levels (about $1400 an ounce in early 2011), meaning mining

the uranium is less profitable. Second, a combination of the post-Cold War era and a decline in nuclear power production has seen a fall in demand for uranium. Move forward to 2016, gold prices are about $200 less per ounce and the South African government are promising more nuclear power production.

Questions

1 Assuming the uranium by-product of a gold mine could be sold, how would an accountant consider whether or not it is worthwhile financially?

2 What factors apart from cost might be considered in the decision?

Reference
www.enca.com/south-africa/uranium-mining-karoo-south-africas-new-gold

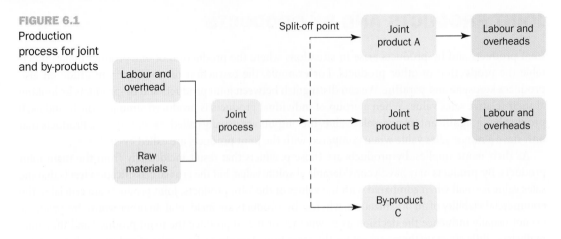

are added to the joint products before sale, and these costs can be specifically allocated to them. In this example, by-product C is sold at the split-off point without further processing, although sometimes by-products may be further processed after the split-off point before they are sold on the outside market.

Later in this chapter, we will examine the accounting treatment of by-products. First, we will concentrate our attention on the allocation of joint costs to joint products.

METHODS OF ALLOCATING JOINT COSTS

If all the production for a particular period is sold, the problem of allocating joint costs to products for inventory valuation and profit measurement does not arise. Inventory valuations are not necessary, and the calculation of profit merely requires the deduction of total cost from total sales. However, if some inventory remains unsold, inventories will exist at the end of the period and it is necessary to allocate costs to particular products. There is more than one method of making this allocation and, as you will see, the choice of method can have significant implications for the calculation of profit and the valuation of inventories. This area will involve the accountant in making subjective decisions that can be among the most difficult to defend. All one can do is attempt to choose an allocation method that seems to provide a rational and reasonable method of cost distribution. The most frequently used methods that are used to allocate joint costs up to split-off point can be divided into the following two categories:

1 Methods based on physical measures such as weight, volume, etc.

2 Methods based on allocating joint costs relative to the market values of the products.

We shall now look at four methods that are used for allocating joint costs using the information given in Example 6.1. Products X, Y and Z all become finished products at the split-off point. We must decide how much of the £600 000 joint costs should be allocated to each individual product. The £600 000 cannot be specifically identified with any of the individual products, since the products themselves were not separated before the split-off point, but some method must be used to split the £600 000 among the products X, Y and Z so that inventories can be valued and the profit for the period calculated.

Physical measures method

Using the physical measures method, we simply allocate the joint cost in proportion to volume. Each product is assumed to receive similar benefits from the joint cost, and is therefore

EXAMPLE 6.1

During the month of July the Van Nostrand Company processes a basic raw material through a manufacturing process that yields three products – products X, Y and Z. There were no opening inventories and the products are sold at the split-off point without further processing. We shall initially assume that all of the output is sold during the period. Details of the production process and the sales revenues are given in the following diagram.

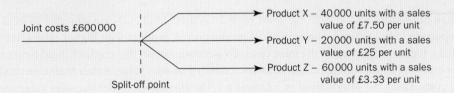

Joint costs £600 000

Split-off point

Product X – 40 000 units with a sales value of £7.50 per unit

Product Y – 20 000 units with a sales value of £25 per unit

Product Z – 60 000 units with a sales value of £3.33 per unit

charged with its proportionate share of the total cost. The cost allocations using this method are as follows:

Product	Units produced	Proportion to total	Joint costs allocated (£)	Cost per unit (£)
X	40 000	$1/3$	200 000	5
Y	20 000	$1/6$	100 000	5
Z	60 000	$1/2$	300 000	5
	120 000		600 000	

Note that this method assumes that the cost per unit is the same for each of the products. To calculate the cost per unit, we simply divide the total cost by the number of units:

$$\text{cost per unit} = £5 \; (£600\,000/120\,000)$$

Thus the joint cost allocations are:

$$\text{Product X: } 40\,000 \times £5 = £200\,000$$
$$\text{Product Y: } 20\,000 \times £5 = £100\,000$$
$$\text{Product Z: } 60\,000 \times £5 = £300\,000$$

Where market prices of the joint products differ, the assumption of identical costs per unit for each joint product will result in some products showing high profits while others may show losses. This can give misleading profit calculations. Let us look at the product profit calculations using the information given in Example 6.1:

Product	Sales revenue (£)	Total cost (£)	Profit (loss) (£)	Profit/sales (%)
X	300 000	200 000	100 000	33 1/3
Y	500 000	100 000	400 000	80
Z	200 000	300 000	(100 000)	(50)
	1 000 000	600 000	400 000	40

You will see from these figures that the allocation of the joint costs bears no relationship to the revenue-producing power of the individual products. Product Z is allocated with the largest share of the joint costs but has the lowest total sales revenue; product Y is allocated with the lowest share of the joint costs but has the highest total sales revenue. This illustrates a significant problem with the physical measures method.

A further problem is that the joint products must be measurable by the same unit of measurement. Sometimes, the products emerging from the joint process consist of solids, liquids and gases, and it can be difficult to find a common base to measure them on. The main advantage of using the physical measures method is simplicity, but this is outweighed by its many disadvantages.

Sales value at split-off point method

When the sales value at split-off point method is used, joint costs are allocated to joint products in proportion to the estimated sales value of production. A product with higher sales value will be allocated a higher proportion of the joint costs. To a certain extent, this method could better be described as a means of apportioning profits or losses according to sales value, rather than a method for allocating costs. Using the information in Example 6.1, the allocations under the sales value method would be as follows:

Product	Units produced	Sales value (£)	Proportion of sales value to total (%)	Joint costs allocated (£)
X	40 000	300 000	30	180 000
Y	20 000	500 000	50	300 000
Z	60 000	200 000	20	120 000
		1 000 000		600 000

The revised product profit calculations would be as follows:

Product	Sales revenue	Total cost (£)	Profit (loss) (£)	Profit/sales (%)
X	300 000	180 000	120 000	40
Y	500 000	300 000	200 000	40
Z	200 000	120 000	80 000	40
	1 000 000	600 000	400 000	

The sales value method ensures that joint costs are allocated based on a product's ability to absorb the joint costs but it can itself be criticized because it is based on the assumption that sales revenue determines prior costs. This can result in an unprofitable product with low sales revenue being allocated with a small share of joint cost, thus mistakenly giving the impression that it is generating profits.

Net realizable value method

In Example 6.1, we assumed that all products are sold at the split-off point and that no additional costs are incurred beyond that point. In practice, it is likely that joint products will each require further processing after the split-off point, and market values may not exist for the products before this processing has taken place. To estimate the sales value at the split-off point, it is therefore necessary to use the estimated sales value at the point of sale and work backwards. This method is called the net realizable value method. The net realizable value at split-off point can be estimated by deducting the further processing costs from the sales revenues. This approach is illustrated with the data given in Example 6.2, which are the same as Example 6.1 except that further processing costs beyond split-off point are now assumed to exist. You should now refer to Example 6.2.

EXAMPLE 6.2

ssume the same situation as Example 6.1 except that further processing costs now apply. Details of the production process and sales revenues are given in the following diagram:

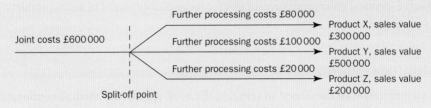

The calculation of the net realizable value and the allocation of joint costs using this method is as follows:

Product	Sales value (£)	Costs beyond split-off point (£)	Estimated net realizable value at split-off point (£)	Proportion to total (%)	Joint costs allocated (£)	Profit (£)	Gross profit (%)
X	300 000	80 000	220 000	27.5	165 000	55 000	18.33
Y	500 000	100 000	400 000	50.0	300 000	100 000	20.00
Z	200 000	20 000	180 000	22.5	135 000	45 000	22.50
	1 000 000	200 000	800 000		600 000	200 000	20.00

Note that the joint costs are now allocated in proportion to each product's net realizable value at split-off point.

Constant gross profit percentage method

When joint products are subject to further processing after split-off point and the net realizable method is used, the gross profit percentages are different for each product. In the above illustration, they are 18.33 per cent for product X, 20 per cent for Y and 22.5 per cent for Z. It could be argued that, since the three products arise from a single productive process, they should earn identical gross profit percentages. The constant gross profit percentage method allocates joint costs so that the overall gross profit percentage is identical for each individual product.

From the information contained in Example 6.2, the joint costs would be allocated in such a way that the resulting gross profit percentage for each of the three products is equal to the overall gross profit percentage of 20 per cent. Note that the gross profit percentage is calculated by deducting the *total* costs of the three products (£800 000) from the *total* sales (£1 000 000) and expressing the profit (£200 000) as a percentage of sales (i.e. 20 per cent). The calculations are as follows:

	Product X (£)	Product Y (£)	Product Z (£)	Total (£)
Sales value	300 000	500 000	200 000	1 000 000
Gross profit (20 per cent)	60 000	100 000	40 000	200 000
Cost of goods sold	240 000	400 000	160 000	800 000
Less separable further processing costs	80 000	100 000	20 000	200 000
Allocated joint costs	160 000	300 000	140 000	600 000

You can see that the required gross profit percentage of 20 per cent is computed for each product. The additional further processing costs for each product are then deducted, and the balance represents the allocated joint costs.

The constant gross profit percentage method assumes that there is a uniform relationship between cost and sales value for each individual product. However, this assumption is questionable, since we do not observe identical gross profit percentages for individual products in multi-product companies that do not involve joint costs.

Comparison of methods

What factors should be considered in selecting the most appropriate method of allocating joint costs? The cause-and-effect criterion, described in Chapter 3, cannot be used because there is no cause-and-effect relationship between the *individual* products and the incurrence of joint costs. Joint costs are caused by *all* products and not by individual products.

Where cause-and-effect relationships cannot be established, allocations should be based on the benefits received criterion. If benefits received cannot be measured, costs should be allocated based on the principle of equity or fairness. The net realizable method and the sales value at split-off point are the methods that best meet the benefits received criterion. If sales values at the split-off point exist, the latter also has the added advantage of simplicity. It is also difficult to estimate the net realizable value in industries where there are numerous subsequent further processing stages and multiple split-off points. As we have discussed, similar measurement problems can also apply with the physical measures method. A summary of the advantages and disadvantages of each allocation method is presented in Exhibit 6.1.

What methods do companies actually use? Little empirical evidence exists apart from a UK survey undertaken many years ago by Slater and Wootton (1984). They reported that 76 per cent of the responding organizations used a physical measures method. In practice, firms are likely to use a method where the output from the joint process can be measured without too much difficulty.

EXHIBIT 6.1 Advantages and disadvantages of the different allocation methods

Method	Advantages	Disadvantages
Physical measurement	Simple to operate where there is a common unit of measurement	• Can distort profit reporting and inventory valuation • Can be difficult to find a common unit of measurement
Sales value at split-off point	Provides more realistic inventory valuations	• Assumes that sales value determines prior costs • Assumes that a sales value at split-off point can be determined
Net realizable value	Takes further processing costs into account Simple to apply if there is only one split-off point	Can be difficult to calculate for a complex process with many split-off points
Constant gross profit percentage	Appropriate only if a constant gross profit for each joint product is a logical assumption	Only appropriate if a constant gross profit for each product makes sense

IRRELEVANCE OF JOINT COST ALLOCATIONS FOR DECISION-MAKING

So far, we have concentrated on the allocation of joint costs for the purposes of inventory valuation and profit measurement. Joint product costs that have been computed for inventory valuation are normally inappropriate for decision-making. You will remember from Chapter 2 that for decision-making, only relevant costs should be used and that these represent the incremental costs relating to a decision. Costs that will be unaffected by a decision are classed as irrelevant. Joint cost allocations are thus irrelevant for decision-making. Consider the information presented in Example 6.3, which shows the additional revenue and costs involved in converting product Y into product Z.

A joint cost of £1 000 000 will be incurred irrespective of which decision is taken, and is not relevant for this decision. The information that is required for the decision is a comparison of the additional costs with the additional revenues from converting product Y into product Z. The following information should therefore be provided:

Additional revenue and costs from converting product Y into product Z	(£)
Additional revenues (50 000 × £2)	100 000
Additional conversion costs	60 000
Additional profit from conversion	40 000

The proof that profits will increase by £40 000 if conversion takes place is as follows:

	Convert to product Z (£)	Do not convert (£)
Sales	1 300 000	1 200 000
Total costs	1 060 000	1 000 000
Profits	240 000	200 000

EXAMPLE 6.3

The Adriatic Company incurs joint product costs of £1 000 000 for the production of two joint products, X and Y. Both products can be sold at split-off point. However, if additional costs of £60 000 are incurred on product Y then it can be converted into product Z and sold for £10 per unit. The joint costs and the sales revenue at split-off point are illustrated in the following diagram:

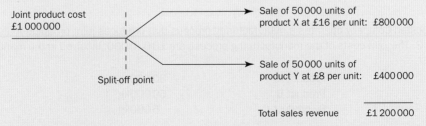

You are requested to advise management whether or not product Y should be converted into product Z.

The general rule is that it will be profitable to extend the processing of a joint product as long as the additional revenues exceed the additional costs, but note that the variable portion of the joint costs will be relevant for some decisions. You should refer to Learning Note 6.1 on the digital support resources (see Preface for details) for an illustration of a situation where joint variable costs are relevant for decision-making.

ACCOUNTING FOR BY-PRODUCTS

By-products are products that have a minor sales value and that emerge incidentally from the production of the major product. As the major objective of the company is to produce the joint products, it can justifiably be argued that the joint costs should be allocated only to the joint products and that the by-products should not be allocated with any portion of the joint cost that are incurred before the split-off point. Any further costs that are incurred in producing by-products after the split-off point can justifiably be charged to the by-product, since such costs are incurred for the benefit of the by-product only.

By-product revenues or by-product net revenues (the sales revenue of the by-product less the additional further processing costs after the split-off point) should be deducted from the cost of the joint products or the main product from which it emerges. Consider Example 6.4.

None of the joint costs shown in Example 6.4 is allocated to the by-product but the further processing costs of £5000 (5000kg × £1) are charged to the by-product. The net revenues from the by-product of £20 000 (sales revenue of £25 000 less further processing costs of £5000) are deducted from the costs of the joint process (£3 020 000). Thus joint costs of £3 000 000 will be allocated to joint products A and B using one of the allocation methods described in this chapter. The accounting entries for the by-product will be as follows:

Dr By-product inventory (5000 × £4)	20 000	
Cr Joint process WIP account		20 000

With the net revenue due from the production of the by-product:

Dr By-product inventory	5 000	
Cr Cash		5 000

With the separable manufacturing costs incurred:

Dr Cash	25 000	
Cr By-product inventory		25 000

With the value of by-products sales for the period.

EXAMPLE 6.4

The Neopolitan Company operates a manufacturing process that produces joint products A and B and by-product C. The joint costs of the manufacturing process are £3 020 000, incurred in the manufacture of:

Product A	30 000kg
Product B	50 000kg
By-product C	5 000kg

By-product C requires further processing at a cost of £1 per kg, after which it can be sold at £5 per kg.

REAL WORLD VIEWS 6.2

Environmentally friendly products from paper mill sludge

Each year, the paper and pulp industry produces millions of tonnes of sludge in the production of paper. This sludge is typically disposed of in land-fill sites or incinerated. Both disposal methods are costly and environmentally undesirable. How-ever, some firms are now transforming undesirable by-products into commercially viable consumer and industrial products. One such firm is Kadant Grantek Inc., based in Wisconsin, USA. Kadant Grantek processes paper mill sludge from local paper mills to make several cellulose-based prod-ucts. The sludge is dried and granulated to make an agricultural seed carrier called Biodac, an indus-trial absorbent called Gran-sorb and a premium cat litter product. The process is clean, releasing only steam into the atmosphere. No waste or further by-products are produced. Kadant Grantek collects the paper mill sludge free of charge from the paper mills. The paper mills in turn do not incur landfill or incineration costs and can portray a greener image. A win–win situation for both parties.

Questions

1 Assuming paper mills decide to sell their sludge for a small fee, how might they account for the revenue generated?

2 Can you think of any other 'waste' by-products that are re-used rather than disposed of?

References
www.biodac.net
www.gran-sorb.net

SUMMARY

The following items relate to the learning objectives listed at the beginning of the chapter.

● **Distinguish between joint products and by-products.**

Both joint products and by-products arise from a joint production process whereby they are not separately identifiable until after they have emerged from this joint process. Joint products have a relatively high sales value while by-products have a low sales value compared with the sales value of a joint product. Joint products are also crucial to the commercial viability of an organization, whereas by-products are incidental.

● **Explain and identify the split-off point in a joint cost situation.**

The split-off point is the point in the process at which products become separately identifiable.

● **Explain the alternative methods of allocating joint costs to products.**

Four different methods of allocating joint costs to products are described: physical measures, sales value at split-off point, net realizable value and gross profit percentage methods. The physical measures method simply allocates joint costs to individual products in proportion to their production volumes. The sales value at split-off point method allocates joint costs to indi-vidual products based on their sales value at split-off point. If market prices of products at the split-off point do not exist, the sales value can be estimated using the net realizable method. Here, the net realizable values of the joint products at split-off point are estimated by deducting the further processing costs from the sales value at the point of sale. The gross profit percent-age method allocates joint costs so that the overall gross profit percentage is identical for each product.

● **Discuss the arguments for and against each of the methods of allocating joint costs to products.**

Cost should be allocated based on cause-and-effect relationships. Such relationships cannot be observed with joint products. When this situation occurs it is recommended that joint costs should be allocated based on the benefits received criterion. The advantage of the physical measures method is its simplicity but it suffers from the disadvantage that it can lead to a situation in which the recorded joint cost inventory valuation for a product is in excess of its net realizable value. The sales value at split-off point suffers from the disadvantage that sales values for many joint products do not exist at the split-off point. The gross profit percentage method assumes that there is a uniform relationship between cost and sales value for each product. However, such a relationship is questionable since identical gross profit percentages for individual products in multi-product companies that do not have joint costs are not observed. Both the sales value at split-off point and the net realizable value methods most closely meet the benefits received criterion but the latter is likely to be the preferred method if sales values at the split-off point do not exist.

● **Present relevant financial information for a decision as to whether a product should be sold at a particular stage or further processed.**

The joint costs allocated to products are irrelevant for decisions relating to further processing. Such decisions should be based on a comparison of the incremental costs with the incremental revenues arising from further processing. The presentation of relevant financial information for further processing decisions was illustrated using the data presented in Example 6.3.

● **Describe the accounting treatment of by-products.**

By-product net revenues should be deducted from the cost of the joint production process prior to allocating these costs to the individual joint products. The accounting treatment of by-products was illustrated with the data presented in Example 6.4.

KEY TERMS AND CONCEPTS

By-products Products that are incidental to the production of joint products and have a low relative sales value.

Constant gross profit percentage method A method of allocating joint costs so that the overall gross profit percentage is the same for each product.

Further processing costs Costs incurred by a joint product or by-product after the split-off point that can be traced to the product involved.

Joint products Products that have a high relative sales value and are crucial to the commercial viability of the organization.

Net realizable value method A method of allocating joint costs on the basis of net realizable value at the split-off point, which is calculated by deducting further processing costs from sales revenues.

Physical measures method A method of allocating joint costs in proportion to volume.

Sales value at split-off point method A method of allocating joint costs in proportion to the estimated sales value of production.

Split-off point The point in a production process at which a joint product or by-product separates from the other products.

RECOMMENDED READING

For additional reading relating to joint product costs you should refer to an article that can be accessed from the ACCA Student Accountant technical article archive at www.accaglobal.com/gb/en/student/exam-support -resources/fundamentals-exams-study-resources/f2 /technical-articles.html. A research publication relating to the accounting of joint blood product costs in a hospital is reported in Trenchard and Dixon (2003).

KEY EXAMINATION POINTS

It is necessary to apportion joint costs to joint products for inventory valuation and profit measurement purposes. Remember that the costs calculated for inventory valuation purposes should not be used for decision-making purposes. Examination questions normally require joint product cost calculations and the presentation of information as to whether a product should be sold at split-off point or further processed (see the answers to Review problems 6.14 and 6.15). A common mistake with the latter requirement is to include joint cost apportionments. You should compare incremental revenues with incremental costs and indicate that, in the short term, joint costs are not relevant to the decision to sell at the split-off point or process further.

ASSESSMENT MATERIAL

The review questions are short questions that enable you to assess your understanding of the main topics included in the chapter. The numbers in parentheses provide you with the page numbers to refer to if you cannot answer a specific question.

The review problems are more complex and require you to relate and apply the content to various business problems. The problems are graded by their level of difficulty. Solutions to review problems that are not preceded by the term 'IM' are provided in a separate section at the end of the book. Solutions to problems preceded by the term 'IM' are provided in the Instructor's Manual accompanying this book that can be downloaded from the lecturer's digital support resources. Additional review problems with fully worked solutions are provided in the *Student Manual* that accompanies this book.

REVIEW QUESTIONS

6.1 Define joint costs, split-off point and further processing costs. (p. 133)

6.2 Distinguish between joint products and by-products. (p. 133)

6.3 Provide examples of industries that produce both joint products and by-products. (p. 132)

6.4 Explain why it is necessary to allocate joint costs to products. (p. 134)

6.5 Describe the four different methods of allocating joint costs to products. (pp. 134–138)

6.6 Why is the physical measure method considered to be an unsatisfactory joint cost allocation method? (p. 135)

6.7 Explain the factors that should influence the choice of method when allocating joint costs to products. (p. 138)

6.8 Explain the financial information that should be included in a decision as to whether a product should be sold at the split-off point or further processed. (pp. 139–140)

6.9 Describe the accounting treatment of by-products. (p. 140)

REVIEW PROBLEMS

6.10 **Basic.** Two products G and H are created from a joint process. G can be sold immediately after split-off. H requires further processing into product HH before it is in a saleable condition. There are no opening inventories and no work in progress of products G, H or HH. The following data are available for last period:

	($)
Total joint production costs	350 000
Further processing costs of product H	66 000

Product	Production units	Closing inventory
G	420 000	20 000
HH	330 000	30 000

Using the physical unit method for apportioning joint production costs, what was the cost value of the closing inventory of product HH for last period?

(a) $16 640
(b) $18 625
(c) $20 000
(d) $21 600

ACCA F2 Management Accounting

6.11 **Basic.** Two joint products A and B are produced in a process. Data for the process for the last period are as follows:

Product	A Tonnes	B Tonnes
Sales	480	320
Production	600	400

Common production costs in the period were $12 000. There was no opening inventory. Both products had a gross profit margin of 40 per cent. Common production costs were apportioned on a physical basis.

What was the gross profit for product A in the period?

(a) $2304
(b) $2880

(c) $3840
(d) $4800

ACCA F2 Management Accounting

6.12 Basic. In a process in which there are no work in progress stocks, two joint products (J and K) are created. Information (in units) relating to last month is as follows:

Product	Sales	Opening stock of finished goods	Closing stock of finished goods
J	6000	100	300
K	4000	400	200

Joint production costs last month were £110 000 and these were apportioned to the joint products based on the number of units produced.

What were the joint production costs apportioned to product J for last month?

(a) £63 800
(b) £64 000
(c) £66 000
(d) £68 200

ACCA Financial Information for Management

6.13 Basic. Two products (W and X) are created from a joint process. Both products can be sold immediately after split-off. There are no opening inventories or work in progress.

The following information is available for last period:
Total joint production costs $776 160

Product	Production units	Sales units	Selling price per unit
W	12 000	10 000	$10
X	10 000	8 000	$12

Using the sales value method of apportioning joint production costs, what was the value of the closing inventory of product X for last period?

(a) $68 992
(b) $70 560
(c) $76 032
(d) £77 616

ACCA F2 Management Accounting

6.14 Intermediate: Process costing and a decision on further processing. Corcoran Ltd operate several manufacturing processes. In process G, joint products (P1 and P2) are created in the ratio 5:3 by volume from the raw materials input. In this process, a normal loss of 5 per cent of the raw material input is expected. Losses have a realizable value of £5 per litre. The company holds no work in progress. The joint costs are apportioned to the joint products using the physical measure basis.

The following information relates to process G for last month:

Raw materials input	60 000 litres (at a cost of £381 000)
Abnormal gain	1 000 litres

Other costs incurred:

Direct labour	£180 000
Direct expenses	£54 000
Production Overheads	110% of direct labour cost

(a) Prepare the process G account for last month in which both the output volumes and values for each of the joint products are shown separately. *(7 marks)*

The company can sell product P1 for £20 per litre at the end of process G. It is considering a proposal to further process P1 in process H in order to create product PP1. Process H has sufficient spare capacity to do this work. The further processing in process H would cost £4 per litre input from process G. In process H, there would be a normal loss in volume of 10 per cent of the input to that process. This loss has no realizable value. Product PP1 could then be sold for £26 per litre.

(b) Determine, based on financial considerations only, whether product P1 should be further processed to create product PP1. *(3 marks)*
(c) In the context of process G in Corcoran Ltd, explain the difference between 'direct expenses' and 'production overheads'. *(2 marks)*

(Total 12 marks)

ACCA Financial Information for Management

6.15 Intermediate: Process costing and a decision on further processing. Luiz Ltd operates several manufacturing processes in which stocks of work in progress are never held. In process K, joint products (P1 and P2) are created in the ratio 2:1 by volume from the raw materials input. In this process, a normal loss of 4 per cent of the raw materials input is expected. Losses have a realizable value of £5 per litre. The joint costs of the process are apportioned to the joint products using the sales value basis. At the end of process K, P1 and P2 can be sold for £25 and £40 per litre respectively.

The following information relates to process K for last month:

Raw material input	90 000 litres at a total cost of £450 000
Actual loss incurred	4800 litres
Conversion costs incurred	£216 000

Required:

(a) Prepare the process K account for last month in which both the output volumes and values for each joint product are shown separately. *(7 marks)*
The company could further process product P1 in process L to create product XP1 at an incremental cost of £3 per litre input. Process L is an existing process with spare capacity. In process L, a normal loss of 8 per cent of input is incurred which has no value. Product XP1 could be sold for £30 per litre.

Required:

(b) Based on financial considerations only, determine, with supporting calculations, whether product P1 should be further processed in process L to create product XP1. *(3 marks)*

(Total 10 marks)

ACCA Financial Information for Management

6.16 Advanced: Calculation of joint product costs and the evaluation of an incremental order. Rayman Company produces three chemical products, J1X, J2Y and B1Z. Raw materials are processed in a single plant to produce two intermediate products, J1 and J2, in fixed proportions. There is no market for these two intermediate products. J1 is processed further through process X to yield the product J1X, product J2 is converted into J2Y by a separate finishing process Y. The Y finishing process produces both J2Y and a waste material, B1, which has no market value. The Rayman Company can convert B1, after additional processing through process Z, into a saleable by-product, B1Z. The company can sell as much B1Z as it can produce at a price of £1.50 per kg.

At normal levels of production and sales, 600 000kg of the common input material are processed each month. There are 440 000kg and 110 000kg respectively, of the intermediate products J1 and J2, produced from this level of input. After the separate finishing processes, fixed proportions of J1X, J2Y and B1Z emerge, as shown below with current market prices (all losses are normal losses):

Product	Quantity kg	Market price per kg
J1X	400 000	£2.425
J2Y	100 000	£4.50
B1Z	10 000	£1.50

At these normal volumes, materials and processing costs are as follows:

	Common plant facility (£000)	X (£000)	Separate finishing processes Y (£000)	Z (£000)
Direct materials	320	110	15	1.0
Direct labour	150	225	90	5.5
Variable overhead	30	50	25	0.5
Fixed overhead	50	25	5	3.0
Total	550	410	135	10.0

Selling and administrative costs are entirely fixed and cannot be traced to any of the three products.

Required:

(a) Draw a diagram that shows the flow of these products, through the processes, label the diagram and show the quantities involved in normal operation. (2 marks)
(b) Calculate the *cost per unit* of the finished products J1X and J2Y and the *total manufacturing profit,* for the month, attributed to each product assuming all joint costs are allocated based on:

(i) physical units (3 marks)
(ii) net realizable value (4 marks)

and comment briefly on the two methods. (3 marks)
NB All losses are normal losses.
(c) A new customer has approached Rayman wishing to purchase 10 000kg of J2Y for £4.00 per kg. This is extra to the present level of business indicated above.

Advise the management how they may respond to this approach by:

(i) Developing a financial evaluation of the offer. (4 marks)
(ii) Clarifying any assumptions and further questions that may apply. (4 marks)

ACCA Paper 8 Managerial Finance

IM6.1 Intermediate.

(a) Explain briefly the term 'joint products' in the context of process costing. (2 marks)
(b) Discuss whether, and if so how, joint process costs should be shared among joint products. (Assume that no further processing is required after the split-off point.) (11 marks)
(c) Explain briefly the concept of 'equivalent units' in process costing. (4 marks)

ACCA Level 1 Costing

IM6.2 Intermediate.

(a) Discuss the problems that joint products and by-products pose the management accountant, especially in his attempts to produce useful product profitability reports. Outline the usual accounting treatments of joint and by-products and indicate the extent to which these treatments are effective in overcoming the problems you have discussed. In your answer, clearly describe the differences between joint and by-products and provide an example of each. (14 marks)
(b) A common process produces several joint products. After the common process has been completed each product requires further specific, and directly attributable, expenditure in order to 'finish off' the product and put it in a saleable condition. Specify the conditions under which it is rational to undertake:

(i) the common process, and
(ii) the final 'finishing off' of each of the products which are the output from the common process.

Illustrate your answer with a single numerical example. (6 marks)

ACCA P2 Management Accounting

IM6.3 Intermediate. Explain how the apportionment of those costs incurred up to the separation point of two or more joint products could give information that is unacceptable for (i) stock valuation and (ii) decision-making. Use figures of your own choice to illustrate your answer. (9 marks)

ACCA Level 2 Management Accounting

IM6.4 Intermediate: Preparation of joint and by-product process account. XYZ plc, a paint manufacturer, operates a process costing system. The following details related to process 2 for the month of October:

Opening work in progress	5000 litres fully complete as to transfers from process 1 and 40% complete as to labour and overhead, valued at £60 000
Transfer from process 1	65 000 litres valued at cost of £578 500
Direct labour	£101 400
Variable overhead	£80 000
Fixed overhead	£40 000
Normal loss	5% of volume transferred from process 1, scrap value £2.00 per litre
Actual output	30 000 litres of paint X (a joint product) 25 000 litres of paint Y (a joint product) 7 000 litres of by-product Z
Closing work in progress	6000 litres fully complete as to transfers from process 1 and 60% complete as to labour and overhead

The final selling price of products X, Y and Z are:

Paint X	£15.00 per litre
Paint Y	£18.00 per litre
Product Z	£4.00 per litre

There are no further processing costs associated with either paint X or the by-product, but paint Y requires further processing at a cost of £1.50 per litre.

All three products incur packaging costs of £0.50 per litre before they can be sold.

Required:

(a) Prepare the process 2 account for the month of October, apportioning the common costs between the joint products, based on their values at the point of separation. (20 marks)
(b) Prepare the abnormal loss/gain account, showing clearly the amount to be transferred to the profit and loss account. (4 marks)

(c) Describe one other method of apportioning the common costs between the joint products, *and* explain why it is necessary to make such apportionments, and their usefulness when measuring product profitability.   *(6 marks)*

CIMA Stage 2 Operational Cost Accounting

IM6.5 Intermediate: Joint cost apportionment and a decision on further processing. QR Limited operates a chemical process that produces four different products Q, R, S and T from the input of one raw material plus water. Budget information for the forthcoming financial year is as follows:

	(£000)
Raw materials cost	268
Initial processing cost	464

Product	Output in litres	Sales (£1000)	Additional processing cost *(£000)*
Q	400 000	768	160
R	90 000	232	128
S	5 000	32	—
T	9 000	240	8

The company policy is to apportion the costs prior to the split-off point on a method based on net sales value.

Currently, the intention is to sell product S without further processing but to process the other three products after the split-off point. However, it has been proposed that an alternative strategy would be to sell all four products at the split-off point without further processing. If this were done the selling prices obtainable would be as follows:

	Per litre *(£)*
Q	1.28
R	1.60
S	6.40
T	20.00

You are required:

(a) to prepare budgeted profit statement showing the profit or loss for each product, and in total, if the current intention is proceeded with;   *(10 marks)*
(b) to show the profit or loss by product, and in total, if the alternative strategy were to be adopted;   *(6 marks)*
(c) to recommend what should be done and why, assuming that there is no more profitable alternative use for the plant.   *(4 marks)*

CIMA Stage 2 Cost Accounting

IM6.6 Intermediate: Joint cost apportionment and decision on further processing. A company manufactures four products from an input of a raw material to process 1. Following this process, product A is processed in process 2, product B in process 3, product C in process 4 and product D in process 5.

The normal loss in process 1 is 10 per cent of input, and there are no expected losses in the other processes. Scrap value in process 1 is £0.50 per litre. The costs incurred in process 1 are apportioned to each product according to the volume of output of each product. Production overhead is absorbed as a percentage of direct wages.

Data in respect of the month of October are:

	Process					
	1 (£000)	*2 (£000)*	*3 (£000)*	*4 (£000)*	*5 (£000)*	*Total (£000)*
Direct materials at £1.25 per litre	100					100
Direct wages	48	12	8	4	16	88
Production overhead						66

	Product			
	A	*B*	*C*	*D*
Output (litres)	22 000	20 000	10 000	18 000
Selling price (£)	4.00	3.00	2.00	5.00
Estimated sales value at end of process 1 (£)	2.50	2.80	1.20	3.00

You are required to:

(a) calculate the profit or loss for each product for the month, assuming all output is sold at the normal selling price;   *(4 marks)*
(b) suggest and evaluate an alternative production strategy that would optimize profit for the month. It should not be assumed that the output of process 1 can be changed;   *(12 marks)*
(c) suggest to what management should devote its attention, if it is to achieve the potential benefit indicated in (b).   *(4 marks)*

CIMA P1 Cost Accounting 2

IM6.7 Advanced: Joint cost stock valuation and decision-making. Milo plc has a number of chemical processing plants in the UK.

At one of these plants, it takes an annual input of 400 000 gallons of raw material A and converts it into two liquid products, B and C.

The standard yield from one gallon of material A is 0.65 gallons of B and 0.3 gallons of C. Product B is processed further, without volume loss, and then sold as product D. Product C has hitherto been sold without further processing. In the year ended 31 July 2017, the cost of material A was £20 per gallon. The selling price of product C was £5 per gallon and transport costs from plant to customer were £74 000.

Negotiations are taking place with Takeup Ltd, which would purchase the total production of product C for the years ending 31 July 2018 and 2019 provided it were converted to product E by further processing. It is unlikely that the contract would be renewed after 31 July 2019. New specialized transport costing £120 000 and special vats costing £80 000 will have to be acquired if the contract is to be undertaken. The vats will be installed in part of the existing factory that is presently unused and for which no use has been forecast for the next three years. Both transport and vats will have no residual value at the end of the contract. The company uses straight line depreciation.

Projected data for 2018 and 2019 are as follows:

	Liquid A	Liquid D	Liquid E
Amount processed (gallons)	400 000		
Processing costs (£):			
Cost of liquid A per gallon	20		
Wages to split-off	400 000 p.a.		

(Continued)

	Liquid A	Liquid D	Liquid E
Overheads to split-off	250 000 p.a.		
Further processing materials per gallon		3.50	3.30
Wages per gallon		2.50	1.70
Overheads		52 000 p.a.	37 000 p.a.
Selling costs (£):			
Total expenses	—	125 000 p.a.	—
Selling price per gallon (£)		40.00	15.50

Total plant administration costs are £95 000 p.a.

You are required to:

(a) Show whether or not Milo plc should accept the contract and produce liquid E in 2018 and 2019. *(5 marks)*

(b) Prepare a pro forma income statement which can be used to evaluate the performance of the individual products sold, assuming all liquid processed is sold, in the financial year to 31 July 2018:

(i) assuming liquids D and C are sold,
(ii) assuming liquids D and E are sold.

Give reasons for the layout adopted and comment on the apportionment of pre-separation costs. *(12 marks)*

(c) Calculate, assuming that 10 000 gallons of liquid C remain unsold at 31 July 2017, and using the FIFO basis for inventory valuation, what would be the valuation of:

(i) the stock of liquid C, and
(ii) 10 000 gallons of liquid E after conversion from liquid C. *(4 marks)*

(d) Calculate an inventory valuation at replacement cost of 10 000 gallons of liquid E in stock at 31 July 2018, assuming that the cost of material A is to be increased by 25 per cent from that date; and comment on the advisability of using replacement cost for:

inventory valuation purposes in the monthly management accounts. *(4 marks)*

Note: Ignore taxation.

ICAEW P2 Management Accounting

IM6.8 Advanced: Cost per unit calculation and decision-making. A chemical company has a contract to supply annually 3600 tonnes of product A at £24 a tonne and 4000 tonnes of product B at £14.50 a tonne. The basic components for these products are obtained from a joint initial distillation process. From this joint distillation a residue is produced which is processed to yield 380 tonnes of by-product Z. By-product Z is sold locally at £5 a tonne and the net income is credited to the joint distillation process.

The budget for the year ending 30 June includes the following data:

		Separable cost		
	Joint process	Product A	Product B	By-product Z
Variable cost per tonne of input (£)	5	11	2	1
Fixed costs for year (£)	5000	4000	8000	500
Evaporation loss in process (% of input)	6	10	20	5

Since the budget was compiled it has been decided that an extensive five-week overhaul of the joint distillation plant will be necessary during the year. This will cost an additional £17 000 in repair costs and reduce all production in the year by 10 per cent. Supplies of the products can be imported to meet the contract commitment at a cost of £25 a tonne for A and £15 a tonne for B.

Experiments have also shown that the joint distillation plant operations could be changed during the year such that either:

(i) The output of distillate for product A would increase by 200 tonnes with a corresponding reduction in product B distillate. This change would increase the joint distillation variable costs for the whole of that operation by 2 per cent.

(ii) Or the residue for by-product Z could be mixed with distillate for products A and B proportionate to the present output of these products. By intensifying the subsequent processing for products A and B, acceptable quality could be obtained. The intensified operation would increase product A and B separable fixed costs by 5 per cent and increase the evaporation loss for the whole operation to 11 per cent and 21 per cent respectively.

You are required to:

(a) calculate on the basis of the original budget:

(i) the unit costs of products A and B, and
(ii) the total profit for the year;

(b) calculate the change in the unit costs of products A and B based on the reduced production;

(c) calculate the profit for the year if the shortfall of production is made up by imported products;

(d) advise management whether either of the alternative distillation operations would improve the profitability calculated under (c) and whether you recommend the use of either. *(30 marks)*

CIMA P3 Management Accounting

IM6.9 Advanced: Calculation of cost per unit, break-even point and a recommended selling price. A chemical company produces among its product range two industrial cleaning fluids, A and B. These products are manufactured jointly. Total sales are expected to be restricted because home trade outlets for fluid B are limited to 54 000 gallons for the year. At this level plant capacity will be under-utilized by 25 per cent.

From the information given below you are required to:

(a) draw a flow diagram of the operations;

(b) calculate separately for fluids A and B for the year:

(i) total manufacturing cost;
(ii) manufacturing cost per gallon;
(iii) list price per gallon;
(iv) profit for the year.

(c) calculate the break-even price per gallon to manufacture an extra 3000 gallons of fluid B for export and which would incur selling, distribution and administration costs of £1260;

(d) state the price you would recommend the company should quote per gallon for this export business, with a brief explanation for your decision.

The following data are given:

1 Description of processes:

Process 1: Raw materials L and M are mixed together and filtered. There is an evaporation loss of 10 per cent.
Process 2: The mixture from Process 1 is boiled and this reduces the volume by 20 per cent. The remaining liquid distils into 50 per cent extract A, 25 per cent extract B, and 25 per cent by-product C.
Process 3: Two parts of extract A are blended with one part of raw material N, and one part of extract B with one part of raw material N, to form respectively fluids A and B.
Process 4: Fluid A is filled into one-gallon labelled bottles and fluid B into six-gallon preprinted drums and they are then both ready for sale. One per cent wastage in labels occurs in this process.

2   Costs:

	Cost per gallon (£)
Raw material L	0.20
Raw material M	0.50
Raw material N	2.00

	Cost (£)
Containers: one-gallon bottles	0.27 each
Containers: six-gallon drums	5.80 each
Bottle labels, per thousand	2.20

Per gallon of input processed

Direct wages:	(£)
Process 1	0.11
Process 2	0.15
Process 3	0.20
Process 4	0.30

Manufacturing overhead:

	Fixed process per annum (£)	Variable, per gallon of input processed (£)
1	6000	0.04
2	20250	0.20
3	19500	0.10
4	14250	0.10

By-product C is collected in bulk by a local company which pays £0.50 per gallon for it and the income is credited to process 2.

Process costs are apportioned entirely to the two main products on the basis of their output from each process.

No inventories of part-finished materials are held at any time.

Fluid A is sold through agents on the basis of list price less 20 per cent and fluid B at list price less 33 1/3 per cent.

Of the net selling price, profit amounts to 8 per cent, selling and distribution costs to 12 per cent and administration costs to 5 per cent. Taxation should be ignored.

CIMA P3 Management Accounting

7
INCOME EFFECTS OF ALTERNATIVE COST ACCUMULATION SYSTEMS

LEARNING OBJECTIVES After studying this chapter, you should be able to:

- explain the differences between an absorption costing and a variable costing system;
- prepare profit statements based on a variable costing and absorption costing system;
- explain the difference in profits between variable and absorption costing profit calculations;
- explain the arguments for and against variable and absorption costing;
- describe the various denominator levels that can be used with an absorption costing system;
- explain why the choice of an appropriate denominator level is important.

In the previous chapters, we looked at the procedures necessary to ascertain product or job costs for inventory valuation to meet the requirements of external reporting. The approach that we adopted was to allocate all manufacturing cost to products, and to value unsold inventories at their total cost of manufacture. Non-manufacturing costs were not allocated to the products but were charged directly to the profit statement and excluded from the inventory valuation. A costing system based on these principles is known as an absorption or full costing system.

In this chapter, we are going to look at an alternative costing system known as variable costing, marginal costing or direct costing. Under this system, only variable manufacturing costs are assigned to products and included in the inventory valuation. Fixed manufacturing costs are not allocated to the product, but are considered as period costs and charged directly to the profit statement. With both systems, non-manufacturing costs are treated as period costs. The difference between the systems lies in whether or not manufacturing fixed overhead should be regarded as a period cost or a product cost. An illustration of the contrasting treatment of fixed manufacturing overhead for both absorption and variable costing systems is shown in Exhibit 7.1. You should note that here direct labour is assumed to be a variable cost. Generally, direct labour is not a short-term variable cost that varies in direct proportion to the volume of activity. It is a step fixed cost (see Chapter 2) that varies in the longer term. In other words, it is a longer-term variable cost. Because of this, variable costing systems generally assume that direct labour is a variable cost.

A discussion as to whether an absorption or variable costing system is preferable depends on the impact each system has on profit measurement and inventory (stock) valuation. The allocation of costs to products/services for inventory valuation is not an issue for many non-manufacturing organizations.

EXHIBIT 7.1
Absorption and
variable costing
systems

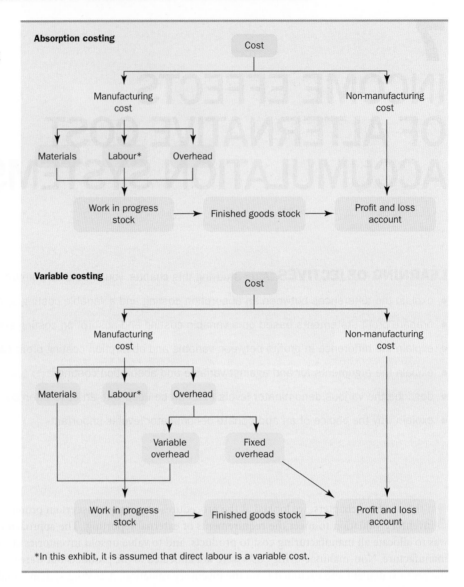

*In this exhibit, it is assumed that direct labour is a variable cost.

The inventories of merchandising companies consist of goods purchased for resale and all overheads are treated as period costs. Some service organizations do have work in progress but, compared with manufacturing organizations, the values of inventories are relatively small so the choice of absorption or variable costing systems tends not to be an important issue. Therefore the remainder of this chapter concentrates on manufacturing organizations. As with the previous three chapters this chapter can be omitted if you are pursuing a management accounting course that does not require you to focus on cost accumulation for inventory valuation and profit measurement (see 'Guidelines for using this book' in Chapter 1).

EXTERNAL AND INTERNAL REPORTING

There are arguments for and against the use of variable costing for inventory valuation for the purpose of external reporting. One important requirement for external reporting is consistency. It would be unacceptable if companies changed their methods of inventory valuation from year-to-year and inter-company comparison would be difficult if some companies valued their inventories on an absorption

REAL WORLD VIEWS 7.1

Variable costing – use of variable costing
According to a recent survey undertaken by CIMA, variable (or marginal) costing is used by almost 40 per cent of firms. Management accountants from a wide range of sectors, including manufacturing and service firms, were queried on how they use traditional techniques to cost products, set prices, analyse and report revenues/profit and allocate resources. Absorption costing was used by approximately 45 per cent of respondent firms. It also reports that variable costing is widely used across organizations of all sizes. Based on this quite recent research, it would seem variable costing is a widely used internal reporting and analysis tool.

Bloomfield (2015) urges a rethink of managerial reporting, particularly in how some management accounting courses are taught. He highlights how costs are recorded in the double entry system of accounting, which leads to costs which are not necessarily the best for decision-making purposes. He notes 'without a knowledge of double-entry bookkeeping, it is hard to understand why absorption costing systems do a better job of reporting the income associated with each operating period' (2015, p.147).

Questions

1 Do you think variable costing is more likely to be used by manufacturing or service sector firms?

2 Do you think integrated accounting information system would be able to produce internal profit statements using variable costing?

Reference
Bloomfield, R. (2015) 'Rethinking managerial reporting', *Journal of Management Accounting Research*, 27(1): 139–150.

cost basis while others did so on a variable cost basis. Furthermore, the users of external accounting reports need the reassurance that the published financial statements have been prepared in accordance with generally accepted standards of good accounting practice. Therefore, there is a strong case for the acceptance of one method of inventory valuation for external reporting. In the UK, Financial Reporting Standard 102 (FRS 102) states:

> In order to match costs and revenue, cost of stocks (inventories) and work in progress should comprise that expenditure which has been incurred in the normal course of business in bringing the product or service to its present location and condition. Such costs will include all related production overheads, even though these may accrue on a time basis.

The effect of this statement was to require absorption costing for external reporting and for non-manufacturing costs to be treated as period costs. The International Accounting Standard on Inventories (IAS2) also requires that companies in other countries adopt absorption costing.

In spite of the fact that absorption costing is required for external reporting, the variable costing versus absorption costing debate is still of considerable importance for internal reporting. Management normally requires profit statements at monthly or quarterly intervals, and will demand separate profit statements for each major product group or segment of the business. This information is particularly useful in evaluating the performance of divisional managers. Management must therefore decide whether absorption costing or variable costing provides the more meaningful information in assessing the economic and managerial performance of the different segments of the business.

Before discussing the arguments for and against absorption and variable costing, let us look at an illustration of both methods using Example 7.1. To keep things simple, we shall assume that the company in this example produces only one product using a single overhead rate for the company as a whole, with units of output being used as the allocation base. These assumptions are very simplistic but the same general principles can be applied in more complex product settings.

EXAMPLE 7.1

The following information is available for periods 1–6 for the Hoque Company:

	(£)
Unit selling price	10
Unit variable cost	6
Fixed costs per each period	300 000

The company produces only one product. Budgeted activity is expected to average 150 000 units per period and production and sales for each period are as follows:

	Period 1	Period 2	Period 3	Period 4	Period 5	Period 6
Units sold (000s)	150	120	180	150	140	160
Units produced (000s)	150	150	150	150	170	140

There were no opening inventories at the start of period 1 and the actual manufacturing fixed overhead incurred was £300 000 per period. We shall also assume that non-manufacturing overheads are £100 000 per period.

VARIABLE COSTING

The variable costing profit statements are shown in Exhibit 7.2. You will see that when a system of variable costing is used, the product cost is £6 per unit, and includes variable costs only. In period 1, production is 150 000 units at a variable cost of £6 per unit. The total fixed costs are then added separately to produce a total manufacturing cost of £1 200 000. Note that the fixed costs of £300 000 are assigned to the period in which they are incurred.

In period 2, 150 000 units are produced but only 120 000 are sold. Therefore 30 000 units remain in inventory at the end of the period. In order to match costs with revenues, the sales of 120 000 units should be matched with costs for 120 000. As 150 000 units were produced, we need to value the 30 000 units in inventory and deduct this sum from the production cost. Using the variable costing system, the 30 000 units in inventory are valued at £6 per unit. A closing inventory of £180 000 will then be deducted

EXHIBIT 7.2 Variable costing statements

	Period 1 (£000s)	Period 2 (£000s)	Period 3 (£000s)	Period 4 (£000s)	Period 5 (£000s)	Period 6 (£000s)
Opening stock	—	—	180	—	—	180
Production cost	900	900	900	900	1020	840
Closing stock	—	(180)	—	—	(180)	(60)
Cost of sales	900	720	1080	900	840	960
Fixed costs	300	300	300	300	300	300
Total costs	1200	1020	1380	1200	1140	1260
Sales	1500	1200	1800	1500	1400	1600
Gross profit	300	180	420	300	260	340
Less non-manufacturing costs	100	100	100	100	100	100
Net profit	200	80	320	200	160	240

from the production costs, giving a cost of sales figure of £720 000. Note that the closing inventory valuation does not include any fixed overheads.

The 30 000 units of closing inventory in period 2 becomes the opening inventory for period 3 and therefore an expense for this period. The production cost for the 150 000 units made in period 3 is added to this opening inventory valuation. The overall effect is that costs for 180 000 units are matched against sales for 180 000 units. The profits for periods 4–6 are calculated in the same way.

ABSORPTION COSTING

Let us now consider, in Exhibit 7.3, the profit calculations when closing inventories are valued on an absorption costing basis. With the absorption costing method, a share of the fixed production overheads are allocated to individual products and are included in their production cost. Fixed overheads are assigned to products by establishing overhead absorption rates as described in Chapter 3. To establish the overhead rate, we must divide the fixed overheads of £300 000 for the period by an appropriate denominator level. Most companies use an annual budgeted activity measure of the overhead allocation base as the denominator level. Our allocation base in Example 7.1 is units of output and we shall assume that the annual budgeted output is 1 800 000 units giving an average for each monthly period of 150 000 units. Therefore, the budgeted fixed overhead rate is £2 per unit (£300 000/150 000 units). The product cost now consists of a variable cost (£6) plus a fixed manufacturing cost (£2), making a total of £8 per unit. Hence, the production cost for period 1 is £1 200 000 (150 000 units at £8).

Now compare the absorption costing statement (Exhibit 7.3) with the variable costing statement (Exhibit 7.2) for period 1. With absorption costing, the fixed cost is included in the production cost figure, whereas with variable costing only the variable cost is included. With variable costing, the fixed cost is allocated separately as a lump sum and is not included in the cost of sales figure. Note also that the closing inventory of 30 000 units for period 2 is valued at £8 per unit in the absorption costing statement, whereas the closing inventory is valued at only £6 in the variable costing statement.

In calculating profits, the matching principle that has been applied in the absorption costing statement is the same as that described for variable costing. However, complications arise in periods 5 and 6; in period 5, 170 000 units were produced, so the production cost of £1 360 000 includes fixed overheads of £340 000 (170 000 units at £2). The total fixed overheads incurred for the period are only £300 000, so £40 000 too much has been allocated. This over-recovery of fixed overhead arising from actual activity differing from budgeted activity is recorded as a period cost adjustment. (A full explanation of under- and over-recoveries of overheads and the reasons for period cost adjustments was presented in Chapter 3; if you are unsure of this concept, please refer back now to the section headed 'Under- and over-recovery of overheads'.)

EXHIBIT 7.3 Absorption costing statements

	Period 1 (£000s)	Period 2 (£000s)	Period 3 (£000s)	Period 4 (£000s)	Period 5 (£000s)	Period 6 (£000s)
Opening stock	—	—	240	—	—	240
Production cost	1200	1200	1200	1200	1360	1120
Closing stock	—	(240)	—	—	(240)	(80)
Cost of sales	1200	960	1440	1200	1120	1280
Adjustments for under-/(over-) recovery of overhead	—	—	—	—	(40)	20
Total costs	1200	960	1440	1200	1080	1300
Sales	1500	1200	1800	1500	1400	1600
Gross profit	300	240	360	300	320	300
Less non-manufacturing costs	100	100	100	100	100	100
Net profit	200	140	260	200	220	200

In period 6, 140 000 units were produced at a cost of £1 120 000, which included only £280 000 (140 000 units at £2) for fixed overheads. As a result, there is an under-recovery of £20 000 arising from actual activity differing from budgeted activity, which is written off as a period cost. You can see that an under- or over-recovery of fixed overhead occurs whenever actual production differs from the budgeted average level of activity of 150 000 units, since the calculation of the fixed overhead rate of £2 per unit was based on the assumption that actual production would be 150 000 units per period. Note that both variable and absorption costing systems do not assign non-manufacturing costs to products for inventory valuation.

VARIABLE COSTING AND ABSORPTION COSTING: A COMPARISON OF THEIR IMPACT ON PROFIT

A comparison of the variable costing and absorption costing statements produced from the information contained in Example 7.1 reveals the following differences in profit calculations:

(a) The profits calculated under the absorption costing and variable costing systems are identical for periods 1 and 4.

(b) The absorption costing profits are higher than the variable costing profits in periods 2 and 5.

(c) The variable costing profits are higher than the absorption costing profits in periods 3 and 6.

Let us now consider each of these in a little more detail.

Production equals sales

In periods 1 and 4, the profits are the same for both methods of costing; in both periods, production is equal to sales, and inventories will neither increase nor decrease. Therefore, if opening inventories exist, the same amount of fixed overhead will be carried forward as an expense to be included in the current period in the opening inventory valuation as will be deducted in the closing inventory valuation from the production cost figure. The overall effect is that, with an absorption costing system, the only fixed overhead that will be included as an expense for the period will be the amount of fixed overhead that is incurred for the period. Thus, whenever sales are equal to production the profits will be the same for both the absorption costing and variable costing systems.

Production exceeds sales

In periods 2 and 5, the absorption costing system produces higher profits; in both periods, production exceeds sales. Profits are higher for absorption costing when production is in excess of sales, because inventories are increasing. A greater amount of fixed overheads in the closing inventory is being deducted from the expenses of the period than is being brought forward in the opening inventory for the period. For example, in period 2, the opening inventory is zero and no fixed overheads are brought forward from the previous period. However, a closing inventory of 30 000 units means that £60 000 fixed overhead has to be deducted from the production cost for the period. In other words, only £240 000 is being allocated for fixed overhead with the absorption costing system, whereas the variable costing system allocates the £300 000 fixed overhead incurred for the period. The effect of this is that profits are £60 000 greater with the absorption costing system. As a general rule, if production is in excess of sales, the absorption costing system will show a higher profit than the variable costing system.

Sales exceed production

In periods 3 and 6, the variable costing system produces higher profits; in both periods, sales exceed production. When this situation occurs, inventories decline and with an absorption costing system a greater amount of fixed overheads will need to be brought forward as an expense in the opening inventory than is being deducted in the closing inventory adjustment. With the absorption costing system, in period 6, 30 000 units of opening inventory are brought forward, so that fixed costs of £60 000 are included in the inventory valuation. However, a closing inventory of 10 000 units requires a deduction of £20 000 fixed overheads from the production costs. The overall effect is that an additional £40 000 fixed overheads is included as an expense within the inventory movements, and a total of £340 000 fixed overheads is allocated for the period. In contrast, the variable costing system would allocate fixed overheads for the period of only £300 000. As a result, profits are £40 000 greater with the variable costing system. As a general rule, if sales are in excess of production, the variable costing system will show a higher profit than the absorption costing system.

Impact of sales fluctuations

The profit calculations for an absorption costing system can produce some strange results. For example, in period 6, the sales volume has increased but profits have declined, in spite of the fact that both the selling price and the cost structure have remained unchanged. A manager whose performance is being judged in period 6 is likely to have little confidence in an accounting system that produces this information. The opposite occurs in period 5, when the sales volume declines but profit increases. The situations in periods 5 and 6 arise because the under- or over-recovery of fixed overhead is treated as a period cost and such adjustments can at times give a misleading picture of profits.

In contrast, the variable costing profit calculations show that when sales volume increases profit also increases. Alternatively, when sales volume decreases, profit also decreases. These relationships continue as long as the selling price and cost structure remain unchanged. Looking again at the variable costing profit calculations, you will note that profit declines in period 5 when the sales volume declines, and increases in period 6 when the sales volume also increases. The reasons for these changes are that, with a system of variable costing, profit is a function of sales volume only, when the selling price and cost structure remain unchanged. However, with absorption costing, profit is a function of both sales volume and production volume.

SOME ARGUMENTS IN SUPPORT OF VARIABLE COSTING

Variable costing provides more useful information for decision-making

The separation of fixed and variable costs helps to provide relevant information about costs for making decisions. Relevant costs are required for a variety of short-term decisions, for example whether to make a component internally or to purchase externally, as well as problems relating to product mix. These decisions will be discussed in Chapter 9. In addition, the estimation of costs for different levels of activity requires that costs be split into their fixed and variable elements. Supporters of variable costing contend that the projection of future costs and revenues for different activity levels and the use of relevant cost decision-making techniques are possible only if a variable costing system is adopted. There is no reason, however, why an absorption costing system cannot be used for profit measurement and inventory valuation and costs can be analysed into their fixed and variable elements for decision-making. The advantage of variable costing is that the analysis of variable and fixed costs is highlighted while such an analysis is not a required feature of an absorption costing system.

Variable costing removes from profit the effect of inventory changes

We have seen that, with variable costing, profit is a function of sales volume, whereas, with absorption costing, profit is a function of both sales and production. We have also learned, using absorption costing principles, that it is possible for profit to decline when sales volumes increase. Where inventory levels are likely to fluctuate significantly, profits may be distorted when they are calculated on an absorption costing basis, since the inventory changes will significantly affect the amount of fixed overheads allocated to an accounting period.

REAL WORLD VIEWS 7.2

Maintaining and improving profits at M-real

Finnish paper company M-real produced paper and packaging products, the demand for which is highly influenced by the demand for end consumer products. Global demand decreased due to the global economic recession and during this same time energy and fuel costs increased. In efforts to maintain and improve profits, M-real embarked on a programme of reducing fixed and variable costs. The programme aimed to reduce variable costs across all businesses. The variable costs to be tackled were 'primarily chemical, energy and logistic costs', according to Mikko Helander, CEO of M-real. The planned measures aimed to increase profits by around €70 million per annum in a full year. On top of the cost reduction programme, the company also planned to increase profitability, by increasing profit margins.

Questions

1 If your business wanted to improve profits by focusing on first fixed costs and then variable costs, what form of profit report might you use internally: one based on absorption costing or one based on variable costing?

2 What do you think would be the main variable cost for a paper company like M-real? Are there any ways in which a paper company might control this variable cost? Do some internet research on other paper companies to help you decide.

Reference

'M-real starts a new internal profit improvement programme for 2011', press release 13 January 2011, available at www.m-real.com/press/Pages/Default.aspx

---

Fluctuating inventory levels are less likely to occur when one measures profits on an annual basis, but on a monthly or quarterly basis, seasonal variations in sales may cause significant fluctuations. As profits are likely to be distorted by an absorption costing system, there are strong arguments for using variable costing methods when profits are measured at frequent intervals and inventory levels fluctuate from month to month. Because frequent profit statements are presented only for management, the argument for variable costing is stronger for management accounting. A survey by Drury and Tayles (2006) relating to 187 UK companies reported that 84 per cent of the companies prepared profit statements at monthly or quarterly intervals. Financial accounts are presented for public release annually or at half-yearly intervals; because significant changes in inventory levels are less likely on an annual basis, the argument for the use of variable costing in financial accounting is not as strong.

A further argument for using variable costing for internal reporting is that the internal profit statements may be used as a basis for measuring managerial performance and absorption costing provides opportunities for unscrupulous managers to manipulate the figures. For example, it would be possible for a manager to deliberately defer some of the fixed overhead allocation by unnecessarily increasing inventories over successive periods.

However, there is a limit to how long managers can continue to increase inventories, and eventually the situation will arise when it is necessary to reduce them, and the deferred fixed overheads will eventually be allocated to the periods when the inventories are reduced. Senior management can also implement control performance measures to guard against such behaviour. Nevertheless, there is likely to remain some scope for distorting profits in the short term.

Variable costing avoids fixed overheads being capitalized in unsaleable inventories

In a period when sales demand decreases, a company can end up with surplus inventories on hand. With an absorption costing system, only a portion of the fixed overheads incurred during the period will be allocated as an expense because the remainder of the fixed overhead will be included in the valuation of the surplus inventories. If these surplus inventories cannot be disposed of, the profit calculation for the current period will be misleading, since fixed overheads will have been deferred to later accounting periods. However, there may be some delay before management concludes that the inventories cannot be sold without a very large reduction in the selling price. In the meantime, the inventories will be over-valued and the overall effect may be that the current period's profits will be overstated.

SOME ARGUMENTS IN SUPPORT OF ABSORPTION COSTING

Absorption costing does not understate the importance of fixed costs

Some people argue that decisions based on a variable costing system may concentrate only on sales revenues and variable costs and ignore the fact that fixed costs must be met in the long run. For example, if a pricing decision is based on variable costs only, then sales revenue may be insufficient to cover all the costs. It is also argued that the use of an absorption costing system, by allocating fixed costs to a product, ensures that fixed costs will be covered. In fact, these arguments are incorrect. Absorption costing will not ensure that fixed costs will be recovered if actual sales volume is less than the estimate used to calculate the fixed overhead rate. For example, consider a situation where fixed costs are £100 000 and an estimated normal activity of 10 000 units is used to calculate the overhead rate. Fixed costs are recovered at £10 per unit. Assume that variable cost is £5 per unit and selling price is set at £20 (total cost plus one-third). If actual sales volume is 5000 units then total sales revenue will be £100 000 and total costs will be £125 000. Total costs therefore exceed total sales revenue. The argument that a variable costing system will cause managers to ignore fixed costs is based on the assumption that such managers are not very bright! A failure to consider fixed costs is due to faulty management and not to a faulty accounting system. Furthermore, using variable costing for inventory valuation and profit measurement still enables full cost information to be extracted for pricing decisions.

Absorption costing avoids fictitious losses being reported

In a business that relies on seasonal sales and in which production is built up outside the sales season to meet demand, the full amount of fixed overheads incurred will be charged, in a variable costing system, against sales. However, in those periods where production is being built up for sales in a later season, sales revenue will be low but fixed costs will be recorded as an expense. The result is that losses will be reported during out-of-season periods and large profits will be reported in the periods when the goods are sold.

By contrast, in an absorption costing system fixed overheads will be deferred and included in the closing inventory valuation, and will be recorded as an expense only in the period in which the goods are sold. Losses are therefore unlikely to be reported in the periods when inventories are being built up. In these circumstances, absorption costing appears to provide the more logical profit calculation.

Fixed overheads are essential for production

The proponents of absorption costing argue that the production of goods is not possible if fixed manu-facturing costs are not incurred. Consequently, fixed manufacturing overheads should be allocated to units produced and included in the inventory valuation.

Consistency with external reporting

Top management may prefer their internal profit reporting systems to be consistent with the external financial accounting absorption costing systems so that they will be congruent with the measures used by financial markets to appraise overall company performance. In a pilot study of six UK companies Hopper *et al.* (1992) observed that senior managers are primarily interested in financial accounting information because it is perceived as having a major influence on how financial markets evaluate companies and their management. If top management believes that financial accounting information does influence share prices then it is likely to use the same rules and procedures for both internal and external profit measurement and inventory valuation so that managers will focus on the same measures as those used by financial markets. The fact that managerial rewards are often linked to external financial measures provides a further motivation to ensure that internal accounting systems do not conflict with external financial accounting reporting requirements.

ALTERNATIVE DENOMINATOR-LEVEL MEASURES

When absorption costing systems are used, estimated fixed overhead rates must be calculated. These rates will be significantly influenced by the choice of the activity level: that is, the denominator activity level that is used to calculate the overhead rate. This problem applies only to fixed overheads, and the greater the proportion of fixed overheads in an organization's cost structure the more acute is the problem. Fixed costs arise from situations where resources must be acquired in discrete, not continuous, amounts in such a way that the supply of resources cannot be continuously adjusted to match the usage of resources. For example, a machine might be purchased that provides an annual capacity of 5000 machine hours but changes in sales demand may cause the annual usage to vary from 2500 to 5000 hours. It is not possible to match the supply and usage of the resource, and unused capacity will arise in those periods where the resources used are less than the 5000 hours of capacity supplied.

In contrast, variable costs arise in those situations where the supply of resources can be continually adjusted to match the usage of resources. For example, the spending on energy costs associated with running machinery (i.e. the supply and resources) can be immediately reduced by 50 per cent if resources used decline by 50 per cent say, from 5000 hours to 2500 hours. There is no unused capacity in respect of variable costs. Consequently, with variable cost the cost per unit of resource used will be constant.

With fixed overheads, the cost per unit of resource used will fluctuate with changes in estimates of activity usage because fixed overhead spending remains constant over a wide range of activity. For example, if the estimated annual fixed overheads associated with the machine referred to above are £192 000, and annual activity is estimated to be 5000 hours, then the machine hour rate will be £38.40 (£192 000/5000 hours). Alternatively, if annual activity is estimated to be 2500 hours then the rate will be £76.80 (£192 000/2500 hours). Therefore the choice of the denominator capacity level can have a profound effect on product cost calculations.

Several choices are available for determining the denominator activity level when calculating overhead rates. Consider the situation described in Example 7.2.

EXAMPLE 7.2

The Green Company has established a separate cost centre for one of its machines. The annual budgeted fixed overheads assigned to the cost centre are £192 000. Green operates three shifts per day of 8 hours, five days per week for 50 weeks per year (the company closes down for holiday periods for two weeks per year). The maximum machine operating hours are 6000 hours per annum (50 weeks × 24 hrs × 5 days) but because of preventive maintenance the maximum practical operating usage is 5000 hours per annum. It is estimated that normal sales demand over the next three years will result in the machine being required for 4800 hours per annum. However, because of current adverse economic conditions budgeted usage for the coming year is 4000 hours. Assume that actual fixed overheads incurred are identical to the estimated fixed overheads and that there are no opening inventories at the start of the budget period.

There are four different denominator activity levels that can be used in Example 7.2. They are:

1 Theoretical maximum capacity of 6000 hours = £32 per hour (£192 000/6000 hours).

2 Practical capacity of 5000 hours = £38.40 per hour (£192 000/5000 hours).

3 Normal average long-run activity of 4800 hours = £40 per hour (£192 000/4800 hours).

4 Budgeted activity of 4000 hours = £48 per hour (£192 000/4000 hours).

Theoretical maximum capacity is a measure of maximum operating capacity based on 100 per cent efficiency with no interruptions for maintenance or other factors. We can reject this measure on the grounds that it represents an activity level that is most unlikely to be achieved. The capacity was acquired with the expectation of supplying a maximum of 5000 hours rather than a theoretical maximum of 6000 hours. This former measure is called practical capacity. Practical capacity represents the maximum capacity that is likely to be supplied by the machine after taking into account unavoidable interruptions arising from machine maintenance and plant holiday closures. In other words, practical capacity is defined as theoretical capacity less activity lost arising from unavoidable interruptions. Normal activity is a measure of capacity required to satisfy average customer demand over a longer term period of, say, approximately three years after taking into account seasonal and cyclical fluctuations. Finally, budgeted activity is the activity level based on the capacity utilization required for the next budget period.

Assuming in Example 7.2 that actual activity and expenditure are identical to budget then, for each of the above denominator activity levels, the annual costs of £192 000 will be allocated as follows:

	Allocated to products	Volume variance (i.e. cost of unused capacity)	Total
Practical capacity	4000 hours × £38.40 = £153 600	1000 hours × £38.40 = £38 400	£192 000
Normal activity	4000 hours × £40 = £160 000	800 hours × £40 = £32 000	£192 000
Budgeted activity	4000 hours × £48 = £192 000	Nil	£192 000

Note that the overheads allocated to products consist of 4000 hours worked on products during the year multiplied by the appropriate overhead rate. The cost of unused capacity (known as the volume variance) is the under-recovery of overheads arising from actual activity being different from the activity level used to calculate the overhead rate. If practical capacity is used, the cost highlights that part of total capacity supplied (5000 hours) has not been utilized. With normal activity the under-recovery of £32 000 represents the cost of failing to utilize the normal activity of 4800 hours. In Example 7.2, we assumed that actual activity was equivalent to budgeted activity. However, if actual activity is less than budgeted activity, then the under-recovery can be interpreted as the cost of failing to achieve budgeted activity.

Impact on inventory valuation of profit computations

The choice of an appropriate activity level can have a significant effect on the inventory valuation and profit computation. Assume in Example 7.2 that 90 per cent of the output was sold and the remaining 10 per cent unsold and that there were no inventories at the start of the period. Thus, 90 per cent of the overheads allocated to products will be allocated to cost of sales and 10 per cent will be allocated to inventories. The volume variance arising from the under- or over-recovery of fixed overheads (i.e. the cost of unused capacity) is recorded as a period cost and therefore charged as an expense against the current period. It is not included in the inventory valuation. The computations are as follows:

	Expenses recorded for the period[a] (£)	Allocated to inventories[b] (£)	Total (£)
Practical capacity	176 640	15 360	192 000
Normal activity	176 000	16 000	192 000
Budgeted activity	172 800	19 200	192 000

Notes
[a]90 per cent of overhead allocated to products plus cost of unused capacity.
[b]10 per cent of overhead allocated to products.

In the above illustration, the choice of the denominator level has not had an important impact on the inventory valuation and the cost of sales (and therefore the profit computation). Nevertheless, the impact can be material when inventories are of significant value. Many service organizations, however, do not hold inventories and just-in-time manufacturing firms aim to maintain minimal inventory levels. In these situations, virtually all the expenses incurred during a period will be recorded as a period expense whatever denominator activity level is selected to calculate the overhead rate. We can therefore conclude that, for many organizations, the choice of the denominator activity level has little impact on profit measurement and inventory valuation. Therefore the impact of the chosen denominator level depends on the circumstances.

Even where the choice of the denominator level is not of significant importance for profit measurement and inventory valuation, it can be of crucial importance for other purposes, such as pricing decisions and managing the cost of unused capacity. Since our objective in this chapter is to focus on the impact of the choice of denominator level on profit measurement and inventory measurement we shall defer a discussion of these other issues until Chapter 11.

Finally, what denominator levels do firms actually use? Little empirical evidence exists relating to current practices but a study of UK organizations by Drury and Tayles (2000) reported that 86 per cent of the respondents used budgeted annual activity. The popularity of this method is that budgeted annual activity is readily available, being determined as part of the annual budgeting process.

SUMMARY

The following items relate to the learning objectives listed at the beginning of the chapter.

- **Explain the differences between an absorption costing and a variable costing system.**

With an absorption costing system, fixed manufacturing overheads are allocated to the products and these are included in the inventory valuations. With a variable costing system, only variable manufacturing costs are assigned to the product; fixed manufacturing costs are regarded as period costs and written off as a lump sum to the profit and loss account. Both variable and absorption costing systems treat non-manufacturing overheads as period costs.

- **Prepare profit statements based on a variable costing and absorption costing system.**

With a variable costing system, manufacturing fixed costs are added to the variable manufacturing cost of sales to determine total manufacturing costs to be deducted from sales revenues. Manufacturing fixed costs are assigned to products with an absorption costing system. Therefore, manufacturing cost of sales is valued at full cost (manufacturing variable costs plus manufacturing fixed costs). With an absorption costing system, fixed manufacturing costs are unitized by dividing the total manufacturing costs by estimated output. If actual output differs from estimated output an under- or over-recovery of overheads arises. This is recorded as a period cost adjustment in the current accounting period.

- **Explain the difference in profits between variable and absorption costing profit calculations.**

When production exceeds sales, absorption costing systems report higher profits. Variable costing systems yield higher profits when sales exceed production. Nevertheless, total profits over the life of the business will be the same for both systems. Differences arise merely in the profits attributed to each accounting period.

- **Explain the arguments for and against variable and absorption costing.**

The proponents of variable costing claim that it enables more useful information to be presented for decision-making, but such claims are questionable since similar relevant cost information can easily be extracted from an absorption costing system. The major advantage of variable costing is that profit is reflected as a function of sales, whereas, with an absorption costing system, profit is a function of both sales and production. It is possible with absorption costing, when all other factors remain unchanged, for sales to increase and profit to decline. In contrast, with a variable costing system, when sales increase, profits also increase. A further advantage of variable costing is that fixed overheads are not capitalized in unsaleable inventories. The arguments that have been made supporting absorption costing include: (a) absorption costing does not understate the importance of fixed costs; (b) absorption costing avoids the possibility of fictitious losses being reported; (c) fixed manufacturing overheads are essential to production and therefore should be incorporated in the product costs; and (d) internal profit measurement should be consistent with absorption costing profit measurement that is used for external reporting requirements.

- **Describe the various denominator levels that can be used with an absorption costing system.**

Four different denominator levels were described. Theoretical maximum capacity is a measure of maximum operating capacity based on 100 per cent efficiency with no interruptions for maintenance or machine breakdowns. Practical capacity represents the maximum capacity that is likely to be supplied after taking into account unavoidable interruptions such as machine maintenance and plant holiday closures. Normal capacity is a measure of capacity required to satisfy average demand over a long-term period (e.g. 3–5 years). Budgeted activity is the activity based on capacity utilization required for the next budget period.

- **Explain why the choice of an appropriate denominator level is important.**

The use of each alternative measure results in the computation of a different overhead rate. This can result in significantly different reported product costs, profit levels and inventory.

APPENDIX 7.1: DERIVATION OF THE PROFIT FUNCTION FOR AN ABSORPTION COSTING SYSTEM

Using the notation listed in Exhibit 7A.1, the variable costing profit function can be expressed in equation form as follows:

$$
\begin{aligned}
\text{OPBT}_{VC} &= \text{Sales} - \text{Variable manufacturing costs of goods sold} \\
&\quad - \text{non-manufacturing variable costs} - \text{All fixed costs} \\
&= \text{usp} \cdot Q_s - \text{uvmc} \cdot Q_s - \text{uvnmc} \cdot Q_s - \text{FC} \qquad (7.A1) \\
&= \text{ucm} \cdot Q_s - \text{FC (Note that the term contribution margin is used to} \\
&\quad \text{describe unit selling price less unit variable cost.)}
\end{aligned}
$$

EXHIBIT 7A.1 Summary of notation used

ucm	=	Contribution margin per unit (i.e. selling price per unit – variable cost per unit)
usp	=	Selling price per unit
uvmc	=	Variable manufacturing cost per unit
uvnmc	=	Variable non-manufacturing cost per unit
ufmc	=	Predetermined fixed manufacturing overhead per unit of output
Q_p	=	Number of units produced
Q_s	=	Number of units sold
FC	=	Total fixed costs (manufacturing and non-manufacturing)
$OPBT_{AC}$	=	Operating profit before taxes for the period (Absorption costing)
$OPBT_{VC}$	=	Operating profit before taxes for the period (Variable costing)

The distinguishable feature between absorption costing and variable costing relates to the timing of the recognition of fixed manufacturing overheads (FC_m) as an expense. Variable and absorption costing reported profits will differ by the amount of fixed manufacturing overheads that are included in the change in opening and closing inventories. This is equivalent to the difference between production and sales volumes multiplied by the manufacturing fixed overhead absorption rate.

We can therefore use equation (7.A1) as the basis for establishing the equation for the absorption costing profit function:

$$\begin{aligned}
OPBT_{AC} &= ucm \cdot Q_s - FC + (Q_p - Q_s)ufmc \\
&= ucm \cdot Q_s - FC + (Q_p \times ufmc) - (Q_s \times ufmc) \qquad (7.A2) \\
&= (ucm - ufmc)Q_s + (ufmc \times Q_p) - FC
\end{aligned}$$

Applying formula 7.A2 to the data given in Example 7.1 in the main body of the chapter gives the following profit function:

$$(£4 - £2)Q_s + (£2 \times Q_p) - £400\,000 = £2Q_s + £2Q_p - £400\,000$$

Applying the above profit function to periods 4–6 we get:

$$\begin{aligned}
\text{Period 4} &= £2(150\,000) + £2(150\,000) - £400\,000 = £200\,000 \\
\text{Period 5} &= £2(140\,000) + £2(170\,000) - £400\,000 = £220\,000 \\
\text{Period 6} &= £2(160\,000) + £2(140\,000) - £400\,000 = £200\,000
\end{aligned}$$

The variable costing profit calculations using formula 7A.1 for Example 7.1:

$$£4Q_s - £400\,000$$

so that:

$$\begin{aligned}
\text{Period 4} &= £4(150\,000) - £400\,000 = £200\,000 \\
\text{Period 5} &= £4(140\,000) - £400\,000 = £160\,000 \\
\text{Period 6} &= £4(160\,000) - £400\,000 = £240\,000
\end{aligned}$$

The difference between the reported operating profits for an absorption costing and a variable costing system can be derived by deducting formula 7.A1 from formula 7.A2 giving:

$$ufmc(Q_p - Q_s) \qquad (7.A3)$$

If you look closely at formula 7A.3, you will see that it represents the inventory change (in units) multiplied by the fixed manufacturing overhead rate. Applying formula 7A.3 to period 5, the inventory change ($Q_p - Q_s$) is 30 000 units (positive) so that absorption costing profits exceed variable costing profits by £60 000 (30 000 units at £2 fixed overhead rate).

KEY TERMS AND CONCEPTS

Absorption costing system A costing system that allocates all manufacturing costs, including fixed manufacturing costs, to products and values unsold stocks at their total cost of manufacture.

Budgeted activity The activity level based on the capacity utilization required for the next budget period.

Direct costing system A costing system that assigns only variable manufacturing costs, not fixed manufacturing costs, to products and includes them in the inventory valuation, also known as variable costing system or marginal costing system.

Full costing system A costing system that allocates all manufacturing costs, including fixed manufacturing costs, to products and values unsold stocks at their total cost of manufacture.

Marginal costing system A costing system that assigns only variable manufacturing costs, not fixed manufacturing costs, to products and includes them in the inventory valuation, also known as variable costing system or direct costing system.

Normal activity A measure of capacity required to satisfy average customer demand over a longer term period after taking into account seasonal and cyclical fluctuations.

Period cost adjustment The record of under- and over- recovery of fixed overheads at the end of a period.

Practical capacity Theoretical capacity less activity lost arising from unavoidable interruptions.

Theoretical maximum capacity A measure of maximum operating capacity based on 100 per cent efficiency with no interruptions for maintenance or other factors.

Variable costing system A costing system that assigns only variable manufacturing costs, not fixed manufacturing costs, to products and includes them in the inventory valuation, also known as marginal costing system or direct costing system.

Volume variance Another term used to refer to the under- or over-recovery of fixed overheads arising from actual activity being different from the activity level used to calculate the fixed overhead rate.

KEY EXAMINATION POINTS

A common mistake is for students to calculate *actual* overhead rates when preparing absorption costing profit statements. Normal or budgeted activity should be used to calculate overhead absorption rates, and this rate should be used to calculate the production overhead cost for all periods given in the question. Do not calculate different actual overhead rates for each accounting period.

Remember not to include non-manufacturing overheads in the inventory valuations for both variable and absorption costing. Also note that variable selling overheads will vary with sales and not production. Another common mistake is not to include an adjustment for under- or over-recovery of fixed overheads when actual production deviates from the normal or budgeted production. You should note that under- or over-recovery of overhead arises only with fixed overheads and when an absorption costing system is used.

ASSESSMENT MATERIAL

The review questions are short questions that enable you to assess your understanding of the main topics included in the chapter. The numbers in parentheses provide you with the page numbers to refer to if you cannot answer a specific question.

The review problems are more complex and require you to relate and apply the content to various business problems. The problems are graded by their level of difficulty. Solutions to review problems that are not preceded by the term 'IM' are provided in a separate section at the end of the book. Solutions to problems preceded by the term 'IM' are provided in the Instructor's Manual accompanying this book that can be downloaded from the lecturer's digital support resources. Additional review problems with fully worked solutions are provided in the *Student Manual* that accompanies this book.

REVIEW QUESTIONS

7.1 Distinguish between variable costing and absorption costing. (pp. 149–150)

7.2 How are non-manufacturing fixed costs treated under absorption and variable costing systems? (pp. 149–150)

7.3 Describe the circumstances when variable and absorption costing systems will report identical profits. (p. 154)

7.4 Under what circumstances will absorption costing report higher profits than variable costing? (p. 154)

7.5 Under what circumstances will variable costing report higher profits than absorption costing? (p. 154)

7.6 What arguments can be advanced in favour of variable costing? (pp. 155–157)

7.7 What arguments can be advanced in favour of absorption costing? (pp. 157–158)

7.8 Explain how absorption costing can encourage managers to engage in behaviour that is harmful to the organization. (p. 156)

7.9 Why is it necessary to select an appropriate denominator level measure only with absorption costing systems? (pp. 158–159)

7.10 Identify and describe the four different denominator level measures that can be used to estimate fixed overhead rates. (p. 159)

7.11 Explain why the choice of an appropriate denominator level is important. (p. 160)

7.12 Why is budgeted activity the most widely used denominator measure? (p. 160)

REVIEW PROBLEMS

7.13 Basic. A company has the following budgeted costs and revenues:

	$ per unit
Sales price	50
Variable production cost	18
Fixed production cost	10

In the most recent period, 2000 units were produced and 1000 units were sold. Actual sales price, variable production cost per unit and total fixed production costs were all as budgeted. Fixed production costs were over-absorbed by $4000. There was no opening inventory for the period.

What would be the reduction in profit for the period if the company had used marginal costing rather than absorption costing?

(a) $4000
(b) $6000
(c) $10000
(d) $14000

ACCA F2 Management Accounting

7.14 Basic. A company uses standard absorption costing to value inventory. Its fixed overhead absorption rate is $12 per labour hour and each unit of production should take four labour hours. In a recent period when there was no opening inventory of finished goods, 20000 units were produced using 100000 labour hours. 18000 units were sold. The actual profit was $464000.

What profit would have been earned under a standard marginal costing system?

(a) $368000
(b) $440000
(c) $344000
(d) $560000

ACCA F2 Management Accounting

7.15 Basic. A company manufactures and sells a single product. In two consecutive months the following levels of production and sales (in units) occurred:

	Month 1	Month 2
Sales	3800	4400
Production	3900	4200

The opening inventory for Month 1 was 400 units. Profits or losses have been calculated for each month using both absorption and marginal costing principles.

Which of the following combination of profits and losses for the two months is consistent with the above data?

	Absorption costing profit/(loss)		Marginal costing profit/(loss)	
	Month 1 ($)	Month 2 ($)	Month 1 ($)	Month 2 ($)
(a)	200	4400	(400)	3200
(b)	(400)	4400	200	3200
(c)	200	3200	(400)	4400
(d)	(400)	3200	200	4400

ACCA F2 Management Accounting

7.16 Basic. The following details have been extracted from KL's budget:

Selling price per unit	$140
Variable production costs per unit	$45
Fixed production costs per unit	$32

The budgeted fixed production cost per unit was based on a normal capacity of 11000 units per month.

Actual details for the months of January and February are given below:

	January	February
Production volume (units)	10000	11500
Sales volume (units)	9800	11200
Selling price per unit	$135	$140
Variable production cost per unit	$45	$45
Total fixed production costs	$350000	$340000

There was no closing inventory at the end of December.

Required:

(i) Calculate the actual profit for January and February using absorption costing. You should assume that any under-/over-absorption of fixed overheads is debited/credited to the income statement each month.

(3 marks)

(ii) The actual profit figure for the month of January using marginal costing was $532000.

Explain, using appropriate calculations, why there is a difference between the actual profit figures for January using marginal costing and using absorption costing.

(2 marks)

CIMA P1 Performance Operations

7.17 Basic. A newly formed company has drawn up the following budgets for its first two accounting periods:

	Period 1	Period 2
Sales units	9 500	10 300
Production units (equivalent to normal capacity)	10 000	10 000

The following budgeted information applies to both periods:

	$
Selling price per unit	6.40
Variable cost per unit	3.60
Fixed production overhead per period	15 000

(a) In period 1, the budgeted profit will be:

  (i) the same under both absorption costing and marginal costing;

  (ii) $750 higher under marginal costing;

  (iii) $750 higher under absorption costing;

  (iv) $1400 higher under absorption costing.

(b) In period 2, everything was as budgeted, except for the fixed production overhead, which was $15 700.

The reported profit, using absorption costing in period 2, would be:

  (i) $12 300

  (ii) $12 690

  (iii) $13 140

  (iv) $13 840

CIMA – Management Accounting Fundamentals

7.18 Intermediate: Preparation of variable and absorption costing statements and an explanation of the differences in profits. Bittern Ltd manufactures and sells a single product at a unit selling price of £25 in constant price level terms. Its cost structure is as follows:

Variable costs:	
Production materials	£10 per unit produced
Distribution	£1 per unit sold
Semi-variable costs:	
Labour	£5000 per annum, plus £2 per unit produced
Fixed costs:	
Overheads	£5000 per annum

For several years Bittern has operated a system of variable costing for management accounting purposes. It has been decided to review the system and to compare it for management accounting purposes with an absorption costing system.

As part of the review, you have been asked to prepare estimates of Bittern's profits in constant- price- level terms over a three-year period in three different hypothetical situations and to compare the two types of system generally for management accounting purposes.

(a) In each of the following three sets of hypothetical circumstances, calculate Bittern's profit in each of years t_1, t_2 and t_3, and also in total over the three-year period t_1 to t_3, using first a variable costing system and then a full-cost absorption costing system with fixed cost recovery based on a normal production level of 1000 units per annum:

  (i) Stable unit levels of production, sales and inventory

	t_1	t_2	t_3
Opening stock	100	100	100
Production	1000	1000	1000
Sales	1000	1000	1000
Closing stock	100	100	100

(5 marks)

  (ii) Stable unit level of sales, but fluctuating unit levels of production and inventory

	t_1	t_2	t_3
Opening stock	100	600	400
Production	1500	800	700
Sales	1000	1000	1000
Closing stock	600	400	100

(5 marks)

  (iii) Stable unit level of production, but fluctuating unit levels of sales and inventory

	t_1	t_2	t_3
Opening stock	100	600	400
Production	1000	1000	1000
Sales	500	1200	1300
Closing stock	600	400	100

(5 marks)

(Note that all the data in (i)–(iii) are volumes, not values.)

(b) Write a short comparative evaluation of variable and absorption costing systems for management accounting purposes, paying particular attention to profit measurement, and using your answer to (a) to illustrate your arguments if you wish. *(10 marks)*

ICAEW Management Accounting

IM7.1 Intermediate. In product costing, the costs attributed to each unit of production may be calculated by using either:

  (i) absorption costing, or

  (ii) marginal (or direct or variable) costing.

Similarly, in departmental cost or profit reports the fixed costs of overhead or service departments may be allocated to production departments as an integral part of the production departments' costs or else segregated in some form.

Required:

Describe absorption and marginal (or direct or variable) costing and outline the strengths and weaknesses of each method. *(11 marks)*

ACCA P2 Management Accounting

IM7.2 Intermediate. Discuss the arguments for and against the inclusion of fixed overheads in stock valuation for the purpose of internal profit measurement.

IM7.3 Intermediate: Preparation of variable and absorption costing statements. Solo Limited makes and sells a single product. The following data relate to periods 1 to 4:

	(£)
Variable cost per unit	30
Selling price per unit	55
Fixed costs per period	6000

Normal activity is 500 units and production and sales for the four periods are as follows:

	Period 1 units	Period 2 units	Period 3 units	Period 4 units
Sales	500	400	550	450
Production	500	500	450	500

There were no opening stocks at the start of period 1.

Required:

(a) Prepare operating statements for EACH of the periods 1 to 4, based on marginal costing principles. *(4 marks)*

(b) Prepare operating statements for EACH of the periods 1 to 4, based on absorption costing principles. *(6 marks)*

(c) Comment briefly on the results obtained in each period AND in total by the two systems. *(5 marks)*

CIMA Stage 1 Cost Accounting

IM7.4 Intermediate: Preparation of variable and absorption costing profit statements and comments in support of a variable costing system. A manufacturer of glass bottles has been affected by competition from plastic bottles and is currently operating at between 65 and 70 per cent of maximum capacity.

The company at present reports profits on an absorption costing basis but with the high fixed costs associated with the glass container industry and a substantial difference between sales volumes and production in some months, the accountant has been criticized for reporting widely different profits from month to month. To counteract this criticism, he is proposing in future to report profits based on marginal costing and in his proposal to management lists the following reasons for wishing to change:

1　Marginal costing provides for the complete segregation of fixed costs, thus facilitating closer control of production costs.

2　It eliminates the distortion of interim profit statements which occur when there are seasonal fluctuations in sales volume although production is at a fairly constant level.

3　It results in cost information which is more helpful in determining the sales policy necessary to maximize profits.

From the accounting records, the following figures were extracted: Standard cost per gross (a gross is 144 bottles and is the cost unit used within the business):

	(£)
Direct materials	8.00
Direct labour	7.20
Variable production overhead	3.36
Total variable production cost	18.56
Fixed production overhead	7.52*
Total production standard cost	26.08

*The fixed production overhead rate was based on the following computations:

Total annual fixed production overhead was budgeted at £7 584 000 or £632 000 per month. Production volume was set at 1 008 000 gross bottles or 70 per cent of maximum capacity.

There is a slight difference in budgeted fixed production overhead at different levels of operating:

Activity level (per cent of maximum capacity)	Amount per month (£000)
50–75	632
76–90	648
91–100	656

You may assume that actual fixed production overhead incurred was as budgeted.

Additional information:

	September	October
Gross sold	87 000	101 000
Gross produced	115 000	78 000
Sales price, per gross	£32	£32
Fixed selling costs	£120 000	£120 000
Fixed administrative costs	£80 000	£80 000

There were no finished goods in stock at 1 September.

You are required:

(a) to prepare monthly profit statements for September and October using

　(i)　absorption costing; and

　(ii)　marginal costing; *(16 marks)*

(b) to comment briefly on the accountant's three reasons that he listed to support his proposal. *(9 marks)*

CIMA Stage 2 Cost Accounting

IM7.5 Intermediate: Calculation of overhead absorption rates and an explanation of the differences in profits. A company manufactures a single product with the following variable costs per unit:

Direct materials	£7.00
Direct labour	£5.50
Manufacturing overhead	£2.00

The selling price of the product is £36.00 per unit. Fixed manufacturing costs are expected to be £1 340 000 for a period. Fixed non-manufacturing costs are expected to be £875 000. Fixed manufacturing costs can be analysed as follows:

Production 1	Department 2	Service department	General factory
£380 000	£465 000	£265 000	£230 000

'General factory' costs represent space costs, for example rates, lighting and heating. Space utilization is as follows:

Production department 1	40%
Production department 2	50%
Service department	10%

Sixty per cent of service department costs are labour related and the remaining 40 per cent machine related.

Normal production department activity is:

	Direct labour hours	Machine hours	Production units
Department 1	80 000	2 400	120 000
Department 2	100 000	2 400	120 000

Fixed manufacturing overheads are absorbed at a predetermined rate per unit of production for each production department, based upon normal activity.

Required:

(a) Prepare a profit statement for a period using the full absorption costing system described above and showing each element of cost separately. Costs for the period were as per expectation, except for additional expenditure of £20 000 on fixed manufacturing overhead in Production Department 1. Production and sales were 116 000 and 114 000 units respectively for the period. *(14 marks)*

(b) Prepare a profit statement for the period using marginal costing principles instead. *(5 marks)*

(c) Contrast the general effect on profit of using absorption and marginal costing systems, respectively. (Use the figures calculated in (a) and (b) above to illustrate your answer.) *(6 marks)*

ACCA Cost and Management Accounting 1

IM7.6 Advanced: Preparation and comments on variable and absorption costing profit statements. Synchrodot Ltd manufactures two standard products, product 1 selling at £15 and product 2 selling at £18. A standard absorption costing system is in operation and summarized details of the unit cost standards are as follows:

	Standard cost data – summary	
	Product 1 (£)	Product 2 (£)
Direct material cost	2	3
Direct labour cost	1	2
Overhead (fixed and variable)	7	9
	£10	£14

The budgeted fixed factory overhead for Synchrodot Ltd is £180 000 (per quarter) for product 1 and £480 000 (per quarter) for product 2. This apportionment to product lines is achieved by using a variety of 'appropriate' bases for individual expense categories, e.g. floor space for rates, number of workstaff for supervisory salaries, etc. The fixed overhead is absorbed into production using practical capacity as the basis and any volume variance is written off (or credited) to the profit and loss account in the quarter in which it occurs. Any planned volume variance in the quarterly budgets is dealt with similarly. The practical capacity per quarter is 30 000 units for product 1 and 60 000 units for product 2.

At the March board meeting the draft budgeted income statement for the April/May/June quarter is presented for consideration. This shows the following:

Budgeted income statement for April, May and June

		Product 1	Product 2
Budgeted sales quantity		30 000 units	57 000 units
Budgeted production quantity		24 000 units	60 000 units
Budgeted sales revenue		£450 000	£1 026 000
Budgeted production costs			
Direct material		£48 000	£180 000
Direct labour		24 000	120 000
Factory overhead		204 000	540 000
		£276 000	£840 000
Add:			
Budgeted opening Finished goods Stock at 1 April	(8000 units)	80 000 (3000 units)	42 000
		356 000	£882 000
Less:			
Budgeted closing Finished goods Stock at 30 June	(2000 units)	20 000 (6000 units)	84 000
Budgeted manufacturing Cost of budgeted sales		£336 000	£798 000
Budgeted manufacturing profit		£114 000	£228 000
Budgeted Administrative and selling costs (fixed)		30 000	48 000
Budgeted profit		£84 000	£180 000

The statement causes consternation at the board meeting because it seems to show that product 2 contributes much more profit than product 1 and yet this has not previously been apparent.

The sales director is perplexed and he points out that the budgeted sales programme for the forthcoming quarter is identical with that accepted for the current quarter (January/February/March) and yet the budget for the current quarter shows a budgeted profit of £120 000 for each product line and the actual results seem to be in line with the budget.

The production director emphasizes that identical assumptions, as to unit variable costs, selling prices and manufacturing efficiency, underlie both budgets but there has

been a change in the budgeted production pattern. He produces the following table:

Budgeted production	Product 1	Product 2
January/February/March	30 000 units	52 500 units
April/May/June	24 000 units	60 000 units

He urges that the company's budgeting procedures be overhauled as he can see no reason why the quarter's profit should be £24 000 up on the previous quarter and why the net profit for product 1 should fall from £4.00 to £2.80 per unit sold, whereas, for product 2 it should rise from £2.11 to £3.16.

You are required:

(a) To reconstruct the company's budget for the January/February/March quarter.   (6 marks)
(b) To restate the budgets (for both quarters) using standard marginal cost as the stock valuation basis.   (8 marks)
(c) To comment on the queries raised by the sales director and the production director and on the varying profit figures disclosed by the alternative budgets.   (8 marks)

ACCA Level 2 Management Accounting

IM7.7 Advanced: Explanation of difference between absorption and variable costing profit statements. The accountant of Minerva Ltd, a small company manufacturing only one product, wishes to decide how to present the company's monthly management accounts. To date, only actual information has been presented on an historic cost basis, with stocks valued at average cost. Standard costs have now been derived for the costs of production. The practical capacity (also known as full capacity) for annual production is 160 000 units, and this has been used as the basis for the allocation of production overheads. Selling and administration fixed overheads have been allocated assuming all 160 000 units are sold. The expected production capacity for net year is 140 000 units. It is anticipated now that, for the 12 months to 31 December, production and sales volume will equal 120 000 units, compared to the forecast sales and production volumes of 140 000 units. The standard cost and standard profit per unit based on practical capacity is:

	(£ per unit)	(£ per unit)
Selling price		25.00
Production costs:		
Variable	8.00	
Fixed	6.00	
	14.00	
Variable selling costs	1.00	15.00
		10.00
Other fixed costs:		
Administration	2.10	
Selling	1.20	3.30
Standard profit per unit		6.70

The accountant has prepared the following three drafts (see below) of Minerva Ltd's profit and loss account for the month of November using three different accounting methods. The drafts are based on data relating to production, sales and stock for November which are given below:

Production and sales quantities November

	(units)
Opening stock	20 000
Production	8 000
	28 000
Less Sales	10 000
Closing stock	18 000

The accountant is trying to choose the best method of presenting the financial information to the directors. The present method is shown under the actual costs column; the two other methods are based on the standard costs derived above.

The following estimated figures for the month of December have just come to hand:

Sales 12 000 units at £25
Production costs:
  variable £116 000
  fixed £90 000

Production 14 000 units
Administration costs £24 500
Selling costs:
  variable £12 000
  fixed £15 000

Draft profit and loss accounts for the month ended 30 November:

	Actual costs (£000) (£000)	Absorption cost method (£000) (£000)	Variable cost method (£000) (£000)
Sales (10 000 units at £25)	250	250	250
Opening stock	280	280	160
Production costs:			
variable	60	112[a]	64
fixed	66	—	—
	406	392	224
Closing stock	261 145	252 140	144 80
	105	110	170
Variable selling costs	—	—	10
Gross profit/ contribution	105	110	160
Other expenses:			
Production – fixed	—	—	80
Administration – fixed	23	21	28
Selling:			
variable	11	10	—
fixed	14 48	12 43	16 124
	57	67	36

	Actual costs (£000) (£000)	Absorption cost method (£000) (£000)	Variable cost method (£000) (£000)
Variances			
Production			
variable		(4)	(4)
– expenditure			
fixed – volume		32	—
– expenditure		(14)	(14)
Administration			
– volume		7	—
– expenditure		(5)	(5)
Selling:			
variable		1	1
– expenditure			
fixed – volume		4	—
– expenditure	— (2)	19 (2)	(24)
Net profit	57	48	60

Note

[a] Sum of variable and fixed costs.

Requirements:

(a) Prepare a schedule explaining the main difference(s) between the net profit figures for November under the three different allocation methods.   (8 marks)

(b) Discuss the relative merits of the two suggested alternative methods as a means of providing useful information to the company's senior management.   (8 marks)

(c) Draw up a short report for senior management presenting your recommendations for the choice of method of preparing the monthly accounts, incorporating in your report the profit and loss account for November and the projected profit and loss account for December as examples of your recommendations.   (9 marks)

ICAEW P2 Management Accounting

PART THREE

INFORMATION FOR DECISION-MAKING

The objective of this part, which contains seven chapters, is to consider the provision of financial information that will help managers to make better decisions. Chapters 8–12 are concerned mainly with short-term decisions based on the environment of today and the physical, human and financial resources that are presently available to a firm; these decisions are determined to a considerable extent by the quality of the firm's long-term decisions. An important distinction between the long-term and short-term decisions is that the former cannot easily be reversed whereas the latter can often be changed. The actions that follow short-term decisions are frequently repeated and it is possible for different actions to be taken in the future. For example, the setting of a particular selling price or product mix can often be changed fairly quickly. With regard to long-term decisions, such as capital investment, which involves, for example, the purchase of new plant and machinery, it is not easy to change a decision in the short term. Resources may only be available for major investments in plant and machinery at lengthy intervals, and it is unlikely that plant replacement decisions will be repeated in the short term.

Chapters 8–12 concentrate mainly on how accounting information can be applied to different forms of short-term decision. Chapter 8 focuses on what will happen to the financial results if a specific level of activity or volume fluctuates. This information is required for making optimal short-term output decisions. Chapter 9 examines how costs and revenues should be measured for a range of non-routine short-term and long-term decisions. Chapter 10 is concerned with profitability analysis and the provision of financial information for pricing decisions. Chapter 11 focuses on an alternative approach for measuring resources consumed by cost objects. This approach is called activity-based costing. Chapters 8–11 assume a world of certainty, whereas Chapter 12 introduces methods of incorporating uncertainty into the analysis, and the topics covered in Chapters 8–11 are re-examined under conditions of uncertainty.

The final two chapters in this part are concerned with long-term decisions. Chapter 13 looks at the appraisal methods that are used for evaluating capital investment decisions and introduces the concept of the time value of money. Chapter 14 examines more complex issues relating to capital investment decisions. In particular, the impact of capital rationing, taxation, inflation and risk is examined.

8
COST–VOLUME–PROFIT ANALYSIS

LEARNING OBJECTIVES After studying this chapter, you should be able to:

- justify the use of linear cost and revenue functions;

- apply the numerical approach to answer questions similar to those listed in Example 8.1;

- construct break-even, contribution and profit–volume graphs;

- apply cost–volume–profit analysis in a multi-product setting;

- explain the meaning of operating leverage and describe how it influences profits;

- identify and explain the assumptions on which cost–volume–profit analysis is based.

You will remember from Chapter 1 that the decision-making process involves selecting from a range of possible courses of action. Before they make their choice, managers need to compare the likely effects of the options they are considering. This chapter looks at one technique that allows them to consider the consequences of particular courses of action. It provides answers to questions such as:

- How many units must be sold to break even?

- What would be the effect on profits if we reduce our selling price and sell more units?

- What sales volume is required to meet the additional fixed charges arising from an advertising campaign?

- Should we pay our sales people on the basis of a salary only, on the basis of a commission only or by a combination of the two?

These and other questions can be answered using cost–volume–profit (CVP) analysis.

CVP analysis examines the relationship between changes in activity (i.e. output) and changes in total sales revenue, costs and net profit. It allows us to predict what will happen to the financial results if a specified level of activity or volume fluctuates. This information is vital to management, since one of the most important variables influencing total sales revenue, total costs and profits is output or volume. Knowledge of this relationship enables management to identify critical output levels, such as the level at which neither a profit nor a loss will occur (i.e. the break-even point).

CVP analysis is based on the relationship between volume and sales revenue, costs and profit in the *short run*. This is normally a period of one year, or less, a time in which the output of a firm is likely to be restricted to that available from the current operating capacity. In the short run some inputs can be increased, but others cannot. Additional supplies of materials and unskilled labour may be obtained at short notice, but operating capacity cannot be significantly changed. For example, it is not possible for a hospital to expand its facilities in the short run in order to increase the number of beds. Similarly, a hotel cannot increase the number of rooms in the short run to increase the number of guests. It is also important to remember that most of the costs and prices of a firm's products or services will already have been predetermined over a short-run period, and the major area of uncertainty will be sales volume. Short-run profitability will, therefore, be most sensitive to sales volume. CVP analysis thus highlights the effects of changes in sales volume on the level of profits in the short run.

The term 'volume' is used within CVP analysis but this has multiple meanings. Different measures can be used to represent the term. For example, sales revenue is a generic term that can be used by most organizations. However, units of output, or activity, tend to be the most widely used terms. This raises the question of what constitutes a unit of output or activity. For a manufacturing organization, such as a car manufacturer, determining units of output is straightforward. It is the number of cars produced. For a computer manufacturer, it is the number of computers produced. Service organizations face a more difficult choice. Hotels may define units as the number of guest nights, leisure centres may use the number of visitors as a measure of output/activity and airlines might use the number of passenger miles.

CVP analysis is dependent on the ability to estimate costs at different activity levels and to do this requires that costs are analysed into their fixed and variable elements. Cost estimation techniques are explained in Chapter 24 in Part Six of this book which focuses on the application of quantitative methods to management accounting. Alternatively, if you require a knowledge of cost estimation techniques now you may prefer to read Chapter 24 immediately after you have read this chapter.

CURVILINEAR CVP RELATIONSHIPS

A diagram showing CVP behaviour is presented in Figure 8.1. You will see that the total revenue and total cost lines are curvilinear. The total revenue line (0–E) initially resembles a straight line but then begins to rise less steeply and eventually starts to decline. This arises because the firm is only able to sell increasing quantities of output by reducing the selling price per unit; thus the total revenue line does not increase proportionately with output. To increase the quantity of sales, it is necessary to reduce the unit selling price, which results in the total revenue line rising less steeply, and eventually beginning to decline. The decline occurs because the adverse effect of price reductions outweighs the benefits of increased sales volume.

The total cost line (A–D) illustrates cost behaviour in a manufacturing firm but similar cost behaviour also applies in non-manufacturing firms. Between points A and B, total costs rise steeply at first as the firm operates at the lower levels of the volume range. This reflects the difficulties of efficiently using manufacturing facilities designed for much larger volume levels. Between points B and C, the total cost line begins to level out and rise less steeply because the firm is now able to operate its manufacturing facilities within the efficient operating range and can take advantage of economies of scale (e.g. specialization of labour, smooth production schedules and discounts from bulk purchases). Economists describe this situation as increasing returns to scale. In the upper portion of the volume range, the total cost line between points C and D rises more steeply as the cost per unit increases. This is because manufacturing facilities are being operated beyond their capacity. Bottlenecks develop, production schedules become more complex and equipment breakdowns begin to occur. The overall effect is that the cost per unit of output increases and causes the total cost line to rise steeply. Economists describe this situation as decreasing returns to scale.

It is also clear from Figure 8.1 that the shape of the total revenue line is such that it crosses the total cost line at two points. In other words, there are two output levels at which the total costs are equal to the total revenues; or, more simply, there are two break-even points.

FIGURE 8.1
Curvilinear CVP relationships

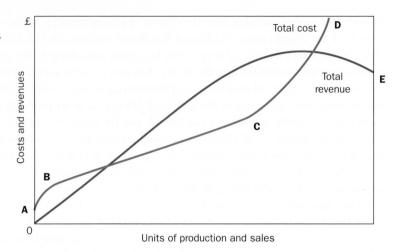

LINEAR CVP RELATIONSHIPS

In Figure 8.2, the total cost line X–Y and the total revenue line 0–V assume that variable cost and selling price are constant per unit of output. This results in a linear relationship (i.e. a straight line) for total revenue and total cost as output/volume changes. If you look at these two lines, you will see that a linear relationship results in only one break-even point. You can also see that the profit area (i.e. the difference between the total revenue line O–V and the total cost line X–Y) widens as volume increases. For comparative purposes, the curvilinear relationships shown in Figure 8.1 are also reproduced in Figure 8.2 (with line A–D and line 0–E showing, respectively, curvilinear total cost and total revenue relationships).

Management accounting assumes linear CVP relationships when applying CVP analysis to short-run business problems. Curvilinear relationships appear to be more realistic of cost and revenue behaviour, so how can we justify CVP analysis based on the assumption of linear relationships? The answers are provided in the following sections.

Relevant range

Linear relationships are not intended to provide an accurate representation of total cost and total revenue throughout all ranges of output. The objective is to represent the behaviour of total cost and revenue over the range of output at which a firm expects to be operating within a short-term planning horizon.

FIGURE 8.2
Linear CVP relationships

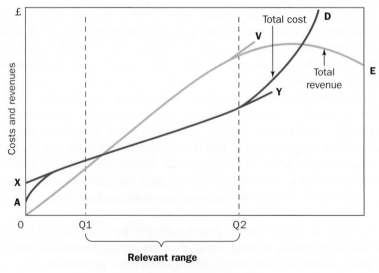

FIGURE 8.3

Fixed costs applicable within the relevant range

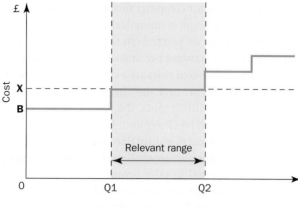

Units of production and sales

This range of output is represented by the output range between points Q1 and Q2 in Figure 8.2. The term relevant range is used to refer to the output range at which the firm expects to be operating within a short-term planning horizon. This relevant range also broadly represents the output levels that the firm has had experience of operating in the past and for which cost information is available.

It is clear from Figure 8.2 that, between points Q1 and Q2, the cost and revenue relationships are more or less linear. It would be unwise, however, to make this assumption for output levels outside the relevant range. CVP analysis should therefore only be applied within the relevant range. If the relevant range changes, different fixed and variable costs and selling prices must be used.

Fixed cost function

Figure 8.2 indicates that at zero output level fixed costs equivalent to 0X would be incurred. This fixed cost level of 0X is assumed to be applicable to activity level Q1 to Q2, shown in Figure 8.3. If there were to be a prolonged economic recession then output might fall below Q1, and this could result in redundancies and shutdowns. Therefore, fixed costs may be reduced to 0B if there is a prolonged and a significant decline in sales demand. Alternatively, additional fixed costs will be incurred if long-term sales volume is expected to be greater than Q2. Over a longer-term time horizon, the fixed cost line will consist of a series of step functions as shown in Figure 8.3. However, since within its short-term planning horizon the firm expects to be operating between output levels Q1 and Q2 (i.e. the relevant range), it will be committed, in the short term, to fixed costs of 0X. Thus the fixed cost of 0X shown in Figures 8.2 and 8.3 represent the fixed costs that would be incurred only for the relevant range.

Total revenue function

Linear CVP relationships assume that selling price is constant over the relevant range of output, and therefore the total revenue line is a straight line. This is a realistic assumption in those firms that operate in industries where selling prices tend to be fixed in the short term. Beyond the relevant range, increases in output may only be possible by offering substantial reductions in price. As it is not the intention of firms to operate outside the relevant range, it is appropriate to assume constant selling prices.

A NUMERICAL APPROACH TO COST–VOLUME–PROFIT ANALYSIS

As an alternative to using diagrams for CVP analysis we can also use a numerical approach. Diagrams are useful for presenting the outcomes in a more visual form to non-accounting managers, but the numerical approach is often a quicker and more flexible method for producing the appropriate information. Indeed, it is possible to express CVP relationships in a simple mathematical equation format so that they can form an input for computer financial models. To keep things simple we shall avoid mathematical formulae and use a simple numerical approach.

In the previous sections, we pointed out that CVP analysis is based on the assumption that selling price and variable cost are constant per unit of output. In contrast, you will remember from Chapter 2 that over a short-run period fixed costs are a constant total amount whereas unit cost changes with output levels. As a result, profit per unit also changes with volume. For example, if fixed costs are £10 000 for a period and output is 10 000 units, the fixed cost will be £1 per unit. Alternatively, if output is 5000 units, the fixed cost will be £2 per unit. Profit per unit will not therefore be constant over varying output levels and it is incorrect to unitize fixed costs for CVP decisions.

Instead of using profit per unit, we shall use contribution margins to apply the numerical approach. Contribution margin is equal to sales revenue minus variable costs. Because the variable cost per unit and the selling price per unit are assumed to be constant the contribution margin per unit is also assumed to be constant. We will use Example 8.1 to illustrate the application of the numerical approach to CVP analysis.

Example 8.1 calculations

1 Break-even point in units (i.e. number of tickets sold)

You will see from Example 8.1 that each ticket sold generates a contribution of £10 (£20 selling price – £10 variable cost), which is available to cover fixed costs and, after they are covered, to contribute to profit. When we have obtained sufficient total contribution to cover fixed costs, the break-even point is achieved, and so:

$$\text{Break-even point in units} = \frac{\text{Fixed costs (£60 000)}}{\text{Contribution per unit (£10)}}$$
$$= 6000 \text{ tickets}$$

2 Units to be sold to obtain a £30 000 profit

To achieve a profit of any size we must first obtain sufficient contribution to cover the fixed costs (i.e. the break-even point). If the total contribution is not sufficient to cover the fixed costs then a loss will occur. Once a sufficient total contribution has been achieved any excess contribution represents profit.

EXAMPLE 8.1

Lee Enterprises operates in the leisure and entertainment industry and one of its activities is to promote concerts at locations throughout the world. The company is examining the viability of a concert in Singapore. Estimated fixed costs are £60 000. These include the fees paid to performers, the hire of the venue and advertising costs. Variable costs consist of the cost of a pre-packed buffet that will be provided by a firm of caterers at a price, which is currently being negotiated, but it is likely to be in the region of £10 per ticket sold. The proposed price for the sale of a ticket is £20.

The management of Lee has requested the following information:

1 The number of tickets that must be sold to break even (that is, the point at which there is neither a profit nor a loss).

2 How many tickets must be sold to earn £30 000 target profit?

3 What profit would result if 8000 tickets were sold?

4 What selling price would have to be charged to give a profit of £30 000 on sales of 8000 tickets, fixed costs of £60 000 and variable costs of £10 per ticket?

5 How many additional tickets must be sold to cover the extra cost of television advertising of £8000?

REAL WORLD VIEWS 8.1

Airbus A380 likely to break even in 2015

The Airbus A380 was the world's first double-decker aircraft. It can accommodate from 555 to 853 passengers depending on the class configuration. Long haul airlines such as Singapore Airlines were early adopters of the aircraft back in 2007.

The 2016 list price of an A380 is approximately $433 million. According to the company website, there are over 120 A380 aircraft in service with 13 airlines. Each aircraft is built to order and airlines often place orders years in advance. According to the *FlightGlobal* website, the Airbus A380 will breakeven in 2015. The site quotes Chief executive, Tom Enders, who says 'Most importantly, we confirm the A380 break-even for 2015.' As of early 2015, €42 billion in revenue has been raised from A380 sales. It also has an order book for 319 A380 aircraft as of the end of March 2016.

Questions

1 Is it true to say that any A380 aircraft sold before break-even has been achieved is making a loss?

2 Can you think of some major fixed costs likely to be incurred on the A380 by Airbus?

References

www.flightglobal.com/news/articles/airbus-a380-aircraft
-profile-205274/

www.airbus.com/presscentre/pressreleases/press
-release-detail/detail/new-airbus-aircraft-list-prices
-for-2016/

www.flightglobal.com/news/articles/airbus-assures-on
-a380-break-even-this-year-409534/

Thus to determine the total contribution to obtain a target profit we simply add the target profit to the fixed costs and divide by the contribution per unit, so that:

$$\text{Units sold for the target profit} = \frac{\text{Fixed costs (£60\,000)} + \text{Target profit (£30\,000)}}{\text{Contribution per unit (£10)}}$$
$$= 9000 \text{ tickets}$$

3 Profit from the sale of 8000 tickets

The total contribution from the sale of 8000 tickets is £80 000 (8000 × £10). To ascertain the profit, we deduct the fixed costs of £60 000, giving a net profit of £20 000. Let us now assume that we wish to ascertain the impact on profit if a further 1000 tickets are sold so that sales volume increases from 8000 to 9000 tickets. Assuming that fixed costs remain unchanged, the impact on a firm's profits resulting from a change in the number of units sold can be determined by multiplying the unit contribution margin by the change in units sold. Therefore the increase in profits will be £10 000 (1000 units times a unit contribution margin of £10).

4 Selling price to be charged to show a profit of £30 000 on sales of 8000 tickets

First, we must determine the total required revenue to obtain a profit of £30 000. This is £170 000, which is derived from the sum of the fixed costs (£60 000), variable costs (8000 × £10) and the target profit (£30 000). Dividing the required sales revenues of £170 000 by the sales volume (8000 tickets) gives a selling price of £21.25.

5 Additional sales volume to meet £8000 additional fixed advertisement charges

The contribution per unit is £10 and fixed costs will increase by £8000. Therefore an extra 800 tickets must be sold to cover the additional fixed costs of £8000.

THE PROFIT–VOLUME RATIO

The profit–volume ratio (also known as the contribution margin ratio) is the contribution divided by sales. It represents the proportion of each £1 of sales available to cover fixed costs and provide for profit. In Example 8.1, the contribution is £10 per unit and the selling price is £20 per unit; the profit–volume ratio is 0.5. This means that for each £1 sale a contribution of £0.50 is earned. Because we assume that selling price and contribution per unit are constant, the profit–volume ratio is also assumed to be constant. This means that the profit–volume ratio can be computed using either unit figures or total figures. Given an estimate of total sales revenue, it is possible to use the profit–volume ratio to estimate total contribution. For example, if total sales revenue is estimated to be £200 000, the total contribution will be £100 000 (£200 000 × 0.5). To calculate the profit, we deduct fixed costs of £60 000; thus a profit of £40 000 will be obtained from total sales revenue of £200 000.

This computation can be expressed in equation form:

$$\text{Profit} = (\text{Sales revenue} \times \text{PV ratio}) - \text{Fixed costs}$$

REAL WORLD VIEWS 8.2

Why is the break-even price of crude oil so important?

The break-even price of crude oil includes production costs, exploring or finding costs, oil well development costs, transportation costs, and selling and general administration expenses. A survey published in 2015 showed some interesting insights into the break-even price for producing crude oil. Petroleum extraction in the Arctic region shows the highest break-even price of $75 per barrel. On the other hand, Middle Eastern countries have the lowest price at $27 per barrel. US shale oil producers have a break-even price of $65 per barrel. These estimates are average break-even prices. The costs may vary depending on the oil well and its location. The chart below describes the break-even price for crude oil.

According to a publication in *Market Realist* by Gordon Kristopher WTI (West Texas Intermediate) crude oil was currently trading at $45 per barrel at the time of the publication and Brent crude oil was trading at $46.4 per barrel. This massive price decline in the last six months will impact oil producers with high break-even prices. The margins of high break-even-price US shale oil producers will be impacted the most. As long as crude oil prices are around the break-even range of US shale oil, then US oil production growth will be slow. Production will likely decline over the long term, which in turn will have a positive impact on oil prices.

Questions

1 Why will a decline in production have a positive impact on oil prices?

2 Why does the break-even price in the above chart differ according to the location of the oil wells?

3 Is the break-even price of crude oil more important than the break-even volume?

Reference

Kristopher, G. (2015) A key investor's guide to the crude oil market (Part 4 of 1 of 15 *Market Monitor*). Available at marketrealist.com/2015/01/crude-oil-market-key-overview/

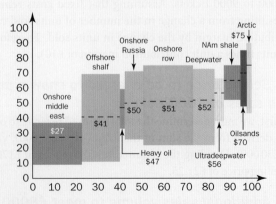

Breakeven Price of Crude Oil

Note: *Market Realist*
Source: Seadrill, Morgan Stanley Equity Research, International Energy Agency

We can rearrange this equation:

$$\text{Profit} + \text{Fixed costs} = \text{Sales revenue} \times \text{PV ratio}$$

Therefore the break-even sales revenue (where profit = 0) = Fixed costs/PV ratio.

If we apply this approach to Example 8.1, the break-even sales revenue is £120 000 (£60 000 fixed costs/ 0.5 PV ratio).

RELEVANT RANGE

It is vital to remember that CVP analysis can only be used for decisions that result in outcomes within the relevant range. Outside this range, the unit selling price and the variable cost are no longer deemed to be constant per unit and any results obtained from the formulae that fall outside the relevant range will be incorrect. The concept of the relevant range is more appropriate for production settings but it can apply within non-production settings. Returning to Lee Enterprises in Example 8.1, we shall now assume that the caterers' charges will be higher per ticket if ticket sales are below 4000 but lower if sales exceed 12 000 tickets. Thus, the £10 variable cost relates only to a sales volume within a range of 4000 to 12 000 tickets. Outside this range, other costs apply. In other words, we will assume that the relevant range is a sales volume of 4000 to 12 000 tickets and outside this range the results of our CVP analysis do not apply.

MARGIN OF SAFETY

The margin of safety indicates by how much sales may decrease before a loss occurs. Using Example 8.1, where unit selling price and variable cost were £20 and £10 respectively and fixed costs were £60 000, we noted that the break-even point was 6000 tickets or £120 000 sales value. If sales are expected to

---

REAL WORLD VIEWS 8.3

Airlines struggling to break even will make 'less than £4 profit per passenger'

According to the International Air and Transport Association (IATA) conference airlines were expected to make around £3.18 profit from each passenger in 2014. Although carriers were expecting net profits of £11 billion, margins were so thin the air industry was expected to make less money than the oil industry makes from selling the fuel it consumes. Tony Tyler, the director general of IATA, said the headline figures masked 'a daily struggle for airlines to break even. The brutal economic reality is that on revenues of $746 billion (£445bn), we will earn an average net margin of 2.4 per cent.'

IATA research revealed that carriers would spend an estimated $212 billion (£126bn) on jet fuel over the next 12 months, representing almost 30 per cent of their total operating costs. Intense competition from low-cost carriers has seen air fares fall in real terms by 3.5 per cent this year,

with the number of passengers worldwide reaching 3.3 billion. Planes are flying fuller than ever before but lower fares mean that a higher percentage of occupied seats is needed to break even. IATA's chief economist, Brian Pearce, said, 'It's remarkable that the industry is generating any profit at all.'

Questions

1 Is break even a good performance monitor over the longer term?

2 How do decreasing margins affect the break-even point and margin of safety?

Reference

Catherine Eade (2014) 'Airlines struggling to break even will make "less than £4 profit per passenger" this year'. *Daily Mail*, 3 June. Available at www.dailymail .co.uk/travel/article-2647105/Airlines-struggling-break -make-4-profit-passenger-year.html#ixzz3UjUsCZm4

be 8000 tickets or £160000, the margin of safety will be 2000 tickets or £40000. Alternatively, we can express the margin of safety in a percentage form based on the following ratio:

$$\text{Percentage margin of safety} = \frac{\text{Expected sales} - \text{Break-even sales}}{\text{Expected sales}}$$

$$= \frac{£160\,000 - £120\,000}{£160\,000} = 25\%$$

Note that higher margins of safety are associated with less risky activities.

CONSTRUCTING THE BREAK-EVEN CHART

Managers may obtain a clearer understanding of CVP behaviour if the information is presented in graphical format. Using the data in Example 8.1, we can construct the break-even chart for Lee Enterprises (Figure 8.4). Note that activity/output is plotted on the horizontal axis and monetary amounts for total costs, total revenues and total profits (or loss) are recorded on the vertical axis. In constructing the graph, the fixed costs are plotted as a single horizontal line at the £60000 level. Variable costs at the rate of £10 per unit of volume are added to the fixed costs to enable the total cost line to be plotted. Two points are required to insert the total cost line. At zero sales, volume total cost will be equal to the fixed costs of £60000. At 12000 units, sales volume total costs will be £180000 consisting of £120000 variable costs plus £60000 fixed costs. The total revenue line is plotted at the rate of £20 per unit of volume. At zero output, total sales are zero and at 12000 units, total sales revenue is £240000. The total revenues for these two points are plotted on the graph and a straight line is drawn that joins these points. The constraints of the relevant range consisting of two vertical lines are then added to the graph; beyond these lines, we have little assurance that the CVP relationships are valid.

FIGURE 8.4

Break-even chart for Example 8.1

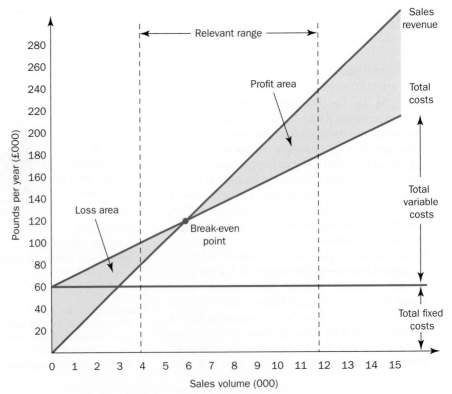

The point at which the total sales revenue line cuts the total cost line is the point where the concert makes neither a profit nor a loss. This is the break-even point and is 6000 tickets or £120 000 total sales revenue. The distance between the total sales revenue line and the total cost line at a volume below the break-even point represents losses that will occur for sales levels below 6000 tickets. Similarly, if the company operates at a sales volume above the break-even point, the difference between the total revenue and the total cost lines represents the profit that results from sales levels above 6000 tickets.

ALTERNATIVE PRESENTATION OF COST–VOLUME–PROFIT ANALYSIS

Contribution graph

In Figure 8.4, the fixed cost line is drawn parallel to the horizontal axis, and the variable cost is the difference between the total cost line and the fixed cost line. An alternative to Figure 8.4 for the data contained in Example 8.1 is illustrated in Figure 8.5. This alternative presentation is called a contribution graph. In Figure 8.5, the variable cost line is drawn first at £10 per unit of volume. The fixed costs are represented by the difference between the total cost line and the variable cost line. Because fixed costs are assumed to be a constant sum throughout the entire output range, a constant sum of £60 000 for fixed costs is added to the variable cost line, which results in the total cost line being drawn parallel to the variable cost line. The advantage of this form of presentation is that it emphasizes the total contribution, which is represented by the difference between the total sales revenue line and the total variable cost line.

Profit–volume graph

Neither the break-even nor the contribution graphs highlight the profit or loss at different volume levels. To ascertain the profit or loss figures from a break-even graph, it is necessary to determine

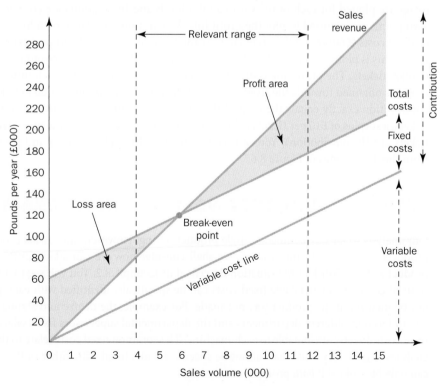

FIGURE 8.5
Contribution chart
for Example 8.1

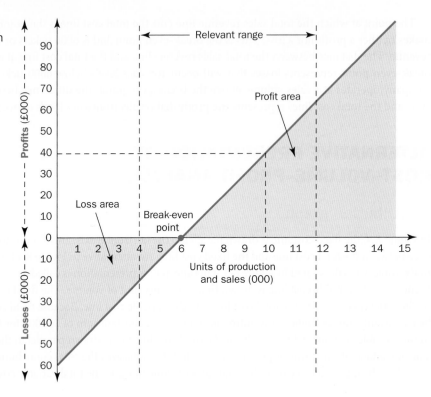

FIGURE 8.6

Profit–volume graph for Example 8.1

the difference between the total cost and total revenue lines. The **profit–volume graph** is a more convenient method of showing the impact of changes in volume on profit. Such a graph is illustrated in Figure 8.6. The horizontal axis represents the various levels of sales volume, and the profits and losses for the period are recorded on the vertical scale. You will see from Figure 8.6 that profits or losses are plotted for each of the various sales levels and these points are connected by a profit line. Two points are required to plot the profit line. When units sold are zero, a loss equal to the amount of fixed costs (£60 000) will be reported. At the break-even point (zero profits) sales volume is 6000 units. This is plotted at the point where the profit line intersects the horizontal line at a sales volume of 6000 tickets. The profit line is drawn between the two points. With each unit sold, a contribution of £10 is obtained towards the fixed costs, and the break-even point is at 6000 tickets, when the total contribution exactly equals the total of the fixed costs. With each additional unit sold beyond 6000 tickets, a surplus of £10 per ticket is obtained. If 10 000 tickets are sold, the profit will be £40 000 (4000 tickets at £10 contribution). You can see this relationship between sales and profit at 10 000 tickets from the dotted lines in Figure 8.6.

MULTI-PRODUCT COST–VOLUME–PROFIT ANALYSIS

Our analysis so far has assumed a single product setting. However, most firms produce and sell many products or services. In this section, we shall consider how we can adapt CVP analysis to a multi-product setting. Consider the situation described in Example 8.2. You will see that there are two types of fixed costs. Direct avoidable fixed costs can be specifically identified with each product and would not be incurred if the product was not made. For example, the deluxe and standard machines might be produced in different departments and the departmental supervisors fixed salaries would represent fixed costs directly attributable to each machine. The common fixed costs relate to the costs of common facilities (e.g. factory rent) that cannot be specifically identified with either of the products since they can only be avoided if *both* products are not sold.

EXAMPLE 8.2

The Super Bright Company sells two types of washing machine – a deluxe model and a standard model. The financial controller has prepared the following information based on the sales forecast for the period:

Sales volume (units)	Deluxe machine 1200 (£)	Standard machine 600 (£)	Total (£)
Unit selling price	300	200	
Unit variable cost	150	110	
Unit contribution	150	90	
Total sales revenues	360 000	120 000	480 000
Less: Total variable cost	180 000	66 000	246 000
Contribution to direct and common fixed costs[a]	180 000	54 000	234 000
Less: Direct avoidable fixed costs	90 000	27 000	117 000
Contribution to common fixed costs[a]	90 000	27 000	117 000
Less common (indirect) fixed costs			39 000
Operating profit			78 000

The common fixed costs relate to the costs of common facilities and can only be avoided if neither of the products is sold. The managing director is concerned that sales may be less than forecast and has requested information relating to the break-even point for the activities for the period.

Note

[a]Contribution was defined earlier in this chapter as sales less variable costs. Where fixed costs are divided into direct and common (indirect) fixed costs it is possible to identify two separate contribution categories. The first is described as contribution to direct and common fixed costs and this is identical to the conventional definition, being equivalent to sales less variable costs. The second is after a further deduction of direct fixed costs and is described as 'contribution to common or indirect fixed costs'.

You might think that the break-even point for the firm as a whole can be derived if we allocate the common fixed costs to each individual product. However, this approach is inappropriate because the allocation will be arbitrary. The common fixed costs cannot be specifically identified with either of the products and can only be avoided if *both* products are not sold. The solution to our problem is to convert the sales volume measure of the individual products into standard batches of products based on the planned sales mix. You will see from Example 8.2 that Super Bright plans to sell 1200 deluxe and 600 standard machines giving a sales mix of 1200:600. Reducing this sales mix to the smallest whole number gives a mix of 2:1. In other words, for the sale of every two deluxe machines one standard machine is expected to be sold. We therefore define our standard batch of products as comprising two deluxe and one standard machine giving a contribution of £390 per batch (two deluxe machines at a contribution of £150 per unit sold plus one standard machine at a contribution of £90).

The break-even point in standard batches can be calculated by using the same break-even equation that we used for a single product, so that:

$$\text{Break-even number of batches} = \frac{\text{Total fixed costs (£156 000)}}{\text{Contribution margin per batch (£390)}}$$
$$= 400 \text{ batches}$$

The sales mix used to define a standard batch (2:1) can now be used to convert the break-even point (measured in standard batches) into a break-even point expressed in terms of the required combination of individual products sold. Thus, 800 deluxe machines (2 × 400) and 400 (1 × 400) standard machines must be sold to break even. The following profit statement verifies this outcome:

Units sold	Deluxe machine 800 (£)	Standard machine 400 (£)	Total (£)
Unit contribution margin	150	90	
Contribution to direct and common fixed costs	120 000	36 000	156 000
Less: Direct fixed costs	90 000	27 000	117 000
Contribution to common fixed costs	30 000	9 000	39 000
Less: Common fixed costs			39 000
Operating profit			0

Let us now assume that the actual sales volume for the period was 1200 units, the same total volume as the break-even volume, but consisting of a sales mix of 600 units of each machine. Thus, the actual sales mix is 1:1 compared with a planned sales mix of 2:1. The total contribution to direct and common fixed costs will be £144 000 ([£150 × 600 for deluxe] + [£90 × 600 for standard]) and a loss of £12 000 (£144 000 contribution − £156 000 total fixed costs) will occur. It should now be apparent to you that *the break-even point (or the sales volumes required to achieve a target profit) is not a unique number: it varies depending on the composition of the sales mix*. Because the actual sales mix differs from the planned sales mix, the sales mix used to define a standard batch has changed from 2:1 to 1:1 and the contribution per batch changes from £390 to £240 ([1 × £150] + [1 × £90]). This means that the revised break-even point will be 650 batches (£156 000 total fixed costs/£240 contribution per batch), which converts to a sales volume of 650 units of each machine based on a 1:1 sales mix. Generally, an increase in the proportion of sales of higher contribution margin products will decrease the break-even point whereas increases in sales of the lower margin products will increase the break-even point.

OPERATING LEVERAGE

Companies can sometimes influence the proportion of fixed and variable expenses in their cost structures. For example, they may choose to rely heavily either on automated facilities (involving high fixed and low variable costs) or on manual systems (involving high variable costs and low fixed costs). The chosen cost structure can have a significant impact on profits. Consider the situation presented in Exhibit 8.1 where the managers of an airline company are considering an investment in automated ticketing equipment.

You will see from Exhibit 8.1 that it is unclear which system should be chosen. If periodic sales exceed £960 000, the automated system will result in higher profits. Automation enables the company to lower its variable costs by increasing fixed costs. This cost structure results in greater increases in profits as sales increase compared with the manual system. Unfortunately, it is also true that a high fixed cost and lower variable cost structure will result in a greater reduction in profits as sales decrease. The term operating leverage is used as a measure of the sensitivity of profits to changes in sales. The greater the degree of operating leverage, the more that changes in sales activity will affect profits. The degree of operating leverage can be measured for a given level of sales by the following formula:

$$\text{Degree of operating leverage} = \text{Contribution margin}/\text{Profit}$$

REAL WORLD VIEWS 8.4

Operating leverage captures relationships

Operating leverage can tell investors a lot about a company's risk profile, and although high operating leverage can often benefit companies, firms with high operating leverage are also vulnerable to sharp economic and business cycle swings. In good times, high operating leverage can supercharge profit. But companies with a lot of costs tied up in machinery, plants, real estate and distribution networks cannot easily cut expenses to adjust to a change in demand. So, if there is a downturn in the economy, earnings do not just fall, they can plummet.

Consider the software developer Inktomi. During the 1990s investors marvelled at the nature of its software business. The company spent tens of millions of dollars to develop each of its digital delivery and storage software programs. But thanks to the internet, Inktomi's software could be distributed to customers at almost no cost. In other words, the company had close to zero cost of goods sold. After its fixed development costs were recovered, each additional sale was almost pure profit.

After the collapse of dotcom technology market demand in 2000, Inktomi suffered the dark side of operating leverage. As sales took a nosedive, profits swung dramatically to a staggering $58 million loss in a single quarter – plunging down from the $1 million profit the company had enjoyed in Q1 of the previous year. The high leverage involved in counting on sales to repay fixed costs can put companies and their shareholders at risk. High operating leverage during a downturn (such as the recession following the 2008 financial crisis) can be an Achilles heel, putting pressure on profit margins and making a contraction in earnings unavoidable.

Indeed, companies such as Inktomi with high operating leverage typically have larger volatility in their operating earnings and share prices. As a result, investors need to treat these companies with caution.

Question

1 Provide examples of other companies that have high and low degrees of operating leverage.

Reference

www.investopedia.com/articles/stocks/06/opleverage.asp

The degree of operating leverage in Exhibit 8.1 for sales of £1 million is 7 (£700 000/£100 000) for the automated system and 2.5 (£200 000/£80 000) for the manual system. This means that profits change by seven times more than the change in sales for the automated system and 2.5 times for the manual system. Thus, for a 10 per cent increase in sales from £1 million to £1.1 million, profits increase by 70 per cent for the automated system (from £100 000 to £170 000) and by 25 per cent for the manual system (from £80 000 to £100 000). In contrast, you will see in Exhibit 8.1 that if sales decline by 10 per cent from £1 million to £0.9 million, profits decrease by 70 per cent (from £100 000 to £30 000) for the automated system and by 25 per cent from (£80 000 to £60 000) for the manual system.

The degree of operating leverage provides useful information for the airline company in choosing between the two systems. Higher degrees of operating leverage can provide significantly greater profits when sales are increasing but higher percentage decreases will also occur when sales are declining. Higher operating leverage also results in a greater volatility in profits. The manual system has a break-even point of £600 000 sales (£120 000 fixed expenses/PV ratio of 0.2) whereas the break-even point for the automated system is £857 143 (£600 000 fixed expenses/PV ratio of 0.7). Thus, the automated system has a lower margin of safety. High operating leverage leads to higher risk arising from the greater volatility of profits and higher break-even point. Contrariwise, the increase in risk provides the potential for higher profit levels (as long as sales exceed £960 000). We can conclude that if management is confident that sales will exceed £960 000, the automated system is preferable.

It is apparent from the above discussion that labour intensive organizations, such as McDonald's and Pizza Hut have high variable costs and low fixed costs, and thus have low operating leverage. These companies can continue to report profits even when they experience wide fluctuations in sales levels.

EXHIBIT 8.1 Sensitivity of profits arising from changes in sales for an automated and manual system

An airline company is considering investing in automated ticketing equipment. The estimated sales revenues and costs for the current manual system and the proposed automated system for a typical period are as follows:

	Automated system (£)		Manual system (£)	
Sales revenue	1 000 000		1 000 000	
Less: Variable expenses	300 000		800 000	
Contribution	700 000	(70%)	200 000	(20%)
Less: Fixed expenses	600 000		120 000	
Profit	100 000		80 000	

The above cost structure suggests that the automated system yields the higher profits. However, if sales decline by 10 per cent the following calculations show that the manual system will result in the higher profits:

	Automated system (£)		Manual system (£)	
Sales revenue	900 000		900 000	
Less: Variable expenses	270 000		720 000	
Contribution	630 000	(70%)	180 000	(20%)
Less: Fixed expenses	600 000		120 000	
Profit	30 000		60 000	

What will happen if sales are 10 per cent higher than the predicted sales for the period?

	Automated system (£)		Manual system (£)	
Sales revenue	1 100 000		1 100 000	
Less: Variable expenses	330 000		880 000	
Contribution	770 000	(70%)	220 000	(20%)
Less: Fixed expenses	600 000		120 000	
Profit	170 000		100 000	

The sales revenue where both systems result in the same profits is £960 000. The automated system yields higher profits when periodic sales revenue exceeds £960 000 whereas the manual system gives higher profits when sales revenue is below £960 000.[a]

	Automated system (£)		Manual system (£)	
Sales revenue	960 000		960 000	
Less: Variable expenses	288 000		768 000	
Contribution	672 000	(70%)	192 000	(20%)
Less: Fixed expenses	600 000		120 000	
Profit	72 000		72 000	

Note

[a]The profit–volume ratio is 0.7 for the automated system and 0.2 for the manual system. Let x = periodic sales revenue: the indifference point is where $0.7x - £600 000 = 0.2x - £120 000$, so $x = £960 000$.

Conversely, organizations that are highly capital intensive, such as easyJet and Volkswagen, have high operating leverage. These companies must generate high sales volumes to cover fixed costs, but sales above the break-even point produce high profits. In general, these companies tend to be more vulnerable to sharp economic and business cycle swings.

COST–VOLUME–PROFIT ANALYSIS ASSUMPTIONS

It is essential that anyone preparing or interpreting CVP information is aware of the underlying assumptions on which the information has been prepared. If these assumptions are not recognized, or the analysis is modified, errors may result and incorrect conclusions may be drawn from the analysis. We shall now consider these important assumptions. They are as follows:

1 All other variables remain constant.

2 A single product or constant sales mix.

3 Total costs and total revenue are linear functions of output.

4 Profits are calculated on a variable costing basis.

5 Costs can be accurately divided into their fixed and variable elements.

6 The analysis applies only to the relevant range.

7 The analysis applies only to a short-term time horizon.

1 All other variables remain constant

It has been assumed that all variables other than the particular one under consideration have remained constant throughout the analysis. In other words, it is assumed that volume is the only factor that will cause costs and revenues to change. However, changes in other variables such as production efficiency, sales mix and price levels can have an important influence on sales revenue and costs. If significant changes in these other variables occur, the CVP analysis presentation will be incorrect and it will be necessary to revise the CVP calculations based on the projected changes to the other variables.

2 Single product or constant sales mix

CVP analysis assumes that either a single product is sold or, if a range of products is sold, that sales will be in accordance with a predetermined sales mix. When a predetermined sales mix is used, it can be depicted in the CVP analysis by measuring sales volume using standard batch sizes based on a planned sales mix. As we have discussed, any CVP analysis must be interpreted carefully if the initial product mix assumptions do not hold.

3 Total costs and total revenue are linear functions of output

The analysis assumes that unit variable cost and selling price are constant. This assumption is only likely to be valid within the relevant range of production described earlier in this chapter.

4 Profits are calculated on a variable costing basis

The analysis assumes that the fixed costs incurred during the period are charged as an expense for that period. Therefore variable-costing profit calculations are assumed. If absorption-costing profit calculations are used, it is necessary to assume that production is equal to sales for the analysis to predict absorption costing profits. For the application of CVP analysis with an absorption costing system, you should refer to Learning Note 8.1 on the dedicated digital support resources (see Preface for details).

5 Costs can be accurately divided into their fixed and variable elements

CVP analysis assumes that costs can be accurately analysed into their fixed and variable elements. In practice, you will see in Chapter 24 that the separation of semi-variable costs into their fixed and variable elements is extremely difficult. Nevertheless, a reasonably accurate analysis is necessary if CVP analysis is to provide relevant information for decision-making.

6 Analysis applies only to the relevant range

Earlier in this chapter we noted that CVP analysis is appropriate only for decisions taken within the relevant production range and that it is incorrect to project cost and revenue figures beyond the relevant range.

7 Analysis applies only to a short-term time horizon

CVP analysis is based on the relationship between volume and sales revenue, costs and profit in the short run, typically a period of one year, in which the output of a firm is likely to be restricted to that available from the current operating capacity. During this period significant changes cannot be made to selling prices and fixed and variable costs. CVP analysis thus examines the effects of changes in sales volume on the level of profits in the short run. It is inappropriate to extend the analysis to long-term decision-making.

THE IMPACT OF INFORMATION TECHNOLOGY

The output from a CVP model is only as good as the input. The analysis will include assumptions about sales mix, production efficiency, price levels, total fixed costs, variable costs and selling price per unit. In practice, estimates regarding these variables will be subject to varying degrees of uncertainty.

Sensitivity analysis is one approach for coping with changes in the values of the variables. Sensitivity analysis focuses on how a result will be changed if the original estimates or the underlying assumptions change. With regard to CVP analysis, sensitivity analysis answers questions such as the following:

1 What will the profit be if the sales mix changes from that originally predicted?
2 What will the profit be if fixed costs increase by 10 per cent and variable costs decline by 5 per cent?

Today's information technology enables management accountants to build CVP computerized models and consider alternative plans by keying the information into a computer, which can quickly show changes both graphically and numerically. Thus, managers can study various combinations of change in selling prices, fixed costs, variable costs and product mix and can react quickly without waiting for formal reports from the management accountant.

SUMMARY

The following items relate to the learning objectives listed at the beginning of the chapter.

- **Justify the use of linear cost and revenue functions.**

Within the relevant range, it is generally assumed that cost and revenue functions are approximately linear. Outside the relevant range linearity is unlikely to apply. Care is therefore required in interpreting CVP relationships outside the relevant range.

- **Apply the numerical approach to answer questions similar to those listed in Example 8.1.**

In Example 8.1, the break-even point was derived by dividing fixed costs by the contribution per unit. To ascertain the number of units sold to achieve a target profit, the sum of the fixed costs and the target profit is divided by the contribution per unit.

- **Construct break-even, contribution and profit–volume graphs.**

Managers may obtain a clearer understanding of CVP behaviour if the information is presented in graphical format. With the break-even chart, the fixed costs are plotted as a single horizontal line. The total cost line is plotted by adding variable costs to fixed costs. The reverse situation applies with a contribution graph. The variable costs are plotted first and the fixed costs are added to variable costs to plot the total cost line. Because fixed costs are assumed to be a constant sum throughout the output range, the total cost line is drawn parallel to the variable cost line. The break-even and contribution graphs do not highlight the profit or loss at different output levels and must be ascertained by comparing the differences between the total cost and total revenue lines. The profit–volume graph shows the impact of changes in volume on profits. The profits and losses are plotted for each of the various sales levels and these are connected by a profit line. You should refer to Figures 8.4–8.6 for an illustration of the graphs.

- **Apply cost–volume–profit analysis in a multi-product setting.**

Multi-product CVP analysis requires that an assumption is made concerning the expected sales mix. The approach that is used is to convert the multi-product CVP analysis into a single product analysis based on the assumption that output consists of standard batches of the multiple products based on the expected sales mix. However, you should note that the answers change as the sales mix changes.

- **Explain the meaning of operating leverage and describe how it influences profits.**

Operating leverage measures the sensitivity of profits in relation to fluctuations in sales. It is measured by dividing total contribution by total profit. An operating leverage of four indicates that profits change by four times more than the change in sales. Therefore, if sales increase/decrease by 10 per cent, profits will increase/decrease by 40 per cent. High levels of operating leverage lead to higher risk arising from highly volatile profits but the increase in risk also provides the potential for higher profit levels when sales are expanding.

- **Identify and explain the assumptions on which cost–volume–profit analysis is based.**

Cost–volume–profit analysis is based on the following assumptions: (a) all variables, other than volume, remain constant; (b) the sales mix remains constant; (c) total costs and revenues are linear functions of output; (d) profits are calculated on a variable costing basis; (e) the analysis applies only to the relevant range; (f) the analysis applies only to a short-term horizon; and (g) costs can be accurately divided into their fixed and variable elements. The techniques that can be used to divide costs into their fixed and variable elements are explained in Chapter 24 in Part Six of this book which focuses on the application of quantitative methods to management accounting. Alternatively, if you require a knowledge of cost estimation techniques now you may prefer to read Chapter 24 immediately after you have completed this chapter.

KEY TERMS AND CONCEPTS

Break-even chart A chart that plots total costs and total revenues against sales volume and indicates the break-even point.

Break-even point The level of output at which costs are balanced by sales revenue and neither a profit nor a loss will occur.

Contribution graph A graph that plots variable costs and total costs against sales volume and fixed costs represent the difference between the total cost line and the variable cost line.

Contribution margin The margin calculated by deducting variable expenses from sales revenue.

Contribution margin ratio The proportion of sales available to cover fixed costs and provide for profit, calculated by dividing the contribution margin by the sales revenue, also known as profit–volume ratio.

Decreasing returns to scale A situation that arises when unit costs rise as volume increases.

Degree of operating leverage The contribution margin divided by the profit for a given level of sales.

Increasing returns to scale A situation that arises when unit costs fall as volume increases.

Margin of safety The amount by which sales may decrease before a loss occurs.

Operating leverage A measure of the sensitivity of profits to changes in sales.

Profit–volume graph A graph that plots profit/losses against volume.

Profit–volume ratio The proportion of sales available to cover fixed costs and provide for profit, calculated by dividing the contribution margin by the sales revenue, also known as contribution margin ratio.

Relevant range The output range at which an organization expects to be operating with a short-term planning horizon.

Sensitivity analysis Analysis that shows how a result will be changed if the original estimates or underlying assumption changes.

RECOMMENDED READING

For additional reading relating to CVP analysis, you should refer to an article that can be accessed from the ACCA Student Accountant www.accaglobal.com/gb /en/student/exam-support-resources/fundamentals -exams-study-resources/f2/technical-articles.html

KEY EXAMINATION POINTS

Students tend to experience little difficulty in preparing break-even charts, but many cannot construct profit–volume charts. Remember that the horizontal axis represents the level of activity, while profit/losses are shown on the vertical axis. The maximum loss is at zero activity, and is equal to fixed costs. For practice on preparing a profit–volume chart, you should attempt Review problem 8.16 and compare your answer with the solution. Students also experience difficulty with the following:

1 coping with multi-product situations;

2 calculating the break-even point when total sales and costs are given but no information is given on the unit costs;

3 explaining the assumptions of CVP analysis.

For multi-product situations you should base your answer on the average contribution per unit, using the approach shown in Example 8.2. Review problem 8.19 requires the computation of a break-even point in a multi-product setting. When unit costs are not given, the break-even point in sales value can be calculated as follows:

$$\text{Fixed costs} \times \frac{\text{total estimated sales}}{\text{total estimated contribution}}$$

or

$$\frac{\text{Fixed costs}}{\text{Profit/volume ratio}}$$

You should refer to the solutions to Review problem 8.17 for an illustration of the application of the above approach. Sometimes questions will give details of costs but not the split into the fixed and variable elements. You can separate the total costs into their fixed and variable elements using the high–low method described in Chapter 24. This approach is required for Review problem 8.17.

ASSESSMENT MATERIAL

The review questions are short questions that enable you to assess your understanding of the main topics included in the chapter. The numbers in parentheses provide you with the page numbers to refer to if you cannot answer a specific question.

The review problems are more complex and require you to relate and apply the content to various business problems. The problems are graded by their level of difficulty. Solutions to review problems that are not preceded by the term 'IM' are provided in a separate section at the end of the book. Solutions to problems preceded by the term 'IM' are provided in the Instructor's Manual accompanying this book that can be downloaded from the lecturer's digital support resources. Additional review problems with fully worked solutions are provided in the *Student Manual* that accompanies this book.

REVIEW QUESTIONS

8.1 Provide examples of how cost–volume–profit analysis can be used for decision-making. (p. 172)

8.2 Explain what is meant by the term 'relevant range'. (pp. 174–175)

8.3 Define the term 'contribution margin'. (p. 176)

8.4 Define the term 'profit–volume ratio' and explain how it can be used for cost–volume–profit analysis. (p. 178)

8.5 Describe and distinguish between the three different approaches to presenting cost–volume–profit relationships in graphical format. (pp. 180–182)

8.6 How can a company with multiple products use cost–volume–profit analysis? (pp. 182–184)

8.7 Explain why the break-even point changes when there is a change in sales mix. (p. 184)

8.8 Describe the assumptions underlying cost–volume–profit analysis. (pp. 187–188)

8.9 Define the term 'operating leverage' and explain how the degree of operating leverage can influence future profits. (pp. 184–187)

8.10 How can sensitivity analysis be used in conjunction with cost–volume–profit analysis? (p. 188)

REVIEW PROBLEMS

8.11 **Basic.** Z plc currently sells products Aye, Bee and Cee in equal quantities and at the same selling price per unit. The contribution to sales ratio for product Aye is 40 per cent; for product Bee it is 50 per cent and the total is 48 per cent. If fixed costs are unaffected by mix and are currently 20 per cent of sales, the effect of changing the product mix to:

Aye 40%
Bee 25%
Cee 35%

is that the total contribution/total sales ratio changes to:

(a) 27.4%
(b) 45.3%
(c) 47.4%
(d) 48.4%
(e) 68.4%

CIMA Stage 2

8.12 **Intermediate.** A company's budget for the next period shows that it would break even at sales revenue of $800 000 and fixed costs of $320 000.

The sales revenue needed to achieve a profit of $200 000 in the next period would be:

(a) $1 000 000
(b) $1 300 000
(c) $1 320 000
(d) $866 667　　　　　　　　　*(2 marks)*

CIMA P1 Performance Operations

8.13 **Intermediate.** RT plc sells three products.

Product R has a contribution to sales ratio of 30%.
Product S has a contribution to sales ratio of 20%.
Product T has a contribution to sales ratio of 25%.

Monthly fixed costs are £100 000. If the products are sold in the ratio:

R: 2 S: 5 T: 3

the monthly break-even sales revenue, to the nearest £1, is:

(a) £400 000
(b) £411 107
(c) £425 532
(d) impossible to calculate without further information.　　　　　*(2 marks)*

CIMA Management Accounting – Performance Management

8.14 **Intermediate.** A company manufactures a single product. Budget and standard cost details for next year include:

Selling price per unit	$24.00
Variable production cost per unit	$8.60
Fixed production costs	$650 000
Fixed selling and distribution costs	$230 400
Sales commission	5% of selling price
Sales	90 000 units

Required:

(i) Calculate the break-even point in units.

(ii) Calculate the percentage by which the budgeted sales can fall before the company begins to make a loss.

The marketing manager has suggested that the selling price per unit can be increased to $25.00 if the sales commission is increased to 8 per cent of selling price and a further $10 000 is spent on advertising.

(iii) Calculate the revised break-even point based on the marketing manager's suggestion.   *(5 marks)*

CIMA P1 Performance Operations

8.15 Intermediate. A break-even chart is shown below for Windhurst Ltd.

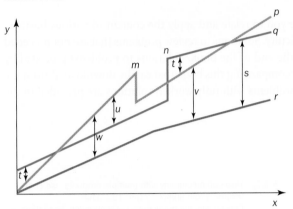

You are required:

(i) to identify the components of the break-even chart labelled p, q, r, s, t, u, v, w, x and y;   *(5 marks)*

(ii) to suggest what events are represented at the values of x that are labelled m and n on the chart;   *(3 marks)*

(iii) to assess the usefulness of break-even analysis to senior management of a small company.   *(7 marks)*

ICAEW Management Accounting

8.16 Intermediate: Preparation of break-even and profit–volume graphs. ZED plc manufactures one standard product, which sells at £10. You are required to:

(a) prepare from the data given below, a break-even and profit–volume graph showing the results for the six months ending 30 April and to determine:

(i) the fixed costs;

(ii) the variable cost per unit;

(iii) the profit–volume ratio;

(iv) the break-even point;

(v) the margin of safety;

Month	Sales (units)	Profit/(loss) (£)
November	30000	40000
December	35000	60000
January	15000	(20000)
February	24000	16000
March	26000	24000
April	18000	(8000)

(b) discuss the limitations of such a graph;

(c) explain the use of the relevant range in such a graph.   *(20 marks)*

CIMA Cost Accounting 2

8.17 Intermediate: Preparation of a contribution graph. Z plc operates a single retail outlet selling direct to the public. Profit statements for August and September are as follows:

	August	September
Sales	80000	90000
Cost of sales	50000	55000
Gross profit	30000	35000

Less:		
Selling and distribution	8000	9000
Administration	15000	15000
Net profit	7000	11000

Required:

(a) Use the high–low method (see Chapter 24 for an explanation) to identify the behaviour of:

(i) cost of sales;

(ii) selling and distribution costs;

(iii) administration costs.   *(4 marks)*

(b) Draw a contribution break-even chart and identify the monthly break-even sales value and area of contribution.   *(10 marks)*

(c) Assuming a margin of safety equal to 30 per cent of the break-even value, calculate Z plc's annual profit.   *(2 marks)*

(d) Z plc is now considering opening another retail outlet selling the same products. Z plc plans to use the same profit margins in both outlets and has estimated that the specific fixed costs of the second outlet will be £100000 per annum.

Z plc also expects that 10 per cent of its annual sales from its existing outlet would transfer to this second outlet if it were to be opened.

Calculate the annual value of sales required from the new outlet in order to achieve the same annual profit as previously obtained from the single outlet.   *(5 marks)*

(e) Briefly describe the cost accounting requirements of organizations of this type.   *(4 marks)*

Chartered Institute of Management Accountants Operational Cost Accounting Stage 2

8.18 Intermediate: Preparation of a break-even chart with step fixed costs. Toowomba manufactures various products and uses CVP analysis to establish the minimum level of production to ensure profitability.

Fixed costs of £50000 have been allocated to a specific product but are expected to increase to £100000 once production exceeds 30000 units, as a new factory will need to be rented in order to produce the extra units. Variable costs per unit are stable at £5 per unit over all levels of activity. Revenue from this product will be £7.50 per unit.

Required:

(a) Formulate the equations for the total cost at:

(i) less than or equal to 30000 units;

(ii) more than 30000 units.   *(2 marks)*

(b) Prepare a break-even chart and clearly identify the break-even point or points.   *(6 marks)*

(c) Discuss the implications of the results from your graph in (b) with regard to Toowomba's production plans.   *(2 marks)*

ACCA Paper 1.2 – Financial Information for Management

8.19 Intermediate: Multi-product CVP analysis. Cardio Co manufactures three types of fitness equipment: treadmills (T), cross-trainers (C) and rowing machines (R). The budgeted sales prices and volumes for the next year are as follows:

	T	C	R
Selling price	$1600	$1800	$1400
Units	420	400	380

The standard cost card for each product is shown below.

	T ($)	C ($)	R ($)
Material	430	500	360
Labour	220	240	190
Variable overheads	110	120	95

Labour costs are 60 per cent fixed and 40 per cent variable. General fixed overheads excluding any fixed labour costs are expected to be $55000 for the next year.

Required:

(a) Calculate the weighted average contribution to sales ratio for Cardio Co. *(4 marks)*

(b) Calculate the margin of safety in $ revenue for Cardio Co. *(3 marks)*

(c) Using the graph paper provided and assuming that the products are sold in a CONSTANT MIX, draw a multi-product break even chart for Cardio Co. Label fully both axes, any lines drawn on the graph and the break even point. *(6 marks)*

(d) Explain what would happen to the break even point if the products were sold in order of the most profitable products first.

Note: You are NOT required to demonstrate this on the graph drawn in part (c). *(2 marks)*

ACCA F5 Performance Management

8.20 Intermediate: Non-graphical CVP behaviour. Tweed Ltd is a company engaged solely in the manufacture of sweaters, which are bought mainly for sporting activities. Present sales are direct to retailers, but in recent years there has been a steady decline in output because of increased foreign competition. In the last trading year the accounting report indicated that the company produced the lowest profit for ten years. The forecast for next year indicates that the present deterioration in profits is likely to continue. The company considers that a profit of £80000 should be achieved to provide an adequate return on capital. The managing director has asked that a review be made of the present pricing and marketing policies. The marketing director has completed this review, and passes the proposals on to you for evaluation and recommendation, together with the profit and loss account for year ending 31 December last year.

Tweed Ltd profit and loss account for year ending 31 December

	(£)	(£)	(£)
Sales revenue			
(100000 sweaters at £10)			1000000
Factory cost of goods sold:			
Direct materials	100000		
Direct labour	350000		
Variable factory overheads	60000		
Fixed factory overheads	220000	730000	
Administration overhead		140000	
Selling and distribution overhead			
Sales commission (2% of sales)	20000		
Delivery costs (variable per unit sold)	50000		
Fixed costs	40000	110000	980000
Profit			20000

The information to be submitted to the managing director includes the following three proposals:

(i) To proceed on the basis of analyses of market research studies which indicate that the demand for the sweaters is such that a 10 per cent reduction in selling price would increase demand by 40 per cent.

(ii) To proceed with an enquiry that the marketing director has had from a mail order company about the possibility of purchasing 50000 units annually if the selling price is right. The mail order company would transport the sweaters from Tweed Ltd to its own warehouse and no sales commission would be paid on these sales by Tweed Ltd. However, if an acceptable price can be negotiated, Tweed Ltd would be expected to contribute £60000 per annum towards the cost of producing the mail order catalogue. It would also be necessary for Tweed Ltd to provide special additional packaging at a cost of £0.50 per sweater. The marketing director considers that for the next year sales from existing business would remain unchanged at 100000 units, based on a selling price of £10 if the mail order contract is undertaken.

(iii) To proceed on the basis of a view by the marketing director that a 10 per cent price reduction, together with a national advertising campaign costing £30000 may increase sales to the maximum capacity of 160000 sweaters.

Required:

(a) The calculation of break-even sales value based on the accounts for last year.

(b) A financial evaluation of proposal (i) and a calculation of the number of units Tweed Ltd would need to sell at £9 each to earn the target profit of £80000.

(c) A calculation of the minimum prices that would have to be quoted to the mail order company, first, to ensure that Tweed Ltd would, at least, break even on the mail order contract, second, to ensure that the same overall profit is earned as proposal (i) and, third, to ensure that the overall target profit is earned.

(d) A financial evaluation of proposal (iii).

IM8.1 Intermediate. Shown below is a typical cost–volume–profit chart:

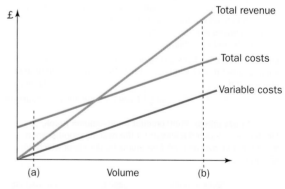

Required:

(a) Explain to a colleague who is not an accountant the reasons for the change in result on this cost–volume–profit chart from a loss at point (a) to a profit at point (b). *(3 marks)*

(b) Identify and critically examine the underlying assumptions of this type of cost–volume–profit analysis and consider whether such analyses are useful to the management of an organization. *(14 marks)*
(Total 17 marks)

ACCA Level 1 Costing

IM8.2 Intermediate. The graphs shown below show cost–volume–profit relationships as they are typically represented in (i) management accounting and (ii) economic theory. In each graph, T = total revenue, TC = total cost, and P = profit. You are required to compare these different representations of cost–volume–profit relationships, identifying, explaining and commenting on points of similarity and also differences.

(15 marks)

ICAEW Management Accounting

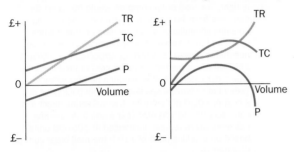

IM8.3 Intermediate. 'A break-even chart must be interpreted in the light of the limitations of its underlying assumptions …'
(From *Cost Accounting: A Managerial Emphasis,* by C.T. Horngren.)

Required:

(a) Discuss the extent to which the above statement is valid and both describe and briefly appraise the reasons for five of the most important underlying assumptions of break-even analysis. *(14 marks)*

(b) For any *three* of the underlying assumptions provided in answer to (a) above, give an example of circumstances in which that assumption is violated. Indicate the nature of the violation and the extent to which the break-even chart can be adapted to allow for this violation. *(6 marks)*

ACCA P2 Management Accounting

IM8.4 Advanced. The accountant's approach to cost–volume–profit analysis has been criticized in that, among other matters, it does not deal with the following:

(a) situations where sales volume differs radically from production volume;

(b) situations where the sales revenue and the total cost functions are markedly non-linear;

(c) changes in product mix;

(d) risk and uncertainty.

Explain these objections to the accountant's conventional cost–volume–profit model and suggest how they can be overcome or ameliorated. *(17 marks)*

ACCA Level 2 Management Accounting

IM8.5 Intermediate: Multi-product profit–volume graph. JK Limited has prepared a budget for the next 12 months when it intends to make and sell four products, details of which are shown below:

Product	Sales in units (thousands)	Selling price per unit (£)	Variable cost per unit (£)
J	10	20	14.00
K	10	40	8.00
L	50	4	4.20
M	20	10	7.00

Budgeted fixed costs are £240 000 per annum and total assets employed are £570 000. You are required:

(a) to calculate the total contribution earned by each product and their combined total contributions; *(2 marks)*

(b) to plot the data of your answer to (a) above in the form of a contribution to sales graph (sometimes referred to as a profit–volume graph) on the graph paper provided; *(6 marks)*

(c) to explain your graph to management, to comment on the results shown and to state the break-even point; *(4 marks)*

(d) to describe briefly three ways in which the overall contribution to sales ratio could be improved. *(3 marks)*

CIMA Stage 2 Cost Accounting

IM8.6 Intermediate: Break-even chart with increases in fixed costs.

(a) Identify and discuss briefly *five* assumptions underlying cost–volume–profit analysis. *(10 marks)*

(b) A local authority, whose area includes a holiday resort situated on the east coast, operates, for 30 weeks each year, a holiday home which is let to visiting parties of children in care from other authorities. The children are accompanied by their own house mothers who supervise them throughout their holiday. From six to 15 guests are accepted on terms of £100 per person per week. No differential charges exist for adults and children.

Weekly costs incurred by the host authority are:

	(£ per guest)
Food	25
Electricity for heating and cooking	3
Domestic (laundry, cleaning etc.) expenses	5
Use of minibus	10

Seasonal staff supervise and carry out the necessary duties at the home at a cost of £11 000 for the 30-week period. This provides staffing sufficient for six to ten guests per week but if 11 or more guests are to be accommodated, additional staff at a total cost of £200 per week are engaged for the whole of the 30-week period.

Rent, including rates for the property, is £4000 per annum and the garden of the home is maintained by the council's recreation department which charges a nominal fee of £1000 per annum.

You are required to:

(i) tabulate the appropriate figures in such a way as to show the break-even point(s) and to comment on your figures; *(8 marks)*

(ii) draw, on the graph paper provided, a chart to illustrate your answer to (b)(i) above. *(7 marks)*

CIMA Cost Accounting Stage 2

IM8.7 Intermediate: Analysis of costs into fixed and variable elements and break-even point calculation.

(a) 'The analysis of total cost into its behavioural elements is essential for effective cost and management accounting.'
Required:
Comment on the statement above, illustrating your answer with examples of cost behaviour patterns. *(5 marks)*

(b) The total costs incurred at various output levels, for a process operation in a factory, have been measured as follows:

Output (units)	Total cost (£)
11 500	102 476
12 000	104 730
12 500	106 263
13 000	108 021
13 500	110 727
14 000	113 201

Required:

Using the high–low method, analyse the costs of the process operation into fixed and variable components. *(4 marks)*

(c) Calculate, and comment on, the break-even output level of the process operation in (b) above, based on the fixed and variable costs identified and assuming a selling price of £10.60 per unit. *(5 marks)*

ACCA Foundation Paper 3

IM8.8 Intermediate: Non-graphical CVP analysis and the acceptance of a special order. Video Technology Plc was established in 1987 to assemble video cassette recorders (VCRs). There is now increased competition in its markets and the company expects to find it difficult to make an acceptable profit next year. You have been appointed as an accounting technician at the company, and have been given a copy of the draft budget for the next financial year.

Draft budget for 12 months to 30 November

	(£m)	(£m)
Sales income		960.0
Cost of sales:		
Variable assembly materials	374.4	
Variable labour	192.0	
Factory overheads – variable	172.8	
– fixed	43.0	(782.2)
		177.8
Gross profit		
Selling overheads – commission	38.4	
– fixed	108.0	
Administration overheads – fixed	20.0	(166.4)
Net profit		11.4

The following information is also supplied to you by the company's financial controller, Edward Davies:

1 planned sales for the draft budget in the year to 30 November are expected to be 25 per cent less than the total of 3.2 million VCR units sold in the previous financial year;

2 the company operates a just-in-time stock control system, which means it holds no stocks of any kind;

3 if more than three million VCR units are made and sold, the unit cost of material falls by £4 per unit;

4 sales commission is based on the number of units sold and not on turnover;

5 the draft budget assumes that the factory will only be working at two-thirds of maximum capacity;

6 sales above maximum capacity are not possible.

Edward Davies explains that the board is not happy with the profit projected in the draft budget, and that the sales director, Anne Williams, has produced three proposals to try and improve matters:

1 Proposal A involves launching an aggressive marketing campaign:

(i) this would involve a single additional fixed cost of £14 million for advertising;

(ii) there would be a revised commission payment of £18 per unit sold;

(iii) sales volume would be expected to increase by 10 per cent above the level projected in the draft budget, with no change in the unit selling price.

2 Proposal B involves a 5 per cent reduction in the unit selling price:

(i) this is estimated to bring the sales volume back to the level in the previous financial year.

3 Proposal C involves a 10 per cent reduction in the unit selling price:

(i) fixed selling overheads would also be reduced by £45 million;

(ii) if proposal C is accepted, the sales director believes sales volume will be 3.8 million units.

Task 1

(a) For each of the three proposals, calculate the:

(i) change in profits compared with the draft budget;

(ii) break-even point in units and turnover.

(b) Recommend which proposal, if any, should be accepted on financial grounds.

(c) Identify *three* non-financial issues to be considered before a final decision is made.

Edward Davies now tells you that the company is considering a new export order with a proposed selling price of £3 million. He provides you with the following information:

1 The order will require two types of material:

(i) material A is in regular use by the company. The amount in stock originally cost £0.85 million, but its standard cost is £0.9 million. The amount in stock is sufficient for the order. The current market price of material A to be used in the order is £0.8 million;

(ii) material B is no longer used by the company and cannot be used elsewhere if not used on the order. The amount in stock originally cost £0.2 million although its current purchase price is £0.3 million. The amount of material B in stock is only half the amount required on the order. If not used on the order, the amount in stock could be sold for £0.1 million;

2 Direct labour of £1.0 million will be charged to the order. This includes £0.2 million for idle time, as a result of insufficient orders to keep the workforce fully employed. The company has a policy of no redundancies and spreads the resulting cost of idle time across all orders.

3 Variable factory overheads are expected to be £0.9 million.

4 Fixed factory overheads are apportioned against the order at the rate of 50 per cent of variable factory overheads.

5 No sales commission will be paid.

Task 2

Prepare a memo for Edward Davies:

(a) showing whether or not the order should be accepted at the proposed selling price;

(b) identifying the technique(s) you have used in reaching this conclusion.

AAT Technicians Stage

IM8.9 Intermediate: Decision-making and non-graphical CVP analysis. York plc was formed three years ago by a group of research scientists to market a new medicine that they had developed. The technology involved in the medicine's manufacture is both complex and expensive. Because of this, the company is faced with a high level of fixed costs.

This is of particular concern to Dr Harper, the company's chief executive. She recently arranged a conference of all management staff to discuss company profitability. Dr Harper showed the managers how average unit cost fell as production volume increased and explained that this was due to the company's heavy fixed cost base. 'It is clear,' she said, 'that as we produce closer to the plant's maximum capacity of 70 000 packs the average cost per pack falls. Producing and selling as close to that limit as possible must be good for company profitability.' The data she used are reproduced below:

Production volume (packs)	40 000	50 000	60 000	70 000
Average cost per unit[a]	£430	£388	£360	£340
Current sales and production volume:	65 000 packs			
Selling price per pack:	£420			

[a]Defined as the total of fixed and variable costs, divided by the production volume.

You are a member of York plc's management accounting team and shortly after the conference you are called to a meeting with Ben Cooper, the company's marketing director. He is interested in knowing how profitability changes with production.

Task 1

Ben Cooper asks you to calculate:

(a) the amount of York plc's fixed costs;
(b) the profit of the company at its current sales volume of 65 000 packs;
(c) the break-even point in units;
(d) the margin of safety expressed as a percentage.

Ben Cooper now tells you of a discussion he has recently had with Dr Harper. Dr Harper had once more emphasized the need to produce as close as possible to the maximum capacity of 70 000 packs. Ben Cooper has the possibility of obtaining an export order for an extra 5000 packs but, because the competition is strong, the selling price would only be £330. Dr Harper has suggested that this order should be rejected as it is below cost and so will reduce company profitability. However, she would be prepared, on this occasion, to sell the packs on a cost basis for £340 each, provided the order was increased to 15 000 packs.

Task 2

Write a memo to Ben Cooper. Your memo should:

(a) calculate the change in profits from accepting the order for 5000 packs at £330;
(b) calculate the change in profits from accepting an order for 15 000 packs at £340;
(c) briefly explain and justify which proposal, if either, should be accepted;
(d) identify two non-financial factors that should be taken into account before making a final decision.

AAT Technicians Stage

IM8.10 Intermediate: Marginal costing and absorption costing profit computations and calculation of break-even point for a given sales mix. A company has two products with the following unit costs for a period:

	Product A (£/unit)	Product B (£/unit)
Direct materials	1.20	2.03
Direct labour	1.40	1.50
Variable production overheads	0.70	0.80
Fixed production overheads	1.10	1.10
Variable other overheads	0.15	0.20
Fixed other overheads	0.50	0.50

Production and sales of the two products for the period were:

	Product A (000 units)	Product B (000 units)
Production	250	100
Sales	225	110

Production was at normal levels. Unit costs in opening stock were the same as those for the period listed above.

Required:

(a) State whether, and why, absorption or marginal costing would show a higher company profit for the period, and calculate the difference in profit depending on which method is used.   *(4 marks)*
(b) Calculate the break-even sales revenue for the period (to the nearest £000) based on the above mix of sales. The selling prices of products A and B were £5.70 and £6.90 per unit, respectively.   *(7 marks)*

ACCA Foundation Stage Paper 3

IM8.11 Advanced: CVP analysis based on capacity usage in a leisure centre. A local government authority owns and operates a leisure centre with numerous sporting facilities, residential accommodation, a cafeteria and a sports shop. The summer season lasts for 20 weeks including a peak period of six weeks corresponding to the school holidays. The following budgets have been prepared for the next summer season:

Accommodation
60 single rooms let on a daily basis.
35 double rooms let on a daily basis at 160 per cent of the single room rate.
Fixed costs £29 900.
Variable costs £4 per single room per day and £6.40 per double room per day.

Sports centre
Residential guests each pay £2 per day and casual visitors £3 per day for the use of facilities.
Fixed costs £15 500.

Sports shop
Estimated contribution £1 per person per day.
Fixed costs £8250.

Cafeteria
Estimated contribution £1.50 per person per day.
Fixed costs £12 750.

During the summer season the centre is open seven days a week and the following activity levels are anticipated:
Double rooms fully booked for the whole season.
Single rooms fully booked for the peak period but at only 80 per cent of capacity during the rest of the season.
30 casual visitors per day on average.

You are required to:

(a) calculate the charges for single and double rooms assuming that the authority wishes to make a £10 000 profit on accommodation;
(b) calculate the anticipated total profit for the leisure centre as a whole for the season;   *(10 marks)*
(c) advise the authority whether an offer of £250 000 from a private leisure company to operate the centre for five years is worthwhile, assuming that the authority uses a 10 per cent cost of capital and operations continue as outlined above.   *(4 marks)*

CIMA Stage 3 Management Accounting Techniques

9

MEASURING RELEVANT COSTS AND REVENUES FOR DECISION-MAKING

LEARNING OBJECTIVES After studying this chapter, you should be able to:

- distinguish between relevant and irrelevant costs and revenues;

- explain the importance of qualitative factors;

- distinguish between the relevant and irrelevant costs and revenues for the five decision-making problems described;

- describe the key concept that should be applied for presenting information for product mix decisions when capacity constraints apply;

- explain why the book value of equipment is irrelevant when making equipment replacement decisions;

- describe the opportunity cost concept;

- explain the misconceptions relating to relevant costs and revenues.

The provision of relevant information for decision-making is one of the most important functions of management accounting. Decision-making involves choosing between alternatives. For example, managers may be faced with decisions as to whether to discontinue a product or a channel of distribution, make a component within the company or buy from an outside supplier, introduce a new product or service and/or replace existing equipment. Something that these decisions have in common is that they are not routine. When decisions of this kind are being considered, special studies are undertaken.

Making decisions requires that only those costs and revenues that are relevant to the alternatives are considered. If irrelevant cost and revenue data are included, the wrong decisions may be made. It is therefore essential to identify the relevant costs and revenues that are applicable to the alternatives being considered. The purpose of this chapter is to enable you to distinguish between relevant costs and revenues for various decision-making situations.

Special studies focus on whatever planning time horizon the decision-maker considers appropriate for a given situation. However, it is important not to focus excessively on the short term, because the objective is to maximize long-term benefits. We begin by explaining the concept of relevant cost and applying this principle to special studies relating to the following:

1 special selling price decisions;

2 product mix decisions when capacity constraints exist;

3 decisions on replacement of equipment;

4 outsourcing (make or buy) decisions;

5 discontinuation decisions.

IDENTIFYING RELEVANT COSTS AND REVENUES

The relevant costs and revenues required for decision-making are only those that will be affected by the decision. Costs and revenues that are independent of a decision are not relevant and need not be considered when making that decision. The relevant financial inputs for decision-making purposes are therefore future cash flows, which will differ between the various alternatives being considered. In other words, only differential (or incremental) cash flows should be taken into account, and cash flows that will be the same for all alternatives are irrelevant. To keep things simple, we shall focus on relevant costs. You should remember, however, that exactly the same principles apply to relevant revenues.

Because decision-making is concerned with choosing between future alternative courses of action, and nothing can be done to alter the past, past costs (also known as sunk costs) are not relevant for decision-making. In Chapter 2, it was pointed out that sunk costs have already been incurred and cannot be avoided, regardless of the alternatives being considered.

Allocated common fixed costs are also irrelevant for decision-making. Facility sustaining costs, such as general administrative and property costs, are examples of common costs. They are incurred to support the organization as a whole and generally will not change whichever alternative is chosen. They will only change if there is a dramatic change in organizational activity resulting in an expansion or contraction in the business facilities. Common fixed costs may be allocated (i.e. apportioned) to cost objects but they should be disregarded for decision-making. This is because decisions merely lead to a redistribution of the same sunk cost between cost objects – they do not affect the level of cost to the company as a whole.

We can illustrate the identification of relevant costs in a non-business setting. Consider a situation in which an individual is uncertain as to whether he or she should purchase a monthly rail ticket to travel to work or use the car. Assuming that the individual already owns and will keep the car, whether or not he or she travels to work by train, the cost of the road fund licence and insurance will be irrelevant. They are sunk costs and will remain the same irrespective of the mode of travel. The cost of fuel will, however, be relevant, because this is a future cost that will differ depending on which alternative method of transport is chosen.

The following general principles can therefore be applied in identifying relevant and irrelevant costs:

1 relevant costs are future costs that differ between alternatives;

2 irrelevant costs consist of sunk costs, allocated costs and future costs that do not differ between alternatives.

IMPORTANCE OF QUALITATIVE/NON-FINANCIAL FACTORS

In many situations, it is difficult to quantify all the important elements of a decision in monetary terms. Those factors that cannot be expressed in monetary terms are classified as qualitative or non-financial factors. An example might be the decline in employee morale that results from redundancies arising from a closure decision. It is essential that qualitative factors be brought to the attention of management during the decision-making process, because otherwise there may be a danger that a wrong decision will be made. For example, the cost of manufacturing a component internally may be more expensive than purchasing from an outside supplier. However, the decision to purchase from an outside supplier could result in the closing down of the company's facilities for manufacturing the component. The effect of such a decision might lead to redundancies and a decline in employee morale, which could affect future output. In addition, the company will now be at the mercy of the supplier who might seek to increase prices on subsequent contracts and/or may not always deliver on time. The company may not then be in a position to meet customers' requirements. In turn, this could result in a loss of customer goodwill and a decline in future sales.

Qualitative factors such as these must be taken into account in the decision-making process. Management must consider the availability of future supplies and the likely effect on customer goodwill if there is a delay in meeting orders. If the component can be obtained from many suppliers and repeat orders for the company's products from customers are unlikely, then the company may give little weighting to these qualitative factors. However, if the component can be obtained from only one supplier and the company relies heavily on repeat sales to existing customers, then the qualitative factors will be of considerable importance. In the latter situation, the company may consider that the quantifiable cost savings from purchasing the component from an outside supplier are insufficient to cover the risk of the qualitative factors occurring.

We shall now move on to apply the relevant cost approach to a variety of decision-making problems. We shall concentrate on measuring the financial outcomes but you should remember that they do not always provide the full story. Qualitative factors should also be taken into account in the decision-making process.

SPECIAL PRICING DECISIONS

Special pricing decisions relate to pricing decisions outside the main market. Typically, they involve one-time-only orders or orders at a price below the prevailing market price. Consider the information presented in Example 9.1.

At first glance, it looks as if the order should be rejected since the proposed selling price of £20 is less than the total unit cost of £33. A study of the cost estimates, however, indicates that for the next quarter direct labour will remain unchanged. It is therefore a fixed cost for the period under consideration. Manufacturing fixed overheads and the marketing and distribution costs are also fixed costs for the period under consideration. These costs will thus remain the same, irrespective of whether or not the order is accepted. Hence they are irrelevant for this decision. All of the variable costs (i.e. the direct material costs, variable manufacturing overheads and the cost of adding the leisure company's logo) will be different if the order is accepted. Therefore, they are relevant costs for making the decision. The relevant revenue and costs per unit for the decision are:

Selling price		20
Less: Direct materials	8	
Variable overheads	2	
Inserting company logo	1	11
Contribution to fixed costs and profit		9

For sales of 15000 sweaters, Caledonian will obtain an additional contribution of £135 000 per month (15000 × £9). In Example 9.1, none of the fixed costs is relevant for the decision. It is appropriate to unitize variable costs because they are constant per unit but fixed costs should not be unitized since (you will recall from Chapter 2) they are not constant per unit of output. You should present unit relevant costs and revenues (as shown above) only when all fixed costs are irrelevant for decision-making. In most circumstances, you are likely to be faced with situations where some of the fixed costs are relevant. Therefore it is recommended that you avoid using unit costs for decision-making and instead adopt the approach presented in Exhibit 9.1, where total costs are used.

EXAMPLE 9.1

The Caledonian Company is a manufacturer of clothing that sells its output directly to clothing retailers in the UK. One of its departments manufactures sweaters. The department has a production capacity of 50 000 sweaters per month. Because of the liquidation of one of its major customers, the company has excess capacity. For the next quarter, current monthly production and sales volume is expected to be 35 000 sweaters at a selling price of £40 per sweater. Expected *monthly* costs and revenues for an activity level of 35 000 sweaters are as follows:

	(£)	(£ per unit)
Direct labour	420 000	12
Direct materials	280 000	8
Variable manufacturing overheads	70 000	2
Manufacturing fixed (non-variable) overheads	280 000	8
Marketing and distribution fixed (non-variable) costs	105 000	3
Total costs	1 155 000	33
Sales	1 400 000	40
Profit	245 000	7

Caledonian is expecting an upsurge in demand and considers that the excess capacity is temporary. Therefore, even though there is sufficient direct labour capacity to produce 50 000 sweaters, Caledonian intends to retain the temporary excess supply of direct labour for the expected upsurge in demand. A leisure company located overseas has offered to buy 15 000 sweaters each month for the next three months at a price of £20 per sweater. The company would pay for the transportation costs and thus no additional marketing and distribution costs will be incurred. No subsequent sales to this customer are anticipated. The company would require its company logo inserting on the sweater and Caledonian has predicted that this will cost £1 per sweater. Should Caledonian accept the offer from the company?

EXHIBIT 9.1 Evaluation of three-month order from the company in the leisure industry

	(1) Do not accept order 35 000 (£)	(2) Accept the order 50 000 (£)	(3) Difference in relevant costs/(revenues) 15 000 (£)
Monthly sales and production in units			
Direct labour	420 000	420 000	—
Direct materials	280 000	400 000	120 000
Variable manufacturing overheads	70 000	100 000	30 000
Manufacturing non-variable overheads	280 000	280 000	—
Inserting company logo		15 000	15 000
Marketing and distribution costs	105 000	105 000	—
Total costs	1 155 000	1 320 000	165 000
Sales revenues	1 400 000	1 700 000	(300 000)
Profit per month	245 000	380 000	135 000
Difference in favour of accepting the order		135 000	

Most developed economies have well-developed road and highway networks. From time to time new highways are built to relieve congested cities, but by and large most developed countries are not embarking on major road-building projects. Reducing government expenditures in developed countries post the 2008 economic crisis prohibited many major new projects. The opposite happened in many developing countries, with foreign contractors doing most of the work. One project in Kenya delivered 50 km of four-lane highway from Nairobi to Thika at a cost of 27 billion Kenyan Shillings (about $270 million), which was completed in early 2012. In early 2015, the Kenyan government announced a plan to double the paved road in the country within 5 years through public–private partnerships. The total value of these contracts was noted as approximately $3 billion. While some money is from exchequer funding and Kenyan banks, some is to be provided by foreign development aid partners. This means competitive tendering and cost controls are an integral part of the bidding and construction process. Contractors will be required to submit tenders and cost reports to government departments or agencies, which in turn are likely to be closely monitored by funding providers. Based on a report from the *Standard* in mid-2016, Chinese firms had successfully bid for a highway project valued at 10.4 billion Kenya Shillings (about $104 million). They had previously worked on the Thika highway mentioned above.

Questions

1 Assuming a non-African construction company is submitting its first ever price to bid for a road construction project  in Africa, what special considerations might it need to consider in forming the price?

2 Assuming less profitable road maintenance projects are available in its home country, how would the firm evaluate on the basis of costs/revenues alone, whether or not to pursue a project like those described above?

References

Doya, D.M. (2015) Kenya beckons banks with $3.2 billion of road-building deals. BloombergBusiness. Available at www.bloomberg.com/news/articles /2015-03-16/kenya-beckons-banks-with-3-2-billion -of-road-building-contracts

Lugaria, P. (2012) 'Thika Road construction project overview'. *Kenya Construction Business Review*. Available at www.constructionkenya.com/1676 /thika-road-construction-design/

Omondi, D. (2016) Chinese firm wins yet another lucrative project available at www.standardmedia.co .ke/business/article/2000207244/chinese-firm -wins-yet-another-lucrative-project

Note from Exhibit 9.1 that in columns (1) and (2) both relevant and irrelevant *total* costs are shown for all alternatives under consideration. If this approach is adopted the *same* amounts for the irrelevant items (i.e. those items that remain unchanged as a result of the decision, which are direct labour, and manufacturing and marketing non-variable overheads) are included for all alternatives, thus making them irrelevant for decision-making. Alternatively, you can omit the irrelevant costs in columns (1) and (2) because they are the same for both alternatives. A third approach, which is shown in column (3), involves presenting only the relevant (i.e. differential) costs and revenues.

Note that column (3) represents the difference between columns (1) and (2). You will see that a comparison of columns (1) and (2), or presenting only the relevant items in column (3), shows that the company is better off by £135 000 per month if the order is accepted.

Four important factors must be considered before recommending acceptance of the order. Most of them relate to the assumption that there are no long-run consequences of accepting the offer at a selling price of £20 per sweater. First, it is assumed that the future selling price will not be affected by selling some of the output at a price below the going market price. If this assumption is incorrect, then competitors may engage in similar practices of reducing their selling prices in an attempt to unload spare capacity. This may lead to a fall in the market price, which, in turn, would lead to a fall in profits from future sales. The loss of future profits may be greater than the short-term gain obtained from accepting special orders at prices below the existing market price. However, given that Caledonian has found a customer outside its normal market, it is unlikely that the market price would be affected. However, if the customer had been within Caledonian's normal retail market there would be a real danger that the market price would be affected. Second, the decision to accept the order prevents the company from accepting other orders that may be obtained during the period at the going price. In other words, it is assumed that no better opportunities will present themselves during the period. Third, it is assumed that the company has unused resources that have no alternative uses that will yield a contribution to profits in excess of £135 000 *per month*. Finally, it is assumed that the fixed costs are unavoidable for the period under consideration. In other words, we assume that the direct labour force and the fixed overheads cannot be reduced in the short term or that they are to be retained for an upsurge in demand, which is expected to occur in the longer term.

Evaluation of a longer-term order

In Example 9.1, we focused on a short-term time horizon of three months. Capacity could not easily be altered in the short term and therefore direct labour and fixed costs were irrelevant costs with respect to the short-term decision. In the longer term, however, it may be possible to reduce capacity and spending on fixed costs and direct labour. Example 9.2 uses the same cost data as Example 9.1, but presents a revised scenario of a longer time horizon so that some of the costs that were fixed in the short term in Example 9.1 can now be changed in the longer term. You will see from Example 9.2 that Caledonian is faced with the following two alternatives:

1 do not accept the overseas order and reduce monthly capacity from 50 000 to 35 000 sweaters;

2 accept the overseas order of 15 000 sweaters per month and retain capacity at 50 000 sweaters per month.

EXAMPLE 9.2

Assume that the department within Caledonian Company has a *monthly* production capacity of 50 000 sweaters. Liquidation of a major customer has resulted in expected future demand being 35 000 sweaters per *month*. Caledonian has not been able to find any customers for the excess capacity of 15 000 sweaters apart from a company located overseas that would be prepared to enter into a contractual agreement for a three-year period for a supply of 15 000 sweaters per month at an agreed price of £25 per sweater. The company would require that a motif be added to each sweater and Caledonian has predicted that will cost £1 per sweater. The company would pay for the transportation costs and thus no additional marketing and distribution costs will be incurred.

Direct materials and variable overheads are predicted to be £8 and £2, respectively, per sweater (the same as Example 9.1) and fixed manufacturing (£280 000), marketing and distribution costs (£105 000) and direct labour (£420 000) are also currently the same as the costs used in Example 9.1. However, if Caledonian does not enter into a contractual agreement, it will reduce the direct labour force by 30 per cent (to reflect a capacity reduction from 50 000 to 35 000 sweaters). Therefore monthly direct labour costs will decline by 30 per cent, from £420 000 to £294 000. Further investigations indicate that manufacturing non-variable costs of £70 000 per month could be saved if a decision was made to reduce capacity by 15 000 sweaters per month. For example, the rental contracts for some of the machinery will not be renewed. Also some savings will be made in supervisory labour and support costs. Savings in marketing and distribution costs would be £20 000 per month. Assume also that if the capacity were reduced, factory rearrangements would result in part of the facilities being rented out at £25 000 per month. Should Caledonian accept the offer from the overseas company?

EXHIBIT 9.2 Evaluation of orders for the unutilized capacity over a three-year time horizon

	(1)	(2)	(3)
			Difference
	Do not	Accept	in relevant
	accept order	the order	costs/(revenues)
Monthly sales and	35 000	50 000	15 000
production in units	(£)	(£)	(£)
Direct labour	294 000	420 000	126 000
Direct materials	280 000	400 000	120 000
Variable manufacturing overheads	70 000	100 000	30 000
Manufacturing non-variable overheads	210 000	280 000	70 000
Inserting motif		15 000	15 000
Marketing and distribution costs	85 000	105 000	20 000
Total costs	939 000	1 320 000	381 000
Revenues from rental of facilities	25 000		25 000
Sales revenues	1 400 000	1 775 000	(375 000)
Profit per month	486 000	455 000	31 000
Difference in favour of rejecting the order		31 000	

The appropriate financial data for the analysis are shown in Exhibit 9.2. Note that column (1) incorporates the reduction in direct labour and fixed costs if capacity is reduced from 50 000 to 35 000 sweaters. A comparison of the monthly outcomes reported in columns (1) and (2) of Exhibit 9.2 shows that the company is better off by £31 000 per month if it reduces capacity to 35 000 sweaters, assuming that there are no qualitative factors to be taken into consideration. Column (3) presents only the differential (relevant) costs and revenues. This approach also indicates that the company is better off by £31 000 per month.

Note that the entry in column (3) of £25 000 is the lost revenues from the rent of the unutilized capacity if the company accepts the orders. This represents the opportunity cost of accepting the orders. In Chapter 2, it was pointed out that where the choice of one course of action requires that an alternative course of action is given up, the financial benefits that are foregone or sacrificed are known as opportunity costs. They only arise when resources are scarce *and* have alternative uses. Thus, in our illustration, the capacity allocated to producing 15 000 sweaters results in an opportunity cost (i.e. the lost revenues from the rent of the capacity) of £25 000 per month.

In Exhibit 9.2, all of the costs and revenues are relevant to the decision because some of the costs that were fixed in the short term could be changed in the longer term. The relevance of a cost often depends on the time horizon under consideration. It is therefore important to make sure that the information presented for decision-making relates to the appropriate time horizon. If inappropriate time horizons are selected, there is a danger that misleading information will be presented. Remember that our aim should always be to maximize *long-term* net cash inflows.

PRODUCT MIX DECISIONS WHEN CAPACITY CONSTRAINTS EXIST

In the short term, sales demand may be in excess of current productive capacity. For example, output may be restricted by a shortage of skilled labour, materials, equipment or space. When sales demand is in excess of a company's productive capacity, the resources responsible for limiting the output should be identified. These scarce resources are known as limiting factors. Within a short-term time period it is unlikely that constraints can be removed and additional resources acquired. Where limiting factors

EXAMPLE 9.3

A farmer in Ruritania has 240 000 square metres (m^2) of land on which he grows maize, potatoes, barley and wheat. He is planning his production for the next growing season. The following information is provided relating to the anticipated demand and productive capacity for the next season:

	Maize	Potatoes	Barley	Wheat
Contribution per tonne of output in Ruritanian dollars				
m^2 required per tonne of output	$160	$112	$96	$80
Estimated sales demand (tonnes)	80	32	24	16
Required area to meet sales	3000	3000	3000	3000
demand (m^2)	240 000	96 000	72 000	48 000

It is not possible in the short run to increase the area of land beyond 240 000m^2 for growing the above crops. You have been asked to advise on the mix of crops that should be produced during the period.

apply, profit is maximized when the greatest possible contribution to profit is obtained each time the scarce or limiting factor is used. Consider Example 9.3.

In Example 9.3 the farmer's ability to increase output and profits/net cash inflows is limited in the short term by the availability of land for growing crops. At first glance, you may think that the farmer should give top priority to producing maize, since this yields the highest contribution per tonne sold, but this assumption would be incorrect. To produce a tonne of maize, 80 scarce m^2 are required, whereas potatoes, barley and wheat require only 32m^2, 24m^2 and 16m^2, respectively of scarce land. By concentrating on growing potatoes, barley and wheat, the farmer can sell 3000 tonnes of each crop and still have some land left to grow maize. Contrariwise, if the farmer concentrates on growing maize, it will only be possible to meet the maximum sales demand of maize and there will be no land available to grow the remaining crops. The way in which you should determine the optimum output to maximize profits is to calculate the contribution per limiting factor for each crop and then to rank the crops in order of profitability based on this calculation.

Using the figures in the present example the result would be as follows:

	Maize	Potatoes	Barley	Wheat
Contribution per tonne of output	$160	$112	$96	$80
m^2 required per tonne of output	80	32	24	16
Contribution per m^2	$2	$3.50	$4	$5
Ranking	4	3	2	1

The farmer can now allocate the 240 000m^2 of land in accordance with the above rankings. The first choice should be to produce as much wheat as possible. The maximum sales are 3000 tonnes, and production of this quantity will result in 48 000m^2 of land being used. The second choice should be to grow barley and the maximum sales demand of 3000 tonnes will result in a further 72 000m^2 of land being used. The third choice is to grow potatoes. To meet the maximum sales demand for potatoes a further 96 000m^2 of land will be required. Growing 3000 tonnes of wheat, barley and potatoes requires 2 16 000m^2 of land, leaving a balance of 24 000m^2 for growing maize, which will enable 300 tonnes of maize to be grown.

REAL WORLD VIEWS 9.2

Multi-product quality competition: impact of resource constraints

According to an article authored by Yayla-Küllü *et al.*, multi-product firms account for 91 per cent of the output in US manufacturing and they often make short- to medium-term adjustments in their product-lines. For many of these product-line decisions, supply capacity constraints must be taken into account when making product-line decisions. The authors provide the following examples of supply capacity constraints.

Many furniture manufacturers produce custom and standard furniture using the same fixed capacity. In another example, the available capacity of a flexible machine (machining time) is allocated between high-and low-quality products where a higher-quality product requires slower machining speeds thereby taking a longer time to produce. The authors also provide an example of a firm in Finland that produces both mass-produced and custom-tailored suits in its factory where a custom-tailored suit uses more of the available limited factory time compared with a mass-produced suit.

The cruise line industry is another example where differentiated product lines are the norm. They provide a wide range of staterooms ranging from small rooms to large luxurious suites. In this industry, supply capacity is limited because it takes time to refurbish existing ships or build new ships. In another example, airlines offer differentiated products such as economy, business and first-class seats. For airlines, changing the product mix by changing the seating configuration in an aircraft is a common short- to medium-term solution to increasing profitability without making investments for new aircrafts.

In all of the above-mentioned examples ignoring supply capacity while deciding the product line can be sub-optimal. The authors point out that many firms often do not determine product-line decisions taking supply capacity constraints into account and provide evidence that shows when resources are limited firms' product lines should be determined by considering the margin per unit capacity.

Questions

1 Provide examples of firms in the retail and merchandising sectors where supply capacity constraints should be taken into account when making product mix decisions.

2 What are the scarce/limiting factors that apply in the examples cited above?

Reference

Yayla-Küllü, H.M., Parlaktürk, A.K. and Swaminathan, J.M. (2013) 'Multiproduct quality competition: impact of resource constraints', *Production and Operations Management* 22(3), 603–614. Available at onlinelibrary.wiley.com.libaccess.hud.ac.uk/doi /10.1111/j.1937-5956.2012.01379.x/abstract

We can now summarize the allocation of the 240 000m^2 of land:

Production	m^2 of land used	Balance of unused land (m^2)
3000 tonnes of wheat	48 000	192 000
3000 tonnes of barley	72 000	120 000
3000 tonnes of potatoes	96 000	24 000
300 tonnes of maize	24 000	—

The above allocation results in the following total contribution:

	$
3000 tonnes of wheat at $80 per tonne contribution	240 000
3000 tonnes of barley at $96 per tonne contribution	288 000
3000 tonnes of potatoes at $112 per tonne contribution	336 000
300 tonnes of maize at $160 per tonne contribution	48 000
Total contribution	912 000

Contrast the above contribution with the contribution that would have been obtained had the farmer ranked crop profitability by their contributions per tonne of output. This would have resulted in maize being ranked as the most profitable crop and all of the available land would have been used to grow 3000 tonnes of maize, giving a total contribution of $480 000 (3000 tonnes × $160).

Always remember to consider other qualitative factors before the final production programme is determined. For example, customer goodwill may be lost causing a fall in future sales if the farm is unable to supply all four crops to, say, 50 of its regular customers. Difficulties may arise in applying this procedure when there is more than one scarce resource. It could not be applied if, for example, labour hours were also scarce and maize had the highest contribution per scarce labour hour. In situations where more than one resource is scarce, it is necessary to resort to linear programming methods in order to determine the optimal production programme. For an explanation of how linear programming can be applied when there is more than one scarce resource, you should refer to Chapter 26.

Finally, it is important that you remember that the approach outlined in this section applies only to those situations in which capacity constraints cannot be removed in the short term. In the longer term additional resources should be acquired if the contribution from the extra capacity exceeds the cost of acquisition.

REPLACEMENT OF EQUIPMENT – THE IRRELEVANCE OF PAST COSTS

Replacement of equipment is a capital investment or long-term decision but one aspect of asset replacement decisions that we will consider at this stage is how to deal with the book value (i.e. the written-down value) of old equipment. This is a problem that has been known to cause difficulty, but the correct approach is to apply relevant cost principles (i.e. past or sunk costs are irrelevant for decision-making). We shall now use Example 9.4 to illustrate the irrelevance of the book value of old equipment in a replacement decision.

You will see from an examination of Example 9.4 that the total costs over a period of three years for each of the alternatives are as follows:

	(1) Retain present machine (£)	(2) Buy replacement machine (£)	(3) Difference relevant costs/(benefits) (£)
Variable/incremental operating costs:			
£50 000 for three years	150 000		
£30 000 for three years		90 000	(60 000)
Old machine book value:			
Three-year annual depreciation charge	60 000		
Lump sum write-off		60 000	
Old machine disposal value		(5 000)	(5 000)
Initial purchase price of new machine		50 000	50 000
Total cost	210 000	195 000	(15 000)

You can see from the above analysis that the £60 000 book value of the old machine is irrelevant to the decision. Book values are not relevant costs because they are past or sunk costs and are therefore the same for all potential courses of action. If the present machine is retained, three years' depreciation at £20 000 per annum will be written off annually, whereas if the new machine is purchased the £60 000 will be written off as a lump sum if it is replaced. Note that depreciation charges for the new machine are not included in the analysis since the cost of purchasing the machine is already included.

EXAMPLE 9.4

Three years ago the Anytime Bank purchased a cheque sorting machine for £120000. Depreciation using the straight line basis, assuming a life of six years and no salvage value, has been recorded each year in the financial accounts. The present written-down value of the machine is £60000 and it has a remaining life of three years. Recently a new sorting and imaging machine has been marketed that will cost £50000 and have an expected life of three years with no scrap value. It is estimated that the new machine will reduce variable operating costs from £50000 to £30000 per annum. The current sales value of the old machine is £5000 and will be zero in three years' time.

The sum of the annual depreciation charges is equivalent to the purchase cost. Thus, including both items would amount to double counting.

The above analysis shows that the costs of operating the replacement machine are £15000 less than the costs of operating the existing machine over the three-year period. Again there are several different methods of presenting the information. They all show a £15000 advantage in favour of replacing the machine. You can present the information shown in columns (1) and (2) above, as long as you ensure that the same amount for the irrelevant items is included for all alternatives. Alternatively, you can present columns (1) and (2) with the irrelevant item (i.e. the £60000) omitted or you can present the differential items listed in column (3). However, if you adopt the last approach you will probably find it more meaningful to restate column (3) as follows:

	£
Savings on variable operating costs (three years)	60000
Sale proceeds of existing machine	5000
	65000
Less purchase cost of replacement machine	50000
Savings on purchasing replacement machine	15000

OUTSOURCING AND MAKE-OR-BUY DECISIONS

Outsourcing is the process of obtaining goods or services from outside suppliers instead of producing the same goods or providing the same services within the organization. Decisions on whether to produce components or provide services within the organization or to acquire them from outside suppliers, are called outsourcing or 'make-or-buy' decisions. Many organizations outsource some of their activities such as their payroll and purchasing functions or the purchase of speciality components. Increasingly, municipal local services such as waste disposal, highways and property maintenance are being outsourced. Consider the information presented in Example 9.5 (Case A).

At first glance, it appears that the component should be outsourced since the purchase price of £30 is less than the current total unit cost of manufacturing. However, the unit costs include some costs that will be unchanged whether or not the components are outsourced. These costs are therefore not relevant to the decision. We are also assuming that there are no alternative uses of the released capacity if the components are outsourced. The appropriate cost information is presented in Exhibit 9.3 (Section A). Alternative approaches to presenting relevant cost and revenue information are presented. In columns (1) and (2) of Exhibit 9.3, cost information is presented that includes both relevant and irrelevant costs for both alternatives under consideration. The same amount for non-manufacturing overheads, which are irrelevant, is included for both alternatives. By including the same amount in both columns, the cost is made irrelevant. Alternatively, you can present cost information in columns (1) and (2) that excludes any irrelevant costs and revenues. Adopting either approach will result in a difference of £60000 in favour of making component A.

EXAMPLE 9.5

Case A

One of the divisions within Rhine Autos is currently negotiating with another supplier regarding outsourcing component A that it manufactures. The division currently manufactures 10 000 units per annum of the component. The costs currently assigned to the components are as follows:

	Total costs of producing 10 000 components (£)	Unit cost (£)
Direct materials AB	120 000	12
Direct labour	100 000	10
Variable manufacturing overhead costs		
(power and utilities)	10 000	1
Fixed manufacturing overhead costs	80 000	8
Share of non-manufacturing overheads	50 000	5
Total costs	360 000	36

The above costs are expected to remain unchanged in the foreseeable future if the Rhine Autos division continues to manufacture the components. The supplier has offered to supply 10 000 components per annum at a price of £30 per unit guaranteed for a minimum of three years. If Rhine Autos outsources component A, the direct labour force currently employed in producing the components will be made redundant. No redundancy costs will be incurred. Direct materials and variable overheads are avoidable if component A is outsourced. Fixed manufacturing overhead costs would be reduced by £10 000 per annum but non-manufacturing costs would remain unchanged. Assume initially that the capacity that is required for component A has no alternative use. Should the division of Rhine Autos make or buy the component?

Case B

Assume now that the extra capacity that will be made available from outsourcing component A can be used to manufacture and sell 10 000 units of component Z at a price of £34 per unit. All of the labour force required to manufacture component A would be used to make component Z. The variable manufacturing overheads, the fixed manufacturing overheads and non-manufacturing overheads would be the same as the costs incurred for manufacturing component A. Materials AB required to manufacture component A would not be required but additional materials XY required for making component Z would cost £13 per unit. Should Rhine Autos outsource component A?

As in earlier exhibits, the third approach is to list only the relevant costs, cost savings and any relevant revenues. This approach is shown in column (3) of Exhibit 9.3 (Section A). This column represents the differential costs or revenues and it is derived from the differences between columns (1) and (2). In column (3), only the information that is relevant to the decision is presented. This approach shows that the additional costs of buying component A are £300 000 but this enables costs of £240 000 associated with making component A to be saved. Therefore the company incurs an extra cost of £60 000 if it buys component A from the outside supplier.

We shall now explore what happens when the extra capacity created from not producing component A has an alternative use. Consider the information presented in Example 9.5 (Case B). The management of Rhine Autos should now consider the following alternatives:

1   make component A and do not make component Z;

2   outsource component A and make and sell component Z.

EXHIBIT 9.3 Evaluating a make-or-buy decision

Section A – Assuming there is no alternative use of the released capacity

	Total cost of continuing to make 10000 components (1) (£ per annum)	Total cost of buying 10000 components (2) (£ per annum)	Difference = Extra costs/ (savings) of buying (3) (£ per annum)
Direct materials AB	120000		(120000)
Direct labour	100000		(100000)
Variable manufacturing overhead costs (power and utilities)	10000		(10000)
Fixed manufacturing overhead costs	80000	70000	(10000)
Non-manufacturing overheads	50000	50000	
Outside purchase cost incurred/(saved)		300000	300000
Total costs incurred/(saved) per annum	360000	420000	60000

Extra costs of buying = £60000

Section B – Assuming the released capacity can be used to make component Z

	(1) Make component A and do not make component Z (£ per annum)	(2) Buy component A and make component Z (£ per annum)	(3) Difference = Extra costs/ (benefits) of buying component A (£ per annum)
Direct materials XY		130000	130000
Direct materials AB	120000		(120000)
Direct labour	100000	100000	
Variable manufacturing overhead costs	10000	10000	
Fixed manufacturing overhead costs	80000	80000	
Non-manufacturing overheads	50000	50000	
Outside purchase cost incurred		300000	300000
Revenue from sales of component Z		(340000)	(340000)
Total net costs	360000	330000	(30000)

Extra benefits from buying component A and using the released capacity to make component Z = £30000

It is assumed that there is insufficient capacity to make both components A and Z. The appropriate financial information is shown in Exhibit 9.3 (Section B). You will see that the same costs will be incurred for both alternatives for direct labour and all of the overhead costs. Therefore these items are irrelevant and the same amount can be entered in columns (1) and (2) or they can be omitted from both columns. Note that direct materials AB (£120000) will be incurred only if the company makes component A, so an entry of £120000 is shown in column (1) and no entry is made in column (2). However, if component A is bought from the supplier the capacity will be used to produce component Z and this will result in a purchase cost of £130000 being incurred for materials XY that are required to produce product Z. Thus £130000 is entered in column (2) and no entry is made in column (1) in respect of materials XY. Also note that the sales revenue arising from the sale of component Z is shown in parentheses in column (2). A comparison of the totals of columns (1) and (2) indicates that that there is a net benefit of £30000 from buying component A if the released capacity is used to make component Z.

**REAL WORLD
VIEWS 9.3**

Manufacturing rethinks outsourcing

The economic recession has resulted in original equipment manufacturers (OEMs) seeking to drive down costs by re-examining their manufacturing strategy, with many companies increasing their level of outsourcing, writes Ronnie Darroch, Plexus regional president (EMEA) in *Electronics Weekly*. He argues that OEMs can be of benefit to electronic manufacturing service (EMS) providers (like Plexus who provide electronics design, manufacturing and after-market services to companies with high complexity products) as OEMs undertake strategic reviews and decide to outsource manufacturing to an EMS provider. Outsourcing all or a portion of their manufacturing allows OEMs to convert internal fixed costs to external variable costs, leaving it more able to deal with changes in end market demand, particularly during periods of economic instability. This can create a win–win for both companies with growth opportunities for the EMS provider and the OEM left to focus on its core competencies.

Questions

1 How can outsourcing change the cost structure of an organization?

2 What are the major benefits and limitations of outsourcing?

Reference

Darroch, R. (2013) 'Manufacturers rethink outsourcing, says Plexus, president EMEA', *Electronics Weekly*, 11 June, p. 4. Available at www.electronicsweekly.com/news/business/viewpoints/manufacturers-rethink-outsourcing-says-plexus-president-emea-2013-12/

Instead of presenting the information in columns (1) and (2), you can present the relevant costs and benefits as shown by the differential items in column (3). This column indicates that the extra costs of buying component A and using the released capacity to make component Z are:

	(£)
Outside purchase cost incurred	300 000
Purchase of materials XY for component Z	130 000
	430 000

The extra benefits are:

	(£)
Revenues from the sale of component Z	340 000
Savings from not purchasing materials AB	120 000
	460 000

The above alternative analysis also shows that there is a net benefit of £30 000 from buying component A if the released capacity is used to make component Z.

DISCONTINUATION DECISIONS

Most organizations periodically analyse profits by one or more cost objects, such as products or services, customers and locations. Periodic profitability analysis can highlight unprofitable activities that require a more detailed appraisal (sometimes referred to as a special study) to ascertain whether or not they should be discontinued. In this section, we shall illustrate how the principle of relevant costs can be applied to discontinuation decisions. Consider Example 9.6. You will see that it focuses on a decision

EXAMPLE 9.6

The Aero Company is a wholesaler that sells its products to retailers throughout the Far East. Aero's head-quarters is in Hong Kong. The company has adopted a regional structure with each region consisting of three to five sales territories. Each region has its own regional office and a warehouse that distributes the goods directly to the customers. Each sales territory also has an office where the marketing staff are located. The South East Asian region consists of three sales territories with offices located in Singapore, Kuala Lumpur and Bangkok. The budgeted results for the next quarter are as follows:

	Singapore (£000)	Kuala Lumpur (£000)	Bangkok (£000)	Total (£000)
Cost of goods sold	920	1002	1186	3108
Sales persons' salaries	160	200	240	600
Sales office rent	60	90	120	270
Depreciation of sales office equipment	20	30	40	90
Apportionment of warehouse rent	24	24	24	72
Depreciation of warehouse equipment	20	16	22	58
Regional and headquarters costs	360	400	340	1100
Total costs assigned to each location	1564	1762	1972	5298
Reported profit/(loss)	236	238	(272)	202
Sales	1800	2000	1700	5500

Assuming that the above results are likely to be typical of future quarterly performance, should the Bangkok territory be discontinued?

REAL WORLD VIEWS 9.4

Opening and closing new stores

Asda is staging a major push south opening 11 new stores in the greater London region over the next few months with plans for a further 150 by 2018. Two of the new stores will be a trial of a new smaller format. These will be Asda's first 'High Street' stores, set on main thoroughfares at a time when many retailers are abandoning the heart of towns for retail parks. The retailer will also open seven standalone petrol filling stations, not attached to any existing stores, and two new superstores.

Arch rival Tesco has announced 43 store closures, Morrisons 23 stores and Sainsbury's has abandoned 40 new supermarket projects and cut 500 jobs. Discounters Aldi and Lidl are still growing. Aldi plans to open around 60 new shops.

Craig Bonnar, the Asda director responsible for store development, said: 'We have set out a clear five-year strategy which includes expanding further into London and the South East, and we anticipate this will include opening 150 petrol stations and 1000 Click and Collect sites by 2018'.

Questions

1 How might management of the above supermarkets determine which stores should be closed?

2 How might Asda management determine which stores to open?

References

Steiner, R. (2015) Asda in push south with smaller stores. *Daily Mail*, 23 Mar. 60. ISSN 03077578.

whether to discontinue operating a sales territory, but the same principles can also be applied to discontinuing products, services or customers.

In Example 9.6, Aero Company analyses profits by locations. Profits are analysed by regions, which are then further analysed by sales territories within each region. It is apparent from Example 9.6 that the South East Asian region is profitable (showing a budgeted quarterly profit of £202 000) but the profitability analysis suggests that the Bangkok sales territory is unprofitable. A more detailed study is required to ascertain whether it should be discontinued. Let us assume that this study indicates that:

1 Discontinuing the Bangkok sales territory will eliminate cost of goods sold, salespersons' salaries and sales office rent.

2 Discontinuing the Bangkok sales territory will have no effect on depreciation of sales office equipment, warehouse rent, depreciation of warehouse equipment and regional and headquarters expenses. The same costs will be incurred by the company for all of these items even if the sales territory is discontinued.

Note that, in the event of discontinuation, the sales office will not be required and the rental will be eliminated, whereas the warehouse rent relates to the warehouse for the region as a whole and, unless the company moves to a smaller warehouse, the rental will remain unchanged. It is therefore not a relevant cost. Discontinuation will result in the creation of additional space and if the extra space remains unused, there are no financial consequences to take into account. However, if the additional space can be sublet to generate rental income, this income would be incorporated as an opportunity cost for the alternative of keeping the Bangkok territory.

Exhibit 9.4 shows the relevant cost and revenue computations. Column (1) shows the costs incurred and revenues derived by the company if the sales territory is kept open (i.e. the items listed in the final column of Example 9.6) and column (2) shows the costs and revenues that will occur if a decision is taken to drop the sales territory. Therefore in column (2) only those costs that would be eliminated (i.e. those in item (1) on our list shown above) are deducted from column (1). For example, Example 9.6 specifies that £240 000 sales persons' salaries will be eliminated if the Bangkok territory is closed so the entry in column (2) is £360000 (£600 000 − £240000).

EXHIBIT 9.4 Relevant cost analysis relating to the discontinuation of the Bangkok territory

	Total costs and revenues to be assigned		
	(1)	(2)	(3)
			Difference in
	Keep Bangkok	Discontinue	incremental
	territory	Bangkok	costs and
	open	territory	revenues
	(£000)	(£000)	(£000)
Cost of goods sold	3108	1922	1186
Sales persons' salaries	600	360	240
Sales office rent	270	150	120
Depreciation of sales office equipment	90	90	
Apportionment of warehouse rent	72	72	
Depreciation of warehouse equipment	58	58	
Regional and headquarters costs	1100	1100	
Total costs to be assigned	5298	3752	1546
Reported profit	202	48	154
Sales	5500	3800	1700

You can see that the company will continue to incur some of the costs (i.e. those in item (2) on our list shown on the previous page) even if the Bangkok territory is closed and these costs are therefore irrelevant to the decision. Again you can either include, or exclude, the irrelevant costs in columns (1) and (2) as long as you ensure that the same amount of irrelevant costs is included for both alternatives if you adopt the first approach. Both approaches will show that future profits will decline by £154 000 if the Bangkok territory is closed. Alternatively, you can present just the relevant costs and revenues shown in column (3). This approach indicates that keeping the sales territory open results in additional sales revenues of £1 700 000 but additional costs of £1 546 000 are incurred giving a contribution of £154 000 towards fixed costs and profits. We can conclude that the Bangkok sales territory should not be closed.

DETERMINING THE RELEVANT COSTS OF DIRECT MATERIALS

So far in this chapter we have assumed, when considering various decisions, that any materials required would not be taken from existing inventories but would be purchased at a later date, and so the estimated purchase price would be the relevant material cost. Where materials are taken from existing inventories you should remember that the original purchase price represents a past or sunk cost and is therefore irrelevant for decision-making. However, if the materials are to be replaced then the decision to use them on an activity will result in additional acquisition costs compared with the situation if the materials were not used on that particular activity. Therefore the future replacement cost represents the relevant cost of the materials.

Consider now the situation where the materials have no further use apart from being used on a particular activity. If the materials have some realizable value, the use of the materials will result in lost sales revenues, and this lost sales revenue will represent an opportunity cost that must be assigned to the activity. Alternatively, if the materials have no realizable value the relevant cost of the materials will be zero.

DETERMINING THE RELEVANT COSTS OF DIRECT LABOUR

Determining the direct labour costs that are relevant to short-term decisions depends on the circumstances. Where a company has temporary spare capacity and the labour force is to be maintained in the short term, the direct labour cost incurred will remain the same for all alternative decisions. The direct labour cost will therefore be irrelevant for short-term decision-making purposes. However, in a situation where casual labour is used and where workers can be hired on a daily basis, a company may then adjust the employment of labour to exactly the amount required to meet the production requirements. The labour cost will increase if the company accepts additional work, and will decrease if production is reduced. In this situation, the labour cost will be a relevant cost for decision-making purposes.

In a situation where full capacity exists and additional labour supplies are unavailable in the short term, and where no further overtime working is possible, the only way that labour resources could then be obtained for a specific order would be to reduce existing production. This would release labour for the order, but the reduced production would result in a lost contribution, and this lost contribution must be taken into account when ascertaining the relevant cost for the specific order. The relevant labour cost per hour where full capacity exists is therefore the hourly labour rate plus an opportunity cost consisting of the contribution per hour that is lost by accepting the order. For a more detailed illustration explaining why this is the appropriate cost, you should refer to Learning Note 9.1 on the digital support resources (see Preface for details).

SUMMARY

The following items relate to the learning objectives listed at the beginning of the chapter.

● **Distinguish between relevant and irrelevant costs and revenues.**

Relevant costs/revenues represent those future costs/revenues that will be changed by a particular decision, whereas irrelevant costs/revenues will not be affected by that decision. In the short term, total profits will be increased (or total losses decreased) if a course of action is chosen where relevant revenues are in excess of relevant costs.

● **Explain the importance of qualitative factors.**

Quantitative factors refer to outcomes that can be measured in numerical terms. In many situations, it is difficult to quantify all the important elements of a decision. Those factors that cannot be expressed in numerical terms are called qualitative factors. Examples of qualitative factors include changes in employee morale and the impact of being at the mercy of a supplier when a decision is made to close a company's facilities and subcontract components. Although qualitative factors cannot be quantified it is essential that they are taken into account in the decision-making process.

● **Distinguish between the relevant and irrelevant costs and revenues for the five decision-making problems described.**

The five decision-making problems described were: (a) special selling price decisions; (b) product mix decisions when capacity constraints apply; (c) decisions on the replacement of equipment; (d) outsourcing (make-or-buy) decisions; and (e) discontinuation decisions. Different approaches can be used for presenting relevant cost and revenue information. Information can be presented that includes both relevant and irrelevant items for all alternatives under consideration. If this approach is adopted, the same amount for the irrelevant items (i.e. those items that remain unchanged as a result of the decision) are included for all alternatives, thus making them irrelevant for the decision. Alternatively, information can be presented that lists only the relevant costs for the alternatives under consideration. Where only two alternatives are being considered, a third approach is to present only the relevant (differential) items. You can adopt any of these three approaches. It is a matter of personal preference. All three approaches were illustrated for the five decision-making problems.

● **Describe the key concept that should be applied for presenting information for product mix decisions when capacity constraints apply.**

The information presented should rank the products by the contribution per unit of the constraining or limiting factor (i.e. the scarce resource). The capacity of the scarce resource should be allocated according to this ranking.

● **Explain why the book value of equipment is irrelevant when making equipment replacement decisions.**

The book value of equipment is a past (sunk) cost that cannot be changed for any alternative under consideration. Only future costs or revenues that will differ between alternatives are relevant for replacement decisions.

● **Describe the opportunity cost concept.**

Where the choice of one course of action requires that an alternative course of action be given up the financial benefits that are foregone or sacrificed are known as opportunity costs. Opportunity costs thus represent the lost contribution to profits arising from the best alternative foregone. They arise only when the resources are scarce and have alternative uses. Opportunity costs must therefore be included in the analysis when presenting relevant information for decision-making.

- **Explain the misconceptions relating to relevant costs and revenues.**

  The main misconception relates to the assumption that only sales revenues and variable costs are relevant and that fixed costs are irrelevant for decision-making. Sometimes variable costs are irrelevant. For example, they are irrelevant when they are the same for all alternatives under consideration. Fixed costs are also relevant when they differ among the alternatives. For a more detailed discussion explaining the misconceptions relating to relevant costs and revenues you should refer to Learning Note 9.2 on the digital support resources (see Preface for details).

- **Additional learning objective presented in Appendix 9.1**

  The appendix to this chapter includes the following additional learning objective: describe the theory of constraints and throughput accounting. This topic has been presented in the appendix because it is not vital to understanding the principles of measuring relevant costs and revenues for decision-making. The topic also tends to be covered on more advanced courses and may not form part of your course curriculum. You should therefore check with your course curriculum to ascertain whether you need to study this topic.

APPENDIX 9.1: THE THEORY OF CONSTRAINTS AND THROUGHPUT ACCOUNTING

During the 1980s Goldratt and Cox (1984) advocated a new approach to production management called optimized production technology (OPT). OPT is based on the principle that profits are expanded by increasing the throughput of the plant. The OPT approach determines what prevents throughput being higher by distinguishing between bottleneck and non-bottleneck resources. A bottleneck might be a machine (or any resource/limiting factor) whose capacity limits the throughput of the whole production process. The aim is to identify bottlenecks and remove them or, if this is not possible, ensure that they are fully utilized at all times. Non-bottleneck resources should be scheduled and operated based on constraints within the system and should not be used to produce more than the bottlenecks can absorb. The OPT philosophy therefore advocates that non-bottleneck resources should not be utilized to 100 per cent of their capacity, since this would merely result in an increase in inventory. Thus idle time in non-bottleneck areas is not considered detrimental to the efficiency of the organization. If it were utilized, it would result in increased inventory without a corresponding increase in throughput for sale.

Goldratt and Cox (1992) describe the process of maximizing operating profit when faced with bottleneck and non-bottleneck operations as the theory of constraints (TOC). The process involves five steps:

1. identify the system's bottlenecks;
2. decide how to exploit the bottlenecks;
3. subordinate everything else to the decision in step 2;
4. elevate the system's bottlenecks;
5. if, in the previous steps a bottleneck has been broken, go back to step 1.

The first step involves identifying the constraint that restricts output from being expanded. Having identified the bottleneck it becomes the focus of attention since only the bottleneck can restrict or enhance the flow of products. It is therefore essential to ensure that the bottleneck activity is fully utilized. Decisions regarding the optimum mix of products to be produced by the bottleneck activity must be made. Step 3 requires that the optimum production of the bottleneck activity determines the production schedule of the non-bottleneck activities. In other words, the output of the non-bottleneck operations are linked to the needs of the bottleneck activity. There is no point in a non-bottleneck activity supplying more than the bottleneck activity can consume. This would merely result in an increase in WIP inventories and no increase in sales volume. The TOC is a process of continuous improvement to clear the throughput chain of all constraints. Thus, step 4 involves taking action to remove (that is, elevate) the constraint. This might involve replacing a bottleneck machine with a faster one, increasing the bottleneck efficiency or changing the design of the product to reduce the processing time required by the activity. When a bottleneck activity has been elevated and replaced by a new bottleneck it is necessary to return to step 1 and repeat the process.

To apply TOC ideas Goldratt and Cox advocate the use of three key measures:

1 *Throughput contribution*, which is the rate at which the system generates profit through sales. It is defined as sales less direct materials.

2 *Investments* (inventory), which is the sum of inventories, research and development costs and the costs of equipment and buildings.

3 *Other operational expenses* (also known as *total factory cost*), which include all operating costs (other than direct materials) incurred to earn throughput contribution.

The TOC aims to increase throughput contribution while simultaneously reducing inventory and operational expenses. However, the scope for reducing the latter is limited since they must be maintained at some minimum level for production to take place at all. In other words, other operational expenses are assumed to be fixed costs. Goldratt and Cox argue that traditional management accounting is obsessed

REAL WORLD VIEWS 9A.1

Throughput accounting: the Garrett Automative experience

Garrett Automative Ltd (GAL) is a UK subsidiary of a American parent company that manufactures turbochargers for the automative industry. GAL decided to begin its profit improvement programme by examining its factory throughput. Throughput was defined as the rate at which raw materials were turned into sales. In other words, throughput was defined as sales less material costs per period of time. All operating costs, other than direct materials, were considered to be fixed in the short run. In conjunction with its new OPT scheduling system, factory bottlenecks, defined as an activity within the organization where demand for the resource outstrips the capacity to supply, were identified. The bottlenecks became certain machines in the factory. The mechanism to improve profitability was to maximize throughput contribution by optimizing the use of bottleneck resources.

Management sought to alleviate the bottlenecks by making additional investments to improve bottleneck capacity and by shifting some of the operations from bottleneck to non-bottleneck machines. New investments to improve efficiency at non-bottleneck machines were rejected because this greater efficiency did nothing to improve throughput

contribution. Priority was given to investments in bottlenecks. To motivate the employees to increase throughput, the performance reporting system was changed. Less emphasis was given to labour efficiency and schedule adherence was introduced as a key performance measure. Employees at non-bottleneck operations were requested not to produce more than the scheduled quantity and use any surplus time on training and TQM initiatives.

GAL has found throughput accounting to be extremely helpful in its particular situation. By concentrating on managing its bottlenecks, GAL has been able to increase its production to meet its sales demand of many different types of turbochargers in relatively small batch sizes.

Question

1 How could the approach described above be applied in a service organization, such as the National Health Service?

References

Darlington, J. (1992) 'Throughput accounting: the Garrett Automative experience', *Management Accounting* (UK), April.

Coughlan and Darlington (1993) 'As fast as the slowest operations: the theory of constraints', *Management Accounting* (UK), June.

by the need to reduce operational expenses, which results in a declining spiral of cost-cutting, followed by falling production and a further round of cost-cutting. Instead, they advocate a throughput orientation whereby throughput must be given first priority, inventories second and operational expenses last.

The TOC adopts a short-run time horizon and treats all operating expenses (including direct labour but excluding direct materials) as fixed, thus implying that variable costing should be used for decision-making, profit measurement and inventory valuation. It emphasizes the management of bottleneck activities as the key to improving performance by focusing on the short-run maximization of throughput contribution. Adopting the throughput approach to implement the TOC, however, appears to be merely a restatement of the contribution per limiting factor that was described in this chapter. Consider the situation outlined in Example 9A.1.

You can see from Example 9A.1 that the required machine utilization is as follows:

Machine			
	1	112%	$(18000/16000 \times 100)$
	2	169%	$(27000/16000 \times 100)$
	3	56%	$(9000/16000 \times 100)$

Machine 2 represents the bottleneck activity because it has the highest machine utilization. To ascertain the optimum use of the bottleneck activity we can use the approach advocated for limiting factors in the main body of the chapter but with throughput contribution defined as selling price less direct materials rather than selling price less variable cost that assumes that labour is a variable cost. The throughput contribution per hour for machine 2 is calculated for each product and the products are ranked in order of profitability based on this calculation. Using the figures in the present example the result would be as follows:

	Product X	Product Y	Product Z
Contribution per unit	£120	£100	£60
Machine 2 hours required	9	3	1.5
Contribution per machine hour	£13.33	£33.33	£40
Ranking	3	2	1

EXAMPLE 9A.1

A company produces three products using three different machines. The following information is available for a period:

Product	X	Y	Z	Total
Throughput contribution (Sales – direct materials)	£120	£100	£60	
Machine hours required per unit:				
Machine 1	6	2	1	
Machine 2	9	3	1.5	
Machine 3	3	1	0.5	
Estimated sales demand	2000	2000	2000	
Required machine hours				
Machine 1	12000	4000	2000	18000
Machine 2	18000	6000	3000	27000
Machine 3	6000	2000	1000	9000

Machine capacity is limited to 16000 hours for each machine and total factory cost (i.e. other operational expenses) is £320000. It is assumed that all direct labour costs are fixed for the period under consideration.

The allocation of the 16 000 hours for the bottleneck activity is:

	Machine hours used	Balance of hours available
Production		
2000 units of Z	3 000	13 000
2000 units of Y	6 000	7 000
777 units of X (7000 hours/9 hours per unit)	7 000	—

Following the five-step TOC process outlined earlier, action should be taken to remove the constraint. Let us assume that a financial analysis indicates that the purchase of a second 'Type 2' machine is justified. Machine capacity will now be increased by 16 000 hours to 32 000 hours and Machine 2 will no longer be a constraint. In other words, the bottleneck will have been elevated and Machine 1 will now become the constraint. The above process must now be repeated to determine the optimum output for Machine 1.

Galloway and Waldron (1988) advocate an approach called **throughput accounting** to apply the TOC philosophy. To ascertain the optimum use of the bottleneck activity, they rank the products according to a measure they have devised called the throughput accounting (TA) ratio. They define the TA ratio as:

$$\text{TA ratio} = \frac{\text{Throughput contribution per hour of the bottleneck resource}}{\text{Cost per factory hour}}$$

$$\text{where Throughput contribution per factory hour} = \frac{\text{Sales price} - \text{Material cost of each product for the bottleneck resource}}{\text{Time on the bottleneck resource}}$$

$$\text{and Cost per factory hour} = \frac{\text{Total factory cost (i.e. other operational expenses)}}{\text{Total time available on bottleneck resource}}$$

Note that sales less direct material cost is equal to throughput contribution, total factory cost is defined in exactly the same way as other operational expenses (see TOC measures described earlier) and return per factory hour is identical to the throughput contribution per hour of the bottleneck activity. Example 9A.1 indicates that the total factory cost (i.e. other operational expenses) for the period is £320 000. The TA ratios and product rankings for the bottleneck activity (Machine 2), using the data shown in Example 9A.1, are as follows:

	Product X	Product Y	Product Z
1 Throughput contribution per factory hour	£13.33	£33.33	£40
2 Cost per factory hour (£320 000/16 000 hours)	£20	£20	£20
3 TA ratio (Row 1/Row 2)	0.6665	1.6665	2.0
4 Ranking	3	2	1

The rankings are identical to the contribution per bottleneck hour calculated earlier. Given that the TA ratio is calculated by dividing the contribution per bottleneck hour by a constant amount (cost per factory hour), the TA ratio appears merely to represent a restatement of the contribution per limiting factor described in the main body of this chapter. Contribution and throughput accounting differ in terms of their definition of variable cost. Contribution treats direct materials, direct labour and variable overheads as variable costs, whereas throughput accounting assumes that only direct materials represent variable costs. Throughput accounting is thus more short-term oriented and assumes that direct labour and variable overheads cannot be avoided within a very short term period. In contrast, contribution assumes that the short term represents a longer period than that assumed with throughput accounting and thus classifies direct labour and variable overheads as variable costs that vary with output in the longer term. For a more detailed discussion of the TOC and throughput accounting you should refer to Dugdale and Jones (1998), Jones and Dugdale (1998) and the solution to Review problems 9.25 and 9.26.

KEY TERMS AND CONCEPTS

Differential cash flows The cash flows that will be affected by a decision that is to be taken, also known as incremental cash flows.

Facility sustaining costs Common costs that are incurred to support the organization as a whole and which are normally not affected by a decision that is to be taken.

Incremental cash flows The cash flows that will be affected by a decision that is to be taken, also known as differential cash flows.

Limiting factors Scarce resources that constrain the level of output.

Opportunity costs Costs that measure the opportunity that is sacrificed when the choice of one course of action requires that an alternative is given up.

Optimized production technology (OPT) An approach to production management that is based on the principle that profits are expanded by increasing the throughput of the plant, which it aims to achieve by identifying and dealing with bottlenecks.

Outsourcing The process of obtaining goods or services from outside suppliers instead of producing the same goods or providing the same services within the organization.

Qualitative or non-financial factors Non-monetary factors that may affect a decision.

Relevant costs and revenues Future costs and revenues that will be changed by a particular decision, whereas irrelevant costs and revenues will not be affected by that decision.

Special studies A detailed non-routine study that is undertaken relating to choosing between alternative courses of action.

Sunk costs Costs that have been incurred by a decision made in the past and that cannot be changed by any decision that will be made in the future.

Theory of constraints (TOC) A five-step process of maximizing operating profit when faced with bottleneck and non-bottleneck operations.

Throughput accounting A management accounting methodology that gives priority to throughput over inventories and operational expenses.

Written-down value The original cost of an asset minus depreciation.

RECOMMENDED READING

For a discussion of the arguments for and against using the contribution analysis approach you should refer to the *Journal of Management Accounting Research* (USA) Fall 1990, 1–32, 'Contribution margin analysis: no longer relevant. Strategic cost management: the new paradigm', which reproduces the contributions from a panel of speakers at the American Accounting Association Annual Meeting: Ferrara (pp. 1–2), Kaplan (pp. 2–15), Shank (pp. 15–21), Horngren (pp. 21–4), Boer (pp. 24–7), together with concluding remarks (pp. 27–32). For a detailed discussion of the theory of constraints and throughput accounting you should refer to Jones and Dugdale (1998) and Dugdale and Jones (1998). You can also refer to articles that provide a general description of the theory of constraints and throughput accounting by referring to articles that can be accessed from the ACCA Student Accountant www.accaglobal.com/gb/en/student/exam-support-resources/fundamentals-exams-study-resources/f2/technical-articles.html

KEY EXAMINATION POINTS

A common mistake that students make when presenting information for decision-making is to compare unit costs. With this approach, there is a danger that fixed costs will be unitized and treated as variable costs. In most cases, you should compare total amounts of costs and revenues rather than unit amounts. Many students do not present the information clearly and concisely. There are many alternative ways of presenting the information, but the simplest approach is to list future costs and revenues for each alternative in a format similar to Exhibit 9.1. You should exclude irrelevant items or ensure that the same amount for irrelevant items is included for each alternative. To determine the amount to be entered for each alternative, you should ask yourself what difference it will make if the alternative is selected.

Never allocate common fixed costs to the alternatives. You should focus on how each alternative will affect future cash flows of the organization. Changes in the apportionment of fixed costs will not alter future cash flows of the company. Remember that if a resource is scarce, your analysis should recommend the alternative that yields the largest contribution per limiting factor.

You should now attempt the review problems and compare your answers with the solutions that are provided. These problems will test your understanding of a variety of decision problems that have been covered in Chapter 9.

ASSESSMENT MATERIAL

The review questions are short questions that enable you to assess your understanding of the main topics included in the chapter. The numbers in parentheses provide you with the page numbers to refer to if you cannot answer a specific question.

The review problems are more complex and require you to relate and apply the content to various business problems. The problems are graded by their level of difficulty. Solutions to review problems that are not preceded by the term 'IM' are provided in a separate section at the end of the book. Solutions to problems preceded by the term 'IM' are provided in the Instructor's Manual accompanying this book that can be downloaded from the lecturer's digital support resources. Additional review problems with fully worked solutions are provided in the *Student Manual* that accompanies this book.

REVIEW QUESTIONS

9.1   What is a relevant cost? (p. 198)

9.2   Why is it important to recognize qualitative factors when presenting information for decision-making? Provide examples of qualitative factors. (pp. 198–199)

9.3   What underlying principle should be followed in determining relevant costs for decision-making? (p. 198)

9.4   Explain what is meant by special pricing decisions. (p. 199)

9.5   Describe the important factors that must be taken into account when making special pricing decisions. (pp. 201–202)

9.6   Describe the dangers involved in focusing excessively on a short-run decision-making time horizon. (p. 203)

9.7   Define limiting factors. (p. 203)

9.8   How should a company determine its optimal product mix when a limiting factor exists? (p. 204)

9.9   Why is the written-down value and depreciation of an asset being considered for replacement irrelevant when making replacement decisions? (p. 206)

9.10   Explain the importance of opportunity costs for decision-making. (p. 203)

9.11   Explain the circumstances when the original purchase price of materials are irrelevant for decision-making. (p. 213)

9.12   Why does the relevant cost of labour differ depending on the circumstances? (p. 213)

9.13   Describe the five steps involved in applying the theory of constraints. (p. 215)

9.14   Describe throughput accounting and explain how it can be used to determine the optimum use of a bottleneck activity. (p. 218)

REVIEW PROBLEMS

9.15 Basic. A company has the following production planned for the next four weeks. The figures reflect the full capacity level of operations. Planned output is equal to the maximum demand per product.

Product	A	B	C	D
	$	$	$	$
	per unit	per unit	per unit	per unit
Selling price	160	214	100	140
Raw material cost	24	56	22	40
Direct labour cost	66	88	33	22
Variable overhead cost	24	18	24	18
Fixed overhead cost	16	10	8	12
Profit	30	42	13	48
Planned output	300	125	240	400
Direct labour hours per unit	6	8	3	2

The direct labour force is threatening to go on strike for two weeks out of the coming four. This means that only 2160 hours will be available for production rather than the usual 4320 hours.

If the strike goes ahead, which product or products should be produced if profits are to be maximized?

(a) D and A

(b) B and D

(c) D only

(d) B and C

ACCA F5 Performance Management

9.16 Basic. A company has just secured a new contract which requires 500 hours of labour.

There are 400 hours of spare labour capacity. The remaining hours could be worked as overtime at time-and-a-half or labour could be diverted from the production of product X. Product X currently earns a contribution of £4 in two labour hours and direct labour is currently paid at a rate of £12 per normal hour.

What is the relevant cost of labour for the contract?

(a) £200

(b) £1200

(c) £1400

(d) £1800

ACCA – Financial Information for Management

9.17 Basic. X plc intends to use relevant costs as the basis of the selling price for a special order: the printing of a brochure. The brochure requires a particular type of paper that is not regularly used by X plc although a limited amount is in X plc's inventory which was left over from a previous job. The cost when X plc bought this paper last year was $15 per ream and there are 100 reams in inventory. The brochure requires 250 reams. The current market price of the paper is $26 per ream, and the resale value of the paper in inventory is $10 per ream.

The relevant cost of the paper to be used in printing the brochure is:

(a) $2500
(b) $4900
(c) $5400
(d) $6500

CIMA P2 Management Accounting: Decision Management

9.18 Basic. All of a company's skilled labour, which is paid £8 per hour, is fully employed manufacturing a product to which the following data refer:

		£ per unit	£ per unit
	Selling price		60
Less	Variable costs:		
	Skilled labour	20	
	Others	15	
			(35)
Contribution			25

The company is evaluating a contract which requires 90 skilled labour hours to complete. No other supplies of skilled labour are available.

What is the total relevant skilled labour cost of the contract?

(a) £720
(b) £900
(c) £1620
(d) £2160   *ACCA – Financial Information for Management*

9.19 Basic. A company has three shops (R, S and T) to which the following budgeted information relates:

	Shop R £000	Shop S £000	Shop T £000	Total £000
Sales	400	500	600	1500
Contribution	100	60	120	280
Less: Fixed costs	(60)	(70)	(70)	(200)
Profit/loss	40	(10)	50	80

Sixty per cent of the total fixed costs are general company overheads. These are apportioned to the shops on the basis of sales value. The other fixed costs are specific to each shop and are avoidable if the shop closes down.

If shop S closed down and the sales of the other two shops remained unchanged, what would be the revised budgeted profit for the company?

(a) £50000
(b) £60000
(c) £70000
(d) £90000

ACCA – Financial Information for Management

9.20 Basic. A company manufactures two products A and B. The budget statement below was produced using a traditional absorption costing approach. It shows the profit per unit for each product based on the estimated sales demand for the period.

	Product A $	Product B $
Selling price per unit	46	62
Production costs per unit:		
Material costs	18	16
Labour costs	4	10
Overhead costs	8	12
Profit per unit	16	24
Additional information:		
Estimated sales demand (units)	6000	8000
Machine hours per unit	0.5	0.8

It has now become apparent that the machine which is used to produce both products has a maximum capacity of 8000 hours and the estimated sales demand cannot be met in full. Total production costs for the period, excluding direct material cost, are $248000. No inventories are held of either product.

Required:

(i) Calculate the return per machine hour for each product if a throughput accounting approach is used.
(2 marks)

(ii) Calculate the profit for the period, using a throughput accounting approach, assuming the company prioritizes Product B.
(3 marks)

CIMA P1 Performance Operations

9.21 Intermediate: Relevant cost for minimum price for a contract. The Telephone Co. (T Co.) is a company specializing in the provision of telephone systems for commercial clients. There are two parts to the business:

– installing telephone systems in businesses, either first time installations or replacement installations;
– supporting the telephone systems with annually renewable maintenance contracts.

T Co. has been approached by a potential customer, Push Co. who wants to install a telephone system in new offices it is opening. While the job is not a particularly large one, T Co. is hopeful of future business in the form of replacement systems and support contracts for Push Co. T Co. is therefore keen to quote a competitive price for the job. The following information should be considered:

1 One of the company's salesmen has already been to visit Push Co. to give them a demonstration of the new system, together with a complementary lunch, the costs of which totalled $400.

2 The installation is expected to take one week to complete and would require three engineers, each of whom is paid a monthly salary of $4000. The engineers have just had their annually renewable contract renewed with T Co. One of the three engineers has spare capacity to complete the work, but the other two would have to be moved from contract X in order to complete this one. Contract X generates a contribution of $5 per engineer hour. There are no other engineers available to continue with Contract X if these two engineers are taken off the job. It would mean that T Co. would miss its contractual completion deadline on Contract X by one week. As a result, T Co. would have to pay a one-off penalty of $500. Since there is no other work scheduled for their engineers in one week's time, it will not be a problem for them to complete Contract X at this point.

3 T Co.'s technical advisor would also need to dedicate eight hours of his time to the job. He is working at full capacity, so he would have to work overtime in order to do this. He is paid an hourly rate of $40 and is paid for all overtime at a premium of 50 per cent above his usual hourly rate.

4 Two visits would need to be made by the site inspector to approve the completed work. He is an independent contractor who is not employed by T Co., and charges Push Co. directly for the work. His cost is $200 for each visit made.

5 T Co's system trainer would need to spend one day at Push Co. delivering training. He is paid a monthly salary of $1500 but also receives commission of $125 for each day spent delivering training at a client's site.

6 120 telephone handsets would need to be supplied to Push Co. The current cost of these is $18.20 each, although T Co. already has 80 handsets in inventory. These were bought at a price of $16.80 each. The handsets are the most popular model on the market and frequently requested by T Co.'s customers.

7 Push Co. would also need a computerized control system called 'Swipe 2'. The current market price of Swipe 2 is $10 800, although T Co. has an older version of the system, 'Swipe 1', in inventory, which could be modified at a cost of $4600. T Co. paid $5400 for Swipe 1 when it ordered it in error two months ago and has no other use for it. The current market price of Swipe 1 is $5450, although if T Co. tried to sell the one they have, it would be deemed to be 'used' and therefore only worth $3000.

8 1000 metres of cable would be required to wire up the system. The cable is used frequently by T Co. and it has 200 metres in inventory, which cost $1.20 per metre. The current market price for the cable is $1.30 per metre.

9 You should assume that there are four weeks in each month and that the standard working week is 40 hours long.

Required:

(a) Prepare a cost statement, using relevant costing principles, showing the minimum cost that T Co. should charge for the contract. Make DETAILED notes showing how each cost has been arrived at and EXPLAINING why each of the costs above has been included or excluded from your cost statement.   (14 marks)

(b) Explain the relevant costing principles used in part (a) and explain the implications of the minimum price that has been calculated in relation to the final price agreed with Push Co.   (6 marks)

ACCA F5 Performance Management

9.22 Advanced: Make or buy decision and limiting factors.

Robber Co. manufactures control panels for burglar alarms, a very profitable product. Every product comes with a one year warranty offering free repairs if any faults arise in this period.

It currently produces and sells 80 000 units per annum, with production of them being restricted by the short supply of labour. Each control panel includes two main components – one key pad and one display screen. At present, Robber Co. manufactures both of these components in-house. However, the company is currently considering outsourcing the production of keypads and/or display screens. A newly established company based in Burgistan is keen to secure a place in the market, and has offered to supply the keypads for the equivalent of $4.10 per unit and the display screens for the equivalent of $4.30 per unit. This price has been guaranteed for two years.

The current total annual costs of producing the keypads and the display screens are:

	Keypads	Display screen
Production	80 000 units	80 000 units
	$000	$000
Direct materials	160	116
Direct labour	40	60
Heat and powder costs	64	88
Machine costs	26	30
Depreciation and insurance costs	84	96
Total annual production costs	374	390

Notes:

1 Materials costs for keypads are expected to increase by 5 per cent in six months' time; materials costs for display screens are only expected to increase by 2 per cent, but with immediate effect.

2 Direct labour costs are purely variable and not expected to change over the next year.

3 Heat and power costs include an apportionment of the general factory overhead for heat and power as well as the costs of heat and power directly used for the production of keypads and display screens. The general apportionment included is calculated using 50 per cent

of the direct labour cost for each component and would be incurred irrespective of whether the components are manufactured in-house or not.

4 Machine costs are semi-variable; the variable element relates to set up costs, which are based on the number of batches made, The keypads' machine has fixed costs of $4000 per annum and the display screens' machine has fixed costs of $6000 per annum, While both components are currently made in batches of 500, this would need to change, with immediate effect, to batches of 400.

5 60 per cent of depreciation and insurance costs relate to an apportionment of the general factory depreciation and insurance costs; the remaining 40 per cent is specific to the manufacture of keypads and display screens.

Required:

(a) Advise Robber Co. whether it should continue to manufacture the keypads and display screens in-house or whether it should outsource their manufacture to the supplier in Burgistan, assuming it continues to adopt a policy to limit manufacture and sales to 80 000 control panels in the coming year.   (8 marks)

(b) Robber Co. takes 0.5 labour hours to produce a keypad and 0.75 labour hours to produce a display screen. Labour hours are restricted to 100 000 hours and labour is paid at $1 per hour. Robber Co. wishes to increase its supply to 100 000 control panels (i.e. 100 000 each of keypads and display screens).

Advise Robber Co. as to how many units of keypads and display panels they should either manufacture and/or outsource in order to minimize their costs.   (7 marks)

(c) Discuss the non-financial factors that Robber Co. should consider when making a decision about outsourcing the manufacture of keypads and display screens.   (5 marks)

ACCA F5 Performance Management

9.23 Advanced: Limiting factors and CVP analysis.

GF is a company that manufactures clothes for the fashion industry. The fashion industry is fast moving and consumer demand can change quickly due to the emergence of new trends.

GF manufactures three items of clothing: the S, the T and the B using the same resources but in different amounts.

Budget information per unit is as follows:

	S ($)	T ($)	B ($)
Selling price	250	40	100
Direct materials ($20 per m²)	100	10	30
Direct labour ($12 per hour)	36	12	27
Variable overhead ($3 per machine hour)	9	3	6.75

Total fixed costs are $300 000 per month.

Included in the original budget constructed at the start of the year, was the sales demand for the month of March as shown below:

	S	T	B
Demand in March (units)	2000	6000	4000

After the original budget had been constructed, items of clothing S, T and B have featured in a fashion magazine. As a result of this, a new customer (a fashion retailer), has ordered 1000 units each of S, T and B for delivery in March. The budgeted demand shown above does not include this order from the new customer.

In March there will be limited resources available. Resources will be limited to:

Direct materials	14 500 m²
Direct labour	30 000 hours

There will be no opening inventory of material, work in progress or finished goods in March.

Required:

(a) Produce a statement that shows the optimal production plan and the resulting profit or loss for March.

Note: you should assume that the new customer's order must be supplied in full. *(10 marks)*

(b) Explain TWO issues that should be considered before the production plan that you produced in part (a) is implemented. *(4 marks)*

The Board of Directors have now addressed the shortage of key resources at GF to ensure that production will meet demand in April. The production plan for the month of April is shown below:

	S	T	B
Production (units)	4000	5000	4000

Required:

(c) For April,

(i) Calculate the break even sales revenue for the given product mix in the production plan. *(4 marks)*
(ii) Calculate the margin of safety percentage. *(2 marks)*
(iii) Explain THREE limitations of breakeven analysis for GF. *(5 marks)*

CIMA P2 Performance Management

9.24 Advanced: Limiting factors, shadow prices and multi-product break-even analysis.
Scenario for parts (a) and (b)
Company WX manufactures a number of finished products and two components. Three finished products (P1, P2, and P3) and two components (C1 and C2) are made using the same resources (but in different quantities). The components are used internally by the company when producing other products but they are not used in the manufacture of P1, P2 or P3.

Budgeted data for December for P1, P2, P3, C1 and C2 are as follows:

	P1	P2	P3	C1	C2
	500	400	600	250	150
Units demanded	$/unit	$/unit	$/unit	$/unit	$/unit
Selling price	155	125	175	—	—
Direct labour ($10 hour)	25	15	30	10	15
Direct material ($50/kg)	10	20	20	5	10
Variable production overhead ($40 machine hour)	10	15	20	10	20
Fixed production overhead ($20/labour hour)	50	30	60	20	30
Gross profit	60	45	45	—	—

Further information for December:

Direct labour: 4300 hours are available.

Direct material: 420kgs are available.

Machine hours: no restrictions apply.

Components: C1 and C2 are readily available from external suppliers for $50 and $80 per unit respectively. The external suppliers are reliable and the quality of the components is similar to that of those manufactured by the company.

Required:

(a) Produce calculations to determine the optimal production plan for P1, P2, P3, C1 and C2 during December.

Note: it is not possible to produce partly finished units or to hold inventory of any of these products or components. *(10 marks)*

(b) There is a possibility that more of the direct material may become available during December. The shadow price per kg of the direct material has been calculated to be $200, $187.50 and $175 depending on how much extra becomes available.

Required:

Explain the shadow prices of $200, $187.50 and $175 for the direct material. Your answer should show the changes to the resource usage and the production plan for each of the shadow prices. *(6 marks)*

Scenario for parts [c] and (d)

Company YZ manufactures products L, M and N. These products are always sold in the rate 9L:6M:5N. The budgeted sales volume for December is a total of 14 000 units. The budgeted sales volumes, selling price per unit and variable cost per unit for each of the products are shown below:

	L	M	N
Sales budget (units)	6300	4200	3500
	$	$	$
Selling price per unit	300	600	230
Variable cost per unit	100	300	50

The budgeted fixed costs of the company for December are $2.7 million.

Required:

(c) Calculate the number of units of each product that must be sold for Company YZ to break even in December given the current sales mix ratio. *(4 marks)*

(d) The sales manager has now said that to be able to sell 6300 units of product L in December it will be necessary to reduce the selling price of product L.

Calculate the sensitivity of Company YZ's total budgeted profit for December to a change in the selling price per unit of product L. *(5 marks)*

CIMA P2 Performance Management

9.25 Advanced: Throughput accounting. Solar Systems Co (S Co) makes two types of solar panels at its manufacturing plant: large panels for commercial customers and small panels for domestic customers. All panels are produced using the same materials, machinery and a skilled labour force. Production takes place for five days per week, from 7 am until 8 pm (13 hours), 50 weeks of the year. Each panel has to be cut, moulded and then assembled using a cutting machine (Machine C), a moulding machine (Machine M) and an assembly machine (Machine A).

As part of a government scheme to increase renewable energy sources, S Co has guaranteed not to increase the price of small or large panels for the next three years. It has also agreed to supply a minimum of 1000 small panels each year to domestic customers for this three-year period.

Due to poor productivity levels, late orders and declining profits over recent years, the finance director has suggested the introduction of throughput accounting within the organization, together with a 'Just in Time' system of production. Material costs and selling prices for each type of panel are shown below.

	Large panels ($)	Small panels ($)
Selling price per unit	12 600	3 800
Material costs per unit	4 300	1 160

Total factory costs, which include the cost of labour and all factory overheads, are $12 million each year at the plant.

Out of the 13 hours available for production each day, workers take a one hour lunch break. For the remaining 12 hours, Machine C is utilized 85 per cent of the time and Machines M and A are utilized 90 per cent of the time. The unproductive time arises either as a result of routine maintenance or because of staff absenteeism, as each machine needs to be manned by skilled workers in order for the machine to run. The skilled workers are currently only trained to work on one type of machine each. Maintenance work is carried out by external contractors who provide a round-the-clock service (that is, they are available 24 hours a day, seven days a week), should it be required.

The following information is available for Machine M, which has been identified as the bottleneck resource:

	Large panels Hours per unit	Small panels Hours per unit
Machine M	1.4	0.6

There is currently plenty of spare capacity on Machines C and A. Maximum demand for large panels and small panels is 1800 units and 1700 units respectively.

Required:

(a) Calculate the throughput accounting ratio for large panels and for small panels and explain what they indicate to S Co about production of large and small panels. *(9 marks)*

(b) Assume that your calculations in part (a) have shown that large panels have a higher throughput accounting ratio than small panels.

Required:
Using throughput accounting, prepare calculations to determine the optimum production mix and maximum profit of S Co for the next year. *(5 marks)*

(c) Suggest and discuss THREE ways in which S Co could try to increase its production capacity and hence increase throughput in the next year without making any additional investment in machinery. *(6 marks)*

ACCA F5 Performance Management

9.26 Throughput accounting. Thin Co. is a private hospital offering three types of surgical procedure known as A, B and C. Each of them uses a pre-operative injection given by a nurse before the surgery. Thin Co. currently rent an operating theatre from a neighbouring government hospital. Thin Co. does have an operating theatre on its premises, but it has never been put into use since it would cost $750000 to equip. The managing director of Thin, Co. is keen to maximize profits and has heard of something called 'throughput accounting', which may help him to do this. The following information is avaiable:

1 All patients go through a five step process, irrespective of which procedure they are having:
  – step 1: consultation with the advisor;
  – step 2: pre-operative injection given by the nurse;
  – step 3: anaesthetic given by anaesthetist;
  – step 4: procedure performed in theatre by the surgeon;
  – step 5: recovery with the recovery specialist.

2 The price of each of procedure A, B and C is $2700, $3500 and $4250 respectively.

3 The only materials' costs relating to the procedure are for the pre-operative injections given by the nurse, the anaesthetic and the dressings. These are as follows:

	Procedure A $ per procedure	Procedure B $ per procedure	Procedure C $ per procedure
Pre-operative nurse's injections	700	800	1000
Anaesthetic	35	40	45
Dressings	5.60	5.60	5.60

4 There are five members of staff employed by Thin Co. Each works a standard 40-hour week for 47 weeks of the year, a total of 1880 hours each per annum. Their salaries are as follows:
  – Advisor: $45000 per annum;
  – Nurse: $38000 per annum;
  – Anaesthetist: $75000 per annum;
  – Surgeon: $90000 per annum;
  – Recovery specialist: $50000 per annum.

The only other hospital costs (comparable to 'factory costs' in a traditional manufacturing environment) are general overheads, which include the theatre rental costs, and amount to $250000 per annum.

5 Maximum annual demand for A, B and C is 600800 and 1200 procedure respectively. Time spent by each of the five different staff members on each procedure is as follows:

	Procedure A Hours per procedure	Procedure B Hours per procedure	Procedure C Hours per procedure
Advisor	0.24	0.24	0.24
Nurse	0.27	0.28	0.30
Anaesthetist	0.25	0.28	0.33
Surgeon	0.75	1	1.25
Recovery specialist	0.60	0.70	0.74

Part hours are shown as decimals e.g. 0.24 hours = 14.4 minutes (0.24 × 60).

Surgeon's hours have been correctly identified as the bottleneck resource.

Required:

(a) Calculate the throughput accounting ratio for procedure C.
Note: It is recommended that you work in hours as provided in the table rather than minutes. *(6 marks)*

(b) The return per factory hour for products A and B has been calculated and is $2612.53 and $2654.40 respectively. The throughput accounting ratio for A and B has also been calculated and is 8.96 and 9.11 respectively.
Calculate the optimum product mix and the maximum profit per annum. *(7 marks)*

(c) Assume that your calculations in part (b) showed that, if the optimum product mix is adhered to, there will be excess demand for procedure C of 696 procedure per annum. In order to satisfy this excess demand, the company is considering equipping and using its own theatre, as well as continuing to rent the existing theatre. The company cannot rent any more theatre time at either the existing theatre or any other theatres in the area, so equipping its own theatre is the only option. An additional surgeon would be employed to work in the newly equipped theatre.

Required:
Discuss whether the overall profit of the company could be improved by equipping and using the extra theatre.
Note: Some basic calculations may help your discussion. *(7 marks)*

ACCA F5 Performance Management

IM9.1 Advanced. 'I remember being told about the useful decision-making technique of limiting factor analysis (also known as "contribution per unit of the key factor"). If an organization is prepared to believe that, in the short run, all costs other than direct materials are fixed costs, is this not the same thing that throughput accounting is talking about? Why rename limiting factor analysis as throughput accounting?'

Requirements:

(a) Explain what a limiting (or 'key') factor is and what sort of things can become limiting factors in a business situation. Which of the factors in the scenario could become a limiting factor? (8 marks)

(b) Explain the techniques that have been developed to assist in business decision-making when single or multiple limiting factors are encountered. (7 marks)

(c) Explain the management idea known as throughput accounting. State and justify your opinion on whether or not throughput accounting and limiting factor analysis are the same thing. Briefly comment on whether throughput accounting is likely to be of relevance to a company. (10 marks)

CIMA Stage 3 Management Accounting Applications

IM9.2 Intermediate: Acceptance of a contract. JB Limited is a small specialist manufacturer of electronic components and much of its output is used by the makers of aircraft for both civil and military purposes. One of the few aircraft manufacturers has offered a contract to JB Limited for the supply, over the next 12 months, of 400 identical components.

The data relating to the production of each component are as follows:

(i) Material requirements:
   3kg material M1 – see note 1 below
   2kg material P2 – see note 2 below
   1 Part No. 678 – see note 3 below
   Note 1. Material M1 is in continuous use by the company. 1000kg are currently held in stock at a book value of £4.70 per kg but it is known that future purchases will cost £5.50 per kg.

   Note 2. 1200kg of material P2 are held in stock. The original cost of this material was £4.30 per kg but as the material has not been required for the last two years it has been written down to £1.50 per kg scrap value. The only foreseeable alternative use is as a substitute for material P4 (in current use) but this would involve further processing costs of £1.60 per kg. The current cost of material P4 is £3.60 per kg.

   Note 3. It is estimated that Part No. 678 could be bought for £50 each.

(ii) Labour requirements: Each component would require five hours of skilled labour and five hours of semi-skilled. An employee possessing the necessary skills is available and is currently paid £12 per hour. A replacement would, however, have to be obtained at a rate of £13 per hour for the work which would otherwise be done by the skilled employee. The current rate for semi-skilled work is £10 per hour and an additional employee could be appointed for this work.

(iii) Overhead: JB Limited absorbs overhead by a machine hour rate, currently £20 per hour of which £7 is for variable overhead and £13 for fixed overhead. If this contract is undertaken it is estimated that fixed costs will increase for the duration of the contract by £3200. Spare machine capacity is available and each component would require four machine hours.

A price of £250 per component has been suggested by the large company which makes aircraft.

You are required to:

(a) state whether or not the contract should be accepted and support your conclusion with appropriate figures for presentation to management; (16 marks)

(b) comment briefly on *three* factors that management ought to consider and which may influence their decision. (9 marks)

CIMA Cost Accounting Stage 2

IM9.3 Intermediate: Preparation of a cost estimate involving the identification of relevant costs. You are the management accountant of a publishing and printing company that has been asked to quote for the production of a programme for the local village fair. The work would be carried out in addition to the normal work of the company. Because of existing commitments, some weekend working would be required to complete the printing of the programme. A trainee accountant has produced the following cost estimate based on the resources as specified by the production manager:

	(£)
Direct materials:	
paper (book value)	5 000
inks (purchase price)	2 400
Direct labour:	
skilled 250 hours at £14.00	3 500
unskilled 100 hours at £12.00	1 200
Variable overhead 350 hours at £4.00	1 400
Printing press depreciation 200 hours at £2.50	500
Fixed production costs 350 hours at £6.00	2 100
Estimating department costs	400
	16 500

You are aware that considerable publicity could be obtained for the company if you are able to win this order and the price quoted must be very competitive.

The following are relevant to the cost estimate above:

1 The paper to be used is currently in stock at a value of £5000. It is of an unusual colour which has not been used for some time. The replacement price of the paper is £8000, while the scrap value of that in stock is £2500. The production manager does not foresee any alternative use for the paper if it is not used for the village fair programmes.

2 The inks required are not held in stock. They would have to be purchased in bulk at a cost of £3000. Eighty per cent of the ink purchased would be used in printing the programme. No other use is foreseen for the remainder.

3 Skilled direct labour is in short supply, and to accommodate the printing of the programmes, 50 per cent of the time required would be worked at weekends, for which a premium of 25 per cent above the normal hourly rate is paid. The normal hourly rate is £14.00 per hour.

4 Unskilled labour is presently under-utilized, and at present 200 hours per week are recorded as idle time. If the printing work is carried out at a weekend, 25 unskilled hours would have to occur at this time, but the employees concerned would be given two hours' time off (for which they would be paid) in lieu of each hour worked.

5 Variable overhead represents the cost of operating the printing press and binding machines.

6 When not being used by the company, the printing press is hired to outside companies for £6.00 per hour. This earns a contribution of £3.00 per hour. There is unlimited demand for this facility.

7 Fixed production costs are those incurred by and absorbed into production, using an hourly rate based on budgeted activity.

8 The cost of the estimating department represents time spent in discussion with the village fair committee concerning the printing of its programme.

Required:

(a) Prepare a revised cost estimate using the opportunity cost approach, showing clearly the minimum price that the company should accept for the order. Give reasons for each resource valuation in your cost estimate. (16 marks)

(b) Explain why contribution theory is used as a basis for providing information relevant to decision-making.

(4 marks)

(c) Explain the relevance of opportunity costs in decision-making.

(5 marks)

CIMA Stage 2 Operational Costs Accounting

IM9.4 Intermediate: Decision on whether to launch a new product. A company is currently manufacturing at only 60 per cent of full practical capacity, in each of its two production departments, due to a reduction in market share. The company is seeking to launch a new product which, it is hoped, will recover some lost sales.

The estimated direct costs of the new product, Product X, are to be established from the following information:

Direct materials:

Every 100 units of the product will require 30 kilos net of Material A. Losses of 10 per cent of materials input are to be expected. Material A costs £5.40 per kilo before discount. A quantity discount of 5 per cent is given on all purchases if the monthly purchase quantity exceeds 25 000 kilos. Other materials are expected to cost £1.34 per unit of Product X.

Direct labour (per 100 units):

Department 1: 40 hours at £12.00 per hour.

Department 2: 15 hours at £13.00 per hour.

Separate overhead absorption rates are established for each production department. Department 1 overheads are absorbed at 130 per cent of direct wages, which is based on the expected overhead costs and usage of capacity if Product X is launched. The rate in Department 2 is to be established as a rate per direct labour hour also based on expected usage of capacity. The following annual figures for Department 2 are based on full practical capacity:

Overhead	£5 424 000
Direct labour hours	2 200 000

Variable overheads in Department 1 are assessed at 40 per cent of direct wages and in Department 2 are £1 980 000 (at full practical capacity).

Non-production overheads are estimated as follows (per unit of Product X):

Variable	£0.70
Fixed	£1.95

The selling price for Product X is expected to be £16 per unit, with annual sales of 2 400 000 units.

Required:

(a) Determine the estimated cost per unit of Product X.

(13 marks)

(b) Comment on the viability of Product X. *(7 marks)*

(c) Market research indicates that an alternative selling price for Product X could be £15.50 per unit, at which price annual sales would be expected to be 2 900 000 units. Determine, and comment briefly on, the optimum selling price.

(5 marks)

ACCA Cost and Management Accounting 1

IM9.5 Intermediate: Limiting key factors. PDR plc manufactures four products using the same machinery. The following details relate to its products:

	Product A £ per unit	Product B £ per unit	Product C £ per unit	Product D £ per unit
Selling price	28	30	45	42
Direct material	5	6	8	6
Direct labour	4	4	8	8
Variable overhead	3	3	6	6
Fixed overhead*	8	8	16	16

	Product A £ per unit	Product B £ per unit	Product C £ per unit	Product D £ per unit
Profit	8	9	7	6
Labour hours	0.25	0.25	0.50	0.50
Machine hours	4	3	4	5
	Units	Units	Units	Units
Maximum demand per week	200	180	250	100

*Fixed costs are £8000 per week.

There is a maximum of 2000 machine hours available per week.

Requirement:

(a) Determine the production plan which will maximize the weekly profit of PDR plc and prepare a profit statement showing the profit your plan will yield. *(10 marks)*

(b) The marketing director of PDR plc is concerned at the company's inability to meet the quantity demanded by its customers.

Two alternative strategies are being considered to overcome this:

(i) To increase the number of hours worked using the existing machinery by working overtime. Such overtime would be paid at a premium of 50 per cent above normal labour rates, and variable overhead costs would be expected to increase in proportion to labour costs.

(ii) To buy product B from an overseas supplier at a cost of £19 per unit including carriage. This would need to be repackaged at a cost of £1 per unit before it could be sold.

Requirement:

Evaluate each of the two alternative strategies and, as management accountant, prepare a report to the marketing director, stating your reasons (quantitative and qualitative) as to which, if either, should be adopted. *(15 marks)*

CIMA Stage 2 Operational Cost Accounting

IM9.6 Intermediate: Allocation of scarce capacity and make-or-buy decision where scarce capacity exists. PQR Limited is an engineering company engaged in the manufacture of components and finished products.

The company is highly mechanized and each of the components and finished products requires the use of one or more types of machine in its machining department. The following costs and revenues (where appropriate) relate to a single component or unit of the finished product:

	Components		Finished products	
	A £	B £	C £	D £
Selling price			127	161
Direct materials	8	29	33	38
Direct wages	10	30	20	25
Variable overhead:				
Drilling	6	3	9	12
Grinding	8	16	4	12
Fixed overhead:				
Drilling	12	6	18	24
Grinding	10	20	5	15
Total cost	54	104	89	126

Notes

1 Overhead absorption rates per machine hour are as follows:

	Variable £	Fixed £
Drilling (per hour)	3	6
Grinding (per hour)	4	5

2 Components A and B are NOT used in finished products C and D. They are used in the company's other products, none of which uses the drilling or grinding machines. The company does not manufacture any other components.

3 The number of machine drilling hours available is limited to 1650 per week. There are 2500 machine grinding hours available per week. These numbers of hours have been used to calculate the absorption rates stated above.

4 The maximum demand in units per week for each of the finished products has been estimated by the marketing director as:

Product C	250 units
Product D	500 units

5 The internal demand for components A and B each week is as follows:

Component A	50 units
Component B	100 units

6 There is no external market for components A and B.

7 PQR Limited has a contract to supply 50 units of each of its finished products to a major customer each week. These quantities are included in the maximum units of demand given in note 5 above.

Requirement:

(a) Calculate the number of units of each finished product that PQR Limited should produce in order to maximize its profits, and the profit per week that this should yield.
(12 marks)

(b) (i) The production director has now discovered that he can obtain unlimited quantities of components identical to A and B for £50 and £96 per unit respectively. State whether this information changes the production plan of the company if it wishes to continue to maximize its profits per week. If appropriate, state the revised production plan and the net benefit per week caused by the change to the production plan. *(7 marks)*

(ii) The solution of problems involving more than one limiting factor requires the use of linear programming.

Explain why this technique must be used in such circumstances, and the steps used to solve such a problem when using the graphical linear programming technique. *(6 marks)*

CIMA Stage 2 Operational Cost Accounting

IM9.7 Intermediate: Limiting/key factors and a decision whether it is profitable to expand output by overtime. B Ltd manufactures a range of products which are sold to a limited number of wholesale outlets. Four of these products are manufactured in a particular department on common equipment. No other facilities are available for the manufacture of these products.

Owing to greater than expected increases in demand, normal single shift working is rapidly becoming insufficient to meet sales requirements. Overtime and, in the longer term, expansion of facilities are being considered.

Selling prices and product costs, based on single shift working utilizing practical capacity to the full, are as follows:

	Product (£/unit)			
	W	X	Y	Z
Selling price	3.650	3.900	2.250	2.950
Product costs:				
Direct materials	0.805	0.996	0.450	0.647
Direct labour	0.604	0.651	0.405	0.509
Variable manufacturing overhead	0.240	0.247	0.201	0.217
Fixed manufacturing overhead	0.855	0.950	0.475	0.760
Variable selling and admin. overhead	0.216	0.216	0.216	0.216
Fixed selling and admin. overhead	0.365	0.390	0.225	0.295

Fixed manufacturing overheads are absorbed on the basis of machine hours which, at practical capacity, are 2250 per period. Total fixed manufacturing overhead per period is £427500. Fixed selling and administration overhead, which totals £190000 per period, is shared among products at a rate of 10 per cent of sales.

The sales forecast for the following period (in thousands of units) is:

Product W	190
Product X	125
Product Y	144
Product Z	142

Overtime could be worked to make up any production shortfall in normal time. Direct labour would be paid at a premium of 50 per cent above basic rate. Other variable costs would be expected to remain unchanged per unit of output. Fixed costs would increase by £24570 per period.

Required:

(a) If overtime is not worked in the following period, recommend the quantity of each product that should be manufactured in order to maximize profit. *(12 marks)*

(b) Calculate the expected profit in the following period if overtime is worked as necessary to meet sales requirements. *(7 marks)*

(c) Consider the factors which should influence the decision whether or not to work overtime in such a situation. *(6 marks)*

ACCA Cost and Management Accounting 1

IM9.8 Advanced: Allocation of land to four different types of vegetable based on key factor principles. A South American farmer has 960 hectares of land on which he grows squash, kale, lettuce and beans. Of the total, 680 hectares are suitable for all four vegetables, but the remaining 280 hectares are suitable only for kale and lettuce. Labour for all kinds of farm work is plentiful.

The market requires that all four types of vegetable must be produced with a minimum of 10000 boxes of any one line. The farmer has decided that the area devoted to any crop should be in terms of complete hectares and not in fractions of a hectare. The only other limitation is that not more than 227500 boxes of any one crop should be produced.

Data concerning production, market prices and costs are as follows:

	Squash	Kale	Lettuce	Beans
Annual yield				
(boxes per hectare)	350	100	70	180
	(Pesos)	(Pesos)	(Pesos)	(Pesos)
Costs				
Direct:				
Materials per hectare	476	216	192	312
Labour:				
Growing, per hectare	896	608	372	528
Harvesting and packing, per box	3.60	3.28	4.40	5.20
Transport, per box	5.20	5.20	4.00	9.60
Market price, per box	15.38	15.87	18.38	22.27

Fixed overhead per annum:

	(Pesos)
Growing	122000
Harvesting	74000
Transport	74000
General administration	100000
Notional rent	74000

It is possible to make the entire farm viable for all four vegetables if certain drainage work is undertaken. This would involve capital investment and it would have the following effects on direct harvesting costs of some of the vegetables:

| | | Change from normal harvesting costs | |
		Squash	Beans
	Capital cost (Pesos)	(Pesos per box)	
First lot of 10 hectares	19 000 total	+1.2	−1.2
Next lot of 10 hectares	17 500 total	+1.3	−1.3
Next lot of 10 hectares	15 000 total	+1.4	−1.4
Remaining land (per hectare)	1 850	+1.5	−1.5

The farmer is willing to undertake such investment only if he can obtain a return of 15 per cent DCF for a four-year period.

You are required to:

(a) Advise the farmer, within the given constraints:

   (i) the area to be cultivated with each crop if he is to achieve the largest total profit;   *(13 marks)*

   (ii) the amount of this total profit;   *(3 marks)*

   (iii) the number of hectares it is worth draining and the use to which they would be put.   *(10 marks)*

(b) Comment briefly on four of the financial dangers of going ahead with the drainage work.   *(4 marks)*

Notes

Show all relevant calculations in arriving at your answer. Ignore tax and inflation.

CIMA Stage 4 Management Accounting – Decision Making

IM9.9 Advanced: Relevant costs for a pricing decision.
Johnson trades as a chandler at the Savoy Marina. His profit in this business during the year to 30 June was £12 000. Johnson also undertakes occasional contracts to build pleasure cruisers, and is considering the price at which to bid for the contract to build the *Blue Blood* for Mr B.W. Dunn, delivery to be in one year's time. He has no other contract in hand, or under consideration, for at least the next few months.

Johnson expects that if he undertakes the contract he would devote one-quarter of his time to it. To facilitate this, he would employ G. Harrison, an unqualified practitioner, to undertake his book-keeping and other paperwork, at a cost of £2000.

He would also have to employ on the contract one supervisor at a cost of £11 000 and two craftsmen at a cost of £8800 each; these costs include Johnson's normal apportionment of the fixed overheads of his business at the rate of 10 per cent of labour cost.

During spells of bad weather one of the craftsmen could be employed for the equivalent of up to three months full time during the winter in maintenance and painting work in the chandler's business. He would use materials costing £1000. Johnson already has two inclusive quotations from jobbing builders for this maintenance and painting work, one for £2500 and the other for £3500, the work to start immediately.

The equipment that would be used on the *Blue Blood* contract was bought nine years ago for £21 000. Depreciation has been written off on a straight line basis, assuming a ten-year life and a scrap value of £1000. The current replacement cost of similar new equipment is £60 000, and is expected to be £66 000 in one year's time. Johnson has recently been offered £6000 for the equipment, and considers that in a year's time he would have little difficulty in obtaining £3000 for it. The plant is useful to Johnson only for contract work.

In order to build the *Blue Blood* Johnson will need six types of material, as follows:

| | No. of units | | Price per unit (£) | | |
Material code	In stock	Needed for contract	Purchase price of stock items	Current purchase price	Current resale price
A	100	1000	1.10	3.00	2.00
B	1 100	1000	2.00	0.90	1.00
C	—	100	—	6.00	—
D	100	200	4.00	3.00	2.00
E	50 000	5000	0.18	0.20	0.25
F	1 000	3000	0.90	2.00	1.00

Materials B and E are sold regularly in the chandler's business. Material A could be sold to a local sculptor, if not used for the contract. Materials A and E can be used for other purposes, such as property maintenance. Johnson has no other use for materials D and F, the stocks of which are obsolete.

The *Blue Blood* would be built in a yard held on a lease with four years remaining at a fixed annual rental of £5000. It would occupy half of this yard, which is useful to Johnson only for contract work. Johnson anticipates that the direct expenses of the contract, other than those noted above, would be £6500.

Johnson has recently been offered a one-year appointment at a fee of £15 000 to manage a boat building firm on the Isle of Wight. If he accepted the offer he would be unable to take on the contract to build *Blue Blood* or any other contract. He would have to employ a manager to run the chandler's business at an annual cost (including fidelity insurance) of £10 000, and would incur additional personal living costs of £2000.

You are required:

(a) to calculate the price at which Johnson should be willing to take on the contract in order to break even, based exclusively on the information given above;   *(15 marks)*

(b) to set out any further considerations which you think that Johnson should take into account in setting the price at which he would tender for the contract.   *(10 marks)*

Ignore taxation.

ICAEW Management Accounting

IM9.10 Advanced: Decision on whether a department should be closed. Shortflower Ltd currently publish, print and distribute a range of catalogues and instruction manuals. The management has now decided to discontinue printing and distribution and concentrate solely on publishing. Longplant Ltd will print and distribute the range of catalogues and instruction manuals on behalf of Shortflower Ltd commencing either at 30 June or 30 November. Longplant Ltd will receive £65 000 per month for a contract which will commence either at 30 June or 30 November. The results of Shortflower Ltd for a typical month are as follows:

	Publishing (£000)	Printing (£000)	Distribution (£000)
Salaries and wages	28	18	4
Materials and supplies	5.5	31	1.1
Occupancy costs	7	8.5	1.2
Depreciation	0.8	4.2	0.7

Other information has been gathered relating to the possible closure proposals:

   (i) Two specialist staff from printing will be retained at their present salary of £1500 each per month in order to fulfil a link function with Longplant Ltd. One further staff member will be transferred to publishing to fill a staff vacancy through staff turnover, anticipated in July. This staff member will be paid at his present salary of £1400 per month, which is £100 more than that of the staff member who is expected to leave. On closure, all other printing and distribution staff will be made redundant and paid an average of two months' redundancy pay.

(ii) The printing department has a supply of materials (already paid for) which cost £18 000 and which will be sold to Longplant Ltd for £10 000 if closure takes place on 30 June. Otherwise the material will be used as part of the July printing requirements. The distribution department has a contract to purchase pallets at a cost of £500 per month for July and August. A cancellation clause allows for non-delivery of the pallets for July and August for a one-off payment of £300. Non-delivery for August only will require a payment of £100. If the pallets are taken from the supplier, Longplant Ltd has agreed to purchase them at a price of £380 for each month's supply that is available. Pallet costs are included in the distribution material and supplies cost stated for a typical month.

(iii) Company expenditure on apportioned occupancy costs to printing and distribution will be reduced by 15 per cent per month if printing and distribution departments are closed. At present, 30 per cent of printing and 25 per cent of distribution occupancy costs are directly attributable costs which are avoidable on closure, while the remainder are apportioned costs.

(iv) Closure of the printing and distribution departments will make it possible to sub-let part of the building for a monthly fee of £2500 when space is available.

(v) Printing plant and machinery has an estimated net book value of £48 000 at 30 June. It is anticipated that it will be sold at a loss of £21 000 on 30 June. If sold on 30 November the prospective buyer will pay £25 000.

(vi) The net book value of distribution vehicles at 30 June is estimated as £80 000. They could be sold to the original supplier at £48 000 on 30 June. The original supplier would purchase the vehicles on 30 November for a price of £44 000.

Required:

Using the above information, prepare a summary to show whether Shortflower Ltd should close the printing and distribution departments on financial grounds on 30 June or on 30 November. Explanatory notes and calculations should be shown. Ignore taxation. *(22 marks)*

ACCA Level 2 Cost and Management Accounting

IM9.11 Advanced: Throughput accounting.

(a) Flopro plc makes and sells two products A and B, each of which passes through the same automated production operations. The following estimated information is available for period 1:

(i) Product unit data:

	A	B
Direct material cost (£)	2	40
Variable production overhead cost (£)	28	4
Overall hours per product unit (hours)	0.25	0.15

(ii) Production/sales of products A and B are 120 000 units and 45 000 units respectively. The selling prices per unit for A and B are £60 and £70 respectively.

(iii) Maximum demand for each product is 20 per cent above the estimated sales levels.

(iv) Total fixed production overhead cost is £1 470 000. This is absorbed by products A and B at an average rate per hour based on the estimated production levels.

Required:

Using net profit as the decision measure, show why the management of Flopro plc argues that it is indifferent on financial grounds as to the mix of products A and B which should be produced and sold, and calculate the total net profit for period 1. *(6 marks)*

(b) One of the production operations has a maximum capacity of 3075 hours which has been identified as a bottleneck that limits the overall production/sales of products A and B. The bottleneck hours required per product unit for products A and B are 0.02 and 0.015 respectively.
All other information detailed in (a) still applies.

Required:

Calculate the mix (units) of products A and B which will maximize net profit and the value (£) of the maximum net profit. *(8 marks)*

(c) The bottleneck situation detailed in (b) still applies. Flopro plc has decided to determine the profit maximizing mix of products A and B based on the throughput accounting principle of maximizing the throughput return per production hour of the bottleneck resource. This may be measured as:

$$\text{Throughput return per production hour} = \frac{(\text{selling price} - \text{material cost})}{\text{bottleneck hours per unit}}$$

All other information detailed in (a) and (b) still applies, except that the variable overhead cost as per (a) is now considered to be fixed for the short/intermediate term, based on the value (£) which applied to the product mix in (a).

Required:

(i) Calculate the mix (units) of products A and B which will maximize net profit and the value of that net profit. *(8 marks)*

(ii) Calculate the throughput accounting ratio for product B which is calculated as: *(3 marks)*

$$\frac{\text{throughput return per hour of bottleneck resource for product B}}{\text{overall total overhead cost per hour of bottleneck resource}}$$

(iii) Comment on the interpretation of throughput accounting ratios and their use as a control device. You should refer to the ratio for product B in your answer. *(6 marks)*

(iv) It is estimated that the direct material cost per unit of product B may increase by 20 per cent due to shortage of supply.
Calculate the revised throughput accounting ratio for product B and comment on it. *(4 marks)*

ACCA Paper 9 Information for Control and Decision Making

10
PRICING DECISIONS AND PROFITABILITY ANALYSIS

LEARNING OBJECTIVES After studying this chapter, you should be able to:

- explain the relevant cost information that should be presented in price-setting firms for both short- term and long-term decisions;

- describe product and customer profitability analysis and the information that should be included for managing the product and customer mix;

- describe the target costing approach to pricing;

- describe the different cost-plus pricing methods for deriving selling prices;

- explain the limitations of cost-plus pricing;

- justify why cost-plus pricing is widely used;

- identify and describe the different pricing policies.

Accounting information is often an important input to pricing decisions. Organizations that sell products or services that are highly customized or differentiated from another by special features, or who are market leaders, have some discretion in setting selling prices. In these organizations, the pricing decision will be influenced by the cost of the product. The cost information that is accumulated and presented is therefore important for pricing decisions. In other organizations, prices are set by overall market and supply and demand forces and they have little influence over the selling prices of their products and services. Nevertheless, cost information is still of considerable importance in these organizations for determining the relative profitability of different products and services so that management can determine the target product mix to which its marketing effort should be directed.

In this chapter, we shall focus on both of the above situations. We shall consider the role that accounting information plays in determining the selling price by a price-setting firm. Where prices are set by the market, our emphasis will be on examining the cost information that is required for product mix decisions. In particular, we shall focus on both product and customer profitability analysis. The same approaches, however, can be applied to the provision of services such as financial or legal.

The theoretical solution to pricing decisions is derived from economic theory, which explains how the optimal selling price is determined. A knowledge of economic theory is not essential for understanding the content of this chapter but it does provide a theoretical background for the principles influencing pricing decisions. For a discussion of economic theory relating to pricing decisions you should refer to Learning Note 10.1 on the dedicated digital support resources (see Preface for details).

THE ROLE OF COST INFORMATION IN PRICING DECISIONS

Most organizations need to make decisions about setting or accepting selling prices for their products or services. In some firms, prices are set by overall market supply and demand forces and the firm has little or no influence over the selling prices of its products or services. This situation is likely to occur where there are many firms in an industry and there is little to distinguish their products from each other. No one firm can influence prices significantly by its own actions. For example, in commodity markets such as wheat, coffee, rice and sugar, prices are set for the market as a whole based on the forces of supply and demand. Also, small firms operating in an industry where prices are set by the dominant market leaders will have little influence over the price of their products or services. Firms that have little or no influence over the prices of their products or services are described as **price takers**.

In contrast, firms selling products or services that are highly customized or differentiated from one another by special features, or who are market leaders, have some discretion in setting prices. Here, the pricing decision will be influenced by the cost of the product, the actions of competitors and the extent to which customers value the product. We shall describe those firms that have some discretion over setting the selling price of their products or services as **price setters**. In practice, firms may be price setters for some of their products and price takers for others.

Where firms are price setters, cost information is often an important input into the pricing decision. Cost information is also of vital importance to price takers in deciding on the output and mix of products and services to which their marketing effort should be directed, given their market prices. For both price takers and price setters, the decision time horizon determines the cost information that is relevant for product pricing or output mix decisions. We shall therefore consider the following four different situations:

1 a price-setting firm facing short-run pricing decisions;
2 a price-setting firm facing long-run pricing decisions;
3 a price-taking firm facing short-run product mix decisions;
4 a price-taking firm facing long-run product mix decisions.

A PRICE-SETTING FIRM FACING SHORT-RUN PRICING DECISIONS

Companies can encounter situations where they have temporary unutilized capacity and are faced with the opportunity of bidding for a one-time special order in competition with other suppliers. In this situation, only the incremental costs of undertaking the order should be taken into account. It is likely that most of the resources required to fill the order will have already been acquired and the cost of these resources will be incurred whether or not the bid is accepted by the customer. Typically, the incremental costs are likely to consist of:

● extra materials that are required to fulfil the order;
● any extra part-time labour, overtime or other labour costs;
● the extra energy and maintenance costs for the machinery and equipment required to complete the order.

The incremental costs of one-off special orders in service companies are likely to be minimal. For example, the incremental cost of accepting one-off special business for a hotel may consist of only the cost of additional meals, laundering and bathroom facilities.

Bids should be made at prices that exceed incremental costs. Any excess of revenues over incremental costs will provide a contribution to committed fixed costs that would not otherwise have been obtained. Given the short-term nature of the decision, long-term considerations are likely to be non-existent and, apart from the consideration of bids by competitors, cost data are likely to be the dominant factor in determining the bid price.

Any bid for one-time special orders that is based on covering only short-term incremental costs must meet all of the following conditions:

- Sufficient capacity is available for all resources that are required to fulfil the order. If some resources are fully utilized, opportunity costs of the scarce resources must be covered by the bid price (see Chapter 9 for an illustration).

- The bid price will not affect the future selling prices and the customer will not expect repeat business to be priced to cover short-term incremental costs.

- The order will utilize unused capacity for only a short period and capacity will be released for use on more profitable opportunities. If more profitable opportunities do not exist and a short-term focus is always adopted to utilize unused capacity, then the effect of pricing a series of special orders over several periods to cover incremental costs constitutes a long-term decision. Thus, the situation arises whereby the decision to reduce capacity is continually deferred and short-term incremental costs are used for long-term decisions.

A PRICE-SETTING FIRM FACING LONG-RUN PRICING DECISIONS

In this section, we shall focus on three approaches that are relevant to a price-setting firm facing long-run pricing decisions. They are:

1 pricing customized products/services;

2 pricing non-customized products/services;

3 target costing for pricing non-customized products/services.

Pricing customized products/services

Customized products or services relate to situations in which products or services tend to be unique so that no comparable market prices exist for them. Since sales revenues must cover costs for a firm to make a profit, many companies use product costs as an input to establish selling prices. Product costs are calculated and a desired profit margin is added to determine the selling price. This approach is called cost-plus pricing. For example, garages undertaking vehicle repairs establish the prices charged to customers using cost-plus pricing. Similarly, firms of accountants use cost-plus pricing to determine the price for the accountancy services that they have provided for their customers. Companies use different cost bases and mark-ups (i.e. the desired profit margin) to determine their selling prices. Consider the following information:

Cost base		Mark-up percentage %	Cost-plus selling price (£)
(1) Direct variable costs	200	150	500
(2) Direct fixed (non-variable) costs	100		
(3) Total direct costs	300	70	510
(4) Indirect (overhead) costs	80		
(5) Total cost	380	35	513

REAL WORLD VIEWS 10.1

A price-setting firm facing long-run pricing decisions – pricing cloud computing

Cloud computing is a term used to describe the delivery of information systems without, for example, the purchase of physical hardware or even software in some instances. What this means for an average business is that they can purchase processing capability, data storage or content delivery of large-scale computer systems, but at a fraction of the purchase price of the same equipment. Thus, expenditures move from a capital nature to an operational nature.

Amazon Web Services (aws.amazon.com) has been one of the pace setting firms in cloud computing. An arm of the well-known online retailer, the web services division offers a broad range of services from computing to database services, payments and billing, data storage and even a staffed support service. The pricing depends on the services offered, and until recently the competition was scarce. Until around 2010, Amazon was the market leader in cloud service provision. Then Microsoft released its cloud computing (Azure) and the immediate response of Amazon was to reduce all prices by $0.02 per gigabyte, which at the highest usage levels represented a price drop of 40 per cent. Pricing of most cloud providers now operates on a pay-as-you-use basis – the more services used, the higher the cost – and there are many more operators such as Rackspace, Google Cloud and IBM.

In the accounting field, a number of providers offer cloud-based software services, charging a small monthly fee. For example, Quickbooks Online (quickbooksonline.intuit.com) is available from $10–40 per month depending on the product. Other examples include Billfaster (www.billfaster.com) at €20/£16 per month, and Kashflow (www.kashflow.com) ranging from £7–18 per month. Increasingly, such cloud software providers are providing more and more add-ons (e.g. Paypal integration) to retain customers. Almost all providers also offer a free trial period, typically 30 days. Some even offer totally free products, such as Wave Accounting (see www.waveapps.com/invoice)

Questions

1 Do you think large-scale providers like Amazon, Microsoft and IBM can influence prices of cloud computing in the longer term?

2 What is your opinion on a long-term price of zero, as currently offered by some cloud providers of accounting software? Is this model sustainable in the long run?

References

Rosenberg, D. (2010) Amazon Web Services continues to take the lead in cloud services, including pricing. Will 'free' be the only way to beat AWS?, cnet, 3 February. Available at www.cnet.com/news/already-a-pacesetter-amazon-drops-cloud-pricing

Intuit Inc. (2016) Available at quickbooks.intuit.com/pricing

---

In the above illustration, three different cost bases are used resulting in three different selling prices. In row (1), only direct variable costs are assigned to products for cost-plus pricing and a high percentage mark-up (150 per cent) is added to cover direct fixed costs and indirect costs and also provide a contribution towards profit. The second cost base is row (3) that incorporates both direct variable and fixed costs. Here a smaller percentage margin (70 per cent) is added to cover indirect overhead costs and a profit contribution. The final cost base, shown in row (5), includes the assignment of a share of company indirect (overhead) costs to each product, and when this is added to direct costs a total product cost is computed. This cost (also known as full cost or long-run cost) is the estimated sum of all those resources that are committed to a product in the long run. It represents an attempt to allocate a share of all costs to products to ensure that all costs are covered in the cost base. The lowest percentage mark-up (35 per cent) is therefore added since the aim is to provide only a profit contribution.

The above illustration is applicable to both manufacturing and non-manufacturing organizations. However, manufacturing organizations generally divide overhead costs (row 4) into manufacturing and non-manufacturing overheads. For example, if the overheads of £80 consist of £60 manufacturing and £20 non-manufacturing, then £60 would be added to row (3) above to produce a total manufacturing cost of £360. Assuming that a profit margin of 40 per cent is added to the total manufacturing cost to provide a contribution to non-manufacturing costs and profit, the selling price would be £504.

Mark-ups are related to the demand for a product. A firm is able to command a higher mark-up for a product that has a high demand. Mark-ups are also likely to decrease when competition is intensive. Target mark-up percentages tend to vary from product line to product line to correspond with well-established differences in custom, competitive position and likely demand. For example, luxury goods with a low sales turnover may attract high profit margins whereas non-luxury goods with a high sales turnover may attract low profit margins.

Note that once the target selling price has been calculated, it is rarely adopted without amendment. The price is adjusted upwards or downwards depending on such factors as the future capacity that is available, the extent of competition from other firms and management's general knowledge of the market. For example, if the price calculation is much lower than that which management considers the customer will be prepared to pay, the price may be increased.

We may ask ourselves the question, 'Why should cost-based pricing formulae be used when the final price is likely to be altered by management?' The answer is that cost-based pricing formulae provide an initial approximation of the selling price. It is a target price and is important information, although by no means the only information that should be used when the final pricing decision is made. Management should use this information, together with their knowledge of the market and their intended pricing strategies, before the final price is set.

Pricing non-customized products/services

With highly customized products or services, sales are likely to be to a single customer with the pricing decision being based on direct negotiations with the customer for a known quantity. In contrast, a market leader must make a pricing decision, normally for large and unknown volumes of a single product, that is sold to thousands of different customers. To apply cost-plus pricing in this situation an estimate is required of sales volume to determine a unit cost, which will determine the cost-plus selling price. This circular process occurs because we are now faced with two unknowns that have a cause-and-effect relationship, namely selling price and sales volume. In this situation, it is recommended that cost-plus selling prices are estimated for a range of potential sales volumes. Consider the information presented in Example 10.1 (Case A).

You will see that the Auckland Company has produced estimates of total costs for a range of activity levels. Instead of adding a percentage profit margin, the Auckland Company has added a fixed lump sum target contribution of £2 million to cover fixed costs and provide a profit contribution.

The information presented indicates to management the sales volumes, and their accompanying selling prices, that are required to generate the required profit contribution. The unit cost calculation indicates the break-even selling price at each sales volume that is required to cover the cost of the resources committed at that particular volume. Management must assess the likelihood of selling the specified volumes at the designated prices and choose the price that they consider has the highest probability of generating at least the specified sales volume. If none of the sales volumes is likely to be achieved at the designated selling prices management must consider how demand can be stimulated and/or costs reduced to make the product viable. If neither of these is successful the product should not be launched; and the same goes if other strategies were to be used. The final decision must be based on management judgement and knowledge of the market.

The situation presented in Example 10.1 represents the most extreme example of the lack of market data for making a pricing decision. If we reconsider the pricing decision faced by the company, it is likely that similar products are already marketed and information may be available relating to their market shares and sales volumes. Assuming that Auckland's product is differentiated from other similar products, a relative comparison should be possible of its strengths and weaknesses and whether customers would be prepared to pay a price in excess of the prices of similar products. It is therefore possible that Auckland may be able to undertake market research to obtain rough approximations of demand levels at a range of potential selling prices as illustrated in Example 10.1 (Case B). Let us assume that Auckland adopts this approach, and apart from this, the facts are the same as those given in Example 10.1 (Case A).

Now look at Case B in Example 10.1. The demand estimates are given for a range of selling prices. In addition, the projected costs, sales revenues and profit contribution are shown. You can see that profits

EXAMPLE 10.1

Case A

The Auckland Company is launching a new product. Sales volume will be dependent on the selling price and customer acceptance but because the product differs substantially from other products within the same product category it has not been possible to obtain any meaningful estimates of price/demand relationships. The best estimate is that demand is likely to range between 100000 and 200000 units provided that the selling price is less than £100. Based on this information the company has produced the following cost estimates and selling prices required to generate a target profit contribution of £2 million from the product.

Sales volume (000s)	100	120	140	160	180	200
Total cost (£000s)	10000	10800	11200	11600	12600	13000
Required profit contribution (£000s)	2000	2000	2000	2000	2000	2000
Required sales revenues (£000s)	12000	12800	13200	13600	14600	15000
Required selling price to achieve target profit contribution (£)	120.00	106.67	94.29	85.00	81.11	75.00
Unit cost (£)	100.00	90.00	80.00	72.50	70.00	65.00

Case B

Assume now an alternative scenario for the product in Case A. The same cost schedule applies but the £2 million minimum contribution no longer applies. In addition, Auckland now undertakes market research. Based on this research, and comparisons with similar product types and their current selling prices and sales volumes, estimates of sales demand at different selling prices have been made. These estimates, together with the estimates of total costs obtained in Case A are shown below:

Potential selling price	£100	£90	£80	£70	£60
Estimated sales volume at the potential selling price (000s)	120	140	180	190	200
Estimated total sales revenue (£000s)	12000	12600	14400	13300	12000
Estimated total cost (£000s)	10800	11200	12600	12800	13000
Estimated profit (loss) contribution (£000s)	1200	1400	1800	500	(1000)

are maximized at a selling price of £80. The information also shows the effect of pursuing other pricing policies. For example, a lower selling price of £70 might be selected to discourage competition and ensure that a larger share of the market is obtained in the future.

Pricing non-customized products/services using target costing

Instead of using the cost-plus pricing approach described in Example 10.1 (Case A) whereby cost is used as the starting point to determine the selling price, target costing is the reverse of this process. With target costing, the starting point is the determination of the target selling price. Next, a standard or desired profit margin is deducted to get a target cost for the product. The aim is to ensure that the future cost will not be higher than the target cost. The stages involved in target costing can be summarized as follows:

Stage 1: determine the target price that customers will be prepared to pay for the product.

Stage 2: deduct a target profit margin from the target price to determine the target cost.

Stage 3: estimate the actual cost of the product.

Stage 4: if estimated actual cost exceeds the target cost investigate ways of driving down the actual cost to the target cost.

The first stage requires market research to determine customers' perceived value of the product, its differentiation value relative to competing products and the price of competing products. The target profit margin depends on the planned return on investment for the organization as a whole and profit as a percentage of sales. This is then decomposed into a target profit for each product that is then deducted from the target price to give the target cost. The target cost is compared with the predicted actual cost. If the predicted actual cost is above the target cost, intensive efforts are made to close the gap. Product designers focus on modifying the design of the product so that it becomes cheaper to produce. Manufacturing engineers also concentrate on methods of improving production processes and efficiencies.

The aim is to drive the predicted actual cost down to the target cost but if the target cost cannot be achieved at the pre-production stage the product may still be launched if management is confident that the process of continuous improvement will enable the target cost to be achieved early in the product's life. If this is not possible, the product will not be launched.

The major attraction of target costing is that marketing factors and customer research provide the basis for determining selling price, whereas cost tends to be the dominant factor with cost-plus pricing. A further attraction is that the approach requires the collaboration of product designers, production engineers, marketing and finance staff whose focus is on managing costs at the product design stage. At this stage costs can be most effectively managed because a decision committing the firm to incur costs will not have been made.

Target costing is most suited for setting prices for non-customized and high sales volume products. It is also an important mechanism for managing the cost of future products. We shall therefore look at target costing in more detail when we focus on cost management in Chapter 22.

A PRICE-TAKING FIRM FACING SHORT-RUN PRODUCT MIX DECISIONS

Price-taking firms with a temporary excess capacity may be faced with opportunities of taking on short-term business *at a market-determined selling price*. In this situation, the cost information that is required is no different from that of a price-setting firm making a short-run pricing decision. In other words, accepting short-term business where the market-determined incremental sales revenues exceed incremental short-run costs will provide a contribution towards committed fixed costs that would not otherwise have been obtained. However, such business is acceptable only if the same conditions as those specified for a price-setting firm apply. You should remember that in these conditions:

- Sufficient capacity is available for all resources that are required from undertaking the business (if some resources are fully utilized, opportunity costs of the scarce resources must be covered by the selling price).

- The company will not commit itself to repeat longer term business that is priced to cover only short-term incremental costs.

- The order will utilize unused capacity for only a short period and capacity will be released for use on more profitable opportunities.

A PRICE-TAKING FIRM FACING LONG-RUN PRODUCT MIX DECISIONS

When prices are set by the market a firm has to decide which products or services to sell given their market prices. In the longer term, a firm can adjust the supply of resources committed to a product. Therefore the sales revenue from a product should exceed the cost of all the resources that are committed to it. Hence there is a need to undertake periodic profitability analysis to distinguish between profitable and unprofitable products in order to ensure that only profitable products are sold. Exhibit 10.1

EXHIBIT 10.1 An illustration of hierarchical profitability analysis

	Product line A				Product line B				Product line C				Company total
	A1 £000s	A2 £000s	A3 £000s	Total £000s	B1 £000s	B2 £000s	B3 £000s	Total £000s	C1 £000s	C2 £000s	C3 £000s	Total £000s	£000s
(1) Sales	100	200	300	600	400	500	600	1500	700	800	900	2400	
(2) Less direct variable and fixed costs	20	60	120	200	200	550	360	1110	680	240	600	1520	
(3) Contribution to product line fixed costs	80	140	180	400	200	(50)	240	390	20	560	300	880	1670
(4) Fixed costs directly attributable to the product line				350				300				500	1150
(5) Contribution to business sustaining fixed costs				50				90				380	520
(6) Business/facility sustaining fixed costs													200
(7) Overall company profit													320

presents an illustration of hierarchical profitability analysis for a company that has three product lines and three individual products within each product line. For example, product line A has three individual products called A1, A2 and A3 within its product line. A similar format has been applied to product lines B and C. A product line consists of a group of similar products. For example, banks have product lines such as savings accounts, lending services, currency services, insurance services and brokering services. Each product line contains individual product variants. The savings product line would include low-balance/low-interest savings accounts, high balance/high interest accounts, postal and internet savings accounts and other product variants. The lending services product line would include personal loans, house mortgage loans, business loans and other product variants within the product line.

You will see in Exhibit 10.1 that three different hierarchical levels have been identified. In row (3), the contribution to product line fixed costs is derived for each individual product by deducting direct variable and direct fixed costs (e.g. advertising for a specific individual product) from sales revenue. Next, in row (4), avoidable fixed costs that can be directly traced to each product line, but not the individual products, are deducted to derive the total contribution for each product line that is reported in row (5). Finally, in row (6), the costs of sustaining the business that cannot be specifically identified with individual products or product lines are deducted from the sum of the product line contributions to compute the profit for the company as a whole. Business sustaining costs, such as general administrative and property costs, are incurred to support the organization as a whole and cannot be directly attributed to individual products or product lines.

To illustrate how profitability analysis can be used, look at product B2. It provides a negative contribution of £50 000 to product line fixed costs. The analysis indicates that the contribution of product line B will increase by £50 000 if product B2 is discontinued. However, periodic profitability analysis as illustrated in Exhibit 10.1 should not be used directly for decision-making. Instead, the profitability analysis represents a periodical strategic review of the costs and profitability of a firm's products/services (or other cost objects, such as customers and sales outlets). In particular, profitability analysis should be used to highlight those products or services that require more detailed special studies.

Before discontinuing product B2, other alternatives or considerations must be taken into account at the special study stage. In some situations, it is important to maintain a full product line for marketing reasons. For example, if customers are not offered a full product line to choose from they may migrate to competitors who offer a wider choice. By reporting individual product profitability, the cost of maintaining a full product line, being the sum of unprofitable products within the product line, is highlighted. Where maintaining a full product line is not required, managers should consider other options before dropping unprofitable products. They should consider reengineering or redesigning the products to reduce their resource consumption.

You will see from the profitability analysis shown in Exhibit 10.1 that product C1 generates a very small contribution margin (£20 000) relative to other products within the product line. This low contribution margin might trigger the need to undertake a special study. Such a study might reveal that although none of product line C direct fixed costs of £500 000 is traceable to individual products, a decision to discontinue product C1 would enable the product line fixed costs to be reduced by £50 000. Thus, discontinuing product C1 would result in the product line contribution (shown in row (5)) and total company profits increasing by £30 000 (£50 000 − £20 000).

The profitability analysis shown in Exhibit 10.1 is based on direct costing principles (see Chapter 7) whereby all costs can be specifically identified with a cost objective at a particular level within the hierarchy of reported profits. Those fixed costs (row 4) that cannot be specifically identified with individual products, but which can be identified with product lines, are only assigned at the product line level. Similarly those fixed costs (row 6) that cannot be specifically identified with individual products or product lines are assigned at the overall company level. Therefore none of the costs is categorized as indirect within the profit reporting hierarchy. An alternative absorption costing system (see Chapter 7) is used by many companies whereby the product line fixed costs (row 4) and the business/facility sustaining fixed costs (row 6) are allocated to the individual products, often on an arbitrary basis. Where absorption costing principles are used, such costs represent indirect costs at the individual product level.

Finally, you should note that, in practice, firms may have hundreds of products and many individual product lines. It will not be feasible to present a product profitability analysis, similar to that shown in Exhibit 10.1, in hard copy format. Instead, the necessary information will be maintained on a database. With hundreds of products, managers will seek to avoid information overload and may extract the relevant information that they require only when they are examining the profitability of a particular product line. In addition, the database may be designed so that periodically only individual loss-making products are routinely reported. Managers can then decide whether they need to initiate more detailed studies to ascertain if such products are viable in the long run.

SURVEYS OF PRACTICE RELATING TO PRICING DECISIONS

Generally, companies should concentrate on long-run pricing decisions and short-run decisions should be viewed as representing abnormal situations. In the previous sections, cost-plus pricing and periodic profitability analysis were examined for price-setting and price-taking firms facing long-run pricing and product mix decisions. To what extent are these approaches used in practice? Exhibit 10.2 summarizes surveys that have been undertaken relating to pricing practices and profitability analysis. A survey of 186 UK companies by Drury and Tayles (2006) reported that 91 per cent of respondents used periodic profitability analysis to monitor the profitability of products, services or customers. The study also indicated that 60 per cent of the respondents used cost-plus pricing even though this practice has been widely criticized. A more recent survey by the Chartered Institute of Management Accountants (2009) based on the responses of 439 respondents located world-wide, reported that approximately 75 per cent of manufacturing organizations and 60 per cent of service organizations used cost-plus pricing. In the following sections, the criticisms of cost-plus pricing and the reasons for its widespread use are examined.

EXHIBIT 10.2 Surveys of practice

A survey of 187 UK organizations by Drury and Tayles (2006) indicated that 91 per cent of respondents analysed profits at least on an annual basis and that 60 per cent used cost-plus pricing. Most of the organizations that used cost-plus pricing indicated that it was applied selectively. It accounted for less than 10 per cent of total sales revenues for 26 per cent of the respondents and more than 50 per cent for 39 per cent of the organizations. Most of the firms (85 per cent) used full cost and the remaining 15 per cent used direct cost as the pricing base. The survey also indicated that 74 per cent analysed profits either by customers or customer categories. In terms of factors influencing the importance of cost-plus pricing, a survey of UK and Australian companies by Guilding, Drury and Tales (2005) reported that the intensity of competition was positively related to the importance of cost-plus pricing.

An earlier UK study by Innes and Mitchell (1995a) reported that 50 per cent of respondents had used customer profitability analysis and a further 12 per cent planned to do so in the future. Of those respondents that ranked customer profitability, 60 per cent indicated that the Pareto 80/20 rule broadly applied (that, is 20 per cent of the customers were generating 80 per cent of the profits).

Dekker and Smidt (2003) undertook a survey of 32 Dutch firms on the use of costing practices that resembled the Japanese target costing concept. They reported that 19 out of the 32 firms used these practices, although they used different names for them. Adoption was highest among assembling firms and was related to a competitive and unpredictable environment.

LIMITATIONS OF COST-PLUS PRICING

The main criticism that has been made against cost-plus pricing is that demand is ignored. The price is set by adding a mark-up to cost and this may bear no relationship to the price–demand relationship. It is assumed that prices should depend solely on costs. For example, a cost-plus formula may suggest a price of £20 for a product where the demand is 100 000 units, whereas at a price of £25 the demand might be 80 000 units. Assuming that the variable cost for each unit sold is £15, the total contribution will be £500 000 at a selling price of £20, compared with a total contribution of £800 000 at a selling price of £25. Thus, cost-plus pricing formulae might lead to incorrect decisions.

It is often claimed that cost-based pricing formulae serve as a pricing 'floor' shielding the seller from a loss. This argument, however, is incorrect since it is quite possible for a firm to lose money even though every product is priced higher than the estimated unit cost. The reason for this is that if sales demand falls below the activity level that was used to calculate the fixed cost per unit, the total sales revenue may be insufficient to cover the total fixed costs. Cost-plus pricing will only ensure that all the costs will be met, and the target profits earned, if the sales volume is equal to, or more than, the activity level that was used to estimate total unit costs.

Consider a hypothetical situation where all of the costs attributable to a product are fixed in the short term and amount to £1 million. Assume that the cost per unit is £100 derived from an estimated volume of 10 000 units. The selling price is set at £130 using the cost-plus method and a mark-up of 30 per cent. If actual sales volume is 7000 units, sales revenues will be £910 000 compared with total costs of £1 million. Therefore the product will incur a loss of £90 000 even though it is priced above full cost.

REASONS FOR USING COST-PLUS PRICING

Considering the limitations of cost-plus pricing, why is it that these techniques are frequently used in practice? The most frequently cited reasons were made by Baxter and Oxenfeldt (1961) in a classic article that remains pertinent many years later. They suggest the following reasons:

Cost-plus pricing offers a means by which plausible prices can be found with ease and speed, no matter how many products the firm handles. Moreover, its imposing computations look factual and precise, and its prices may well seem more defensible on moral grounds than prices established by other means. Thus a monopolist threatened by a public inquiry might reasonably feel that he is safeguarding his case by cost-plus pricing.

Another major reason for the widespread use of cost-plus pricing methods is that they may help a firm to predict the prices of other firms. For example, if a firm has been operating in an industry where average mark-ups have been 40 per cent in the past, it may be possible to predict that competitors will be adding a 40 per cent mark-up to their costs. Assuming that all the firms in the industry have similar cost structures, it will be possible to predict the price range within which competitors may price their products. If all the firms in an industry price their products in this way, it may encourage price stability.

In response to the main objection that cost-based pricing formulae ignore demand, we have noted that the actual price that is calculated by the formula is rarely adopted without amendments. The price is adjusted upwards or downwards after taking account of the number of sales orders on hand, the extent of competition from other firms, the importance of the customer in terms of future sales and the policy relating to customer relations. Therefore it is argued that management attempts to adjust the mark-up based on the state of sales demand and other factors that are of vital importance in the pricing decision.

PRICING POLICIES

Cost information is only one of many variables that must be considered in the pricing decision. The final price that is selected will depend on the pricing policy of the company. A price-skimming or penetration pricing policy might be selected.

A price-skimming policy is an attempt to exploit those sections of the market that are relatively insensitive to price changes. For example, high initial prices may be charged to take advantage of the novelty appeal of a new product when demand is not very sensitive to price changes. A skimming pricing policy offers a safeguard against unexpected future increases in costs or a large fall in demand after the novelty appeal has declined. Once the market becomes saturated, the price can be reduced to attract that part of the market that has not yet been exploited. A skimming pricing policy should not, however, be adopted when a number of close substitutes are already being marketed. Here demand is likely to be very sensitive to price changes and any price in excess of that being charged for a substitute product by a competitor is likely to lead to a large reduction in sales.

A penetration pricing policy is based on the concept of charging low prices initially with the intention of gaining rapid acceptance of the product. Such a policy is appropriate when close substitutes are available or when the market is easy to enter. The low price discourages potential competitors from entering the market and enables a company to establish a large share of the market. This can be achieved more easily when the product is new rather than later on when buying habits have become established.

Many products have a product life cycle consisting of four stages: introductory, growth, maturity and decline. At the introductory stage, the product is launched and there is minimal awareness and acceptance of it. Sales begin to expand rapidly at the growth stage, because of introductory promotions and greater customer awareness, but this begins to taper off at the maturity stage as potential new customers are exhausted. At the decline stage, sales diminish as the product is gradually replaced with new and better versions.

Sizer (1989) suggests that in the introductory stage it may be appropriate to shade upwards or downwards the price found by normal analysis to create a more favourable demand in future years. For example, he suggests that if there is no production capacity constraint, a lower price than that suggested by normal analysis may be preferred. Such a price may result in a higher sales volume and a slow

REAL WORLD VIEWS 10.2

Pricing policies – pricing iPhones and similar devices

Apple Inc. is well known for developing innovative products like the iPhone, iPad and iPod. Such devices are manufactured with complex electronic components and incur substantial design and development costs. The actual cost of manufacture of these products is a closely guarded secret. While the manufacture and distribution costs are important factors in setting a price for such devices, other factors affect pricing policy too, according to industry analysts and reviewers.

Taking the iPhone as an example, the first factor is the features and capability of the device, whereby, for example, the price increases according to the storage capacity or screen quality. As the iPhone has developed through to the current iPhone 7 (launched September 2016), additional functionality has been offered. For example, the iPhone 7 introduced better battery life, is water resistant and has improved stereo speakers. Such additional functionality has increased manufacturing costs, but in general end-consumer pricing has remained relatively static for each new iPhone model, including the iPhone 7, at about $600–700. How has Apple kept prices low, despite increasing costs? The answer lies, at least partly, in a pricing policy which forces mobile phone operators to offer heavy subsidies to new customers wanting an iPhone. And operators typically comply as the demand for iPhones remains high – the iPhone 6/6s sold almost 50 million units in the first half of 2016, with iPhone 7 sales remaining steady, helped no doubt by defects with the Galaxy Note 7.

Questions

1 Do devices like iPhones have differing prices during various stages of their life cycle?

2 Can companies like Apple adopt price-skimming policies? Why or why not?

References

Solomon, B. (2016) Apple Earnings, iPhone Sales Keep Falling, Forbes, 25 October, Available at www.forbes.com/sites/briansolomon/2016/10/25/apple-reports-4th-quarter-earnings-iphone-7

Su, J.B (2016) Apple iPhone 6s Crowned World's Best-Selling Smartphone, Forbes, 7 September. Available at www.forbes.com/sites/jeanbaptiste/2016/09/07/apple-iphone-6s-was-worlds-top-selling-smartphone-last-quarter-report

Zimbardo, P. (2010) What's behind Apple's iPhone pricing strategy?, Seeking Alpha, 21 June. Available at seekingalpha.com/article/211063-whats-behind-apples-iphone-pricing-strategy

competitive reaction, which will enable the company to establish a large market share and to earn higher profits in the long term.

When the product moves from the introduction to the growth stage, the product will have less of a novelty appeal as competitors introduce their versions of the product. Competitors can be discouraged from entering the market by lowering the price. The move from the introduction to the growth stage should also result in a reduction in unit costs because of reduced material costs from bulk buying, reduced labour costs arising from increased efficiency due to the learning effect and lower unit fixed costs arising from fixed production costs being spread over a greater volume.

The move from the growth stage to the maturity stage means that the product has become established and the selling price is likely to be fairly constant, but periodically special offers may be made to tempt customers to buy the product. Unit production costs are likely to be fairly constant as there will be no further benefits arising from economies of scale. At the maturity stage a firm will also be less concerned with the future effects of current selling prices and should adopt a selling price that maximizes short-run profits.

to maintain sales revenues and retain customers. Also, the Group incurred some fixed expenses that did not vary according to a decrease in revenues.

Cost-plus pricing at City Steel in Thailand
In the first quarter of the year 2015/2016, City Steel's total revenues (THB 135.44 million) decreased by 35 per cent compared with the previous year. Adverse economic conditions caused the Group's products to decrease substantially and made price competition become more intense. A drop in steel price of more than 30 per cent from the previous year had contributed to a decrease in the Group's total revenues. Since the Group employed cost-plus pricing strategy to determine products selling prices, once material costs decreased, the Group's sales revenues would decline, which caused the Group's net profits to decrease correspondingly.   The Group had to reduce some mark-ups on the selling price in order

Questions

1 To what extent did cost-plus pricing contribute to the decline in total sales revenues?

2 How might City Steel determine the price at which it sells steel?

References
Anonymous (2015) Thailand: CITY – Management Discussion and Analysis Quarter 1 Ending 31 Oct 2015. *Asia News Monitor* 16 Dec. search.proquest .com.libaccess.hud.ac.uk/docview/1749007079? pq-origsite=summon

CUSTOMER PROFITABILITY ANALYSIS

In the past, management accounting reports have tended to concentrate on analysing profits by products. Increasing attention is now being given to analysing profits by customers using an activity-based costing approach. Customer profitability analysis provides important information that can be used to determine which classes of customers should be emphasized or de-emphasized and the price to charge for customer services. Let us now look at an illustration of customer profitability analysis. Consider the information presented in Example 10.2. Note that the cost driver rate referred to in Example 10.2 represents the costing rates that have been computed by the company for the different activities. An explanation of how these rates are derived was provided in chapter 3. The profitability analysis in respect of the four customers is as follows:

	A	B	Y	Z
Customer attributable costs:				
Sales order processing	60 000	30 000	15 000	9 000
Sales visits	4 000	2 000	1 000	1 000
Normal deliveries	30 000	10 000	2 500	1 250
Special (urgent) deliveries	10 000	2 500	0	0
Credit collection[a]	24 658	8 220	1 370	5 480
	128 658	52 720	19 870	16 730
Operating profit contribution	90 000	120 000	70 000	200 000
Contribution to higher level sustaining expenses	(38 658)	67 280	50 130	183 270

Note
[a](Annual sales revenue × 10%) × (Average collection period/365)

You can see from the above analysis that A and B are high cost to serve whereas Y and Z are low cost to serve customers. Customer A provides a positive operating profit contribution but is unprofitable when customer attributable costs are taken into account. This is because customer A requires more sales orders, sales visits, and normal and urgent deliveries than the other customers. In addition, the customer is slow to pay and has higher delivery costs than the other customers. Customer profitability analysis identifies

EXAMPLE 10.2

The Darwin Company has recently adopted customer profitability analysis. It has undertaken a customer profitability review for the past 12 months. Details of the activities and the cost driver rates relating to those expenses that can be attributed to customers are as follows:

Activity	Cost driver rate
Sales order processing	£300 per sales order
Sales visits	£200 per sales visit
Normal delivery costs	£1 per delivery kilometre travelled
Special (urgent) deliveries	£500 per special delivery
Credit collection costs	10% per annum on average payment time

Details relating to four of the firm's customers are as follows:

Customer	A	B	Y	Z
Number of sales orders	200	100	50	30
Number of sales visits	20	10	5	5
Kilometres per delivery	300	200	100	50
Number of deliveries	100	50	25	25
Total delivery kilometres	30 000	10 000	2 500	1 250
Special (urgent deliveries)	20	5	0	0
Average collection period (days)	90	30	10	10
Annual sales	£1 million	£1 million	£0.5 million	£ 2 million
Annual operating profit contribution[a]	£90 000	£120 000	£70 000	£200 000

Note
[a]Consists of sales revenues less variable cost of sales.

the characteristics of high-cost and low-cost-to-serve customers and shows how customer profitability can be increased. The information should be used to persuade high-cost-to-serve customers to modify their buying behaviour away from placing numerous small orders and/or purchasing non-standard items that are costly to make. For example, customer A can be made profitable if action is taken to persuade the customer to place a smaller number of larger quantity orders, avoid special deliveries and reduce the credit period. If unprofitable customers cannot be persuaded to change their buying behaviour, selling prices should be increased (or discounts on list prices reduced) to cover the extra resources consumed.

Customer profitability analysis can also be used to rank customers by order of profitability using Pareto analysis. This type of analysis is based on observations by Pareto that a very small proportion of items usually account for the majority of the value. For example, the Darwin Company (Example 10.2) might find that 20 per cent of customers account for 80 per cent of profits. Special attention can then be given to enhancing the relationships with the most profitable customers to ensure that they do not migrate to other competitors. In addition, greater emphasis can be given to attracting new customers that have the same attributes as the most profitable customers.

Organizations such as banks, often with a large customer base in excess of one million customers, cannot apply customer profitability analysis at the individual customer level. Instead, they concentrate on customer segment profitability analysis by combining groups of customers into meaningful segments. This enables profitable segments to be highlighted where customer retention is particularly important and provides an input for determining the appropriate marketing strategies for attracting the new customers that have the most profit potential. Segment groupings that are used by banks include income classes, age bands, socioeconomic categories and family units.

REAL WORLD VIEWS 10.4

Measuring and managing customer profitability

In an article in *Strategic Finance*, Garry Cokins states that many companies' managerial accounting systems are not able to report customer profitability information to support analysis for how to rationalize which types of customers to retain, grow or win back, and which types of new customers to acquire. Some customers purchase a mix of mainly low-profit margin products and, after adding the non-product-related costs to serve for those customers to the product costs, they may be unprofitable. Conversely, customers who purchase a mix of relatively high-profit-margin products may demand so much in extra services that they may be unprofitable. The danger of maintaining unprofitable customers is further exacerbated by basing compensation incentives to the sales force that are based exclusively on sales revenues rather than profitable sales after taking into account the associated costs to serve the customers.

Cokins distinguishes between low-maintenance 'good' customers who place standard orders with no fuss, and high-maintenance 'bad' customers who demand non-standard offers and services, such as special delivery requirements. The extra expenses for high-maintenance customers add up. Cokins advocates the use of activity-based customer profitability analysis (see Chapter 11) to turn loss-making customers into profit-making customers.

Questions

1 Can you think of any reason why two customers who purchase equal volumes of equivalent products might be more or less profitable?

2 What actions should a company take with its unprofitable customers?

References

Cokins, G. (2015) Measuring and managing customer profitability, *Strategic Finance*, 23–29 February. Available at www.imanet.org/resources-publications/ strategic-finance-magazine/issues/February%202015

SUMMARY

The following items relate to the learning objectives listed at the beginning of the chapter.

- **Explain the relevant cost information that should be presented in price-setting firms for both short-term and long-term decisions.**

For *short-term* decisions, the incremental costs of accepting an order should be presented. Bids should then be made at prices that exceed incremental costs. For short-term decisions many costs are likely to be fixed and irrelevant. Short-term pricing decisions should meet the following conditions: (a) spare capacity should be available for all of the resources that are required to fulfil an order; (b) the bid price should represent a one-off price that will not be repeated for future orders; and (c) the order will utilize unused capacity for only a short period and capacity will be released for use on more profitable opportunities. For *long-term* decisions, a firm can adjust the supply of virtually all of the resources. Therefore, cost information should be presented providing details of all of the resources that are committed to a product or service. Since business facility sustaining costs should be covered in the long term by sales revenues, there are strong arguments for allocating such costs for long-run pricing decisions. To determine an appropriate selling price a mark-up is added to the total cost of the resources assigned to the product/service to provide a contribution to profits. If facility sustaining costs are not allocated, the mark-up must be sufficient to provide a contribution to covering facility sustaining costs and a contribution to profit.

- **Describe product and customer profitability analysis and the information that should be included for managing the product and customer mix.**

Price-taking firms have to decide which products to sell, given their market prices. A mechanism is therefore required that ascertains whether or not the sales revenues from a product/service (or customer) exceeds the cost of resources that are committed to it. Periodic profitability analysis meets this requirement. Ideally, hierarchical profitability analysis should be used that categorizes costs according to their variability at different hierarchical levels to report different hierarchical contribution levels. The aim of the hierarchical analysis should be to directly assign all organizational expenses to the particular hierarchical or organizational level where they become avoidable, so that arbitrary apportionments are avoided. The approach is illustrated in Exhibit 10.1.

● **Describe the target costing approach to pricing.**

Target costing is the reverse of cost-plus pricing. With target costing the starting point is the determination of the target selling price – the price that customers are willing to pay for the product (or service). Next a target profit margin is deducted to derive a target cost. The target cost represents the estimated long-run cost of the product (or service) that enables the target profit to be achieved. Predicted actual costs are compared with the target cost. If the target cost is not achieved the product/service is unlikely to be launched.

● **Describe the different cost-plus pricing methods for deriving selling prices.**

Different cost bases can be used for cost-plus pricing. Bases include direct variable costs, total direct costs and total cost based on an assignment of a share of all organizational costs to the product or service. Different percentage profit margins are added depending on the cost base that is used. If direct variable cost is used as the cost base, a high percentage margin will be added to provide a contribution to cover a share of all of those costs that are not included in the cost base plus profits. Alternatively if total cost is used as the cost base a lower percentage margin will be added to provide only a contribution to profits.

● **Explain the limitations of cost-plus pricing.**

Cost-plus pricing has three major limitations. First, demand is ignored. Second, the approach requires that some assumption be made about future volume prior to ascertaining the cost and calculating the cost-plus selling prices. This can lead to an increase in the derived cost-plus selling price when demand is falling and vice versa. Third, there is no guarantee that total sales revenue will be in excess of total costs even when each product is priced above 'cost'.

● **Justify why cost-plus pricing is widely used.**

There are several reasons why cost-plus pricing is widely used. First, it offers a means by which prices can be determined with ease and speed in organizations that produce hundreds of products. Cost-plus pricing is likely to be particularly applicable to those products that generate relatively minor revenues that are not critical to an organization's success. A second justification is that cost-based pricing methods may encourage price stability by enabling firms to predict the prices of their competitors. Also, target mark-ups can be adjusted upwards or downwards according to expected demand, thus ensuring that demand is indirectly taken into account.

● **Identify and describe the different pricing policies.**

Cost information is only one of the many variables that must be considered in the pricing decision. The final price that is selected will depend on the pricing policy of a company. A price-skimming policy or a penetration pricing policy might be selected. A price-skimming policy attempts to charge high initial prices to exploit those sections of the market where demand is initially insensitive to pricing changes. In contrast, a penetration pricing policy is based on the concept of charging low prices, initially with the intention of gaining rapid acceptance of the product (or service).

● **Additional learning objective presented in Appendix 10.1**

The appendix to this chapter includes an additional learning objective: to calculate the optimal selling price using differential calculus. This topic is included in the appendix because it is not included in the syllabus requirements of many courses. However, the examinations set by some professional accountancy bodies do require a knowledge of this topic. You should therefore check your course curriculum to ascertain whether you need to read Appendix 10.1

APPENDIX 10.1: CALCULATING OPTIMAL SELLING PRICES USING DIFFERENTIAL CALCULUS

The optimal output is determined at the point where marginal revenue equals marginal cost (see Chapter 2 for a definition of these terms). The highest selling price at which the optimum output can be sold determines the optimal selling price. If demand and cost schedules are known, it is possible to derive simultaneously the optimum output level and selling price using differential calculus. Consider Example 10A.1.

The first step when calculating the optimum selling price is to calculate total cost and revenue functions. The total cost (TC) function is:

$$TC = £700\,000 + £70x$$

where x is the annual level of demand and output and £700 000 represents non-variable (fixed) costs.

At present the selling price is £160 and demand is 10 000 units. Each increase or decrease in price of £2 results in a corresponding decrease or increase in demand of 500 units. Therefore, if the selling price were increased to £200, demand would be zero. To increase demand by one unit, selling price must be reduced by £0.004 (£2/500 units). Thus, the maximum selling price (SP) for an output of x units is:

$$SP = £200 - £0.004x$$

Assuming that the output demanded is 10 000 units SP = £200 − £0.004 (10 000) = £160. Therefore, if demand is 10 000 units, the maximum selling price is £160, the same selling price given in Example 10A.1. We shall now use differential calculus to derive the optimal selling price:

$$TC = £700\,000 + £70x$$
$$SP = £200 - £0.004x$$

Therefore, total revenue (TR) for an output of x units = $£200x - £0.004x^2$:

$$\text{marginal cost(MC)} = \frac{dTC}{dx} = £70$$

$$\text{marginal revenue(MR)} = \frac{dTR}{dx} = £200 - £0.008x$$

At the optimum output level:

$$\frac{dTC}{dx} = \frac{dTR}{dx}$$

EXAMPLE 10A.1

A division within the Caspian Company sells a single product. Divisional fixed costs are £700 000 per annum and a variable cost of £70 is incurred for each additional unit produced and sold over a very large range of outputs. The current selling price for the product is £160 and at this price 10 000 units are demanded per annum. It is estimated that for each successive increase in price of £2, annual demand will be reduced by 500 units. Alternatively, for each £2 reduction in price, demand will increase by 500 units.

Calculate the optimum output and price for the product assuming that if prices are set within each £2 range there will be a proportionate change in demand.

And so:

$$£70 = £200 - £0.008x$$
$$x = 16\,250 \text{ units}$$

The highest selling price at which this output can be sold is:

$$SP = £200 - £0.004(16\,250)$$

so:

$$SP = £135$$

Thus optimum selling price and output are £135 and 16 250 units, respectively.

For a more detailed example of setting optimal selling prices using differential calculus you should refer to Review problems 10.17 and 10.18 at the end of this chapter and to their solutions.

KEY TERMS AND CONCEPTS

Absorption costing system A costing system that allocates all manufacturing costs, including fixed manufacturing costs, to products and values unsold stocks at their total cost of manufacture.

Cost-plus pricing An approach to pricing customized products and services that involves calculating product costs and adding the desired profit margin.

Customer profitability analysis The analysis of profits by individual customers or customer categories.

Direct costing A costing system that assigns only direct costs to products or services and includes them in the inventory valuation.

Full cost The estimated sum of all resources that are committed to a product or service in the long run, also known as long-run cost.

Long-run cost The estimated sum of all resources that are committed to a product or service in the long run, also known as full cost.

Pareto analysis A type of analysis based on the observation that a very small proportion of items account for the majority of value.

Penetration pricing policy An approach to pricing that involves charging low prices initially with the intention of gaining rapid acceptance of the product.

Price setters Firms that have some discretion over setting the selling price of their products or services.

Price takers Firms that have little or no influence over setting the selling price of their products or services.

Price-skimming policy An approach to pricing that attempts to exploit sections of the market that are relatively insensitive to price changes.

Product life cycle The period of time from initial expenditure on research and development to the withdrawal of support to customers.

Target costing A technique that focuses on managing costs during a product's planning and design phase by establishing the target cost for a product or service that is derived from starting with the target selling price and deducting a desired profit margin.

RECOMMENDED READING

You should refer to Lucas (2003) for an evaluation of research supporting the accountants' and economists' respective positions to pricing. See Ansari et al. (2008) and Burrows and Chenhall (2012) for a review of the history of target costing and for a survey of target costing in Dutch firms you should refer to Dekker and Smidt (2003). You can also refer to an article by Kohli and Suri (2011) that examines the relationship between pricing and enhanced profitability.

KEY EXAMINATION POINTS

Questions requiring the use of differential calculus are sometimes set by the professional accountancy examination bodies (e.g. Review problems 10.17 and 10.18).

Where demand information is given you should avoid calculating and recommending cost-plus selling prices. Wherever possible, incorporate estimated revenues and costs for different demand levels and recommend the selling price that yields the maximum profit. You should also be prepared to discuss the limitations of cost-plus pricing and indicate why it is widely used in spite of these limitations.

ASSESSMENT MATERIAL

The review questions are short questions that enable you to assess your understanding of the main topics included in the chapter. The numbers in parentheses provide you with the page numbers to refer to if you cannot answer a specific question.

The review problems are more complex and require you to relate and apply the content to various business problems. The problems are graded by their level of difficulty. Solutions to review problems that are not preceded by the term 'IM' are provided in a separate section at the end of the book. Solutions to problems preceded by the term 'IM' are provided in the Instructor's Manual accompanying this book that can be downloaded from the lecturer's digital support resources. Additional review problems with fully worked solutions are provided in the *Student Manual* that accompanies this book.

REVIEW QUESTIONS

10.1 Distinguish between a price taker and a price setter. (p. 231)

10.2 What costs are likely to be relevant for (a) a short-run pricing decision, and (b) a long-run pricing decision? (pp. 231–238)

10.3 What is meant by the term 'full cost'? (p. 233)

10.4 What is meant by cost-plus pricing? (pp. 232, 239)

10.5 Distinguish between cost-plus pricing and target costing. (p. 235)

10.6 Describe the four stages involved with target costing. (p. 235)

10.7 What role does cost information play in price-taking firms? (pp. 236–238)

10.8 Describe the alternative cost bases that can be used with cost-plus pricing. (p. 232)

10.9 What are the limitations of cost-plus pricing? (p. 239)

10.10 Why is cost-plus pricing frequently used in practice? (pp. 239–240)

10.11 Describe the different kinds of pricing policy that an organization can apply. (pp. 240–241)

10.12 Why is customer profitability analysis important? (pp. 242–244)

REVIEW PROBLEMS

10.13 Intermediate: Calculation of an optimal selling price. A company manufactures a single product, product Y. It has documented levels of demand at certain selling prices for this product as follows:

Demand	Selling price per unit	Cost per unit
Units	£	£
1100	48	22
1200	46	21
1300	45	20
1400	42	19

Required:
Using a tabular approach, calculate the marginal revenues and marginal costs for product Y at the different levels of demand, and so determine the selling price at which the company profits are maximized. (10 marks)

ACCA – Financial Information for Management

10.14 Intermediate: Calculation of different cost-plus prices. Albany has recently spent some time on researching and developing a new product for which they are trying to establish a suitable price. Previously they have used cost-plus 20 per cent to set the selling price.

The standard cost per unit has been estimated as follows:

	£	
Direct materials		
Material 1	10	(4kg at £2.50/kg)
Material 2	7	(1kg at £7/kg)
Direct labour	13	(two hours at £6.50/hour)
Fixed overheads	7	(two hours at £3.50/hour)
	37	

Required:

(a) Using the standard costs calculate two different cost-plus prices using two different bases and explain an advantage and disadvantage of each method. (6 marks)

(b) Give two other possible pricing strategies that could be adopted and describe the impact of each one on the price of the product. (4 marks)

ACCA Paper 1.2 – Financial Information for Management

10.15 Advanced: Customer profitability analysis. ST is a distribution company that buys a product in bulk from manufacturers, repackages the product into smaller packs and then sells the packs to retail customers. ST's customers vary in size and consequently the size and frequency of their orders also varies. Some customers order large quantities from ST each time they place an order. Other customers order only a few packs each time.

The current accounting system of ST produces very basic management information that reports only the overall company profit. ST is therefore unaware of the costs of servicing individual customers. However, the company has now decided to investigate the use of direct customer profitability analysis (DCPA).

ST would like to see the results from a small sample of customers before it decides whether to fully introduce DCPA.

The information for two customers, and for the whole company, for the previous period was as follows:

	Customer		
	B	D	Company
Factory contribution ($000)	75	40.5	450
Number of:			
Packs sold (000)	50	27	300
Sales visits to customers	24	12	200
Orders placed by customers	75	20	700
Normal deliveries to customers	45	15	240
Urgent deliveries to customers	5	0	30

Activity costs:	$000s
Sales visits to customers	50
Processing orders placed by customers	70
Normal deliveries to customers	120
Urgent deliveries to customers	60

Required:

(a) Prepare a direct customer profitability analysis for each of the two customers. *(6 marks)*

(b) Explain how ST could use DCPA to increase its profits.

(4 marks)

CIMA P2 Performance Management

10.16 Advanced: Minimum selling price based on relevant costs. DLW is a company that builds innovative, environmentally friendly housing. DLW's houses use high quality materials and the unique patented energy saving technology used in the houses has been the result of the company's own extensive research in the area.

DLW is planning to expand into another country and has been asked by a prominent person in that country for a price quotation to build them a house. The Board of Directors believes that securing the contract will help to launch their houses in the country and have agreed to quote a price for the house that will exactly cover its relevant cost.

The following information has been obtained in relation to the contract:

1 The Chief Executive and Marketing Director recently met with the potential client to discuss the house. The meeting was held at a restaurant and DLW provided food and drinks at a cost of $375.

2 1200kg of Material Z will be required for the house. DLW currently has 550kg of Material Z in its inventory purchased at a price of $58 per kg. Material Z is regularly used by DLW in its houses and has a current replacement cost of $65 per kg. The resale value of the Material Z in inventory is $35 per kg.

3 400 hours of construction worker time are required to build the house. DLW's construction workers are paid an hourly rate of $22 under a guaranteed wage agreement and currently have spare capacity to build the house.

4 The house will require 90 hours of engineer time. DLW engineers are paid a monthly salary of $4750 each and do not have any spare capacity. In order to meet the engineering requirement for the house, DLW can choose one of two options:

(i) Pay the engineers an overtime rate of $52 per hour to perform the additional work.

(ii) Reduce the number of engineers' hours available for their existing job, the building of Product Y. This would result in lost sales of Product Y.

Summary details of the existing job the engineers are working on:

Information for one unit of Product Y	
Sales revenue	$4860
Variable costs	$3365
Engineers' time required per unit	30 hours

5 A specialist machine would be required for 7 weeks for the house build. DLW have 4 weeks remaining on the 15 week specialist machine rental contract that cost $15000. The machine is currently not in use. The machine can be rented for an additional 15 weeks at a cost of $15250. The specialist machine can only be rented in blocks of 15 weeks.

Alternatively, a machine can be purchased for $160000 and sold after the work on the house has been completed for $140000.

6 The windows required for the house have recently been developed by DLW and use the latest environmentally friendly insulating material. DLW produced the windows at a cost of $34950 and they are currently the only ones of their type. DLW were planning to exhibit the windows at a house building conference. The windows would only be used for display purposes at the conference and would not be for sale to prospective clients.

DLW has had assurances from three separate clients that they would place an order for 25 windows each if they saw the technology demonstrated at the conference. The contribution from each window is $10450. If the windows are used for the contract, DLW would not be able to attend the conference. The conference organisers will charge a penalty fee of $1500 for non-attendance by DLW. The Chief Executive of DLW can meet the clients directly and still secure the orders for the windows. The meetings would require two days of the Chief Executive's time. The Chief Executive is paid an annual salary of $414000 and contracted to work 260 days per year.

7 The house build requires 400kg of other materials. DLW currently has none of these materials in its inventory. The total current purchase price for these other materials is $6000.

8 DLW's fixed overhead absorption rate is $37 per construction worker hour.

9 DLW's normal policy is to add a 12 per cent mark-up to the cost of each house.

Required:

(a) Produce a schedule that shows the minimum price that could be quoted for the contract to build the house.

Your schedule should show the relevant cost of each of the nine items identified above. You should also explain each relevant cost value you have included in your schedule and why any values you have excluded are not relevant. *(17 marks)*

(b) Explain TWO reasons why relevant costing may not be a suitable approach to pricing houses in the longer term for DLW. *(4 marks)*

(c) Recommend, with justifications, a pricing strategy for DLW to use to price the innovative, environmentally friendly houses when they are launched in the new country. *(4 marks)*

CIMA P2 Performance Management

10.17 Advanced: Change in optimum price arising from a change in cost structure and sensitivity analysis. PPP is a theme park. The following information is available for the forthcoming month:

Forecast daily ticket sales and prices

	Ticket sales	Price per ticket
Pre-booked discounted ticket	1500	$29
Standard ticket	8000	$39
Premium family ticket (admits four people)	675	$185

The theme park will be open for 30 days in the month.

Costs

Variable costs per person per day are forecast to be $12.50. Fixed costs for the month are forecast to be $6 500 000.

Pricing information

The sales of pre-booked discounted tickets and standard tickets will be restricted to 1500 and 8000 per day respectively for the forthcoming month. It is forecast that all of these tickets will be sold.

A premium family ticket admits four people to the theme park and allows them to go to the front of the queues in the theme park. The price of a premium family ticket has been set at $185 in order to maximize the profit from the sale of these tickets for the month. Market information shows that for every $5 increase in the selling price of a premium family ticket the demand would reduce by 25 tickets, and that for every $5 decrease in the selling price the demand would increase by 25 tickets.

The theme park has adequate capacity to accommodate any level of demand for premium family tickets. It is to be assumed that four people would always be admitted on every premium family ticket sold.

Sales of the different ticket types are independent of each other.

Equipment hire

PPP is considering hiring some automated ticket reading equipment for the forthcoming month. The hire of this equipment would increase fixed costs by $250 000 for the month. However, variable costs per person would be reduced by 8 per cent during the period of the hire.

Required:

(a) Calculate the financial benefit of hiring the equipment for the forthcoming month given its impact on variable cost and therefore the price charged for premium family tickets.

Note: If $P = a - bx$ then $MR = a - 2bx$. *(13 marks)*

It has now been realized that a competing theme park is planning to offer discounted ticket prices during the forthcoming months. It is thought that this will reduce the demand for PPP's standard tickets. PPP will not be able to reduce the price of the standard tickets for the forthcoming month.

(b) Discuss the sensitivity of the decision to hire the equipment to a change in the number of standard tickets sold per day. (Note: your answer should include the calculation of the sensitivity). *(4 marks)*

PPP produces an annual budget. The annual budget includes details of budgeted ticket sales volumes, revenues and costs for each month. Each month PPP compares actual performance against the budget for that month.

At the start of every month, PPP conducts a review of its competitors to produce a revised forecast for ticket sales. This revised sales forecast is used to devise pricing policies and promotional campaigns to ensure that budgeted targets are met.

Required:

(c) Compare and contrast the use of feedforward control and feedback control, using the information given above about PPP to illustrate your answer. *(8 marks)*

CIMA P2 Performance Management

10.18 Advanced: Calculation of optimum selling price and discussion of price skimming. ALG Co is launching a new, innovative product on to the market and is trying to decide on the right launch price for the product. The product's expected life is three years. Given the high level of costs which have been incurred in developing the product, ALG Co wants to ensure that it sets its price at the right level and has therefore consulted a market research company to help it do this. The research, which relates to similar but not identical products launched by other companies, has revealed that at a price of $60, annual demand would be expected to be 250 000 units. However, for every $2 increase in selling price, demand would be expected to fall by 2000 units and for every $2 decrease in selling price, demand would be expected to increase by 2000 units.

A forecast of the annual production costs which would be incurred by ALG Co in relation to the new product are as follows:

Annual production (units)	200 000	250 000	300 000	350 000
	($)	($)	($)	($)
Direct material	2 400 000	3 000 000	3 600 000	4 200 000
Direct labour	1 200 000	1 500 000	1 800 000	2 100 000
Overheads	1 400 000	1 550 000	1 700 000	1 850 000

Required:

(a) Calculate the total variable cost per unit and total fixed overheads. *(3 marks)*

(b) Calculate the optimum (profit maximizing) selling price for the new product AND calculate the resulting profit for the period.

Note: If $P = a - bx$ then $MR = a - 2bx$. *(7 marks)*

(c) The sales director is unconvinced that the sales price calculated in (b) above is the right one to charge on the initial launch of the product. He believes that a high price should be charged at launch so that those customers prepared to pay a higher price for the product can be 'skimmed off' first.

Required:

Discuss the conditions which would make market skimming a more suitable pricing strategy for ALG, and recommend whether ALG should adopt this approach instead. *(5 marks)*

ACCA F5 Performance Management

10.19 Advanced: Profit-maximizing pricing decision based on demand/price relationships. The McIntyre Resort (MR), which is privately owned, is a world-famous luxury hotel and golf complex. It has been chosen as the venue to stage 'The Robyn Cup', a golf tournament which is contested by teams of golfers from across the globe, which is scheduled to take place during July 2019. MR will offer accommodation for each of the five nights on which guests would require accommodation.

The following information is available regarding the period of the tournament

1 Hotel data:

Total rooms	2400

Room mix:

Double rooms	75%
Single rooms	15%
Family rooms	10%

Fee per room per night ($):

Double rooms	400
Single rooms	300
Family rooms	600

Number of guests per room:

Double rooms	2
Single rooms	1
Family rooms	4

When occupied, all rooms will contain the number of guests as above.

Costs:

Variable cost per guest per night	$100

Attributable fixed costs for the five-day period:

Double rooms	$516 000
Single and family rooms (total)	$300 000

2 Accommodation for guests is provided on an all-inclusive basis (meals, drinks, entertainment etc.).

3 The objective of the hotel management is to maximize profit.

4 The hotel management expect all single and family rooms to be 'sold out' for each of the five nights of the tournament. However, they are unsure whether the fee in respect of double rooms should be increased or decreased. At a price of $400 per room per night they expect an occupancy rate of 80 per cent of available double rooms. For each $10 increase/decrease they expect the number of rooms to decrease/increase by 40.

Required:

(a) (i) Calculate the profit-maximizing fee per double room that MR should charge per night during the tournament;   (6 marks)

(ii) Calculate how much profit would be earned from staging the tournament as a consequence of charging that fee.   (4 marks)

(b) The management of the hotel is concerned by the level of variable costs per guest night to be incurred in respect of the tournament, A recent review of proposed operational activities has concluded that variable cost per guest per night in **all rooms** in the hotel would be reduced by 20 per cent if proposed changes in operational activities were made. However, this would result in additional attributable fixed costs amounting to $200 000 in respect of the five-day period.

Required:

Advise management whether, on purely financial grounds, it should make the proposed changes in operational activities.   (6 marks)

(c) Discuss TWO initiatives that management might consider in order to further improve the profit from staging the golf tournament.   (4 marks)

ACCA P5 Performance Management

10.20 Advanced. A company has carried out extensive product research and as a result has just launched a new innovative product unlike anything else that is currently available on the market. The company has launched this product using a market-skimming pricing policy.

The market in which it operates is highly competitive and historically success has been achieved by being the first to market with new products. Only a small number of companies have survived in the market and those that remain are constantly aiming to develop new products either by improving those already in the market or by extensive product research.

Required:
Explain, with reasons, the changes that the company may need to make to the unit selling price of the product as it moves through each of the four stages of its product life cycle.

(10 marks)

CIMA P2 Performance Management

10.21 Intermediate: Discussion of marginal and absorption cost approaches to pricing. ML is an engineering company that specializes in providing engineering facilities to businesses that cannot justify operating their own facilities in-house. ML employs a number of engineers who are skilled in different engineering techniques that enable ML to provide a full range of engineering facilities to its customers. Most of the work undertaken by ML is unique to each of its customers, often requiring the manufacture of spare parts for its customers' equipment, or the building of new equipment from customer drawings. As a result most of ML's work is short term, with some jobs being completed within hours while others may take a few days.

To date ML has adopted a cost-plus approach to setting its prices. This is based on an absorption costing system that uses machine hours as the basis of absorbing overhead costs into individual job costs. The managing director is concerned that over recent months ML has been unsuccessful when quoting for work with the consequence that there has been an increase in the level of unused capacity. It has been suggested that ML should adopt an alternative approach to its pricing based on marginal costing since *any price that exceeds variable costs is better than no work*.

Required:
With reference to the above scenario:

(i) briefly explain absorption and marginal cost approaches to pricing;

(ii) discuss the validity of the comment *any price that exceeds variable costs is better than no work*.

(10 marks)

CIMA P2 Management Accounting: Decision Management

IM10.1 Advanced. A company supplying capital equipment to the engineering industry is part of a large group of diverse companies. It determines its tender prices by adding a standard profit margin as a percentage of its prime cost.

Although it is working at full capacity the group managing director considers the company's annual return on capital employed as inadequate.

You are required, as the group assistant management accountant, to provide him with the following information:

(a) why the return-on-prime-cost (ROPC) approach to tendering would be likely to yield an inadequate return on capital employed;   (7 marks)

(b) the steps involved in calculating a return on capital employed (ROCE) tendering rate for a particular contract;   (7 marks)

(c) three problems likely to be encountered in meeting a pre-set profit target on a ROCE basis.   (6 marks)

CIMA P3 Management Accounting

IM10.2 Advanced. It has been stated that companies do not have profitable products, only profitable customers. Many companies have placed emphasis on the concept of customer account profitability (CAP) analysis in order to increase their earnings and returns to shareholders. Much of the theory of CAP draws from the view that the main strategic thrust operated by many companies is to encourage the development and sale of new products to existing customers.

Requirements:

(a) Briefly explain the concept of CAP analysis.   *(5 marks)*
(b) Critically appraise the value of CAP analysis as a means of increasing earnings per share and returns to shareholders.   *(15 marks)*

CIMA Stage 4 Strategic Management Accounting and Marketing

IM10.3 Advanced: Discussion of pricing strategies. A producer of high-quality executive motor cars has developed a new model that it knows to be very advanced both technically and in style by comparison with the competition in its market segment.

The company's reputation for high quality is well established and its servicing network in its major markets is excellent. However, its record in timely delivery has not been so good in previous years, although this has been improving considerably.

In the past few years it has introduced annual variations/improvements in its major models. When it launched a major new vehicle some six years ago, the recommended retail price was so low in relation to the excellent specification of the car that a tremendous demand built up quickly and a two-year queue for the car developed within six months. Within three months a second-hand model had been sold at an auction for nearly 50 per cent more than the list price and even after a year of production a sizeable premium above list price was being obtained.

The company considers that, in relation to the competition, the proposed new model will be as attractive as was its predecessor six years ago. Control of costs is very good so that accurate cost data for the new model are to hand. For the previous model, the company assessed the long-term targeted annual production level and calculated its prices on that basis. In the first year, production was 30 per cent of that total.

For the present model, the company expects that the relationship between first-year production and longer term annual production will also be about 30 per cent, although the absolute levels in both cases are expected to be higher than previously.

The senior management committee, of which you are a member, has been asked to recommend the pricing approach that the company should adopt for the new model.

You are required:

(a) to list the major pricing approaches available in this situation and discuss in some detail the relative merits and disadvantages to the company of each approach in the context of the new model;   *(15 marks)*
(b) to recommend which approach you would propose, giving your reasons;   *(5 marks)*
(c) to outline briefly in which ways, if any, your answers to (a) and (b) above would differ if, instead of a high-quality executive car, you were pricing a new family model of car with some unusual features that the company might introduce.   *(5 marks)*

CIMA Stage 4 Management Accounting Decision Making

IM10.4 Advanced: Cost-plus and relevant cost information for pricing decisions. Josun plc manufactures cereal-based foods, including various breakfast cereals under private brand labels. In March the company had been approached by Cohin plc, a large national supermarket chain, to tender for the manufacture and supply of a crunchy-style breakfast cereal made from oats, nuts, raisins, etc. The tender required Josun to quote prices for a 1.5kg packet at three different weekly volumes: 50000, 60000 and 70000. Josun plc had, at present, excess capacity on some of its machines and could make a maximum of 80000 packets of cereal a week.

Josun's management accountant is asked to prepare a costing for the Cohin tender. The company prepares its tender prices on the basis of full cost plus 15 per cent of cost as a profit margin. The full cost is made up of five elements: raw materials per packet of £0.30; operating wages £0.12 per packet; manufacturing overheads costed at 200 per cent of operating wages; administration and other corporate overheads at 100 per cent of operating wages; and packaging and transport costing £0.10 per packet. The sales manager has suggested that as an incentive to Cohin, the profit margin be cut on the 60000 and 70000 tenders by ½ per cent and 1 per cent to 14½ per cent and 14 per cent respectively. The manufacturing and administration overheads are forecast as fixed at £12500 per week, unless output drops to 50000 units or below per week, when a saving of £1000 per week can be made. If no contract is undertaken then all the manufacturing and administration overheads will be saved except for £600 per week. If the tender is accepted the volume produced and sold will be determined by the sales achieved by Cohin.

A week before the Cohin tender is to be presented for negotiation, Josun receives an enquiry from Stamford plc, a rival supermarket chain, to produce, weekly, 60000 packets of a similar type of breakfast cereal of slightly superior quality at a price of £1.20 per 1.5kg packet, the quality and mix of the cereal constituents being laid down by Stamford. This product will fill a gap in Stamford's private label range of cereals. The estimated variable costs for this contract would be: raw materials £0.40p per packet, operating labour £0.15 per packet and packaging and transport £0.12 per packet. None of the 80000 weekly capacity could be used for another product if either of these contracts was taken up.

You are required to:

(a) compute the three selling prices per packet for the Cohin tender using Josun's normal pricing method;   *(3 marks)*
(b) advise Josun, giving your financial reasons, on the relative merits of the two contracts;   *(6 marks)*
(c) discuss the merits of full-cost pricing as a method of arriving at selling prices;   *(5 marks)*
(d) make recommendations to Josun as to the method it might use to derive its selling prices in future;   *(3 marks)*
(e) calculate the expected value of each tender given the following information and recommend which potential customer should receive the greater sales effort. It is estimated that there is a 70 per cent chance of Stamford signing the contract for the weekly production of 60000 packets, while there is a 20 per cent chance of Cohin not accepting the tender. It is also estimated that the probabilities of Cohin achieving weekly sales volumes of 50000, 60000 or 70000 are 0.3, 0.5 and 0.2 respectively. The two sets of negotiations are completely independent of one another;   *(4 marks)*
(f) provide, with reasons, for each of the two contracts under negotiation, a minimum and a recommended price that Josun could ask for the extra quantity that could be produced under each contract and which would ensure the full utilization of Josun's weekly capacity of 80000 packets.   *(4 marks)*

ICAEW P2 Management Accounting

IM10.5 Advanced: Selection of optimal selling price based on demand and cost schedules. Sniwe plc intend to launch a commemorative product on 1 August 2017 for a sports event commencing in 2019. The product will have variable costs of £16 per unit.

Production capacity available for the product is sufficient for 2000 units per annum. Sniwe plc has made a policy decision to produce to the maximum available capacity during the year to 31 July 2018.

Demand for the product during the year to 31 July 2018 is expected to be price dependent, as follows:

Selling price per unit (£)	Annual sales (units)
20	2000
30	1600
40	1200
50	1100
60	1000
70	700
80	400

It is anticipated that in the year to 31 July 2019 the availability of similar competitor products will lead to a market price of £40 per unit for the product during that year.

During the year to 31 July 2019, Sniwe plc intend to produce only at the activity level required to enable them to satisfy demand, with stocks being run down to zero if possible. This policy is intended as a precaution against a sudden collapse of the market for the product by 31 July 2019.

Required:
(Ignore tax and the time value of money.)

(a) Determine the launch price at 1 August 2017 which will maximize the net benefit to Sniwe plc during the two-year period to 31 July 2019 where the demand potential for the year to 31 July 2019 is estimated as (i) 3600 units and (ii) 1000 units.   *(12 marks)*

(b) Identify which of the launch strategies detailed in (a)(i) and (a)(ii) above will result in unsold stock remaining at 31 July 2019. Advise management of the minimum price at which such unsold stock should be able to be sold in order to alter the initial launch price strategy which will maximize the net benefit to Sniwe plc over the life of the product.   *(6 marks)*

(c) Comment on any other factors that might influence the initial launch price strategy where the demand in the year to 31 July 2019 is estimated at 1000 units.   *(4 marks)*

ACCA Level 2 Management Accounting

IM10.6 Advanced: Calculation of unit costs and optimum selling price. French Ltd is about to commence operations utilizing a simple production process to produce two products X and Y. It is the policy of French to operate the new factory at its maximum output in the first year of operations. Cost and production details estimated for the first year's operations are:

Product	Labour hours	Machine hours	Direct labour (£)	Direct materials (£)	Fixed production overheads directly attributable to product (£000)	Maximum production (000 units)
X	1	4	5	6	120	40
Y	8	2	28	16	280	10

There are also general fixed production overheads concerned in the manufacture of both products but which cannot be directly attributed to either. This general fixed production overhead is estimated at £720 000 for the first year of operations. It is thought that the cost structure of the first year will also be operative in the second year.

Both products are new and French is one of the first firms to produce them. Hence, in the first year of operations the sales price can be set by French. In the second and subsequent years it is felt that the market for X and Y will have become

more settled and French will largely conform to the competitive market prices that will become established. The sales manager has researched the first year's market potential and has estimated sales volumes for various ranges of selling price. The details are:

Product X		Product Y	
Range of per unit sales prices (£) (£)	Sales volume (000)	Range of per unit sales prices (£) (£)	Sales volume (000)
Up to 24.00	36	Up to 96.00	11
24.01 to 30.00	32	96.01 to 108.00	10
30.01 to 36.00	18	108.01 to 120.00	9
36.01 to 42.00*	8	120.01 to 132.00	8
		132.01 to 144.00	7
		144.01 to 156.00*	5

*Maximum price.

The managing director of French wishes to ascertain the total production cost of X and Y as, he says, 'Until we know the per unit cost of production we cannot properly determine the first year's sales price. Price must always ensure that total cost is covered and there is an element of profit – therefore I feel that the price should be total cost plus 20 per cent. The determination of cost is fairly simple as most costs are clearly attributable to either X or Y. The general factory overhead will probably be allocated to the products in accordance with some measure of usage of factory resources such as labour or machine hours. The choice between labour and machine hours is the only problem in determining the cost of each product – but the problem is minor and so, therefore, is the problem of pricing.'

Required:

(a) Produce statements showing the effect the cost allocation and pricing methods mentioned by the managing director will have on
  (i) unit costs,
  (ii) closing stock values; and
  (iii) disclosed profit for the first year of operation.
    (8 marks)

(b) Briefly comment on the results in (a) above and advise the managing director on the validity of using the per unit cost figures produced for pricing decisions.   *(4 marks)*

(c) Provide appropriate statements to the management of French Ltd that will be of direct relevance in assisting the determination of the optimum prices of X and Y for the first year of operations.

  The statements should be designed to provide assistance in each of the following, separate, cases:
  (i) year II demand will be below productive capacity;
  (ii) year II demand will be substantially in excess of productive capacity.
  In both cases, the competitive market sales prices per unit for year II are expected to be:

  X – £30 per unit

  Y – £130 per unit

  Clearly specify, and explain, your advice to French for each of the cases described. (Ignore taxation and the time value of money.)   *(8 marks)*

ACCA P2 Management Accounting

IM10.7 Advanced: Calculation of optimal output level adopting a limiting factor approach and the computation of optimum selling prices using differential calculus. AB plc makes two products, Alpha and Beta. The company made a £500 000 profit last year and proposes an identical plan for the coming year. The relevant data for last year are summarized in Table 1.

Table 1: Actuals for last year

	Product Alpha	Product Beta
Actual production and sales (units)	20 000	40 000
Total costs per unit	£20	£40
Selling prices per unit (25% on cost)	£25	£50
Machining time per unit (hours)	2	1
Potential demand at above selling prices (units)	30 000	50 000

Fixed costs were £480 000 for the year, absorbed on machining hours which were fully utilized for the production achieved.

A new managing director has been appointed and he is somewhat sceptical about the plan being proposed. Furthermore, he thinks that additional machining capacity should be installed to remove any production bottlenecks and wonders whether a more flexible pricing policy should be adopted.

Table 2 summarizes the changes in costs involved for the extra capacity and gives price/demand data, supplied by the marketing department, applicable to the conditions expected in the next period.

Table 2: Costs
Extra machining capacity would increase fixed costs by 10 per cent in total. Variable costs and machining times per unit would remain unchanged.

	Product Alpha	Product Beta
Price/demand data		
Price range (per unit)	£20–30	£45–55
Expected demand (000 units)	45–15	70–30

You are required to:

(a) calculate the plan to maximize profits for the coming year based on the data and selling prices in Table 1; *(7 marks)*

(b) comment on the pricing system for the existing plan used in Table 1; *(3 marks)*

(c) calculate the best selling prices and production plan based on the data in Table 2; *(7 marks)*

(d) comment on the methods you have used in part (c) to find the optimum prices and production levels. *(3 marks)*

Any assumptions made must be clearly stated.

CIMA Stage 3 Management Accounting Techniques

IM10.8 Advanced: Calculation of optimum quantity and prices for joint products using differential calculus plus a discussion of joint cost allocations. Nuts plc produces alpha and beta in two stages. The separation process produces crude alpha and beta from a raw material costing £170 per tonne. The cost of the separation process is £100 per tonne of raw material. Each tonne of raw material generates 0.4 tonne of crude alpha and 0.6 tonne of crude beta. Neither product can be sold in its crude state.

The refining process costs £125 per tonne for alpha and £50 per tonne for beta; no weight is lost in refining. The demand functions for refined alpha and refined beta are independent of one another, and the corresponding price equations are:

$$P_A = 1250 - \frac{1000Q_A}{32}$$

$$P_B = 666\tfrac{2}{3} - \frac{1000Q_B}{18}$$

where
P_A = price per tonne of refined alpha
P_B = price per tonne of refined beta
Q_A = quantity of refined alpha
Q_B = quantity of refined beta

The company is considering whether any part of the production of crude alpha or crude beta should be treated as a by-product. The by-product would be taken away free of charge by a large-scale pig farming enterprise.

Requirements:

(a) If all the output of the separation process is refined and sold:
  (i) calculate the optimal quantity of raw material to be processed and the quantities and prices of the refined products; and
  (ii) determine the 'major' product which is worth refining and the 'minor' product which deserves consideration as a potential by-product, but do not attempt to calculate at this stage how much of the 'minor' product would be refined. *(10 marks)*

(b) Calculate:
  (i) the optimal quantity of the 'major' product which would be worth producing regardless of the value of the 'minor' product; and
  (ii) the quantity of the resulting 'minor' product that would be worth refining. *(6 marks)*

(c) Evaluate the principal methods and problems of joint-cost allocation for stock valuation, referring to Nuts plc where appropriate. *(9 marks)*

ICAEW P2 Management Accounting

IM10.9 Advanced: Calculation of optimum selling prices using differential calculus. Cassidy Computers plc sells one of its products, a plug-in card for personal computer systems, in both the UK and Ruritania. The relationship between price and demand is different in the two markets, and can be represented as follows:

Home market: Price (in £) = $68 - 8Q1$

Export market: Price (in $) = $110 - 10Q2$

where Q1 is the quantity demanded (in 000) in the home market and Q2 is the quantity demanded (in 000) in the export market. The current exchange rate is two Ruritanian dollars to the pound.

The variable cost of producing the cards is subject to economies of scale, and can be represented as:

Unit variable cost (in £) = $19 - Q$ (where $Q = Q1 + Q2$).

Requirements:

(a) Calculate the optimum selling price and total contribution made by the product if it can be sold:
  (i) only in the home market
  (ii) only in the export market
  (iii) in both markets. *(10 marks)*

(b) Calculate the optimum selling prices and total contribution made by the product if it can be sold in both markets, but subject to a constraint imposed by the Ruritanian government that the company can sell no more cards in Ruritania than it sells in its home market. How sensitive are the prices to be charged in each market and the total contribution, to changes in the exchange rate over the range $1 = £0.25 to $1 = £1.00? *(8 marks)*

(c) How does the volatility of foreign exchange rates affect the ways in which export sales are priced in practice? *(7 marks)*

ICAEW P2 Management Accounting

11
ACTIVITY-BASED COSTING

LEARNING OBJECTIVES After studying this chapter, you should be able to:

- explain why a cost accumulation system is required for generating relevant cost information for decision-making;

- describe the differences between activity-based and traditional costing systems;

- explain why traditional costing systems can provide misleading information for decision-making;

- identify and explain each of the four stages involved in designing ABC systems;

- describe the ABC cost hierarchy;

- distinguish between traditional ABC and time-driven ABC;

- describe the ABC profitability analysis hierarchy;

- describe the ABC resource consumption model.

The aim of the two previous chapters was to provide you with an understanding of the principles that should be used to identify relevant costs and revenues for various types of decision. It was assumed that relevant costs could easily be measured but, in reality, it was pointed out that indirect relevant costs can be difficult to identify and measure. The measurement of indirect relevant costs for decision-making using activity-based costing (ABC) techniques will be examined in this chapter. The aim of this chapter is to provide you with a conceptual understanding of ABC. Some of the issues explored are complex and therefore much of the content of this chapter is appropriate for a second year management accounting course. If you are pursuing a first year course the content relating to ABC that was presented in Chapter 3 should meet your requirements. In addition, you may wish to read this chapter and omit those sections that are labelled advanced reading. Because this chapter extends the material covered in Chapter 3, it is recommended that you refresh your memory by reading pages 51–59 prior to reading this chapter.

Our focus will be on an organization's *existing* products or services. There is also a need to manage *future* activities to ensure that only profitable products and services are launched. Here the emphasis is on providing strategic cost information using techniques such as target costing, life cycle costing and value engineering. These issues will be explored in Chapter 22 and the mechanisms for appraising investments in new products, services or locations will be described in Chapters 13 and 14.

Unless otherwise stated, we shall assume that products are the cost objects but the techniques used, and the principles established, can also be applied to other cost objects such as customers, services and locations. We begin with an examination of the role that a cost accumulation system plays in generating relevant cost information for decision-making.

THE NEED FOR A COST ACCUMULATION SYSTEM IN GENERATING RELEVANT COST INFORMATION FOR DECISION-MAKING

There are three main reasons why a cost accumulation system is required to generate relevant cost information for decision-making. They are:

1 many indirect costs are relevant for decision-making;

2 an attention-directing information system is required that periodically identifies those potentially unprofitable products that require more detailed special studies;

3 product decisions are not independent.

There is a danger that only those incremental costs that are uniquely attributable to individual products will be classified as relevant, and indirect costs will be classified as irrelevant for decision-making. Direct costs are transparent and how they will be affected by decisions is clearly observable. In contrast, how indirect costs will be affected by decisions is not clearly observable.

The costs of many joint resources are indirect but fluctuate in the long term according to the demand for them. The cost of support functions fall within this category. They include activities such as materials procurement, materials handling, production scheduling, warehousing, expediting and customer order processing. Product introduction, discontinuation, redesign and mix decisions determine the demand for support function resources. For example, if a decision results in a 10 per cent reduction in the demand for the resources of a support activity then we would expect, in the long term, for some of the costs of that support activity to decline by 10 per cent. Therefore, to estimate the impact that decisions will have on the support activities (and their future costs) a cost accumulation system is required that assigns those indirect costs, using cause-and-effect allocations, to products.

The second reason relates to the need for a periodic attention-directing reporting system. Periodic product profitability analysis meets this requirement. A cost accumulation system is therefore required to assign costs to products for periodic profitability analysis to identify those potentially unprofitable products/services that require more detailed special studies to ascertain if they are likely to be profitable in the future.

The third reason for using a cost accumulation system is that many product-related decisions are not independent. Consider again those joint resources shared by most products that fluctuate in the longer term according to the demand for them. If we focus only on individual products and assume that they are independent, decisions will be taken in isolation of decisions made on other products. For joint resources, the incremental/avoidable costs relating to a decision to add or drop a *single* product may be zero. Assuming that 20 products are viewed in this manner then the sum of the incremental costs will be zero. However, if the 20 products are viewed as a *whole* there may be a significant change in resource usage and incremental costs for those joint resources that fluctuate according to the demand for them.

Cooper (1990b) also argues that decisions should not be viewed independently. He states:

The decision to drop one product will typically not change 'fixed' overhead spending. In contrast, dropping 50 products might allow considerable changes to be made. Stated somewhat tritely, the sum of the parts (the decision to drop individual products) is not equal to the sum of the whole (the realizable savings from having dropped 50 products). To help them make effective decisions, managers require cost systems that provide insights into the whole, not just isolated individual parts (p. 58).

TYPES OF COST SYSTEM

Costing systems can vary in terms of which costs are assigned to cost objects and their level of sophistication. Typically, cost systems are classified as follows:

1 direct costing systems;

2 traditional absorption costing systems;

3 activity-based costing systems.

Direct costing systems only assign direct costs to cost objects. Because they do not assign indirect costs to cost objects they report contributions to indirect costs. Periodic profitability analysis would thus be used to highlight negative or low contribution products. An estimate of those indirect costs that are relevant to the decision should be incorporated within the analysis at the special study stage. The disadvantage of direct costing systems is that systems are not in place to measure and assign indirect costs to cost objects. Direct costing systems can only be recommended where indirect costs are a low proportion of an organization's total costs.

Both traditional and ABC systems assign indirect costs to cost objects. The major features of these systems were described in Chapter 3 and the assignment of costs to products was illustrated for both systems. In the next section, the major features that were described in Chapter 3 are briefly summarized but the assignment of costs to products will not be repeated. If you wish to renew your understanding of the detailed cost assignment process you should refer back to Chapter 3 for an illustration of the application of the two-stage allocation process for both traditional and ABC systems.

A COMPARISON OF TRADITIONAL AND ABC SYSTEMS

Figure 3.3 was used in Chapter 3 to illustrate the major differences between traditional costing and ABC systems. This diagram is repeated in the form of Figure 11.1 to provide you with an overview of both systems. Both use a two-stage allocation process. In the first stage, a traditional system allocates overheads to production and service cost centres (typically departments) and then reallocates service department cost centre costs to the production departments. You will see from the lower panel of Figure 11.1 that an ABC system assigns overheads to each major activity (rather than cost centres or departments). With ABC systems, many activity-based cost centres (alternatively known as activity cost pools) are established, whereas with traditional systems overheads tend to be pooled by departments, although they are normally described as cost centres.

Activities consist of the aggregation of many different tasks, events or units of work that cause the consumption of resources. They tend to consists of verbs associated with objects. Typical support activities include: scheduling production, set up machines, move materials, purchase materials, inspect items, process supplier records, expedite and process customer orders. Production process activities include machine products and assemble products. Within the production process, activity cost centres are sometimes identical to the cost centres used by traditional cost systems. Support activities are also sometimes identical to cost centres used by traditional systems, such as when the purchasing department and activity are both treated as cost centres. Overall, however, ABC systems will normally have a greater number of activity cost centres compared with traditional systems.

You will see from Figure 11.1 that stage two of the two-stage allocation process allocates costs from cost centres (pools) to products or other chosen cost objects. Traditional costing systems trace overheads to products using a small number of second stage allocation bases (normally described as overhead allocation rates), which vary directly with the volume produced. Instead of using the terms 'allocation bases' or 'overhead allocation rates' the term cost driver is used by ABC systems. You should be able to remember that a cost driver represents a measure that exerts the major influence on the cost of a particular activity. Direct labour and machine hours are the allocation bases that are

(a) Traditional costing systems

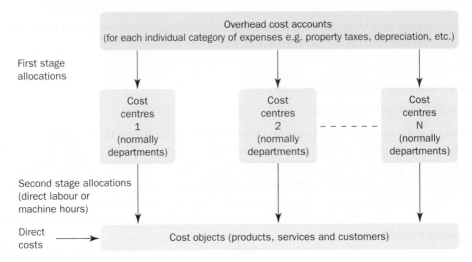

(b) Activity-based costing systems

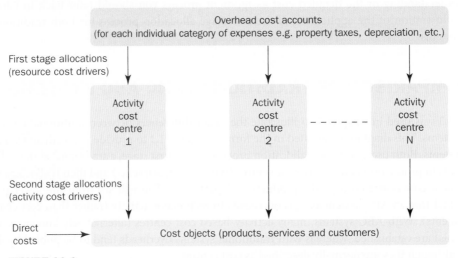

FIGURE 11.1
An illustration of the two-stage allocation process for traditional and activity-based systems

normally used by traditional costing systems. In contrast, ABC systems use many different types of second stage cost drivers, including non-volume-based drivers, such as the number of production runs for production scheduling and the number of purchase orders for the purchasing activity.

Therefore the major distinguishing features of ABC systems are that within the two-stage allocation process they rely on:

1 a greater number of cost centres;

2 a greater number and variety of second stage cost drivers.

By using a greater number of cost centres and different types of cost drivers that cause activity resource consumption, and assigning activity costs to cost objects on the basis of cost driver usage, ABC systems can more accurately measure the resources consumed by cost objects. Traditional cost systems tend to report less accurate costs because they use cost drivers where no cause-and-effect relationships exist to assign support costs to cost objects.

THE EMERGENCE OF ABC SYSTEMS

During the 1990s the limitations of traditional product costing systems began to be widely publicized. These systems were designed decades ago when most companies manufactured a narrow range of products, and direct labour and materials were the dominant factory costs. Overhead costs were relatively small, and the distortions arising from inappropriate overhead allocations were not significant. Information processing costs were high, and it was therefore difficult to justify more sophisticated overhead allocation methods.

Today, companies produce a wide range of products; direct labour often represents only a small fraction of total costs, and overhead costs are of considerable importance. Simplistic overhead allocations cannot be justified, particularly when information processing costs are no longer a barrier to introducing more sophisticated cost systems. Furthermore, today's intense global competition has made decision errors due to poor cost information more probable and more costly.

During the late 1980s a few firms in the USA and Europe implemented ABC type systems. In a series of articles based on observations of innovative ABC-type systems, Cooper and Kaplan (1988) conceptualized the ideas underpinning these systems and coined the term ABC. The articles generated a considerable amount of publicity and consultants began to market and implement ABC systems. Surveys (see Exhibit 11.1) report that approximately 25 per cent of companies in various countries have implemented ABC. Based on their experience of working with early US adopters, Cooper and Kaplan articulated their ideas and reported further theoretical advances in articles published between 1990 and 1992. These ideas and the theoretical advances are described in the remainder of this chapter. ABC ideas have now become firmly embedded in the management accounting literature and educational courses.

REAL WORLD VIEWS 11.1

ABC in China – Xu Ji Electric Co Ltd

Until recently, Xu Ji Electric Co Ltd was a typical stateowned Chinese enterprise manufacturing electrical products such as relays. From an accounting point of view, this implied a manual book-keeping system which was primarily designed to meet external reporting requirements. This was to the detriment of management accounting information, and product costing was not accurate.

The company underwent several changes under Chinese free market developments. If the company were to compete and introduce new products, it needed to invest in more modern production control and testing methods, increase its marketing, increase its research and development, as well as improve its costing system. It decided to adopt an activity-based costing (ABC) system which would trace labour costs directly to products and customer contracts and allocate manufacturing overheads. It took some years for Xu Ji Electric Co Ltd to get the ABC system up and running, but the eventual result was monthly ABC cost reports in some divisions. For example, at the Relays Division which manufactures many types of electrical relay, these reports allocated costs like after-sales service, technical support, warehousing, marketing and production planning to products and customer contracts. At the Relays Division, the activity cost centres included activities such as wiring, labelling, installation, electrical testing and materials management. The Relays division operated in a highly competitive and saturated market and the resulting ABC system assisted the division managers in obtaining more accurate costs and improving divisional performance.

Questions

1 Do you think Xu Ji Electric Co Ltd is a good example of a business where ABC might be useful?

2 Can you think of some activities of Xu Ji Electric Co Ltd other than those stated above?

Reference

Liu, L.Y.J. and Pan, F. (2011) 'Activity based costing in China: A case study of Xu Ji Electric Co. Ltd', *Research Executive Summary* Series, Vol. 7, No. 13, CIMA, London. Available at www.cimaglobal.com/Thought -leadership/Research-topics/Management-accounting -in-different-sectors/Activity-based-costing-in-China/

EXHIBIT 11.1 Surveys of company practice

> Surveys indicate that service companies are more likely to implement ABC than manufacturing companies. This is because most of the costs in service organizations are indirect. In contrast, manufacturing companies can trace important components (such as direct materials and direct labour) of costs to individual products. Therefore, indirect costs are likely to be a much smaller proportion of total costs.
>
> A UK survey by Drury and Tayles (2005) reported that 51 per cent of the financial and service organizations surveyed, compared with 15 per cent of manufacturing organizations, had implemented ABC. The international survey by the Chartered Institute of Management (2009) reported that approximately 28 per cent of the respondents used ABC. Both surveys report a higher rate of adoption in larger companies compared with smaller companies.
>
> A more recent survey by Al-Sayed and Dugdale (2016) adopted a wider definition of ABC and focused on activity-based innovations (defined as 'any management accounting practice that uses the concept of "activities" as its hard core'). They reported that 32 per cent were serious users of activity-based innovations (ABI) and that 72 per cent of the business units sampled have had experience or interest in ABI. Based on these findings the authors concluded that ABI can now be regarded as mainstream management accounting practice.

VOLUME-BASED AND NON-VOLUME-BASED COST DRIVERS

Our comparison of ABC systems with traditional costing systems indicated that ABC systems rely on a greater number and variety of second stage cost drivers. The term 'variety of cost drivers' refers to the fact that ABC systems use both volume-based and non-volume-based cost drivers. In contrast, traditional systems use only volume-based cost drivers. Volume-based cost drivers assume that a product's consumption of overhead resources is directly related to units produced. In other words, they assume that the overhead consumed by products is highly correlated with the number of units produced. Typical volume-based cost drivers used by traditional systems are units of output, direct labour hours and machine hours. These cost drivers are appropriate for measuring the consumption of expenses such as machine energy costs, depreciation related to machine usage, indirect labour employed in production centres and inspection costs where each item produced is subject to final inspection. For example, machine hours are an appropriate cost driver for energy costs since if volume is increased by 10 per cent, machine hours are likely to increase by 10 per cent, thus causing 10 per cent more energy costs to be consumed. Similarly, an increase in volume of 10 per cent is likely to increase the consumption of direct labour hours by 10 per cent and, assuming that indirect labour hours are correlated with direct labour hours, 10 per cent more indirect labour costs will be consumed.

Volume-based drivers are appropriate in the above circumstances because activities are performed each time a unit of the product or service is produced. In contrast, non-volume related activities are not performed each time a unit of the product or service is produced. Consider, for example, two activities – setting up a machine and re-engineering products. Set-up resources are consumed each time a machine is changed from one product to another. It costs the same to set up a machine for 10 or 5000 items. As more set-ups are done more set-up resources are consumed. It is the number of set-ups, rather than the number of units produced, that is a more appropriate measure of the resources consumed by the set-up activity. Similarly, product re-engineering costs may depend on the number of different engineering works orders and not the number of units produced. For both activities, non-volume-based cost drivers such as number of set-ups and engineering orders are needed for the accurate assignment of the costs of these activities.

Using only volume-based cost drivers to assign non-volume related overhead costs can result in the reporting of distorted product costs. The extent of distortion depends on what proportion of total overhead costs the non-volume based overheads represent and the level of product diversity. If a large proportion of an organization's costs are unrelated to volume there is danger that inaccurate product costs will be reported with a traditional costing system. Conversely, if non-volume related overhead costs are only a small proportion of total overhead costs, the distortion of product costs will not be significant. In these circumstances, traditional product costing systems are likely to be acceptable.

Product diversity applies when products consume different overhead activities in dissimilar proportions. Differences in product size, product complexity, sizes of batches and set-up times cause product diversity. If all products consume overhead resources in similar proportions, product diversity will be low and products will consume non-volume-related activities in the same proportion as volume-related activities. Hence, product cost distortion will not occur with traditional product costing systems. Two conditions are therefore necessary for product cost distortion:

- non-volume-related overhead costs are a large proportion of total overhead costs; and
- product diversity applies.

Where these two conditions exist, traditional product costing systems can result in the overcosting of high volume products and undercosting of low volume products. Consider the information presented in Example 11.1.

The reported product costs and profits for the two products are as follows:

| | Traditional system | | ABC system | |
| | Product HV | Product LV | Product HV | Product LV |
	(£)	(£)	(£)	(£)
Direct costs	310 000	40 000	310 000	40 000
Overheads allocated[a]	300 000 (30%)	50 000 (5%)	150 000 (15%)	150 000 (15%)
Reported profits/(losses)	(10 000)	60 000	140 000	(40 000)
Sales revenues	600 000	150 000	600 000	150 000

Note
[a]Allocation of £1 million overheads using direct labour hours as the allocation base for the traditional system and number of batches processed as the cost driver for the ABC system.

Because product HV is a high volume product that consumes 30 per cent of the direct labour hours whereas product LV, the low volume product consumes only 5 per cent, the traditional system that uses direct labour hours as the allocation base allocates six times more overheads to product HV. However, ABC systems recognize that overheads are caused by other factors, besides volume. In our example, all of the overheads are assumed to be volume unrelated. They are caused by the number of batches processed and the ABC system establishes a cause-and-effect allocation relationship by using the number of batches processed as the cost driver. Both products require 15 per cent of the total number of batches so they are allocated with an equal amount of overheads.

It is apparent from the consumption ratios of the two products that the traditional system based on direct labour hours will overcost high volume products and undercost low volume products. Consumption ratios represent the proportion of each activity consumed by a product. The consumption ratios if direct labour hours are used as the cost driver are 0.30 for product HV and 0.05 for product LV so that six times more overheads will be assigned to product HV. When the number of batches processed are used as the cost driver the consumption ratios are 0.15 for each product and an equal amount of overhead will be assigned to each product. Distorted product costs are reported with the traditional costing system that uses the volume-based cost driver because the two conditions specified above apply:

1 non-volume related overheads are a large proportion of total overheads, being 100 per cent in our example.

2 product diversity exists because the product consumption ratios for the two identified cost drivers are significantly different.

EXAMPLE 11.1

Assume that the Balearic company has only one overhead cost centre or cost pool. It currently operates a traditional costing system using direct labour hours to allocate overheads to products. The company produces several products, two of which are products HV and LV. Product HV is made in high volumes whereas product LV is made in low volumes. Product HV consumes 30 per cent of the direct labour hours and product LV consumes only 5 per cent. Because of the high volume production, product HV can be made in large production batches but the irregular and low level of demand for product LV requires it to be made in small batches. A detailed investigation indicates that the number of batches processed causes the demand for overhead resources. The traditional system is therefore replaced with an ABC system using the number of batches processed as the cost driver. You ascertain that each product accounts for 15 per cent of the batches processed during the period and the overheads assigned to the cost centre that fluctuate in the long term according to the demand for them amount to £1 million. The direct costs and sales revenues assigned to the products are as follows:

	Product HV (£)	Product LV (£)
Direct costs	310 000	40 000
Sales revenues	600 000	150 000

Show the product profitability analysis for products HV and LV using the traditional and ABC systems.

The illustration above shows that if the consumption ratios for batches processed had been the same as the ratios for direct labour the traditional and ABC systems would report identical product costs.

With the traditional costing system misleading information is reported. A small loss is reported for product HV and if it were discontinued the costing system mistakenly gives the impression that overheads will decline in the longer term by £300 000. The message from the costing system is to concentrate on the more profitable speciality products such as product LV. In reality, this strategy would be disastrous because low volume products such as product LV are made in small batches and require more people for scheduling production, performing set-ups, inspection of the batches and handling a large number of customer requests for small orders. The long-term effect would be escalating overhead costs.

In contrast, the ABC system allocates overheads on a cause-and-effect basis and more accurately measures the relatively high level of overhead resources consumed by product LV. The message from the profitability analysis is the opposite from the traditional system; that is, product HV is profitable and product LV is unprofitable. If product LV is discontinued, and assuming that the cost driver (number of batches processed) is the cause of all the overheads, then a decision to discontinue product LV should result in the reduction in resource spending on overheads by £150 000.

Example 11.1 is very simplistic. It is assumed that the organization has established only a single cost centre or cost pool, when, in reality, many will be established with a traditional system, and even more with an ABC system. Furthermore, the data have been deliberately biased to show the superiority of ABC. The aim of the illustration has been to highlight the potential cost of errors that can occur when information extracted from simplistic and inaccurate cost systems is used for decision-making.

DESIGNING ABC SYSTEMS

The discussion so far has provided a broad overview of ABC. We shall now examine ABC in more detail by looking at the design of ABC systems. Four steps are involved. They are:

1 identifying the major activities that take place in an organization;

2 assigning costs to cost pools/cost centres for each activity;

3 determining the cost driver for each major activity;

4 assigning the cost of activities to products according to the product's demand for activities.

The first two steps relate to the first stage, and the final two steps to the second stage of the two-stage allocation process shown in Figure 11.1. Let us now consider each of these stages in more detail.

Step 1: Identifying activities

Activities are the aggregation of many different tasks, events or units of work that cause the consumption of resources. For example, purchasing materials might be identified as a separate activity. This activity consists of the aggregation of many different tasks, such as receiving a purchase request, identifying suppliers, preparing purchase orders, mailing purchase orders and performing follow-ups.

REAL WORLD VIEWS 11.2

Activity-based costing in restaurants

Raab, Shoemaker and Mayer (2007) developed a workable ABC model for a restaurant operation in the USA that enabled previously undistributed indirect operating expenses to be traced to individual menu items. Menu prices were previously determined on a cost-plus basis using variable cost as the cost base. In recent years, indirect operating expenses had become a larger percentage of the total cost structure of the restaurant.

The ABC study only examined the restaurant's dinner entrée and beverage service and its lunch menu was not included in the study. The ABC analysis revealed that 11 out of the 14 dinner entrées were unprofitable and were thus a major contributor to the restaurant's negative operating profit. These results reflect the restaurant's relatively high overhead costs which were not taken into account when determining menu prices. The authors conclude that menu ABC profitability analyses that goes beyond the simple analysis of food costs can be applied in the restaurant industry and that a restaurant manager's menu management decisions will differ dramatically if he or she is confronted with the differing results arising from an ABC approach.

Questions

1 The first step in designing an ABC system is to identify the major activities in an organization. What are the major activities in a restaurant?

2 What action should an organization take when the ABC analysis identifies loss-making activities?

3 What are the factors that might prevent the restaurant industry from using ABC?

Reference

Raab, C., Shoemaker, S. and Mayer, K.J. (2007) Activity-based costing – A more accurate way to estimate costs for a restaurant menu, *International Journal of Hospitality & Tourism Administration*, 8(3), 1–15. Available at dx.doi.org/10.1300/J149v08n03_01

The activities chosen should be at a reasonable level of aggregation based on costs versus benefits criteria. For example, rather than classifying purchasing of materials as an activity, each of its constituent tasks could be classified as separate activities. However, this level of decomposition would involve the collection of a vast amount of data and is likely to be too costly for product costing purposes. Alternatively, the purchasing activity might be merged with the materials receiving, storage and issuing activities to form a single materials procurement and handling activity. This is likely to represent too high a level of aggregation because a single cost driver is unlikely to provide a satisfactory determinant of the cost of the activity. For example, selecting the number of purchase orders as a cost driver may provide a good explanation of purchasing costs but may be entirely inappropriate for explaining costs relating to receiving and issuing. Therefore, instead of establishing materials procurement and handling as a single activity it may be preferable to decompose it into three separate activities; namely purchasing, receiving and issuing activities, and establish separate cost drivers for each activity.

The final choice of activities must be a matter of judgement but it is likely to be influenced by factors such as the total cost of the activity centre (it must be of significance to justify separate treatment) and the ability of a single driver to provide a satisfactory determinant of the cost of the activity. Where the latter is not possible, further decomposition of the activity will be necessary. Activities with the same product consumption ratios can use the same cost driver to assign costs to products. Thus, all activities that have the same cost driver can be merged to form a single activity cost centre.

Step 2: Assigning costs to activity cost centres

After the activities have been identified the cost of resources consumed over a specified period must be assigned to each activity. The aim is to determine how much the organization is spending on each of its activities. Many of the resources will be directly attributable to specific activity centres but others (such as labour and lighting and heating costs) may be indirect and jointly shared by several activities. These costs should be assigned to activities on the basis of cause-and-effect cost drivers, or interviews with staff who can provide reasonable estimates of the resources consumed by different activities. Arbitrary allocations should be minimized. The greater the amount of costs traced to activity centres by cost apportionments at this stage the more arbitrary and less reliable will be the product cost information generated by ABC systems. Cause-and-effect cost drivers used at this stage to allocate shared resources to individual activities are called resource cost drivers. Employee surveys are frequently used to estimate the amount of time they spend on different activities in order to assign costs to activities. In large organizations this process can be very time-consuming and expensive and has deterred many organizations from adopting ABC.

Step 3: Selecting appropriate cost drivers for assigning the cost of activities to cost objects

In order to assign the costs attached to each activity cost centre to products, a cost driver must be selected for each activity centre. Cost drivers used at this stage are called activity cost drivers. Several factors must be borne in mind when selecting a suitable cost driver. First, it should provide a good explanation of costs in each activity cost pool. Second, a cost driver should be easily measurable, the data should be relatively easy to obtain and be identifiable with products. The costs of measurement should therefore be taken into account.

Activity cost drivers consist of transaction and duration drivers. Transaction drivers, such as the number of purchase orders processed, number of customer orders processed, number of inspections performed and the number of set-ups undertaken, all count the number of times an activity is performed. Transaction drivers are the least expensive type of cost driver to measure but they are also likely to be the least accurate because they assume that the same quantity of resources is required every time an activity is performed. However, if the variation in the amount of resources required by individual cost objects is not great, transaction drivers will provide a reasonably accurate measurement of activity resources consumed. If this condition does not apply then duration cost drivers should be used.

Duration drivers represent the amount of time required to perform an activity. Examples of duration drivers include set-up hours and inspection hours. For example, if one product requires a short set-up time and another requires a long time then using set-up hours as the cost driver will more accurately measure activity resource consumption than the transaction driver (number of set-ups) which assumes that an equal amount of activity resources are consumed by both products. Using the number of set-ups will result in the product that requires a long set-up time being undercosted whereas the product that requires a short set-up will be overcosted. This problem can be overcome by using set-up hours as the cost driver, but this will increase the measurement costs.

Step 4: Assigning the cost of the activities to products

The final step involves applying the cost driver rates to products. This means that the cost driver must be measurable in a way that enables it to be identified with individual products. Thus, if set-up hours are selected as a cost driver, there must be a mechanism for measuring the set-up hours consumed by each product. Alternatively, if the number of set-ups is selected as the cost driver, measurements by products are not required since all products that require a set-up are charged with a constant set-up cost. The ease and cost of obtaining data on cost driver consumption by products is therefore a factor that must be considered during the third step when an appropriate cost driver is being selected.

ACTIVITY HIERARCHIES

Manufacturing activities can be classified along a cost hierarchy dimension consisting of:

1 unit-level activities;
2 batch-level activities;
3 product-sustaining activities;
4 facility-sustaining activities.

Unit-level activities (also known as volume-related activities) are performed each time a unit of the product or service is produced. Expenses in this category include direct labour, direct materials, energy costs and expenses that are consumed in proportion to machine processing time (such as maintenance). Unit-level activities consume resources in proportion to the number of units of production and sales volume. For example, if a firm produces 10 per cent more units it will consume 10 per cent more labour cost, 10 per cent more machine hours and 10 per cent more energy costs. Typical cost drivers for unit level activities include labour hours, machine hours and the quantity of materials processed. These cost drivers are also used by traditional costing systems. Traditional systems are therefore also appropriate for assigning the costs of unit-level activities to cost objects.

Batch-related activities, such as setting up a machine or processing a purchase order, are performed each time a batch of goods is produced. The cost of batch-related activities varies with the number of batches made, but is common (or fixed) for all units within the batch. For example, set-up resources are consumed when a machine is changed from one product to another. As more batches are produced, more set-up resources are consumed. It costs the same to set up a machine for 10 or 5000 items. Thus the demands for the set-up resources are not determined by the number of units produced after completing the set-up. Similarly, purchasing resources are consumed each time a purchasing order is processed, but the resources consumed are not determined by the number of units included in the purchase order. Other examples of batch-related costs include resources devoted to production scheduling, first-item inspection and materials movement. Traditional costing systems treat batch-related expenses as fixed costs, whereas ABC systems assume that batch-related expenses vary with the number of batches processed.

REAL WORLD VIEWS 11.3

ABC in healthcare

The remuneration system that is applied in health-care organizations in several countries (e.g. Australia, the USA, Switzerland, Spain and Italy) enables ABC profitability analysis to be applied in hospitals. These countries apply the Diagnosis Related Groups (DRGs) reimbursement system to fund hospital activities. With this system, diagnoses requiring similar treatments are assumed to require similar resources resulting in reimbursement at a standard unit price by the National Health System for the healthcare services. Diagnostic-Therapeutic Pathways (DTPs) identify all the services needed to diagnose and treat a specific disease from the first access of the patient into the healthcare system and are made comparable with the DRG.

Cannavacciuolo et al. (2015) report on how ABC was used in an Italian hospital to determine the amount of resources used by each activity included in the DTP and thus develop a DTP cost. The DTP cost was derived from the sum of activity cost pools needed to perform a DTP. Thus it is possible to determine the profitability of each DTP by comparing its cost with the DRG tariff. Where the DTP cost exceeded the DRG tariff, activities are examined with a view to performing them more efficiently. ABC also enabled the most cost-consuming activities to be identified. The determination of the cost of each activity of a DTP also provided the potential to compare the costs of DTPs with those

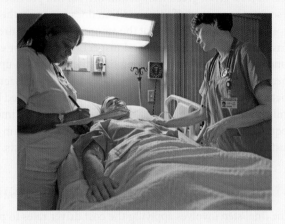

in other hospitals and thus highlight potential for carrying out the activities more effectively and efficiently.

Questions

1 In some countries revenues may be received in a lump sum and are not assignable to individual diagnosis related groups. What role can ABC play in such organizations?

2 Do you think many business organizations utilize ABC techniques? Why or why not?

Reference

Cannavacciuolo, L., Illario, M., Ippolito, A. and Ponsiglione, C. (2015) 'An activity-based costing approach for detecting inefficiencies of healthcare processes', *Business Process Management Journal*, 21(1), 55–79. Available at dx.doi.org/10.1108/BPMJ-11-2013-0144

Product-sustaining activities or **service-sustaining activities** are performed to enable the production and sale of individual products (or services). Examples of product-sustaining activities include maintaining and updating product specifications and the technical support provided for individual products and services. Other examples are the resources to prepare and implement engineering change notices (ECNs), to design processes and test routines for individual products, and to perform product enhancements. The costs of product-sustaining activities are incurred irrespective of the number of units of output or the number of batches processed and their expenses will tend to increase as the number of products manufactured is increased. ABC uses product-level bases such as number of active part numbers and number of ECNs to assign these costs to products. Where customers are the cost objects the equivalent term for product sustaining is **customer-sustaining activities**. Customer market research and support for an individual customer, or groups of customers if they represent the cost object, are examples of customer-sustaining activities.

The final activity category is **facility-sustaining** (or **business-sustaining**) **activities**. They are performed to support the facility's general manufacturing process and include general administrative staff, plant management and property costs. They are incurred to support the organization as a whole and are common and joint to all products manufactured in the plant. There would have to be a dramatic change in activity, resulting in an expansion or contraction in the size of the plant, for facility-sustaining costs to change. Such events are most unlikely in most organizations. Therefore these costs should not be assigned to products since they are unavoidable and irrelevant for most decisions. Instead, they are regarded as common costs to *all* products made in the plant and deducted as a lump sum from the total of the operating margins from *all* products.

COST VERSUS BENEFITS CONSIDERATIONS

In Chapter 3, it was pointed out that the design of a cost system should be based on cost versus benefit considerations. A sophisticated ABC system should generate the most accurate product costs. The cost of implementing and operating an ABC system is significantly more expensive than operating a direct costing or a traditional costing system. In particular, the training and software requirements may prohibit its adoption by small organizations. However, the partial costs reported by direct costing systems, and the distorted costs reported by traditional systems (unsophisticated), may result in significant mistakes in decisions (such as selling unprofitable products or dropping profitable products) arising from the use of this information. If the cost of errors arising from using partial or distorted information generated from using these systems exceeds the additional costs of implementing and operating an ABC system, then an ABC (sophisticated) system ought to be implemented.

The optimal costing system is different for different organizations. A simplistic traditional costing system may report reasonably accurate product costs in organizations that have the following characteristics:

1 low levels of competition;

2 non-volume-related indirect costs that are a low proportion of total indirect costs;

3 a fairly standardized product range all consuming organizational resources in similar proportions (i.e. low product diversity).

In contrast, a sophisticated (ABC) system may be optimal for organizations having the following characteristics:

1 intensive competition;

2 non-volume-related indirect costs that are a high proportion of total indirect costs;

3 a diverse range of products, all consuming organizational resources in significantly different proportions (i.e. high product diversity).

TIME-DRIVEN ABC

The survey evidence summarized in Exhibit 11.1 indicates that the ABC adoption rate has been fairly low. The costly design, implementation and operation of such systems have been the major contributory factors explaining the low rate of adoption. Kaplan and Anderson (2004) conclude that many companies have abandoned ABC systems because they took too long to implement and were too expensive to build and implement. To overcome these problems they advocate adapting traditional ABC by using a more simplistic approach called time-driven ABC.

Kaplan and Anderson present the data shown in the upper section of Exhibit 11.2 to illustrate a traditional ABC system for a customer services department with a quarterly total expenditure of £560 000 (consisting of the cost of personnel, information technology and other fixed expenses) involving three activities – processing customers orders, handling customer orders and performing credit checks. Employees are surveyed to estimate the percentage of time they expect to spend on the three activities and the department's expenses are assigned to the activities based on the average percentages

EXHIBIT 11.2 Traditional and time-driven ABC

Calculation of cost driver rates using the traditional ABC approach

Activity	% of time spent	Assigned cost (£)	Cost driver quantity	Cost driver rate (£)
Process customer orders	70	392 000	49 000	8 per order
Handle customer enquiries	10	56 000	1 400	40 per enquiry
Perform credit checks	20	112 000	2 500	44.80 per credit check
		560 000		

Time-driven ABC reporting

Activity	Cost driver quantity	Unit time (minutes)	Total time used (minutes)	Cost driver rate (£)	Total cost assigned (£)
Process customer orders	49 000	8	392 000	6.40	313 600
Handle customer enquiries	1 400	44	61 600	35.20	49 280
Perform credit checks	2 500	50	125 000	40.00	100 000
Total used			578 600		462 880
Total supplied			700 000		560 000
Unused capacity			121 400		97 120

Adapted from Kaplan and Anderson (2004).

derived from the survey. The quantities of work for the three activities are obtained in order to derive the cost driver rates shown in the upper section of Exhibit 11.2. These cost driver rates are used to assign the department's resources to the customers or products that use the activities. The traditional ABC approach can be easily applied to the simplistic illustration shown in Exhibit 11.2 but applying this approach in a large organization with thousands of employees and activities that requires surveying how employees spend their time can be prohibitively time-consuming and expensive.

Kaplan and Anderson illustrate how time-driven ABC can be applied to the situation presented in the lower section of Exhibit 11.2. With this approach managers directly estimate the resource demands required by each product, customer or service instead of assigning resource costs to each activity and then to products or customers. This simplified approach requires estimates of only two items:

1 the cost per time unit of supplying resource capacity, and

2 unit times of consumption of resource capacity by products, services or customers.

Estimates of the cost per time unit of supplying resource capacity avoids the need to undertake the very time-consuming approach of surveying employees on how they spend their time. Instead Kaplan and Anderson advocate that managers should first directly estimate the practical capacity of the resources supplied as a percentage of maximum theoretical capacity. An approximate approach is to assume that practical full capacity is around 80 per cent of theoretical maximum capacity so that if an employee works 40 hours per week this theoretical maximum capacity will be reduced to a practical full capacity of 32 hours using an 80 per cent conversion rate. Applying this approach to the customer service department Kaplan and Anderson assume that there are 28 workers in the department working 8 hours per day resulting in each worker supplying 10 560 minutes per month (22 days × 8 hours × 60 minutes) or 31 680 minutes per quarter. Assuming that practical capacity is about 79 per cent of theoretical capacity, around 25 000 hours of practical capacity will be supplied per worker per quarter resulting in a total practical capacity supplied of 700 000 hours

(28 workers $\times$ 25 000 hours). The cost per minute of supplying capacity in the department is therefore £0.80 (£560 000 total expenditure/700 000 hours).

The next stage is to *determine the time it takes to perform one unit of each kind of activity.* Kaplan and Anderson suggest that this information can be derived from interviews with employees or direct observation and that reasonable approximations rather than precise observations will suffice. They assume that it takes 8 minutes to process an order, 44 minutes to handle an enquiry and 50 minutes to perform a credit check. Cost driver rates are calculated by multiplying the cost per minute of supplying capacity by the time it takes to perform one unit of each kind of activity. The cost driver rates are £6.40 for processing customer orders (8 $\times$ £0.80), £35.20 for handling enquiries (44 $\times$ £0.80) and £40 for performing a credit check (50 $\times$ £0.80). These rates can now be used to assign cost to individual customers, products or services that use each activity.

The lower part of Exhibit 11.2 shows the time-driven ABC report for the period. The report provides essential information relating to both the quantity and cost of the unused practical capacity. Management should investigate the cost of the unused capacity and decide if or how to reduce the cost of supplying unused resources in future periods. The lower part of Exhibit 11.2 also indicates why the cost driver rates for time-driven ABC are lower than the traditional ABC rates. The traditional ABC cost driver rates are derived from the actual capacity *used* shown in the lower part of Exhibit 11.2 whereas the time-driven approach is derived from the practical capacity *supplied*. Therefore the cost of unused capacity is buried within the traditional ABC cost driver rates.

Besides simplifying the operation of an ABC system, time-driven ABC can capture the complexity of real world operations. The example outlined above assumed that all transactions for each activity were the same and required the same amount of time to process. Kaplan and Anderson illustrate how time equations can be established to capture more complex operations. They provide an example of

REAL WORLD VIEWS 11.4

Time-driven activity-based costing for public services

Public sector organizations increasingly must account for their performance and provide quality services at lower costs. To accomplish this many local authorities and public sector organizations have used ABC systems but many have tried ABC and abandoned it because they were time-consuming and expensive to operate. Rather than abandoning ABC a possible solution is to improve it using time-driven ABC (TDABC). An article published in *Public Money and Management* authored by Stouthuysen *et. al* (2014) illustrates the application TDABC to two indoor swimming pools in a medium-sized Belgian city and financed by the same local authority.

The TDABC model used 'types of pool visitors' as cost objects broken down into four distinct cost object categories. Six main activities were identified. To calculate the cost per time unit spent on an activity, the total annual operating expenses (i.e. the cost of supplied capacity) for each pool was calculated. Next, practical capacity supplied using an annual time measure availability based on the number of full-time equivalent workers at each pool was calculated. Finally, total cost per pool was divided by the practical capacity to obtain the cost per minute of supplying capacity in each pool. Cost driver rates were calculated by multiplying the cost per minute by the time involved for each kind of activity and then assigned cost objects according to their use of each activity.

Questions

1 Can you provide some examples of cost objects and activities that might be applicable to a swimming pool?

2 How might the information produced by an ABC system be used in a leisure centre?

References

Stouthuysen, K., Schierhout, K., Roodhooft, F. and Reusen, E. (2014) 'Time-driven activity-based costing for public services', *Public Money & Management*, 34(4): 289–296. dx.doi.org/10.1080/09540962.2014.920202

processing a chemical for transportation where standard packaging takes 0.5 minutes, special packaging requires an additional 6.5 minutes and if the item is to be transported by air a further 2 minutes are required for the package to be placed in a container that is suitable for air travel. The estimated total time for the packaging process can be determined by multiplying the different types of packaging by the time required for each type of packaging. The resulting cost driver rate per minute would be multiplied by the number of minutes required for the specific type of packaging. In contrast, the traditional ABC approach requires that the varying transaction times are captured by treating each variant of the process as a separate activity and thus increasing the complexity of the ABC system.

Presumably Kaplan and Anderson use the term 'time-driven ABC' for the simplified version of ABC because the capacity of most resources is measured in terms of time availability but they point out that the approach can also be used for resources whose capacity is measured in other units. They illustrate how the capacity of a warehouse or vehicles could be measured by the space provided and memory storage by the megabytes supplied.

ACTIVITY-BASED COSTING PROFITABILITY ANALYSIS

In the previous chapter, a hierarchical approach to profitability analysis was illustrated using direct costing principles. In this section, we shall examine how Cooper and Kaplan (1991) have applied the ABC hierarchical activity classification to profitability analysis. At this stage, you will find it helpful to refer back to Exhibit 10.1 in the previous chapter so that you can compare the less complex direct costing hierarchical analysis with the more complex ABC hierarchical analysis. The general principles of activity profitability analysis applied to different cost objects is illustrated in Figure 11.2. This approach categorizes costs according to the causes of their variability at different hierarchical levels. Hierarchies identify the lowest level to which cost can meaningfully be assigned without relying on arbitrary allocations. In Figure 11.2, the lowest hierarchical levels (shown at the top of the diagram) are product, customer and branch contributions after deducting unit level costs and, ignoring the business unit level the highest hierarchical levels (shown in the penultimate row prior to the overall business unit) are product lines, distribution channels and country profits.

Let us initially focus on products as the cost object. Look at the column for products as the cost object in Figure 11.2. You will see that a unit-level contribution margin is calculated for each *individual* product. This is derived by deducting the cost of unit-level activities from sales revenues. From this, unit-level contribution expenses relating to batch-related activities are deducted. Next the cost of product-sustaining activities are deducted. Thus, three different contribution levels are reported at the *individual* product level. Differentiating contributions at these levels provides a better understanding of the implications of product mix and discontinuation decisions in terms of cost and profit behaviour.

In Figure 11.2, there are two further levels within the product hierarchy. They are the product brand level and the product line level. Some organizations do not market their products by brands and therefore have only one further level (i.e. the product line) within the product hierarchy. A product line consists of a group of similar products. For example, banks have product lines such as savings accounts, lending services, currency services, insurance services and brokering services. Each product line contains individual product variants. The savings product line would include low balance/low interest savings accounts, high balance/high interest accounts, postal and internet savings accounts and other product variants. The lending services product line would include personal loans, house mortgage loans, business loans and other product variants within the product line. Some expenses such as marketing, research and development, and distribution expenses might be incurred for the benefit of the whole product line and not for any products within the line. Therefore these product line-sustaining expenses should be attributed to the product line but no attempt should be made to allocate them to individual products. Finally, the profit for the organizational unit as a whole can be determined by deducting facility-sustaining expenses from the sum of the individual product line contributions.

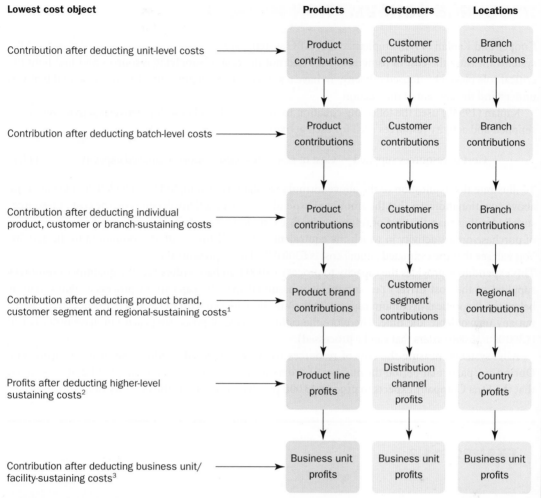

Lowest cost object	Products	Customers	Locations
Contribution after deducting unit-level costs	Product contributions	Customer contributions	Branch contributions
Contribution after deducting batch-level costs	Product contributions	Customer contributions	Branch contributions
Contribution after deducting individual product, customer or branch-sustaining costs	Product contributions	Customer contributions	Branch contributions
Contribution after deducting product brand, customer segment and regional-sustaining costs[1]	Product brand contributions	Customer segment contributions	Regional contributions
Profits after deducting higher-level sustaining costs[2]	Product line profits	Distribution channel profits	Country profits
Contribution after deducting business unit/facility-sustaining costs[3]	Business unit profits	Business unit profits	Business unit profits

Notes

[1]Consists of expenses dedicated to sustaining specific product brands or customer segments or regions but which cannot be attributed to individual products, customers or branches.

[2]Consists of expenses dedicated to sustaining the product lines or distribution channels or countries but which cannot be attributed to lower items within the hierarchy.

[3]Consists of expenses dedicated to the business as a whole and not attributable to any lower items within the hierarchy.

FIGURE 11.2

An illustration of hierarchical profitability analysis

A similar approach to the one described above for products can also be applied to other cost objects. The two final columns shown in Figure 11.2 illustrate how the approach can be applied to customers and locations. The aim of ABC hierarchical profitability analysis is to assign all organizational expenses to a particular hierarchical or organizational level where cause-and-effect cost assignments can be established so that arbitrary allocations are non-existent. The hierarchical approach helps to identify the impact on resource consumption by adding or dropping items at each level of the hierarchy. For example, if a product line is dropped, activities at the product line level and below (i.e. above the product line profits row in Figure 11.2) which are uniquely associated with the product line will be affected, but higher level activities (i.e. at the business unit level) will be unaffected. Similarly, if a product within a particular product line is dropped then all unit, batch and product-sustaining activities uniquely associated with that product will be affected but higher level product-level and business unit level activities will be unaffected.

RESOURCE CONSUMPTION MODELS

Cooper and Kaplan (1992) emphasize that ABC systems are models of resource consumption. ABC systems measure the cost of using resources and not the cost of supplying resources and highlight the critical role played by unused capacity. To have a good conceptual grasp of ABC, it is essential that you understand the content of this section.

Kaplan (1994b) used the following equation to formalize the relationship between activity resources supplied and activity resources used for each activity:

$$\text{Cost of resources supplied} = \text{Cost of resources used} + \text{Cost of unused capacity} \qquad (11.1)$$

To illustrate the application of the above formula we shall use Example 11.2. The left-hand side of the above equation indicates that the amount of expenditure on an activity depends on the cost of resources supplied rather than the cost of resources used. Example 11.2 contains data relating to the processing of purchase orders activity in which the equivalent of ten full-time staff are committed to the activity. You will see that the estimated annual cost is £300 000. This represents the cost of resources supplied. This expenditure provides the capacity to process 15 000 purchase orders (i.e. the quantity of resources supplied of the cost driver) per annum. It is assumed that the capacity to process 15 000 orders is below the theoretical maximum capacity that could be achieved working at 100 per cent activity without any unavoidable idle time. Therefore the estimated cost of processing each purchase order is £20 (£300 000/15 000 orders that can be processed).

ABC systems measure the cost of resources used by individual products, services or customers. During any particular period the number of orders processed will vary. In Example 11.2, it is assumed that the Etna Company expects to process 13 000 purchase orders (i.e. the quantity of resources used).

EXAMPLE 11.2

The following information relates to the purchasing activity in a division of the Etna Company for the next year:

(1) Resources supplied

Ten full-time staff at £30 000 per year (including employment costs)	= £300 000 annual activity cost
Cost driver	= Number of purchase orders processed
Quantity of cost driver supplied per year: (Each member of staff can process 1500 orders per year)	= 15 000 purchase orders
Estimated cost driver rate	= £20 per purchase order (£300 000/15 000 orders)

(2) Resources used

Estimated number of purchase orders to be processed during the year	= 13 000
Estimated cost of resources used assigned to parts and materials	= £260 000 (13 000 × £20)

(3) Cost of unused capacity

Resources supplied (15 000) − Resources used (13 000) at £20 per order	= £40 000 (2000 × £20)

The ABC system will therefore assign £26 0000 (13 000 orders at £20 per order) to the parts and materials ordered during the year. This represents the cost of resources used.

The cost of unused capacity represents the difference between the cost of resources supplied and the cost of resources used. Resources have been acquired to enable 15 000 purchase orders to be processed, but during the year only 13 000 orders will be processed giving an unused capacity of 2000 purchase orders. Hence the predicted cost of the unused capacity will be £40 000 (2000 orders at £20 per order).

Unused capacity arises because the supply of some resources has to be acquired in discrete amounts in advance of usage such that the supply cannot be continually adjusted in the short run to match exactly the usage of resources. Typical expenses in this category include the acquisition of equipment or the employment of non-piecework employees. The expenses of supplying these resources are incurred independently of usage in the short run and this independence has led to them being categorized as fixed costs. Kaplan and Cooper (1998) describe such resources as committed resources. In contrast, there are other types of resource whose supply can be continually adjusted to match exactly the usage of resources. For example, materials, casual labour and the supply of energy for running machinery can be continually adjusted to match the exact demand. Thus, the cost of supplying these resources will generally equal the cost of resources used and the resources will have no unused capacity. Kaplan and Cooper classify these resources as flexible resources although they have traditionally been categorized as variable costs.

The problem of adjusting the supply of resources to match the usage of resources and eliminating unused capacity therefore applies only to committed resources. Where the cost of supplying resources in the short run is fixed, the quantity used will fluctuate each period based on the activities performed for the output produced. Activity-based systems measure the cost of *using* these resources, even though the cost of supplying them will not vary with short-run usage.

Managers make decisions (for example, changes in output volume and mix, process changes and improvements and changes in product and process design) that result in changes in activity resource usage. Assuming that such decisions result in a decline in the demand for activity resources, then the first term on the right-hand side of equation (11.1) will decline (the cost of resources used) but the cost of unused capacity (the second term on the right-hand side of the equation) will increase to offset exactly the lower resource usage cost. To translate the benefits of reduced activity demands into cash flow savings management action is required. They must permanently remove the unused capacity by reducing spending on the supply of the resources. Thus, to make a resource variable in the downward direction requires two management decisions, first to reduce the demand for the resource and, second, to lower the spending on the resource.

Demands for activity resources can also increase because of decisions to introduce new products, expand output and create greater product variety. Such decisions can lead to situations where activity resource usage exceeds the supply of resources. In the short term, the excess demand might be absorbed by people working longer or faster or delaying production. Eventually, however, additional spending will be required to increase the supply of activity resources. Thus, even if permanent changes in activity resource consumption occur that result in either unused or excess capacity, there may be a significant time lag before the supply of activity resources is adjusted to match the revised predicted activity usage. Indeed, there is always a danger that managers may not act to reduce the spending on the supply of resources to match a reduction in demand. They may keep existing resources in place even when there has been a substantial decline in demands for the activities consuming the resources. Consequently, there will be no benefits arising from actions to reduce activity usage. However, if decisions are made based on reported ABC costs, it is implicitly assumed that predicted changes in activity resource usage will be translated into equivalent cash flow changes for the resources supplied.

A major feature of ABC systems is therefore that reported product, service or customer costs represent estimates of the cost of resources used. In a period, many decisions are made that affect the usage of resources. It is not feasible to link the required changes in the supply of resources with the change in usage predicted by each *individual* decision. The periodic reporting of both the predicted quantity and the cost of unused capacity for each activity signals the need for management to investigate the potential for reducing the activity resources supplied. In the case of committed resources performing one less set-up, ordering one less batch of materials or undertaking one fewer engineering change notice, will not result in an automatic reduction in spending. It will create additional capacity, and changes in spending on the supply of resources will often be the outcome of the totality of many decisions rather than focusing on a one-off product decision. Such ideas are considered to be of such vital importance by Kaplan and Cooper that they conclude that managing used and unused capacity is the central focus of ABC.

PERIODIC REVIEW OF AN ABC DATABASE

The detailed tracking of costs is unnecessary when ABC information is used for decision-making. A database should be maintained that is reviewed periodically, say once or twice a year. In addition, periodic cost and profitability audits (similar to that illustrated in Figure 11.2) should be undertaken to provide a strategic review of the costs and profitability of a firm's products, customers and sales outlets. Rather than focusing on the past it is preferable to concentrate on the future profitability of products and customers using estimated activity-based costs. It is therefore recommended that an activity cost database is maintained at estimated standard costs that are updated on an annual or semi-annual basis.

ABC COST MANAGEMENT APPLICATIONS

Our aim in this chapter has been to look at how ABC can be used to provide information for decision-making by more accurately assigning costs to cost objects, such as products, customers and locations. In addition, ABC can be used for a range of strategic cost management applications. These include cost reduction, activity-based budgeting, performance measurement, benchmarking of activities, process management and business process re-engineering.

The decision to implement ABC should not, therefore, be based only on its ability to produce more accurate and relevant decision-making information. A survey by Innes, Mitchell and Sinclear (2000) on ABC applications reported that the cost management applications tend to outweigh the product costing applications which were central to ABC's initial development. We shall examine ABC applications to strategic cost management in Chapter 22. Finally, you should note that care should be exercised when using unit costs derived from ABC systems. For a discussion of the limitations of ABC unit costs, you should refer to Learning Note 10.2 on the digital support resources.

SUMMARY

The following items relate to the learning objectives listed at the beginning of the chapter.

- **Explain why a cost accumulation system is required for generating relevant cost information for decision-making.**

There are three main reasons why a cost accumulation system is required for generating relevant cost information. First, many indirect costs are relevant for decision-making and a costing system is therefore required that provides an estimate of resources consumed by cost objects using cause- and-effect allocations to allocate indirect costs. Second, an attention-directing information system is required that periodically identifies those potentially unprofitable products that require more detailed special studies. Third, many product decisions are not independent and to capture product interdependencies those joint resources that fluctuate in the longer term according to the demand for them should be assigned to products.

● **Describe the differences between activity-based and traditional costing systems.**

The major differences relate to the two-stage allocation process. In the first stage, traditional systems allocate indirect costs to cost centres (normally departments), whereas activity-based systems allocate indirect costs to cost centres based on activities rather than departments. Since there are many more activities than departments a distinguishing feature is that activity-based systems will have a greater number of cost centres in the first stage of the allocation process. In the second stage, traditional systems use a limited number of different types of second stage volume-based allocation bases (cost drivers) whereas activity-based systems use many different types of volume-based and non-volume-based cause-and-effect second stage drivers.

● **Explain why traditional costing systems can provide misleading information for decision-making.**

Traditional systems often tend to rely on arbitrary allocations of indirect costs. In particular, they rely extensively on volume-based allocations. Many indirect costs are not volume-based but, if volume-based allocation bases are used, high volume products are likely to be assigned with a greater proportion of indirect costs than they have consumed, whereas low volume products will be assigned a lower proportion. In these circumstances traditional systems will overcost high volume products and undercost low volume products. In contrast, ABC systems recognize that many indirect costs vary in proportion to changes other than production volume. By identifying the cost drivers that cause the costs to change and assigning costs to cost objects on the basis of cost driver usage, costs can be more accurately traced. It is claimed that this cause-and-effect relationship provides a superior way of determining relevant costs.

● **Identify and explain each of the four stages involved in designing ABC systems.**

The design of ABC systems involves the following four stages: (a) identify the major activities that take place in the organization; (b) create a cost centre/cost pool for each activity; (c) determine the cost driver for each major activity; and (d) trace the cost of activities to the product according to a product's demand (using cost drivers as a measure of demand) for activities.

● **Describe the ABC cost hierarchy.**

ABC systems classify activities along a cost hierarchy consisting of unit-level, batch-level, product-sustaining and facility-sustaining activities. Unit-level activities are performed each time a unit of the product or service is produced. Examples include direct labour and energy costs. Batch-level activities are performed each time a batch is produced. Examples include setting up a machine or processing a purchase order. Product-sustaining activities are performed to enable the production and sale of individual products. Examples include the technical support provided for individual products and the resources required for performing product enhancements. Facility-sustaining activities are performed to support the facility's general manufacturing process. They include general administrative staff and property support costs.

● **Distinguish between traditional ABC and time-driven ABC.**

Traditional ABC allocates resource costs to activities using resource cost drivers and then allocates the cost of activities to cost objects using activity cost drivers. With time-driven ABC the cost per time unit of supplying capacity for a department or process is estimated by dividing the total cost of the process by the practical capacity supplied (usually estimated as a percentage of theoretical capacity). The next stage is to determine the time it takes to perform one unit of each kind of activity. The cost driver rates for each activity are calculated by multiplying the time taken to perform each activity by the cost per time unit of supplying capacity. These rates are used to assign costs to the cost objects that use each activity.

● **Describe the ABC profitability analysis hierarchy.**

The ABC profitability analysis hierarchy categorizes costs according to their variability at different hierarchical levels to report different hierarchical contribution levels. At the final level, facility or business-sustaining costs are deducted from the sum of the product contributions to derive a profit at the business unit level. In other words, facility/business-sustaining costs are not allocated to individual products. The aim of hierarchical profitability analysis is to assign all organizational expenses to a particular hierarchical or organizational level where cause-and-effect cost assignments can be established so that arbitrary apportionments are non-existent.

● **Describe the ABC resource consumption model.**

ABC systems are models of resource consumption. They measure the cost of using resources and not the cost of supplying resources. The difference between the cost of resources supplied and the cost of resources used represents the cost of unused capacity. The cost of unused capacity for each activity is the reporting mechanism for identifying the need to adjust the supply of resources to match the usage of resources. However, to translate the benefits of reduced activity demands into cash flow savings, management action is required to remove the unused capacity by reducing the spending on the supply of resources.

KEY TERMS AND CONCEPTS

Activities The aggregation of many different tasks, events or units of work that cause the consumption of resources.

Activity cost drivers A cost driver used to assign the costs assigned to an activity cost centre to products.

Batch-related activities Activities that are performed each time a batch of goods is produced.

Business-sustaining activities Activities performed to support the organization as a whole, also known as facility-sustaining activities.

Committed resources Resources that have to be acquired in discrete amounts in advance of usage, where the supply cannot be continually adjusted in the short run to match exactly the usage of resources.

Consumption ratio The proportion of each activity consumed by a product.

Cost driver The basis used to allocate costs to cost objects in an ABC system. It is also a measure that exerts a major influence on the cost of a particular activity.

Cost of resources supplied The cost of resources supplied for an activity, whether or not all these resources are actually required, which may include the cost of some unused capacity.

Cost of resources used The cost of resources actually used for an activity, which excludes the cost of any unused capacity.

Cost of unused capacity The difference between the cost of resources supplied and the cost of resources used.

Customer-sustaining activities Activities that are performed to support the relationship with customers.

Duration drivers A cost driver used to assign the costs assigned to an activity cost centre to products that is based on the amount of time required to perform an activity.

Facility-sustaining activities Activities performed to support the organization as a whole, which are normally not affected by a decision that is to be taken. Also known as business-sustaining activities.

Flexible resources Types of resource whose supply can be continually adjusted to match exactly the usage of resources.

Model of resource consumption A model that focuses on the cost of using resources, as opposed to the cost of supplying resources.

Non-volume-based cost drivers A method of allocating indirect costs to cost objects that uses alternative measures instead of assuming that a product's consumption of overhead resources is directly related to the number of units produced.

Product line-sustaining expenses Expenses relating to supporting a product line rather than a specific brand or product within that product line.

Product-sustaining activities Support activities that are performed to enable the production and sale of individual products and that are not related to the volume of each product.

Resource cost driver A cause-and-effect cost driver used to allocate shared resources to individual activities.

Service-sustaining activities Support activities that are performed to enable the production and sale of individual services and that are not related to the volume of each service provided.

Time-driven ABC A simplified approach for operating ABC in large organizations where employees are surveyed to estimate the percentage of time they expect to spend on activities and expenses are assigned to the activities based on the average percentages derived from the survey. The quantities of work for activities are obtained in order to derive the cost driver rates, which are then used to assign to resources the customers or products that use the activities.

Transaction drivers A cost driver used to assign the costs assigned to an activity cost centre to products that is based on the number of times an activity is performed.

Unit-level activities Activities that are performed each time a unit of the product or service is produced.

Volume-based cost drivers A method of allocating indirect costs to cost objects that correlates a product's consumption of overhead resources with the number of units produced.

RECOMMENDED READING

For an illustration of the calculation of product costs using an ABC systems, you can refer to an ABC article that can be accessed from the ACCA Student Accountant technical article archive at http://www.accaglobal.com/gb/en/student/exam-support-resources/fundamentals-exams-study-resources/f2/technical-articles.html. Kaplan and Cooper have been the major contributors to the development of activity-based costing. Much of this chapter has therefore drawn off their ideas. For a detailed description of their ideas should consult their book *Cost and Effect: Using Integrated Systems to Drive Profitability and Performance* (1998). For a survey of the factors influencing the choice of product costing systems in UK organizations, see Al-Omiri and Drury (2007), and Al-Sayed and Dugdale (2016) for factors influencing activity-based innovations. The time-driven ABC content covered in this chapter was derived from Kaplan and Anderson (2004 and 2007) and you should refer to these articles for a more detailed explanation of this topic.

KEY EXAMINATION POINTS

Questions often require you to compute product costs for a traditional system and an activity-based system and explain the difference between the product costs.

Questions also often require you to outline the circumstances where ABC systems are likely to prove most beneficial.

ASSESSMENT MATERIAL

The review questions are short questions that enable you to assess your understanding of the main topics included in the chapter. The numbers in parentheses provide you with the page numbers to refer to if you cannot answer a specific question.

The review problems are more complex and require you to relate and apply the content to various business problems. The problems are graded by their level of difficulty. Solutions to review problems that are not preceded by the term 'IM' are provided in a separate section at the end of the book. Solutions to problems preceded by the term 'IM' are provided in the Instructor's Manual accompanying this book that can be downloaded from the lecturer's digital support resources. Additional review problems with fully worked solutions are provided in the *Student Manual* that accompanies this book.

REVIEW QUESTIONS

11.1 Explain why a cost accumulation system is required for generating relevant cost information for decision-making. (p. 256)

11.2 Describe the three different types of cost system that can be used to assign costs to cost objects. (p. 257)

11.3 What are the fundamental differences between a traditional and an ABC system? (pp. 257–258)

11.4 Define activities and cost drivers. (p. 257)

11.5 What factors led to the emergence of ABC systems? (p. 259)

11.6   Distinguish between volume-based and non-volume-based cost drivers. (pp. 260–262)

11.7   Describe the circumstances when traditional costing systems are likely to report distorted costs. (pp. 261–262)

11.8   Explain how low volume products can be undercosted and high volume products overcosted when traditional costing systems are used. (pp. 261–262)

11.9   What is meant by 'product diversity' and why is it important for product costing? (pp. 261–262)

11.10   Describe each of the four stages involved in designing ABC systems. (pp. 263–265)

11.11   Distinguish between resource cost drivers and activity cost drivers. (p. 264)

11.12   Distinguish between transaction and duration cost drivers. (pp. 264–265)

11.13   Describe the ABC manufacturing cost hierarchy. (pp. 265–267)

11.14   Describe the ABC profitability analysis hierarchy. (pp. 270–271)

11.15   What is an ABC resource consumption model? (p. 272)

11.16   Distinguish between the cost of resources supplied, the cost of resources used and the cost of unused capacity. (p. 273)

11.17   Explain the circumstances in which ABC is likely to be preferred to traditional costing systems. (p. 261)

11.18   Explain how time-driven ABC differs from traditional ABC (pp. 267–270)

REVIEW PROBLEMS

11.19 Advanced. Large service organizations, such as banks and hospitals, used to be noted for their lack of standard costing systems, and their relatively unsophisticated budgeting and control systems compared with large manufacturing organizations. But this is changing and many large service organizations are now revising their use of management accounting techniques.

Requirements:

(a) Explain which features of large-scale service organizations encourage the application of activity-based approaches to the analysis of cost information. *(6 marks)*

(b) Explain which features of service organizations may create problems for the application of activity-based costing. *(4 marks)*
Explain the uses for activity-based cost information in service industries. *(4 marks)*

(c) Many large service organizations were at one time state owned, but have now been privatized. Examples in some countries include electricity supply and telecommunications. They are often regulated. Similar systems of regulation of prices by an independent authority exist in many countries and are designed to act as a surrogate for market competition in industries where it is difficult to ensure a genuinely competitive market.

Explain which aspects of cost information and systems in service organizations would particularly interest a regulator, and why these features would be of interest. *(6 marks)*

CIMA Stage 4 Management Accounting Control Systems

11.20 Intermediate: Calculation of traditional and ABC product costs and a discussion of their impact on selling prices and sales volume. Duff Co manufactures three products, X, Y and Z. Demand for products X and Y is relatively elastic whilst demand for product Z is relatively inelastic. Each product uses the same materials and the same type of direct labour but in different quantities. For many years, the company has been using full absorption costing and absorbing overheads on the basis of direct labour hours. Selling prices are then determined using cost plus pricing. This is common within this industry, with most competitors applying a standard mark-up.

Budgeted production and sales volumes for X, Y and Z for the next year are 20 000 units, 16 000 units and 22 000 units respectively.

The budgeted direct costs of the three products are shown below:

Product	X $ per unit	Y $ per unit	Z $ per unit
Direct materials	25	28	22
Direct labour ($12 per hour)	30	36	24

In the next year, Duff Co also expects to incur indirect production costs of $1 377 400, which are analysed as follows:

Cost pools	$	Cost drivers
Machine set up costs	280 000	Number of batches
Material ordering costs	316 000	Number of purchase orders
Machine running costs	420 000	Number of machine hours
General facility costs	361 400	Number of machine hours
	1 377 400	

The following additional data relate to each product:

Product	X	Y	Z
Batch size (units)	500	800	400
No of purchase orders per batch	4	5	4
Machine hours per unit	1.5	1.25	1.4

Duff Co wants to boost sales revenue in order to increase profits but its capacity to do this is limited because of its use of cost plus pricing and the application of the standard mark-up. The finance director has suggested using activity based costing (ABC) instead of full absorption costing, since this will alter the cost of the products and may therefore enable a different price to be charged.

Required:

(a) Calculate the budgeted full production cost per unit of each product using Duff Co's current method of absorption costing. All workings should be to two decimal places. *(3 marks)*

(b) Calculate the budgeted full production cost per unit of each product using activity-based costing. All workings should be to two decimal places. *(11 marks)*

(c) Discuss the impact on the selling prices and the sales volumes OF EACH PRODUCT which a change to activity based costing would be expected to bring about. *(6 marks)*

ACCA F5 Performance Management

11.21 Intermediate: Traditional and ABC profitability analysis comparisons. FG specializes in the manufacture of tablets, laptops and desktop PCs. FG currently operates a standard absorption costing system. Budgeted information for next year is given below:

Products	Tablets $000	Laptops $000	Desktop PCs $000	Total $000
Sales revenue	3640	12480	9880	26000
Direct material	800	2800	2200	5800

(Continued)

Products	Tablets $000	Laptops $000	Desktop PCs $000	Total $000
Direct labour	300	1200	800	2300
Fixed production overheads	1456	4992	3952	10400
Gross profit	1084	3488	2928	7500

Fixed production overheads are currently absorbed based on a percentage of sales revenue.

FG is considering changing to an activity-based costing system. The main activities and their associated cost drivers and overhead cost have been identified as follows:

Activity	Cost driver	Production overhead cost $000
Manufacturing scheduling	Number of orders	162
Parts handling	Number of parts	2464
Assembly	Assembly time	4472
Software installation and testing	Number of software applications	2000
Packaging	Number of units	1302
		10400

Further details have also been ascertained as follows:

	Tablets	Laptops	Desktop PCs
Budgeted production for next year (units)	10000	12000	6000
Average number of units per order	10	6	4
Number of parts per unit	20	35	25
Assembly time per unit (minutes)	20	40	30
Number of software applications per unit	2	3	4

Required:

(a) Calculate the total gross profit for each product using the proposed activity-based costing system. *(13 marks)*

(b) Discuss the differences between the gross profit figures calculated in part (a) compared with those calculated under the current absorption costing system. *(8 marks)*

(c) Explain how the information obtained from the activity-based costing system could be used for cost management purposes. *(4 marks)*

CIMA P1 Performance Operations

11.22 Advanced: Evaluation of traditional and ABC systems plus beyond budgeting discussion. Robust Laptops Co. (RL) make laptop computers for use in dangerous environments. The company's main customers are organizations like oil companies and the military that require a laptop that can survive rough handling in transport to a site and can be made to their unique requirements.

The company started as a basic laptop manufacturer but its competitors grew much larger and RL had to find a niche market where its small size would not hinder its ability to compete. It is now considered one of the best quality producers in this sector.

RL had the same finance director for many years who preferred to develop its systems organically. However, due to fall in profitability, a new chief executive officer (CEO) has been appointed who wishes to review RL's financial control systems in order to get better information with which to tackle the profit issue.

The CEO wants to begin by thinking about the pricing of the laptops to ensure that selling expensive products at the wrong price is not compromising profit margins. The laptops are individually specified by customers for each order and pricing has been on a production cost plus basis with a mark-up of 45 per cent. The company uses an absorption costing system based on labour hours in order to calculate the production cost per unit.

The main control system used within the company is the annual budget. It is set before the start of the financial year and variances are monitored and acted on by line managers. The CEO has been reading about major companies that have stopped using budgets and wants to know how such a radical move works and why a company might take such a step. He has been worried by moves by competitors into RL's market with impressive new products. This has created unrest among the staff at RL with two experienced managers leaving the company.

Financial and other information for Robust Laptops

Data for the year ended 30 September

Volume (units)	23800	Total $000
Direct variable costs		
Material		40650
Labour		3879
Packaging and transport		2118
Subtotal		46647
Overhead costs		
Customer service		7735
Purchasing and receiving		2451
Inventory management		1467
Administration of production		2537
Subtotal		14190
Total		60837
Labour time per unit	3 hours	
Data collected for the year:		
No. of minutes on calls to customer	899600	
No of purchase orders raised	21400	
No of components used in production	618800	

Order 11784

Units ordered	16	
Direct costs for this order:		$
Material		27328
Labour		2608
Packaging and transport		1424
Other activities relating to this order:		
No. of minutes on calls to customer	1104	
No. of purchase orders raised	64	
No. of components used in production	512	
Administration of production (absorbed as general overhead)	3 labour hrs per unit	

Required:
Write a report to the CEO to include:

(a) An evaluation of the current method of costing against an activity-based costing (ABC) system. You should provide illustrative calculations using the information provided on the above costs and Order 11784. Briefly state what action management might take in the light of your results with respect to this order. *(15 marks)*

(b) An explanation of the operation of a beyond budgeting approach and an evaluation of the potential of such a change at RL. *(10 marks)*

ACCA P5 Advanced Performance Management

11.23 Advanced: Traditional and ABC profitability analysis.
Abkaber plc assembles three types of motorcycle at the same factory: the 50cc Sunshine; the 250cc Roadster and the 1000cc Fireball. It sells the motorcycles throughout the world. In response to market pressures, Abkaber plc has invested heavily in new manufacturing technology in recent years and, as a result, has significantly reduced the size of its workforce.

Historically, the company has allocated all overhead costs using total direct labour hours, but is now considering introducing activity-based costing (ABC). Abkaber plc's accountant has produced the following analysis.

	Annual output (units)	Annual direct labour hours	Selling price (£ per unit)	Raw material cost (£ per unit)
Sunshine	2 000	200 000	4 000	400
Roadster	1 600	220 000	6 000	600
Fireball	400	80 000	8 000	900

The three cost drivers that generate overheads are:

Deliveries to retailers – the number of deliveries of motorcycles to retail showrooms

Set-ups – the number of times the assembly line process is re-set to accommodate a production run of a different type of motorcycle

Purchase orders – the number of purchase orders.

The annual cost driver volumes relating to each activity and for each type of motorcycle are as follows:

	Number of deliveries to retailers	Number of set-ups	Number of purchase orders
Sunshine	100	35	400
Roadster	80	40	300
Fireball	70	25	100

The annual overhead costs relating to these activities are as follows:

	£
Deliveries to retailers	2 400 000
Set-up costs	6 000 000
Purchase orders	3 600 000

All direct labour is paid at £5 per hour. The company holds no stocks. At a board meeting there was some concern over the introduction of activity-based costing.

The finance director argued: 'I very much doubt whether selling the Fireball is viable but I am not convinced that activity-based costing would tell us any more than the use of labour hours in assessing the viability of each product.'

The marketing director argued: 'I am in the process of negotiating a major new contract with a motorcycle rental company for the Sunshine model. For such a big order, they will not pay our normal prices but we need to at least cover our incremental costs. I am not convinced that activity-based costing would achieve this as it merely averages costs for our entire production.'

The managing director argued: 'I believe that activity-based costing would be an improvement but it still has its problems. For instance, if we carry out an activity many times surely we get better at it, and costs fall rather than remain constant. Similarly, some costs are fixed and do not vary either with labour hours or any other cost driver.'

The chairman argued: 'I cannot see the problem. The overall profit for the company is the same no matter which method of allocating overheads we use. It seems to make no difference to me.'

Required:

(a) Calculate the total profit on each of Abkaber plc's three types of product using each of the following methods to attribute overheads:
 (i) the existing method based on labour hours; and
 (ii) activity-based costing.   (13 marks)

(b) Write a report to the directors of Abkaber plc, as its management accountant. The report should:
 (i) evaluate the labour hours and the activity-based costing methods in the circumstances of Abkaber plc; and
 (ii) examine the implications of activity-based costing for Abkaber plc, and in so doing evaluate the issues raised by each of the directors.

Refer to your calculations in requirement (a) above where appropriate.   (12 marks)

ACCA 2.4 Financial Management and Control

11.24 Advanced: Hierarchical profitability analysis. WTL manufactures and sells four products: W, X, Y, and Z from a single factory. Each of the products is manufactured in batches of 100 units using a just-in-time manufacturing process and consequently there is no inventory of any product. This batch size of 100 units cannot be altered without significant cost implications. Although the products are manufactured in batches of 100 units, they are sold as single units at the market price. WTL has a significant number of competitors and is forced to accept the market price for each of its products. It is currently reviewing the profit it makes from each product, and for the business as a whole, and has produced the following statement for the latest period:

Product	W	X	Y	Z	Total
Number of: units sold	100 000	130 000	80 000	150 000	
Machine hours	200 000	195 000	80 000	300 000	775 000
Direct labour hours	50 000	130 000	80 000	75 000	335 000
	$	$	$	$	$
Sales	1 300 000	2 260 000	2 120 000	1 600 000	7 280 000
Direct materials	300 000	910 000	940 000	500 000	2 650 000
Direct labour	400 000	1 040 000	640 000	600 000	2 680 000
Overhead costs	400 000	390 000	160 000	600 000	1 550 000
Profit/(Loss)	200 000	(80 000)	380 000	(100 000)	400 000

WTL is concerned that two of its products are loss making and has carried out an analysis of its products and costs. This analysis shows:

1 The sales of each product are completely independent of each other.

2 The overhead costs have been absorbed into the above product costs using an absorption rate of $2 per machine hour.

3 Further analysis of the overhead cost shows that some of it is caused by the number of machine hours used, some is caused by the number of batches produced and some of the costs are product specific fixed overheads that would be avoided if the product were discontinued. Other general fixed overhead costs would be avoided only by the closure of the factory. Details of this analysis are as follows:

	$000	$000
Machine hour related		310
Batch related		230
Product specific fixed overhead:		
Product W	500	
Product X	50	
Product Y	100	
Product Z	50	700
General fixed overhead		310
		1550

Required:

(a) Prepare a columnar statement that is more useful for decision-making than the profit statement prepared by WTL. Your statement should also show the current total profit for the business. *(8 marks)*

(b) Prepare a report to the board of WTL that:

(i) Explains why your statement is suitable for decision-making; *(4 marks)*

(ii) Advises WTL which, if any, of its four products should be discontinued in order to maximize its company profits. *(4 marks)*

(c) Calculate the break-even volume (in batches) for Product W. *(4 marks)*

(d) Explain how WTL could use Value Analysis to improve its profits. *(5 marks)*

CIMA P2 Performance Management

11.25 Advanced: ABC hierarchical cost computations. GMB Co. designs, produces and sells a number of products. Functions are recognized from design through to the distribution of products. Within each function, a number of activities may be distinguished and a principal driver identified for each activity.

Each sales order will normally comprise a number of batches of any one of a range of products. The company is active in promoting, where possible, a product focus for design, dedicated production lines and product marketing. It also recognizes that a considerable level of expenditure will relate to supporting the overall business operation.

It is known that many costs may initially be recognized at the unit, batch, product-sustaining (order) or business/facility-sustaining (overall) levels. A list of expense items relating to Order Number 377 of product Zeta is shown below. The methods of calculating the values for Order Number 377 shown below are given in brackets alongside each expense item. These methods also indicate whether the expense items should be regarded as product unit, batch, product-sustaining (order) or business/facility-sustaining (overall) level costs. The expense items are not listed in any particular sequence. Each expense item should be adjusted to reflect its total cost for Order Number 377.

Order Number 377 comprises 5000 units of product Zeta. The order will be provided in batches of 1000 product units.

Order Number 377	$
Production scheduling (rate per hour × hours per batch)	60 000
Direct material cost (per unit material specification)	180
Selling – batch expediting (at rate per batch)	60 000
Engineering design and support (rate per hour × hours per order)	350 000
Direct labour cost (rate per hour × hours per unit)	150
Machine set-up (rate per set-up × number of set-ups per batch)	34 000
Production line maintenance (rate per hour × hours per order)	1 100 000
Business/facility sustaining cost (at 30% of all other costs)	1 500 000
Marketing (rate per visit to client × number of visits per order)	200 000
Distribution (tonne miles × rate per tonne mile per batch)	12 000
Power cost (rate per kilowatt hour × kilowatts per unit)	120
Design work (rate per hour × hours per batch)	30 000
Administration – invoicing and accounting (at rate per batch)	24 000

Required:

(a) Prepare a statement of total cost for Order Number 377, which analyses the expense items into sections for each of four levels, with sub-totals for each level where appropriate. The four levels are:

(i) unit-based costs;

(ii) batch-related costs;

(iii) product-sustaining (order level) costs; and

(iv) business/facility-sustaining (overall level) costs. *(5 marks)*

(b) Identify and discuss the appropriateness of the cost driven of any TWO expense values in EACH of levels (i) to (iii) above and ONE value that relates to level (iv).

In addition, suggest a likely cause of the cost driver for any ONE value in EACH of levels (i) to (iii), and comment on possible benefits from the identification of the cause of each cost driver. *(10 marks)*

(c) Discuss the practical problems that may be encountered in the implementation of an activity-based system of product cost management. *(5 marks)*

(Total 20 marks)

ACCA Advanced Performance Advanced Performance Management

IM11.1 Intermediate. The traditional methods of cost allocation, cost apportionment and absorption into products are being challenged by some writers who claim that much information given to management is misleading when these methods of dealing with fixed overheads are used to determine product costs.

You are required to explain what is meant by *cost allocation*, *cost apportionment* and *absorption* and to describe briefly the alternative approach of *activity-based costing* in order to ascertain total product costs. *(15 marks)*

CIMA Stage 2 Cost Accounting

IM11.2 Intermediate. 'Attributing direct costs and absorbing overhead costs to the product/service through an activity-based costing approach will result in a better understanding of the true cost of the final output.'

(*Source*: a recent CIMA publication on costing in a service environment.)

You are required to explain and comment on the above statement.   (15 marks)

CIMA Stage 2 Cost Accounting

IM11.3 Advanced. The basic ideas justifying the use of activity-based costing (ABC) and activity-based budgeting (ABB) are well publicized, and the number of applications has increased. However, there are apparently still significant problems in changing from existing systems.

Requirements:

(a) Explain which characteristics of an organization, such as its structure, product range, or environment, may make the use of activity-based techniques particularly useful.
                                                    (5 marks)

(b) Explain the problems that may cause an organization to decide not to use, or to abandon use of, activity-based techniques.   (8 marks)

(c) Some categorizations of cost drivers provide hierarchical models:

   (i)   unit-level activities;
   (ii) batch activities;
   (iii) product-sustaining activities;
   (iv) facility-sustaining activities.

Other analyses focus on 'value adding' and 'non-value adding' activities.

Requirement:

Explain what is meant by 'non-value adding activities', and discuss the usefulness of this form of analysis.   (7 marks)

CIMA Stage 4 Management Accounting Control Systems

IM11.4 Intermediate: Calculation of ABC product costs and a discussion of the usefulness of ABC. Trimake Limited makes three main products, using broadly the same production methods and equipment for each. A conventional product costing system is used at present, although an activity-based costing (ABC) system is being considered. Details of the three products for a typical period are:

	Labour hours	Machine unit	Materials per unit £	Volumes units
	Labour hours	*Machine unit*	*Materials per unit £*	*Volumes units*
Product X	½	1½	20	750
Product Y	1½	1	12	1250
Product Z	1	3	25	7000

Hours per unit

Direct labour costs £14 per hour and production overheads are absorbed on a machine hour basis. The rate for the period is £28 per machine hour.

(a) You are required to calculate the cost per unit for each product using conventional methods.   (4 marks)

Further analysis shows that the total of production overheads can be divided as follows:

	(%)
Costs relating to set-ups	35
Costs relating to machinery	20
Costs relating to materials handling	15
Costs relating to inspection	30
Total production overhead	100%

The following activity volumes are associated with the product line for the period as a whole.

Total activities for the period:

	Number of set-ups	Number of movements of materials	Number of inspections
Product X	75	12	150
Product Y	115	21	180
Product Z	480	87	670
	670	120	1000

You are required:

(b) to calculate the cost per unit for each product using ABC principles;   (15 marks)

(c) to comment on the reasons for any differences in the costs in your answers to (a) and (b).   (3 marks)

CIMA Stage 3 Management Accounting Techniques

IM11.5 Advanced: Comparison of traditional product costing with ABC. Duo plc produces two products, A and B. Each has two components specified as sequentially numbered parts, i.e. product A (parts 1 and 2) and product B (parts 3 and 4). Two production departments (machinery and fitting) are supported by five service activities (material procurement, material handling, maintenance, quality control and set-up). Product A is a uniform product manufactured each year in 12 monthly high volume production runs. Product B is manufactured in low volume customized batches involving 25 separate production runs each month. Additional information is as follows:

	Product A	Product B
Production details:		
Components	Parts 1, 2	Parts 3, 4
Annual volume produced	300000 units	300000 units
Annual direct labour hours:		
Machinery department	500000 DLH	600000 DLH
Fitting department	150000 DLH	200000 DLH

Overhead cost analysis[a]

	(£000s)
Material handling	1500
Material procurement	2000
Set-up	1500
Maintenance	2500
Quality control	3000
Machinery (machinery power, depreciation etc.)[b]	2500
Fitting (machine, depreciation, power etc.)[b]	2000
	15000

[a] It may be assumed that these represent fairly homogeneous activity-based cost pools.

[b] It is assumed these costs (depreciation, power etc.) are primarily production volume driven and that direct labour hours are an appropriate surrogate measure of this.

Cost driver analysis

Cost driver	Part 1	Part 2	Part 3	Part 4
	Annual cost driver Volume per component			
Material movements	180	160	1000	1200
Number of orders	200	300	2000	4000
Number of set-ups	12	12	300	300
Maintenance hours	7000	5000	10000	8000
Number of inspections	360	360	2400	1000
Direct labour hours	150000	350000	200000	400000
Direct labour hours	50000	100000	60000	140000

You are required to compute the unit costs for products A and B using (i) a traditional volume-based product costing system and (ii) an activity-based costing system.   *(20 marks)*

IM11.6 Advanced: Profitability analysis using ABC as traditional cost allocation bases. ABC plc, a group operating retail stores, is compiling its budget statements for the next year. In this exercise, revenues and costs at each store A, B and C are predicted. Additionally, all central costs of warehousing and a head office are allocated across the three stores in order to arrive at a total cost and net profit of each store operation.

In earlier years the central costs were allocated in total based on the total sales value of each store. But, as a result of dissatisfaction expressed by some store managers, alternative methods are to be evaluated.

The predicted results before any re-allocation of central costs are as follows:

	A (£000)	B (£000)	C (000)
Sales	5000	4000	3000
Costs of sales	2800	2300	1900
Gross margin	2200	1700	1100
Local operating expenses			
Variable	660	730	310
Fixed	700	600	500
Operating profit	840	370	290

The central costs that are to be allocated are:

	(£000)
Warehouse costs:	
Depreciation	100
Storage	80
Operating and despatch	120
Delivery	300
Head office:	
Salaries	200
Advertising	80
Establishment	120
Total	1000

The management accountant has carried out discussions with staff at all locations in order to identify more suitable 'cost drivers' of some of the central costs. So far the following has been revealed.

	A	B	C
Number of despatches	550	450	520
Total delivery distances (thousand miles)	70	50	90
Storage space occupied (%)	40	30	30

1   An analysis of senior management time revealed that 10 per cent of their time was devoted to warehouse issues with the remainder shared equally between the three stores.
2   It was agreed that the only basis on which to allocate the advertising costs was sales revenue.
3   Establishment costs were mainly occupancy costs of senior management.

This analysis has been carried out against a background of developments in the company, for example, automated warehousing and greater integration with suppliers.

Required:

(a) As the management accountant, prepare a report for the management of the group which:

(i) Computes the budgeted net profit of each store based on the *sales value* allocation base originally adopted and explains 'cost driver', 'volume' and 'complexity' issues in relation to cost allocation commenting on the possible implications of the dissatisfaction expressed.   *(6 marks)*
(ii) Computes the budgeted net profit of each store using the additional information provided, discusses the extent to which an improvement has been achieved in the information on the costs and profitability of running the stores and comments on the results.   *(11 marks)*

(b) Explain briefly how regression analysis and coefficient of determination (r^2) could be used in confirming the delivery mileage allocation method used in (a) above.   *(3 marks)*

ACCA Paper 8 Managerial Finance

IM11.7 Advanced: Unit cost computation based on traditional and ABC systems. Excel Ltd make and sell two products, VG4U and VG2. Both products are manufactured through two consecutive processes – making and packing. Raw material is input at the commencement of the making process. The following estimated information is available for the period ending 31 March:

(i)

	Making (£000)	Packing (£000)
Conversion costs:		
Variable	350	280
Fixed	210	140

Forty per cent of fixed costs are product specific, the remainder are company fixed costs. Fixed costs will remain unchanged throughout a wide activity range.

(ii)

Product information:	VG4U	VG2
Production time per unit:		
Making (minutes)	5.25	5.25
Packing (minutes)	6	4
Production sales (units)	5000	3000
Selling price per unit (£)	150	180
Direct material cost per unit (£)	30	30

(iii) Conversion costs are absorbed by products using estimated time-based rates.

Required:

(a) Using the above information:

(i) Calculate unit costs for each product, analysed as relevant.   *(10 marks)*
(ii) Comment on a management suggestion that the production and sale of one of the products should not proceed in the period ending 31 March.   *(4 marks)*

(b) Additional information is gathered for the period ending 31 March as follows:

(i) The making process consists of two consecutive activities, moulding and trimming. The moulding variable conversion costs are incurred in proportion to the temperature required in the moulds. The variable trimming conversion costs are incurred in proportion to the consistency of the material when it emerges from the moulds. The variable packing process conversion costs are incurred in proportion to the time required for each product. Packing materials (which are part of the variable packing cost) requirement depends on the complexity of packing specified for each product.

(ii) The proportions of product specific conversion costs (variable and fixed) are analysed as follows: Making process: moulding (60 per cent); trimming (40 per cent) Packing process: conversion (70 per cent); packing material (30 per cent).

(iii) An investigation into the effect of the cost drivers on costs has indicated that the proportions in which the total product specific conversion costs are attributable to VG4U and VG2 are as follows:

	VG4U	VG2
Temperature (moulding)	2	1
Material consistency (trimming)	2	5
Time (packing)	3	2
Packing (complexity)	1	3

(iv) Company fixed costs are apportioned to products at an overall average rate per product unit based on the estimated figures.

Required:
Calculate amended unit costs for each product where activity-based costing is used and company fixed costs are apportioned as detailed above. *(12 marks)*

(c) Comment on the relevance of the amended unit costs in evaluating the management suggestion that one of the products be discontinued in the period ending 31 March. *(4 marks)*

(d) Management wishes to achieve an overall net profit margin of 15 per cent on sales in the period ending 31 March in order to meet return on capital targets.

Required:
Explain how target costing may be used in achieving the required return and suggest specific areas of investigation. *(5 marks)*

ACCA Paper 9 Information for Control and Decision-Making

IM11.8 **Advanced: ABC profitability analysis.** A company sells and services photocopying machines. Its sales department sells the machines and consumables, including ink and paper, and its service department provides an after-sales service to its customers. The after-sales service includes planned maintenance of the machine and repairs in the event of a machine breakdown. Service department customers are charged an amount per copy that differs depending on the size of the machine.

The company's existing costing system uses a single overhead rate, based on total sales revenue from copy charges, to charge the cost of the service department's support activities to each size of machine. The service manager has suggested that the copy charge should more accurately reflect the costs involved. The company's accountant has decided to implement an activity-based costing system and has obtained the following information about the support activities of the service department:

Activity	Cost driver	Overheads per annum $000
Customer account handling	Number of customers	126
Planned maintenance scheduling	Number of planned maintenance visits	480
Unplanned maintenance scheduling	Number of unplanned maintenance visits	147
Spare part procurement	Number of purchase orders	243
Other overheads	Number of machines	600
Total overheads		1596

The following data have also been collected for each machine size:

	Small photocopiers	Medium photocopiers	Large photocopiers
Charge per copy	$0.03	$0.04	$0.05
Average number of copies per year per machine	60 000	120 000	180 000
Number of machines	300	800	500
Planned maintenance visits per machine per year	4	6	12
Unplanned maintenance visits per machine per year	1	1	2
Total number of purchase orders per year	500	1 200	1 000
Cost of parts per maintenance visit	$100	$300	$400
Labour cost per maintenance visit	$60	$80	$100

Each customer has a service contract for two machines on average.

Required:
(a) **Calculate** the annual profit per machine for each of the three sizes of machine, using the current basis for charging the costs of support activities to machines. *(4 marks)*

(b) **Calculate** the annual profit per machine for each of the three sizes of machine using activity-based costing. *(14 marks)*

(c) **Explain** the potential benefits to the company of using an activity-based costing system. *(7 marks)*

12
DECISION-MAKING UNDER CONDITIONS OF RISK AND UNCERTAINTY

LEARNING OBJECTIVES After studying this chapter, you should be able to:

- calculate and explain the meaning of expected values;

- explain the meaning of the terms standard deviation and coefficient of variation as measures of risk and outline their limitations;

- construct a decision tree when there is a range of alternatives and possible outcomes;

- describe and calculate the value of perfect and imperfect information;

- explain and apply the maximin, maximax and regret criteria;

- explain the implications of pursuing a diversification strategy.

In Chapters 8–11, we considered the use of a single representative set of estimates for predicting future costs and revenues when alternative courses of action are followed. For example, in Chapter 10, we used a single representative estimate of demand for each selling price. However, the outcome of a particular decision may be affected by an uncertain environment that cannot be predicted and a single representative estimate does not therefore convey all the information that might reasonably influence a decision.

Consider a situation in which a company has two mutually exclusive potential alternatives, A and B, each of which yields receipts of £500 000. The estimated costs of alternative A can be predicted with considerable confidence and are expected to fall in the range of £400 000–£420 000; £410 000 might be considered a reasonable estimate of cost. The estimate for alternative B is subject to much greater uncertainty, since this alternative requires high-precision work involving operations that are unfamiliar to the company's labour force. The estimated costs are between £350 000 and £450 000, but £400 000 is selected as a representative estimate. If we consider single representative estimates, alternative B appears preferable, since the estimated profit is £100 000 compared with an estimated profit of £90 000 for alternative A; but a different picture may emerge if we take into account the range of possible outcomes.

Alternative A is expected to yield a profit of between £80 000 and £100 000 whereas the range of profits for alternative B is between £50 000 and £150 000. Management may consider it preferable to opt for a fairly certain profit of between £80 000 and £100 00 for alternative A rather than take the chance of earning a profit of £50 000 from alternative B (even though there is the possibility of earning a profit of £150 000 at the other extreme).

This example demonstrates that there is a need to incorporate the uncertainty relating to each alternative into the decision-making process and in this chapter, we shall consider the various methods of doing this.

RISK AND UNCERTAINTY

A distinction is often drawn by decision theorists between risk and uncertainty. Risk is applied to a situation where there are several possible outcomes and there is relevant past experience to enable statistical evidence to be produced for predicting the possible outcomes. The approaches that rely on specifying the probabilities for alternative courses of action that are described in the earlier part of this chapter represent attempts to measure the risk of the alternative courses of action. Uncertainty exists where there are several possible outcomes, but there is little previous statistical evidence to enable the possible outcomes to be predicted. Therefore the methods that do not entail the use of probabilities that are described later in the chapter are used. However, the distinction between risk and uncertainty is not essential for our analysis and you should note that the terms are often used interchangeably.

Probabilities

Because decision problems exist in an uncertain environment, it is necessary to consider those uncontrollable factors that are outside the decision-maker's control and that may occur for alternative courses of action. These uncontrollable factors are called events or states of nature. For example, in

REAL WORLD VIEWS 12.1

A risk management toolkit

The CGMA website offers management accountants a collection of tools and resources which are useful to identify, assess and respond to (or manage) various types of risk faced by an organization. For example, it identifies risks in four categories – extended enterprise risk, cyber risk, ethics and governance risk, and fraud. In accessing risk, it offers resources on tools such as heat map and scenario planning. On risk management, resources on financial risk, process risk and innovation risk are also available.

The role of the board in managing organizational risk is also mentioned. Many management accountants sit on boards, and those who do not are invariably information providers and advisors to boards. It is noted that risk and strategy are intertwined, and as boards are responsible for strategy, they are by default responsible for risk. The top reasons why boards may not be adequately informed on organizational risk include gaps in the board's skills, risk blindness, poor communication to the board and the complexity of the business environment the organization operates in. The website also notes that boards should not be involved in the daily detail of risk management, but they have an extremely important role to set the risk agenda, embody risk assessment with the organization's culture and oversee implementation of actions to reduce risk.

Questions

1 Can management accountants/managers always identify and assess all risks a business may face?

2 How can management accountants help boards better understand the risks an organization may face?

References

CGMA Risk Management Toolkit, available at www.cgma .org/Resources/Tools/Pages/Risk-management -toolkit.aspx

a product launch situation, possible states of nature could consist of events such as a similar product being launched by a competitor at a lower price, at the same price, at a higher price or no similar product being launched at all.

The likelihood that an event or state of nature will occur is known as its probability, and this is normally expressed in decimal form with a value between 0 and 1. A value of 0 denotes a nil likelihood of occurrence, whereas a value of 1 signifies absolute certainty – a definite occurrence. A probability of 0.4 means that the event is expected to occur four times out of ten. The total of the probabilities for events that can possibly occur must sum to 1.0. For example, if a tutor indicates that the probability of a student passing an examination is 0.7 then this means that the student has a 70 per cent chance of passing the examination. Given that the pass/fail alternatives represent an exhaustive listing of all possible outcomes of the event, the probability of not passing the examination is 0.3.

The information can be presented in a probability distribution. A probability distribution is a list of all possible outcomes for an event and the probability that each will occur. The probability distribution for the above illustration is as follows:

Outcome	Probability
Pass examination	0.7
Do not pass examination	0.3
Total	1.0

Some probabilities are known as objective probabilities because they can be established mathematically or compiled from historical data. Tossing a coin and throwing a dice are examples of objective probabilities. For example, the probability of heads occurring when tossing a coin logically must be 0.5. This can be proved by tossing the coin many times and observing the results. Similarly, the probability of obtaining number 1 when a dice is thrown is 0.166 (i.e. one-sixth). This again can be ascertained from logical reasoning or recording the results obtained from repeated throws of the dice.

It is unlikely that objective probabilities can be established for business decisions, since many past observations or repeated experiments for particular decisions are not possible; the probabilities will have to be estimated based on managerial judgement. Probabilities established in this way are known as subjective probabilities because no two individuals will necessarily assign the same probabilities to a particular outcome. Subjective probabilities are based on an individual's expert knowledge, past experience and observations of current variables that are likely to have an impact on future events. Such probabilities are unlikely to be estimated correctly, but any estimate of a future uncertain event is bound to be subject to error.

The advantage of this approach is that it provides more meaningful information than stating the most likely outcome. Consider, for example, a situation where a tutor is asked to state whether student A and student B will pass an examination. The tutor may reply that both students are expected to pass the examination. This is the tutor's estimate of the most likely outcome. However, the following probability distributions are preferable:

Outcome	Student A probability	Student B probability
Pass examination	0.9	0.6
Do not pass examination	0.1	0.4
Total	1.0	1.0

Such a probability distribution requires the tutor to specify the degree of confidence in his or her estimate of the likely outcome of a future event. This information is clearly more meaningful than a mere estimate of the most likely outcome that both students are expected to pass the examination, because it indicates that it is most unlikely that A will fail, whereas there is a possibility that B will fail. Let us now apply the principles of probability theory to business decision-making.

PROBABILITY DISTRIBUTIONS AND EXPECTED VALUE

The presentation of a probability distribution for each alternative course of action can provide useful additional information to management, since the distribution indicates the degree of uncertainty that exists for each alternative course of action. Probability distributions enable management to consider not only the possible profits (i.e. the payoff) from each alternative course of action, but also the amount of uncertainty that applies to each alternative. Let us now consider the situation presented in Example 12.1.

From the probability distributions shown in Example 12.1, you will see that there is a one in ten chance that profits will be £600 000 for product A, but there is also a four in ten chance that profits will be £800 000. A more useful way of reading the probability distribution is to state that there is a seven in ten chance that profits will be £800 000 or less. This is obtained by adding together the probabilities for profits of £600 000, £700 000 and £800 000. Similarly, there is a three in ten chance that profits will be £900 000 or more.

EXAMPLE 12.1

A manager is considering whether to make product A or product B, but only one can be produced. The estimated sales demand for each product is uncertain. A detailed investigation of the possible sales demand for each product gives the following probability distribution of the profits for each product.

Product A probability distribution

(1) Outcome	(2) Estimated probability	(3) Weighted (col. 1 amount × col. 2) (£)
Profits of £600 000	0.10	60 000
Profits of £700 000	0.20	140 000
Profits of £800 000	0.40	320 000
Profits of £900 000	0.20	180 000
Profits of £1 000 000	0.10	100 000
	1.00	
	Expected value	800 000

Product B probability distribution

(1) Outcome	(2) Estimated probability	(3) Weighted (col. 1 amount × col. 2) (£)
Profits of £400 000	0.05	20 000
Profits of £600 000	0.10	60 000
Profits of £800 000	0.40	320 000
Profits of £1 000 000	0.25	250 000
Profits of £1 200 000	0.20	240 000
	1.00	
	Expected value	890 000

Which product should the company make?

Expected values

The expected value (sometimes called expected payoff) is calculated by weighting each of the profit levels (i.e. possible outcomes) in Example 12.1 by its associated probability. The sum of these weighted amounts is called the expected value of the probability distribution. In other words, the expected value is the weighted arithmetic mean of the possible outcomes. The expected values of £800 000 and £890 000 calculated for products A and B take into account a range of possible outcomes rather than using a single most likely estimate. For example, the single most likely estimate is the profit level with the highest probability attached to it. For both products A and B in Example 12.1, the single most likely estimate is £800 000, which appears to indicate that we may be indifferent as to which product should be made. However, the expected value calculation takes into account the possibility that a range of different profits are possible and weights these profits by the probability of their occurrence. The weighted calculation indicates that product B is expected to produce the highest average profits in the future.

The expected value of a decision represents the long-run average outcome that is expected to occur if a particular course of action is undertaken many times. For example, if the decision to make products A and B is repeated on, say, 100 occasions in the future then product A will be expected to give an average profit of £800 000 whereas product B would be expected to give an average profit of £890 000. The expected values are the averages of the possible outcomes based on management estimates. There is no guarantee that the actual outcome will equal the expected value. Indeed, the expected value for product B does not appear in the probability distribution.

MEASURING THE AMOUNT OF RISK

In addition to the expected values of the profits for the various alternatives, management is also interested in the degree of uncertainty of the expected future profits. For example, let us assume that another alternative course of action, say, product C, is added to the alternatives in Example 12.1 and that the probability distribution is as follows:

Product C probability distribution

Outcome	Estimated probability	Weighted amount (£)
Loss of £400 000	0.5	(200 000)
Profit of £2 200 000	0.5	1 100 000
	Expected value	900 000

Product C has a higher expected value than either product A or product B, but it is unlikely that management will prefer product C to product B, because of the greater variability of the possible outcomes. In other words, there is a greater degree of uncertainty attached to product C.

The conventional measure of the dispersion of a probability distribution is the standard deviation. The standard deviation (σ) is the square root of the mean of the squared deviations from the expected value and is calculated from the following formula:

$$\sigma = \sqrt{\sum_{x=1}^{n}(A_x - \overline{A})^2 P_x} \tag{12.1}$$

where A_x are the profit-level observations, $\overline{A}$ is the expected or mean value, P_x is the probability of each outcome and the summation is over all possible observations, where n is the total number of possibilities.

The calculations of the standard deviations are £109 540 for product A and £214 240 for product B. If we are comparing the standard deviations of two probability distributions with different expected values, we cannot make a direct comparison. Can you see why this should be so? Consider the following probability distribution for another product, say product D.

Product D probability distribution

Outcome (£ million)	Estimated probability	Weighted amount (£ million)
Profits of £4.0	0.05	0.2
Profits of £6.0	0.10	0.6
Profits of £8.0	0.40	3.2
Profits of £10.0	0.25	2.5
Profits of £12.0	0.20	2.4
	Expected value	8.9

The standard deviation for product D is £2 142 400, but all of the possible outcomes are ten times as large as the corresponding outcomes for product B. The outcomes for product D also have the same pattern of probabilities as product B so that the standard deviation for product D is ten times as large as that for product B. This scale effect can be removed be replacing the standard deviation with a relative measure of dispersion. The relative amount of dispersion can be expressed by the coefficient of variation, which is simply the standard deviation divided by the expected value. The coefficient of variation for product B is 214 240/890 000 = 0.241 (or 24.1 per cent), and for product D it is also 0.241 (2.1424m/8.9m), thus indicating that the relative amount of dispersion is the same for both products.

Measures such as expected values, standard deviations or coefficient of variations are used to summarize the characteristics of alternative courses of action, but they are poor substitutes for representing the probability distributions, since they do not provide the decision-maker with all the relevant information. There is an argument for presenting the entire probability distribution directly to the decision-maker. Such an approach is appropriate when management must select one from a small number of alternatives, but in situations where many alternatives need to be considered the examination of many probability distributions is likely to be difficult and time consuming. In such situations, management may have no alternative but to compare the expected values and coefficients of variation.

ATTITUDES TO RISK BY INDIVIDUALS

How do we determine whether or not a risky course of action should be undertaken? The answer to this question depends on the decision-maker's attitude to risk. We can identify three possible attitudes: an aversion to risk, a desire for risk and an indifference to risk. Consider two alternatives, A and B, which have the following possible outcomes, depending on the state of the economy (i.e. the state of nature):

Possible returns

State of the economy	A (£000)	B (£000)
Recession	90	0
Normal	100	100
Boom	110	200

If we assume that the three states of the economy are equally likely then the expected value for each alternative is £100 000. A risk seeker is one who, given a choice between more or less risky alternatives with identical expected values, prefers the riskier alternative (alternative B). A risk seeker would generally choose the alternative that has the highest expected value and is unlikely to be put off by the low probability of any of the potential adverse outcomes. Faced with the same choice, a risk averter would choose to avoid risk and select the less risky alternative (alternative A). The person who is indifferent to risk (risk neutral) would be indifferent to both alternatives because they have the same expected values and will choose a course of action that gives the highest expected value. With regard to investors in general, studies of the securities markets provide convincing evidence that the majority of investors are risk averse.

Let us now reconsider how useful expected value calculations are for choosing between alternative courses of action. Expected values represent a long-run average solution, but decisions should not be made on the basis of expected values alone, since they do not enable the decision-maker's attitude towards risk to be taken into account. Consider, for example, a situation where two individuals play a coin-tossing game, with the loser giving the winner £5000. The expected value to the player who calls heads is as follows:

Outcome	Cash flow (£)	Probability	Weighted amount (£)
Heads	+5000	0.5	+2500
Tails	−5000	0.5	−2500
		Expected value	0

The expected value is zero, but this will not be the actual outcome if only one game is played. The expected value calculation represents the average outcome only if the game is repeated on many occasions. However, because the game is to be played only once, it is unlikely that each player will find the expected value calculation on its own to be a useful calculation for decision-making. In fact, the expected value calculation implies that each player is indifferent to playing the game, but this indifference will only apply if the two players are neutral to risk. However, a risk averter will find the game most unattractive. As most business managers are unlikely to be neutral towards risk, and business

---

REAL WORLD VIEWS 12.2

Risk and uncertainty – what risks do management accountants need to consider?
According to Gillian Lees, a blogger on www.cimaglobal.com, the typical risk assessment model for a management accountant reads like this: identify risks, assess their impact and probability, and develop risk responses. This seems a reasonable approach, but Lees wonders how specific management accountants need to be in their efforts to identify risks. Some risks are readily identifiable, for example risks of fire or flood. However, as Lees points out, not all risks are identifiable. The volcanic ash from an Icelandic volcano that caused major disruption to air traffic over Europe in 2010 was a risk not many could have foreseen. It was probably a surprise even to airlines that would normally include such risks in their 'risk register' as they fly close to or over volcanoes regularly. A key point raised by Lees based on the volcanic ash example is that all assessments of risk will have an element of 'unknown unknowns'. In other words, it is not possible to identify every single risk. What

is important, according to Lees, is to try to think about the processes to deal with unknown risks. For example, a major disruption to fuel supplies would equally ground aircraft in the same way as a volcanic eruption. The risk assessment should, in the airline example, assess not what might cause aircraft to be grounded for a week or more, but how to deal with the event were it to happen.

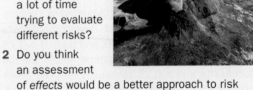

Questions

1 Do you think management accountants should spend a lot of time trying to evaluate different risks?

2 Do you think an assessment of *effects* would be a better approach to risk assessment and management?

Reference
community.cimaglobal.com/blogs/gillian-lees-blog/did-you-have-volcanoes-your-riskregister

decisions are rarely repeated, it is unwise for decisions to be made solely on the basis of expected values. At the very least, expected values should be supplemented with measures of dispersion and, where possible, decisions should be made after comparing the probability distributions of the various alternative courses of action.

DECISION TREE ANALYSIS

In the examples given earlier in this chapter, we have assumed that profits were uncertain because of the uncertainty of sales demand. In practice, more than one variable may be uncertain (e.g. sales and costs), and also the value of some variables may be dependent on the values of other variables. Many outcomes may therefore be possible and some outcomes may be dependent on previous outcomes. A useful analytical tool for clarifying the range of alternative courses of action and their possible outcomes is a decision tree.

A decision tree is a diagram showing several possible courses of action and possible events (i.e. states of nature) and the potential outcomes for each course of action. Each alternative course of action or event is represented by a branch, which leads to subsidiary branches for further courses of action or possible events. Decision trees are designed to illustrate the full range of alternatives and events that can occur, under all envisaged conditions. The value of a decision tree is that its logical analysis of a problem enables a complete strategy to be drawn up to cover all eventualities before a firm becomes committed to a scheme. Let us now consider Example 12.2. This will be used to illustrate how decision trees can be applied to decision-making under conditions of uncertainty.

The decision tree for Example 12.2 is set out in Figure 12.1. The box indicates the point at which decisions have to be taken and the branches emanating from it indicate the available alternative courses of action. The circles indicate the points at which there are environmental changes that affect the consequences of prior decisions. The branches from these points indicate the possible types of environment (states of nature) that may occur.

Note that the joint probability of two events occurring together is the probability of one event times the probability of the other event. For example, the probability of the development effort succeeding and the product being very successful consists of the products of the probabilities of these two events, i.e. 0.75×0.4, giving a probability of 0.30. Similarly, the probability of the development effort being successful and the product being moderately successful is 0.225 (0.75×0.3). The total expected value for the decision to develop the product consists of the sum of all the items in the expected value column on the 'Develop product' branch of the decision tree, i.e. £49 500. If we assume that there are no other alternatives

---

EXAMPLE 12.2

A company is considering whether to develop and market a new product. Development costs are estimated to be £180 000, and there is a 0.75 probability that the development effort will be successful and a 0.25 probability that the development effort will be unsuccessful. If the development is successful, the product will be marketed and it is estimated that:

1 if the product is very successful profits will be £540 000;

2 if the product is moderately successful profits will be £100 000;

3 if the product is a failure, there will be a loss of £400 000.

Each of the above profit and loss calculations is after taking into account the development costs of £180 000. The estimated probabilities of each of the above events are as follows:

1 Very successful	0.4
2 Moderately successful	0.3
3 Failure	0.3

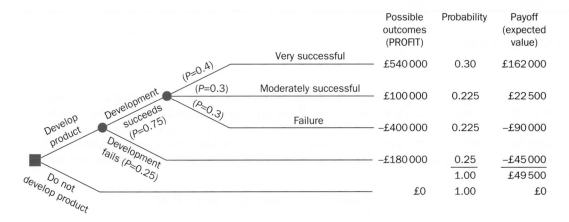

			Possible outcomes (PROFIT)	Probability	Payoff (expected value)
Very successful			£540 000	0.30	£162 000
Moderately successful			£100 000	0.225	£22 500
Failure			−£400 000	0.225	−£90 000
			−£180 000	0.25	−£45 000
				1.00	£49 500
			£0	1.00	£0

■ Decision point ● Possible events

FIGURE 12.1
A simple decision tree

available, other than the decision not to develop, the expected value of £49 500 for developing the product can be compared with the expected value of zero for not developing the product. Decision theory would suggest that the product should be developed because a positive expected value occurs. However, this does not mean that an outcome of £49 500 profit is guaranteed. The expected value calculation indicates that if the probabilities are correct and this decision was repeated on many occasions, an average profit of £49 500 would result.

Unfortunately, the decision will not be repeated on many occasions, and a run of repeated losses could force a company out of business before it has the chance to repeat similar decisions. Management may therefore prefer to examine the following probability distribution for developing the product shown in Figure 12.1:

Outcome	Probability
Loss of £400 000	0.225
Loss of £180 000	0.25
Profit of £100 000	0.225
Profit of £540 000	0.30

Management may decide that the project is too risky, since there is nearly a 0.5 probability of a loss occurring.

The decision tree provides a convenient means of identifying all the possible alternative courses of action and their interdependencies. This approach is particularly useful for assisting in the construction of probability distributions when many combinations of events are possible.

BUYING PERFECT AND IMPERFECT INFORMATION

When a decision-maker is faced with a series of uncertain events that might occur, he or she should consider the possibility of obtaining additional information about which event is likely to occur. This section considers how we can calculate the maximum amount it would be worth paying to acquire additional information from a particular source. The approach we shall take is to compare the expected value of a decision if the information is acquired, against the expected value with the absence of the information. The difference represents the maximum amount it is worth paying for the additional information. Consider Example 12.3.

EXAMPLE 12.3

The Boston Company must choose between one of two machines – machine A has low fixed costs and high unit variable costs, whereas machine B has high fixed costs and low unit variable costs. Consequently, machine A is most suited to low-level demand whereas machine B is suited to high-level demand. For simplicity, assume that there are only two possible demand levels – low and high – and the estimated probability of each of these events is 0.5. The estimated profits for each demand level are as follows:

	Low demand (£)	High demand (£)	Expected value (£)
Machine A	500 000	800 000	650 000
Machine B	50 000	1 000 000	525 000

There is a possibility of employing a firm of market consultants who would be able to provide a perfect prediction of the actual demand. What is the maximum amount the company should be prepared to pay the consultants for the additional information?

Without the additional information, machine A will be purchased using the expected value decision rule. If the additional information is obtained then this will give a perfect prediction of the level of demand, and the size of the machine can be matched with the level of demand. Therefore, if demand is predicted to be low, machine A will be purchased, whereas if demand is predicted to be high, machine B will be purchased. The revised expected value is:

$$(0.5 \times £500\,000) + (0.5 \times £1\,000\,000) = £750\,000$$

You can see that the expected value is calculated by taking the highest profit in the case of low and high demand. When the decision to employ the market consultants is being taken, it is not known which level of demand will be predicted. Therefore the best estimate of the outcome from obtaining the additional information is a 0.5 probability that it will predict a low demand and a 0.5 probability that it will predict a high demand. (These are the probabilities that are currently associated with low and high demand.) Note that without the survey the company will choose machine A resulting in an expected value of £650 000.

The value of the additional information is ascertained by deducting the expected value without the market survey (£650 000) from the expected value with the survey (£750 000). Thus the additional information increases expected value from £650 000 to £750 000 and the expected value of perfect information is £100 000. As long as the cost of obtaining the information is less than £100 000, the firm of market consultants should be employed.

In the above illustration, it was assumed that the additional information would give a 100 per cent accurate prediction of the expected demand. In practice, it is unlikely that perfect information is obtainable, but *imperfect* information (for example, predictions of future demand may be only 80 per cent reliable) may still be worth obtaining. However, the value of imperfect information will always be less than the value of perfect information except when both equal zero. This would occur where the additional information would not change the decision. Note that the principles that are applied for calculating the value of imperfect information are the same as those we applied for calculating the value of perfect information, but the calculations are more complex. For an illustration, see Pogue (2009).

MAXIMIN, MAXIMAX AND REGRET CRITERIA

In situations where uncertainty exists it is not possible to assign meaningful estimates of probabilities to possible outcomes. Where this situation occurs managers might use any of the following criteria to make decisions: maximin, maximax or the criterion of regret.

The assumption underlying the maximin criterion is that the worst possible outcome will always occur and the decision-maker should therefore select the largest payoff under this assumption. Consider the Boston Company in Example 12.3. You can see that the worst outcomes are £500 000 for machine A and £50 000 for machine B. Consequently, machine A should be purchased using the maximin decision rule.

The maximax criterion is the opposite of maximin, and is based on the assumption that the best payoff will occur. Referring again to Example 12.3, the highest payoffs are £800 000 for machine A and £1 000 000 for machine B. Therefore machine B will be selected under the maximax criterion.

The regret criterion is based on the fact that, having selected an alternative that does not turn out to be the best, the decision-maker will regret not having chosen another alternative when he or she had the opportunity. Thus, if in Example 12.3, machine B has been selected on the assumption that the high level of demand would occur, and the high level of demand actually did occur, there would be no regret. However, if machine A has been selected, the company would lose £200 000 (£1 000 000 − £800 000). This measures the amount of the regret. Similarly, if machine A were selected on the assumption that

---

REAL WORLD VIEWS 12.3

Risk appetite and tolerance – insights from the Institute of Risk Management

A 2011 guidance paper commissioned by the Institute of Risk Management gives some useful detail on what risk appetite is and how to manage it – either in a corporate governance sense or to inform how the organization is run. The report notes the term risk appetite is similar to risk attitude or risk capacity, but it suggests risk appetite is the most commonly used term in practice. For example, ISO 31000 defines it as the 'amount and type of risk that an organization is willing to pursue or retain'. The appetite for risk is typically determined by management and/or the board of directors.

The level of risk appetite in an organization depends on its context, but the paper suggests the capacity for risk depends on four board items: the business context, people and knowledge, reputation and infrastructure of the organization. It gives an example of GEC, who in the 1990s came under new management and with a change of name to Marconi, moved away from a traditional manufacturing and defence business towards telecoms and internet businesses. Given the subsequent failure of the group, they may have lacked the risk capacity to move into new areas that the management team had little knowledge of.

Although all organizations may have a particular risk appetite, banks are a good example of organizations who often publish risk appetite statements. For example, the Reserve Bank of Australia notes:

> In terms of operational issues, the Bank has a low appetite for risk. The Bank makes resources available to control operational risks to acceptable levels. The Bank recognizes that it is not possible or necessarily desirable to eliminate some of the risks inherent in its activities. Acceptance of some risk is often necessary to foster innovation and efficiencies within business practices.

The above shows even central banks must accept some levels of risk, but it does not in general engage in anything other than low risk courses of action.

Questions

1 What do you think would be the risk appetite of a high-technology company?

2 What role might management accountants have in preparing a risk appetite statement?

References

Risk appetite and tolerance – guidance paper, Institute of Risk Management/Crowe Horwath, 2011.

Reserve Bank of Australia, Risk Attitude Statement, available at www.rba.gov.au/about-rba/risk-appetite-statement.html

demand would be low, and the low level of demand actually did occur, there would be no regret; but if machine B were selected, the amount of the regret would be £450 000 (£500 000 − £50 000). This information is summarized in the following regret matrix:

	State of nature	
	Low demand (£)	High demand (£)
Choose machine A	0	200 000
Choose machine B	450 000	0

The aim of the regret criterion is to minimize the maximum possible regret. The maximum regret for machine A is £200 000 while that for Machine B is £450 000. Machine A would therefore be selected using the regret criterion.

RISK REDUCTION AND DIVERSIFICATION

It is unwise for a firm to invest all its funds in a single project, since an unfavourable event may occur that will affect this project and have a dramatic effect on the firm's total financial position. A better approach would be for the firm to adopt a diversification strategy and invest in a number of different projects. If this diversification strategy is followed, an unfavourable event that affects one project may have a relatively lesser effect on the remaining projects and thus have only a small impact on the firm's overall financial position. That is, a firm should not put all its eggs in one basket, but should try to minimize risk by spreading its investments over a variety of projects.

The objective in pursuing a diversification strategy is to achieve certain desirable characteristics regarding risk and expected return. Let us now consider Example 12.4. From Example 12.4, it can be seen that both the existing activities (umbrella manufacturing) and the proposed new project (ice-cream manufacturing) are risky when considered on their own, but when they are combined, the risk is eliminated because whatever the outcome the cash inflow will be £100 000. Example 12.4 tells us that we should not only consider the risk of individual projects but should also take into account how the risks of potential new projects and existing activities co-vary with each other. Risk is eliminated completely in Example 12.4 because perfect negative correlation (i.e. where the correlation coefficient is −1) exists between the cash flows of the proposed project and the cash

EXAMPLE 12.4

A firm that currently manufactures umbrellas is considering diversifying and investing in the manufacture of ice-cream. The predicted cash flows for the existing activities and the new project are shown below:

States of nature	Existing activities (Umbrella manufacturing) (£)	Proposed project (Ice-cream manufacturing) (£)	Combination of existing activities and the proposed project (£)
Sunshine	−200 000	+300 000	+100 000
Rain	+300 000	−200 000	+100 000

To simplify the illustration, it is assumed that only two states of nature exist (rain or sunshine) and each has a probability of 0.5.

flows of the existing activities. When the cash flows are perfectly positively correlated (where the correlation is +1), risk reduction cannot be achieved when the projects are combined. For all other correlation values, risk reduction advantages can be obtained by investing in projects that are not perfectly correlated with existing activities.

The important point that emerges from the above discussion is that it is not the risk of individual projects in isolation that is of interest but rather the incremental risk that each project will contribute to the overall risk of the firm.

SUMMARY

The following items relate to the learning objectives listed at the beginning of the chapter.

● **Calculate and explain the meaning of expected values.**

The expected value is calculated by weighting each of the possible outcomes by its associated probability. The sum of these weighted outcomes is called the expected value of the probability distribution. In other words, the expected value is the weighted arithmetic mean of the possible outcomes.

● **Explain the meaning of the terms standard deviation and coefficient of variation as measures of risk and outline their limitations.**

Standard deviation measures the dispersion of the possible outcomes. It is an absolute measure. In contrast, the coefficient of variation is a relative measure derived from dividing the standard deviation by the expected value. Both measures attempt to summarize the risk associated with a probability distribution. They assume that risk is measured in terms of the spread of possible outcomes. Decision-makers are probably more interested in a downside measure of risk that measures the possibility of risk being less than the expected value. Because of this there are strong arguments for presenting the entire probability distribution to the decision-maker.

● **Construct a decision tree when there is a range of alternatives and possible outcomes.**

Where there are many possible outcomes for various alternatives, and some outcomes are dependent on previous outcomes, a decision tree is a useful analytical tool for clarifying the range of alternative courses of actions and their possible outcomes. A decision tree is a diagram that shows the possible courses of actions, the potential events (states of nature for each outcome) together with their potential outcomes and associated probabilities. A decision tree thus represents an analytical tool for deriving expected values and a probability distribution in more complex situations.

● **Describe and calculate the value of perfect and imperfect information.**

The value of perfect and imperfect information relates to determining the value of the maximum amount it is worth paying for additional information. The approach involves comparing the expected value of a decision if the information is acquired, against the expected value with the absence of the information. The difference represents the maximum value that it is worth paying for the additional information. You should refer to the section in the chapter on buying perfect and imperfect information for an illustration of the calculation of the value of perfect information.

● **Explain and apply the maximin, maximax and regret criteria.**

In situations in which uncertainty applies, it is not possible to assign meaningful estimates of probabilities to possible outcomes. When this situation occurs, either the maximin, maximax or regret criteria may be used. The maximin criterion assumes that the worst possible outcome will occur and that the decision should be based on the largest payoff under this assumption. The maximax is the opposite to maximin and is based on the assumption that the best possible payoff will occur. The regret criterion is based on the fact that, having selected an alternative that does not turn out to be the best, the decision-maker will regret not having chosen another alternative when he or she had the opportunity. The aim is to minimize the maximum possible regret. The application of the criteria was illustrated using Example 12.3.

● **Explain the implication of pursuing a diversification strategy.**

The implication of diversification is that the degree of uncertainty attached to various alternatives should not be considered in isolation. Instead, how an alternative interacts with existing activities should be considered. The aim should be to measure incremental, rather than the total risk, of a project.

KEY TERMS AND CONCEPTS

Coefficient of variation A ratio measure of dispersion derived by dividing the standard deviation by the expected value.

Decision tree A diagram showing several possible courses of action and possible events and the potential outcomes for each of them.

Diversification strategy A strategy of investing in a range of different projects in order to minimize risk.

Events In the context of risk and uncertainty, factors that are outside the decision-maker's control, also known as states of nature.

Expected value A figure calculated by weighting each of the possible outcomes by its associated probability.

Expected value of perfect information The maximum amount it is worth paying for additional information in an uncertain situation, calculated by comparing the expected value of a decision if the information is acquired against the expected value in the absence of the information.

Maximax criterion A decision rule based on the assumption that the best possible outcome will always occur and the decision-maker should therefore select the largest payoff.

Maximin criterion A decision rule based on the assumption that the worst possible outcome will always occur and the decision-maker should therefore select the largest payoff under this assumption.

Objective probabilities Probabilities that can be established mathematically or compiled from historical data.

Probability In the context of risk, the likelihood that an event or state of nature will occur, normally expressed in decimal form with a value between 0 and 1.

Probability distribution A list of all possible outcomes for an event and the probability that each will occur.

Regret criterion A decision rule based on the fact that if a decision-maker selects an alternative that does not turn out to be the best, he or she will experience regret and therefore decisions should be made that will minimize the maximum possible regret.

Risk A term applied to a situation where there are several possible outcomes and there is relevant past experience to enable statistical evidence to be produced for predicting the possible outcomes.

Risk averter An individual who, given a choice between more or less risky alternatives with identical expected values, prefers the less risky option.

Risk neutral An individual who, given a choice between more or less risky alternatives with identical expected values, would be indifferent to both alternatives because they have the same expected values.

Risk seeker An individual who, given a choice between more or less risky alternatives with identical expected values, prefers the riskier option.

Single most likely estimate The outcome with the highest probability attached to it.

Standard deviation The square root of the mean of the squared deviations from the expected value.

States of nature In the context of risk and uncertainty, factors that are outside the decision-maker's control, also known as events.

Subjective probabilities Probabilities that are based on an individual's expert knowledge, past experience, and on observations of current variables which are likely to affect future events.

Uncertainty A term applied to a situation where there are several possible outcomes and but there is little previous statistical evidence to enable probabilities to be attached to possible outcomes.

RECOMMENDED READING

For a discussion of the topics covered in this chapter, you should refer to articles that can be accessed from the ACCA Student Accountant technical articles archive. For an article relating to the value of imperfect information see www.accaglobal.com/gb/en/student/exam-support -resources/professional-exams-study-resources/p5 /technical-articles/risks-of-uncertainty---part-2.html and articles relating to decision trees and uncertainty in general see www.accaglobal.com/gb/en/student /exam-support-resources/fundamentals-exams-study -resources/f5/technical-articles.html

KEY EXAMINATION POINTS

When you are faced with problems requiring an evaluation of alternatives with uncertain outcomes, you should calculate expected values and present probability distributions.

Note that expected values on their own are unlikely to be particularly useful and there is a need to supplement this measure with a probability distribution. Avoid calculating standard deviations, since they are rarely required and are a poor substitute for probability distributions.

It is particularly important with this topic that you plan your answer carefully. Once you have started your answer, it is difficult to remedy the situation if you initially adopt the wrong approach. A rough sketch of a decision tree at the start of your answer will force you to analyse the problem and identify all the alternatives and possible outcomes.

Examination questions on this topic sometimes also include a requirement as to whether additional perfect information should be purchased. Do make sure that you understand how to calculate the value of perfect information.

ASSESSMENT MATERIAL

The review questions are short questions that enable you to assess your understanding of the main topics included in the chapter. The numbers in parentheses provide you with the page numbers to refer to if you cannot answer a specific question.

The review problems are more complex and require you to relate and apply the content to various business problems. The problems are graded by their level of difficulty. Solutions to review problems that are not preceded by the term 'IM' are provided in a separate section at the end of the book. Solutions to problems preceded by the term 'IM' are provided in the Instructor's Manual accompanying this book that can be downloaded from the lecturer's digital support resources. Additional review problems with fully worked solutions are provided in the *Student Manual* that accompanies this book.

REVIEW QUESTIONS

12.1 Distinguish between risk and uncertainty. (p. 286)

12.2 What is a probability distribution? (p. 287)

12.3 How do subjective probabilities differ from objective probabilities? (p. 287)

12.4 Distinguish between expected value and the single most likely estimate. (p. 289)

12.5 Distinguish between the standard deviation and the coefficient of variation. (pp. 289–290)

12.6 What are the disadvantages of the standard deviation as a measure of risk? (p. 290)

12.7 What is a decision tree and what purpose does it serve? (pp. 292–293)

12.8 What is the expected value of perfect information and how can it be determined? (pp. 293–294)

12.9 Distinguish between maximin, maximax and regret criteria. When might it be appropriate to apply these criteria? (p. 295)

12.10 How does diversification impact on measuring risk? (pp. 296–297)

REVIEW PROBLEMS

12.11 **Intermediate.** Darwin uses decision tree analysis in order to evaluate potential projects. The company has been looking at the launch of a new product which it believes has a 70 per cent probability of success. The company is, however, considering undertaking an advertising campaign costing £50 000, which would increase the probability of success to 95 per cent.

If successful, the product would generate income of £200 000, otherwise £70 000 would be received.

What is the maximum that the company would be prepared to pay for the advertising?

(a) £32 500
(b) £29 000
(c) £17 500
(d) £50 000.

ACCA Paper 1.2 – Financial Information for Management

12.12 Intermediate. A company uses decision tree analysis to evaluate potential options. The management accountant for the company has established the following:

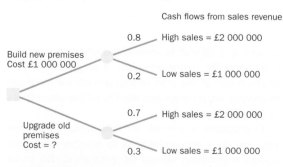

Cash flows from sales revenue

Build new premises Cost £1 000 000

0.8 — High sales = £2 000 000
0.2 — Low sales = £1 000 000

Upgrade old premises Cost = ?

0.7 — High sales = £2 000 000
0.3 — Low sales = £1 000 000

What would be the cost of the upgrade that would make the company financially indifferent between building new premises and upgrading the old one?

(a) £100 000
(b) £900 000
(c) £1 000 000
(d) £1 700 000

ACCA Paper 1.2 – Financial Information for Management

12.13 Intermediate. A company is planning to launch a new product. The price at which it will sell the product will be determined by the level of competition in the market which is currently uncertain. The possible selling prices and variable costs and their respective associated probabilities are as follows:

Selling price per unit		Variable cost per unit	
$	Probability	$	Probability
60	0.30	20	0.25
64	0.25	24	0.40
68	0.45	26	0.35

Selling price and variable cost per unit are independent of each other.

Required:
Calculate the probability of the contribution per unit being equal to or greater than $40. *(3 marks)*

CIMA P1 Performance Operations

12.14 Intermediate. A marketing manager is deciding which of four potential selling prices to charge for a new product. The market for the product is uncertain and reaction from competitors may be strong, medium or weak. The manager has prepared a payoff table showing the forecast profit for each of the possible outcomes.

Competitor reaction	Selling price			
	$80	$90	$100	$110
Strong	$70 000	$80 000	$70 000	$75 000
Medium	$50 000	$60 000	$70 000	$80 000
Weak	$90 000	$100 000	$90 000	$80 000

Required:

(i) Identify the selling price that would be chosen if the manager applies the maximin criterion to make the decision.

(ii) Identify, using a regret matrix, the selling price that would be chosen if the manager applies the minimax regret criterion to make the decision. *(4 marks)*

CIMA P1 Performance Operations

12.15 Intermediate. A company has to decide which of three mutually exclusive projects to invest in next year. The directors believe that the success of the projects will vary depending on economic conditions. There is a 30 per cent chance that conditions will be good, a 20 per cent chance that conditions will be fair and a 50 per cent chance that conditions will be poor. The company uses expected value to make this type of decision.

The net present value for each of the possible outcomes is as follows:

Economic conditions	Project A $000	Project B $000	Project C $000
Good	700	800	700
Fair	400	500	600
Poor	300	400	500

A firm of economic analysts believes it can provide perfect information on economic conditions.

Required:
Calculate the maximum amount that should be paid for the information from the firm of economic analysts. *(5 marks)*

CIMA P1 Performance Operations

12.16 Intermediate. A company has to decide which of three machines to purchase to manufacture a product. Each machine has the same purchase price but the operating costs of the machines differ. Machine A has low fixed costs and high variable costs; Machine B has average fixed costs and average variable costs whilst Machine C has high fixed costs and low variable costs. Machine A would consequently be preferable if demand was low and Machine C would be preferable if demand was high. There is a 35 per cent chance that demand will be high, a 40 per cent chance that demand will be medium and a 25 per cent chance that demand will be low. The company uses expected value to make this type of decision.

The estimated net present values for each of the possible outcomes are as follows:

Demand	Machine A $	Machine B $	Machine C $
High	100 000	140 000	180 000
Medium	150 000	160 000	140 000
Low	200 000	100 000	80 000

A market research company believes it can provide perfect information on product demand.

Required:
Calculate the maximum amount that should be paid for the information from the market research company. *(5 marks)*

CIMA P1 Performance Operations

12.17 Intermediate. A company uses a third party delivery service to deliver goods to customers. The current average cost per delivery is $12.50. The company is trying to decide whether to establish an in-house delivery service. A number of factors could affect the average total cost per delivery for the in-house delivery service. The table below shows the possible average total costs and the probability of each one occurring:

Average total cost	Probability
$10.50	0.05
$10.70	0.10
$11.00	0.08
$12.10	0.12
$12.50	0.14
$12.60	0.16
$14.20	0 12
$15.60	0.18
$15.80	0.05

The expected value of the average total cost, based on the probability distribution above, is $13.

Required:
Explain the decision that the company manager is likely to make, based on the probability distribution and the current delivery cost of $12.50 per delivery, if the manager is:

(i) risk neutral
(ii) risk averse
(iii) risk seeking   (5 marks)

CIMA P1 Performance Operations

12.18 Intermediate. XY has developed two new products, Product X and Product Y, but has insufficient resources to launch both products. The success of the products will depend on the extent of competitor reaction. There is a 20 per cent chance that competitors will take no action, a 50 per cent chance that they will launch a similar product and a 30 per cent chance that they will launch a better product.

The profit/loss that will be earned by each of the products depending on the extent of competitor reaction is as follows:

Competitor reaction	Product X	Product Y
No action	$540000	$620000
Launch a similar product	$320000	$380000
Launch a better product	($150000)	($200000)

Another option for XY would be to launch neither product. If it chooses this course of action there is a 60 per cent chance that competitors will take no action and there will be no effect on the company's profit. There is a 40 per cent chance that competitors will launch a new product and company profits will reduce by $100000.

Required:
Demonstrate, using a decision tree and based on expected value, the best course of action for the company.   (5 marks)

CIMA P1 Performance Operations

12.19 Intermediate: Calculation of payoffs and expected value.
Gam Co sells electronic equipment and is about to launch a new product onto the market. It needs to prepare its budget for the coming year and is trying to decide whether to launch the product at a price of $30 or $35 per unit. The following information has been obtained from market research:

Price per unit $30 Probability	Sales volume	Price per unit $35 Probability	Sales volume
0.4	120000	0.3	108000
0.5	110000	0.3	100000
0.1	140000	0.4	94000

Notes

1 Variable production costs would be $12 per unit for production volumes up to and including 100000 units each year. However, if production exceeds 100000 units each

year, the variable production cost per unit would fall to $11 for all units produced.
2 Advertising costs would be $900000 per annum at a selling price of $30 and $970000 per annum at a price of $35.
3 Fixed production costs would be $450000 per annum.

Required:

(a) Calculate each of the six possible profit outcomes which could arise for Gam Co in the coming year.   (8 marks)
(b) Calculate the expected value of profit for each of the two price options and recommend, on this basis, which option Gam Co would choose.   (3 marks)
(c) Briefly explain the maximin decision rule and identify which price should be chosen by management if they use this rule to decide which price should be charged.   (3 marks)
(d) Discuss the factors which may give rise to uncertainty when setting budgets.   (6 marks)

ACCA F5 Performance Management

12.20 Advanced: Evaluation of a project using different risk measures. Mackerel Contracting (Mackerel) is a listed defence contractor working mainly for its domestic government in Zedland. At present, Mackerel is considering tendering for a contract to design and develop a new armoured personnel vehicle (APV) for the army to protect its soldiers during transport around a battlefield. The invitation to tender from the government specifies that the APV should take two years to develop and test, and be delivered for a full cost to Mackerel of no more than $70000 per unit at current prices before Mackerel's profit element. Normally, government contracts are approximately priced on a cost plus basis with Mackerel aiming to make a 19 per cent mark-up.

At the last briefing meeting, the institutional shareholders of Mackerel expressed concern about the volatility of the company's earnings (currently a $20.4m operating profit per annum) especially during the economic downturn which is affecting Zedland at present. They are also concerned by cuts in government expenditure resulting from this recession. The Zedland minister for procurement has declared 'In the current difficult economic conditions, we are preparing a wide ranging review of all defence contracts with a view to deciding on what is desirable within the overall priorities for Zedland and what is possible within our budget'. The government procurement manager has indicated that the government would be willing to commit to purchase 500 APVs within the price limit set but with the possibility of increasing this to 750 or 1000 depending on defence commitments. In the invitation to tender document, the government has stated it will pay a fixed sum of $7.5m towards development and then a 19 per cent mark-up on budgeted variable costs.

Mackerel's risk management committee (RMC) is considering how much to spend on design and development. It has three proposals from the engineering team: a basic design package (Type 1) and two other improved design packages (Type 2 and Type 3). The design packages will have different total fixed costs but are structured to give the same variable cost per unit. The basic design package will cost $7.5m to develop which will satisfy the contract specification. It is believed that the improved design packages will increase the chances of gaining a larger government order but it has been very difficult to ascertain the relevant probabilities of different order volumes. The RMC need a full appraisal of the situation using all suitable methods.

The risk manager has gathered information on the APV contract which is contained in appendix A. She has identified that a major uncertainty in pricing the vehicle is the price of steel, as each APV requires 9.4 tonnes of steel. However, she has been successful in negotiating a fixed price contract for all the steel that might be required at $1214 per tonne. The risk manager has tried to estimate the effect of choosing different design packages but is unsure of how to proceed to evaluate the different options.

You are a consultant brought in to advise Mackerel on the new contract. The RMC need a report which outlines the external factors affecting the profitability of the project and how these factors can be built into the choice of the design budget which is ultimately set.

Appendix A

Budgeted cost for APV

Variable cost per unit

	$	
Steel	11 412	9–4 tonnes at contracted prices
Engine/transmission	9 500	
Electronics	8 450	
Other	4 810	
Labour	13 800	

Design and development (fixed total)	$
Package	
Type 1	7 500 000
Type 2	8 750 000
Type 3	10 000 000

Risk manager's assessment of likely government order:

		Probability	
Demand	Type 1	Type 2	Type 3
500	85%	25%	20%
750	10%	50%	50%
1000	5%	25%	30%

Required:

Write a report to the risk management committee to:

(i) Analyse the risks facing trie management of Mackerel and discuss how the management team's attitude to risk might affect their response.   (9 marks)

(ii) Evaluate the APV project using metrics and methods for decision-making under risk and uncertainty and assess the suitability of the different methods used.   (19 marks)

(iii) Recommend an appropriate choice of method of assessing the project and, therefore, a course of action for the APV contract.   (3 marks)

ACCA P5 Advanced Performance Management

12.21 Advanced: Risk assessment based on a joint probability distribution. The Equine Management Academy (EMA) which was founded in 1990 is a privately owned organization located in Hartland, a developing country which has a large agricultural sector and where much transportation is provided by horses. EMA operates an equine college which provides a range of undergraduate and postgraduate courses for students who wish to pursue a career in one of the following disciplines:

Equine (horse) surgery
Equine dentistry, and
Equine business management.

The equine college which has a maximum capacity of 1200 students per annum is currently the only equine college in Hartland.

The following information is available:

(1) A total of 1200 students attended the equine college during the year ended 31 May 2018. Student mix and fees paid were as per the following table:

Student category	% of total number of students	Fee ($) per student, per annum
Surgery	30	12 000
Dentistry	25	10 000
Business management	45	6 000

(2) Total operating costs (all fixed) during the year amounted to $6 500 000.

(3) Operating costs of the equine college are expected to increase by 4 per cent during the year ending 31 May 2019. This led to a decision by the management to increase the fees of all students by 5 per cent with effect from 1 June 2018. The management expect the number of students and the mix of students during the year ending 31 May 2019 to remain unchanged from those of the year ended 31 May 2018.

(4) EMA also operates a riding school at which 240 horses are stabled. The riding school is open for business on 360 days per annum. Each horse is available for four horse-riding lessons per day other than on the 40 days per annum that each horse is rested, i.e. not available for the provision of riding lessons. During the year ended 31 May 2018, the riding school operated at 80 per cent of full capacity.

(5) Horse-riding lessons are provided for riders in three different skill categories. These are 'Beginner', 'Competent' and 'Advanced'.

During the year ended 31 May 2018, the fee per riding lesson was as follows:

Skill category of horse rider	Lesson mix	Fee ($) per lesson
Beginner	50%	15
Competent	25%	30
Advanced	25%	50

(6) Total operating costs of the riding school (all fixed) amounted to $5 750 000 during the year ended 31 May 2018,

(7) It is anticipated that the operating costs of the riding school will increase by 6 per cent in the year ending 31 May 2019. The management have decided to increase the charge per lesson, in respect of 'Competent' and 'Advanced' riders by 10 per cent with effect from 1 June 2018. There will be no increase in the charge per lesson for 'Beginner' riders.

(8) The lesson mix and capacity utilization of the riding school will remain the same during the year ending 31 May 2019.

Required:

(a) Prepare a statement showing the budgeted net profit or loss for the year ending 31 May 2019.   (7 marks)

Some time ago the government of Hartland, which actively promotes environmental initiatives, announced its intention to open an academy comprising an equine college and riding school. The management of EMA are uncertain of the impact that this will have on the budgeted number of students and riders during the year ending 31 May 2019, although they consider that due to the excellent reputation of the instructors at the riding school, capacity utilization could remain uncharged or even increase, in spite of the opening of the government funded academy. Current estimates of the number of students entering the academy and the average capacity utilization of the riding school are as follows:

	Equine college		Riding school	
Student fees	Probability	Capacity utilization	Probability
No change	0.20	90%	0·10
Decrease by 10%	0.60	80%	0·60
Decrease by 20%	0.20	70%	0·30

Required:

(b) (i) Prepare a summary table which shows the possible net profit or loss outcomes, and the combined probability of each potential outcome for the year ending 31 May 2019. The table should also show the expected value of net profit or loss for the year; *(9 marks)*

(ii) Comment briefly on the use of expected values by the management of EMA; *(3 marks)*

(iii) Suggest three reasons why the government of Hartland might have decided to open an academy comprising an equine college and a riding school. *(6 marks)*

ACCA P5 Advanced Performance Management

12.22 Advanced: Decision tree, expected value and value of perfect information. Gym Bunnies (GB) is a health club. It currently has 6000 members, with each member paying a subscription fee of $720 per annum. The club is comprised of a gym, a swimming pool and a small exercise studio.

A competitor company is opening a new gym in GB's local area, and this is expected to cause a fall in GB's membership numbers, unless GB can improve its own facilities. Consequently, GB is considering whether or not to expand its exercise studio in a hope to improve its membership numbers. Any improvements are expected to last for three years.

Option 1
No expansion. In this case, membership numbers would be expected to fall to 5250 per annum for the next three years. Operational costs would stay at their current level of $80 per member per annum.

Option 2
Expand the exercise studio. The capital cost of this would be $360000. The expected effect on membership numbers for the next three years is as follows:

Probability	Effect on membership numbers
0.4	Remain at their current level of 6000 members per annum
0.6	Increase to 6500 members per annum

The effect on operational costs for the next three years is expected to be:

Probability	Effect on operational costs
0.5	Increase to $120 per member per annum
0.5	Increase to $180 per member per annum

Required:

(a) Using the criterion of expected value, prepare and fully label a decision tree that shows the two options available to GB. Recommend the decision that GB should make.

Note: Ignore time value of money. *(12 marks)*

(b) Calculate the maximum price that GB should pay for perfect information about the expansion's exact effect on MEMBERSHIP NUMBERS. *(6 marks)*

(c) Briefly discuss the problems of using expected values for decisions of this nature. *(2 marks)*

ACCA F5 Performance Management

12.23 Advanced: Decision tree, expected value and maximin criterion.

(a) The Alternative Sustenance Company is considering introducing a new franchised product, Wholefood Waffles. Existing ovens now used for making some of the present 'Half-baked' range of products could be used instead for baking the Wholefood Waffles. However, new specialized batch mixing equipment would be needed. This cannot be purchased, but can be hired

from the franchiser in three alternative specifications, for batch sizes of 200, 300 and 600 units respectively. The annual cost of hiring the mixing equipment would be £5000, £15000 and £21500 respectively.

The 'Half-baked' product, which would be dropped from the range currently earns a contribution of £90000 per annum, which it is confidently expected could be continued if the product were retained in the range.

The company's marketing manager considers that, at the market price for Wholefood Waffles of £0.40 per unit, it is equally probable that the demand for this product would be 600000 or 1000000 units per annum.

The company's production manager has estimated the variable costs per unit of making Wholefood Waffles and the probabilities of those costs being incurred, as follows:

Batch size: Cost per unit (pence)	200 units Probability if annual sales are either 600000 or 1000000 units	300 units Probability if annual sales are either 600000 or 1000000 units	600 units Probability if annual sales are 600000 units	600 units Probability if annual sales are 1000000 units
£0.20	0.1	0.2	0.3	0.5
£0.25	0.1	0.5	0.1	0.2
£0.30	0.8	0.3	0.6	0.3

You are required:

(i) to draw a decision tree setting out the problem faced by the company; *(12 marks)*

(ii) to show in each of the following three independent situations which size of mixing machine, if any, the company should hire:

1 to satisfy a 'maximin' (or 'minimax' criterion);

2 to maximize the expected value of contribution per annum;

3 to minimize the probability of earning an annual contribution of less than £100000. *(7 marks)*

(b) You are required to outline briefly the strengths and limitations of the methods of analysis which you have used in part (a) above. *(6 marks)*

ICAEW Management Accounting

IM12.1 Advanced: Preparation of project statements for different demand levels and calculations of expected profit. Seeprint Limited is negotiating an initial one-year contract with an important customer for the supply of a specialized printed colour catalogue at a fixed contract price of £16 per catalogue. Seeprint's normal capacity for producing such catalogues is 50000 per annum.

Last year Seeprint Limited earned £11000 profit per month from a number of small accounts requiring specialized colour catalogues. If the contract under negotiation is not undertaken, then a similar profit might be obtained from these customers next year, but, if it is undertaken, there will be no profit from such customers.

The estimated costs of producing colour catalogues of a specialized nature are given below.

The costs below are considered certain with the exception of the direct materials price.

Cost data:

	(£)
Variable costs per catalogue	
Direct materials	4.50
Direct wages	3.00
Direct expenses	1.30

Semi-variable costs	Output levels (capacity utilization)		
	80% (£)	100% (£)	120% (£)
Indirect materials	46800	47000	74400
Indirect wages	51200	55000	72000
Indirect expenses	6000	8000	9600

Estimated fixed costs per annum:

Depreciation of specialist equipment	£8000
Supervisory and management salaries	£20000
Other fixed costs allocated to specialist colour catalogues production	£32000

You are required to:

(a) Tabulate the costs and profits per unit and in total and the annual profits, assuming that the contract orders in the year are:
(i) 40000, (ii) 50000 and (iii) 60000 catalogues, at a direct material cost of £4.50 per catalogue. Comment on the tabulation you have prepared.   *(10 marks)*

(b) Calculate the expected profit for the year if it is assumed that the probability of the total order is:
0.4 for 40000 catalogues
0.4 for 50000 catalogues
0.1 for 60000 catalogues

and that the probability of direct material cost is:
0.5 at £4.50 per catalogue
0.3 at £5.00 per catalogue
0.2 at £5.50 per catalogue.   *(6 marks)*

(c) Discuss the implications for Seeprint Limited of the acceptance or otherwise of the contract with the important customer.   *(6 marks)*

ACCA Level 2 Management Accounting

IM12.2 Advanced: CVP analysis and uncertainty. The accountant of Laburnum Ltd is preparing documents for a forthcoming meeting of the budget committee. Currently, variable cost is 40 per cent of selling price and total fixed costs are £40000 per year.

The company uses an historical cost accounting system. There is concern that the level of costs may rise during the ensuing year and the chairman of the budget committee has expressed interest in a probabilistic approach to an investigation of the effect that this will have on historic cost profits. The accountant is attempting to prepare the documents in a way that will be most helpful to the committee members. He or she has obtained the following estimates from his colleagues:

	Average inflation rate over ensuing year	Probability
Pessimistic	10%	0.4
Most likely	5%	0.5
Optimistic	1%	0.1
		1.0

	Demand at current selling prices	Probability
Pessimistic	£50000	0.3
Most likely	£75000	0.6
Optimistic	£100000	0.1
		1.0

The demand figures are given in terms of sales value at the current level of selling prices but it is considered that the company could adjust its selling prices in line with the inflation rate without affecting customer demand in real terms.

Some of the company's fixed costs are contractually fixed and some are apportionments of past costs; of the total fixed costs, an estimated 85 per cent will remain constant irrespective of the inflation rate.

You are required to analyse the foregoing information in a way which you consider will assist management with its budgeting problem. Although you should assume that the directors of Laburnum Ltd are solely interested in the effect of inflation on historic cost profits, you should comment on the validity of the accountant's intended approach. As part of your analysis you are required to calculate:

(i) the probability of at least breaking even, and
(ii) the probability of achieving a profit of at least £20000.   *(16 marks)*

ACCA Level 2 Management Accounting

IM12.3 Advanced: Output decision based on expected values. A ticket agent has an arrangement with a concert hall that holds pop concerts on 60 nights a year whereby he receives discounts as follows per concert:

For purchase of:	He receives a discount of:
200 tickets	20%
300 tickets	25%
400 tickets	30%
500 tickets or more	40%

Purchases must be in full hundreds. The average price per ticket is £3.

He must decide in advance each year the number of tickets he will purchase. If he has any tickets unsold by the afternoon of the concert he must return them to the box office. If the box office sells any of these he receives 60 per cent of their price.

His sales records over a few years show that for a concert with extremely popular artistes he can be confident of selling 500 tickets, for one with lesser known artistes 350 tickets, and for one with relatively unknown artistes 200 tickets.

His records also show that 10 per cent of tickets he returns are sold by the box office.

His administration costs incurred in selling tickets are the same per concert irrespective of the popularity of the artistes.

There are two possible scenarios in which his sales records can be viewed:

Scenario 1:   that, on average, he can expect concerts with lesser known artistes

Scenario 2:   that the frequency of concerts will be:

	(%)
with popular artistes	45
with lesser known artistes	30
with unknown artistes	25
	100

You are required to calculate:

Separately for each of Scenarios 1 and 2:

(a) the expected demand for tickets per concert;

(b) (i) the level of his purchases of tickets per concert that will give him the largest profit over a long period of time;
(ii) the profit per concert that this level of purchases of tickets will yield.

For Scenario 2 only: the maximum sum per annum that the ticket agent should pay to a pop concert specialist for 100 per cent correct predictions as to the likely success of each concert. *(25 marks)*

CIMA P3 Management Accounting

IM12.4 Advanced: Contracting hotel accommodation based on uncertain demand. Crabbe, the owner of the Ocean Hotel, is concerned about the hotel's finances and has asked your advice. Crabbe gives you the following information:

'We have rooms for 80 guests. When the hotel is open, whatever the level of business, we have to meet the following each month':

	(£)
Staff wages and benefits	12 500
General overheads (rates, electricity, etc.)	8 000
Depreciation	2 200
Interest on mortgage and bank loan	1 800
Repayments on mortgage and bank loan	2 500
Drawings for my own needs	1 000
	28 000

'For our normal business we charge an average of £20 per night for each guest. Each guest night involves variable costs of £4 for laundry and cleaning. Guests also spend money in the restaurant, which on average brings us another £5 per guest night after meeting variable costs.'

'I need advice on two problems; one concerns the month of September and the other relates to the winter.'

1 'Normal business in September will depend on weather conditions, and the probabilities of occupancy from normal business are':

For month of September

Weather condition	A	B	C
Probability	0.3	0.4	0.3
Occupancy (total guest nights)	1440	1680	1920

'Airtravel Tours has enquired about a block booking at a discount in September. I intend to quote a discount of 40 per cent on our normal guest night charge. In the restaurant Airtravels package tourists will only bring us £3 per guest night after variable costs. Airtravel could take all our capacity, but I have to decide how many guest nights to offer. The contract will mean that I agree in advance to take the same number of Airtravel tourists every night throughout September. If they won't accept my price, I would be prepared to go as far as a 60 per cent discount.'

2 'When we come to the winter, trade is usually so bad that we close for three months. We retain only a skeleton staff, costing £1500 per month, and general overheads are reduced from £8000 to £2000. I am trying to find ways of keeping open this winter, but staying open will incur the full monthly outgoings.'

'If we remained open for all three months I estimate our basic winter trade at reduced prices, together with income from conferences, would be as follows':

	Average number of guests per night	Charge per guest night (£)	Restaurant revenue per guest night net of variable costs (£)
Basic winter trade	12	14	5
Conferences etc.	30	13	4

'Alternatively, I am considering offering a series of language courses. We could not take any other guests, and I estimate the total demand for the three months as follows':

Market condition	X	Y	Z
Probability	0.3	0.4	0.3
Occupancy (total guest nights)	2160	4320	6480

'If the courses are offered we shall have to run them for the full three months, irrespective of the take-up. The charge per night would be £24, and the revenue from the restaurant net of variable cost would only be £1 per guest night.

'We would have to spend about £5000 per month on tutors, and the courses would also have to be advertised beforehand at a cost of £1500.'

Assume 30-day months throughout.

Requirements:

(a) Calculate the number of guest nights Crabbe should contract to Airtravel Tours at the quoted 40 per cent discount. *(6 marks)*

(b) Determine the minimum price per guest night at which it would be worthwhile for Crabbe to do business with Airtravel, and the maximum number of guest nights it would be worthwhile to contract at this price. *(4 marks)*

(c) Assess which of the winter options Crabbe should undertake and state any reservation you may have about your assessment. *(9 marks)*

(d) Briefly explain the criteria on which you have identified costs to assess Crabbe's business options in requirements (a) to (c). *(6 marks)*

ICAEW P2 Management Accounting

IM12.5 Advanced: Pricing and purchase contract decisions based on uncertain demand and calculation of maximum price to pay for perfect information. Z Ltd is considering various product pricing and material purchasing options with regard to a new product it has in development. Estimates of demand and costs are as follows:

		£15 per unit Sales volume	£20 per unit Sales volume
If selling price per unit is			
Forecasts	Probability	(000 units)	(000 units)
Optimistic	0.3	36	28
Most likely	0.5	28	23
Pessimistic	0.2	18	13
Variable manufacturing costs (excluding materials) per unit		£3	£3
Advertising and selling costs		£25 000	£96 000
General fixed costs		£40 000	£40 000

Each unit requires 3kg of material and because of storage problems any unused material must be sold at £1 per kg. The sole suppliers of the material offer three purchase options, which must be decided at the outset, as follows:

(i) any quantity at £3 per kg;
(ii) a price of £2.75 per kg for a minimum quantity of 50 000 kg; or
(iii) a price of £2.50 per kg for a minimum quantity of 70 000kg.

You are required, assuming that the company is risk neutral, to;

(a) prepare calculations to show what pricing and purchasing decisions the company should make, clearly indicating the recommended decisions;   (15 marks)

(b) calculate the maximum price you would pay for perfect information as to whether the demand would be optimistic or most likely pessimistic.   (5 marks)

CIMA Stage 3 Management Accounting Techniques

IM12.6 Advanced: Selling price decision based on expected values and value of additional information. Warren Ltd is to produce a new product in a short-term venture which will utilize some obsolete materials and expected spare capacity. The new product will be advertised in quarter I with production and sales taking place in quarter II. No further production or sales are anticipated.

Sales volumes are uncertain but will, to some extent, be a function of sales price. The possible sales volumes and the advertising costs associated with each potential sales price are as follows:

Sales price £20 per unit		Sales price £25 per unit		Sales price £40 per unit	
Sales volume units (000)	Probability	Sales volume units (000)	Probability	Sales volume units (000)	Probability
4	0.1	2	0.1	0	0.2
6	0.4	5	0.2	3	0.5
8	0.5	6	0.2	10	0.2
		8	0.5	15	0.1

Advertising Costs	£20 000	£50 000	£100 000

The resources used in the production of each unit of the product are:

Production labour:	grade 1	0.4 hours
	grade 2	0.2 hour

Materials: X	1 unit
Y	2 units

The normal cost per hour of labour is

grade 1	£10
grade 2	£15

However, before considering the effects of the current venture, there is expected to be 800 hours of idle time for each grade of labour in quarter II. Idle time is paid at the normal rates.

Material X is in stock at a book value of £8 per unit, but is widely used within the firm and any usage for the purposes of this venture will require replacing. Replacement cost is £9 per unit.

Material Y is obsolete stock. There are 16 000 units in stock at a book value of £3.50 per unit and any stock not used will have to be disposed of at a cost, to Warren, of £2 per unit. Further quantities of Y can be purchased for £4 per unit.

Overhead recovery rates are:

Variable overhead	£10 per direct labour hour worked
Fixed overhead	£3 per direct labour hour worked

Total fixed overheads will not alter as a result of the current venture.

Feedback from advertising will enable the exact demand to be determined at the end of quarter I and production in quarter II will be set to equal that demand. However, it is necessary to decide now on the sales price in order that it can be incorporated into the advertising campaign.

Required:

(a) Calculate the expected money value of the venture at each sales price and on the basis of this advise Warren of its best course of action.   (12 marks)

(b) Briefly explain why the management of Warren might rationally reject the sales price leading to the highest expected money value and prefer one of the other sales prices.   (4 marks)

(c) It will be possible, for the sales price of £40 per unit only, to ascertain which of the four levels of demand will eventuate. If the indications are that the demand will be low then the advertising campaign can be cancelled at a cost of £10 000 but it would then not be possible to continue the venture at another sales price. This accurate information concerning demand will cost £5000 to obtain.

Indicate whether it is worthwhile obtaining the information and ascertain whether it would alter the advice given in (a) above.   (4 marks)

ACCA Level 2 Management Accounting

IM12.7 Advanced: Hire of machine based on uncertain demand and value of perfect information. The Ruddle Co. Ltd had planned to install and, with effect from next April, commence operating sophisticated machinery for the production of a new product – product Zed. However, the supplier of the machinery has just announced that delivery of the machinery will be delayed by six months and this will mean that Ruddle will not now be able to undertake production using that machinery until October.

'The first six months of production' stated the commercial manager of Ruddle, 'are particularly crucial as we have already contracted to supply several national supermarket groups with whatever quantities of Zed they require during that period at a price of £40 per unit. Their demand is, at this stage, uncertain but would have been well within the capacity of the permanent machinery we were to have installed. The best estimates of the total demand for the first period are thought to be':

Estimated demand – first six months	
Quantity (000 units)	Probability
10	0.5
14	0.3
16	0.2

'Whatever the level of demand, we are going to meet it in full even if it means operating at a loss for the first half year. Therefore I suggest we consider the possibility of hiring equipment on which temporary production can take place.' Details of the only machines which could be hired are:

	Machine A	Machine B	Machine C
Productive capacity per six month period (units)	10 000	12 000	16 000
Variable production cost for each unit produced	£6.5	£6	£5
Other 'fixed' costs total for six months	£320 000	£350 000	£400 000

In addition to the above costs, there will be a variable material cost of £5 per unit. For purchases greater than 10 000 units a discount of 20 per cent per unit will be given, but this only applies to the excess over 10 000 units.

Should production capacity be less than demand then Ruddle could subcontract production of up to 6000 units but would be required to supply raw materials. Subcontracting costs are:

up to 4000 units subcontracted £30 per unit

any excess over 4000 units subcontracted £35 per unit.

These subcontracting costs relate only to the work carried out by the subcontractor and exclude the costs of raw materials.

The commercial manager makes the following further points, 'Due to the lead time required for setting up production, the choice of which machine to hire must be made before the precise demand is known. However, demand will be known in time for production to be scheduled so that an equal number of units can be produced each month. We will, of course, only produce sufficient to meet demand.

'We need to decide which machine to hire. However, I wonder whether it would be worthwhile seeking the assistance of a firm of market researchers? Their reputation suggests that they are very accurate and they may be able to inform us whether demand is to be 10, 14 or 16 thousand units.'

Required:

(a) For each of the three machines that could be hired show the possible monetary outcomes and, using expected values, advise Ruddle on its best course of action.

(12 marks)

(b) (i) Calculate the maximum amount which it would be worthwhile to pay to the firm of market researchers to ascertain details of demand. (You are required to assume that the market researchers will produce an absolutely accurate forecast and that demand will be exactly equal to one of the three demand figures given.) *(4 marks)*

(ii) Comment on the view that as perfect information is never obtainable the calculation of the expected value of perfect information is not worthwhile. Briefly explain any uses such a calculation may have.

(4 marks)

Ignore taxation and the time value of money.

ACCA P2 Management Accounting

IM12.8 Advanced: Calculation of expected value of perfect and imperfect information. Butterfield Ltd manufactures a single brand of dog food called 'Lots O Grissle' (LOG). Sales have stabilized for several years at a level of £20 million per annum at current prices. This level is not expected to change in the foreseeable future (except as indicated below). It is well below the capacity of the plant. The managing director, Mr Rover, is considering how to stimulate growth in the company's turnover and profits. After rejecting all of the alternative possibilities that he can imagine, or that have been suggested to him, he is reviewing a proposal to introduce a new luxury dog food product. It would be called 'Before Eight Mince' (BEM), and would have a recommended retail price of £0.50 per tin. It would require no new investment, and would incur no additional fixed costs.

Mr Rover has decided that he will undertake this new development only if he can anticipate that it will at least break even in the first year of operation.

(a) Mr Rover estimates that BEM has a 75 per cent chance of gaining acceptance in the marketplace. His best estimate is that if the product gains acceptance it will have sales in the forthcoming year of £3.2 million at retail prices, given a contribution of £1 million after meeting the variable costs of manufacture and distribution. If, by the same token, the product fails to gain acceptance, sales for the year will, he thinks, be only £800 000 at retail prices, and for various reasons there would be a negative contribution of £400 000 in that year.

You are required to show whether, on the basis of these preliminary estimates, Mr Rover should give the BEM project further consideration. *(4 marks)*

(b) Mr Rover discusses the new project informally with his sales director, Mr Khoo Chee Khoo, who suggests that some of the sales achieved for the new product would cause lost sales of LOG. In terms of retail values he estimates the likelihood of this as follows:

There is a 50 per cent chance that sales of LOG will fall by half of the sales of BEM.

There is a 25 per cent chance that sales of LOG will fall by one-quarter of the sales of BEM.

There is a 25 per cent chance that sales of LOG will fall by three-quarters of the sales of BEM.

The contribution margin ratio of LOG is 25 per cent at all relevant levels of sales and output. You are required to show whether, after accepting these further estimates, Mr Rover should give the BEM project further consideration. *(5 marks)*

(c) Mr Rover wonders also whether, before attempting to proceed any further, he should have some market research undertaken. He approaches Delphi Associates, a firm of market research consultants for whom he has a high regard. On previous occasions he has found them to be always right in their forecasts, and he considers that their advice will give him as near perfect information as it is possible to get. He decides to ask Delphi to advise him only on whether or not BEM will gain acceptance in the marketplace in the sense in which he has defined it; he will back Mr Khoo Chee Khoo's judgement about the effects of the introduction of BEM on the sales of LOG. If Delphi advise him that the product will not be accepted he will not proceed further. Delphi have told him that their fee for this work would be £100 000.

You are required to show whether Mr Rover should instruct Delphi Associates to carry out the market research proposals. *(5 marks)*

(d) Preliminary discussions with Delphi suggest that Delphi's forecast will not be entirely reliable. They believe that, if they indicate that BEM will gain acceptance, there is only a 90 per cent chance that they will be right; and, if they indicate failure to gain acceptance, there is only a 70 per cent chance that they will be right. This implies a 75 per cent chance overall that Delphi will indicate acceptance, in line with Mr Rover's estimate.

You are required to show the maximum amount that Mr Rover should be prepared to pay Delphi to undertake the market research, given the new estimates of the reliability of their advice. *(5 marks)*

(e) You are required to outline briefly the strengths and limitations of your methods of analysis in (a)–(d) above.

(6 marks)

ICAEW Management Accounting

13
CAPITAL INVESTMENT DECISIONS: APPRAISAL METHODS

LEARNING OBJECTIVES After studying this chapter, you should be able to:

- explain the opportunity cost of an investment;

- distinguish between compounding and discounting;

- explain the concepts of net present value (NPV), internal rate of return (IRR), payback method and accounting rate of return (ARR);

- calculate NPV, IRR, the payback period and ARR;

- justify the superiority of NPV over the IRR;

- explain the limitations of payback and ARR;

- justify why the payback and ARR methods are widely used in practice;

- describe the effect of performance measurement on capital investment decisions.

Capital investment decisions are those decisions that involve current outlays in return for a stream of benefits in future years. It is true to say that all of the firm's expenditures are made in expectation of realizing future benefits. The distinguishing feature between short-term decisions and capital investment (long-term) decisions is time. Generally, we can classify short-term decisions as those that involve a relatively short time horizon, say one year, from the commitment of funds to the receipt of the benefits. Contrariwise, capital investment decisions are those decisions in which a significant period of time elapses between the outlay and the recoupment of the investment. We shall see that this commitment of funds for a significant period of time involves an interest cost, which must be brought into the analysis. With short-term decisions, funds are committed only for short periods of time, and the interest cost is normally so small that it can be ignored.

Capital investment decisions normally represent the most important decisions that an organization makes, since they commit a substantial proportion of a firm's resources to actions that are likely to be irreversible. For example, the projected capital expenditure for Sainsbury plc and Tesco plc (two UK supermarket chains) for 2016 were £1.0 and £2.6 billion, respectively.

Capital investment decisions are applicable to all sectors of society. Business firms' investment decisions include investments in plant and machinery, research and development, advertising and

REAL WORLD VIEWS 13.1

Capital investment in energy generation

All businesses have to continually engage in capital investment to improve and maintain processes, equipment and facilities. Governments also invest in infrastructure projects like roads, rail and utilities provision. Whether a private or public organization, when capital investment is not undertaken, the effects will cause problems.

In South Africa, no power generation plants had been built for about 20 years from the early 1990s. With a growing economy since then, this has caused problems for many businesses. In 2008, the country exceeded its generation capability which caused power blackouts. The power problems hit one business sector particularly hard, namely the mining sector. Ore smelters and mines consume vast quantities of power and the South African economy is hugely dependent on this sector. Why no investment in new generation capacity? The *Financial Times* website (10 April 2010), stated that a major problem was low electricity prices, which in turn implied little cash for re-investment. According to a Bloomberg article, investment of R500 billion from 2013 to 2017 was needed to overcome an electricity shortage. To help overcome this issue, electricity prices were increased from just under 20 cent per kw/h to 75 cent between 2008 and 2016. However, additional power generation capacity takes time to build and Eskom, who produce 95 per cent of South Africa's power, had spent R265 billion up to 2015. In response, smelting operations like International Ferro Metals invested in their own onsite generation facility. The company produces some of its power requirements by recycling heat from its smelters. This not only helps protect the company from power outages, but also protects to some degree against rising costs. A sound investment in the longer term it would seem.

Questions

1 When evaluating an investment in energy generation solely on cost considerations, can a manager make the right decision?

2 Thinking about the International Ferro Metals example given above, what non-financial benefits might arise other than protecting against power outages?

References

Deloitte (2012) The economic impact of electricity price increases on various sectors of the South African economy. Available at www.eskom.co.za /CustomerCare/MYPD3/Documents/Economic _Impact_of_Electrcity_Price_Increases_Document1.pdf

Eskom Price Tariff, available at www.eskom.co.za /CustomerCare/TariffsAndCharges/Pages /Tariff_History.aspx

Eskom 2015 annual report results summary, available at www.eskom.co.za/IR2015/Documents /Eskom_advert_2015.pdf

MacNamara, W. (2010) Energy crisis: Big push to make sure that power stays on, Financial Times, 10 April. Available at www.ft.com/content/aaaec744-4c0e -11df-a217-00144feab49a

warehouse facilities. Investment decisions in the public sector include new roads, schools and airports. Individuals' investment decisions include house buying and the purchase of consumer durables. In this and the following chapter, we shall examine the economic evaluation of the desirability of investment proposals. We shall concentrate on the investment decisions of business firms, but the same principles, with modifications, apply both to individuals and the public sector.

To simplify the introduction to capital investment decision, we shall assume initially that all cash inflows and outflows are known with certainty and that sufficient funds are available to undertake all profitable investments. We will also assume a world in which there are no taxes and where there is an absence of inflation. These factors will be brought into the analysis in the next chapter. It is important that you check your course curriculum to ascertain whether this chapter is relevant to your course. In some courses, capital investment decisions are included in a corporate financial management course rather than a management accounting course.

THE OPPORTUNITY COST OF AN INVESTMENT

Investors can invest in securities traded in financial markets. If you prefer to avoid risk, you can invest in government securities, which will yield a *fixed* return. By the same token, you may prefer to invest in *risky* securities such as the ordinary shares of companies quoted on the stock exchange. If you invest in the ordinary shares of a company, you will find that the return will vary from year to year, depending on the performance of the company and its future expectations. Investors normally prefer to avoid risk if possible, and will generally invest in risky securities only if they believe that they will obtain a greater return for the increased risk. In the past risk-free gilt-edged securities issued by the government have yielded returns varying from 0.5 to 15 per cent and in 2017 were less than 1 per cent. To simplify the calculations, we shall assume that government securities yield a return of 10 per cent. You will therefore be prepared to invest in ordinary shares only if you expect the return to be greater than 10 per cent; let us assume that you require an *expected* return of 15 per cent to induce you to invest in ordinary shares in preference to a risk-free security. Note that expected return means the estimated average future return. You would expect to earn, on average, 15 per cent, but in some years you might earn more and in others considerably less.

Suppose you invest in company X ordinary shares. Would you want company X to invest your money in a capital project that gives less than 15 per cent? Surely not, assuming the project has the same risk as the alternative investments in shares of other companies that are yielding a return of 15 per cent. You would prefer company X to invest in other companies' ordinary shares at 15 per cent or, alternatively, to repay your investment so that you could invest it yourself at 15 per cent.

The rates of return that are available from investments in securities in financial markets such as ordinary shares and government gilt-edged securities represent the opportunity cost of an investment in capital projects; that is, if cash is invested in the capital project, it cannot be invested elsewhere to earn a return. A firm should therefore invest in capital projects only if they yield a return in excess of the opportunity cost of the investment. The opportunity cost of the investment is also known as the minimum required rate of return, cost of capital, discount rate or interest rate.

The return on securities traded in financial markets provides us with the opportunity costs, that is the required rates of return available on securities. The expected returns that investors require from the ordinary shares of different companies vary because some companies' shares are more risky than others. The greater the risk, the greater the expected returns. Consider Figure 13.1. You can see that as the risk of a security increases, the return that investors require to compensate for the extra risk increases. Consequently, investors will expect to receive a return in excess of 15 per cent if they invest in securities that have a higher risk than company X ordinary shares. If this return were not forthcoming, investors would not purchase high risk securities. It is therefore important that companies investing in high risk capital projects earn higher returns to compensate investors for this risk. You can also see that a risk-free security such as a gilt-edged government security yields the lowest return, i.e. 10 per cent. Consequently, if a firm invests in a project with zero risk, it should earn a return in excess of 10 per cent. If the project does not yield this return and no other projects are available, then the funds earmarked for the project should be repaid to the shareholders as dividends. The shareholders could then invest the funds themselves at 10 per cent.

FIGURE 13.1
Risk–return
trade-off

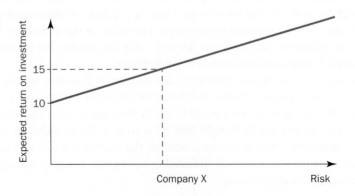

COMPOUNDING AND DISCOUNTING

Our objective is to calculate and compare returns on an investment in a capital project with an alternative equal risk investment in securities traded in the financial markets. This comparison is made using a technique called discounted cash flow (DCF) analysis. Because a DCF analysis is the opposite of the concept of compounding interest, we shall initially focus on compound interest calculations.

Suppose you are investing £100000 in a risk-free security yielding a return of 10 per cent payable at the end of each year. Exhibit 13.1 shows that if the interest is reinvested, your investment will accumulate to £146410 by the end of year 4. Period 0 in the first column of Exhibit 13.1 means that no time has elapsed or the time is *now*, period 1 means one year later and so on. The values in Exhibit 13.1 can also be obtained by using the formula:

$$FV_n = V_0(1 + K)^n \qquad\qquad (13.1)$$

where FV_n denotes the future value of an investment in n years, V_0 denotes the amount invested at the beginning of the period (year 0), K denotes the rate of return on the investment and n denotes the number of years for which the money is invested. The calculation for £100000 invested at 10 per cent for two years is:

$$FV_2 = £100000(1 + 0.10)^2 = £121000$$

In Exhibit 13.1, all of the year-end values are equal as far as the time value of money is concerned. For example, £121000 received at the end of year 2 is equivalent to £100000 received today and invested at 10 per cent. Similarly, £133100 received at the end of year 3 is equivalent to £121000 received at the end of year 2, since £121000 can be invested at the end of year 2 to accumulate to £133100. Unfortunately, none of the amounts is directly comparable at any single moment in time, because each amount is expressed at a different point in time.

When making capital investment decisions, we must convert cash inflows and outflows for different years into a common value. This is achieved by converting the cash flows into their respective values at the same point in time. Mathematically, any point in time can be chosen, since all four figures in Exhibit 13.1 are equal to £100000 at year 0, £110000 at year 1, £121000 at year 2 and so on. However, it is preferable to choose the point in time at which the decision is implemented and this is the present time or year 0. All of the values in Exhibit 13.1 can therefore be expressed in values at the present time (i.e. present value) of £100000.

The process of converting cash to be received in the future into a value at the present time by the use of an interest rate is termed discounting and the resulting present value is the discounted present value. Compounding is the opposite of discounting, since it is the future value of present

EXHIBIT 13.1 The value of £100000 invested at 10 per cent, compounded annually, for four years

End of year	Interest earned (£)	Total investment (£)
0		100000
	0.10 × 100000	10000
1		110000
	0.10 × 110000	11000
2		121000
	0.10 × 121000	12100
3		133100
	0.10 × 133100	13310
4		146410

value cash flows. Equation (13.1) for calculating future values can be rearranged to produce the present value formula:

$$V_0 \text{ (present value)} = \frac{FV_n}{(1 + K)^n} \tag{13.2}$$

By applying this equation, the calculation for £121 000 received at the end of year 2 can be expressed as:

$$\text{present value} = \frac{£121\,000}{(1 + 0.10)^2} = £100\,000$$

You should now be aware that £1 received today is not equal to £1 received one year from today. No rational person will be equally satisfied with receiving £1 a year from now as opposed to receiving it today, because money received today can be used to earn interest over the ensuing year. Thus, one year from now an investor can have the original £1 plus one year's interest on it. For example, if the interest rate is 10 per cent each £1 invested now will yield £1.10 one year from now. That is, £1 received today is equal to £1.10 one year from today at 10 per cent interest. Alternatively, £1 one year from today is equal to £0.9091 today, its present value, because £0.9091 plus 10 per cent interest for one year amounts to £1. The concept that £1 received in the future is not equal to £1 received today is known as the time value of money.

We shall now consider four different methods of appraising capital investments: the net present value, internal rate of return, accounting rate of return and payback methods. We shall see that the first two methods take into account the time value of money whereas the accounting rate of return and payback methods ignore this factor.

THE CONCEPT OF NET PRESENT VALUE

By using discounted cash flow techniques and calculating present values, we can compare the return on an investment in capital projects with an alternative equal risk investment in securities traded in the financial market. Suppose a firm is considering four projects (all of which are risk free) shown in Exhibit 13.2. You can see that each of the projects is identical with the investment in the risk-free security shown in Exhibit 13.1 because you can cash in this investment for £110 000 in year 1, £121 000 in year 2, £133 100 in year 3 and £146 410 in year 4. In other words, your potential cash receipts from the risk-free security are identical to the net cash flows for projects A, B, C and D shown in Exhibit 13.2. Consequently, the firm should be indifferent as to whether it uses the funds to invest in the projects or invests the funds in securities of identical risk traded in the financial markets.

The most straightforward way of determining whether a project yields a return in excess of the alternative equal risk investment in traded securities is to calculate the net present value (NPV). This is

EXHIBIT 13.2 Evaluation of four risk-free projects

	A (£)	B (£)	C (£)	D (£)
Project investment outlay	100 000	100 000	100 000	100 000
End of year cash flows:				
Year 1	110 000	0	0	0
2	0	121 000	0	0
3	0	0	133 100	0
4	0	0	0	146 410
present value =	$\dfrac{110\,000}{1.10}$	$\dfrac{121\,000}{(1.10)^2}$	$\dfrac{133\,100}{(1.10)^3}$	$\dfrac{146\,410}{(1.10)^4}$
	= 100 000	= 100 000	= 100 000	= 100 000

the present value of the net cash inflows less the project's initial investment outlay. If the rate of return from the project is greater than the return from an equivalent risk investment in securities traded in the financial market, the NPV will be positive. Alternatively, if the rate of return is lower, the NPV will be negative. A positive NPV therefore indicates that an investment should be accepted, while a negative value indicates that it should be rejected. A zero NPV calculation indicates that the firm should be indifferent to whether the project is accepted or rejected.

You can see that the present value of each of the projects shown in Exhibit 13.2 is £100 000. You should now deduct the investment cost of £100 000 to calculate the project's NPV. The NPV for each project is zero. The firm should therefore be indifferent to whether it accepts any of the projects or invests the funds in an equivalent risk-free security. This was our conclusion when we compared the cash flows of the projects with the investments in a risk-free security shown in Exhibit 13.1.

You can see that it is better for the firm to invest in any of the projects shown in Exhibit 13.2 if their initial investment outlays are less than £100 000. This is because we have to pay £100 000 to obtain an equivalent stream of cash flows from a security traded in the financial markets. Conversely, we should reject the investment in the projects if their initial investment outlays are greater than £100 000. You should now see that the NPV rule leads to a direct comparison of a project with an equivalent risk security traded in the financial market. Given that the present value of the net cash inflows for each project is £100 000, their NPVs will be positive (thus signifying acceptance) if the initial investment outlay is less than £100 000, and negative (thus signifying rejection) if the initial outlay is greater than £100 000.

CALCULATING NET PRESENT VALUES

You should now have an intuitive understanding of the NPV rule. We shall now learn how to calculate NPVs. The NPV can be expressed as:

$$NPV = \frac{FV_1}{1 + K} + \frac{FV_2}{(1 + K)^2} + \frac{FV_3}{(1 + K)^3} + \cdots + \frac{FV_n}{(1 + K)^n} - I_0 \tag{13.3}$$

where I_0 represents the investment outlay and FV represents the future values received in years 1 to n. The rate of return K used is the return available on an equivalent risk security in the financial market. Consider the situation in Example 13.1.

EXAMPLE 13.1

The Bothnia Company is evaluating two projects with an expected life of three years and an investment outlay of £1 million. The estimated net cash inflows for each project are as follows:

	Project A (£)	Project B (£)
Year 1	300 000	600 000
Year 2	1 000 000	600 000
Year 3	400 000	600 000

The opportunity cost of capital for both projects is 10 per cent. You are required to calculate the net present value for each project.

The net present value calculation for Project A is:

$$NPV = \frac{£300\,000}{(1.10)} + \frac{£1\,000\,000}{(1.10)^2} + \frac{£400\,000}{(1.10)^3} - £1\,000\,000 = +£399\,700$$

Alternatively, the net present value can be calculated by referring to a published table of present values. You will find examples of such a table if you refer to Appendix A (see page 737). To use the table, simply find the discount factors by referring to each year of the cash flows and the appropriate interest rate.

For example, if you refer to year 1 in Appendix A, and the 10 per cent column, this will show a discount factor of 0.909. For years 2 and 3, the discount factors are 0.826 and 0.751. You then multiply the cash flows by the discount factors to find the present value of the cash flows. The calculation is as follows:

Year	Amount (£000s)	Discount factor	Present value (£)
1	300	0.9091	272 730
2	1 000	0.8264	826 400
3	400	0.7513	300 520
			1 399 650
		Less initial outlay	1 000 000
		Net present value	399 650

In order to reconcile the NPV calculations derived from formula 13.3 and the discount tables, the discount factors used in this chapter are based on four decimal places. Normally, the factors given in Appendix A based on three decimal places will suffice. The difference between the two calculations shown above is due to rounding differences.

Note that the discount factors in the present value table are based on £1 received in n years time calculated according to the present value formula (equation 13.2). For example, £1 received in years 1, 2 and 3 when the interest rate is 10 per cent is calculated (based on four decimal places) as follows:

$$Year\ 1 = £1/1.10 = 0.9091$$
$$Year\ 2 = £1(1.10)^2 = 0.8264$$
$$Year\ 3 = £1(1.10)^3 = 0.7513$$

The positive net present value from the investment indicates the increase in the market value of the shareholders' funds which should occur once the stock market becomes aware of the acceptance of the project. The net present value also represents the potential increase in present consumption that the project makes available to the ordinary shareholders, after any funds used have been repaid with interest. For example, assume that the firm finances the investment of £1 million in Example 13.1 by borrowing £1 399 700 at 10 per cent and repays the loan and interest out of the project's proceeds as they occur. You can see from the repayment schedule in Exhibit 13.3 that £399 700 received from the loan is available for current consumption, and the remaining £1 000 000 can be invested in the project. The cash flows from the project are just sufficient to repay the loan. Therefore, acceptance of the project enables the ordinary shareholders' present consumption to be increased by the net present value of £399 700. Hence the acceptance of all available projects with a positive net present value should lead to the maximization of shareholders' wealth.

We shall now calculate the net present value for Project B shown in Example 13.1. The cash flows for project B represent an annuity. An annuity is an asset that pays a fixed sum each period for a specific number of periods. You can see for project B that the cash flows are £600 000 per annum for three years. When the annual cash flows are equivalent to an annuity, the calculation of net present value is simplified. The discount factors for an annuity are set out in Appendix B (see page 738). We need to find

EXHIBIT 13.3 The pattern of cash flows assuming that the loan is repaid out of the proceeds of the project

Year	Loan outstanding at start of year (1) (£)	Interest at 10% (2) (£)	Total amount owed before repayment (3) = (1) + (2) (£)	Proceeds from project (4) (£)	Loan outstanding at year end (5) = (3) − (4) (£)
1	1 399 700	139 970	1 539 670	300 000	1 239 670
2	1 239 670	123 967	1 363 637	1 000 000	363 637
3	363 637	36 363	400 000	400 000	0

the discount factor for 10 per cent for three years. If you refer to Appendix B, you will see that it is 2.487. The NPV is calculated as follows:

Annual cash inflow	Discount factor	Present value (£)
£600 000	2.487	1 492 200
	Less investment cost	1 000 000
	Net present value	492 200

You will see that the total present value for the period is calculated by multiplying the cash inflow by the discount factor. It is important to note that the annuity tables shown in Appendix B can only be applied when the annual cash flows are the same each year. Annuities are also based on the assumption that cash flows for the first period are received at the end of the period, and not at the start of the period, and that all subsequent cash flows are received at the end of each period. Note that the discount factors shown in Appendix B are derived from the following formula for an annuity:

$$\text{Present value} = \frac{A}{r}\left(1 - \frac{1}{(1+r)^n}\right) \qquad (13.4)$$

where A is the annuity amount and r (also denoted by K) is the interest/discount rate per period.

Therefore, the annuity factor for the present value for £1 received in each of three periods at a cost of capital (discount rate) of 10 per cent is:

$$\text{PV} = \frac{£1}{0.10}\left(1 - \frac{1}{(1+0.10)^3}\right) = 10\,(0.24868) = 2.847$$

Sometimes, to simplify the calculations, examination questions are set based on the assumption that constant cash flows occur into perpetuity (i.e. for a very long time, typically over 50 years). In this situation, the present value is determined by dividing the cash flow by the discount rate. For example, the present value of a cash flow of £100 per annum into perpetuity at a discount rate of 10 per cent is £1000 (£100/0.10). Again, the present value calculation is based on the assumption that the first cash flow is received one period hence.

THE INTERNAL RATE OF RETURN

The **internal rate of return (IRR)** is an alternative technique for use in making capital investment decisions that also takes into account the time value of money. The internal rate of return represents the true interest rate earned on an investment over the course of its economic life. This measure is sometimes referred to as the **discounted rate of return**. The internal rate of return is the interest rate

K that when used to discount all cash flows resulting from an investment, will equate the present value of the cash receipts to the present value of the cash outlays. In other words, it is the discount rate that will cause the net present value of an investment to be zero. Alternatively, the internal rate of return can be described as the maximum cost of capital that can be applied to finance a project without causing harm to the shareholders. The internal rate of return is found by solving for the value of *K* from the following formula:

$$I_0 = \frac{FV_1}{1 + K} + \frac{FV_2}{(1 + K)^2} + \frac{FV_3}{(1 + K)^3} + \cdots + \frac{FV_n}{(1 + K)^n} \tag{13.5}$$

It is easier, however, to use the discount tables. Let us now calculate the internal rate of return (using discount factors based on four decimal places) for Project A in Example 13.1.

The IRR can be found by trial and error by using a number of discount factors until the NPV equals zero. For example, if we use a 25 per cent discount factor, we get a positive NPV of £84 800. We must therefore try a higher figure. Applying 35 per cent gives a negative NPV of £66 530. We know then that the NPV will be zero somewhere between 25 per cent and 35 per cent. In fact, the IRR is between 30 per cent and 31 per cent but closest to 30 per cent, as indicated by the following calculation:

Year	Net cash flow (£)	Discount factor (30%)	Present value of cash flow (£)
1	300 000	0.7692	230 760
2	1 000 000	0.5917	591 700
3	400 000	0.4552	182 080
		Net present value	1 004 540
		Less initial outlay	1 000 000
		Net present value	4 540

It is claimed that the calculation of the IRR does not require the prior specification of the cost of capital. The decision rule is that if the IRR is greater than the opportunity cost of capital, the investment is profitable and will yield a positive NPV. Alternatively, if the IRR is less than the cost of capital, the investment is unprofitable and will result in a negative NPV. Therefore any interpretation of the significance of the IRR will still require that we estimate the cost of capital. The calculation of the IRR is illustrated in Figure 13.2.

The dots in the graph represent the NPV at different discount rates. The point where the line joining the dots cuts the horizontal axis indicates the IRR (the point at which the NPV is zero). Figure 13.2 indicates that the IRR is approximately 30 per cent, and you can see from this diagram that the interpolation method can be used to calculate the IRR without carrying out trial-and-error calculations. When we use interpolation, we infer the missing term (in this case the discount rate at which NPV is zero) from a known series of numbers. For example, at a discount rate of 25 per cent the NPV is +£84 800 and for a discount rate of 35 per cent the NPV is −£66 530. The total distance between these points is £151 330 (+£84 800 and −£66 530). The calculation for the approximate IRR is therefore:

$$25\% + \frac{84\,800}{151\,330} \times (35\% - 25\%) = 30.60\%$$

In other words, if you move down line A in Figure 13.2 from a discount rate of 25 per cent by £84 800, you will reach the point at which NPV is zero. The distance between the two points on line A is £151 330, and we are given the discount rates of 25 per cent and 35 per cent for these points. Therefore 84 800/151 330 represents the distance that we must move between these two points for the NPV to be zero. This distance in terms of the discount rate is 5.60 per cent [(84 800/151 330) × 10 per cent], which,

FIGURE 13.2

Interpretation of the internal rate of return

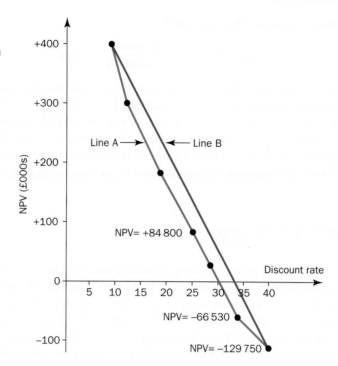

when added to the starting point of 25 per cent, produces an IRR of 30.60 per cent. The formula using the interpolation method is as follows:

$$A + \frac{C}{C - D}(B - A) \tag{13.6}$$

where A is the discount rate of the low trial, B is the discount rate of the high trial, C is the NPV of cash inflow of the low trial and D is the NPV of cash inflow of the high trial. Thus:

$$25\% + \left[\frac{84\,800}{84\,800 - (-66\,530)} \times 10\% \right]$$

$$= 25\% + \left[\frac{84\,800}{151\,300} \times 10\% \right]$$

$$= 30.60\%$$

Note that the interpolation method only gives an approximation of the IRR. The greater the distance between any two points that have a positive and a negative NPV, the less accurate is the IRR calculation. Consider line B in Figure 13.2. The point where it cuts the horizontal axis is approximately 33 per cent, whereas the actual IRR is 30.60 per cent.

The calculation of the IRR is easier when the cash flows are of a constant amount each year. Let us now calculate the internal rate of return for project B in Example 13.1. Because the cash flows are equal each year, we can use the annuity table in Appendix B. When the cash flows are discounted at the IRR, the NPV will be zero. The IRR will therefore be at the point at which:

$$[\text{annual cash flow}] \times \left[\begin{array}{c} \text{discount factor for number of years} \\ \text{for which cash flow is received} \end{array} \right] - \left[\begin{array}{c} \text{investment} \\ \text{cost} \end{array} \right] = 0$$

Rearranging this formula, the internal rate of return will be at the point at which:

$$\text{Discount factor} = \frac{\text{investment cost}}{\text{annual cash flow}}$$

Substituting the figures for project B in Example 13.1:

$$\text{Discount factor} = \frac{£1\,000\,000}{£600\,000} = 1.666$$

We now examine the entries for the year 3 row in Appendix B to find the figures closest to 1.666. They are 1.673 (entered in the 36 per cent column) and 1.652 (entered in the 37 per cent column). We can therefore conclude that the IRR is between 36 per cent and 37 per cent. However, because the cost of capital is 10 per cent, an accurate calculation is unnecessary; the IRR is far in excess of the cost of capital. The calculation of the IRR can be rather tedious (as the cited examples show), but the trial-and-error approach can be programmed for fast and accurate solution by a computer or calculator.

RELEVANT CASH FLOWS

Investment decisions, like all other decisions, should be analysed in terms of the cash flows that can be directly attributable to them. These cash flows should include the incremental cash flows that will occur in the future following acceptance of the investment. The cash flows will include cash inflows and outflows, or the inflows may be represented by savings in cash outflows. For example, a decision to purchase new machinery may generate cash savings in the form of reduced out-of-pocket operating costs. For all practical purposes, such cost savings are equivalent to cash receipts.

It is important to note that depreciation is not included in the cash flow estimates for capital investment decisions, since it is a non-cash expense. This is because the capital investment cost of the asset to be depreciated is included as a cash outflow at the start of the project and depreciation is merely a financial accounting method for allocating past capital costs to future accounting periods. Any inclusion of depreciation will lead to double-counting.

REAL WORLD VIEWS 13.2

The results of a prefeasibility study by Ironveld plc in South Africa

The *Africa Research Bulletin* reported the results of a prefeasibility study by Ironveld plc stating that the grades for pig iron and ferro vanadium were better than expected at its project on the Northern Limb of the Bushveld Complex in South Africa. The prefeasibility study demonstrated the viability of developing the Ironveld pig-iron project delivering 1 Mt/y of pig iron and 9670 t/y of ferro vanadium production for 25 years starting from 2019. The capital cost of the project is estimated at about US$938 million. The prefeasibility study estimated a post-tax internal rate of return of 28.8 per cent and a net present value of US$1.07 billion, assuming a 10 per cent discount rate. The prefeasibility study was based on pig-iron prices of US$450/t and US$35/kg for ferro vanadium, yielding total annual revenue of R6500 million (US$657 million) at full production.

Questions

1 Why has the company used both net present value and internal rate of return, but ignored the payback, when undertaking the prefeasibility study?

2 What steps can the company take to ensure that there is less likelihood that incorrect estimates will result in the project not having an acceptable net present value and internal rate of return?

Reference

Iron Ore: South Africa (2013) Africa Research Bulletin: Economic, Financial and Technical Series, 50(5): 19999B–20000A. Available at onlinelibrary.wiley.com /doi/10.1111/j.1467-6346.2013.05209.x/pdf

TIMING OF CASH FLOWS

To simplify the presentation our calculations have been based on the assumption that any cash flows in future years will occur in one lump sum at the year end. Obviously, this is an unrealistic assumption, since cash flows are likely to occur at various times throughout the year, and a more realistic assumption is to assume that cash flows occur at the end of each month and use monthly discount rates. Typically, discount and interest rates are quoted as rates per annum using the term annual percentage rate (APR). Discount tables, such as those provided in the appendix at the end of this book also assume that cash flows occur in one lump sum at the end of the year. If you wish to use monthly discount rates it is necessary to convert annual discount rates to monthly rates. An approximation of the monthly discount rate can be obtained by dividing the annual rate by 12. However, this simplified calculation ignores the compounding effect whereby each monthly interest payment is reinvested to earn more interest each month. To convert the annual discount rate to a monthly discount rate that takes into account the compounding effect we must use the following formula:

$$\text{Monthly discount rate} = (_{12}\sqrt{1 + APR}) - 1 \qquad (13.7)$$

Assume that the annual percentage discount rate is 12.68 per cent. Applying formula 13.7 gives a monthly discount rate of:

$$(_{12}\sqrt{1.1268}) - 1 = 1.01 - 1 = .01 \text{ (i.e. 1 per cent per month)}.$$

Therefore the monthly cash flows would be discounted at 1 per cent. In other words, 1 per cent compounded monthly is equivalent to 12.68 per cent compounded annually. Formula 13.2 can be used to ascertain the present value using monthly discount rates with k denoting the monthly discount rate and n denoting the number of months. Note that the monthly discount rates can also be converted to annual percentage rates using the formula:

$$(1 + k)^{12} - 1 \text{ (where } k = \text{the monthly discount rate)} \qquad (13.8)$$

Assuming a monthly rate of 1 per cent the annual rate is $(1.01)^{12} - 1 = 0.1268$ (i.e. 12.68 per cent per annum). Instead of using formulae (13.7) and (13.8), you can divide the annual percentage rate by 12 to obtain an approximation of the monthly discount rate or multiply the monthly discount rate by 12 to approximate the annual percentage rate.

COMPARISON OF NET PRESENT VALUE AND INTERNAL RATE OF RETURN

In many situations the internal rate of return method will result in the same decision as the net present value method. In the case of conventional projects (in which an initial cash outflow is followed by a series of cash inflows) that are independent of each other (i.e. where the selection of a particular project does not preclude the choice of the other), both NPV and IRR rules will lead to the same accept/reject decisions. However, there are also situations where the IRR method may lead to different decisions being made from those that would follow the adoption of the NPV procedure.

Mutually exclusive projects

Where projects are mutually exclusive, it is possible for the NPV and the IRR methods to suggest different rankings as to which project should be given priority. Mutually exclusive projects exist where the acceptance of one project excludes the acceptance of another project, for example the choice of one of several possible factory locations, or the choice of one of many different possible machines.

When evaluating mutually exclusive projects, the IRR method can incorrectly rank projects, because of its reinvestment assumptions, and, in these circumstances, it is recommended, that the NPV method is used.

Percentage returns

Another problem with the IRR rule is that it expresses the result as a percentage rather than in monetary terms. Comparison of percentage returns can be misleading; for example, compare an investment of £10 000 that yields a return of 50 per cent with an investment of £100 000 that yields a return of 25 per cent. If only one of the investments can be undertaken, the first investment will yield £5000 but the second will yield £25 000. If we assume that the cost of capital is 10 per cent, and that no other suitable investments are available, any surplus funds will be invested at the cost of capital (i.e. the returns available from equal risk securities traded in financial markets). Choosing the first investment will leave a further £90 000 to be invested, but this can only be invested at 10 per cent, yielding a return of £9000. Adding this to the return of £5000 from the £10 000 investment gives a total return of £14 000. Clearly, the second investment, which yields a return of £25 000, is preferable. Thus, if the objective is to maximize the shareholders' wealth then NPV provides the correct measure.

Reinvestment assumptions

The assumption concerning the reinvestment of interim cash flows from the acceptance of projects provides another reason for supporting the superiority of the NPV method. The implicit assumption if the NPV method is adopted is that the cash flows generated from an investment will be reinvested immediately at the cost of capital (i.e. the returns available from equal risk securities traded in financial markets). However, the IRR method makes a different implicit assumption about the reinvestment of the cash flows. It assumes that all the proceeds from a project can be reinvested immediately to earn a return equal to the IRR of the original project. This assumption is likely to be unrealistic because a firm should have accepted all projects that offer a return in excess of the cost of capital and any other funds that become available can only be reinvested at the cost of capital. This is the assumption that is implicit in the NPV rule.

Unconventional cash flows

Where a project has unconventional cash flows, the IRR has a technical shortcoming. Most projects have conventional cash flows that consist of an initial negative cash flow followed by positive cash inflows in later years. In this situation, the algebraic sign changes, being negative at the start and positive in all future periods. If the sign of the net cash flows changes in successive periods, it is possible for the calculations to produce as many internal rates of return as there are sign changes. While multiple rates of return are mathematically possible, only one rate of return is economically significant in determining whether or not the investment is profitable.

Fortunately, the majority of investment decisions consist of conventional cash flows that produce a single IRR calculation. However, the problem cannot be ignored, since unconventional cash flows are possible (such as open cast mining where cash outflows occur at the end of the project arising from the need to rectify the land after mining) and, if the decision-maker is unaware of the situation, serious errors may occur at the decision-making stage. Example 13.2 illustrates a situation where two internal rates of return occur.

You will find that the cash flows in Example 13.2 give internal rates of return of 5 per cent and 50 per cent. The effect of multiple rates of return on the NPV calculations is illustrated in Figure 13.3. When the cost of capital is between 5 per cent and 50 per cent, the NPV is positive and, following the NPV rule, the project should be accepted. However, if the IRR calculation of 5 per cent is used, the project may be incorrectly rejected if the cost of capital is in excess of 5 per cent. You can see that the graph of

EXAMPLE 13.2

The Bothnia Company has the following series of cash flows for a specific project:

Year 0	−£400 000 (Investment outlay)
Year 1	+£1 020 000 (Net cash inflows)
Year 2	−£630 000 (Environmental and disposal costs)

You are required to calculate the internal rate of return.

FIGURE 13.3
Net present values for
unconventional cash flows

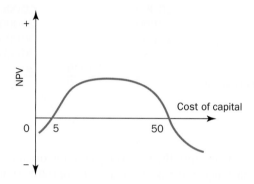

the NPV in Figure 13.3 indicates that this is an incorrect decision when the cost of capital is between 5 per cent and 50 per cent. Alternatively, if the IRR of 50 per cent is used, this will lead to the same decision being made as if the NPV rule were adopted, provided that the cost of capital is greater than 5 per cent.

TECHNIQUES THAT IGNORE THE TIME VALUE OF MONEY

In addition to those methods that take into account the time value of money, two other methods that ignore this factor are frequently used in practice. These are the payback method and the accounting rate of return method. Methods that ignore the time value of money are theoretically weak and they will not necessarily lead to the maximization of the market value of ordinary shares. Nevertheless, the fact that they are frequently used in practice means that we should be aware of these techniques and their limitations.

PAYBACK METHOD

The **payback method** is one of the simplest and most frequently used methods of capital investment appraisal. It is defined as the length of time that is required for a stream of cash proceeds from an investment to recover the original cash outlay required by the investment. If the stream of cash flows from the investment is constant each year, the payback period can be calculated by dividing the total initial cash outlay by the amount of the expected annual cash proceeds. Therefore, if an investment requires an initial outlay of £60 000 and is expected to produce annual cash inflows of £20 000 per year for five years, the payback period will be £60 000 divided by £20 000, or three years. If the stream of expected proceeds is not constant from year to year, the payback period is determined by adding up the cash

EXAMPLE 13.3

The cash flows and NPV calculations for two projects are as follows:

	Project A		Project B	
	(£)	(£)	(£)	(£)
Initial cost		50 000		50 000
Net cash inflows				
Year 1	10 000		10 000	
Year 2	20 000		10 000	
Year 3	20 000		10 000	
Year 4	20 000		20 000	
Year 5	10 000		30 000	
Year 6	—		30 000	
Year 7	—	80 000	30 000	140 000
NPV at a 10 per cent cost of capital		10 500		39 460

inflows expected in successive years until the total is equal to the original outlay. Example 13.3 illustrates two projects, A and B, that require the same initial outlay of £50 000 but that display different time profiles of benefits.

In Example 13.3, project A pays back its initial investment cost in three years, whereas project B pays back its initial cost in four years. Therefore, project A would be ranked in preference to project B because it has a faster payback period. However, project B has a higher NPV, and the payback method incorrectly ranks project A in preference to project B. Two obvious deficiencies are apparent from these calculations. First, the payback method does not take into account cash flows that are earned after the payback period and, second, it fails to take into account the differences in the timing of the proceeds that are earned before the payback period. Payback computations ignore the important fact that future cash receipts cannot be validly compared with an initial outlay until they are discounted to their present values. Not only does the payback period incorrectly rank project A in preference to project B, but the method can also result in the acceptance of projects that have a negative NPV. Consider the cash flows for project C in Example 13.4.

The payback period for project C is three years and if this were within the time limit set by management, the project would be accepted in spite of its negative NPV. Note also that the payback method would rank project C in preference to project B in Example 13.3, in spite of the fact that B would yield a positive NPV.

The payback period can only be a valid indicator of the time that an investment requires to pay for itself, if all cash flows are first discounted to their present values and the discounted values are then used to calculate the payback period. This adjustment gives rise to what is known as the adjusted or discounted payback method. Even when such an adjustment is made, the adjusted payback method cannot be a complete measure of an investment's profitability. It can estimate whether an investment is likely to be profitable, but it cannot estimate how profitable the investment will be.

Despite the theoretical limitations of the payback method, it is widely used in practice (see Exhibit 13.4). Why, then, is payback a widely applied formal investment appraisal technique? It is a particularly useful approach for ranking projects where a firm faces liquidity constraints and requires a fast repayment of investments. The payback method may also be appropriate in situations where risky

REAL WORLD VIEWS 13.3

Payback method – payback from domestic wind and solar energy

Increasingly, householders and small businesses are considering renewable power generation systems to decrease their costs. Most of the UK, Ireland and Scandinavia are suited to generating energy from wind, whereas more central European countries tend to opt for solar power. While larger businesses typically appraise all investments using solid techniques and criteria, smaller businesses (and households) do not have either the knowledge or resources to do a full investment appraisal.

For wind energy generation, an investment outlay is necessary. This may range from a few thousand pounds for a small domestic type wind turbine to about £70000 for a 15kW turbine capable of meeting the power requirements of a small farm or office complex. In terms of measuring whether an investment is worthwhile, the typical evaluation method used is the payback period. Most suppliers of wind turbines provide payback calculators on their websites. The UK's Energy Saving Trust also provides such a tool (see the link below). According to its calculator a

wind turbine rated with a 15kW generation capability, assuming 75 per cent of the power is sold to the national grid will have a lifetime benefit of just over £81000 at 2016 rates. If the cost is £70000, the net gain is thus £11000, giving a payback period of about 17 years assuming a 20-year lifespan.

Questions

1 What might affect the payback calculations on wind energy investments for a business and/or a household?

2 In making a decision, should the business or householder look beyond the payback period?

References

Energy Saving Trust (2016) Cashback calculator. Available at www.nonpvfitcalculator.energysavingtrust.org.uk/, accessed 20 November, 2016.
The Renewable Energy Hub, www.renewableenergyhub.co.uk/wind-turbines/how-much-does-wind-turbines-cost.html, accessed 20 November, 2016.

EXAMPLE 13.4

The cash flows and NPV calculation for project C are as follows:

	(£)	(£)
Initial cost		50000
Net cash inflows		
Year 1	10000	
Year 2	20000	
Year 3	20000	
Year 4	3500	
Year 5	3500	
Year 6	3500	
Year 7	3500	64000
NPV (at 10 per cent cost of capital)		(−1036)

EXHIBIT 13.4 Surveys of practice

A survey by Brounen, de Jong and Koedijk (2004) in mainland Europe reported that the usage of the payback method was 65 per cent in the Netherlands, 50 per cent in Germany and 51 per cent in France. NPV was used by 70 per cent of the German respondents compared with 56 per cent using IRR. Usage of IRR exceeded that of NPV in both the Netherlands and France. A more recent survey based on 439 respondents (60 per cent UK and 40 per cent non-UK) by the Chartered Institute of Management Accountants (2009) reported that net present value was used by 62 per cent of the companies surveyed, followed by 55 per cent using payback, 42 per cent using internal rate of return, 34 per cent using discounted payback and 18 per cent using accounting rate of return. The larger companies used all of the appraisal techniques to a greater extent than the smaller companies.

investments are made in uncertain markets that are subject to fast design and product changes or where future cash flows are extremely difficult to predict. The payback method assumes that risk is time related: the longer the period, the greater the chance of failure. By concentrating on the early cash flows, payback uses data in which managers have greater confidence. Thus, the payback period can be used as a rough measure of risk, based on the assumption that the longer it takes for a project to pay for itself, the riskier it is. Managers may also choose projects with quick payback periods because of self-interest. If a manager's performance is measured using short-term criteria, such as net profits, there is a danger that he or she may choose projects with quick paybacks to show improved net profits as soon as possible. The payback method is also frequently used in conjunction with the NPV or IRR methods. It serves as a simple first-level screening device that identifies those projects that should be subject to more rigorous investigation. A further attraction of payback is that it is easily understood by all levels of management and provides an important summary measure: how quickly will the project recover its initial outlay? Ideally, the payback method should be used in conjunction with the NPV method, and the cash flows discounted before the payback period is calculated.

REAL WORLD VIEWS 13.4

Appraising water irrigation systems

The globe is facing an increase in water demand resulting in the need for additional agricultural land and irrigation water. Elyamany and El-Nashar (2013) provided an illustration of a financial appraisal of four alternative methods of water irrigation in Egypt. They were a traditional system of open canals which allow a high percentage of water dissipation and evaporation, a pipeline with one pump at the canal head, a pipeline with one pump at the head and one pump at the middle, and a lined open canal. Three appraisal methods were used to evaluate the alternatives. They were NPV, IRR and the payback method. All three methods provide the same conclusion and support the

decision that the best design alternative was one pump at the intake of the canal.

Questions

1 Can you provide some examples of the costs and benefits that would be included in the investment appraisal?

2 What are the disadvantages of using IRR and payback to evaluate the above alternatives?

Reference
Elnashar, W. and Elyamany, A.H. (2013), 'Estimating Life Cycle Cost of Improved Field Irrigation Canal', *Water Resource Management*, 30, 99–113

ACCOUNTING RATE OF RETURN

The accounting rate of return (also known as the return on investment and return on capital employed) is calculated by dividing the average annual profits from a project into the average investment cost. It differs from other methods in that profits rather than cash flows are used. Assuming that depreciation represents the only non-cash expense, profit is equivalent to cash flows less depreciation. The use of accounting rate of return can be attributed to the wide use of the return on investment measure in financial statement analysis.

When the average annual net profits are calculated, only additional revenues and costs that follow from the investment are included in the calculation. The average annual net profit is therefore calculated by dividing the difference between incremental revenues and costs by the estimated life of the investment. The incremental costs include either the *net* investment cost or the total depreciation charges, these figures being identical. The average investment figure that is used in the calculation depends on the method employed to calculate depreciation. If straight line depreciation is used, it is presumed that investment will decline in a linear fashion as the asset ages. The average investment under this assumption is one-half of the amount of the initial investment plus one-half of the scrap value at the end of the project's life (see note 1 at the end of the chapter for an explanation).

For example, the three projects described in Examples 13.3 and 13.4 for which the payback period was computed, required an initial outlay of £50 000. If we assume that the projects have no scrap values and that straight line depreciation is used, the average investment for each project will be £25 000. The calculation of the accounting rate of return for each of these projects is as follows:

$$\text{accounting rate of return} = \frac{\text{average annual profits}}{\text{average investment}}$$

$$\text{Project A} = \frac{6\,000}{25\,000} = 24\%$$

$$\text{Project B} = \frac{12\,857}{25\,000} = 51\%$$

$$\text{Project C} = \frac{2\,000}{25\,000} = 8\%$$

For project A the total profit over its five-year life is £30 000 (£80 000 − £50 000), giving an average annual profit of £6000. The average annual profits for projects B and C are calculated in a similar manner.

It follows that the accounting rate of return is superior to the payback method in one respect; that is, it allows for differences in the useful lives of the assets being compared. For example, the calculations set out above reflect the high earnings of project B over the whole life of the project, and consequently it is ranked in preference to project A. Also, projects A and C have the same payback periods, but the accounting rate of return correctly indicates that project A is preferable to project C.

However, the accounting rate of return suffers from the serious defect that it ignores the time value of money. When the method is used in relation to a project where the cash inflows do not occur until near the end of its life, it will show the same accounting rate of return as it would for a project where the cash inflows occur early in its life, providing that the average cash inflows are the same. For this reason, the accounting rate of return cannot be recommended. Nevertheless, the accounting rate of return is used in practice (see Exhibit 13.4). This is probably due to the fact that the annual accounting rate of return is frequently used to measure the managerial performance of different business units within a company. Therefore, managers are likely to be interested in how any new investment contributes to the business unit's overall accounting rate of return.

THE EFFECT OF PERFORMANCE MEASUREMENT ON CAPITAL INVESTMENT DECISIONS

The way that the performance of a manager is measured is likely to have a profound effect on the decisions he or she will make. There is a danger that, because of the way performance is measured, a manager may be motivated to take the wrong decision and not follow the NPV rule. Consider the information presented in Exhibit 13.5 in respect of the net cash inflows and the annual reported profits or losses for projects J and K. The figures without the parentheses refer to the cash inflows whereas the figures within the parentheses refer to annual reported profit. You will see that the total cash inflows over the five-year lives for projects J and K are £11 million and £5 million respectively. Both projects require an initial outlay of £5 million. Assuming a cost of capital of 10 per cent, without undertaking any calculations it is clear that project J will have a positive NPV and project K will have a negative NPV.

If the straight line method of depreciation is used, the annual depreciation for both projects will be £1 million (£5 million investment cost/five years). Therefore the reported profits (shown in parentheses) are derived from deducting the annual depreciation charge from the annual net cash inflows. For decision-making the focus is on the entire life of the projects. Our objective is to ascertain whether the present value of the cash inflows exceeds the present value of the cash outflows over the entire life of a project, and not allocate the NPV to different accounting periods as indicated by the dashed vertical lines in Exhibit 13.5. In other words, we require an answer to this question: Will the project add value?

In contrast, a company is required to report on its performance externally at annual intervals and managerial performance is also often evaluated on an annual or more frequent basis. Evaluating managerial performance at the end of the five-year project lives is clearly too long a time scale since managers are unlikely to remain in the same job for such lengthy periods. Therefore, if a manager's performance is measured using short-term criteria, such as annual profits, he or she may choose projects that have a favourable impact on short-term financial performance. Because Project J will have a negative impact on performance in its early years (i.e. it contributes losses) there is a danger that a manager who is anxious to improve his or her short-term performance might reject project J even though it has a positive impact on the performance measure in the long-term.

The reverse may happen with project K. This has a favourable impact on the short-term profit performance measure in years one and two but a negative impact in the longer term so the manager might accept the project to improve his or her short-term performance measure.

EXHIBIT 13.5 Annual net cash inflows (profits/losses) for two projects each with an initial outlay of £5 million

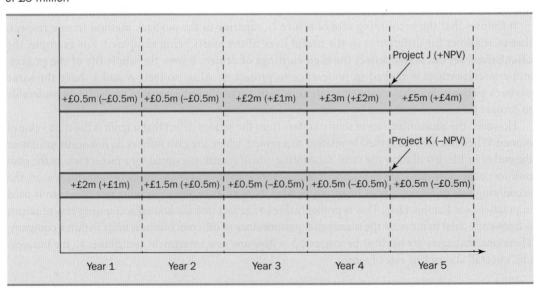

It is thus important to avoid an excessive focus on short-term profitability measures since this can have a negative impact on long-term profitability. Emphasis should also be given to measuring a manager's contribution to an organization's long-term objectives. These issues are discussed in Chapter 19 when we shall look at performance measurement in more detail. However, at this point you should note that the way in which managerial performance is measured will influence their decisions and may motivate them to work in their own best interests, even when this is not in the best interest of the organization.

QUALITATIVE FACTORS

Not all investment projects can be described completely in terms of monetary costs and benefits (e.g. expenditure on facilities for employees, or expenditure to avoid unpleasant environmental effects from the company's manufacturing process). There is a danger that those aspects of a new investment that are difficult to quantify may be omitted from the financial appraisal.

One approach that has been suggested for overcoming these difficulties is not to attempt to place a value on those benefits that are difficult to quantify. Instead, the process can be reversed by estimating how large these benefits must be in order to justify the proposed investment. Assume that a project with an estimated life of ten years and a cost of capital of 20 per cent has a negative NPV of £1 million. To achieve a positive NPV, or in other words to obtain the required rate of return of 20 per cent, additional cash flows would need to be achieved that when discounted at 20 per cent, would amount to at least £1 million. The project lasts for ten years, and the discount factor for an annuity over ten years at 20 per cent is 4.192. Therefore the additional cash flows from the benefits that have not been quantified must be greater than £238 550 per annum (note that £1 million divided by an annuity factor (Appendix B) for ten years at 20 per cent (4.192) equals £238 550) in order to justify the proposed investment. Discussions should then take place to consider whether benefits that have not been quantified, such as improved flexibility, rapid customer service, market adaptability and reduction in environmental impact are worth more than £238 550 per year.

Capital investment decisions are particularly difficult in non-profit organizations such as public sector organizations, since it is not always possible to quantify the costs and benefits of a project. Cost–benefit analysis (CBA) has been developed to resolve this problem. It is an investment appraisal technique for analysing and measuring the costs and benefits to the community arising from capital projects. CBA defines the costs and benefits in much wider terms than those that would be included in investment appraisals undertaken in the pursuit of profit maximization. For example, the application of CBA to an investment in a public transportation system would incorporate the benefits of the travelling time saved by users of the system.

SUMMARY

The following items relate to the learning objectives listed at the beginning of the chapter.

● **Explain the opportunity cost of an investment.**

The rates of return that are available from investments in financial markets in securities with different levels of risk (e.g. company shares, company and government bonds) represent the opportunity cost of an investment. In other words, if cash is invested in a capital project it cannot be invested elsewhere to earn a return. A firm should therefore only invest in projects that yield a return in excess of the opportunity cost of investment.

● **Distinguish between compounding and discounting.**

The process of converting cash invested today at a specific interest rate into a future value is known as compounding. Discounting is the opposite of compounding and refers to the process of converting cash to be received in the future into the value at the present time. The resulting present value is called the discounted present value.

● **Explain the concepts of net present value (NPV), internal rate of return (IRR), payback method and accounting rate of return (ARR).**

Both NPV and IRR are methods of determining whether a project yields a return in excess of an equal risk investment in traded financial securities. A positive NPV provides an absolute value of the amount by which an investment exceeds the return available from an alternative investment in financial securities of equal risk. Conversely, a negative value indicates the amount by which an investment fails to match an equal risk investment in financial securities. In contrast, the IRR indicates the true percentage return from an investment after taking into account the time value of money. To ascertain whether an investment should be undertaken, the percentage internal rate of return on investment should be compared with the returns available from investing in equal risk in financial securities. Investing in all projects that have positive NPVs or IRRs in excess of the opportunity cost of capital should maximize shareholder value. The payback method is the length of time that is required for a stream of cash proceeds from an investment to recover the original cash outflow required by the investment. The ARR expresses the annual average profits arising from a project as a percentage return on the average investment required for the project.

● **Calculate NPV, IRR, the payback period and ARR.**

The NPV is calculated by discounting the net cash inflows from a project and deducting the investment outlay. The IRR is calculated by ascertaining the discount rate that will cause the NPV of a project to be zero. The payback period is calculated by adding up the cash flows expected in successive years until the total is equal to the original outlay. The ARR is calculated by dividing the average annual profits estimated from a project by the average investment cost. The calculation of NPV and IRR was illustrated using Example 13.1 and Examples 13.3 and 13.4 were used to illustrate the calculations of the payback period and the ARR.

● **Justify the superiority of NPV over IRR.**

NPV is considered to be theoretically superior to IRR because: (a) unlike the NPV method the IRR method cannot be guaranteed to rank mutually exclusive projects correctly; (b) the percentage returns generated by the IRR method can be misleading when choosing between alternatives; (c) the IRR method makes incorrect reinvestment assumptions by assuming that the interim cash flows can be reinvested at the IRR rather than the cost of capital; and (d) where unconventional cash flows occur multiple IRRs are possible.

● **Explain the limitations of payback and ARR.**

The major limitations of the payback method are that it ignores the time value of money and it does not take into account the cash flows that are earned after the payback period. The ARR also fails to take into account the time value of money and relies on a percentage return rather than an absolute value.

● **Justify why the payback and ARR methods are widely used in practice.**

The payback method is frequently used in practice because (a) it is considered useful when firms face liquidity constraints and require a fast repayment of their investments; (b) it serves as a simple first-level screening device that identifies those projects that should be subject to more rigorous investigations; and (c) it provides a rough measure of risk, based on the assumption that the longer it takes for a project to pay for itself, the riskier it is. The ARR is a widely used financial accounting measure of managerial and company performance. Therefore, managers are likely to be interested in how any new investment contributes to the business unit's overall accounting rate of return.

● **Describe the effect of performance measurement on capital investment decisions.**

Managerial and company performance is normally evaluated using short-term financial criteria whereas investment appraisal decisions should be based on the cash flows over the whole life of the projects. Thus, the way that performance is evaluated can have a profound influence on investment decisions and there is a danger that managers will make decisions on the basis of an investment's impact on the short-term financial performance evaluation criteria rather than using the NPV decision rule.

NOTE

1 Consider a project that costs £10000 and has a life of four years and an estimated scrap value of £2000. The following diagram using straight line depreciation to calculate the written-down values (WDV) illustrates why the project's scrap value is added to the initial outlay to calculate the average capital employed. You can see that at the mid-point of the project's life the capital employed is equal to £6000 (i.e. ½ (10000 + £2000)).

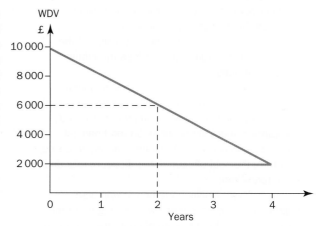

KEY TERMS AND CONCEPTS

Accounting rate of return A method of appraising capital investments where the average annual profits from a project are divided into the average investment cost, also known as return on investment and return on capital employed.

Annual percentage rate (APR) A discount or interest rate quoted as a rate per annum.

Annuity An asset that pays a fixed sum each period for a specific number of periods.

Compounding interest The concept of adding the interest earned to the original capital invested so that further interest is generated.

Cost of capital The financial return that an organization could receive if, instead of investing cash in a capital project, it invested the same amount in securities on the financial markets, also known as the opportunity cost of an investment, the minimum required rate of return, the discount rate and the interest rate.

Cost–benefit analysis (CBA) An investment appraisal technique developed for use by non-profit-making organizations that defines the costs and benefits of a project in much wider terms than those included in investment appraisals undertaken in the pursuit of profit maximization.

Discount rate The financial return that an organization could receive if, instead of investing cash in a capital project, it invested the same amount in securities on the financial markets, also known as the opportunity cost of an investment, the minimum required rate of return, the cost of capital and the interest rate.

Discounted cash flow (DCF) A technique used to compare returns on investments that takes account of the time value of money.

Discounted payback method A version of the payback method of appraising capital investments in which future cash flows are discounted to their present values.

Discounted present value The value today of cash to be received in the future, calculated by discounting.

Discounted rate of return A technique used to make capital investment decisions that takes into account the time value of money, representing the true interest rate earned on an investment over the course of its economic life, also known as internal rate of return (IRR).

Discounting The process of converting cash to be received in the future into a value at the present time by the use of an interest rate.

Interest rate The financial return that an organization could receive if, instead of investing cash in a capital project, it invested the same amount in securities on the financial markets, also known as the opportunity cost of an investment, the minimum required rate of return, the cost of capital and the discount rate.

Internal rate of return (IRR) A technique used to make capital investment decisions that takes into account the time value of money, representing the true interest rate earned on an investment over the course of its economic life, also known as discounted rate of return.

Minimum required rate of return The financial return that an organization could receive if, instead of investing cash in a capital project, it invested the same amount in securities on the financial markets, also known as the opportunity cost of an investment, the cost of capital, the discount rate and the interest rate.

Mutually exclusive In the context of comparing capital investments, a term used to describe projects where the acceptance of one project excludes the acceptance of another.

Net present value (NPV) The present value of the net cash inflows from a project less the initial investment outlay.

Opportunity cost of an investment The financial return that an organization could receive if, instead of investing cash in a capital project, it invested the same amount in securities on the financial markets, also known as the minimum required rate of return, the cost of capital, the discount rate and the interest rate.

Payback method A simple method to appraise capital investments, defined as the length of time that is required for a stream of cash proceeds from an investment to recover the original cash outlay.

Present value The value today of cash to be received in the future.

Return on capital employed A method of appraising capital investments where the average annual profits from a project are divided into the average investment cost, also known as the accounting rate of return and return on investment.

Return on investment A method of appraising capital investments where the average annual profits from a project are divided into the average investment cost, also known as the accounting rate of return and return on capital employed.

Risk-free gilt-edged securities Bonds issued by the UK government for set periods of time with fixed interest rates.

Time value of money The concept that a specific amount of cash is worth more now than it will be in the future.

RECOMMENDED READING

The financing of capital projects is normally part of a corporate finance course. If you wish to undertake further reading relating to the financing of capital investments, you should refer to Pike, Neale and Linsley (2015) or Brealey, Myers and Allen (2016).

KEY EXAMINATION POINTS

A common mistake is a failure to distinguish between relevant and irrelevant cash flows. Remember to include only incremental cash flows in a DCF analysis. Depreciation and reapportionments of overheads should not be included. If you are required to evaluate mutually exclusive projects, use NPV, since IRR can give incorrect rankings. Where IRR calculations are required, check that the cash flows are conventional. For unconventional cash flows, it is necessary to calculate more than one IRR. Normally, very accurate calculations of the IRR will not be required, and an approximate answer using the interpolation method should be appropriate.

Note that the examination questions set by the professional accountancy examining bodies normally provide you with the formulae for annuities for both present and future values. Sometimes examination questions require you to use formula 13.4, shown within the chapter, to determine the constant cash flow per period (i.e. the annuity amount) required to produce a given *present* value. You should refer to the answer to Review problem 13.22 for an illustration of how the annuity value is calculated. Examinations questions may also require you to use the annuity formula for *future* values, rather than the present value formula presented in the text. The following future value annuity formula is normally provided:

$$\text{Future value} = A \left(\frac{(1 + r)^n - 1}{r} \right)$$

where r (also denoted by k) is the rate of interest per period and A is the annuity amount.

Typical examination questions require you to calculate the future value of an annuity or the annuity value where the future value is given.

ASSESSMENT MATERIAL

The review questions are short questions that enable you to assess your understanding of the main topics included in the chapter. The numbers in parentheses provide you with the page numbers to refer to if you cannot answer a specific question.

The review problems are more complex and require you to relate and apply the content to various business problems. The problems are graded by their level of difficulty. Solutions to review problems that are not preceded by the term 'IM' are provided in a separate section at the end of the book. Solutions to problems preceded by the term 'IM' are provided in the Instructor's Manual accompanying this book that can be downloaded from the lecturer's digital support resources. Additional review problems with fully worked solutions are provided in the *Student Manual* that accompanies this book.

REVIEW QUESTIONS

13.1 What is meant by the opportunity cost of an investment? What role does it play in capital investment decisions? (p. 310)

13.2 Distinguish between compounding and discounting. (pp. 311–312)

13.3 Explain what is meant by the term 'time value of money'. (p. 312)

13.4 Describe the concept of net present value (NPV). (pp. 312–313)

13.5 Explain what is meant by the internal rate of return (IRR). (pp. 315–316)

13.6 Distinguish between independent and mutually exclusive projects. (pp. 319–320)

13.7 Explain the theoretical arguments for preferring NPV to IRR when choosing among mutually exclusive projects. (p. 320)

13.8 Why might managers choose to use IRR in preference to NPV? (p. 317)

13.9 Describe the payback method. What are its main strengths and weaknesses? (pp. 321–324)

13.10 Describe the accounting rate of return. What are its main strengths and weaknesses? (p. 325)

13.11 Distinguish between the payback method and discounted payback method. (pp. 321–322)

13.12 What impact can the way in which a manager's performance is measured have on capital investment decisions? (pp. 326–327)

REVIEW PROBLEMS

13.13 Intermediate. A company is considering investing in manufacturing equipment that has a three-year life. The purchase price of the equipment is $70 000 and at the end of the three-year period it will be sold for cash of $10 000. The equipment will be used to produce 6000 units each year of a product which earns a contribution per unit of $7. Incremental fixed costs are expected to be $12 000 per annum.

The company has a cost of capital of 8 per cent per annum. Ignore tax. and inflation.

Required:
Calculate the sensitivity of the investment decision to a change in the cost of capital. *(5 marks)*

CIMA P1 Performance Operations

13.14 Intermediate. Cab Co. owns and runs 350 taxis and had sales of $10 million in the last year. Cab Co. is considering introducing a new computerized taxi tracking system.

The expected costs and benefits of the new computerized tracking system are as follows:

(i) The system would cost $2 100 000 to implement.

(ii) Depreciation would be provided at $420 000 per annum.

(iii) $75 000 has already been spent on staff training in order to evaluate the potential of the new system. Further training costs of $425 000 would be required in the first year if the new system is implemented.

(iv) Sales are expected to rise to $11 million in year 1 if the new system is implemented, thereafter increasing by 5 per cent per annum. If the new system is not implemented, sales would be expected to increase by $200 000 per annum.

(v) Despite increased sales, savings in vehicle running costs are expected as a result of the new system. These are estimated at 1 per cent of total sales.

(vi) Six new members of staff would be recruited to manage the new system at a total cost of $120 000 per annum.

(vii) Cab Co. would have to take out a maintenance contract for the new system at a cost of $75 000 per annum for five years.

(viii) Interest on money borrowed to finance the project would cost $150 000 per annum.

(ix) Cab Co.'s cost of capital is 10 per cent per annum.

Required:

(a) State whether each of the following items are relevant or irrelevant cashflows for a net present value (NPV) evaluation of whether to introduce the computerized tracking system.

(i) Computerized tracking system investment of $2 100 000;

(ii) Depreciation of $420 000 in each of the five years;

(iii) Staff training costs of $425 000;

(iv) New staff total salary of $120 000 per annum;

(v) Staff training costs of $75 000;

(vi) Interest cost of $150 000 per annum. *(5 marks)*

(b) Calculate the following values if the computerized tracking system is implemented.

(i) Incremental sales in year 1;

(ii) Savings in vehicle running costs in year 1;

(iii) Present value of the maintenance costs over the life of the contract. *(3 marks)*

ACCA F2 Performance Management

13.15 Intermediate. A company is considering offering its customers an early settlement discount. The company currently receives payments from customers on average 65 days after the invoice date. The company is considering offering a 2 per cent early settlement discount for payment within 30 days of the invoice date.

The effective annual interest rate of the early settlement discount using compound interest methodology and assuming a 365 day year is:

(a) 22.94%
(b) 20.86%
(c) 23.45%
(d) 27.85% *(2 marks)*

CIMA P1 Performance Operations

13.16 Intermediate. The details of four short-term investments are as follows:

Investment A pays interest of 1.7 per cent every 3 months
Investment B pays interest of 3.4 per cent every 6 months
Investment C pays interest of 5.4 per cent every 9 months
Investment D pays interest of 7.0 per cent every 12 months

The investment that gives the highest effective annual rate of interest, assuming that the interest is reinvested, is:

(a) Investment A
(b) Investment B
(c) Investment C
(d) Investment D   (2 marks)

CIMA P1 Performance Operations

13.17 Intermediate. A $100 bond has a coupon rate of 8 per cent per annum and is due to mature in four years' time. The next interest payment is due in one year's time. Similar bonds have a yield to maturity of 10 per cent.

Required:

Calculate the expected purchase price of the bond at today's date.
(3 marks)

CIMA P1 Performance Operations

13.18 Intermediate. A bond has a coupon rate of 6 per cent and will repay its nominal value of $100 when it matures after four years.

The bond will be purchased today for $103 ex-interest and held until maturity.

Required:

Calculate, to 0.01 per cent, the yield to maturity for the bond based on today's purchase price.   (5 marks)

CIMA P1 Performance Operations

13.19 Intermediate. PQ is purchasing the lease on a property which has an annual lease payment of $300 in perpetuity. The lease payments will be paid annually in advance.

PQ has a cost of capital of 12 per cent per annum.

The present value of the lease payments is:

(a) $2500
(b) $2800
(c) $3600
(d) $3900   (2 marks)

CIMA P1 Performance Operations

13.20 Intermediate. Sydney is considering making a monthly investment for her son who will be five years old on his next birthday. She wishes to make payments until his 18th birthday and intends to pay £50 per month into an account yielding an APR of 12.68 per cent. She plans to start making payments into the account the month after her son's fifth birthday.

How much will be in the account immediately after the final payment has been made?

(a) £18 847
(b) £18 377
(c) £17 606
(d) £18 610.

ACCA Paper 1.2 – Financial Information for Management

13.21 Intermediate. Sydney wishes to make an investment on a monthly basis starting next month for five years. The payments into the fund would be made on the first day of each month. The interest rate will be 0.5 per cent per month. Sydney needs a terminal value of £7000.

What should be the monthly payments into the fund to the nearest £?

(a) £75
(b) £86
(c) £100
(d) £117

ACCA Paper 1.2 – Financial Information for Management

13.22 Intermediate. Augustine wishes to take out a loan for £2000. The interest rate on this loan would be 10 per cent per annum and Augustine wishes to make equal monthly repayments, comprising interest and principal, over three years starting one month after the loan is taken out.

What would be the monthly repayment on the loan (to the nearest £)?

(a) £56
(b) £64
(c) £66
(d) £67

ACCA Paper 1.2 – Financial Information for Management

13.23 Intermediate: Calculation of terminal values and monthly repayments.

(a) James is considering paying £50 into a fund on a monthly basis for ten years starting in one year's time. The interest earned will be 1 per cent per month. Once all of these payments have been made the investment will be transferred immediately to an account that will earn interest at 15 per cent per annum until maturity. The fund matures five years after the last payment is made into the fund.

Required:

Calculate the terminal value of the fund in 15 years' time to the nearest pound.   (3 marks)

(b) Doug wishes to take out a loan for £2000. He has the choice of two loans:

Loan 1: monthly payments for 36 months at an APR of 9.38 per cent

Loan 2: monthly payments for 24 months at an APR of 12.68 per cent

Required:

(i) Calculate the monthly repayments for loans 1 and 2 to two decimal places.   (5 marks)

(ii) Calculate the total amount repaid under each loan and purely on the basis of this information recommend which loan Doug should choose.   (2 marks)

ACCA Paper 1.2 – Financial Information for Management

13.24 Advanced: Relevant cash flows and calculation of NPV and IRR. A car manufacturer has been experiencing financial difficulties over the past few years. Sales have reduced significantly as a result of the worldwide economic recession. Costs have increased due to quality issues that led to a recall of some models of its cars.

Production volume last year was 50 000 cars and it is expected that this will increase by 4 per cent per annum each year for the next five years.

The company directors are concerned to improve profitability and are considering two potential investment projects.

Project 1 – implement a new quality control process
The company has paid a consultant process engineer $50 000 to review the company's quality processes. The consultant recommended that the company implement a new quality control process. The new process will require a machine costing $20 000 000. The machine is expected to have a useful life of five years and no residual value.

It is estimated that raw material costs will be reduced by $62 per car and that both internal and external failure costs from quality failures will be reduced by 80 per cent.

Estimated internal and external failure costs per year without the new process, based on last year's production volume of 50 000 cars, and their associated probabilities are shown below:

Internal failure costs		External failure costs	
$	Probability	$	Probability
300 000	50%	1 300 000	60%
500 000	30%	1 900 000	30%
700 000	20%	3 000 000	10%

Internal and external failure costs are expected to increase each year in line with the number of cars produced.

The company's accountant has calculated that this investment will result in a net present value (NPV) of $13 38 000 and an internal rate of return of 10.5 per cent.

Project 2 – in-house component manufacturing

The company could invest in new machinery to enable in-house manufacturing of a component that is currently made by outside suppliers. The new machinery is expected to cost $15 000 000 and have a useful life of five years and no residual value. Additional working capital of $1 000 000 will also be required as a result of producing the component in-house.

The price paid to the current supplier is $370 per component. It is estimated that the in-house variable cost of production will be $260 per component. Each car requires one component. Fixed production costs, including machinery depreciation, are estimated to increase by $5 000 000 per annum as a result of manufacturing the component in-house.

Depreciation is calculated on a straight line basis.

Additional information

The company is unable to raise enough capital to carry out both projects. The company will therefore have to choose between the two alternatives.

Taxation and inflation should be ignored.

The company uses a cost of capital of 8 per cent per annum.

Required:

(a) Calculate for Project 1 the relevant cash flows that the accountant should have used for year 1 when appraising the project.
   All workings should be shown in $000.   *(6 marks)*

(b) Calculate for Project 2:
   (i) the net present value (NPV)
   (ii) the internal rate of return (IRR).

   All workings should be shown in $000.   *(10 marks)*

(c) Advise the company directors which of the two investment projects should be undertaken.   *(4 marks)*

(d) A company is considering two alternative investment projects both of which have a positive net present value. The projects have been ranked on the basis of both net present value (NPV) and internal rate of return (IRR). The result of the ranking is shown below:

	Project A	Project B
NPV	1st	2nd
IRR	2nd	1st

Discuss potential reasons why the conflict between the NPV and IRR ranking may have arisen.   *(5 marks)*

CIMA P1 Performance operations

13.25 Advanced: Calculation of NPV and IRR with taxes and inflation. DP is considering whether to purchase a piece of land close to a major city airport. The land will be used to provide 600 car parking spaces. The cost of the land is $6 000 000 but further expenditure of $2 000 000 will be required immediately to develop the land to provide access roads and suitable surfacing for car parking. DP is planning to operate the car park for five years after which the land will be sold for $10 000 000 at Year 5 prices. A consultant has prepared a report detailing projected revenues and costs.

Revenues

It is estimated that the car park will operate at 75 per cent capacity during each year of the project.

Car parking charges will depend on the prices being charged by competitors. There is a 40 per cent chance that the price will be $60 per week, a 25 per cent chance the price will be $50 per week and a 35 per cent chance that the price will be $70 per week.

DP expects that it will earn a contribution to sales ratio of 80 per cent.

Fixed operating costs

DP will lease a number of vehicles to be used to transport passengers to and from the airport. It is expected that the lease costs will be $50 000 per annum.

Staff costs are estimated to be $350 000 per annum.

The company will hire a security system at a cost of $100 000 per annum.

Inflation

All of the values above, other than the amount for the sale of the land at the end of the five-year period, have been expressed in terms of current prices. The vehicle leasing costs of $50 000 per annum will apply throughout the five years and are not subject to inflation.

Car parking charges and variable costs are expected to increase at a rate of 5 per cent per annum starting in Year 1.

All fixed operating costs excluding the vehicle leasing costs are expected to increase at a rate of 4 per cent per annum starting in Year 1.

Other information

The company uses net present value based on the expected values of cash flow when evaluating projects of this type.

DP has a money cost of capital of 8 per cent per annum.

DP's financial director has provided the following taxation information:

- Tax depreciation is not available on either the initial cost of the land or the development costs.
- Taxation rate: 30 per cent of taxable profits. Half of the tax is payable in the year in which it arises, the balance is payable in the following year.

All cash flows apart from the initial investment of $8 000 000 should be assumed to occur at the end of the year.

Required:

(a) Evaluate the project from a financial perspective. You should use net present value as the basis of your evaluation and show your workings in $000.   *(14 marks)*

(b) Calculate the internal rate of return (IRR) of the project.
    (5 marks)

The main reason why discounted cash flow methods of investment appraisal are considered theoretically superior is that they take account of the time value of money.

Required:

(c) Explain the THREE elements that determine the 'time value of money' and why it is important to take it into consideration when appraising investment projects.
    (6 marks)

CIMA P1 Performance Operations

13.26 Advanced: Calculation of payback, ARR and NPV.
Stadler is an ambitious young executive who has recently been appointed to the position of financial director of Paradis plc, a small listed company. Stadler regards this appointment as a temporary one, enabling him to gain experience before moving to a larger organization. His intention is to leave Paradis plc in three years' time, with its share price standing high. As a consequence, he is particularly concerned that the reported profits of Paradis plc should be as high as possible in his third and final year with the company.

Paradis plc has recently raised £350 000 from a rights issue, and the directors are considering three ways of using these funds. Three projects (A, B and C) are being considered, each involving the immediate purchase of equipment costing £350 000. One project only can be undertaken, and the equipment for each project will have a useful life equal to that of the project, with no scrap value. Stadler favours project C because it is expected to show the highest accounting profit in the third year. However, he does not wish to reveal his real reasons for favouring project C, and so, in his report to the chairman, he recommends project C because it shows the highest internal rate of return. The following summary is taken from his report:

Project	Net cash flows (£000) Years									Internal rate of return (%)
	0	1	2	3	4	5	6	7	8	
A	−350	100	110	104	112	138	160	180	—	27.5
B	−350	40	100	210	260	160	—	—	—	26.4
C	−350	200	150	240	40	—	—	—	—	33.0

The chairman of the company is accustomed to projects being appraised in terms of payback and accounting rate of return, and he is consequently suspicious of the use of internal rate of return as a method of project selection. Accordingly, the chairman has asked for an independent report on the choice of project. The company's cost of capital is 20 per cent and a policy of straight line depreciation is used to write off the cost of equipment in the financial statements.

Requirements:

(a) Calculate the payback period for each project.   *(3 marks)*
(b) Calculate the accounting rate of return for each project.

                                                        (5 marks)
(c) Prepare a report for the chairman with supporting calculations indicating which project should be preferred by the ordinary shareholders of Paradis plc.   *(12 marks)*
(d) Discuss the assumptions about the reactions of the stock market that are implicit in Stadler's choice of project C.   *(5 marks)*

Note: ignore taxation.   *ICAEW P2 Financial Management*

IM13.1 Advanced. The evidence of many recent studies suggests that there are major differences between current theories of investment appraisal and the methods which firms actually use in evaluating long-term investments.

You are required to:

(a) present theoretical arguments for the choice of net present value as the best method of investment appraisal;
(b) explain why in practice other methods of evaluating investment projects have proved to be more popular with decision-makers than the net present value method.

IM13.2 Intermediate: Payback, accounting rate of return and net present value calculations plus a discussion of qualitative factors. The following information relates to three possible capital expenditure projects. Because of capital rationing only one project can be accepted:

	Project		
	A	B	C
Initial cost	£200 000	£230 000	£180 000
Expected life	5 years	5 years	4 years
Scrap value expected	£10 000	£15 000	£8 000
Expected cash inflows	(£)	(£)	(£)
End year 1	80 000	100 000	55 000
2	70 000	70 000	65 000
3	65 000	50 000	95 000
4	60 000	50 000	100 000
5	55 000	50 000	

The company estimates its cost of capital is 18 per cent.

Calculate:

(a) The payback period for each project.   *(4 marks)*
(b) The accounting rate of return for each project.   *(4 marks)*
(c) The net present value of each project.   *(8 marks)*
(d) Which project should be accepted – give reasons.   *(5 marks)*
(e) Explain the factors management would need to consider, in addition to the financial factors, before making a final decision on a project.   *(4 marks)*

                        AAT Stage 3 Cost Accounting and Budgeting

IM13.3 Intermediate: Calculation of payback, NPV and ARR for mutually exclusive projects. Your company is considering investing in its own transport fleet. The present position is that carriage is contracted to an outside organization. The life of the transport fleet would be five years, after which time the vehicles would have to be disposed of. The cost to your company of using the outside organization for its carriage needs is £250 000 for this year. This cost, it is projected, will rise 10 per cent per annum over the life of the project. The initial cost of the transport fleet would be £750 000 and it is estimated that the following costs would be incurred over the next five years:

	Drivers' costs (£)	Repairs and maintenance (£)	Other costs (£)
Year 1	33 000	8 000	130 000
Year 2	35 000	13 000	135 000
Year 3	36 000	15 000	140 000
Year 4	38 000	16 000	136 000
Year 5	40 000	18 000	142 000

Other costs include depreciation. It is projected that the fleet would be sold for £150 000 at the end of year 5. It has been agreed to depreciate the fleet on a straight line basis.

To raise funds for the project your company is proposing to raise a long-term loan at 12 per cent interest rate per annum.

You are told that there is an alternative project that could be invested in using the funds raised, which has the following projected results:

        Payback = three years
        Accounting rate of return = 30 per cent
        Net present value = £140 000.

As funds are limited, investment can only be made in one project.

Note: The transport fleet would be purchased at the beginning of the project and all other expenditure would be incurred at the end of each relevant year.

Required:

(a) Prepare a table showing the net cash savings to be made by the firm over the life of the transport fleet project. *(5 marks)*

(b) Calculate the following for the transport fleet project:

(i) payback period;
(ii) accounting rate of return;
(iii) net present value. *(13 marks)*

(c) Write a short report to the investment manager in your company outlining whether investment should be committed to the transport fleet or the alternative project outlined. Clearly state the reasons for your decision. *(7 marks)*

AAT Cost Accounting and Budgeting

IM13.4 Intermediate: NPV and payback calculations. You are employed as the assistant accountant in your company and you are currently working on an appraisal of a project to purchase a new machine. The machine will cost £55 000 and will have a useful life of three years. You have already estimated the cash flows from the project and their taxation effect and the results of your estimates can be summarized as follows:

	Year 1	Year 2	Year 3
Post-tax cash inflow	£18 000	£29 000	£31 000

Your company uses a post-tax cost of capital of 8 per cent to appraise all projects of this type.

Task 1

(a) Calculate the net present value of the proposal to purchase the machine. Ignore the effects of inflation and assume that all cash flows occur at the end of the year.

(b) Calculate the payback period for the investment in the machine.

Task 2

The marketing director has asked you to let her know as soon as you have completed your appraisal of the project. She has asked you to provide her with some explanation of your calculations and of how taxation affects the proposal.

Prepare a memorandum to the marketing director which answers her queries. Your memorandum should contain the following:

(a) your recommendation concerning the proposal;
(b) an explanation of the meaning of the net present value and the payback period;
(c) an explanation of the effects of taxation on the cash flows arising from capital expenditure.

AAT Technicians Stage

IM13.5 Intermediate: Present value of purchasing or renting machinery. The Portsmere Hospital operates its own laundry. Last year the laundry processed 120 000 kilograms of washing and this year the total is forecast to grow to 132 000 kilograms. This growth in laundry processed is forecast to continue at the same percentage rate for the next seven years. Because of this, the hospital must immediately replace its existing laundry equipment. Currently, it is considering two options, the purchase of machine A or the rental of machine B. Information on both options is given below:

Machine A – purchase

Annual capacity (kilograms)	£180 000
Material cost per kilogram	£2.00
Labour cost per kilogram	£3.00
Fixed costs per annum	£20 000
Life of machine	3 years
Capital cost	£60 000
Depreciation per annum	£20 000

Machine B – rent

Annual capacity (kilograms)	£170 000
Material cost per kilogram	£1.80
Labour cost per kilogram	£3.40
Fixed costs per annum	£18 000
Rental per annum	£20 000
Rental agreement	3 years
Depreciation per annum	nil

Other information:

1 The hospital is able to call on an outside laundry if there is either a breakdown or any other reason why the washing cannot be undertaken in-house. The charge would be £10 per kilogram of washing.

2 Machine A, if purchased, would have to be paid for immediately. All other cash flows can be assumed to occur at the end of the year.

3 Machine A will have no residual value at any time.

4 The existing laundry equipment could be sold for £10 000 cash.

5 The fixed costs are a direct cost of operating the laundry.

6 The hospital's discount rate for projects of this nature is 15 per cent.

You are an accounting technician employed by the Portsmere Hospital and you are asked to write a brief report to its chief executive. Your report should:

(a) evaluate the two options for operating the laundry, using discounted cash flow techniques;
(b) recommend the preferred option and identify one possible non-financial benefit;
(c) justify your treatment of the £10 000 cash value of the existing equipment;
(d) explain what is meant by discounted cashflow.

Note: Inflation can be ignored.   *AAT Technicians Stage*

IM13.6 Advanced: Comparison of NPV and IRR. Using the discounted cash flow yield (internal rate of return) for evaluating investment opportunities has the basic weakness that it does not give attention to the amount of the capital investment, in that a return of 20 per cent on an investment of £1000 may be given a higher ranking than a return of 15 per cent on an investment of £10 000.

Comment in general on the above statement and refer in particular to the problem of giving priorities to (ranking) investment proposals. Your answers should make use of the following information:

	Project A cash flow (£)	Project B cash flow (£)
Year 0 (Capital investments)	1000	10 000
1 Cash flows	240	2 300
2 Cash flows	288	2 640
3 Cash flows	346	3 040
4 Cash flows	414	3 500
5 Cash flows	498	4 020
Cost of capital	10%	10%

Taxation can be ignored. *(20 marks)*

ACCA P3 Financial Management

IM13.7 Advanced: Calculation of NPV and additional cash flows which will result in a zero NPV. Losrock Housing Association is considering the implementation of a refurbishment programme on one of its housing estates which would reduce maintenance and heating costs and enable a rent increase to be made.

Relevant data are as follows:

(i)   Number of houses: 300.

(ii) Annual maintenance cost per house: £300. This will be reduced by 25 per cent on completion of the refurbishment of each house.

(iii) Annual heating cost per house: £500. This will be reduced by 30 per cent on completion of the refurbishment of each house.

(iv) Annual rental income per house: £2100. This will be increased by 15 per cent on completion of the refurbishment of each house.

(v)   Two contractors A and B have each quoted a price of £2000 per house to implement the refurbishment work.

(vi) The quoted completion profiles for each contractor are as follows:

Number of houses refurbished

	Year 1	Year 2	Year 3
Contractor A	90	90	120
Contractor B	150	90	60

(vii) Contractor A requires £100 000 at the commencement of the work and the balance of the contract price in proportion to the number of houses completed in each of years 1 to 3. Contractor B requires £300 000 at the commencement of the work and the balance of the contract price in proportion to the number of houses completed in each of years 1 to 3.

(viii) An eight-year period from the commencement of the work should be used as the time horizon for the evaluation of the viability of the refurbishment programme.

Assume that all events and cash flows arise at year end points. Savings and rent increases will commence in the year following refurbishment.
Ignore taxation.

Required:

(a) Prepare financial summaries and hence advise management whether to accept the quote from contractor A or contractor B in each of the following situations:

(i)   ignoring the discounting of cash flows; and
(ii) where the cost of capital is determined as 14 per cent.
(14 marks)

(b) For contractor A only, calculate the maximum refurbishment price per house at which the work would be acceptable to Losrock Housing Association on financial grounds using discounted cash flows as the decision base, where the initial payment remains at £100 000 and the balance is paid in proportion to the houses completed in each of years 1 to 3.   *(5 marks)*

(c) Suggest additional information relating to maintenance and heating costs which might affect the acceptability of the existing quotes per house where discounted cash flows are used as the decision base.   *(3 marks)*

ACCA Level 2 Management Accounting

IM13.8 Advanced: Replacement decision and the conflict between decision-making and performance evaluation models.
Paragon Products plc has a factory that manufactures a wide range of plastic household utensils. One of these is a plastic brush that is made from a special raw material used only for this purpose. The brush is moulded on a purpose-built machine that was installed in January 2015 at a cost of £210 000 with an expected useful life of seven years. This machine was

assumed to have zero scrap value at the end of its life and was depreciated on the same straight line basis that the company used for all equipment.

Recently an improved machine has become available, at a price of £130 000, which requires two men to operate it rather than the five men required for the existing machine. It also uses a coarser grade of raw material costing £70 per tonne (1000 kg), compared with £75 per tonne for the present material. Further, it would use only 60 per cent of the power consumed by the existing machine. However, it has an expected life of only three years and an expected scrap value of £10 000.

The factory manager is considering replacing the existing machine immediately with the new one as the suppliers have offered him £40 000 for the existing machine, which is substantially more than could be obtained on the second-hand market, provided the new machine is installed by 1 January 2019. Unfortunately, this would leave stocks of the old raw material (sufficient to make 40 000 brushes) which could not be used and which would fetch only £25 per tonne on resale.

The brush department is treated as a profit centre. Current production amounts to 200 000 brushes a year which are sold at a wholesale price of £1 each. The production of each brush uses 2 kg of the raw material, consumes 1 kW hour of electricity costing £0.05, and incurs direct labour costs amounting to £0.25 per brush. Overhead costs amount to £60 000 per annum and include £10 000 relating to supervision costs which vary according to the number of employees. The men no longer required to operate the new machine could be found employment elsewhere in the factory and would be paid their current wage although they would be performing less skilled work normally paid at 80 per cent of their current rate.

Requirements:

(a) Evaluate the proposal to replace the existing machine with the new model, ignoring the time value of money in your analysis.   *(10 marks)*

(b) Construct brush department profit and loss accounts for each alternative for 2019, 2020 and 2021. Indicate how the factory manager's decision might be influenced by these figures.   *(8 marks)*

(c) Explain how your analysis would be affected if the new machine had a longer expected life and the time value of money was to be taken into account.   *(7 marks)*

Note: Ignore taxation.   *ICAEW P2 Management Accounting*

IM13.9 Advanced: Calculation of a contract price involving monthly discounting and compounding. Franzl is a contract engineer working for a division of a large construction company. He is responsible for the negotiation of contract prices and the subsequent collection of instalment monies from customers. It is company policy to achieve a mark-up of at least 10 per cent on the direct production costs of a contract, but there is no company policy on the speed of customer payment. Franzl usually attempts to persuade customers to pay in six-monthly instalments in arrears.

Franzl is presently engaged in deciding on the minimum acceptable price for contract K491, which will last for 24 months. He has estimated that the following direct production costs will be incurred:

	(£)
Raw material	168 000
Labour	120 000
Plant depreciation	18 400
Equipment rental	30 000
	336 400

On the basis of these costs, Franzl estimates that the minimum contract price should be £370 000. The raw material and labour costs are expected to rise evenly over the period of the contract and to be paid monthly in arrears. Plant depreciation has been calculated as the difference between the cost of the new plant (£32 400) which will be purchased for the contract and its realizable value (£14 000) at the end of contract. Special equipment will be rented for the first year of the contract, the rent being paid in two six-monthly instalments in advance. The contract will be financed from head office funds, on which interest of 1 per cent per month is charged or credited according to whether the construction division is a net borrower or net lender.

Requirements:

(a) Calculate the net present value of contract K491 assuming that Franzl's minimum price and normal payment terms are accepted.
(5 marks)

(b) Assuming that the customer agrees to pay the instalments in advance rather than arrears, calculate the new contract price and mark-up that Franzl could accept so as to leave the net value of the contract unchanged.
(5 marks)

(c) Prepare two statements to show that the eventual cash surpluses generated in (a) and (b) are identical. The statements need show *only* the total cash received and paid for each category of revenue and expense.
(6 marks)

(d) Discuss the factors that should influence the tender price for a long-term contract.
(9 marks)

Note: Ignore taxation.   *ICAEW Financial Management*

14

CAPITAL INVESTMENT DECISIONS: THE IMPACT OF CAPITAL RATIONING, TAXATION, INFLATION AND RISK

LEARNING OBJECTIVES After studying this chapter, you should be able to:

- explain capital rationing and select the optimum combination of investments when capital is rationed for a single period;
- calculate the incremental taxation payments arising from a proposed investment;
- describe the two approaches for adjusting for inflation when appraising capital projects;
- explain how risk-adjusted discount rates are calculated;
- explain how sensitivity analysis can be applied to investment appraisal;
- describe the initiation, authorization and review procedures for the investment process.

In the previous chapter, the major techniques that can be used for appraising capital investment decisions were introduced and their relative merits were assessed. To simplify the discussion, we made a number of assumptions: first, that cash inflows and outflows were known with certainty; second, that sufficient funds were available to enable acceptance of all those projects with positive net present values; third, that firms operated in an environment where there was no taxation and no inflation; and, finally, that the cost of capital was the risk-free rate.

In this chapter, we shall relax these assumptions and discuss how capital investment techniques can be applied to more complicated situations. In addition, we shall look at the procedures that should be in place for initiating, authorizing and reviewing project investments. Many of the topics included in this chapter are complex and more appropriate to a second year management accounting course. You should note that these topics are highlighted using a vertical green line at the side of the page. Also some of the topics may be incorporated in a corporate finance course rather than a management accounting course. Therefore, you should check whether the topics are included in your course curriculum prior to reading this chapter.

CAPITAL RATIONING

In our previous discussions, it has been suggested that all investments with positive net present values (NPV) should be undertaken. For mutually exclusive projects, the project with the highest net present value should be chosen. However, situations may occur where there are insufficient funds available to enable a firm to undertake all those projects that yield a positive net present value. The situation is described as capital rationing. Capital rationing occurs whenever there is a budget ceiling or a market constraint on the amount of funds that can be invested during a specific period of time. For various reasons, top management may pursue a policy of limiting the amount of funds available for investment in any one period. Such policies may apply to firms that finance all their capital investment with internal funds. Alternatively, in a large decentralized organization, top management may limit the funds available to the divisional managers for investment.

The term soft capital rationing is often used to refer to situations where, for various reasons the firm *internally* imposes a budget ceiling on the amount of capital expenditure. By way of contrast, where the amount of capital investment is restricted because of *external* constraints such as the inability to obtain funds from the financial markets, the term hard capital rationing is used.

Whenever capital rationing exists, management should allocate the limited available capital in a way that maximizes the NPVs of the firm. Thus it is necessary to rank all investment opportunities so that the NPV can be maximized from the use of the available funds. Ranking in terms of absolute NPVs will normally give incorrect results, since this method leads to the selection of large projects, each of which has a high individual NPV but that have in total a lower NPV than a large number of smaller projects with lower individual NPVs. For example, the ranking of projects by NPV will favour a project that yields an NPV of £100 000, for an investment of £1 million, over two projects of £500 000 that each yield an individual NPV of £80 000. Clearly, if funds are restricted to £1 million, it is better to accept the two smaller projects, which will yield a total NPV of £160 000. Consider the situation presented in Example 14.1.

Our aim is to select the projects in descending order of profitability until the investment funds of £20 million have been exhausted. If we use the net present value method of ranking, the following projects will be selected:

Projects selected in order of ranking	Investment cost (£m)	New present value (£m)
C	5	2.575
D	10	2.350
G	5	0.900
	Total net present value	5.825

EXAMPLE 14.1

A division of the Bothnia Company that operates under the constraint of capital rationing has identified seven independent investments from which to choose. The company has £20 million available for capital investment during the current period. Which projects should the company choose? The net present values and profitability index ratios for each of the projects are as follows:

Projects	Investment required (£m)	Present value, PV (£m)	Net present value (£m)	Profitability index (PV/ investment cost)	Ranking as per NPVs	Ranking as per profitability index
A	2.5	3.25	0.75	1.30	6	2
B	10.0	10.825	0.825	1.08	5	6
C	5.0	7.575	2.575	1.51	1	1
D	10.0	12.35	2.35	1.23	2	3
E	12.5	13.35	0.85	1.07	4	7
F	2.5	3.0	0.5	1.20	7	4
G	5.0	5.9	0.9	1.18	3	5

Instead of ranking by NPVs, projects should be ranked by their profitability index. The profitability index is defined as the present value of a project divided by its investment outlay. The profitability index represents the application of the approach outlined in Chapter 9 for allocating scarce resources (i.e. with investment funds being the scarce resource in Example 14.1). Only projects with a profitability index in excess of 1.0 are acceptable since they have positive NPVs. For ranking purposes, projects should be accepted in descending order based on their profitability index. Therefore, if we adopt the rankings by the profitability index, the selected projects will be as follows:

Projects selected in order of ranking	Investment cost (£m)	Net present value (£)
C	5.0	2.575
A	2.5	0.750
D	10.0	2.350
F	2.5	0.500
	Total net present value	6.175

You can see that the ranking of projects by the profitability index gives the highest NPV. Our discussion so far has assumed that investment funds are restricted for one period only. To extend the analysis to multi-period capital rationing, it is necessary to adopt the mathematical programming techniques described in Chapter 26.

TAXATION AND INVESTMENT DECISIONS

In our discussions so far, we have ignored the impact of taxation. Taxation rules differ between countries but in most countries similar principles tend to apply relating to the taxation allowances available on capital investment expenditure. Companies rarely pay taxes on the profits that are disclosed in their annual published accounts, since certain expenses that are deducted in the published accounts are

REAL WORLD VIEWS 14.1

Taxation and investment decisions – encouraging investment with lower tax rates

Writing in *The Australian Financial Review* Jack Mintz states that for investment decisions, taxes matter, and Australia's company tax rate (30 per cent) is too high in international terms to be competitive for capital. Australia now imposes a higher tax burden on new investments than most countries it competes with. In 2015 Australia had the sixth-highest tax rate among the 34 OECD countries. Over the past decade the average tax rate in the OECD has fallen from 28.2 per cent to 25.3 per cent. The British rate has fallen from 30 per cent to 20 per cent, with further reductions to a recently announced 17 per cent tax rate planned by 2020. Canada has reduced its company tax rate from 34.2 per cent in 2005 to 26.6 per cent in 2015.

Australia now has the fourth-highest tax burden on capital investment among OECD countries. So why have other countries seen fit to reduce company tax? Moving to a lower tax burden on capital does more than encourage investment. It results in a faster adoption of new technologies. It means businesses are more cost-competitive to export their products and to compete with imports.

Questions

1 Should low tax rates be the sole concern of businesses engaging in capital investments? List some other important factors.

2 Should a company consider evaluating investments based on differing tax rates, assuming all other factors being equal?

Reference

Mintz, J. (2016) 'Regressive company tax is well above world rates', *The Australian Financial Review*, 39. Mar 29, ISSN 04042018.

not allowable deductions for taxation purposes. For example, depreciation is not an allowable deduction; instead, taxation legislation enables capital allowances (also known as writing-down allowances (WDAs) or depreciation tax shields) to be claimed on capital expenditure that is incurred on plant and machinery and other fixed assets. Capital allowances represent standardized depreciation allowances granted by the tax authorities. These allowances vary from country to country but their common aim is to enable the *net* cost of assets to be deducted as an allowable expense, either throughout their economic life or on an accelerated basis which is shorter than an asset's economic life.

Taxation laws in different countries typically specify the amount of capital expenditure that is allowable (sometimes this exceeds the cost of the asset where a government wishes to stimulate investment), the time period over which the capital allowances can be claimed and the depreciation method to be employed. For many years UK companies could claim annual capital/writing down allowances of 25 per cent on the written-down value of plant and equipment based on the reducing balance method of depreciation. Different percentage capital allowances were also available on other assets such as industrial buildings where an allowance of 4 per cent per annum based on straight line depreciation could be claimed.

Let us now consider how taxation affects the NPV calculations. You will see that the calculation must include the incremental tax cash flows arising from the investment. Consider the information presented in Example 14.2.

The first stage is to calculate the annual writing-down allowances (i.e. the capital allowances). The calculations are as follows:

End of year	Annual writing-down allowance (£)	Written-down value (£)
0	0	1 000 000
1	250 000 (25% × £1 000 000)	750 000
2	187 500 (25% × £750 000)	562 500
3	140 630 (25% × £562 500)	421 870
4	105 470 (25% × £421 870)	316 400
	683 600	

Next we calculate the additional taxable profits arising from the project. The calculations are as follows:

	Year 1 (£)	Year 2 (£)	Year 3 (£)	Year 4 (£)
Incremental annual profits	500 000	500 000	500 000	500 000
Less annual writing-down allowance	250 000	187 500	140 630	105 470
Incremental taxable profits	250 000	312 500	359 370	394 530
Incremental tax at 35%	87 500	109 370	125 780	138 090

EXAMPLE 14.2

The Sentosa Company operates in Ruritania where investments in plant and machinery are eligible for 25 per cent annual writing-down allowances on the written-down value using the reducing balance method of depreciation. The corporate tax rate is 35 per cent. The company is considering whether to purchase some machinery which will cost £1 million and which is expected to result in additional net cash inflows and profits of £500 000 per annum for four years. It is anticipated that the machinery will be sold at the end of year 4 for its written-down value for taxation purposes. Assume a one-year lag in the payment of taxes. Calculate the net present value.

You can see that for each year the incremental tax payment is calculated as follows:

$$\text{corporate tax rate} \times (\text{incremental profits} - \text{capital/writing down allowances})$$

Note that depreciation charges should not be included in the calculation of incremental cash flows or taxable profits. We must now consider the timing of the taxation payments. In many countries, taxation payment dates vary depending on the end of the accounting year, but they are generally paid approximately one year after the end of the company's accounting year. We shall apply this rule to our example. This means that the tax payment of £87 500 for year 1 will be paid at the end of year 2, £109 370 tax will be paid at the end of year 3 and so on.

The incremental tax payments are now included in the NPV calculation:

Year	Cash flow (£)	Taxation	Net cash flow (£)	Discount factor	Present value (£)
0	−1 000 000	0	−1 000 000	1.0000	−1 000 000
1	+500 000	0	+500 000	0.9091	+454 550
2	+500 000	−87 500	+412 500	0.8264	+340 890
3	+500 000	−109 370	+390 630	0.7513	+293 480
4	+500 000 ⎱ +316 400[a] ⎰	−125 780	+690 620	0.6830	+471 690
5	0	−138 090	−138 090	0.6209	−85 740
				Net present value	+474 870

[a]Sale of machinery for written-down value of £316 400 as shown in the above calculation of the writing-down allowances.

The taxation rules in most countries allow capital allowances to be claimed on the *net* cost of the asset. In our example, the machine will be purchased for £1 million and the estimated realizable value at the end of its life is its written-down value of £316 400. Therefore the estimated net cost of the machine is £683 600. You will see from the calculation of the writing-down allowances at the start of this section that the total of the allowances amounts to the net cost. How would the analysis change if the estimated realizable value for the machine was different from its written-down value, say £450 000? The company will have claimed allowances of £683 600 but the estimated net cost of the machine is £550 000 (£1 million − £450 000 estimated net realizable value). Therefore excess allowances of £133 600 (£683 600 − £550 000) will have been claimed and an adjustment must be made at the end of year 4 so that the tax authorities can claim back the excess allowance. This adjustment is called a balancing charge.

Note that the above calculation of taxable profits for year 4 (payable in year 5) will now be as follows:

Incremental annual profits	500 000
Less annual writing-down allowance	(105 470)
Add balancing charge	133 600
Incremental taxable profits	528 130
Incremental taxation at 35%	184 845

An alternative calculation is to assume that a writing-down allowance will not be claimed in year 4. The balancing charge is now calculated by deducting the written-down value at the end of year 3 of £421 870 from the *actual* sales value at the time of sale (i.e. £450 000 sale proceeds). The balancing charge is now £28 130. This is the same as the net charge incorporated in the above calculation (£133 600 balancing charge − £105 470 WDA = £28 130). You can adopt either method. It is a matter of personal preference.

Let us now assume that the estimated disposal value is less than the written-down value for tax purposes, say £250 000. The net investment cost is £750 000 (£1 000 000 − £250 000), but you will see that our calculations at the start of this section indicate that estimated taxation capital allowances of £683 600 will have been claimed by the end of year 4. Therefore an adjustment of £66 400 (£750 000 − £683 600) must be made at the end of year 4 to reflect the fact that insufficient capital allowances have been claimed. This adjustment is called a balancing allowance.

Thus in year 4, the total capital allowance will consist of an annual writing-down allowance of £105 470 plus a balancing allowance of £66 400, giving a total of £171 870. Taxable profits for year 4 are now £328 130 (500 000 − £171 870) and tax at the rate of 35 per cent on these profits will be paid at the end of year 5.

Do note that in the UK, and some other countries, it is possible to combine similar types of asset into asset pools, and purchases and sales of assets are added to the pool so that balancing allowances and charges on individual assets do not arise. However, similar outcomes are likely to occur. Accordingly, it is essential when appraising investment proposals to be fully aware of the specific taxation legislation that applies so that you can precisely determine the taxation impact. In most cases, taxation is likely to have an important effect on the NPV calculation. For an illustration of the treatment of asset acquisitions and disposals when asset are incorporated into a general pool, you should refer to the article by Franklin (1998).

THE EFFECT OF INFLATION ON CAPITAL INVESTMENT APPRAISAL

ADVANCED READING

What impact does inflation have on capital investment decisions? We shall see that inflation affects *future cash flows* and *the return* that shareholders require on the investment (i.e. the discount rate). How does inflation affect the *required rate of return* on an investment? According to Fisher (1930), the rates quoted on financial securities such as treasury bills, fully reflect anticipated inflation. Note that the rates quoted on securities are known as nominal or money rates of return, whereas the real rate of return represents the rate that would be required in the absence of inflation. Fisher proposed the following equation relating to the nominal rate of return to the real rate of return and the rate of inflation:

$$\left(1 + \begin{array}{c}\text{nominal rate} \\ \text{of return}\end{array}\right) = \left(1 + \begin{array}{c}\text{real rate} \\ \text{of return}\end{array}\right) \times \left(1 + \begin{array}{c}\text{expected rate} \\ \text{of inflation}\end{array}\right) \qquad (14.1)$$

Suppose that the real rate of return is expected to be 2 per cent and the anticipated rate of inflation 8 per cent. Applying Fisher's equation, the nominal or money rate of return would be:

$$(1 + 0.02)(1 + 0.08) = 1.1016$$

The nominal rate of return would therefore be 10.16 per cent (i.e. 1.1016 − 1). In the absence of inflation, an individual who invests £100 in a risk-free security will require a 2 per cent return of £102 to compensate for the time value of money. Assuming that the expected rate of inflation is 8 per cent, then to maintain the return of £102 in real terms, this return will have to grow by 8 per cent to £110.16 (i.e. £102 + 8 per cent). Therefore a real rate of return of 2 per cent requires a nominal rate of return of 10.16 per cent when the expected rate of inflation is 8 per cent.

Inflation also affects *future cash flows*. For example, assume that you expect a cash flow of £100 in one year's time when there is no inflation. Now assume that that the predicted annual inflation rate is 10 per cent. Your expected cash flow at the end of the year will now be £110, instead of £100. However, you will be no better off as a result of the 10 per cent increase in cash flows. Assume that you can buy physical goods, say widgets, at £1 each when there is no inflation so that at the start of the year you can buy 100 widgets. With an annual inflation rate of 10 per cent the cost of a widget will increase to £1.10 and your cash flow will be £110, but your purchasing power will remain unchanged because you will still only be able to buy 100 widgets.

The increase in cash flows from £100 to £110 is an illusion because it is offset by a decline in the purchasing power of the monetary unit. Rather than expressing cash flows in year one as monetary units, it is more meaningful to express the cash flows in today's purchasing power or monetary unit (that is, in real cash flows). Thus, £110 receivable at the end of year one is equivalent to £100 in today's purchasing power. When cash flows are expressed in monetary units at the time when they are received they are described as nominal or money cash flows, whereas cash flows expressed in today's (that is, time zero) purchasing power are known as real cash flows. Therefore the £110 cash flow is a nominal cash flow but if it is expressed in today's purchasing power it will be equivalent to a real cash flow of £100.

Real cash flows can be converted to nominal cash flows using the following formula:

$$\text{Nominal cash flow} = \text{Real cash flow } (1 + \text{the anticipated rate of inflation})^n \qquad (14.2)$$

where n = the number of periods that the cash flows are subject to inflation.

Alternatively, we can rearrange formula (14.2) to restate it in terms of real cash flows:

$$\text{Real cash flow} = \text{Nominal cash flow}/(1 + \text{the anticipated rate of inflation})^n \qquad (14.3)$$

Therefore, if a real cash flow expressed in today's purchasing power is £100 and the anticipated annual rate of inflation is 10 per cent then the nominal value at the end of year 2 will be:

$$£100(1 + 0.10)^2 = £121$$

or a nominal cash flow of £121 receivable at the end of year 2 will be equivalent to a real cash flow of:

$$£121/(1 + 0.10)^2 = £100$$

The average rate of inflation for all goods and services traded in an economy is known as the general rate of inflation. Assume that your cash flow of £100 has increased at exactly the same rate as the general rate of inflation (in other words, the general rate of inflation is 10 per cent). Therefore your purchasing power has remained unchanged and you will be no better or worse off if all your cash flows increase at the general rate of inflation. Indeed, we would expect the same result to apply when we calculate NPVs. If project cash flows increase at exactly the same rate as the general rate of inflation, we would expect NPV to be identical to what the NPV would be if there was no inflation. Consider Example 14.3.

You should recall from Chapter 13 that the NPV can be expressed in formula terms as:

$$\frac{FV_1}{1 + K} + \frac{FV_2}{(1 + K)^2} + \frac{FV_3}{(1 + K)^3} + \cdots + \frac{FV_n}{(1 + K)^n} = I_0$$

where FV_n are future values, K is the cost of capital and I_0 is the initial investment cost. The NPV calculation is:

$$\frac{£600\,000}{1.10} + \frac{£400\,000}{(1.10)^2} + \frac{£1\,000\,000}{(1.10)^3} - £1\,000\,000 = £627\,347$$

Let us now adjust Example 14.3 and incorporate the effects of inflation. Suppose that an annual inflation rate of 8 per cent is expected during the three years of the project. In this situation, the stock market data that are used to calculate the rate of return required by investors will include a premium for anticipated inflation. Hence this premium will be incorporated in the required rate of return on the project (i.e. the applicable cost of capital for the project).

EXAMPLE 14.3

Year 1	£600 000
Year 2	£400 000
Year 3	£1 000 000

A division within the Bothnia Company is considering whether to undertake a project that will cost £1 million and will have the following cash inflows:

The cost of capital (i.e. the required rate of return) is 10 per cent and the expected rate of inflation is zero. Ignore taxation. Calculate the net present value. Initially assume zero inflation.

The revised required rate of return (RRR) is calculated using Fisher's formula:

$$1 + \text{nominal RRR} = [1 + \text{real RRR } (0.10)] \times [1 + \text{rate of inflation } (0.08)]$$
$$= (1 + 0.10)(1 + 0.08)$$
$$= 1.188$$

Therefore the RRR is now 18.8 per cent (i.e. $1.188 - 1$). It is also necessary to adjust the cash flows for inflation. The revised NPV calculation is:

$$\frac{£600\,000(1.08)}{1.10(1.08)} + \frac{£400\,000(1.08)^2}{(1.10)^2\,(1.08)^2} + \frac{£1\,000\,000(1.08)^3}{(1.10)^3\,(1.08)^3} - £1\,000\,000 = £627\,347$$

You can see in the numerator of the NPV calculation that the real cash flows are adjusted at the compound rate of inflation of 8 per cent. In the denominators of the calculation, Fisher's equation is shown to calculate the discount rate assuming an expected inflation rate of 8 per cent. Consequently, the inflation factors of 1.08 cancel out. Therefore if the cash flows and the required rate of return are subject to the same rate of inflation, then the project's NPV will be unaffected by expected changes in the level of inflation. For example, if inflation is now expected to be 5 per cent instead of 8 per cent then the inflation factor of 1.08 in the numerator and denominator of the NPV calculation would be replaced by 1.05. However, the revised inflation factors would still cancel out and NPV would remain unchanged.

Looking at the NPV calculation, you should see that there are two correct approaches for adjusting for inflation which will lead to the same answer. They are:

Method 1: Predict *nominal cash flows* (i.e. adjust the cash flows for inflation) and use a *nominal discount rate.*

Method 2: Predict *real cash flows* at today's prices and use a *real discount rate.*

You will have noted that the approach outlined above used Method 1. Can you see that if we use Method 2 the inflation factors of 1.08 will be omitted from the numerator and denominator in the above NPV calculation but the NPV will remain unchanged? The NPV calculation will thus be identical to the calculation shown earlier, which assumed zero inflation.

The correct treatment of inflation therefore requires that the assumptions about inflation that enter the cash flow forecasts are consistent with those that enter into the discount rate calculation. You must avoid the mistakes that are commonly made of discounting real cash flows at nominal discount rates or the discounting of nominal cash flows at real discount rates.

CALCULATING RISK-ADJUSTED DISCOUNT RATES

In Chapter 13, we noted that a company should only invest in new projects if the returns are greater than those that the shareholders could obtain from investing in securities of the same risk traded in the financial markets. If we can measure the returns that investors require for different levels of risk, we can use these rates of return as the discount rates for calculating net present values and thus incorporate risk into investment appraisal.

Studies of past average returns from investing in securities listed on the UK and USA stock exchanges indicate returns of approximately 4 per cent for treasury bills and 13 per cent for ordinary shares (i.e. common stocks). Investing in treasury bills is nearly risk free, but investing in ordinary shares is risky (see note 1 at the end of the chapter). There is a possibility that you could earn very low or very high returns if you invest in ordinary shares. The studies of past returns indicate that the safest investment has yielded the lowest average rate of return. The evidence indicates that investors require higher expected returns for investing in risky securities.

The average return from investing in ordinary shares represents the average return you would have obtained from investing in all shares listed on the UK or USA stock exchange. A portfolio containing all

Use your crystal ball

An article published in *The Irish Times* by Olive Keogh cites the following comments by Patrick Gibbons, professor of strategic management at the UCD Michael Smurfit Graduate Business School:

The one thing we know about most forecasts is that they are wrong. At a minimum, in making forecasts, firms should think about a range of key parameters, such as market shares, growth rates and so on, as opposed to single-point estimates. The amount of resources devoted to forecasting are predicated on how easily reversible the decisions are. Where investment requirements are low, the investment/capital is extremely flexible, or the payback period is very fast, then extensive market forecasting may not be required. Where investment requirements

are high, capital is extremely specialized and inflexible, and where the lead-time to bring investment on-stream is very long, then more extensive forecasting is necessary.

Questions

1 How can more extensive and less extensive forms of forecasting be applied to appraising capital investment projects?

2 What is the difference between estimates based on a range of key parameters and single-point estimates?

Reference

Keogh, O. (2012) 'Use your crystal ball', *Irish Times*, 30 March. Available at www.irishtimes.com/business /economy/ireland/use-your-crystal-ball-1.492272

shares, or a representative sample, listed on a national stock exchange is termed the market portfolio. It is possible for investors to invest in a portfolio of shares (or a unit trust) that in terms of risk and return is virtually identical to the market portfolio.

The extra average return in the past from investing in the market portfolio compared with the risk-free investment has been 9 per cent (13 per cent − 4 per cent). This extra return is called the risk premium. Suppose a firm has a project that in terms of risk is identical with the market portfolio. What is the *current* required rate of return on this project? We calculate this by taking the current interest rate on treasury bill securities (called the risk-free rate) and adding the average past risk premium of 9 per cent. Assume that the current interest rate is 4 per cent. The required rate of return (RRR) is calculated as follows:

$$\text{RRR on an equivalent investment to the market portfolio} = \text{risk-free rate (4\%)} + \text{average past risk premium (9\%)} \qquad (14.4)$$

Therefore the project's cash flows should be discounted at 13 per cent and a project that is risk free should be discounted at the same rate as that available from investing in treasury bills (i.e. 4 per cent).

We have now established two benchmarks: the discount rate for risk-free projects and the discount rate for investments that have a risk equivalent to the market portfolio. However, we have not established how discount rates can be estimated for projects that do not fall into these categories. To do this, we must consider the relationship between risk and return.

Let us consider the risk and return from holding the market portfolio. Assume that the expected return from holding the market portfolio is 13 per cent and the risk-free rate of interest is 4 per cent. Therefore the risk premium required for holding the market portfolio is 9 per cent. We shall also assume that risk measured by the standard deviation from investing in the market portfolio is 16 per cent and that from investing in the risk-free security is zero. These risk–return relationships are plotted in Figure 14.1. Note that the return on the market portfolio is represented by R_m and the return on the risk-free security as R_f.

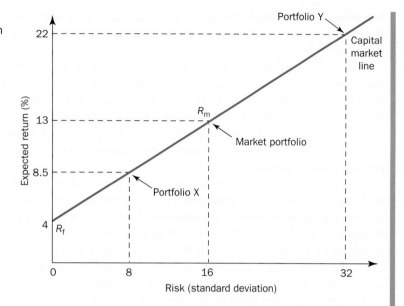

FIGURE 14.1

Risk–return relationship from combining borrowing and lending with the market portfolio

You can see that an investor can invest in any portfolio that falls on the line between points R_f and R_m. For example, if you invest in portfolio X consisting of £500 in the market portfolio and £500 in the risk-free investment, your *expected* return will be 8.5 per cent (£500 at 4 per cent plus £500 at 13 per cent). Note that the standard deviation from investing in portfolio X is:

$$\left(\begin{array}{c} 1/2 \times \text{standard deviation of} \\ \text{risk-free security (0)} \end{array}\right) + \left(\begin{array}{c} 1/2 \times \text{standard deviation of} \\ \text{market portfolio (16\%)} \end{array}\right) = 8\% \qquad (14.5)$$

In other words, investing in portfolio X is half as risky as investing in the market portfolio. We can now establish a formula for calculating the *expected* return on portfolios of different levels of risk:

$$\text{expected return} = \text{risk-free return} + \left(\text{risk premium} \times \frac{\text{risk of selected portfolio}}{\text{risk of market portfolio}}\right) \qquad (14.6)$$

$$= 4 + (9\% \times 8/16) = 8.5\%$$

Using this formula, we can calculate the expected return for any point along the line R_f to R_m in Figure 14.1. How can you invest in a portfolio that falls on the line above R_m? Such a position is achieved by borrowing and investing your funds in the market portfolio. Suppose you invest £1000 of your own funds and borrow £1000 at the risk-free rate of 4 per cent and invest the combined funds of £2000 in the market portfolio. We shall call this portfolio Y. Your *expected* annual return will be £260 from investing in the market portfolio (£2000 × 13 per cent) less £40 interest on the £1000 loan. Therefore your return will be £220 from investing £1000 of your own funds, i.e. 22 per cent. However, this is the *expected* return, and there is a possibility that the return on the market portfolio could be zero, but you would have to repay the borrowed funds. In other words, by borrowing you increase the variability of your potential returns and therefore the standard deviation. The calculation of the standard deviation for portfolio Y is:

$$\frac{(£2000 \times 16\%) - (£1000 \times 0\%)}{£1000} = 32\%$$

We can also use equation (14.6) to calculate the expected return on portfolio Y. It is:

$$4\% + (9\% \times 32/16) = 22\%$$

We have now established that an investor can achieve any point along the sloping line in Figure 14.1 by combining lending (i.e. investing in the risk-free security) and investing in the market portfolio or borrowing and investing in the market portfolio. The sloping line shown in Figure 14.1 that indicates the risk return relationship from combining lending or borrowing with the market portfolio is called the capital market line.

The market portfolio can now be used as a benchmark for determining the expected return on *individual* securities, rather than portfolios of securities. Consider three securities – the ordinary shares of companies A, B and C. Let us assume that, relative to the variability of the market portfolio, the risk of security A is identical, B is half as risky and C is twice as risky. In other words, in terms of risk, security A is identical with the market portfolio, B is equivalent to portfolio X and C is equivalent to portfolio Y. Consequently, the required rates of return are 13 per cent for A, 8.5 per cent for B and 22 per cent for C.

The returns available from combining investing in the market portfolio with borrowing and lending represent the most efficient investment portfolios, and determine the risk/return relationships for all securities traded in the market. The relationship between the risk of a security and the risk of the market portfolio is called beta. The beta of the market portfolio is 1.0 and the beta of a security that is half as risky as the market is 0.5, whereas the beta of a security that is twice as risky as the market portfolio is 2.0. The relationship between risk (measured in terms of beta) and expected return is shown by the sloping line in Figure 14.2. This sloping line is called the security market line.

The model described above is called the capital asset pricing model (CAPM). The equation for the CAPM is the equation for the security market line shown in Figure 14.2 and can be used to establish the expected return on any security. The equation is:

$$\begin{matrix} \text{expected} \\ \text{return on a} \\ \text{security} \end{matrix} = \begin{matrix} \text{risk-free} \\ \text{rate} \end{matrix} + \left(\begin{matrix} \text{expected return} \\ \text{on the market} \\ \text{portfolio} \end{matrix} - \begin{matrix} \text{risk-free} \\ \text{rate} \end{matrix} \right) \times \text{beta} \tag{14.7}$$

Therefore

$$\text{security A} = 4\% + (13\% - 4\%) \times 1.0 = 13\%$$
$$\text{security B} = 4\% + (13\% - 4\%) \times 0.5 = 8.5\%$$
$$\text{security C} = 4\% + (13\% - 4\%) \times 2.0 = 22\%$$

FIGURE 14.2
Risk–return relationship expressed in terms of beta

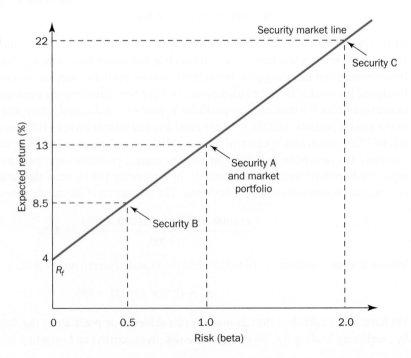

How is beta calculated? For the answer to this question you should consult the business finance literature (see Recommended reading at the end of the chapter). Calculating betas in practice is very tedious. Fortunately, it is unnecessary to calculate betas, since their values are published in various risk measurement publications relating to securities traded in financial markets. You should now know how to calculate the required rates of returns for a firm's securities: simply multiply the average risk premium from investing in the market portfolio (9 per cent) by the beta for the security, and add this to the current interest rate on treasury bills. The required rate of return for a firm can now be used as the discount rate to appraise investment projects provided that the project is of equivalent risk to the firm's existing assets. Where the risk differs from average firm risk the required rate of return for a proxy firm of similar risk should be calculated and used as the appropriate discount rate.

WEIGHTED AVERAGE COST OF CAPITAL

So far we have assumed that firms are financed only by equity finance (i.e. ordinary share capital and retained earnings). However, most companies are likely to be financed by a combination of debt and equity capital. These companies aim to maintain target proportions of debt and equity.

The cost of *new* debt capital is simply the after tax interest cost of raising new debt. Assume that the after tax cost of new debt capital is 6 per cent and the required rate of return on equity capital is 14 per cent and that the company intends to maintain a capital structure of 50 per cent debt and 50 per cent equity. The overall cost of capital for the company is calculated as follows:

$$\left(\begin{array}{c} \text{proportion of debt capital} \\ \times \text{ cost of debt capital} \\ (0.5 \times 6\%) \end{array}\right) + \left(\begin{array}{c} \text{proportion of equity capital} \\ \times \text{ cost of equity capital} \\ (0.5 \times 14\%) \end{array}\right) = 10\% \qquad (14.8)$$

The overall cost of capital is also called the weighted average cost of capital. Can we use the weighted average cost of capital as the discount rate to calculate a project's NPV? The answer is yes, provided that the project is of equivalent risk to the firm's existing assets and the firm intends to maintain its target capital structure of 50 per cent debt and 50 per cent equity.

We have now established how to calculate the discount rate for projects that are of similar risk to the firm's existing assets and to incorporate the financing aspects. It is the weighted average cost of equity and debt capital.

SENSITIVITY ANALYSIS

The aim of sensitivity analysis is not to quantify risk but to assess how responsive the NPV is to changes in the variables that are used to calculate it. Thus it is assumed that risk-adjusted discount rates are derived using the approach described in the preceding sections. Figure 14.3 illustrates that the NPV calculation is dependent on several independent variables, all of which are uncertain. The approach requires that the NPVs are calculated under alternative assumptions to determine how sensitive they are to changing conditions.

The application of sensitivity analysis can indicate those variables to which the NPV is most sensitive and the extent to which these variables may change before the investment results in a negative NPV. In other words, sensitivity analysis indicates why a project might fail. Management should review any critical variables to assess whether or not there is a strong possibility of events occurring that will lead to a negative NPV. Management should also pay particular attention to controlling those variables to which NPV is particularly sensitive, once the decision has been taken to accept the investment. Sensitivity analysis is illustrated with Example 14.4.

REAL WORLD VIEWS 14.3

Sensitivity analysis – oil and gas exploration, the sensitivity of return on investment

According to Industrial Info Resources, a leading provider of industrial intelligence data, the sustained high prices for oil and natural gas that existed at the time prompted an increasing interest in drilling in locations that were previously not considered. For example, oil is being extracted from sands in countries such as Canada, where the deposits are second in size to Saudi Arabia, at approximately 170 billion barrels. In the US, 'wet gas' is being extracted, as well as 'dry gas' from shale deposits. Wet gas refers to natural gas, which has a lower methane content, typically less than 85 per cent. This lower methane content increases the processing costs. Nevertheless, according to Industrial Info Resources, with natural gas prices at $4 per thousand cubic feet, New York based Seneca Resources achieved a return in investment of 20–40 per cent in extracting dry gas from shale deposits. In comparison, the report also mentions Range Resources Corporation, which achieved a 40–60 per cent return on a well in south western Pennsylvania, which had higher gas content. The cost of both wells was estimated at $4m.

Questions

1 Other than the volume of oil or gas found, what factors might affect the return on investment for a particular drill site?

2 Do you think oil and gas exploration companies are likely to continuously use sensitivity analysis in exploration activities, developing oil/gas finds or both?

References

www.industrialinfo.com/showAbstract.jsp
  ?newsitemID=171455
www.canadasoilsands.ca/en/overview/index.aspx

Some of the variables referred to in Example 14.4 to which sensitivity analysis can be applied are as follows:

1 *Sales volume*: The net cash flows will have to fall to £876 040 (£2 000 000/2.283 discount factor) for the NPV to be zero, because it will be zero when the present value of the future cash flows is equal to the investment cost of £2 000 000. As the cash flows are equal each year, the cumulative discount

FIGURE 14.3
Sensitivity of NPV to changes in independent variables

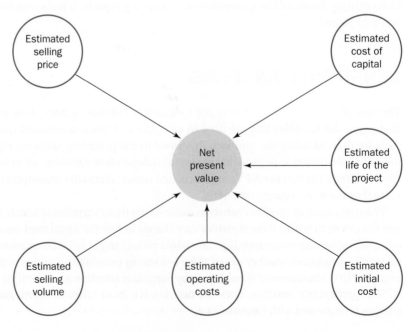

EXAMPLE 14.4

One of the divisions of the Bothnia Company is considering the purchase of a new machine and estimates of the most likely cash flows are as follows:

	Year 0 (£)	Year 1 (£)	Year 2 (£)	Year 3 (£)
Initial outlay	−2 000 000			
Cash inflows				
(100 000 units at £30 per unit)		3 000 000	3 000 000	3 000 000
Variable costs		2 000 000	2 000 000	2 000 000
Net cash flows	−2 000 000	+1 000 000	+1 000 000	+1 000 000

The cost of capital is 15 per cent and the net present value is £283 000.

tables in Appendix B can be used. The discount factor for 15 per cent and year 3 is 2.283. If the discount factor is divided into the required present value of £2 000 000, we get an annual cash flow of £876 040. Given that the most likely *net* cash flow is £1 000 000, the *net* cash flow may decline by approximately £124 000 each year (£1 million − £876 040) before the NPV becomes zero. Total sales revenue may therefore decline by £372 000 (assuming that net cash flow is 33.1/3 per cent of sales). At a selling price of £30 per unit, this represents 12 400 units, or alternatively we may state that the sales volume may decline by 12.4 per cent before the NPV becomes negative.

2 *Selling price*: When the sales volume is 100 000 units per annum, total annual sales revenue can fall to approximately £2 876 000 (£3 000 000 − £124 000) before the NPV becomes negative (note that it is assumed that total variable costs and units sold will remain unchanged). This represents a selling price per unit of £28.76, or a reduction of £1.24 per unit, which represents a 4.1 per cent reduction in the selling price.

3 *Variable costs*: The total annual variable costs can increase by £124 000 or £1.24 per unit before NPV becomes zero. This represents an increase of 6.2 per cent.

4 *Initial outlay*: The initial outlay can rise by the NPV before the investment breaks even. The initial outlay may therefore increase by £283 000 or 14.15 per cent.

5 *Cost of capital*: We calculate the internal rate of return for the project, which is 23 per cent. Consequently, the cost of capital can increase by 53 per cent before the NPV becomes negative.

The elements to which the NPV appears to be most sensitive are the items with the lowest percentage changes. They are selling price followed by the variable costs, and it is important that management pay particular attention to these items so that they can be carefully monitored.

Sensitivity analysis can take various forms. In our example, for the selected variables, we focused on the extent to which each could change for NPV to become zero. Another form of sensitivity analysis is to examine the impact on NPV of a specified percentage change in a selected variable. For example, what is the impact on NPV if sales volume falls by 10 per cent? A third approach is to examine the impact on NPV of pessimistic, most likely and optimistic estimates for each selected variable.

Sensitivity analysis has a number of limitations. In particular, the method requires that changes in each key variable be isolated, but management is more interested in the combination of the effect of changes in two or more key variables. According to the international survey by the Chartered Institute of Management Accountants (2009) around 63 per cent of larger companies and 45 per cent of smaller companies used sensitivity analysis to appraise capital investments.

INITIATION, AUTHORIZATION AND REVIEW OF PROJECTS

The capital investment process should ensure that procedures are in place so that new projects are initiated, investigated and evaluated using the approaches described in this and the previous chapter. It is also necessary to ensure that projects that are accepted contribute to achieving an organization's objectives and support its strategies. In addition, once a project has been authorized, procedures should be established for reviewing and controlling new investments. The capital investment process involves several stages including:

1 the search for investment opportunities;
2 initial screening;
3 project authorizations;
4 controlling the capital expenditure during the installation stage;
5 post-completion audit of the cash flows.

Search for investment opportunities

Potential investment projects are not just born – someone has to suggest them. Without a creative search of new investment opportunities, even the most sophisticated appraisal techniques are worthless. A firm's prosperity depends far more on its ability to create investments than on its ability to appraise them. Thus it is important that a firm scans the environment for potential opportunities or takes action to protect itself against potential threats. This process is closely linked to the strategies of an organization. An important task of senior management is therefore to promote a culture that encourages the search for and promotion of new investment opportunities.

Initial screening

During this stage, projects are examined and subject to preliminary assessment to ascertain if they are likely to warrant further attention through the application of more sophisticated analysis. Projects that are not considered to warrant further attention are normally discarded. The preliminary assessment involves an examination of whether projects satisfy strategic criteria and conform to initial risk requirements. At this stage projects may also be subject to an assessment as to whether they satisfy simplistic financial criteria, such as meeting required payback periods. For most large firms, those projects that meet the initial screening requirements are included in an annual capital budget, which is a list of projects planned for the coming year. However, it should be noted that the inclusion of a project in the capital budget does not provide an authorization for the final go-ahead for the investment.

Project authorizations

Many organizations require that project proposals are presented in a formalized manner by submitting capital appropriation request forms for each project. These requests include descriptions of the projects, detailed cash flow forecasts, the investment required and a financial appraisal incorporating discounted cash flow analyses. Because investment decisions are of vital importance, appropriation requests are generally submitted for approval to a top management committee. Companies normally set ceilings for investments so that only those projects that exceed the ceiling are submitted to the top management committee. Investments below the ceiling are normally of less strategic importance and of lower value and are therefore subject to approval at lower management levels.

Controlling the capital expenditure during the installation stage

Comparisons should be made between actual and estimated expenditures at periodic intervals during the installation and construction stage of the project. Reports should be prepared giving details of the percentage completion, over- or under-spending relative to the stage of completion, the estimated costs to complete compared with the original estimate, the time taken compared with the estimate for the current stage of completion and also the estimated completion date compared with the original estimate. This information will enable management to take corrective cost-saving action such as changing the construction schedule.

Post-completion audit of cash flows

When the investment is in operation, post-completion audits should be undertaken whereby the actual results are compared with the estimated results that were included in the investment proposal. Whenever possible, actual cash flows plus estimated cash flows for the remainder of the project's life should be compared with the cash flows that were included in the original estimate. However, the feasibility of making such a comparison will depend on the ease and cost of estimating future cash flows.

A major problem is that, except for the very large projects, the portion of cash flows that stem from a specific capital investment is very difficult to isolate. All one can do in such situations is to scrutinize carefully the investment at the approval stage and incorporate the estimated results into departmental operating budgets. Although the results of individual projects cannot be isolated, their combined effect can be examined as part of the conventional periodic performance review.

A post-audit of capital investment decisions is a very difficult task, and any past investment decisions that have proved to be wrong should not be interpreted in isolation. It is important to remind oneself that capital investment decisions are made under uncertainty. For example, a good decision may turn out to be unsuccessful yet may still have been the correct decision in the light of the information and alternatives available at the time.

Care should be taken to ensure that post-audits are not conducted as recriminatory 'post mortem'. Adopting such an approach can discourage initiative and produce a policy of over-caution. There is a danger that managers will submit only safe investment proposals. The problem is likely to be reduced if managers know their selections will be fairly judged.

In spite of all the problems, a post-audit comparison should be undertaken. A record of past performance and mistakes is one way of improving future performance and ensuring that fewer mistakes are made. In addition, the fact that the proposers of capital investment projects are aware that their estimates will be compared with actual results encourages them to exercise restraint and submit more thorough and realistic appraisals of future investment projects. According to the international survey by the Chartered Institute of Management Accountants (2009) around 47 per cent of larger companies and 32 per cent of smaller companies conducted post-completion audits of capital expenditure.

SUMMARY

The following items relate to the learning objectives listed at the beginning of the chapter.

- **Explain capital rationing and select the optimum combination of investments when capital is rationed for a single period.**

Capital rationing applies to a situation where there is a constraint on the amount of funds that can be invested during a specific period of time. In this situation, the net present value is maximized by adopting the profitability index method (i.e. the present value of cash flows divided by the investment outlay) of ranking, and using this ranking to select investments up to the total investment funds that are available for the period.

● **Calculate the incremental taxation payments arising from a proposed investment.**

The cash flows from a project must be reduced by the amount of taxation payable on these cash flows. However, the taxation savings arising from the capital allowances (i.e. annual writing-down allowances) reduce the taxation payments. Because taxation payments do not occur at the same time as the associated cash flows, the precise timing of the taxation payments should be identified to calculate NPV. You should refer to the section headed 'Taxation and investment decisions' for an illustration of the computation of the incremental taxation payment.

● **Describe the two approaches for adjusting for inflation when appraising capital projects.**

The net present value can be adjusted by two basic ways to take inflation into account. First, a discount rate can be used, based on the required rate of return, that includes an allowance for inflation. Remember that cash flows must also be adjusted for inflation. Second, the anticipated rate of inflation can be excluded from the discount rate and the cash flows can be expressed in real terms. In other words, the first method discounts nominal cash flows at a nominal discount rate and the second method discounts real cash flows at a real discount rate.

● **Explain how risk-adjusted discount rates are calculated.**

Risk-adjusted discount rates for a firm can be calculated using the capital asset pricing model (CAPM). The CAPM uses beta as a measure of risk. Beta is a measure of the sensitivity of the returns on a firm's securities relative to a proxy market portfolio (e.g. the *Financial Times* All-Share Index). The risk-adjusted return is derived by adding a risk premium for a firm's securities to a risk-free rate (normally represented by government treasury bills). The risk premium is derived by estimating the return on the market portfolio over the risk-free rate and multiplying this premium by the beta of a firm's shares.

● **Explain how sensitivity analysis can be applied to investment appraisal.**

Sensitivity analysis can take many forms but the most popular form is to independently ascertain the percentage change in each of the variables used to calculate NPV for the NPV to become zero.

● **Describe the initiation, authorization and review procedures for the investment process.**

The capital investment process entails several stages including: (a) the search for investment opportunities; (b) initial screening of the projects; (c) project authorizations; (d) controlling the capital expenditure during the installation stage; and (e) a post-completion audit of the cash flows. You should refer to the section in Chapter 14 titled 'Initiation, authorization and review of capital projects' for an explanation of each of these stages.

● **Additional learning objective specified in Learning Note 14.1.**

The learning note accompanying this chapter includes an additional learning objective: to evaluate mutually exclusive investments with unequal lives. Because this topic does not form part of the curriculum for many courses, it is presented as a learning note. You should check your course curriculum to ascertain if you need to read Learning Note 14.1 that can be accessed from the digital resources accompanying this book (see Preface for details).

NOTE

1 Future payments of interest and the principal repayment on maturity are fixed and known with certainty. Gilt-edged securities, such as treasury bills, are therefore risk free in nominal terms. However, they are not risk free in real terms because changes in interest rates will result in changes in the market values.

KEY TERMS AND CONCEPTS

Balancing allowance An adjusting payment made by the tax authorities when the estimated realizable value of an asset is less than its written-down value, reflecting insufficient allowances that have been claimed.

Balancing charge An adjusting payment made to the tax authorities when the estimated realizable value of an asset exceeds its written-down value, reflecting excess allowances that have been claimed.

Beta The relationship between the risk of a security and the risk of the market portfolio.

Capital allowances Standardized depreciation allowances granted by the tax authorities with the aim of enabling the net cost of assets to be deducted as an allowable expense over a given time period, also known as writing-down allowances (WDAs) and depreciation tax shields.

Capital asset pricing model (CAPM) A model that shows the relationship between risk and expected rate of return on an investment.

Capital market line A graphical representation of the risk return relationship from combining lending or borrowing with the market portfolio.

Capital rationing The limiting of capital available for investment that occurs whenever there is a budget ceiling or a market constraint on the amount of funds that can be invested during a specific period of time.

Depreciation tax shields Standardized depreciation allowances granted by the tax authorities with the aim of enabling the net cost of assets to be deducted as an allowable expense over a given time period, also known as capital allowances and writing-down allowances (WDAs).

General rate of inflation The average rate of inflation for all goods and services traded in an economy.

Hard capital rationing A term used to refer to situations where the amount of capital investment is restricted because of external constraints such as the inability to obtain funds from the financial markets.

Market portfolio A portfolio containing all shares, or a representative sample of shares, listed on a national stock exchange.

Money cash flows Cash flows expressed in monetary units at the time when they are received.

Money rates of return The rates of return quoted on securities that reflect anticipated inflation, also known as nominal rates of return.

Nominal or **money cash flows** Cash flows expressed in monetary units at the time when they are received.

Nominal rates of return The rates of return quoted on securities that reflect anticipated inflation, also known as money rates of return.

Post-completion audits Audits that are undertaken when an investment is in operation, comparing actual results with the estimated results that were included in the investment proposal.

Profitability index The present value of a project divided by its investment outlay.

Real cash flows Cash flows expressed in terms of today's purchasing power, assuming no future inflation.

Real rate of return The rate of return on an investment that would be required in the absence of inflation.

Risk premium The extra average return from investing in the market portfolio compared with a risk-free investment.

Security market line A graphical representation of the relationship between risk (measured in terms of beta) and expected return for securities with different levels of risk.

Sensitivity analysis Analysis that shows how a result will be changed if the original estimates or underlying assumption changes.

Soft capital rationing A term used to refer to situations where an organization imposes an internal budget ceiling on the amount of capital expenditure.

Weighted average cost of capital The overall cost of capital to an organization, taking into account the proportion of capital raised from debt and equity.

Writing-down allowances (WDAs) Standardized depreciation allowances granted by the tax authorities with the aim of enabling the net cost of assets to be deducted as an allowable expense over a given time period, also known as capital allowances and depreciation tax shields.

RECOMMENDED READING

This chapter has provided an outline of the capital asset pricing model and the calculation of risk-adjusted discount rate. These topics are dealt with in more depth in the business finance literature. You should refer to Brealey, Myers and Allen (2016) for a description of the capital asset pricing model and risk-adjusted discount rates. For a discussion of the differences between company, divisional and project cost of capital and an explanation of how project discount rates can be calculated when project risk is different from average overall firm risk, see Pike, Neale and Linsley (2015).

KEY EXAMINATION POINTS

A common error is for students to include depreciation and apportioned overheads in the DCF analysis. Remember that only incremental cash flows should be included in the analysis. Where a question includes taxation, you should separately calculate the incremental taxable profits and then work out the tax payment. You should then include the tax payment in the DCF analysis. Incremental taxable profits are normally incremental cash flows less capital allowances on the project. To simplify the calculations, questions sometimes indicate that capital allowances should be calculated on a straight line depreciation method.

Do not use accounting profits instead of taxable profits to work out the tax payment. Taxable profits are calculated by adding back depreciation to accounting profits and then deducting capital allowances. Make sure that you include any balancing allowance or charge and disposal value in the DCF analysis if the asset is sold.

With inflation, you should discount nominal cash flows at the nominal discount rate. Most questions give the nominal discount rate (also called the money discount rate). You should then adjust the cash flows for inflation. If you are required to choose between alternative projects, check that they have equal lives. If not, use one of the methods described in Learning Note 14.1 on the digital support resources (see Preface for details).

ASSESSMENT MATERIAL

The review questions are short questions that enable you to assess your understanding of the main topics included in the chapter. The numbers in parentheses provide you with the page numbers to refer to if you cannot answer a specific question.

The review problems are more complex and require you to relate and apply the content to various business problems. The problems are graded by their level of difficulty. Solutions to review problems that are not preceded by the term 'IM' are provided in a separate section at the end of the book. Solutions to problems preceded by the term 'IM' are provided in the Instructor's Manual accompanying this book that can be downloaded from the lecturer's digital support resources. Additional review problems with fully worked solutions are provided in the *Student Manual* that accompanies this book.

REVIEW QUESTIONS

14.1 What is capital rationing? Distinguish between hard and soft capital rationing. (pp. 338–339)

14.2 Explain how the optimum investment programme should be determined when capital is rationed for a single period. (pp. 339–340)

14.3 How does taxation affect the appraisal of capital investments? (pp. 340–341)

14.4 Define writing-down allowances (also known as depreciation tax shields or capital allowances), balancing allowances and balancing charges. (pp. 342–343)

14.5 How does the presence of inflation affect the appraisal of capital investments? (pp. 343–344)

14.6 Distinguish between nominal cash flows and real cash flows and nominal discount rates and real discount rates. (p. 344)

14.7 Why is it necessary to use risk-adjusted discount rates to appraise capital investments? (pp. 345–346)

14.8 Explain how risk-adjusted discount rates are calculated. (pp. 345–349)

14.9 How can sensitivity analysis help in appraising capital investments? What are the limitations of sensitivity analysis? (pp. 349–351)

14.10 Describe the different forms of sensitivity analysis. (p. 351)

14.11 Describe the stages involved in the initiation, authorization and review of projects. (pp. 352–353)

14.12 Explain what a post-completion audit is and how it can provide useful benefits. (p. 353)

REVIEW PROBLEMS

14.13 **Intermediate.** A company has a real cost of capital of 6 per cent per annum and inflation is 3 per cent per annum. The company's money cost of capital per annum is:

(a) 9.00%
(b) 2.91%

(c) 3.00%
(d) 9.18%

(2 marks)

CIMA P1 Performance Operations

14.14 Intermediate. A project requires an initial investment of $150000 and has an expected life of five years. The required rate of return on the project is 12 per cent per annum.

The project's estimated cash flows each year are as follows:

	$000
Sales revenue	101
Variable costs	30
Incremental fixed costs	5

The selling price, costs and activity levels are expected to remain the same for each year of the project.

Ignore taxation and inflation.

Required:

Calculate the percentage change in the selling price that would result in the project being rejected. *(4 marks)*

CIMA P1 Performance Operations

14.15 A capital investment project has the following estimated cash flows and present values:

Year		Cash flow $	Discount factor @ 12%	Present value $
0	Initial investment	(100000)	1.0	(100000)
1–5	Contribution per annum	52000	3.605	187460
1–5	Fixed costs per annum	(25000)	3.605	(90125)
5	Residual value	20000	0.567	11340

Required:

(i) Calculate the sensitivity of the investment decision to a change in the annual fixed costs. *(3 marks)*

(ii) State TWO benefits to a company of using sensitivity analysis in investment appraisal. *(2 marks)*

CIMA P1 Performance Operations

14.16 A company is considering investing in a project with an expected life of four years. The project has a positive net present value of $280000 when cash flows are discounted at 12 per cent per annum. The project's estimated cash flows include net cash inflows of $320000 for each of the four years. No tax is payable on projects of this type.

The percentage decrease in the estimated annual net cash inflows that would cause the company's management to reject the project from a financial perspective is, to the nearest 0.1 per cent:

(a) 87.5%
(b) 21.9%
(c) 3.5%
(d) 28.8% *(2 marks)*

CIMA P1 Performance Operations

14.17 A company is considering five investment projects as follows:

Project	Investment $	Profitability index
A	12000	0.20
B	8000	0.05
C	20000	0.60
D	16000	0.40
E	14000	0.30

The company has $40000 available for investment. Projects C and D are mutually exclusive. All projects can be undertaken only once and are divisible.

Required:

Calculate the maximum net present value (NPV) that can be earned from the projects given that there is only $40000 available for investment. *(5 marks)*

CIMA P1 Performance Operations

14.18 TS operates a fleet of vehicles and is considering whether to replace the vehicles on a one, two or three year cycle.

Each vehicle costs $25000. The operating costs per vehicle for each year and the resale value at the end of each year are as follows:

	Year 1 $	Year 2 $	Year 3 $
Operating costs	5000	8000	11000
Resale value	18000	15000	5000

The cost of capital is 6 per cent per annum.

Required:

Calculate the optimum replacement cycle for the vehicles. You should assume that the initial investment is incurred at the beginning of year 1 and that all other cash flows arise at the end of the year. *(5 marks)*

CIMA P1 Performance Operations

14.19 Advanced. The following data relate to both questions (a) and (b). A company is considering investing in a manufacturing project that would have a three-year life span. The investment would involve an immediate cash outflow of £50000 and have a zero residual value. In each of the three years, 4000 units would be produced and sold. The contribution per unit, based on current prices, is £5. The company has an annual cost of capital of 8 per cent. It is expected that the inflation rate will be 3 per cent in each of the next three years.

(a) The net present value of the project (to the nearest £500) is:

(a) £4500
(b) £5000
(c) £5500
(d) £6000
(e) £6500 *(3 marks)*

(b) If the annual inflation rate is now projected to be 4 per cent, the maximum monetary cost of capital for this project to remain viable, is (to the nearest 0.5 per cent):

(a) 13.0%
(b) 13.5%
(c) 14.0%
(d) 14.5%
(e) 15.0% *(2 marks)*

CIMA Management Accounting – Decision Making

14.20 Advanced: NPV, taxation and optimal replacement period (see Learning Note 14.1 for an explanation of optimal replacement period). LM is a supermarket chain that operates 500 stores. The company's sales have fallen behind its competitors as it currently does not offer its customers an online shopping service.

It is considering a proposal to establish an online shopping service using the technology of PQ, an existing online retailer.

Sales revenue and gross profit

The number of customers using the online delivery service in the first five years is estimated to be as follows:

Year 1	100 000 customers per week
Year 2	120 000 customers per week
Year 3	150 000 customers per week
Year 4	160 000 customers per week
Year 5	170 000 customers per week

Customers are expected to spend an average of $200 per week. Delivery to customers will be free of charge. The expected gross profit margin is 20 per cent of selling price.

Loss of existing in-store sales

It is estimated that 30 per cent of customers purchasing online would have purchased in store if the online facility was not available. The sales revenue per customer and gross profit margin on online sales will be the same as that for instore sales.

Capital expenditure

LM will purchase a fleet of delivery vehicles costing $15 million. The vehicles will have a useful life of five years and will be depreciated on a straight line basis. They will have no residual value at the end of the five year period. The vehicles will be eligible for tax depreciation.

Contract with the online retailer

The contract with PQ will be for an initial period of 5 years. LM will pay $340 million to buy one of PQ's existing warehouses. LM will also invest $90 million to expand the facility. The expanded warehouse will then be leased back to PQ for five years for a fee of $20 million per annum. The cost of purchasing the warehouse and the expansion costs will not be eligible for tax depreciation. The warehouse will have a realizable value of $350 million at the end of the five-year period.

LM will pay 1 per cent of gross profit from the online business to PQ. LM will also pay a fee of $30 million per annum to license the technology and as a contribution towards PQ's research and development costs.

Other operating costs

The online operation will result in additional costs in the first year of $60 million, including delivery costs but excluding depreciation. This amount will rise by $5 million each year as the customer numbers increase.

Taxation

LM's financial director has provided the following taxation information:

- Tax depreciation: 25 per cent per annum of the reducing balance, with a balancing adjustment in the year of disposal.
- Taxation rate: 30 per cent of taxable profits. Half of the tax is payable in the year in which it arises, the balance is paid in the following year.
- LM has sufficient taxable profits from other parts of its business to enable the offset of any pre-tax losses on this project.

Other information

- A cost of capital of 12 per cent per annum is used to evaluate projects of this type.
- Ignore inflation.

Required:

(a) Evaluate whether LM should go ahead with the proposal to establish an online shopping service. You should use net present value as the basis of your evaluation. Your workings should be rounded to the nearest $ million.

(14 marks)

(b) Explain TWO other factors that LM should consider before deciding whether to go ahead with the contract.

(4 marks)

(c) LM is concerned that replacing the delivery vehicles every five years will result in breakdowns and customer complaints. It is therefore considering whether to replace the vehicles on a one, two or three-year cycle. The proposed contract with the online retailer expires after five years, however at the end of this period LM will continue to operate the online business. The delivery vehicles will therefore require to be continually replaced.

Each vehicle costs $25 000. The operating costs per vehicle for each year and the resale value at the end of each year are estimated as follows:

	Year 1 $	Year 2 $	Year 3 $
Operating costs	6 000	8 000	12 000
Resale value	16 000	10 000	4 000

Required:
Calculate, using the annualized equivalent method, whether the vehicles should be replaced on a one, two or three year cycle. You should assume that the initial investment is incurred at the beginning of year 1 and that all other cash flows arise at the end of the year. Ignore taxation and inflation and use a cost of capital of 12 per cent.

(7 marks)

CIMA P1 Performance Operations

14.21 Advanced: Inflation and taxation. Assume that you have been appointed finance director of Breckall plc. The company is considering investing in the production of an electronic security device, with an expected market life of five years.

The previous finance director has undertaken an analysis of the proposed project; the main features of his analysis are shown below. He has recommended that the project should not be undertaken because the estimated annual accounting rate of return is only 12.3 per cent:

Proposed electronic security device project

	Year 0 (£000)	Year 1 (£000)	Year 2 (£000)	Year 3 (£000)	Year 4 (£000)	Year 5 (£000)
Investment in depreciable fixed assets	4 500					
Cumulative investment in working capital	300	400	500	600	700	700
Sales		3 500	4 900	5 320	5 740	5 320
Materials		535	750	900	1 050	900
Labour		1 070	1 500	1 800	2 100	1 800
Overhead		50	100	100	100	100
Interest		576	576	576	576	576
Depreciation		900	900	900	900	900
		3 131	3 826	4 276	4 726	4 276
Taxable profit		369	1 074	1 044	1 014	1 044
Taxation		129	376	365	355	365
Profit after tax		240	698	679	659	679

Total initial investment is £4 800 000.
Average annual after tax profit is £591 000.

All the above cash flow and profit estimates have been prepared in terms of present-day costs and prices, since the previous finance director assumed that the sales price could be increased to compensate for any increase in costs.

You have available the following additional information:

(a) Selling prices, working capital requirements and overhead expenses are expected to increase by 5 per cent per year.

(b) Material costs and labour costs are expected to increase by 10 per cent per year.

(c) Capital allowances (tax depreciation) are allowable for taxation purposes against profits at 25 per cent per year on a reducing balance basis.

(d) Taxation on profits is at a rate of 35 per cent, payable one year in arrears.

(e) The fixed assets have no expected salvage value at the end of five years.

(f) The company's real after-tax weighted average cost of capital is estimated to be 8 per cent per year, and nominal after-tax weighted average cost of capital 15 per cent per year.

Assume that all receipts and payments arise at the end of the year to which they relate, except those in year 0, which occur immediately.

Required:

(a) Estimate the net present value of the proposed project. State clearly any assumptions that you make. *(13 marks)*

(b) Calculate by how much the discount rate would have to change to result in a net present value of approximately zero. *(4 marks)*

(c) Describe how sensitivity analysis might be used to assist in assessing this project. What are the weaknesses of sensitivity analysis in capital investment appraisal? Briefly outline alternative techniques of incorporating risk into capital investment appraisal. *(8 marks)*

ACCA Level 3 Financial Management

14.22 Advanced: NPV, IRR, inflation and taxation. PT is a major international computer manufacturing company. It is considering investing in the production of microcomputers. These computers will be targeted at the education market with the specific aim of encouraging children to learn computer science at an early age.

Sales of the microcomputers are expected to be 100 000 units in Year 1 and then to increase at the rate of 20 per cent per annum for the remainder of the project life. The project has a life of five years.

The company's research and development division has already spent $250 000 in developing the product. A further investment of $10 million in a new manufacturing facility will be required at the beginning of year 1. It is expected that the new manufacturing facility could be sold for cash of $1.5 million, at year 5 prices, at the end of the life of the project. The manufacturing facility will be depreciated over 5 years using the straight line method.

The project will also require an investment of $3 million in working capital at the beginning of the project. The amount of the investment in working capital is expected to increase by the rate of inflation each year.

The selling price of the new product in year 1 will be $45 and the variable cost per unit will be $25. The selling price and the variable cost per unit are expected to increase by the rate of inflation each year.

The microcomputers will be exclusively produced in the new manufacturing facility. The total fixed costs in year 1 will be $2.5 million including depreciation. The fixed costs are expected to increase thereafter by the rate of inflation each year.

Taxation

PT's financial director has provided the following taxation information:

- Tax depreciation: 25 per cent per annum of the reducing balance, with a balancing adjustment in the year of disposal.
- Taxation rate: 30 per cent of taxable profits. Half of the tax is payable in the year in which it arises, the balance is paid in the following year.

- PT has sufficient taxable profits from other parts of its business to enable the offset of any pre-tax losses.

Other information

- A cost of capital of 12 per cent per annum is used to evaluate projects of this type.
- Inflation is expected to be 4 per cent per annum throughout the life of the project.

Required:

(a) Evaluate whether PT should go ahead with the investment project. You should use net present value as the basis of your evaluation. Your workings should be rounded to the nearest $000. *(14 marks)*

(b) Calculate the following for the investment project:

(i) The internal rate of return (IRR); *(5 marks)*

(ii) The increase or decrease in the cost of capital, expressed as a percentage of the original cost of capital, which would change the decision about whether to accept or reject the project. *(2 marks)*

CIMA P1 Performance Operations

14.23 Advanced: Single period capital rationing. Banden Ltd is a highly geared company that wishes to expand its operations. Six possible capital investments have been identified, but the company only has access to a total of £620 000. The projects are not divisible and may not be postponed until a future period. After the projects end it is unlikely that similar investment opportunities will occur:

	Expected net cash inflows (including salvage value)					
	Year 1	2	3	4	5	Initial outlay
Project	(£)	(£)	(£)	(£)	(£)	(£)
A	70 000	70 000	70 000	70 000	70 000	246 000
B	75 000	87 000	64 000			180 000
C	48 000	48 000	63 000	73 000		175 000
D	62 000	62 000	62 000	62 000		180 000
E	40 000	50 000	60 000	70 000	40 000	180 000
F	35 000	82 000	82 000			150 000

Projects A and E are mutually exclusive. All projects are believed to be of similar risk to the company's existing capital investments.

Any surplus funds may be invested in the money market to earn a return of 9 per cent per year. The money market may be assumed to be an efficient market.

Banden's cost of capital is 12 per cent per year.

Required:

(a) Calculate:

(i) The expected net present value.

(ii) The expected profitability index associated with each of the six projects, and rank the projects according to both of these investment appraisal methods.

Explain briefly why these rankings differ. *(8 marks)*

(b) Give reasoned advice to Banden Ltd recommending which projects should be selected. *(6 marks)*

(c) A director of the company has suggested that using the company's normal cost of capital might not be appropriate in a capital rationing situation. Explain whether you agree with the director. *(4 marks)*

(d) The director has also suggested the use of linear or integer programming to assist with the selection of projects. Discuss the advantages and disadvantages of these mathematical programming methods to Banden Ltd. *(7 marks)*

ACCA Level 3 Financial Management

14.24 Advanced: Investment appraisal, expected values and sensitivity analysis. Umunat plc is considering investing £50000 in a new machine with an expected life of five years. The machine will have no scrap value at the end of five years. It is expected that 20000 units will be sold each year at a selling price of £3.00 per unit. Variable production costs are expected to be £1.65 per unit, while incremental fixed costs, mainly the wages of a maintenance engineer, are expected to be £10000 per year. Umunat plc uses a discount rate of 12 per cent for investment appraisal purposes and expects investment projects to recover their initial investment within two years.

Required:

(a) Explain why risk and uncertainty should be considered in the investment appraisal process. *(5 marks)*

(b) Calculate and comment on the payback period of the project. *(4 marks)*

(c) Evaluate the sensitivity of the project's net present value to a change in the following project variables:

(i) sales volume;

(ii) sales price;

(iii) variable cost;

and discuss the use of sensitivity analysis as a way of evaluating project risk. *(10 marks)*

(d) On further investigation, it is found that there is a significant chance that the expected sales volume of 20000 units per year will not be achieved. The sales manager of Umunat plc suggests that sales volumes could depend on expected economic states that could be assigned the following probabilities:

Economic state	Poor	Normal	Good
Probability	0.3	0.6	0.1
Annual sales volume (units)	17500	20000	22500

Calculate and comment on the expected net present value of the project. *(6 marks)*

ACCA 2.4 Financial Management and Control

IM14.1 Advanced. You have been appointed as chief management accountant of a well-established company with a brief to improve the quality of information supplied for management decision-making. As a first task you have decided to examine the system used for providing information for capital investment decisions. You find that discounted cash flow techniques are used but in a mechanical fashion with no apparent understanding of the figures produced. The most recent example of an investment appraisal produced by the accounting department showed a positive net present value of £35000 for a five-year life project when discounted at 14 per cent which you are informed 'was the rate charged on the bank loan raised to finance the investment'. You note that the appraisal did not include any consideration of the effects of inflation, neither was there any form of risk analysis.

You are required to:

(a) explain the meaning of a positive net present value of £35000; *(4 marks)*

(b) comment on the appropriateness or otherwise of the discounting rate used; *(4 marks)*

(c) state whether you agree with the treatment of inflation and, if not, explain how you would deal with inflation in investment appraisals; *(6 marks)*

(d) explain what is meant by 'risk analysis' and describe ways this could be carried out in investment appraisals and what benefits (if any) this would bring. *(6 marks)*

CIMA Stage 3 Management Accounting Techniques Pilot Paper

IM14.2 Intermediate: NPV calculation and taxation.

Data

Tilsley Ltd manufactures motor vehicle components. It is considering introducing a new product. Helen Foster, the production director, has already prepared the following projections for this proposal:

	Year			
	1	2	3	4
	(£000)	(£000)	(£000)	(£000)
Sales	8750	12250	13300	14350
Direct materials	1340	1875	2250	2625
Direct labour	2675	3750	4500	5250
Direct overheads	185	250	250	250
Depreciation	2500	2500	2500	2500
Interest	1012	1012	1012	1012
Profit before tax	1038	2863	2788	2713
Corporation tax @ 30%	311	859	836	814
Profit after tax	727	2004	1952	1899

Helen Foster has recommended to the board that the project is not worthwhile because the cumulative after tax profit over the four years is less than the capital cost of the project.

As an assistant accountant at the company, you have been asked by Philip Knowles, the chief accountant, to carry out a full financial appraisal of the proposal. He does not agree with Helen Foster's analysis and provides you with the following information:

- the initial capital investment and working capital will be incurred at the beginning of the first year. All other receipts and payments will occur at the end of each year;
- the equipment will cost £10 million;
- additional working capital of £1 million;
- this additional working capital will be recovered in full as cash at the end of the four-year period;
- the equipment will qualify for a 25 per cent per annum reducing balance writing-down allowance;
- any outstanding capital allowances at the end of the project can be claimed as a balancing allowance;
- at the end of the four-year period the equipment will be scrapped, with no expected residual value;
- the additional working capital required does not qualify for capital allowances, neither is it an allowable expense in calculating taxable profit;
- Tilsley Ltd pays corporation tax at 30 per cent of chargeable profits;
- there is a one-year delay in paying tax;
- the company's cost of capital is 17 per cent.

Task

Write a report to Philip Knowles. Your report should:

(a) evaluate the project using net present value techniques;

(b) recommend whether the project is worthwhile;

(c) explain how you have treated taxation in your appraisal;

(d) give *three* reasons why your analysis is different from that produced by Helen Foster, the production director.

Note:

Risk and inflation can be ignored. *AAT Technicians Stage*

IM14.3 Advanced: Calculation of IRR and incremental yield involving identification of relevant cash flows. LF Ltd wishes to manufacture a new product. The company is evaluating two mutually exclusive machines, the Reclo and the Bunger. Each machine is expected to have a working life of four years and is capable of a maximum annual output of 150000 units.

Cost estimates associated with the two machines include:

	Reclo £000	Bunger £000
Purchase price	175	90
Scrap value	10	9
Incremental working capital	40	40
Maintenance (per year)	40 (20 in year 1)	
Supervisor	20	
Allocated central overhead	35	
Labour costs (per unit)	£1.30	
Material costs (per unit)	£0.80	

The Reclo requires 120 square metres of operating space. LF Ltd currently pays £35 per square metre to rent a factory which has adequate spare space for the new product. There is no alternative use for this spare space. £5000 has been spent on a feasibility survey of the Reclo.

The marketing department will charge a fee of £75 000 per year for promoting the product, which will be incorporated into existing plans for catalogues and advertising. Two new salesmen will be employed by the marketing department solely for the new product, at a cost of £22 500 per year each. There are no other incremental marketing costs.

The selling price in year one is expected to be £3.50 per unit, with annual production and sales estimated at 130 000 units throughout the four year period. Prices and costs after the first year are expected to rise by 5 per cent per year. Working capital will be increased by this amount from year one onwards.

Taxation is payable at 25 per cent per year one year in arrears and a writing-down allowance of 25 per cent per year is available on a reducing balance basis.

The company's accountant has already estimated the taxable operating cash flows (sales less relevant labour costs, materials costs, etc., but before taking into account any writing-down allowances) of the second machine, the Bunger. These are:

	Bunger – £000			
Year	1	2	3	4
Taxable operating cash flows	50	53	55	59

Required:

(a) Calculate the expected internal rate of return (IRR) of each of the machines. State clearly any assumptions that you make. *(14 marks)*

(b) Evaluate, using the incremental yield method, which, if either, of the two machines should be selected. *(6 marks)*

(c) Explain briefly why the internal rate of return is regarded as a relatively poor method of investment appraisal. *(5 marks)*

ACCA Level 3 Financial Management

IM14.4 Advanced: Net present value calculation for the replacement of a machine and a discussion of the conflict between ROI and NPV. Eckard plc is a large, all-equity financed, divisionalized textile company whose shares are listed on the London Stock Exchange. It has a current cost of capital of 15 per cent. The annual performance of its four divisions is assessed by their return on investment (ROI), i.e. net profit after tax divided by the closing level of capital employed. It is expected that the overall ROI for the company for the year ending 31 December 2018 will be 18 per cent, with the towelling division having the highest ROI of 25 per cent. The towelling division has a young, ambitious managing director who is anxious to maintain its ROI for the next two

years, by which time he expects to be able to obtain a more prestigious job either within Eckard plc or elsewhere. He has recently turned down a proposal by his division's finance director to replace an old machine with a more modern one, on the grounds that the old one has an estimated useful life of four years and should be kept for that period. The finance director has appealed to the main board of directors of Eckard plc to reverse her managing director's decision.

The following estimates have been prepared by the finance director for the new machine:

Investment cost: £256 000, payable on 2 January 2019.

Expected life: four years to 31 December 2022.

Disposal value: equal to its tax written down value on 1 January 2022 and receivable on 31 December 2022.

Expected cash flow savings: £60 000 in 2019, rising by 10 per cent in each of the next three years. These cash flows can be assumed to occur at the end of the year in which they arise.

Tax position: the company is expected to pay 35 per cent corporation tax over the next four years. The machine is eligible for a 25 per cent per annum writing-down allowance. Corporation tax can be assumed to be paid 12 months after the accounting year end on 31 December. No provision for deferred tax is considered to be necessary.

Old machine to be replaced: this would be sold on 2 January 2019 with an accounting net book value of £50 000 and a tax written-down value of nil. Sale proceeds would be £40 000, which would give rise to a balancing charge. If retained for a further four years, the disposal value would be zero.

Relevant accounting policies: the company uses the straight line depreciation method with a full year's depreciation being charged in both the year of acquisition and the year of disposal. The capital employed figure for the division comprises all assets excluding cash.

Requirements:

(a) Calculate the net present value to Eckard plc of the proposed replacement of the old machine by the new one. *(8 marks)*

(b) Calculate, for the years 2019 and 2020 only, the effect of the decision to replace the old machine on the ROI of the towelling division. *(7 marks)*

(c) Prepare a report for the main board of directors recommending whether the new machine should be purchased. Your report should include a discussion of the effects that performance measurement systems can have on capital investment decisions. *(10 marks)*

ICAEW P2 Financial Management

IM14.5 Advanced: Determining the optimum replacement period for a fleet of taxis. Eltern plc is an unlisted company with a turnover of £6 million which runs a small fleet of taxis as part of its business. The managers of the company wish to estimate how regularly to replace the taxis. The fleet costs a total of £55 000 and the company has just purchased a new fleet. Operating costs and maintenance costs increase as the taxis get older. Estimates of these costs and the likely resale value of the fleet at the end of various years are presented below:

Year	1 (£)	2 (£)	3 (£)	4 (£)	5 (£)
Operating costs	23 000	24 500	26 000	28 000	44 000
Maintenance costs	6 800	9 200	13 000	17 000	28 000
Resale value	35 000	24 000	12 000	2 000	200

The company's cost of capital is 13 per cent per year.

Required:

(a) Evaluate how regularly the company should replace its fleet of taxis. Assume all cash flows occur at the year end and are after taxation (where relevant). Inflation may be ignored. *(10 marks)*

(b) Briefly discuss the main problems of this type of evaluation. *(4 marks)*

ACCA Level 3 Financial Management

IM14.6 Advanced: Relevant cash flows and taxation plus unequal lives (see Learning Note 14.1). Pavgrange plc is considering expanding its operations. The company accountant has produced *pro forma* profit and loss accounts for the next three years assuming that:

(a) The company undertakes no new investment.
(b) The company invests in Project 1.
(c) The company invests in Project 2.

Both projects have expected lives of three years, and the projects are mutually exclusive.

The *pro forma* accounts are shown below:

(a) *No new investment*

Years	1 (£000)	2 (£000)	3 (£000)
Sales	6500	6950	7460
Operating costs	4300	4650	5070
Depreciation	960	720	540
Interest	780	800	800
Profit before tax	460	780	1050
Taxation	161	273	367
Profit after tax	299	507	683
Dividends	200	200	230
Retained earnings	99	307	453

(b) *Investment in Project 1*

Years	1 (£000)	2 (£000)	3 (£000)
Sales	(7340)	8790	9636
Operating costs	4869	5620	6385
Depreciation	1460	1095	821
Interest	1000	1030	1030
Profit before tax	11	1045	1400
Taxation	4	366	490
Profit after tax	7	679	910
Dividends	200	200	230
Retained earnings	(193)	479	680

(c) *Investment in Project 2*

Years	1 (£000)	2 (£000)	3 (£000)
Sales	8430	9826	11314
Operating costs	5680	6470	7230
Depreciation	1835	1376	1032
Interest	1165	1205	1205
Profit before tax	(250)	775	1847
Taxation	0	184	646
Profit after tax	(250)	591	1201
Dividends	200	200	230
Retained earnings	(450)	391	971

The initial outlay for Project 1 is £2 million and for Project 2 £3½ million.

Tax-allowable depreciation is at the rate of 25 per cent on a reducing balance basis. The company does not expect to acquire or dispose of any fixed assets during the next three years other than in connection with Projects 1 or 2. Any investment in Project 1 or 2 would commence at the start of the company's next financial year.

The expected salvage value associated with the investments at the end of three years is £750000 for Project 1, and £1500000 for Project 2.

Corporate taxes are levied at the rate of 35 per cent and are payable one year in arrears.

Pavgrange would finance either investment with a three-year term loan at a gross interest payment of 11 per cent per year. The company's weighted average cost of capital is estimated to be 8 per cent per annum.

Required:

(a) Advise the company which project (if either) it should undertake. Give the reasons for your choice and support it with calculations. *(12 marks)*

(b) What further information might be helpful to the company accountant in the evaluation of these investments? *(3 marks)*

(c) If Project 1 had been for four years' duration rather than three years, and the new net cash flows of the project (after tax and allowing for the scrap value) for years four and five were £77000 and (£188000), respectively, evaluate whether your advice to Pavgrange would change. *(5 marks)*

(d) Explain why the payback period and the internal rate of return might not lead to the correct decision when appraising mutually exclusive capital investments. *(5 marks)*

ACCA Level 3 Financial Management

IM14.7 Advanced: Adjusting cash flows for inflation and the calculation of NPV and ROI. The general manager of the nationalized postal service of a small country, Zedland, wishes to introduce a new service. This service would offer same-day delivery of letters and parcels posted before 10am within a distance of 150 kilometres. The service would require 100 new vans costing $8000 each and 20 trucks costing $18000 each. 180 new workers would be employed at an average annual wage of $13000 and five managers at average annual salaries of $20000 would be moved from their existing duties, where they would not be replaced.

Two postal rates are proposed. In the first year of operation letters will cost $0.525 and parcels $5.25. Market research undertaken at a cost of $50000 forecasts that demand will average 15000 letters per working day and 500 parcels per working day during the first year and 20000 letters per day and 750 parcels per day thereafter. There is a five-day working week. Annual running and maintenance costs on similar new vans and trucks are currently estimated in the first year of operation to be $2000 per van and $4000 per truck, respectively. These costs will increase by 20 per cent per year (excluding the effects of inflation). Vehicles are depreciated over a five-year period on a straight line basis. Depreciation is tax allowable and the vehicles will have negligible scrap value at the end of five years. Advertising in year one will cost $500000 and in year two $250000. There will be no advertising after year two. Existing premises will be used for the new service but additional costs of $150000 per year will be incurred.

All the above cost data are current estimates and exclude any inflation effects. Wage and salary costs and all other costs are expected to rise because of inflation by approximately 5 per cent per year during the five-year planning horizon of the postal service. The government of Zedland will not permit annual price increases within nationalized industries to exceed the level of inflation.

Nationalized industries are normally required by the government to earn at least an annual after tax return of

5 per cent on average investment and to achieve, on average, at least zero net present value on their investments.

The new service would be financed half with internally generated funds and half by borrowing on the capital market at an interest rate of 12 per cent per year. The opportunity cost of capital for the postal service is estimated to be 14 per cent per year. Corporate taxes in Zedland, to which the postal service is subject, are at the rate of 30 per cent for annual profits of up to $500000 and 40 per cent for the balance in excess of $500000. Tax is payable one year in arrears. All transactions may be assumed to be on a cash basis and to occur at the end of the year with the exception of the initial investment which would be required almost immediately.

Required:
Acting as an independent consultant prepare a report advising whether the new postal service should be introduced. Include in your report a discussion of other factors that might need to be taken into account before a final decision was made with respect to the introduction of the new postal service. State clearly any assumptions that you make.　*(18 marks)*

ACCA Level 3 Financial Management

IM14.8 Advanced: Calculation of discounted payback and NPV incorporating inflation, tax and financing costs. The board of directors of Portand Ltd are considering two *mutually exclusive* investments each of which is expected to have a life of five years. The company does not have the physical capacity to undertake both investments. The first investment is relatively capital intensive while the second is relatively labour intensive. Forecast profits of the two investments are:

Investment 1 (requires four new workers)

Year		0	1	2	3	4	5
				(£000)			
Initial cost	(500)						
Projected sales			400	450	500	550	600
Production costs			260	300	350	450	500
Finance charges			21	21	21	21	21
Depreciation[1]			125	94	70	53	40
Profit before tax			(6)	35	59	26	39

Average profit
  before tax £30600.

Investment 2 (requires nine new workers)

Year		0	1	2	3	4	5
				(£000)			
Initial cost	(175)						
Projected sales			500	600	640	640	700
Production costs			460	520	550	590	630
Depreciation[1]			44	33	25	18	14
Profit before tax			(4)	47	65	32	56

Average profit
  before tax £39200.

[1]Depreciation is a tax-allowable expense and is at 25 per cent per year on a reducing balance basis. Both investments are of similar risk to the company's existing operations.

Additional information

(i)　Tax and depreciation allowances are payable/receivable one year in arrears. Tax is at 25 per cent per year.

(ii)　Investment 2 would be financed from internal funds, which the managing director states have no cost to the company. Investment 1 would be financed by internal funds plus a £150000, 14 per cent fixed rate term loan.

(iii)　The data contain no adjustments for price changes. These have been ignored by the board of directors as both sales and production costs are expected to increase by 9 per cent per year, after year one.

(iv)　The company's real overall cost of capital is 7 per cent per year and the inflation rate is expected to be 8 per cent per year for the foreseeable future.

(v)　All cash flows may be assumed to occur at the end of the year unless otherwise stated.

(vi)　The company currently receives interest of 10 per cent per year on short-term money market deposits of £350000.

(vii)　Both investments are expected to have negligible scrap value at the end of five years.

Director A favours Investment 2 as it has a larger average profit.

Director B favours Investment 1, which she believes has a quicker discounted payback period, based on cash flows.

Director C argues that the company can make £35000 per year on its money market investments and that, when risk is taken into account, there is little point in investing in either project.

Required:

(a) Discuss the validity of the arguments of each of Directors A, B and C with respect to the decision to select Investment 1, Investment 2 or neither.　*(7 marks)*

(b) Verify whether or not Director B is correct in stating that Investment 1 has the quicker discounted payback period. Evaluate which investment, if any, should be selected. All calculations must be shown. Marks will not be deducted for sensible rounding. State clearly any assumptions that you make.　*(14 marks)*

(c) Discuss briefly what non-financial factors might influence the choice of investment.　*(4 marks)*

ACCA Level 3 Financial Management

IM14.9 Advanced: Sensitivity analysis and alternative methods of adjusting for risk. Parsifal Ltd is a private company whose ordinary shares are all held by its directors. The chairman has recently been impressed by the arguments advanced by a computer salesman, who has told him that Parsifal will be able to install a fully operational computer system for £161500. This new system will provide all the data currently being prepared by a local data processing service. This local service has a current annual cost of £46000. According to the salesman, annual maintenance costs will be only £2000 and if properly maintained the equipment can be expected to last 'indefinitely'.

The chairman has asked the company accountant to evaluate whether purchase of the computer system is worthwhile. The accountant has spoken to a friend who works for a firm of management consultants. She has told him that Parsifal would probably have to employ two additional members of staff at a total cost of about £15000 per annum and that there would be increased stationery and other related costs of approximately £4000 per annum if Parsifal purchased the computer system. She also estimates that the useful life of the system would be between six and ten years, depending on the rate of technological change and changes in the pattern of the business of Parsifal. The system would have no scrap or resale value at the end of its useful life.

The company accountant has prepared a net present value calculation by assuming that all the annual costs and savings were expressed in real terms and that the company had a real cost of capital of 5 per cent per annum. He chose this course of action because he did not know either the expected rate of inflation of the cash flows or the cost of capital of Parsifal Ltd. All cash flows, except the initial cost of the system, will arise at the end of the year to which they relate.

You are required to:

(a) estimate, using the company accountant's assumptions, the life of the system which produces a zero net present value; *(3 marks)*

(b) estimate the internal real rate of return arising from purchase of the computer system, assuming that the system will last:

  (i) for six years, and
  (ii) indefinitely; *(5 marks)*

(c) estimate the value of the annual running costs (maintenance, extra staff, stationery and other related costs) that will produce a net present value of zero, assuming that the system will last for ten years; *(3 marks)*

(d) discuss how the company accountant should incorporate the information from parts (a), (b) and (c) above in his recommendation to the directors of Parsifal Ltd as to whether the proposed computer system should be purchased; *(7 marks)*

(e) discuss how the company accountant could improve the quality of his advice. *(7 marks)*

Ignore taxation *ICAEW P2 Financial Management*

IM14.10 Advanced: Calculation of expected net present value plus a discussion of whether expected values is an appropriate way of evaluating risk. Galuppi plc is considering whether to scrap some highly specialized old plant or to refurbish it for the production of drive mechanisms, sales of which will last for only three years. Scrapping the plant will yield £25 000 immediately, whereas refurbishment will require an immediate outlay of £375 000.

Each drive mechanism will sell for £50 and, if manufactured entirely by Galuppi plc, give a contribution at current prices of £10. All internal company costs and selling prices are predicted to increase from the start of each year by 5 per cent. Refurbishment of the plant will also entail fixed costs of

£10 000, £12 500 and £15 000 for the first, second and third years respectively.

Estimates of product demand depend on different economic conditions. Three have been identified as follows:

Economic condition	Probability of occurrence	Demand in the first year (units)
A	0.25	10 000
B	0.45	15 000
C	0.3	20 000

Demand in subsequent years is expected to increase at 20 per cent per annum, regardless of the initial level demanded.

The plant can produce up to 20 000 drive mechanisms per year, but Galuppi plc can supply more by contracting to buy partially completed mechanisms from an overseas supplier at a fixed price of £20 per unit. To convert a partially completed mechanism into the finished product requires additional work amounting, at current prices, to £25 per unit. For a variety of reasons the supplier is only willing to negotiate contracts in batches of 2000 units.

All contracts to purchase the partially completed units must be signed one year in advance, and payment made by Galuppi plc at the start of the year in which they are to be used.

Galuppi plc has a cost of capital of 15 per cent per annum and you may assume that all cash flows arise at the end of the year, unless you are told otherwise.

Requirements:

(a) Determine whether refurbishment of the plant is worthwhile. *(17 marks)*

(b) Discuss whether the expected value method is an appropriate way of evaluating the different risks inherent in the refurbishment decision of Galuppi plc. *(8 marks)*

ICAEW P2 Financial Management

PART FOUR

INFORMATION FOR PLANNING, CONTROL AND PERFORMANCE MEASUREMENT

The objective in this section is to consider the implementation of decisions through the planning and control process. Planning involves systematically looking at the future, so that decisions can be made today that will bring the company its desired results. Control can be defined as the process of measuring and correcting actual performance to ensure that plans for implementing the chosen course of action are carried out.

Part Four contains six chapters. Chapter 15 considers the role of budgeting within the planning process and the relationship between the long-range plan and the budgeting process. The budgeting process in profit-oriented organizations is compared with that in non-profit organizations.

Chapters 16 to 18 are concerned with the control process. To fully understand the role that management accounting control systems play in the control process, it is necessary to be aware of how they relate to the entire array of control mechanisms used by organizations. Chapter 16 describes the different types of control that are used by companies. The elements of management accounting control systems are described within the context of the overall control process. Chapters 17 and 18 focus on the technical aspects of accounting control systems. They describe the major features of a standard costing system: a system that enables the differences between the planned and actual outcomes to be analysed in detail. Chapter 17 describes the operation of a standard costing system and explains the procedure for calculating the variances. Chapter 18 examines more complex aspects relating to standard costing.

Chapters 16–18 focus on management accounting control systems within cost centres at lower management levels within an organization rather than at the business unit level. Chapter 19 considers financial performance measurement at higher organization levels relating to divisionalized business units. Our focus in this chapter is on financial measures of divisional performance but you should note at this point that financial measures alone cannot adequately measure all those factors that are critical to the success of a division. Emphasis should also be given to reporting key non-financial measures relating to such areas as competitiveness, quality, delivery performance, innovation and flexibility to respond to changes in demand. In particular, a range of financial and non-financial performance measures should be developed that support the objectives and strategies of the organization. We shall examine these aspects in Chapter 21 where our focus will be on strategic performance management. A major feature of divisionalized companies is that they engage in interdivisional trading of goods and services involving financial transactions with each other, which creates the need to establish transfer prices. The established transfer price is a cost to the receiving division and revenue to the suppling division, which means that whatever transfer price is set will affect the divisional financial performance measures. Chapter 20 focuses on the transfer pricing problem and examines how transfer prices can be established that will motivate managers to make optimal decisions and also ensure that the performance measures derived from using the transfer prices represent a fair reflection of managerial performance.

15
THE BUDGETING PROCESS

LEARNING OBJECTIVES After studying this chapter, you should be able to:

- explain how budgeting fits into the overall planning and control framework;
- identify and describe the six different purposes of budgeting;
- identify and describe the various stages in the budget process;
- prepare functional and master budgets;
- describe the use of computer-based financial models for budgeting;
- describe activity-based budgeting;
- describe zero-based budgeting (ZBB);
- describe the criticisms relating to traditional budgeting.

In the previous seven chapters, we have considered how management accounting can assist managers in making decisions. The actions that follow managerial decisions normally involve several aspects of the business, such as the marketing, production, purchasing and finance functions, and it is important that management should coordinate these various interrelated aspects of decision-making. If they fail to do this, there is a danger that managers may each make decisions that they believe are in the best interests of the organization when, in fact, taken together they are not; for example, the marketing department may introduce a promotional campaign that is designed to increase sales demand to a level beyond that which the production department can handle. The various activities within a company should be coordinated by the preparation of plans of actions for future periods. These detailed plans are usually referred to as budgets. Our objective in this chapter is to examine the planning process within a business organization and to consider the role of budgeting within this process.

THE STRATEGIC PLANNING, BUDGETING AND CONTROL PROCESS

To help you understand the budgetary process, we shall begin by looking at how it fits into an overall general framework of planning and control. The framework outlined in Figure 15.1 provides an overview of an organization's planning and control process. The first stage involves establishing the objectives and supporting strategies of the organization within the strategic planning process.

Strategic planning process

Before the budgeting process begins, an organization should have prepared a long-term plan (also known as a strategic plan). Strategic planning begins with the specification of an organization's vision, mission and objectives towards which future operations should be directed. The vision and mission of an organization are normally specified in short statements that consist of a few sentences (see Exhibit 15.1 for an illustration). A vision statement clarifies the beliefs and governing principles of an organization: what it wants to be in the future or how it wants the world in which it operates to be. In contrast, a mission statement is more action oriented. It includes a description in very general terms of what the organization does to achieve its vision, its broad purpose and reason for existence, the nature of the business(es) it is in and the customers it seeks to serve and satisfy. Both vision and mission statements are a visionary projection of the central and overriding concepts on which the organization is based.

Corporate objectives relate to the organization as a whole. Objectives tend to be more specific and represent desired states or results to be achieved. They are normally measurable and are expressed in financial terms such as desired profits or sales levels, return on capital employed, rates of growth or market share. Objectives must also be developed for the different parts of an organization. Unit objectives relate to the specific objectives of individual units within the organization, such as a division or one company within a holding company. Corporate objectives are normally set for the organization as a whole and are

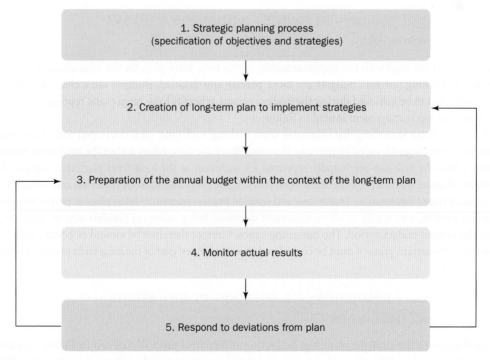

FIGURE 15.1
Strategic planning, budgeting and control process

EXHIBIT 15.1 Vision and mission statements for Singapore Airlines

---

Singapore Airlines vision statement

Singapore Airlines has a responsibility not only to be an excellent company, but also to be an excellent citizen of the world by enhancing the lives of the people we touch. With that aim in mind, we have made many commitments to the arts and education, to our communities and to the health and welfare of our country's citizens and of those in countries we fly to. With this goal in mind, we've also made a strong commitment to preserving the environment – and our world for future generations.

Singapore Airlines mission statement

Singapore Airlines is a global company dedicated to providing air transportation services of the highest quality and to maximizing returns for the benefit of its shareholders and employees.

---

then translated into unit objectives, which become the targets for the individual business units within the organization. It is important that senior managers in an organization understand clearly where their company is going and why and how their own role contributes to the attainment of corporate objectives. The strategic planning process should also specify how the objectives of the organization will be achieved.

Creation of long-term plan

The term strategy is used to describe the courses of action that need to be taken to achieve the objectives set. When management has identified those strategic options that have the greatest potential for achieving the company's objectives, long-term plans should be created to implement the strategies. A long-term plan is a statement of the preliminary targets and activities required by an organization to achieve its strategic plan, together with a broad estimate for each year of the resources required and revenues expected. Because long-term planning involves 'looking into the future' for several years ahead (typically at least five years) the plans tend to be uncertain, general in nature, imprecise and subject to change.

Preparation of the annual budget within the context of the long-term plan

Budgeting is concerned with the implementation of the long-term plan for the year ahead. Because of the shorter planning horizon, budgets are more precise and detailed. Budgets are a clear indication of what is expected to be achieved during the budget period, whereas long-term plans represent the broad directions that top management intend to follow.

The budget is not something that originates 'from nothing' each year – it is developed within the context of ongoing business and is ruled by previous decisions that have been taken within the long-term planning process. When the activities are initially approved for inclusion in the long-term plan, they are based on uncertain estimates that are projected for several years. These proposals must be reviewed and revised in the light of more recent information. This review and revision process frequently takes place as part of the annual budgeting process, and it may result in important decisions being taken on possible activity adjustments within the current budget period. The budgeting process cannot therefore be viewed as being purely concerned with the current year – it must be considered as an integrated part of the long-term planning process.

Monitor actual outcomes and respond to deviations from planned outcomes

The final stages in the strategic planning, budgeting and control process outlined in Figure 15.1 are to compare the actual and the planned outcomes, and to respond to any deviations from the plan. These stages represent the budgetary control process. Planning and control are closely linked. Planning involves looking ahead to determine the actions required to achieve the objectives of the organization. Control involves looking back to ascertain what actually happened and comparing it with the planned outcomes. Effective control requires that corrective action is taken so that actual outcomes conform to planned outcomes. Alternatively, the plans may require modification if the comparisons indicate that the plans are no longer attainable. The corrective action is indicated by the arrowed lines in Figure 15.1 linking stages 5 and 2 and 5 and 3. These arrowed lines represent feedback loops. They signify that the process is dynamic and stress the interdependencies between the various stages in the process. The feedback loops between the stages indicate that the plans should be regularly reviewed and, if they are no longer attainable, alternative courses of action must be considered for achieving the organization's objectives. The loop between stages 5 and 3 also stresses the corrective action that may be taken so that actual outcomes conform to planned outcomes.

A detailed discussion of the control process will be deferred until the next chapter. We shall now consider the short-term budgeting process in more detail.

THE MULTIPLE FUNCTIONS OF BUDGETS

Budgets serve a number of useful purposes. They include:

1 *planning* annual operations;
2 *coordinating* the activities of the various parts of the organization and ensuring that the parts are in harmony with each other;
3 *communicating* plans to the various responsibility centre managers;
4 *motivating* managers to strive to achieve the organizational goals;
5 *controlling* activities;
6 *evaluating* the performance of managers.

Let us now examine each of these six factors.

Planning

The major planning decisions will already have been made as part of the long-term planning process. However, the annual budgeting process leads to the refinement of those plans, since managers must produce detailed plans for the implementation of the long-range plan. Without the annual budgeting process, the pressures of day-to-day operating problems may tempt managers not to plan for future operations. The budgeting process ensures that managers do plan for future operations and that they consider how conditions in the next year might change and what steps they should take now to respond to these changed conditions. This process encourages managers to anticipate problems before they arise and to respond to changing conditions with reasoned judgement, instead of making hasty decisions that are based on expediency.

Coordination

The budget serves as a vehicle through which the actions of the different parts of an organization can be brought together and reconciled into a common plan. Without any guidance, managers may each make their own decisions, believing that they are working in the best interests of the organization. For example, the purchasing manager may prefer to place large orders so as to obtain large discounts; the production manager will be concerned with avoiding high inventory levels; and the accountant will be concerned with the impact of the decision on the cash resources of the business. It is the aim of budgeting to reconcile these differences for the good of the organization as a whole, rather than for the benefit of any individual area. Budgeting therefore compels managers to examine the relationship between their own operations and those of other departments and, in the process, to identify and resolve conflicts.

Communication

If an organization is to function effectively, there must be definite lines of communication so that all the parts will be kept fully informed of the plans and the policies, and constraints, to which the organization is expected to conform. Everyone in the organization should have a clear understanding of the part he/she is expected to play in achieving the annual budget. This process will ensure that the appropriate individuals are made accountable for implementing the budget. Through the budget, top management communicates its expectations to lower level management, so that all members of the organization may understand these expectations and can coordinate their activities to attain them. It is not just the budget itself that facilitates communication – much vital information is communicated in the actual act of preparing it.

Motivation

The budget can be a useful device for influencing managerial behaviour and motivating managers to perform in line with the organizational objectives. A budget provides a standard that under the right circumstances, a manager will be motivated to strive to achieve. However, budgets can also encourage inefficiency and conflict between managers. If individuals have actively participated in preparing the budget, and it is used as a tool to assist managers in managing their departments, it can act as a strong motivational device by providing a challenge. However, if the budget is dictated from above, and imposes a threat rather than a challenge, it may be resisted and do more harm than good. We shall discuss the dysfunctional motivational consequence of budgets in Chapter 16.

Control

A budget assists managers in managing and controlling the activities for which they are responsible. By comparing the actual results with the budgeted amounts for different categories of expenses, managers can identify costs that do not conform to the original plan and thus require their attention. This process enables management to operate a system of management by exception, which means that a manager's attention and effort can be concentrated on significant deviations from the expected results. By investigating the reasons for the deviations, managers may be able to identify inefficiencies such as the purchase of inferior quality materials. When the reasons for the inefficiencies have been found, appropriate control action should be taken to remedy the situation.

Performance evaluation

A manager's performance is often evaluated by measuring his or her success in meeting the budgets. In some companies, bonuses are awarded on the basis of an employee's ability to achieve the targets specified in the periodic budgets, or promotion may be partly dependent on a manager's budget record. In addition, the manager may wish to evaluate his or her own performance. The budget thus provides a useful means of informing managers of how well they are performing in meeting targets that they have previously helped to set. The use of budgets as a method of performance evaluation also influences human behaviour and, for this reason, we shall consider the behavioural aspects of performance evaluation in Chapter 16.

CONFLICTING ROLES OF BUDGETS

Because a single budget system is normally used to serve several purposes there is a danger that these purposes may conflict with one another. For instance, the planning and motivation roles may be in conflict. Demanding budgets that may not be achieved may be appropriate to motivate maximum performance, but they are unsuitable for planning purposes. For these, a budget should be set based on easier and more realistic targets that are expected to be met.

There can also be a conflict between the planning and performance evaluation roles. For planning purposes, budgets are set in advance of the budget period and are based on an anticipated set of circumstances or environment. Performance evaluation should be based on a comparison of actual performance with an adjusted budget to reflect the circumstances under which managers actually operated. In practice, many firms compare actual performance with the original budget (adjusted to the actual level of activity, i.e. a flexible budget), but if the circumstances envisaged when the original budget was set have changed then there will be a planning and evaluation conflict.

THE BUDGET PERIOD

The conventional approach is that once a year the manager of each budget centre prepares a detailed budget for one year. For control purposes, the budget is divided into either 12 monthly or 13 four-weekly periods. The preparation of budgets on an annual basis has been strongly criticized on the grounds that it is too rigid and ties a company to a 12-month commitment, which can be risky because the budget is based on uncertain forecasts.

An alternative approach is for the annual budget to be broken down by months for the first three months and by quarters for the remaining nine. The quarterly budgets are then developed on a monthly basis as the year proceeds. For example, during the first quarter, the monthly budgets for the second quarter will be prepared; and during the second quarter, the monthly budgets for the third quarter will be prepared. The quarterly budgets may also be reviewed as the year unfolds. For example, during the first quarter, the budget for the next three quarters may be changed as new information becomes available. A new budget for a fifth quarter will also be prepared. This process is known as continuous or rolling budgeting, and ensures that a 12-month budget is always available by adding a quarter in the future as the quarter just ended is dropped. Contrast this with a budget prepared once per year. As the year goes by, the period for which a budget is available will shorten until the budget for next year is prepared. Rolling budgets also ensure that planning is not something that takes place once a year when the budget is being formulated. Instead, budgeting is a continuous process, and managers are encouraged to constantly look ahead and review future plans. Another advantage is that it is likely that actual performance will be compared with a more realistic target, because budgets are being constantly reviewed and updated. The main disadvantage of a rolling budget is that it can create uncertainty for managers because the budget is constantly being changed.

Irrespective of whether the budget is prepared on an annual or a continuous basis, it is important that monthly or four-weekly budgets are normally used for *control* purposes.

ADMINISTRATION OF THE BUDGETING PROCESS

It is important that suitable administration procedures exist to ensure that the budget process works effectively. In practice, the procedures should be tailor made to the requirements of the organization, but as a general rule a firm should ensure that procedures are established for approving the budgets and that the appropriate staff support is available for assisting managers in preparing their budgets.

The budget committee

The budget committee should consist of high-level executives who represent the major segments of the business. Its major task is to ensure that budgets are realistic and that they are coordinated satisfactorily. The normal procedure is for the functional heads to present their budget to the committee for approval. If the budget does not reflect a reasonable level of performance, it will not be approved and the

functional head will be required to adjust the budget and re-submit it for approval. It is important that
the person whose performance is being measured should agree that the revised budget can be achieved
or it will not act as a motivational device. If budget revisions are made, the budgetees should at least feel
that they were given a fair hearing by the committee. We shall discuss budget negotiation in more detail
later in this chapter.

Accounting staff

The accounting staff will normally circulate instructions and offer advice about budget preparation,
provide past information that may be useful for preparing the present budget and ensure that managers
submit their budgets on time. The accounting staff do not determine the content of the various budgets,
but they do provide a valuable advisory service for the line managers. They will also coordinate the
individual budgets into a budget for the whole organization.

STAGES IN THE BUDGETING PROCESS

The important stages are as follows:

1 communicating details of budget policy and guidelines to those people responsible for the
preparation of budgets;

2 determining the factor that restricts output;

3 preparation of the sales budget;

4 initial preparation of various budgets;

5 negotiation of budgets with superiors;

6 coordination and review of budgets;

7 final acceptance of budgets;

8 ongoing review of budgets.

Let us now consider each of these stages in more detail.

Communicating details of the budget policy

Many decisions affecting the budget year will already have been taken as part of the long-term planning process. The long-range plan is therefore the starting point for the preparation of the annual budget. Thus, top management must communicate the policy effects of the long-term plan to those responsible for preparing the current year's budgets. Policy effects might include planned changes in sales mix, or the expansion or contraction of certain activities. Any other important guidelines that are to govern the preparation of the budget should also be specified – for example the allowances that are to be made for price and wage increases, and expected changes in productivity. Also, any expected changes in the environment such as industry demand and output should be communicated by top management to the managers responsible for budget preparation.

Determining the factor that restricts performance

In every organization, there is some factor that restricts performance for a given period. In the majority of organizations, this factor will be sales demand. However, it is possible for production capacity to restrict performance when sales demand is in excess of available capacity. Prior to the preparation of the budgets, top management needs to determine the factor that restricts performance, since this factor will in turn determine the point at which the annual budgeting process should begin.

Preparation of the sales budget

When sales demand is the factor that restricts output, it is the volume of sales and sales mix that determines the level of a company's operations. For this reason, the sales budget is the most important plan in the annual budgeting process. This budget is also the most difficult plan to produce, because sales demand will be influenced by the state of the economy or the actions of competitors.

Initial preparation of budgets

The managers who are responsible for meeting the budgeted performance should prepare the budget for those areas for which they are responsible. The preparation of the budget should be a 'bottom-up' process. This means that the budget should originate at the lowest levels of management and be refined and coordinated at higher levels. The justification for this approach is that it enables managers to participate in the preparation of their budgets and increases the probability that they will accept the budget and strive to achieve the budget targets.

Negotiation of budgets

Budgets should be a participative process. The budget should be originated at the lowest level of management and managers at this level should submit their budget to their superiors for approval. The superior should then incorporate this budget with other budgets for which he or she is responsible and then submit this budget for approval to his or her superior. The manager who is the superior then becomes the budgetee at the next higher level. The process is illustrated in Figure 15.2. Sizer (1989) describes this approach as a two-way process of a top-down statement of objectives and strategies, bottom-up budget preparation and top-down approval by senior management.

The lower-level managers are represented by boxes 1–8. Managers 1 and 2 will prepare their budgets in accordance with the budget policy and the guidelines laid down by top management. The managers will submit their budget to their supervisor, who is in charge of the whole department (department A). Once these budgets have been agreed by the manager of department A, they will be combined by the departmental manager, who will then present this budget to his or her superior (manager of plant 1)

FIGURE 15.2
An illustration of budgets
moving up the organization
hierarchy

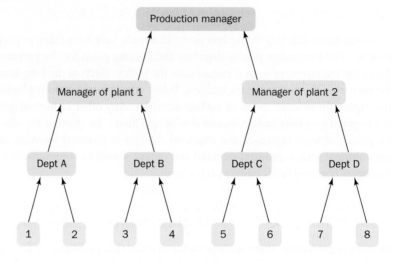

FIGURE 15.2
An illustration of budgets moving up the organization hierarchy

for approval. The manager of plant 1 is also responsible for department B and will combine the agreed budgets for departments A and B before presenting the combined budget to his or her supervisor (the production manager). The production manager will merge the budget for plants 1 and 2, and this final budget will represent the production budget that will be presented to the budget committee for approval.

At each of these stages, the budgets will be negotiated between the budgetees and their superiors, and eventually be agreed by both parties. Hence the figures that are included in the budget are the result of a bargaining process between a manager and his or her superior. It is important that the budgetees should participate in arriving at the final budget and that the superior does not revise the budget without giving full consideration to the subordinates' arguments for including any of the budgeted items. Otherwise, real participation will not be taking place and it is unlikely that the subordinate will be motivated to achieve a budget that he or she did not accept.

It is also necessary to be watchful that budgetees do not deliberately attempt to obtain approval for easily attainable budgets. It is equally unsatisfactory for a superior to impose difficult targets in the hope that an authoritarian approach will produce the desired results. The desired results may be achieved in the short term, but only at the cost of a loss of morale and increased labour turnover in the future.

Coordination and review of budgets

As the individual budgets move up the organizational hierarchy in the negotiation process, they must be examined in relation to each other. This examination may reveal that some budgets are out of balance with others and need modifying so that they will be compatible with conditions, constraints and plans that are beyond a manager's knowledge or control. This process may lead to the budgets being recycled from the bottom to the top for a second or even a third time until all the budgets are coordinated and are acceptable to all the parties involved. During the coordination process, a budgeted profit statement, a balance sheet and a cash flow statement should be prepared to ensure that all the parts combine to produce an acceptable whole. Otherwise, further adjustments and budget recycling will be necessary until the final outcome is acceptable.

Final acceptance of the budgets

When all the budgets are in harmony with one another, they are summarized into a **master budget** consisting of a budgeted profit statement, a balance sheet and a cash flow statement. After the master budget has been approved, the budgets are then passed down through the organization to the appropriate responsibility centres. The approval of the master budget is the authority for the manager of each responsibility centre to carry out the plans contained in each budget.

Budget review

The budget process should not stop when the budgets have been agreed. Periodically, the actual results should be compared with the budgeted results in the form of a periodic performance report. These comparisons should normally be made on a weekly or monthly basis and a report should be available online immediately following the period end so that management can identify the items that are not proceeding according to plan and investigate the reasons for the differences. If these differences are within the control of management, corrective action can be taken to avoid similar inefficiencies occurring again in the future. However, the differences may be due to changes in the actual conditions being different from those originally expected. This will mean that the budget plans should be adjusted. This revised budget then represents a revised statement of formal operating plans for the remaining portion of the budget period. The important point to note is that the budgetary process does not end for the current year once the budget has begun; budgeting should be seen as a continuous and dynamic process.

A DETAILED ILLUSTRATION

Let us now look at an illustration of the procedure for constructing budgets in a manufacturing company, using the information contained in Example 15.1. Note that the level of detail included here is much less than that which would be presented in practice. A truly realistic illustration would fill many pages, with detailed budgets being analysed in various ways. We shall consider an annual budget, whereas a realistic illustration would analyse the annual budget into 12 monthly periods. Monthly analysis would considerably increase the size of the illustration, but would not give any further insight into the basic concepts or procedures. In addition, we shall assume in this example that the budgets are prepared for only two responsibility centres (namely departments 1 and 2). In practice, many responsibility centres are likely to exist.

Sales budget

The sales budget shows the quantities of each product that the company plans to sell and the intended selling price. It provides the predictions of total revenue from which cash receipts from customers will be estimated and it also supplies the basic data for constructing budgets for production costs and for selling, distribution and administrative expenses. The sales budget is therefore the foundation of all other budgets, since all expenditure is ultimately dependent on the volume of sales. If the sales budget is not accurate, the other budget estimates will also be unreliable. We will assume that the Enterprise Company has completed a marketing analysis and that the following annual sales budget is based on the result:

Schedule 1 – Sales budget for year

Product	Units sold	Selling price (£)	Total revenue (£)
Alpha	8 500	400	3 400 000
Sigma	1 600	560	896 000
			4 296 000

EXAMPLE 15.1

The Enterprise Company manufactures two products, known as alpha and sigma. Alpha is produced in department 1 and sigma in department 2. The company is preparing the annual budget for the next financial year based on the following budgeted information:

	(£)
Material X	7.20 per unit
Material Y	16.00 per unit
Direct labour	12.00 per hour

Overhead is recovered on a direct labour hour basis.

The standard material and labour usage for each product is as follows:

	Model alpha	Model sigma
Material X	10 units	8 units
Material Y	5 units	9 units
Direct labour	10 hours	15 hours

The balance sheet for the previous year end was as follows:

	(£)	(£)	(£)
Fixed assets:			
Land		170 000	
Buildings and equipment	1 292 000		
Less depreciation	255 000	1 037 000	1 207 000
Current assets:			
Inventories, finished goods	99 076		
raw materials	189 200		
Debtors	289 000		
Cash	34 000		
	611 276		
Less current liabilities			
Creditors	248 800		362 476
Net assets			1 569 476
Represented by shareholder's interest:			
1 200 000 ordinary shares of £1 each		1 200 000	
Reserves		369 476	
			1 569 476

Other relevant budgeted data are as follows for the year:

	Finished product	
	Model alpha	Model sigma
Forecast sales (units)	8 500	1 600
Selling price per unit	£400	£560
Ending inventory required (units)	1 870	90
Beginning inventory (units)	170	85

(Continued on the next page) ➔

	Direct material	
	Material X	Material Y
Beginning inventory (units)	8500	8000
Ending inventory required (units)	10200	1700

	Department 1 (£)	Department 2 (£)
Budgeted variable overhead rates (per direct labour hour):		
Indirect materials	1.20	0.80
Indirect labour	1.20	1.20
Power (variable portion)	0.60	0.40
Maintenance (variable portion)	0.20	0.40
Budgeted fixed overheads		
Depreciation	100000	80000
Supervision	100000	40000
Power (fixed portion)	40000	2000
Maintenance (fixed portion)	45600	3196

	(£)
Estimated non-manufacturing overheads: Stationery etc. (Administration)	4000
Salaries	
Sales	74000
Office	28000
Commissions	60000
Car expenses (Sales)	22000
Advertising	80000
Miscellaneous (Office)	8000
	276000

Budgeted cash flows are as follows:

	Quarter 1 (£)	Quarter 2 (£)	Quarter 3 (£)	Quarter 4 (£)
Receipts from customers	1000000	1200000	1120000	985000
Payments:				
Materials	400000	480000	440000	547984
Payments for wages	400000	440000	480000	646188
Other costs and expenses	120000	100000	72016	13642

You are required to prepare a master budget for the next year and the following budgets:

1 sales budget;

2 production budget;

3 direct materials usage budget;

4 direct materials purchase budget;

5 direct labour budget;

6 production overhead budget;

7 selling and administration budget;

8 cash budget.

Schedule 1 represents the *total* sales budget for the year. In practice, the *total* sales budget will be supported by detailed *subsidiary* sales budgets where sales are analysed by areas of responsibility, such as sales territories and into monthly periods analysed by products.

Production budget and budgeted inventory levels

When the sales budget has been completed, the next stage is to prepare the production budget. This budget is expressed in *quantities only* and is the responsibility of the production manager. The objective is to ensure that production is sufficient to meet sales demand and that economic inventory levels are maintained. The production budget (schedule 2) for the year will be as follows:

Schedule 2 – Annual production budget

	Department 1 (alpha)	Department 2 (sigma)
Units to be sold	8 500	1 600
Planned closing inventory	1 870	90
Total units required for sales and inventories	10 370	1 690
Less planned opening inventories	170	85
Units to be produced	10 200	1 605

The total production for each department should also be analysed on a monthly basis.

Direct materials usage budget

The supervisors of departments 1 and 2 will prepare estimates of the materials that are required to meet the production budget. The materials usage budget for the year will be as follows:

Schedule 3 – Annual direct material usage budget

	Department 1			Department 2					
	Units	Unit price (£)	Total (£)	Units	Unit price (£)	Total (£)	Total units	Total unit price (£)	Total (£)
Material X	102 000[a]	7.20	734 400	12 840[c]	7.20	92 448	114 840	7.20	826 848
Material Y	51 000[b]	16.00	816 000	14 445[d]	16.00	231 120	65 445	16.00	1 047 120
			1 550 400			323 568			1 873 968

[a]10 200 units production at ten units per unit of production.
[b]10 200 units production at five units per unit of production.
[c]1605 units production at eight units per unit of production.
[d]1605 units production at nine units per unit of production.

Direct materials purchase budget

The direct materials purchase budget is the responsibility of the purchasing manager, since it will be he or she who is responsible for obtaining the planned quantities of raw materials to meet the production requirements. The objective is to purchase these materials at the right time at the planned purchase price. In addition, it is necessary to take into account the planned raw material inventory levels. The annual materials purchase budget for the year will be as follows:

Schedule 4 – Direct materials purchase budget

	Material X (units)	Material Y (units)
Quantity necessary to meet production requirements as per material usage budget	114 840	65 445
Planned closing inventory	10 200	1 700
	125 040	67 145
Less planned opening inventory	8 500	8 000
Total units to be purchased	116 540	59 145
Planned unit purchase price	£7.20	£16
Total purchases	£839 088	£946 320

Note that this budget is a summary budget for the year, but for detailed planning and control it will be necessary to analyse the annual budget on a monthly basis.

Direct labour budget

The direct labour budget is the responsibility of the respective managers of departments 1 and 2. They will prepare estimates of their departments' labour hours required to meet the planned production. Where different grades of labour exist, these should be specified separately in the budget. The budget rate per hour should be determined by the industrial relations department. The direct labour budget will be as follows:

Schedule 5 – Annual direct labour budget

	Department 1	Department 2	Total
Budgeted production (units)	10 200	1 605	
Hours per unit	10	15	
Total budgeted hours	102 000	24 075	126 075
Budgeted wage rate per hour	£12	£12	
Total wages	£1 224 000	£288 900	£1 512 900

Production overhead budget

The production overhead budget is also the responsibility of the respective production department managers. The total of the overhead budget will depend on the behaviour of the costs of the individual overhead items in relation to the anticipated level of production. The overheads must also be analysed according to whether they are controllable or non-controllable for the purpose of cost control. The production overhead budget will be as follows:

Schedule 6 – Annual production overhead budget
Anticipated activity – 102 000 direct labour hours (department 1)
24 075 direct labour hours (department 2)

	Variable overhead rate per direct labour hour		Overheads		
	Department 1 (£)	Department 2 (£)	Department 1 (£)	Department 2 (£)	Total (£)
Controllable overheads:					
Indirect material	1.20	0.80	122 400	19 260	
Indirect labour	1.20	1.20	122 400	28 890	

Power (variable portion)	0.60	0.40	61 200	9 630
Maintenance (variable portion)	0.20	0.40	20 400	9 630
			326 400	67 410	393 810

Non-controllable overheads:			
Depreciation	100 000	80 000	
Supervision	100 000	40 000	
Power (fixed portion)	40 000	2 000	
Maintenance (fixed portion)	45 600	3 196	
	285 600	125 196	410 796
Total overhead	612 000	192 606	804 606
Budgeted departmental overhead rate	£6.00[a]	8.00[b]	

[a]£612 000 total overheads divided by 102 000 direct labour hours.
[b]£192 606 total overheads divided by 24 075 direct labour hours.

The budgeted expenditure for the variable overhead items is determined by multiplying the budgeted direct labour hours for each department by the budgeted variable overhead rate per hour. It is assumed that all variable overheads vary in relation to direct labour hours.

Selling and administration budget

The selling and administration budgets have been combined here to simplify the presentation. In practice, separate budgets should be prepared: the sales manager will be responsible for the selling budget, the distribution manager will be responsible for the distribution expenses and the chief administrative officer will be responsible for the administration budget.

Schedule 7 – Annual selling and administration budget

	(£)	(£)
Selling:		
Salaries	74 000	
Commission	60 000	
Car expenses	22 000	
Advertising	80 000	236 000
Administration:		
Stationery	4 000	
Salaries	28 000	
Miscellaneous	8 000	40 000
		276 000

Departmental budgets

For cost control, the direct labour budget, materials usage budget and production overhead budget are combined into separate departmental budgets known as responsibility centres. These budgets are normally broken down into 12 separate monthly budgets, and the actual monthly expenditure is compared with the budgeted amounts for each of the items concerned. This comparison is used for judging how effective managers are in controlling the expenditure for which they are responsible. The departmental budget for department 1 will be as follows:

Department 1 – Annual departmental operating budget

	(£)	Budget (£)	Actual (£)
Direct labour (from schedule 5):			
102 000 hours at £12		1 224 000	
Direct materials (from schedule 3):			
102 000 units of material X at £7.20 per unit	734 400		
51 000 units of material Y at £16 per unit	816 000	1 550 400	
Controllable overheads (from schedule 6):			
Indirect materials	122 400		
Indirect labour	122 400		
Power (variable portion)	61 200		
Maintenance (variable portion)	20 400	326 400	
Uncontrollable overheads (from schedule 6):			
Depreciation	100 000		
Supervision	100 000		
Power (fixed portion)	40 000		
Maintenance (fixed portion)	45 600	285 600	
		3 386 400	

Master budget

When all the budgets have been prepared, the budgeted profit and loss account and balance sheet provide the overall picture of the planned performance for the budget period:

Budgeted profit statement for the year

	(£)	(£)
Sales (schedule 1)		4 296 000
Opening inventory of raw materials (from opening balance sheet)	189 200	
Purchases (schedule 4)	1 785 408[a]	
	1 974 608	
Less closing inventory of raw materials (schedule 4)	100 640[b]	
Cost of raw materials consumed	1 873 968	
Direct labour (schedule 5)	1 512 900	
Production overheads (schedule 6)	804 606	
Total manufacturing cost	4 191 474	
Add opening inventory of finished goods (from opening balance sheet)	99 076	
Less closing inventory of finished goods	665 984[c]	(566 908)
Cost of sales		3 624 566
Gross profit		671 434
Selling and administration expenses (schedule 7)		276 000
Budgeted operating profit for the year		395 434

[a]£839 088 (X) + £946 320 (Y) from schedule 4.
[b]10 200 units at £7.20 plus 1700 units at £16 from schedule 4.

[c]1870 units of alpha valued at £332 per unit, 90 units of sigma valued at £501.60 per unit. The product unit costs are calculated as follows:

	Alpha Units	Alpha (£)	Sigma Units	Sigma (£)
Direct materials				
X	10	72.00	8	57.60
Y	5	80.00	9	144.00
Direct labour	10	120.00	15	180.00
Production overheads:				
Department 1	10	60.00	—	—
Department 2	—	—	15	120.00
		332.00		501.60

Budgeted balance sheet as at 31 December

	(£)	(£)
Fixed assets:		
Land		170 000
Building and equipment	1 292 000	
Less depreciation[a]	435 000	857 000
		1 027 000
Current assets:		
Raw material inventory	100 640	
Finished good inventory	665 984	
Debtors[b]	280 000	
Cash[c]	199 170	
	1 245 794	
Current liabilities:		
Creditors[d]	307 884	937 910
		1 964 910
Represented by shareholders' interest:		
1 200 000 ordinary shares of £1 each	1 200 000	
Reserves	369 476	
Profit and loss account	395 434	1 964 910

[a]£255 000 + £180 000 (schedule 6) = £435 000.
[b]£289 000 opening balance + £4 296 000 sales − £4 305 000 cash.
[c]Closing balance as per cash budget.
[d]£248 800 opening balance + £1 785 408 purchases + £141 660 indirect materials − £1 867 984 cash.

Cash budgets

The objective of the **cash budget** is to ensure that sufficient cash is available at all times to meet the level of operations that are outlined in the various budgets. The cash budget for Example 15.1 is presented below and is analysed by quarters, but, in practice, monthly or weekly budgets will be necessary. Because cash budgeting is subject to uncertainty, it is necessary to provide for more than the minimum amount required, to allow for some margin of error in planning. Cash budgets can help a firm to avoid cash balances that are surplus to its requirements by enabling management to take steps in advance to invest the surplus cash in short-term investments. Cash deficiencies can also be identified in advance, and steps can be taken to ensure that bank loans will be available to meet any temporary shortfalls. For example, when management examines the cash budget for the Enterprise Company, it may consider that the cash balances are higher than necessary in the second and third quarters of the year and it may decide to invest part of the cash balance in short-term investments.

The overall aim should be to manage the cash of the firm to attain maximum cash availability and maximum interest income on any idle funds.

Cash budget for the year

	Quarter 1 (£)	Quarter 2 (£)	Quarter 3 (£)	Quarter 4 (£)	Total (£)
Opening balance	34000	114000	294000	421984	34000
Receipts from debtors	1000000	1200000	1120000	985000	4305000
	1034000	1314000	1414000	1406984	4339000
Payments:					
Purchase of materials	400000	480000	440000	547984	1867984
Payment of wages	400000	440000	480000	646188	1966188
Other costs and expenses	120000	100000	72016	13642	305658
	920000	1020000	992016	1207814	4139830
Closing balance	114000	294000	421984	199170	199170

Final review

The budgeted profit statement, the balance sheet and the cash budget will be submitted by the accountant to the budget committee, together with a number of budgeted financial ratios such as

the return on capital employed, working capital, liquidity and gearing ratios. If these ratios prove to be acceptable, the budgets will be approved. In Example 15.1, the return on capital employed is approximately 20 per cent, but the working capital ratio (current assets:current liabilities) is over 4:1, so management should consider alternative ways of reducing investment in working capital before finally approving the budgets.

COMPUTERIZED BUDGETING

In the past, budgeting was a task dreaded by many management accountants. You will have noted from Example 15.1 that many numerical manipulations are necessary to prepare the budget. In the real world, the process is far more complex, and, as the budget is being formulated, usually revised several times.

In today's world, the budgeting process is computerized instead of being primarily concerned with numerical manipulations, and the accounting staff can now become more involved in the real planning process. Computer-based financial models enable management to evaluate many different options before the budget is finally agreed. 'What-if?' analysis can be employed. For example, answers to the following questions can be displayed in the form of a master budget: What if sales increase or decrease by 10 per cent? What if unit costs increase or decrease by 5 per cent? What if the credit terms for sales were reduced from 30 to 20 days?

In addition, such models can incorporate actual results, period by period, and carry out the necessary calculations to produce budgetary *control* reports. It is also possible to adjust the budgets for the remainder of the year when it is clear that the circumstances on which the budget was originally set have changed.

ACTIVITY-BASED BUDGETING

ADVANCED READING

The conventional approach to budgeting works fine for unit-level activity costs where the consumption of resources varies proportionately with the volume of the final output of products or services. However, for those indirect costs and support activities where there are no clearly defined input–output relationships, and the consumption of resources does not vary with the final output of products or services, conventional budgets merely serve as authorization levels for certain levels of spending for each budgeted item of expense. Budgets that are not based on well-understood relationships between activities and costs are poor indicators of performance, and performance reporting normally implies little more than checking whether the budget has been exceeded. Conventional budgets therefore provide little relevant information for managing the costs of support activities.

With conventional budgeting, indirect costs and support activities are prepared on an incremental basis. This means that existing operations and the current budgeted allowance for existing activities are taken as the starting point for preparing the next annual budget. The base is then adjusted for changes (such as changes in product mix, volumes and prices) that are expected to occur during the new budget period. This approach is called incremental budgeting, since the budget process is concerned mainly with the increment in operations or expenditure that will occur during the forthcoming budget period. For example, the allowance for budgeted expenses may be based on the previous budgeted allowance plus an increase to cover higher prices caused by inflation. The major disadvantage of the incremental approach is that the majority of expenditure, which is associated with the 'base level' of activity, remains unchanged. Thus, the cost of non-unit level activities becomes fixed and past inefficiencies and waste inherent in the current way of doing things is perpetuated.

To manage costs more effectively, organizations have adopted activity-based budgeting (ABB). The aim of ABB is to authorize the supply of only those resources that are needed to perform activities required to meet the budgeted production and sales volume. Whereas ABC assigns resource expenses to activities and then uses activity cost drivers to assign activity costs to cost objects (such as products, services or customers), ABB is the reverse of this process. Cost objects are the starting point. Their budgeted output determines the necessary activities that are then used to estimate the resources that are required for the budget period. ABB involves the following stages:

1. estimate the production and sales volume by individual products or customers;
2. estimate the demand for organizational activities;
3. determine the resources that are required to perform organizational activities;
4. estimate for each resource the quantity that must be supplied to meet the demand;
5. take action to adjust the capacity of resources to match the projected supply.

The first stage is identical to conventional budgeting. Details of budgeted production and sales volumes for individual products and customer types will be contained in the sales and production budgets. Next, ABC extends conventional budgeting to support activities such as ordering, receiving, scheduling production and processing customers' orders. To implement ABB, the activities that are necessary to produce and sell the products and services and service customers must be identified. Estimates of the quantity of activity cost drivers must be derived for each activity. For example, the number of purchase orders, the number of receipts, the number of set-ups and the number of customer orders processed are estimated using the same approach as that used by conventional budgeting to determine the quantity of direct labour and materials that are incorporated into the direct labour and materials purchase budgets. Standard cost data incorporating a bill of activities are maintained for each product indicating the different activities, and the quantity of activity drivers that are required, to produce a specified number of products. Such documentation provides the basic information for building up the activity-based budgets.

The third stage is to estimate the resources that are required for performing the quantity of activity drivers demanded. In particular, estimates are required of each type of resource, and their quantities required, to meet the demanded quantity of activities. For example, if the number of customer orders to be processed is estimated to be 5000 and each order takes 30 minutes processing time then 2500 labour hours of the customer processing activity must be supplied.

In the fourth stage, the resources demanded (derived from the third stage) are converted into an estimate of the total resources that must be supplied for each type of resource used by an activity. The quantity of resources supplied depends on the cost behaviour of the resource. For flexible resources where the supply can be matched exactly to meet demand, such as direct materials and energy costs, the quantity of resources supplied will be identical to the quantity demanded. For example, if customer processing were a flexible resource, exactly 2500 hours would be purchased. However, a more likely assumption is that customer processing labour will be a step-fixed costs function in relation to the volume of the activity (see Chapter 2 for a description of step-fixed costs). Assuming that each person employed is contracted to work 1500 hours per year then 1.67 persons (2500/1500) represents the quantity of resources required, but because resources must be acquired in uneven amounts, two persons must be employed. For other resources, such as equipment, resources will tend to be fixed and committed over a very wide range of volume for the activity. As long as demand is less than the capacity supplied by the committed resource, no additional spending will be required.

The final stage is to compare the estimates of the quantity of resources to be supplied for each resource with the quantity of resources that are currently committed. If the estimated demand for a resource exceeds the current capacity, additional spending must be authorized within the budgeting process to acquire additional resources. Alternatively, if the demand for resources is less than the projected supply, the budgeting process should result in management taking action to either redeploy or reduce those resources that are no longer required.

Exhibit 15.2 illustrates an activity-based budget for an order receiving process or department. You will see that the budget is presented in a matrix format with the major activities being shown for each of the columns and the resource inputs are listed by rows. The cost driver activity levels are also highlighted. A major feature of ABB is the enhanced visibility arising from showing the outcomes, in terms of cost drivers, from the budgeted expenditure. This information is particularly useful for planning and estimating future expenditure.

EXHIBIT 15.2 Activity-based budget for an order receiving process

Activities →	Handle import goods	Execute express orders	Special deliveries	Distribution administration	Order receiving (standard products)	Order receiving (non-standard products)	Execute rush orders	Total cost
Resource expense accounts:								
Office supplies								
Telephone expenses								
Salaries								
Travel/training								
Total cost								
Activity cost driver → measures	Number of customs documents	Number of customer bills	Number of letters of credit	Number of consignment notes	Number of standard orders	Number of non-standard orders	Number of rush orders	

Let us now look at how ABB can be applied using the information presented in Exhibit 15.2. Assume that ABB stages one and two as outlined above result in an estimated annual demand of 2800 orders for the processing of the receipt of the standard customers' order activity (column 6 in Exhibit 15.2). For the staff salaries row (that is, the processing of customers' orders labour resource) assume that each member of staff can process on average 50 orders per month, or 600 per year. Therefore 4.67 (2800 orders/600 orders) persons are required for the supply of this resource (that is, stage three as outlined above). The fourth stage converts the 4.67 staff resources into the amount that must be supplied, that is five members of staff. Let us assume that the current capacity or supply of resources committed to the activity is six members of staff at £25 000 per annum, giving a total annual cost of £150 000. Management is therefore made aware that staff resources can be reduced by £25 000 per annum by transferring one member of staff to other activities where staff resources need to be expanded or, more drastically, making them redundant.

Some of the other resource expenses (such as office supplies and telephone expenses) listed in Exhibit 15.2 for the processing of customers' order activity represent flexible resources that are likely to vary in the short term with the number of orders processed. Assuming that the budget for the forthcoming period represents 80 per cent of the number of orders processed during the previous budget period, then the budget for those resource expenses that vary in the short term with the number of orders processed should be reduced by 20 per cent.

With conventional budgeting, the budgeted expenses for the forthcoming budget for support activities are normally based on the previous year's budget plus an adjustment for inflation. Support costs are therefore considered to be fixed in relation to activity volume. In contrast, ABB provides a framework for understanding the amount of resources that are required to achieve the budgeted level of activity. By comparing the amount of resources that are required with the amount of resources that are in place, upwards or downwards adjustments can be made during the budget setting phase.

THE BUDGETING PROCESS IN NON-PROFIT-MAKING ORGANIZATIONS

The budgeting process in a non-profit-making organization normally adopts an incremental budgeting approach with the managers of the various activities calculating the expected costs of maintaining current ongoing activities and then adding to those costs any further developments of the services that are considered desirable. The available resources for financing the proposed level of public services should be sufficient to cover the total costs of such services. In the case of a municipal authority, the resources will be raised by local taxes and government grants. Similar procedures are followed by churches, hospitals, charities and other non-profit-making organizations, in that they produce estimates for undertaking their activities and then find the means to finance them, or reduce the activities to realistic levels so that they can be financed from available financial resources.

One difficulty encountered in non-profit-making organizations is that precise objectives are difficult to define in a quantifiable way, and the actual accomplishments are even more difficult to measure. In most situations, outputs cannot be measured in monetary terms. By 'outputs' we mean the quality and amount of the services rendered. In profit-oriented organizations output can be measured in terms of sales revenues. The effect of this is that budgets in non-profit organizations, tend to be mainly concerned with the input of resources (i.e. expenditure), whereas budgets in profit organizations focus on the relationships between inputs (expenditure) and outputs (sales revenue). In non-profit organizations, there is not the same emphasis on what was intended to be achieved for a given input of resources. The budgeting process tends to compare what is happening in cash input terms with the estimated cash inputs. In other words, there is little emphasis on measures of managerial performance in terms of the results achieved. The reason for this is that there is no clear relationship between resource inputs and the benefits flowing from the use of these resources.

Line item budgets

The traditional format for budgets in non-profit organizations is referred to as line item budgets. A line item budget is one in which individual expense items are expressed in considerable detail, but the activities being undertaken are given little attention. In other words, line item budgeting shows the nature of the spending but not the purpose.

The amounts in this type of budget are frequently established on the basis of historical costs that have been adjusted for anticipated changes in costs and activity levels. When they are compared with the actual expenditures, line item budgets provide a basis for comparing whether or not the authorized budgeted expenditure has been exceeded or whether underspending has occurred. However, such line item budgets fail to identify the costs of *activities* and the *programmes* to be implemented. In addition, compliance with line item budgets provides no assurance that resources are used wisely, effectively or efficiently in financing the various activities in a non-profit organization. Planning, programming budgeting systems (PPBS) are intended to overcome these deficiencies. For a description and illustration of PPBS, you should refer to Learning Note 15.1 on the digital support resources accompanying this book (see Preface for details).

ZERO-BASED BUDGETING

Zero-based budgeting (also known as priority-based budgeting) emerged as an attempt to overcome the limitations of incremental budgets. This approach requires that projected expenditure for existing activities should start from base zero rather than last year's budget. In other words, managers are required to justify all budgeted expenditure rather than just the changes from the previous year. Besides adopting a 'zero-based' approach, zero-based budgeting (ZBB) also focuses on programmes or activities instead of functional departments based on line items, which is a feature of traditional budgeting. Programmes normally relate to various activities undertaken by municipal or government organizations. Examples include extending childcare facilities, improvement of healthcare for senior citizens and the extension of nursing facilities.

ZBB is best suited to discretionary costs and support activities. With discretionary costs, management has some discretion as to the amount it will budget for the particular activity in question. Examples of discretionary costs include advertising, research and development and training costs. There is no optimum relationship between inputs (as measured by the costs) and outputs (measured by revenues or some other objective function) for these costs. Furthermore, they are not predetermined by some previous

REAL WORLD VIEWS 15.3

ZBB is back

Although the apex of ZBB's popularity in the late 1970s is long past, there has been renewed interest in ZBB in today's environment of fiscal constraint, says Shayne Kavanagh in an article published in *Public Finance*. He cites a recent Government Finance Officers' Association (GFOA) survey that shows that an increasing number of leading public budget practitioners (44 per cent of all respondents) are considering ZBB, and just over 20 per cent of those say they are now using ZBB.

The GFOA's research found that 'textbook' ZBB is extremely rare. Instead, the term ZBB refers to budgeting methods that borrow elements of pure ZBB but do not conform to the theoretical ideal. According to GFOA's research, those describing themselves as using ZBB tend to fall into two major categories. The first category is termed zero-line-item budgeting (i.e. each line in the budget lists the budgeted expenditure by each expenditure category), and focuses on determining if inputs are reasonable given the expected output. This method seeks to create greater transparency in how line items are arrived at by requiring detailed justifications of line-item requests in lieu of pointing to prior years' allocations as the justification. The second category, called service-level budgeting, presents decision-makers with different service levels and asks decision-makers to choose between them, thus focusing on the question of which level of service should be funded within a programme or department. In service-level budgeting, departments concentrate on presenting decision packages and service levels with associated metrics, while there is less emphasis on detailed input estimates.

Question

1 Why has there recently been renewed interest in ZBB?

Reference

Kavanagh, S. (2012) ZBB is back!, *Public Management*, 94(3), 14–17. Available at webapps.icma.org /pm/9403/public/feature2.cfm?title=ZBB%20Is %20Back!&subtitle=&author=Shayne%20Kavanaugh

---

commitment. In effect, management can determine what quantity of service it wishes to purchase and there is no established method for determining the appropriate amount to be spent in particular periods. ZBB has mostly been applied in municipal and government organizations where the predominant costs are of a discretionary nature.

ZBB involves the following three stages:

- a description of each organizational activity in a decision package;
- the evaluation and ranking of decision packages in order of priority;
- allocation of resources based on order of priority up to the spending cut-off level.

Decision packages are identified for each decision unit. Decision units represent separate programmes or groups of activities that an organization undertakes. A decision package represents the operation of a particular programme with incremental packages reflecting different levels of effort that may be expended on a specific function. One package is usually prepared at the 'base' level for each programme. This package represents the minimum level of service or support consistent with the organization's objectives. Service or support higher than the base level is described in one or more incremental packages. For example, managers might be asked to specify the base package in terms of level of service that can be provided at 70 per cent of the current cost level and incremental packages identify higher activity or cost levels.

Once the decision packages have been completed, management is ready to start to review the process. To determine how much to spend and where to spend it, management will rank all packages in order of decreasing benefits to the organization. Theoretically, once management has set the budgeted level of spending, the packages should be accepted down to the spending level based on cost–benefit principles.

The benefits of ZBB over traditional methods of budgeting are claimed to be as follows:

1 Traditional budgeting tends to extrapolate the past by adding a percentage increase to the current year. ZBB avoids the deficiencies of incremental budgeting and represents a move towards the allocation of resources by need or benefit. Thus, unlike traditional budgeting the level of previous funding is not taken for granted.

2 ZBB creates a questioning attitude rather than one that assumes that current practice represents value for money.

3 ZBB focuses attention on outputs in relation to value for money.

ZBB was first applied in Texas Instruments. It quickly became one of the more fashionable management tools of the 1970s. Yet ZBB never achieved the widespread adoption that its proponents envisaged. The major reason for its lack of success would appear to be that it is too costly and time consuming. The process of identifying decision packages and determining their purpose, cost and benefits is extremely time consuming. Furthermore, there are often too many decision packages to evaluate and there is frequently insufficient information to enable them to be ranked.

Research suggests that many organizations tend to approximate the principles of ZBB rather than applying the full-scale approach outlined in the literature. For example, it does not have to be applied throughout the organization. It can be applied selectively to those areas about which management is most concerned and used as a one-off cost reduction programme. Some of the benefits of ZBB can be captured by using priority-based incremental budgets. Priority incremental budgets require managers to specify what incremental activities or changes would occur if their budgets were increased or decreased by a specified percentage (say 10 per cent). Budget allocations are made by comparing the change in costs with the change in benefits. Priority incremental budgets thus represent an economical compromise between ZBB and incremental budgeting.

CRITICISMS OF BUDGETING

In recent years criticisms of traditional budgeting have attracted much publicity. The most outspoken critics of traditional budgeting have been Hope and Fraser. In a series of articles Hope and Fraser (1999a, 1999b, 2001, 2003a, 2003b) have argued that companies should abandon traditional budgeting. They advocate that companies should move beyond budgeting. According to Hope and Fraser (2003a), a number of innovative companies, such as Svenska Handelsbanken (a Swedish bank) and Volvo, had abandoned traditional budgeting. The major criticism is that the annual budgeting process is incapable of meeting the demands of the competitive environment in today's information age. Ekholm and Wallin (2000) and Dugdale and Lyne (2006) have reviewed the literature relating to annual budgets. They have identified the following criticisms relating to the annual budgeting process:

● encouraging rigid planning and incremental thinking whereby budgets are derived from last year's activities plus an adjustment for the current year rather than adopting a zero-based budgeting approach;

● being time consuming i.e. taking up an enormous amount of management time which results in a situation where the benefits may not be worth their cost. Hope and Fraser (2003) claim that budgeting is a protracted and expensive process, absorbing up to 30 per cent of management time. They cite a study indicating that global companies invested more than 25 000 person days per $1 billion of revenue in the planning and performance measurement processes;

● ignoring key drivers of shareholder value (e.g. innovation, developing new products and markets and responding to competitor threats) by focusing too much attention on short-term financial numbers;

● being a yearly rigid ritual that impedes firms from being flexible and adaptive in the increasingly unpredictable environment facing contemporary organizations; indeed, Hope and Fraser argue that budgeting conflicts with the new competitive environment and stifles innovation because, once set, budgets are not typically changed resulting in plans and targets that become quickly out of date;

- tying the company to a 12-month commitment, which is risky since it is based on uncertain forecasts derived from a fast-changing environment;

- meeting only the lowest targets and not attempting to beat the targets; Hope and Fraser argue that budgets often serve as a 'fixed performance contract' whereby targets are set at the beginning of the period. If the actual performance meets or exceeds the pre-specified static budget target, performance is deemed to be satisfactory. They argue that a fixed contract represents a poor standard of performance evaluation when the factors underlying the targets may have changed during the budget period. They also argue that the use of fixed performance contracts encourages managers to engage in dysfunctional behaviour (see 'Harmful side-effects of controls' in Chapter 16) to achieve the budget even if this results in undesirable actions that do not contribute to the organization's objectives;

- spending what is in the budget even if this is not necessary in order to guard against next year's budget being reduced;

- being disconnected from strategy whereby budgets are typically prepared in isolation from, and not aligned with, the strategic objectives of the organization.

Beyond budgeting

The term beyond budgeting is used by Hope and Fraser to relate to alternative approaches that should be used instead of annual budgeting. Beyond budgeting consists of similar activities as budgeting but dispenses with the annual budgeting process whereby resources are allocated in advance only on an annual basis. Instead, rolling forecasts, ambitious target setting, more decentralized decision behaviour and relative external performance evaluation are advocated.

Quarterly rolling forecasts are advocated that typically cover five to eight quarters. Such forecasts are regularly revised thus supporting managers' ability to determine strategies that continuously adapt to the fast changing market conditions. Rolling forecasts are considered to provide more accurate information because they are constantly updated by the latest estimates of economic trends, customer demand and data from the most recent quarter. Hope and Fraser also argue that rolling forecasts avoid the dysfunctional behaviour that occurs with annual budgets because performance evaluation is no longer based on achieving fixed targets since the targets are continuously changed and updated.

Instead of evaluating performance against a static outdated budget, Hope and Fraser advocate abandoning budget targets and replacing them with relative external performance measures. These performance measures are based on comparisons of a small number of key performance indicators with competitors and similar units within the company, thus ensuring that they are based on the economic conditions prevailing at the time. Because the use of relative comparisons means managers do not know how successful they have been until the period is over, they must strive to ensure that their performance (in terms of a comparison of the key performance indicators) is better than the external and internal competitors. Hope and Fraser suggest that this approach results in managers having the confidence to stretch their performance. According to Bourmistrov and Kaarbøe (2013), one of the main problems of budgets is the establishment of 'comfort zones' whereas relative performance evaluation moves managers to so-called 'stretch zones' whereby they strive for continuous improvement.

Advocates of the beyond budgeting philosophy claim that it supports decentralization and employee empowerment initiatives that are required for firms to compete in today's fast changing environment. In empowered organizations, managers have wide discretion in making decisions and can obtain resources more quickly without being dependent on resources being centrally allocated in advance as part of the annual budgeting process. Empowered organizations trust their managers to claim the resources they need to seize the opportunities that they identify in an ever changing environment.

Beyond budgeting also places greater emphasis on team-based (or business unit) rewards rather than individual rewards because of the difficulty in identifying the incremental contribution of individuals and the need to demonstrate that everyone is pulling together in the same direction, each dependent on the other.

Surveys relating to criticisms of budgeting

Because of the criticisms of budgeting, and the beyond budgeting movement, Dugdale and Lyne (2006) surveyed financial and non-financial managers in 40 UK companies. Their main conclusion was that budgeting is alive and well. All of the companies surveyed used budgets and, generally, both financial and non-financial managers thought they were important for planning, control, performance measurement, coordination and communication. To find out how problematic the respondents viewed their budgets, they were asked whether they agreed with 20 critical propositions. The respondents tended to disagree with the propositions. Ekholm and Wallin (2000) also surveyed 168 Finnish companies. They reported that relatively few companies were planning to abandon the annual budget. However, in contrast to the UK findings by Dugdale and Lyne (2006), there was strong agreement with many of the criticisms relating to budgeting. Comments by several respondents also indicated that complementary systems, such as rolling forecasts and monitoring systems similar to the balanced scorecard, already exist and are run in parallel with the annual budget.

A more recent study of budgeting practices in North American organizations was undertaken by Libby and Lindsay (2010). Their findings indicate that budgeting systems continue to play a key role in firms' control systems and that only 5 per cent of the 558 surveyed firms were considering possibly abandoning budgeting, although many were taking steps to improve their systems to overcome some of the common criticisms. They also found that:

- budgets were revised much more often than expected and new resources were allocated outside the budget process in order to respond in changes in the competitive environment;

- the budget was explicitly linked to strategy implementation in the majority of firms surveyed and that the criticism that budgets are not linked to strategy was not supported by the responses by the majority of firms;

- few of the sampled firms used budgets as fixed performance contracts. Instead, subjective considerations and allowances for uncontrollable events were extensively used when using the budget for performance evaluation.

Libby and Lindsay conclude that instead of going beyond budgeting, most firms have chosen to improve the process and that claims that budgets are flawed are probably overstated. The international survey undertaken by the Chartered Institute of Management Accountants (2009) reported that only around 5 per cent of the responding organizations used beyond budgeting and around 90 per cent used annual financial forecasts.

SUMMARY

The following items relate to the learning objectives listed at the beginning of the chapter.

- **Explain how budgeting fits into the overall planning and control framework.**

The annual budget should be set within the context of longer-term plans, which are likely to exist even if they have not been made explicit. A long-term plan is a statement of the preliminary targets and activities required by an organization to achieve its strategic plans, together with a broad estimate for each year of the resources required. Because long-term planning involves 'looking into the future' for several years, the plans tend to be uncertain, general in nature, imprecise and subject to change. Annual budgeting is concerned with the detailed implementation of the long-term plan for the year ahead.

- **Identify and describe the six different purposes of budgeting.**

Budgets are used for the following purposes: (a) planning annual operations; (b) coordinating the activities of the various parts of the organization and ensuring that the parts are in harmony with one another; (c) communicating the plans to the managers of the various responsibility centres; (d) motivating managers to strive to achieve organizational goals; (e) controlling activities; and (f) evaluating the performance of managers.

● Identify and describe the various stages in the budget process.

The important stages are as follows: (a) communicating details of the budget policy and guidelines to those people responsible for the preparation of the budgets; (b) determining the factor that restricts output (normally sales volume); (c) preparation of the sales budget (assuming that sales demand is the factor that restricts output); (d) initial preparation of the various budgets; (e) negotiation of budgets with superiors; (f) coordination and review of budgets; (g) final acceptance of budgets; and (h) ongoing review of budgets. Each of these stages is described in this chapter.

● Prepare functional and master budgets.

When all of the budgets have been prepared, they are summarized into a master budget consisting in a budgeted profit and loss account, a balance sheet and a cash budget statement. The preparation of functional and master budgets was illustrated using Example 15.1.

● Describe the limitations of incremental budgeting.

With incremental budgeting, indirect costs and support activities are prepared on an incremental basis. This means that existing operations and the current budgeted allowance for existing activities are taken as the starting point for preparing the next annual budget. The base is then adjusted for changes which are expected to occur during the new budget period. When this approach is adopted, the concern is mainly with the increment in operations or expenditure that will occur during the forthcoming budget period. The major disadvantage of the incremental approach is that the majority of expenditure, which is associated with the 'base level' of activity, remains unchanged. Thus, past inefficiencies and waste inherent in the current way of doing things are perpetuated.

● Describe activity-based budgeting.

Activity-based budgeting (ABB) aims to manage costs more effectively by authorizing the supply of only those resources that are needed to perform activities required to meet the budgeted production and sales volume. Whereas ABC assigns resource expenses to activities and then uses activity cost drivers to assign activity costs to cost objects (such as products, services or customers), ABB is the reverse of this process. Cost objects are the starting point. Their budgeted output determines the necessary activities that are then used to estimate the resources that are required for the budget period. ABB involves the following stages: (a) estimate the production and sales volume by individual products and customers; (b) estimate the demand for organizational activities; (c) determine the resources that are required to perform organizational activities; (d) estimate for each resource the quantity that must be supplied to meet the demand; and (e) take action to adjust the capacity of resources to match the projected supply.

● Describe zero-based budgeting (ZBB).

ZBB is a method of budgeting that is mainly used in non-profit organizations but it can also be applied to discretionary costs and support activities in profit organizations. It seeks to overcome the deficiencies of incremental budgeting. ZBB works from the premise that projected expenditure for existing programmes should start from base zero, with each year's budgets being compiled as if the programmes were being launched for the first time.

● Describe the criticisms relating to traditional budgeting.

Criticisms relating to traditional budgeting include encouraging rigid planning and incremental thinking, being time consuming, a failure to encourage continuous improvement, achieving the target even if this results in undesirable actions and being a yearly rigid ritual. The beyond budgeting movement advocates that budgeting should be replaced with rolling forecasts that embrace key performance indicators and also incorporate exception-based monitoring and benchmarking.

KEY TERMS AND CONCEPTS

Activity-based budgeting (ABB) An approach to budgeting that takes cost objects as the starting point, determines the necessary activities and then estimates the resources that are required for the budget period.

Beyond budgeting A term used to describe alternative approaches, such as rolling forecasts, that can be used instead of annual budgeting.

Budgeting The implementation of the long-term plan for the year ahead through the development of detailed financial plans.

Budget A financial plan for implementing management decisions.

Budgetary control process The process of comparing actual and planned outcomes, and responding to any deviations from the plan.

Cash budget A budget that aims to ensure that sufficient cash is available at all times to meet the level of operations that are outlined in all other budgets.

Continuous budgeting An approach to budgeting in which the annual budget is broken down into months for the first three months and into quarters for the rest of the year, with a new quarter being added as each quarter ends, also known as rolling budgeting.

Control process The process of comparing actual and planned outcomes, and responding to any deviations from the plan.

Corporate objectives Specific, measurable statements, often expressed in financial terms, of what the organization as a whole wishes to achieve.

Decision packages A decision package represents the incremental packages reflecting different levels of effort that may be expended to undertake a specific group of activities within an organization.

Discretionary costs Costs such as advertising and research where management has some discretion as to the amount it will budget.

Feedback loops Parts of a control system that allow for review and corrective action to ensure that actual outcomes conform with planned outcomes.

Incremental budgeting An approach to budgeting in which existing operations and the current budgeted allowance for existing activities are taken as the starting point for preparing the next annual budget and are then adjusted for anticipated changes.

Incremental budgets Budgets where expenses for an item within the budget are based on the previous budgeted allowance plus an increase to cover higher prices caused by inflation.

Line item budgets The traditional format for budgets in non-profit organizations, in which expenditures are expressed in considerable detail, but the activities being undertaken are given little attention.

Long-term plan A top-level plan that sets out the objectives that an organization's future activities will be directed towards, also known as a strategic plan.

Management by exception A system in which a manager's attention and effort can be concentrated on significant deviations from the expected results.

Master budget A document that brings together and summarizes all lower level budgets and which consists of a budgeted profit and loss account, a balance sheet and cash flow statement.

Mission statement A statement that provides in very general terms what the organization does to achieve its vision, its broad purpose and reason, its existence, the nature of the business(es) it is in and the customers it seeks to serve and satisfy.

Priority-based budgeting An approach to budgeting in which projected expenditure for existing activities starts from base zero rather than last year's budget, forcing managers to justify all budget expenditure, also known as zero-based budgeting.

Priority-based incremental budgets Budgets in which managers specify what incremental activities or changes would occur if their budgets were increased or decreased by a specified percentage, leading to budget allocations being made by comparing the change in costs with the change in benefits.

Rolling budgeting An approach to budgeting in which the annual budget is broken down into months for the first three months and into quarters for the rest of the year, with a new quarter being added as each quarter ends, also known as continuous budgeting.

Strategic plan A top-level plan that sets out the objectives that an organization's future activities will be directed towards, also known as a long-term plan.

Strategy The courses of action that must be taken to achieve an organization's overall objectives.

Unit objectives Specific, measurable statements, often expressed in financial terms, of what individual units within an organization wish to achieve.

Vision statement A statement that clarifies the beliefs and governing principles of an organization, what it wants to be in the future or how it wants the world in which it operates to be.

Zero-based budgeting An approach to budgeting in which projected expenditure for existing activities starts from base zero rather than last year's budget, forcing managers to justify all budget expenditure, also known as priority-based budgeting.

RECOMMENDED READING

In this chapter, we have provided a very brief summary of the process for selecting alternative strategies. A detailed explanation of strategy formulation can be found in the corporate strategy literature. Predominant texts on this area include Johnson, Scholes and Whittington (2017) and Thompson and Martin (2014). For a more detailed discussion of budgeting in the public sector, see Jones and Pendlebury (2010).

Articles relating to the criticisms of budgeting include Ekholm and Wallin (2000), Hope and Fraser (2003a), Dugdale and Lyne (2006) and Ostregen and Stensaker (2011). The articles by Libby and Lindsay (2010) also includes a survey relating to budgeting practices.

KEY EXAMINATION POINTS

Examination questions on budgeting frequently require the preparation of functional or cash budgets. A common mistake is to incorrectly deduct closing inventories and add opening inventories when preparing production and material purchase budgets. Examination questions are also set frequently on zero-based

budgeting (ZBB). Do make sure that you can describe and discuss the advantages and disadvantages of ZBB and distinguish between incremental budgeting and ZBB. You should refer to the solution to Review problem 15.25 for the application of activity-based budgeting.

ASSESSMENT MATERIAL

The review questions are short questions that enable you to assess your understanding of the main topics included in the chapter. The numbers in parentheses provide you with the page numbers to refer to if you cannot answer a specific question.

The review problems are more complex and require you to relate and apply the content to various business problems. The problems are graded by their level of difficulty. Solutions to review problems that are not preceded by the term 'IM' are provided in a separate section at the end of the book. Solutions to problems preceded by the term 'IM' are provided in the Instructor's Manual accompanying this book that can be downloaded from the lecturer's digital support resources. Additional review problems with fully worked solutions are provided in the *Student Manual* that accompanies this book.

REVIEW QUESTIONS

15.1 Define the term 'budget'. How are budgets used in planning? (pp. 368–371)

15.2 Describe the different stages in the planning and control process. (pp. 369–371)

15.3 Distinguish between budgeting and long-range planning. How are they related? (p. 370)

15.4 Describe the different purposes of budgeting. (pp. 371–372)

15.5 Explain what is meant by the term 'management by exception'. (p. 372)

15.6 Describe how the different roles of budgets can conflict with one another. (pp. 372–373)

15.7 Distinguish between continuous and rolling budgets. (p. 373)

15.8 Describe the different stages in the budgeting process. (pp. 374–377)

15.9 All budgets depend on the sales budget. Do you agree? Explain. (p. 375)

15.10 What is a master budget? (p. 377)

15.11 Define incremental budgeting. (p. 386)

15.12 What are the distinguishing features of activity-based budgeting? (pp. 386–388)

15.13 Describe the five different stages that are involved with activity-based budgeting. (pp. 388–390)

15.14 What are the distinguishing features of budgeting in non-profit-making organizations? (pp. 388–389)

15.15 What are line item budgets? (p. 389)

15.16 How does zero-based budgeting differ from traditional budgeting? (pp. 389–391)

15.17 What are discretionary costs? (p. 389)

15.18 Distinguish between zero-based budgeting and priority-based incremental budgeting. (p. 391)

REVIEW PROBLEMS

15.19 **Basic.** X Co uses rolling budgeting, updating its budgets on a quarterly basis. After carrying out the last quarter's update to the cash budget, it projected a forecast

cash deficit of $400 000 at the end of the year. Consequently, the planned purchase of new capital equipment has been postponed.

Which of the following types of control is the sales manager's actions an example of?

- (a) Feedforward control
- (b) Negative feedback control
- (c) Positive feedback control
- (d) Double loop feedback control

ACCA F5 Performance Management

15.20 Basic. A company produces two products, A1 and A2 that are sold to retailers. The budgeted sales volumes for the next quarter are as follows:

Product	Units
A1	32000
A2	56000

The inventory of finished goods is budgeted to increase by 1000 units of A1 and decrease by 2000 units of A2 by the end of the quarter.

Materials B3 and B4 are used in the production of both products. The quantities required of each material to produce one unit of the finished product and the purchase prices are shown in the table below:

	B3	B4
A1	8 kg	4 kg
A2	4 kg	3 kg
Purchase price per kg	$1.25	$1.80
Budgeted opening inventory	30,000 kg	20,000 kg

The company plans to hold inventory of raw materials, at the end of the quarter, of 5 per cent of the quarter's material usage budget.

Required:
Prepare the following budgets for the quarter:

- (i) The production budget (in units)
- (ii) The material usage budget (in kg)
- (iii) The material purchases budget (in kg and $)

(5 marks)

CIMA P1 Performance Operations

15.21 Basic. CH is a building supplies company that sells products to trade and private customers.

Budget data for each of the six months to March are given below:

	Oct $000	Nov $000	Dec $000	Jan $000	Feb $000	March $000
Credit sales	250	250	250	260	260	280
Cash sales	60	60	65	75	80	90
Credit purchases	170	180	180	200	200	200
Other operating costs (excluding depreciation)	90	90	90	122	123	123

Eighty per cent of the value of credit sales is received in the month after sale, 10 per cent two months after sale and 8 per cent three months after sale. The balance is written off as a bad debt.

Seventy five per cent of the value of credit purchases is paid in the month after purchase and the remaining 25 per cent is paid two months after purchase.

All other operating costs are paid in the month they are incurred.

CH has placed an order for four new forklift trucks that willl cost $25000 each. The scheduled payment date is in February.

The cash balance at 1 January is estimated to be $15000.

Required:
Prepare a cash budget far each of the THREE months of January, February and March.   *(5 marks)*

CIMA P1 Performance Operations

15.22 Basic: Rolling budgets. Designit is a small company providing design consultancy to a limited number of large clients. The business is mature and fairly stable year on year. It has 30 employees and is privately owned by its founder. Designit prepares an annual fixed budget. The company's accounts department consists of one part-qualified accountant who has a heavy workload. He prepares the budget using spreadsheets. The company has a November year end.

Designit pays each of its three sales managers an annual salary of $150000, plus an individual bonus based on sales targets set at the beginning of the year. There are always two levels of bonus that can be earned, based on a lower and an upper level of fee income. For the year ended 30 November, for example, each of the sales managers was given a lower target of securing $l.5m of fee income each, to be rewarded by an individual bonus equating to 20 per cent of salary. If any of the managers secured a further $1.5m of fee income, their bonus would increase by 5 per cent to the upper target of 25 per cent. None of the managers achieved the upper target but all of them achieved the lower one.

This is the same every year and Designit finds that often the managers secure work from several major clients early in the year and reach the $1.5m target well before the year has ended. They then make little effort to secure extra fees for the company, knowing that it would be almost impossible to hit the second target. This, together with a few other problems that have arisen, has made the company consider whether its current budgeting process could be improved and whether the bonus scheme should also be changed.

Designit is now considering replacing the fixed budget with a monthly rolling budget, which Designit believes will make the budgeting process more relevant and timely, and encourage managers to focus on the future rather than the past. It would also prevent the problem of targets being met too early on in the year by the sales managers because the targets would be set for monthly performance rather than annual performance. For example, a manager could be given a target of securing $200000 fee income in the first month for a reward of 2 per cent of salary. Then, depending on what is happening both within the business and in the economy as a whole, at the end of the first month, a different target fee income could be set for the second month.

Required:

- (a) Explain what a monthly rolling budget is and how it would operate at Designit.   *(4 marks)*
- (b) Discuss the problems that may be encountered if Designit decides to introduce monthly rolling budgets together with a new bonus scheme, such as the one outlined above.   *(6 marks)*
- (c) Discuss the problems with the current bonus scheme and, assuming that the company decides against introducing rolling budgets, describe and justify an alternative, more effective bonus scheme that could be introduced.   *(6 marks)*
- (d) Discuss the risk of using the company accountant's own spreadsheets for budgeting.   *(4 marks)*

ACCA F5 Performance Management

15.23 Intermediate: Incremental and zero base budgeting. Newtown School's head teacher has prepared the budget for the year ending 31 May. The government pays the school $1050 for each child registered at the beginning of the school year, which is June 1, and $900 for any child joining the school part-way through the year. The school does not have to refund the money to the government if a child leaves the school part-way through the year. The number of pupils registered at the school on 1 June at the beginning of the budget year is 690, which is 10 per cent lower than the previous year. Based on past experience, the probabilities for the number of pupils starting the school part-way through the year are as follows:

Probability	No. of pupils joining late
0.2	50
0.3	20
0.5	26

The head teacher admits to being 'poor with numbers' and does not understand probabilities so, when calculating budgeted revenue, he just calculates a simple average for the number of pupils expected to join late. His budgeted revenue for the year ending 31 May is therefore as follows:

	Pupils	Rate per pupil	Total income
Pupils registered at beginning of school year	690	$1050	$724 500
Average expected number of new joiners	32	$900	$28 800
			$753 300

The head teacher uses incremental budgeting to budget for his expenditure, taking actual expenditure for the previous year as a starting point and simply adjusting it for inflation, as shown below.

	Note	Actual cost for y/e 31 May $	Inflationary adjustment	Budgeted cost for y/e 31 May $
Repairs and maintenance	1	44 000	+3%	45 320
Salaries	2	620 000	+2%	632 400
Capital expenditure	3	65 000	+6%	68 900
Total budgeted expenditure				746 620
Budget surplus				6 680

Notes

1   $30 000 of the costs for the year ended 31 May related to standard maintenance checks and repairs that have to be carried out by the school every year in order to comply with government health and safety standards. These are expected to increase by 3 per cent in the coming year. In the year ended 31 May $14 000 was also spent on redecorating some of the classrooms. No redecorating is planned for the coming year.

2   One teacher earning a salary of $26 000 left the school on 31 May and there are no plans to replace her. However, a 2 per cent pay rise will be given to all staff with effect from 1 December.

3   The full $65 000 actual costs for the year ended 31 May related to improvements made to the school gym. This year, the canteen is going to be substantially improved, although the extent of the improvements and level of service to be offered to pupils is still under discussion. There is a 0.7 probability that the cost will be $145 000 and a 0.3 probability that it will be $80 000. These costs must be paid in full before the end of the year ending 31 May.

The school's board of governors, who review the budget, are concerned that the budget surplus has been calculated incorrectly. They believe that it should have been calculated using expected income, based on the probabilities provided, and using expected expenditure, based on the information provided

in Notes 1 to 3. They believe that incremental budgeting is not proving a reliable tool for budget setting in the school since, for the last three years, there have been shortfalls of cash despite a budget surplus being predicted. Since the school has no other source of funding available to it, these shortfalls have had serious consequences, such as the closure of the school kitchen for a considerable period in the last school year, meaning that no hot meals were available to pupils. This is thought to have been the cause of the 10 per cent fall in the number of pupils registered at the school on 1 June.

Required:

(a) Considering the views of the board of governors, recalculate the budget surplus/deficit for the year ending 31 May.   (6 marks)

(b) Discuss the advantages and disadvantages of using incremental budgeting.   (4 marks)

(c) Briefly outline the three main steps involved in preparing a zero-based budget.   (6 marks)

(d) Discuss the extent to which zero-based budgeting could be used by Newtown School to improve the budgeting process.   (4 marks)

15.24 Incremental and rolling budgets and budget participation.
The Drinks Group (DG) has been created over the last three years by merging three medium sized family businesses. These businesses are all involved in making fruit drinks. Fizzy (F) makes and bottles healthy, fruit-based sparkling drinks. Still (S) makes and bottles fruit-flavoured non-sparkling drinks and Healthy (H) buys fruit and squeezes it to make basic fruit juices. The three companies have been divisionalized within the group structure. A fourth division called Marketing (M) exists to market the products of the other divisions to various large retail chains. Marketing has only recently been set up in order to help the business expand. All of the operations and sales of DG occur in Nordland, which is an economically well-developed country with a strong market for healthy non-alcoholic drinks.

The group has recruited a new finance director (FD), who was asked by the board to perform a review of the efficiency and effectiveness of the finance department as her first task on taking office. The finance director has just presented her report to the board regarding some problems at DG.

Extract from finance director's Report to the Board:

The main area for improvement, which was discussed at the last board meeting, is the need to improve profit margins throughout the business. There is no strong evidence that new products or markets are required but that the most promising area for improvement lies in better internal control practices.

Control

As DG was formed from an integration of the original businesses (F, S, H), there was little initial effort put into optimizing the control systems of these businesses. They have each evolved over time in their own way. Currently, the main method of central control that can be used to drive profit margin improvement is the budget system in each business. The budgeting method used is to take the previous year's figures and simply increment them by estimates of growth in the market that will occur over the next year. These growth estimates are obtained through a discussion between the financial managers at group level and the relevant divisional managers. The management at each division are then given these budgets by head office and their personal targets are set around achieving the relevant budget numbers.

Divisions

H and S divisions are in stable markets where the levels of demand and competition mean that sales growth is unlikely, unless by acquisition of another brand. The main engine for prospective profit growth in these divisions is through margin improvements. The managers at these divisions have been successful in previous years and generally keep to the agreed budgets. As a result, they are usually not comfortable with changing existing practices.

F is faster growing and seen as the star of the Group. However, the Group has been receiving complaints from customers about late deliveries and poor quality control of the F products. The F managers have explained that they are working hard within the budget and capital constraints imposed by the board and have expressed a desire to be less controlled.

The marketing division has only recently been set up and the intention is to run each marketing campaign as an individual project which would be charged to the division whose products are benefiting from the campaign. The managers of the manufacturing divisions are very doubtful of the value of M, as each believes that they have an existing strong reputation with their customers that does not require much additional spending on marketing. However, the board decided at the last meeting that there was scope to create and use a marketing budget effectively at DG, if its costs were carefully controlled. Similar to the other divisions, the marketing division budgets are set by taking the previous year's actual spend and adding a percentage increase. For M, the increase corresponds to the previous year's growth in group turnover.

End of extract

At present, the finance director is harassed by the introduction of a new information system within the finance department which is straining the resources of the department. However, she needs to respond to the issues raised above at the board meeting and so is considering using different budgeting methods at DG. She has asked you, the management accountant at the Group, to do some preliminary work to help her decide whether and how to change the budget methods. The first task that she believes would be useful is to consider the use of rolling budgets. She thinks that fast growing F may prove the easiest division in which to introduce new ideas.

F's incremental budget for the current year is given below. You can assume that cost of sales and distribution costs are variable and administrative costs are fixed:

	Q1 $000	Q2 $000	Q3 $000	Q4 $000	Total $000
Revenue	17520	17958	18407	18867	72752
Cost of sales	9636	9877	10124	10377	40014
Gross profit	7884	8081	8283	8490	32738
Distribution costs	1577	1616	1657	1698	6548
Administration costs	4214	4214	4214	4214	16856
Operating profit	2093	2251	2412	2578	9334

The actual figures for quarter 1 (which has just completed) are:

	$000
Revenue	17932
Cost of sales	9863
Gross profit	8069
Distribution costs	1614
Administration costs	4214
Operating profit	2241

On the basis of the Q1 results, sales volume growth of 3 per cent per quarter is now expected.

The finance director has also heard you talking about bottom-up budgeting and wants you to evaluate its use at DG.

Required:

(a) Evaluate the suitability of incremental budgeting at each division. *(8 marks)*

(b) Recalculate the budget for Fizzy division (F) using rolling budgeting and assess the use of rolling budgeting at F. *(8 marks)*

(c) Recommend any appropriate changes to the budgeting method at the Marketing division (M), providing justifications for your choice. *(4 marks)*

(d) Analyse and recommend the appropriate level of participation in budgeting at Drinks Group (DG). *(6 marks)*

ACCA P5 Advanced Performance Management

15.25 Advanced: Activity-based budgeting. Flosun plc makes and sells a range of products. Management has carried out an analysis of the total cost of production. The information in Appendix 3.1 reflects this analysis of budgeted costs for the six-month period to 30 June. The analysis has identified that the factory is organized in order to permit the operation of three production lines X, Y and Z. Each production line facilitates the production of two or more products. Production line X is only used for the production of products A and B. The products are manufactured in batches on a just-in-time basis in order to fulfil orders from customers. Only one product can be manufactured on the production line at any one time. Materials are purchased and received on a just-in-time basis. Additional information is available for production line X as follows:

(i) Production line machine costs including labour, power, etc., vary in proportion to machine hours.

(ii) Costs incurred for production scheduling, WIP movement, purchasing and receipt of materials are assumed to be incurred in proportion to the number of batches of product which are manufactured. Machine set-up costs vary in proportion to the number of set-ups required and are linked to a batch throughput system.

(iii) Costs for material scheduling systems and design/testing routines are assumed to be incurred by each product in proportion to the total quantity of components purchased and the total number of types of component used, respectively. The number of different components designed/tested for products A and B are 12 and 8, respectively.

(iv) Product line development cost is identified with changes in product design and production method. At present such costs for production line X are apportioned 80 per cent: 20 per cent to products A and B, respectively. Production line maintenance costs are assumed to vary in proportion to the maintenance hours required for each product.

(v) General factory costs are apportioned to each of production lines X, Y and Z in the ratio 25 per cent: 30 per cent: 45 per cent, respectively. Such costs are absorbed by product units at an average rate per unit through each production line.

Required:

(a) Prepare an activity based budget for production line X for the six-month period to 30 June analysed into sub-sets for activities that are product unit based, batch based, product sustaining, production line sustaining and factory sustaining.

The budget should show:

(i) Total cost for each activity sub-set grouped to reflect the differing operational levels at which each sub-set is incurred/controlled.

(ii) Average cost per unit for each of products A and B analysed by activity sub-set. *(24 marks)*

(b) Discuss the incidence and use of each of the following terms in relation to Flosun plc, giving examples from the question to illustrate your answer:

(i) hierarchy of activities;

(ii) cost pools;

(iii) cost drivers. *(6 marks)*

(c) Prepare a sequential set of steps that may be included in an investigation of activities in order to improve company profitability.

This should be a general list of steps and not specifically relating to Flosun plc. *(5 marks)*

Appendix 3.1
Flosun plc – Budget data six months to 30 June

	Product A	Product B
Material cost per product unit	£60	£45
Production line X – machine hours per unit	0.8	0.5
Production batch size (units)	100	200
Total production (units)	9000	15000
Components per product unit (quantity)	20	12
Number of customers	5	10
Number of production line set-ups	15	25
Production line X – maintenance hours	300	150

Cost category	Production line X £	Factory total £
Labour, power, etc.	294000	
Set-up of machines	40000	
Production scheduling	29600	
WIP movement	36400	
Purchasing and receipt of material	49500	
Material scheduling system	18000	
Design/testing routine	16000	
Production line development	25000	
Production line maintenance	9000	
General factory administration		500000
General factory occupancy		268000

ACCA Paper 9 Information for Control and Decision Making

15.26 Advanced. The modern dynamic business environment has been described as a 'buyer's market' in which companies must react to the rapidly changing characteristics of the market and the needs of customers. Many managers have criticized traditional forms of budgeting for being too restrictive and for being of little use for performance management and control.

Required:
Explain how the principles of 'beyond budgeting' promote a cultural framework that is suitable for the modern dynamic business environment. *(10 marks)*

CIMA P1 Performance Operations

15.27 Advanced. Some commentators argue that: 'With continuing pressure to control costs and maintain efficiency, the time has come for all public sector organization to embrace zero-based budgeting. There is no longer a place for incremental budgeting in any organization, particularly public sector ones, where zero-based budgeting is far more suitable anyway.'

Required:

(a) Discuss the particular difficulties encountered when budgeting in public sector organization compared with budgeting in private sector organization, drawing comparisons between the two types of organization. *(5 marks)*
(b) Explain the terms 'incremental budgeting' and 'zero-based budgeting'. *(4 marks)*
(c) State the main stages involved in preparing zero-based budgets. *(3 marks)*
(d) Discuss the view that 'there is no longer a place for incremental budgeting in any organization, particularly public sector ones', highlighting any drawbacks of zero-based budgeting that need to be considered. *(8 marks)*

ACCA P5 Advanced Performance Management

IM15.1 Intermediate. Outline:

(a) the objectives of budgetary planning and control systems;
(b) the organization required for the preparation of a master budget. *(10 marks)*

ACCA Level 1 Costing

IM15.2 Intermediate. The preparation of budgets is a lengthy process which requires great care if the ultimate master budget is to be useful for the purposes of management control within an organization.

You are required:

(a) to identify and to explain briefly the stages involved in the preparation of budgets identifying separately the roles of managers and the budget committee; *(8 marks)*
(b) to explain how the use of spreadsheets may improve the efficiency of the budget preparation process. *(7 marks)*

CIMA Stage 1 Accounting

IM15.3 Advanced. What is zero-based budgeting and how does it differ from other more traditional forms of budgeting? Discuss the applicability of zero-based budgeting to profit-oriented organizations. *ACCA Level 2 Management Accounting*

IM15.4 Advanced. The chief executive of your organization has recently seen a reference to zero-based budgeting. He has asked for more details of the technique.

You are required to prepare a report for him explaining:

(a) what zero-based budgeting is and to which areas it can best be applied;
(b) what advantages the technique has over traditional type budgeting systems;
(c) how the organization might introduce such a technique. *(20 marks)*

CIMA P3 Management Accounting

IM15.5 Advanced. Prepare brief notes about zero-based budgeting covering the following topics:

(a) what zero-based budgeting means;
(b) how zero-based budgeting would operate;
(c) what problems might be met in introducing zero-based budgeting;
(d) what special advantages could be expected from zero-based budgeting, as compared with more traditional budgeting methods, for an organization operating in an economic recession. *(20 marks)*

CIMA P3 Management Accounting

IM15.6 Advanced. A budgetary planning and control system may include many individual budgets which are integrated into a 'master budget'.

You are required to outline and briefly explain with reasons the steps that should normally be taken in the preparation of master budgets in a manufacturing company, indicating the main budgets which you think should normally be prepared. *(12 marks)*

ICAEW Management Accounting

IM15.7 Advanced. The managing director of your company believes that the existing annual budget system is costly to operate and produces unsatisfactory results due to: long preparation period; business decisions being made throughout the year; unpredictable changes in the rate of general inflation; sudden changes in the availability and price of raw materials. He has read about rolling budgets and wonders whether these might be more useful for his decision-making.

You are required, as the management accountant, to prepare a paper for him covering the following areas.

(a) a brief explanation of rolling budgets; *(4 marks)*
(b) how a rolling budget system would operate; *(4 marks)*
(c) *three* significant advantages of a rolling budget system; *(6 marks)*
(d) *three* problems likely to be encountered in using a rolling budget system. *(6 marks)*

CIMA P3 Management Accounting

IM15.8 Advanced. Explain the specific roles of planning, motivation and evaluation in a system of budgetary control.

(7 marks)

ACCA Level 2 Management Accounting

IM15.9 Intermediate: Preparation of functional budgets. X plc manufactures Product X using three different raw materials. The product details are as follows:

Selling price per unit £250

Material A	3kgs	material price £3.50 per kg
Material B	2kgs	material price £5.00 per kg
Material C	4kgs	material price £4.50 per kg
Direct labour	8 hours	labour rate £8.00 per hour

The company is considering its budgets for next year and has made the following estimates of sales demand for Product X for July to October:

July	August	September	October
400 units	300 units	600 units	450 units

It is company policy to hold stocks (inventories) of finished goods at the end of each month equal to 50 per cent of the following month's sales demand and it is expected that the stock at the start of the budget period will meet this policy.

At the end of the production process, the products are tested: it is usual for 10 per cent of those tested to be faulty. It is not possible to rectify these faulty units.

Raw material stocks (inventories) are expected to be as follows on 1 July:

Material A	1000kgs
Material B	400kgs
Material C	600kgs

Stocks are to be increased by 20 per cent in July and then remain at their new level for the foreseeable future.

Labour is paid on an hourly rate based on attendance. In addition to the unit direct labour hours shown above, 20 per cent of *attendance time* is spent on tasks which support production activity.

Requirements:

(a) Prepare the following budgets for the quarter from July to September inclusive:

  (i) sales budget in quantity and value;
  (ii) production budget in units;
  (iii) raw material usage budget in kgs;
  (iv) raw material purchases budget in kgs and value;
  (v) labour requirements budget in hours and value.

(16 marks)

(b) Explain the term 'principal budget factor' and why its identification is an important part of the budget preparation process. *(3 marks)*

(c) Explain clearly, using data from part (a) above, how you would construct a spreadsheet to produce the labour requirements budget for August. Include a specimen cell layout diagram containing formulae that would illustrate the basis for the spreadsheet. *(6 marks)*

CIMA Stage 2 Operational Cost Accounting

IM15.10 Intermediate: Preparation of functional budgets. D Limited is preparing its annual budgets for the year to 31 December. It manufactures and sells one product, which has a selling price of £150. The marketing director believes that the price can be increased to £160 with effect from 1 July and that at this price the sales volume for each quarter will be as follows:

	Sales volume
Quarter 1	40000
Quarter 2	50000
Quarter 3	30000
Quarter 4	45000

Sales for each quarter of the following year are expected to be 40000 units.

Each unit of the finished product which is manufactured requires four units of component R and three units of component T, together with a body shell S. These items are purchased from an outside supplier.

Currently prices are:

Component R	£8.00 each
Component T	5.00 each
Shell S	£30.00 each

The components are expected to increase in price by 10 per cent with effect from 1 April; no change is expected in the price of the shell.

Assembly of the shell and components into the finished product requires six labour hours: labour is currently paid at £10.00 per hour. A 4 per cent increase in wage costs is anticipated to take effect from 1 October.

Variable overhead costs are expected to be £10 per unit for the whole of the year; fixed production overhead costs are expected to be £240000 for the year, and are absorbed on a per unit basis. Opening stocks (inventories) are expected to be as follows:

Finished units	9000 units
Component R	3000 units
Component T	5500 units
Shell S	500 units

Closing stocks (inventories) at the end of each quarter are to be as follows:

Finished units	10% of next quarter's sales
Component R	20% of next quarter's production requirements
Component T	15% of next quarter's production requirements
Shell S	10% of next quarter's production requirements

Requirement:

(a) Prepare the following budgets of D Limited for the year ending 31 December, showing values for each quarter and the year in total:

  (i) sales budget (in £s and units)
  (ii) production budget (in units)
  (iii) material usage budget (in units)
  (iv) production cost budget (in £s). *(15 marks)*

(b) Sales are often considered to be the principal budget factor of an organization.

Requirement:
Explain the meaning of the 'principal budget factor' and, assuming that it is sales, explain how sales may be forecast making appropriate reference to the use of statistical techniques and the use of microcomputers. *(10 marks)*

CIMA Stage 2 Operational Cost Accounting

IM15.11 Intermediate: Preparation of cash budgets. A company is to carry out a major modernization of its factory commencing in two weeks, time. During the modernization, which is expected to take four weeks to complete, no production of the company's single product will be possible.

The following additional information is available:

(i) *Sales/Debtors:* Demand for the product at £100 per unit is expected to continue at 800 units per week, the level of sales achieved for the last four weeks, for one further week. It is then expected to reduce to 700 units per week for three weeks, before rising to a level of 900 units per week where it is expected to remain for several weeks. All sales are on credit, 50 per cent being received in cash in the week following the week of sale and 50 per cent in the week after that.

(ii) *Production/Finished goods stock (inventories):* Production will be at a level of 1200 units per week for the next two weeks. Finished goods stock is 2800 units at the beginning of week 1.

(iii) *Raw material stock:* Raw material stock is £36 000 at the beginning of week 1. This will be increased by the end of week 1 to £40 000 and reduced to £10 000 by the end of week 2.

(iv) *Costs*

	(£ per unit)
Variable:	
Raw material	35
Direct labour	20
Overhead	10
Fixed:	
Overhead	25

Fixed overheads have been apportioned to units on the basis of the normal output level of 800 units per week and include depreciation of £4000 per week.

In addition to the above unit costs, overtime premiums of £5000 per week will be incurred in weeks 1 and 2. During the modernization variable costs will be avoided, apart from direct labour which will be incurred at the level equivalent to 800 units production per week. Outlays on fixed overheads will be reduced by £4000 per week.

(v) *Payments:* Creditors for raw materials, which stand at £27 000 at the beginning of week 1, are paid in the week following purchase. All other payments are made in the week in which the liability is incurred.

(vi) *Liquidity:* The company has a bank overdraft balance of £39 000 at the beginning of week 1 and an overdraft limit of £50 000.

The company is anxious to establish the liquidity situation over the modernization period, excluding the requirements for finance for the modernization itself.

Required:

(a) Prepare a weekly cash budget covering the six-week period up to the planned completion of the modernization.
(15 marks)

(b) Comment briefly on any matters concerning the liquidity situation that you feel should be drawn to the attention of management.
(7 marks)

ACCA Level 1 Costing

15.12 Advanced: Preparation of a cash budget and a decision whether to close a department and subcontract. The Rosrock Housing Association has two types of housing estate in the Rosburgh area (A and B).
The following information is available:

(i) The association has its own squad of painters who carry out painting and decorating work on the housing estates. The estimated cost for each house in which the work will be done in 2019 is as follows:

Painting

	(£)
(a) Direct material cost	75
(b) Direct labour cost	270

(c) In 2019 overhead cost is absorbed at 20 per cent on direct material cost plus 100 per cent on direct labour cost. Only 30 per cent of material related overhead and $33^1/_3$ per cent of labour related overhead is variable, the remainder is fixed overhead and the absorption rate is arrived at using the budgeted number of houses that require painting and decorating each year.

(d) Fixed overhead may be analysed into:

1. Items avoidable on cessation of the service 30%
2. Depreciation of equipment and premises 20%
3. Apportionment of head office costs 50%

(e) Direct material and direct labour cost are wholly variable.

(ii) The total number of houses of each type and the percentage requiring painting and decorating each year is as follows:

	Estate Type A	*Estate Type B*
Total number of houses	500	600
Percentage of houses requiring maintenance each year:	30%	20%

(iii) Where relevant, all future costs are expected to increase each year by a fixed percentage of the previous year's level due to changes in prices and wage rates as follows:

Direct material cost	5%
Direct labour cost	7%
Overhead cost	6%

(iv) Forecast balances at 31 December 2018 and other cash flow timing information is as follows:

(a) Creditors for materials: £2100. Credit purchases are 90 per cent of purchases, the remainder being cash purchases. The credit purchases outstanding at a year end are estimated at 10 per cent of the annual materials purchased on credit. There are no materials on hand on 31 December 2018.

(b) Labour costs accrued: £2800. Labour costs outstanding at a year end are estimated at 4 per cent of the annual total earnings for the year.

(c) Creditors for variable overheads: £600. Variable overheads are paid 60 per cent in the month of incidence and 40 per cent in the month following. Variable overheads are deemed to accrue evenly each month throughout the year.

(d) Fixed overheads are paid in 12 equal amounts with no accruals or prepayments.

Required:

(a) Prepare a cash budget for the existing painting and decorating function for the period 1 January 2019 to 31 December 2021 which shows the cash flows for each of the years 2019, 2020 and 2021. (Calculations should be rounded to the nearest whole £.) *(14 marks)*

(b) An outside company has offered to undertake all painting and decorating work for a three-year period 2019 to 2021 for a fixed fee of £135 000 per annum.

(i) Calculate whether the offer should be accepted on financial grounds using the information available in the question. *(2 marks)*

(ii) List and comment on other factors that should be taken into account by Rosrock Housing Association management when considering this offer. *(6 marks)*

ACCA Level 2 Cost and Management Accounting

16

MANAGEMENT CONTROL SYSTEMS

LEARNING OBJECTIVES After studying this chapter, you should be able to:

- describe the three different types of control used in organizations;

- distinguish between feedback and feed-forward controls;

- explain the potential harmful side-effects of results controls;

- define the four different types of responsibility centre;

- explain the different elements of management accounting control systems;

- describe the controllability principle and the methods of implementing it;

- discuss how the level of difficulty of targets impacts on motivation and performance;

- describe the influence of participation in the budgeting process;

- distinguish between the different approaches that manages use to evaluate budgetees' performance.

Control is the process of ensuring that a firm's activities conform to its plan and that its objectives are achieved. There can be no control without objectives and plans, since these predetermine and specify the desirable behaviour and set out the procedures that should be followed by members of the organization to ensure that a firm is operated in a desired manner.

In an article published many years ago Drucker (1964) distinguished between 'controls' and 'control'. **Controls** are measurement and information, whereas control means direction. In other words, 'controls' are purely a means to an end; and that end is control. **Control** is the function that makes sure that actual work is done to fulfil the original intention and 'controls' are used to provide information to assist in determining the control action to be taken. For example, material costs may be greater than budget. 'Controls' will indicate that costs exceed budget and that this may be because the purchase of inferior quality materials causes excessive wastage. 'Control' is the action that is taken to purchase the correct quality materials in the future to reduce excessive wastage. 'Controls' encompass all the methods and procedures that direct employees towards achieving the organization objectives. Many different control mechanisms are used in organizations and the management accounting control system represents only one aspect of the various control mechanisms that companies use to control their managers and employees. To fully understand the role that management accounting control systems play in the control process, it is necessary to be aware of how they relate to the entire array of control mechanisms used by organizations. Note that the term management control system is used to refer to the entire array of controls used by an organization.

This chapter begins by describing the different types of controls that are used by companies. The elements of management accounting control systems will then be described within the context of the overall control process.

CONTROL AT DIFFERENT ORGANIZATIONAL LEVELS

Control is applied at different levels within an organization. Merchant and Van der Stede (2017) distinguish between strategic control and management control. Strategic control has an external focus. The emphasis is on how a firm, given its strengths and weaknesses and limitations, can compete with other firms in the same industry. We shall explore some of these issues in Chapter 21 within the context of strategic performance management. In this, and the next four chapters, our emphasis will be on management control systems which consist of a collection of control mechanisms that primarily have a shorter-term internal focus. The aim of management control systems is to influence employee behaviours in desirable ways in order to increase the probability that an organization's objectives will be achieved. Merchant and Van der Stede define management control as dealing with employees' behaviour. They state:

> It is people in the organization that make things happen. Management controls are necessary to guard against the possibilities that people will do something the organizations do not want them to do or fail to do something they should do . . . If all employees could always be relied on to do what is best for the organization there would be no need for management control systems.

The terms 'management accounting control systems', 'accounting control systems' and 'management control systems' are often used interchangeably. Both management accounting and accounting control systems refer to the collection of practices such as budgetary planning and control, standard costing and periodic performance reporting that are normally administered by the management accounting function. Management control systems, however, represent a broader term that encompasses management accounting/accounting control systems but also includes other controls such as action, personnel and social controls. These controls are described in the following section.

DIFFERENT TYPES OF CONTROL MECHANISM

Companies use many different control mechanisms to cope with the problem of organizational control. To make sense of the vast number of controls that are used we shall classify them into three categories using approaches that have been adopted by Ouchi (1979) and Merchant and Van der Stede (2017). They are:

1. action (or behavioural) controls;
2. personnel, cultural and social controls;
3. results (or output) controls.

You should note that management accounting systems are normally synonymous with output controls whereas management control systems encompass all the above categories of controls.

Action or behavioural controls

Behavioural controls (also known as action controls) involve observing the actions of individuals as they go about their work. They are appropriate where cause and effect relationships are well understood, so that if the correct actions are followed, the desired outcomes will occur. Under these circumstances, effective control can be achieved by having superiors watch and guide the actions of subordinates. For example, if the supervisor watches the workers on the assembly line and ensures that the work is done exactly as prescribed, then the expected quality and quantity of work should ensue. Forms of action controls described by Merchant and Van der Stede include behavioural constraints, preaction reviews and action accountability.

The aim of *behavioural constraints* is to prevent people from doing things that should not be done. They include physical constraints, such as computer passwords that restrict accessing or updating information sources to authorized personnel, and administrative constraints such as imposing ceilings on the amount of capital expenditure that managers may authorize is an example of an administrative constraint.

Preaction reviews involve the scrutiny and approval of action plans of the individuals being controlled before they can undertake a course of action. Examples include the approval by municipal authorities of plans for the construction of properties prior to building commencing, or the approval by a tutor of a dissertation plan prior to the student being authorized to embark on the dissertation.

Action accountability involves defining actions that are acceptable or unacceptable, observing the actions and rewarding acceptable or punishing unacceptable actions. Examples of action accountability include establishing work rules and procedures and company codes of conduct that employees must follow. Line item budgets that were described in the previous chapter are another form of action accountability whereby an upper limit on an expense category is given for the budget period. If managers exceed these limits they are held accountable and are required to justify their actions.

Action controls that focus on *preventing* undesirable behaviour are the ideal form of control because their aim is to prevent the behaviour from occurring. They are preferable to *detection* controls that are applied after the occurrence of the actions because they avoid the costs of undesirable behaviour. Nevertheless, detection controls can still be useful if they are applied in a timely manner so that they can lead to the early cessation of undesirable actions. Their existence also discourages individuals from engaging in such actions.

Personnel, cultural and social controls

Social or cultural controls involve the selection of people who have already been socialized into adopting particular norms and patterns of behaviour required to achieve an organization's objectives. For example, if the only staff promoted to managerial level are those who display a high commitment to the firm's objectives then the need for other forms of controls can be reduced. Social/cultural controls represent a set of values, social norms and beliefs that are shared by members of the organization and that influence their actions. Control is exercised by individuals over one another – for example, procedures used by groups within an organization to regulate performance of their own members and to bring them into line when they deviate from group norms.

Personnel controls involve helping employees do a good job by building on employees' natural tendencies to control themselves. In particular, they ensure that the employees have the capabilities (in terms of intelligence, qualifications and experience) and the resources needed to do a good job. This requires appropriate training to ensure that employees know how to perform the assigned tasks and to make them fully aware of the results and actions that are expected from them.

Results or output controls

Output or results controls involve collecting and reporting information about the outcomes of work effort. The major advantage of results controls is that senior managers do not have to be knowledgeable about the means required to achieve the desired results or be involved in directly observing the actions of subordinates. They merely rely on performance reports to ascertain whether or not the desired outcomes have been achieved. Management accounting control systems can be described as a form of output controls. They are mostly defined in monetary terms such as revenues, costs, profits and ratios such as return on investment. Results measures also include non-accounting measures such as the number of units of defective production, the number of loan applications processed or ratio measures such as the number of customer deliveries on time as a percentage of total deliveries.

Results controls involve the following stages:

1 establishing performance measures that the organization wishes to monitor;

2 establishing performance targets;

3 measuring performance;

4 providing rewards or punishment.

The *first stage* involves selecting performance measures for those aspects of activities that the organization wishes to monitor. Ideally, desirable behaviour should improve the performance measure and undesirable behaviour should have a detrimental effect on the measure.

The *second stage* requirement of a preset performance target informs individuals what to aim for and enables employees or their superiors to interpret performance. The *third stage* specified above relates to measuring performance. Ability to measure some outputs effectively constrains the use of results measures. In the previous chapter, it was pointed out that the outputs in non-profit organizations are extremely difficult to measure and inhibit the use of results controls. To encourage the right behaviours results, measures should also be timely and understandable. Significant delays in reporting will result in the measures losing most of their motivational impact and a lengthy delay in taking remedial action when outcomes deviate from target. If measures are not understandable it is unlikely that managers will know how their actions will effect the measure and there is a danger that the measures will lose their motivational impact.

The *fourth* and *final stage* of results controls involves encouraging employees to achieve organizational goals by having rewards (or punishments) linked to their success (or failure) in achieving the results measures. Organizational rewards include salary increases, bonuses, promotions and recognition. Employees can also derive intrinsic rewards through a sense of accomplishment and achievement. Punishments include demotions, failure to obtain the rewards and possibly the loss of one's job.

FEEDBACK AND FEED-FORWARD CONTROLS

Feedback control involves monitoring outputs achieved against desired outputs and taking whatever corrective action is necessary if a deviation exists. In feed-forward control, instead of actual outputs being compared against desired outputs, predictions are made of what outputs are expected to be at some future time. If these expectations differ from what is desired, control actions are taken that will minimize these differences. The objective is for control to be achieved before any deviations from desired outputs actually occur. In other words, with feed-forward controls, likely errors can be anticipated and steps taken to avoid them, whereas with feedback controls, actual errors are identified after the event and corrective action is taken to implement future actions to achieve the desired outputs.

A major limitation of feedback control is that errors are allowed to occur. However, this is not usually a significant problem when there is a short time lag between the occurrence of an error and the identification and implementation of corrective action. Feed-forward control is therefore preferable when a significant time lag occurs. The budgeting process is a feed-forward control system. To the extent that outcomes fall short of what is desired, alternatives are considered until a budget is produced that is expected to achieve what is desired. The comparison of actual results with budget, in identifying variances and taking remedial action to ensure that future outcomes will conform with budgeted outcomes, is an illustration of a feedback control system. Thus, accounting control systems consist of both feedback and feed-forward controls.

REAL WORLD VIEWS 16.1

Defining success on what is spent rather than what is achieved

The British government has pledged to spend 0.7 per cent of national aid resulting in £12 billion being allocated to the Department for International Development's (DfID's) aid budget despite the fact that the Independent Commission on Aid Impact published a scathing report on DfID's efforts to help developing countries. It concluded that the programmes had unrealistic targets and their performances were not properly assessed.

'There is almost nothing better designed to perpetuate wastefulness than the knowledge that the overall budget is guaranteed come what may', writes Dominic Lawson in *The Sunday Times* (2015). He cites that in 2012 the House of Lords' economic affairs committee warned that this target 'wrongly prioritizes the amount spent rather than the result achieved; it makes the achievement of the spending target more important than the overall effectiveness of the programme'. In the same article Lawson points out that the Department for International Development spent a quarter of its £12 billion aid budget in the final month of last year as it rushed to meet its spending budget target with the result that multilateral aid organizations were 'being stuffed with British taxpayers' cash more quickly than they knew what to do with it'.

Questions

1 What are the advantages and disadvantages of using a fixed budget as outlined above?

2 What approaches can be taken to overcome the problems relating to fixed budgets?

Reference

Lawson, D. (2015) 'This is one target our armed forces can afford to miss', *Sunday Times*, 8 March.

HARMFUL SIDE-EFFECTS OF CONTROLS

Harmful side-effects occur when the controls motivate employees to engage in behaviour that is not organizationally desirable. In this situation, the control system leads to a lack of goal congruence. Alternatively, when controls motivate behaviour that is organizationally desirable they are described as encouraging goal congruence.

Results controls can lead to a lack of goal congruence if the results that are required can only be partially specified. Here there is a danger that employees will concentrate only on what is monitored by the control system, regardless of whether or not it is organizationally desirable. In other words, they will seek to maximize their individual performance according to the rules of the control system, irrespective of whether their actions contribute to the organization's objectives. In addition, they may ignore other important areas if they are not monitored by the control system. The expression 'What you measure is what you get' applies in these circumstances.

Figure 16.1, derived from Emmanual, Otley and Merchant (1990), illustrates the problems that can arise when the required results can only be partially specified. You will see that those aspects of behaviour on which subordinates are likely to concentrate to achieve their personal goals (circle B) do not necessarily correspond with those necessary for achieving the wider organizational goals (circle A). In an ideal system, the measured behaviour (represented by circle C) should completely cover the area of desired behaviour (represented by circle A). Therefore if a manager maximizes the performance measure, he or she will also maximize his or her contribution to the goals of the organization. In other words, the performance measures encourage goal congruence. In practice, it is unlikely that perfect performance measures can be constructed that measure all desirable organizational behaviour, and so it is unlikely that all of circle C will cover circle A. Assuming that managers desire the rewards offered by circle C, their actual behaviour (represented by circle B) will be altered to include more of circle C and, to the extent that C coincides with A, more of circle A.

However, organizational performance will be improved only to the extent that the performance measure is a good indicator of what is desirable to achieve the firm's goals. Unfortunately, performance

FIGURE 16.1

The measurement and reward process with imperfect measures

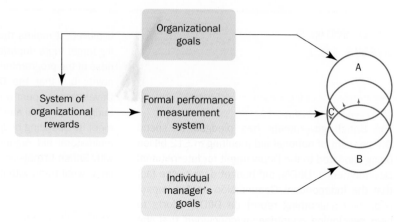

A Behaviour necessary to achieve organizational goals
B Behaviour actually engaged in by an individual manager
C Behaviour formally measured by control systems

measures are not perfect and, as an ideal measure of overall performance, are unlikely to exist. Some measures may encourage goal congruence or organizationally desirable behaviour (the part of circle C that coincides with A), but other measures will not encourage goal congruence (the part of circle C that does not coincide with A). Consequently, there is a danger that subordinates will concentrate only on what is measured, regardless of whether or not it is organizationally desirable. Furthermore, actual behaviour may be modified so that desired results appear to be obtained, although they may have been achieved in an undesirable manner that is detrimental to the firm.

It is clear that flaws in the performance measurement systems used by banks contributed to the financial crisis in the banking sector in 2008. Bonuses and performance measures were based on short-term, rather than long-term performance, that did not take risk into account. These performance measures encouraged managers to take actions to increase sales or profits when such actions resulted in providing high risk loans. The performance measures motivated managers to increase the reported sales revenues and profits, and thus their bonus, without considering the adverse long-term implications of their actions. They were not engaging in organizationally desirable behaviour because the performance measurement and reward system strongly encouraged them not to do so. Many would argue that the managers were acting in an unethical manner but clearly the performance measurement and the reward system was also at fault. We shall discuss how such dysfunctional behaviour may be reduced in Chapters 19 and 21.

MANAGEMENT ACCOUNTING CONTROL SYSTEMS

Up to this point in the chapter, we have been looking at the broad context of management control systems. We shall now concentrate on management accounting control systems that represent the predominant controls in most organizations.

Why are management accounting controls the predominant controls? There are several reasons. First, all organizations need to express and aggregate the results of a wide range of dissimilar activities using a common measure. The monetary measure meets this requirement. Second, profitability and liquidity are essential to the success of all organizations and financial measures relating to these and other areas are closely monitored by stakeholders. It is therefore natural that managers will wish to monitor performance in monetary terms. Third, financial measures also enable a common decision rule to be applied by all managers when considering alternative courses of action. That is, a course of action will normally benefit a firm only if it results in an improvement in its

REAL WORLD VIEWS 16.2

Crime-fighting targets lead to 'dysfunctional' policing says police chief

Government crime-fighting targets are a shambles and should be scrapped, claims Chief Superintendent, Ian Johnston. Mr Johnston was speaking ahead of the Police Superintendents' Association's annual conference, when he asked the police minister to scrap the current targets regime.

'I believe we should abolish the performance framework in its entirety,' Mr Johnston said. 'It sounds radical, but it would be very warmly welcomed by the police service and would allow us, the professionals, to make judgements. We want to reclaim policing for the police.' He added: 'Centrally imposed targets are preventing senior police officers from delivering the policing that the public wants and deserves. We need to restore discretion to senior police officers enabling them to make decisions that relate to local policing issues, ensuring that we deliver a high standard of quality policing.'

The leaders of rank-and-file police officers have made a similar demand to reverse the target-driven culture that has forced them to make 'ludicrous' decisions such as a case where a child was arrested for throwing cream buns at a bus. The Police Federation said judging officers purely on how many arrests, cautions or on-the-spot fines they can deliver was making a mockery of the criminal justice system. The drive to meet Whitehall performance targets was compelling officers to criminalize middle England, they added.

The organization published a dossier of ridiculous cases they claimed resulted from Home Office targets placed on beat bobbies. The cases included a Cheshire man who was cautioned by police for being found in possession of an egg with intent to throw and a West Midlands woman arrested on her wedding day for criminal damage to a car park barrier when her foot slipped on her accelerator.

Today, Mr Johnston said, 'current Home Office targets have made some senior officers seriously ill from the stress of managing a wide range of competing demands. More than 70 per cent of basic command unit commanders believe national targets have had a negative impact on service delivery. We are obliged to count everything and in order to account for our performance we are not addressing a lot of the issues that the public see as far more important.' He added: 'The time has come for someone to say that the performance framework and the red tape and the bureaucracy have got to go. The government's focus on volume crime targets is skewing all police activity in a way that our members see as increasingly dysfunctional.'

Question

1 How might the dysfunctional effects of the performance system in the police force be minimized?

Reference
www.dailymail.co.uk/news, 7 September 2007.

financial performance. Finally, measuring results in financial terms enables managers to be given more autonomy. Focusing on the outcomes of managerial actions, summarized in financial terms, gives managers the freedom to take whatever actions they consider to be appropriate to achieve the desired results.

RESPONSIBILITY CENTRES

The complex environment in which most businesses operate today makes it virtually impossible for most firms to be controlled centrally. It is simply not possible for central management to have all the relevant information and time to determine the detailed plans for the entire organization. Some degree of decentralization is essential for all but the smallest firms. Organizations decentralize by creating responsibility centres. A responsibility centre may be defined as a unit of a firm such as a department or division where an individual manager is held responsible for the unit's performance. There are four types of responsibility centre:

1 cost or expense centres;

2 revenue centres;

3 profit centres;

4 investment centres.

The creation of responsibility centres is a fundamental part of management accounting control systems. It is therefore important that you can distinguish between the various forms of responsibility centre.

Cost or expense centres

Cost or expense centres are responsibility centres whose managers are normally accountable for only those costs that are under their control. We can distinguish between two types of cost centre – standard cost centres and discretionary cost centres. The main features of standard cost centres are that output can be measured and the input required to produce each unit of output can be specified. Control is exercised by comparing the standard cost (that is, the cost of the inputs that *should* have been consumed in producing the output) with the cost that was *actually* incurred. The difference between the actual cost and the standard cost is described as the variance. Standard cost centres and variance analysis will be discussed extensively in the next chapter.

Standard cost centres are best suited to units within manufacturing firms but they can also be established in service industries such as units within banks, where output can be measured in terms of the number of cheques or the number of loan applications processed and there are also well-defined input–output relationships. Although cost centre managers are not accountable for sales revenues, they can affect the amount of sales revenue generated if quality standards are not met and outputs are not produced according to schedule. Therefore quality and timeliness non-financial performance measures are also required besides financial measures.

Discretionary expense centres are those responsibility cost centres where output cannot be measured in financial terms and there are no clearly observable relationships between inputs (the resources consumed) and the outputs (the results achieved). Control normally takes the form of ensuring that actual expenditure adheres to budgeted expenditure for each expense category and also ensuring that the tasks assigned to each centre have been successfully accomplished. Examples of discretionary centres include advertising and publicity and research and development departments. One of the major problems arising in discretionary expense centres is measuring the effectiveness of expenditures. For example, the marketing support department may not have exceeded an advertising budget but this does not mean that the advertising expenditure has been effective. The advertising may have been incorrectly timed, it may have been directed to the wrong audience, or it may have contained the wrong message. Determining the effectiveness and efficiency of discretionary expense centres is one of the most difficult areas of management control.

Revenue centres

Revenue centres are responsibility centres where managers are mainly accountable for financial outputs in the form of generating sales revenues. Typical examples of revenue centres are where regional sales managers are accountable for sales within their regions. Revenue centre managers may also be held accountable for selling expenses, such as sales person salaries, commissions and order getting costs. They are not, however, made accountable for the cost of the goods and services that they sell.

Profit centres

Both cost and revenue centre managers have limited decision-making authority. Cost centre managers are accountable only for managing inputs (costs) of their centres. Revenue centres are accountable for selling the products or services but they have no control over their manufacture. A significant increase in managerial autonomy occurs when unit managers are given responsibility for both production and sales. In this situation, managers are normally free to set selling prices, choose which markets to sell in, make product mix and output decisions and select suppliers. Units within an organization whose managers are accountable for both revenues and costs are called profit centres or business units. As the name implies, profit centres tend to be larger independent units within an organization.

Investment centres

Investment centres are responsibility centres whose managers are responsible for both sales revenues and costs and, in addition, have responsibility and authority to make capital investment decisions. Typical investment centre performance measures include return on investment and economic value added. These measures are influenced by revenues, costs and assets employed and thus reflect the responsibility that managers have for both generating profits and managing the investment base.

Investment centres represent the highest level of managerial autonomy. They include the company as a whole, operating subsidiaries, business units and divisions. You will find that many firms are not precise in their terminology and call their investment centres profit centres. Profit and investment centres will be discussed extensively in Chapter 19.

THE NATURE OF MANAGEMENT ACCOUNTING CONTROL SYSTEMS

Management accounting control systems have two core elements. The first is the formal planning processes such as budgeting and long-term planning that were described in the previous chapter. These processes are used for establishing performance expectations for evaluating performance. The second is responsibility accounting, which involves the creation of responsibility centres. Responsibility centres enable accountability for financial results and outcomes to be allocated to heads of responsibility centres throughout the organization. The objective of responsibility accounting is to accumulate costs and revenues for each individual responsibility centre so that the deviations from a performance target (typically the budget) can be attributed to the individual who is accountable for the responsibility centre. For each responsibility centre, the process involves setting a performance target, measuring performance, comparing performance against the target, analysing the variances and taking action where significant variances exist between actual and target performance. In the remainder of the chapter we shall focus on responsibility accounting within cost centres at lower management levels rather than at the business unit level. We shall consider control and performance measurement at higher organization levels relating to business units (profit centres and investment centres) in chapters 19 and 21 where our focus will be on strategic performance measurement and management.

Responsibility accounting relating to cost and revenue centres at lower management levels is implemented by issuing performance reports at frequent intervals (normally monthly) that inform responsibility centre managers of the deviations from budgets for which they are accountable and are required to take action. An example of a performance report issued to a cost centre manager is presented in the lower section of Exhibit 16.1. You should note that at successively higher levels of management, less detailed information is reported. You can see from the upper sections of Exhibit 16.1 that the information is condensed and summarized as the results relating to the responsibility centre are reported at

EXHIBIT 16.1 Responsibility accounting monthly performance reports

		Budget		Variance[a] F (A)	
		Current month (£)	Year to date (£)	This month (£)	Year to date (£)
Performance report to managing director					
Managing director	Factory A	453 900	6 386 640	80 000(A)	98 000(A)
	Factory B	X	X	X	X
	Factory C	X	X	X	X
	Administration costs	X	X	X	X
	Selling costs	X	X	X	X
	Distribution costs	X	X	X	X
		2 500 000	30 000 000	400 000(A)	600 000(A)
Performance report to production manager of factory A					
Production manager	Works manager's office	X	X	X	X
	Machining department 1	165 600	717 600	32 760(A)	89 180(A)
	Machining department 2	X	X	X	X
	Assembly department	X	X	X	X
	Finishing department	X	X	X	X
		453 900	6 386 640	80 000(A)	98 000(A)
Performance report to head of responsibility centre					
Head of responsibility centre	Direct materials	X	X	X	X
	Direct labour	X	X	X	X
	Indirect labour	X	X	X	X
	Indirect materials	X	X	X	X
	Power	X	X	X	X
	Maintenance	X	X	X	X
	Idle time	X	X	X	X
	Other	X	X	X	X
		165 600	717 600	32 760(A)	89 180(A)

[a]F indicates a favourable variance (actual cost less than budgeted cost) and (A) indicates an adverse budget (actual cost greater than budget cost). Note that, at the lowest level of reporting, the responsibility centre head's performance report contains detailed information on operating costs. At successively higher levels of management, less detail is reported. For example, the managing director's information on the control of activities consists of examining those variances that represent significant departures from the budget for each factory and functional area of the business and requesting explanations from the appropriate managers.

higher levels. Exhibit 16.1 includes only financial information. In addition, important non-financial measures such as those relating to quality and timeliness may be reported.

Responsibility accounting involves:

- distinguishing between those items that managers can control and for which they should be held accountable and those items over which they have no control and for which they are not held accountable (i.e. applying the controllability principle);
- setting performance targets and determining how challenging the targets should be;
- determining how much influence managers should have in the setting of targets.

We shall now examine each of these items in detail.

THE CONTROLLABILITY PRINCIPLE

Responsibility accounting is based on the application of the controllability principle, which means that it is appropriate to assign only those costs to responsibility centres that can be significantly influenced by the manager of that responsibility centre. The controllability principle can be implemented by either eliminating the uncontrollable items from the areas for which managers are held accountable or calculating their effects so that the reports distinguish between controllable and uncontrollable items.

Applying the controllability principle is difficult in practice because many areas do not fit neatly into either controllable and uncontrollable categories. Instead, they are partially controllable. Even when outcomes are affected by occurrences outside a manager's control, such as competitors' actions, price changes and supply shortages, a competent manager can take action to reduce their adverse effects. He or she can substitute alternative materials where the prices of raw materials change or monitor and respond to competitors' actions. If these factors are categorized as uncontrollable, managers will not be motivated to try and influence them.

Dealing with the distorting effects of uncontrollable factors before the measurement period

Management can attempt to deal with the distorting effects of uncontrollables by making adjustments either before or after the measurement period. Uncontrollable and controllable factors can be determined prior to the measurement period by specifying which budget line items are to be regarded as controllable and uncontrollable. Uncontrollable items can either be excluded from performance reports or shown in a separate section within the performance report so that they are clearly identifiable. The latter approach has the advantage of drawing managerial attention to those costs that a company incurs to support its activities. Managers may be able to indirectly influence these costs if they are made aware of the sums involved.

Dealing with the distorting effects of uncontrollable factors after the measurement period

Merchant and Van der Stede (2017) identify four methods of removing the effects of uncontrollable factors from the results measures after the measurement period and before the rewards are assigned. They are:

1 variance analysis;
2 flexible performance standards;
3 relative performance evaluations;
4 subjective performance evaluations.

Variance analysis seeks to analyse the factors that cause the actual results to differ from predetermined budgeted targets. In particular, it helps to distinguish between controllable and uncontrollable items and identify those individuals who are accountable for the variances. For example, variances analysed by each type of cost, and by their price and quantity effects, enables variances to be traced to accountable individuals and also to isolate those variances that are due to uncontrollable factors. Variance analysis will be discussed extensively in Chapters 17 and 18.

Flexible performance standards apply when targets are adjusted to reflect variations in uncontrollable factors arising from the circumstances not envisaged when the targets were set. The most widely used flexible performance standard is to use flexible budgets, whereby the uncontrollable volume effects on cost behaviour are removed from the manager's performance reports. Because some costs vary with changes in the level of activity, it is essential when applying the controllability principle to take into account the variability of costs. For example, if the actual level of activity is greater than the

EXAMPLE 16.1

An item of expense that is included in the budget for a responsibility centre varies directly in relation to activity at an estimated cost of £5 per unit of output. The budgeted monthly level of activity was 20 000 units and the actual level of activity was 24 000 units at a cost of £105 000.

budgeted level of activity, then those costs that vary with activity will be greater than the budgeted costs purely because of changes in activity. Let us consider the simplified situation presented in Example 16.1.

Assuming that the increase in activity was due to an increase in sales volume being greater than that anticipated when the budget was set, then the increases in costs arising from the volume change are beyond the control of the responsibility centre manager. It is clearly inappropriate to compare actual *variable* costs of £105 000 from an activity level of 24 000 units with budgeted *variable* costs of £100 000 from an activity level of 20 000 units. This would incorrectly suggest an overspending of £5000. If managers are to be made responsible for their costs, it is essential that they are responsible for performance under the conditions in which they worked and not for a performance based on conditions when the budget was drawn up. In other words, it is misleading to compare actual costs at one level of activity with budgeted costs at another level of activity. At the end of the period, the original budget must be adjusted to the actual level of activity to take into account the impact of the uncontrollable volume change on costs. This procedure is called flexible budgeting. In Example 16.1, the performance report should be as follows:

Budgeted expenditure	*Actual expenditure*
(flexed to 24 000 units)	(24 000 units)
£120 000	£105 000

The budget is adjusted to reflect what the costs should have been for an actual activity of 24 000 units. This indicates that the manager has incurred £15 000 less expenditure than would have been expected for the actual level of activity and a favourable variance of £15 000 should be recorded on the performance report, not an adverse variance of £5000, which would have been recorded had the original budget not been adjusted.

In Example 16.1, it was assumed that there was only one variable item of expense, but, in practice, the budget will include many different expenses including fixed, semi-variable and variable expenses. You should note that fixed expenses do not vary in the short term with activity and therefore the budget should remain unchanged for these expenses. The budget should be flexed only for variable and semi-variable expenses.

Budgets may also be adjusted to reflect other uncontrollable factors besides volume changes. Budgets are normally set based on the environment that is anticipated during the budget setting process. If the budget targets are then used throughout the duration of the annual budget period for performance evaluation, the managers will be held accountable for uncontrollable factors arising from forecasting errors. To remove the managerial exposure to uncontrollable risks arising from forecasting errors, ex post budget adjustments can be made whereby the budget is adjusted to the environmental and economic conditions that the manager's actually faced during the period.

Relative performance evaluation relates to the situations where the performance of a responsibility centre is evaluated relative to the performance of similar centres within the same company or to similar units outside the organization. To be effective, responsibility centres must perform similar tasks and face similar environmental and business conditions with the units that they are being benchmarked against. Such relative comparisons with units facing similar environmental conditions neutralizes the uncontrollable factors because they are in effect held constant when making the relative comparisons.

The major difficulty relating to relative performance evaluations is finding benchmark units that face similar conditions and uncertainties.

Instead of making the formal and quantitative adjustments that are a feature of the methods that have been described so far, subjective judgements can be made in the evaluation process based on the knowledge of the outcome measures and the circumstances faced by the responsibility centre heads. The disadvantages of subjective evaluations are that they are not objective, they tend not to provide the person being evaluated with a clear indication of how performance has been evaluated, they can create conflict with superiors resulting in a loss of morale and a decline in motivation, and they are expensive in terms of management time.

Guidelines for applying the controllability principle

Dealing with uncontrollables represents one of the most difficult areas for the design and operation of management accounting control systems. The following guidelines published by the Report of the Committee of Cost Concepts and Standards by the American Accounting Association in the United States in 1957 still continues to provide useful guidance:

1 If a manager *can control the quantity and price paid* for a service then the manager is responsible for all the expenditure incurred for the service.

2 If the manager *can control the quantity of the service but not the price paid* for the service then only that amount of difference between actual and budgeted expenditure that is due to usage should be identified with the manager.

3 If the manager *cannot control either the quantity or the price paid* for the service then the expenditure is uncontrollable and should not be identified with the manager.

REAL WORLD VIEWS 16.3

Responsibility cost control systems in China
Because of the previous lack of effective control of expenditure by the Han Dan Company, a system of responsibility accounting and standard costing was introduced. The basic principles underlying the responsibility cost control system included: (1) setting cost and profit targets (responsibility standards) that take into account market pressures; (2) assigning target costs to various levels of responsibility centre; (3) evaluating performance based on fulfilment of the responsibility targets; and (4) implementing a reward scheme with built-in incentive mechanisms. In order to facilitate performance measurement and evaluation, non-controllable common costs were excluded from the responsibility costs decomposed within primary production factories. Responsibility contracts between factory managers and managers at lower levels must also be signed. Breakdown of the aggregated responsibility targets to all profit centres and their subordinates are conducted by the Department of Finance and Accounting. In addition, the department is responsible for monthly and yearly reporting of the execution results of the responsibility cost control system. It also reports and analyses the variances between actual outcomes and responsibility targets and determines the necessary bonus rewards (or penalty) for each responsibility centre in terms of the fulfilment of the cost and profit targets signed by managers. If a responsibility centre or individual worker fails to meet the cost targets specified in the responsibility contracts, all bonus and other benefits relating to the responsibility unit or worker will be forfeited.

Question

1 What are the limitations of linking bonuses to meeting cost targets?

Reference
Jun Lin, Z. and Yu, Z. (2002) Responsibility, cost control system in China: A case of management accounting application, *Management Accounting*, 13(4), 447–467.

An example of the last situation is when the costs of an industrial relations department are apportioned to a department on some arbitrary basis; such arbitrary apportionments are likely to result in an allocation of expenses that the managers of responsibility centres may not be able to influence. In addition to the above guidelines, Merchant and Van der Stede's general rule should also be used as a guide – 'Hold employees accountable for the performance areas you want them to pay attention to'.

SETTING PERFORMANCE TARGETS AND DETERMINING HOW CHALLENGING THEY SHOULD BE

There is substantial evidence from a large number of studies that the existence of a defined, quantitative goal or target is more likely to motivate higher levels of performance than when no such target is stated. People perform better when they have a clearly defined goal to aim for and are aware of the standards that will be used to interpret their performance. The fact that a financial target represents a specific quantitative goal gives it a strong motivational potential, but the targets set must be accepted if managers are to be motivated to achieve higher levels of performance. Unfortunately, it is not possible to specify exactly the optimal degree of difficulty for financial targets, since task uncertainty and cultural, organizational and personality factors all affect an individual manager's reaction to a financial target.

Figure 16.2, derived from Emmanuel, Otley and Merchant (1990), shows the theoretical relationship between budget difficulty, aspiration levels and performance. In Figure 16.2, it is *assumed that performance and aspiration levels are identical*. Note that the aspiration level relates to the personal goal of the budgetee (that is, the person who is responsible for the budget). In other words, it is the level of performance that they hope to attain. You will see from Figure 16.2 that, as the level of budget difficulty is increased, both the budgetees' aspiration level and performance increases. However, there becomes a point where the budget is perceived as impossible to achieve and the aspiration level and performance decline dramatically. It can be seen from Figure 16.2 that the budget level that motivates the best level of performance may not be achievable. In contrast, a budget that is set based on what is expected to be achieved (that is, the expectations budget in Figure 16.2) motivates a lower level of performance.

To motivate the highest level of actual performance, demanding budgets should be set and small adverse variances should be regarded as a healthy sign and not as something to be avoided. If budgets are always achieved with no adverse variances, this indicates that the standards are too loose to motivate the best possible results.

It appears from our previous discussion that tight budgets should be established to motivate maximum performance, although this may mean that the budget has a high probability of not being achieved.

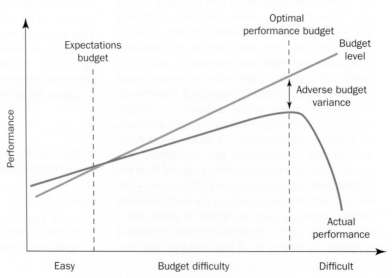

FIGURE 16.2
The effect of budget difficulty on performance

REAL WORLD VIEWS 16.4

Community participation in local budget spend

In a BBC documentary called *Power to the People*, Michael Portillo visited a 'You Decide' session organized by the local council in Tower Hamlets, London. At this session, local people decide what is to be done with £250 000 of council money. They are given fully costed options under headings like healthcare, the elderly and local policing. The options in each category can be debated for a time, then all present 'vote' for their preferred option using an electronic voting system. This continues until all funds are used up. This, it could be argued, saves the council a bit of time and allocates resources to where residents deem most appropriate. Of course £250 000 is a long way off a council's full budget, but at least there is participation in how the money is spent. There is also now a 'You Choose' budget simulator website that encourages the public to consider where council budget cuts might fall, where efficiencies might be made, and where income might be generated. The You Choose software is available to all councils in England and Wales and can be tailored by each council to suit their needs. The results of any input from council area residents are instantly available to the council.

Questions

1 Can you think of any advantages of schemes or tools like those mentioned above?

2 Can you think of any disadvantages?

Reference

You Choose: Budget consultation tool. Available at www.idea.gov.uk/idk/core/page.do?pageId =22436695

However, budgets are not used purely as a motivational device to maximize performance. They are also used for planning purposes and it is most unlikely that tight budgets will be suitable for planning purposes. Why? Tight budgets that have a high probability of not being achieved are most unsuitable for cash budgeting and for harmonizing the company plans in the form of a master budget. Most companies use the same budgets for planning and motivational purposes. If only one set of budgets is used it is most unlikely that one set can, at the same time, perfectly meet both planning and motivational requirements.

Budgets with a high probability of being achieved are widely used in practice. They provide managers with a sense of achievement and self-esteem that can be beneficial to the organization in terms of increased levels of commitment and aspirations. Rewards such as bonuses, promotions and job security are normally linked to budget achievement so that the costs of failing to meet budget targets can be high. The greater the probability of the failure to meet budget targets the greater is the probability that managers will be motivated to distort their performance by engaging in behaviour that will result in the harmful side-effects described earlier in this chapter.

DETERMINING HOW MUCH INFLUENCE MANAGERS SHOULD HAVE IN SETTING TARGETS

Participation relates to the extent that budgetees are able to influence the figures that are incorporated in their budgets or targets. Participation is sometimes referred to as bottom-up budget setting whereas a non-participatory approach whereby subordinates have little influence on the target setting process is sometimes called top-down budget setting.

Allowing individuals to participate in the setting of performance targets has several advantages. First, individuals are more likely to accept the targets and be committed to achieving them if they have been involved in the target setting process. Second, participation can reduce the information asymmetry gap that applies when standards are imposed from above. Budgetees have more information than their superiors on the relationships between outputs and inputs and the constraints that exist at the operating level whereas the superiors have a broader view of the organization as a whole and the resource constraints that apply. This information sharing process enables more effective targets to be set that attempt to deal with both operational and organizational constraints. Finally, imposed standards can encourage negative attitudes and result in demotivation and alienation. This in turn can lead to a rejection of the targets and poor performance.

Participation has been advocated by many writers as a means of making tasks more challenging and giving individuals a greater sense of responsibility. For many years participation in decision-making was thought to be a panacea for effective organizational effort but this school of thought was later challenged. The debate has never been resolved. The believers have never been able to demonstrate that participation really does have a positive effect on productivity and the sceptics have never been able to prove the opposite.

Because of the conflicting findings relating to the effectiveness of participation, research has tended to concentrate on studying how various factors influence the effectiveness of participation. If participation is used selectively in the right circumstances, it has an enormous potential for encouraging the commitment to organizational goals, improving attitudes towards the budgeting system and increasing subsequent performance. Note, however, at this stage that there are some limitations on the positive effects of participation in standard setting and circumstances where top-down budget setting is preferable. They are:

1 Performance is measured by precisely the same standard that the budgetee has been involved in setting. This gives the budgetee the opportunity to negotiate lower targets that increase the probability of target achievement and the accompanying rewards. Therefore an improvement in performance – in terms of comparison with the budget – may result merely from a lowering of the standard.

2 Participation by itself is not adequate in ensuring commitment to standards. The manager must also believe that he or she can significantly influence the results and be given the necessary feedback about them.

3 A top-down approach to budget setting is likely to be preferable where a process is highly programmable and there are clear and stable input–output relationships. Here there is no need to negotiate targets using a bottom-up process.

DIFFERENT APPROACHES THAT MANAGERS USE TO EVALUATE BUDGETEES' PERFORMANCE

Earlier in this chapter we discussed some of the harmful side-effects that can arise from the use of results controls. Some of these effects can be due to the ways in which the output measures are used. A number of studies have been undertaken that examine the side-effects arising from the ways that accounting information is used in performance evaluation. A pioneering study undertaken many years ago by Hopwood (1976) in a manufacturing division of a large UK company is still recognized as providing a suitable description of the different ways managers use budgets to evaluate performance. Three distinct styles of using budget and actual cost information in performance evaluation were observed:

1 **Budget-constrained style:** Despite the many problems in using accounting data as comprehensive measures of managerial performance, the evaluation is based primarily on the cost centre head's ability continually to meet the budget on a short-term basis. This criterion of performance is stressed at the expense of other valued and important criteria and a cost centre head will tend to receive an unfavourable evaluation if his or her actual costs exceed the budgeted costs, regardless of other considerations. Budget data are therefore used in a rigid manner in performance evaluation.

2 **Profit-conscious style:** The performance of the cost centre head is evaluated on the basis of his or her ability to increase the general effectiveness of his or her unit's operations in relation to

EXHIBIT 16.2 Hopwood's findings on the effect of different styles of evaluating budget performance

	Style of evaluation		
	Budget constrained	Profit conscious	Non accounting
Involvement with costs	High	High	Low
Job-related tension	High	Medium	Medium
Manipulation of accounting information	Extensive	Little	Little
Relations with superior	Poor	Good	Good
Relations with colleagues	Poor	Good	Good

the long-term goals of the organization. One important aspect of this at the cost centre level is the head's concern with the minimization of long-run costs. The accounting data must be used with some care and in a rather flexible manner, with the emphasis for performance evaluation in contributing to long-term profitability.

3 **Non-accounting style:** Accounting data play a relatively unimportant part in the supervisor's evaluation of the cost centre head's performance.

The evidence from Hopwood's study indicated that both the budget-constrained and the profit-conscious styles of evaluation led to a higher degree of involvement with costs than the non-accounting style. Only the profit-conscious style, however, succeeded in attaining this involvement without incurring either emotional costs for the managers in charge of the cost centres or defensive behaviour that was undesirable from the company's point of view.

The budget-constrained style gave rise to a belief that the evaluation was unjust, and caused widespread worry and tension, resulting in manipulation of information and undesirable behaviour as methods of relieving tension. In contrast, the profit-conscious style of evaluation avoided these problems, while at the same time it ensured that there was an active involvement with the financial aspects of the operations. A summary of the effect of the three styles of evaluation is given in Exhibit 16.2.

Hopwood's study was based on cost centres having a high degree of interdependence. Rigid measures of performance become less appropriate as the degree of interdependence increases and therefore the managers used the accounting information in a more flexible manner to ensure that the information remained effective. Otley (1978) replicated Hopwood's study in a British firm that consisted of profit centres with a high degree of independence and where accounting information represented a more adequate basis of performance evaluation. He found no significant differences in the levels of job tension and performance reported by managers evaluated on styles initially used by Hopwood. Possible explanations for the differences included the fact that in Otley's study, managers operated more independently of other units within the same organization and the managers in Hopwood's study operated in a less predictable environment than those in Otley's study.

Using a budget-constrained style when managers face high levels of interdependence or uncertainty is likely to be inappropriate because the rigid use of budget data assumes that most of the factors that have an effect on outcomes are within the control of the managers being evaluated. In contrast, the rigid use of budget data may be more acceptable where managers perceive that they are able to exercise control over their performance outcomes. This applies where there is low uncertainty or interdependency.

CONTINGENCY THEORY

To design effective management accounting control systems, it is necessary to consider the circumstances in which they will be used. It should be apparent from this chapter that there is no universally best management accounting control system which can be applied to all organizations.

The applicability of a management accounting control system is contingent on the situational factors faced by organizations. This approach is known as the contingency theory approach to management accounting. The situational factors represent the contingent factors (also known as contingent variables or contextual factors). Examples of the contingent factors that have been examined in the literature include the external environment faced by organizations, the type of competitive strategy they adopt, organizational structure and the nature of the production process. The aspects of the management accounting control systems that contingency theory research has focused on include dimensions of budgeting (participation, importance of meeting budgets), reliance on accounting information for performance evaluation and dimensions of information (e.g. timeliness and level of aggregation). For example, in this chapter it has been pointed out that the appropriateness of participation is dependent on the nature of the production process. In the previous section, it was also suggested that the appropriate style of performance evaluation was influenced by organizational structure and environmental uncertainty.

A considerable amount of literature has emerged focusing on the contingency theory of management accounting. For a detailed summary of this literature you should refer to Learning Note 16.1 in the digital support resources accompanying this book (see Preface for details).

ALTERNATIVE USES OF MANAGEMENT ACCOUNTING INFORMATION

Throughout this book, it is generally assumed that one of the major purposes of management accounting is to aid rational economic decision-making. However, at this stage, it is important that you are aware that accounting information can also be used for other purposes that are not necessarily consistent with rational economic behaviour. Managers can find value in accounting information for symbolic purposes even when the information has little or no relation to decision-making. For example, instead of the information actually being used for decision-making or control purposes, it may be used as a means of signalling to others inside and outside the organization that decisions are being taken rationally and that managers in an organization are accountable. Accounting information is also used for political purposes. Interested parties use the information to promote their own vested interests to achieve political power or a bargaining position. Finally, accounting information may be used for legitimizing purposes in order to justify and legitimize actions that have already been decided on, rather than the information being used as a decision input. For a more detailed discussion of the different purposes for which accounting information is used, you should refer to Learning Note 16.2 in the digital support resources accompanying this book.

SUMMARY

The following items relate to the learning objectives listed at the beginning of the chapter.

● **Describe the three different types of control used in organizations.**

Three different categories of controls are used – action/behavioural controls, personnel and cultural controls and results/output controls. With action controls, the actions themselves are the focus of controls. Personnel controls help employees do a good job by building on employees' natural tendencies to control themselves. They include selection and placement, training and job design. Cultural controls represent a set of values, social norms and beliefs that are shared by members of the organization and that influence their actions. Output or results controls involve collecting and reporting information about the outcomes of work effort.

- **Distinguish between feedback and feed-forward controls.**

Feedback control involves monitoring outputs achieved against desired outputs and taking whatever corrective action is necessary if a deviation exists. In feed-forward control, instead of actual outputs being compared against desired outputs, predictions are made of what outputs are expected to be at some future time. If these expectations differ from what is desired, control actions are taken that will minimize these differences.

- **Explain the potential harmful side-effects of results controls.**

Results controls can promote a number of harmful side-effects. They can lead to a lack of goal congruence when employees seek to achieve the performance targets in a way that is not organizationally desirable. They can also lead to data manipulation and negative attitudes, which can result in a decline in morale and a lack of motivation.

- **Define the four different types of responsibility centre.**

A responsibility centre may be defined as a unit of a firm where an individual manager is held accountable for the unit's performance. There are four types of responsibility centre – cost or expense centres, revenue centres, profit centres and investment centres. Cost or expense centres are responsibility centres where managers are normally accountable for only those costs that are under their control. Revenue centres are responsibility centres where managers are accountable only for financial outputs in the form of generating sales revenues. Units within an organization whose managers are accountable for both revenues and costs are called profit centres. Investment centres are responsibility centres whose managers are responsible for both sales revenues and costs and, in addition, have responsibility and authority to make capital investment decisions.

- **Explain the different elements of management accounting control systems.**

Management accounting control systems have two core elements. The first is the formal planning processes such as budgeting and long-term planning. These processes are used for establishing performance expectations for evaluating performance. The second is responsibility accounting, which involves the creation of responsibility centres. Responsibility centres enable accountability for financial results/outcomes to be allocated to individuals throughout the organization.

- **Describe the controllability principle and the methods of implementing it.**

The controllability principle states that it is appropriate to charge to an area of responsibility only those costs that are significantly influenced by the manager of that responsibility centre. The controllability principle can be implemented by either eliminating the uncontrollable items from the areas that managers are held accountable for or calculating their effects so that the reports distinguish between controllable and uncontrollable items.

- **Discuss how the level of difficulty of targets impacts on motivation and performance.**

Different types of performance target can be set ranging from easily achievable to difficult to achieve. Targets that are considered moderately difficult to achieve (called highly achievable targets) are recommended because they can be used for planning purposes and they also have a motivational impact.

- **Describe the influence of participation in the budgeting process.**

Participation relates to the extent to which budgetees are able to influence the figures that are incorporated in their budgets or targets. Allowing individuals to participate in the setting of performance targets results in individuals being more likely to accept the targets and be committed to achieving them. Participation, however, is subject to the limitation that performance is measured by precisely the same standard that the budgetee has been involved in setting. Participation must be used selectively; but if it is used in the right circumstances, it has an enormous potential for encouraging the commitment to organizational goals.

● **Distinguish between the different approaches that manages use to evaluate budgetees' performance.**

Three distinct styles of performance evaluation have been identified – a budget-constrained style, a profit-conscious style and a non-accounting style. With a budget-constrained style, budget data are used in a rigid manner in performance evaluation. A profit-conscious style uses accounting data in a more flexible manner, with the emphasis for performance evaluation on a unit's contribution to long-term profitability. With a non-accounting style, accounting data play a relatively unimportant part in performance evaluation. Using a budget-constrained style when managers face high levels of interdependence or uncertainty is likely to be inappropriate because the rigid use of budget data assumes that most of the factors that have an effect on outcomes are within the control of the managers being evaluated. In contrast, the rigid use of budget data may be more acceptable where managers perceive that they are able to exercise control over their performance outcomes. This applies where there is low uncertainty or interdependency.

KEY TERMS AND CONCEPTS

Action controls Observing the actions of individuals as they go about their work, also known as behavioural controls.

Aspiration level The level of performance that the person responsible for the budget hopes to attain.

Behavioural controls Controls that involve observing the actions of individuals as they go about their work, also known as action controls.

Bottom-up budget setting Allowing individuals to participate in the setting of budgets and targets.

Contingency theory An approach to management accounting that takes account of situational factors faced by organizations.

Control The process of ensuring that a firm's activities conform to its plan and that its objectives are achieved.

Controllability principle The principle that it is appropriate to charge to an area of responsibility only those costs that are significantly influenced by the manager of that responsibility centre.

Controls Measurement and information used to help determine what control action needs to be taken.

Cost centres Responsibility centres whose managers are normally accountable for only those costs that are under their control, also known as expense centres.

Discretionary expense centres Cost centres where output cannot be measured in financial terms and there are no clearly observable relationships between inputs and outputs.

Ex post budget adjustments The adjustment of a budget to the environmental and economic conditions that the manager's actually faced during the period.

Expense centres Responsibility centres whose managers are normally accountable for only those costs that are under their control, also known as cost centres.

Feedback control Monitoring outputs achieved against desired outputs and taking whatever corrective action is necessary if a deviation exists.

Feed-forward control Comparing predictions of expected outputs with the desired outputs and taking prior corrective action to minimize any differences.

Flexible budgets Budgets in which the uncontrollable volume effects on cost behaviour are removed from the manager's performance reports.

Goal congruence The situation that exists when controls motivate employees to behave in a way that is in tune with the organization's goals.

Investment centres Responsibility centres whose managers are responsible for both sales revenues and costs and also have responsibility and authority to make capital investment decisions.

Management control system The entire array of controls used by an organization.

Output controls Collecting and reporting information about the outcomes of work effort, also known as results controls.

Participation The extent that individuals are able to influence the figures that are incorporated in their budgets or targets.

Performance reports Performance reports show budget and actual performance (normally listed by items of expenses) at frequent intervals (normally monthly) for each responsibility centre.

Personnel controls Helping employees to perform well through the use of selection and placement, training, job design and the provision of necessary resources.

Profit centres Responsibility centres where managers are accountable for both revenues and costs.

Relative performance evaluation The evaluation of the performance of a responsibility centre relative to the performance of similar centres within the same company or of similar units outside the organization.

Responsibility accounting The creation of responsibility centres and the accumulation of costs and revenues so that the deviations from budget can be attributed to the individual who is accountable for the responsibility centre.

Responsibility centre A unit of a firm where an individual manager is held responsible for the unit's performance.

Results controls Collecting and reporting information about the outcomes of work effort, also known as output controls.

Revenue centres Responsibility centres where managers are mainly accountable for financial outputs in the form of generating sales revenues.

Social or cultural controls The selection of people who have already been socialized into adopting particular norms and patterns of behaviour to perform particular tasks.

Standard cost centres Cost centres where output can be measured and the input required to produce each unit of output can be specified.

Strategic control Control that focuses outside the organization, looking at how a firm can compete with other firms in the same industry.

Subjective judgements Judgements made by senior managers of a responsibility head's performance based on the senior manager's own experience, knowledge and interpretation of the performance level achieved.

Top-down budget setting Imposing budgets and targets from above, without the participation of the individuals involved.

Variance The difference between the actual cost and the standard cost.

Variance analysis The analysis of factors that cause the actual results to differ from predetermined budgeted targets.

RECOMMENDED READING

There are a number of important textbooks that specialize in management control. If you wish to study management control in more depth, you are recommended to read Merchant and Van der Stede (2017).

For a broader discussion of how the array of different controls should be viewed as a single package, you should refer to Malmi and Brown (2008).

KEY EXAMINATION POINTS

Essay questions are extensively used in second year management accounting courses but tend not to be widely used for first year courses. The most frequently examined topic on first year courses is to prepare flexible budgets (see solutions to Review problem 16.21). If you are required to prepare flexible budgets, remember to flex the budget on the basis of target cost for actual output rather than input measures, such as direct labour or input hours. Also questions requiring you to comment on, or redraft performance reports, are frequently set at all levels (e.g. Review problem 16.23). It is important that you distinguish between controllable and non-controllable expenses and stress the need to incorporate non-financial measures. A common error is to compare actual performance with an unflexed budget.

ASSESSMENT MATERIAL

The review questions are short questions that enable you to assess your understanding of the main topics included in the chapter. The numbers in parentheses provide you with the page numbers to refer to if you cannot answer a specific question.

The review problems are more complex and require you to relate and apply the chapter content to various business problems. The problems are graded by their level of difficulty. Solutions to review problems that are not preceded by the term 'IM' are provided in a separate section at the end of the book. Solutions to problems preceded by the term 'IM' are provided in the Instructor's Manual accompanying this book that can be downloaded from the lecturer's digital support resources. Additional review problems with fully worked solutions are provided in the *Student Manual* that accompanies this book.

REVIEW QUESTIONS

16.1 Distinguish between 'controls' and 'control'. (p. 403)

16.2 Identify and describe three different types of control mechanism used by companies. (pp. 404–406)

16.3 Provide examples of behavioural, action, social, personnel and cultural controls. (pp. 404–406)

16.4 Describe the different stages that are involved with output/results controls. (pp. 405–406)

16.5 Distinguish between feedback and feed-forward controls. Provide an example of each type of control. (p. 406)

16.6 Describe some of the harmful side-effects that can occur with output/results controls. (pp. 407–408)

16.7 Explain the circumstances in which it is appropriate or inappropriate to use personnel/cultural, behavioural/ action and results/output controls. (pp. 409–410)

16.8 Describe the four different types of responsibility centre. (pp. 410–411)

16.9 Explain what is meant by the term 'responsibility accounting'. (p. 411)

16.10 What factors must be taken into account when operating a responsibility accounting system? (p. 411)

16.11 What is the 'controllability principle'? Describe the different ways in which the principle can be applied. (pp. 411–415)

16.12 What are flexible budgets? Why are they preferred to fixed (static budgets)? (p. 414)

16.13 What is meant by the term 'aspiration level'? (p. 416)

16.14 Describe the effect of the level of budget difficulty on motivation and performance. (pp. 416–417)

16.15 Distinguish between participation and top-down budget setting. (p. 417)

16.16 Describe the factors influencing the effectiveness of participation in the budget process. (p. 418)

16.17 What are the limitations of participation in the budget process? (p. 418)

16.18 Distinguish between budget-constrained, profit-conscious and non-accounting styles of performance evaluation. (pp. 418–419)

16.19 Under what circumstances is it considered appropriate to use (a) the budget-constrained and (b) the profit-conscious style of performance evaluation? (pp. 418–419)

REVIEW PROBLEMS

16.20 Basic. The standard cost card for a company's only product is given below:

	$ per unit
Selling price	118
Direct labour 4 hours at $20 per hour	80
Direct material 3 kg at $7 per hour	21
Fixed production overhead	5
Profit	12

For a period, budgeted production and sales were 8000 units, whilst actual production and sales were 6000 units.

What is the flexed budget profit?

(a) $62 000
(b) $72 000
(c) $96 000
(d) $102 000

(2 marks)

ACCA F5 Performance Management

16.21 Intermediate: Flexible budgets and the motivational role of budgets. Club Atlantic is an all-weather holiday complex providing holidays throughout the year. The fee charged to guests is fully inclusive of accommodation and all meals. However, because the holiday industry is so competitive, Club Atlantic is only able to generate profits by maintaining strict financial control of all activities.

The club's restaurant is one area in which there is a constant need to monitor costs. Susan Green is the manager of the restaurant. At the beginning of each year she is given an annual budget which is then broken down into months. Each month she receives a statement monitoring actual costs against the annual budget and highlighting any variances. The statement for the

month ended 31 October is reproduced below along with a list of assumptions:

*Club Atlantic Restaurant Performance
Statement Month to 31 October*

	Actual	Budget	Variance (over)/under
Number of guest days	11 160	9 600	(1 560)
	(£)	(£)	(£)
Food	20 500	20 160	(340)
Cleaning materials	2 232	1 920	(312)
Heat, light and power	2 050	2 400	350
Catering wages	8 400	7 200	(1 200)
Rent rates, insurance and depreciation	1 860	1 800	(60)
	35 042	33 480	(1 562)

Assumptions:

(a) The budget has been calculated on the basis of a 30-day calendar month with the cost of rents, insurance and depreciation being an apportionment of the fixed annual charge.

(b) The budgeted catering wages assume that:

  (i) there is one member of the catering staff for every 40 guests staying at the complex;

  (ii) the daily cost of a member of the catering staff is £30.

(c) All other budgeted costs are variable costs based on the number of guest days.

Task 1
Using the data above, prepare a revised performance statement using flexible budgeting. Your statement should

show both the revised budget and the revised variances. Club Atlantic uses the existing budgets and performance statements to motivate its managers as well as for financial control. If managers keep expenses below budget they receive a bonus in addition to their salaries. A colleague of Susan is Brian Hilton. Brian is in charge of the swimming pool and golf course, both of which have high levels of fixed costs. Each month he manages to keep expenses below budget and in return enjoys regular bonuses. Under the current reporting system, Susan Green receives a bonus only rarely.

At a recent meeting with Club Atlantic's directors, Susan Green expressed concern that the performance statement was not a valid reflection of her management of the restaurant. You are currently employed by Hall and Co., the club's auditors, and the directors of Club Atlantic have asked you to advise them whether there is any justification for Susan Green's concern.

At the meeting with the Club's directors, you were asked the following questions:

(a) Do budgets motivate managers to achieve objectives?
(b) Does motivating managers lead to improved performance?
(c) Does the current method of reporting performance motivate Susan Green and Brian Hilton to be more efficient? (10 marks)

Task 2
Write a brief letter to the directors of Club Atlantic addressing their question and justifying your answers.
Note: You should make use of the data given in this task plus your findings in Task 1. (10 marks)

AAT Technicians Stage

16.22 Advanced: Discussion of the weaknesses of a budget system and beyond budgeting. Perkin manufactures electronic components for export worldwide, from factories in Ceeland, for use in smartphones and hand held gaming devices. These two markets are supplied with similar components by two divisions, Phones Division (P) and Gaming Division (G). Each division has its own selling, purchasing, IT and research and development functions, but separate IT systems. Some manufacturing facilities, however, are shared between the two divisions.

Perkin's corporate objective is to maximize shareholder wealth through innovation and continuous technological improvement in its products. The manufacturers of smartphones and gaming devices, who use Perkin's components, update their products frequently and constantly compete with each other to launch models which are technically superior.

Perkin has a well-established incremental budgeting process. Divisional managers forecast sales volumes and costs months in advance of the budget year. These divisional budgets are then scrutinized by the main board, and revised significantly by them in line with targets they have set for the business. The finalized budgets are often approved after the start of the accounting year. Under pressure to deliver consistent returns to institutional shareholders, the board does not tolerate failure by either division to achieve the planned net profit for the year once the budget is approved. Last year's results were poor compared to the annual budget. Divisional managers, who are appraised on the financial performance of their own division, have complained about the length of time that the budgeting process takes and that the performance of their divisions could have been better but was constrained by the budgets which were set for them.

In P Division, managers had failed to anticipate the high popularity of a new smartphone model incorporating a large screen designed for playing games, and had not made the necessary technical modifications to the division's own components. This was due to the high costs of doing so, which had not been budgeted for. Based on the original sales forecast, P Division had already committed to manufacturing large quantities of the existing version of the component and so had to heavily discount these in order to achieve the planned sales volumes.

A critical material in the manufacture of Perkin's products is silver, which is a commodity which changes materially in price according to worldwide supply and demand. During the year, supplies of silver were reduced significantly for a short period of time and G Division paid high prices to ensure continued supply. Managers of G Division were unaware that P Division held large inventories of silver which they had purchased when the price was much lower.

Initially, G Division accurately forecasted demand for its components based on the previous years' sales volumes plus the historic annual growth rate of 5 per cent. However, overall sales volumes were much lower than budgeted. This was due to a fire at the factory of their main customer, which was then closed for part of the year. Reacting to this news, managers at G Division took action to reduce costs, including closing one of the three R&D facilities in the division.

However, when the customer's factory reopened, G Division was unwilling to recruit extra staff to cope with increased demand; nor would P Division re-allocate shared manufacturing facilities to them, in case demand increased for its own products later in the year. As a result, Perkin lost the prestigious preferred supplier status from their main customer who was unhappy with G Division's failure to effectively respond to the additional demand. The customer had been forced to purchase a more expensive, though technically superior, component from an alternative manufacturer.

The institutional shareholders' representative, recently appointed to the board, has asked you as a performance management expert for your advice. 'We need to know whether Perkin's budgeting process is appropriate for the business, and how this contributed to last year's poor performance', she said, 'and more importantly, how do we need to change the process to prevent this happening in the future, such as a move to beyond budgeting.'

Required:

(a) Evaluate the weaknesses in Perkin's current budgeting system and whether it is suitable for the environment in which Perkin operates. (13 marks)
(b) Evaluate the impact on Perkin of moving to beyond budgeting. (12 marks)

ACCA P5 Advanced Performance Management

16.23 Advanced: Comments on a performance assessment system and style of performance evaluation. Albacore Chess Stores (Albacore) is a chain of 12 shops specializing in selling items associated with the game of chess: boards, pieces, clocks, software and books. Three years ago, the company was the subject of a venture capital buyout from a larger group. A new senior management team was put in place after the buyout. They have the aim of running the business in order to maximize profits.

The chief financial officer (CFO), along with the other members of senior management, sets the annual budget and uses a standard costing approach with variance analysis in order to control individual shop performance. The head office handles all capital purchases and brand marketing. All inventory purchasing is done centrally and the shop opening times are set as standard across the company. As an illustration of senior management attitude, the CFO had set the budget for staff costs at $7 per hour for part-time staff and this was rigorously observed in the period.

Each shop is run by a manager who reports their financial results to head office. The shop managers recruit and manage the staffing of their shop. They have some autonomy in setting prices locally and have been given authority to vary prices by up to 10 per cent from a master list produced by the CFO. They also have a local marketing budget agreed each year by the shop's manager and the marketing director as part of the annual appraisal process.

The shop managers have approached the chairman of Albacore to complain about the way that they are managed and their remuneration. They feel that their efforts are unrecognized by senior management. One manager commented, 'I have had a successful year in hard economic circumstances. I have run a number of promotions in the shop that have been well received by the customers. However, the budgets that are set are impossible to achieve and as a result I have not been paid any bonus although I feel that I have done everything in my power to bring in good profits.'

The shop managers at Albacore are paid a basic salary of $27 000 with bonuses of up to 30 per cent of basic salary dependent on two factors: performance above budget and the operational director's performance assessment. The budget for the next year is prepared by the CFO and presented at the shop manager's annual appraisal.

The chairman has come to you to ask if you can consider the system of performance assessment for the shop managers and give an independent perspective on the reward systems at Albacore. She has provided the following illustrative information from the previous year for one shop:

Albacore Chess Stores

Tunny Branch Budget for Year to Sept

	Budget $	Actual $	Variance $
Sales	266 000	237 100	−28 900
Cost of sales	106 400	94 840	11 560
Gross profit	159 600	142 260	−17 340
Marketing	12 000	11 500	500
Staff costs			
Manager	27 000	27 000	0
Part-time staff	38 000	34 000	4 000
Property costs	26 600	26 600	0
Shop profit	56 000	43 160	−12 840

Notes:
Property costs includes heating, lighting and rental.
Positive variances are favourable.

The manager of this shop commented at the appraisal meeting that she felt that the assessment was unfair since her failure to make budget was due to general economic conditions. The industry as a whole saw a 12 per cent fall in revenues during the period and the budget for the period was set to be the same as the previous period. She was not paid a bonus for the period.

Required:

(a) Assess the suitability of the branch information given as a means of assessing the shop manager's performance for this store, providing suitable additional calculations.
(8 marks)
(b) Analyse the performance management style and evaluate the performance appraisal system at Albacore. Suggest suitable improvements to its reward system for the shop managers. (12 marks)

ACCA P5 Advanced Performance Management

16.24 Advanced: Comments on budget and control practices.
The Rubber Group (TRG) manufactures and sells a number of rubber-based products. Its strategic focus is channelled through profit centres that sell products transferred from production divisions that are operated as cost centres. The profit centres are the primary value-adding part of the business, whose commercial profit centre managers are responsible for the generation of a contribution margin sufficient to earn the target return of TRG. The target return is calculated after allowing for the sum of the agreed budgeted cost of production at production divisions, plus the cost of marketing, selling and distribution costs and central services costs.

The Bettamould Division is part of TRG and manufactures moulded products that it transfers to profit centres at an agreed cost per tonne. The agreed cost per tonne is set following discussion between management of the Bettamould Division and senior management of TRG.

The following information relates to the agreed budget for the Bettamould Division for the year ending 30 June:

1　The budgeted output of moulded products to be transferred to profit centres is 100 000 tonnes. The budgeted transfer cost has been agreed on a two-part basis as follows:

　(i)　a standard variable cost of $200 per tonne of moulded products;
　(ii)　a lump sum annual charge of $50 000 000 in respect of fixed costs, which is charged to profit centres, at $500 per tonne of moulded products.

2　Budgeted standard variable costs (as quoted in 1 above) have been set after incorporating each of the following:

　(i)　A provision in respect of processing losses amounting to 15 per cent of material inputs. Materials are sourced on a JIT basis from chosen suppliers who have been used for some years. It is felt that the 15 per cent level of losses is necessary because the ageing of the machinery will lead to a reduction in the efficiency of output levels.
　(ii)　A provision in respect of machine idle time amounting to 5 per cent. This is incorporated into variable machine costs. The idle time allowance is held at the 5 per cent level partly through elements of 'real-time' maintenance undertaken by the machine operating teams as part of their job specification.

3　Quality checks are carried out on a daily basis on 25 per cent of throughput tonnes of moulded products.
4　All employees and management have contracts based on fixed annual salary agreements. In addition, a bonus of 5 per cent of salary is payable as long as the budgeted output of 100 000 tonnes has been achieved;
5　Additional information relating to the points in (2) above (but NOT included in the budget for the year ending 30 June) is as follows:

　(i)　There is evidence that materials of an equivalent specification could be sourced for 40 per cent of the annual requirement at the Bettamould Division, from another division within TRG that has spare capacity.
　(ii)　There is evidence that a move to machine maintenance being outsourced from a specialist company could help reduce machine idle time and hence allow the possibility of annual output in excess of 100 000 tonnes of moulded products.
　(iii)　It is thought that the current level of quality checks (25 per cent of throughput on a daily basis) is vital, although current evidence shows that some competitor companies are able to achieve consistent acceptable quality with a quality check level of only 10 per cent of throughput on a daily basis.

The directors of TRG have decided to investigate claims relating to the use of budgeting within organizations which have featured in recent literature. A summary of relevant points from the literature is contained in the following statement:

'The use of budgets as part of a "performance contract" between an organization and its managers may be seen as a practice that causes management action which might lead to the following problems:

(a) Meeting only the lowest targets
(b) Using more resources than necessary
(c) Making the bonus — whatever it takes
(d) Competing against other divisions, business units and departments
(e) Ensuring that what is in the budget is spent

(f) Providing inaccurate forecasts
(g) Meeting the target, but not beating it
(h) Avoiding risks.'

Required:

(a) Explain the nature of any SIX of the eight problems listed above relating to the use of budgeting. *(12 marks)*
(b) Illustrate EACH of the six problems chosen in (a) using the data from the Bettamould Division TRG scenario. *(6 marks)*
(c) Suggest ways in which each of the six problems chosen in (a) above may be overcome. *(6 marks)*

ACCA Advanced Performance Management

16.25 Advanced. A transport company is preparing its cost budgets for the coming year. It has been set both social objectives and cost targets by (the government which it must achieve in order to receive a subsidy. Part of the subsidy is paid when acceptable budgets have been submitted to the government's transport office and the balance is payable at the end of the year provided the company has achieved its social objectives and cost targets.

The first draft of the cost budgets has been completed and submitted to the budget committee.

Required:

Explain to the board of directors how (i) feed-forward control and (ii) feedback control should be used in the transport company. (You should use examples from the company's budgeting system in your answer.) *(10 marks)*

CIMA P2 Performance Management

16.26 Advanced. A college is preparing its budget for next year. In previous years the director of the college has prepared the college budget without the participation of senior staff and presented it to the college board for approval.

Last year the college board criticized the director over the lack of participation of his senior staff in the preparation of the budget and requested that for next year's budget the senior staff were to be involved.

Required:

Discuss the potential advantages and disadvantages to the college of involving the senior staff in the budget preparation process. *(10 marks)*

CIMA P2 Performance Management

16.27 Advanced. 'Responsibility accounting is based on the application of the controllability principle.'

Required:

(a) Explain the 'controllability' principle and why its application is difficult in practice. *(6 marks)*
(b) Explain how the management of an organization can attempt to overcome the difficulties inherent in the practical application of the controllability principle. *(8 marks)*
(c) Explain the following approaches that can be used to set financial targets within an organization:

(i) engineered approach
(ii) historical approach
(iii) negotiated approach. *(6 marks)*

ACCA P3 Performance Measurement

16.28 Advanced. 'A competent management accounting system should endeavour to enhance the performance of a company. It should, in particular, consider the behavioural consequences of the system.'

Required:

(a) Explain why it is necessary when designing a management accounting system to consider the behavioural consequences of its application. *(5 marks)*

(b) Explain the potential behavioural issues that may arise in the application of performance monitoring, budgeting and transfer pricing and suggest how problems may be overcome. *(15 marks)*

ACCA P3 Performance Measurement

16.29 Advanced. A firm of solicitors is using budgetary control. The senior partner estimated the demand for the year for each of the firm's four divisions: civil, criminal, corporate and property. A separate partner is responsible for each division.

Each divisional partner then prepared a cost budget based on the senior partner's demand estimate for the division. These budgets were then submitted to the senior partner for his approval. He then amended them as he thought appropriate before issuing each divisional partner with the final budget for the division. He did not discuss these amendments with the respective divisional partners. Actual performance is then measured against the final budgets for each month and each divisional partner's performance is appraised by asking the divisional partner to explain the reasons for any variances that occur.

The corporate partner has been asked to explain why her staff costs exceeded the budgeted costs for last month while the chargeable time was less than budgeted. Her reply is as follows:

'My own original estimate of staff costs was higher than the final budgeted costs shown on my divisional performance report. In my own cost budget, I allowed for time to be spent developing new services for the firm's corporate clients and improving the clients access to their own case files. This would improve the quality of our services to clients and therefore increase client satisfaction. The trouble with our present system is that it focuses on financial performance and ignores the other performance indicators found in modem performance management systems.'

Required:

(a) Discuss the present budgeting system and its likely effect on divisional partner motivation. *(6 marks)*
(b) Explain two non-financial performance indicators (other than client satisfaction and service quality) that could be used by the firm. *(4 marks)*

CIMA P2 Performance Management

IM16.1 Intermediate. Explain the meaning of each of the undernoted terms, comment on their likely impact on cash budgeting and profit planning and suggest ways in which any adverse effects of each may be reduced.

(a) Budgetary slack. *(7 marks)*
(b) Incremental budgets. *(7 marks)*
(c) Fixed budgets. *(6 marks)*

ACCA Level 2 Cost and Management Accounting II

IM16.2 Advanced.

(a) Discuss the use of the following as aids to *each* of planning and control:

(i) rolling budgets;
(ii) flexible budgets;
(iii) planning and operational variances. *(9 marks)*

(b) Discuss the extent to which the incidence of budgetary slack is likely to be affected by the use of each of the techniques listed in (a). *(6 marks)*

ACCA Paper 9 Information for Control and Decision Making

IM16.3 Advanced. In the context of budgetary control, certain costs are not amenable to the use of flexible budgets. These include some costs which are often called 'discretionary' (or 'programmed').

You are required to explain:

(a) the nature of discretionary (or programmed) costs and give two examples;

(b) how the treatment of these costs differs from that of other types of cost in the process of preparing and using budgets for control purposes. *(20 marks)*

CIMA P3 Management Accounting

IM16.4 Advanced.

(a) In the context of budgeting, provide definitions for *four* of the following terms:
aspiration level;
budgetary slack;
feedback;
zero-base budgeting;
responsibility accounting. *(8 marks)*

(b) Discuss the motivational implications of the level of efficiency assumed in establishing a budget. *(9 marks)*

ACCA Level 2 Management Accounting

IM16.5 Advanced. 'Budgeting is too often looked on from a purely mechanistic viewpoint. The human factors in budgeting are more important than the accounting techniques. The success of a budgetary system depends on its acceptance by the company members who are affected by the budgets.'

Discuss the validity of the above statement from the viewpoint of both the planning and the control aspects of budgeting. In the course of your discussion, present at least one practical illustration to support your conclusions. *(20 marks)*

ACCA P2 Management Accounting

IM16.6 Advanced. 'The major reason for introducing budgetary control and standard costing systems is to influence human behaviour and to motivate the managers to achieve the goals of the organization. However, the accounting literature provides many illustrations of accounting control systems that fail to give sufficient attention to influencing human behaviour towards the achievement of organization goals.'

You are required:

(a) To identify and discuss four situations in which accounting control systems might not motivate desirable behaviour.

(b) To briefly discuss the improvements you would suggest in order to ensure that some of the dysfunctional behavioural consequences of accounting control systems are avoided.

IM16.7 Advanced. 'The final impact which any accounting system has on managerial and employee behaviour is dependent not only upon its design and technical characteristics but also in the precise manner in which the resulting information is used.'
(A. Hopwood, *Accountancy and Human Behaviour*).

Discuss this statement in relation to budgeting and standard costing.

IM16.8 Advanced. 'Motivation is the over-riding consideration that should influence management in formulating and using performance measures, and in designing management control systems.'

Discuss this statement in relation to the design and implementation of budgetary control systems.

IM16.9 Advanced.

(a) Discuss the behavioural arguments for and against involving those members of management who are responsible for the implementation of the budget in the annual budget setting process. *(10 marks)*

(b) Explain how the methods by which annual budgets are formulated might help to overcome behavioural factors likely to limit the efficiency and effectiveness of the budget. *(7 marks)*

IM16.10 Advanced. An article in *Management Accounting* concluded that there will always be some budgetary padding in any organization.

Requirements:

(a) As management accountant, write a report to your finance director, explaining what steps can be taken by you, and by senior management when approving budgets, to minimize budgetary slack. *(8 marks)*

(b) The finance director, having read the report referred to in part (a), discussed the problem with the managing director and suggested that appropriate action be taken to reduce budgetary slack.

The managing director expressed doubts, stating that in his opinion removing all budget padding could cause considerable problems.

Requirement:
Explain the arguments that can be advanced for accepting some budgetary slack and the advantages of this to the manager being appraised and to the organization. Discuss whether the budget review and approval process should permit managers to build in some budgetary slack. *(12 marks)*

CIMA Stage 4 Management Accounting Control Systems

IM16.11 Intermediate: Preparation of flexible budgets and an explanation of variances. You have been provided with the following operating statement, which represents an attempt to compare the actual performance for the quarter which has just ended with the budget:

	Budget	Actual	Variance
Number of units sold (000s)	640	720	80
	£000	£000	£000
Sales	1024	1071	47
Cost of sales (all variable)			
Materials	168	144	
Labour	240	288	
Overheads	32	36	
	440	468	(28)
Fixed labour cost	100	94	6
Selling and distribution costs:			
Fixed	72	83	(11)
Variable	144	153	(9)
Administration costs:			
Fixed	184	176	8
Variable	48	54	(6)
	548	560	(12)
Net profit	36	43	7

Required:

(a) Using a flexible budgeting approach, re-draft the operating statement so as to provide a more realistic indication of the variances and comment briefly on the possible reasons (other than inflation) why they have occurred. *(12 marks)*

(b) Explain why the original operating statement was of little use to management. *(2 marks)*

(c) Discuss the problems associated with the forecasting of figures that are to be used in flexible budgeting. *(6 marks)*

ACCA Paper 8 Managerial Finance

IM16.12 Intermediate: Responsibility centre performance reports.
Data
Jim Smith has recently been appointed as the headteacher of Mayfield School in Midshire. The age of the pupils ranges from 11 years to 18 years. For many years, Midshire County Council

was responsible for preparing and reporting on the school budget. From June, however, these responsibilities passed to the headteacher of Mayfield School.

You have recently accepted a part-time appointment as the accountant to Mayfield School, although your previous accounting experience has been gained in commercial organizations. Jim Smith is hoping that you will be able to apply that experience to improving the financial reporting procedures at Mayfield School.

The last budget statement prepared by Midshire County Council is reproduced below. It covers the ten months to the end of May and all figures refer to cash payments made.

Midshire County Council Mayfield School
Statement of school expenditure against budget: 10 months ending May

	Expenditure to date	Budget to date	Under-/ over-spend	Total budget for year
Teachers full time	1 680 250	1 682 500	2 250 Cr	2 019 000
Teachers part time	35 238	34 600	638	41 520
Other employee expenses	5 792	15 000	9 208 Cr	18 000
Administrative staff	69 137	68 450	687	82 140
Caretaker and cleaning	49 267	57 205	7 938 Cr	68 646
Resources (books etc.)	120 673	100 000	20 673	120 000
Repairs and maintenance	458	0	458	0
Lighting and heating	59 720	66 720	7 000 Cr	80 064
Rates	23 826	19 855	3 971	23 826
Fixed assets: furniture and equipment	84 721	100 000	15 279 Cr	120 000
Stationery, postage and phone	1 945	0	1 945	0
Miscellaneous expenses	9 450	6 750	2 700	8 100
Total	2 140 477	2 151 080	10 603 Cr	2 581 296

Task 1
Write a memo to Jim Smith. Your memo should:

(a) identify *four* weaknesses of the existing statement as a management report;
(b) include an improved *outline* statement format showing revised column headings and a more meaningful classification of costs which will help Jim Smith to manage his school effectively (figures are not required);
(c) give *two* advantages of your proposed format over the existing format.

Data
The income of Mayfield School is based on the number of pupils at the school. Jim Smith provides you with the following breakdown of student numbers.

Mayfield School:
Student numbers as at 31 May

School year	Age range	Current number of pupils
1	11–12	300
2	12–13	350
3	13–14	325
4	14–15	360
5	15–16	380
6	16–17	240
7	17–18	220
Total number of students		2 175

Jim also provides you with the following information relating to existing pupils:

- pupils move up one school year at the end of July;
- for those pupils entering year 6, there is an option to leave the school. As a result, only 80 per cent of the current school year 5 pupils go on to enter school year 6;

- of those currently in school-year 6 only 95 per cent continue into school year 7;
- pupils currently in school year 7 leave to go on to higher education or employment;
- the annual income per pupil is £1200 in years 1 to 5 and £1500 in years 6 to 7.

The new year 1 pupils come from the final year at four junior schools. Not all pupils, however, elect to go to Mayfield School. Jim has investigated this matter and derived accurate estimates of the proportion of final year pupils at each of the four junior schools who go on to attend Mayfield School.

The number of pupils in the final year at each of the four junior schools is given below along with Jim's estimate of the proportion likely to choose Mayfield School:

Junior School	Number in final year at 31 May	Proportion choosing Mayfield School
Ranmoor	60	0.9
Hallamshire	120	0.8
Broomhill	140	0.9
Endcliffe	80	0.5

Task 2
(a) Forecast the number of pupils and the income of Mayfield School for the next year from August to July. *(15 marks)*
(b) Assuming expenditure next year is 5 per cent more than the current annual budgeted expenditure, calculate the budgeted surplus or deficit of Mayfield School for next year. *(10 marks)*

AAT Technicians Stage

IM16.13 Advanced: Comments on an existing performance measurement and bonus system and recommendations for improvement. 1. You are the group management accountant of a large divisionalized group.

There has been extensive board discussion of the existing system of rewarding divisional general managers with substantial bonuses based on the comparison of the divisional profit with budget.

The scheme is simple: the divisional profit (PBIT) is compared with the budget for the year. If budget is not achieved no bonus is paid. If budget is achieved a bonus of 20 per cent of salary is earned. If twice budgeted profit is achieved, a bonus of 100 per cent of salary is paid, which is the upper limit of the bonus scheme. Intermediate achievements are calculated *pro rata*.

The finance director has been asked to prepare a number of reports on the issues involved and has asked you to prepare some of these.

He has decided to use the results for Division X as an example on which the various discussions could be based. A schedule of summary available data is given below:

Division X
Summary of management accounting data

	Strategic plan 2019 Prepared Aug 2018	Budget 2019 Prepared Oct 2018	Latest estimate 2019 Prepared April 2019
Sales of units by Division X	35 000	36 000	35 800
Sales	28 000	28 800	28 100
Marginal costs	14 350	15 300	14 900
Fixed factory cost	6 500	6 800	7 200
Product development	2 000	2 000	1 400
Marketing	3 500	3 200	2 600
PBIT	1 650	1 500	2 000

Division X manufactures and sells branded consumer durables in competitive markets. High expenditure is required on product development and advertising, as the maintenance of market share depends on a flow of well-promoted new models.

Reliable statistics on market size are available annually. Based on the market size for 2018, where stronger than anticipated growth had occurred, a revised market estimate of 165000 units for 2019 is agreed by group and divisional staff in May 2019. This is a significant increase on the estimate of 150000 units made in May 2018 and used since.

The divisional general manager has commented that action now, almost halfway through the year, is unlikely to produce significant results during this year. However, had he known last year, at the time of producing the budget, that the market was growing faster, he could have taken the necessary action to maintain the strategic plan market share. The actions would have been:

- cutting prices by £10 per unit below the price at present charged and used in the latest estimate for 2019;
- increasing marketing expenditure by £300000 compared with the strategic plan.

The group managing director, commenting on the same data, said that the divisional general manager could have maintained both strategic plan market share and selling prices by an alternative approach.

The approach, he thought, should have been:

- maintaining expenditure on product development and marketing at 20 per cent of sales over the years;
- spending his time controlling production costs instead of worrying about annual bonuses.

You are required:

(a) To analyse and comment on the results of Division X, making appropriate comparisons with budget, with plan and with new available data. Present the results in such a form that the board can easily understand the problems involved. *(17 marks)*

(b) To comment on the advantages and problems of the existing bonus system for the divisional general manager and the way in which the present bonus scheme may motivate the divisional general manager. *(8 marks)*

(c) To make specific proposals, showing calculations if appropriate, for an alternative bonus scheme, reflecting your analysis in (a). *(8 marks)*

A non-executive director has commented that he can understand the case for linking executive directors' rewards to group results. He is not convinced that this should be extended to divisional managers and certainly not to senior managers below this level in divisions and head office.

(d) Explain and discuss the case for extending bonus schemes widely throughout the organization. *(7 marks)*

CIMA Stage 4 Management Accounting – Control and Audit

IM16.14 Advanced: Budget use and performance reporting.
A new private hospital of 100 beds was opened to receive patients on 2 January although many senior staff members including the supervisor of the laundry department had been *in situ* for some time previously. The first months were expected to be a settling-in period; the hospital facilities being used to full capacity only in the second and subsequent months.

In May the supervisor of the laundry department received her first monthly performance report from the hospital administrator, together with an explanatory memorandum. Copies of both documents are set out below.

The supervisor had never seen the original budget, neither had she been informed that there would be a monthly performance report. She knew she was responsible for her department and had made every endeavour to run it as efficiently as possible. It had been made clear to her that there

would be a slow build-up in the number of patients accepted by the hospital and so she would need only three members of staff, but she had had to take on a fourth during the month due to the extra work. This extra hiring had been anticipated for May, not late February.

Rockingham Private Patients Hospital Ltd
MEMORANDUM　　　　　　　　　　　　　　　　　　30 April
To:　　　All Department Heads/Supervisors
From:　Hospital Administrator

Attached is the Monthly Performance Report for your department. The hospital has adopted a responsibility accounting system so you will be receiving one of these reports monthly. Responsibility accounting means that you are accountable for ensuring that the expenses of running your department are kept in line with the budget. Each report compares the actual expenses of running your department for the month with our budget for the same period. The difference between the actual and forecast will be highlighted so that you can identify the important variations from budget and take corrective action to get back on budget. Any variation in excess of 5 per cent from budget should be investigated and an explanatory memo sent to me giving reasons for the variations and the proposed corrective actions.

Performance report – laundry department
month ending to 31 March

	Actual	Budget	Variation (Over) Under	% Variation
Patient days	8000	6500	(1500)	(23)
Weight of laundry processed (kg)	101170	81250	(19920)	(24.5)
	(£)	(£)	(£)	
Department: Expenses				
Wages	4125	3450	(675)	(19.5)
Supervisor salary	1490	1495	5	—
Washing materials	920	770	(150)	(19.5)
Heating and power	560	510	(50)	(10)
Equipment depreciation	250	250	—	—
Allocated administration costs	2460	2000	(460)	(23)
Equipment maintenance	10	45	35	78
	9815	8520	(1295)	(15)

Comment: We need to have a discussion about the overexpenditure of the department.

You are required to:

(a) Discuss in detail the various possible effects on the behaviour of the laundry supervisor of the way that her budget was prepared and the form and content of the performance report, having in mind the published research findings in this area. *(15 marks)*

(b) Re-draft, giving explanations, the performance report and supporting memorandum in a way which, in your opinion, would make them more effective management tools. *(10 marks)*

ICAEW P2 Management Accounting

IM16.15 Advanced: Advantages and disadvantages of participation and comments on a new performance measurement and evaluation system. Incorporated Finance plc is a finance company that has 100 branch offices in major towns and cities throughout the UK. These offer a variety of hire purchase and loan facilities to personal customers both directly and through schemes operated on behalf of major retailers. The main function of the branches is to sell loans and to ensure that repayments are collected; the head office is responsible for raising the capital required, which it provides to branches at a current rate of interest.

Each year branch managers are invited to provide estimates of the following items for the forthcoming year, as the start of the budgetary process:

Value of new loans (by category e.g. direct, retail, motor)
Margin percentage (i.e. loan rate of interest less cost of capital provided by head office)
Gross margin (i.e. value of new loans × margin percentage)
Branch operating expenses
Net margin (i.e. gross margin less operating expenses).

The main branch expenses relate to the cost of sales and administrative staff and to the cost of renting and maintaining branch premises, but also include the cost of bad debts on outstanding loans.

These estimates are then passed to headquarters by area and regional managers and are used, together with other information such as that relating to general economic conditions, to set an overall company budget. This is then broken down by headquarters into regional figures; regional managers then set the area budgets and area managers finally set branch budgets. However, a common complaint of branch managers is that the budgets they are set often bear little resemblance to the estimates they originally submitted.

Budget targets are set for the five items specified above, with managers receiving a bonus based on the average percentage achievement of all five targets, weighted equally.

Requirements:

(a) Discuss the advantages and disadvantages of allowing managers to participate in budget setting, and suggest how Incorporated Finance plc should operate its budgetary system. *(15 marks)*

(b) The managing director is considering changing the performance evaluation and bonus scheme so that branch managers are set only a net margin target. Prepare a report for him outlining the advantages and disadvantages of making such a change. *(10 marks)*

ICAEW P2 Management Accounting

17

STANDARD COSTING AND VARIANCE ANALYSIS 1

LEARNING OBJECTIVES After studying this chapter, you should be able to:

- explain how a standard costing system operates;

- explain how standard costs are set;

- explain the meaning of standard hours produced;

- identify and describe the purposes of a standard costing system;

- calculate labour, material, overhead and sales margin variances and reconcile actual profit with budgeted profit;

- identify the causes of labour, material, overhead and sales margin variances;

- distinguish between standard variable costing and standard absorption costing.

In the previous chapter we examined the major features of management accounting control systems. The different types of management control used by companies were described so that the elements of management accounting control systems could be described within the context of the overall control process. A broad approach to control was adopted and the detailed procedures of financial controls were not examined. In this chapter, we shall focus on the detailed financial controls that are used by organizations.

We shall describe a financial control system that enables the deviations from budget to be analysed in detail, thus enabling costs to be controlled more effectively. This system of control is called standard costing. In particular, we shall examine how a standard costing system operates and how the variances are calculated. Standard costing systems are applied in standard cost centres, which were described in the previous chapter. You will recall that the main features of standard cost centres are that output can be measured and the input required to produce each unit of output can be specified. Therefore standard costing is generally applied to manufacturing activities and non-manufacturing activities are not incorporated within the standard costing system. However, the sales variances that are described in this chapter can also be applied in revenue centres. In Chapter 19, we shall look at financial performance measures that are appropriate for measuring the performance of profit and investment centres.

Standard costs are predetermined costs; they are target costs that should be incurred under efficient operating conditions. They are not the same as budgeted costs. A budget relates to an entire activity or operation; a standard presents the same information on a *per unit* basis. A standard therefore provides cost expectations per unit of activity and a budget provides the cost expectation for the total activity. If the budget output for a product is for 10 000 units and the standard cost is £3 per unit, budgeted cost will be £30 000. We shall see that establishing standard costs for each unit produced enables a detailed analysis to be made of the difference between the budgeted cost and the actual cost so that costs can be controlled more effectively.

In the first part of the chapter (pages 440–441), we shall concentrate on those variances that are likely to be useful for cost control purposes. The final part describes those variances that are required for financial accounting purposes but that are not particularly useful for cost control. If your course does not relate to the disposition of variances for financial accounting purposes, you can omit pages 451–455.

OPERATION OF A STANDARD COSTING SYSTEM

Standard costing is most suited to an organization whose activities consist of a series of *common* or *repetitive* operations where the input required to produce each unit of output can be specified. It is therefore relevant in manufacturing companies, since the processes involved are often of a repetitive nature. Standard costing procedures can also be applied in service industries such as units within banks, where output can be measured in terms of the number of cheques or the number of loan applications processed, and there are also well-defined input–output relationships (see Exhibit 17.2 for surveys relating to the usage of standard costing systems). In fastfood restaurants, such as Burger King, the standard input required to produce a single hamburger can be specified. It is therefore possible to specify the standard inputs required for a given output of hamburgers because there is a physical relationship between ingredients such as meats, buns, condiments and packaging and the number of hamburgers made. Standard costing cannot, however, be applied to activities of a non-repetitive nature, since there is no basis for observing repetitive operations and consequently standards cannot be set.

A standard costing system can be applied to organizations that produce many different products, as long as production consists of a series of common operations. For example, if the output from a factory is the result of five common operations, it is possible to produce many different product variations from these operations. It is therefore possible that a large product range may result from a small number of common operations. Standard costs are developed for repetitive operations and product standard costs can be derived simply by combining the standard costs from the operations which are necessary to make the product. This process is illustrated in Exhibit 17.1.

It is assumed that the standard costs are £200, £300, £400 and £500 for each of the operations 1 to 4. The standard cost for *product* 100 is therefore £1100, which consists of £200 for operation 1, plus £400 and £500 for operations 3 and 4. The standard costs for each of the other products are calculated in a similar manner. In addition, the total standard cost for the total output of each operation for the period has been calculated. For example, six items of operation number 1 have been completed, giving a total standard cost of £1200 for this operation (six items at £200 each). Three items of operation 2 have been completed, giving a total standard cost of £900 and so on.

EXHIBIT 17.1 Standard costs analysed by operations and products

Responsibility centre	No.	(£)	100	101	102	103	104	105	106	Total standard cost (£)	Actual cost
A	1	200	✓	✓		✓	✓	✓	✓	1200	
B	2	300		✓		✓	✓	✓		900	
C	3	400	✓		✓		✓			1200	
D	4	500	✓	✓	✓				✓	2000	
Standard product cost			£1100	£1000	£900	£500	£600	£500	£700	5300	

Since its introduction in the early 1900s standard costing has flourished and is still one of the most widely used management accounting techniques. Surveys of UK manufacturing companies by Drury *et al.* (1993) and New Zealand companies by Guilding *et al.* (1998) reported that approximately 75 per cent of the companies used standard costing. A CIMA sponsored study of 41 UK manufacturing organizations by Dugdale, Jones and Green (2006) reported that 30 of the firms employed standard costing. The majority of these firms (26) set standard costs for materials and labour and a smaller majority (20) also set standard overhead costs. They conclude that despite huge changes in the manufacturing environment, standard costing is alive and well. The international survey conducted by the Chartered Institute of Management Accountants (2009) reported that approximately 45 per cent of the respondents used standard costing but the survey included manufacturing and non-manufacturing companies so it is likely that the usage rate was much higher for manufacturing companies.

Variances allocated to responsibility centres

You can see from Exhibit 17.1 that different responsibility centres are responsible for each operation. For example, responsibility centre A is responsible for operation 1, responsibility centre B for operation 2, and so on. Consequently, there is no point in comparing the actual cost of *product* 100 with the standard cost of £1100 for the purposes of control, since responsibility centres A, C and D are responsible for the variance. None of the responsibility centres is solely answerable for the variance. Cost control requires that responsibility centres be identified with the standard cost for the output achieved. Therefore, if the actual costs for responsibility centre A are compared with the standard cost of £1200 for the production of the six items (see first row of Exhibit 17.1), the manager of this responsibility centre will be answerable for the full amount of the variance. Only by comparing total actual costs with total standard costs *for each operation or responsibility centre* for a period can control be effectively achieved. A comparison of standard product costs (i.e. the columns in Exhibit 17.1) with actual costs that involves several different responsibility centres is clearly inappropriate.

Figure 17.1 provides an overview of the operation of a standard costing system. You will see that the standard costs for the actual output for a particular period are traced to the managers of responsibility centres who are responsible for the various operations. The actual costs for the same period are also charged to the responsibility centres. Standard and actual costs are compared and the variance is reported.

FIGURE 17.1
An overview of a standard costing system

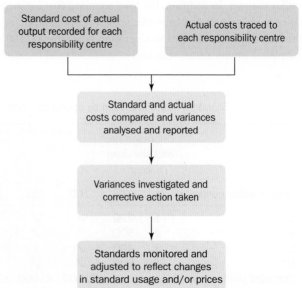

For example, if the actual cost for the output of the six items produced in responsibility centre A during the period is £1300 and the standard cost is £1200 (Exhibit 17.1), a variance of £100 will be reported.

Detailed analysis of variances

The box below the first arrow in Figure 17.1 indicates that the operation of a standard costing system also enables a detailed analysis of the variances to be reported. Variances for each responsibility centre can be identified by each element of cost and analysed according to the price and quantity content because different managers may be responsible for the price and quantity elements. For example, the purchasing manager may be responsible for material prices whereas the production manager may be responsible for the quantities used. The accountant assists managers by pinpointing where the variances have arisen and the responsibility managers can undertake to carry out the appropriate investigations to identify the reasons for the variance. For example, the accountant might identify the reason for a direct materials variance as being excessive usage of a certain material in a particular process, but the responsibility centre manager would then investigate this process and identify the reasons for the excessive usage. Such an investigation should result in appropriate remedial action being taken or, if it is found that the variance is due to a permanent change in the standard, the standard should be changed.

Actual product costs are not required

It is questionable whether the allocation of actual costs to products serves any useful purpose. Because standard costs represent *future* target costs, they are preferable to actual *past* costs for decision-making. Also, the external financial accounting regulations in most countries specify that if standard product costs provide a reasonable approximation of actual product costs, they are acceptable for inventory valuation calculations for external reporting.

There are therefore strong arguments for not producing actual *product* costs when a standard costing system exists, since this will lead to large administrative savings. However, it must be stressed that actual costs must be accumulated periodically for each operation or responsibility centre, so that comparisons can be made with standard costs. Nevertheless, there will be considerably fewer responsibility centres than products, and the accumulation of actual costs is therefore much less time consuming.

ESTABLISHING COST STANDARDS

Control over costs is best effected through action at the point where the costs are incurred. Hence the standards should be set for the quantities of material, labour and services to be consumed in performing an *operation*, rather than the complete *product* cost standards. Variances from these standards should be reported to show causes and responsibilities for deviations from standard. Product cost standards are derived by listing and adding the standard costs of operations required to produce a particular product. For example, you will see by referring to Exhibit 17.1 that the standard cost of product 100 is £1100 and is derived from the sum of the standard costs of operations 1, 3 and 4.

There are two approaches that can be used to set standard costs. First, past historical records can be used to estimate labour and material usage. Second, standards can be set based on engineering studies. This involves a detailed study of each operation based on careful specifications of materials, labour and equipment and on controlled observations of operations. If historical records are used to set standards, there is a danger that past inefficiencies will affect the standards. If historical standards are used, standards are set based on average past performance for the same or similar operations. The disadvantage of this method is that, unlike the engineering method, it does not focus attention on finding the best combination of resources, production methods and product quality. Nevertheless, standards derived from average historical usage do appear to be widely used in practice.

We shall now consider how standards are established for each operation for direct labour, direct materials and overheads using the engineering studies approach. Note that the standard cost for each

REAL WORLD VIEWS 17.1

Establishing standard costs – using an ERP to update standard costs
Once standard costs have been established and used by a business, they should be updated on a regular basis. Actual costs are frequently used as a basis for any updates. SAP, a leading enterprise resource planning (ERP) system, provides tools and data with which actual costs can be used to establish and update standards. A component of SAP called product costing (PC) is a very useful starting point for the exercise. This module captures the cost of manufacture and the costs of goods sold (including sales and administration overhead). Cost of manufacture as defined by SAP is composed of material and production costs, process costs and production overhead. The PC module can feed actual data to another component of SAP called cost object controlling (COO). This module in turn is used to calculate material usage costs, value work in progress and calculate variances. The PC module can also pass actual material cost data to material records in the system, thereby keeping the standard cost of material up-to-date automatically.

Questions

1 Can you think of any type of business that might need to frequently update the standard cost of its materials?

2 Do you think variance reporting would be more relevant to managers if standard costs are regularly updated?

References
Duncan, T. (2013) '5 steps to understanding product costing – Part 3 quantity structure', SAP Community Network, 2 January. Available at scn.sap.com /community/erp/financials/controlling/blog/2013 /01/02/5-steps-to-understanding-product-costing -part-3-quantity-structure
SAP (2015) 'Product cost by period', SAP. Available at help.sap.com/saphelp_470/helpdata/en/90 /ba60bc446711d189420000e829fbbd/content.htm

operation is derived from multiplying the quantity of input that should be used per unit of output (i.e. the quantity standard) by the amount that should be paid for each unit of input (i.e. the price standard).

Direct material standards

These are based on product specifications derived from an intensive study of the input *quantity* necessary for each operation. This study should establish the most suitable materials for each product/ operation, based on product design and quality policy, and also the optimal quantity that should be used after taking into account any unavoidable wastage or loss. Material quantity standards are usually recorded on a bill of materials. This states the required quantity of materials for each operation to complete the product. A separate bill of materials is maintained for each product. The standard material product cost is then found by multiplying the standard quantities by the appropriate standard prices.

The standard *prices* are obtained from the purchasing department. The standard material prices are based on the assumption that the purchasing department has carried out a suitable search of alternative suppliers and has selected suppliers who can provide the required quantity of sound quality materials at the most competitive price. Standard prices then provide a suitable base against which actual prices paid for materials can be evaluated.

Direct labour standards

To set labour standards, activities should be analysed by the different operations. Each operation is studied and an allowed time computed. The normal procedure for such a study is to analyse each operation to eliminate any unnecessary elements and to determine the most efficient production method. The most efficient methods of production, equipment and operating conditions are then standardized.

This is followed by an estimate of the number of standard hours required by an average worker to complete the job. Unavoidable delays such as machine breakdowns and routine maintenance are included in the standard time. The contractual wage rates are applied to the standard time allowed to determine the standard labour cost for each operation. Where an operation requires a mix of workers paid at different wage rates the average wage rate may be used.

Overhead standards

The procedure for establishing standard manufacturing overhead rates for a standard costing system is the same as that which is used for establishing predetermined overhead rates as described in Chapter 3. Separate rates for fixed and variable overheads are essential for planning and control. With traditional costing systems, the standard overhead rate will be based on a rate per direct labour hour or machine hour of input.

Fixed overheads are largely independent of changes in activity and remain constant over wide ranges of activity in the short term. It is therefore inappropriate to unitize fixed overheads for short-term cost control purposes. However, in order to meet the external financial reporting inventory valuation requirements, fixed manufacturing overheads must be traced to products. It is therefore necessary to unitize fixed overheads for inventory valuation purposes.

The main difference with the treatment of overheads under a standard costing system as opposed to a non-standard costing system is that the product overhead cost is based on the hourly overhead rates multiplied by the *standard hours* (that is, hours which should have been used) rather than the *actual hours* used.

A standard cost card should be maintained for each product and operation. It reveals the quantity of each unit of input that should be used to produce one unit of output. A typical product standard cost card is illustrated in Exhibit 17.3. In most organizations, standard cost cards will be stored on a computerized

EXHIBIT 17.3 An illustration of a standard cost card

Date standard set						Product: Sigma		
Direct materials								
		Quantity	Standard price		Department			Totals
Operation no.	Item code	(kg)	(£)	A	B	C	D	(£)
1	5.001	5	3		£15			
2	7.003	4	4			£16		
Direct labour								31
Operation no.	Standard hours	Standard rate (£)						
1	7	9			£63			
2	8	9				£72		
								135
Factory overhead								
Department	Standard hours	Standard rate (£)						
B	7	3			£21			
C	8	4				£32		
								53
Total manufacturing cost per unit (£)								219

database. Standards should be continuously reviewed and, where significant changes in production methods or input prices occur, they should be changed in order to ensure that standards reflect current targets.

Standard hours produced

It is not possible to measure *output* in terms of units produced for a department making several different products or operations. For example, if a department produces 100 units of product X, 200 units of product Y and 300 units of product Z, it is not possible to add the production of these items together, since they are not homogeneous. This problem can be overcome by ascertaining the amount of time, working under efficient conditions, it should take to make each product. This time calculation is called standard hours produced. In other words, standard hours are an *output* measure that can act as a common denominator for adding together the production of unlike items.

Let us assume that the following standard times are established for the production of one unit of each product:

Product X	five standard hours
Product Y	two standard hours
Product Z	three standard hours

This means that it should take five hours to produce one unit of product X under efficient production conditions. Similar comments apply to products Y and Z. The production for the department will be calculated in standard hours as follows:

Product	Standard time per unit produced (hours)	Actual output (units)	Standard hours produced
X	5	100	500
Y	2	200	400
Z	3	300	900
			1800

Remember that standard hours produced is an output measure and flexible budget allowances should be based on this. In the illustration, we should expect the *output* of 1800 standard hours to take 1800 direct labour hours of *input* if the department works at the prescribed level of efficiency. The department will be inefficient if 1800 standard hours of output are produced using, say, 2000 direct labour hours of input. The flexible budget allowance should therefore be based on 1800 standard hours produced to ensure that no extra allowance is given for the 200 excess hours of input. Otherwise, a manager will obtain a higher budget allowance through being inefficient.

PURPOSES OF STANDARD COSTING

Standard costing systems are widely used because they provide cost information for many different purposes (see Figure 17.2), such as the following:

● Providing a prediction of future costs that can be used for *decision-making purposes*. Standard costs can be derived from either traditional or activity-based costing systems. Because standard costs represent *future* target costs based on the elimination of avoidable inefficiencies, they are preferable to estimates based on adjusted past costs which may incorporate inefficiencies. For example, in markets where competitive prices do not exist, products may be priced on a bid basis. In these situations, standard costs provide more appropriate information because efficient competitors will seek to eliminate avoidable costs. It is therefore unwise to assume that inefficiencies are recoverable within the bid price.

FIGURE 17.2
Standard costs for inventory valuation and profit measurement

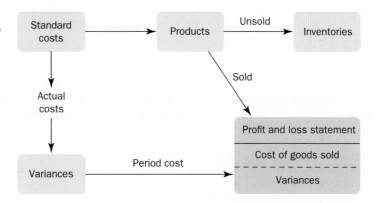

- Providing a *challenging target* which individuals are motivated to achieve. For example, research evidence suggests that the existence of a defined quantitative goal or target is likely to motivate higher levels of performance than would be achieved if no such target were set.

- Assisting in *setting budgets* and evaluating managerial performance. Standard costs are particularly valuable for budgeting because they provide a reliable and convenient source of data for converting budgeted production into physical and monetary resource requirements. Budgetary preparation time is considerably reduced if standard costs are available because the standard costs of operations and products can be readily built up into total costs of any budgeted volume and product mix.

- Acting as a *control device* by highlighting those activities which do not conform to plan and thus alerting managers to those situations that may be 'out of control' and in need of corrective action. With a standard costing system variances are analysed in great detail such as by element of cost, and price and quantity elements. Useful feedback is therefore provided to help to pinpoint the areas in which variances have arisen.

- Simplifying the task of tracing costs to products for *profit measurement and inventory valuation* purposes. In addition to preparing annual financial accounting profit statements, most organizations also prepare monthly internal profit statements. If actual costs are used, a considerable amount of time is required in tracking costs so that monthly costs can be allocated between cost of sales and inventories. A data processing system is required which can track monthly costs in a resource efficient manner. Standard costing systems meet this requirement. You will see from Figure 17.2 that product costs are maintained at standard cost. Inventories and cost of goods sold are recorded at standard cost and a conversion to actual cost is made by writing off all variances arising during the period as a period cost. Note that the variances from standard cost are extracted by comparing actual with standard costs at the responsibility centre level, and not at the product level, so that actual costs are not assigned to individual products.

A SUMMARY OF VARIANCE ANALYSIS FOR A VARIABLE COSTING SYSTEM

It is possible to compute variances simply by committing to memory a series of variance formulae. If you adopt this approach, however, it will not help you to understand what a variance is intended to depict and what the relevant variables represent. In our discussion, we shall therefore concentrate on the fundamental meaning of the variance, so that you can logically deduce the variance formulae as we go along.

All of the variances presented in this chapter are illustrated from the information contained in Example 17.1. Note that the level of detail presented is highly simplified. A truly realistic situation would involve many products, operations and responsibility centres but would not give any further insights into the basic concepts or procedures.

EXAMPLE 17.1

Alpha manufacturing company produces a single product, which is known as sigma. The product requires a single operation and the standard cost for this operation is presented in the following standard cost card:

Standard cost card for product sigma	(£)
Direct materials:	
2kg of A at £10 per kg	20.00
1kg of B at £15 per kg	15.00
Direct labour (three hours at £9 per hour)	27.00
Variable overhead (three hours at £2 per direct labour hour)	6.00
Total standard variable cost	68.00
Standard contribution margin	20.00
Standard selling price	88.00

Alpha Ltd plan to produce 10 000 units of sigma in the month of April and the budgeted costs based on the information contained in the standard cost card are as follows:

Budget based on the above standard costs and an output of 10 000 units	(£)	(£)	(£)
Sales (10 000 units of sigma at £88 per unit)			880 000
Direct materials:			
A: 20 000kg at £10 per kg	200 000		
B: 10 000kg at £15 per kg	150 000	350 000	
Direct labour (30 000 hours at £9 per hour)		270 000	
Variable overheads (30 000 hours at			
£2 per direct labour hour)		60 000	680 000
Budgeted contribution			200 000
Fixed overheads			120 000
Budgeted profit			80 000

Annual budgeted fixed overheads are £1 440 000 and are assumed to be incurred evenly throughout the year. The company *uses a variable costing system* for internal profit measurement purposes.
    The actual results for April are:

	(£)	(£)
Sales (9000 units at £90)		810 000
Direct materials:		
A: 19 000kg at £11 per kg	209 000	
B: 10 100kg at £14 per kg	141 400	
Direct labour (28 500 hours at £9.60 per hour)	273 600	
Variable overheads	52 000	676 000
Contribution		134 000
Fixed overheads		116 000
Profit		18 000

Manufacturing overheads are charged to production on the basis of direct labour hours. Actual production and sales for the period were 9000 units.

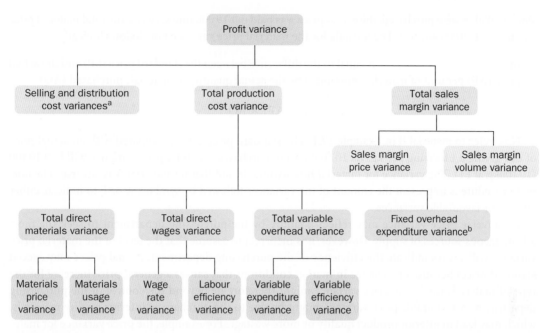

[a]Selling and distribution cost variances are not presented in this chapter. If activities are of a repetitive nature, standards can be established and variances can be calculated in a similar manner to production cost variances. If standards cannot be established, costs should be controlled by comparing budgeted and actual costs.

[b]With an absorption costing system, the summary of fixed overhead variances presented in Exhibit 17.5 would replace this box.

FIGURE 17.3
Variance analysis for a variable costing system

Figure 17.3 shows the breakdown of the profit variance (the difference between budgeted and actual profit) into the component cost and revenue variances that can be calculated for a standard variable costing system. We shall now calculate the variances set out in Figure 17.3 using the data presented in Example 17.1.

MATERIAL VARIANCES

The costs of the materials that are used in a manufactured product are determined by two basic factors: the price paid for the materials, and the quantity of materials used in production. This gives rise to the possibility that the actual cost will differ from the standard cost because the *actual price* paid will be different from the *standard price* and/or that the *actual quantity* of materials used will be different from the *standard quantity*. We can therefore calculate a price variance (called a material price variance for materials) and a quantity variance (called a material usage variance).

Material price variances

The starting point for calculating this variance is simply to compare the standard price per unit of materials with the actual price per unit. You should now read Example 17.1. You will see that the standard price for material A is £10 per kg, but the actual price paid was £11 per kg. The price variance is £1 per kg. This is of little consequence if the excess purchase price has been paid only for a small number of units or purchases. But the consequences are important if the excess purchase price has been paid for a large number of units, since the effect of the variance will be greater.

The difference between the standard material price and the actual price per unit should therefore be multiplied by the quantity of materials purchased. For material A, the price variance is £1 per unit; but since 19 000kg were purchased, the excess price was paid out 19 000 times. Hence the total material price variance is £19 000 adverse. The formula for the material price variance now follows logically:

the material price variance is equal to the difference between the standard price (SP) and the actual price (AP) per unit of materials multiplied by the actual quantity of materials purchased (AQ):

$$(SP - AP) \times AQ$$

Now refer to material B in Example 17.1. The standard price is £15, compared with an actual price of £14 giving a £1 saving per kg. As 10 100kg were purchased, the total price variance will be £10 100 (10 100kg at £1). The variance for material B is favourable and that for material A is adverse. The normal procedure is to present the amount of the variances followed by symbols A or F to indicate either adverse or favourable variances.

An adverse price variance may reflect a failure by the purchasing department to seek the most advantageous sources of supply. However, it is incorrect to assume that the level of the material price variance will always indicate the efficiency of the purchasing department. Actual prices may exceed standard prices because of a change in market conditions that causes a general price increase for the type of materials used. The price variance might therefore be beyond the control of the purchasing department. A favourable price variance might be due to the purchase of inferior quality materials, which may lead to inferior product quality or more wastage. For example, the price variance for material B is favourable, but we shall see in the next section that this is offset by excess usage. If the reason for this excess usage is the purchase of inferior quality materials then the material usage variance should be assigned to the purchasing department.

Calculation on quantity purchased or quantity used

It is important that variances are reported as quickly as possible so that any inefficiencies can be identified and remedial action taken. A problem occurs, however, with material purchases in that there may be a considerable delay before materials are actually used; materials may be purchased in one period and used in subsequent periods. For example, if 10 000 units of a material are purchased in period 1 at a price of £1 per unit over standard and 2000 units are used in each of periods 1 to 5, the following alternatives are available for calculating the price variance:

1 The full amount of the price variance of £10 000 is reported in *period 1* with quantity being defined as the *actual quantity purchased*.

2 The price variance is calculated with quantity being defined as the *actual quantity used*. The unit price variance of £1 is multiplied by the quantity used (i.e. 2000 units), which means that a price variance of £2000 will be reported for each of *periods 1 to 5*.

Method 1 is recommended, because the price variance can be reported in the period in which it is incurred and reporting of the total price variance is not delayed until months later when the materials are used. Also, adopting this approach enables corrective action to be taken earlier. For the sake of simplicity, we shall assume in Example 17.1 that the actual purchases are identical with the actual usage.

Material usage variance

The starting point for calculating this quantity variance is simply to compare the standard quantity that should have been used with the actual quantity which has been used. Refer again to Example 17.1. You will see that the standard usage for the production of one unit of sigma is 2kg for material A. As 9000 units of sigma are produced, 18 000kg of material A should have been used; however, 19 000kg are actually used, which means there has been an excess usage of 1000kg.

The importance of this excess usage depends on the price of the materials. For example, if the price is £0.01 per kg then an excess usage of 1000kg will not be very significant, but if the price is £10 per unit then an excess usage of 1000kg will be very significant indeed. It follows that to assess the importance of the excess usage, the variance should be expressed in monetary terms.

Should the standard material price per kg or the actual material price per kg be used to calculate the variance? The answer is the standard price. If the *actual* material price is used, the usage variance will be affected by the efficiency of the purchasing department, since any excess purchase price will be assigned to the excess usage. It is therefore necessary to remove the price effects from the usage variance calculation and this is achieved by valuing the variance at the standard price. Hence the 1000kg excess usage of material A is multiplied by the standard price of £10 per unit, which gives an adverse usage variance of £10 000. The formula for the variance is:

the material usage variance is equal to the difference between the standard quantity (SQ) required for actual production and the actual quantity (AQ) used multiplied by the standard material price (SP):

$$(SQ - AQ) \times SP$$

For material B, you will see from Example 17.1 that the standard quantity is 9000kg (9000 units × 1kg), but 10 100kg have been used. The excess usage of 1100kg is multiplied by the standard price of £15 per kg, which gives an adverse variance of £16 500. Note that the principles of flexible budgeting described in the previous chapter also apply here, with *standard quantity being based on actual production and not budgeted production*. This ensures that a manager is evaluated under the conditions in which he or she actually worked and not those envisaged at the time the budget was prepared.

The material usage variance is normally controllable by the manager of the appropriate production responsibility centre. Common causes of material usage variances include the careless handling of materials by production personnel, the purchase of inferior quality materials, pilferage, changes in quality control requirements or changes in methods of production. Separate material usage variances should be calculated for each type of material used and allocated to each responsibility centre.

Joint price usage variance

Note that the analysis of the material variance into the price and usage elements is not theoretically correct, since there may be a joint mutual price/quantity effect. The following information is extracted from Example 17.1 for material A:

1 18 000kg of material A are required, at a standard price of £10 per kg.

2 19 000kg are used, at a price of £11 per kg.

The purchasing officer might readily accept responsibility for the price variance of £1 per kg for 18 000kg, but may claim that the extra 1000kg at £1 is more the responsibility of the production manager. It may be argued that if the production manager had produced in accordance with the standard then the extra 1000kg would not have been needed.

The production manager, contrariwise, will accept responsibility for the 1000kg excess usage at a standard price of £10, but will argue that he should not be held accountable for the additional purchase price of £1 per unit.

One possible way of dealing with this would be to report the joint price/quantity variance of £1000 (1000kg at £1) separately and not charge it to either manager. In other words, the original price variance of £19 000 would be analysed as follows:

	(£)
1. Pure price variance (18 000kg at £1 per kg)	18 000A
2. Joint price/quantity variance (1 000kg at £1 per kg)	1 000A
	19 000A

Nevertheless, it is recommended that you adopt the approach outlined in the earlier section and calculate the material price variance by multiplying the difference between the standard and actual prices by the actual quantity, rather than the standard quantity. Adopting this approach results in the joint price/quantity variance being assigned to the materials price variance. This approach can be justified on the ground that the purchasing manager ought to be responsible for the efficient purchase of all material requirements, irrespective of whether or not the materials are used efficiently by the production departments.

Total material variance

From Figure 17.3, you will see that this variance is the total variance before it is analysed into the price and usage elements. The formula for the variance is:

> the **total material variance** is the difference between the standard material cost (SC) for the actual production and the actual cost (AC):

$$SC - AC$$

For material A, the standard material cost is £20 per unit (see Example 17.1), giving a total standard material cost of £180 000 (9000 units $\times$ £20). The actual cost is £209 000, and therefore the variance is £29 000 adverse. The price variance of £19 000 plus the usage variance of £10 000 agrees with the total material variance. Similarly, the total material variance for material B is £6400, consisting of a favourable price variance of £10 100 and an adverse usage variance of £16 500.

Note that if the price variance is calculated on the actual quantity *purchased* instead of the actual quantity *used*, the price variance plus the usage variance will agree with the total variance only when the quantity purchased is equal to the quantity that is used in the particular accounting period. Reconciling the price and usage variance with the total variance is merely a reconciliation exercise, and you should not be concerned if reconciliation of the sub-variances with the total variance is not possible.

LABOUR VARIANCES

The cost of labour is determined by the price paid for labour and the quantity of labour used. Thus a price variance (wage rate variance) and a quantity variance (labour efficiency variance) will also arise for labour.

Wage rate variance

The price (wage rate) variance is calculated by comparing the standard price per hour with the actual price paid per hour. In Example 17.1, the standard wage rate per hour is £9 and the actual wage rate is £9.60 per hour, giving a wage rate variance of £0.60 per hour. To determine the importance of the variance, it is necessary to ascertain how many times the excess payment of £0.60 per hour is paid. As 28 500 labour hours are used (see Example 17.1), we multiply 28 500 hours by £0.60. This gives an adverse wage rate variance of £17 100. The formula for the wage rate variance is:

> the **wage rate variance** is equal to the difference between the standard wage rate per hour (SR) and the actual wage rate (AR) multiplied by the actual number of hours worked (AH):

$$(SR - AR) \times AH$$

Note the similarity between this variance and the material price variance. Both variances multiply the difference between the standard price and the actual price paid for a unit of a resource by the actual quantity of resources used. The wage rate variance is probably the one that is least subject to control by management. In most cases, the variance is due to wage rate standards not being kept in line with changes in actual wage rates and for this reason it is not normally controllable by departmental managers.

Labour efficiency variance

The labour efficiency variance represents the quantity variance for direct labour. The quantity of labour that should be used for the actual output is expressed in terms of *standard hours produced*. In Example 17.1, the standard time for the production of one unit of sigma is three hours. Thus a production level of 9000 units results in an output of 27 000 standard hours. In other words, working at the prescribed level of efficiency, it should take 27 000 hours to produce 9000 units. However, 28 500 direct labour hours are actually required to produce this output, which means that 1500 excess direct labour hours are used. We multiply the excess direct labour hours by the *standard* wage rate to calculate the variance. This gives an adverse variance of £13500. The formula for calculating the labour efficiency variance is:

the labour efficiency variance is equal to the difference between the standard labour hours for actual production (SH) and the actual labour hours worked (AH) during the period multiplied by the standard wage rate per hour (SR):

$$(SH - AH) \times SR$$

This variance is similar to the material usage variance. Both variances multiply the difference between the standard quantity and actual quantity of resources consumed by the standard price. The labour efficiency variance is normally controllable by the manager of the appropriate production responsibility centre and may be due to a variety of reasons. For example, the use of inferior quality materials, different grades of labour, failure to maintain machinery in proper condition, the introduction of new equipment or tools and changes in the production processes will all affect the efficiency of labour. An efficiency variance may not always be controllable by a production manager; it may be due, for example, to poor production scheduling by the planning department, or to a change in quality control standards.

Total labour variance

From Figure 17.3, you will see that this variance represents the total variance before analysis into the price and quantity elements. The formula for the variance is:

the total labour variance is the difference between the standard labour cost (SC) for the actual production and the actual labour cost (AC):

$$SC - AC$$

In Example 17.1, the actual production was 9000 units, and, with a standard labour cost of £27 per unit, the standard cost is £243 000. The actual cost is £273 600, which gives an adverse variance of £30 600.

VARIABLE OVERHEAD VARIANCES

A total variable overhead variance is calculated in the same way as the total direct labour and material variances. In Example 17.1, the output is 9000 units and the standard variable overhead cost is £6 *per unit* produced. The standard cost of production for variable overheads is thus £54 000. The actual variable overheads incurred are £52 000, giving a favourable variance of £2000. The formula for the variance is:

the total variable overhead variance is the difference between the standard variable overheads charged to production (SC) and the actual variable overheads incurred (AC):

$$SC - AC$$

Where variable overheads vary with direct labour or machine hours of *input* the total variable overhead variance will be due to one or both of the following:

1 A *price* variance arising from actual expenditure being different from budgeted expenditure.

2 A *quantity* variance arising from actual direct labour or machine hours of input being different from the hours of input, which *should* have been used.

These reasons give rise to the two sub-variances, which are shown in Figure 17.3: the variable overhead expenditure variance and the variable overhead efficiency variance.

Variable overhead expenditure variance

To compare the actual overhead expenditure with the budgeted expenditure, it is necessary to flex the budget (see Chapter 16 for an explanation of flexible budgeting). Because it is assumed in Example 17.1 that variable overheads will vary with direct labour hours of *input*, the budget is flexed on this basis. Actual variable overhead expenditure is £52000, resulting from 28500 direct labour hours of input. For this level of activity, variable overheads of £57000, which consist of 28500 input hours at £2 per hour, should have been spent. Spending was £5000 less than it should have been and the result is a favourable variance.

If we compare the budgeted and the actual overhead costs for 28500 direct labour hours of input, we shall ensure that any efficiency content is removed from the variance. This means that any difference must be due to actual variable overhead spending being different from the budgeted variable overhead spending. The formula for the variance is:

the **variable overhead expenditure variance** is equal to the difference between the budgeted flexed variable overheads (BFVO) for the actual direct labour hours of input and the actual variable overhead costs incurred (AVO):

$$BFVO - AVO$$

Because it is assumed that variable overheads vary with the actual direct labour hours of input the budgeted flexed variable overheads (BFVO) has been derived from multiplying the actual quantity of direct labour hours of input by the standard variable overhead rate.

Variable overhead represents the aggregation of a large number of individual items, such as indirect labour, indirect materials, electricity, maintenance and so on. The variable overhead variance can arise because the prices of individual items have changed. It can also be affected by how efficiently the individual variable overhead items are used. Waste or inefficiency, such as using more kilowatt hours of power than should have been used, will increase the cost of power and, thus, the total cost of variable overhead. The variable overhead expenditure on its own is therefore not very informative. Any meaningful analysis of this variance requires a comparison of the actual expenditure for each individual item of variable overhead expenditure against the budget.

Variable overhead efficiency variance

In Example 17.1, it is assumed that variable overheads vary with direct labour hours of input. The variable overhead efficiency variance arises because 28500 direct labour hours of input were required to produce 9000 units. Working at the prescribed level of efficiency, it should take 27000 hours to produce 9000 units of output. Therefore an extra 1500 direct labour hours of input were required. Because variable overheads are assumed to vary with direct labour hours of input, an additional £3000 (1500 hours at £2) variable overheads will be incurred. The formula for the variance is:

the **variable overhead efficiency variance** is the difference between the standard hours of output (SH) and the actual hours of input (AH) for the period multiplied by the standard variable overhead rate (SR):

$$(SH - AH) \times SR$$

You should note that if it is assumed that variable overheads vary with direct labour hours of input, this variance is identical to the labour efficiency variance, apart from the fact that the standard variable overhead rate is used instead of the wage rate.

A GENERIC ROUTINE APPROACH TO VARIANCE ANALYSIS FOR VARIABLE COSTS

In our discussion of each of the variable cost variances in the preceding sections, a theoretical approach was adopted that began by explaining the fundamental meaning of each variance so that you could logically deduce the formula for each variance. Although it is the author's recommendation that you adopt this approach, feedback indicates that some readers prefer to use an alternative routine generic approach that is presented in Appendix 17.A1. You should only read Appendix 17.A1 if you have found the variance calculations is the previous section confusing and wish to adopt the alternative routine generic approach.

FIXED OVERHEAD EXPENDITURE OR SPENDING VARIANCE

The final production variance shown in Figure 17.3 is the fixed overhead expenditure variance. With a variable costing system, fixed manufacturing overheads are not unitized and allocated to products. Instead, the total fixed overheads for the period are charged as an expense to the period in which they are incurred. Fixed overheads are assumed to remain unchanged in the short term in response to changes in the level of activity, but they may change in response to other factors. For example, price increases may cause expenditure on fixed overheads to increase. The fixed overhead expenditure variance therefore explains the difference between budgeted fixed overheads and the actual fixed overheads incurred. The formula for the fixed overhead expenditure variance is the difference between the budgeted fixed overheads (BFO) and the actual fixed overhead (AFO) spending:

$$BFO - AFO$$

In Example 17.1, budgeted fixed overhead expenditure is £120000 and actual fixed overhead spending £116000. Therefore the fixed overhead expenditure variance is £4000. Whenever the actual fixed overheads are less than the budgeted fixed overheads, the variance will be favourable. The total of the fixed overhead expenditure variance on its own is not particularly informative. Any meaningful analysis of this variance requires a comparison of the actual expenditure for each individual item of fixed overhead expenditure against the budget. The difference may be due to a variety of causes, such as changes in salaries paid to employees, or the appointment of additional supervisors. Only by comparing individual items of expenditure and ascertaining the reasons for the variances can one determine whether the variance is controllable or uncontrollable. Generally, this variance is likely to be uncontrollable in the short term.

SALES VARIANCES

Sales variances can be used to analyse the performance of the sales function or revenue centres on broadly similar terms to those for manufacturing costs. The most significant feature of sales variance calculations is that they are calculated in terms of profit or contribution margins rather than sales values. Consider Example 17.2.

You will see that when the variances are calculated on the basis of sales value, it is necessary to compare the budgeted sales *value* of £110000 with the actual sales of £120000. This gives a favourable variance of £10000. This calculation, however, ignores the impact of the sales effort on profit. The budgeted profit contribution is £40000, which consists of 10000 units at £4 per unit, but the actual impact of the

EXAMPLE 17.2

The budgeted sales for a company are £110000 consisting of 10000 units at £11 per unit. The standard cost per unit is £7. Actual sales are £120000 (12000 units at £10 per unit) and the actual cost per unit is £7.

sales effort in terms of profit margins indicates a profit contribution of £36000, which consists of 12000 units at £3 per unit, indicating an adverse variance of £4000.

If we examine Example 17.2, we can see that the selling prices have been reduced and that this has led not only to an increase in the total sales revenue but also to a reduction in total profits. The objective of the selling function is to influence total profits favourably. Thus a more meaningful performance measure will be obtained by comparing the results of the sales function in terms of profit or contribution margins rather than sales revenues. Let us now calculate the sales variances for a standard variable costing system from the information contained in Example 17.1.

Total sales margin variance

Where a variable costing approach is adopted, the total sales *margin* variance seeks to identify the influence of the sales function on the difference between budget and actual profit contribution.

REAL WORLD VIEWS 17.2

The effect of standards on product and service quality

Setting standards in an organization may be primarily to assist in the calculation of a standard cost for the product or service for management accounting purposes. Standards are also relevant for operational and customer service managers as they may affect the manufacture of the product or the quality of the service.

Take McDonald's, Burger King or Coca-Cola for example. All three companies produce products that adhere to standard ingredients, albeit with some minimal regional variation. A BigMac or Whopper for example, will contain a beef pattie that is manufactured to an exact uncooked weight. Similarly, every bottle of Coca-Cola will contain a similar amount of cola concentrate. As the ingredients are standardized according to 'recipes', a standard cost can be readily calculated and used for cost control and performance reporting. Perhaps more importantly, the customer is confident of getting a similar product on each purchase.

In comparison, consider a car-hire company like Hertz or a bank like HSBC. Most service

organizations will have a customer care (HSBC) or reservations (Hertz) call centre. Staff at these centres will have a standard customer handling time to adhere to — perhaps three minutes. It is not always possible to deal with customer issues or make a sale in the allotted time. Exceeding the standard handling time ultimately increases cost as more staff may be needed to handle customer call volume. By the same token, by strictly adhering to a standard handling time, customer satisfaction and quality of service may be reduced. Thus, in a service company scenario, a fine balance between standards and quality must be achieved to ensure customer satisfaction in the longer term.

Discussion points

1 Do you think it is plausible to set standards for delivery of services, which are primarily dictated by cost?

2 Is it possible to measure the delivery of a service (e.g. a mortgage application) against a set standard?

In Example 17.1, the budgeted contribution to fixed overheads and profit is £200 000, which consists of budgeted sales of 10 000 units at a contribution of £20 per unit. This is compared with a contribution derived from the actual sales volume of 9000 units. Because the sales function is responsible for the sales volume and the unit selling price, but not the unit manufacturing costs, *the standard cost of sales and not the actual cost of sales is deducted from the actual sales revenue*. The calculation of the contribution for ascertaining the total sales margin variance will therefore be as follows:

	(£)
Actual sales revenue (9000 units at £90)	810 000
Standard variable cost of sales for actual sales volume (9000 units at £68)	612 000
Profit contribution margin	198 000

To calculate the total sales margin variance, we deduct the budgeted contribution for the period of £200 000 from the above profit contribution of £198 000. This gives an adverse variance of £2000.

The formula for calculating the variance is as follows:

the **total sales margin variance** is the difference between actual sales revenue (ASR) less the standard variable cost of sales (SCOS) and the budgeted contribution (BC):

$$(ASR - SCOS) - BC$$

Using the standard cost of sales in the above formula and calculation ensures that production variances do not distort the calculation of the sales variances. This means that sales variances arise only because of changes in those variables controlled by the sales function (i.e. selling prices and sales quantity). Figure 17.3 indicates that it is possible to analyse the total sales margin variance into two sub-variances – a sales margin price variance and a sales margin volume variance.

Sales margin price variance

In Example 17.1, the actual selling price is £90 and the standard selling price is £88. In order to ensure that production variances do not distort the calculation of the sales margin price variance, the standard unit variable cost of £68 should be deducted from both the actual and the standard selling prices. This gives a contribution of £22 that is derived from the actual selling price and a contribution of £20 derived from the standard selling price. Because the actual sales volume is 9000 units, the increase in selling price means that the increase in contribution of £2 per unit is obtained 9000 times giving a favourable sales margin variance of £18 000. In formula terms, the variance is calculated as follows:

$$[(\text{Actual selling price} - \text{standard variable cost}) - (\text{Standard selling price} - \text{standard variable cost})] \times \text{Actual sales volume}$$

Since the standard variable cost is deducted from both the actual and standard selling price, the above formula can be simplified by omitting standard variable cost so that:

the **sales margin price variance** is the difference between the actual selling price (ASP) and the standard selling price (SSP) multiplied by the actual sales volume (AV):

$$(ASP - SSP) \times AV$$

Sales margin volume variance

To ascertain the effect of changes in the sales volume on the difference between the budgeted and the actual contribution, we must compare the budgeted sales volume with the actual sales volume. You will see from Example 17.1 that the budgeted sales are 10 000 units but the actual sales are 9000 units and to enable us to determine the impact of this reduction in sales volume on profit, we must multiply the 1000 units by the standard contribution margin of £20. This gives an adverse variance of £20 000.

The use of the standard margin (standard selling price less standard cost) ensures that the volume variance will not be affected by any *changes* in the actual selling prices. The formula for calculating the variance is:

the sales margin volume variance is the difference between the actual sales volume (AV) and the budgeted volume (BV) multiplied by the standard contribution margin (SM):

$$(AV - BV) \times SM$$

Difficulties in interpreting sales margin variances

The favourable sales margin price variance of £18 000 plus the adverse volume variance of £20 000 add up to the total adverse sales margin variance of £2000. It may be argued that it is not very meaningful to analyse the total sales margin variance into price and volume components, since changes in selling prices are likely to affect sales volume. A favourable price variance will tend to be associated with an adverse volume variance and vice versa. It may be unrealistic to expect to sell more than the budgeted volume when selling prices have increased.

A further problem with sales variances is that the variances may arise from external factors and may not be controllable by management. For example, changes in selling prices may be a reaction to changes in selling prices of competitors. Alternatively, a reduction in both selling prices and sales volume may be the result of an economic recession that was not foreseen when the budget was prepared. For control and performance appraisal, it may be preferable to compare actual market share with target market share for each product. In addition, the trend in market shares should be monitored and selling prices should be compared with competitors' prices.

REAL WORLD VIEWS 17.3

Standard costing in healthcare

Meditech South Africa (Pty) Ltd provides software solutions to meet the information needs of healthcare organizations in Africa and the Middle East. According to their website, the software can encompass all areas of healthcare from doctor's offices to hospitals. While their software products are generally patient centric, healthcare cost management also features in some of their products.

For example, the software designed for hospitals includes some functionality for finance managers on cost accounting. The functions include budgets and standard cost definition. Costs can be defined for labour, materials and overhead and can draw cost information from other Meditech software modules. With standard costs defined, actual costs can be compared to standard/budget. Standard costs can also be used as a basis to reimburse costs from health insurers, or actual costs of providing the services can be compared to reimbursement levels.

The software also includes several reports such as variance reports by department, labour cost variances and flexible budget reports – all of which are useful for budgetary control and future budget preparation. Integration with other Meditech software modules and other systems implies cost data can be calculated at a departmental, procedure or patient level. For example, the cost accounting module can integrate with payroll systems 'report on labour variance using labour productive hours and dollars'.

Questions

1 Do you think standards can be applied to procedures in hospitals?

2 Do you think standard cost variance reports are useful in healthcare?

Reference

Meditech website at www.meditech.co.za/products /hospitals/executives-and-finance/cost-accounting

STANDARD ABSORPTION COSTING

RECONCILING BUDGETED PROFIT AND ACTUAL PROFIT

Top management will be interested in the reason for the actual profit being different from the budgeted profit. By adding the favourable production and sales variances to the budgeted profit and deducting the adverse variances, the reconciliation of budgeted and actual profit shown in Exhibit 17.4 can be presented in respect of Example 17.1.

Example 17.1 assumes that Alpha Ltd produces a single product consisting of a single operation and that the activities are performed by one responsibility centre. In practice, most companies make many products, which require operations to be carried out in different responsibility centres. A reconciliation statement such as that presented in Exhibit 17.4 will therefore normally represent a summary of the variances for many responsibility centres. The reconciliation statement thus represents a broad picture to top management that explains the major reasons for any difference between the budgeted and actual profits.

STANDARD ABSORPTION COSTING

The external financial accounting regulations in most countries require that companies should value inventories at full absorption manufacturing cost. The effect of this is that fixed overheads should be allocated to products and included in the closing inventory valuations. With the variable costing system, fixed overheads are not allocated to products. Instead, the total fixed costs are charged as an expense to the period in which they are incurred. (For a discussion of the differences between variable and absorption costing systems, you should refer back to Chapter 7.) With an absorption costing system, an additional fixed overhead variance is calculated. This variance is called a volume variance. In addition, the sales margin variances must be expressed in unit *profit* margins instead of *contribution* margins. These variances are not particularly useful for control purposes but are required for profit measurement and inventory valuation purposes. If your course does not relate to the disposition of variances to meet financial accounting requirements, you can omit pages 451–455.

With a standard absorption costing system, predetermined fixed overhead rates are established by dividing annual budgeted fixed overheads by the budgeted annual level of activity. We shall assume that, in respect of Example 17.1, budgeted annual fixed overheads are £1 440 000 (£120 000 per month) and

EXHIBIT 17.4 Reconciliation of budgeted and actual profits for a standard variable costing system

	(£)	(£)	(£)
Budgeted net profit			80 000
Sales variances:			
Sales margin price	18 000F		
Sales margin volume	20 000A	2 000A	
Direct cost variances:			
Material: Price	8 900A		
Usage	26 500A	35 400A	
Labour: Rate	17 100A		
Efficiency	13 500A	30 600A	
Manufacturing overhead variances:			
Fixed overhead expenditure	4 000F		
Variable overhead expenditure	5 000F		
Variable overhead efficiency	3 000A	6 000F	62 000A
Actual profit			18 000

budgeted annual activity is 120 000 units (10 000 units per month). The fixed overhead rate *per unit* of output is calculated as follows:

$$\frac{\text{budgeted fixed overheads (£1 440 000)}}{\text{budgeted activity (120 000 units)}} = £12 \text{ per unit of sigma produced}$$

Where different products are produced, units of output should be converted to standard hours. In Example 17.1, the output of one unit of sigma requires three direct labour hours. Therefore, the budgeted output in standard hours is 360 000 hours (120 000 × three hours). The fixed overhead rate *per standard hour* of output is:

$$\frac{\text{budgeted fixed overheads (£1 440 000)}}{\text{budgeted standard hours (360 000)}} = £4 \text{ per standard hour}$$

By multiplying the number of hours required to produce one unit of sigma by £4 per hour, we also get a fixed overhead allocation of £12 for one unit of sigma (three hours × £4). *For the remainder of this chapter, output will be measured in terms of standard hours produced.*

We shall assume that production is expected to occur evenly throughout the year. Monthly budgeted production output is therefore 10 000 units, or 30 000 standard direct labour hours. At the planning stage, an input of 30 000 direct labour hours (10 000 × three hours) will also be planned, as the company will budget at the level of efficiency specified in the calculation of the product standard cost. Thus the *budgeted hours of input* and the *budgeted hours of output* (i.e. the standard hours for the products produced) will be the same at the planning stage. In contrast, the *actual* hours of input may differ from the standard hours for the actual output of the products produced. In Example 17.1, the actual direct labour hours of input are 28 500, and 27 000 standard hours should have been used for the products actually produced.

With an absorption costing system, fixed overheads of £108 000 (27 000 standard hours for an actual output of 9000 units at a standard rate of £4 per hour) will have been charged/allocated to products for the month of April. Actual fixed overhead expenditure was £116 000. Therefore, £8 000 (£116 000 – £108 000) has not been allocated to products. In other words, there has been an under-recovery of fixed overheads. Where the fixed overheads allocated to products exceeds the overhead incurred, there will be an over-recovery of fixed overheads. The under- or over-recovery of fixed overheads represents the total fixed overhead variance for the period. The total fixed overhead variance is calculated using a formula similar to those for the total direct labour and total direct materials variances:

the total fixed overhead variance is the difference between the standard fixed overhead charged to production (SC) and the actual fixed overhead incurred (AC):

$$\text{SC (£108 000)} - \text{AC (£116 000)} = £8000\text{A}$$

Note that the standard cost for the actual production can be calculated by measuring production in standard hours of output (27 000 hours × £4 per hour) or units of output (9000 units × £12 per unit).

The under- or over-recovery of fixed overheads (i.e. the fixed overhead variance) arises because the fixed overhead rate is calculated by dividing *budgeted* fixed overheads by *budgeted* output. If actual output or actual fixed overhead expenditure differs from budget, an under- or over-recovery of fixed overheads will arise. In other words, the under- or over-recovery may be due to the following:

1 A fixed overhead expenditure variance of £4000 arising from actual *expenditure* (£116 000) being different from budgeted *expenditure* (£120 000).

2 A fixed overhead volume variance arising from actual *production* differing from budgeted *production*.

The fixed overhead expenditure variance also occurs with a variable costing system. The favourable variance of £4000 was explained earlier in this chapter. The volume variance arises only when *inventories are valued on an absorption costing basis*.

Volume variance

This variance seeks to identify the portion of the total fixed overhead variance that is due to actual production being different from budgeted production. In Example 17.1, the standard fixed overhead rate of £4 per hour is calculated on the basis of a normal activity of 30 000 standard hours per month. Only when standard hours for the products actually produced are 30 000 will the budgeted monthly fixed overheads of £120 000 be exactly recovered. Actual output, however, is only 9 000 units or 27 000 standard hours. The fact that the actual production is 3000 standard hours less than the budgeted output hours will lead to a failure to recover £12 000 fixed overhead (3000 hours at £4 fixed overhead rate per hour). The formula for the variance is:

the **volume variance** is the difference between the standard hours for the actual production (SH) and the budgeted hours for the budgeted production (BH) for a period multiplied by the standard fixed overhead rate (SR):

$$(SH - BH) \times SR$$

The volume variance reflects the fact that fixed overheads do not fluctuate in relation to output in the short term. Whenever actual production is less than budgeted production, the fixed overhead charged to production will be less than the budgeted cost and the volume variance will be adverse. Conversely, if the actual production is greater than the budgeted production, the volume variance will be favourable.

When the adverse volume variance of £12 000 is netted with the favourable expenditure variance of £4000, the result is equal to the total fixed overhead adverse variance of £8000. It is also possible to analyse the volume variance into two further sub-variances — the volume efficiency variance and the capacity variance.

Volume efficiency variance

If we wish to identify the reasons for the volume variance, we may ask why the actual production was different from the budgeted production. One possible reason may be that the labour force worked at a different level of efficiency from that anticipated in the budget.

The actual number of direct labour hours of input was 28 500. Hence one would have expected 28 500 hours of output (i.e. standard hours produced) from this input, but only 27 000 standard hours were actually produced. Thus one reason for the failure to meet the budgeted output was that output in standard hours was 1500 hours fewer than it should have been. If the labour force had worked at the prescribed level of efficiency, an additional 1500 standard hours would have been produced and this would have led to a total of £6000 (£1500 hours at £4 per standard hour) fixed overheads being absorbed. The inefficiency of labour is therefore one of the reasons why the actual production was less than the budgeted production and this gives an adverse variance of £6000. The formula for the variance is:

the **volume efficiency variance** is the difference between the standard hours of output (SH) and the actual hours of input (AH) for the period multiplied by the standard fixed overhead rate (SR):

$$(SH - AH) \times SR$$

You may have noted that the physical content of this variance is a measure of labour efficiency and is identical with the labour efficiency variance. Consequently, the reasons for this variance will be identical with those previously described for the labour efficiency variance.

Volume capacity variance

This variance indicates the second reason why the actual production might be different from the budgeted production. The budget is based on the assumption that the direct labour hours of input will be 30 000 hours, but the actual hours of input are 28 500 hours. The difference of 1500 hours reflects the fact that the company has failed to utilize the planned capacity. If we assume that the 1500 hours would have been worked at the prescribed level of efficiency, an additional 1500 standard hours could have been produced and an additional £6000 fixed overhead could have been absorbed. Hence the capacity variance is £6000 adverse. Whereas the volume efficiency variance indicated a failure to utilize capacity *efficiently*, the volume capacity variance indicates a failure to utilize capacity *at all*. The formula is:

the **volume capacity variance** is the difference between the actual hours of input (AH) and the budgeted hours of input (BH) for the period multiplied by the standard fixed overhead rate (SR):

$$(AH - BH) \times SR$$

A failure to achieve the budgeted capacity may be for a variety of reasons. Machine breakdowns, material shortages, poor production scheduling, labour disputes and a reduction in sales demand are all possible causes of an adverse volume capacity variance. The volume efficiency variance is £6000 adverse and the volume capacity variance is also £6000 adverse. When these two variances are added together, they agree with the fixed overhead volume variance of £12000. Exhibit 17.5 summarizes the variances we have calculated in this section.

You should note that the volume variance and two sub-variances (capacity and efficiency) are sometimes restated in non-monetary terms as follows:

$$\text{production volume ratio} = \frac{\text{standard hours of actual output (27000)}}{\text{budgeted hours of output (30000)}} \times 100$$

$$= 90\%$$

$$\text{production efficiency ratio} = \frac{\text{standard hours of actual output (27000)}}{\text{actual hours worked (28500)}} \times 100$$

$$= 94.7\%$$

$$\text{capacity usage ratio} = \frac{\text{actual hours worked (28500)}}{\text{budgeted hours of input (30000)}} \times 100$$

$$= 95\%$$

EXHIBIT 17.5 Diagram of fixed overhead variances

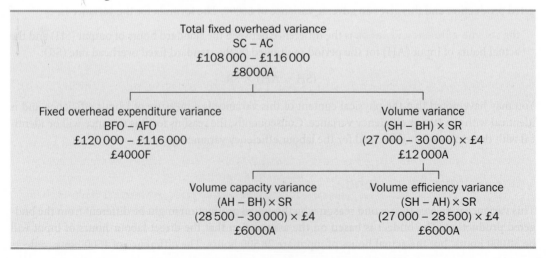

EXHIBIT 17.6 Reconciliation of budgeted and actual profit for a standard absorption costing system

	(£)	(£)	(£)	(£)
Budgeted net profit				80 000
Sales variances:				
Sales margin price		18 000F		
Sales margin volume		8 000A	10 000F	
Direct cost variances:				
Material – Price: Material A	19 000A			
Material B	10 100F	8 900A		
– Usage: Material A	10 000A			
Material B	16 500A	26 500A	35 400A	
Labour – Rate		17 100A		
Efficiency		13 500A	30 600A	
Manufacturing overhead variances:				
Fixed – Expenditure	4 000F			
Volume	12 000A	8 000A		
Variable – Expenditure	5 000F			
Efficiency	3 000A	2 000F	6 000A	62 000A
Actual profit				18 000

RECONCILIATION OF BUDGETED AND ACTUAL PROFIT FOR A STANDARD ABSORPTION COSTING SYSTEM

The reconciliation of the budgeted and actual profits is shown in Exhibit 17.6. You will see that the reconciliation statement is identical with the variable costing reconciliation statement, apart from the fact that the absorption costing statement includes the fixed overhead volume variance and values the sales margin volume variance at the standard profit margin per unit instead of the contribution per unit. If you refer back to Example 17.1 (page 440), you will see that the contribution margin for sigma is £20 per unit sold whereas the profit margin per unit after deducting fixed overhead cost (£12 per unit) is £8. Multiplying the difference in budgeted and actual sales volumes of 1000 units by the standard profit margin gives a sales volume margin variance of £8000. Note that the sales margin price variance is identical for both systems.

SUMMARY

The following items relate to the learning objectives listed at the beginning of the chapter.

● **Explain how a standard costing system operates.**

Standard costing is most suited to an organization whose activities consist of a series of repetitive operations and the input required to produce each unit of output can be specified. A standard costing system involves the following: (a) the standard costs for the actual output are recorded for each operation for each responsibility centre; (b) actual costs for each operation are traced to each responsibility centre; (c) the standard and actual costs are compared; (d) variances are investigated and corrective action is taken where appropriate; and (e) standards are monitored and adjusted to reflect changes in standard usage and/or prices.

● **Explain how standard costs are set.**

Standards should be set for the quantities and prices of materials, labour and services to be consumed in performing each operation associated with a product. Product standard costs are derived by listing and adding the standard costs of operations required to produce a particular product. Two approaches are used for setting standard costs. First, past historical records can be used to estimate labour and material usage. Second, standards can be set based on engineering studies. With engineering studies, a detailed study of each operation is undertaken under controlled conditions, based on high levels of efficiency, to ascertain the quantities of labour and materials required. Target prices are then applied based on efficient purchasing to ascertain the standard costs.

● **Explain the meaning of standard hours produced.**

It is not possible to measure output in terms of units produced for a department making several different products or operations. This problem is overcome by ascertaining the amount of time, working under efficient operating conditions, it should take to make each product. This time calculation is called standard hours produced. Standard hours thus represents an output measure that acts as a common denominator for adding together the production of unlike items.

● **Identify and describe the purposes of a standard costing system.**

Standard costing systems can be used for the following purposes: (a) providing a prediction of future costs that can be used for decision-making; (b) providing a challenging target which individuals are motivated to achieve; (c) providing a reliable and convenient source of data for budget preparation; (d) acting as a control device by highlighting those activities that do not conform to plan and thus alerting managers to those situations that may be 'out of control' and in need of corrective action; and (e) simplifying the task of tracing costs to products for profit measurement and inventory valuation purpose.

● **Calculate labour, material, overhead and sales margin variances and reconcile actual profit with budgeted profit.**

To reconcile actual profit with budget profit, the favourable variances are added to the budgeted profit and adverse variances are deducted. The end result should be the actual profit. A summary of the formulae for the computation of the variances is presented in Exhibit 17.7. In each case, the formula is presented so that a positive variance is favourable and a negative variance unfavourable. Alternatively, you can use the routine generic approach shown in Appendix 17.1.

● **Identify the causes of labour, material, overhead and sales margin variances.**

Quantities cost variances arise because the actual quantity of resources consumed exceed actual usage. Examples include excess usage of materials and labour arising from the usage of inferior materials, careless handling of materials and failure to maintain machinery in proper condition. Price variances arise when the actual prices paid for resources exceed the standard prices. Examples include the failure of the purchasing function to seek the most efficient sources of supply or the use of a different grade of labour from that incorporated in the standard costs.

● **Distinguish between standard variable costing and standard absorption costing.**

With a standard variable costing system, fixed overheads are not allocated to products. Sales margin variances are therefore reported in terms of contribution margins and a single fixed overhead variance, that is, the fixed overhead expenditure variance is reported. With a standard absorption costing system, fixed overheads are allocated to products and this process leads to the creation of a fixed overhead volume variance and the reporting of sales margin variances measured in terms of profit margins. The fixed overhead volume variance is not particularly helpful for cost control purposes, but this variance is required for financial accounting purposes.

EXHIBIT 17.7 Summary of the formulae for the computation of the variances

The following variances are reported for both variable and absorption costing systems:

Materials and labour

1   Material price
    variance
    = (standard price per unit of material − actual price) × quantity of
    materials purchased

2   Material usage
    variance
    = (standard quantity of materials for actual production − actual
    quantity used) × standard price per unit

3   Total materials
    cost variance
    = (actual production × standard material cost per unit of
    production) − actual materials cost

4   Wage rate variance
    = (standard wage rate per hour − actual wage rate) × actual labour
    hours worked

5   Labour efficiency
    variance
    = (standard quantity of labour hours for actual production
    − actual labour hours) × standard wage rate

6   Total labour cost
    variance
    = (actual production × standard labour cost per unit of production)
    − actual labour cost

Fixed production overhead

7   Fixed overhead
    expenditure
    = budgeted fixed overheads − actual fixed overheads

Variable production overhead

8   Variable overhead
    expenditure variance
    = (budgeted variable overheads br actual input volume
    − actual variable overhead cost)

9   Variable overhead
    efficiency variance
    = (standard quantity of input hours for actual production
    − actual input hours) × variable overhead rate

10 Total variable
    overhead variance
    = (actual production × standard variable overhead rate per unit)
    − actual variable overhead cost

Sales margins

11 Sales margin
    price variance
    = (actual selling price − budgeted selling price)
    × actual sales volume

12 Sales margin
    volume variance
    = (actual sales volume − budgeted sales volume)
    × standard contribution margin

13 Total sales margin
    variance
    = (actual sales revenue − standard variable cost of sales)
    − total budgeted contribution

*With a standard absorption costing system, profit margins are used instead of contribution margins to
calculate the sales margin variances and the following additional variances can be reported:*

14 Fixed overhead
    volume variance
    = (Standard hours for actual production − budgeted hours for
    budgeted production) × standard fixed overhead rate

15 Volume efficiency
    variance
    = (standard quantity of input hours for actual production
    − actual input hours) × standard fixed overhead rate

16 Volume capacity
    variance
    = (actual hours of input − budgeted hours of input)
    × standard fixed overhead rate

17 Total fixed overhead
    variance
    = (actual production × standard fixed overhead rate per unit)
    − actual fixed overhead cost

APPENDIX 17.1: A GENERIC ROUTINE APPROACH TO VARIANCE ANALYSIS

In this appendix an alternative approach is presented for calculating the materials, labour and variable cost variances. The disadvantage with adopting this alternative approach is that you will not have a theoretical understanding of each variance. The advantage of the alternative approach is its simplicity because all of the variable cost variances can be derived from a single worksheet. You should therefore only read this section and Exhibit 17.A1 if you found the theoretical approach confusing and your preference is to use the generic approach.

To compute the price variances (material price, wage rate and variable overhead expenditure variances) we noted that the price variances were due to the differences between the standard prices (SP) and the actual prices (AP) multiplied by the actual quantity (AQ) of the resource used giving the formula:

$$(SP - AP) \times AQ \text{ which can be restated as:}$$
$$(AQ \times SP) - (AQ \times AP)$$

The first term in the above formula is entered in the first column of Exhibit 17.A1 and the second term is entered in the second column so that the variance is the difference between columns 1 and 2. Adopting this approach for material A the actual quantity of materials purchased (19 000kg) at the standard price (£10) is entered in column 1 and the actual quantity of materials purchased (19 000kg) at the actual price (£11) is entered in column 2. The difference between columns 1 and 2 is the adverse price variance of £19 000 (£190 000 − £209 000). If you now refer to Exhibit 17.A1 you will see that the same approach is used to compute the price variances for labour and variable overhead. All of the variances are derived from the differences between columns 1 and 2. In order to present a generic approach the terms 'actual

EXHIBIT 17.A1 Variance analysis adopting the generic routine approach

	(1) Actual quantity of inputs at standard price (AQ × SP)	(2) Actual quantity of inputs at actual price (AQ × AP)	(3) Standard inputs required for actual output at standard prices (SQ × SP)
	Price variance = (1 − 2)		Quantity variance (3 − 1)
Material A price and usage variances	19 000 kg × £10 = £190 000	19 000 kg × £11 = £209 000 = £19 000A	(9 000 × 2 kg) × £10 = £180 000 = £10 000A
Material B price and usage variances	10 100 kg × £15 = £151 500	10 100 kg × £14 = £141 400 = £10 100F	(9 000 × 1 kg) × £15 = £135 000 = £16 500A
Wage rate and labour efficiency variance	28 500 hours × £9 = £256 500	28 500 hours × £9.60 = £273 600 = £17 100A	(9 000 × 3 hours) × £9 = £243 000 = £13 500A
Variable overhead expenditure and efficiency variance	28 500 hours × £2 = £57 000	£52 000 = £5 000F	(9 000 × 3 hours) × £2 = £54 000 = £3 000A

Total variances (3 − 2)
Material A (£180 000 − £209 000) = £29 000A
Material B (£135 000 − £141 400) = £6 400A
Labour (£243 000 − £273 600) = £30 600A
Variable overheads (£54 000 − £52 000) = £2 000F

quantity of materials purchased' and 'actual hours' have been replaced with the generic term 'actual quantity of inputs' in Exhibit 17.A1.

We shall now calculate the quantity variances (material usage, labour and overhead efficiency) using the generic approach. Look at the material usage variance. We used the following formula:

$$(SQ - AQ) \times SP \text{ which can be restated as:}$$
$$(SQ \times SP) - (AQ \times SP)$$

The first term in the above formula is entered in the third column of Exhibit 17.A1 and the second term is already entered in the first column so the variance is the difference between columns 3 and 1. Adopting this approach for material A the standard quantity required for the actual production (9000 × 2kg) at the standard price (£10) is entered in column 3 and the actual quantity used (19 000kg) at the standard price (£10) is entered in column 1. The difference between column 3 and column 1 is the adverse usage variance of £10 000 (£180 000 − £190 000). You will see by referring to Exhibit 17.A1 that the same approach has also been used to calculate the usage variances for labour and variable overheads (labour and variable overhead efficiency). All of the quantity variances are therefore derived from the differences between columns 3 and 1.

In our earlier calculations in the main body of the chapter we noted that the total variances for materials, labour and variable overheads were the difference between the standard cost for the actual production and the actual cost. The first item is shown in column 3 of Exhibit 17.A1 and the second in column 2. Therefore the total variance for each element of cost is the difference between columns 3 and 2.

KEY TERMS AND CONCEPTS

Bill of materials A document stating the required quantity of materials for each operation to complete the product.

Budgeted costs Expected costs for an entire activity or operation.

Engineering studies Detailed studies of each operation, based on careful specifications of materials, labour and equipment and on controlled observations of operations.

Fixed overhead expenditure variance The difference between the budgeted fixed overheads and the actual fixed overhead spending.

Labour efficiency variance The difference between the standard labour hours for actual production and the actual labour hours worked during the period multiplied by the standard wage rate per hour.

Material price variance The difference between the standard price and the actual price per unit of materials multiplied by the quantity of materials purchased.

Material usage variance The difference between the standard quantity required for actual production and the actual quantity used multiplied by the standard material price.

Sales margin price variance The difference between the actual selling price and the standard selling price multiplied by the actual sales volume.

Sales margin volume variance The difference between the actual sales volume and the budgeted volume multiplied by the standard contribution margin.

Standard costs Target costs that are predetermined and should be incurred under efficient operating conditions.

Standard hours The number of hours a skilled worker should take working under efficient conditions to complete a given job.

Standard hours produced A calculation of the amount of time, working under efficient conditions, it should take to make each product.

Total fixed overhead variance The difference between the standard fixed overhead charged to production and the actual fixed overhead incurred.

Total labour variance The difference between the standard labour cost for the actual production and the actual labour cost.

Total material variance The difference between the standard material cost for the actual production and the actual cost.

Total sales margin variance The difference between actual sales revenue less the standard variable cost of sales and the budgeted contribution.

Total variable overhead variance The difference between the standard variable overheads charged to production and the actual variable overheads incurred.

Variable overhead efficiency variance The difference between the standard hours of output and the actual hours of input for the period multiplied by the standard variable overhead rate.

Variable overhead expenditure variance The difference between the budgeted flexed variable overheads for the actual direct labour hours of input and the actual variable overhead costs incurred.

Volume capacity variance The difference between the actual hours of input and the budgeted hours of input for the period, multiplied by the standard fixed overhead rate.

Volume efficiency variance The difference between the standard hours of output and the actual hours

of input for the period, multiplied by the standard fixed overhead rate.

Volume variance The difference between actual production and budgeted production for a period, multiplied by the standard fixed overhead rate.

Wage rate variance The difference between the standard wage rate per hour and the actual wage rate, multiplied by the actual number of hours worked.

KEY EXAMINATION POINTS

A common error that students make is to calculate variances based on the original fixed budget. Remember to flex the budget. Therefore the starting point when answering a standard costing question should be to calculate actual production. If more than one product is produced, output should be expressed in standard hours. If standard overhead rates are not given, you can calculate the rates by dividing budgeted fixed and variable overheads by the budgeted output. Remember that output can be measured by units produced or standard hours produced. Make sure you are consistent and use overhead rates per standard hours if production is measured in standard hours or overhead rates per unit produced if output is measured in terms of units produced. You should always express output in

standard hours if the question requires the calculation of overhead efficiency variances. If the question does not specify whether you should calculate the variances on an absorption costing or variable costing basis, choose your preferred method and state the approach you have selected in your answer.

Frequently, questions are set that give you the variances but require calculations of actual costs and inputs (see Review problem 17.18). Students who calculate variances simply by committing to memory a series of variance formulae experience difficulties in answering these questions. Make sure you understand how the variances are calculated, and check your answers with the solutions to the review problems.

ASSESSMENT MATERIAL

The review questions are short questions that enable you to assess your understanding of the main topics included in the chapter. The numbers in parentheses provide you with the page numbers to refer to if you cannot answer a specific question.

The review problems are more complex and require you to relate and apply the content to various business problems. The problems are graded by their level of difficulty. Solutions to review problems that are not preceded by the term 'IM' are provided in a separate section at the end of the book. Solutions to problems preceded by the term 'IM' are provided in the Instructor's Manual accompanying this book that can be downloaded from the lecturer's digital support resources. Additional review problems with fully worked solutions are provided in the *Student Manual* that accompanies this book.

REVIEW QUESTIONS

17.1 Describe the difference between budgeted and standard costs. (p. 432)

17.2 Explain how a standard costing system operates. (pp. 433–434)

17.3 Describe how standard costs are established using engineering studies. (pp. 435–437)

17.4 What are standard hours produced? What purpose do they serve? (p. 438)

17.5 Describe the different purposes of a standard costing system. (pp. 438–439)

17.6 What are the possible causes of (a) material price and (b) material usage variances? (pp. 442–443)

17.7 Explain why it is preferable for the material price variance to be computed at the point of purchase rather than the point of issue. (p. 442)

17.8 What are the possible causes of (a) wage rate and (b) labour efficiency variances? (pp. 444–445)

17.9 Explain how variable overhead efficiency and expenditure variances are computed. What are the possible causes of each of these variances? (pp. 446–447)

17.10 Why are sales variances based on contribution margins rather than sales revenues? (pp. 447–448)

17.11 Distinguish between a standard absorption and a standard variable costing system. (p. 451)

17.12 What additional variance arises with a standard absorption costing system? Why? (pp. 451–454)

17.13 How do sales variances differ between a standard absorption and marginal costing system? (p. 455)

17.14 Explain what is meant by a volume variance. Does the volume variance provide any meaningful information for cost control? (pp. 453–454)

REVIEW PROBLEMS

17.15 Basic. Q plc uses standard costing. The details for April were as follows:

Budgeted output	15000 units
Budgeted labour hours	60000 hours
Budgeted labour cost	£540000
Actual output	14650 units
Actual labour hours paid	61500 hours
Productive labour hours	56000 hours
Actual labour cost	£522750

Calculate the idle time and labour efficiency variances for April.

(4 marks)

CIMA P1 Management Accounting: Performance Evaluation

17.16 Basic. A company's actual profit for a period was $27000. The only variances for the period were.

	$
Sales price	5000 adverse
Fixed overhead volume	3000 favourable
Fixed overhead capacity	4000 favourable
Fixed overhead efficiency	1000 adverse

What was the budgeted profit for the period?

(a) $25000
(b) $26000
(c) $28000
(d) $29000

(2 marks)

ACCAF2 Management Accounting

17.17 Basic. A company uses standard absorption costing. The following information was recorded by the company for October:

	Budget	Actual
Output and sales (units)	8700	8200
Selling price per unit	£26	£31
Variable cost per unit	£10	£10
Total fixed overheads	£34800	£37000

(a) The sales price variance for October was:

(i) £38500 favourable
(ii) £41000 favourable
(iii) £41000 adverse
(iv) £65600 adverse

(b) The sales volume profit variance for October was:

(i) £6000 adverse
(ii) £6000 favourable
(iii) £8000 adverse
(iv) £8000 favourable

(c) The fixed overhead volume variance for October was:

(i) £2000 adverse
(ii) £2200 adverse

(iii) £2200 favourable
(iv) £4200 adverse

(4 marks)

CIMA P1 Management Accounting: Performance Evaluation

17.18 Intermediate: Calculation of actual quantities working backwards from variances. The following profit reconciliation statement summarizes the performance of one of SEWs products for March.

	(£)
Budgeted profit	4250
Sales volume variance	850A
Standard profit on actual sales	3400
Selling price variance	4000A
	(600)

Cost variances:	Adverse (£)	Favourable (£)	
Direct material price		1000	
Direct material usage	150		
Direct labour rate	200		
Direct labour efficiency	150		
Variable overhead expenditure	600		
Variable overhead efficiency	75		
Fixed overhead efficiency		2500	
Fixed overhead volume		150	
Actual profit	1175	3650	2475F
			1875

The budget for the same period contained the following data:

Sales volume		1500 units
Sales revenue	£20000	
Production volume		1500 units
Direct materials purchased		750kg
Direct materials used		750kg
Direct material cost	£4500	
Direct labour hours		1125
Direct labour cost	£4500	
Variable overhead cost	£2250	
Fixed overhead cost	£4500	

Additional information:

- stocks of raw materials and finished goods are valued at standard cost;
- during the month the actual number of units produced was 1550;
- the actual sales revenue was £12000;
- the direct materials purchased were 1000kg.

Required:

(a) Calculate

(i) the actual sales volume;
(ii) the actual quantity of materials used;

(iii) the actual direct material cost;
(iv) the actual direct labour hours;
(v) the actual direct labour cost;
(vi) the actual variable overhead cost;
(vii) the actual fixed overhead cost.   *(19 marks)*

(b) Explain the possible causes of the direct materials usage variance, direct labour rate variance and sales volume variance.   *(6 marks)*

CIMA Operational Cost Accounting Stage 2

17.19 Intermediate: Interpretation of variances and calculation of materials, labour and sales variances. Sticky Wicket (SW) manufactures cricket bats using high quality wood and skilled labour using mainly traditional manual techniques. The manufacturing department is a cost centre within the business and operates a standard costing system based on marginal costs.

At the beginning of April the production director attempted to reduce the cost of the bats by sourcing wood from a new supplier and deskilling the process a little by using lower grade staff on parts of the production process. The standards were not adjusted to reflect these changes.

The variance report for April is shown below (extract):

Variances	Adverse $	Favourable $
Material price		5100
Material usage	7500	
Labour rate		43600
Labour efficiency	48800	
Labour idle time	5400	

The production director pointed out in his April board report that the new grade of labour required significant training in April and this meant that productive time was lower than usual. He accepted that the workers were a little slow at the moment but expected that an improvement would be seen in May. He also mentioned that the new wood being used was proving difficult to cut cleanly resulting in increased waste levels.

Sales for April were down 10 per cent on budget and returns of faulty bats were up 20 per cent on the previous month. The sales director resigned after the board meeting stating that SW had always produced quality products but the new strategy was bound to upset customers and damage the brand of the business.

Required:

(a) Assess the performance of the production director using all the information above taking into account both the decision to use a new supplier and the decision to deskill the process.   *(7 marks)*

In May the budgeted sales were 19000 bats and the standard cost card is as follows:

	Std cost $	Std cost $
Materials (2kg at $5/kg)	10	
Labour (3 hrs at $12/hr)	36	
Marginal cost		46
Selling price		68
Contribution		22

In May the following results were achieved:

40000kg of wood were bought at a cost of $196000, this produced 19200 cricket bats. No inventory of raw materials is held. The labour was paid for 62000 hours and the total cost was $694000. Labour worked for 61500 hours.

The sales price was reduced to protect the sales levels. However, only 18000 cricket bats were sold at an average price of $65.

Required:

(b) Calculate the materials, labour and sales variances for May in as much detail as the information allows. You are not required to comment on the performance of the business.   *(13 marks)*

ACCA F5 Performance Management

17.20 Intermediate: Variable costing reconciliation statement. HB makes and sells a single product. The company operates a standard marginal costing system and a just-in-time purchasing and production system. No inventory of raw materials or finished goods is held.

Details of the budget and actual data for the previous period are given below:

Budget data

Standard production costs per unit:

		$
Direct material	8kg @ $10.80 per kg	86.40
Direct labour	1.25 hours @	
	$18.00 per hour	22.50
Variable overheads	1.25 hours @	7.50
	$6.00 per direct labour hour	

Standard selling price: $180 per unit
Budgeted fixed production overheads: $170000
Budgeted production and sales: 10000 units

Actual data

Direct material: 74000kg @ $11.20 per kg
Direct labour: 10800 hours @ $19.00 per hour
Variable overheads: $70000

Actual selling price: $184 per unit
Actual fixed production overheads: $168000
Actual production and sales: 9000 units

Required:

(a) Prepare a statement using marginal costing principles that reconciles the budgeted profit and the actual profit. Your statement should show the variances in as much detail as possible.   *(11 marks)*

(b) (i) Explain why the variances used to reconcile profit in a standard marginal casting system are different from those used in a standard absorption costing system.   *(4 marks)*

(ii) Calculate the variances that would be different and any additional variances that would be required if the reconciliation statement was prepared using standard absorption costing.

Note: Preparation of a revised statement is not required.   *(4 marks)*

(c) Explain the arguments for the use of traditional absorption costing rather than marginal costing for profit reporting and inventory valuation.   *(6 marks)*

CIMA Performance Operations

17.21 Advanced: Performance reporting and variable costing variance analysis. Woodeezer Ltd makes quality wooden benches for both indoor and outdoor use. Results have been disappointing in recent years and a new managing director, Peter Beech, was appointed to raise production volumes. After an initial assessment, Peter Beech considered that budgets had been set at levels that made it easy for employees to achieve. He argued that employees would be better motivated by setting budgets that challenged them more in terms of higher expected output.

Other than changing the overall budgeted output, Mr Beech has not yet altered any part of the standard cost card. Thus, the budgeted output and sales for November was 4000 benches and the standard cost card below was calculated on this basis:

		£
Wood	25kg at £3.20 per kg	80.00
Labour	4 hours at £8 per hour	32.00
Variable overhead	4 hours at £4 per hour	16.00
Fixed overhead	4 hours at £16 per hour	64.00
		192.00
Selling price		220.00
Standard profit		28.00

Overheads are absorbed on the basis of labour hours and the company uses an absorption costing system. There were no stocks at the beginning of November. Stocks are valued at standard cost.

Actual results for November were as follows:

		£
Wood	80 000kg at £3.50	280 000
Labour	16 000 hours at £7	112 000
Variable overhead		60 000
Fixed overhead		196 000
Total production cost (3600 benches)		648 000
Closing stock (400 benches at £192)		76 800
Cost of sales		571 200
Sales (3200 benches)		720 000
Actual profit		148 800

The average monthly production and sales for some years prior to November had been 3400 units and budgets had previously been set at this level. Very few operating variances had historically been generated by the standard costs used.

Mr Beech has made some significant changes to the operations of the company. However, the other directors are now concerned that Mr Beech has been too ambitious in raising production targets. Mr Beech had also changed suppliers of raw materials to improve quality, increased selling prices, begun to introduce less skilled labour and significantly reduced fixed overheads.

The finance director suggested that an absorption costing system is misleading and that a marginal costing system should be considered at some stage in the future to guide decision-making.

Required:

(a) Prepare an operating statement for November. This should show all operating variances and should reconcile budgeted and actual profit for the month for Woodeezer Ltd. *(14 marks)*

(b) In so far as the information permits, examine the impact of the operational changes made by Mr Beech on the profitability of the company. In your answer, consider each of the following:

(i) motivation and budget setting;
(ii) possible causes of variances. *(6 marks)*

(c) Re-assess the impact of your comments in part (b), using a marginal costing approach to evaluating the impact of the operational changes made by Mr Beech.

Show any relevant calculations to support your arguments. *(5 marks)*

ACCA 2.4 Financial Management and Control

17.22 Advanced: Calculation and interpretation of variances for a variable costing system. Chaff Co. processes and sells brown rice. It buys unprocessed rice seeds and then, using a relatively simple process, removes the outer husk of the rice to produce the brown rice. This means that there is substantial loss of weight in the process. The market for the purchase of seeds and the sales of brown rice has been, and is expected to be, stable. Chaff Co. uses a variance analysis system to monitor its performance.

There has been some concern about the interpretation of the variances that have been calculated in month 1:

1. The purchasing manager is adamant, despite criticism from the production director, that he has purchased wisely and saved the company thousands of dollars in purchase costs by buying the required quantity of cheaper seeds from a new supplier.

2. The production director is upset at being criticized for increasing the wage rates for month 1; he feels the decision was the right one, considering all the implications of the increase. Morale was poor and he felt he had to do something about it.

3. The maintenance manager feels that saving $8000 on fixed overhead has helped the profitability of the business. He argues that the machines' annual maintenance can wait for another month without a problem as the machines have been running well.

The variances for month 1 are as follows:

	$
Material price	48 000 (Fav.)
Material usage	52 000 (Adv.)
Labour rate	15 000 (Adv.)
Labour efficiency	18 000 (Fav.)
Labour idle time	12 000 (Fav.)
Variable overhead expenditure	18 000 (Adv.)
Variable overhead efficiency	30 000 (Fav.)
Fixed overhead expenditure	8 000 (Fav.)
Sales price	85 000 (Adv.)
Sales volume	21 000 (Adv.)

Fav. = Favourable, Adv. = Adverse
Chaff Co. uses labour hours to absorb the variable overhead.

Required:

(a) Comment on the performance of the purchasing manager, the production director and the maintenance manager using the variances and other information above and reach a conclusion as to whether or not they have each performed well. *(9 marks)*

In month 2 the following data apply:
Standard costs for 1 tonne of brown rice

– one to four tonnes of rice seeds are needed at a cost of $60 per tonne
– it takes two labour hours of work to produce one tonne of brown rice and labour is normally paid $18 per hour. Idle time is expected to be 10 per cent of hours paid; this is not reflected in the rate of $18 above
– two hours of variable overhead at a cost of $30 per hour
– the standard selling price is $240 per tonne
– the standard contribution per tonne is $56 per tonne

Budget information for month 2 is

– fixed costs were budgeted at $210 000 for the month
– budgeted production and sales were 8400 tonnes

The actual results for month 2 were as follows:
Actual production and sales were 8000 tonnes

- 12 000 tonnes of rice seeds were bought and used, costing $660 000
- 15 800 labour hours were paid for, costing $303 360
- 15 000 labour hours were worked
- variable production overhead cost $480 000
- fixed costs were $200 000
- sales revenue achieved was $1 800 000

Required:

(b) Calculate the variances for month 2 in as much detail as the information allows and reconcile the budget profit to the actual profit using marginal costing principles. You are not required to comment on the performance of the business or its managers for their performance in month 2. *(16 marks)*

(Total 25 marks)

ACCA Performance Management

17.23 Intermediate. A major information source within many businesses is a system of standard costing and variance analysis.

Required:

(a) Describe briefly four purposes of a system of standard costing. *(4 marks)*

(b) Explain three different levels of performance that may be incorporated into a system of standard costing and comment on how these may relate to the purposes set out in (a) above. *(6 marks)*

(c) Comment on whether standard costing applies in both manufacturing and service businesses and how it may be affected by modern initiatives of continuous performance improvement and cost reduction. *(4 marks)*

(d) A standard costing system enables variances for direct costs, variable and fixed overheads to be extracted. Identify and briefly discuss some of the complexities and practical problems in calculation which may limit the usefulness of those variances. *(6 marks)*

ACCA Paper 8 – Managerial Finance

IM17.1 Intermediate: Flexible budgets and computation of labour and material variances.

(a) JB plc operates a standard marginal cost accounting system. Information relating to product J, which is made in one of the company departments, is given below:

Product J	Standard marginal product cost Unit (£)
Direct material	
six kilograms at £4 per kg	24
Direct labour	
one hour at £7 per hour	7
Variable production overhead[a]	3
	34

[a] Variable production overhead varies with units produced.

Budgeted fixed production overhead, per month: £100 000.

Budgeted production for product J: 20 000 units per month.

Actual production and costs for month 6 were as follows:

Units of J produced	18 500 (£)
Direct materials purchased and used: 113 500kg	442 650
Direct labour: 17 800 hours	129 940
Variable production overhead incurred	58 800
Fixed production overhead incurred	104 000
	735 390

You are required to:

(i) prepare a columnar statement showing, by element of cost, the:

  (i) original budget;
  (ii) flexed budget;
  (iii) actual;
  (iv) total variances; *(9 marks)*

(ii) subdivide the variances for direct material and direct labour shown in your answer to (a) (i)−(iv) above to be more informative for managerial purposes. *(4 marks)*

(b) Explain the meaning and use of a 'rolling forecast'. *(2 marks)*

CIMA State 2 Cost Accounting

IM17.2 Intermediate: Reconciliation of standard and actual cost for a variable costing system.

Data

You are employed as the assistant management accountant in the group accountant's office of Hampstead plc. Hampstead recently acquired Finchley Ltd, a small company making a specialist product called the Alpha. Standard marginal costing is used by all the companies within the group and, from 1 August, Finchley Ltd will also be required to use standard marginal costing in its management reports. Part of your job is to manage the implementation of standard marginal costing at Finchley Ltd.

John Wade, the managing director of Finchley, is not clear how the change will help him as a manager. He has always found Finchley's existing absorption costing system sufficient. By way of example, he shows you a summary of its management accounts for the three months to 31 May. These are reproduced below:

Statement of budgeted and actual cost of Alpha production – 3 months ended 31 May

Alpha production (units)	Actual Inputs	10 000 (£)	Budget Inputs	12 000 (£)	Variance (£)
Materials	32 000 metres	377 600	36 000 metres	432 000	54 400
Labour	70 000 hours	845 600	72 000 hours	900 000	54 400
Fixed overhead absorbed		330 000		396 000	66 000
Fixed overhead unabsorbed		75 000		0	(75 000)
		1 628 200		1 728 000	99 800

John Wade is not convinced that standard marginal costing will help him to manage Finchley. 'My current system tells me all I need to know', he said. 'As you can see, we are £99 800 below budget which is really excellent given that we lost production as a result of a serious machine breakdown.'

To help John Wade understand the benefits of standard marginal costing, you agree to prepare a statement for the three months ended 31 May reconciling the standard cost of production to the actual cost of production.

Task 1

(a) Use the budget data to determine:

  (i) the standard marginal cost per Alpha;
  (ii) the standard cost of actual Alpha production for the three months to 31 May.

(b) Calculate the following variances:

  (i) material price variance;
  (ii) material usage variance;
  (iii) labour rate variance;
  (iv) labour efficiency variance;
  (v) fixed overhead expenditure variance.

(c) Write a *short* memo to John Wade. Your memo should:

(i) include a statement reconciling the actual cost of production to the standard cost of production;

(ii) give *two* reasons why your variances might differ from those in his original management accounting statement despite using the same basic data;

(iii) *briefly* discuss *one* further reason why your reconciliation statement provides improved management information.

Data

On receiving your memo, John Wade informs you that:

- the machine breakdown resulted in the workforce having to be paid for 12000 hours even though no production took place;
- an index of material prices stood at 466.70 when the budget was prepared but at 420.03 when the material was purchased.   *(10 marks)*

Task 2

Using this new information, prepare a revised statement reconciling the standard cost of production to the actual cost of production. Your statement should subdivide:

- both the labour variances into those parts arising from the machine breakdown and those parts arising from normal production;
- the material price variance into that part due to the change in the index and that part arising for other reasons.

Data

Barnet Ltd is another small company owned by Hampstead plc. Barnet operates a job costing system making a specialist, expensive piece of hospital equipment.

Existing system

Currently, employees are assigned to individual jobs and materials are requisitioned from stores as needed. The standard and actual costs of labour and material are recorded for each job. These job costs are totalled to produce the marginal cost of production. Fixed production costs − including the cost of storekeeping and inspection of deliveries and finished equipment − are then added to determine the standard and actual cost of production. Any costs of remedial work are included in the materials and labour for each job.

Proposed system

Carol Johnson, the chief executive of Barnet, has recently been to a seminar on modern manufacturing techniques. As a result, she is considering introducing just-in-time stock deliveries and total quality management. Barnet would offer suppliers a long-term contract at a fixed price but suppliers would have to guarantee the quality of their materials. In addition, she proposes that the workforce is organized as a single team with flexible work practices. This would mean employees helping each other as necessary, with no employee being allocated a particular job. If a job were delayed, the workforce would work overtime without payment in order for the job to be completed on time. In exchange, employees would be guaranteed a fixed weekly wage and time off when production was slack to make up for any overtime incurred.

Cost of quality

Carol has asked to meet you to discuss the implications of her proposals on the existing accounting system. She is particularly concerned to monitor the *cost of quality*. This is defined as the total of all costs incurred in preventing defects plus those costs involved in remedying defects once they have occurred. It is a single figure measuring all the explicit costs of quality, that is, those costs collected within the accounting system.   *(10 marks)*

Task 3

In preparation for the meeting, produce *brief* notes. Your notes should:

(a) identify *four* general headings (or classifications) which make up the *cost of quality*;

(b) give one example of a type of cost likely to be found within each category;

(c) assuming Carol Johnson's proposals are accepted, state, with reasons, whether or not:

(i) a standard marginal costing system would still be of help to the managers;

(ii) it would still be meaningful to collect costs by each individual job;

(d) identify *one* cost saving in Carol Johnson's proposals that would not be recorded in the existing costing system.

(10 marks)

AAT Technicians Stage

IM17.3 Intermediate: Calculation of labour, material and overhead variances and reconciliation of budgeted and actual profit. You are the management accountant of T plc. The following computer printout shows details relating to April:

	Actual	Budget
Sales volume	4900 units	5000 units
Selling price per unit	£15.00	£14.00
Production volume	5400 units	5000 units
Direct materials		
kgs	10600	10000
price per kg	£0.60	£0.50
Direct labour		
hours per unit	0.55	0.50
rate per hour	£11.40	£12.00
Fixed overhead:		
Production	£10300	£10000
Administration	£3100	£3000

T plc uses a standard absorption costing system. There was no opening or closing work in progress.

Requirements:

(a) Prepare a statement that reconciles the budgeted profit with the actual profit for April, showing individual variances in as much detail as the above data permit.

(20 marks)

(b) Explain briefly the possible causes of:

(i) the material usage variance;

(ii) the labour rate variance;

(iii) the sales volume profit variance.   *(6 marks)*

(c) Explain the meaning and relevance of interdependence of variances when reporting to managers.   *(4 marks)*

CIMA Stage 2 Operational Cost Accounting

IM17.4 Intermediate: Computation of fixed overhead variances. A manufacturing company has provided you with the following data, which relate to component RYX for the period which has just ended:

	Budget	Actual
Number of labour hours	8400	7980
Production units	1200	1100
Overhead cost (all fixed)	£22260	£25536

Overheads are absorbed at a rate per standard labour hour.

Required:

(a) (i) Calculate the fixed production overhead cost variance and the following subsidiary variances:

expenditure
efficiency
capacity

(ii) Provide a summary statement of these four variances.   (7 marks)

(b) Briefly discuss the possible reasons why adverse fixed production overhead expenditure, efficiency and capacity variances occur.   (10 marks)

(c) Briefly discuss two examples of interrelationships between the fixed production overhead efficiency variances and the material and labour variances.   (3 marks)

ACCA Paper 8 Managerial Finance

IM17.5 Intermediate: Labour and overhead variances and ex post wage rate analysis.

Data
The Eastern Division of Countryside Communications plc assembles a single product, the Beta. The Eastern Division has a fixed price contract with the supplier of the materials used in the Beta. The contract also specifies that the materials should be free of any faults. Because of these clauses in the contract, the Eastern Division has no material variances when reporting any differences between standard and actual production.

You have recently accepted the position of assistant management accountant in the Eastern Division. One of your tasks is to report variances in production costs on a four-weekly basis. Fixed overheads are absorbed on the basis of standard labour hours. A colleague provides you with the following data:

*Standard costs and budgeted production –
four weeks ended 27 November*

	Quantity	Unit price	Standard cost per Beta
Material	30 metres	£12.00	£360.00
Labour	10 hours	£12.00	£120.00
Fixed overhead	10 hours	£15.25	£157.50
Standard cost per Beta			£637.50
Budgeted production	1200 Betas	£637.50	£765000

Actual production – four weeks ended 27 November

	Quantity	Total cost
Actual cost of material	31200 metres	£374400
Actual cost of labour	11440 hours	£136708
Actual fixed cost overheads		£207000
Actual cost of actual production		£718108
Actual production	1040 Betas	

Task 1

(a) Calculate the following variances:

(i) the labour rate variance;
(ii) the labour efficiency variance (sometimes called the utilization variance);
(iii) the fixed overhead expenditure variance (sometimes known as the price variance);
(iv) the fixed overhead volume variance;
(v) the fixed overhead capacity variance;
(vi) the fixed overhead efficiency variance (sometimes known as the usage variance).

(b) Prepare a statement reconciling the standard cost of actual production with the actual cost of actual production.

Data
When the Eastern Division's budget for the four weeks ended 27 November was originally prepared, a national index of labour rates stood at 102.00. In preparing the budget, Eastern Division had allowed for a 5 per cent increase in labour rates. For the actual four weeks ended 27 November, the index stood at 104.04.

Because of this, Ann Green, Eastern Division's production director, is having difficulty understanding the meaning of the labour rate variance calculated in task 1.   (13 marks)

Task 2
Write a memo to Ann Green. Your memo should:

(a) identify the original labour rate before allowing for the 5 per cent increase;
(b) calculate the revised standard hourly rate using the index of 104.04;
(c) subdivide the labour rate variance calculated in task 1(a) into that part due to the change in the index and that part arising for other reasons;
(d) *briefly* interpret the possible meaning of these two subdivisions of the labour rate variance;
(e) give two reasons why the index of labour rates might not be valid in explaining part of the labour rate variance;
(f) *briefly* explain the meaning of the following variances calculated in task 1 and for each variance suggest one reason why it may have occurred;

(i) the fixed overhead expenditure (or price) variance;
(ii) the fixed overhead capacity variance;
(iii) the fixed overhead efficiency (or usage) variance.
                                        (12 marks)

AAT Technicians Stage

IM17.6 Calculation of actual input data working back from variances. The following profit reconciliation statement has been prepared by the management accountant of ABC Limited for March:

		(£)
Budgeted profit		30000
Sales volume profit variance		5250A
Selling price variance		6375F
		31125

Cost variances:	A (£)	F (£)
Material		
price	1985	
usage		400
Labour:		
rate		9800
efficiency	12000	
Variable overhead:		
expenditure		1000
efficiency	1500	
Fixed overhead:		
expenditure		500
volume	24500	
	39985	11700
		28285A
Actual profit		2840

The standard cost card for the company's only product is as follows:

		(£)
Materials	5 litres at £0.20	1.00
Labour	4 hours at £12.00	48.00
Variable overhead	4 hours at £1.50	6.00
Fixed overhead	4 hours at £3.50	14.00
		69.00
Standard profit		300
Standard selling price		72.00

The following information is also available:

1 There was no change in the level of finished goods stock during the month.
2 Budgeted production and sales volumes for March were equal.
3 Stocks of materials, which are valued at standard price, decreased by 800 litres during the month.
4 The actual labour rate was £0.28 lower than the standard hourly rate.

Required:

(a) Calculate the following:

(i)   the actual production/sales volume;   (4 marks)
(ii) the actual number of hours worked;   (4 marks)
(iii) the actual quantity of materials purchased; (4 marks)
(iv) the actual variable overhead cost incurred; (2 marks)
(v)   the actual fixed overhead cost incurred.   (2 marks)

(b) ABC Limited uses a standard costing system whereas other organizations use a system of budgetary control. Explain the reasons why a system of budgetary control is often preferred to the use of standard costing in non-manufacturing environments.   (9 marks)

CIMA Stage 2 Operational Cost Accounting

IM17.7 Intermediate: Calculation of inputs working backwards from variances. The following data have been collected for the month of April by a company which operates a standard absorption costing system:

Actual production of product EM	600 units
Actual costs incurred:	(£)
Direct material E 660 metres	6270
Direct material M 200 metres	650
Direct wages 3200 hours	23200
Variable production overhead	6720
(which varied with hours worked)	
Fixed production overhead	27000
Variances	(£)
Direct material price:	
Material E	330 F
Material M	50 A
Direct material usage:	
Material E	600 A
Material M	nil
Direct labour rate	800 A
Direct labour efficiency	1400 A
Variable production overhead:	
expenditure	320 A
efficiency	400 A
Fixed production overhead:	
expenditure	500 F
volume	2500 F

Opening and closing work in progress figures were identical, so can be ignored.

You are required to:

(a) prepare for the month of April a statement of total standard costs for product EM;   (3 marks)
(b) prepare a standard product cost sheet for one unit of product EM;   (7 marks)
(c) calculate the number of units of product EM that were budgeted for April;   (2 marks)
(d) state how the material and labour cost standards for product EM would originally have been determined.   (3 marks)

CIMA Stage 2 Cost Accounting

IM17.8 Advanced: Variance calculations and reconciliation of budgeted and actual profit. Bamfram plc is a well-established manufacturer of a specialized product, a Wallop, which has the following specifications for production:

Components	Standard quantity	Standard price (£)
WALS	15	60
LOPS	8	75

The standard direct labour hours to produce a Wallop at the standard wage rate of £10.50 per hour has been established at 60 hours per Wallop.

The annual fixed overhead budget is divided into calendar months with equal production per month. The budgeted annual fixed overheads are £504000 for the budgeted output of 2400 Wallops per annum.

Mr Jones, a marketing person, is now the managing director of Bamfram plc and must report to the board of directors later this day and he seeks your advice in respect of the following operating information for the month of May:

	(£)	(£)
Sales		504000
Cost of sales:		
Direct materials	281520	
Direct labour	112329	
	393840	
Fixed production overheads	42600	436440
Gross profit		67560
Administration expenses		11150
Selling and distribution expenses		17290
Net profit		39120

The sales manager informs Mr Jones that despite adverse trading conditions his sales staff have been able to sell 180 Wallops at the expected standard selling price.

The production manager along with the purchasing department manager are also pleased that prices for components have been stable for the whole of the current year and they are able to provide the following information:

Stocks for May are as follows:

	1 May	31 May
Component WALS	600	750
Component LOPS	920	450

The actual number of direct labour hours worked in May was 11700, considerably less than the production manager had budgeted. Further, the purchasing manager advised that WALS had cost £171000 at a price of £57 per unit in the month of May and 1000 LOPS had been acquired for £81000.

Mr Jones, eager to please the board of directors, requests you, as the newly appointed management accountant, to prepare appropriate statements to highlight the following information that is to be presented to the board:

(a) The standard product cost of a Wallop.   (3 marks)
(b) (i) The direct material variances for both price and usage for each component used in the month of May assuming that prices were stable throughout the relevant period.
    (ii) The direct labour efficiency and wage rate variances for the month of May.
    (iii) The fixed production overhead expenditure and volume variances.

    Note: You may assume that during the month of May there is no change in the level of finished goods stocks.   (10 marks)
(c) A detailed reconciliation statement of the standard gross profit with the actual gross profit for the month of May.
                                                   (4 marks)
(d) Draft a brief report for Mr Jones that he could present to the board of directors on the usefulness, or otherwise, of the statement you have prepared in your answer to (c) above.   (5 marks)

ACCA Level 2 Management Accounting

IM17.9 Advanced: Computation of variances and the reconciliation of budgeted and actual profits for a taxi firm.
Tardy Taxis operates a fleet of taxis in a provincial town. In planning its operations for November, it estimated that it would carry fare-paying passengers for 40 000 miles at an average price of £1 per mile. However, past experience suggested that the total miles run would amount to 250 per cent of the fare-paid miles. At the beginning of November it employed ten drivers and decided that this number would be adequate for the month ahead.

The following cost estimates were available:

Employment costs of a driver	£1000 per month
Fuel costs	£0.08 per mile run
Variable overhead costs	£0.05 per mile run
Fixed overhead costs	£9000 per month

In November revenue of £36 100 was generated by carrying passengers for 38 000 miles. The total actual mileage was 105 000 miles. Other costs amounted to:

Employment costs of drivers	£9600
Fuel costs	£8820
Variable overhead costs	£5040
Fixed overhead costs	£9300

The saving in the cost of drivers was due to one driver leaving during the month; she was not replaced until early December.

Requirements:

(a) Prepare a budgeted and actual profit and loss account for November, indicating the total profit variance.
                                                   (6 marks)
(b) Using a flexible budget approach, construct a set of detailed variances to explain the total profit variance as effectively as possible. Present your analysis in a report to the owner of Tardy Taxis including suggested reasons for the variances.   (14 marks)
(c) Outline any further variances you think would improve your explanation, indicating the additional information you would require to produce these.   (5 marks)

ICAEW P2 Management Accounting

18
STANDARD COSTING AND VARIANCE ANALYSIS 2: FURTHER ASPECTS

LEARNING OBJECTIVES After studying this chapter, you should be able to:

- prepare a set of accounts for a standard costing system;

- explain and calculate material mix and yield and sales mix and quantity variances;

- explain and calculate planning and operating variances;

- explain the factors that influence the decision to investigate a variance and describe the different methods that can be used to determine whether an investigation is warranted;

- explain the role of standard costing within an ABC system.

In the previous chapter the principles of a standard costing system and variance analysis were explained. In this chapter, we are going to consider further aspects of standard costing. First, we shall look at the accounting entries that are necessary to record the variances. Next, we shall look at how the material usage variance and sales margin variances can further analysed. We shall then turn our attention to how variance analysis can be adapted to reflect changes in the environment and the factors that should be taken into account in deciding whether it is worthwhile investigating variances. Finally, we shall consider how standard costing variance analysis can be modified when an ABC system has been implemented.

It is possible that many, or all of the above topics, do not form part of your course curriculum. The accounting entries for recording the variances and the further analysis of the material usage and sales margin variances tend to be covered only on specialist accounting courses. Therefore if you are pursuing a non-specialist accounting course, it is likely that you can omit reading those sections of the chapter relating to these topics. The remaining topics are likely to be appropriate for both specialist and non-specialist courses, but they tend to be covered only on second level courses. It is therefore very important that you refer to your course curriculum to determine which sections within this chapter you should read.

RECORDING STANDARD COSTS IN THE ACCOUNTS

If you are not studying for a specialist accounting qualification, it is possible that your curriculum may not include the recording of standard costs. You should therefore check whether or not this topic is included in your curriculum to ascertain if you need to read this section. Standard costs can be used for planning, control and decision-making purposes without being entered into the books. However, the incorporation of standard costs into the cost accounting system greatly simplifies the task of tracing costs for inventory valuation and saves a considerable amount of data processing time. For example, if raw material inventories are valued at standard cost, the inventory records may be maintained in terms of physical quantities only. The value of raw materials inventory may be obtained simply by multiplying the physical quantities of raw materials in inventory by the standard cost per unit. This avoids the need to record inventories on a first in, first out or average cost basis. The financial accounting regulations in most countries specify that inventory valuations based on standard costs may be included in externally published financial statements, provided the standard costs used are current and attainable. Most companies that have established standard costs therefore incorporate them into their cost accounting recording system.

Variations exist in the data accumulation methods adopted for recording standard costs, but these variations are merely procedural and the actual inventory valuations and profit calculations will be the same whichever method is adopted. In this chapter, we shall illustrate a standard absorption costing system that values all inventories at standard cost and all entries that are recorded in the inventory accounts will therefore be at *standard prices*. Any differences between standard costs and actual costs are debited or credited to variance accounts. Adverse variances will appear as debit balances, since they are additional costs in excess of standard. Conversely, favourable variances will appear as credit balances. Only production variances are recorded and sales variances are not entered in the accounts.

Let us now consider the cost accounting records that we examined in Example 17.1 (p. 440) (see Chapter 17). The variances recorded in the accounts are those for an absorption costing system, presented in Exhibit 17.6 (p. 455). The appropriate ledger entries are now presented in Exhibit 18.1. Each ledger entry and journal entry has been labelled with numbers from 1 to 13 to try to give you a clear understanding of each accounting entry. You will need to refer back to Example 17.1 and Exhibit 17.6 in order to understand the explanation of the accounting procedures.

Purchase of materials

A purchase of 19 000kg of raw material A at £11 per kg and 10 100kg of raw material B at £14 per kg was made. This gives a total purchase cost of £209 000 for A and £141 400 for B. The standard prices were £10 per kg for A and £15 per kg for B. The accounting entries for material A are:

1. Dr Stores ledger control account (AQ × SP)	190 000	
1. Dr Material price variance account	19 000	
1. Cr Creditors control account (AQ × AP)		209 000

You will see that the stores ledger control account shown in Exhibit 18.1 is debited with the standard price (SP) for the actual quantity purchased (AQ), and the actual price (AP) to be paid is credited to the creditors control account. The difference is the material price variance. The accounting entries for material B are:

2. Dr Stores ledger control account (AQ × SP)	151 500	
2. Cr Material price variance account		10 100
2. Cr Creditors (AQ × AP)		141 400

Usage of materials

The actual issue amounts were 19 000kg of A and 10 100kg of B and the standard usage (SQ) was 18 000 and 9000kg at standard prices of £10 and £15. The accounting entries for material A are:

3. Dr Work in progress (SQ × SP)	180 000	
3. Dr Material usage variance	10 000	
3. Cr Stores ledger control account (AQ × SP)		190 000

EXHIBIT 18.1 Accounting entries for a standard costing system

Stores ledger control account			
1. Creditors (material A)	190000	3. Work in progress (material A)	180000
2. Creditors (material B)	151500	3. Material usage variance (material A)	10000
		4. Work in progress (material B)	135000
		4. Material usage variance (material B)	16500
	341500		341500

Creditors control account			
2. Material price variance (material B)	10100	1. Stores ledger control (material A)	190000
		1. Material price variance (material A)	19000
		2. Stores ledger control (material B)	151500

Variance accounts			
1. Creditors (material A)	19000	2. Creditors (material price B)	10100
3. Stores ledger control (material A usage)	10000	8. Fixed factory overhead (expenditure)	4000
4. Stores ledger control (material B usage)	16500	9. Variable factory overhead (expenditure)	5000
6. Wages control (wage rate)	17100		19100
6. Wages control (lab. effic'y)	13500	13. Costing P + L a/c (balance)	72000
8. Fixed factory overhead (volume)	12000		
9. Variable factory overhead (effic'y)	3000		
	91100		91100

Work in progress control account			
3. Stores ledger (material A)	180000	10. Finished goods inventory account	720000
4. Stores ledger (material B)	135000		
6. Wages control	243000		
8. Fixed factory overhead	108000		
9. Variable factory overhead	54000		
	720000		720000

Wages control account			
5. Wages accrued account	273600	6. WIP	243000
		6. Wage rate variance	17100
		6. Labour efficiency variance	13500
	273600		273600

Fixed factory overhead control account			
7. Expense creditors	116000	8. WIP	108000
8. Expenditure variance	4000	8. Volume variance	12000
	120000		120000

Variable factory overhead control account			
7. Expense creditors	52000	9. WIP	54000
9. Expenditure	5000	9. Efficiency variance	3000
	57000		57000

Finished goods inventory control account			
10. WIP	720000	12. Cost of sales	720000

Cost of sales account			
12. Finish goods inventory	720000	13. Costing P + L a/c	720000

➡

Costing P + L Account			
12. Cost of sales at standard cost	720 000	11. Sales	810 000
13. Variance account (net variances)	72 000		
Profit for period	18 000		
	810 000		810 000

Work in progress is debited with the standard quantity of materials at the standard price and the stores ledger account is credited with the actual quantity issued at the standard price. The difference is the material usage variance. The accounting entries for material B are:

4. Dr Work in progress (SQ × SP)	135 000	
4. Dr Material usage variance	16 500	
4. Cr Stores ledger control account (AQ × SP)		151 500

Direct wages

The actual hours worked were 28 500 hours for the month. The standard hours produced were 27 000. The actual wage rate paid was £9.60 per hour, compared with a standard rate of £9 per hour. The actual wages cost is recorded in the same way in a standard costing system as an actual costing system. The accounting entry for the actual wages paid is:

5. Dr Wages control account	273 600	
5. Cr Wages accrued account		273 600

The wages control account is then cleared as follows:

6. Dr Work in progress (SQ × SP)	243 000	
6. Cr Wages control account		243 000
6. Dr Wage rate variance	17 100	
6. Dr Labour efficiency variance	13 500	
6. Cr Wages control account		30 600

The wages control account is credited and the work in progress account is debited with the standard cost (i.e. standard hours produced times the standard wage rate). The wage rate and labour efficiency variance accounts are debited, since they are both adverse variances and account for the difference between the actual wages cost (recorded as a debit in the wages control account) and the standard wages cost (recorded as a credit in the wages control account).

Manufacturing overhead costs incurred

The actual manufacturing overhead incurred is £52 000 for variable overheads and £116 000 for fixed overheads. The accounting entries for actual overhead *incurred* are recorded in the same way in a standard costing system as in an actual costing system. That is:

7. Dr Factory variable overhead control account	52 000	
7. Dr Factory fixed overhead control account	116 000	
7. Cr Expense creditors		168 000

Absorption of manufacturing overheads and recording the variances

Work in progress is debited with the standard manufacturing overhead cost for the output produced. The standard overhead rates were £4 per standard hour for fixed overhead and £2 per standard hour for variable overheads. The actual output was 27 000 standard hours. The standard fixed overhead cost is therefore £108 000 (27 000 standard hours at £4 per hour) and the variable overhead cost is £54 000. The accounting entries for fixed overheads are:

8. Dr Work in progress (SQ × SP)	108 000	
8. Dr Volume variance	12 000	
8. Cr Factory fixed overhead control account		120 000
8. Dr Factory fixed overhead control account	4 000	
8. Cr Fixed overhead expenditure variance		4 000

You will see that the debit of £108 000 to the work in progress account and the corresponding credit to the factory fixed overhead control account represents the standard fixed overhead cost of production. The difference between the debit entry of £116 000 in the factory fixed overhead control account in Exhibit 18.1 for the *actual* fixed overheads incurred, and the credit entry of £108 000 for the *standard* fixed overhead cost of production, is the total fixed overhead variance which consists of an adverse volume variance of £12 000 and a favourable expenditure variance of £4000. This is recorded as a debit to the volume variance account and a credit to the expenditure variance account. The accounting entries for variable overheads are:

9. Dr Work in progress account (SQ × SP)	54 000	
9. Dr Variable overhead efficiency variance	3 000	
9. Cr Factory variable overhead control account		57 000
9. Dr Factory variable overhead control account	5 000	
9. Cr Variable overhead expenditure variance account		5 000

The same principles apply with variable overheads. The debit to work in progress account and the corresponding credit to the factory variable overhead control account of £54 000 is the standard variable overhead cost of production. The difference between the debit entry of £52 000 in the factory variable overhead account in Exhibit 18.1 for the *actual* variable overheads incurred, and the credit entry of £54 000 for the *standard* variable overhead cost of production, is the total variable overhead variance which consists of an adverse efficiency variance of £3000 and a favourable expenditure variance of £5000.

Completion of production

In Exhibit 18.1, the total amount recorded on the debit side of the work in progress account is £720 000. As there are no opening or closing inventories, this represents the total standard cost of production for the period, which consists of 9000 units at £80 per unit. When the completed production is transferred from work in progress to finished goods inventory, the accounting entries will be as follows:

10. Dr Finished inventory account	720 000	
10. Cr Work in progress account		720 000

Because there are no opening or closing inventories, both the work in progress account and the stores ledger account will show a nil balance.

Sales

Sales variances are not recorded in the accounts, so actual sales of £810 000 for 9000 units will be recorded as:

11. Dr Debtors	810 000	
11. Cr Sales		810 000

As all the production for the period has been sold, there will be no closing inventory of finished goods and the standard cost of production for the 9000 units will be transferred from the finished goods account to the cost of sales account:

12. Dr Cost of sales account	288 000	
12. Cr Finished goods account		288 000

Finally, the cost of sales account and the variance accounts will be closed by a transfer to the costing profit and loss account (the item labelled 13 in Exhibit 18.1). The balance of the costing profit and loss account will be the *actual* profit for the period.

Calculation of profit

To calculate the profit, we must add the adverse variances and deduct the favourable variances from the standard cost of sales, which is obtained from the cost of sales account. This calculation gives the actual cost of sales for the period, which is then deducted from the actual sales to produce the actual profit for the period. The calculations are as follows:

	(£)	(£)	(£)
Sales			810 000
Less standard cost of sales		720 000	
Plus adverse variances:			
Material A price variance	19 000		
Material usage variance	26 500		
Wage rate variance	17 100		
Labour efficiency variance	13 500		
Volume variance	12 000		
Variable overhead efficiency variance	3 000	91 100	
		811 100	
Less favourable variances:			
Material B price variance	10 100		
Fixed overhead expenditure variance	4 000		
Variable overhead expenditure variance	5 000	19 100	
Actual cost of sales			792 000
Actual profit			18 000

ADVANCED READING

DIRECT MATERIALS MIX AND YIELD VARIANCES

In many industries, particularly of the process type, it is possible to vary the mix of input materials and affect the yield. Where it is possible to combine two or more raw materials, input standards should be established to indicate the target mix of materials required to produce a unit, or a specified number of units, of output. Laboratory and engineering studies are necessary in order to determine the standard mix.

The costs of the different material mixes are estimated, and a standard mix is determined based on the mix of materials that minimizes the cost per unit of output but still meets the quality requirements.

By deviating from the standard mix of input materials, operating managers can affect the yield and cost per unit of output. Such deviations can occur as a result of a conscious response to changes in material prices, or alternatively may arise from inefficiencies and a failure to adhere to the standard mix. By computing mix and yield variances, we can provide an indication of the cost of deviating from the standard mix.

Mix variance

The material mix variance arises when the mix of materials used differs from the predetermined mix included in the calculation of the standard cost of an operation. If the mixture is varied so that a larger than standard proportion of more expensive materials is used, there will be an unfavourable variance. When a larger proportion of cheaper materials is included in the mixture, there will be a favourable variance. Consider Example 18.1.

The total input for the period is 100 000 litres, and, using the standard mix, an input of 50 000 litres of X (5/10 × 100 000), 30 000 litres of Y (3/10 × 100 000) and 20 000 litres of Z (2/10 × 10 0000) should have been used. However, 53 000 litres of X, 28 000 litres of Y and 19 000 litres of Z were used. Therefore 3000 additional litres of X at a standard price of £7 per litre were substituted for 2000 litres of Y (at a standard price of £5 per litre) and 1000 litres of Z (at a standard price of £2 per litre). An adverse material mix variance of £9000 will therefore be reported. The formula for the material mix variance is as follows:

(actual quantity in standard mix proportions − actual quantity used) × standard price

If we apply this formula, the calculation is as follows:

Actual usage in standard proportions:

		(£)
X = 50 000 litres (5/10 × 100 000) at	£7	350 000
Y = 30 000 litres (3/10 × 100 000) at	£5	150 000
Z = 20 000 litres (2/10 × 100 000) at	£2	40 000
		540 000

Actual usage in actual proportions:

	(£)
X = 53 000 litres at £7	371 000
Y = 28 000 litres at £5	140 000
Z = 19 000 litres at £2	38 000
	549 000
mix variance =	£9 000 A

Note that standard prices are used to calculate the mix variance to ensure that the price effects are removed from the calculation. An adverse mix variance will result from substituting more expensive higher quality materials for cheaper materials. Substituting more expensive materials may result in a boost in output and a favourable yield variance. Contrariwise, a favourable mix variance will result from substituting cheaper materials for more expensive materials – but this may not always be in a company's best interests, since the quality of the product may suffer or output might be reduced. Generally, the use of a less expensive mix of inputs will mean the production of fewer units of output than standard. This may be because of excessive evaporation of the input units, an increase in rejects due to imperfections in the lower quality inputs or other similar factors. To analyse the effect of changes in the quantity of outputs from a given mix of inputs, a yield variance can be calculated. It is important that the standard mix be continuously reviewed and adjusted where necessary, since price changes may lead to a revised standard mix.

Direct materials yield variance

The materials yield variance arises because there is a difference between the standard output for a given level of inputs and the actual output attained. In Example 18.1, an input of 100 000 litres should have given an output of 90 000 litres of product A. (Every ten litres of input should produce nine litres of output.) In fact, 92 700 litres were produced, which means that the output was 2700 litres greater than

standard. This output is valued at the average standard cost per unit of *output*, which is calculated as follows:

Each ten litres of *input* is expected to yield nine litres of *output*.

The standard cost for this output is £54.

Therefore the standard cost for one litre of *output* = 54 × 1/9 = £6.

The yield variance will be £6 × 2700 = £16 200F. The formula is as follows:

$$(\text{actual yield} - \text{standard yield from actual input of material})$$
$$\times \text{standard cost per unit of output}$$
$$= (92\,700 \text{ litres} - 90\,000 \text{ litres}) \times £6 = £16\,200F$$

An adverse yield variance may arise from a failure to follow standard procedures. For example, in the steel industry a yield variance may indicate that the practice that was followed for pouring molten metal may have been different from that which was determined as being the most efficient when the standard yield was calculated. Alternatively, the use of inferior quality materials may result in an adverse yield variance.

The material mix variance in Example 18.1 is £9000 adverse, while the material yield variance is £16 200 favourable. There was a trade-off in the material mix, which boosted the yield. This trade-off may have arisen because the prices of materials Y and Z have increased, whereas the actual price paid for material X is identical with the standard price. The manager of the production process may have responded to the different relative prices by substituting material X for materials Y and Z. This substitution process has resulted in an adverse mix variance and a favourable yield variance.

EXAMPLE 18.1

The Milano company has established the following standard mix for producing nine litres of product A:

	(£)
five litres of material X at £7 per litre	35
three litres of material Y at £5 per litre	15
two litres of material Z at £2 per litre	4
	£54

A standard loss of 10 per cent of input is expected to occur. Actual input was:

	(£)
53000 litres of material X at £7 per litre	371000
28000 litres of material Y at £5.30 per litre	148400
19000 litres of material Z at £2.20 per litre	41800
100000	£561200

Actual output for the period was 92700 litres of product A.

Material usage variance

The material usage variance consists of the mix variance and the yield variance. The material usage variance is therefore a favourable variance of £7200, consisting of an adverse mix variance of £9000 and a favourable yield variance of £16 200. To calculate the material usage variance, we compare the standard quantity of materials for the actual production with the actual quantity of materials used and multiply by the standard material prices in the normal way. The calculations are as follows:

Standard quantity for actual production at standard prices

Actual production of 92 700 litres requires an input of 103 000 litres (92 700 × 10/9), consisting of:

	(£)
51 500 litres of X (103 000 × 5/10) at £7 per litre	= 360 500
30 900 litres of Y (103 000 × 3/10) at £5 per litre	= 154 500
20 600 litres of Z (103 000 × 2/10) at £2 per litre	= 41 200
	556 200 (i)

Actual quantity at standard prices

	(£)
53 000 litres of X at £7 per litre	= 371 000
28 000 litres of Y at £5 per litre	= 140 000
19 000 litres of Z at £2 per litre	= 38 000
	549 000 (ii)
Material usage variance (i) – (ii)	= £7 200 F

Note that the standard quantity for actual production at standard prices can also be calculated by multiplying the actual output by the standard cost per unit of output (92 700 × £6 = £556 200).

SALES MIX AND SALES QUANTITY VARIANCES

Where a company sells several different products that have different profit margins, the sales volume margin variance can be divided into a sales quantity (sometimes called a sales yield variance) and sales mix variance. For example, multinational telecomm companies are interested in the impact of the sales mix on profits arising from international calls where different tariffs apply for calls made between different countries. The quantity variance measures the effect of changes in physical volume on total profits and the mix variance measures the impact arising from the actual sales mix being different from the budgeted sales mix. The variances can be measured either in terms of contribution margins or profit margins. However, contribution margins are recommended because changes in sales volume affect profits by the contribution per unit sold and not the profit per unit sold. Let us now calculate the sales margin mix and quantity variances. Consider Example 18.2.

The **total sales margin variance** is £4000 adverse, and is calculated by comparing the difference between the budgeted total contribution and the actual contribution. Contribution margins for the three products were exactly as budgeted. The total sales margin for the period therefore consists of a zero **sales margin price variance** and an adverse **sales margin volume variance** of £4000. Even though more units were sold than anticipated (22 000 rather than the budgeted 20 000), and budgeted and actual contribution margins were the same, the sales volume variance is £4000 adverse. The reasons for this arise from having sold fewer units of product X, the high margin product, and more units of product Z, which has the lowest margin.

We can explain how the sales volume margin variance was affected by the change in sales mix by calculating the **sales margin mix variance**. The formula for calculating this variance is:

$$(\text{actual sales quantity} - \text{actual sales quantity in budgeted proportions})$$
$$\times \text{ standard margin}$$

EXAMPLE 18.2

The budgeted sales for the Milano company for a period were:

	Units	Unit contribution margin (£)	Total contribution (£)
Product X	8 000 (40%)	20	160 000
Y	7 000 (35%)	12	84 000
Z	5 000 (25%)	9	45 000
	20 000		289 000

and the actual sales were:

	Units (£)	Unit contribution margin (£)	Total contribution
Product X	6 000	20	120 000
Y	7 000	12	84 000
Z	9 000	9	81 000
	22 000		285 000

Assume that actual selling prices and unit costs are identical to standard costs/prices. You are required to calculate the sales margin variances.

If we apply this formula, we will obtain the following calculations:

	Actual sales quantity	Actual sales in budgeted proportions	Difference	Standard margin (£)	Sales margin mix variance (£)
Product X	6 000 (27%)	8 800 (40%) =	−2 800	20	56 000A
Y	7 000 (32%)	7 700 (35%) =	−700	12	8 400A
Z	9 000 (41%)	5 500 (25%) =	+3 500	9	31 500F
	22 000	22 000			32 900A

To compute the sales quantity component of the sales volume variance, we compare the budgeted and actual sales volumes (holding the product mix constant). The formula for calculating the sales quantity variance is:

$$(\text{actual sales quantity in budgeted proportion} - \text{budgeted sales quantity})$$
$$\times \text{standard margin}$$

Applying this formula gives the following calculations:

	Actual sales in budgeted proportions	Budgeted sales quantity	Difference	Standard margin (£)	Sales margin quantity variance (£)
Product X	8 800 (40%)	8 000 (40%)	+800	20	16 000F
Y	7 700 (35%)	7 000 (35%)	+700	12	8 400F
Z	5 500 (25%)	5 000 (20%)	+500	9	4 500F
	22 000	20 000			28 900F

By separating the sales volume variance into quantity and mix variances, we can explain how the sales volume variance is affected by a shift in the total physical volume of sales and a shift in the relative mix of products. The sales volume quantity variance indicates that if the original planned sales mix of 40 per cent of X, 35 per cent of Y and 25 per cent of Z had been maintained then, for the actual sales volume of 22 000 units, profits would have increased by £28 900. In other words, the sales volume variance would have been £28 900 favourable instead of £4000 adverse. However, because the actual sales mix was not in accordance with the budgeted sales mix, an adverse mix variance of £32 900 occurred. The adverse sales mix variance has arisen because of an increase in the percentage of units sold of product Z, which has the lowest contribution margin, and a decrease in the percentage sold of units of product X, which has the highest contribution margin. An adverse mix variance will occur whenever there is an increase in the percentage sold of units with below average contribution margins or a decrease in the percentage sold of units with above average contribution margins. The division of the sales volume variance into quantity and mix components demonstrates that increasing or maximizing sales volume may not be as desirable as promoting the sales of the most desirable mix of products.

The sales quantity variance is sometimes further divided into a market size and a market share variance. For an explanation of these variances, you should refer to Learning Note 18.1 in the digital support resources accompanying this book (see Preface for details).

DISTINGUISHING BETWEEN PLANNING AND OPERATING VARIANCES

Standards or plans are normally based on the environment that is anticipated when the targets are set. However, if the environment is different from that anticipated, actual performance should be compared with a standard that reflects these changed conditions (i.e. an ex post variance analysis approach).

EXAMPLE 18.3

The standard cost per unit of raw material was estimated to be £10 per unit. The general market price at the time of purchase was £10.50 per unit and the actual price paid was £10.45 per unit. A purchase of 100 000 units of the raw materials was made during the period.

Clearly, to measure managerial performance, we should compare like with like and compare actual results with adjusted standards based on the conditions that managers actually operated during the period. Let us now apply this principle to the material price variance. Consider Example 18.3.

The conventional material price variance is £45 000 adverse (100 000 units at £0.45). However, this variance consists of an adverse *planning variance* of £50 000 that is due to incorrect estimates of the target buying price and a favourable *purchasing efficiency (operational) variance* of £5 000. The planning variance is calculated as follows:

purchasing planning variance

= (original target price − general market price at the time of purchase)
$$\times \text{ quantity purchased}$$
= (£10 − 10.50) × 100 000
= £50 000A

This planning variance is not controllable, but it does provide useful feedback information to management on how effective the company's planning process has been and thus provide feedback to improve future planning.

The efficiency of the purchasing department is assessed by a purchasing efficiency (operational) variance. This variance measures the purchasing department's efficiency for the conditions that actually prevailed during the reporting period and is calculated as follows:

purchasing efficiency variance

= (general market price − actual price paid) × quantity purchased
= (£10.50 − £10.45) × 100 000
= £5000F

Hence the conventional price variance of £45 000A adverse can be divided into an *uncontrollable* adverse material planning variance of £50 000 and a *controllable* favourable purchasing efficiency variance of £5000. This analysis gives a clearer indication of the efficiency of the purchasing function, and avoids including adverse uncontrollable price variances in the performance reports that are beyond the control of managers. If an adverse price variance of £50 000 is reported, this is likely to lead to dysfunctional motivation effects if the purchasing department has performed the purchasing function efficiently.

The same approach as that described above can also be applied to labour, overhead and sales variances. For example, the approach can be applied to usage variances with separate uncontrollable planning and operational usage variances being reported. For a more detailed discussion of distinguishing between planning and operating variances, you should refer to Learning Note 18.2 in the digital support resources accompanying this book. The solutions to Review problems 18.15 and 18.16 also provides a further illustration of planning and operating variances.

THE INVESTIGATION OF VARIANCES

After the variances have been reported, management must decide which variances should be investigated. They could adopt a policy of investigating every reported variance. Such a policy would, however, be very expensive and time consuming, and would lead to investigating some variances that would not result in improvements in operations even if the cause of the variance was determined. If, by way of contrast, management does not investigate reported variances, the control function would be ignored. The optimal policy lies somewhere between these two extremes. In other words, the objective is to investigate only those variances that yield benefits in excess of the cost of investigation.

There are several reasons why actual performance might differ from standard performance. A variance may arise when frequent changes in prices of inputs occur, resulting in standard prices becoming out of date. Consequently, any investigation of price variances will indicate a general change in market prices rather than any efficiencies or inefficiencies in acquiring the resources. Standards can also become out of date where operations are subject to frequent technological changes. Investigation of variances falling into this category will provide feedback on the inaccuracy of the standards and highlight the need to update the standard. Where standards are revised, it may be necessary to alter some of the firm's output or input decisions. Ideally, standards ought to be frequently reviewed and, where appropriate, updated in order to minimize variances being reported that are due to standards being out of date.

Variances can also result from inefficient operations due to a failure to follow prescribed procedures, faulty machinery or human errors. Investigation of variances in this category should pinpoint the cause of the inefficiency and lead to corrective action to eliminate the inefficiency being repeated.

Finally, variances can be due to random or chance fluctuations for which no cause can be found. These may occur when a particular process is performed by the same worker under the same conditions, yet performance varies. When no known cause is present to account for this variability, it is said to be due to random or uncontrollable factors. A standard is determined from a series of observations of a particular operation. A representative reading from these observations is chosen to determine a standard. Frequently, the representative reading that is chosen is the average or some other measure of central tendency. The important point to note is that one summary reading has been chosen to represent the standard when, in reality, a range of outcomes is possible when the process is *under control*. Any observation that differs from the chosen standard when the process is under control can be described as a random uncontrollable variation around the standard.

Any investigation of variances due to random uncontrollable factors will involve a cost and will not yield any benefits because no assignable cause for the variance is present. Furthermore, those variances arising from assignable causes (such as out-of-date standards or out-of-control operations) do not necessarily warrant investigation. For example, such variances may only be worthy of investigation if the benefits expected from the investigation exceed the costs of searching for and correcting the sources of the variance.

Variances may therefore be due to the following causes:

1 random uncontrollable factors when the operation is under control;

2 assignable causes, but with the costs of investigation exceeding the benefits;

3 assignable causes, but with the benefits from investigation exceeding the cost of investigation.

A perfect cost investigation model would investigate only those variances falling into the third category.

In many companies, managers use simple rule of thumb models based on arbitrary criteria such as investigating if the absolute size of a variance is greater than a certain amount or if the variance exceeds the standard cost by some predetermined percentage (say 10 per cent). The advantages of using simple arbitrary rules are their simplicity and ease of implementation. There are, however, several disadvantages. Simple rule of thumb models do not consider the costs and benefits of an investigation. For example, investigating all variances that exceed the standard cost by a fixed percentage can lead to investigating many variances of small amounts.

Some of these difficulties can be overcome by applying different percentages or amounts for different expense items as the basis for the investigation decision. For example, smaller percentages might be used as a signal to investigate key expense items and a higher percentage applied to less important items of expense.

As an alternative to using simple rule of thumb investigation models, more sophisticated statistical models can be used that rely on statistical quality control theory to determine the statistical probability of an observed variance being out of control and requiring further investigation. For a description and illustration of these models you should refer to Learning Note 18.3 in the digital support resources accompanying this book.

THE ROLE OF STANDARD COSTING WHEN ABC HAS BEEN IMPLEMENTED

For those organizations that have implemented activity-based systems, standard costing still has an important role to play in controlling the costs of unit-level activities. Unit-level activities can be defined as those activities that are performed each time a unit of product or service is produced. These activities consume resources in proportion to the number of units produced. For example, if a firm produces 10 per cent more units, it will consume 10 per cent more labour cost, 10 per cent more materials, 10 per cent more machine hours and 10 per cent more energy costs. Expenses in this category include direct labour, direct materials, energy costs and expenses that are consumed in proportion to machine processing times (such as machine maintenance). Therefore traditional variance analysis can be applied for direct labour, direct materials and those variable overheads that vary with output, machine hours and direct labour hours.

Variance analysis is most suited to controlling the costs of unit-level activities but it can also provide meaningful information for managing those overhead costs that are fixed in the short term but variable in the longer term if traditional volume-based cost drivers are replaced with activity-based cost drivers that better reflect the causes of resource consumption. Variance analysis, however, cannot be used to manage all overhead costs. It is inappropriate for the control of facility-sustaining (infrastructure) costs because the costs of these resources do not fluctuate in the longer term according to the demand for them.

Mak and Roush (1994) and Kaplan (1994b) have considered how variance analysis can be applied to incorporate activity costs and cost drivers for those overheads that are fixed in the short term but variable in the long term. The data presented in Example 18.4 illustrate their ideas relating to ABC overhead variance analysis for a set-up activity. You will see from this example that budgeted *fixed* costs of £80 000 provide a practical capacity to perform 2000 set-ups during the period. Assuming that the number of set-ups has been identified as the appropriate cost driver, a cost of £40 per set-up (£80 000/2000) will be charged to products. Since budgeted capacity usage is 1600 set-ups, not all of the capacity provided (2000 set-ups) will be used, and a budgeted cost of unused capacity of £16 000 (400 × £40), will be highlighted during the budget process. The actual number of set-ups performed was 1500 compared with a budget of 1600 and an unexpected capacity utilization variance of £4000 (100 × £40) will be reported at the end of the period. The traditional spending (expenditure) variance is £10 000, being the difference between budgeted and actual fixed costs incurred. We can now reconcile the *fixed* set-up expenses charged to products with the actual expenses incurred that are recorded in the financial accounts:

	£
Set-up expenses charged to products (1500 × £40)	60 000
Budgeted unused capacity variance (400 × £40)	16 000A
Capacity utilization variance (100 × £40)	4 000A
Expenditure variance	10 000F
Total actual expenses	70 000

The above capacity variances highlight for management attention the £20 000 unused capacity (£16 000 expected and £4000 unexpected) and thus signals the opportunity for actions such as reducing the supply of resources or using the surplus resources to generate additional revenues.

In Example 18.4, it is assumed that the *variable* set-up costs, such as the cost of supplies used in the set-up activity, varies with the number of set-ups. The variable cost driver rate of £25 per set-up has

EXAMPLE 18.4

A ssume the following information for the set-up activity for a period:

Budget	Actual
Activity level: 1600 set-ups	Total fixed costs: £70 000
Practical capacity supplied: 2000 set-ups	Total variable costs: £39 000
Total fixed costs: £80 000	
Total variable costs: £40 000	Number of set-ups 1 500
Cost driver rates (variable): £25 per set-up	
(fixed): £40 per set-up	

been calculated by dividing the budgeted variable cost of £40 000 by the budgeted number of set-ups of 1600. Note that the budgeted variable cost per set-up will be £25 for all activity levels. Thus the estimated set-up costs at the practical capacity of 2000 set-ups would be £50 000 (2500 × £25) but the cost per set-up would remain at £25. To calculate the set-up variable cost variance, we must flex the budget. The actual number of set-ups performed was 1500 and the flexible budget allowance is £37 500 (1500 × £25). Actual expenditure is £39 000 and therefore an adverse variable cost variance of £1500 will be reported. The reconciliation between the variable set-up expenses charged to products and the actual expenses incurred is as follows:

Variable set-up expenses charged to products	
(1500 × £25)	37 500
Variable overhead variance	1 500A
Total actual expenses	39 000

In Example 18.4, we assumed that the number of set-ups was the cost driver. If set-ups take varying amounts of time they will not represent an homogeneous measure of output and thus may not provide a satisfactory measure of the cost of activity. To overcome this problem, it may be preferable to use the number of set-up hours as the cost driver. Let us now assume in Example 18.4 that the cost driver is set-up hours and that the quantity of set-up hours is the same for all of set-ups. Therefore the variance analysis based on set-up hours will be identical to the variances that were computed when the number of set-ups was the cost driver.

Where cost drivers that capture the duration of the activity are used, Mak and Roush (1994) advocate the reporting of separate efficiency variances for each activity. Assume in Example 18.4 that the standard activity level for the actual number of set-ups performed during the period was 1500 hours but the actual number of set-up hours required was 1660. The standard activity level represents the number of set-up hours that should have been required for the actual number of set-ups. The difference between the standard and the actual set-up hours thus arises because of efficiencies/inefficiencies in performing the set-up activities. Assuming that variable costs vary with the number of set-up hours then inefficiency in performing set-up activities has resulted in an extra 160 set-up hours (1660 − 1500) being used, thus causing additional spending of £4000 (160 hours × £25). In addition, a favourable variable overhead expenditure variance of £2500 will be reported. This figure is derived in a manner similar to the traditional analysis by deducting the actual variable overhead expenditure of £39 000 from the flexible budget based on actual set-up hours (1660 × £25 = £41 500). Note that the sum of the efficiency variance (£4000A) and the expenditure variance (£2500F) is the same as the variable overhead variance of £1500 reported when the number of set-ups was used as the cost driver.

SUMMARY

The following items relate to the learning objectives listed at the beginning of the chapter.

● **Prepare a set of accounts for a standard costing system.**

The method used in the chapter to illustrate the recording of standard costs valued all inventories at standard cost with all entries being recorded in the inventory accounts at standard prices. Any differences between standard costs and actual costs are debited or credited to variance accounts. Adverse variances appear as debit balances and favourable variances as credit balances. The preparation of a set of accounts for a standard costing system was illustrated in Exhibit 18.1.

● **Explain and calculate material mix and yield and sales mix and quantity variances.**

In some production processes it is possible to vary the mix of materials used to make the final product. Any deviations from the standard mix will lead to a materials mix variance. A favourable mix variance will occur when cheaper materials are substituted for more expensive ones. This may not always be in the company's best interest, since product quality may suffer or output may be reduced, leading to an adverse yield variance. The yield variance arises because there is a difference between the standard output for a given level of input and the actual output attained. Part of the sales margin volume variance may be accounted for because the actual sales mix differs from the budgeted sales mix. Calculating a sales margin mix variance can isolate this element. The remaining part of the sales margin volume variance represents the sales quantity variance.

● **Explain and calculate planning and operating variances.**

One of the criticisms of standard costing is that standards are normally based on the environment that was anticipated when the targets were set. To overcome this problem, whenever the actual environment is different from the anticipated environment, performance should be compared with a standard that reflects the changed conditions. One possible solution is to extract an uncontrollable planning or forecasting variance and report operating variances based on the changed conditions that applied during the period. The calculations of planning and operating variances were illustrated using Example 18.3.

● **Explain the factors that influence the decision to investigate a variance and describe the different methods that can be used to determine whether an investigation is warranted.**

The decision to investigate a variance should depend on whether the expected benefits are likely to exceed the costs of carrying out the investigation. Variances may be due to: (a) random uncontrollable variations when the variance is under control; (b) assignable causes but the costs of investigation exceed the benefits of investigation; and (c) assignable causes but the benefits from investigation exceed the costs of investigation. The aim should be only to investigate those variances that fall into the last category.

● **Explain the role of standard costing within an ABC system.**

Within an ABC system, variance analysis is most suited to controlling the costs of unit-level activities. It can also provide meaningful information for managing those overhead costs that are fixed in the short term but variable in the longer term if traditional volume-based cost drivers are replaced with activity-based cost drivers that better reflect the causes of resource consumption. Variance analysis, however, cannot be used to manage all overhead costs. It is inappropriate for the control of facility-sustaining (infrastructure) costs because the cost of these resources does not fluctuate in the longer term according to the demand for them.

KEY TERMS AND CONCEPTS

Assignable causes Variances that can be assigned to a known cause, which may or may not be worth investigating further.

Ex post variance analysis approach An approach to variance analysis in which actual results are compared with adjusted standards based on the conditions in which managers actually operated during the period.

Material mix variance The difference between the mix of materials actually used and the predetermined mix included in the calculation of the standard cost of an operation.

Materials yield variance The difference between the standard output for a given level of inputs and the actual output attained.

Purchasing efficiency variance The general market price less the actual price paid, multiplied by the quantity purchased.

Purchasing planning variance The original target price less the general market price at the time of purchase, multiplied by the quantity purchased.

Random or uncontrollable factors Factors that cannot be assigned to a known cause.

Sales margin mix variance The actual sales quantity less the actual sales quantity in budgeted proportions, divided by the standard margin.

Sales margin price variance The difference between the actual contribution margin and the standard margin multiplied by the actual sales volume.

Sales margin volume variance The difference between the actual sales volume and the budgeted sales volume multiplied by the standard contribution margin.

Sales quantity variance The actual sales quantity in budgeted proportion less the budgeted sales quantity, multiplied by the standard margin.

Total sales margin variance The difference between actual sales revenue less the standard variable cost of sales and the budgeted contribution.

RECOMMENDED READING

For additional reading relating to planning and operating variances and mix and yield variances, you should refer to articles that can be accessed from the ACCA Student Accountant technical article archive at www.accaglobal.com/gb/en/student/exam-support-resources/fundamentals-exams-study-resources/f5/technical-articles.html. For further reading on ABC variance analysis see Kaplan (1994a) and Mak and Roush (1994, 1996).

KEY EXAMINATION POINTS

Questions on mix and yield variances, variance investigation models and calculating planning and operating variance tend to be included only in advanced management accounting examinations. Make sure you understand these topics and attempt the review problems that relate to these topics. You should compare your answers with the solutions to the review problems. Note that, besides adopting the approach described in the chapter, Review problem 18.14 also presents an alternative approach for calculating direct material yield variances. Sometimes examination questions require you to discuss the usefulness of standard costing variance analysis in today's business environment and/or the future role of standard costing. These topics are discussed in Learning Notes 18.4 and 18.5 in the digital support resources accompanying this book (see Preface for details).

ASSESSMENT MATERIAL

The review questions are short questions that enable you to assess your understanding of the main topics included in the chapter. The numbers in parentheses provide you with the page numbers to refer to if you cannot answer a specific question.

The review problems are more complex and require you to relate and apply the content to various business problems. The problems are graded by their level of difficulty. Solutions to review problems that are not preceded by the term 'IM' are provided in a separate section at the end of the book. Solutions to problems preceded by the term 'IM' are provided in the Instructor's Manual accompanying this book that can be downloaded from the lecturer's digital support resources. Additional review problems with fully worked solutions are provided in the *Student Manual* that accompanies this book.

REVIEW QUESTIONS

18.1 Under what circumstances will a (a) material mix and (b) material yield variances arise? (pp. 474–476)

18.2 Distinguish between a sales margin mix and sales margin quantity variance. (pp. 478–479)

18.3 What are planning variances? Why are they separately identified? (pp. 479–480)

18.4 Describe the approaches for determining when a variance should be investigated. (pp. 480–482)

18.5 Explain why actual performance might differ from standard performance. (pp. 480–482)

18.6 When should a standard cost variance be investigated? (p. 481)

18.7 What is a statistical control chart? How can it be applied to determining when a variance should be investigated? (pp. 481–482)

18.8 How can standard costing be used when ABC has been implemented? (pp. 482–483)

18.9 Why is standard costing more suitable for controlling the cost of unit-level activities? (p. 482)

REVIEW PROBLEMS

18.10 Advanced. The following data relate to both questions (a) and (b). A company has budgeted to produce and sell 15 000 units per annum of a single product. The budgeted market size for this product is 75 000 units per annum. The budgeted information per unit is as follows:

	£
Selling price	125
Standard cost:	
Direct materials	20
Direct labour	15
Variable overhead	10
Fixed overhead	5
Standard profit	75

In the period covered by the budget, the following actual results were recorded:

Production and sales	13 000 units
Industry sales	10 per cent lower than previously forecast

(a) The market size variance, calculated on a contribution per unit basis is:

(A) £40 000 adverse
(B) £40 000 favourable
(C) £120 000 adverse
(D) £120 000 favourable
(E) £160 000 adverse

(b) The market share variance, calculated on a contribution per unit basis is:

(A) £40 000 adverse
(B) £40 000 favourable
(C) £120 000 adverse
(D) £120 000 favourable
(E) £160 000 favourable   *(3 marks)*

CIMA Management Accounting – Decision Making

18.11 Intermediate: Accounting entries for a standard costing system. Bronte Ltd manufactures a single product, a laminated kitchen unit with a standard cost of £110 made up as follows:

	(£)
Direct materials (15 sq. metres at £3 per sq. metre)	45
Direct labour (five hours at £10 per hour)	50

Variable overheads (five hours at £2 per hour)	10
Fixed overheads (five hours at £1 per hour)	5
	110

The standard selling price of the kitchen unit is £130. The monthly budget projects production and sales of 1000 units. Actual figures for the month of April are as follows:

Sales 1200 units at £132
Production 1400 units
Direct materials 22 000 sq. metres at £4 per sq. metre
Direct wages 6800 hours at £11
Variable overheads £11 000
Fixed overheads £6000

You are required to prepare:

(a) a trading account reconciling actual and budgeted profit and showing all the appropriate variances;   *(13 marks)*
(b) ledger accounts in respect of the above transactions.
(10 marks)

ICAEW Accounting Techniques*

18.12 Advanced: Sales mix and yield variances. Valet Co is a car valeting (cleaning) company. It operates in the country of Strappia, which has been badly affected by the global financial crisis. Petrol and food prices have increased substantially in the last year and the average disposable household income has decreased by 30 per cent. Recent studies have shown that the average car owner keeps their car for five years before replacing it, rather than three years as was previously the case. Figures over recent years also show that car sales in Strappia are declining whilst business for car repairs is on the increase.

Valet Co offers two types of valet – a full valet and a mini valet. A full valet is an extensive clean of the vehicle, inside and out; a mini valet is a more basic clean of the vehicle. Until recently, four similar businesses operated in Valet Co's local area, but one of these closed down three months ago after a serious fire on its premises. Valet Co charges customers $50 for each full valet and $30 for each mini valet and this price never changes. Their budget and actual figures for the last year were as follows:

	Budget	Actual
Number of valets:		
Full valets	3600	4000
Mini valets	2000	3980

(Continued)

	$	$	$	$
Revenue		240000		319400
Variable costs:				
Staff wages	(114000)		(122000)	
Cleaning materials	(6200)		(12400)	
Energy costs	(6520)		(9200)	
		(126720)		(143600)
Contribution		113280		175800
Fixed costs:				
Rent, rates and depreciation		(36800)		(36800)
Operating profit		76480		139000

The budgeted contribution to sales ratios for the two types of valet are 44.6 per cent for full valets and 55 per cent for mini valets.

Required:

(a) Using the data provided for full valets and mini valets, calculate:

    (i) The total sales mix contribution variance; *(4 marks)*
    (ii) The total sales quantity contribution variance. *(4 marks)*

(b) Briefly describe the sales mix contribution variance and the sales quantity contribution variance. *(2 marks)*

(c) Discuss the SALES performance of the business for the period, taking into account your calculations from part (a) AND the information provided in the scenario. *(10 marks)*

ACCA F5 Performance Management

18.13 Advanced: Material mix and yield variances. The Safe Soap Co makes environmentally-friendly soap using three basic ingredients. The standard cost card for one batch of soap for the month of September was as follows:

Material	Kilograms	Price per kilogram ($)
Lye	0.25	10
Coconut oil	0.6	4
Shea butter	0.5	3

The budget for production and sales in September was 120000 batches. Actual production and sales were 136000 batches. The actual ingredients used were as follows:

Material	Kilograms
Lye	34080
Coconut oil	83232
Shea butter	64200

Required:

(a) Calculate the total material mix variance and the total material yield variance for September. *(8 marks)*

(b) In October the materials mix and yield variances were as follows:

Mix: $6000 adverse
Yield: $10000 favourable

The production manager is pleased with the results overall, stating:

'At the beginning of September I made some changes to the mix of ingredients used for the soaps. As I expected, the mix variance is adverse in both months because we haven't yet updated our standard cost card but, in both months, the favourable yield variance more than makes up for this. Overall, I think we can be satisfied that the changes made to the product mix are producing good results and now we are able to produce more batches and meet the growing demand for our product.'

The sales manager, however, holds a different view and says:

'I'm not happy with this change in the ingredients mix. I've had to explain to the board why the sales volume variance for October was $22000 adverse. I've tried to explain that the quality of the soap has declined slightly and some of my customers have realized this and simply aren't happy but no-one seems to be listening. Some customers are even demanding that the price of the soap be reduced and threatening to go elsewhere if the problem isn't sorted out.'

Required:

(i) Briefly explain what the adverse materials mix and favourable materials yield variances indicate about production at Safe Soap Co in October.

    Note: You are NOT required to discuss revision of standards or operational and planning variances. *(4 marks)*

(ii) Discuss whether the sales manager could be justified in claiming that the change in the materials mix has caused an adverse sales volume variance in October. *(3 marks)*

ACCA F5 Performance Management

18.14 Advanced: Material mix and yield variances and ABC variance analysis. Choc Co is a company which manufactures and sells three types of biscuit in packets. One of them is called 'Ooze' and contains three types of sweetener: honey, sugar and syrup. The standard materials usage and cost for one unit of 'Ooze' (one packet) is as follows:

		$
Honey	20 grams at $0.02 per gram	0.40
Sugar	15 grams at $0.03 per gram	0.45
Syrup	10 grams at $0.025 per gram	0.25
		1.10

In the three months ended 30 November, Choc Co. produced 101000 units of 'Ooze' using 2200kg of honey, 1400kg of sugar and 1050kg of syrup. Note: there are 1000 grams in a kilogram (kg).

Choc Co. has used activity-based costing to allocate its overheads for a number of years. One of its main overheads is machine set-up costs. In the three months ended 30 November, the following information was available in relation to set-up costs:

Budget

Total number of units produced	264000
Total number of set-ups	330
Total set-up costs	$52800

Actual

total number of unite produced	320000
total number of set-ups	360
total set-up costs	$60000

Required:

(a) Calculate the following variances for materials in Ooze:

    (i) Total materials usage variance; *(4 marks)*
    (ii) Total materials mix variance; *(4 marks)*
    (iii) Total materials quantity (yield) variance. *(4 marks)*

(b) Calculate the following activity-based variances in relation to the set-up cost of the machines:

    (i) The expenditure variance; *(3 marks)*
    (ii) The efficiency variance. *(3 marks)*

(c) Briefly outline the steps involved in allocating overheads using activity-based costing. *(2 marks)*

ACCA F5 Performance Management

18.15 Advanced: Planning and operating variances. A company has produced the following performance report for April. The budget shown in the report was based on an original assumption that the total market size for April would be 40 million units. Since the performance report was produced, more accurate market size information has become available. The actual market size for April was lower than estimated at 37.5 million units.

	Budget	Actual	Variance
Sales and production units	2 000 000	1 650 000	(350 000)

	Budget $000	Actual $000	Variance $000
Revenue	7 000	5 643.0	(1 357.0)
Variable costs	4 220	3 580.5	639.5
Fixed costs	1 050	1 100.0	(50.0)
Profit	1 730	962.5	(767.5)

Required:

(a) Produce a statement that reconciles budget profit to actual profit for April in as much detail as possible.
(6 marks)

(b) Discuss the advantages and disadvantages of your statement with regard to responsibility accounting.
(4 marks)

CIMA P2 Performance Management

18.16 Intermediate: Planning and operating variances. Bedco manufactures bed sheets and pillowcases which it supplies to a major hotel chain. It uses a just-in-time system and holds no inventories.

The standard cost for the cotton which is used to make the bed sheets and pillowcases is $5 per m². Each bed sheet uses 2 m² of cotton and each pillowcase uses 0.5 m². Production levels for bed sheets and pillowcases for November were as follows:

	Budgeted production levels (units)	Actual production levels (units)
Bed sheets	120 000	120 000
Pillowcases	190 000	180 000

The actual cost of the cotton in November was $5.80 per m². 248 000 m² of cotton was used to make the bed sheets and 95 000 m² was used to make the pillowcases.

The world commodity prices for cotton increased by 20 per cent in the month of November. At the beginning of the month, the hotel chain made an unexpected request for an immediate design change to the pillowcases. The new design required 10 per cent more cotton than previously. It also resulted in production delays and therefore a shortfall in production of 10 000 pillowcases in total that month.

The production manager at Bedco is responsible for all buying and any production issues which occur, although he is not responsible for the setting of standard costs.

Required:

(a) Calculate the following variances for the month of November, for both bed sheets and pillow cases, and in total:

(i) Material price planning variance; (3 marks)
(ii) Material price operational variance; (3 marks)
(iii) Material usage planning variance; (3 marks)
(iv) Material usage operational variance. (3 marks)

(b) Assess the performance of the production manager for the month of November. (8 marks)

ACCA F5 Performance Management

18.17 Advanced: Planning and operating variances. Linsil has produced the following operating statement reconciling budgeted and actual gross profit for the last three months, based on actual sales of 122 000 units of its single product:

Operating statement	£	£	£
Budgeted gross profit			800 000
Budgeted fixed production overhead			352 000
			1 152 000
Budgeted contribution			
Sales volume contribution variance		19 200	
Sales price variance		(61 000)	
			(41 800)
			1 110 200
Actual sales less standard variable cost of sales			
Planning variances			
Variable cost variances	Favourable	Adverse	
Direct material price		23 570	
Direct material usage	42 090		
Direct labour rate		76 128	
Direct labour efficiency		203 333	
	42 090	303 031	(260 941)
Operational variances			
Variable cost variances	Favourable	Adverse	
Direct material price		31 086	
Direct material usage	14 030		
Direct labour rate		19 032	
Direct labour efficiency	130 133		
	144 163	50 118	94 045
Actual contribution			943 304
Budgeted fixed production overhead		(352 000)	
Fixed production overhead expenditure variance		27 000	
Actual fixed production overhead			(325 000)
Actual gross profit			618 304

The standard direct costs and selling price applied during the three-month period and the actual direct costs and selling price for the period were as follows:

	Standard	Actual
Selling price (£/unit)	31.50	31.00
Direct material usage (kg/unit)	3.00	2.80
Direct material price (£/kg)	2.30	2.46
Direct labour efficiency (hrs/unit)	1.25	1.30
Direct labour rate (£/hr)	12.00	12.60

After the end of the three-month period and prior to the preparation of the above operating statement, it was decided to revise the standard costs retrospectively to take account of the following:

1 a 3 per cent increase in the direct material price per kilogram;
2 a labour rate increase of 4 per cent;

3 the standard for labour efficiency had anticipated buying a new machine leading to a 10 per cent decrease in labour hours; instead of buying a new machine, existing machines had been improved, giving an expected 5 per cent saving in material usage.

Required:

(a) Using the information provided, demonstrate how each planning and operational variance in the operating statement has been calculated.   (11 marks)

(b) Calculate direct labour and direct material variances based on the standard cost data applied during the three-month period.   (4 marks)

(c) Explain the significance of separating variances into planning and operational elements, using the operating statement above to illustrate your answer.   (5 marks)

(d) Discuss the factors to be considered in deciding whether a variance should be investigated.   (5 marks)

ACCA 2.4 Financial Management and Control

18.18 Advanced: Traditional and activity-based variance analysis. Frolin Chemicals Ltd produces FDN. The standard ingredients of 1kg of FDN are:

0.65kg of ingredient F	@ £4.00 per kg
0.30kg of ingredient D	@ £6.00 per kg
0.20kg of ingredient N	@ £2.50 per kg
1.15kg	

Production of 4000kg of FDN was budgeted for April. The production of FDN is entirely automated and production costs attributed to FDN production comprise only direct materials and overheads. The FDN production operation works on a JIT basis and no ingredient or FDN inventories are held.

Overheads were budgeted for April for the FDN production operation as follows:

Activity		Total amount
Receipt of deliveries from suppliers	(standard delivery quantity is 460kg)	£4 000
Despatch of goods to customers	(standard dispatch quantity is 100kg)	£8 000
		£12 000

In April, 4200kg of FDN were produced and cost details were as follows:

- *Materials used:*
  2840kg of F, 1210kg of D and 860kg of N
  total cost £20 380

- *Actual overhead costs:*
  12 supplier deliveries (cost £4800) were made, and 38 customer despatches (cost £7800) were processed.

Frolin Chemicals Ltd's budget committee met recently to discuss the preparation of the financial control report for April, and the following discussion occurred:

Chief accountant: 'The overheads do not vary directly with output and are therefore by definition "fixed". They should be analysed and reported accordingly.'

Management accountant: 'The overheads do not vary with output, but they are certainly not fixed. They should be analysed and reported on an activity basis.'

Requirements:

Having regard to this discussion,

(a) prepare a variance analysis for FDN production costs in April: separate the material cost variance into price, mixture and yield components; separate the overhead cost variance into expenditure, capacity and efficiency components using consumption of ingredient F as the overhead absorption base;   (11 marks)

(b) prepare a variance analysis for FDN production overhead costs in April on an activity basis;   (9 marks)

(c) explain how, in the design of an activity-based costing system, you would identify and select the most appropriate activities and cost drivers.   (5 marks)

CIMA Stage 3 Management Accounting Applications

18.19 Advanced: Investigation of variances. From past experience a company operating a standard cost system has accumulated the following information in relation to variances in its monthly management accounts:

Percentage of total number of variances

1 Its variances fall into two categories:

Category 1: those that are not worth investigating	64
Category 2: those that are worth investigating	36
	100

2 Of Category 2, corrective action has eliminated 70 per cent of the variances, but the remainder have continued.

3 The cost of investigation averages £350 and that of correcting variances averages £550.

4 The average size of any variance not corrected is £525 per month and the company's policy is to assess the present value of such costs at 2 per cent per month for a period of five months.

You are required to:

(a) prepare *two* decision trees, to represent the position if an investigation is:
  (i) carried out;
  (ii) not carried out;   (12 marks)

(b) recommend, with supporting calculations, whether or not the company should follow a policy of investigating variances as a matter of routine;   (3 marks)

(c) explain briefly *two* types of circumstance that would give rise to variances in Category 1 and *two* to those in Category 2;   (6 marks)

(d) mention any *one* variation in the information used that you feel would be beneficial to the company if you wished to improve the quality of the decision-making rule recommended in (b) above. Explain briefly why you have suggested it.   (4 marks)

CIMA P3 Management Accounting

18.20 Advanced (N.B. Relates to material covered in digital support resources Learning Notes 18.4 and 18.5.)

(a) In high technology small batch manufacture, accountants sometimes take the view that standard costing cannot be applied. The move into high technology is generally accompanied by a shift away from labour-dominated to capital-intensive processes.

  You are required to appraise the application of standard costing in the circumstance described above.   (12 marks)

(b) In order to secure and direct employee motivation towards the achievement of a firm's goals, it may be considered that budget centres should be created at the lowest defined management level.

  You are required to discuss the advantages and disadvantages of creating budget centres at such a level.   (12 marks)

CIMA Stage 4 Management Accounting – Control and Audit

18.21 Advanced (N.B. Relates to material covered in digital support resources Learning Notes 18.4 and 18.5.) In recent years, writers have argued that standard costing and variance analysis should not be used for cost control and performance evaluation purposes in today's manufacturing world. Its use, they argue, is likely to induce behaviour that is inconsistent with the strategic manufacturing objectives that companies need to achieve in order to survive in today's intensely competitive international economic environment.

Requirements:

(a) Explain the arguments referred to in the above paragraph concerning the relevance of standard costing and variance analysis. *(10 marks)*

(b) Explain the arguments in favour of the relevance of standard costing and variance analysis in the modern manufacturing environment. *(8 marks)*

(c) Suggest methods that might be used by management accountants to control costs and evaluate efficiency as alternatives or complements to standard costing and variance analysis. *(7 marks)*

CIMA Stage 3 Management Accounting Applications

18.22 Advanced.

(a) The investigation of a variance is a fundamental element in the effective exercise of control through budgetary control and standard costing systems. The systems for identifying the variances may be well defined and detailed yet the procedures adopted to determine whether to pursue the investigation of variances may well not be formalized.

Critically examine this situation, discussing possible effective approaches to the investigation of variances. *(15 marks)*

(b) Explain the major motivational factors that influence managers in their actions to eliminate variances from budget. *(10 marks)*

CIMA Stage 4 Management Accounting Control and Audit

IM18.1 Advanced. In the new industrial environment, the usefulness of standard costing is being challenged and new approaches sought.

One approach, pioneered by the Japanese, is to replace standard costs by target costs.

You are required:

(a) to describe the problems associated with standard costing in the new industrial environment; *(6 marks)*

(b) to explain what target costs are and how they are developed and used; *(6 marks)*

(c) to contrast standard and target costs. *(5 marks)*

CIMA Management Accounting Techniques

IM18.2 Advanced. Variance investigation decisions are normally explained in textbooks by simple models, which assume the availability of a significant amount of information.

An example of this approach is as follows.

The managers estimate the probability of any variance being due to a controllable, and therefore correctable, cause at 25 per cent. They estimate the cost of investigating a variance at £1400, and the cost of correcting the cause of a correctable variance at £400. The investigation process is regarded as 100 per cent reliable in that a correctable cause of the variance will be found if it exists.

Managers estimate the loss due to not investigating, and hence not discovering, a correctable cause of the variance, averages 75 per cent of the size of the variance. For example, the loss from the failure to discover a correctable £4000 variance would be £3000.

Requirement:

(a) Calculate the minimum size of variance that would justify investigation. *(8 marks)*

(b) In addition to the approach described above, alternative approaches exist to decide whether to investigate variances by using criteria related to the absolute size of the variance and criteria based on the percentage from standard.

(i) Explain why these approaches are taken rather than the approach described in (a) above.

(ii) Comment on the appropriateness of the alternative approaches described above. *(12 marks)*

CIMA Stage 4 Management Accounting Control Systems

IM18.3 Intermediate: Accounting entries for a standard costing system. Fischer Ltd manufactures a range of chess sets, and operates a standard costing system. Information relating to the Spassky design for the month of March is as follows:

1   Standard costs per 100 sets

	(£)
Raw materials:	
Plaster of Paris, 20kg at £8 per kg	160
Paint, half-a-litre at £30 per litre	15
Direct wages, two-and-a-half hours at £10 per hour	25
Fixed production overheads, 400 per cent of direct wages	100
	300

2   Standard selling price per set £3.80.

3   Raw materials, work in progress and finished goods stock records are maintained at standard cost.

4   Stock levels at the beginning and end of March were as follows:

	1 March	31 March
Plaster of Paris	2 800kg	2 780kg
Paint	140 litres	170 litres
Finished sets	900 sets	1 100 sets

There was no work in progress at either date.

5   Budgeted production and sales during the month were 30 000 sets. Actual sales, all made at standard selling price, and actual production were 28 400 and 28 600 sets respectively.

6   Raw materials purchased during the month were 5400kg of plaster of Paris at a cost of £43 200 and 173 litres of paint at a cost of £5800.

7   Direct wages were 730 hours at an average rate of £11 per hour.

8   Fixed production overheads amounted to £34 120.

Requirement:

Prepare for the month of March:

(a) the cost ledger accounts for raw materials, work in progress and finished goods; *(10 marks)*

(b) (i) budget trading statement;
(ii) standard cost trading statement;
(iii) financial trading statement;
(iv) a reconciliation between these statements identifying all relevant variances. *(14 marks)*

ICAEW Accounting Techniques

IM18.4 Advanced: Mix variances and reconciliation as actual and budgeted profit. A company operates a number of hairdressing establishments that are managed on a franchise arrangement. The franchisor offers support using a PC package that deals with profit budgeting and control information.

Budget extracts of one franchisee for November are shown below, analysed by male and female clients. For the purposes of budget projections, average revenue rates are used. At the month end these are compared with the average monthly rates actually achieved using variance analysis. Sales price, sales quantity, sales mix and cost variances are routinely produced in order to compare the budget and actual results.

Staff working in this business are paid on a commission basis in order to act as an incentive to attract and retain clients. The labour rate variance is based on the commission payments, any basic pay is part of the monthly fixed cost.

Budget

	Male	Female
Clients	4000	1000
	(£)	(£)
Average revenue (per client)	7.5	18.0
Average commission (per client)	3.0	10.0
Total monthly fixed cost		£20 000

Actual results

	Male	Female
Clients	2000	2000
	(£)	(£)
Average revenue (per client)	8.0	20.0
Average commission (per client)	3.5	11.0
Total monthly fixed cost		£24 000

Required:

(a) Reconcile the budgeted and actual profit for November by calculating appropriate price, quantity, mix and cost variances, presenting the information in good form. You should adopt a contribution style, with mix variances based on units (i.e. clients). *(10 marks)*

(b) Write a short memorandum to the manager of the business commenting on the result in (a) above. *(4 marks)*

(c) Comment on the limitations associated with generating sales variances as in (a) above. *(6 marks)*

ACCA Paper 8 Managerial Finance

IM18.5 Advanced: Detailed variance analysis (including revision variances) plus an explanation of the meaning of operating statement variances. Tungach Ltd makes and sells a single product. Demand for the product exceeds the expected production capacity of Tungach Ltd. The holding of stocks of the finished product is avoided if possible because the physical nature of the product is such that it deteriorates quickly and stocks may become unsaleable.

A standard marginal cost system is in operation. Feedback reporting takes planning and operational variances into consideration.

The management accountant has produced the following operating statement for period 9:

Tungach Ltd
Operating statement – Period 9

	(£)	(£)
Original budgeted contribution		36 000
Revision variances:		
Material usage	9600(A)	
Material price	3600(F)	
Wage rate	1600(F)	4400(A)
Revised budgeted contribution		31 600
Sales volume variance:		
Causal factor		
Extra capacity	4740(F)	

Productivity drop	987.5(A)	
Idle time	592.5(A)	
Stock increase	2370(A)	790(F)
Revised standard contribution for sales achieved		32 390
Other variances:		
Material usage	900(F)	
Material price	3120(A)	
Labour efficiency	2950(A)	
Labour idle time	1770(A)	
Wage rate	2760(A)	
		9 700(A)
Actual contribution		22 690

(F) = favourable   (A) = adverse

Other data are available as follows:

(i) The original standard contribution per product unit as determined at period 1 was:

	(£)	(£)
Selling price		45
Less: Direct material one-and-a-half kilos at £8	12	
Direct labour two hours at £12.00	24	36
Contribution		9

(ii) A permanent change in the product specification was implemented from period 7 onwards. It was estimated that this change would require 20 per cent additional material per product unit. The current efficient price of the material has settled at £7.50 per kilo.

(iii) Actual direct material used during period 9 was 7800 kilos at £7.90 per kilo. Any residual variances are due to operational problems.

(iv) The original standard wage rate overestimated the degree of trade union pressure during negotiations and was £0.20 higher than the rate subsequently agreed. Tungach Ltd made a short-term operational decision to pay the workforce at £12.10 per hour during periods 7 to 9 in an attempt to minimize the drop in efficiency likely because of the product specification change. Management succeeded in extending the production capacity during period 9 and the total labour hours paid for were 9200 hours. These included 150 hours of idle time.

(v) Budgeted production and sales
quantity (period 9)   4000 units
Actual sales quantity (period 9)   4100 units
Actual production quantity (period 9) 4400 units

(vi) Stocks of finished goods are valued at the current efficient standard cost.

Required:

(a) Prepare detailed figures showing how the material and labour variances in the operating statement have been calculated. *(8 marks)*

(b) Prepare detailed figures showing how the sales volume variance has been calculated for each causal factor shown in the operating statement. *(6 marks)*

(c) Prepare a report to the management of Tungach Ltd explaining the meaning and relevance of the figures given in the operating statement for period 9. The report should contain specific comments for any two of the sales volume variance causal factors and any two of the 'other variances'. The comments should suggest possible reasons for each variance, the management member likely to be answerable for each variance and possible corrective action. *(8 marks)*

ACCA Level 2 Management Accounting

IM18.6 Advanced: Reconciliation of budgeted and actual profit including operating and planning variances plus an interpretation of the reconciliation statement. Casement Ltd makes windows with two types of frame: plastic and mahogany. Products using the two types of material are made in separate premises under the supervision of separate production managers.

Data for the three months ended 30 November are shown below.

	Plastic		Mahogany		Totals	
	Budget	Actual	Budget	Actual	Budget	Actual
	3000	2500	1000	1250	4000	3750
Sales units	(£000)	(£000)	(£000)	(£000)	(£000)	(£000)
Sales revenue	660	520	340	460	1000	980
Materials	(147)	(120)	(131)	(160)	(278)	(280)
Labour	(108)	(105)	(84)	(85)	(192)	(190)
Fixed production overheads	(162)	(166)	(79)	(83)	(241)	(249)
Sales commissions	(33)	(26)	(17)	(23)	(50)	(49)
Other selling and administration costs					(128)	(133)
Net profit					111	79

Casement Ltd sells to a wide variety of users, so that window sizes and shapes vary widely; consequently a square metre of window is adopted as the standard unit for pricing and costing.

Sales budgets were based on the expectation that the company's share of the regional market in windows would be 12 per cent. The Window Federation's quarterly report reveals that sales in the regional market totalled 25000 units in the three months ended 30 November. The managing director of Casement Ltd is concerned that the company's sales and profit are below budget; she wants a full analysis of sales variances as well as an analysis of the cost variances that can be obtained from the data.

Labour costs comprise the wages of shop-floor employees who receive a fixed wage for a 40-hour week; no overtime is worked. Production managers receive a fixed monthly salary that is included in production overheads, plus an annual personal performance bonus (excluded from the above data) that is decided by the board of directors at the end of each year. Sales representatives are paid a monthly retainer plus commission of 5 per cent on all sales.

The management of Casement Ltd is keen to improve performance and is reviewing the company's reward structure. One possibility under consideration is that the company should adopt a profit-related pay scheme. The scheme would replace all the existing arrangements and would give every employee a basic remuneration equal to 90 per cent of his or her earnings last year. In addition, every employee would receive a share in the company's profit; on the basis of the past year's trading, this payment would amount to about 17 per cent of basic remuneration for each employee.

Requirements:

(a) Prepare a variance report for the managing director on the results for the quarter ended 30 November, providing market share and market volume (or size) variances, sales mix variance and basic cost variances, from the available information. *(10 marks)*

(b) Interpret your results in part (a) for the benefit of the managing director. *(7 marks)*

(c) Examine the issues (excluding taxation) which should be considered by the management of Casement Ltd in relation to the company's reward structure, with particular reference to the proposal to move to a profit-related pay scheme. *(8 marks)*

ICAEW P2 Management Accounting

IM18.7 Advanced: Performance reports for sales and product managers. Zits Ltd makes two models for rotary lawn mowers, the Quicut and the Powacut. The company has a sales director and, reporting to her, two product managers, each responsible for the profitability of one of the two models. The company's financial year ended on 31 March. The budgeted and actual results for the two models for the year ended on 31 March are given below:

	Quicut		Powacut		Total	
	Budget	Actual	Budget	Actual	Budget	Actual
Sales units	240	280	120	110	360	390
(000 units)	(£000)	(£000)	(£000)	(£000)	(£000)	(£000)
Sales revenue	28800	32200	24000	24200	52800	56400
Costs:						
Variable	9600	11480	7200	6820	16800	18300
Traceable fixed manufacturing	8200	7600	6800	6800	15000	14400
Period costs:						
Manufacturing					5700	6000
Administration and selling					4300	4500
					41800	43200
Net profit before tax					£11000	£13200

The accountant had drawn up a series of flexed budgets at the beginning of the year should the actual volume differ from budget. The variable costs were unchanged, but the budgeted fixed costs, assuming a constant sales mix for the different output ranges, were as given below:

Output range (000 units)	300–360 (£000)	361–420 (£000)
Traceable fixed manufacturing costs	15000	16000
Period cost – manufacturing	5700	6000
– administration and selling	4300	4500
	£25000	£26000

The sales director has just received information from the trade association that industry rotary lawn mower sales for the 12 months ended on 31 March were one-and-a-third million units as against a forecast of one million.

Requirements:

(a) Prepare a schedule of variances that will be helpful to the sales director and a schedule of more detailed variances that will be appropriate to the two product managers who are treated as profit centres. *(16 marks)*

(b) Discuss the results scheduled in (a) above identifying which of the variances are planning and which are operating variances. *(9 marks)*

ICAEW Management Accounting

IM18.8 Advanced: Investigation of variances.

(a) Describe and comment briefly on the basis and limitations of the control chart approach to variance investigation decisions. *(6 marks)*

(b) The following analysis is available for the month of April for Department A:

	(£)
Standard direct material	72000
Material usage variance	4500 adverse
Material mix variance	2500 adverse

The following estimates have also been made for Department A:

	(£)
Estimated cost of investigating the total material variance	1000
Estimated cost of correcting the total variance if investigated and found to be out of control	2000
Estimated cost of permitting out-of-control material variances to continue	10000

Maximum probability of a given total variance:

Probability Total	0.99	0.98	0.96	0.93	0.89	0.85	0.8	0.75
Variance £000	1	2	3	4	5	6	7	8

You are required to determine, using a payoff table, whether the variance should be investigated.   *(6 marks)*

(c) You are uncertain of the estimated probability in (b). Calculate the probability estimate at which you would be indifferent between investigating and not investigating the variance.   *(6 marks)*

(d) Discuss the use of mathematical models for the variance investigation decision.   *(7 marks)*

CIMA Stage 4 Management Accounting Control and Audit

19

DIVISIONAL FINANCIAL PERFORMANCE MEASURES

LEARNING OBJECTIVES After studying this chapter, you should be able to:

- distinguish between non-divisionalized and divisionalized organizational structures;

- explain why it is preferable to distinguish between managerial and economic performance;

- explain the factors that should be considered in designing financial performance measures for evaluating divisional managers;

- explain the meaning of return on investment (ROI), residual income and economic value added (EVA$^{(TM)}$);

- compute economic value added (EVA$^{(TM)}$);

- explain why performance measures may conflict with the net present value decision model;

- identify and explain the approaches that can be used to reduce the dysfunctional consequences of short-term financial measures.

Large global companies produce and sell a wide variety of products throughout the world. Because of the complexity of their operations, it is difficult for top management to control operations directly. It may therefore be appropriate to divide a company into separate self-contained segments or divisions and to allow divisional managers to operate with a great deal of independence. Divisional managers have responsibility for both the production and marketing activities of the division. Consistent with this greater independence each division is a profit or investment centre. The danger in creating autonomous divisions is that divisional managers might not pursue goals that are in the best interests of the company as a whole. The objective of this chapter is to consider divisional financial performance measures that aim to motivate managers to pursue those goals that will best benefit the company as a whole. In other words, the objective is to develop divisional financial performance measures that will achieve goal congruence.

A major feature of divisionalized companies is that they engage in inter-divisional trading of goods and services involving financial transactions with each other, which creates the need to establish transfer prices. The established transfer price is a cost to the receiving division and revenue to the suppling division, which means that whatever transfer price is set will affect the divisional financial performance measures. In the next chapter, we shall examine the various approaches that can be adopted to arrive at transfer prices between divisions. Our focus in this chapter is on financial measures of divisional performance but you should note at this point that financial measures alone cannot adequately measure all those factors that are critical to the success of a division. Emphasis should also be given to reporting key non-financial measures relating to such areas as competitiveness, quality, delivery performance, innovation and flexibility to respond to changes in demand. In particular, a range of financial and non-financial performance measures should be developed that support the objectives and strategies of the organization. We shall examine these aspects in Chapter 21 where our focus will be on strategic performance management.

DIVISIONAL ORGANIZATIONAL STRUCTURES

A functional organizational structure is one in which all activities of a similar type within a company are placed under the control of the appropriate departmental head. A simplified organization chart for a functional organizational structure is illustrated in Figure 19.1(a). It is assumed that the company illustrated consists of five separate departments – production, marketing, financial administration, purchasing and research, and development. In a typical functional organization none of the managers of the five

FIGURE 19.1
A functional and divisionalized organizational structure

(a) Functional organizational structure

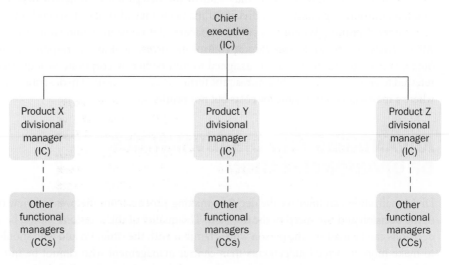

(b) Divisionalized organizational structure

IC = Investment centres, CC = Cost centres, RC = Revenue centres

departments is responsible for more than a part of the process of acquiring the raw materials, converting them into finished products, selling to customers, and administering the financial aspects of this process. You will see from Figure 19.1(a) that the marketing function is a revenue centre and the remaining departments are cost centres. Revenues and costs (including the cost of investments) are combined together only at the chief executive, or corporate level, which is classified as an investment centre.

Let us now consider Figure 19.1(b), which shows a simplified **divisionalized organizational structure**, which is split up into divisions in accordance with the products that are made. Alternatively many global companies may establish divisions according to geographical regions (e.g. European division, North African division, Asian division etc.). You will see from the diagram that each divisional manager is responsible for all of the operations relating to his or her particular product. To reflect this greater autonomy, each division is either an investment centre or a profit centre. Note that there are also multiple cost and revenue centres at lower management levels within each division. The planning and control systems described in the four previous chapters should be applied to the cost and revenue centres. Also, in practice, only parts of a company may be divisionalized. For example, in the simplified structure shown in Figure 19.1(b) the administration and shared services is a cost centre with responsibility for providing services to all of the divisions. In practice, rather than combining all shared services under one centre there would be several centres such as research and development, legal services, financial services etc. all reporting to the chief executive and providing services to all divisions. Figure 19.1(b) also shows that each divisional manager reports to a chief executive or top management team, normally located at corporate headquarters, who is responsible for the activities of all of the divisions. In this chapter, we shall focus on financial measures and controls at the profit or investment centre (i.e. divisional) level.

Generally, a divisionalized organizational structure will lead to decentralization of the decision-making process. For example, divisional managers will normally be free to set selling prices, choose which market to sell in, make product mix and output decisions, and select suppliers (this may include buying from other divisions within the company or from other companies). In non-divisionalized organizations, pricing, product mix and output decisions will be made by central management. Consequently, managers in non-divisionalized organizations will have far less independence than divisional managers. Thus divisional managers have profit responsibility whereas managers in non-divisionalized companies do not have profit responsibility.

Profit centres and investment centres

The creation of separate divisions may lead to the delegation of different degrees of authority; for example, in some organizations a divisional manager may also have responsibility for making capital investment decisions. Where this situation occurs, the division is known as an **investment centre**. Alternatively, where a manager cannot control the investment and is responsible only for the profits obtained from operating the assets assigned to him or her by corporate headquarters, the segment is referred to as a **profit centre**. In contrast, the term **cost centre** is used to describe a responsibility centre where a manager is responsible for costs but not profits.

ADVANTAGES AND DISADVANTAGES OF DIVISIONALIZATION

Divisionalization can improve the decision-making process from the point of view of both the quality of the decision and the speed of the decision. The quality of the decisions should be improved because decisions can be made by the person who is familiar with the situation and who should therefore be able to make more informed judgements than central management who cannot be intimately acquainted with all the activities of the various segments of the business. Speedier decisions should also occur because information does not have to pass along the chain of command to and from top management.

Decisions can be made on the spot by those who are familiar with the product lines and production processes and who can react to changes in local conditions in a speedy and efficient manner. In addition, delegation of responsibility to divisional managers provides them with greater freedom, thus making their activities more challenging and providing the opportunity to achieve self-fulfilment. This process should mean that motivation will be increased not just at the divisional manager level but throughout the whole division.

The major potential disadvantage of divisionalization is that there is a danger that divisions may compete with one another excessively and that divisional managers may be encouraged to take action that will increase their own profits at the expense of the profits of other divisions and the company as a whole. This may adversely affect cooperation between the divisions and lead to a lack of harmony in achieving the overall organizational goals of the company.

PRE-REQUISITES FOR SUCCESSFUL DIVISIONALIZATION

A divisionalized structure is most suited to large companies that are engaged in several dissimilar activities. Examples of companies with divisionalized structures include Unilever, Siemens AG, Mitsubishi Group and Samsung. The reason is that it is difficult for top management to be intimately acquainted with all the diverse activities of the various segments of the business. Contrariwise, when the major activities of a company are closely related, these activities should be carefully coordinated and this coordination is more easily achieved in a centralized organizational structure.

For successful divisionalization, it is important that the activities of a division be as independent as possible of other activities. However, the comments by Solomons (1965) many years ago are still relevant today. He states that, even though substantial independence of divisions from each other is a necessary condition for divisionalization, if carried to the limit it would destroy the very idea that such divisions are an integral part of any single business. Divisions should be more than investments – they should contribute not only to the success of the company but to the success of one another.

DISTINGUISHING BETWEEN THE MANAGERIAL AND ECONOMIC PERFORMANCE OF THE DIVISION

Before discussing the factors to be considered in determining how divisional profitability should be measured, we must decide whether the primary purpose is to measure the performance of the division or that of the divisional manager. The messages transmitted from these two measures may be quite different. For example, a manager may be assigned to an ailing division to improve performance, and might succeed in substantially improving the performance of the division. However, the division might still be unprofitable because of industry factors, such as overcapacity and a declining market. The future of the division might be uncertain, but the divisional manager may well be promoted as a result of the outstanding managerial performance. Conversely, a division might report significant profits but, because of management deficiencies, the performance may be unsatisfactory when the favourable economic environment is taken into account.

If the purpose is to evaluate the divisional manager then only those items directly controllable by the manager should be included in the divisional financial performance measure. Thus all allocations of indirect costs, such as central service and central administration costs, which cannot be influenced by divisional managers, ought not to be included in the profitability measure. Such costs can only be controlled where they are incurred; which means that central service managers should be held accountable for them.

Corporate headquarters, however, will also be interested in evaluating a division's economic performance for decision-making purposes, such as expansion, contraction and divestment decisions. In this situation, a measure that includes only those amounts directly controllable by the divisional manager would overstate the economic performance of the division. This over-statement occurs because, if the

*Pre-requisites for successful
divisionalization – divisions at Siemens AG*

German global company Siemens AG had a turnover of almost €76 billion in 2015, recording a profit after taxes of €7.4 billion, according to its annual report. The company operates globally, with 351 000 employees globally. Siemens is a diverse organization. Looking at the home page of the company's website, we get an idea of how diverse. The web page lists ten divisions:

- Power and gas
- Wind power and renewables
- Power generation services
- Energy management
- Building technologies
- Mobility
- Digital factory
- Process industries and drives
- Healthcare
- Financial services

Each division is further broken down. For example, the process industries and drives division includes process automation, sensor systems, integrated drive systems and plant engineering software. This level of information suggests a quite detailed organizational structure. While the website does not tell us the exact internal structures, we could expect that some activities (e.g. financial services) may be cross-sector and/or cross-divisional. The 2015 Annual Report confirms this, noting 'The Division Financial Services (SFS) supports the activities of our Industrial Business and also conducts its own business with external customers' (p. 2).

Questions

1 What advantages does a divisionalized structure have for decision-making at Siemens?
2 Would a divisionalized structure be suited to fast-food giant McDonalds?

References

Siemens (2015) Annual Report 2015, Siemens AG. Available at www.siemens.com/investor/pool/en /investor_relations/Siemens_AR2015.pdf
Siemens (2016) Siemens at a Glance. Available at www .siemens.com/investor/en/company_overview.htm

divisions were independent companies, they would have to incur the costs of those services provided by head office. Therefore, to measure the economic performance of the division many items that the divisional manager cannot influence, such as interest expenses, taxes and the allocation of central administrative staff expenses, should be included in the profitability measure.

ALTERNATIVE DIVISIONAL PROFIT MEASURES

There are strong arguments for two measures of divisional profitability – one to evaluate managerial performance and the other to evaluate the economic performance of the division. In this chapter, we focus on both measures. Exhibit 19.1 presents a divisional profit statement that contains three different measures we can use to measure divisional performance. For measuring *managerial performance,* the application of the controllability principle (see Chapter 16) suggests that controllable profit is the most appropriate measure. This is computed by deducting from divisional revenues all those costs that are controllable by a divisional manager. Controllable profit provides a measure of divisional managerial performance based on its ability to use only those resources under its control effectively. It should not be interpreted in isolation if it is used to evaluate the performance of a divisional manager. Instead, it should be evaluated relative to a budgeted performance, so that market conditions and size (in terms of assets employed) are taken into account.

Controllable profit provides an incomplete measure of the *economic performance* of a division, since it does not include those costs that are attributable to the division but, by the same token, are not controllable by the divisional manager. For example, depreciation of divisional assets, and head office finance and legal staff who are assigned to providing services for specific divisions, would fall into this

REAL WORLD VIEWS 19.2

Distinguishing between the managerial and economic performance of the division – performance at Siemens

From Real World View 19.1, you know that Siemens operates in many countries and has quite a diverse product offering. With such complex and broad operations, there are many factors that can affect the performance of a business sector or division. In its 2015 Annual Report, Siemens refers to its performance under a number of headings derived from Vision 2020. The performance measures are under seven headings: stringent corporate governance, sustainable value creation, financial, global management, partner of choice for customers, be employer of choice and an ownership culture. Throughout the 2015 and 2014 Annual Report, the targets set under the Vision 2020 programme are mentioned, and in the former

performance is reported on. For example, under the financial heading, revenue growth is referred to as follows: 'our primary measure for managing and controlling our revenue growth is comparable growth, which excludes currency translation and portfolio effects'.

Questions

1 If the performance of a divisional manager at Siemens falls short of target due to external factors such as economic recession, should the manager be held accountable?

2 How might the actual assessment of divisional performance differ in recessionary times?

References

Siemens (2015) Annual Report 2015, Siemens AG. Available at www.siemens.com/investor/pool/en /investor_relations/Siemens_AR2015.pdf

Siemens (2016) Strategy overview. Available at www .siemens.com/about/en/strategic-overview.htm

category. These expenses would be avoidable if a decision were taken to close the division. Those non-controllable expenses that are attributable to a division, and which would be avoidable if the division were closed, are deducted from controllable profit to derive the divisional profit contribution. This is clearly a useful figure for evaluating the *economic contribution* of the division, since it represents the contribution that a division is making to corporate profits and overheads. It should not be used, however, to evaluate managerial performance, because it includes costs that are not controllable by divisional managers.

Many companies allocate all corporate general and administrative expenses to divisions to derive a divisional net profit before taxes. From a theoretical point of view, it is difficult to justify such allocations since they tend to be arbitrary and do not have any connection with the manner in which divisional activities influence the level of these corporate expenses. Divisional profit contribution would therefore seem to be the most appropriate measure of the *economic* performance of divisions, because it is not distorted by arbitrary allocations. We have noted, however, that corporate headquarters may wish to compare a division's economic performance with that of comparable firms operating in the same industry. The divisional profit contribution would overstate the performance of the division, because, if the division were independent, it would have to incur the costs of those services performed

EXHIBIT 19.1 Alternative divisional profit measures

	£
Total sales revenues	xxx
Less controllable costs	xxx
1 *Controllable profit*	xxx
Less non-controllable avoidable costs	xxx
2 *Divisional profit contribution*	xxx
Less allocated corporate expenses	xxx
3 *Divisional net profit before taxes*	xxx

by head office. The apportioned head office costs are an approximation of the costs that the division would have to incur if it traded as a separate company. Consequently, companies may prefer to use divisional net profit when comparing the economic performance of a division with similar companies.

SURVEYS OF PRACTICE

Despite the many theoretical arguments against divisional net profit, survey evidence indicates that this measure is used widely to evaluate both divisional economic and managerial performance (Drury and El-Shishini, 2005; Chartered Institute of Management Accountants, 2009). The CIMA study also reported profit before tax was the most widely used performance measurement tool, being used by approximately 90 per cent of the organization. The UK study by Drury and El-Shishini (2005) asked the respondents to rank in order of importance the factors influencing organizations to allocate the cost of shared corporate resources to divisions. In rank order, the highest rankings were attributed to the following factors:

1 to show divisional managers the total costs of operating their divisions;

2 to make divisional managers aware that such costs exist and must be covered by divisional profits;

3 divisional managers would incur such costs if they were independent units.

The counter-argument to item 2 above is that if central management wishes to inform managers that divisions must be profitable enough to cover not only its own operations but corporate expenses as well, it is preferable to set a high budgeted controllable profit target that takes account of these factors. Divisional managers can then concentrate on increasing controllable profit by focusing on those costs and revenues that are under their control, and not be concerned with costs that they cannot control.

There is also some evidence to suggest that companies hold managers accountable for divisional net profit because this is equivalent to the measure that financial markets focus on to evaluate the performance of the company as a whole (Joseph *et al.*, 1996; Ezzamel *et al.*, 2008). Top management therefore requires its divisional managers to concentrate on the same measures as those used by financial markets. A further reason to justify the use of divisional net profit as a managerial performance measure is that it represents the application of the controllability principle by the use of relative performance evaluations that were described in Chapter 16. You should remember from Chapter 16 that with relative performance evaluations the performance of a responsibility centre is evaluated relative to the performance of similar centres within the same company or to similar units outside the organization.

RETURN ON INVESTMENT

Instead of focusing purely on the absolute size of a division's profits, most organizations focus on the return on investment (ROI) of a division. Note that ROI is synonymous with accounting rate of return (ARR) described as an investment appraisal technique in Chapter 13. In Chapter 13, our focus was on future estimates (i.e. an *ex ante* measure) for making investment decisions. In this chapter, we are focusing on an historic after-the-event (i.e. *ex post*) performance measure. ROI expresses divisional profit as a percentage of the assets employed in the division. Assets employed can be defined as total divisional assets, assets controllable by the divisional manager or net assets. We shall consider the alternative measures of assets employed later in the chapter.

To illustrate the attraction of ROI consider a situation in which division A earns a profit of £10 million and division B a profit of £20 million. Can we conclude that Division B is more profitable than Division A? The answer is no, since we should consider whether the divisions are returning a sufficiently high return on the capital invested in the division. Assume that £40 million capital is invested in division A and £200 million in division B. Division A's ROI is 25 per cent (£10m/£40m) whereas the return for division B is 10 per cent (£20m/£200m). Capital invested has alternative uses and corporate management will wish to ascertain whether the returns being earned on the capital invested in a particular division exceed the division's opportunity cost of capital (i.e. the returns available from the alternative use of the capital). If, in the above illustration, the return available on similar investments to that in Division B is 15 per cent, then the economic viability of Division B is questionable if profitability cannot be improved. In contrast, the ROI measure suggests that Division A is very profitable.

A major attraction of ROI is that it can be used as a common denominator for comparing the returns of dissimilar businesses, such as other divisions within the group or outside competitors. ROI has been widely used for many years in all types of organization so that most managers understand what the measure reflects and consider it to be of considerable importance.

Despite the widespread use of ROI, a number of problems exist when this measure is used to evaluate the performance of divisional managers. For example, it is possible that divisional ROI can be increased by actions that will make the company as a whole worse off and, conversely, actions that decrease the divisional ROI may make the company as a whole better off. In other words, evaluating divisional managers on the basis of ROI may not encourage goal congruence. Consider the following example:

	Division X	Division Y
Investment project available	£10 million	£10 million
Controllable contribution	£2 million	£1.3 million
Return on the proposed project	20%	13%
ROI of divisions at present	25%	9%

It is assumed that neither project will result in any changes in non-controllable costs and that the overall cost of capital for the company is 15 per cent. The manager of Division X would be reluctant to invest the additional £10 million because the return on the proposed project is 20 per cent, and this would reduce the existing overall ROI of 25 per cent. The manager of Division Y would, however, wish to invest the £10 million because the return on the proposed project of 13 per cent is in excess of the present return of 9 per cent and it would increase the division's overall ROI. Consequently, the managers of both divisions would make decisions that would not be in the best interests of the company. The company should accept only those projects where the return is in excess of the cost of capital of 15 per cent, but the manager of Division X would reject a potential return of 20 per cent and the manager of Division Y would accept a potential return of 13 per cent. ROI can therefore lead to a lack of goal congruence.

RESIDUAL INCOME

To overcome some of the dysfunctional consequences of ROI, the residual income approach can be used. For the purpose of evaluating the performance of *divisional managers*, residual income is defined as controllable profit less a cost of capital charge on the investment controllable by the divisional manager. For evaluating the *economic performance* of the division, residual income can be defined as divisional profit contribution (see Exhibit 19.1) less a cost of capital charge on the total investment in assets employed by the division. If residual income is used to measure the managerial performance of investment centres, there is a greater probability that managers will be encouraged, when acting in their own best interests, also to act in the best interests of the company. Returning to our previous illustration in respect of the investment decision for Divisions X and Y, the residual income calculations are as follows:

	Division X (£)	Division Y (£)
Proposed investment	10 million	10 million
Controllable contribution	2 million	1.3 million
Cost of capital charge (15 per cent of the investment cost)	1.5 million	1.5 million
Residual income	0.5 million	−0.2 million

This calculation indicates that the residual income of Division X will increase and that of division Y will decrease if both managers accept the project. Therefore the manager of Division X would invest, whereas the manager of Division Y would not. These actions are in the best interests of the company as a whole.

A further reason cited in favour of residual income over the ROI measure is that residual income is more flexible, because different cost of capital percentage rates can be applied to investments that have different levels of risk. Not only will the cost of capital of divisions that have different levels of risk differ – so may the risk and cost of capital of assets within the *same* division. The residual income measure enables different risk-adjusted capital costs to be incorporated in the calculation, whereas the ROI cannot incorporate these differences.

Residual income suffers from the disadvantages of being an absolute measure, which means that it is difficult to compare the performance of a division with that of other divisions or companies of a different size. For example, a large division is more likely to earn a larger residual income than a small division. To overcome this deficiency, targeted or budgeted levels of residual income should be set for each division that are consistent with asset size and the market conditions of the divisions.

Surveys of methods used by companies to evaluate the performance of divisional managers indicate a strong preference for ROI over residual income. For example, the international CIMA survey (2009) reported that approximately 70 per cent of the respondents' organizations used ROI compared with around 10 per cent using residual income.

Why is ROI preferred to residual income? Skinner (1990) found evidence to suggest that firms prefer to use ROI because, being a ratio, it can be used for interdivision and interfirm comparisons where the size of the divisions or firms differs. ROI for a division can be compared with the return from other divisions within the group or with whole companies outside the group, whereas absolute monetary measures such as residual income are not appropriate in making such comparisons. A second possible reason for the preference for ROI is that 'outsiders' tend to use ROI as a measure of a company's overall performance. Corporate managers therefore want their divisional managers to focus on ROI so that their performance measure is congruent with outsiders' measure of the company's overall economic performance. A further reason, suggested by Kaplan and Atkinson (1998), is that managers find percentage measures of profitability such as ROI more convenient, since they enable a division's profitability to be compared with other financial measures (such as inflation rates, interest rates and the ROI rates of other divisions and comparable companies outside the group).

ECONOMIC VALUE ADDED (EVA(TM))

During the 1990s residual income was refined, improved and renamed as economic value added (EVA(TM)) by the Stern Stewart consulting organization and it registered EVA(TM) as its trademark. Stern Stewart advocate that EVA(TM) can be used to measure the performance of companies as a whole or different divisions within a divisionalized company. *The Economist* (1997) reported that more than 300 firms worldwide had adopted EVA(TM) including Coca-Cola, AT&T, ICL, Siemens, Boots and the Burton Group. A UK study by Drury and El-Shishini (2005) reported that 23 per cent of the responding organizations used EVA(TM) to evaluate divisional performance. More recently the CIMA (2009) international survey reported a usage rate of around 15–20 per cent.

Stern Stewart developed EVA(TM) with the aim of producing an overall financial measure that encourages senior managers to concentrate on the delivery of shareholder value. They consider that the major aim of managers of companies, whose shares are traded in the stock market, should be to maximize shareholder value. This management principle of maximizing shareholder value is also known as value-based-management (VBM). VBM states that management should first and foremost consider the interests of shareholders in its business decisions. It is therefore important that the key financial measure that is used to measure divisional or company performance should be congruent with shareholder value. VBM focuses on value as opposed to profit thus reducing the tendency to make decisions which have positive short-term impact but may be detrimental in the long term. Stern Stewart claims that, compared with other financial measures, EVA$^{\text{(TM)}}$ is more likely to meet this requirement than traditional profit measures.

The EVA$^{\text{(TM)}}$ concept extends the traditional residual income measure by incorporating adjustments to the traditional profit performance measure for distortions that can arise from measuring profit using generally accepted accounting principles (GAAP). EVA$^{\text{(TM)}}$ can be defined as:

$$\text{EVA}^{\text{(TM)}} = \text{Conventional divisional profit} \pm \text{accounting adjustments} - \text{cost of capital}$$
$$\text{charge on divisional assets}$$

The cost of capital charge is incorporated in the above calculation because traditional profit measures ignore the cost of equity capital (i.e. the opportunity cost of funds provided by shareholders). Companies create shareholder value only when they generate a return in excess of the return required by the providers of capital (i.e. both debt and equity). Traditional profit measures include the cost of debt finance but ignore the cost of equity finance. Also by making the cost of capital visible managers are made aware that capital has a cost so that they need to generate sufficient income to cover their cost of capital.

Adjustments are made to the chosen conventional divisional profit measure in order to replace historic accounting data that do not reflect the shareholder wealth that has been created with a measure that attempts to approximate economic value that has been generated during the period. Stern Stewart have stated that they have developed approximately 160 accounting adjustments that may need to be made to convert the conventional accounting profit into a sound measure of EVA$^{\text{(TM)}}$ but they have indicated that most organizations will only need to use about ten of the adjustments. These adjustments result in the capitalization of many discretionary expenditures, such as research and development, marketing and advertising, by spreading these costs over the periods in which the benefits are received. Therefore, managers will not bear the full costs of the discretionary expenditures in the period in which they are incurred. Instead, the cost will be spread across the periods when the benefits from the expenditure are estimated to be received.

AN ILLUSTRATION OF THE CALCULATION OF EVA$^{\text{(TM)}}$

We shall now compute EVA$^{\text{(TM)}}$ using the information shown in Example 19.1. To compute EVA$^{\text{(TM)}}$, an amended accounting profit is calculated by making adjustments to the conventional accounting profit and then deducting a cost of capital charge. The cost of capital charge is derived from multiplying the percentage cost of capital by an amended capital employed computation that incorporates adjustments of historical accounting values to estimate economic values. Given that capital employed should relate to the investment for the full period our aim is to estimate the capital employed *at the start* of the period. The calculations of adjusted profit, adjusted capital employed and EVA$^{\text{(TM)}}$ are shown in Exhibit 19.2. An explanation of the calculations in Exhibit 19.2 is shown below:

● The EVA$^{\text{(TM)}}$ calculation seeks to ascertain whether value is being added for shareholders in terms of whether the funds invested in the business generate a return in excess of the cost of capital. To do this, the adjusted profit excludes any cost of capital charges (e.g. interest on debt capital) because it is incorporated in the EVA$^{\text{(TM)}}$ cost of capital adjustment. The tax charge should also be adjusted because it includes the tax benefit arising from interest being a tax-deductible expense. The inclusion of interest in the profit statement results in the tax charge being lower. Since the adjusted profit excludes the interest cost, it is also necessary to remove the interest tax benefit from the taxation charge. You will see from Exhibit 19.2 that, instead of making profit before interest and tax (£15m), the starting point for the above adjustment could also have been incorporated by making profit after tax (£11.2m) the starting point in the adjusted profit calculation and adding back the after-tax cost of interest of £0.8m (£1m × (1 − the tax rate)). This agrees with the subtotal of £12m shown by the approach adopted in Exhibit 19.2.

EXAMPLE 19.1

The summarized profit statement for the past year for Atlantic plc is shown below:

	£000
Operating profit before tax and interest	15 000
Interest expenses	1 000
Profit before tax	14 000
Taxation	2 800
Profit after tax and interest	11 200

Further information is as follows:

1 Research and development costs of £500 000 were incurred during the current financial year and £400 000 in the previous financial year and the full amount was included in the profit computations for both years. The expenditure in both years is expected to yield benefits in future years.

2 The only other research and development costs were £1m incurred six years ago and charged as an expense in the profit statement. It is considered that equal benefits will be derived from this investment over a five-year period that started from the beginning of the previous financial year.

3 Non-cash expenses were £50 000 in the current year and £40 000 in the previous year were included in the calculation of operating profit.

4 The provision for doubtful debts was increased from £250 000 at the start of the year to £350 000.

5 The taxation charge for the year includes a provision for deferred tax of £180 000. There was no provision for deferred tax balance prior to the current year.

6 Economic depreciation is estimated to be £210 000 in the current financial year whereas historical depreciation included in the above profit calculation was £160 000. In previous years it can be assumed that economic and accounting depreciation were the same.

7 The capital employed (debt plus equity capital) recorded in the published financial statements at the start of the financial year was £80m.

8 The before tax cost of debt was 5 per cent and the estimated cost of equity was 10 per cent. The rate of corporation tax was 20 per cent.

9 The company's capital structure was 60 per cent equity and 40 per cent debt. You are required to calculate the EVA$^{(TM)}$ for the period.

- The expenses on research and development (£500 000) incurred in the current period represent an investment that yields future benefits so the costs should be assigned to the future periods that benefit from this expenditure. Therefore £500 000 should be added back to profit and capitalized by adding to capital employed in the year in which the expenses were incurred. This means that capital employed will be increased by £500 000 in the *current accounting period* but our objective is to calculate the adjusted capital employed at *the start of the current accounting period* so the research and development expenses incurred in the previous period (£400 000) are added back to determine the adjusted capital employed at the start of the period.

- Benefits derived from research and development expenditure incurred in previous periods should be assigned to the future periods that benefit from the expenditure. Therefore the expenditure of £1m incurred six years ago should be assigned to the periods that benefited so

EXHIBIT 19.2 Calculation of EVA(TM) for Example 19.1

Adjusted profit	
	£000
Operating profit before tax and interest	15000
Less: Tax charges adjusted to exclude the tax benefit on interest (£2800 +	
(£1000 × 20 per cent)	(3000)
	12000
Add: Research and development costs recorded as an expense	500
Non-cash expenses	50
Increase in provision for doubtful debts	100
Increase in deferred taxation	180
Accounting depreciation	160
	12990
Less: Economic depreciation	(210)
Benefit received from research and development costs incurred five years ago	(200)
Adjusted profit	12580

Adjusted capital employed	
	£000
Capital employed at the *start* of the year (see Note 7 in Example 19.1)	80000
Add: Capitalization of research and development (incurred in the previous	
financial year)	400
Capitalization of research and development (incurred five years ago)	800
Non-cash expenses incurred in the previous financial year	40
Provision for doubtful debts	250
Adjusted capital employed at the start of the year	81490

Weighted average cost of capital
Cost of equity (60% × 10%) + After-tax cost of debt (40% × 5% × (1 − 20%) = 7.6%

Economic value added EVA(TM)
Adjusted profit (£12.580m) − cost of capital charge (7.6% × £81.49m) = £6.387m

£200 000 (one-fifth – see note 2 in Example 19.1) is deemed to be the benefit received in the current accounting period so it is shown as a deduction to derive the adjusted profit. The first year of benefits from the £1m investment in research and development were received in the previous accounting period so the future benefits at the *start of the accounting period* from the investment of £1m will have declined from £1m to £800 000. Therefore £800 000 is added back to the unadjusted capital employed.

- Non-cash expenses (£50 000), increases in provisions for bad debts (£100 000) and the increase in deferred taxation provision (£180 000) that are recorded as expenses in the current accounting period are added back to current profits since EVA(TM) seeks to convert figures derived from accrual accounting to cash flows because cash flows provide a better measure of economic value added. These items should also be capitalized so the previous year's non-cash expense (£40 000) is added back to determine the adjusted capital employed at the *start of the current accounting period*. The provision for doubtful debts at the start of the year (£250 000) represents the sum of provisions made in previous years is also capitalized and added back to compute the adjusted capital employed. However, note 5 of Example 19.1 indicates that there was no deferred tax balance at the start of the financial period so no adjustment is required.

- Economic depreciation represents an estimate of the true change in the value of assets during a period. Therefore, depreciation of £160 000 based on historical book values is added back to profits. Instead, a charge for economic depreciation of £210 000 based on economic values, rather than historical values, is deducted in the adjusted profit calculation. Given that note 6 in Example 19.1 indicates that economic and accounting depreciation were the same in previous years, no adjustment is required to the adjusted capital employed at the start of the current accounting period.

● Finally, a cost of capital charge consisting of the weighted average cost of capital (see Chapter 14) is applied to the adjusted capital employed and deducted from the adjusted profit to calculate EVA$^{(TM)}$.

● Instead of adding back the provision for deferred taxation of £180 000 you could have made the adjustment within the tax charges in Exhibit 19.2. Our aim is to exclude non-cash payments and we are informed in note 5 that the taxation charge of £2.8m includes a provision for deferred tax of £180 000 so to ascertain the tax cash payment we deduct the £180 000 giving a payment of £2.62m. Adding the tax benefit of interest shown in Exhibit 1 of £200 000 results in an adjusted tax charge of £2.82m. Inserting an adjusted taxation charge of £2.82 m in Exhibit 19.2 instead of £3m and omitting adding the provision for deferred taxation results in the same adjusted profit of £12.58m.

Our earlier discussion relating to which of the conventional alternative divisional profit measures listed in Exhibit 19.1 should be used to evaluate managerial performance, also applies to the calculation of EVA$^{(TM)}$. There are strong theoretical arguments for using controllable profit as the starting point for calculating EVA$^{(TM)}$ for evaluating managerial performance. Many companies, however, use divisional net profit (after allocated costs) to calculate EVA$^{(TM)}$ and use this measure to evaluate both divisional, managerial and economic performance.

DETERMINING WHICH ASSETS SHOULD BE INCLUDED IN THE INVESTMENT BASE

We must determine which assets to include in a division's asset base to compute ROI, residual income and EVA$^{(TM)}$. If the purpose is to evaluate the performance of the divisional manager then only those assets that can be directly traced to the division and that are controllable by the divisional manager should be included in the asset base. Assets managed by central headquarters should not be included. For example, if debtors (accounts receivable) and cash are administered and controlled centrally, they should not be included as part of the asset base. By way of contrast, if a divisional manager can influence these amounts, they should be included in the investment base. If they were not included, divisional managers could improve their profits by granting over-generous credit terms to customers; they would obtain the rewards of the additional sales without being charged with any cost for the additional capital that would be tied up in debtors.

Any liabilities that are within the control of the division should be deducted from the asset base. The term **controllable investment** is used to refer to the net asset base that is controllable or strongly influenced by divisional managers. Our overall aim in analysing controllable and non-controllable investment is to produce performance measures that will encourage a manager to behave in the best interests of the organization and also to provide a good approximation of managerial performance. It is therefore appropriate to include in the investment base only those assets that a manager can influence and any arbitrary apportionments should be excluded.

If the purpose is to evaluate the economic performance of the division, the profitability of the division will be overstated if controllable investment is used. This is because a division could not operate without the benefit of corporate assets such as buildings, cash and debtors managed at the corporate level. These assets would be included in the investment base if the divisions were separate independent companies. Therefore many divisionalized companies allocate corporate assets to divisions when comparing divisional profitability with comparable firms in the same industry.

REAL WORLD VIEWS 19.3

How the use of EVA$^{(TM)}$ analysis transformed Armstrong's financial performance

The financial mission of a company should be to invest and create cash flows in excess of the cost of capital. If an investment is announced that is expected to earn in excess of the cost of capital, then the value of the firm will immediately rise by the present value of that excess – as long as the market understands and believes the available projections. The question is: What is the best way to measure this?

Traditional measures of return, such as ROI, actually could unwittingly motivate and reward managers to shrink the value of the company. Therefore, the concept EVA$^{(TM)}$ was developed. In a nutshell, EVA$^{(TM)}$ is designed to measure the degree to which a company's after-tax operating profits exceed – or fall short of – the cost of capital invested in the business. It makes managers think more about the use of capital and the amount of capital in each business.

Armstrong World Industries Inc. is a multibillion-dollar manufacturer and supplier of floor coverings, insulation products, ceiling and wall systems and installation products. The decision was made to discontinue the ROI concept and use EVA$^{(TM)}$ for strategic planning, performance measurement, and compensation. EVA$^{(TM)}$ is computed from straightforward adjustments to convert book values on the income statement and balance sheet to an economic basis. Armstrong used about a dozen adjustments.

Armstrong considered EVA$^{(TM)}$ to be the best financial measure for accurately linking accounting measures to stock market value and performance, making it ideal for setting financial targets. Changes in behaviour have become focused on three basic actions: (1) improving profit without more capital; (2) investing in projects earning above the cost of capital; and (3) eliminating operations unable to earn above the cost of capital.

On a higher strategic level, EVA$^{(TM)}$ allowed Armstrong to step back to see where the company was losing value. In what the company called its 'sunken ship' chart it was clear that businesses earning above the cost of capital were providing huge amounts of EVA$^{(TM)}$. However, the ship was being dragged down because of negative EVA$^{(TM)}$ businesses and corporate overhead. By selling or combining negative EVA$^{(TM)}$ businesses, and by growing and further reducing costs in its positive EVA$^{(TM)}$ businesses, the company provided the potential to more than double its EVA$^{(TM)}$.

Questions

1 Can you provide examples of accounting adjustments required to compute EVA$^{(TM)}$?

2 Why is EVA$^{(TM)}$ preferred to ROI?

Reference

Institute of Management & Administration (2002) 'Report on Financial Analysis Planning and Reporting', Institute of Management & Administration, September, London.

THE IMPACT OF DEPRECIATION

It is common to find fixed assets valued at either their original cost or their written down value (WDV) for the purpose of calculating return on investment and residual income, but both of these valuation methods are weak. Consider, for example, an investment in an asset of £1 million with a life of five years with annual cash flows of £350 000 and a cost of capital of 10 per cent. This investment has a positive NPV of £326 850 and should be accepted. You can see from Exhibit 19.3 that the annual profit is £150 000 when straight line depreciation is used. If the asset is *valued at original cost*, there will be a return of 15 per cent per annum for five years. This will understate the true return, because the economic valuation is unlikely to remain at £1 million each year for five years and then immediately fall to zero. If ROI is based on the *written-down value*, you can see from Exhibit 19.3 that the investment base will decline each year – and, with constant profits, the effect will be to show a steady increase in return on investment. This steady increase in return on investment will suggest an improvement in managerial performance when the economic facts indicate that performance has remained unchanged over the five-year period.

EXHIBIT 19.3 Profitability measures using straight line depreciation

	1 (£)	2 (£)	3 (£)	4 (£)	5 (£)
Net cash flow	350 000	350 000	350 000	350 000	350 000
Depreciation	200 000	200 000	200 000	200 000	200 000
Profit	150 000	150 000	150 000	150 000	150 000
Cost of capital (10% of WDV)	100 000	80 000	60 000	40 000	20 000
EVA$^{(TM)}$	50 000	70 000	90 000	110 000	130 000
Opening WDV of the asset	1 000 000	800 000	600 000	400 000	200 000
ROI	15%	18.75%	25%	37.5%	75%

Similar inconsistencies will also occur if conventional depreciation methods are used to measure EVA$^{(TM)}$. If the asset is valued at the original cost, EVA$^{(TM)}$ of £50 000 will be reported each year (£150 000 profit − (10 per cent cost of capital × 1 million)). Contrariwise, if the cost of capital charge is based on the written-down value of the asset, the investment base will decline each year and EVA$^{(TM)}$ will increase. You will remember from the calculation of EVA$^{(TM)}$ that, to overcome problems that arise from using financial accounting depreciation, it was adjusted and replaced with economic depreciation to compute the adjusted profit and capital employed.

Exhibit 19.3 serves to illustrate that if asset written-down values derived from using financial accounting depreciation methods are used to determine the division's investment base, managers can improve their ROI or EVA$^{(TM)}$ by postponing new investments and operating with older assets with low written-down values. In contrast, divisional managers who invest in new equipment will have a lower ROI or EVA$^{(TM)}$. This situation arises because financial accounting depreciation methods (including the reducing balance method) produce lower profitability measures in the earlier years of an asset's life.

To overcome this problem, it has been suggested that ROI or EVA$^{(TM)}$ calculations should be based on the original cost (i.e. gross book value) of the assets. When assets are measured at gross book value, managers will have an incentive to replace existing assets with new assets. This is because the increase in the investment base is only the difference between the original cost of the old asset and the purchase cost of the new asset. This difference is likely to be significantly less than the incremental cash flow (purchase cost less sale proceeds of the old asset) of the new asset. Managers may therefore be motivated to replace old assets with new ones that have a negative NPV. To overcome the problems created by using financial accounting depreciation methods, alternative depreciation models have been recommended and adjustments for depreciation based on these methods is included in the computation of adjusted profit and capital employed to calculate EVA$^{(TM)}$. These alternative depreciation methods are discussed in Learning Note 19.1 in the digital support resources accompanying this book (see Preface for details).

THE EFFECT OF PERFORMANCE MEASUREMENT ON CAPITAL INVESTMENT DECISIONS

We noted in Chapter 13 that capital investment decisions should be taken on the basis of the net present value (NPV) decision rule. The way in which the performance of the divisional manager is measured, however, is likely to have a profound effect on the decisions that he or she will make. There is a danger that, because of the way in which divisional performance is measured, the manager may be motivated to take the wrong decision and not follow the NPV rule. We noted earlier in this chapter that the residual income (or EVA$^{(TM)}$) method of evaluation appeared to encourage a divisional manager to make capital investment decisions that are consistent with the NPV rule, but there is no guarantee that this or any

EXHIBIT 19.4 Mutually exclusive capital projects NPV ranking[1]

	X (£000s)	Y (£000s)	Z (£000s)
Machine cost initial outlay (time zero)	861	861	861
Estimated net cash flow (year 1)	250	390	50
Estimated net cash flow (year 2)	370	250	50
Estimated net cash flow (year 3)	540	330	1100
Estimated net present value at 10% cost of capital[a]	77	(52)	52
Ranking on the basis of NPV	1	3	2

Note
[a]The net present value calculations are to the nearest £000.

other financial measure will, in fact, motivate the manager to act in this way. Consider the information presented in Exhibit 19.4, which relates to three mutually exclusive projects: X, Y and Z. Applying the NPV rule, you will see from the information presented that the *manager should choose project X in preference to project Z, and should reject project Y.*

Profits and return on investment

Divisional managers are likely to estimate the outcomes from alternative investments and choose the investment that maximizes their performance measure. Exhibit 19.5 shows the estimated profits and ROI's for projects X, Y and Z. The calculations in Exhibit 19.5 are based on the net cash flows for each year presented in Exhibit 19.4, less straight line depreciation of £287 000 per year (£861 000/3years). The ROI is calculated on the *opening* written-down value at the start of the year. From the calculation in Exhibit 19.5, you will see that a manager who is anxious to improve his or her *short-term* performance will choose project Y if he or she is evaluated on total profits or return on investment, since project Y earns the largest profits and ROI in year 1; but project Y has a negative net present value, and should be rejected. Alternatively, a manager who assesses the impact of the project on his or her performance measure *over the three years* will choose project Z, because this yields the highest total profits and average ROI.

EXHIBIT 19.5 Estimated profit and ROI from mutually exclusive projects

Profits	X (£000s)	Y (000s)	Z (£000s)
Year 1	(37)	103	(237)
Year 2	83	(37)	(237)
Year 3	253	43	813
Total profits	299	109	339

ROI	X (%)	Y (%)	Z (%)
Year 1	(4.3)	11.9	(27.5)
Year 2	14.5	(6.4)	(41.3)
Year 3	88.1	15.0	283.2
Average	32.8	6.8	71.5

REAL WORLD
VIEWS 19.4

Tesco fiasco fuels fears that executive pay equation can skew priorities

As a result of the recent financial troubles at Tesco its shares declined to an 11-year low in 2014. Terry Smith, chief executive of investment house Fundsmith, stated in an article published in *The Financial Times* that investors had long ignored warning signs that Tesco's return on capital employed/return on investment (ROCE/ROI) had fallen sharply between 1995 and 2011. Instead, during this period the investors had reacted favourably to Tesco's reported results because they had become fixated on its rising earnings per share (EPS) which had quadrupled. This raises questions about the metrics Tesco uses to calculate executive remuneration, and whether this might have led managers to prioritize EPS over ROCE. Deloitte's annual review of FTSE 100 directors' executive remuneration reported an 'over-emphasis on measures such as EPS, total shareholder return (a combination of share price changes and dividend payouts over a period of time) and return measures such as ROCE/ROI'.

The article highlights comments from a major asset management company for Dutch pension scheme members (APG) and Homes Equity Ownership Services which advises more than 30 institutional investors. APG recently issued remuneration guidelines for the companies it invests in. The guidelines express concerns about incentives that seem vulnerable to the risk of manipulation of corporate activity to improve payouts. 'In the most basic terms, we believe that long-term value creation to shareholders is the added economic value over and above the cost of capital. We believe pay policies should be set to reflect and support this.' APG is also in favour of the additional use of non-financial factors, such as customer satisfaction, human capital, health and safety, and sustainability performance, in determining pay.

The director of Homes Equity Ownership Services stated that ROCE can produce 'a very profitable business, but a very small business. For instance, if a company has a ROCE of 30 per cent, this figure will fall if it embarks on a project with an estimated ROCE of 20 per cent. A ROCE maximizer would therefore avoid this investment. Yet if the company's cost of capital is 10 per cent, taking on this project would still increase its profitability.' The director recommends that ROCE should be used in combination with a measure of profit, such as economic value added or economic profit.

Questions

1 Why might measures such as ROCE (also called ROI) continue to be used to determine executive remuneration even though the limitations of such measures have been highlighted for many years?

2 Why is the use of additional non-financial measures recommended to determine executive remuneration and what are the disadvantages of incorporating such measures?

Reference

Collis, S., McGee, H. and Carswell, S. (2014) *Irish Times*, 29 September.

Economic value added (EVA$^{(TM)}$)

Let us now consider whether the EVA$^{(TM)}$ calculations are consistent with the NPV calculations. Exhibit 19.6 presents the estimated EVA$^{(TM)}$ calculations for project X using conventional financial accounting depreciation methods. The total present value of EVA$^{(TM)}$ for project X is £77000 and this is identical with the NPV of project X, which was calculated in Exhibit 19.4. EVA$^{(TM)}$ is therefore the long-term counterpart of the discounted NPV. Thus, given that maximizing NPV is equivalent to maximizing shareholder value, then maximizing the present value of EVA$^{(TM)}$ is also equivalent to maximizing shareholder value and Stern Stewart's claim that EVA$^{(TM)}$ is congruent with shareholder value would appear to be justified. Consequently, if divisional managers are evaluated on the basis of the long-run present value of EVA$^{(TM)}$, their capital investment decisions should be consistent with the decisions that would be taken using the NPV rule.

However, there is no guarantee that the short-run EVA$^{(TM)}$ measure will be consistent with the longer run measure if conventional depreciation methods are used. To ensure consistency with the long-run measure and NPV, an adjustment must be made within the EVA$^{(TM)}$ accountancy adjustments so

EXHIBIT 19.6 Estimated EVA$^{(TM)}$ calculations for project X[a]

	Year 1 (£000s)	Year 2 (£000s)	Year 3 (£000s)	Total (£000s)
Profit before interest	(37)	83	253	
10% interest on opening written-down value	86	57	29	
EVA$^{(TM)}$	(123)	26	224	
PV of EVA$^{(TM)}$	(112)	21	168	77

Note
[a]All calculations are to the nearest £000.

that depreciation is based on economic values and not historic book values. For example, if conventional depreciation is used the EVA$^{(TM)}$ for year 1 for each of the projects will be as follows:

	(£000s)[a]
Project X	(−123)
Project Y	17
Project Z	(−323)

Note
[a]Derived from deducting 10 per cent interest (£86 000) on opening WDV from Year 1 profits shown in Exhibit 19.5.

The *short-term* measure of EVA$^{(TM)}$ may lead to acceptance of project Y. In addition, a manager concerned about a possible deterioration in his or her expected EVA$^{(TM)}$ may reject project X even when he or she is aware that acceptance will mean an increase in long-term EVA$^{(TM)}$.

We can therefore conclude that the short-run EVA$^{(TM)}$ measure will be consistent with the longer run measure only if alternative unconventional depreciation methods are used. These methods are described in Learning Note 19.1 in the digital support resources accompanying this book (see Preface for details).

ADDRESSING THE DYSFUNCTIONAL CONSEQUENCES OF SHORT-TERM FINANCIAL PERFORMANCE MEASURES

Ideally, divisional financial performance measures should report economic income rather than accounting profit. To calculate economic income, all future cash flows should be estimated and discounted to their present value. This calculation should be made for a division at the beginning and end of a measurement period. The difference between the beginning and ending values represents economic income. Economic income represents a theoretical ideal since, in practice, it is extremely difficult to approximate. The main problem with using estimates of economic income to evaluate performance is that it lacks precision and objectivity. It is also inconsistent with external financial accounting information that is used by financial markets to evaluate the performance of the company as a whole. It is likely that corporate managers may prefer their divisional managers to focus on the same financial reporting measures that are used by financial markets to evaluate the company as a whole.

The financial performance measures described in this chapter are used as surrogates for economic income. Their main weaknesses are that they are backward looking and short term oriented. Such weaknesses have been widely publicized in recent years and highlighted as a major contributory factor to the collapse of the banking sector in 2008. The performance measures encouraged senior bankers to engage in risky behaviour because risk was not reflected in the short-term performance measures. Indeed, the short-term impact of marketing high risk loans and trading in high risk complex financial products can initially result in the reporting of favourable performance measures. The longer the measurement

REAL WORLD VIEWS 19.5

Airport security performance measurements – and bonus payments

Following events of September 2001, airport security screening in the US and globally increased dramatically. As we all know, this led to increasing queues at airports which while inconvenient, are paramount to the safety and security of passengers.

Since 2001, many airports have used technology to speed things up to some extent at airport security. For example, automated conveyors delivering crates for our hand luggage through x-ray machines and full body scanners are now quite common. Anonymous tracking of smart devices (smart phones and tablets) in the security queue is also a commonly-used method of predicting the length of the queue. With such developments, as you may imagine, the time spent at security has become a performance measurement at many airports. For example, Heathrow Airport in London reported less than 5 minutes' security waiting time at least 96 per cent of the time in October 2016.

While waiting time is an important measurement, is it the correct measure to consider in the longer term? An article on revealnews.org provides some insights. In the US, the Transportation Security Administration (TSA) are responsible for airport security. The article reports how undercover officials were able to get weapons and other items through security undetected 95 per cent of the time. The article mentions how 'the findings weren't surprising to current and former TSA officials, who say that the security operations office had come to focus on efficiency and reduced wait times'. It also suggests that managers in charge received bonuses for achieving these targets.

Questions

1 Based on the above, is time waiting for or being processed through airport security a shorter term target or longer term? Could it ever be a shorter term performance measure?

2 Do you think performance on an issue such as airport security should be measured and rewarded by performance-based bonus payments?

References

Becker, A (2016) TSA official responsible for security lapses earned big bonuses, reveal.com, available at www.revealnews.org/article/tsa-official-responsible-for-security-lapses-earned-big-bonuses

October 2016 Central Security Performance Report, available at www.heathrow.com/file_source/Company/Static/PDF/Companynewsandinformation/Central_Security_Performance_Oct16.pdf

---

period, the more congruent financial measures of performance are with economic income. For example, profits over a three-year measurement period are a better indicator of economic income than profits over a six-month period. The longer the measurement period, the more likely the adverse long-term consequences of the risky activities of the banks would have been reflected in the performance measurement system. The disadvantage of lengthening the measurement period is that rewards are often tied to the performance evaluation and, if they are provided a long time after actions are taken, there is a danger that they will lose much of their motivational effects. Also, feedback information is required at frequent intervals to enable managers to respond to deviations from plan.

Probably the most widely used approach to mitigate against the dysfunctional consequences that can arise from relying excessively on short-term financial performance measures is to supplement them with non-financial measures that measure those factors that are critical to the long-term success and profits of the organization. These measures focus on areas such as competitiveness, product/service leadership, productivity, quality, delivery performance, innovation and flexibility in responding to changes in demand. If managers focus excessively on the short term, the benefits from improved short-term financial performance may be counter-balanced by a deterioration in the non-financial measures. Such non-financial measures should provide a broad indication of the contribution of a divisional manager's current actions to the long-term success of the organization.

The incorporation of non-financial measures creates the need to link financial and non-financial measures of performance. The balanced scorecard emerged in the 1990s to meet this requirement. The balanced scorecard will be covered extensively in Chapter 21 where our focus will be on strategic performance management but, at this stage, you should note that the divisional financial performance evaluation measures discussed in this chapter ought to be seen as one of the elements within the balanced scorecard. Divisional performance evaluation should be based on a combination of financial and non-financial measures.

SUMMARY

The following items relate to the learning objectives listed at the beginning of the chapter.

- **Distinguish between non-divisionalized and divisionalized organizational structures.**

In non-divisionalized organizations, the organization as a whole is an investment centre. With a divisionalized structure, the organization is split up into divisions that consist of either investment centres or profit centres. Thus, the distinguishing feature is that in a non-divisionalized structure only the organization as a whole is an investment centre and below this level a functional structure consisting of cost centres and revenue centres applies throughout. In contrast, in a divisionalized structure the organization is divided into separate profit or investment centres and a functional structure consisting of cost centres and revenues applies below this level.

- **Explain why it is preferable to distinguish between managerial and economic performance.**

Divisional economic performance can be influenced by many factors beyond the control of divisional managers. For example, good or bad economic performance may arise mainly from a favourable or unfavourable economic climate faced by the division rather than the specific contribution of the divisional manager. To evaluate the performance of divisional managers, an attempt ought to be made to distinguish between the economic and managerial performance.

- **Explain the factors that should be considered in designing financial performance measures for evaluating divisional managers.**

To evaluate the performance of a divisional manager only those items directly controllable by the manager should be included in the divisional managerial performance financial measures. Thus, all allocations of indirect costs, such as those central service and administration costs that cannot be influenced by divisional managers, ought not to be included in the performance measure. Such costs can only be controlled where they are incurred, which means those central service managers should be held accountable for them.

- **Explain the meaning of return on investment (ROI), residual income and economic value added (EVA$^{(TM)}$).**

ROI expresses divisional profit as a percentage of the assets employed in a division. Residual income is defined as divisional profit less a cost of capital charge on divisional investment (e.g. net assets or total assets). During the 1990s residual income was refined and renamed as EVA$^{(TM)}$. It extends the traditional residual income measure by incorporating adjustments to the divisional financial performance measure for distortions introduced by using generally accepted accounting principles that are used for external financial reporting. Thus, EVA$^{(TM)}$ consists of a divisional profit measure plus or minus the accounting adjustments less a cost of capital charge. All three measures can be used as measures of managerial or economic performance.

- **Compute economic value added (EVA$^{(TM)}$).**

EVA$^{(TM)}$ is computed by starting with a conventional divisional profit measure and (a) adding or deducting adjustments for any distortions to divisional profit measures arising from using generally accepted accounting principles for external reporting; and (b) deducting a cost of capital charge on divisional assets. Typical accounting adjustments include the capitalization of discretionary expenditures, such as research and development expenditure. A detailed calculation of EVA$^{(TM)}$ was provided in Example 19.1.

- **Explain why performance measures may conflict with the net present value decision model.**

Divisional managerial and economic performance are normally evaluated using short-term financial criteria whereas investment appraisal decisions using NPV are based on the cash flows over the whole life of the projects. Thus, the way in which performance is evaluated can have a profound influence on investment decisions and there is a danger that managers will make decisions on the basis of an investment's impact on the short-term financial performance evaluation criteria rather than using the NPV decision rule. A conflict may arise between the measures because performance measures are short term, multi-period and historical whereas NPV is a future single period measure over the whole life of the investment.

- **Identify and explain the approaches that can be used to reduce the dysfunctional consequences of short-term financial measures.**

Methods suggested for reducing the dysfunctional consequences include (a) the use of improved financial performance measures such as EVA$^{(TM)}$ that incorporate accounting adjustments that attempt to overcome the deficiencies of conventional accounting measures; (b) lengthening the performance measurement period; and (c) focusing on both financial and non-financial measures using the balanced scorecard approach described in Chapter 21.

KEY TERMS AND CONCEPTS

Balanced scorecard A strategic management tool that integrates financial and non-financial measures of performance in a single concise report, with the aim of incorporating performance measurement within the strategic management process.

Controllable investment The net asset base that is controllable or strongly influenced by divisional managers.

Controllable profit A profit figure that is computed by deducting from divisional revenues all those costs that are controllable by a divisional manager.

Cost centre A location to which costs are assigned, also known as a cost pool.

Divisional net profit before taxes A profit figure obtained by allocating all general and administrative expenses to divisions.

Divisional profit contribution Controllable profit, less any non-controllable expenses that are attributable to a division, and which would be avoidable if the division were closed.

Divisionalized organizational structure A decentralized organizational structure in which a firm is split into separate divisions.

Economic value added (EVA$^{(TM)}$) A refinement of the residual income measure that incorporates adjustments to the divisional financial performance measure for distortions introduced by generally accepted accounting principles, trademarked by the Stern Stewart consulting organization.

Functional organizational structure An organizational structure that is split by all activities of a similar type within a company being placed under the control of appropriate departmental heads.

Investment centre Responsibility centres whose managers are responsible for both sales revenues and costs and also have responsibility and authority to make capital investment decisions.

Profit centre A division or part of an organization in which the manager does not control the investment and is responsible only for the profits obtained from operating the assets assigned by corporate headquarters.

Residual income Controllable profit less a cost of capital charge on the investment controllable by the divisional manager.

Return on investment (ROI) A method of appraising capital investments where the average annual profits from a project are divided into the average investment cost, also known as the accounting rate of return and return on capital employed.

Value-based-management (VBM) A management principle that states that management should first and foremost consider the interests of shareholders in its business decisions.

RECOMMENDED READING

You should refer to two articles written by Ryan (2011) relating to a description, calculation and discussion of economic value added that can be accessed from the www.accaglobal.com/gb/en/student/exam-support -resources/professional-exams-study-resources/p5 /technical-articles.html. See also Keef and Roush (2002) for a discussion of the criticisms of economic value added and Lovata and Costigan (2002) for a survey relating to the adopters of economic value added. For a theoretical review of economic value added, see O'Hanlon and Peasnell (1998).

KEY EXAMINATION POINTS

Most examination questions include a comparison of residual income (RI) (or EVA$^{(TM)}$) and return on investment (ROI). Make sure you can calculate these measures and discuss the merits and deficiencies of RI and ROI. You should emphasize that when evaluating short-term divisional performance, it is virtually impossible to capture in one financial measure all the variables required to measure the performance of a divisional manager. It is also necessary to include in the performance reports other non-financial performance measures.

Examination questions may also require you to compare the change in RI or ROI when the assets are valued at original cost or written-down value (see Exhibit 19.3). Note that neither method of valuation is satisfactory (you should therefore pay particular attention to the section in the chapter on 'The impact of depreciation'). You should refer to the solution to review problem 19.22 for an illustration of the computation of EVA$^{(TM)}$.

ASSESSMENT MATERIAL

The review questions are short questions that enable you to assess your understanding of the main topics included in the chapter. The numbers in parentheses provide you with the page numbers to refer to if you cannot answer a specific question.

The review problems are more complex and require you to relate and apply the content to various business problems. The problems are graded by their level of difficulty. Solutions to review problems that are not preceded by the term 'IM' are provided in a separate section at the end of the book. Solutions to problems preceded by the term 'IM' are provided in the Instructor's Manual accompanying this book that can be downloaded from the lecturer's digital support resources. Additional review problems with fully worked solutions are provided in the *Student Manual* that accompanies this book.

REVIEW QUESTIONS

19.1 Distinguish between divisionalized and non-divisionalized organizational structure. (pp. 495–496)

19.2 Distinguish between profit centres and investment centres. (p. 496)

19.3 What are the advantages and disadvantages of divisionalization? (p. 496)

19.4 What are the pre-requisites for successful divisionalization? (p. 497)

19.5 Why might it be appropriate to distinguish between the managerial and economic performance of a division? (pp. 497–498)

19.6 Describe three alternative profit measures that can be used to measure divisional performance. Which measures are preferable for (a) measuring divisional *managerial* performance and (b) measuring divisional *economic* performance? (pp. 499–500)

19.7 Why is it common practice not to distinguish between managerial and economic performance? (p. 500)

19.8 Why is it common practice to allocate central costs to measure divisional managerial performance? (p. 500)

19.9 Distinguish between return on investment, residual income and economic value added. (pp. 500–503)

19.10 How does the use of return on investment as a performance measure lead to bad decisions? How do residual income and economic value added overcome this problem? (pp. 500–503)

19.11 Explain how economic value added is calculated. (pp. 503–506)

19.12 Describe the effect of performance measurement on capital investment decisions. (pp. 509–511)

19.13 Explain the approaches that can be used to reduce the dysfunctional consequences of short-term financial measures. (pp. 511–513)

REVIEW PROBLEMS

19.14 Intermediate. A company has reported annual operating profits for the year of £89.2m after charging £9.6m for the full development costs of a new product that is expected to last for the current year and two further years. The cost of capital is 13 per cent per annum. The balance sheet for the company shows fixed assets with a historical cost of £120m. A note to the balance sheet estimates that the replacement cost of these fixed assets at the beginning of the year is £168m. The assets have been depreciated at 20 per cent per year.

The company has a working capital of £27.2m.

Ignore the effects of taxation.

The economic valued added® (EVA$^{(TM)}$) of the company is closest to:

(a) 64.16m
(b) 70.56m
(c) 83.36m
(d) 100.96m   *(2 marks)*

CIMA P1 Management Accounting: Performance Evaluation

19.15 Intermediate. Division L has reported a net profit after tax of £8.6m for the year ended 30 April 2018. Included in the costs used to calculate this profit are the following items:

- interest payable of £2.3m;
- development costs of £6.3m for a new product that was launched in May 2017, and is expected to have a life of three years;
- advertising expenses of £1.6m that relate to the relaunch of a product in June 2018.

The net assets invested in Division L are £30m.

The cost of capital for Division L is 13 per cent per year.

Calculate the economic valued added® for Division L for the year ended 30 April 2018.   *(3 marks)*

CIMA P1 Management Accounting: Performance Evaluation

19.16 Intermediate. A division is considering investing in capital equipment costing $2.7m. The useful economic life of the equipment is expected to be 50 years, with no resale value at the end of the period. The forecast return on the initial investment is 15 per cent per annum before depreciation. The division's cost of capital is 7 per cent.

What is the expected annual residual income of the initial investment?

(a) $0
(b) ($270000)
(c) $162000
(d) $216000   *(2 marks)*

ACCA Performance Management

19.17 Advanced: Calculation of ROI and RI and conflict between NPV and performance measurement. The Biscuits division (Division B) and the Cakes division (Division C) are two divisions of a large, manufacturing company. While both divisions operate in almost identical markets, each division operates separately as an investment centre. Each month, operating statements must be prepared by each division and these are used as a basis for performance measurement for the divisions.

Last month, senior management decided to recharge head office costs to the divisions. Consequently, each division is now going to be required to deduct a share of head office costs in its operating statement before arriving at 'net profit', which is then used to calculate return on investment (ROI). Prior to this, ROI has been calculated using controllable profit only. The company's target ROI, however, remains unchanged at 20 per cent per annum. For each of the last three months, Divisions B and C have maintained ROIs of 22 per cent per annum and 23 per cent per annum respectively, resulting in healthy bonuses being awarded to staff. The company has a cost of capital of 10 per cent.

The budgeted operating statement for the month of July is shown below:

	B $000	C $000
Sales revenue	1300	1500
Less variable costs	(700)	(800)
Contribution	600	700
Less controllable fixed costs	(134)	(228)
Controllable profit	466	472
Less apportionment of head office costs	(155)	(180)
Net profit	311	292
Divisional net assets	$23.2m	$22.6m

Required:

(a) Calculate the expected annualized return on investment (ROI) using the new method as preferred by senior management, based on the above budgeted operating statements, for each of the divisions.   *(2 marks)*

(b) The divisional managing directors are unhappy about the results produced by your calculations in (a) and have heard that a performance measured called 'residual income' may provide more information.

   Calculate the annualized residual income (RI) for each of the divisions, based on the net profit figures for the month of July.   *(3 marks)*

(c) Discuss the expected performance of each of the two divisions, using both ROI and, RI and making any additional calculations deemed necessary. Conclude as to whether, in your opinion, the two divisions have performed well.   *(6 marks)*

(d) Division B has now been offered an immediate opportunity to invest in new machinery at a cost of $2.12 million. The machinery is expected to have a useful economic life of four years, after which it could be sold for $200000. Division B's policy is to depreciate all of its machinery on a straight line basis over the life of the asset. The machinery would be expected to expand Division B's production capacity, resulting in an 8.5 per cent increase in contribution per month.

   Recalculate Division B's expected annualized ROI and annualized RI, based on July's budgeted operating statement after adjusting for the investment. State whether the managing director will be making a decision that is in the best interests of the company as a whole if ROI is used as the basis of the decision.
                                                  (5 marks)

(e) Explain any behavioural problems that will result if the company's senior management insist on using solely ROI, based on net profit rather than controllable profit, to assess divisional performance and reward staff.
                                                  (4 marks)

ACCA F5 Performance Measurement

19.18 Advanced: Value based management and EVA$^{(TM)}$. LOL Co. is a chain of shops selling cards and gifts throughout its country. It has been listed on the stock exchange for ten years and enjoys a fairly high profile in the retail sector of the national economy. You have been asked by the chief executive officer (CEO) to advise the company on value-based management (VBM), as a different approach to performance management. The CEO has read about this method as a way of focusing on shareholder interests and in the current tough economic climate, she thinks that it may be a useful development for LOL.

The company has traditionally used earnings per share (EPS) growth and share price in order to assess performance. The changes being proposed are considered significant and the CEO wants to be briefed on the implications of the new analysis and also how to convince both the board and the major investors of the benefits.

Financial data for LOL:

	2017 $m	2018 $m
Profit before interest and tax	50.7	43.5
Interest paid	4.0	7.8
Profit after interest and tax	35.0	26.8
Average number of shares in issue (millions)	160	160

Capital employed at the end of the year was	(in $m)
2016	99.2
2017	104.1
2018	97.8

LOL aims for a capital structure of 50:50 debt to equity.

Costs of capital:

	2017	2018
Equity	12.70%	15.30%
Debt (post-tax cost)	4.20%	3.90%

Corporation tax is at the rate of 25%.

Stock market information

	2017	2018
Stock market all-share index	2225.4	1448.9
Retailing sector index	1225.6	907.1
LOL (average share price) ($)	12.20	10.70

Required:

(a) Explain to the CEO what value-based management involves and how it can be used to focus the company on shareholder interest. *(4 marks)*

(b) Perform an assessment of the financial performance of LOL using economic value added (EVA™) and evaluate your results compared with those of earnings per share (EPS) growth and share price performance. You should state any assumptions made *(12 marks)*

(c) Evaluate VBM measures against traditional profit-based measures of performance. *(4 marks)*

ACCA P5 Advanced Performance Measurement

19.19 Advanced: Discussion of EVA™, calculation of RI and ROI and recommendation whether divisions should be treated as cost, profit or investment centres. Beach Foods (Beach) is a family-owned business which has grown strongly over its 100-year history. The objective of the business is to maximize the family's wealth through their shareholdings. Beach has three divisions. It manufactures a variety of foods in two of the divisions: Beach Baby Foods (Baby) and Beach Chocolate Foods (Chocolate). Each of these divisions knows its own market and sets prices accordingly. The third division (R&D) researches new products on the instructions of the other divisions and is considered to be vital to the survival and growth of Beach. The board of Beach has been considering the impact of using a divisional structure and has come to you as a performance management consultant to ask for your advice.

There is disagreement at board level about the correct choice of divisional performance measure to be used in the two manufacturing divisions. Currently, the business uses EVA™ but two directors have been questioning its value, complaining that it is complicated to understand. These directors have been promoting the use of either residual income (RI) or return on investment (ROI) as alternatives. The board wants to use the same measure for each division. As well as qualitatively evaluating these different measures, the board needs an assessment of the impact of a change in performance measure on their perception of these divisions' performance. Therefore, as an example, they require you to calculate and discuss the use of ROI and RI at Baby division, given the data in Appendix 1.

The chief executive officer (CEO) of Beach has engaged a business analyst to perform a study of the portfolio of manufacturing businesses which make up Beach. This has been completed in Appendix 2. The CEO wants your comments (based on the categorization given in Appendix 2) on how this work will impact on the performance management of the divisions. Specifically, the CEO has asked for your recommendations on how to control each division; that is, whether each division should be treated as a cost/profit/investment centre and also, the appropriate management style to use for handling staff in each division. The CEO commented to you:

'I have heard of different approaches to the use of budget information in assessing performance: budget-constrained, profit-conscious and also a non-accounting style. I need to know how these approaches might apply to each division given your other comments.'

All of this work has been partly prompted by complaints from the divisional managers. The Chocolate divisional managers complain that they had to wait for a year to get approval to upgrade their main production line. This production line upgrade has reduced wastage and boosted Chocolate's profit margin by 10 percentage points. The Baby division has been very successful in using the ideas of the R&D division, although Baby's managers do complain about the recharging of R&D costs to their division. Head office managers are worried about Chocolate as it has seemed to be drifting recently with a lack of strategic direction. Chocolate's managers are considered to be good but possibly not sufficiently focused on what benefits Beach as a whole.

Required:

(a) Assess the use of EVA™ as a divisional performance measure for the manufacturing divisions at Beach.
(8 marks)

(b) Using Appendix 1, calculate the ROI and RI for Baby and assess the impact of the assumptions made when calculating these metrics on the evaluation of the performance of this division and its management.
(7 marks)

(c) Provide justified recommendations for each division's control and management style as requested by the CEO.
(10 marks)

Appendix 1

Figures from Beach management accounts for year ended 31 March:

Bab division

	$m
Revenue	220
Costs	
Divisional operating costs	121
R&D costs recharged	11
Allocated head office management fees	28
Profit before tax	60
Capital employed	424

Notes:

1. Baby launched a new product with a large publicity campaign during the year.

2. The notional cost of capital for Baby is estimated by the chief financial officer at 11 per cent. WACC for Beach is 7.5 per cent.

3. ROI for similar entities is 20 per cent.

4. EVA™ for Baby is calculated as $35m.

Appendix 2

Star	Problem child
Baby:	
Market growth	18%	
Relative market share	105%	

Cash cow	Dog
Chocolate:	
Market growth	3%	
Relative market share	120%	

Relative market share is the market share of the division compared to that of the market leader. If an organization is a market leader, then its market share is compared to the next largest competitor.

Note: You may assume that the calculations and this categorization are accurate.

ACCA Advanced Performance Management

19.20 Advanced: Calculation of residual income and economic added value. Alpha Division, which is part of the Delta Group, is considering an investment opportunity to which the following estimated information relates:

1 An initial investment of $45m in equipment at the beginning of year 1 will be depreciated on a straight line basis over a three-year period with a nil residual value at the end of year 3.

2 Net operating cash inflows in each of years 1 to 3 will be $12.5m, $18.5m and $27m respectively.

3 The management accountant of Alpha Division has estimated that the NPV of the investment would be $1.937m using a cost of capital of 10 per cent.

4 A bonus scheme that is based on short-term performance evaluation is in operation in all divisions within the Delta Group.

Required:

(a) (i) Calculate the residual income of the proposed investment and comment briefly (using ONLY the above information) on the values obtained in reconciling the short-term and long-term decision views likely to be adopted by divisional management regarding the viability of the proposed investment.
(6 marks)

(ii) A possible analysis of divisional profit measurement at Alpha Division might be as follows:

	$m
Sales revenue	xxx
Less: variable costs	xxx
1. Variable short run contribution margin	xxx
Less: controllable fixed costs	xxx
2. Controllable profit	xxx
Less: non-controllable avoidable costs	xxx
3. Divisional profit	xxx

Required:

Discuss the relevance of each of the divisional profit measures 1, 2 and 3 in the above analysis as an acceptable measure of divisional management performance and/or divisional economic performance at Alpha Division.

You should use appropriate items from the following list relating to Alpha Division in order to illustrate your discussion:

(i) Sales to customers external to the Delta Group.

(ii) Interdivisional transfers to other divisions within the Delta Group at adjusted market price.

(iii) Labour costs or equipment rental costs that are fixed in the short term.

(iv) Depreciation of non-current assets at Alpha Division.

(v) Head office finance and legal staff costs for services provided to Alpha Division.   *(8 marks)*

(b) Summary financial information for the Gamma Group (which is not connected with the Delta Group) is as follows:

Income statements/financial information:

	2019 $m	2020 $m
Revenue	400	450
Profit before tax	96	117
Income tax expense	(29)	(35)
Profit for the period	67	82
Dividends	(23)	(27)
Retained earnings	44	55

Balance sheets:

	2019 $m	2020 $m
Non-current assets	160	180
Current assets	180	215
	340	395
Financed by:		
Total equity	270	325
Long-term debt	70	70
	340	395

Other information is as follows:

1 Capital employed at the end of 2018 amounted to $279m.

2 The Gamma Group had non-capitalized leases valued at $16m in each of the years 2018 to 2020 which were not subject to amortization.

3 Amortization of goodwill amounted to $5m per year in both 2019 and 2020. The amount of goodwill written off against reserves on acquisitions in years prior to 2019 amounted to $45m.

4 The Group's pre-tax cost of debt was estimated to be 10 per cent.

5 The Group's cost of equity was estimated to be 16 per cent in 2019 and 18 per cent in 2020.

6 The target capital structure is 50 per cent equity, 50 per cent debt.

7 The rate of taxation is 30 per cent in both 2019 and 2020.

8 Economic depreciation amounted to $40m in 2019 and $45m in 2020. These amounts were equal to the depreciation used for tax purposes and depreciation charged in the income statements.

9 Interest payable amounted to $6m per year in both 2019 and 2020.

10 Other non-cash expenses amounted to $12m per year in both 2019 and 2020.

Required:

(i) Stating clearly any assumptions that you make, estimate the economic value added (EVA™) of the Gamma Group for both 2019 and 2020 and comment briefly on the performance of the Group.   *(8 marks)*

(ii) Briefly discuss THREE disadvantages of using EVA™ in the measurement of financial performance.   *(3 marks)*
(Total 25 marks)

ACCA Advanced Performance Management

19.21 Advanced: Divisional performance evaluation using ROI, RI and EVA(TM). The Health and Fitness Group (HFG), which is privately owned, operates three centres in the country of Mayland. Each centre offers dietary plans and fitness programmes to clients under the supervision of dieticians and fitness trainers. Residential accommodation is also available at each centre. The centres are located in the towns of Ayetown, Beetown and Ceetown.

The following information is available:

1 Summary financial data for HFG in respect of the year ended 31 May 2018.

	Ayetown $000	Beetown $000	Ceetown $000	Total $000
Revenue:				
Fees received	1800	2100	4500	8400
Variable costs	(468)	(567)	(1395)	(2430)
Contribution	1332	1533	3105	5970
Fixed costs	(936)	(1092)	(2402)	(4430)
Operating profit	396	441	703	1540
Interest costs on long-term debt at 10%				(180)
Profit before tax				1360
Income tax expense				(408)
Profit for the year				952
Average book values for 2018:				
Assets				
Non-current assets	1000	2500	3300	6800
Current assets	800	900	1000	2700
Total assets	1800	3400	4300	9500
Equity and liabilities:				
Share capital				2500
Retained earnings				4400
Total equity				6900
Non-current liabilities				
Long-term borrowings				1800
Total non-current liabilities				1800
Current liabilities	80	240	480	800
Total current liabilities	80	240	480	800
Total liabilities				2600
Total equity and liabilities				9500

2 HFG defines residual income (RI) for each centre as operating profit minus a required rate of return of 12 per cent of the total assets of each centre.

3 At present HFG does not allocate the long-term borrowings of the group to the three separate centres.

4 Each centre faces similar risks.

5 Tax is payable at a rate of 30 per cent.

6 The market value of the equity capital of HFG is $9 million. The cost of equity of HFG is 15 per cent.

7 The market value of the long-term borrowings of HFG is equal to the book value.

8 The directors are concerned about the return on investment (ROI) generated by the Beetown centre and they are considering using sensitivity analysis in order to show how a target ROI of 20 per cent might be achieved.

9 The marketing director stated at a recent board meeting that 'The Group's success depends on the quality of service provided to our clients. In my opinion, we need only to concern ourselves with the number of complaints received from clients during each period as this is the most important performance measure for our business. The number of complaints received from clients is a

perfect performance measure. As long as the number of complaints received from clients is not increasing from period to period, then we can be confident about our future prospects.'

Required:

(a) The directors of HFG have asked you, as management accountant, to prepare a report providing them with explanations as to the following:

(i) Which of the three centres is the most 'successful'? Your report should include a commentary on return on investment (ROI), residual income (RI) and economic value added (EVA(TM)) as measures of financial performance. Detailed calculations regarding each of these three measures must be included as part of your report;

Note: a maximum of seven marks is available for detailed calculations. *(14 marks)*

(ii) The percentage change in revenue, total costs and net assets during the year ended 31 May 2018 that would have been required in order to have achieved a target ROI of 20 per cent by the Beetown centre. Your answer should consider each of these three variables in isolation. State any assumptions that you make.

(6 marks)

(iii) Whether or not you agree with the statement of the marketing director in note (9) above. *(5 marks)*

Professional marks for appropriateness of format, style and structure of the report. *(4 marks)*

(b) The Superior Fitness Co. (SFC), which is well established in Mayland, operates nine centres. Each of SFC's centres is similar in size to those of HFG. SFC also provides dietary plans and fitness programmes to its clients. The directors of HFG have decided that they wish to benchmark the performance of HFG with that of SFC.

Required:

Discuss the problems that the directors of HFG might experience in their wish to benchmark the performance of HFG with the performance of SFC, and recommend how such problems might be successfully addressed. *(7 marks)*

(Total 36 marks)

ACCA Advanced Performance Management

19.22 Advanced: Evaluation performance using EVA(TM). Stillwater Services (SS) is a listed water utility company providing water and sewage services to the public and businesses of a region of Teeland. The company was formed when the government-owned Public Water Company of Teeland was broken up into regional utility companies (one of which was SS) and sold into private ownership over four years ago.

As a vital utility for the economy of Teeland, water services are a government-regulated industry. The regulator is principally concerned that SS does not abuse its monopoly position in the regional market to unjustifiably increase price. The majority of services (80 per cent) are controlled by the regulator who sets an acceptable return on capital employed (ROCE) level and ensures that the pricing of SS within these areas does not breach this level. The remaining services, such as a bottled water operation and a contract repairs service, are unregulated and SS can charge a market rate for these. The regulator calculates its ROCE figure based on its own valuation of the capital assets being used in regulated services and the operating profit from those regulated services.

The target pre-tax ROCE set by the regulator is 6 per cent. If SS were to breach this figure, then the regulator could fine the company. In the past, other such companies have seen fines amounting to millions of dollars.

The board of SS is trying to drive the performance for the benefit of the shareholders. This is a new experience for many at SS, having been in the public sector until four years ago. In order to try to better communicate the objective of maximizing shareholder wealth, the board have decided to introduce economic value added (EVA^{TM}) as the key performance indicator.

The finance director has asked you to calculate EVA^{TM} for the company, based on the following financial information for the year ending 30 September 2018:

Stillwater Services

	Regulated $m	Non-regulated $m	2018 Total $m
Revenue	276.0	69.0	345.0
Operating costs	230.0	47.0	277.0
Operating profit	46.0	22.0	68.0
Finance charges			23.0
Profit before tax			45.0
Tax at 25%			9.5
Profit after tax			35.5

Capital employed:		2018 $m	2017 $m
Measured from published accounts		657.0	637.0
Measured by regulator (for regulated services only)		779.0	761.0

Notes:

1. Total operating costs include

	2018 $m	2017 $m
Depreciation	59	57
Provision for doubtful debts	2	0.5
Research and development	12	—
Other non-cash items	7	6

2. Economic depreciation is assessed to be $83m in 2018.

    Economic depreciation includes any appropriate amortization adjustment.

    In previous years, it can be assumed that economic and accounting depreciation were the same.

3. Tax is the cash paid in the current year ($9m) and an adjustment of $0.5m for deferred tax provisions. There was no deferred tax balance prior to 2018.

4. The provision for doubtful debts was $4.5m on the 2018 statement of financial position.

5. Research and development is not capitalized in the accounts.

    It relates to a new project that will be developed over five years and is expected to be of long-term benefit to the company. 2018 is the first year of this project.

6. Cost of capital of SS

	Equity	16%
	Debt (pre-tax)	5%

7. Gearing of SS   40% Equity
                     60% Debt

Required:

(a) Evaluate the performance of SS using EVA^{TM}. *(13 marks)*
(b) Assess whether SS meets its regulatory ROCE target and comment on the impact of such a constraint on performance management at SS. *(7 marks)*

ACCA P5 Advanced Performance Measurement

19.23 Advanced: Accounting, motivational and ethical issues arising from divisional actions. Within a large group, divisional managers are paid a bonus that can represent a large proportion of their annual earnings. The bonus is paid when the budgeted divisional profit for the financial year is achieved or exceeded.

Meetings of divisional boards are held monthly and attended by the senior management of the division, and senior members of group management.

With the aid of the financial year approaching, there had been discussion in all divisional board meetings of forecast profit for the year, and whether budgeted profit would be achieved. In three board meetings, for divisions that were having difficulty in achieving budgeted profits, the following divisional actions had been discussed. In each case, the amounts involved would have been material in determining whether the division would achieve its budget:

- Division A had severely cut spending on training, and postponed routine re-painting of premises.
- Division B had renegotiated a contract for consultancy services. It was in the process of installing total quality management (TQM) systems and had originally agreed to pay progress payments to the consultants, and had budgeted to make these payments. It had renegotiated that the consultancy would invoice the division with the total cost only when the work was completed in the next financial year.
- Division C had persuaded some major customers to take early delivery, in the current financial year, of products originally ordered for delivery early in the next financial year. This would ensure virtually nil stock at year end.

Requirement:
Discuss the financial accounting, budgeting, ethical and motivational issues that arise from these divisional actions.

Comment on whether any group management action is necessary. *(20 marks)*

CIMA Stage 4 Management Accounting Control Systems

IM19.1 Advanced. A large organization, with a well-developed cost centre system, is considering the introduction of profit centres and/or investment centres throughout the organization, where appropriate. As management accountant, you will be providing technical advice and assistance for the proposed scheme.

You are required:

(a) to describe the main characteristics and objectives of profit centres and investment centres; *(4 marks)*
(b) to explain what conditions are necessary for the successful introduction of such centres; *(5 marks)*
(c) to describe the main behavioural and control consequences that may arise if such centres are introduced; *(4 marks)*
(d) to compare two performance appraisal measures that might be used if investment centres are introduced. *(4 marks)*

CIMA Stage 3 Management Accounting Techniques

IM19.2 Advanced. 'In the control of divisional operations within a large company, conflicts often arise between the aims of the organization as a whole and the aspirations of the individual divisions.'

What forms may these conflicts take, and how would you expect the finance function to assist in the resolution of such conflicts?

IM19.3 Advanced. Divisionalized structures are normal in large firms, and occur even when centralized structures would be feasible.

Requirements:

(a) Explain and discuss the arguments for divisionalized structures in large firms. *(6 marks)*

(b) Explain the costs and potential inefficiencies of a divisionalized structure. *(6 marks)*

(c) Explain how adoption of a divisionalized structure changes the role of top management and their control of subordinates. *(8 marks)*

CIMA Stage 4 Management Accounting Control Systems

IM19.4 Advanced: Establishing a system of divisional performance measurement in a hospital.

(a) Briefly explain how the measurement of divisional performance differs when assessing the achievement of strategic targets as distinct from operational targets.

(5 marks)

(b) J is a hospital supplying a wide range of healthcare services. The government has created a competitive internal market for healthcare by separating the function of service delivery from purchasing. The government provides funds for local health organizations to identify healthcare needs and to purchase services from different organizations that actually supply the service. The service suppliers are mainly hospitals.

J is service supplier and has established contracts with some purchasing organizations. The healthcare purchasing organizations are free to contract with any supplier for the provision of their healthcare requirements.

Previously, J was organized and controlled on the basis of functional responsibility. This meant that each specialist patient function, such as medical, nursing and pharmacy services, was led by a manager who held operational and financial responsibility for its activities throughout the hospital. J now operates a system of control based on devolved financial accountability. Divisions comprising different functions have been established and are responsible for particular categories of patient care such as general medical or general surgical services. Each division is managed by a senior medical officer.

J's board recognizes that it exists in a competitive environment. It believes there is a need to introduce a system of divisional appraisal. This measures performance against strategic as well as operational targets, using both financial and non-financial criteria. The board is concerned to develop a system that improves the motivation of divisional managers. This will encourage them to accept responsibility for achieving strategic as well as operational organizational targets. In particular, the board wishes to encourage more contractual work to supply services to healthcare purchasing organizations from both within and outside its local geographical area. It is a clear aim of the board that a cultural change in the management of the organization will result from the implementation of such a system.

Requirement:
Discuss the issues which the board of J should take into consideration in establishing a system of performance measurement for divisional managers in order to ensure the attainment of its strategic targets. *(15 marks)*

CIMA Stage 4 Strategic Management Accounting and Marketing

IM19.5 Advanced: Calculation of NPV and ROI and a discussion as to whether a goal congruence exists. J plc's business is organized into divisions. For operating purposes, each division is regarded as an investment centre, with divisional managers enjoying substantial autonomy in their selection of investment projects. Divisional managers are rewarded via a remuneration package which is linked to a return on investment (ROI) performance measure. The ROI calculation is based on the net book value of assets at the beginning of the

year. Although there is a high degree of autonomy in investment selection, approval to go ahead has to be obtained from group management at the head office in order to release the finance.

Division X is currently investigating three independent investment proposals. If they appear acceptable, it wishes to assign each a priority in the event that funds may not be available to cover all three. Group finance staff assess the cost of capital to the company at 15 per cent.

The details of the three proposals are:

	Project A (000)	Project B (£000)	Project C (£000)
Initial cash outlay on fixed assets	60	60	60
Net cash inflow in year 1	21	25	10
Net cash inflow in year 2	21	20	20
Net cash inflow in year 3	21	20	30
Net cash inflow in year 4	21	15	40

Ignore tax and residual values.

Depreciation is straight line over asset life, which is four years in each case.

You are required:

(a) to give an appraisal of the *three* investment proposals from a divisional and from a company point of view; *(13 marks)*

(b) to explain any divergence between these two points of view and to demonstrate techniques by which the views of both the division and the company can be brought into line. *(12 marks)*

CIMA Stage 4 Management Accounting Control and Audit

M19.6 Advanced: Merits and problems associated with three proposed divisional performance measures. Sliced Bread plc is a divisionalized company. Among its divisions are Grain and Bakery. Grain's operations include granaries, milling and dealings in the grain markets; Bakery operates a number of bakeries.

The following data relate to the year ended 30 November:

	Grain (£000)	Bakery (£000)
Sales	44000	25900
Gain on sale of plant	—	900
	44000	26800
Direct labour	8700	7950
Direct materials	25600	10200
Depreciation	700	1100
Divisional overhead	5300	4550
Head office costs (allocated)	440	268
	40740	24068
Fixed assets (at cost less accumulated depreciation)	7000	9000
Stocks	6350	1800
Trade debtors	4000	2100
Cash at bank	1500	—
Bank overdraft	—	750
Trade creditors	3000	2150

Divisional managements (DMs) are given authority to spend up to £20000 on capital items as long as total spending remains within an amount provided for small projects in the annual budget. Larger projects, as well as sales of assets with book values in excess of £20000, must be submitted to central management (CM). All day-to-day operations are delegated to DMs, whose performance is monitored with the aid of budgets and reports.

The basis for appraising DM performance is currently under review. At present divisions are treated as investment centres for DM performance appraisal, but there is disagreement as to whether return on capital employed or residual income is the better measure. An alternative suggestion has been made that DM performance should be appraised on the basis of controllable profit; this measure would exclude depreciation and gains or losses on sale of assets, treating investment in fixed assets as a CM responsibility.

The cost of capital of Sliced Bread plc is 15 per cent per annum.

Requirements:

(a) Calculate for both divisions the three measures (return on capital employed, residual income and controllable profit) which are being considered by Sliced Bread plc, and state any assumptions or reservations about the data you have used in your calculations.   (5 marks)

(b) Examine the merits and problems of Sliced Bread plc's three contemplated approaches to DM performance appraisal, and briefly suggest how CM could determine the required level of performance in each case.   (15 marks)

(c) Discuss briefly whether further measures are needed for the effective appraisal of DM performance.   (5 marks)

IM19.7 Advanced: Discussion of residual income and ROI and the problems with using these measures. Indico Ltd is a well established company that has operated in a sound but static market for many years where it has been the dominant supplier. Over the past three years it has diversified into three new product areas that are unrelated to each other and to the original business.

Indico Ltd has organized the operation of its four activities on a divisional basis with four divisional general managers having overall responsibility for all aspects of running each business except for finance. All finance is provided centrally with routine accounting and cash management, including invoicing, debt collection and bill payments, being handled by the head office. Head office operating costs were £1 million in the year ending 31 December. The total capital employed at mid-year amounted to £50 million, of which £20 million was debt capital financed at an average annual interest rate of 10 per cent. Head office assets comprise 50 per cent fixed assets and 50 per cent working capital. To date, the company has financed its expansion without raising additional equity capital, but it may soon require to do so if further expansion is undertaken. It has estimated that the cost of new equity capital would be 20 per cent per annum. No new investment was undertaken in during the year pending a review of the performance of each division.

The results for the divisions for the year to 31 December are as follows:

Division

	A (£m)	B (£m)	C (£m)	D (£m)
Sales	110.0	31.0	18.0	13.0
Trading profit	2.0	1.1	1.2	0.5
Exchange gain (1)	2.0	—	—	—
Profit after currency movement	4.0	1.1	1.2	0.5
Exceptional charge (2)	—	—	(1.8)	—
Profit(loss) after exceptional charges	4.0	1.1	(0.6)	0.5
Group interest charge (3)	(1.1)	(0.3)	(0.2)	(0.1)
Net divisional profit(loss)	2.9	0.8	(0.8)	0.4
Depreciation charged above	3.0	1.0	2.0	0.4
Net assets (at year end)	23.5	9.5	4.0	1.8

1   The exchange gain represents the difference between the original sterling value of an overseas contract and the eventual receipts in sterling.

2   The exceptional charge relates to the closure of a factory in January.

3   Group interest is purely a notional charge from head office based on a percentage of sales.

Requirements:

(a) Calculate the return on investment and residual income for each division, ignoring the head office costs and stating any assumptions you consider appropriate. Explain how this information is useful in evaluating divisional performance, and outline the main standards of comparison you would use.   (13 marks)

(b) Explain how you would deal with the head office costs in measuring divisional performance within Indico Ltd.
     (4 marks)

(c) Discuss the problems arising from using return on investment and residual income to evaluate a speculative new division operating in a high technology industry. State how you could improve these measures to enable better divisional comparisons to be made.   (8 marks)

ICAEW P2 Management Accounting

IM19.8 Advanced: Performance reporting and a discussion of key measurement issues for a divisionalized company. A recently incorporated power company, set up after the privatization of the electricity and coal industries, owns the following assets:

An electricity generating station, capable of being fuelled either by coal or by oil.
    Three coal mines, located some 10 to 20 miles from the generating station, connected to a coal preparation plant.
    A coal preparation plant, which takes the coal from the three mines and cleans it into a form suitable for use in the generating plant. As a by-product, a quantity of high-quality coal is produced that can be sold on the industrial market. The plant has a rail link to the generating station.

The electricity generated is distributed via power lines owned by a separate company, which has an obligation to provide the distribution service on pre-set terms. The market for electricity is highly competitive with demand varying both by the time of day (in the short term) and by season of the year (in the medium term).

The power company is in the process of developing a management accounting system which will be used to provide information to assist in setting electricity tariffs for customers and to hold managers within the company accountable for their performance. Initially, there are five main operating units, with a manager responsible for each, namely the generating station, the three coal mines and the coal preparation plant.

Requirements:

(a) Outline, using *pro forma* (i.e. without figures) reports where necessary, the accounting statements you would recommend as a basis for the evaluation of the performance of each of the unit managers.   (10 marks)

(b) Discuss the key measurement issues that need to be resolved in designing such a responsibility accounting system.   (8 marks)

(c) Explain how the information required for tariff setting purposes might differ from that used for performance evaluation.   (7 marks)

ICAEW P2 Management Accounting

IM19.9 Advanced: Calculations of residual income using straight line and annuity depreciation.

(a) Meldo Division is part of a vertically integrated group where all divisions sell externally and transfer goods to other divisions within the group. Meldo Division management performance is measured using controllable profit before tax as the performance measurement criterion.

(i) Show the cost and revenue elements that should be included in the calculation of controllable divisional profit before tax. *(3 marks)*

(ii) Discuss ways in which the degree of autonomy allowed to Meldo Division may affect the absolute value of controllable profit reported. *(9 marks)*

(b) Kitbul Division management performance is measured using controllable residual income as the performance criterion. Explain why the management of Kitbul Division may make a different decision about an additional investment opportunity where residual income is measured using:

(i) straight line depreciation or

(ii) annuity depreciation based on the cost of capital rate of the division.

Use the following investment information to illustrate your answer:

Investment of £900 000 with a three-year life and nil residual value.

Net cash inflow each year of £380 000.

Cost of capital is 10 per cent. Imputed interest is calculated on the written-down value of the investment at the start of each year. Present value of an annuity of £1 for three years at 10 per cent interest is £2.487. *(8 marks)*

ACCA Level 2 Cost Accounting II

IM19.10 Advanced: Impact of transactions on divisional performance measures and various issues relating to divisional performance measurement.

Scenario

Frantisek Precision Engineering plc (FPE) is an engineering company that makes tools and equipment for a wide range of applications. FPE has 12 operating divisions, each of which is responsible for a particular product group. In the past, divisional performance has been assessed on the basis of residual income (RI). RI is calculated by making a finance charge (at bank base rate + 2 per cent) on net assets (excluding cash) as at the end of the year to each division.

Rapier Management Consultants has recently been engaged to review the management accounting systems of FPE. In regard to the performance evaluation system, Rapier has reported as follows:

RI is a very partial and imperfect performance indicator. What you need is a more comprehensive system that reflects the mission, strategy and technology of each individual division. Further, executives should each be paid a performance bonus linked to an indicator relating to their own personal effectiveness.

FPE's directors provisionally accepted the Rapier recommendation and have carried out a pilot scheme in the diving equipment (DE) division. DE division manufactures assorted equipment used by sport and industrial divers. Safety is a critical factor in this sector. Customers will not readily accept new products, design features and technologies, and therefore many remain unexploited.

At the start of 2018, Rapier designed a performance evaluation system for DE division as follows:

Factor	Calculated
Return on capital employed (ROCE)	Operating profit for the year divided by book value of net assets (excluding cash) at the end of the year
Cash conversion period (CCP)	Number of days' debtors plus days' stock minus days' creditors outstanding at the end of the year
Strategy	Number of new products and major design features (innovations) successfully brought to market

Under the terms of DEs new performance evaluation system, the bases of bonuses for individual divisional managers are:

ROCE over 10 per cent	chief executive, production manager, sales manager
CCP less than 40 days	accountant, office manager
more than four innovations	chief executive, design manager

DE divisions accounting office currently consists of four employees. The division does not have its own bank account. All main accounting systems are operated by FPE's head office. DE's accounting staff draw information from the main accounting system in order to prepare weekly budgetary control reports which are submitted to head office. The reports prompt regular visits by head office accountants to investigate reported cost variances.

Part One

In November 2018 DE's accountant predicts that DE's results for 2018 will be as follows:

	2018		End 2018
Sales	£6 900 000	Stock	£530 000
Purchases	£2 920 000	Debtors	£1 035 000
Operating profit	£450 000	Creditors	£320 000
Number of innovations	four	Net assets	£4 800 000

The accountant further forecasts that in the absence of some change in policy or new investment, the corresponding figures for 2019 and end 2019 will be similar to those shown above for 2018. On receiving this forecast, DE division's chief executive convenes a meeting of his managers to discuss strategy for the rest of 2018 and for 2019. Several proposals are made, including:

From the office manager

I propose that we immediately dispose of £160 000 of stock at cost and defer a creditor payment of £180 000 due 16 December 2018 until 2 January 2019. The first measure will reduce profit by £16 500 a year from 2019 onwards. The second measure will incur an immediate £2 000 penalty.

From the production manager

I recommend we invest £400 000 in new equipment, either immediately or in early 2019. This will increase operation profit by £25 000 per year for eight years and the equipment will have a residual value of £40 000 at the end of its life.

From the design manager

I propose we introduce a new electronic digital depth gauge to the market. This will involve an initial investment of £100 000 in new equipment, either immediately or in early 2019, which will have a life of at least ten years. Sales will have to be on six months' 'buy or return' credit in order to overcome market resistance. I forecast that the new depth gauge will generate £20 000 extra operating profit per year with purchases, sales, stock and creditors all increasing in proportion.

Requirements:

(a) Explain the impact of each proposal on the reported performance of DE division in 2016 and 2019, having regard to the new performance evaluation criteria stated in the scenario.

State whether or not each proposal is likely to be acceptable to members of DE management. *(15 marks)*

(b) State your views (supported by financial evaluation) on the inherent merits of each proposal, having regard to factors you consider relevant. *(10 marks)*

Note: Where relevant, you may assume that depreciation is on a straight line basis and DCF evaluation is carried out using an 8 per cent discount rate and ten-year time horizon.

Part Two

A great deal of management accounting practice (including divisional performance evaluation) can be carried out with varying degrees of sophistication. Many new techniques have been developed in recent years. The degree of sophistication adopted in any case is partly influenced by the imagination and knowledge of the management accountant and partly by the availability of management information technology.

Requirements:

(a) In the light of this quotation, state your views on the advantages and disadvantages to FPE of using a firm of consultants to advise on the design of management accounting systems.

Explain your opinion on the merits of the statement quoted above. *(10 marks)*

(b) Explain the main purpose of divisional organization and the main features of the management accounting systems that are used to support it. *(5 marks)*

(c) Explain the changes that might be required in the management accounting operation of DE division if that division became an independent business. *(10 marks)*

Part Three

There is nothing inherently wrong with the factors used in DE's new performance evaluation system. The problem is what those factors are used for – in particular, their use as a basis for management remuneration.

For one thing, almost any factor is highly vulnerable to manipulation: for another thing, they can seriously distort business decision making.

Requirements:

Having regard to this statement:

(a) explain the strengths and weaknesses of RI and ROCE as divisional business performance indicators as far as FPE is concerned; *(5 marks)*

(b) comment critically on the statement made by Rapier (quoted in the scenario). In particular, explain the problems connected with linking management pay to performance, and the measures that management accountants might take to deal with these problems; *(7 marks)*

(c) explain what just-in-time (JIT) philosophy is, in the light of a proposal to adopt JIT practices in the DE division. Write a report for FPE management on whether or not DE division's production manager should be paid a bonus linked to CCP instead of one linked to ROCE (see scenario), in the light of the proposal to adopt JIT practices in the DE division.

(13 marks)

CIMA State 3 Management Accounting Applications

20
TRANSFER PRICING IN DIVISIONALIZED COMPANIES

LEARNING OBJECTIVES After studying this chapter, you should be able to:

- describe the different purposes of a transfer pricing system;

- identify and describe five different transfer pricing methods;

- explain why the correct transfer price is the external market price when there is a perfectly competitive market for the intermediate product;

- explain why cost-plus transfer prices will not result in the optimum output being achieved;

- explain two methods of transfer pricing that have been advocated to resolve the conflicts between the decision-making and performance evaluation objectives;

- describe the additional factors that must be considered when setting transfer prices for multinational transactions.

In the previous chapter, alternative financial measures for evaluating divisional performance were examined. However, all of the financial measure outcomes will be significantly affected when divisions transfer goods and services to each other. The established transfer price is a cost to the receiving division and revenue to the supplying division, which means that whatever transfer price is set will affect the profitability of each division. In addition, this transfer price will also significantly influence each division's input and output decisions, and thus total company profits.

In this chapter, we shall examine the various approaches that can be adopted to arrive at transfer prices between divisions. Although our focus will be on transfer pricing between divisions (i.e. profit or investment centres), transfer pricing can also apply between cost centres (typically support/service centres) or from cost centres to profit/investment centres. Look at Figure 19.1 in the previous chapter. You will see that the administration and shared services support cost centres provide services to all of the other divisions. The cost of support centres might be reallocated to the division based on cost allocations or the divisions may be charged for the services based on their usage at an appropriate transfer price. The same basic principles apply as those that apply between divisions, the only difference being that there is no need for a profit element to be included in the transfer price to reimburse the supplying cost centre. A more rigorous economic analysis of the transfer pricing problem is provided in the Appendix at the end of this chapter.

PURPOSE OF TRANSFER PRICING

A transfer pricing system can be used to meet the following purposes:

1 To provide information that motivates divisional managers to make good economic decisions. This will happen when actions that divisional managers take to improve the reported profit of their divisions also improves the profit of the company as a whole.

2 To provide information that is useful for evaluating the managerial and economic performance of the divisions.

3 To ensure that divisional autonomy is not undermined.

4 To intentionally move profits between divisions or locations for shifting taxable profits to divisions located in different countries.

Providing information for making good economic decisions

Goods transferred from a supplying division to a receiving division are known as intermediate products. The products sold by a receiving division to the outside world are known as final products. The objective of the receiving division is to subject the intermediate product to further processing before it is sold as a final product in the outside market. The transfer price of the intermediate product represents a cost to the receiving division and a revenue to the supplying division. Therefore transfer prices are used to determine how much of the intermediate product will be produced by the supplying division and how much will be acquired by the receiving division. In a centralized company, the decision as to whether an intermediate product should be sold or processed further is determined by comparing the incremental cost of, and the revenues from, further processing. In a divisionalized organization structure, however, the manager of the receiving division will treat the price at which the intermediate product is transferred as an incremental cost and this may lead to incorrect decisions being made.

For example, let us assume that the incremental cost of the intermediate product is £100, and the additional further processing costs of the receiving division are £60. The incremental cost of producing the final product will therefore be £160. Let us also assume that the supplying division has a temporary excess capacity, which is being maintained in order to meet an expected resurgence in demand, and that the market price of the final product is £200. To simplify the illustration, we assume there is no market for the intermediate product. The correct short-term decision would be to convert the intermediate product into the final product. In a centralized company this decision would be taken, but in a divisionalized organization structure where the transfer price for the intermediate product is £150 based on full cost plus a profit margin, the incremental cost of the receiving division will be £210 (£150 + £60). The divisional manager would therefore incorrectly decide not to purchase the intermediate product for further processing. This problem can be overcome if the transfer price is set at the incremental cost of the supplying division, which in this example is £100.

Evaluating divisional performance

When goods are transferred from one division to another, the transfer price represents revenue to the supplying division and a cost to the receiving division. Consequently, the prices at which goods are transferred can influence each division's reported profits, and there is a danger that an unsound transfer price will result in a misleading performance measure that may cause divisional managers to believe that the transfer price is affecting their performance rather unfairly. This may lead to disagreement and negative motivational consequences.

Conflict of objectives

Unfortunately, no single transfer price is likely to perfectly serve all of the specified purposes. They often conflict and managers are forced to make trade-offs. In particular, the decision-making and the performance evaluation purposes may conflict with one another. For example, in some situations, the transfer price that motivates the short-run optimal economic decision is incremental cost. If the supplying division in our earlier example has excess capacity, the incremental cost will probably equal variable cost. The supplying division will fail to cover any of its fixed costs when transfers are made at variable cost, and will therefore report a loss. Furthermore, if a transfer price equal to variable cost (£100 in the above example) is imposed on the manager of the supplying division, the concept of divisional autonomy and decentralization is undermined. By way of contrast, a transfer price that may be satisfactory for evaluating divisional performance (£150 in the above example) may lead divisions to make suboptimal decisions when viewed from the overall company perspective.

ALTERNATIVE TRANSFER PRICING METHODS

The management accounting literature identifies many different types of transfer price that companies can use to transfer goods and services. The most notable ones are:

1 market-based transfer prices;

2 cost plus a profit mark-up transfer prices;

3 marginal/variable cost transfer prices;

4 full cost transfer prices;

5 negotiated transfer prices;

6 marginal/variable cost plus opportunity cost transfer prices.

Exhibit 20.1 indicates that transfer pricing is widely used and that the majority of firms use full cost-based transfer pricing and only around 10 per cent of the responding firms use variable cost-based transfer pricing. The following sections describe in detail each of the transfer pricing methods.

MARKET-BASED TRANSFER PRICES

In most circumstances, where a perfectly competitive market for an intermediate product exists, it is optimal for both decision-making and performance evaluation purposes to set transfer prices at competitive market prices. A perfectly competitive market exists in which products sold are identical and no individual buyer or seller can affect the market prices.

EXHIBIT 20.1 Surveys of company practice

The international survey by the Chartered Institute of Management Accountants (2009) reported that around 70 per cent of large manufacturing companies and 40 per cent of service companies used transfer pricing. A UK survey by Abu Serdaneh (2004) based on responses from 170 companies reported the percentage of companies that used particular transfer pricing methods to a considerable extent. The percentage usage was as follows:

	%	%
Prevailing market price	16	
Adjusted market price	15	31
Unit full manufacturing cost	24	
Unit full manufacturing cost plus a profit margin	38	62
Unit variable manufacturing cost	2	
Unit variable manufacturing cost plus a profit margin	6	
Unit variable manufacturing cost plus a fixed fee	1	9
Negotiated transfer price		8

The findings indicated that a minority of companies used more than one transfer price.

When transfers are recorded at market prices, divisional performance is more likely to represent the real economic contribution of the division to total company profits. If the supplying division did not exist, the intermediate product would have to be purchased on the outside market at the current market price. Alternatively, if the receiving division did not exist, the intermediate product would have to be sold on the outside market at the current market price. Divisional profits are therefore likely to be similar to the profits that would be calculated if the divisions were separate organizations. Consequently, divisional profitability can be compared directly with the profitability of similar companies operating in the same type of business.

Where the selling costs for internal transfers of the intermediate product are identical with those that arise from sales in the outside market, it will not matter whether the supplying division's output is sold internally or externally. To illustrate this, we shall consider two alternatives. First, assume initially that the output of the supplying division is sold *externally* and that the receiving division purchases its requirements externally. Now consider a second situation where the output of the intermediate product is transferred *internally* at the market price and is not sold on the outside market. You should now refer to Exhibit 20.2. The aim of this diagram is to show that divisional and total profits are not affected, whichever of these two alternatives is chosen.

Exhibit 20.2 illustrates a situation where the receiving division sells 1000 units of the final product in the external market. The incremental costs of the supplying division for the production of 1000 units of the intermediate product are £5000, with a market price for the output of £8000. The incremental costs of the receiving division for the additional processing of the 1000 units of the intermediate product are £4000. This output can be sold for £18 000. You will see that it does not matter whether the intermediate product is transferred internally or sold externally – profits of each division and total company profits remain unchanged.

EXHIBIT 20.2 Profit impact using market-based transfer prices

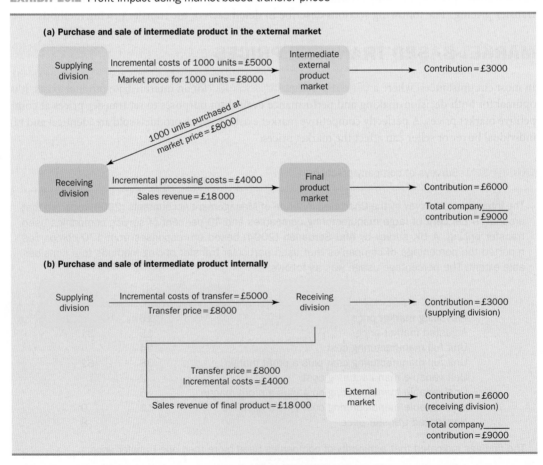

COST PLUS A MARK-UP TRANSFER PRICE

Before we discuss different cost-based transfer prices you should read Example 20.1 and then look at Exhibit 20.3. This exhibit shows the profit for the Baltic Group as a whole using the data given in Example 20.1. The profit maximizing output is 5000 units. The aim of the transfer pricing system should be to motivate both the supplying division (Oslo) and the receiving division (Bergen) to operate at the optimum output level of 5000 units. Assuming that the cost base for the cost plus a mark-up transfer price is full cost, the fixed costs of the supplying division will be unitized by dividing the fixed costs of £60 000 for the period by the estimated output. The resulting unitized fixed cost will be added to the unit variable cost to derive a full cost per unit of output. A profit mark-up is then added to full cost to derive the transfer price.

Let us assume that £35 per unit (or £35 000 per 1000 units) is the full cost plus a mark-up transfer price based on a unit fixed cost of £12 derived from dividing £60 000 fixed costs by an estimated output of 5000 units plus a unit variable cost of £11 plus a mark-up of £12. At this transfer price the profit computations for each division will be as follows:

Oslo division (Supplying division)

Output level (units)	Transfer price revenues	Variable costs	Fixed costs	Total profit/(loss)
1000	35 000	11 000	60 000	(36 000)
2000	70 000	22 000	60 000	(12 000)
3000	105 000	33 000	60 000	12 000
4000	140 000	44 000	60 000	36 000
5000	175 000	55 000	60 000	60 000
6000	210 000	66 000	60 000	84 000

EXAMPLE 20.1

The Oslo division and the Bergen division are divisions within the Baltic Group. One of the products manufactured by the Oslo division is an intermediate product for which there is no external market. This intermediate product is transferred to the Bergen division where it is converted into a final product for sale on the external market. One unit of the intermediate product is used in the production of the final product. The expected units of the final product that the Bergen division estimates it can sell at various selling prices are as follows:

Net selling price (£)	Quantity sold (units)
100	1000
90	2000
80	3000
70	4000
60	5000
50	6000

The costs of each division are as follows:

(£)	Oslo (£)	Bergen (£)
Variable cost per unit	11	7
Fixed costs attributable to the products	60 000	90 000

Bergen division (Receiving divisions)

Output level (units)	Total revenues	Variable costs	Total cost of transfers	Fixed costs	Total profit/ (loss)
1000	100 000	7 000	35 000	90 000	(32 000)
2000	180 000	14 000	70 000	90 000	6 000
3000	240 000	21 000	105 000	90 000	24 000
4000	280 000	28 000	140 000	90 000	22 000
5000	300 000	35 000	175 000	90 000	0
6000	300 000	42 000	210 000	90 000	(42 000)

The supplying division maximizes profits at an output level of 6000 units whereas the receiving division maximizes profits at 3000 units so neither division will be motivated to operate at the optimal output level for the company as a whole of 5000 units. The receiving division will therefore choose to purchase 3000 units from the supplying division. This is because the Bergen division will compare its net marginal revenue with the transfer price and expand output as long as the net marginal revenue of the additional output exceeds the transfer price. Note that net marginal revenue is defined as the marginal (incremental) revenue from the sale of an extra unit (or a specified number of incremental units) of the final product less the marginal/incremental conversion costs (excluding the transfer price). The calculations of net marginal revenues are as follows for increments of 1000 units:

Units	Net marginal revenue (£)
1000	93 000 (100 000 − 7 000)
2000	73 000 (80 000 − 7 000)
3000	53 000 (60 000 − 7 000)
4000	33 000 (40 000 − 7 000)
5000	13 000 (20 000 − 7 000)
6000	−7 000 (0 − 7 000)

If you refer to the receiving division (Bergen) in the schedule of profit calculations, you will see that expanding output from 1000 to 2000 units results in total revenues increasing from £100 000 to £180 000 so the marginal revenue is £80 000. Also variable conversion costs increase from £7000 to £14 000 so marginal cost is £7000. Therefore net marginal revenue is £73 000 (£80 000 − £7000). Faced with a transfer price of £35 000 per 1000 units, the Bergen division will not expand output beyond 3000 units because the transfer price paid for each batch (£35 000) exceeds the net marginal revenue.

EXHIBIT 20.3 Profit computations for the Baltic Group

Note that the following profit computations for the company as a whole do not incorporate the transfer price since it represents inter company trading with the transfer pricing revenues of the supplying division cancelling out the transfer pricing costs incurred by the receiving division.

Whole company profit computations

Output level (units)	Total revenues	Company variable costs	Company fixed costs	Company profit/(loss)
1000	100 000	18 000	150 000	(68 000)
2000	180 000	36 000	150 000	(6 000)
3000	240 000	54 000	150 000	36 000
4000	280 000	72 000	150 000	58 000
5000	300 000	90 000	150 000	60 000

MARGINAL/VARIABLE COST TRANSFER PRICES

Marginal cost is a term that is used by economists. It refers to the additional cost of one extra unit of output. Accountants generally assume that marginal cost is the same as variable cost. When the market for the intermediate product is imperfect or non-existent, transfer prices set at the variable/marginal cost of the supplying division can motivate both the supplying and receiving division managers to operate at output levels that will maximize overall company profits. Using the data given in Example 20.1, the variable cost transfer price is £11 per unit or £11 000 for each batch of 1000 units. The receiving division will expand output as long as net marginal revenue exceeds the transfer price. Now look at the net marginal revenue that we calculated for the receiving division in the previous section to illustrate cost plus a mark-up transfer pricing. You will see that the net marginal revenue from expanding output from 4000 to 5000 units is £13 000 and the transfer price that the receiving division must pay to acquire this batch of 1000 units is £11 000. Therefore expanding the output will increase the profits of the receiving division. Will the manager of the receiving division be motivated to expand output from 5000 to 6000 units? The answer is no, because the net marginal revenue (−£7000) is less than the transfer price of purchasing the 1000 units.

Setting the transfer price at the unit variable cost of the supplying division will motivate the divisional managers to operate at the optimum output level for the company as a whole, provided that the supplying division manager is instructed to meet the demand of the receiving division at this transfer price. Although the variable cost transfer price encourages overall company optimality, it is a poor measure of divisional performance. At a variable cost transfer price of £11 per unit the profit computations for each division will be as follows:

Oslo division (Supplying division)

Output level (units)	Transfer price revenues	Variable costs	Fixed costs	Total profit/ (loss)
1000	11 000	11 000	60 000	(60 000)
2000	22 000	22 000	60 000	(60 000)
3000	33 000	33 000	60 000	(60 000)
4000	44 000	44 000	60 000	(60 000)
5000	55 000	55 000	60 000	(60 000)
6000	66 000	66 000	60 000	(60 000)

Bergen division (Receiving division)

Output level (units)	Total revenues	Variable costs	Total cost of transfers	Fixed costs	Total profit/ (loss)
1000	100 000	7 000	11 000	90 000	(8 000)
2000	180 000	14 000	22 000	90 000	54 000
3000	240 000	21 000	33 000	90 000	96 000
4000	280 000	28 000	44 000	90 000	118 000
5000	300 000	35 000	55 000	90 000	120 000
6000	300 000	42 000	66 000	90 000	102 000

You can see that the supplying division reports a loss equal to £60 000 at all output levels. In the short term, fixed costs are unavoidable and therefore the division manager is no worse off since fixed costs will still be incurred. Note also that the Oslo division also produces other products so the overall divisional profit (excluding the inter divisional transfers with Bergen) may be positive. In contrast, the receiving division maximizes its profits at the optimal output level of 5000 units with a reported profit of £120 000. We can conclude that the variable cost transfer price motivates managers to choose the optimal output level for the company as a whole but it results in a poor measure of divisional performance since the allocation of the £60 000 profits from inter divisional profits results in the supplying division reporting a loss of £60 000 and the receiving division reporting a profit of £120 000.

FULL COST TRANSFER PRICES WITHOUT A MARK-UP

In Chapter 3, it was pointed out that full costs require that predetermined fixed overhead rates should be established. Let us assume that the 5000 units optimal output level for the company as a whole is used to determine the fixed overhead rate per unit. Therefore the fixed cost per unit for the intermediate product will be £12 per unit (£60 000 fixed costs/5000 units) giving a full cost of £23 (£11 variable cost plus £12 fixed cost). If the transfer price is set at £23 per unit (i.e. £23 000 per 1000 batch) the receiving division manager will expand output as long as net marginal revenue exceeds the transfer price. If you refer to the net marginal revenue schedule shown in the section describing cost plus a mark-up transfer prices, you will see that the receiving division manager will choose to purchase 4000 units. For each 1000 units increment in output up to 4000 units, net marginal revenue exceeds the transfer cost of £23 000 per thousand unit batch. The manager will choose not to expand output to the 5000 units optimal level for the company as a whole because the transfer cost of £23 000 exceeds the net marginal revenue of £13 000. Also, at the selected output level of 4000 units the total transfer price revenues of the supplying division will be £92 000 (4000 units at £23), but you will see from the profit calculations shown earlier for the Oslo division that the total costs are £104 000 (£44 000 variable cost + £60 000 fixed cost). Therefore the supplying division will report a loss because all of its fixed costs have not been recovered. Hence the transfer price is suitable for neither performance evaluation nor ensuring that optimal output decisions are made.

NEGOTIATED TRANSFER PRICES

The difficulties encountered in establishing a sound system of transfer pricing have led to suggestions that negotiated transfer prices should be used. Negotiated transfer prices are most appropriate in situations where some market imperfections exist for the intermediate product, such as where there are several different market prices. When there are such imperfections in the market, the respective divisional managers must have the freedom to buy and sell outside the company to enable them to engage in a bargaining process. It is claimed that if this is the case then the friction and bad feeling that may arise from a centrally controlled market transfer price will be eliminated without incurring a misallocation of resources.

For negotiation to work effectively, it is important that managers have equal bargaining power. If the receiving division has many sourcing possibilities for the intermediate product or service, but the supplying division has limited outlets, the bargaining power of the managers will be unequal. Unequal bargaining power can also occur if the transfers are a relatively small proportion of the business for one of the divisions and a relatively large proportion of the business of the other. A further difficulty with negotiation is that it is time consuming for the managers concerned, particularly where a large number of transactions are involved.

Will the managers of the Baltic Group be able to negotiate a transfer price that meets the decision-making and performance evaluation requirements of a transfer pricing system? If the manager of the supplying division cannot avoid the fixed costs in the short run, he or she will have no bargaining power because there is no external market for the intermediate product. The manager will therefore accept any price as long as it is not below variable cost. Meaningful negotiation is not possible. If the fixed costs are avoidable the manager has some negotiating power since he or she can avoid £60 000 by not producing the intermediate product. The manager will try and negotiate a selling price in excess of full cost. If an output level of 5000 units is used to calculate the full cost, the unit cost from our earlier calculations was £23 and the manager will try and negotiate a price in excess of £23. If you examine the net marginal revenue of the receiving division shown on page 530, you will see that the manager of the receiving division will not expand output to 5000 units if the transfer price is set above £23 per unit. As indicated earlier, negotiation is only likely to work when there is an imperfect external market for the intermediate product.

MARGINAL/VARIABLE COST PLUS OPPORTUNITY COST TRANSFER PRICES

Setting transfer prices at the marginal/variable cost of the supplying division per unit transferred plus the opportunity cost per unit of the supplying division is often cited as a general rule that should lead to optimum decisions for the company as a whole. Opportunity cost is defined as the contribution foregone by the supplying division from transferring internally the intermediate product. This rule will result in the transfer price being set at the variable cost per unit when there is no market for the intermediate product. Why? If the facilities are dedicated to the production of the intermediate product they will have no alternative use, so the opportunity cost will be zero. Consider now a situation in which there is a perfectly competitive external market for the intermediate product. Assume that the market price for the intermediate product is £20 per unit and the variable cost per unit of output is £5. If the supplying division has no spare capacity, the contribution foregone from transferring the intermediate product is £15. Adding this to the variable cost per unit will result in the transfer price being set at the market price of £20 per unit. What is the transfer price if the supplying division has temporary spare capacity? In this situation, there will be no foregone contribution and the transfer price will be set at the variable cost per unit of £5.

You should have noted that applying the above general rule leads to the same transfer price as was recommended earlier in this chapter. In other words, if there is a perfectly competitive external market for the intermediate product, the market price is the optimal transfer price. When there is no market for the intermediate product, transfers should be made at the variable cost per unit of output of the intermediate product. Thus, the general rule is merely a restatement of the principles that have been established earlier. The major problem with this general rule is that it is difficult to apply in more complex situations such as when there is an imperfect market for the intermediate product.

COMPARISON OF COST-BASED TRANSFER PRICING METHODS

Figure 20.1 enables us to compare the cost-based transfer pricing methods in terms of whether they result in the optimal output levels for the company as a whole. Note that it is assumed that there is no market for the intermediate product. You will see that the variable (marginal) cost of the intermediate

FIGURE 20.1
A comparison of marginal cost and full cost or cost-plus transfer pricing

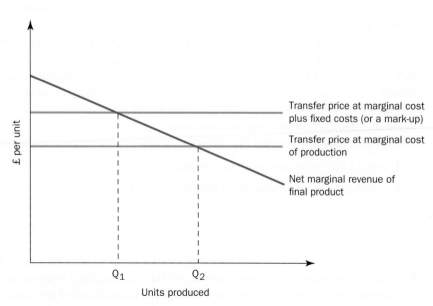

Transfer price at marginal cost plus fixed costs (or a mark-up)

Transfer price at marginal cost of production

Net marginal revenue of final product

product is assumed to be constant throughout the entire production range and that the net marginal revenue for the final product declines to reflect the fact that to sell more the price must be lowered. Remember it was pointed out earlier that the term 'net marginal revenue' refers to the marginal revenue of the final product less the marginal/variable conversion costs (excluding the transfer price) incurred by the receiving division. Economic theory indicates that the optimal output for the company as a whole is where the marginal cost of producing the intermediate product is equal to the net marginal revenue from the sale of the final product. That is an output level of Q_2.

If the transfer price is set at the variable cost per unit of the intermediate product, the receiving division will purchase the intermediate product up to the point where net marginal revenue equals its marginal/variable costs. It will therefore result in the optimal output from the overall company perspective (Q_2). If a higher transfer price is set (as indicated by the green line) to cover full cost, or a mark-up is added to full cost, then the supplying division will restrict output to suboptimal levels such as Q_1.

It is apparent from our discussion of the different transfer pricing methods using the data in Example 20.1 and the diagrammatic presentation in Figure 20.1 that the theoretically correct transfer to encourage divisions to choose the optimal output for the company as a whole is the variable/marginal cost of producing the intermediate product. To simplify our analysis, we have assumed that there is no market for the intermediate product.

Transfer pricing becomes even more complex when we introduce an imperfect market for the intermediate product. You should note, however, that *where there is an imperfect market for the intermediate product the theoretically correct transfer price is still the variable/marginal cost of producing the intermediate product at the optimal output for the company as a whole.* (See the Appendix to this chapter for a more detailed explanation of how the theoretically correct transfer price is determined when there is an imperfect market for the intermediate product.)

PROPOSALS FOR RESOLVING TRANSFER PRICING CONFLICTS

Our discussion so far has indicated that in the absence of a perfect market for the intermediate product none of the transfer pricing methods can perfectly meet both the decision-making and performance evaluation requirements and also not undermine divisional autonomy. It has been suggested that if the external market for the intermediate product does not approximate closely those of perfect competition, then if long-run marginal cost can be accurately estimated, transfers at marginal cost should motivate decisions that are optimal from the overall company's perspective. However, transfers at marginal cost are unsuitable for performance evaluation since they do not provide an incentive for the supplying division to transfer goods and services internally. This is because they do not contain a profit margin for the supplying division. Central headquarters intervention may be necessary to instruct the supplying division to meet the receiving division's demand at the marginal cost of the transfers. Thus, divisional autonomy will be undermined. Transferring at cost plus a mark-up creates the opposite conflict. Here the transfer price meets the performance evaluation requirement but will not induce managers to make optimal decisions.

To resolve the above conflicts the following transfer pricing methods have been suggested:

1 adopt a dual-rate transfer pricing system;

2 transfer at a marginal cost plus a fixed lump-sum fee.

Dual-rate transfer pricing system

Dual-rate transfer pricing uses two separate transfer prices to price each inter divisional transaction. For example, the supplying division may receive the full cost plus a mark-up on each transaction and the receiving division may be charged at the marginal (variable) cost of the transfers. The full cost plus a

EXHIBIT 20.4 Projected financial statement from inter group trading

	(£)	(£)
Sale of final product: 100 000 units at £50		5 000 000
Marginal (variable) costs:		
Supplying division processing costs (100 000 units at £10)	1 000 000	
Receiving division conversion costs (100 000 units at £30)	3 000 000	4 000 000
Total contribution from interdivisional trading		1 000 000

mark-up transfer price is intended to approximate the market price of the goods or services transferred. Exhibit 20.4, which relates to inter divisional trading between two divisions in respect of 100 000 units of an intermediate product, is used to illustrate the application of a dual-rate transfer pricing system. You will see that if the transfer price is set at the supplying division's variable cost of £10 per unit for the intermediate product, the supplying division will be credited with a zero contribution from the transfers, and all of the total contribution of £1 million from inter divisional trading will be assigned to the receiving division.

Dual-rate transfer pricing can be implemented by setting the *transfer price to be charged to the receiving division* at the variable cost of the supplying division (£10 per unit). To keep things simple here, the transfer price that the *supplying division receives* is set at variable cost plus 50 per cent, giving a price of £15. It is assumed that the mark-up added will be sufficient to cover the supplying division's fixed costs and also provide a profit contribution. Therefore the receiving division manager will use the variable cost of the supplying division, which should ensure that decisions are made that are optimal from the company's perspective. The transfer price should also meet the performance evaluation requirements of the supplying division since each unit transferred generates a profit. Thus the supplying division manager is motivated to transfer the intermediate product internally. The reported outcomes for each division using the above dual-rate transfer prices, and the information shown in Exhibit 20.4 would be as follows.

Supplying division	(£)	Receiving division	(£)
Transfers to the supplying division at £15 (100 000 units at £10 plus 50 per cent)	1 500 000	Sales of the final product at £50 (100 000 units)	5 000 000
Less: variable processing costs	(1 000 000)	Less variable costs:	
		Supplying division transfers	
		(100 000 units at £10)	(1 000 000)
		Conversion costs	
		(100 000 units at £30)	(3 000 000)
Profit contribution	500 000	Profit contribution	1 000 000

Note that the contribution for the company as a whole shown in Exhibit 20.4 is less than the sum of the divisional profits by £500 000, but this can be resolved by a simple accounting adjustment when calculating the profits for the group as a whole.

Dual-rate transfer prices are not widely used in practice for several reasons. First, the use of different transfer prices causes confusion, particularly when the transfers spread beyond two divisions. Second, they are considered to be artificial. Third, they reduce divisional incentives to compete effectively. For example, the supplying division can easily generate internal sales to the receiving divisions when they are charged at variable cost. This protects them from competition and gives them little incentive to improve their productivity. Finally, top-level managers do not like to double-count internal profits because this can result in misleading information and create a false impression of divisional profits. Furthermore, the inter divisional profits can be considerably in excess of total company profits where a sequence of transfers involves several divisions. At the extreme, all of the divisions may report profits when the company as a whole is losing money.

Marginal costs plus a fixed lump-sum fee

A solution that has been proposed where the market for the intermediate product is imperfect or non-existent, and where the supplying division has no capacity constraints, is to price all transfers at the short-run marginal cost (assumed to be equivalent to variable cost per unit of output) and for the supplying division to also charge the receiving division a fixed fee for the privilege of obtaining these transfers at short-run variable cost. This approach is sometimes described as a two-part transfer pricing system. With this system, the receiving division acquires additional units of the intermediate product at the variable cost of production. Therefore, when it equates its marginal (variable) costs with its net marginal revenues to determine the optimum profit-maximizing output level, it will use the appropriate variable costs of the supplying division. The supplying division can recover its fixed costs and earn a profit on the inter divisional transfers through the fixed fee charged each period. The fixed fee is intended to compensate the supplying division for tying up some of its fixed capacity for providing products or services that are transferred internally. The fixed fee should cover a share of fixed costs of the supplying division and also provide a return on capital. For example, it can be based on the receiving division's budgeted use of the average capacity of the supplying division. Therefore if a particular receiving division plans to use 25 per cent of a supplying division's average capacity, the division would be charged 25 per cent of the fixed costs plus a further charge to reflect the required return on capital. The fixed fee plus the short-run variable cost represents an estimate of long-run marginal cost.

The advantage of this approach is that transfers will be made at the variable cost of the supplying division and both divisions should also be able to report profits from inter divisional trading. Furthermore, the receiving divisions are made aware, and charged for the full cost of obtaining intermediate products from other divisions, through the two components of the two-part transfer pricing system. It also stimulates planning, communication and coordination among the divisions because the supplying and receiving divisions must agree on the capacity requirements in order to determine the bases for the fixed fee.

If you refer back to Example 20.1 you will see that this proposal would result in a transfer price at the short-run marginal (variable) cost of £11 per unit for the intermediate product plus a fixed fee lump-sum payment of £60 000 to cover the fixed costs of the capacity allocated to producing the intermediate product. In addition, a fixed sum to reflect the required return on the capital employed would be added to the £60 000. Adopting this approach the receiving division will use the short-run variable cost to equate with its net marginal revenue and choose to purchase the optimal output level for the company as a whole (5000 units). For longer term decisions, the receiving division will be made aware that the revenues must be sufficient to cover the full cost of producing the intermediate product (£11 unit variable cost plus £60 000 fixed costs plus the opportunity cost of capital). When the lump-sum fixed fee is added to the short-run transfer price, you will see that the supplying division will report a profit at all output levels. Assume, for example, that the fixed fee is £75 000 (£60 000 fixed costs plus £15 000 to provide a satisfactory return on capital). Now refer back to the divisional profit calculations shown on page 531 for the variable cost transfer pricing system. You will see that the supplying division will report a profit of £15 000 (the revenues from the fixed fee of £75 000 less the £60 000 loss equal to the fixed costs). The receiving division's reported profits will be reduced by the £75 000 fixed fee for all output levels but its profits will still be maximized at the optimal output level of 5000 units.

Kaplan and Cooper (1998) advocate the two-part pricing system approach using an activity-based costing (ABC) system to calculate long-run marginal cost. The short-run element of the marginal cost consists of the cost of the supplying division's unit-level and batch-level activities assigned to the intermediate product or service. You should be able to recall from Chapter 11 that unit-level activities consume resources in proportion to the number of units of production and sales volume and typically include direct labour and material costs. Batch-level activities, such as setting up a machine or processing a purchase order, are performed each time a batch of goods is produced. Therefore the costs of batch-related activities vary with the number of batches made. They are treated as fixed costs by traditional costing systems.

The fixed fee is added to approximate long-run marginal cost. It consists of an annual fee derived from the product-related and facility sustaining costs. Remember from Chapter 11 that product sustaining costs are performed to enable the production and sale of individual products (or services) and include the technical support provided for individual products or services. Facility sustaining costs are the costs incurred to support a facility's manufacturing process and include general administrative, plant management and property costs. The fixed fee should be based on the user's planned use of the supplying division's products and facilities. For example, if a receiving division plans to use 20 per cent

REAL WORLD VIEWS 20.1

How a multinational pharmaceutical company solved its transfer pricing problems using ABC

Teva Pharmaceutical Industries Ltd reorganized its pharmaceutical operations into decentralized cost and profit centres. Teva proposed a transfer pricing system based on marginal costs. But the proposed transfer pricing system generated a storm of controversy. First, some executives observed that the marketing divisions would report extremely high profits because they were being charged for the variable costs only. Second, the operations division would get 'credit' only for the variable expenses. There would be little pressure and motivation to control non-variable expenses. Third, if Teva's plants were less efficient than outside manufacturers of the pharmaceutical products, the marginal cost transfer price would give the marketing divisions no incentive to shift their source of supply. An alternative approach had to be found.

Teva's managers considered, but rejected, several traditional methods for establishing a new transfer pricing system. Market price was not feasible because no market existed for Teva's manufactured and packaged pharmaceutical products that had not already been marketed to customers. Senior executives also believed strongly that negotiated transfer prices would lead to endless arguments among managers in the different divisions, which would consume excessive time on non-productive discussions.

Teva solved its transfer pricing problem by using ABC. Transfer prices are calculated in two different procedures. The first one assigns unit- and batch-level costs and the second assigns product-specific and plant-level costs. The marketing divisions are charged for unit-level costs (principally materials and labour) based on the actual quantities of each individual product they acquire. In addition, they are charged batch-level costs based on the actual number of production and packaging batches of each product they order. The product-specific and

plant-level expenses are charged to marketing divisions annually in lump sums based on budgeted information.

What about unused capacity? To foster a sense of responsibility among marketing managers for the cost of supplying capacity resources, Teva charges the marketing division that experienced the decline in demand a lump-sum assignment for the cost of maintaining the unused production capacity in an existing line. The assignment of the plant-level costs receives much attention, particularly from the managers of the marketing divisions. They want to verify that these costs do indeed stay 'fixed' and don't creep upward each period. The marketing managers make sure that increases in plant-level costs occur only when they request a change in production capacity.

Marketing managers now distinguish between products that cover all manufacturing costs versus those that cover only the unit- and batch-level expenses but not their annual product sustaining and plant-level expenses. Because of the assignment of unused capacity expenses to the responsible marketing division, the marketing managers incorporate information about available capacity when they make decisions about pricing, product mix and product introduction.

Questions

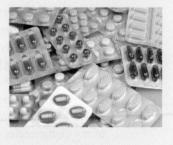

1 How does the transfer pricing system overcome the limitations of marginal cost transfer pricing?

2 Why is it important that capacity costs are taken into account when making pricing and product mix decisions?

Reference
Kaplan, R.S., Weiss, D. and Deseh, E. (1997), 'Transfer pricing with ABC', *Management Accounting* (USA), May, 20–8.

of the average capacity of the supplying division and 30 per cent of the output of a particular product then the fixed fee would be 20 per cent of the facility sustaining costs plus 30 per cent of the product's sustaining costs.

The prepaid capacity would be reserved for the user paying for that capacity. Kaplan and Atkinson (2013) suggest that the approach has two desirable economic traits. First, in the short run, transfers will take place at short-run marginal costs (which consist of unit- and batch-related costs) as specified by economic theory. Second, managers will be more honest in negotiations at the capacity acquisition stage. If they overstate their estimated requirements in order to ensure adequate capacity for their own use, they will pay a higher fixed fee. Alternatively, if they understate their estimated requirements to reduce their fixed fee, they may not have sufficient capacity for their needs as the capacity may have been reserved for others who have expressed a willingness to pay for the capacity. When capacity expectations are not realized, there is a danger that capacity allocations based on expectations may no longer be assigned to their most profitable current uses. This problem can be overcome by allowing divisions to subcontract with each other so that divisions facing better opportunities can rent the excess capacity from other divisions that they have previously reserved.

DOMESTIC TRANSFER PRICING RECOMMENDATIONS

This chapter has described the various approaches that can be adopted to arrive at transfer prices for transactions between different units within an organization and the circumstances in which they are appropriate. The following is a summary of the recommendations that can be derived from our discussion of the different transfer pricing methods:

1 Where a competitive market exists for the intermediate product, the market price (less any adjustments to reflect additional selling and distribution and collection expenses to outside customers) should be used as the transfer price.

2 Where no external market exists for the intermediate product, transfers should be made at the long-run marginal cost of producing a product or delivering a service. The long-run marginal cost should consist of two elements – the variable cost per unit of the product or service transferred and a fixed lump-sum fee based on the receiving division's budgeted use of the average capacity of the supplying division. The variable cost per unit plus the lump-sum fixed fee ensures that the receiving division incorporates the full costs of the supplying division's resources required to produce the intermediate product and also motivates the supplying divisions because they are reimbursed for the capacity utilized.

3 Where an imperfect market for the intermediate product or service exists and a small number of products, or transactions, are involved, a negotiated transfer pricing system is likely to be the most suitable method. Here some form of external benchmark price is likely to be available to enable a meaningful bargaining process to take place between the supplying and receiving divisional managers.

4 Where cost-based transfer prices are used, standard costs and not actual costs per unit of output, should be used. If actual costs are used the supplying divisions will be able to pass on the cost of any inefficiencies to the receiving divisions. Using standard costs ensures that the cost of inefficiencies are borne by the supplying divisions.

INTERNATIONAL TRANSFER PRICING

So far we have concentrated on domestic transfer pricing. International transfer pricing is concerned with the prices that an organization uses to transfer products between divisions in different countries. The rise of multinational organizations introduces additional issues that must be considered when setting transfer prices.

When the supplying and the receiving divisions are located in different countries with different taxation rates, and the taxation rates in one country are much lower than those in the other, it would be in the company's interest if most of the profits were allocated to the division operating in the low taxation country. For example, consider an organization that manufactures products in Country A, which has a marginal tax rate of 25 per cent and sells those products to Country B, which has a marginal tax rate of 40 per cent. It is in the company's best interests to locate most of its profits in Country A, where the tax rate is lowest. Therefore it will wish to use the highest possible transfer price so that the receiving division operating in Country B will have higher costs and report lower profits, whereas the supplying division operating in Country A will be credited with higher revenues and thus report the higher profits. In many multinational organizations, the taxation issues outweigh other transfer pricing issues and the dominant consideration in the setting of transfer prices is the minimization of global taxes.

Taxation authorities in each country are aware that companies can use the transfer pricing system to manipulate the taxable profits that are declared in different countries and investigate the transfer pricing mechanisms of companies to ensure that they are not using the transfer pricing system to avoid paying local taxes. In an attempt to provide a worldwide consensus on the pricing of international intrafirm transactions, the Organization for Economic Cooperation and Development (OECD) issues guideline statements. These statements are important because the taxation authorities in most countries have used them as the basis for regulating transfer pricing behaviour of international intra-firm transactions. The OECD guidelines are based on the arm's length price principle which relates to the price that would have resulted if the prices had actually been used between two unrelated parties. The arm's length principle can be implemented using one of the following methods:

1 the comparable uncontrolled price method (which uses externally verified prices of similar transactions involving unrelated prices);

2 the resale price method (which deducts a percentage from the selling price from the final product to allow for profit);

3 the cost-plus method.

The OECD guidelines state that, whenever possible the comparable uncontrolled price method should be used and if there is no market price, preference should be given to cost plus. Where the cost-plus method is used, considerable variations in costing practices exist that provide some flexibility for a company to engage in opportunistic behaviour to reduce their taxation burden when determining the cost-plus transfer price. A considerable amount of publicity has been recently given highlighting how multinational companies are moving revenues around the world to minimize tax liabilities. For example: Apple, Facebook, Amazon, eBay and Google reported revenue of £2.7 billion in the UK between 2014 and 2015 but many more billions of pounds of cash spent by UK consumers are recorded every year and moved around the world to their sister companies located in tax havens like Luxembourg, Ireland and Bermuda. Industry experts estimate the true UK sales of the five firms to be nearly £18 billion but less than £100 million is paid in UK taxes.

There is a general agreement that regulation of global transfer pricing tax rules needs to be substantially improved to cope with today's intangible products such as electronic books, mp3 files, computer games and other digital media. Even the man in charge of global tax policy at the OECD, the body that crafts international rules on taxation, has stated that the current system is rotten and that aggressive tax planning needs to be replaced with firmer rules. Unfortunately, there appears to be slow progress on how this should be done.

The process of multinational companies acting aggressively to minimize global taxes has attracted a considerable amount of negative publicity on the grounds that the behaviour is unethical. There is evidence to suggest that consumers are penalizing such behaviour by migrating from firms engaged in unethical behaviour to their competitors. For example, many consumers of Starbucks in the UK migrated to its rival, Costa, because of their perception that Starbucks did not pay a fair amount of UK taxes. Because of the concern that its customers perceived it to be engaged in unethical behaviour, Starbucks responded by volunteering to add an extra £10m corporation tax liability.

REAL WORLD VIEWS 20.2

UK tax authority doubles its tax income from investigations of multinational transfer pricing

According to an article in the *Financial Times* the UK tax authority (HMRC – HM Revenue & Customs) raised £1.1bn from challenging the pricing of multinational companies' internal deals in 2013–14 – more than twice as much as in the previous year. The increase came as HMRC stepped up its 'transfer-pricing' investigations – scrutinizing the prices charged on transactions between different parts of the same company – following a public outcry over multinational tax planning. The Treasury has intensified action against multinationals' tax avoidance by launching a new 'diverted profits tax' as well as contributing to an overhaul of the transfer-pricing rules by the OECD group of mostly wealthy nations.

The transfer-pricing rules permit HMRC to adjust the profits on transactions between companies in the same corporate group where it appears that the transaction did not take place at 'arm's length', on the same terms as for an unrelated company. In the year to 2014, the amount of extra tax secured from transfer-pricing inquiries aimed at large businesses more than tripled.

Questions

1 Do you think it is always possible to establish an arm's length/ market price?

2 Would an arms' length price be more difficult to establish in the provision of services?

References

Houlder, V. (2015, Mar 06). 'HMRC nets pound(s)1.1bn as it doubles take from pricing probes at multinationals'. *Financial Times*, 3. ISSN 03071766. search.proquest.com.libaccess.hud.ac.uk /docview/1669776097?pq-origsite=summon

REAL WORLD VIEWS 20.3

The ethics of tax avoidance

Across Europe, just how much – or little – US multinational firms are paying in taxes is coming under intense scrutiny according to an article published in the *Washington Post*. Most of the investigations revolve around the issue of 'transfer pricing', when one part of a large company sells goods or services to another part of the company. While the US companies say they are paying what they owe, European authorities have argued that many firms have developed complex tax strategies to lower their tax bills, sometimes with the help of countries hungry for the jobs they can bring.

Many US multinational corporations have established European headquarters in low-tax countries. Apple runs its European operations from Ireland, which has a 12.5 per cent corporate tax rate. In 2005, Amazon set up its European operations in Luxembourg, which is known for striking generous tax arrangements. It is argued that the profits have often been routed through low-tax European countries, potentially cheating others nations in which the companies operate. The European Parliamentary Research Service estimates that corporate tax avoidance results in a loss of tax revenue to the EU of about €50 billion to €70 billion each year.

Questions

1 Do you think management accountants are involved in tax planning decisions such as those referred to above?

2 Do you think tax avoidance is ever ethical? Is it sustainable?

References

Merle, R. (2016) 'Business News: Why McDonald's and Google are in trouble in Europe'. *Wall Street Journal*, May 31 www.washingtonpost.com/business/economy /why-mcdonalds-and-google-are-in-trouble-in -europe/2016/05/

It would appear that multinational companies should use two transfer pricing systems – one for internal purposes based on our discussion in the earlier part of this chapter and another for taxation purposes. However, evidence of two transfer pricing systems is likely to attract the attention of the taxation authorities. It is easier for companies to claim that they are not manipulating profits to evade taxes if they use the same transfer pricing method for taxation and internal purposes. For this reason, and the greater simplicity, multinational companies tend to use the same transfer pricing method for both domestic and international transfers.

Transfer pricing can also have an impact on import duties and dividend repatriations. Import duties can be minimized by transferring products at low prices to a division located in a country with high import duties. Some countries also restrict the repatriation of income and dividends. By increasing the transfer prices of goods transferred into divisions operating with these restrictions, it is possible to increase the funds repatriated without appearing to violate dividend restrictions.

Finally, you should note that international transfer pricing is a complex topic and this section has only provided an introduction to the topic. For a more detailed explanation of international taxation you should refer to the recommended reading at the end of the chapter.

SUMMARY

The following items relate to the learning objectives listed at the beginning of the chapter.

- **Describe the different purposes of a transfer pricing system.**

Transfer pricing can be used for the following purposes: (a) to provide information that motivates divisional managers to make good economic decisions; (b) to provide information that is useful for evaluating the managerial and economic performance of a division; (c) to intentionally move profits between divisions or locations; and (d) to ensure that divisional autonomy is not undermined.

- **Identify and describe five different transfer pricing methods.**

The five main transfer pricing methods are (a) market-based transfer prices; (b) marginal cost transfer prices; (c) full cost transfer prices; (d) cost plus a mark-up transfer prices; and (e) negotiated transfer prices.

- **Explain why the correct transfer price is the external market price when there is a perfectly competitive market for the intermediate product.**

If there is a perfectly competitive market for the intermediate product, transfers recorded at market prices are likely to represent the real economic contribution to total company profits. If the supplying division did not exist, the intermediate product would have to be purchased on the outside market at the current market price. Alternatively, if the receiving division did not exist, the intermediate product would have to be sold on the outside market at the current market price. Divisional profits are therefore likely to be similar to the profits that would be calculated if the divisions were separate organizations. For decision-making, if the receiving division does not acquire the intermediate product internally, it would be able to acquire the product at the competitive external market price. Similarly, if the supplying division does transfer internally, it will be able to sell the product at the external market price. Thus, the market price represents the opportunity cost of internal transfers.

- **Explain why cost-plus transfer prices will not result in the optimum output being achieved.**

If cost-plus transfer prices are used, the receiving division will determine its optimal output at the point where the marginal cost of its transfers is equal to its net marginal revenue (i.e. marginal revenue less marginal conversion costs, excluding the transfer price). However, the marginal cost of the transfers (i.e. the cost-plus transfer price) will be in excess of the marginal cost of producing the intermediate product for the company as a whole. Thus, marginal cost will be overstated and the receiving division manager will restrict output to the point where net marginal revenue equals the transfer price, rather than the marginal cost to the company of producing the intermediate product.

- **Explain the two methods of transfer pricing that have been advocated to resolve the conflicts between the decision-making and performance evaluation objectives.**

To overcome the decision-making and performance evaluation conflicts that can occur with cost-based transfer pricing two methods have been proposed – a dual-rate transfer pricing system and a two-part transfer pricing system. With a dual rate transfer pricing system, the receiving division is charged with the marginal (variable) cost of the intermediate product and the supplying division is credited with the full cost per unit plus a profit margin. Any inter-divisional profits are written off by an accounting adjustment. The two-part transfer pricing system involves transfers being made at the variable cost per unit of output of the supplying division plus a lump-sum fixed fee charged by the supplying division to the receiving division for the use of the capacity allocated to the intermediate product. This transfer pricing system should also motivate the receiving division to choose the optimal output level and enable the supplying division to obtain a profit on inter divisional trading.

- **Describe the additional factors that must be considered when setting transfer prices for multinational transactions.**

When divisions operate in different countries, taxation implications can be a dominant influence. The aim is to set transfer prices at levels that will ensure that most of the profits are allocated to divisions operating in low taxation counties. However, taxation authorities in the countries where the divisions are located and the OECD have introduced guidelines and legislation to ensure that companies do not use the transfer prices for taxation manipulation purposes. Transfer pricing can also have an impact on import duties and dividend repatriations.

- **Additional learning objective presented in Appendix 20.1: To explain how optimal transfer prices can be determined based on economic theory.**

The theoretically correct transfer price when there are no capacity constraints is the marginal cost of producing the intermediate product at the optimum output level for the company as a whole. The application of this rule is illustrated with Exhibits 20.A1 and 20.A2 when there is no external market and with Exhibits 20.A3 and 20.A4 when there is an imperfect market for the intermediate product.

APPENDIX 20.1: ECONOMIC THEORY OF TRANSFER PRICING

Throughout this chapter, it has been pointed out that economic theory indicates that the *theoretically correct transfer price to encourage total organizational optimality is, in the absence of capacity constraints, the marginal cost of producing the intermediate product at the optimal output level for the company as a whole.* No attempt has been made to explain or illustrate the theory because the explanation is fairly complex and a knowledge of the theory is not essential for you to understand the transfer pricing mechanisms described in this chapter. Indeed, it is unlikely to form part of the curriculum for many readers. However, for those readers pursuing advanced courses for the examinations of the professional accountancy bodies, an understanding of economic theory may be necessary. Questions relating to an understanding of theory are sometimes included in the examinations of the professional accountancy bodies (see for example questions 20.22–20.23 at the end of the chapter). If you are not pursing the examinations of the professional accountancy bodies, and your curriculum does not require a detailed understanding of economic theory, you may wish to omit this section.

Setting transfer prices when there is no market for the intermediate product

To simplify the presentation, we shall initially assume there is no market for the intermediate product. In this situation, a responsibility centre may still be classified as a profit or investment centre if it has other activities that involve external sales, and is not dependent on sales revenues only from internal transfers. Besides applying to situations where there is no market for the intermediate product, the theoretically correct transfer price (that is, the marginal cost of producing the intermediate product for the optimal output for the company as a whole) also applies to situations where there is an imperfect market for the intermediate product.

Assuming that there is no market for the intermediate product the optimal output for the company as a whole is the level at which:

$$\left(\begin{array}{c}\text{marginal cost of}\\\text{supplying division}\end{array}\right) + \left(\begin{array}{c}\text{marginal cost of}\\\text{receiving division}\end{array}\right) = \left(\begin{array}{c}\text{marginal revenue}\\\text{of receiving division}\end{array}\right) \qquad (20.1)$$

This equation can be rewritten as

$$\left(\begin{array}{c}\text{marginal cost of}\\\text{supplying division}\end{array}\right) = \left(\begin{array}{c}\text{marginal revenue of}\\\text{receiving division}\end{array}\right) - \left(\begin{array}{c}\text{marginal cost of}\\\text{receiving division}\end{array}\right) \qquad (20.2)$$

The right-hand side of equation (20.2) is known as **net marginal revenue**. This is defined as the marginal revenue derived by the receiving division from the sale of an additional unit less the marginal cost of converting the intermediate product into the final product; so the net marginal revenue therefore excludes the transfer price. The optimum output level can therefore be re-expressed as the output level where:

$$\begin{array}{c}\text{marginal cost of}\\\text{the supplying division}\end{array} = \begin{array}{c}\text{net marginal revenue of}\\\text{the receiving division}\end{array}$$

This transfer pricing rule is illustrated in Exhibit 20.A1. To simplify the analysis, we shall assume that output can be produced and sold only in 1000-unit batches. You can see that the optimal output level where marginal cost equals net marginal revenue is 7000 units. At this output level profits for the company as a whole are maximized (see column 7). The theoretically correct transfer price for batches of 1000 units is the marginal cost of the supplying division at this output level (i.e. £4000). The receiving division will compare this transfer price with its net marginal revenue (column 6 in Exhibit 20.A1) for each output level and will be motivated to expand output up to the level where the transfer price equals its net marginal revenue (i.e. 7000 units). The transfer price of £4000 will also induce the supplying division to produce 7000 units. At an output level below 7000 units, the supplying division will be motivated to expand output, because the transfer price received from the receiving division will be in excess of its marginal cost. However, the supplying division will not be motivated to produce beyond 7000 units, since the marginal cost will be in excess of the transfer price.

The profits for each division at the various output levels based on a transfer price of £4000 per batch of 1000 units are presented in Exhibit 20.A2. You can see that at the optimal transfer price both divisions will arrive at the correct optimal solution. In other words, they will be motivated to operate at output levels that will maximize overall company profits. Note that overall company profits and divisional profits are maximized at an output level of 6000 or 7000 units. This is because marginal cost equals net marginal revenue when output is expanded from 6000 to 7000 units. Overall company profits therefore remain unchanged.

EXHIBIT 20.A1 Optimum transfer price for an imperfect final market and no market for the intermediate product

	Supplying division			Receiving division			
(1)	(2)	(3)	(4)	(5)	(6)	(7)	
					Net	Overall	
				Total net	marginal	company	
Units	Total cost	Marginal cost	Units	revenue	revenue	profit (loss):	
produced	(£)	(£)	produced	(£)[a]	(£)	(5)–(2) (£)	
1000	4000	4000	1000	10000	10000	6000
2000	7000	3000	2000	19000	9000	12000
3000	10000	3000	3000	27000	8000	17000
4000	11000	1000	4000	34000	7000	23000
5000	13000	2000	5000	40000	6000	27000
6000	15000	2000	6000	45000	5000	30000
7000	19000	4000	7000	49000	4000	30000
8000	24000	5000	8000	52000	3000	28000
9000	31000	7000	9000	54000	2000	23000
10000	39000	8000	10000	55000	1000	16000
11000	48000	9000	11000	55000	0	7000
12000	58000	10000	12000	54000	–1000	(4000)

[a]Net revenue is defined as total revenue from the sale of the final product less the conversion costs incurred. It does not include the transfer price.

Earlier in this chapter, it was pointed out that most accountants assume that marginal cost is constant per unit of output within the relevant output range. In other words, for *short-term* output decisions marginal cost is usually interpreted as being equivalent to variable cost per unit of output.

Assume now that in Exhibit 20.A1 marginal cost is equivalent to variable cost and is £6000 per batch of 1000 units so that the total costs of the supplying division will increase in increments of £6000. In other words, the marginal cost (column 3 in Exhibit 20.A1) would be £6000 for all output levels, and the total cost column would increase in increments of £6000. The optimum output level

EXHIBIT 20.A2 Reported profits at a transfer price of £4000 per batch

	Supplying division				Receiving division		
		Transfer			Transfer		Total
Units	Total	price	Profit	Total net	price		company
produced	cost	received	(loss)	revenue	paid	Profit (loss)	profit (loss)
(£)	(£)	(£)	(£)	(£)	(£)	(£)	(£)
1000	4000	4000	0	10000	4000	6000	6000
2000	7000	8000	1000	19000	8000	11000	12000
3000	10000	12000	2000	27000	12000	15000	17000
4000	11000	16000	5000	34000	16000	18000	23000
5000	13000	20000	7000	40000	20000	20000	27000
6000	15000	24000	9000	45000	24000	21000	30000
7000	19000	28000	9000	49000	28000	21000	30000
8000	24000	32000	8000	52000	32000	20000	28000
9000	31000	36000	5000	54000	36000	18000	23000
10000	39000	40000	1000	55000	40000	15000	16000
11000	48000	44000	(4000)	55000	44000	11000	7000
12000	58000	48000	(10000)	54000	48000	6000	(4000)

will be at 5000 units, the level at which marginal cost equals net marginal revenue. Where marginal cost is constant, the marginal cost of producing the intermediate product at the optimum output level will be equivalent to variable cost. Therefore, in the absence of capacity constraints, the theoretically correct transfer price will be equivalent to variable cost per unit of output assuming that marginal cost is constant throughout the entire output range. Applying this rule to Exhibit 20.A1, the correct transfer price is £6000 per batch.

At a transfer price of £6000 per batch the manager of the receiving division will expand output until the transfer price is equal to its net marginal revenue. Hence the receiving division will be motivated to produce 5000 units, which is the optimal output level of the company as a whole. However, the supplying division will be indifferent to the amount it supplies to the receiving division if transfers are priced at a variable cost of £6000 per batch, because it will earn a zero contribution on each batch transferred. Contrariwise, all of the total company contribution of £10 000 (£40 000 net revenue less £30 000 total cost of the supplying division) arising from inter divisional trading will be allocated to the receiving division.

This example illustrates the conflicts between the role of a transfer price in motivating optimal decisions and its role in evaluating divisional performance. Where marginal cost is equal to variable costs, the theoretically correct transfer price that motivates optimizing behaviour results in the supplying division earning zero contribution and failing to recover any of its fixed costs on the inter divisional transfers. Note, however, that where marginal cost is not constant the supplying division will report profits arising from inter dimensional trading (see Exhibit 20.A2).

Imperfect market for the intermediate product

Where there is an imperfect market for the intermediate product, we can apply the same approach that we used to derive transfer prices when there was no market for the intermediate product. The theoretically correct transfer price, in the absence of capacity constraints, is therefore the marginal cost of producing the intermediate product at the optimal output level for the company as a whole. Consider Exhibit 20.A3 (see note 1).

Column 4 shows the marginal revenue that can be obtained from selling the intermediate product in the external market, and column 6 shows the net marginal revenue from converting the intermediate product into a final product and selling in the external final product market.

EXHIBIT 20.A3 Optimum transfer price for an imperfect intermediate market

Supplying division			Receiving division		
(1) Units produced	(2) Total cost (£)	(3) Marginal cost (£)	(4) Marginal revenue (£)	(5) Units produced	(6) Net marginal revenue (£)
1	19	19	40 (1)	1	35.00 (3)
2	37	18	37 (2)	2	33.50 (5)
3	54	17	34 (4)	3	32.00 (6)
4	69	15	31 (7)	4	30.50 (8)
5	83	14	28 (10)	5	29.00 (9)
6	98	15	25 (13)	6	27.50 (11)
7	114	16	22	7	26.00 (12)
8	132	18	19	8	24.50
9	152	20	16	9	23.00
10	175	23	13	10	21.50
11	202	27	10	11	20.00
12	234	32	7	12	18.50
13	271	37	4	13	17.00

To determine the optimal output level, we must allocate the output of the intermediate product between sales in the intermediate product market and the final product market. The sale of the first unit in the intermediate external market gives a marginal revenue (MR) of £40 compared with a net marginal revenue (NMR) of £35 if the first unit is transferred to the receiving division and sold as a final product. Consequently, the first unit of output of the supplying division should be sold in the intermediate external market. The second unit of output should also be sold in the intermediate market because the MR of £37 is in excess of the NMR of £35 if the unit is sold as a final product. The third unit of output of the intermediate product should be sold in the final product market, since the NMR of £35 is in excess of the MR of £34 that can be obtained from selling in the intermediate market. The fourth unit of output yields an MR of £34 if sold in the intermediate market, compared with £33.50 if sold in the final product market. Therefore the fourth unit should be allocated to the intermediate market. The remaining output of the supplying division should be allocated in a similar manner.

The numbers in parentheses in columns 4 and 6 of Exhibit 20.A3 refer to the ranking of the 13 units of output of the supplying division on the basis of MR from the sale of the intermediate product and NMR from the sale of the final product. The allocation of the output of the supplying division based on these rankings is shown in column 3 of Exhibit 20.A4.

We can now determine the optimal output for the company as a whole by comparing the marginal cost of the supplying division (column 2 of Exhibit 20.A4) with the MR/NMR derived from either selling the intermediate product or converting it into a final product for sale (column 4 of Exhibit 20.A4). By comparing these two columns, you will see that the optimal output is 11 units. The twelfth unit should not be produced, because the marginal cost of the supplying division is in excess of the MR/NMR that can be obtained from its most profitable use.

The theoretically correct transfer price is the marginal cost of the supplying division at the optimal output level (i.e. £27). To be more precise, the optimal output level is just in excess of 11 units, and the marginal cost will be between £27 and £27.50 at the optimal output level. In other words, if we were to graph the data in Exhibit 20.A4, the marginal cost and MR/NMR schedules would intersect at a point above £27 and below £27.50. Therefore the transfer price should be set at any point between £27.01 and £27.49.

If you refer to column 4 of Exhibit 20.A3, you will see that if the transfer price is set between £27.01 and £27.49 then the manager of the supplying division will choose to sell the first five units of the intermediate product on the external market (this is because marginal revenue is in excess of the transfer price) and transfer the remaining output to the receiving division (this is because the transfer price is in

EXHIBIT 20.A4 Allocation of output of supplying division between intermediate and external market

(1) Output (units)	(2) Marginal cost of supplying division (£)	(3) Allocation per ranking in Exhibit 21.6	(4) Marginal revenue/ net marginal revenue (£)
1	19	Intermediate market	40.00
2	18	Intermediate market	37.00
3	17	Final market	35.00
4	15	Intermediate market	34.00
5	14	Final market	33.50
6	15	Final market	32.00
7	16	Intermediate market	31.00
8	18	Final market	30.50
9	20	Final market	29.00
10	23	Intermediate market	28.00
11	27	Final market	27.50
12	32	No allocation	26.00

excess of marginal revenue). You will also see that the manager of the supplying division will select an output level of 11 units based on the principle that he or she will not manufacture any units when the marginal cost is in excess of the transfer price.

If the transfer price is set between £27.01 and £27.49, the manager of the receiving division will choose to sell six units (see column 6 of Exhibit 20.A3) because NMR is in excess of the transfer price. A transfer price set within this range will therefore induce the supplying division to produce 11 units, sell five units to the external market and transfer six units to the receiving division; the receiving division will also wish to purchase six units from the supplying division. This is identical with the optimal output schedule for the company as a whole shown in Exhibit 20.A4.

What would be the correct transfer price if the marginal cost per unit of the intermediate product were constant throughout the entire output range (i.e. marginal cost equals variable cost)? The answer is that applying the marginal cost rule will result in the transfer price being set at the variable cost per unit of the supplying division. You can see that if the variable/marginal cost of the supplying division was £29 throughout the entire output schedule in Exhibits 20.A3 and 20.A4 then applying the above procedure would result in the transfer price being set at £29.

Capacity constraints

When there is a capacity constraint, a transfer price based on the marginal cost rule will not ensure that the optimum output levels are achieved. For example, let us assume that in Exhibits 20.A3 and 20.A4 the capacity of the supplying division is restricted to 6 units. You will see from the ranking (see columns 4 and 6 of Exhibit 20.A3) that the scarce capacity of six units should be allocated so that three units are transferred to the receiving division and three units are sold on the intermediate external market. However, column 4 of Exhibit 20.A3 indicates that at a transfer price between £27.01 and £27.49, the supplying division will maximize its own profits by selling five units of the intermediate product in the external market and transferring one unit to the receiving division. Alternatively, by referring to column 6, you will see that the receiving division will maximize its own profits by taking the entire output of six units from the supplying division and selling them as final products (see note 1 at the end of the chapter). This situation will also apply if the transfer price is set at the marginal cost of the supplying division at the capacity level of six units.

Both divisions pursuing their own best interests in isolation will not therefore arrive at the optimal company solution that is, the sale of three units of the intermediate product and three units of the final product. A conflict occurs because what is in the best interests of a specific division is not in the best interests of the company as a whole. One way of ensuring that the optimal solution is achieved is for central headquarters to obtain information from the supplying and the receiving divisions and to work out the optimal production programme for each division. However, such an approach strikes at the very heart of the transfer price problem, because the optimal production programme has been achieved by an infringement of divisional autonomy.

Summary relating to an imperfect market for the intermediate product

Let us now summarize our findings where there is an imperfect market for the intermediate product. Where the supplying division has no capacity constraints, the theoretically correct transfer price is the marginal cost of producing the intermediate product at the optimal output level for the company as a whole. Where unit marginal cost is constant (and thus equals variable cost) and fixed costs remain unchanged, this rule will give a transfer price equal to the variable cost per unit of the supplying division. However, when capacity constraints apply and the profit maximizing output cannot be achieved, transfer prices based on marginal cost will not ensure that optimal output is achieved and, in this situation, it may be necessary for staff at the central headquarters to establish the optimum production programme for each division based on the output derived from a linear programming model. The application of linear programming to management accounting is presented in Chapter 26.

It is difficult to provide a rigorous analysis of transfer pricing in non-diagrammatic form. To overcome this difficulty, a number of theoretical transfer pricing models applicable to different situations are presented in diagrammatic form in Learning Note 20.1 in the digital support resources accompanying this book (see Preface for details).

NOTE

1 The supplying division will obtain marginal revenue in excess of the transfer price of £27.01/£27.49 for the sale of the first five units on the external market and it will not be motivated to follow the optimal company plan for the company as a whole.

Similarly, the receiving division will maximize its own profits by accepting all transfers until the net marginal revenue equals the transfer price and it will therefore wish to sell six units of the final product.

KEY TERMS AND CONCEPTS

Dual-rate transfer pricing A method of transfer pricing that uses two separate transfer prices to price each inter divisional transaction.

Final products Products sold by a receiving division to the outside world.

Intermediate products Goods transferred from the supplying division to the receiving division.

Net marginal revenue The marginal (incremental) revenue from the sale of an extra unit (or a specified number of incremental units) of the final

product less the marginal/incremental conversion costs (excluding the transfer price).

Perfectly competitive market A market where the product is homogeneous and no individual buyer or seller can affect the market prices.

Two-part transfer pricing system A method of transfer pricing where the receiving division acquires intermediate products at the variable cost of production and the supplying division also charges a fixed fee.

RECOMMENDED READING

See Bartelsman and Beetsma (2003) for a discussion of corporate tax avoidance through transfer pricing, Cools and Emmanuel (2007) for a discussion of the implications of transfer pricing fiscal compliance and KPMG (2011) for transfer pricing being applied to digital

media. You can also refer to PWC (2015/16) for an on-line publication (www.pwc.com/gx/en/services/tax/transfer-pricing/itp-download.html) relating to rules and regulations for international transfer pricing compliance.

KEY EXAMINATION POINTS

When discussing a transfer pricing system, you should indicate that the proposed system should motivate managers to make correct decisions, provide a reasonable measure of performance and ensure that divisional autonomy is not undermined. It is not possible for a single transfer price to meet all three of

these requirements. Examination questions may also require you to recommend an optimal transfer price. It is particularly important that you understand how optimal transfer prices should be set when there is an imperfect market or no market for the intermediate product.

ASSESSMENT MATERIAL

The review questions are short questions that enable you to assess your understanding of the main topics included in the chapter. The numbers in parentheses provide you with the page numbers to refer to if you cannot answer a specific question.

The review problems are more complex and require you to relate and apply the content to various business problems. The problems are graded by their level of difficulty. Solutions to review problems that are not preceded by the term 'IM' are provided in a separate section at the end of the book. Solutions to problems preceded by the term 'IM' are provided in the Instructor's Manual accompanying this book that can be downloaded from the lecturer's digital support resources. Additional review problems with fully worked solutions are provided in the *Student Manual* that accompanies this book.

REVIEW QUESTIONS

20.1 Distinguish between intermediate products and final products. (p. 526)

20.2 Explain the four purposes for which transfer pricing can be used. (pp. 526–527)

20.3 Explain why a single transfer pricing method cannot serve all four purposes. (pp. 526–527)

20.4 If an external, perfectly competitive market exists for an intermediate product what should be the transfer price? Why? (pp. 527–528)

20.5 Define the term 'net marginal revenue'. (p. 530)

20.6 If there is no external market for the intermediate product what is the optimal transfer price? Why? (p. 531)

20.7 Why are full cost and cost plus a mark-up transfer prices unlikely to result in the optimum output? (pp. 532)

20.8 Why are marginal cost transfer prices not widely used in practice? (p. 533)

20.9 Why are transfer prices based on full cost widely used in practice? (p. 532)

20.10 Discuss the advantages and disadvantages of negotiated transfer prices. (p. 532)

20.11 What are the circumstances that favour the use of negotiated transfer prices? (p. 532)

20.12 Describe the two proposals that have been recommended for resolving transfer pricing conflicts. (pp. 534–537)

20.13 What are the special considerations that must be taken into account with international transfer pricing? (pp. 539–541)

20.14 When there is an imperfect market for the intermediate product what is the optimal transfer price? (pp. 542–543)

REVIEW PROBLEMS

20.15 Advanced: Determining optimal transfer price range and volume. Mobe Co manufactures electronic mobility scooters. The company is split into two divisions: the scooter division (Division S) and the motor division (Division M). Division M supplies electronic motors to both Division S and to external customers. The two divisions run as autonomously as possible, subject to the group's current policy that Division M must make internal sales first before selling outside the group; and that Division S must always buy its motors from Division M. However, this company policy, together with the transfer price which Division M charges Division S, is currently under review.

Details of the two divisions are given below.

Division S

Division S's budget for the coming year shows that 35 000 electronic motors will be needed. An external supplier could supply these to Division S for $800 each.

Division M

Division M has the capacity to produce a total of 60 000 electronic motors per year. Details of Division M's budget, which has just been prepared for the forthcoming year, are as follows:

Budgeted sales volume (units)	60 000
Selling price per unit for external sales of motors	$850
Variable costs per unit for external sales of motors	$770

The variable cost per unit for motors sold to Division S is $30 per unit lower due to cost savings on distribution and packaging.

Maximum external demand for the motors is 30 000 units per year.

Required:
Assuming that the group's current policy could be changed, advise, using suitable calculations, the number of motors which Division M should supply to Division S in order to maximize group profits. Recommend the transfer price or prices at which these internal sales should take place.

Note: All relevant workings must be shown. *(10 marks)*

ACCA F5 Performance Management

20.16 Advanced: Interdivisional profit statements and optimal transfer prices. Bath Co. is a company specializing in the manufacture and sale of baths. Each bath consists of a main unit plus a set of bath fittings. The company is split into two divisions, A and B. Division A manufactures the bath and Division B manufactures sets of bath fittings, Currently, all of Division A's sales are made externally. Division B, however, sells to Division A as well as to external customers. Both of the divisions are profit centres.

The following data are available for both divisions:

Division A

Current selling price for each bath	$450
Costs per bath:	
Fittings from Division B	$75
Other materials from external suppliers	$200
Labour costs	$45
Annual fixed overheads	$7 440 000
Annual production and sales of baths (units)	80 000
Maximum annual market demand for baths (units)	80 000

Division B

Current external selling price per set of fittings	$80
Current price for sales to Division A	$75
Costs per set of fittings:	
Materials	$5
Labour costs	$15
Annual fixed overheads	$4 400 000
Maximum annual production and sales of sets of fittings (units) (including internal and external sales)	200 000
Maximum annual external demand for sets of fittings (units)	180 000
Maximum annual internal demand for sets of fittings (units)	80 000

The transfer price charged by Division B to Division A was negotiated some years ago between the previous divisional managers, who have now both been replaced by new managers. Head office only allows Division A to purchase its fittings from Division B, although the new manager of Division A believes that he could obtain fittings of the same quality and appearance for $65 per set, if he were given autonomy to purchase from outside the company. Division B makes no cost savings from supplying internally to Division A rather than selling externally.

Required:

(a) Under the current transfer pricing system, prepare a profit statement showing the profit for each of the divisions and for Bath Co. as a whole. Your sales and costs figures should be split into external sales and interdivisional transfers, where appropriate. *(6 marks)*

(b) Head office is considering changing the transfer pricing policy to ensure maximization of company profits without demotivating either of the divisional managers. Division A will be given autonomy to buy from external suppliers and Division B to supply external customers in priority to supplying to Division A.

Calculate the maximum profit that could be earned by Bath Co. if transfer pricing is optimized. *(8 marks)*

(c) Discuss the issues of encouraging divisional managers to take decisions in the interests of the company as a whole, where transfer pricing is used. Provide a reasoned recommendation of a policy Bath Co. should adopt. *(6 marks)*

ACCA F5 Performance Management

20.17 Advanced: Impact of transfer prices on inter-divisional profit statements. SBA is a company that produces televisions and components for televisions. The company has two divisions, Division S and Division B.

Division S manufactures components for televisions. Division S sells components to Division B and to external customers. Division B uses five of the components in each of the televisions that it manufactures, and sells televisions directly to external customers.

Division S

Budgeted variable manufacturing cost per component:	$
Direct material	14
Direct labour	18
Variable overhead	12

The following information relating to next year is also available:

Fixed costs	$560 000
Production capacity	175 000 components
External demand	150 000 components
Potential demand from Division B	80 000 components

The anticipated external market price for a component is $50.

Division B

	$
Sales price	450
Budgeted variable manufacturing cost per television	
Direct material	40
Direct labour	62
Variable overhead	16

In addition to the variable costs above, each television produced needs five components.

Fixed costs are budgeted to be $1 460 000 for next year. Annual sales of televisions are expected to be 16 000 units.

Transfer pricing policy

Transfer prices are set at opportunity cost.

Division S must satisfy the demand of Division B before selling components externally.

Division B is allowed to purchase components from Division S or from external suppliers.

Required:

(a) Assuming that Division B buys all the components it requires from Division S:

Produce a profit statement for each division detailing sales and costs, showing external sales and internal company transfers separately where appropriate. *(7 marks)*

(b) A specialist external supplier has approached Division B and offered to supply 80 000 components at a price of $42 each. The components fulfil the same function as those manufactured by Division S. The manager of Division B has accepted the offer and has agreed to buy all the components it requires from this supplier.

(i) Produce a revised profit statement for each division and for the total SBA company. *(6 marks)*

Division S has just received an enquiry from a new customer for the production of 25 000 components. The manager of Division S requires a total profit for the year for the division of $450 000.

(ii) Calculate the minimum price per component to sell the 25,000 components to the new customer that would enable the manager of Division S to meet the profit target.

Note: this order will have no effect on the divisional fixed costs and no impact on the 150 000 components Division S sells to its existing external customers at $50 per component. Division B will continue to purchase the 80 000 components it requires from the specialist external supplier. *(4 marks)*

(c) Discuss the potential implications for SBA of outsourcing the production of one type of component that it manufactures. *(8 marks)*

CIMA P2 Performance Management

20.18 Advanced: Calculating the effects of a transfer pricing system on divisional and company profits. Division A of a large divisionalized organization manufactures a single standardized product. Some of the output is sold externally while the remainder is transferred to Division B where it is a sub-assembly in the manufacture of that division's product. The unit costs of Division A's product are as follows:

	(£)
Direct material	4
Direct labour	2
Direct expense	2
Variable manufacturing overheads	2
Fixed manufacturing overheads	4
Selling and packing expense – variable	1
	15

Annually 10000 units of the product are sold externally at the standard price of £30.

In addition to the external sales, 5000 units are transferred annually to Division B at an internal transfer charge of £29 per unit. This transfer price is obtained by deducting variable selling and packing expense from the external price since this expense is not incurred for internal transfers.

Division B incorporates the transferred-in goods into a more advanced product. The unit costs of this product are as follows:

	(£)
Transferred-in item (from Division A)	29
Direct material and components	23
Direct labour	3
Variable overheads	12
Fixed overheads	12
Selling and packing expense – variable	1
	80

Division B's manager disagrees with the basis used to set the transfer price. He argues that the transfers should be made at variable cost plus an agreed (minimal) mark-up since he claims that his division is taking output that Division A would be unable to sell at the price of £30.

Partly because of this disagreement, a study of the relationship between selling price and demand has recently been made for each division by the company's sales director. The resulting report contains the following table:

Customer demand at various selling prices:

Division A			
Selling price	£20	£30	£40
Demand	15000	10000	5000
Division B			
Selling price	£80	£90	£100
Demand	7200	5000	2800

The manager of Division B claims that this study supports his case. He suggests that a transfer price of £12 would give Division A a reasonable contribution to its fixed overheads while allowing Division B to earn a reasonable profit. He also believes that it would lead to an increase of output and an improvement in the overall level of company profits.

You are required:

(a) to calculate the effect that the transfer pricing system has had on the company's profits;   (16 marks)
(b) to establish the likely effect on profits of adopting the suggestion by the manager of Division B of a transfer price of £12.   (6 marks)

ACCA Level 2 Management Accounting

20.19 Advanced: Comments on proposed transfer price policy and recommended changes. You are the management accountant of the SSA Group that manufactures an innovative range of products to provide support for injuries to various joints in the body. The group has adopted a divisional structure. Each division is encouraged to maximize its reported profit.

Division A, which is based in a country called Nearland, manufactures joint support appliances that incorporate a 'one-size-fits-all people' feature. A different appliance is manufactured for each of knee, ankle, elbow and wrist joints.

Budget information in respect of Division A for the year ended 31 December 2018 is as follows:

Support appliance	Knee	Ankle	Elbow	Wrist
Sales units (000s)	20	50	20	60
Selling price per unit ($)	24	15	18	9
Total variable cost of sales ($000)	200	350	160	240

Each of the four support products uses the same quantity of manufacturing capacity. This gives Division A management the flexibility to alter the product mix as desired. During the year to 31 December 2018, it is estimated that a maximum of 160000 support products could be manufactured.

The following information relates to Division B which is also part of the SSA group and is based in Distantland:

1 Division B purchases products from various sources, including from other divisions in SSA group, for subsequent resale to customers.
2 The management of Division B has requested two alternative quotations from Division A in respect of the year ended 31 December 2018 as follows:

Quotation 1 – Purchase of 10000 ankle supports.
Quotation 2 – Purchase of 18000 ankle supports.

The management of the SSA Group has decided that a minimum of 50000 ankle supports must be reserved for customers in Nearland in order to ensure that customer demand can be satisfied and the product's competitive position is maintained in the Nearland market.

The management of the SSA Group is willing, if necessary, to reduce the budgeted sales quantities of other types of joint support in order to satisfy the requirements of Division B for ankle supports. They wish, however, to minimize the loss of contribution to the Group.

The management of Division B is aware of another joint support product, which is produced in Distantland, that competes with the Division A version of the ankle support and which could be purchased at a local currency price that is equivalent to $9 per support. SSA Group policy is that all divisions are allowed autonomy to set transfer prices and purchase from whatever sources they choose. The management of Division A intends to use market price less 30 per cent as the basis for each of quotations 1 and 2.

Required:

(a) (i) The management of the SSA Group has asked you to advise regarding the appropriateness of the decision by the management of Division A to use an adjusted market price as the basis for the preparation of each quotation and the implications of the likely sourcing decisions by the management of Division B.
Your answer should cite relevant quantitative data and incorporate your recommendation of the prices that should be quoted by Division A for the ankle supports in respect of quotations 1 and 2, which will ensure that the profitability of SSA Group as a whole is not adversely affected by the decision of the management of Division B.   (8 marks)
(ii) Advise the management of Divisions A and B regarding the basis of transfer pricing that should be employed in order to ensure that the profit of the SSA Group is maximized.   (4 marks)
(b) After considerable internal discussion concerning Quotation 2 by the management of SSA Group, Division A is not prepared to supply 18000 ankle supports to Division B at any price lower than 30 per cent below market price. All profits in Distantland are subject to taxation at a rate of 20 per cent. Division A pays tax in Nearland at a rate of 40 per cent on all profit.

Advise the management of SSA Group whether the management of Division B should be directed to purchase the ankle supports from Division A or to purchase a similar product from a local supplier in Distantland. Supporting calculations should be provided.

(8 marks)

ACCA Advanced Performance Management

20.20 Advanced: Interdivisional profit statements and international transfer pricing. HPR harvests, processes and roasts coffee beans. The company has two divisions:

Division P is located in Country Y. It harvests and processes coffee beans. The processed coffee beans are sold to Division R and external customers.

Division R is located in Country Z. It roasts processed coffee beans and then sells them to external customers.

Countries Y and Z use the same currency but have different taxation rates.

The budgeted information for the next year is as follows:

Division P

Capacity	1 000 tonnes
External demand for processed coffee beans	800 tonnes
Demand from Division R for processed coffee beans	625 tonnes
External market selling price for processed coffee beans	$11 000 per tonne
Variable costs	$7 000 per tonne
Annual fixed costs	$1 500 000

Division R

Sales of roasted coffee beans	500 tonnes
Market selling price for roasted coffee beans	$20 000 per tonne

The production of one tonne of roasted coffee beans requires an input of one-and-a-quarter tonnes of processed coffee beans. The cost of roasting is $2 000 per tonne of input plus annual fixed costs of $1 000 000.

Transfer pricing policy of HPR

Division P must satisfy the demand from Division R for processed coffee beans before selling any to external customers.

The transfer price for the processed coffee beans is variable cost plus 10 per cent per tonne.

Taxation

The rate of taxation on company profits is 45 per cent in Country Y and 25 per cent in Country Z.

Required:

(a) (i) Produce statements that show the budgeted profit after tax for the next year for each of the two divisions. Your profit statements should show sales and costs split into external sales and internal transfers where appropriate. *(8 marks)*

(ii) Discuss the potential tax consequences of HPR's current transfer pricing policy. *(6 marks)*

(b) Produce statements that show the budgeted contributions that would be earned by each of the two divisions if HPR's head office changed its policy to state that transfers must be made at opportunity cost. Your statements should show sales and costs split into external sales and internal transfers where appropriate. *(6 marks)*

(c) Explain TWO behavioural issues that could arise as a result of the head office of HPR imposing transfer prices instead of allowing the divisional managers to set the prices. *(5 marks)*

CIMA P2 Performance Management

20.21 Advanced: Impact of transfer prices on divisional performance reporting and discussion whether divisions should be profit or cost centres. Landual Lamps (Landual) manufactures and delivers floor and table lamps for homes and offices in Beeland. The company sells through its website and uses commercial logistics firms to deliver their products. The markets for its products are highly competitive. The company has traditionally relied on the high quality of its designs to drive demand for its products.

The company is divided into two divisions (components and assembly), plus a head office that provides design, administrative and marketing support. The manufacturing process involves:

1. the components division making the housing components and electrical components for the lamp. This is an intricate process as it depends on the specific design of the lamp and so serves as a significant source of competitive advantage for Landual;
2. the assembly division assembling the various components into a finished lamp ready for shipment. This is a simple process.

The finance director (FD) of Landual is currently overloaded with work due to changes in financial accounting policies that are being considered at board level. As a result, she has been unable to look at certain management accounting aspects of the business and has asked you to do a review of the transfer pricing policy between the components and assembly divisions.

The current transfer pricing policy at Landual is as follows:

(a) market prices for electrical components are used as these are generic components for which there is a competitive external market; and

(b) prices for housing components based on total actual production costs to the components division are used as there is no external market for these components since they are specially designed for Landual's products.

Currently, the components division produces only for the assembly division in order to meet overall demand without the use of external suppliers for housing and electrical components. If the components division were to sell its electrical components externally, then additional costs of $269 000 would arise for transport, marketing and bad debts.

The FD is considering two separate changes within Landual: one to the transfer pricing policy and a second one to the divisional structure.

First, the transfer pricing policy for housing components would change to use variable cost to the components division. The FD wants to know the impact of the change in transfer pricing policy on the existing results of the two divisions and the company. (No change is proposed to the transfer price of the electrical components.)

Second, as can be seen from the divisional performance report below, the two divisions are currently treated as profit centres. The FD is considering splitting the components division into two further separate divisions: an electrical components division and a housing components division. If the board agrees to this proposal, then the housing components division will be treated as a cost centre only, charging its total production cost to the assembly division. The electrical components and assembly divisions will remain as profit centres.

The FD needs to understand the impact of this proposed new divisional structure on divisional performance assessment and on the company as a whole. She has asked that, in order to keep the discussion on the new divisional structure simple, you use the existing transfer pricing policy to do illustrative calculations. She stated that she would reallocate head office costs to the two new components divisions in proportion to their cost of sales.

You are provided with the following financial and other information for Landual Lamps.

Actual data for Landual Lamps for the year ended 31 March

	Components division $'000	Assembly division $'000	Landual Lamps $'000
Sales			
Electrical	1557		
Housing	8204		
sub-total	9761	15794	15794
Cost of sales			
Electrical	804	1557	
Housing	6902	8204	
sub-total	7706	9761	7706
Fixed production costs			
Electrical	370		
Housing	1302		
sub-total	1672	1268	2940
Allocated head office costs	461	2046	2507
Profit	(78)	2719	2641

Note:

1 The components division has had problems meeting budgets recently, with an adverse variance of $575000 in the last year. This variance arises in relation to the cost of sales for housing component production.

Required:

(a) Evaluate the current system of transfer pricing at Landual, using illustrative calculations as appropriate. *(10 marks)*

(b) Advise the finance director (FD) on the impact of changing the transfer pricing policy for housing components as suggested by the FD and comment on your results, using illustrative calculations as appropriate. *(6 marks)*

(c) Evaluate the impact of the change in proposed divisional structure on the profit in the divisions and the company as directed by the FD. *(9 marks)*

ACCA P5 Advanced Performance Management

20.22 Advanced: Evaluation of divisional performance using EVA™ and evaluation of transfer prices. JHK Coffee Machines Co. (JHK) manufactures coffee makers for use in bars and cafes. It has been successful over the last five years and has built and maintained a loyal customer base by making a high-quality machine backed by a three-year warranty. The warranty states that JHK will recover and repair any machine that breaks down in the warranty period at no cost. Additionally, JHK always maintains sufficient spare parts to be able to quote for a repair of any of its machines made within the previous ten years.

JHK is structured into two divisions: manufacturing/sales (M/S) and service. The board is now considering ways to improve coordination of the activities of the divisions for the benefit of the company as a whole.

The company's mission is to maximize shareholder wealth. Currently, the board use total shareholder return (TSR) as an overall corporate measure of performance and return on investment (ROI) as its main relative measure of performance between the two divisions. The board's main concern is that the divisional managers' performance is not being properly assessed by the divisional performance measure used. It now wants to consider other measures of divisional performance. Residual income (RI) and economic value added (EVA™) have been suggested.

A colleague has collected the following data which will allow calculation of ROI, RI and EVA™.

	Manufacturing/ sales $m	Service $m
Revenue	880	17.0
Operating costs	494	11.0

Operating profit	386	6.0
Apportioned head office costs	85	1.0
Profit before tax	301	5.0
Capital employed	1294	38.0
The notional cost of capital used is	9% pa	
The current cost of debt is	5.5%	
The tax rate is	30%	

Operating costs include:

	Manufacturing/ sales $m	Service $m
Depreciation	88	2.7
Other non-cash expenses	4	0.3

All operating costs are tax deductible.

In addition to the divisional performance measures, the board wants to consider the position of the service division.

The standard costs within the service division are as follows:

	$
Labour (per hour)	18
Variable divisional overhead (per hour)	12
Fixed divisional overhead (per hour)	25

Overheads are allocated by work hours

Currently, the service division does two types of work. There are repairs that are covered by JHK's warranty and there are repairs done outside warranty at the customer's request. The service division is paid by the customer for the out-of-warranty repairs while the repairs under warranty generate an annual fee of $10m, which is a recharge from the M/S division. The company sells 440000 units per year and in the past, 9 per cent of these have needed a repair within the three-year warranty. Parts are charged by the M/S division to the service division at cost and average $75 per repair. A repair takes two hours, on average, to complete.

The board is considering amending this existing $10m internal recharge agreement between M/S and service. There has been some discussion of tailoring one of the two transfer pricing approaches (market price or cost plus) to meet the company's objectives.

Although the service division has the capacity to cover all of the existing work available, it could outsource the warranty service work, as it is usually straightforward. It would retain the out-of-warranty service work as this is a higher margin business. It would then begin looking for other opportunities to earn revenue using its engineering experience. A local engineering firm has quoted a flat price of $200 per warranty service repair provided that it obtains a contract for all of the warranty repairs from JHK.

Finally, the board is also considering a change to the information systems at JHK, The existing systems are based in the individual functions (production, sales, service, finance and human resources). The board is considering the implementation of a new system based on an integrated, single database that would be accessible at any of the company's five sites. The company network would be upgraded to allow real-time input and update of the database. The database would support a detailed management information system and a high-level executive information system.

Required:

Write a report to the finance director to:

(a) Evaluate the divisional performance at JHK and critically discuss the proposed measures of divisional performance. *(12 marks)*

(b) Outline the criteria for designing a transfer pricing system and evaluate the two methods discussed for calculating the transfer price between the service and M/S divisions. (Perform appropriate calculations.) *(12 marks)*

(c) Evaluate the potential impact of the introduction of the new executive information system at JHK on performance management. *(5 marks)*

ACCA F5 Performance Management

20.23 Advanced: Calculation of optimal selling price using calculus and impact of optimal transfer prices on profits. The GHYD company comprises two divisions: GH and YD.

GH manufactures components using a specialized machine. It sells the same components both externally and to YD. The variable costs of producing the component are as follows:

	$/unit
Direct materials	25.00
Direct labour	35.00
Variable overhead	10.00
	70.00

GH currently sells its components to the external market for $125 per unit.

GH also sells 4000 components per month to YD. These are transferred at the same price as the external selling price.

YD uses two of these components in each unit of its CX product. The current selling price of the CX product is $375 per unit and at this selling price the demand for the CX is 2000 units per month. The variable costs of producing a unit of CX are as follows:

	$/unit
Direct materials	35.00
Components transferred from GH @ $125 each	250.00
Direct labour	15.00
Variable overhead	10.00

At this level of activity, the total monthly contribution earned by YD from the sale of the CX product is £130 000.

An analysis of the demand for the CX product indicates that for every $25 increase in its selling price the monthly demand would reduce by 500 units, and that for every $25 decrease in its selling price, demand would increase by 500 units.

Note: If $P = a - bx$ then $MR = a - 2bx$

Required:

(a) (i) Calculate the selling price per unit of CX that would maximize the profits generated by that product for the YD division. *(4 marks)*
(ii) Calculate, based on the selling price you calculated in (a)(i) above, the monthly contribution that CX would generate for:
- GHYD as a whole
- GH division
- YD division

Note: Your answer should show three separate amounts. *(6 marks)*

(b) GHYD has now reviewed its transfer pricing policy and decided that all transfer prices should be set so as to lead to optimal decision-making for the company as a whole. Assuming that the transfer price for the component is changed to reflect this new policy:

(i) Calculate the selling price per unit of CX that would maximize the profits earned by CX for the company as a whole. Note: you should assume that there is sufficient capacity within the company. *(4 marks)*
(ii) Calculate, based on the selling price you calculated in (b) (i) above, the monthly contribution that CX would generate for:
- GHYD as a whole
- GH division
- YD division

Note: Your answer should show three separate amounts. *(3 marks)*

(c) Discuss, using your answers to (a) and (b) above, the impact that alternative transfer prices have on the divisional profits of GH and YD and on the company as a whole. *(8 marks)*

CIMA P2 Performance Management

IM20.1 Advanced. Exel Division is part of the Supeer Group. It produces a basic fabric that is then converted in other divisions within the group.

The fabric is also produced in other divisions within the Supeer Group and a limited quantity can be purchased from outside the group. The fabric is currently charged out by Exel Division at total actual cost plus 20 per cent profit mark-up.

(a) Explain why the current transfer pricing method used by Exel Division is unlikely to lead to:

(i) maximization of group profit
(ii) and effective divisional performance measurement. *(6 marks)*

(b) If the supply of basic fabric is insufficient to meet the needs of the divisions that convert it for sale outside the group, explain a procedure that should lead to a transfer pricing and deployment policy for the basic fabric for group profit maximization. *(6 marks)*
(c) Show how the procedure explained in (b) may be in conflict with other objectives of transfer pricing and suggest how this conflict may be overcome. *(5 marks)*

ACCA Level 2 – Cost and Management Accounting II

IM20.2 Advanced: Discussion of transfer price where there is an external market for the intermediate product. Fabri Division is part of the Multo Group. Fabri Division produces a single product for which it has an external market that utilizes 70 per cent of its production capacity. Gini Division, which is also part of the Multo Group requires units of the product available from Fabri Division, which it will then convert and sell to an external customer. Gini Division's requirements are equal to 50 per cent of Fabri Division's production capacity. Gini Division has a potential source of supply from outside the Multo Group. It is not yet known if this source is willing to supply on the basis of (i) only supplying *all* of Gini Division's requirements or (ii) supplying any part of Gini Division's requirements as requested.

(a) Discuss the transfer pricing method by which Fabri Division should offer to transfer its product to Gini Division in order that group profit maximization is likely to follow. You may illustrate your answer with figures of your choice. *(14 marks)*
(b) Explain ways in which (i) the degree of divisional autonomy allowed and (ii) the divisional performance measure in use by Multo Group may affect the transfer pricing policy of Fabri Division. *(6 marks)*

ACCA Level 2 Cost and Management Accounting II

IM20.3 Advanced.

(a) Spiro Division is part of a vertically integrated group of divisions allocated in one country. All divisions sell externally and also transfer goods to other divisions within the group. Spiro Division performance is measured using profit before tax as a performance measure:

(i) Prepare an outline statement showing the costs and revenue elements that should be included in the calculation of divisional profit before tax. *(4 marks)*
(ii) The degree of autonomy that is allowed to divisions may affect the absolute value of profit reported. Discuss the statement in relation to Spiro Division. *(6 marks)*

(b) Discuss the pricing basis on which divisions should offer to transfer goods in order that corporate profit maximizing decisions should take place. *(5 marks)*

ACCA Paper 9 Information for Control and Decision Making

IM20.4 Advanced.

(a) The transfer pricing method used for the transfer of an intermediate product between two divisions in a group has been agreed at standard cost plus 30 per cent profit mark-up. The transfer price may be altered after taking into consideration the planning and operational variance analysis at the transferor division. Discuss the acceptability of this transfer pricing method to the transferor and transferee divisions. *(5 marks)*

(b) Division A has an external market for product X that fully utilizes its production capacity. Explain the circumstances in which Division A should be willing to transfer product X to Division B of the same group at a price that is less than the existing market price. *(5 marks)*

(c) An intermediate product, which is converted in divisions L, M and N of a group, is available in limited quantities from other divisions within the group and from an external source. The total available quantity of the intermediate product is insufficient to satisfy demand. Explain the procedure that should lead to a transfer pricing and deployment policy resulting in group profit maximization. *(5 marks)*

ACCA Paper 9 Information for Control and Decision Making

IM20.5 Advanced: Resolving a transfer price conflict. Alton division (A) and Birmingham division (B) are two manufacturing divisions of Conglom plc. Both of these divisions make a single standardized product; A makes product I and B makes product J. Every unit of J requires one unit of I.

The required input of I is normally purchased from division A but sometimes it is purchased from an outside source.

The following table gives details of selling price and cost for each product:

	Product I (£)	Product J (£)
Established selling price	30	50
Variable costs		
Direct material	8	5
Transfers from A	—	30
Direct labour	5	3
Variable overhead	2	2
	15	40
Divisional fixed cost (per annum)	£500 000	£225 000
Annual outside demand with current selling prices (units)	100 000	25 000
Capacity of plant (units)	130 000	30 000
Investment in division	£6 625 000	£1 250 000

Division B is currently achieving a rate of return well below the target set by the central office. Its manager blames this situation on the high transfer price of product I. Division A charges Division B for the transfers of I at the outside supply price of £30. The manager of division A claims that this is appropriate since this is the price 'determined by market forces'. The manager of B has consistently argued that intra-group transfers should be charged at a lower price based on the costs of the producing division plus a 'reasonable' mark-up.

The board of Conglom plc is concerned about B's low rate of return and the divisional manager has been asked to submit proposals for improving the situation. The board has now received a report from B's manager in which he asks the board to intervene to reduce the transfer price charged for product I. The manager of B also informs the board that he is considering the possibility of opening a branch office in rented premises in a nearby town, which should enlarge the market for product J by 5000 units per year at the existing price. He estimates that the branch office establishment costs would be £50 000 per annum.

You have been asked to write a report advising the board on the response that it should make to the plans and proposals put forward by the manager of division B. Incorporate in your report a calculation of the rates of return currently being earned on the capital employed by each division and the changes to these that should follow from an implementation of any proposals that you would recommend. *(22 marks)*

ACCA Level 2 Management Accounting

IM20.6 Advanced: Apportionment of company profit to various departments. AB Limited which buys and sells machinery has three departments:

New machines (manager, Newman)
Second-hand machines (manager, Handley)
Repair workshops (manager, Walker)

In selling new machines. Newman is often asked to accept an old machine in part-exchange. In such cases, the old machine is disposed of by Handley.

The workshops do work both for outside customers and also for the other two departments. Walker charges his outside customers for materials at cost and for labour time at £8 per hour. This £8 is made up as follows:

	Per hour (£)	
Fixed costs	2.00	(10000 budgeted hours per annum)
Variable costs	4.50	
Profit	1.50	
	£8.00	

AB Limited wishes to go over to a profit centre basis of calculations so as to be able to reward its three managers according to their results. It wishes to assess the situation in the context of the following transaction:

Newman sold to PQ Limited a new machine at list price of £16 000, the cost of which to AB Limited was £12 000.

To make the sale, however, Newman had to allow PQ Limited £5000 for its old machine in part-exchange.

PQ Limited's old machine was in need of repair before it could be resold and Newman and Handley were agreed in their estimate of those repairs as £50 in materials and 100 hours of workshop's labour time. That estimate was proved to be correct when the workshops undertook the repair.

At the time of taking PQ Limited's machine in part-exchange Handley would have been able to buy a similar machine from other dealers for £3700 without the need for any repair. When the machine had been repaired, he sold it to ST Limited for £4200.

You are required to:

(a) Show how you would calculate the profit contribution for each of the three departments from the above transaction.

(b) Recalculate the profit contribution for each department if there were the following alternative changes of circumstances:

(i) When the workshops came to repair the old machine they found that they required an extra 50 hours of labour time because of a fault not previously noticed.

(ii) Before deciding on the figure he would allow PQ Limited for their old machine, Newman asks Walker to estimate the cost of repairs. This estimate is £50 in materials and 100 hours of workshops labour time. When, however, workshops came to repair the old machine, it took them 50 per cent longer than estimated.

(c) Recommend briefly how to deal with the following situations in the context of profit centre calculation:

(i) The manufacturer of the new machines allows AB Limited £200 per machine for which AB Limited undertakes to do all warranty repairs. Over the year the total cost of repairs under warranty exceeds the amount allowed by the supplier.

(ii) Although 4000 hours of workshop time were budgeted to be reserved for the other two departments, their load increases over the year by 20 per cent (at standard efficiency). The load from outside customers, however, stays as budgeted.

(25 marks)

CIMA P3 Management Accounting

IM20.7 Advanced: Computation of three different transfer prices and the extent to which each price encourages goal congruence. English Allied Traders plc has a wide range of manufacturing activities, principally within the UK. The company operates on the divisionalized basis with each division being responsible for its own manufacturing, sales and marketing, and working capital management. Divisional chief executives are expected to achieve a target 20 per cent return on sales.

A disagreement has arisen between two divisions which operate on adjacent sites. The Office Products Division (OPD) has the opportunity to manufacture a printer using a new linear motor which has recently been developed by the Electric Motor Division (EMD). Currently, there is no other source of supply for an equivalent motor in the required quantity of 30 000 units a year, although a foreign manufacturer has offered to supply up to 10 000 units in the coming year at a price of £9 each. EMD's current selling price for the motor is £12. Although EMD's production line for this motor is currently operating at only 50 per cent of its capacity, sales are encouraging and EMD confidently expects to sell 100 000 units in for the next year, and its maximum output of 120 000 units in the following year.

EMD has offered to supply OPD's requirements for the next year at a transfer price equal to the normal selling price, less the variable selling and distribution costs that it would not incur on this internal order. OPD responded by offering an alternative transfer price of the standard variable manufacturing cost plus a 20 per cent profit margin. The two divisions have been unable to agree, so the corporate operations director has suggested a third transfer price equal to the standard full manufacturing cost plus 15 per cent. However, neither divisional chief executive regards such a price as fair.

EMD's budget for the next year for the production and sale of motors, based on its standard costs for the forecast 100 000 units sales, but excluding the possible sales to OPD, is as follows:

	(£000)
Sales revenue (100 000 units at £12.00 each)	1200
Direct manufacturing costs	
Bought-in materials	360
Labour	230
Packaging	40
Indirect manufacturing costs	
Variable overheads	10
Line production managers	30
Depreciation	
Capital equipment	150
Capitalized development costs	60
Total manufacturing costs	880

Sales and distribution costs	
Salaries of sales force	50
Carriage	20
General overhead	50
Total costs	1000
Profit	200

Notes

1 The costs of the sales force and indirect production staff are not expected to increase up to the current production capacity.

2 General overhead includes allocations of divisional administrative expenses and corporate charges of £20 000 specifically related to this product.

3 Depreciation for all assets is charged on a straight line basis using a five-year life and no residual value.

4 Carriage is provided by an outside contractor.

Required:

(a) Calculate each of the three proposed transfer prices and comment on how each might affect the willingness of EMD's chief executive to engage in inter divisional trade.

(10 marks)

(b) Outline an alternative method of setting transfer prices that you consider to be appropriate for this situation, and explain why it is an improvement on the other proposals.

(5 marks)

ICAEW P2 Management Accounting and Financial Management 2

IM20.8 Advanced: Optimal output and transfer price where the market for the intermediate product is imperfect. Engcorp and Flotilla are UK divisions of Griffin plc, a multinational company. Both divisions have a wide range of activities. You are an accountant employed by Griffin plc and the finance director has asked you to investigate a transfer pricing problem.

Engcorp makes an engine, the Z80, which it has been selling to external customers at £1350 per unit. Flotilla wanted to buy Z80 engines to use in its own production of dories; each dory requires one engine. Engcorp would only sell if Flotilla paid £1350 per unit. The managing director of Engcorp commented:

'We have developed a good market for this engine and £1350 is the current market price. Just because Flotilla is not efficient enough to make a profit is no reason for us to give a subsidy.'

Flotilla has now found that engines suitable for its purpose can be bought for £1300 per unit from another manufacturer. Flotilla is preparing to buy engines from this source.

From information supplied by the divisions, you have derived the following production and revenue schedules that are applicable over the capacity range of the two divisions:

	Engcorp's data for Z80 engines		Flotilla's data for dories	
Annual number of units	Total manufacturing cost (£000)	Total revenue from outside sales (£000)	Total cost of producing dories excluding engine costs (£000)	Total revenue from sales of dories (£000)
100	115	204	570	703
200	185	362	1120	1375
300	261	486	1670	2036
400	344	598	2220	2676
500	435	703	2770	3305
600	535	803	3320	3923
700	645	898	3870	4530
800	766	988	4420	5126

Required:

(a) Ignoring the possibility that Flotilla could buy engines from another manufacturer, calculate to the nearest 100 units:

(i) the quantity of Z80 production that would maximize profits for Griffin plc;

(ii) the consequent quantity of Z80 units that would be sold to external customers and the quantity that would be transferred to Flotilla. *(8 marks)*

(b) Explain the issues raised by the problems of transfer pricing between Engcorp and Flotilla, and discuss the advantages and disadvantages of the courses of action that could be taken. *(10 marks)*

(c) Discuss the major considerations in setting transfer prices for a profit-maximizing international group. *(7 marks)*

ICAEW P2 Management Accounting

IM20.9 Advanced: Calculation of optimum selling price using calculus as the effect of using the imperfect market price as the transfer price. HKI plc has an Engineering Division and a Motorcycle Division. The Engineering Division produces engines that it sells to 'outside' customers and transfers to the Motorcycle Division. The Motorcycle Division produces a powerful motorbike called the 'Beast', which incorporates an HKI engine in its design.

The divisional managers have full control over the commercial policy of their respective divisions and are each paid 1 per cent of the profit that is earned by their divisions as an incentive bonus. Details of the Engineering Division's production operation for the next year are expected to be as follows:

Annual fixed costs	£3 000 000
Variable cost per engine	£350

Details of the Motorcycle Division's production operation for the next year are expected to be as follows:

Annual fixed costs	£50 000
Variable cost per Beast	£700*

*Note: this figure excludes transfer costs.

Both divisions have significant surplus capacity.

Market research has indicated that demand from 'outside' customers for HKI plcs products is as follows:

- 9000 engines are sold at a unit selling price of £700; sales change by an average of ten engines for each £1 change in the selling price per engine;
- 1000 Beasts are sold at a unit selling price of £2200; sales change by an average of 125 Beasts for each £100 change in the selling price per Beast.

It is established practice for the Engineering Division to transfer engines to the Motorcycle Division at 'market selling price'.

You are required:

(a) to calculate the unit selling price of the Beast (accurate to the nearest penny) that should be set in order to maximize HKI plc's profit; *(7 marks)*

(b) to calculate the selling price of the Beast (accurate to the nearest penny) that is likely to emerge if the Engineering Division Manager sets a market selling price for the engine that is calculated to maximize profit from engine sales to outside customers. You may assume that both divisional managers are aware of the information given above. Explain your reasoning and show your workings; *(8 marks)*

(c) to explain why you agree or disagree with the following statement made by the financial director of HKI plc:

'Pricing policy is a difficult area that offers considerable scope for dysfunctional behaviour. Decisions about selling prices should be removed from the control of divisional managers and made the responsibility of a head office department.' *(12 marks)*

CIMA Stage 4 Management Accounting – Decision Making

PART FIVE

STRATEGIC PERFORMANCE AND COST MANAGEMENT AND CHALLENGES FOR THE FUTURE

P art Five focuses on strategic aspects of performance management and control. Increasing emphasis is now being placed on the need for management accounting to support an organization's competitive strategies. To encourage behaviour that is consistent with an organization's strategy, attention is focusing on an integrated framework of performance management that can be used to clarify, communicate and manage strategy. Chapter 21 describes the recent developments that seek to incorporate performance measurement and management within the strategic management process.

In Part Four, the major features of traditional management accounting control systems and the mechanisms that can be used to control costs were described. Traditional cost control systems tend to be based on the preservation of the status quo and the ways of performing existing activities are not reviewed. The emphasis is on cost containment rather than cost reduction. In contrast, strategic cost management focuses on cost reduction rather than cost containment. Chapter 22 examines the various approaches that fall within the area of strategic cost management and value creation. Ideally, cost management should also incorporate value creation where the aims should be not only to take actions that will reduce costs but also to enhance customer satisfaction and value. Customer value may be increased by either reducing the cost without sacrificing product/service functionality or by increasing functionality without increasing cost. Reducing cost is important because it enables a company to remain competitive by reducing or maintaining selling prices and thus increasing customer satisfaction and value. Increasing customer satisfaction is generally associated with an increase in sales revenues and profits which should ultimately be reflected in creating additional shareholder value.

The content covered in Chapters 21 and 22 describes practices that have only become widely used in the past two decades. In Chapter 23 we shall concentrate on the emerging issues that are likely to have an impact on management accounting and consider some potential future developments in management accounting. This chapter is intended to be the concluding chapter to this book, even though three other chapters follow in Part Six. These three chapters in Part Six focus on the application of quantitative methods to management accounting but are intended to be addendum chapters relating to topics included earlier rather than concluding chapters. For an explanation justifying this approach you should refer to the introduction to Part Six.

21
STRATEGIC PERFORMANCE MANAGEMENT

LEARNING OBJECTIVES After studying this chapter, you should be able to:

- describe three competitive strategies that a firm can adopt to achieve sustainable competitive advantage and explain how they influence performance management systems;

- describe the balanced scorecard;

- explain each of the four perspectives of the balanced scorecard;

- provide illustrations of performance measures for each of the four perspectives;

- explain how the balanced scorecard links strategy formulation to financial outcomes;

- distinguish between lead and lag measures;

- outline the benefits and criticisms of the balanced scorecard.

Prior to the late 1980s management accounting performance management systems tended to focus mainly on financial measures of performance. The inclusion of only those items that could be expressed in monetary terms motivated managers to focus excessively on cost reduction and ignore other important variables that were necessary to compete in the global competitive environment that emerged during the 1990s. Product quality, delivery, reliability, after-sales service and customer satisfaction became key competitive variables but none of these was given sufficient importance measured by the traditional management accounting performance management system.

During the late 1980s much greater emphasis was given to incorporating into the management reporting system those non-financial performance measures that provided feedback on the key variables that are required to compete successfully in a global economic environment. However, a proliferation of performance measures emerged. This resulted in confusion when some of the measures conflicted with one another and it was possible to enhance one measure at the expense of another. It was also not clear to managers how the non-financial measures they were evaluated on contributed to the whole picture of achieving success in financial terms. According to Kaplan and Norton (2001a) previous performance management systems that incorporated non-financial measurements used ad hoc collections of such measures, more like checklists of measures for managers to keep track of and improve rather than a comprehensive system of linked measurements.

During the 1990s strategic performance management systems emerged that not only integrated financial and non-financial measures of performance but also facilitated strategy implementation and contributed to enhanced performance. The aim of this chapter is to describe the major features of these systems.

THE PERFORMANCE MANAGEMENT FRAMEWORK

Otley (1999) identifies five main sets of issues that need to be addressed in developing a framework for managing organizational performance. He suggests that these issues can be represented by the following set of questions:

1 What are the key objectives that are central to the organization's overall future success and how does it go about evaluating its achievement for each of these objectives?

2 What strategies and plans has the organization adopted and what are the processes and activities that it has decided will be required for it to successfully implement these? How does it assess and measure the performance of these activities?

3 What level of performance does the organization need to achieve in each of the areas defined in the above two questions and how does it go about setting appropriate performance targets for them?

4 What rewards will managers (and other employees) gain by achieving these performance targets (or, conversely, what penalties will they suffer by failing to achieve them)? Because the human resources function is often responsible for the rewards systems in many organizations, the linking of rewards to performance targets tends not to be sufficiently emphasized in performance management systems.

5 What are the information flows (feedback and feed-forward loops) that are necessary to enable the organization to learn from its experience and to adapt its current behaviour in the light of that experience? These feedback and feed-forward controls (see Chapter 16) provide information about the extent to which a company is achieving its key strategic aims. This process can range from simple corrective action through to the revision of a corporate strategy if it becomes apparent that the current strategy is proving ineffective.

STRATEGY AND STRATEGIC POSITIONING

A major aim of strategic performance management systems is to facilitate strategy implementation. Strategies can be defined as the means by which an organization plans to achieve its objectives. The chosen strategies have an important influence in determining what performance measures might be appropriate. The linking of strategies and performance measures thus promotes organizational behaviour that supports the implementation of the chosen strategies. Various typologies of strategy (known as strategic positioning) that firms may choose have been identified in the strategic management literature. Porter (1985) suggests that a firm has a choice of three generic strategies in order to achieve competitive advantage. They are:

● A cost leadership strategy, whereby an enterprise aims to be the lowest cost producer within the industry thus enabling it to compete on the basis of lower selling prices rather than providing unique products or services. The source of this competitive advantage may arise from factors such as economies of scale, access to favourable raw materials prices and superior technology (Langfield-Smith, 1997).

● A differentiation strategy, whereby the enterprise seeks to offer products or services that are considered by its customers to be superior and unique relative to its competitors. Examples include the quality or dependability of the product, after-sales service, the wide availability of the product and product flexibility (Langfield-Smith, 1997).

● A focusing strategy, which involves seeking competitive advantage by focusing on a narrow segment of the market that has special needs that are poorly served by other competitors in the industry. A focusing strategy recognizes that differences can exist within segments (e.g. customers and geographical regions) of the same market. Competitive advantage is based on adopting either a cost leadership or product differentiation strategy within the chosen segment.

In practice, firms may choose a combination of the three strategies within the different markets in which they operate. Strategic positioning relates to the choice of the optimal mix of the three general strategies.

Miles and Snow (1978) distinguish between defender and prospector strategies. Defender organizations perceive a great deal of stability in their external environment and concentrate on a narrow and limited mix of products and customers. They compete on product price, quality and customer service rather than innovation and product and market development and do this by focusing on making operations efficient through cost, quality and service leadership. They engage in little product/market development. Prospectors perceive high uncertainty in their environment and are continually searching for new market opportunities. They are the creators of change. They compete through new product innovations and market development. The marketing and research and development functions dominate finance and production, so efficiency and profit performance are not as important as maintaining industry leadership in product innovation.

A firm's choice of performance measures and the emphasis given to them will be influenced by the strategic position it adopts. For example, a firm pursuing a cost leadership or defender strategy will give greater emphasis to cost-based measures and quality and output/input efficiency measures. In contrast, a firm pursuing a differentiation or prospector strategy will give greater emphasis to marketing measures such as percentage market share, percentage of sales from new products, percentage of sales from new markets etc. The performance management system is most effective when it fits with business strategy. Without such a fit, what is being measured (and communicated as important) and what is actually important to the firm are not synchronized with one another (Melnyk *et al.*, 2014).

PERFORMANCE MEASUREMENT AND PERFORMANCE MANAGEMENT SYSTEMS

The terms 'performance measurement system' and 'performance management system' tend to be used interchangeably in the literature but it is possible to distinguish between them. The performance measurement system encompasses the processes for setting goals and collecting, analysing and interpreting performance data. The objective of the process is to convert data into information and to assess the effectiveness and efficiency of action (Neely *et al.*, 1995).

Melnyk *et al.* (2014) state that although performance measurement is important, it is not sufficient to manage an enterprise. There is a complementary need for a performance management system. The performance management system encompasses the processes of assessing the differences between actual and desired outcomes, identifying and flagging those differences that are critical (thereby warranting management intervention), understanding if and why the deficiencies have taken place, and, when necessary, introducing (and monitoring) corrective actions aimed at closing the significant performance gaps.

ALTERNATIVE PERFORMANCE MANAGEMENT FRAMEWORKS

Several different strategic performance management frameworks have been presented in the literature that seek to integrate financial and non-financial measures of performance and also facilitate strategy implementation and enhanced performance. The major strategic performance frameworks that have emerged are:

- a results/determinants framework (Fitzgerald *et al.*, 1991) which the authors apply to the service industry;
- the performance pyramid (Lynch and Cross, 1991a,b);
- the balanced scorecard (Kaplan and Norton, 1992);
- the performance prism framework (Neely *et al.*, 2002).

REAL WORLD VIEWS 21.1

Seven myths about managing performance

The Globe and Mail (Canada) quotes an article written by Professor Pietro Micheli in *Industry Week* in which he listed seven myths about performance management that promote the wrong behaviours. The following is a summary of these myths:

Myth 1: Numbers are objective
Numbers are open to interpretation and manipulation, so there is a danger that the numbers may not be accepted as valid. It is important to communicate what the numbers mean, and why they should be trusted.

Myth 2: Data are accurate
Compiling data is expensive so performance measures must meet cost/benefits criteria.

Myth 3: More measures add more value
Too many performance measures do not provide value since they can confuse and there is no time to use them. Find the measures that are important that tell you something you can act upon and then use just them.

Myth 4: Everyone should be aligned
The typical way in which managers try to create alignment can end up generating bureaucracy and negatively impacting on staff morale. Managers and employees need some discretion to adjust targets to fit their situation. For example, in a provincial health department it would be unwise to expect ambulances in urban and rural areas to hit the same targets.

Myth 5: Incentives do the trick
Managers believe that by setting targets and rewards, they will motivate employees to achieve organizational goals. There is a danger that employees become so fixated on the measures they forget the broader picture.

Myth 6: Performance measures foster change
Organizations often bring in performance indicators to point employees in new directions during periods of change. A dynamic system is required where performance measures are revised regularly.

Myth 7: Control leads to improvements
If you want to make improvements, the system must be dynamic, cost-effective, and encourage learning rather than control. If people feel the effort is really about control, they will be suspicious and disengage and will not result in improvements.

Questions

1 Provide examples of how performance measures might promote the wrong behaviours.

2 Why must performance measures be regularly reviewed and updated?

References
Micheli, P. (2012) 'The seven myths of performance management', 18 December, *Industry Week*. Available at www.industryweek.com/compensation-strategies/seven-myths-performance-management

Schachter, H. (2013) 'Seven myths about managing performance', *The Globe and Mail*, 4 February. Available at www.theglobeandmail.com/report-on-business/careers/management/seven-myths-about-managing-performance/article8122362/

The balanced scorecard has become the dominant strategic performance management framework and has tended to overshadow the other frameworks that have emerged. Indeed, its diffusion was so rapid that, as early as 1997, it was labelled as one of the most influential management instruments of the twentieth century (Sibbet, 1997, p. 12). Therefore, because of its widespread use and popularity, we shall concentrate on the balanced scorecard in the remainder of this chapter. The other performance management frameworks have many similarities to the balanced scorecard and describing these frameworks would tend to involve undue repetition. An understanding of these alternative frameworks is unlikely to be essential for most readers but some of the specialist accounting bodies do set examination questions requiring an understanding of these alternative performance frameworks. To meet the requirements of all readers, these alternative performance management frameworks are presented in Learning Note 21.1 in the digital support resources accompanying this book (see Preface for details). You should check your course curriculum to ascertain if you need to read Learning Note 21.1.

THE BALANCED SCORECARD

The need to integrate financial and non-financial measures of performance and identify key performance measures that link measurements to strategy led to the emergence of the balanced scorecard. The balanced scorecard was devised by Kaplan and Norton (1992) and refined in later publications (Kaplan and Norton, 1993, 1996a, 1996b, 2001a, 2001b). The following discussion is a summary of Kaplan and Norton's writings on this topic. Figure 21.1 illustrates how the balanced scorecard provides a framework for implementing an organization's strategy into specific objectives and linked performance measures (specified in terms of targets and actual measures) that are required to achieve each of the specific objectives.

Figure 21.1 emphasizes that the balanced scorecard philosophy creates a strategic focus by translating an organization's strategy into operational objectives and performance measures for the following four perspectives:

1 Financial perspective (How do we look to shareholders?).

2 Customer perspective (How do customers see us?).

3 Internal business perspective (What must we excel at to satisfy our shareholders and customers?).

4 Learning and growth perspective (How can we continue to improve and create value?).

The balanced scorecard is a strategic management technique for communicating and evaluating the achievement of the mission and strategy of the organization. Kaplan and Norton define strategy as:

> Choosing the market and customer segments the business unit intends to serve, identifying the critical internal and business processes that the unit must excel at to deliver the value propositions to customers in the targeted market segments, and selecting the individual and organizational capabilities required for the internal and financial objectives.

You will see by referring to Figure 21.1 that strategy is implemented by specifying the major *objectives* for each of the four perspectives and translating them into specific *performance measures,*

FIGURE 21.1
The balanced scorecard

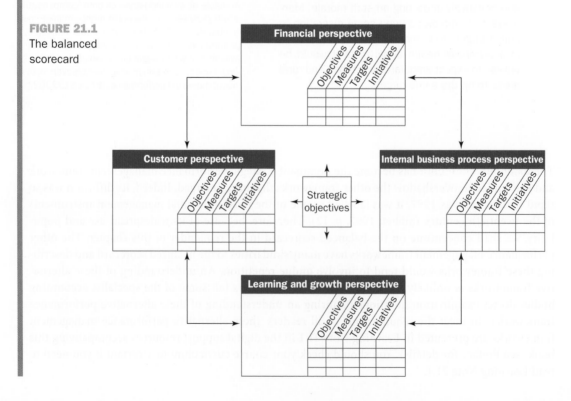

REAL WORLD VIEWS 21.2

How Southwest Airlines developed its balanced scorecard analysis

Southwest Airlines set 'operating efficiency' as its strategic theme. The four perspectives embodied in the balanced scorecard were linked together by a series of relatively simple questions and answers:

Financial: What will drive operating efficiency?
Answer: More customers on fewer planes.
Customer: How will we get more customers on fewer planes?
Answer: Attract targeted segments of customers who value price and on-time arrivals.
Internal: What must our internal focus be?
Answer: Fast aircraft turnaround time.
Learning: How will our people accomplish fast turnaround?
Answer: Educate and compensate the ground crew regarding how they contribute to the firm's success. Also, use the employee stockholder programme.

The chart below shows how Southwest used this framework to lay out its balanced scorecard model. The first column of the chart contains the 'strategy map', that illustrates the cause-and-effect relationships between strategic objectives. The Objectives column shows what each strategy must achieve and what is critical to its success. The Measurement column shows how success in achieving each strategy will be measured and tracked. The Target column spells out the level of performance or rate of improvement that is needed. The Initiative column contains key action programmes required to achieve objectives. Note that all of the measures, targets and initiatives are all aligned to one an objective.

The company extended the effort to the department level and the degree of development varied between departments. The goal was to identify key performance measures in each segment for the operating personnel. Some of the non-financial metrics that have emerged on a departmental level include: load factor (percentage of seats occupied); utilization factors on aircraft and personnel; on-time performance; available seat miles; denied-boarding rate; lost bag reports per 10 000 passengers; flight cancellation rate; employee head count; and customer complaints per 10 000 passengers filed with the Department of Transportation.

Questions

1 Looking at the internal key answer of 'fast turnaround time', can Southwest always control this?

2 Do you think performance measures like those in the Southwest scorecard are more useful to non-accountants and managers?

Southwest Airlines' balanced scorecard framework

Strategic theme: operating efficiency	Objectives	Measurement	Target	Initiative
Financial — Profitability, Fewer planes, More customers	Profitability	Market value	30% CAGR	
	More customers	Seat revenue	20% CAGR	
	Fewer planes	Plane lease cost	5% CAGR	
Customer — Flight is on time, Lowest prices	Flight is on time	FAA on-time arrival rating	#1	Quality management
	Lowest prices	Customer ranking (market survey)	#1	Customer loyalty programme
Internal — Fast ground turnaround	Fast ground turnaround	On ground time	30 minutes	Cycle time optimization
		On-time departure	90%	
Learning — Ground crew alignment	Ground crew alignment	% ground crew trained	Yr. 1 70%	ESOP Ground crew training
			Yr. 3 90%	
		% ground crew stockholders	Yr. 5 100%	

Balanced Scorecard Collaborative, Institute of Management & Administration Report on Financial Analysis Planning and Reporting, July 2002

targets and initiatives. There may be one or more objectives for each perspective and one or more performance measures linked to each objective. The balanced scorecard does not focus solely on achieving financial objectives. It also highlights non-financial objectives that an organization must achieve in order to meet its financial objectives in the future. Only the critical performance measures are incorporated in the scorecard. To minimize information overload and avoid a proliferation of measures, each perspective ought to comprise four to five separate measures. Thus, the scorecard can provide *top* management with a fast but comprehensive view in tracking the extent that the organizational unit (i.e. a division/strategic business unit) is implementing strategy. A balanced scorecard should be established for the entire organization and also at lower levels such as divisions and responsibility centres below the divisional level. It is important that scorecards at lower levels within an organization consist of items that the responsibility centre manager can influence, and not by the actions of others, and that relate directly to the performance measures of the entire organization.

We shall now examine each of the four perspectives presented in Figure 21.1. Typical generic objectives and performance measures applicable to each perspective are presented in Exhibits 21.1–21.4 but in practice each organization will customize the objectives and performance measures to fit their own specific strategies. You should also note that Exhibits 21.1–21.4 focus only on core generic objectives and appropriate performance measures but the Balanced Scorecard should also incorporate target values for the measures associated with each objective. In addition, the major initiatives that are required to achieve each objective and the associated performance measure should be described.

The financial perspective

The financial perspective specifies the financial performance objectives anticipated from pursuing the organization's strategy and also the economic consequences of the outcomes expected from achieving the objectives specified from the other three perspectives. Therefore the objectives and measures from the other perspectives should be selected to ensure that the financial outcomes will be achieved. Kaplan and Norton state that they have observed three core financial themes that drive the business strategy: revenue growth and mix, cost reduction and asset utilization.

Generic objectives and possible measures for these themes are shown in Exhibit 21.1. Typical *revenue growth* objectives for a business pursuing a growth strategy include increasing the number of new products, developing new customers and markets and changing to a more profitable product or service mix. Once the objectives have been determined, performance measures should be established that are linked to each objective. Possible measures are listed against each objective in Exhibit 21.1. They are

EXHIBIT 21.1 Financial perspective objectives and measures

Objectives	Measures
Revenue growth:	
Increase the number of new products	Percentage of revenues from new products
Develop new customers and markets	Percentage of revenues from new customers/markets
Change to a more profitable product (or service) mix	Sales growth percentage for targeted segments
Cost reduction:	
Reduce product/service cost per unit	Percentage reduction in cost per unit
Reduce selling/general administration costs	Percentage to total revenues of selling and administration costs
Asset utilization:	
Improve asset utilization	Return on investment
	Economic value added

percentage revenues from new products, percentage revenues from new customers/markets and growth of sales in the targeted segments.

The *cost reduction* objectives may include reduction in unit product costs and a reduction in selling and general and administration costs. Thus the percentage reduction in costs per unit of output for the selected cost objects and the percentage to total revenues of selling and administrative costs represent possible performance measures.

Exhibit 21.1 lists the improvement of *asset utilization* as the major objective of the asset utilization theme. Financial performance measures such as return on investment and economic value added that were described in Chapter 19 provide overall outcome measures of success for the overall financial objectives of revenue growth, cost reduction and asset utilization.

The customer perspective

The customer perspective should identify the customer and market segments in which the business unit will compete. The customer perspective underpins the revenue element for the financial perspective objectives. Therefore the achievement of customer objectives should ensure that target revenues will be generated. Exhibit 21.2 lists five typical core or generic objectives. They are: increasing market share, increasing customer retention, increasing customer acquisition, increasing customer satisfaction and increasing customer profitability. Typical core measures for these objectives (see Exhibit 21.2) are, respectively: percentage market share, percentage growth of business with existing customers, number of new customers or total sales to new customers, ratings from customer satisfaction surveys and profitability analysis by customer segments. The first four measures relate to the means required to achieve customer profitability but they do not measure the outcome. Customer profitability measures meet this requirement. In other words, a company does not want just satisfied customers, it also wants profitable customers.

In addition to the core objectives and measures, additional measures (Kaplan and Norton use the term **customer value propositions**) are needed that represent the attributes that drive the creation of customer value and thus drive the core outcomes relating to the customer perspective. Common product/service attributes encompass the functionality of the products/services, their price and quality and for the customer dimension the delivery time attribute. Focusing on these attributes or measures has the potential to increase customer value and thus have a favourable impact on the core objectives. Typical objectives relating to the above attributes are listed in Exhibit 21.2. They are, respectively: improve product functionality, decrease price relative to competitors, improve quality and improve delivery time. Possible measures for these objectives include, respectively: customer surveys satisfaction scores relating to product functionality, price relative to competitors, percentage of returns from customers and percentage of on-time deliveries.

EXHIBIT 21.2 Customer perspective objectives and measures

Objectives	Measures
Core:	
Increase market share	Percentage market share
Increase customer retention	Percentage growth in business from existing customers
Increase customer acquisition	Total sales to new customers
Increase customer satisfaction	Customer survey satisfaction ratings
Increase customer profitability	Customer profitability analysis
Customer value propositions:	
Improve product functionality	Customer survey product functionality rating scores
Decrease price relative to competitors	Price relative to competitors
Improve product/service quality	Percentage returns from customers
Improve delivery time	Percentage on-time deliveries

The internal business perspective

The internal business perspective requires that managers identify the critical internal processes for which the organization must excel in implementing its strategy. Critical processes should be identified that are required to achieve the organization's customer and financial objectives. Kaplan and Norton identify a generic process value chain that provides guidance for companies applying the internal process perspective. The process value chain consists of three processes: the innovation process, the operations process and the post-sales process.

In the *innovation process*, managers research the needs of customers and then create the products or services that will meet those needs. It represents the longer-term aspect of value creation in which companies first identify new markets, new customers and the emerging and latent needs of existing customers. Then continuing on this long wave of value creation companies design and develop new products and services that enable them to reach these new markets and customers. Typical objectives for the innovation process are listed in Exhibit 21.3. They are increasing the number of new products, developing new markets and customers and decreasing the time taken to develop new products. Supporting performance measures are, respectively: percentage of sales from new products (also new product introductions versus competitors), percentage of sales from new markets and development cycle time (e.g. time to the market).

The *operations process* represents the shorter-term aspect of value creation. It is concerned with producing and delivering existing products and services to customers. Objectives of the operation process listed in Exhibit 21.3 include, increasing process efficiency, increasing process quality, decreasing process cost and decreasing process time. Historically, the operations process has been the major focus of most of an organization's performance management system and many possible measures exist. Typical measures associated with each of the objectives for the operations process are listed in Exhibit 21.3.

Process efficiency measures tend to focus on output/input measures such as the production efficiency ratio (standard hours of output/actual hours of input) or capacity measures such as the capacity usage ratio (actual hours utilized/budgeted hours to be utilized). Quality measures include total quality costs as a percentage of sales derived from the cost of quality report (see Chapter 22), process parts per million defect rates, percentage of defective units and percentage of processes under statistical control.

EXHIBIT 21.3 Internal business perspective objectives and measures

Objectives	Measures
Innovation:	
Increase the number of new products	Percentage of sales from new products
	New product introductions versus competitors
Develop new markets and customers	Percentage of sales from new markets
Decrease the time taken to develop new products	Development cycle time (time to the market)
Operations:	
Increase process efficiency	Output/inputs ratios
Increase process quality	Total quality costs as a percentage of sales
	Percentage of defective output
Decrease process cost	Unit cost trends
Decrease process time	Manufacturing cycle efficiency
Post-sales service:	
Increase service quality	Percentage of customer requests that are handled with a single call
Increase service efficiency	Output/inputs ratios
Decrease service time	Cycle time in resolving customer problems
Decrease service cost	Unit cost trends

Process cost measures include unit cost trend measures relating to key processes and cycle time measures have evolved that support the objective of decreasing process time.

The total manufacturing cycle time consists of the sum of processing time, inspection time, wait time and move time. Only processing time adds value and the remaining activities are non-value-added activities. The aim is to reduce the time spent on non-value-added activities and thus minimize manufacturing cycle time. A measure of cycle time that has been adopted is manufacturing cycle efficiency (MCE):

$$MCE = \frac{\text{processing time}}{\text{processing time} + \text{inspection time} + \text{wait time} + \text{move time}}$$

The generic performance measures that have been illustrated above relate to manufacturing operations but similar measures can be adopted for service companies. For example, many customers are forced to queue to receive a service. Companies that can eliminate waiting time for a service will find it easier to attract customers. The time taken to process mortgage and loan applications by financial institutions can involve a considerable amount of non-value-added waiting time. Thus, reducing the time to process the applications enhances customer satisfaction and creates the potential for increasing sales revenues. Therefore service companies should also develop cycle time measures that support their specific customer processing activity objectives.

The *post-sales service process* represents the final item in the process value chain for the operations process perspective. It focuses on how responsive the organization is to customers after the product or service has been delivered. Post-sales services include warranty and repair activities, treatment of defects and returns and the process and administration of customer payments. Increasing quality, increasing efficiency and decreasing process time and cost are also objectives that apply to the post-sales service. Performance can be measured by some of the time, quality and cost measurements that have been suggested for the operations process. For example, service quality can be measured by first-pass yields defined as the percentage of customer requests that are handled with a single service call, rather than requiring multiple calls to resolve the problem. Increasing efficiency can be measured by appropriate output/input ratios and decreasing process time can be measured by cycle time where the process starts with the receipt of a customer request and ends with the ultimate resolution of the problem. Finally, the trend in unit costs can be used to measure the key post-sale service processes.

The learning and growth perspective

To ensure that an organization will continue to have loyal and satisfied customers in the future and continue to make excellent use of its resources, the organization and its employees must keep learning and developing. Hence there is a need for a perspective that focuses on the capabilities that an organization needs to create long-term growth and improvement. This perspective stresses the importance of organizations investing in their infrastructure (people, systems and organizational procedures) to provide the capabilities that enable the accomplishment of the other three perspectives' objectives. Kaplan and Norton have identified three major enabling factors for this perspective. They are: employee capabilities, information systems capabilities and the organizational climate for motivation, empowerment and alignment. Thus this perspective has three major core objectives: increase employee capabilities, increase information system capabilities and increase motivation, empowerment and alignment. The objectives and associated performance measures for this perspective are listed in Exhibit 21.4.

Core measures for the *employee capabilities* objective are concerned with employee satisfaction, employee retention and employee productivity. Many companies periodically measure employee satisfaction using surveys to derive employee satisfaction ratings. Employee retention can be measured by the annual percentage of key staff that resigns and many different methods can be used to measure employee productivity. A generic measure of employee productivity that can be applied throughout the organization and compared with different divisions is the sales revenue per employee.

EXHIBIT 21.4 Learning and growth perspective objectives and measures

Objectives	Measures
Increase employee capabilities	Employee satisfaction survey ratings
	Annual percentage of key staff leaving
	Sales revenue per employee
Increase information system capabilities	Percentage of processes with real time feedback capabilities
	Percentage of customer-facing employees having online access to customer and product information
Increase motivation, empowerment and alignment	Number of suggested improvements per employee
	Number of suggestions implemented per employee
	Percentage of employees with personal goals aligned to the balanced scorecard
	Percentage of employees who achieve personal goals

For employees to be effective in today's competitive environment, they need accurate and timely information on customers, internal processes and the financial consequences of their decisions. Measures of *strategic information system capabilities* suggested by Kaplan and Norton include percentage of processes with real time quality, cycle time and cost feedback capabilities available and the percentage of customer facing employees having online access to customer and product information.

The number of suggested improvements per employee and the number of suggestions implemented per employee are proposed measures relating to the objective having *motivated and empowered employees*. Suggested measures relating to the objective of increasing individual and organizational alignment are the percentage of employees with personal goals aligned to the balanced scorecard and the percentage of employees who achieve personal goals.

Lag and lead measures

The balanced scorecard is not simply a collection of critical performance measures. The performance measures are derived from a company's strategy and objectives. The balanced scorecard consists of two types of performance measure. The first consists of lag measures. These are the *outcome measures* that mostly fall within the financial perspective and are the results of past actions. Outcome (lag) measures are important because they indicate whether strategy is being implemented successfully with the desired financial consequences. Outcome measures, such as economic value added and return on investment, are normally generic and therefore tend to be common to most strategies and organizations. Lag measures generally do not incorporate the effect of decisions when they are made. Instead, they show the financial impact of the decisions as their impact materializes and this can be long after the decisions were made. The second type of performance measures are lead measures, which are the *performance drivers* of future financial performance. They cause the outcome and usually distinguish one strategy from another. They are normally unique to a particular strategy and thus support the objective of linking measures to strategy. Lead measures tend to be the non-financial measures relating to the customer, internal business process and learning and growth perspectives.

Cause-and-effect relationships

One critical assumption of the balanced scorecard is that each performance measure is part of a cause-and-effect relationship involving a linkage from strategy formulation to financial outcomes.

Cause-and-effect relationships are the means by which lead and lag measures are integrated and thus serve as the mechanism for communicating strategy. The chain of cause and effect should permeate all four perspectives of the balanced scorecard. Measures of organizational learning and growth are assumed to be the drivers of the internal business processes. The measures of these processes are, in turn, assumed to be the drivers of measures of customer perspective, while these measures are the driver of the financial perspective. The assumption that there is a cause-and-effect relationship is necessary because it allows the measurements relating to the non-financial perspectives to be used to predict future financial performance.

Kaplan and Norton (1996b) state that strategy can be viewed as a set of hypotheses about cause and effect, thus enabling a scorecard to tell the story of a business unit's strategy through a sequence of cause-and-effect relationships. The measurement system should make relationships (hypotheses) among objectives (and measures) in the various perspectives explicit so that they can be managed and validated. Every measure selected for a balanced scorecard should be an element of a chain of cause-and-effect relationships that communicates the meaning of the business unit's strategy to the organization.

Cause-and-effect relationships can be expressed by a sequence of if-then statements. For example, a link between improved training of workers to perform multiple tasks and higher profits can be established through the following sequence of if-then statements:

> If employee skills are upgraded to perform multiple tasks by undertaking support activities such as duties relating to set-ups, minor repairs, preventive maintenance, quality inspection and operating different machines within the cell, then manufacturing processes can be redesigned by moving from a batch production functional layout to a cellular JIT manufacturing system. If the manufacturing processes are redesigned then cycle time will decrease; if cycle time decreases, then delivery time will decrease; if delivery time decreases, then customer satisfaction will increase; if customer satisfaction increases, then market share will increase; if market share increases, then sales revenues will increase; if sales revenues increase then profits will increase.

The strategy map shown in Figure 21.2 illustrates the process redesign strategy as described by the above sequence of if-then statements, and indicates that the chain of cause-and-effect relationships encompasses all four perspectives of the balanced scorecard. Also note that a performance measure can

FIGURE 21.2
Strategy map

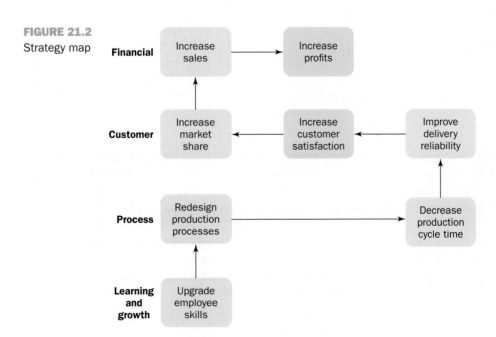

REAL WORLD VIEWS 21.3

How ZYSCO uses the balanced scorecard (BSC)

An article by Chen *et al.* (2015) published in *Strategic Finance* described how Zhongyuan Special Steel Co. (ZYSCO), a typical Chinese state-owned company, introduced a new strategic management system that would integrate its value creation strategy into everyone's day-to-day job. The BSC was the core of this new system. The foundation for implementing a balanced scorecard (BSC) was ZYSCO's strategy map. The BSC task force first drew the strategy map shown in Figure 1. Next, the BSC was developed based on ZYSCO's strategy map. Figure 2 shows the BSC and indicates how the strategic objectives were translated into performance measures.

Since the steel industry in China had large overcapacity problems, the company downplayed revenue growth and production capacity as financial measures and focused on increasing net income by controlling costs and expenses. For the customer perspective, customer satisfaction rate is based on a customer survey, which includes evaluation of product quality, on-time delivery, after-sale service and so on.

ZYSCO's BSC was then decomposed by departments creating BSCs using the company's strategy map and BSC as a guide. The authors concluded that ZYSCO's compensation system should be linked to the new system and new measures.

Questions

1 Based on ZYSCO's BSC and strategy map, create a BSC for either the finance or sales departments.

2 What problems might arise with ZYSCO seeking to link its compensation system with its new system and measures?

Reference

Chen, Y., Lu, Z. and Lin., T.W. (2015) 'How ZYSCO uses the balanced scorecard', *Strategic Finance*. Available at sfmagazine.com/past-issues/past-issues-archive-detail/?monthNumber=1&yearNumber=2015

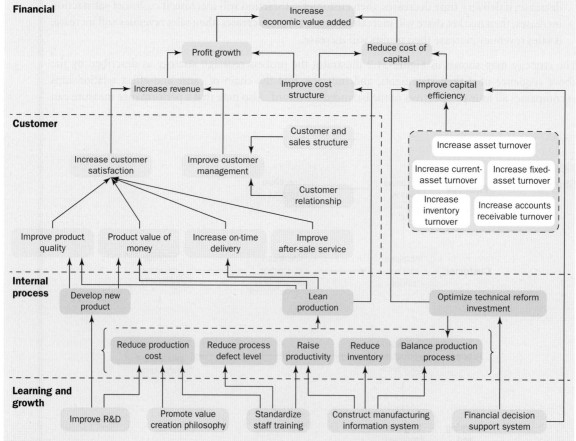

FIGURE 1

ZYSCO strategy map

KEY STRATEGIC OBJECTIVES	MEASURES	WEIGHT	TARGET
FINANCIAL PERSPECTIVE			
Increase revenue	Net income	18%	Budget
	Gross profit margin	10%	Budget
Improve cost structure	Costs and expenses	15%	Budget
Improve capital efficiency	Assets turnover	10%	Budget
CUSTOMER PERSPECTIVE			
Increase customer satisfaction	Customer satisfaction rate (based on customer survey)	6%	95%
Improve customer management	Customer retention rate	6%	100%
	Percentage of sales from high-profit products	5%	Budget
INTERNAL PROCESS PERSPECTIVE			
Develop new product	Number of new products	2%	As planned
Lean production	Implementation of lean production (evaluated by board)	5%	95%
	Manufacturing cost reduction	5%	Budget
	Capacity balance	5%	As planned
Optimize technical reform investment	Return on technical reform investment	5%	Budget
LEARNING AND GROWTH PERSPECTIVE			
Improve R&D	Number of new patents	1%	As planned
Promote value creation philosophy	Promotion of value creation (evaluated by board)	1%	95%
Standardize staff training	Training evaluation (evaluated by board)	2%	95%
Manufacture information integration system	System coverage (evaluated by board)	2%	80%
Financial decision support system	Financial decision support (evaluated by board)	2%	90%

FIGURE 2

ZYSCO balanced scorecard

serve as both a lag indicator and a lead indicator. For example, cycle time is an outcome measure (i.e. a lag measure) arising from improving employee skills and redesigning processes. Improvements in cycle times also serve as a lead indicator in terms of its influence on delivery time measures.

LINKING PERFORMANCE EVALUATION WITH THE BALANCED SCORECARD

Look at Figure 21.1. You will see that, besides objectives and measures, targets and initiatives are also incorporated in the balanced scorecard. Target values should be established for the measures associated with each objective. In addition, the major initiatives for each objective should be described. The scorecard objectives, initiatives and measures become the means for conveying the strategy of the organization to its employees and managers. Responsibility centre objectives and measures should also be aligned with the scorecard objectives and measures.

For feedback reporting, actual performance measures should also be added and compared with target values. The reward system should also be linked to the achievement of the scorecard objectives and measures. Failure to change the reward system may result in managers continuing to focus on short-term financial performance at the expense of concentrating on the strategic objectives of the scorecard. A US study indicates that the balanced scorecard approach is linked to incentive compensation schemes. Epstein and Manzoni (1998) reported that 60 per cent of the 100 large USA organizations surveyed linked the balanced scorecard approach to incentive pay for their senior executives.

Exhibit 21.5 provides an illustration of linking the reward system with objectives, targets and performance measures. Weights expressed as percentages shown in the parentheses are used to indicate the relative importance that management has assigned to each perspective and objective. You will see that each perspective is assigned a weight of 25 per cent. Within each perspective, there are multiple objectives and

EXHIBIT 21.5 Illustration of a target and weighting incentive scheme

Perspectives	Objectives	Measures	Targets
Financial (25%)	Increase economic value added (25%)	Economic value added	20% increase
	Increase return on investment (25%)	Return on investment	20% increase
	Increase revenues (25%)	Sales revenues	25% increase
	Decrease process costs (25%)	Process costs	15% decrease
Customer (25%)	Increase market share (25%)	Market share	20%
	Increase customer retention (35%)	Repeat orders	60%
	Improve delivery time (40%)	On-time delivery (per cent)	100%
Internal processes (25%)	Improve cycle time (70%)	Cycle time	three days
	Increase process quality (30%)	Percentage defects	0.01%
Learning and growth (25%)	Improve employee skills (100%)	Hours of training	35 hours per employee

measures. For example, within the customer perspective there are three performance measures and management has assigned a weight of 25 per cent to increasing market share, 35 per cent to increasing customer retention and 40 per cent to an improvement in on-time delivery. The percentage weightings are used to structure the reward system. Therefore, in Exhibit 21.5, 10 per cent (40% × 25%) of the reward would be assigned to the delivery objective.

Note that the achievement of the objectives and targets shown in Exhibit 21.5 is based on cause-and-effect relationships. For example, increasing economic value added by the targeted 20 per cent is dependent on increasing sales revenues by a target of 25 per cent and decreasing process costs by 15 per cent. These changes are, in turn dependent on other outcomes in other perspectives such as increasing market share and reducing cycle times by the target levels.

The actual values of the measures are compared with the target measures for a given time period. The design of a performance evaluation and reward system that is linked to multiple perspectives and objectives presents a number of difficulties. In Exhibit 21.5, equal percentage weightings have been allocated to each perspective but there is no reason why management may choose to assign different percentage weightings.

A further problem arises when some of the target performance measures are achieved but others are not achieved. For example, in Exhibit 21.5, assume for the customer perspective that the target performance measures of 60 per cent for repeat orders and 100 per cent for on-time delivery were achieved but the actual increase in market share was 15 per cent compared with the target of 20 per cent. Should managers be given rewards when not all of the measures for the objectives within the customer perspective have been achieved? One possible solution is for the rewards to be based on the percentage achievement of each objective. Therefore, because the percentage achievement for increasing market share was 75 per cent (15 per cent actual performance compared with a target of 20 per cent) the percentage of the total reward would be 4.7 per cent (25% × 25% × 75%) compared with 6.25 per cent (25% × 25% × 100%) had the 20 per cent target market share been achieved. There is a danger with this approach that insufficient attention will be given to all the performance measures. To avoid this, the reward system could specify that no reward be given unless and until strategic measures exceed a specified minimum value.

It is also important that the linking of the balanced scorecard to a performance evaluation and reward system incorporate an appropriate time dimension. An adequate amount of time must elapse between the implementation of a strategic initiative and the ascertainment of whether the strategy has been successful. Thus lag measures incorporated in the financial perspective can be expected to have a longer time perspective than the lead measures incorporated in the other perspectives. A possible approach is for the performance evaluation and reward system to incorporate short-term one-year targets and longer term targets (e.g. a three- to five-year time horizon).

Research evidence suggests that companies that use the balanced scorecard may continue to base their incentives mainly on financial measures. A study by Kraus and Lind (2010) of eight of Sweden's largest multinational companies that had adopted the balanced scorecard at the corporate level reported that incentives at this level were largely based on financial measures and that corporate control was also financially focused. The authors conclude that because financial markets focus on financial measures incentives are also based on encouraging managers to focus on the same measures that are used by financial markets. Kraus and Lind point out that their research focused on the impact of the balanced scorecard on control at the corporate level and that there was a need to undertake further research to ascertain whether companies that use balance scorecards at lower business unit levels also link their reward systems mainly to financial measures at these lower levels.

BENEFITS AND LIMITATIONS OF THE BALANCED SCORECARD APPROACH

The following is a summary of the major benefits that can be attributed to the balanced scorecard approach:

1 The approach improves communications within the organization and promotes the active formulation and implementation of organizational strategy by making it highly visible through the linkage of performance measures and targets to business unit strategy.

2 It links financial and non-financial measures by identifying those non-financial measures that are leading indicators of future financial performance.

3 The balanced scorecard limits the number of measures used by focusing on the most critical. It thus avoids a proliferation of measures by focusing management's attention on only those that are vital to the implementation of strategy.

The balanced scorecard has also been subject to frequent criticisms. Most of them question the assumption of the cause-and-effect relationship and the absence of a time dimension. It is argued that the cause-and-effect relationships are merely hypotheses that are too ambiguous and lack a theoretical underpinning or empirical support.

One critical element of the balanced scorecard in guiding strategic improvement is the recognition that an adequate amount of time must elapse between the implementation of a strategic initiative and the determination of whether the strategy has been successful in increasing financial lag measures (Atkinson, 2006). A major criticism of the balanced scorecard is the absence of any time dimension. This presents a problem when there are differences in the timing of the effects of the various lead measures resulting in the outcomes occurring at different points in time. It is therefore difficult to determine the extent to which a particular lead indicator has had an impact on a lag measure when other lead indicators, occurring at different points in time, are also impacting on the lag measures. A number of researchers have commented on the absence of a time dimension in the balanced scorecard (Nørreklit, 2000; Bukh and Malmi, 2005; Franco-Santos and Bourne, 2005). For example, Norreklit argued that the absence of an explicit time dimension as part of the scorecard makes it impossible to establish cause-and-effect relationships. Several studies also suggest that causal linkages between non-financial performance drivers and financial outcome measures were often neither specified nor well understood (Malmi, 2001; Ittner and Larcker, 2003). In a study of the use of balanced scorecards in Finnish companies, Malmi (2001) found that, despite interviewees' claims to the contrary, links between strategy and balanced scorecard measures were weak and causal linkages between multiple measures were difficult to explain.

Other criticisms relate to the omission of important perspectives, the most notable being the environmental/impact on society perspective (see Chapter 23) and an employee perspective. It should be

EXHIBIT 21.6 Surveys of practice relating to balanced scorecard usage

Surveys indicate that even though the balanced scorecard did not emerge until the early 1990s it is now widely used in many countries throughout the world. A Bain & Company survey by Rigby and Biolodeau (2013) of a broad range of international executives in 1221 firms reported a 73 per cent predicted usage rate of the balanced scorecard in 2013. In the UK, a survey of 163 manufacturing companies (annual sales turnover in excess of £50 million) by Zuriekat (2005) reported that 30 per cent had implemented the balanced scorecard. Other studies in mainland Europe indicate significant usage. Pere (1999) reported a 31 per cent usage rate of companies in Finland with a further 30 per cent in the process of implementing it. In Sweden, Kald and Nilsson (2000) reported that 27 per cent of major Swedish companies have implemented the approach. Oliveras and Amat (2002) report widespread usage in Spain and Speckbacher, Bischof and Pfeiffer (2003) report a usage rate of 24 per cent in German-speaking countries (Germany, Austria and Switzerland). Major companies adopting the balanced scorecard include KPMG Peat Marwick, Allstate Insurance and AT&T (Chow, Haddad and Williamson, 1997).

In terms of the perspectives used, Malmi (2001) conducted a study involving semi-structured interviews in 17 companies in Finland. He found that 15 companies used the four perspectives identified by Kaplan and Norton (1992) and two companies added a fifth – an employee's perspective. The UK study by Zuriekat (2005) reported that virtually all of the balanced scorecard respondents used the financial, customer and internal business process perspectives. Other perspectives used were learning and growth, employee, supplier and the environment. The respective percentage usage rates for the balance scorecard adopters were 39 per cent, 45 per cent, 65 per cent and 26 per cent. The study also reported that 35 per cent of the adopters linked their reward systems to the balanced scorecard. A study by Olve, Roy and Wetter (2000) found that 15–20 performance measures are customarily used.

noted, however, that Kaplan and Norton (1996b) presented the four perspectives as a suggested framework rather than a constraining straitjacket. There is nothing to prevent companies adding additional perspectives to meet their own requirements but they must avoid the temptation of creating too many perspectives and performance measures since one of the major benefits of the balanced scorecard is its conciseness and clarity of presentation.

Our discussion relating to the core objectives and measures of the four perspectives has concentrated mainly on the manufacturing organizations. The balance scorecard, however, has been widely adopted in service organizations. Exhibit 21.7 provides an illustration of potential balanced scorecard performance measures for different types of service organization. You will also find it appropriate at this point to refer to Exhibit 21.6 which summarizes surveys of practice relating to the usage of the balanced scorecard.

EXHIBIT 21.7 Potential scorecard measures in different business sectors

	Generic	Healthcare	Airlines	Banking
Financial strength (Looking back)	Market share	Patient census	Revenue/cost	Outstanding loan
	Revenue growth	Unit profitability	per available	balances
	Operating profits	Funds raised	passenger mile	Deposit balances
	Return on equity	for capital	Mix of freight	Non-interest
	Stock market	improvements	Mix of full fare to	income
	performance	Cost per care	discounted	
	Growth in margin	Per cent of	Average age of fleet	
		revenue – new	Available seat miles	
		programmes	and related yields	

EXHIBIT 21.7 *(continued)*

	Generic	Healthcare	Airlines	Banking
Customer service and satisfaction (Looking from the outside in)	Customer satisfaction Customer retention Quality customer service Sales from new products/services	Patient satisfaction survey Patient retention Patient referral rate Admittance or discharge timeliness Medical plan awareness	Lost bag reports per 10 000 passengers Denied boarding rate Flight cancellation rate Customer complaints filed with the DOT	Customer retention Number of new customers Number of products per customer Face time spent between loan officers and customers
Internal operating efficiency (Looking from the inside out)	Delivery time Cost process quality Error rates on shipments Supplier satisfaction	Weekly patient complaints Patient loads Breakthroughs in treatments and medicines Infection rates Readmission rate Length of stay	Load factors (percentage of seats occupied) Utilization factors on aircraft and personnel On-time performance	Sales calls to potential customers Thank you calls or cards to new and existing customers Cross selling statistics
Learning and growth (Looking ahead)	Employee skill level Training availability Employee satisfaction Job retention Amount of overtime worked Amount of vacation time taken	Training hours per caregiver Number of peer reviewed papers published Number of grants awarded (NIH) Referring MDs Employee turnover rate	Employee absenteeism Worker safety statistics Performance appraisals completed Training programme hours for employee	Test results from training knowledge of product offerings, sales and service Employee satisfaction survey

SUMMARY

The following items relate to the learning objectives listed at the beginning of the chapter.

- **Describe three competitive strategies that a firm can adopt to achieve sustainable competitive advantage and explain how they influence performance management systems.**

Porter (1985) suggests that a firm has a choice of three generic strategies to achieve sustainable competitive advantage. A firm adopting a cost leadership strategy seeks to be the lowest cost producer within the industry thus enabling it to compete on the basis of lower selling prices. A differentiation strategy applies when a firm seeks to offer products or services that are considered by its customers to be superior and unique relative to its competitors. Finally, a firm can adopt a focus strategy, which involves focusing on a narrow segment of the market that has special needs that are poorly served by other competitors. More emphasis is likely to be given to cost-based performance measures in firms pursing a low cost strategy whereas firms following a product differentiation strategy are likely to have a greater need for market-based performance measures.

- **Describe the balanced scorecard.**

Recent developments in performance evaluation have sought to integrate financial and non-financial measures and assist in clarifying, communicating and managing strategy. The balanced scorecard attempts to meet these requirements. It requires that managers view the business from the following four different perspectives: (a) financial perspective; (b) customer perspective; (c) internal business process perspective and (d) learning and growth perspective. Organizations should articulate the major goals for each of the four perspectives and then translate these goals into specific initiatives and performance measures. Each organization must decide what its critical performance measures are. The choice will vary over time and should be linked to the strategies that the organization is following.

- **Explain each of the four perspectives of the balanced scorecard.**

The financial perspective provides objectives and associated performance measures relating to the financial outcomes of past actions. Thus, it provides feedback on the success of pursuing the objectives identified for the other three perspectives. In the customer perspective objectives, performance measures and initiatives should be established that track a business unit's ability to create satisfied and loyal customers. They relate to market share, customer retention, new customer acquisition, customer satisfaction and customer profitability. In the internal business perspective, managers identify the critical internal processes for which the organization must excel in implementing its strategy. The principal internal business processes include the innovation processes, operation processes and post-service sales processes. The final perspective on the balanced scorecard identifies the infrastructure that the business must build to create long-term growth and improvement. The following three categories have been identified as falling within this perspective: employee capabilities, information system capabilities and motivation, empowerment and alignment.

- **Provide illustrations of performance measures for each of the four perspectives.**

Within the financial perspective, examples include economic value added and residual income. Market share and customer satisfaction ratings are generic measures within the customer perspective. Typical internal business perspective measures include percentage of sales from new products (innovation processes), cycle time measures such as manufacturing cycle efficiency (operation processes) and percentage returns from customers (post-service sales processes). Measures of employee satisfaction represent generic measures within the learning and growth satisfaction.

- **Explain how the balanced scorecard links strategy formulation to financial outcomes.**

The balanced scorecard philosophy translates an organization's vision and strategy into operational objectives, initiatives and performance measures for each of the four perspectives. Each performance measure is part of a cause-and-effect relationship involving a linkage from strategy formulation to financial outcomes. Measures of organizational learning and growth are assumed to be the drivers of the internal business processes. The measures of these processes are in turn assumed to be the drivers of measures of customer perspective, while these measures are the driver of the financial perspective. Measurements relating to the non-financial perspectives are assumed to be predictors of future financial performance.

- **Distinguish between lead and lag measures.**

Lag measures are outcome measures that mostly fall within the financial perspective and are the results of past actions. Lag measures generally do not incorporate the effect of decisions when they are made. Instead, they show the impact of the decisions as their impact materializes and this can be long after the decisions were made. Lead measures are generally non-financial measures that are the drivers of future financial performance.

- **Outline the benefits and criticisms of the balanced scorecard.**

A major benefit of the balanced scorecard is that it assists in communicating and implementing strategy throughout the organization by translating strategy into a coherent and linked set of understandable and measurable targets and performance. Criticisms relate to the cause-and-effect relationship and the absence of a time dimension. It is argued that the cause-and-effect relationships are merely hypotheses that are too ambiguous and lack a theoretical underpinning or empirical support. The time dimension presents a problem when there are differences in the timing of the effects of the various lead measures resulting in the outcomes occurring at different points in time. It is therefore difficult to determine the extent to which a particular lead indicator has had an impact on a lag measure.

KEY TERMS AND CONCEPTS

Balanced scorecard A strategic management tool that integrates financial and non-financial measures of performance in a single concise report, with the aim of incorporating performance management within the strategic management process.

Capacity usage ratio A measure of capacity calculated by dividing the actual hours utilized by the budgeted hours to be utilized.

Cost leadership strategy A strategy adopted by an organization that aims to be the lowest cost producer within a market segment thus enabling it to compete on the basis of lower selling prices than its competitors.

Customer perspective One of the perspectives considered on the balanced scorecard, focusing on how the organization appears to its customers.

Customer value propositions The attributes that drive core objectives and measures relating to the customer perspective of an organization.

Defender strategy Firms pursuing a defender strategy perceive a great deal of stability in their external environment. They compete on product price, quality and customer service rather than innovation and product and market development.

Differentiation strategy A strategy adopted by an organization that seeks to offer products or services that are considered by its customers to be superior or unique relative to its competitors.

Financial perspective One of the perspectives considered on the balanced scorecard, focusing on how the organization looks to shareholders.

Focusing strategy A strategy that involves seeking competitive advantage by focusing on a narrow segment of the market that has special needs that are poorly served by other competitors in the industry. Competitive advantage is based on adopting either a cost leadership or product/service differentiation strategy within the chosen segment.

Internal business perspective One of the perspectives considered on the balanced scorecard, focusing on what the organization needs to excel at.

Lag measures Outcome measures that mostly fall within the financial perspective and are the results of past actions

Lead measures Non-financial measures that are the drivers of future financial performance.

Learning and growth perspective One of the perspectives considered on the balanced scorecard, focusing on how the organization can continue to improve and create value.

Manufacturing cycle efficiency (MCE) A measure of cycle time that is calculated by dividing processing time by processing time plus the non-value-added activities of inspection time, wait time and move time.

Production efficiency ratio A process efficiency measure calculated by dividing the standard hours of output by the actual hours of input.

Prospector strategy Firms pursuing a prospector strategy perceive high uncertainty in their environment and are continually searching for new market opportunities. They compete through new product innovations and market development.

Strategic positioning The choice of strategies an organization uses to achieve sustainable competitive advantage.

RECOMMENDED READING

This chapter has summarized Kaplan and Norton's writings but for a more detailed description of their work you should refer to the books they have written on the balance scorecard – *The Strategy-Focused Organization* (2001a) and *Alignment: Using the Balanced Scorecard to Create Corporate Synergies* (2006a). See also Kaplan and Norton (2005 and 2006b) and Kaplan (2009) for shorter articles on the balanced scorecard. You should refer to the writings of Norreklit (2000, 2003) for a critique of the balanced scorecard. See also *Journal of Accounting & Organizational Change Special Issue on the Balanced Scorecard* edited by Norreklit, H. and Mitchell, F. (2014). For a broader description of performance management linked to strategy you should refer to Simons (1998). Finally, for a study of the purposes for which managers use the balanced scorecard, see Wiersma (2009).

KEY EXAMINATION POINTS

Some examining bodies set examination questions that use other performance management frameworks that are described in Learning Note 21.1. You should check your course curriculum to ascertain whether you need to read Learning Note 21.1. Sometimes more general questions are set that do not refer to any specific performance measurement framework. You should incorporate the performance frameworks criteria of Otley (1999) shown at the start of this chapter and also adopt a balanced scorecard approach by emphasizing the need to integrate financial and non-financial measures and link performance measurement to an organization's strategies.

ASSESSMENT MATERIAL

The review questions are short questions that enable you to assess your understanding of the main topics included in the chapter. The numbers in parentheses provide you with the page numbers to refer to if you cannot answer a specific question.

The review problems are more complex and require you to relate and apply the content to various business problems. The problems are graded by their level of difficulty. Solutions to review problems that are not preceded by the term 'IM' are provided in a separate section at the end of the book. Solutions to problems preceded by the term 'IM' are provided in the Instructor's Manual accompanying this book that can be downloaded from the lecturer's digital support resources. Additional review problems with fully worked solutions are provided in the Student Manual that accompanies this book.

REVIEW QUESTIONS

21.1 What are the major issues to be addressed in developing a framework for managing organizational performance? (p. 561)

21.2 Describe the various generic strategies that an organization can adopt to achieve organizational competitive advantage (pp. 561–562)

21.3 How do different competitive strategies influence the choice of performance measures? (p. 562)

21.4 What is the purpose of a balanced scorecard? (pp. 564–566)

21.5 Describe the four perspectives of the balanced scorecard. (pp. 566–570)

21.6 Explain the differences between lag measures and lead measures. (p. 570)

21.7 Explain what is meant by cause-and-effect relationships within the balanced scorecard. (pp. 570–571)

21.8 Discuss the benefits and limitations of the balanced scorecard. (pp. 575–576)

21.9 Identify and describe the core objectives of the customer perspective. (p. 567)

21.10 Describe the three principal internal business processes that can be included within the internal business perspective. (pp. 568–569)

21.11 What is manufacturing cycle efficiency? (p. 569)

21.12 Describe three principal categories within the learning and growth perspective. (pp. 569–570)

21.13 Provide examples of performance measures within each of the four perspectives of the balanced scorecard. (pp. 566–570)

REVIEW PROBLEMS

21.14 Advanced: EVA™, key performance indicators for critical success factors, JIT, kaizen costing and zero defects. Iron Chicken (IC) is a multinational business which manufactures commercial building control systems. Building control systems include heating and air-conditioning systems, lighting controls, power and water monitoring and security systems (e.g. keypad access, alarms and CCTV). IC's manufacturing takes place at a number of factory sites where some products have a long product life and are simple and mass-produced while other products are complex and have a short product life due to changing technologies. IC's mission statement is 'to create value for shareholders through control products which improve productivity, save energy and increase comfort and safety'.

A new chief executive officer (CEO) has been appointed to address a decline in IC's share price in the last three years. This CEO has identified that the business has grown through acquisition and as a result she stated, 'Senior management have focused on making corporate deals and not making control systems.' The CEO has declared that the business must focus on optimizing its value generation rather than just getting larger through acquisitions.

You are a performance management expert within IC. The CEO has tasked you with aiding her in aspects of her improvement programme. First, she wants your views on the use of EVA™ as the key performance metric at IC. You have been supplied with the current EVA™ calculation (Appendix 1) but there is some doubt about whether the junior management accountant who has done this work was sufficiently trained in the method. So, the CEO needs you to evaluate its accuracy and the assumptions which form part of the calculation.

Second, the CEO believes that the poor performance of the company can be addressed by ensuring that the mission statement flows down into the performance management of the business. To that end, the following critical success factors (CSFs) have been identified and the CEO wants you to suggest additional key performance indicators (KPIs) for these.

	CSF	Associated current KPI
1	Greater staff productivity	Units produced per labour hour
2	Reduction of wastage in production	Power consumed per unit produced
3	Greater innovation of products	Number of new products launched

Your suggestions should be in addition to these current KPIs.

Third, in order to improve performance, the CEO plans to implement initiatives associated with 'lean' manufacturing. Specifically, there are three projects which have been suggested and the CEO needs your advice on these:

1 Move to just-in-time manufacturing
2 Use kaizen costing
3 Examine the costs of quality in achieving a 'zero defects' approach to manufacturing

The CEO has stated, 'I need to know briefly how the improvement projects will meet the three CSFs and also how they will impact on the existing three KPIs.'

Finally, the CEO requested, 'You must tell me the implications of the improvement projects for our information systems as I feel that they are not currently suitable for the plan that I have.' The current information systems of the company are based around the functional departments of the business such as manufacturing, marketing, finance and logistics. Each department has developed its own system although all feed into the finance system which is the main one used for strategic decision-making. In order that the department systems can all feed through to the current finance system, these current systems only handle quantitative data. The company is considering the implementation of a new information system. This new system will introduce networking technology in order to bring together all of the departmental systems into a new, single, corporate database.

Required:

Write a report to the CEO of Iron Chicken to:

(i) Evaluate the accuracy of the EVA™ calculation and the assumptions in Appendix 1. Advise the CEO on your results, providing calculations as needed. *(15 marks)*

(ii) For each of the three critical success factors at IC, briefly explain a weakness of the current KPI associated with that CSF and then provide a justified alternative KPI. *(6 marks)*

(iii) Explain what the three improvement projects are, how they will help to meet the CSFs at IC and comment on the impact of each project on the existing three KPIs. *(15 marks)*

(iv) Assess the impact of the proposed, new information system on the three improvement projects. *(10 marks)*

Professional marks will be awarded for the format, style and structure of the discussion of your answer. *(4 marks)*

ACCA P5 Advanced Performance Management

Appendix 1

Economic value added

	Year ended 30 June	
	$m	Note
Operating profit	551.4	
Add back		
Non-cash expenses	15.1	
Marketing capitalised	23.1	5
Operating lease expenses	40.0	
Less		
Tax	134.8	6
Lost tax relief on interest	24.5	7
Net operating profit after tax (NOPAT)	470.3	
Capital employed		
From the statement of financial position	2401.0	10
Marketing spend capitalized	23.1	5
Operating leases	115.0	8
Adjusted capital employed	2539.1	

WACC = (1/2 × 16%) + (1/2 × 6.8%) = 11.4%

EVA™ = NOPAT − (WACC × Capital employed) = 181

Assumptions and notes:

1 Debt/Equity — 100.0%
2 Cost of equity — 16.0%
3 Tax Rate — 30.0%
4 Cost of debt (pre-tax) — 6.8%
5 There has been $23.1m of marketing spent each year for the last two years in order to build the brand of IC long term.
6 Tax paid in the year was $130m while the tax charged per the accounts was $134.8m.
7 Interest charged in the period was $81.6m.
   Lost tax relief on this interest was 30% × $81.6m.
8 The operating leases have an average life of four years.
9 The only research and development spending identified in the last five years was $10m expensed during this year on a new product.
   The product has not been launched yet.
10 Capital employed during the period (from the statement of financial position):

Opening	2282.0
Change in period	119.0
Closing	2401.0

21.15 Advanced: Balanced scorecard. Squarize is a large company which, for many years, operated solely as a pay-tv broadcaster. However, five years ago, it started product bundling, offering broadband and telephone services to its pay-tv customers. Customers taking up the offer were then known in the business as 'bundle customers' and they had to take up both the broadband and telephone services together with the pay-tv service. Other customers were still able to subscribe to pay-tv alone but not to broadband and telephone services without the pay-tv service.

All contracts to customers of Squarize are for a minimum three-month period. The pay-tv box is sold to the customer at the beginning of the contract; however, the broadband and telephone equipment is only rented to them.

In the first few years after product bundling was introduced, the company saw a steady increase in profits. Then, Squarize saw its revenues and operating profits fall. Consequently, staff bonuses were not paid, and staff became dissatisfied. Several reasons were identified for the deterioration of results:

1 In the economy as a whole, discretionary spending had been severely hit by rising unemployment and inflation. In a bid to save cash, many pay-tv customers were cancelling their contracts after the minimum three-month period as they were then able to still keep the pay-tv box. The box comes with a number of free channels, which the customer can still continue to receive free of charge, even after the cancellation of their contract.
2 The company's customer service call centre, which is situated in another country, had been the cause of lots of complaints from customers about poor service, and, in particular, the number of calls it sometimes took to resolve an issue.
3 Some bundle customers found that the broadband service that they had subscribed to did not work. As a result, they were immediately cancelling their contracts for all services within the 14 day cancellation period permitted under the contracts.

In a response to the above problems and in an attempt to increase revenues and profits, Squarize made the following changes to the business:

1 It made a strategic decision to withdraw the pay-tv-broadband-telephone package from the market and, instead, offer each service as a standalone product.
2 It guaranteed not to increase prices for a 12-month period for each of its three services.
3 It transferred its call centre back to its home country and increased the level of staff training given for call centre workers.
4 It investigated and resolved the problem with customers' broadband service.

It is now one year since the changes were made and the finance director wants to use a balanced scorecard to assess the extent to which the changes have been successful in improving the performance of the business.

Required:

(a) For each perspective of the balanced scorecard, identify two goals (objectives) together with a corresponding performance measure for each goal which could be used by the company to assess whether the changes have been successful. Justify the use of each of the performance measures that you choose. *(16 marks)*

(b) Discuss how the company could reduce the problem of customers terminating their pay-tv service after only three months. *(4 marks)*

ACCA F5 Performance Management

21.16 Advanced: Balanced scorecard. Pharmaceutical Technologies Co. (PT) is a developer and manufacturer of medical drugs in Beeland, It is one of the 100 largest listed companies on the national stock exchange. The company focuses on buying prospective drugs that have shown initial promise in testing from small bio-engineering companies. PT then leads these through three regulatory stages to launch in the general medical market, The three stages are:

1 to confirm the safety of the drug (does it harm hurnans?), in small scale trials;

2 to test the efficacy of the product (does it help cure?), again in small scale trials; and

3 finally, large-scale trials to definitively decide on the safety and efficacy of the product.

The drugs are then marketed through the company's large sales force to healthcare providers and end users (patients). The healthcare providers are paid by either health insurance companies or the national government dependent on the financial status of the patient.

The Beeland Drug Regulator (BDR) oversees this testing process and makes the final judgement about whether a product can be sold in the country.

Its objectives are to protect, promote and improve public health by ensuring that:

– medicines have an acceptable balance of benefit and risk;

– the users of these medicines understand this risk–benefit profile; and

– new beneficial product development is encouraged.

The regulator is governed by a board of trustees appointed by the government. It is funded directly by the government and also through fees charged to drug companies when granting licences to sell their products in Beeland.

PT has used share price and earnings per share as its principal measures of performance to date. However, the share price has underperformed the market and the health sector in the last two years. The chief executive officer (CEO) has identified that these measures are too narrow and is considering implementing a balanced scorecard approach to address this problem.

A working group has drawn up a suggested balanced scorecard. It began by identifying the objectives from the board's medium term strategy:

– Create shareholder value by bringing commercially viable drugs to market

– Improve the efficiency of drug development

– Increase shareholder value by innovation in the drug approval process

The working group then considered the stakeholder perspectives:

– Shareholders want a competitive return on their investment

– Purchasers (governments, insurers and patients) want to pay a reasonable price for the drugs

– Regulators want an efficient process for the validation of drugs

– Doctors want safe and effective drug products

– Patients want to be cured

Finally, this leads to the proposed scorecard of performance measures:

– Financial – share price and earnings per share

– Customer – number of patients using PT products

– Internal business process – exceed industry standard on design and testing; time to regulatory approval of a product

– Learning and growth – training days undertaken by staff; time to market of new product; percentage of drugs bought by PT that gain final approval.

The balanced scorecard now needs to be reviewed to ensure that it will address the company's objectives and the issues that it faces in its business environment.

Required:

(a) Describe how the implementation of a balanced scorecard delivers a range of performance measures aligned with the corporate strategy. *(4 marks)*

(b) Evaluate the performance measures proposed for PT's balanced scorecard. *(10 marks)*

(c) Identify and analyse the influence of four different external stakeholders on the regulator (BDR). *(6 marks)*

(d) Using your answer from part (c), describe how the application of the balanced scorecard approach at BDR would differ from the approach within PT. *(7 marks)*

ACCA P5 Advanced Performance management

21.17 Advanced: Balanced scorecard (customer perspective) and the reward management system. Victoria-Yeeland Logistics (Victoria) is a logistics support business, which operates a fleet of lorries to deliver packages of goods on behalf of its customers within the country of Yeeland. Victoria collects packages from its customers' manufacturing sites or from the customers' port of importation and delivers to the final user of the goods. The lorries are run and maintained from a set of depots spread throughout Yeeland.

The overall objective of Victoria is to maximize shareholder wealth. The delivery business in Yeeland is dominated by two international companies and one other domestic business and profit margins are extremely tight. The market is saturated by these large operators and a number of smaller operators. The cost base of Victoria is dominated by staff and fuel, with fuel prices being highly volatile in the last few years.

In order to improve performance measurement and management at Victoria, the chief financial officer (CFO) plans to use the balanced scorecard (BSC). However, she has been pulled away from this project in order to deal with an issue with refinancing the business' principal lending facility. The CFO has already identified some suitable metrics but needs you, as her assistant, to complete her work and address any potential questions which might arise when she makes her presentation on the BSC to the board. The CFO has completed the identification of metrics for three of the perspectives (Appendix 1) but has yet to complete the work on the metrics for the customer perspective. This should be done using the data given in Appendix 2.

Additionally, two issues have arisen in the reward management system at Victoria, one in relation to senior management and the other for operational managers. Currently, senior management gets a fixed salary supplemented by an annual bonus awarded by the board. Shareholders have been complaining that these bonuses are not suitable. The operational managers also get bonuses based on their performance as assessed by their management superiors. The operational managers are unhappy with the system. In order to address this, it has been suggested that they should be involved in bonus target setting as otherwise there is a sense of demotivation from such a system. The CFO wants an evaluation of this system of rewards in light of the introduction of the BSC and best practice.

Required:

(a) Discuss how Victoria's success in the customer perspective may impact on the metrics given in the financial perspective. *(5 marks)*

(b) Recommend, with justification, and calculate a suitable performance metric for each customer perspective success factor. Comment on the problems of using customer complaints to measure whether packages are delivered safely and on time. *(11 marks)*

(c) Advise Victoria on the reward management issues outlined by the CFO. *(9 marks)*

Appendix 1

Financial perspective
(How do we appear to our shareholders?)
Return on capital employed
Profit margin
Revenue growth

Customer perspective
(How do we appear to our customers?)
Success factors:
Ability to meet customers' transport needs
Ability to deliver packages quickly
Ability to deliver packages on time
Ability to deliver packages safely

Internal process perspective
(What business processes must excel?)
Time taken to load and unload
Lorry capacity utilization

Learning and growth perspective
(How do we sustain and improve our ability to grow?)
Leadership competence (qualitative judgement)
Training days per employee

Appendix 2

The process: A customer makes a transport request for a package to be collected and delivered to a given destination. The customer is supplied with a time window in which the delivery will occur. Packages are then loaded onto lorries and delivered according to a route specified by the depot's routing manager.

Total number of customer transport requests	610 000
Total number of packages transported	548 000
Total number of lorry journeys	73 000
Total package kilometres	65 760 000
Total package minutes	131 520 000
Number of delivery complaints from customers:	
from damaged packages	8 220
from late delivery (outside agreed time window)	21 920

Notes:

1. All figures are for the last financial year.
2. A package kilometre is defined as a kilometre travelled by one package.
3. A package minute is defined as a minute spent in transit by one package.

ACCA P5 Advanced Performance Management

21.18 Advanced: Balanced scorecard and problems with interpreting performance measures. Soup operates passenger rail services in Deeland, a technologically advanced country, with high demand for fast reliable rail travel from business and leisure passengers. Many passengers choose train travel because they see it as less harmful to the environment than other forms of transport.

Soup's main objective is to maximize shareholder wealth. Since becoming licensed to operate routes in Regions A and B by the Deeland government five years ago, Soup has consistently delivered increased dividends and share prices for investors. In its initial appraisal of the licensing opportunity, Soup expected to operate the routes for at least 15 years, however, their licence may not be renewed when it expires in three years' time. The government has warned Soup it 'is unhappy about high returns to shareholders while there are many reports of poor passenger service, overcrowded trains and unreliable services on certain routes and at busy times'.

Soup owns its fleet of diesel powered trains. Each train in Region A has seven coaches with 70 passenger seats available per coach. In the less busy Region B, each train has six coaches each with 70 seats. As a condition of the licence, Soup runs a set number of services at both busy and quieter times in both regions. Soup has two larger rivals, both operating electric trains, which cause less harm to the environment than diesel powered trains. They run on the same routes in both regions.

The government regulates fares charged to passengers, which are the same per distance travelled for every operator in that region. The railway track, stations and other infrastructure are managed by the government which charges the operators a fee. There are several stations along the route which are only used by Soup trains and others where Soup trains do not stop at all.

Soup's trains are 25 years old, originally purchased cheaply from an operator whose licence was withdrawn by the government. Soup believes the low price it paid is a key competitive advantage enabling them to steadily increase their return on capital employed, the company's main performance measure, to a level well in excess of their rivals. The shareholders are pleased with the growth in passenger numbers over the last five years, which is the other performance measure Soup uses.

Soup's ageing trains spend increasing time undergoing preventative maintenance, safety checks or repairs. A recent television documentary also showed apparently poor conditions on board, such as defective heating and washroom facilities and dirty, torn seating. Passengers complained in the program of difficulties finding a seat, the unreliability of accessing wireless internet services and even that the menu in the on-board cafe had not changed for five years.

Soup's CEO responded that unreliable internet access arose from the rapid growth in passengers expecting to access the internet on trains. She said Soup had never received any formal complaints about the lack of choice in the on-board cafe, nor had she heard of a recent press report that Soup's trains were badly maintained, so causing harm to the environment.

The CEO has asked you, as chief management accountant, for your advice. 'In view of the government's warning, we must develop performance measures balancing the needs of passengers with the requirements of the shareholders', she has said. 'I don't want to know how to improve the actual performance of the business; that is the job of the operational managers, nor do I just want a list of suggested performance measures. Instead I need to know why these performance measures will help to improve the performance of Soup.'

The following data applies to Soup:

	Region A	Region B
Number of services per day		
Peak times	4	4
Other times	6	8
Number of passengers per day		
Peak times	2500	1400
Other times	2450	1850

Required:

(a) Advise the CEO on how the use of the balanced scorecard could improve the performance management system of Soup. *(10 marks)*

(b) Using the performance data given, evaluate the comments of the Deeland government that Soups trains are overcrowded. *(7 marks)*

(c) Assess the problems Soup may encounter in selecting and interpreting performance measures when applying the balanced scorecard to its performance management system. *(8 marks)*

ACCA P5 Advanced Performance Management

21.19 Advanced: Evaluation of a strategic performance report and balanced scorecard and difficulties in interpreting BSC in a service organization. Kolmog Hotels is a large, listed chain of branded hotels in Ostland. Its stated mission is: 'To become the No. 1 hotel chain in Ostland, building the strength of the Kolmog brand by consistently delighting customers, investing in employees, delivering innovative products/services and continuously improving performance.' The subsidiary aims of the company are to maximize shareholder value, create a culture of pride in the brand and strengthen the brand loyalty of all stakeholders.

The hotels in the Kolmog chain include a diverse range of buildings and locations serving different customer groups (large conference venues, city centre business hotels and country house hotels for holidays). For reporting purposes, the company has divided itself into the four geographical regions of Ostland as can be seen in a recent example of the strategic performance report for the company used by the board for their annual review (see Appendix 1). At the operational level, each hotel manager is given an individual budget for their hotel, prepared in the finance department, and is judged by performance against budgeted profit.

Kolmog is planning a strategic change to its current business model. The board has decided to sell many of the hotels in the chain and then rent them back. This is consistent with many other hotel companies who are focusing on the management of their hotels rather than managing a large, property portfolio of hotels.

In order to assist this strategic change, the chief executive officer (CEO) is considering introducing the balanced scorecard (BSC) across Kolmog. He has tasked you, as a management accountant in the head office, with reviewing the preliminary work done on the development of the scorecard in order to ensure that it is consistent with the goal of meeting the strategic objectives of the company by tying operational and strategic performance measurement into a coherent framework.

The CEO is worried that the BSC might be perceived within the organization as a management accounting technique that has been derived from the manufacturing sector. In order to assess its use at Kolmog, he has asked you to explain the characteristics that differentiate service businesses from manufacturing ones.

Senior executives at the head office of Kolmog have drawn up a preliminary list of perspectives and metrics as an outline of the balanced scorecard in Table 1:

Table 1

Key strategic perspective	Metric
Strategic financial performance	– financial performance benchmarked to Kolmog's main competitors (share price and return on capital employed)
Customer satisfaction	– customer satisfaction survey scores
Hotel performance against budget	– variance analysis for each hotel
Employee satisfaction	– staff turnover

The history of rewards at Kolmog has not been good, with only 1 per cent of staff receiving their maximum possible bonus in previous years and 75 per cent of staff receiving no bonus. This has led to many complaints that targets set for the reward system are too challenging.

Under a new performance reward system, employee targets are to be derived from the above BSC strategic measures depending on the employee's area of responsibility. The new system is for hotel managers to be given challenging targets based on their hotel's performance against budgeted profit, industry-wide staff turnover and the company's average customer satisfaction scores. The hotel managers will then get up to 30 per cent of their basic salary as a bonus, based on their regional manager's assessment of their performance against these targets. The CEO wants you to use Fitzgerald and Moon's building block model to assess the new system. He is happy with the dimensions of performance but wants your comments on the standards and rewards being applied here.

Appendix 1

Strategic performance report for review

Kolmog Hotels Year to 31 Mar 2017

	East Region $m	West Region $m	North Region $m	South Region $m	Total $m	Total 2016 $m	As % of revenue for 2017
Revenue	235	244	313	193	985	926	
Cost of sales	28	30	37	21	116	110	11.78%
Gross profit	207	214	276	172	869	816	
Staff costs	61	65	78	54	258	245	26.19%
Other operating costs							
hotels	68	70	97	54	289	270	29.34%
head office					158	150	16.04%
Operating profit	78	79	101	64	164	151	16.60%
Financing costs					78	73	7.92%
Profit before tax					86	78	8.73%

			Growth Year on Year
Capital employed	$1132m	$1065m	6.29%
EPS	$1.36	$1.27	7.09%
Share price	$12.34	$11.76	4.93%
ROCE	14.49%	14.18%	

Required:

Write a report to the CEO to:

(i) explain the characteristics that differentiate service businesses from manufacturing ones, using Kolmog to illustrate your points; *(5 marks)*

(ii) evaluate the current strategic performance report and the choice of performance metrics used (Appendix 1); *(8 marks)*

(iii) evaluate the outline balanced scorecard (Table 1) at Kolmog, suggesting suitable improvements; *(12 marks)*

(iv) describe the difficulties in implementing and using the balanced scorecard at Kolmog; *(7 marks)*

(v) explain the purpose of setting targets which are challenging, and evaluate the standards and rewards for the hotel managers' performance reward system as requested by the CEO. *(14 marks)*

Professional marks will be awarded for the format, style and structure of the discussion of your answer. *(4 marks)*

ACCA P5 Advanced Performance Management

21.20 Advanced: Financial and non-financial performance measurement in a service organization. The owners of the *Eatwell Restaurant* have diversified business interests and operate in a wide range of commercial areas. Since buying the restaurant in 2013 they have carefully recorded the data below:

Recorded data for the Eatwell Restaurant (2014–2017)

	2014	2015	2016	2017
Total meals served	3750	5100	6200	6700
Regular customers attending weekly	5	11	15	26
Number of items on offer per day	4	4	7	9
Reported cases of food poisoning	4	5	7	7
Special theme evenings introduced	0	3	9	13
Annual operating hours with no customers	380	307	187	126
Proposals submitted to cater for special events	10	17	29	38
Contracts won to cater for special events	2	5	15	25
Complimentary letters from satisfied customers	0	4	3	6
Average number of customers at peak times	18	23	37	39
Average service delay at peak time (mins)	32	47	15	35
Maximum seating capacity	25	25	40	40
Weekly opening hours	36	36	40	36
Written complaints received	8	12	14	14
Idle time	570	540	465	187
New meals introduced during the year	16	8	27	11
Financial data	£	£	£	£
Average customer spend on wine	3	4	4	7
Total turnover	83000	124500	137000	185000
Turnover from special events	2000	13000	25000	55000
Profit	11600	21400	43700	57200
Value of food wasted in preparation	1700	1900	3600	1450
Total turnover of all restaurants in locality	895000	1234000	980000	1056000

Required:

(a) Assess the overall performance of the business and submit your comments to the owners. They wish to compare the performance of the restaurant with their other business interests and require your comments to be grouped into the key areas of performance such as those described by Fitzgerald and Moon.
(See Learning Note 21.1 on the digital support resources.)

(14 marks)

(b) Identify any additional information that you would consider of assistance in assessing the performance of the *Eatwell Restaurant* in comparison with another restaurant. Give reasons for your selection and explain how they would relate to the key performance area categories used in (a).

(6 marks)

ACCA Advanced Performance Management

21.21 Advanced: Evaluation of a performance management system using the performance pyramid (see Learning Note 21.1). Cod Electrical Motors (Cod) manufactures electrical

motors for some of the 24 different European domestic appliance manufacturers. Their motors are used in appliances such as washing machines and refrigerators. Cod has been in business for over 50 years and has obtained a reputation for producing reliable, low-cost motors.

Cod has recently rewritten its mission statement, which now reads:

'Cod Electrical Motors is committed to providing competitively priced, high quality products, with service exceeding customer expectations, We will add value to our business relationships by investing in product development and highly trained personnel.'

The board has recognized that its existing key performance indicators (KPIs) do not capture the features of the corporate mission. It is worried that the staff see the mission statement as a public relations exercise rather than the communication of Cod's vision.

The monthly board papers contain a simple performance summary which is used as the key performance measurement system at that level.

Example of board papers for November 2017:

Cod Electrical Motors

Key performance indicators for November 2017

	This month	YTD	Comparative
Profit ($m)	2.1	25.6	1.9
Free cash flow ($m)	3.4	17.6	1.6
Return on capital employed (%)	12.4	11.7	11.8

Notes:

(a) The year end is 31 December.
(b) The comparative figure is for the same month in the previous year.
(c) ROCE is an annualized figure.
(d) YTD means year to date.

There are additional performance indicators not available to the board that line management use for a more detailed picture.

Additional performance information:

	Note	2017	2016
	1		
Activity			
No. of orders		2560	2449
No. of deliveries		1588	1660
Staff			
No. of staff (FTE basis)	2	1229	1226
No. of staff training days		2286	1762
No. of vacant posts	3	11	17
Customers			
No. of orders with a complaint	4		
late delivery		26	25
product quality		39	31
customer service		21	24
other		52	43
Preferential supplier status	5	14	12
Production			
New products			
begun in year to date		2	1
in development at month end		4	3
launched in year to date		1	1
Quality			
internal failure costs ($'000)		3480	2766
external failure costs ($'000)		872	693

Notes:

1   Figures are year to date with comparatives from the previous year quoted on the same basis.
2   FTE = Full-time equivalent staff numbers.
3   Post is considered vacant if unfilled for more than four months,
4   Complaints are logged and classified into the four categories given when received.
5   Number of customers where Cod holds preferred supplier status.

Required:

(a) Assess whether the current key performance indicators (KPIs) meet the expected features of a modern performance measurement system.   *(7 marks)*
(b) Explain how the performance pyramid (Lynch and Cross) can help Cod's board to reach its goal of a coherent set of performance measures.   *(6 marks)*
(c) Evaluate the current system using the performance pyramid and apply the performance pyramid to Cod in order to suggest additional KPIs and a set of operational performance measures for Cod.   *(12 marks)*

ACCA P5 Advanced Performance Management

21.22 Advanced: Evaluation of performance management system using perform pyramid and a discussion of myopia, gaming and ossification. Graviton Clothing (Graviton) is a listed manufacturer of clothing with a strong reputation for producing desirable, fashionable products which can attract high selling prices. The company's objective is to maximize shareholder wealth. Graviton's products are sold through its own chain of stores. Graviton's markets demand designs which are in tune with current fashion trends which can alter every few weeks. Therefore, the business's stated aim is to focus production on these changing market trends by maintaining flexibility to adapt to that market demand through close control of all stages of the supply chain (design, manufacture and distribution).

The chief executive officer (CEO) is unhappy with the current performance measurement system at Graviton. The system was created about five years ago by the finance director who has subsequently retired. The aim of the system was to provide the company with a list of measures which would cover performance at the strategic, tactical and operational levels of management. An example of the most recent performance report is given in Table 1.

Table 1: Graviton Performance Dashboard Report for the year to Sep 2017

	2017	2016	2015	Change 2017/2016
Financial				
Revenue ($m)	1723	1570	1413	9.7%
Operating Profit ($m)	320	314	308	1.9%
ROCE	15.8%	15.9%	15.9%	
Design				
Design awards won	3	2	3	50.0%
Manufacture				
Average time to market (days)	22.2	22.3	22.1	−0.4%
Distribution				
Deliveries on time	87.0%	86.8%	87.3%	0.2%

Commentary:

– The revenue growth of the business remains strong in a difficult market.
– Return on capital employed matches the industry average of about 16%.
– Time to market for new designs has been maintained at 22 days by paying overtime to designers in order to meet production schedules.

Recent press reports about Graviton have been mixed, with positive comments about the innovative new designs and much admiration over the growth of sales which the business has achieved. However, there has been some criticism from customers of the durability of Graviton's clothes and from institutional investors that the dividend growth is not strong.

The CEO believes that there are major gaps in the current list of key metrics used by Graviton. She wants an evaluation of the current system and suggestions for improvements. However, she has warned you that the board wants a reasoned argument for each measure to be included in the list in order to avoid overloading each level of management with too much data.

Although rapidly growing, Graviton has had some problems in the last few years which have appeared on recent internal audit reports. It was found that a senior manager at factory site 1 has been delaying invoicing for completed orders in order to ensure that profit targets are met in both the current and the next accounting period. At factory site 2, there has been excellent return on a low capital employed figure although there is a significant adverse variance in the equipment repairs account.

The board is dominated by long-serving executives who are sceptical of change, given Graviton's growth over the past three years. At a recent board meeting, they have shared the CEO's concern about data overload and also have pointed out a variety of problems with the use of performance measures. They presented the CEO with a list of three common problems (myopia, gaming, ossification) and argued that the current good performance of the business did not justify changing the performance measurement system. The CEO needs to know if these problems apply to Graviton and if they do, then what can be done to manage them.

Required:

(a) Evaluate the current performance measurement system using the Performance Pyramid of Lynch and Cross.
          (15 marks)
(b) Assess whether the three problems listed by the board apply to Graviton and suggest appropriate performance management solutions to them.   *(10 marks)*

ACCA P5 Advanced Performance Management

21.23 Advanced: Performance measurement in non-profit organizations.

(a) The absence of the profit measure in not-for-profit (NFP) organizations causes problems for the measurement of their efficiency and effectiveness.

You are required to explain:

(i)   Why the absence of the profit measure should be a cause of the problems referred to.   *(9 marks)*
(ii) How these problems extend to activities within business entities which have a profit motive. Support your answer with examples.   *(4 marks)*

(b) A public health clinic is the subject of a scheme to measure its efficiency and effectiveness. Among a number of factors, the 'quality of care provided' has been included as an aspect of the clinic's service to be measured. Three features of 'quality of care provided' have been listed:

clinic's adherence to appointment times;
patients' ability to contact the clinic and make appointments without difficulty;
the provision of a comprehensive patient health monitoring programme.

You are required to:

(i)   suggest a set of quantitative measures that can be used to identify the effective level of achievement of each of the features listed;   *(9 marks)*
(ii) indicate how these measures could be combined into a single 'quality of care' measure.   *(3 marks)*

CIMA Stage 4 Management Accounting – Control and Audit

IM21.1 Advanced. Management accounting practice has traditionally focused on techniques to assist organizational decision-making and cost control. In concentrating on the internal environment, the management accounting function has been criticized for not addressing the needs of senior management to enable effective strategic planning. In particular, the criticism has focused on inadequate provision of information which analyses the organization's exposure to environmental change and its progress towards the achievement of corporate objectives.

Requirement:

Explain how strategic management accounting can provide information that meets the requirements of senior managers in seeking to realize corporate objectives. *(20 marks)*

CIMA Stage 4 Strategic Management Accountancy and Marketing

IM21.2 Advanced. The new manufacturing environment is characterized by more flexibility, a readiness to meet customers' requirements, smaller batches, continuous improvements and an emphasis on quality.

In such circumstances, traditional management accounting performance measures are, at best, irrelevant and, at worst, misleading.

You are required:

(a) to discuss the above statement, citing specific examples to support or refute the views expressed; *(10 marks)*

(b) to explain in what ways management accountants can adapt the services they provide to the new environment. *(7 marks)*

CIMA Stage 3 Management Accounting Techniques

IM21.3 Advanced. Research on performance measurement in service businesses, reported in *Management Accounting*, found that 'performance measurement often focuses on easily quantifiable aspects such as cost and productivity whilst neglecting other dimensions which are important to competitive success'.

You are required:

(a) to explain what 'other dimensions' you think are important measures of performance; *(8 marks)*

(b) to describe what changes would be required to traditional information systems to deal with these 'other dimensions'. *(9 marks)*

CIMA Stage 3 Management Accounting

IM21.4 Advanced. The 'balanced scorecard' approach aims to provide information to management to assist strategic policy formulation and achievement. It emphasizes the need to provide the user with a set of information which addresses all relevant areas of performance in an objective and unbiased fashion.

Requirements:

(i) Discuss in general terms the main types of information which would be required by a manager to implement this approach to measuring performance.

(ii) Comment on three specific examples of performance measures that could be used in a company in a service industry, for example a firm of consultants. *(10 marks)*

CIMA Stage 4 Strategic Financial Management

IM21.5 Advanced: Design and discussion of key performance indicators for DIY outlets and regional companies. Duit plc has recently acquired Ucando Ltd which is a regional builders' merchants/DIY company with three outlets all within a radius of 40 miles. Duit plc is building up its national coverage of outlets. Duit plc has set up regional companies each with its own board of directors responsible to the main board situated in London.

It is expected that eventually each regional company will have between ten and 20 outlets under its control. A regional company will take over control of the three Ucando Ltd outlets. Each outlet will have its own manager and new ones have just been appointed to the three Ucando Ltd outlets.

The outlets' managers will be allowed to hire and fire whatever staff they need and the introduction of a head count budget is being considered by head office. Each outlet manager is responsible for his own sales policy, pricing, store layout, advertising, the general running of the outlet and the purchasing of goods for resale, subject to the recommendations below. Duit plc's policy is that all outlet managers have to apply to the regional board for all items of capital expenditure greater than £500, while the regional board can sanction up to £100 000 per capital expenditure project.

The outlets will vary in size of operations, and this will determine the number of trade sales representatives employed per outlet. There will be a minimum of one trade sales representative per outlet under the direction of the outlet manager. Each manager and representative will be entitled to a company car.

Outlet sales are made to both retail and trade on either cash or credit terms. Debtor and cash control is the responsibility of regional office. Cash received is banked locally, and immediately credited to the head office account. Credit sales invoices are raised by the outlet with a copy sent to regional office. Within each outlet it is possible to identify the sales origin, e.g. timber yard, sawmill, building supplies, kitchen furniture, etc.

Timber for resale is supplied to an outlet on request from stocks held at regional office or direct from the ports where Duit (Timber Importers) Ltd has further stocks. Duit Kitchens Ltd provides kitchen furniture that the outlets sell. Duit plc also has a small factory making windows, doors and frames that are sold through the outlets. When purchasing other products for resale, the outlet is requested to use suppliers with which head office has negotiated discount buying arrangements. All invoices for outlet purchases and overheads are passed by the respective outlet manager before being paid by regional office. In existing Duit outlets, a perpetual inventory system is used, with a complete physical check once a year.

Information concerning last year's actual results for one of Ucando Ltd's outlets situated at Birport is given below:

Birport DIY outlet
Trading and profit and loss account for year to 31 March

	(£)	(£)
Sales (1)		1 543 000
Less cost of sales		1 095 530
Prime gross margin (29%)		447 470
Less:		
Wages (2)	87 400	
Salaries (3)	45 000	
Depreciation:		
equipment (4)	9 100	
buildings	3 500	
vehicles (three cars)	6 500	
Vehicle running expenses	6 170	
Leasing of delivery lorry	6 510	
Lorry running expenses	3 100	
Energy costs	9 350	
Telephone/stationery	9 180	
Travel and entertaining	3 490	
Commission on sales	7 770	
Bad debts written off	9 440	

(Continued)

	(£)	(£)
Advertising	25160	
Repairs	6000	
Rates, insurance	13420	
Sundry expenses	10580	
Delivery expenses	7400	269070
	Net profit	£178400
	(11.56%)	

Position at 31 March

	(£)
Debtors	100900
Stock	512000

Notes:

1 Sales can be identified by till code: cash/credit, trade/ retail, timber, kitchen furniture, frames, heavy building supplies, light building supplies, sawmill, etc.
2 Workforce distributed as follows: timber yard (3), sawmill (1), sales (7), general duties (1), administration (3).
3 Paid to sales representatives (2), assistant manager, manager.
4 Equipment used in sales area, sawmill, yard.

Requirements:

(a) Describe a cost centre, a profit centre and an investment centre and discuss the problems of and benefits from using them for management accounting purposes.
(7 marks)

(b) Suggest key performance indicators that can be used either individually or jointly by each member of the management team for the regional outlet network, i.e. those in the regional office, the outlets and their departments, in a responsibility reporting system for their evaluation purposes. *(6 marks)*

(c) Justify the key performance indicators that you have suggested in (b) incorporating, where appropriate, reference to whether the individuals or entities are being treated as cost, profit or investment centres. *(6 marks)*

(d) Design a pro forma monthly report without figures that can be used by both the outlet manager for his management and control needs and by the regional board to evaluate the outlet. The report can include two or more sections if you wish. Provide a brief explanation for the format chosen. *(6 marks)*

Note: The manufacturing companies and the importing company report direct to the main board.

ICAEW Management Accounting

IM21.6 Advanced: Financial and non-financial performance measures. Scotia Health Consultants Ltd provides advice to clients in medical, dietary and fitness matters by offering consultation with specialist staff.

The budget information for the year ended 31 May is as follows:

(i) Quantitative data as per Appendix.
(ii) Clients are charged a fee per consultation at the rate of: medical £75; dietary £50 and fitness £50.
(iii) Health foods are recommended and provided only to dietary clients at an average cost to the company of £10 per consultation. Clients are charged for such health foods at cost plus 100 per cent mark-up.
(iv) Each customer enquiry incurs a variable cost of £3, whether or not it is converted into a consultation.
(v) Consultants are each paid a fixed annual salary as follows: medical £40000; dietary £28000; fitness £25000.
(vi) Sundry other fixed cost: £300000.

Actual results for the year to 31 May incorporate the following additional information:

(i)   Quantitative data as per Appendix.
(ii) A reduction of 10 per cent in health food costs to the company per consultation was achieved through a rationalization of the range of foods made available.
(iii) Medical salary costs were altered through dispensing with the services of two full-time consultants and subcontracting outside specialists as required. A total of 1900 consultations were subcontracted to outside specialists who were paid £50 per consultation.
(iv) Fitness costs were increased by £80000 through the hire of equipment to allow sophisticated cardiovascular testing of clients.
(v)   New computer software has been installed to provide detailed records and scheduling of all client enquiries and consultations. This software has an annual operating cost (including depreciation) of £50000.

Required:

(a) Prepare a statement showing the financial results for the year to 31 May in tabular format. This should show:

(i)   the budget and actual gross margin for each type of consultation and for the company;
(ii) the actual net profit for the company;
(iii) the budget and actual margin (£) per consultation for each type of consultation. (Expenditure for each expense heading should be shown in (i) and (ii) as relevant.)
(15 marks)

(b) Suggest ways in which each of the undernoted performance measures (1 to 5) could be used to supplement the financial results calculated in (a). You should include relevant quantitative analysis from the Appendix below for each performance measure:

1. Competitiveness; 2 Flexibility; 3. Resource utilization; 4. Quality; 5. Innovation. *(20 marks)*

Appendix
Statistics relating to the year ended 31 May

	Budget	Actual
Total client enquiries:		
new business	50000	80000
repeat business	30000	20000
Number of client consultations:		
new business	15000	20000
repeat business	12000	10000
Mix of client consultations:		
medical	6000	5500
		(note 1)
dietary	12000	10000
fitness	9000	14500
Number of consultants employed:		
medical	6	4
		(note 1)
dietary	12	12
fitness	9	12
Number of client complaints:	270	600

Note 1: Client consultations includes those carried out by outside specialists. There are now four full-time consultants carrying out the remainder of client consultations.

ACCA Paper 9 Information for Control and Decision Making

IM21.7 Advanced: Critical success factors. The directors of the Healthy Eating Group (HEG), a successful restaurant chain that commenced trading several years ago, have decided to enter the sandwich market in Homeland, its country of operation. It has set up a separate operation under the name of Healthy Sandwiches Co. (HSC). A management team for HSC has been recruited via a recruitment consultancy that specializes in food sector appointments. Homeland has very high unemployment and the vast majority of its workforce has no experience in a food manufacturing environment. HSC will commence trading on 1 January.

The following information is available:

1 HSC has agreed to make and supply sandwiches to agreed recipes for the Superior Food Group (SFG), which owns a chain of supermarkets in all towns and cities within Homeland. SFG insists that it selects the suppliers of the ingredients that are used in making the sandwiches it sells and therefore HSC would be unable to reduce the costs of the ingredients used in the sandwiches. HSC will be the sole supplier for SFG.

2 The number of sandwiches sold per year in Homeland is 625 million. SFG has a market share of 4 per cent.

3 The average selling price of all sandwiches sold by SFG is $2.40. SFG wishes to make a mark-up of $33^1/3$ per cent on all sandwiches sold. 90 per cent of all sandwiches sold by SFG are sold before 2 pm each day. The majority of the remaining 10 per cent are sold after 8 pm. It is the intention that all sandwiches are sold on the day that they are delivered into SFG's supermarkets.

4 The finance director of HSC has estimated that the average cost of ingredients per sandwich is $0.70. All sandwiches are made by hand.

5 Packaging and labelling costs amount to $0.15 per sandwich.

6 Fixed overheads have been estimated to amount to $5 401 000 per annum. Note that fixed overheads include all wages and salaries costs as all employees are subject to fixed term employment contracts.

7 Distribution costs are expected to amount to 8 per cent of HSC's revenue.

8 The finance director of HSC has stated that he believes the target sales margin of 32 per cent can be achieved, although he is concerned about the effect that an increase in the cost of all ingredients would have on the forecast profits (assuming that all other revenue/cost data remain unchanged).

9 The existing management information system of HEG was purchased at the time that HEG commenced trading. The directors are now considering investing in an enterprise resource planning system (ERPS).

Required:

(a) Using only the above information, show how the finance director of HSC reached his conclusion regarding the expected sales margin and also state whether he was correct to be concerned about an increase in the price of ingredients. *(5 marks)*

(b) Explain FIVE critical success factors to the performance of HSC on which the directors must focus if HSC is to achieve success in its marketplace. *(10 marks)*

(c) Explain how the introduction of an ERPS could impact on the role of management accountants. *(5 marks)*

(Total 20 marks)

ACCA P5 Performance Management

22

STRATEGIC COST MANAGEMENT AND VALUE CREATION

LEARNING OBJECTIVES After studying this chapter, you should be able to:

- distinguish between the features of a traditional management accounting control system and cost management;

- describe the typical pattern of cost commitment and cost incurrence during the three stages of a product's life cycle;

- describe the target costing approach to cost management;

- distinguish between target costing and kaizen costing;

- describe activity-based cost management;

- distinguish between value-added and non-value-added activities;

- explain the role of benchmarking and business process engineering within the cost management framework;

- outline the main features of a just-in-time philosophy.

- explain the purpose of a cost of quality report;

- describe how value chain analysis can be used to increase customer satisfaction and manage costs more effectively.

In Chapters 16–18, the major features of traditional management accounting control systems and the mechanisms that can be used to control costs were described. The focus was on comparing actual results against a preset standard (typically the budget), identifying and analysing variances and taking remedial action to ensure that future outcomes conform with budgeted outcomes. Traditional cost control systems tend to be based on the preservation of the status quo and the ways of performing existing activities are not reviewed. The emphasis is on cost containment rather than cost reduction.

Strategic cost management and value creation seeks to have a more profound effect on reducing an organization's costs and to provide a competitive advantage. It aims to provide a competitive advantage by creating better or equivalent customer satisfaction at a lower cost than that offered by competitors. In particular, strategic cost management is a future oriented approach that focuses on cost reduction and continuous improvement and changes in the ways that activities and processes are performed, rather than just focusing on cost containment. Indeed, the term cost reduction could be used instead of cost management but the former is an evocative term. Therefore cost management is preferred. Whereas traditional cost control systems are routinely applied on a continuous basis, cost management tends to be applied on an ad hoc basis when an opportunity for cost reduction is identified. Also, many of the approaches that are incorporated within the area of cost management do not necessarily involve the use of accounting techniques. In contrast, cost control relies heavily on accounting techniques.

Strategic cost management consists of those actions that are taken by managers to reduce costs, some of which are prioritized on the basis of information extracted from the accounting system. Other actions, however, are undertaken without the use of accounting information. They involve process improvements, where an opportunity has been identified to perform processes more effectively and efficiently, and which have obvious cost reduction outcomes and also the potential to increase customer satisfaction. It is important that you are aware of all the approaches that can be used to reduce costs even if these methods do not rely mainly on accounting information. You should also note that although cost management seeks to reduce costs, it should not be at the expense of customer satisfaction.

Ideally, cost management should also incorporate value creation where the aims should be not only to take actions that will reduce costs but also to enhance customer satisfaction and value. Customer value may be increased by either reducing the cost without sacrificing product/service functionality or by increasing functionality without increasing cost. Reducing cost is important because it enables a company to remain competitive by reducing or maintaining selling prices and thus increasing customer satisfaction and value. Increasing customer satisfaction is generally associated with an increase in sales revenues and profits which should ultimately be reflected in creating additional shareholder value.

LIFE CYCLE COST MANAGEMENT

Identifying the costs incurred during the different stages of a product's life cycle provides an insight into understanding and managing the total costs incurred throughout its life cycle. In particular, life cycle cost management helps management to understand the cost consequences of developing and making a product and to identify areas in which cost reduction efforts are likely to be most effective.

Figure 22.1 illustrates a typical pattern of cost commitment and cost incurrence during the three stages of a product's life cycle – the planning and design stage, the manufacturing stage and the service and abandonment stage. Committed or locked-in costs are those costs that have not been incurred but that will be incurred in the future on the basis of decisions that have already been made. At this stage, costs become committed and broadly determine the future costs that will be incurred during the manufacturing stage.

You will see from Figure 22.1 that approximately 80 per cent of a product's costs are *committed* during the planning and design stage. At this stage, product designers determine the product's design and

ADVANCED READING

FIGURE 22.1

Product life cycle phases: relationship between costs committed and costs incurred

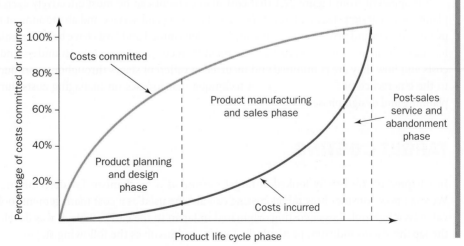

EVA$^{(TM)}$ target costing

Taylor, Woods and Cheng Ge Fang (2014) reported on how one UK company moved its target costing system away from profit targets and focused it on product-level economic value added (EVA$^{(TM)}$) targets. The company, which used the pseudonym Electronics for confidentiality purposes, had been using target costing since the 1990s. Electronics deducted a target EVA$^{(TM)}$ instead of a target profit from the selling price to determine a target cost, thus ensuring that the cost of capital is considered in cost-savings programmes. The incorporation of EVA$^{(TM)}$-based targets into target costing may require a larger reduction in product cost than required under traditional accounting-based profit metrics. At Electronics the reduction needed to meet EVA$^{(TM)}$ targets was 46 per cent. The expected selling price under EVA$^{(TM)}$ target costing did not change and was still determined by customer value so the change did not affect the firm's focus on customers.

Closing the gap between current and target cost involves evaluating the impact of reducing and substituting product components as well as changing assembly methods. The use of EVA$^{(TM)}$ extended the range of cost-reduction opportunities to include capital costs. Alternatives that required more capital were evaluated carefully in order to assess their impact on EVA$^{(TM)}$. At Electronics, EVA$^{(TM)}$-based measures changed how people behaved by, for example, motivating engineers to seek ways of reducing the capital base, since such savings enabled the target EVA$^{(TM)}$ to be achieved. Thus, more attention was focused on capital costs.

Questions

1 What practical difficulties might arise from determining the target cost using EVA$^{(TM)}$ target costing?

2 Does the use of conventional (non-EVA$^{(TM)}$) target costing mean that the cost of capital is ignored?

Reference

Taylor, G, Woods, M. and Cheng Ge Fang (2014) 'Electronics: A case study of economic value added in target costing', *Financial Management*, April, 55–6.

the production process. In contrast, the majority of costs are *incurred* at the manufacturing stage, but they have already become locked in at the planning and design stage and are difficult to alter. During the service and abandonment stage further costs are incurred relating to customer support and the need for a company to discharge its environmental and sustainability responsibilities. For example, Microsoft has provided support for its Windows operating systems after the sales have ceased and mining companies have to rehabilitate the damage they have done to the environment after mining has ceased. Many of these costs also become committed at the planning and design stage.

It is apparent from Figure 22.1 that cost management can be most effectively exercised during the planning and design stage and not at the manufacturing and service and abandonment stages when the product design and processes have already been determined and costs have been committed. At this latter stage, the focus is more on cost containment than cost management. An understanding of life cycle costs and how they are committed and incurred at different stages throughout a product's life cycle led to the emergence of target costing, a technique that focuses on managing costs during a product's planning and design phase.

TARGET COSTING

In Chapter 10, we briefly looked at target costing as a mechanism for determining selling prices. We shall now consider how target costing can also be used as a cost management tool and customer value creation tool. Target costing originated in Japan in the early 1970s. It was developed mainly by the Japanese auto industry, particularly Toyota, and involves the following stages:

Stage 1: Determine the target price that customers will be prepared to pay for the product.

Stage 2: Deduct a target profit margin from the target price to determine the target cost.

Stage 3: Estimate the actual cost of the product.

Stage 4: If estimated actual cost exceeds the target cost investigate ways of driving down the actual cost to the target cost.

The first stage requires market research to determine the *customers' perceived value* of the product, based on its functions and its attributes (i.e. its functionality), its differentiation value relative to competing products and the price of competing products. This process results in the determination of a target selling price. The target profit margin depends on the planned return on investment for the organization as a whole and profit as a percentage of sales. This is then decomposed into a target profit for each product, which is subsequently deducted from the target price to give the target cost. The target cost is compared with the predicted actual cost. If the predicted actual cost is above the target cost, intensive efforts are made to close the gap so that the predicted cost equals the target cost. Instead of designing the product and determining how much it costs, target costing reverses the procedure and determines the target cost for a product and steps are taken to design a product that does not exceed the target cost.

A major feature of target costing is that a team approach is adopted to achieve the target cost. The team members include designers, engineers, purchasing, manufacturing, marketing and management accounting personnel. Their aim is to achieve the target cost specified for the product at the prescribed level of functionality and quality. The discipline of a team approach ensures that no particular group is able to impose their functional preferences. For example, design engineers pursuing their flair for design may design into products features that increase a product's costs but which customers do not value, or features that require the use of unique parts when alternative designs requiring standardized parts may meet customer requirements. Similarly, without a multi-functional team approach, a marketing emphasis might result in the introduction of product features that customers find attractive, but not essential, and so they are not prepared to pay to have them included in the product's design. Therefore, the aim during the product design process is to eliminate product functions that add cost but that do not increase the market price.

In some organizations, representatives from the suppliers are included in the design team in order to obtain their expertise. They can often provide suggestions of design changes that will enable standard parts to replace custom-designed parts, thus reducing the product's cost. Alternatively, suppliers have the expertise to suggest alternative parts or components at the lowest cost for a given level of functionality.

The major advantage of adopting target costing is that it is deployed during a product's design and planning stage so that it can have a maximum impact in determining the level of the locked-in costs. It is an iterative process with the design team, which ideally should result in the design team continuing with its product and process design attempts until it finds designs that give an expected cost that is equal or less than the target cost. If the target cost cannot be attained then the product should not be launched. Design teams should not be allowed to achieve target costs by eliminating desirable product functions. Thus, the aim is to design a product with an expected cost that does not exceed target cost and that also meets the target level of functionality. Design teams use reverse engineering, value analysis and process improvements to achieve the target cost.

Reverse engineering

Reverse engineering (also known as **tear-down analysis**) involves examining a competitor's product in order to identify opportunities for product improvement and/or cost reduction. The competitor's product is dismantled to identify its functionality and design and to provide insights about the processes that are used and the cost to make the product. The aim is to benchmark provisional product designs with the designs of competitors and to incorporate any observed relative advantages of the competitor's approach to product design.

Value analysis

Value analysis (also known as **value engineering**) is a systematic interdisciplinary examination of factors affecting the cost of a product or service in order to devise means of achieving the specified purpose at the required standard of quality and reliability at the target cost. The aim of value analysis is to achieve the assigned target cost by (i) identifying improved product designs that reduce the product's cost without sacrificing functionality and/or (ii) eliminating unnecessary functions that increase the product's costs and for which customers are not prepared to pay extra. A value analysis exercise might involve considering a series of questions such as: What is the function of the part or material? Can it be simplified? Is it necessary? Are all the features necessary? Can the parts be obtained or made at a lower cost? Can the use of material components be standardized to facilitate longer production runs if manufactured internally or to provide bulk buying benefits if purchased?

Value analysis requires the use of **functional analysis**. This process involves decomposing the product into its many elements or attributes. For example, in the case of automobiles, functions might consist of style, comfort, operability, reliability, quality, attractiveness and many others (Kato, 1993). A price, or value, for each element is determined that reflects the amount the customer is prepared to pay. To obtain this information, companies normally conduct surveys and interviews with customers. The cost of each function of a product is compared with the benefits perceived by the customers. If the cost of the function exceeds the benefit to the customer, then the function should be eliminated, modified to reduce its cost or enhanced in terms of its perceived value so that its value exceeds the cost. Also by focusing on the product's functions, the design team will often consider components that perform the same function in other products, thus increasing the possibility of using standard components and reducing costs. It should be noted that the focus is on value to the customer rather than just cost reduction. Therefore value may be increased by either reducing the cost without sacrificing functionality or by increasing functionality without increasing cost.

Process improvements

Both reverse engineering and value analysis focus on product design to achieve cost reductions. The business processes that will be used to produce and market the product are also potential sources of cost reduction. Therefore it is important that processes within the entire value chain (a description of value chain analysis is provided later in the chapter) are intensively studied with a view to eliminating non-value-added activities or increasing their efficiency in order to achieve the needed cost reductions.

The need for accurate cost measurement systems

It is important that target costing is supported by an accurate cost system. In particular, cost drivers should be established that are the significant determinants of the costs of the activities so that cause-and-effect allocations are used. Arbitrary cost allocations should be avoided. If arbitrary cost allocations are used, the allocation base will not be a significant determinant of cost. Let us assume that an arbitrary allocation base, say, direct labour hours, is used to allocate support costs to products. To reduce the projected cost towards the target cost, the target costing team will be motivated to focus on reducing direct labour hours. Why? Because this will result in a smaller proportion of the support costs being assigned to the product. However, the support costs incurred by the organization will not be reduced because there is no cause-and-effect relationship between direct labour hours and the resulting costs. Therefore, the target costing exercise will merely result in a reduction in the costs that are allocated to the product but organizational costs will not be reduced. In contrast, if cause-and-effect allocation bases (i.e. cost drivers) are established, reductions in cost driver usage should be followed by a reduction in organizational support costs.

Therefore it is very important that cost systems use cost drivers that are the determinants of costs so that they will motivate designers to take actions that will reduce organizational costs. Decisions taken at the design stage lead to the committed usage of cost drivers that can be difficult to change in the future.

Surveys of practice

Given that target costing was developed in Japan, it is not surprising that the survey evidence suggests greater usage in Japan. A study of Tani *et al.* (1994) reported that 61 per cent of their sample of 180 listed Japanese manufacturing firms used some form of target costing. In the USA, Ernst & Young and the Institute of Management Accountants (IMA) (2003) reported that 26 per cent of IMA member firms employed target costing. A survey by Dekker and Smidt (2003) of Dutch firms listed at the Amsterdam Stock Exchange on the adoption and use of practices that resemble the Japanese target costing concept reported that 19 out of 32 manufacturing firms claimed to use these practices, although they used different names for them. In Sweden, a study by Ax *et al.* (2008) reported a 25 per cent usage rate. In a comparative study of the implementation of target costing in UK, Australian and New Zealand companies Yazdifar and Askarany (2012) reported similar adoption rates for each country with approximately 18 per cent of companies adopting target costing.

In a review of the literature on the development of target costing, Burrows and Chenhall (2012) point out that the target costing literature has focused on manufacturing organizations and is best suited to new products that are marketed in competitive environments having short product life cycles. However, the study by Yazdifar and Askarany (2012) reported similar usage of target costing by manufacturing and service organizations. In contrast, the survey by Dekker and Smidt (2003) reported that none of the 11 responding non-manufacturing organizations used target costing. However, they do not rule out the possibility that these organizations may have had difficulty relating the target costing definition in the survey to their situation and that different but related methods might be used in these industries in product and service development.

An illustration of target costing

Example 22.1 is used to illustrate the target costing process. You will note from reading the information presented in this example that the projected cost of the product is £700 compared with a target cost of £560. To achieve the target cost, the company establishes a project team to undertake an intense target costing exercise. Example 22.1 indicates that the end result of the target costing exercise is a projected cost of £555 that is marginally below the target cost of £560. Let us now look at how the company has achieved the target cost and also how the costs shown in Example 22.1 have been derived.

In response to the need to reduce the projected cost, the project team starts by purchasing similar types of camcorder from its main competitors and undertaking reverse engineering. This process involves dismantling the camcorders to provide insights into potential design improvements for the new camcorder that will be launched. Reverse engineering is undertaken with the project team working closely with the design engineers. Their objective is to identify new designs that will accomplish the same functions at a lower cost and also to eliminate any functions that are deemed to be unnecessary. This process results in a simplified design, the reduction in the number of parts and the replacement of some customized parts with standard parts. The outcome of the reverse engineering and value analysis activities is a significant reduction in the projected direct materials, labour and rework costs, but the revised cost estimates still indicate that the projected cost exceeds the target cost.

Next the team engages in functional analysis. It identifies the different elements, functions and attributes of the camcorder and potential customers are interviewed to ascertain the values that they place on each of the functions. This process indicates that several functions that have been included in the prototype are not valued by customers. The team therefore decides to eliminate these functions. The functional analysis results in further cost reductions being made, principally in the areas of materials and direct labour assembly costs but the revised cost estimates still indicate that the target cost has not been attained.

The team now turns its attention to redesigning the production and support processes. It decides to redesign the ordering and receiving process by reducing the number of suppliers and working closely with a smaller number of suppliers. The suppliers are prepared to enter into contractual arrangements whereby they are periodically given a predetermined production schedule and in return they will

EXAMPLE 22.1

The Digital Electronics Company manufactures high-quality cameras and video equipment. It is in the process of introducing a 'top of the range' combined camcorder and camera that incorporates today's most advanced technologies. The company has undertaken market research to ascertain customers' perceived value of the product, based on its special features and a comparison with competitors' products. The results of the survey, and a comparison of the new product with competitors' products and market prices, have been used to establish a target selling price and projected lifetime volume. In addition, cost estimates have been prepared based on the proposed product specification. The company has set a target profit margin of 30 per cent on the proposed selling price and this has been deducted from the target selling price to determine the target cost. The following is a summary of the information that has been presented to management:

Projected lifetime sales volume	300 000 units
Target selling price	£800
Target profit margin (30 per cent of selling price)	£240
Target cost (£800 – £240)	£560
Projected cost	£700

The excess of the projected cost over the target cost results in an intensive target costing exercise. After completing the target costing exercise, the projected cost is £555, which is marginally below the target cost of £560. The analysis of the projected cost before and after the target costing exercise is as follows:

	Before		After	
	(£)	(£)	(£)	(£)
Manufacturing cost				
Direct material (bought in parts)	390		325	
Direct labour	100		80	
Direct machining costs	20		20	
Ordering and receiving	8		2	
Quality assurance	60		50	
Rework	15		6	
Engineering and design	10	603	8	491
Non-manufacturing costs				
Marketing	40		25	
Distribution	30		20	
After-sales service and warranty costs	27	97	19	64
Total cost		700		555

inspect the shipments and guarantee quality prior to delivery. In addition, the marketing, distribution and customer after-sales services relating to the product are subject to an intensive review, and process improvements are made that result in further reductions in costs that are attributable to the camcorder. The projected cost after undertaking all of the above activities is £555 compared with the target cost of £560 and at this point the target costing exercise is concluded.

Having described the target costing approach that the Digital Electronics Company has used let us now turn our attention to the derivation of the projected costs shown in Example 22.1. The projected cost for direct materials prior to the target costing exercise is £390 but reverse engineering and the functional analysis have resulted in a reduction in the number of parts that are required to manufacture the camcorder. The elimination of most of the unique parts, and the use of standard parts that the company currently purchases in large volumes, also provides scope for further cost savings. The outcome of the redesign process is a direct material cost of £325.

The simplified product design enables the assembly time to be reduced thus resulting in the reduction of direct labour costs from £100 to £80. The direct machine costs relate to machinery that will be used exclusively for the production of the new product. The estimated cost of acquiring, maintaining and operating the machinery throughout the product's life cycle is £6 million. This is divided by the projected lifetime sales volume of the camera (300 000 units) giving a unit cost of £20. However, it has not been possible to reduce the unit cost because the machinery costs are committed, and fixed, and the target costing exercise has not resulted in a change in the predicted lifetime volume.

Prior to the target costing exercise 80 separate parts were included in the product specification. The estimated number of orders placed for each part throughout the product's life cycle is 150 and the predicted cost per order for the order and receiving activity is £200. Therefore the estimated lifetime costs are £2.4 million (80 parts × 150 orders × £200 per order) giving a unit cost of £8 (£2.4 million/300 000 units). The simplified design and the parts standardization arising from the functional analysis and the value engineering activities have enabled the number of parts to be reduced to 40. The redesign of the ordering and receiving process has also enabled the number of orders and the ordering cost to be reduced (the former from 150 to 100 and the latter from £200 to £150 per order). Thus the projected lifetime ordering and receiving costs after the target costing exercise are £600 000 (40 parts × 100 orders × £150 per order) giving a revised unit cost of £2 (£600 000/300 000 units).

Quality assurance involves inspecting and testing the camcorders. Prior to the target costing exercise the projected cost was £60 (12 hours at £5 per hour) but the simplified design means that the camcorder will be easier to test resulting in revised cost of £50 (10 hours at £5 per hour). Rework costs of £15 represent the average rework costs per camcorder. Past experience with manufacturing similar products suggests that 10 per cent of the output will require rework. Applying this rate to the estimated total lifetime volume of 300 000 camcorders results in 30 000 camcorders requiring rework at an estimated average cost of £150 per reworked camcorder. The total lifetime rework cost is therefore predicted to be £4.5 million (30 000 × £150) giving an average cost per unit of good output of £15 (£4.5 million/300 000). Because of the simplified product design the rework rate and the average rework cost will be reduced. The predicted rework rate is now 5 per cent and the average rework cost will be reduced from £150 to £120. Thus, the revised estimate of the total lifetime cost is £1.8 million (15 000 reworked units at £120 per unit) and the projected unit cost is £6 (£1.8 million/300 000 units).

The predicted total lifetime engineering and design costs and other product sustaining costs are predicted to be £3 million giving a unit cost of £10. The simplified design and reduced number of parts enables the lifetime cost to be reduced by 20 per cent, to £2.4 million, and the unit cost to £8. The planned process improvements have also enabled the predicted marketing, distribution and after-sales service costs to be reduced. In addition, the simplified product design and the use of fewer parts has contributed to the reduction in the after-sales warranty costs. However, to keep our example brief the derivation of the non-manufacturing costs will not be presented, other than to note that the company uses an activity-based costing system. All costs are assigned using cost drivers that are based on established cause-and-effect relationships.

KAIZEN COSTING

In addition to target costing, kaizen costing is widely used by Japanese organizations as a mechanism for reducing and managing costs. Kaizen is the Japanese term for making continuous improvements to processes through small incremental amounts, rather than through major innovations. The major difference between target and kaizen costing is that target costing is normally applied until the design is finalized and then replaced by kaizen costing, which is applied during the manufacturing stage of the product life cycle. With target costing, the focus is on the product, and cost reductions are achieved primarily through product design. In contrast, kaizen costing focuses on the production processes and cost reductions are derived primarily through the increased efficiency of the production process.

Therefore the potential cost reductions are smaller with kaizen costing because the products are already in the manufacturing stage of their life cycles and a significant proportion of the costs will have become locked in.

The aim of kaizen costing is to reduce the cost of components and products by a pre-specified amount. Monden and Hamada (1991) describe the application of kaizen costing in a Japanese automobile plant. Each plant is assigned a target cost reduction ratio and this is applied to the previous year's actual costs to determine the target cost reduction. Kaizen costing relies heavily on employee empowerment. They are assumed to have superior knowledge about how to improve processes because they are closest to the manufacturing processes and customers and are likely to have greater insights into how costs can be reduced. Thus, a major feature of kaizen costing is that workers are given the responsibility to improve processes and reduce costs. Unlike target costing, it is not accompanied by a set of techniques or procedures that are automatically applied to achieve the cost reductions.

The focus on continuous improvement means that once the goals have been attained they not only become permanent but are replaced by new and more ambitious goals. Although the targeted improvements may be small their gradual cumulative improvements over the longer-term can be significant.

ACTIVITY-BASED MANAGEMENT

The early adopters of activity-based costing (ABC) used it to produce more accurate product (or service) costs but it soon became apparent to the users that it could be extended beyond purely product costing to a range of budgeting (see activity-based budgeting in Chapter 15) and cost management applications. The terms activity-based management (ABM) or activity-based cost management (ABCM) are used to describe the cost management applications of ABC. To implement an ABM system, only the first three of the four stages described in Chapter 11 for designing an activity-based product costing system are required. They are:

1 identifying the major activities that take place in an organization (i.e. activity analysis);

2 assigning costs to cost pools/cost centres for each activity;

3 determining the cost driver for each major activity.

Thus, firms can omit the final stage of assigning activity costs to products and adopt ABC solely for cost management without activity-based product costing. Where a firm does use an activity-based system for both cost management and product costing, it may choose to create a large number of activity cost pools to monitor the costs of the many different activities but aggregate the pools so that a smaller number is used for product costing purposes.

ABM views the business as a set of linked activities that ultimately add value to the customer. It focuses on managing the business on the basis of the activities that make up the organization. ABM is based on the premise that every activity consumes costs. Therefore, by managing activities, costs will be managed in the long term. Managing activities requires an understanding of what factors cause activities to be performed and what causes activity costs to change. The goal of ABM is to enable customer needs to be satisfied while making fewer demands on organizational resources (i.e. cost reduction). Besides providing information on what activities are performed, ABM provides information on the cost of activities, why the activities are undertaken, and how well they are performed.

Traditional budget and control reports analyse costs by types of expense for each responsibility centre. In contrast, ABM analyses costs by activities and thus provides management with information on why costs are incurred and the output from the activity (in terms of cost drivers). Exhibit 22.1 illustrates the difference between the conventional analysis and the activity-based analysis in respect of customer order processing a business process. A business process consists of a collection of activities that are linked together in a coordinated manner to achieve a specified objective. The major differences are that the ABM approach reports by *business processes* and *activities* whereas the traditional analysis is by *departments*.

Another distinguishing feature of ABM reporting is that it often reports information on processes and activities that cross departmental boundaries. For example, different production departments and

EXHIBIT 22.1 Customer order processing activity

	(£000s)
Traditional analysis	
Salaries	320
Stationery	40
Travel	140
Telephone	40
Depreciation of equipment	40
	580
ABM analysis	
Preparing quotations	120
Receiving customer orders	190
Assessing the creditworthiness of customers	100
Expediting	80
Resolving customer problems	90
	580

the distribution department might undertake customer processing activities. They may resolve customer problems by expediting late deliveries. The finance department may assess customer credit worthiness and the remaining customer processing activities might be undertaken by the customer service department. Therefore the total cost of the customer processing activity could be considerably in excess of the costs that are assigned to the customer service department. However, to simplify the presentation it is assumed in Exhibit 22.1 that the departmental and activity costs are identical but if the cost of the customer order processing activity was found to be, say, three times the amount assigned to the customer service department, this would be important information because it may change the way in which the managers view the activity. For example, the managers may give more attention to reducing the costs of the customer processing activity.

It is apparent from an examination of Exhibit 22.1 that the ABM approach provides more meaningful information. It gives more visibility to the cost of undertaking the activities that make up the organization and may raise issues for management action that are not highlighted by the traditional analysis. For example, why is £90 000 spent on resolving customer problems? Attention directing information such as this is important for managing the cost of the activities.

Knowing costs by activities is a catalyst that eventually triggers the action necessary to become competitive. Consider a situation in which sales persons, as a result of costing activities, are informed that it costs £50 to process a customer's order. They therefore become aware that it is questionable to pursue orders with a low sales value. By eliminating many small orders, and concentrating on larger value orders, the demand for customer processing activities should decrease, and future spending on this activity should be reduced.

Prior to the introduction of ABM, most organizations have been unaware of the cost of undertaking the activities that make up the organization. Knowing the cost of activities enables those activities with the highest cost to be highlighted so that they can be prioritized for detailed studies to ascertain whether they can be eliminated or performed more efficiently. In a study of a UK-based multinational bank Soin, Seal and Cullen (2002) reported that ABM was used to establish which activities were expensive and why they were being used, and to ascertain whether increased volumes would or would not increase costs. No attempt was made to link costs to products or customers.

Value-added and non-value-added activities

To identify and prioritize the potential for cost reduction many organizations have found it useful to classify activities as either value added or non-value added. Definitions of what constitutes value-added and non-value-added activities vary. A common definition is that a value-added activity is an activity

REAL WORLD
VIEWS 22.2

The impact of ABC at Insteel industries

Insteel Industries decided to implement ABM at the Andrews, South Carolina, plant. The ABM team analysed operations and identified 12 business processes involving a total of 146 activities. The ABM study revealed that the 20 most expensive activities accounted for 87 per cent of Andrew's total physical and people resource of $21.4 million. Activities were further classified into value added and non-value added. Nearly $4.9 million was spent on non-value-added activities such as reactive maintenance, dealing with scrap, moving materials, reworking products and managing customer complaints. Those activities, within the 20 most expensive, were targeted for cost reduction and process improvement.

The company estimates that within a year of the first ABM study, $1.8 million had been saved in quality costs, mainly through a reduction of scrap and reactive maintenance costs. Freight costs were reduced $555 000 in a year in the Andrews plant alone. Non-value-added activities were reduced from 22 per cent of activity costs to 17 per cent.

The ABM study prompted Insteel to start tracking freight cost per pound shipped. This directed attention to ways in which these costs could be reduced. By changing the layout of boxes within each truck, the Andrews plant was able to ship 7400 pounds more per truckload. This represented a 20 per cent reduction in freight expense. When Insteel realized how much they were actually incurring in quality costs, the team probed more deeply into understanding better what was causing the quality costs to be incurred and for suggesting steps to reduce them. Insteel realized that certain foreign suppliers of rods were lower in price but supplied poorer quality rods that caused breakdowns in Insteel's manufacturing process. The lower price of those suppliers did not compensate for the quality costs. Insteel switched to higher quality rod suppliers. Insteel also realized that smaller diameter wire products were more likely to break and disrupt the manufacturing process. Insteel migrated its product mix to more large diameter wire products. Such initiatives led to reduction in quality costs from $6.7 million to $4.9 million in the following year. It is hard to estimate how much of these savings would have been realized had Insteel not conducted an ABM analysis. The activity analysis gave it an appreciation of the scope and quantified the magnitude of the improvement potential, thereby allowing it to prioritize among various process improvement possibilities. Clearly ABM served as a focusing device by providing cost data by activities, directing attention to the top 20 activities, and by labelling some of them as non-value-added activities.

Question

1 How might activity costs for Insteel differ from departmental costs?

Reference
Narayanan, V.G and Sarkar, R.G. (2002) 'The impact of activity-based costing on managerial decisions at Intel Industries: a field study', *Journal of Economics and Management Strategy*, 11(2), 257–288.

that customers perceive as adding usefulness or value to the product or service they purchase. For example, painting a car would be a value-added activity in an organization that manufactures cars. Other definitions are an activity that is being performed as efficiently as possible or an activity that supports the primary objective of producing outputs.

In contrast, a non-value-added activity is an activity where there is an opportunity for cost reduction without reducing the product's service potential to the customer. Examples of non-value-added activities include inspecting, storing and moving raw materials and performing set-ups. The cost of these activities can be reduced without reducing the value of the products to the customers. Non-value-added activities are essentially those activities that customers should not be expected to pay for. Reporting the cost of non-value-added activities draws management's attention to the vast amount of waste that has been tolerated by the organization. This should prioritize those activities with the greatest potential for cost reduction by eliminating or carrying them out more effectively. For example, the activity of inspecting incoming materials is necessary only because of the poor quality of deliveries by suppliers.

By establishing strong relationships with nominated suppliers who can guarantee high-quality deliveries, incoming inspections can be eventually eliminated. Activities can be undertaken more effectively at a lower cost by finding ways of reducing set-up times, material movements and inventory levels and also improving production flows. Taking action to reduce or eliminate non-value-added activities is given top priority because by doing so the organization permanently reduces the cost it incurs without reducing the value of the product to the customer.

Kaplan and Cooper (1998) have criticized the classification of activities by simplistic value-added and non-value-added categories because of the difficulty of clearly defining them and the demotivating impact when employees are informed that they are performing non-value-added activities. They discuss whether the activity of setting up a machine is value added or non-value-added. One view is that customers do not perceive performing set-ups as adding usefulness to products and the activity is non-value added. However, without set-ups a plant can produce only single products. If customers value customized or diverse products, changing machine settings to produce different product varieties creates value for customers.

To overcome the above problems, Kaplan and Cooper advocate that instead of using a value-added/non-value-added classification, the following simple five-point scale should be used to summarize an ABC project team's initial judgement about the current efficiency of an activity:

1 highly efficient, with little (less than 5 per cent) apparent opportunity for improvement;

2 modestly efficient, some (5–15 per cent) opportunity for improvement;

3 average efficiency, good opportunities (15–25 per cent) for improvement;

4 inefficient, major opportunities (25–50 per cent) for improvement;

5 highly inefficient, perhaps should not be done at all such as replacing defective products; 50–100 per cent opportunity for improvement.

By identifying the cost of activities that make up their organization and classifying them into the above five categories, opportunities for cost reduction can be prioritized without giving rise to motivational issues. Cost reduction can be achieved by either eliminating the activities, performing them more efficiently with fewer organizational resources or redesigning them so that they are performed in an entirely different and more cost efficient way. We shall consider how activities can be redesigned later in the chapter.

ABM cost audits

The routine tracking of costs is unnecessary for providing information for ABM. Instead, a cost audit can be undertaken at periodic intervals when the need arises for activity cost analysis. Indeed, activity cost analysis need not be applied throughout the organization. The focus can be on activities within selected business processes such as distribution/logistics, materials procurement and various production processes in manufacturing organizations or non-manufacturing processes such as the accounts payable and customer ordering. ABM has also been widely applied to activities within business processes in the financial sector (e.g. credit card approvals, loan applications in banks and life insurance policy applications in insurance companies).

ABM as behavioural orientated cost systems

Our discussion so far has related to the application of ABM during the manufacturing or service phase of a product's life cycle. However, some organizations have used their activity-based costing systems to influence future costs at the design stage within the target costing process. In particular, they have opted for behaviourally oriented cost systems that are less accurate than costing technology allows in order to induce desired behavioural responses (Merchant and Shields, 1993). For example, the Portable Instruments Division of Tektronix, Inc., in the USA, assigned material support expenses using a single cost driver – number of part numbers. The company wanted to encourage design engineers to focus their attention on reducing the number of part numbers, parts and suppliers in future generations of products. Product timeliness was seen as a critical success factor and this was facilitated by designs that simplified parts procurement and production processes. The cost system motivated engineers to design simpler products requiring less development time because they had fewer parts and part numbers. The cost system designers knew that most of the material support expenses were not incurred in direct proportion to the single cost driver chosen, but the simplified and imprecise cost system focused attention on factors deemed to be most critical to the division's future success.

BENCHMARKING

In order to identify the best way of performing activities and business processes, organizations are turning their attention to benchmarking, which involves comparing key activities or processes with best practices found within and outside the organization. External benchmarking attempts to identify a process, such as customer order processing, that needs to be improved and finding a non-rival organization in which similar processes exist and that is considered to represent world-class best practice for the process and studying how it performs that process. The objective is to find out how the process can be improved and ensure that the improvements are implemented. In contrast, internal benchmarking compares different business units within an organization that perform the same processes. The unit that is considered to represent best practice becomes the target to achieve.

Benchmarking is often used to measure performance compared to others using specific performance metrics such as cost, productivity or cycle time per unit of measure. Sometimes it is carried out collaboratively by comparing subsidiaries of multinational companies in different countries or through their industry trade associations. For example, the UK construction industry has carried out benchmarking since the late 1990s through its industry association.

Benchmarking is widely used in public sector organizations. Unlike private sector organizations, the government acts as a governing body that can force public sector organizations to disclose the relevant information for benchmarking exercises. League tables summarizing selected metrics into a weighted overall score are widely used in the public sector to present the results of benchmarking. For example, published data provide rankings of universities by various metrics that may influence the choice of potential students.

League tables enable many different areas of performance to be summarized into one final score thus providing an indication of how well the organization has performed overall. Ideally, league tables should improve competition among the organizations and provide an incentive for organizations to improve and move up the table.

League tables are often criticized because they do not take into account differences between the organizations being measured. For example, the performance of schools may be influenced more by demographics of the area where the schools are located (with schools in poorer areas typically appearing towards the bottom of the table), rather than the quality of education provided. There is also a danger that too much stress on performance measures and benchmarking can encourage dysfunctional behaviour such as manipulating the performance measures or organizations taking actions to improve their measured scores without improving underlying performance. For example, universities may over-concentrate on improving short-term examination performance in the league tables at the expense of providing a challenging and high-quality education. Another criticism of comparing metrics is that they can become a measuring exercise rather than a learning process because they over-concentrate comparisons with the benchmark when the focus should be on learning from and implementing best practice.

One major advantage of benchmarking is that it is cost beneficial since an organization can save time and money avoiding mistakes that other companies have made and/or the organization can avoid duplicating the efforts of other companies. The overall aim should be to find and implement best practice.

BUSINESS PROCESS REENGINEERING

Business process reengineering involves examining business processes and making substantial changes to how the organization currently operates. It involves the redesign of how work is done through activities. A business process consists of a collection of activities that are linked together in a coordinated manner to achieve a specific objective. For example, material handling might be classed as a business process consisting of separate activities relating to scheduling production, storing materials, processing purchase orders, inspecting materials and paying suppliers.

The aim of business process reengineering is to improve the key business processes in an organization by focusing on simplification, cost reduction, improved quality, enhanced customer satisfaction and to become a world-class competitor. Business process reengineering can be applied not only to manufacturing processes but also to administrative processes. Consider the materials handling process outlined in the above paragraph. The process might be reengineered by sending the production schedule direct to nominated suppliers and entering into contractual agreements to deliver the materials in accordance with the production schedule and also guaranteeing their quality by inspecting them prior to delivery. The end result might be the elimination, or a permanent reduction, of the storing, purchasing and inspection activities. These activities are non-value-added activities since they represent an opportunity for cost reduction without reducing the products' service potentials to customers.

A distinguishing feature of business process reengineering is that it involves radical and dramatic changes in processes by abandoning current practices and reinventing completely new methods of performing business processes. The focus is on major changes rather than marginal improvements. A further example of business process reengineering is moving from a traditional functional plant layout to a just-in-time cellular product layout and adopting a just-in-time philosophy. Adopting a just-in-time (JIT) system and philosophy has important implications for cost management and performance reporting. It is therefore important that you understand the nature of such systems and how they differ from traditional systems. This topic is discussed in the next section.

JUST-IN-TIME SYSTEMS

In the previous section, it was pointed out that reorganizing business processes and adopting a just-in-time (JIT) system was an illustration of business process reengineering. Given that implementing a JIT system is a mechanism for reducing non-value-added costs and long-run costs, it is important that you understand the nature of such a system and its cost management implications.

The success of Japanese firms in international markets in the 1980s and 1990s generated interest among many Western companies as to how this success was achieved. The implementation of **just-in-time (JIT) production methods** (also known as **lean manufacturing systems**) was considered to be one of the major factors contributing to this success. The aims of JIT are to reduce waste by producing the required items, at the required quality and in the required quantities, at the precise time at which they are required. In other words, nothing is purchased or produced until it is needed. JIT manufacturing is a demand **pull manufacturing system** that pulls products through the manufacturing process. Each operation produces only what is necessary to meet the demand of the following operation. Production is not undertaken until there is a signal from the following process indicating a need to produce. The demand pull process starts with customer demand for a finished product and works all the way back to the demand for direct materials that arrive just in time to be used in the production process. JIT production aims to keep the materials moving in a continuous flow with no stoppages and no storage.

The major features of a JIT production system are:

1 The rearrangement of the production process into production cells consisting of different types of equipment that are used to manufacture a given product.

2 Reducing set-up times (i.e. the amount of time required to adjust equipment settings and to retool for the production of a different product).

REAL WORLD VIEWS 22.3

Just-in-time at Boeing

The Boeing 737 jet is the world's most popular and reliable commercial airliner. The company has manufactured over 8000 jets in the 737 family. In 2005, the 737-900ER was launched, which can carry more passengers over a further range than any previous model. According to a press release from the time, Boeing adopted lean manufacturing techniques on this 737 model, the end result of which is one of the shortest assembly times of any commercial aircraft – just 11 days. Lean manufacturing is a production philosophy that treats the use of resources on anything other than value creation as wasteful, e.g. waiting time, transport delays, defects. At Boeing, the assembly time was cut in half between 1999 and 2005. A JIT approach is contained within the principles of lean manufacturing. The techniques were also applied to the manufacture of the 787-Dreamliner aircraft and to more recent models of the 737, such as the 737-MAX. In fact, Boeing plans to increase production of the MAX during 2017, something surely assisted by lean manufacturing and JIT.

Questions

1 Do you think Boeing made changes to its assembly line to assist its lean manufacturing efforts?

2 How might the JIT approach at Boeing help its customers (i.e. airlines)?

References

www.bloomberg.com/news/articles/2014-04-16/boeing-s-737-turns-8-000-the-best-selling-plane-ever-isn-t-slowing, accessed 4 December 2016.

www.airlinereporter.com/2015/12/boeing-shows-off-the-first-737-max-production-line, accessed 4 December 2016.

Arkell, D. (2005) The evolution of creation, Boeing Frontiers, 3(10). Available at www.boeing.com/news/frontiers/archive/2005/march/mainfeature1.html

---

3 Increased emphasis on total quality management that seeks to eliminate defective production.

4 Production cell workers are trained to multitask so that they can perform a variety of operations and tasks.

5 The adoption of JIT purchasing techniques, whereby the delivery of materials immediately precedes demand or use.

6 The modification of management accounting performance measures and product costing systems so that they support the JIT production systems.

Rearrangement of the production process

The first stage in implementing JIT manufacturing techniques is to rearrange the production process away from a **batch production functional layout** towards a product layout using flow lines. With a batch production functional plant layout, products pass through a number of specialist departments that normally contain a group of similar machines. Products are processed in large batches so as to minimize the set-up times when machine settings are changed between processing batches of different products. Batches move via different and complex routes through the various departments, travelling over much of the plant before they are completed. Each process normally involves a considerable amount of waiting time. In addition, much time is taken transporting items from one process to another. A further problem is that it is not easy at any point in time to determine what progress has been made on individual batches. Therefore detailed cost accumulation records are necessary to track work in progress. The consequences of this complex routing process are high work in progress inventory levels, long manufacturing cycle times and high material handling costs.

REAL WORLD VIEWS 22.4

Just-in-time systems at Apple

Every time Apple releases a new device it cannot satisfy immediate demand. This is a result of Apple's precise JIT manufacturing system. Apple does not wish to take the risk of producing more devices than it will sell, so it adjusts manufacturing to match demand based on a pull system. Apple has adopted this system in order to reduce its inventory costs and thus increase its profit, but Apple's production is insufficient to keep up with sudden increases in demand. How can Apple make products faster than it does now? It could set up factories in many different countries and invest in next-generation production capabilities that might produce its devices even faster.

Questions

1 What are the advantages and disadvantages of Apple adopting a JIT system?

2 What should be the main features of a management information system for a company that adopts a JIT manufacturing philosophy?

Reference

Wall Street Journal, Europe (2013) 'Who's right about Apple's cash pile: Cook or Icahn?', 29 October. Available at blogs.wsj.com/digits/2013/10/29/apple-icahn-and-the-cash-pile-manjoo-vs-berman/

The JIT solution is to reorganize the production process by dividing the many different products that an organization makes into families of similar products or components. All of the products in a particular group will have similar production requirements and routings. Production is rearranged so that each product family is manufactured in a well-defined production cell based on flow line principles. In a product flow line, specialist departments containing *similar* machines no longer exist. Instead groups of *dissimilar* machines are organized into product or component family flow lines that function like an assembly line. For each product line, the machines are placed close together in the order in which they are required by the group of products to be processed. Items in each product family can now move, one at a time, from process to process more easily, thereby reducing work in progress inventories and lead times. The ideal layout of each flow line is normally U shaped. This layout is called cellular manufacturing.

JIT manufacturing aims to produce the right parts at the right time, only when they are needed, and only in the quantity needed, using a pull manufacturing system. The pull system is implemented by monitoring the consumption of parts at each operation stage and using various types of visible signalling systems (known as kanbans) to authorize production and movement of the part to the using location. The producing cell cannot run the parts until authorized to do so. The signalling mechanism usually involves the use of kanban containers. These containers hold materials or parts for movement from one work centre to another. The capacity of kanban containers tends to vary from two to five units. They are just big enough to permit the production line to operate smoothly despite minor interruptions to individual work centres within the cell.

To illustrate how the system works, consider three machines forming part of a cell where the parts are first processed by machine A before being further processed on machine B and then machine C. The kanbans are located between the machines. As long as the kanban container is not full, the worker at machine A continues to produce parts, placing them in the kanban container. When the container is full, the worker stops producing and recommences when a part has been removed from the container by the worker operating machine B. A similar process applies between the operations of machines B and C. This process can result in idle time within certain locations within the cell, but the JIT philosophy considers that it is more beneficial to absorb short-run idle time rather than add to inventory during these periods. During idle time the workers perform preventive maintenance on the machines.

With a pull system problems arising in any part of the system will immediately halt the production line because work centres at the earlier stages will not receive the pull signal (because the kanban container is full) if a problem arises at a later stage. Alternatively, work centres at a later stage will not have their pull signal answered (because of empty kanban containers) when problems arise with work centres at the earlier stages of the production cycle. Thus attention is drawn immediately to production problems so that appropriate remedial action can be taken. This is deemed to be preferable to the approach adopted in a traditional manufacturing system where large inventory levels provide a cushion for production to continue.

In contrast, the traditional manufacturing environment is based on a **push manufacturing system**. With this system, machines are grouped into work centres based on the similarity of their functional capabilities. Each manufactured part has a designated routing, and the preceding process supplies parts to the subsequent process without any consideration being given to whether the next process is ready to work on the parts or not. Hence the use of the term 'push through system'.

Demand pull JIT systems are also applied in non-manufacturing organizations. For example, fast-food restaurants such as McDonald's and Burger King use a demand pull system to control their finished inventories. When a customer orders a burger, it is taken from the shelf of completed burgers and the chef does not cook any new burgers until the inventories begin to run out. Customer demand thus pulls the burgers through the system.

Reduced set-up times

Set-up time is the amount of time required to adjust equipment settings and to retool for the production of a different product. Long set-up and changeover times make the production of batches with a small number of units uneconomic. Why? Because larger batches enable the costs of a set-up to be spread over a larger number of units thus reducing the set-up cost per unit. However, the production of large batches leads to substantial throughput delays and the creation of high inventory levels. Throughput delays arise because several lengthy production runs are required to process larger batches through the factory. A further problem with large batches is that they often have to wait for lengthy periods before they are processed by the next process or before they are sold.

The JIT philosophy is to substantially reduce or eliminate the need for set-ups. Set-up times can be reduced by training workers to perform set-ups more quickly. Alternatively, set-ups can be minimized or eliminated entirely by establishing manufacturing cells that are dedicated to the manufacture of a single product or a family of single products rather than multiple dissimilar products. Many firms have also reduced set-up times by investing in advanced manufacturing technologies that enable machine settings to be adjusted automatically instead of manually. By significantly reducing set-up times, small batch sizes become economical. Small batch sizes, combined with short throughput times, also enable a firm to adapt more readily to short-term fluctuations in market demand and respond faster to customer requests, since production is not dependent on long planning lead times.

Total quality management

With a JIT system, a defective part can stop the entire demand pull production flow line. Defective parts represents waste that cannot be tolerated in a production environment that operates without inventories. Therefore total quality management with a never ending quest to a goal of zero defects is an essential part of a JIT production system. In contrast, with a traditional batch production system, WIP inventories are available at each production stage to meet the demands of succeeding operations so defective units are unlikely to halt the production process. Compared with a JIT system, there is less need to eliminate defective output and therefore the same emphasis may not be placed on total quality management.

Multiple-task workforce

Producing on demand can result in workers having free time when there is no demand pull signal from the following operation. There is also a need to respond quickly to any production problems in the flow line so there is a greater emphasis on employee empowerment whereby employees can take actions without requiring authorization at higher management levels. Therefore workers are trained to perform multiple tasks by undertaking support activities such as duties relating to set-ups, minor repairs, preventive maintenance, quality testing and inspection. Workers are also trained to operate different machines within the cell. The ability of workers to multitask enables a smooth production flow within the cell to be achieved.

JIT purchasing arrangements

The JIT philosophy also extends to adopting JIT purchasing techniques, whereby the delivery of materials immediately precedes demand or use. By arranging with suppliers for more frequent deliveries of small batches just before the supplies are needed, inventories can be cut to a minimum. Considerable savings in material handling expenses can be obtained by requiring suppliers to inspect materials before their delivery and guaranteeing their quality. This improved service is obtained by giving more business to fewer highly reliable suppliers and placing longer-term purchasing orders. Therefore the supplier has an assurance of long-term sales, and can plan to meet this demand. Thus, a critical component of JIT purchasing is that strong long-term relationships are established with reliable suppliers based on trust and cooperation.

Companies that have implemented JIT purchasing techniques claim to have substantially reduced their investment in raw materials and work in progress inventories. Other advantages include a substantial saving in factory space, large quantity discounts, savings in time from negotiating with fewer suppliers and a reduction in paperwork arising from issuing blanket long-term orders to a few suppliers rather than individual purchase orders to many suppliers.

JIT and management accounting

Management accountants in many organizations have been strongly criticized because of their failure to alter the management accounting system to reflect the move from a traditional manufacturing to a just-in-time manufacturing system. Conventional management accounting systems can encourage behaviour that is inconsistent with a just-in-time manufacturing philosophy. Management accounting must support just-in-time manufacturing by monitoring, identifying and communicating to decision-makers any delay, error and waste in the system. Modern management accounting systems are now placing greater emphasis on providing information on supplier reliability, set-up times, throughput cycle times, percentage of deliveries that are on time and defect rates.

In a traditional manufacturing environment, many different unrelated products may be subject to processing in a single department. After the products have been processed, they are transferred to other processes located in different departments. Because many products are processed in each department, the costs of each department are common to all products passing through each department. These departmental costs are mostly indirect product costs that are allocated to products using the approaches described in Chapter 3. In a JIT manufacturing system, all of the processes necessary for the manufacture of a single product (or family of similar products) are undertaken in a single cell. Therefore the costs of operating the cell can be directly assigned to the cell's product or family of similar products.

Also with traditional manufacturing systems support departments provide services for all products manufactured by an organization and support costs represent indirect product costs that are allocated to products using the approaches described in Chapter 3. In contrast, we have noted that workers within production cells multitask by performing multiple support activities that are performed by support departments in traditional manufacturing systems. Because production cells are dedicated to the manufacturing of a single product or a family of similar products, many of the support activities can now be directly traced to the product dedicated cells. Thus, with a JIT system a higher proportion of costs can be directly assigned to products compared with a traditional batch production systems. Therefore the benefits from implementing ABC product costing may be lower in JIT organizations.

QUALITY COST MANAGEMENT

To compete successfully in today's global competitive environment companies have become 'customer driven' and have made customer satisfaction an overriding priority. Customers now demand ever improving levels of service regarding cost, quality, reliability, delivery and the choice of innovative new products. Quality has become a key competitive variable in both service and manufacturing organizations and this has created the need for management accountants to become more involved in the

---

REAL WORLD VIEWS 22.5

Cost of quality – BP and Toyota

In recent years, two global companies have had to deal with some quite large costs as a result of quality control failures. First, take the example of Toyota cars in the USA. In late 2009 and early 2010, Toyota recalled several of its US models, the Camry in particular, after several accidents occurred due to a faulty accelerator pedal. The recall involved over 5 million vehicles, and sales and production were suspended for a time in the USA. According to author Paul Ingrassia, the problem occurred because Toyota broke one of its key principles called the 'three nevers' at its US manufacturing plants: never build a new product, in a new facility, with a new workforce. In the case of the Camry in the USA, all three were broken. This cost the company $2 billion before any legal costs. Toyota was fined $1.2 billion in March 2014 by the US Justice Department. The recall woes continued, with a recall of over 6 million vehicles in April 2014, costing the company at least $600 million in repair costs.

In April 2010, the Deepwater Horizon drilling rig, which was ultimately under the control of British Petroleum (BP), exploded in the Gulf of Mexico. An oil slick resulted, which lasted for approximately 3 months and caused extensive damage to the environment and coastlines around the Gulf of Mexico. By September 2010, the total costs had risen to almost $10 billion, with BP setting aside a provision of $20 billion. In January 2011, a US presidential commission squarely laid the blame for the

disaster at the door of BP and its contractors. The report cited several systemic failures, short-cuts and sub-standard materials and workmanship as the cause, all of which it attributed to management failures. By 2016, BP published its final estimate of the total cost at just under $62 billion.

Questions

1 Can management accountants do anything to help engineers and designers focus more on considering the cost of failures in quality and quality control?

2 Can you list some of the internal and external failure costs for the two issues described above?

References

BP Press Release, 14 July 2016, available at www .bp.com/en/global/corporate/press/press-releases /bp-estimates-all-remaining-material-deepwater -horizon-liabilitie.html

CNNMoney (2014) Toyota's huge fine won't dent its $60 billion cash pile. Available at money.cnn .com/2014/03/19/news/companies/toyota-cash -pile/?iid=EL

Ingrassia, P (2010) *Crash Course: The American Automobile Industry's Road from Glory to Disaster*, Random House.

Kollewe, J. (2010) 'BP oil spill cost hits nearly $10bn', 20 September, *The Guardian*. Available at www .guardian.co.uk/environment/2010/sep/20/bp-oil -spill-deepwater-horizon-costs-10bn

Toyota Recalls More Than 6 Million Vehicles Worldwide, Bloomberg, www.bloomberg.com/news /articles/2014-04-09/toyota-recalls-6-76-million -vehicles-worldwide-including-rav4, accessed 4 December, 2016.

provision of information relating to the quality of products and services and activities that produce them. Various studies suggest that costs of quality can be substantial, ranging from 10 per cent to 20 per cent of total sales. Eliminating inferior quality by implementing quality improvement initiatives can therefore result in substantial cost savings and higher revenues and value creation. Companies that do not focus on continuous quality improvement programmes are likely to suffer a decline in market shares, revenues and value. The emphasis on quality has been a key competitive weapon for many years, resulting quality having now shifted from a source of strategic advantage to a competitive necessity.

Total quality management (TQM), a term used to describe a situation where all business functions are involved in a process of continuous quality improvement, has been adopted by many companies. TQM practices emerged as an increasingly fashionable management innovation in response to the lack of competitiveness in Western manufacturing industries during the 1980s and the perceived superiority of Japanese firms in delivering high-quality products and services. It is a customer-oriented process of continuous improvement that focuses on delivering products or services of consistent high quality in a timely fashion. In the past most European and American companies considered quality to be an additional cost of manufacturing, but in the 1990s they realized that focusing on TQM saves money. Prior to the 1990s, companies focused on emphasizing production volume over quality resulting in high levels of inventories at each production stage in order to protect against shortages caused by inferior quality at previous stages. This approach results in excessive expenditure on inspection, rework, scrap and warranty repairs. In the 1990s many companies discovered that it was cheaper to produce the items correctly the first time rather than wasting resources by making substandard items that have to be detected, reworked, scrapped or returned by customers.

In recent years international quality standards have been introduced. The International Organization for Standardization has introduced five standards known as the ISO 9000 family of standards that provide a certification that a company's quality systems meets certain quality standards. The process of obtaining certification is subject to a detailed audit of quality systems and is lengthy and expensive. Many companies now require their suppliers to hold ISO certification and certification has become necessary to compete in the global market. The ISO quality standards have been adopted worldwide by approximately 1.14 million companies. According to the ISO survey (2014) Europe accounted for approximately 42 per cent and China 30 per cent of global ISO 9001 certifications that specify the requirements of a quality management system.

Cost of quality reports

In the 1990s it became apparent that quality practices had become so important that management accounting could no longer ignore TQM. Traditional management accounting focused on cost and production analysis, but ignored quality analysis. Management accounting systems emerged that helped organizations to achieve their quality goals by providing a variety of reports and measures that motivated and evaluated managerial efforts to improve quality. These include financial and non-financial measures. Many companies were not aware of how much they were spending on quality because costs were incurred across many different departments and not accumulated as a separate cost object within the costing system. Managers need to know the costs of quality and how they are changing over time. A cost of quality report should be prepared to indicate the total cost to the organization of producing products or services that do not conform with quality requirements. Four categories of costs should be reported:

1 Prevention costs are the costs incurred in preventing the production of products or services that do not conform to specification. They include the costs of preventive maintenance, quality planning and training, quality reporting and supplier evaluation and selection.

2 Appraisal costs are the costs incurred to ensure that materials, products and services meet quality conformance standards. They include the costs of inspecting purchased parts, work in process and finished goods, quality audits and field tests.

3 Internal failure costs are the costs incurred when products and services fail to meet quality standards or customer needs. They include costs incurred before the product is despatched to the customer, such as the costs of scrap, repair, downtime and work stoppages caused by defects.

4 External failure costs are the costs incurred when products or services fail to conform to requirements or satisfy customer needs after they have been delivered. They include the costs of handling customer complaints, warranty replacement, repairs of returned products, lost market share and the costs arising from a damaged company reputation. Costs within this category can have a dramatic impact on future sales.

Exhibit 22.2 presents a typical cost of quality report. Note that some of the items in the report will have to be estimated. For example, included in the external failure costs category is the foregone contribution from lost sales arising from poor quality. This cost is extremely difficult to estimate. Nevertheless, the lost contribution can be substantial and it is preferable to include an estimate rather than omit it from the report. Because of the difficulty in estimating the opportunity cost of lost sales arising from poor quality, many companies omit this cost from their cost of quality reports. The total costs of quality in these firms will be significantly higher than the costs that are reported in the cost of quality reports. By expressing each category of costs as a percentage of sales revenues, comparisons can be made with previous periods, other organizations and divisions within the same group. Trends in absolute amounts and percentages can therefore be observed and acted upon. Such comparisons can highlight problem areas. For example, comparisons of external failure costs with other companies can provide an indication of the current level of customer satisfaction.

EXHIBIT 22.2 Cost of quality report

	(£000s)	% of sales (£100 million)
Prevention costs		
Quality training	1000	
Supplier reviews	300	
Quality engineering	400	
Preventive maintenance	500	
	2200	2.2
Appraisal costs		
Inspection of materials received	500	
Inspection of WIP and completed units	1000	
Testing equipment	300	
Quality audits	800	
	2600	2.6
Internal failure costs		
Scrap	800	
Rework	1000	
Downtime due to quality problems	600	
Retesting	400	
	2800	2.8
External failure costs		
Returns	2000	
Recalls	1000	
Warranty repairs	800	
Handling customer complaints	500	
Foregone contribution from lost sales	3000	
	7300	7.3
	14900	14.9

The cost of quality report can be used as an attention directing device to make the top management of a company aware of how much is being spent on quality-related costs and the areas where they should focus their attention. Exhibit 22.2 shows that significant savings can be made by reducing the costs of scrap and rework. The report can also draw management's attention to the possibility of reducing total quality costs by a wiser allocation of costs among the four quality categories. For example, by spending more on the prevention costs, the amount of spending in the internal and external failure categories can be substantially reduced and therefore total spending can be lowered. Also, by designing quality into the products and processes, appraisal costs can be reduced, since far less inspection is required.

Prevention and appraisal costs are sometimes referred to as the costs of quality conformance or compliance and internal and external failure costs are also known as the costs of non-conformance or non-compliance. Costs of compliance are incurred with the intention of eliminating the costs of failure. They are discretionary in the sense that they do not have to be incurred, whereas costs of non-compliance are the result of production imperfections and can only be reduced by increasing compliance expenditure. The optimal investment in compliance costs is when total costs of quality reach a minimum. This can occur when 100 per cent quality compliance has not been achieved. It is virtually impossible to measure accurately all quality costs (particularly the lost contribution from foregone sales) and determine the optimal investment in conformance costs. However, some people argue that a failure to achieve 100 per cent quality compliance is non-optimal and that a zero defects policy is optimal. With a zero defects policy, the focus is on continuous improvement with the ultimate aim of achieving zero defects and eliminating all internal and external failure costs.

A zero defects policy does not use percentages as the unit of measurement because a small percentage defect rate can result in a large number of defects. For example, a 1 per cent defect rate from an output of one million units results in 10000 defective units. To overcome this problem, the attainment of a zero defects goal is measured in parts per million (PPM) so that seemingly small numbers can be transferred into large numbers. Thus, instead of reporting a 1 per cent defect rate, a measure of 10000 PPM is more likely to create pressure for action and highlight the trend in defect rates. Cost of quality reports provide a useful summary of quality efforts and progress to top management, but at lower management levels non-financial quality measures provide more timely and appropriate target measures for quality improvement.

Non-financial measures of quality and customer satisfaction

In addition to financial measures, organizations need non-financial measures relating to the quality of the products and services and the activities that produce them. Typical measures provided by the management accounting information system relating to internal processes include:

- process parts per million (PPM) defect rates for each product line;
- the number and percentage of defects for each product line;
- process yields (ratio of good items produced to good items entering the process);
- supplier performance measures such as percentage of defects of incoming materials and the number of late deliveries.

Non-financial measures relating to customer satisfaction include:

- number and percentage of defective goods delivered to customers;
- number and percentage of customer complaints;
- percentage of products that do not meet the warranty requirements;
- percentage of deliveries that are not on time.

In addition, many companies conduct surveys to measure customer satisfaction in relation to product or service quality. In general, cost of quality reports are produced annually but non-financial measures should be reported at more frequent intervals in order to provide earlier warnings of

potential quality problems so that remedial actions can be quickly taken. Managers should examine trends over time and use the measures to highlight areas that require action to improve quality
performance.

Control charts

Cost of quality reports and the above non-financial measures provide top management with an overview of the cost of quality and quality performance but they must be supplemented by techniques for
the detailed daily control of the quality of operations and processes. Statistical quality control charts
are used as a mechanism for distinguishing between random and non-random variations in operating
processes. A control chart is a graph of a series of successive observations of operations taken at regular
intervals of time to test whether a batch of produced items is within preset tolerance limits. Usually,
samples from a particular production process are taken at hourly or daily intervals. The mean, and
sometimes the range, of the sampled items are calculated and plotted on a quality control chart (see
Figure 22.2). Each observation is plotted relative to preset points on the expected distribution. Only
observations beyond specified preset control limits are regarded as worthy of investigation.

The control limits are based on a series of past observations of a process when it is under control,
and thus working efficiently. It is assumed that the past observations can be represented by a normal
distribution. The past observations are used to estimate the population mean and the population standard deviation. Assuming that the distribution of possible outcomes is normal, then, when the process
is under control, we should expect:

68.27 per cent of the observation to fall within the range $+1\sigma$ from the mean;

95.45 per cent of the observation to fall within the range $+2\sigma$ from the mean.

Control limits are now set. For example, if control limits are set based on two standard deviations from
the mean then this would indicate 4.55 per cent (100 per cent $-$ 95.45 per cent) of future observations
would result from pure chance when the process is under control. Therefore there is a high probability
that an observation outside the 2σ control limits is out of control.

Figure 22.2 shows three control charts, with the outer horizontal lines representing a possible control
limit of 2σ so that all observations outside this range are investigated. You will see that for operation A,
the process is deemed to be in control because all observations fall within the control limits. For operation B, the last two observations suggest that the operation is out of control. Therefore both observations
should be investigated. With operation C, the observations would not prompt an investigation because
all the observations are within the control limits. However, the last six observations show a steadily
increasing usage in excess of the mean, and the process may be out of control. Statistical procedures
(called casum procedures) that consider the trend in recent usage as well as daily usage can also be used.

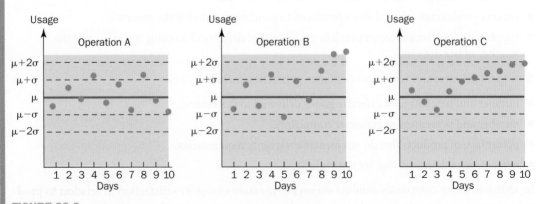

FIGURE 22.2
Statistical quality control charts

COST MANAGEMENT AND THE VALUE CHAIN

The value chain is the linked set of value creating activities all the way from basic raw material sources for component suppliers through to the ultimate end use product or service delivered to the customer. The value chain is illustrated in Figure 22.3. It consists of those activities that add value to customers, products and services. There are two types of linkages: *internal linkages* and *external linkages*. Internal linkages are relationships among activities that are performed within the firm and external linkages relate to activities that are performed with a firm's suppliers and customers. It is important that a company focuses on the entire value chain and not just the internal linkages. Effective management of the value chain is essential to increase customer value at the lowest possible cost.

A value chain analysis is used to analyse, coordinate and optimize linkages in the value chain. Coordinating the individual parts of the value chain together creates the conditions to improve customer satisfaction, particularly in terms of cost efficiency, quality and delivery. A firm that performs the value chain activities more efficiently, and at a lower cost than its competitors, will gain a competitive advantage. Therefore it is necessary to understand how value chain activities are performed and how they interact with each other. The activities are not just a collection of independent activities but a system of interdependent activities in which the performance of one activity affects the performance and cost of other activities.

The linkages in the value chain express the relationships between the performance of one activity and its effects on the performance of another activity. A linkage occurs when interdependence exists between activities and the higher the interdependence between activities the greater is the required coordination. Thus, it is appropriate to view the value chain from the customer's perspective, with each link being seen as the customer of the previous link. If each link in the value chain is designed to meet the needs of its customers, then end customer satisfaction should ensue. Furthermore, by viewing each link in the value chain as a supplier–customer relationship, the opinions of the customers can be used to provide useful feedback information on assessing the quality of service provided by the supplier. Opportunities are thus identified for improving activities throughout the entire value chain.

In the value chain shown in Figure 22.3, the design process activities occur before the production process. Product designs affect production costs and production costs are determined by product cost drivers so that knowing the cost driver rates of the activities required to produce the products is essential for exploiting the linkages between design and production. If designers are made aware that the number of parts is a major cost driver of the various product-related activities, then they will focus on producing products with standard parts thus reducing the number of parts required and the cost of production activities. The design activity is also linked to the customer service activity in the value chain. Producing a product with fewer parts and relying on standard parts reduces the likelihood of product failure and the associated warranty costs besides enhancing customer satisfaction and value.

A cost management system should also provide performance measures relating to the wide variety of activities that span the value chain. Information on supplier reliability, throughput cycle times and percentage of deliveries that are on time provides the feedback that contributes to timely customer deliveries, thus increasing customer value at the lowest possible cost.

Shank and Govindarajan (1992) illustrated how an American automobile company failed to use the entire value chain approach to exploit links with suppliers and enhance profitability. The company had

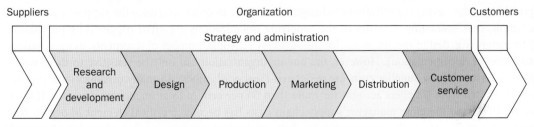

FIGURE 22.3
The value chain

REAL WORLD VIEWS 22.6

Supply chain cost management

For many companies their focus on cost reduction has been limited to the costs of their internal activities. This internal focus has resulted in companies adopting JIT practices and outsourcing in order to reduce costs. The implementing of JIT practices in many cases only shifted costs elsewhere in the supply chain by forcing suppliers or customers to carry that inventory. In these companies the majority of their costs can be determined outside the business. If the majority of an organization's costs lie outside the business then it follows that the biggest opportunities for improvement in their cost position will also be found by focusing on the wider supply chain. This requires companies within the supply chain to share information.

According to an article written by Christopher and Gattorna (2005) published in *Marketing Management* there is now a growing recognition of the importance of shared information in the supply chain in consumer goods distribution involving the adoption of collaborative planning forecasting and replenishment (CPFR). CPFR involves the joint determination of forecasts through pooled knowledge and information. Based on this agreed view of demand over the forecast horizon, the supplier takes responsibility for the replenishment of supplies based upon the actual rate of sale or usage. Significant inventory reductions have been reported in numerous pilot applications along with simultaneous improvement in sales revenue as a result of improved availability.

Question

1 How can an organization reduce its own costs and that of other organizations by sharing information within the value chain?

Reference

Christopher, M. and Gattorna, J. (2005) 'Supply chain cost management and value-based pricing', *Industrial Marketing Management*, 34, 115–121.

made significant internal savings from introducing JIT manufacturing techniques, but, at the same time, price increases from suppliers more than offset these internal cost savings. A value chain perspective revealed that 50 per cent of the firm's costs related to purchases from parts suppliers. As the automobile company reduced its own need for buffer inventories, it placed major new strains on the manufacturing responsiveness of suppliers. The increase in the suppliers' manufacturing costs was greater than the decrease in the automobile company's internal costs. Shank and Govindarajan state:

> For every dollar of manufacturing cost the assembly plants saved by moving towards JIT management concepts, the suppliers' plant spent much more than one dollar extra because of schedule instability arising from the introduction of JIT. Because of its narrow value-added perspective, the auto company had ignored the impact of its changes on its suppliers' costs. Management had ignored the idea that JIT involves a partnership with suppliers.

Managing linkages in the value chain is also the central idea of the concept of supply chain management. By examining potential linkages with suppliers and understanding supplier costs it may be possible for the buying organization to change its activities in order to reduce the supplier's costs. For example, cost generating activities in the supplying organizations are often triggered by purchasing parameters (e.g. design specifications, lot size, delivery schedule, number of shipments, design changes and level of documentation). However, the buying organization can only be sensitive to these issues if it understands how supplier costs are generated (Seal *et al.*, 1999). In many organizations, materials purchased from suppliers account for more than 60 per cent of total manufacturing costs (Drury *et al.*, 1993) and therefore managing supply chain costs has become a critical element in overall cost management. Because of this some companies have established strategic supply partnerships. Seal *et al.* (1999) describe the attempt at a strategic supply partnership between two UK companies and how the buying company was seeking information sharing and research and development collaboration with the supplier for strategic components. In return, the supplier was wishing to develop a higher level of cooperation and trust. Such developments represent an attempt to apply cost management throughout the entire value chain.

SUMMARY

The following items relate to the learning objectives listed at the beginning of the chapter.

- **Distinguish between the features of a traditional management accounting control system and cost management.**

A traditional management accounting control system tends to be based on the preservation of the status quo and the ways of performing existing activities are not reviewed. The emphasis is on cost containment rather than cost reduction. Cost management focuses on cost reduction rather than cost containment. Whereas traditional cost control systems are routinely applied on a continuous basis, cost management tends to be applied on an ad hoc basis when an opportunity for cost reduction is identified. Also many of the approaches that are incorporated within the area of cost management do not involve the use of accounting techniques. In contrast, cost control relies heavily on accounting techniques.

- **Describe the typical pattern of cost commitment and cost incurrence during the three stages of a product's life cycle.**

Three stages of a product's life cycle can be identified – the planning and design stage, the manufacturing stage and the service and abandonment stage. Approximately 80 per cent of a product's costs are committed during the planning and design stage. Cost management can be most effectively exercised during the planning and design stage and not at the manufacturing stage when the product design and processes have already been determined and costs have been committed.

- **Describe the target costing approach to cost management.**

Target costing is a customer-oriented technique that is widely used by Japanese companies and which has recently been adopted by companies in Europe and the USA. The first stage requires market research to determine the target selling price for a product. Next, a standard or desired profit margin is deducted to establish a target cost for the product. The target cost is compared with the predicted actual cost. If the predicted actual cost is above the target cost intensive efforts are made to close the gap. Value engineering and functional analysis are used to drive the predicted actual cost down to the target cost. The major advantage of adopting target costing is that it is deployed during a product's design and planning stage so that it can have a maximum impact in determining the level of the locked-in costs.

- **Distinguish between target costing and kaizen costing.**

The major difference between target and kaizen costing is that target costing is normally applied during the design stage whereas kaizen costing is applied during the manufacturing stage of the product life cycle. With target costing, the focus is on the product and cost reductions are achieved primarily through product design. In contrast, kaizen costing focuses on the production processes.

- **Describe activity-based cost management.**

Activity-based management (ABM) focuses on managing the business on the basis of the activities that make up the organization. It is based on the premise that activities consume costs. Therefore, by managing activities, costs will be managed in the long term. The goal of ABM is to enable customer needs to be satisfied while making fewer demands on organization resources. Knowing the cost of activities enables those activities with the highest cost to be highlighted so that they can be prioritized for detailed studies to ascertain whether they can be eliminated or performed more efficiently.

● **Distinguish between value-added and non-value-added activities.**

A value-added activity is an activity that customers perceive as adding usefulness and value to the product or service they purchase, whereas a non-value-added activity is an activity where there is an opportunity for cost reduction without reducing the product's service potential to the customer. Taking action to reduce or eliminate non-value-added activities is given top priority because by doing so the organization permanently reduces the cost it incurs without reducing the value of the product to the customer.

● **Explain the role of benchmarking and business process engineering within the cost management framework.**

Benchmarking involves comparing key activities and processes with world-class best practices by identifying a process that needs to be improved, finding a non-rival organization that is considered to represent world-class best practice for the process and studying how it performs the process. The objective is to establish how the process can be improved and ensure that the improvements are implemented. The aim of business process reengineering is to improve the key business processes in an organization by focusing on simplification, cost reduction, improved quality and enhanced customer satisfaction. A distinguishing feature of business process reengineering is that it involves radical and dramatic changes in processes by abandoning current practices and reinventing completely new methods of performing business processes.

● **Outline the main features of a just-in-time philosophy.**

Many companies seek to eliminate and/or reduce the costs of non-value-added activities by introducing just-in-time (JIT) systems. The aims of a JIT system are to produce the required items, at the required quality and in the required quantities, at the precise time they are required. In particular, JIT aims to eliminate waste by minimizing inventories and reducing cycle or throughput times (i.e. the time elapsed from when customers place an order until the time when they receive the desired product or service). Adopting a JIT manufacturing system involves moving from a batch production functional layout to a cellular flow line manufacturing system. The JIT philosophy also extends to adopting JIT purchasing techniques, whereby the delivery of materials immediately precedes their use. By arranging with suppliers for more frequent deliveries, inventories can be cut to a minimum.

● **Explain the purpose of a cost of quality report.**

A cost of quality report indicates the total cost to the organization of producing products or services that do not conform with quality requirements. Quality costs are analysed by four categories for reporting purposes (prevention, appraisal and internal and external failure costs). The report draws management's attention to the possibility of reducing total quality costs by a wiser allocation of costs among the four quality categories.

● **Describe how value chain analysis can be used to increase customer satisfaction and manage costs more effectively.**

Increasing attention is now being given to value chain analysis as a means of increasing customer satisfaction and value, and managing costs more effectively. The value chain is the linked set of value creating activities all the way from basic raw material sources from component suppliers through to the ultimate end use product or service delivered to the customer. Understanding how value chain activities are performed and how they interact with each other creates the conditions to improve customer satisfaction and value, particularly in terms of cost efficiency, quality, delivery and customer satisfaction.

KEY TERMS AND CONCEPTS

Activity-based cost management (ABCM) The cost management applications applied to activity-based costing, without the need to assign activity costs to products, also known as activity-based management.

Activity-based management (ABM) The cost management applications applied to activity-based costing, without the need to assign activity costs to products, also known as activity-based cost management.

Appraisal costs The costs incurred to ensure that materials, products and services meet quality conformance standards.

Batch production functional layout A plant layout in which products pass in batches through a number of specialist departments that normally contain a group of similar machines.

Benchmarking A mechanism for achieving continuous improvement by measuring products, services or activities against those of other best performing organizations.

Business process reengineering Examining business processes and making substantial changes to how the organization operates and the redesign of how work is done through activities.

Cellular manufacturing A plant layout based on product flow lines, which are normally U shaped.

Committed costs Costs that have not yet been incurred but that will be incurred in the future on the basis of decisions that have already been made, also known as locked-in costs.

Cost of quality report A report indicating the total cost to the organization of producing products or services that do not conform with quality requirements.

Costs of non-compliance Internal and external failure costs, also known as costs of non-compliance.

Costs of non-conformance Internal and external failure costs, also known as costs of non-compliance.

Costs of quality compliance Prevention and appraisal costs, also known as costs of quality conformance.

Costs of quality conformance Prevention and appraisal costs, also known as costs of quality compliance.

External failure costs The costs incurred when products or services fail to conform to requirements or satisfy customer needs after they have been delivered.

Functional analysis A process that involves decomposing a product into its many elements or attributes and determining a price or value for each element that reflects the amount the customer is prepared to pay.

Internal failure costs The internal costs incurred when products and services fail to meet quality standards or customer needs.

Just-in-time (JIT) production methods The design of the production process that involves producing the required items, at the required quality and in the required quantities, at the precise time they are required.

Kaizen costing Making improvements to a process during the manufacturing phase of the product life cycle through small incremental amounts, rather than through large innovations.

Kanbans Visible signalling systems that authorize the production of parts and their movement to the location where they will be used.

Lean manufacturing systems Systems that seek to reduce waste in manufacturing by implementing just-in-time production systems, focusing on quality, simplifying processes and investing in advanced technologies.

Life cycle cost management The estimation of costs over a product's entire life cycle in order to determine whether profits made during the manufacturing phase will cover the costs incurred during the pre- and post-manufacturing stages.

Locked-in costs Costs that have not yet been incurred but that will be incurred in the future on the basis of decisions that have already been made, also known as committed costs.

Non-value-added activity An activity where there is an opportunity for cost reduction without reducing the product's service potential to the customer.

Prevention costs The costs incurred in preventing the production of products or services that do not conform to specification.

Product flow line A plant layout in which groups of dissimilar machines are organized into product or component family flow lines so that individual items can move from process to process more easily.

Production cell A self-contained area in which a team works on a product family.

Pull manufacturing system A system that pulls products through the manufacturing process so that each operation produces only what is necessary to meet the demand of the following operation.

Push manufacturing system A system in which machines are grouped into work centres based on the similarity of their functional capabilities and one process supplies parts to the subsequent process without any consideration as to whether the next process is ready to work on the parts or not.

Reverse engineering The dismantling and examination of a competitor's product in order to identify opportunities for product improvement and/or cost reduction, also known as tear-down analysis.

Statistical quality control charts A graph of a series of successive observations of operations taken at regular intervals to test whether a batch of produced items is within pre-set tolerance limits.

Supply chain management Managing linkages in the supply chain by examining supplier costs and modifying activities to reduce these costs.

Target costing A technique that focuses on managing costs during a product's planning and design phase by establishing the target cost for a product or service that is derived from starting with the target selling price and deducting a desired profit margin.

Tear down analysis The dismantling and examination of a competitor's product in order to identify opportunities for product improvement and/or cost reduction, also known as reverse engineering.

Total quality management (TQM) A customer-oriented process of continuous improvement that focuses on delivering products or services of consistent high quality in a timely fashion.

Value-added activity An activity that customers perceive as adding usefulness to the product or service they purchase.

Value analysis A systematic interdisciplinary examination of factors affecting the cost of a product or service in order to devise means of achieving the specified purpose at the required standard of quality and reliability at the target cost, also known as value engineering.

Value chain The linked set of value creating activities all the way from basic raw material sources for component suppliers through to the ultimate end use product or service delivered to the customer.

Value engineering A systematic interdisciplinary examination of factors affecting the cost of a product or service in order to devise means of achieving the specified purpose at the required standard of quality and reliability at the target cost, also known as value analysis.

Value chain analysis The analysis, coordination and optimization of the linked set of value creating activities all the way from basic raw material sources for component suppliers through to the ultimate end use product or service delivered to the customer.

Zero defects policy A focus on continuous improvement with the ultimate aim of achieving zero defects and eliminating all internal and external failure costs.

RECOMMENDED READING

You should refer to Ansari et al. (2008) and Burrows and Chenhall (2012) for a review of the history of target costing. A more detailed description of activity-based cost management can be found in Kaplan and Atkinson (2013). For a description of benchmarking in the public sector, see Ryan (2012). See also a paper published by the Chartered Institute of Management Accountants (2014) titled 'Rethinking the value chain' for a discussion of the value chain in today's global environment.

KEY EXAMINATION POINTS

Much of the content of this chapter relates to relatively new topics. Therefore fewer examination questions have been set by the professional examining bodies on the content of this chapter. The questions that follow provide an illustration of the type of questions that have been set.

It is likely that many of the questions that will be set on cost management topics will be essays and will require students to demonstrate that they have read widely on the various topics covered in this chapter. Questions set are likely to be open ended and there will be no one ideal answer.

ASSESSMENT MATERIAL

The review questions are short questions that enable you to assess your understanding of the main topics included in the chapter. The numbers in parentheses provide you with the page numbers to refer to if you cannot answer a specific question.

The review problems are more complex and require you to relate and apply the content to various business problems. The problems are graded by their level of difficulty. Solutions to review problems that are not preceded by the term 'IM' are provided in a separate section at the end of the book. Solutions to problems preceded by the term 'IM' are provided in the Instructor's Manual accompanying this book that can be downloaded from the lecturer's digital support resources. Additional review problems with fully worked solutions are provided in the *Student Manual* that accompanies this book.

REVIEW QUESTIONS

22.1 How does cost management differ from traditional management accounting control systems? (pp. 590–591)

22.2 What are committed (locked-in) costs? (p. 591)

22.3 Explain the essential features of life cycle costing. (pp. 591–592)

22.4 Describe the stages involved with target costing. Describe how costs are reduced so that the target cost can be achieved. (pp. 592–594)

22.5 What is kaizen costing? (pp. 597–598)

22.6 What are the distinguishing features of activity-based management? (pp. 598–601)

22.7 Distinguish between value added and non-value added activities. (pp. 599–601)

22.8 What is business process reengineering? (p. 603)

22.9 Identify and discuss the four kinds of quality costs that are included in a cost of quality report. Give examples of costs that fall within each category. (pp. 609–610)

22.10 Discuss the value of a cost of quality report. (pp. 609–610)

22.11 Describe what is meant by a zero defects policy. (p. 611)

22.12 Explain what is meant by value chain analysis. Illustrate how value chain analysis can be applied. (pp. 613–615)

22.13 Explain how benchmarking can be used to manage costs and improve activity performance. What are the major features of a just-in-time manufacturing philosophy? (pp. 602–607)

22.14 Distinguish between a pull and push manufacturing system. (pp. 605–606)

22.15 What are the essential features of just-in-time purchasing arrangements? (p. 607)

REVIEW PROBLEMS

22.16 Advanced: Life cycle costing and learning curve. Fit Co. specializes in the manufacture of a small range of hi-tech products for the fitness market. They are currently considering the development of a new type of fitness monitor, which would be the first of its kind in the market. It would take one year to develop, with sales then commencing at the beginning of the second year. The product is expected to have a life cycle of two years, before it is replaced with a technologically superior product. The following cost estimates have been made.

	Year 1	Year 2	Year 3
Units manufactured and sold		100 000	200 000
Research and development costs	$160 000		
Product design costs	$800 000		
Marketing costs	$1 200 000	$1 000 000	$1 750 000
Manufacturing costs:			
Variable cost per unit		$40	$42
Fixed production costs		$650 000	$1 290 000
Distribution costs:			
Variable cost per unit		$4	$4·50
Fixed distribution costs		$120 000	$120 000
Selling costs:			
Variable cost per unit		$3	$3·20
Fixed selling costs		$180 000	$180 000
Administration costs	$200 000	$900 000	$1 500 000

Note: You should ignore the time value of money,

Required:

(a) Calculate the life cycle cost per unit. *(6 marks)*

(b) After preparing the cost estimates above, the company realizes that it has not taken into account the effect of the learning curve on the production process. The variable manufacturing cost per unit above, of $40 in year 2 and $42 in year 3, includes a cost for half-an-hour of labour. The remainder of the variable manufacturing cost is not driven by labour hours. The year 2 cost per hour for labour is $24 and the year 3 cost is $26 per hour. Subsequently, it has now been estimated that, although the first unit is expected to take 0.5 hours, a learning curve of 95 per cent is expected to occur until the 100th unit has been completed.

Calculate the revised life cycle cost per unit, taking into account the effect of the learning curve.

Note: the value of the learning co-efficient, b, is -0·0740005.

(10 marks)

(c) Discuss the benefits of life cycle costing. *(4 marks)*

ACCA F5 Performance Management

22.17 Advanced: Target costing and value chain. PBB is a toy manufacturer and retailer. PBB sells toys to consumers through its large network of retail outlets in its home country and via the company's website.

PBB purchases the materials and components that it needs to manufacture toys from a number of different suppliers. All of the purchases are delivered to PBB's raw material store at its factory and are held there until they are needed for production.

Finished toys are transported from the factory to PBB's retail outlets by PBB's fleet of vehicles. The vehicles follow the same schedule each week irrespective of the load they are carrying. Finished toys that are destined for sale via the company's website are transported to PBB's distribution centre.

PBB has recently won the contract to manufacture and sell a new toy. The new toy, Toy Z, is a doll based on a character from a very popular international children's film. PBB is free to set the selling price of Toy Z as it sees fit, but must pay a royalty fee of 15 per cent of the selling price to the film company. PBB intends to sell Toy Z through its network of retail outlets.

PBB plans to adopt a target costing approach for Toy Z. Market research has determined that the selling price will be $25 per Toy Z. PBB requires a profit margin of 25 per cent of the selling price of Toy Z.

The forecast costs per Toy Z are:

	$
Component A	2.15
Component B	1.75
Other materials	see note below for additional information
Labour (0.4 hours at $15 per hour)	6.00
Product-specific production overhead cost	1.89
Product-specific selling and distribution cost	2.38

Note: Each Toy Z requires 0.6kg of 'other materials'. These 'other materials' are purchased from a supplier at a cost of $4 per kg and 4 per cent of all materials purchased are found to be substandard.

Required:

(a) Calculate the cost gap that exists between the forecast total cost per unit and the target cost per unit of Toy Z.
(3 marks)

(b) Discuss how PBB could reduce costs in THREE primary activities in its value chain.
(7 marks)

CIMA P2 Performance Management

22.18 Advanced: Cost of quality reporting. JMM is a car manufacturer. It is a relatively new company and the directors are keen to establish a reputation for high quality. The management of JMM recognizes the need to establish a culture of Total Quality Management (TQM) at the company.

The management accounting team at JMM has collected the following actual information for the most recent quarter of the current year:

Cost data

	$
Customer support centre cost per hour	58
Equipment testing cost per hour	30
Manufacturing rework cost per car	380
Warranty repair cost per car	2600

Volume and activity data

Cars requiring manufacturing rework	800 cars
Cars requiring warranty repair	650 cars
Customer support centre time	500 hours
Production line equipment testing time	400 hours

Additional information

JMM undertook a quality review of its existing suppliers during the quarter at a cost of $60000.

Due to the quality issues in the quarter, the car production line experienced periods of unproductive 'down time' which cost $375000.

Required:

(a) Produce a Cost of Quality report for JMM using the four recognized quality cost headings.
(6 marks)

(b) Explain how a Cost of Quality report would support the development of a TQM culture at JMM.
(4 marks)

CIMA P2 Performance Management

22.19 Advanced: Cost of quality reporting, kaizen costing and just-in-time production and purchasing. Tench Cars (Tench) is a large national car manufacturing business. It is based in Essland, a country that has recently turned from state communism to democratic capitalism. The car industry had been heavily supported and controlled by the bureaucracy of the old regime. The government had stipulated production and employment targets for the business but had ignored profit as a performance measure. Tench is now run by a new generation of capitalist business people intent on rejuvenating the company's fortunes.

The company has a strong position within Essland, which has a population of 200 million and forms the majority of Tench's market. However, the company has also traditionally achieved a good market share in six neighbouring countries due to historic links and shared culture between them and Essland. All of these markets are experiencing growing car ownership as political and market reforms lead to greater wealth in a large proportion of the population. Additionally, the new government in Essland is deregulating markets and opening the country to imports of foreign vehicles.

Tench's management recognizes that it needs to make fundamental changes to its production approach in order to combat increased competition from foreign manufacturers, Tench's cars are now being seen as ugly, polluting and with poor safety features in comparison to the foreign competition. Management plans to address this by improving the quality of its cars through the use of quality management techniques. It plans to improve financial performance through the use of kaizen costing and just-in-time purchasing and production. Tench's existing performance reporting system uses standard costing and budgetary variance analysis in order to monitor and control production activities.

The chief financial officer (CFO) of Tench has commented that he is confused by the terminology associated with quality management and needs a clearer understanding of the different costs associated with quality management. The CFO also wants to know the impact of including quality costs and using the kaizen costing approach on the traditional standard costing approach at Tench.

Required:

Write to the CFO to:

(a) Discuss the impact of collection and use of quality costs on the current costing systems at Tench.
(6 marks)

(b) Discuss and evaluate the impact of the kaizen costing approach on the costing systems and employee management at Tench.
(8 marks)

(c) Briefly evaluate the effect of moving to just-in-time purchasing and production, noting the impact on performance measures at Tench.
(6 marks)

ACCA P5 Advanced Performance Management

22.20 Advanced: Benchmarking. Ganymede University (GU) is one of the three largest universities in Teeland, which has eight universities in total. All of the universities are in the public sector. GU obtains the vast majority of its revenue through government contracts for academic research and payments per head for teaching students. The economy of Teeland has been in recession in the last year and this has caused the government to cut funding for all the universities in the country.

In order to try to improve efficiency, the chancellor of the university, who leads its executive board, has asked the head administrator to undertake an exercise to benchmark GU's administration departments against the other two large universities in the country, AU and BU. The government education ministry has supported this initiative and has required all three universities to cooperate by supplying information.

The following information has been collected regarding administrative costs for the most recent academic year:

	GU $000	AU $000	BU $000
Research			
contract management	14430	14574	14719
laboratory management	41810	42897	42646
Teaching facilities management	26993	27263	26723
Student support services	2002	2022	2132
Teachers' support services	4005	4100	4441
Accounting	1614	1571	1611
Human resources	1236	1203	1559
IT management	6471	6187	6013
General services	17049	16095	18644
Total	115610	115912	118488
Drivers:			
Student numbers	28394	22783	29061
Staff numbers	7920	7709	8157
Research contract value $m	185	167	152

The key drivers of costs and revenues have been assumed to be research contract values supported, student numbers and total staff numbers. The head administrator wants you to complete the benchmarking and make some preliminary comment on your results.

Required:

(a) Assess the progress of the benchmarking exercise to date, explaining the actions that have been undertaken and those that are still required. *(8 marks)*

(b) Evaluate, as far as possible, Ganymede University's bench marked position. *(9 marks)*

ACCA P5 Advanced Performance Management

22.21 Advanced: Preparations of a cost of quality statement.
Telecoms At Work (TAW) manufactures and markets office communications systems. During the year ended 31 May, TAW made an operating profit of $30 million on sales of $360 million. However, the directors are concerned that products do not conform to the required level of quality and TAW is therefore not fulfilling its full potential in terms of turnover and profits achieved.

The following information is available in respect of the year ended 31 May:

1 Production data:

Units manufactured and sold	18000
Units requiring rework	2100
Units requiring warranty repair service	2700
Design engineering hours	48000
Process engineering hours	54000
Inspection hours (manufacturing)	288000

2 Cost data:

	$
Design engineering per hour	96
Process engineering per hour	70
Inspection per hour (manufacturing)	50
Rework per communication system reworked (manufacturing)	4800
Customer support per repaired unit (marketing)	240
Transportation costs per repaired unit (distribution)	280
Warranty repairs per repaired unit (customer service)	4600

3 Staff training costs amounted to $180000 and additional product testing costs of $72000.

4 The marketing director has estimated that sales of 1800 units were lost as a result of public knowledge of poor quality at TAW. The average contribution per communication system is estimated at $7200.

Required:

(a) Prepare a cost analysis that shows actual prevention costs, appraisal costs, internal failure costs and external failure costs for the year ended 31 May. Your statement should show each cost heading as a per cent of turnover and clearly show the total cost of quality. Comment briefly on the inclusion of opportunity costs in such an analysis. *(11 marks)*

(b) A detailed analysis has revealed that the casings in which the communications systems are housed are often subject to mishandling in transit to TAW's manufacturing premises. The directors are considering two alternative solutions proposed by the design engineering team which are aimed at reducing the quality problems that are currently being experienced. These are as follows:

Option 1 – Increase the number of immediate physical inspections of the casings when they are received from the supplier. This will require an additional 10000 inspection hours.

Option 2 – Redesign and strengthen the casings and the containers used to transport them to better withstand mishandling during transportation. Redesign will require an additional 2000 hours of design engineering and an additional 5000 hours of process engineering.

Internal failure costs of rework for each reworked communication system are as follows:

		$
Variable costs	(including direct materials, direct labour rework and supplies)	1920
Allocated fixed costs	(equipment, space and allocated overhead)	2880
Total costs (as per note 2 on cost data)		4800

The directors of TAW believe that, even if it is able to achieve improvements in quality, it will be unable to save any of the fixed costs of internal and external failure.

If TAW chooses to inspect the casings more carefully, it expects to eliminate rework on 720 communication systems whereas if it redesigns the casings it expects to eliminate rework on 960 communication systems.

If incoming casings are inspected more carefully, TAW estimates that 600 fewer communication systems will require warranty repair and that it will be able to sell an additional 300 communication systems. If the casing is redesigned, the directors estimate that 840 fewer communication systems will require warranty repair and that an additional 360 communication systems will be sold.

External failure costs of repair for each repaired communication system are as follows:

	Variable costs $	Fixed costs $	Total costs $
Customer support costs	96	144	240
Transportation costs	210	70	280
Warranty repair costs	1700	2900	4600

Required:

Prepare an estimate of the financial consequences of each option and advise the directors of TAW which option should be chosen. *(9 marks)*

ACCA P5 Advanced Performance Management

22.22 Advanced: ABC cost management. Navier Aerials Co (Navier) manufactures satellite dishes for receiving satellite television signals. Navier supplies the major satellite TV companies who install standard satellite dishes for their customers. The company also manufactures and installs a small number of specialized satellite dishes to individuals or businesses with specific needs resulting from poor reception in their locations.

The chief executive officer (CEO) wants to initiate a programme of cost reduction at Navier. His plan is to use activity-based management (ABM) to allocate costs more accurately and to identify non-value adding activities. The first department to be analysed is the customer care department, as it has been believed for some time that the current method of cost allocation is giving unrealistic results for the two product types.

At present, the finance director (FD) absorbs the cost of customer care into the product cost on a per unit basis using the data in Table 1. He then tries to correct the problem of unrealistic costing by making rough estimates of the costs to be allocated to each product, based on the operations director's impression of the amount of work of the department. In fact, he simply adds $100 above the standard absorbed cost to the cost of a specialized dish to cover the assumed extra work involved at customer care.

The cost accountant has gathered information for the customer care department in Table 2 from interviews with the finance and customer care staff. She has used this information to correctly calculate the total costs of each activity using activity-based costing in Table 3. The CEO wants you, as a senior management accountant, to complete the work required for a comparison of the results of the current standard absorption costing to activity-based costing for the standard and specialized dishes.

Once this is done, the CEO wants you to consider the implications for management of the customer care process of the costs of each activity in that department. The CEO is especially interested in how this information may impact on the identification of non-valued added activities and quality management at Navier.

Navier Dishes (information for the year ending 31 March)

Customer care (CC) department

Table 1: Existing costing data

	$000
Salaries	400
Computer time	165
Telephone	79
Stationery and sundries	27
Depreciation of equipment	36
	707

Note:

(i) CC cost is currently allocated to each dish based on 16 000 orders a year, where each order contains an average of 5.5 dishes.

Table 2: Activity-costing data

Activities of CC dept	Staff time	Comments
Handling enquiries and preparing quotes for potential orders	40%	relates to 35 000 enquiries/quotes per year
Receiving actual orders	10%	relates to 16 000 orders in the year
Customer credit checks	10%	done once an order is received
Supervision of orders through manufacture to delivery	15%	
Complaints handling	25%	relates to 3 200 complaints per year

Notes:

1 Total department cost is allocated using staff time as this drives all of the other costs in the department.
2 90 per cent of both enquiries and orders are for standard dishes. The remainder are for specialized dishes.
3 Handling enquiries and preparing quotes for specialized dishes takes 20 per cent of staff time allocated to this activity.
4 The process for receiving an order, checking customer credit and supervision of the order is the same for both a specialized dish order and a standard dish order.
5 50 per cent of the complaints received are for specialized dish orders.
6 Each standard dish order contains an average of six dishes.
7 Each specialized dish order contains an average of one dish.

Table 3: Activity-based costs

	Total $	Standard $	Specialized $
Handling enquiries and preparing quotes	282 800	226 240	56 560
Receiving actual orders	70 700	63 630	7 070
Customer credit checks	70 700	63 630	7 070
Supervision of order through manufacture to delivery	106 050	95 445	10 605
Complaints handling	176 750	88 375	88 375
Total	707 000	537 320	169 680

Required:

(a) Evaluate the impact of using activity-based costing, compared to the existing costing system for customer care, on the cost of both types of product. *(13 marks)*
(b) Assess how the information on each activity can be used and improved upon at Navier in assisting cost reduction and quality management in the customer care department.

Note: There is no need to make comments on the different product types here. *(12 marks)*

ACCA P5 Advanced Performance Management

22.23 Advanced: Traditional and activity-based budget statements and life cycle costing. The budget for the production, planning and development department of Obba plc, is currently prepared as part of a traditional budgetary planning and control system. The analysis of costs by expense type for the period ended 30 November where this system is in use is as follows:

Expense type	Budget %	Actual %
Salaries	60	63
Supplies	6	5
Travel cost	12	12
Technology cost	10	7
Occupancy cost	12	13

The total budget and actual costs for the department for the period ended 30 November are £1 000 000 and £1 060 000, respectively.

The company now feels that an activity-based budgeting approach should be used. A number of activities have been identified for the production, planning and development department. An investigation has indicated that total budget and actual costs should be attributed to the activities on the following basis:

	Budget %	Actual %
Activities		
1. Routing/scheduling – new products	20	16
2. Routing/scheduling – existing products	40	34
3. Remedial re-routing/scheduling	5	12
4. Special studies – specific orders	10	8
5. Training	10	15
6. Management and administration	15	15

Required:

(a) (i) Prepare two budget control statements for the production planning and development department for the period ended 30 November which compare budget with actual cost and show variances using:

1 a traditional expense-based analysis and
2 an activity-based analysis.   *(6 marks)*

(ii) Identify and comment on four advantages claimed for the use of activity-based budgeting over traditional budgeting using the production planning and development example to illustrate your answer.
           (12 marks)

(iii) Comment on the use of the information provided in the activity-based statement which you prepared in (i) in activity-based performance measurement and suggest additional information that would assist in such performance measurement.   *(8 marks)*

(b) Other activities have been identified and the budget quantified for the three months ended 31 March as follows:

Activities	Cost driver unit basis	Units of cost driver	Cost (£000)
Product design	design hours	8000	2000 (see note 1)
Purchasing	purchase orders	4000	200
Production	machine hours	12000	1500 (see note 2)
Packing	volume (cu.m.)	20000	400
Distribution	weight (kg)	120000	600

Note 1: this includes all design costs for new products released this period.
Note 2: this includes a depreciation provision of £300000 of which £8000 applies to 3 months' depreciation on a straight line basis for a new product (NPD). The remainder applies to other products.

New product NPD is included in the above budget. The following additional information applies to NPD:

(i) Estimated total output over the product life cycle: 5000 units (four years' life cycle).
(ii) Product design requirement: 400 design hours.
(iii) Output in quarter ended 31 March: 250 units.
(iv) Equivalent batch size per purchase order: 50 units.
(v) Other product unit data: production time 0.75 machine hours: volume 0.4 cu. metres; weight 3kg.

Required:

Prepare a unit overhead cost for product NPD using an activity-based approach which includes an appropriate share of life cycle costs using the information provided in (b) above.
           (9 marks)

ACCA Information for Control and Decision Making

22.24 Advanced.

(a) Contrast the features of organizations that would benefit from ABC with those that would not.   *(8 marks)*

(b) Explain in what ways ABC may be used to manage costs, and the limitations of these approaches.   *(11 marks)*

(c) Explain and discuss the use of target costing to control product costs.   *(6 marks)*

CIMA Stage 4 Management Accounting

IM22.1 Advanced. Your managing director, after hearing a talk at a branch meeting on just-in-time (JIT) manufacturing would like the management to consider introducing JIT at your unit which manufactures typewriters and also keyboards for computing systems.

You are required, as the assistant management accountant, to prepare a discussion paper for circulation to the directors and senior management, describing just-in-time manufacturing, the likely benefits which would follow its introduction and the effect its introduction would probably have on the cost accounting system.   *(13 marks)*

CIMA Stage 2 Cost Accounting

IM22.2 Advanced.

(a) Life cycle costing normally refers to costs incurred by the user of major capital equipment over the whole of the useful equipment life. Explain the determination and calculation of these costs and the problems in their calculation.   *(8 marks)*

(b) In the strategy and marketing literature, there is continual discussion of the product life cycle. You are required to explain, for each of the four stages of the product life cycle:

- start-up
- growth
- maturity
- harvest

which system of product costing would be most useful for decision making and control, and why.

Explain briefly in your answer possible alternative organizational structures at each stage in the life cycle.
           (12 marks)

CIMA Stage 4 Management Accounting – Control and Audit

IM22.3 Advanced. Kaplan ('Relevance regained', *Management Accounting*, September 1988) states the view that the 'time-honoured traditions of cost accounting' are 'irrelevant, misleading and wrong'. Variance analysis, product costing and operational control are cited as examples of areas in which information provided by management accountants along traditional lines could well fail to meet today's needs of management in industry.

You are required to:

(a) state what you consider to be the main requirements for effective operational control and product costing in modern industry;   *(10 marks)*

(b) identify which 'traditional cost accounting' methods in the areas quoted in (a) may be considered to be failing to supply the appropriate information to management, and explain why;   *(9 marks)*

(c) recommend changes to the 'traditional cost accounting' methods and information which would serve to meet the problems identified in (b).   *(6 marks)*

CIMA Stage 4 Management Accounting – Control and Audit

IM22.4 Advanced. A company is proposing the introduction of an activity-based costing (ABC) system as a basis for much of its management accounting information:

(a) Briefly describe how ABC is different from a traditional absorption approach to costing and explain why it was developed.   *(8 marks)*

(b) Discuss the advantages and limitations of this 'approach based on activities' for management accounting information in the context of:

(i) preparing plans and budgets
(ii) monitoring and controlling operations
(iii) decision-making, for example, product deletion decisions. *(12 marks)*

ACCA Paper 8 Managerial Finance

IM22.5 Advanced. 'Japanese companies that have used just-in-time (JIT) for five or more years are reporting close to a 30 per cent increase in labour productivity, a 60 per cent reduction in inventories, a 90 per cent reduction in quality rejection rates, and a 15 per cent reduction in necessary plant space. However, implementing a just-in-time system does not occur overnight. It took Toyota over twenty years to develop its system and realize significant benefits from it.'

Requirements:

(a) explain how the benefits claimed for JIT in the above quotation are achieved and why it takes so long to achieve those benefits; *(15 marks)*
(b) explain how management information systems in general (and management accounting systems in particular) should be developed in order to facilitate and make best use of JIT. *(10 marks)*

CIMA Stage 3 Management Accounting Applications

IM22.6 Advanced: Feedback control theory and product quality measurement.

(a) In control theory, a 'feedback control' mechanism is one which supplies information to determine whether corrective action should be taken to re-establish control of a system.

You are required to:

(i) illustrate by means of a diagram how the feedback mechanism operates within a control system, adding a commentary describing how the system functions; *(9 marks)*
(ii) distinguish 'feed-forward' from 'feedback' control, giving two examples of each from within management accounting. *(4 marks)*

(b) Achievement of a high standard of product quality has become a major issue in modern manufacturing industry.

In support of programmes aimed at achieving acceptable quality standards, some companies have introduced detailed 'quality cost' measurement schemes.

In others, the philosophy has been that no measurement procedures should be devoted especially to the measurement of quality costs: quality cost schemes designed to measure performance in this area are considered to add to administrative burdens; in reality 'quality' should be the expected achievement of the required product specification:

Required:

(i) set out a classification of quality costs that would be useful for reporting purposes. Give examples of actual costs that would be represented in each classification; *(7 marks)*
(ii) discuss the reality of the differences of philosophy expressed in the opening statement. Do they represent fundamental differences or may they be reconciled? *(5 marks)*

CIMA Stage 4 Management Accounting – Control and Audit

IM22.7 Advanced: Financial evaluation of implementing a quality management programme. Bushworks Ltd convert synthetic slabs into components AX and BX for use in the car industry. Bushworks Ltd is planning a quality management programme at a cost of £250000. The following information relates to the costs incurred by Bushworks Ltd both before and after the implementation of the quality management programme:

1 *Synthetic slabs*
Synthetic slabs cost £40 per hundred. On average 2.5 per cent of synthetic slabs received are returned to the supplier as scrap because of deterioration in stores. The supplier allows a credit of £1 per hundred slabs for such returns. In addition, on receipt in stores, checks to ensure that the slabs received conform to specification costs £14000 per annum.

A move to a just-in-time purchasing system will eliminate the holding of stocks of synthetic slabs. This has been negotiated with the supplier who will deliver slabs of guaranteed design specification for £44 per hundred units, eliminating all stockholding costs.

2 *Curing/moulding process*
The synthetic slabs are issued to a curing/holding process which has variable conversion costs of £20 per hundred slabs input. This process produces sub-components A and B which have the same cost structure. Losses of 10 per cent of input to the process because of incorrect temperature control during the process are sold as scrap at £5 per hundred units. The quality programme will rectify the temperature control problem thus reducing losses to 1 per cent of input to the process.

3 *Finishing process*
The finishing process has a bank of machines that perform additional operations on type A and B sub-components as required and converts them into final components AX and BX respectively. The variable conversion costs in the finishing process for AX and BX are £15 and £25 per hundred units respectively. At the end of the finishing process, 15 per cent of units are found to be defective.

Defective units are sold for scrap at £10 per hundred units. The quality programme will convert the finishing process into two dedicated cells, one for each of component types AX and BX. The dedicated cell variable costs per hundred sub-components A and B processed will be £12 and £20 respectively. Defective units of components AX and BX are expected to fall to 2.5 per cent of the input to each cell. Defective components will be sold as scrap as at present.

4 *Finished goods*
A finished goods stock of components AX and BX of 15000 and 30000 units respectively is held throughout the year in order to allow for customer demand fluctuations and free replacement of units returned by customers due to specification faults. Customer returns are currently 2.5 per cent of components delivered to customers. Variable stock holding costs are £15 per thousand component units.

The proposed dedicated cell layout of the finishing process will eliminate the need to hold stocks of finished components, other than sufficient to allow for the free replacement of those found to be defective in customer hands. This stock level will be set at one month's free replacement to customers which is estimated at 500 and 1000 units for types AX and BX respectively. Variable stockholding costs will remain at £15 per thousand component units.

5 *Quantitative data*

Some preliminary work has already been carried out in calculating the number of units of synthetic slabs, sub-components A and B and components AX and BX that will be required both before and after the implementation of the quality management programme, making use of the information in the question. Table 1 summarizes the relevant figures:

Table 1

| | Existing situation | | Amended situation | |
	Type A/AX (units)	Type B/BX (units)	Type A/AX (units)	Type B/BX (units)
Sales	800 000	1 200 000	800 000	1 200 000
Customer returns	20 000	30 000	6 000	12 000
Finished goods delivered	820 000	1 230 000	806 000	1 212 000
Finished process losses	144 706	217 059	20 667	31 077
Input to finishing process	964 706	1 447 059	826 667	1 243 077
	2 411 765		2 069 744	
Curing/moulding losses	267 974		20 907	
Input to curing/moulding	2 679 739		2 090 651	
Stores losses	68 711		—	
Purchase of synthetic slabs	2 748 450		2 090 651	

Required:

(a) Evaluate and present a statement showing the net financial benefit or loss per annum of implementing the quality management programme, using the information in the question and the data in Table 1.
(All relevant workings must be shown.)   *(27 marks)*

(b) Explain the meaning of the terms internal failure costs, external failure costs, appraisal costs and prevention costs giving examples of each.   *(8 marks)*

ACCA Information for Control and Decision Making

23
CHALLENGES FOR THE FUTURE

LEARNING OBJECTIVES After studying this chapter you should be able to:

- explain the meaning of sustainable development and shared value;

- describe environmental management accounting;

- explain the role of the management accountant in avoiding unethical behaviour;

- explain how today's information technology is changing the role of the management accountant;

- discuss whether globalization causes management accounting practices to differ across national borders;

- explain the meaning of intellectual capital;

- describe integrated reporting.

In Chapter 1 the important changes that have taken place in the business environment over the past few decades were described. It was pointed out how these changes significantly altered the ways in which firms operated and, throughout the book, the ways in which these changes have influenced management accounting practices were described. In this chapter we shall concentrate on the emerging issues that are likely to have an impact on management accounting and consider some potential future developments in management accounting. To fully understand future developments it is helpful to understand how management accounting has evolved over the years. The chapter therefore begins with a brief history of management accounting.

However, before you start reading this chapter it is important that you note that this chapter is intended to be the concluding chapter to this book, even though three other chapters follow in Part Six. These chapters focus on the application of quantitative methods to management accounting but are intended to be addendum chapters relating to topics included earlier rather than concluding chapters. For an explanation justifying this approach you should refer to the introduction to Part Six.

A BRIEF HISTORICAL REVIEW OF MANAGEMENT ACCOUNTING

The origins of today's management accounting can be traced back to the Industrial Revolution of the nineteenth century. During the late 1980s criticisms of current management accounting practices were widely publicized in the professional and academic accounting literature. In 1987 Johnson and Kaplan's book, entitled *Relevance Lost: The Rise and Fall of Management Accounting*, was published. An enormous amount of publicity was generated by this book as a result of the authors' criticisms of management accounting. Many other commentators also concluded that management accounting was in crisis and that fundamental changes in practice were required.

According to Johnson and Kaplan (1987), most of the management accounting practices that were in use in the mid-1980s had been developed by 1925, and for the next 60 years there was a slow down, or even a halt, in management accounting innovation. They argue that this stagnation could be attributed mainly to the demand for product cost information for external financial accounting reports. The separation of the ownership and management of organizations created a need for the owners of a business to monitor the effective stewardship of their investment. This need led to the development of financial accounting. Statutory obligations were established requiring companies to publish audited annual financial statements. In addition, there was a requirement for these published statements to conform to a set of rules known as generally accepted accounting principles (GAAP), which were developed by regulators.

The preparation of published external financial accounting statements required that costs be allocated between cost of goods sold and inventories. Cost accounting emerged to meet this requirement. Simple procedures were established to allocate costs to products that were objective and verifiable for financial accounting purposes. Such costs, however, were not sufficiently accurate for decision-making purposes and for distinguishing between profitable and unprofitable products and services. Johnson and Kaplan argue that the product costs derived for financial accounting purposes were also being used for management accounting purposes. They conclude that managers did not have to yield the design of management accounting systems to financial accountants and auditors. Separate systems could have been maintained for managerial and financial accounting purposes, but the high cost of information collection meant that the costs of maintaining two systems exceeded the additional benefits. Thus, companies relied primarily on the same information as that used for external financial reporting to manage their internal operations.

Johnson and Kaplan claim that, over the years, organizations had become fixated on the cost systems of the 1920s. Furthermore, when the information systems were automated in the 1960s, the system designers merely automated the manual systems that were developed in the 1920s. Johnson and Kaplan conclude that the lack of management accounting innovation over the decades, and the failure to respond to its changing environment, resulted in a situation in the mid-1980s where firms were using management accounting systems that were obsolete and no longer relevant to the changing competitive and manufacturing environment.

Since the mid-1980s management accounting practitioners and academics have sought to modify and implement new techniques that are relevant to today's environment that will ensure that management accounting regains its relevance. Many new management accounting tools such as activity-based costing, activity-based management and the balanced scorecard emerged in the late 1980s and early 1990s and over the years they have been refined and modified. By the mid-1990s Kaplan (1994a) stated that:

> The past ten years have seen a revolution in management accounting theory and practice. The seeds of the revolution can be seen in publications in the early to mid-1980s that identified the failings and obsolescence of existing cost and performance measurement systems. Since that time we have seen remarkable innovations in management accounting; even more remarkable has been the speed with which the new concepts have become widely known, accepted and implemented in practice and integrated into a large number of educational programmes.

Nevertheless many of the techniques that were developed decades ago such as budgeting, variance analysis, cost-volume-profit analysis and payback investment appraisal are still widely used today. Indeed, if you were to compare the content of the first edition of this book published in 1985 with the current edition you would find a significant overlap in the content of both books. One reason for this is that the techniques have been adapted to respond to the changing environment. What will be the future of management accounting? In the following sections the emerging issues and their possible impact on management accounting will be discussed.

ENVIRONMENTAL AND SUSTAINABILITY ISSUES

Increasing attention is now being given to making companies accountable for ethical, social and environmental issues and the need for organizations to be managed in a sustainable way. There is now a general recognition that environmental resources are limited and should be preserved for future generations. Social factors relating to a company's impact on the community, the provision of employment and safe working conditions and a concern for society as a whole have also emerged as important issues that companies should concentrate on.

Until recently more attention has been given to social responsibility reporting relating to ethical, social and environmental issues within company's annual *external* reports, possibly due to pressures from stakeholders and government regulations requiring more social responsibility reporting. Nevertheless, it has been argued by some that the reporting has been cosmetic, based on public relations

REAL WORLD VIEWS 23.1

BP Gulf of Mexico oil accident

According to a US Congressional enquiry, this accident apparently partly resulted from local decisions within the oil multinational BP and its contractors to save relatively immaterial costs by cutting corners in oil exploration safety measures (National Commission on the BP Deepwater Horizon Oil Spill & Offshore Drilling, 2011). The ensuing accident might have been prevented had more robust safety measures been in place. It directly killed 11 workers employed on the oil drilling exploration rig. It also directly caused large scale oil pollution in the Gulf of Mexico and directly incurred large economic costs for BP and its partners in extinguishing the fire, stopping the oil leak and cleaning up some of the spilt oil.

These direct (and fairly immediate) external impacts on social, environmental and economic factors themselves then caused many other negative impacts in these areas. Thus, for example, the oil pollution killed many fish, prevented many fishermen going to sea to catch fish for a period and damaged the tourist industry in states close to the oil spill (National Commission on the BP Deepwater Horizon Oil Spill & Offshore Drilling, 2011).

The negative environmental impact from the oil spill therefore caused other social and economic impacts on communities in coastal areas close to the oil spill. Several of these and other impacts then fed through into further economic impacts for BP and its contractors who were required to pay compensation to those affected and who suffered reputation damage. In total, BP reported costs of US$40.9 billion in 2010 associated with the Gulf oil spill.

Questions

1 Do you think environmental costs and benefits can be accurately measured?

2 Do issues such as the environment help management accountants become more strategically important members of the organization?

References

Unerman, J. and Chapman, C. (2014) 'Academic contributions to enhancing accounting for sustainable development', *Accounting, Organizations and Society*, 39(6), 385–94.

National Commission on the BP Deepwater Horizon Oil Spill and Offshore Drilling (2011). Deep Water: The Gulf Oil Disaster and the Future of Offshore Drilling: Report to the President, Washington DC, US Independent Agencies and Commissions.

campaigns to publicize the company's social and environmental good deeds. For example, Hopper and Bui (2016) state that for some external corporate reporting will only produce 'greenwashing' that gives the impression of adoption of sustainability practices to gain external legitimacy and to mitigate pressures for environmental reform.

Management accounting has also been criticized for not giving sufficient attention to how social, environmental and sustainability issues can be incorporated within management accounting information systems. In 2013 a major international management accounting research journal (*Management Accounting Research*) published a special issue titled 'Sustainable development, management and accounting: Boundary crossing', edited by Bebbington and Thomson (2013). The editors stated that the aim of the special issue was to provide an impetus for the evolution of a sustainable development-orientated management accounting.

The principle of sustainability requires that companies should operate in ways that secure long-term economic performance by avoiding short-term behaviour that is socially detrimental or environmentally wasteful. The most widely quoted definition of sustainable development is 'An approach to progress which meets the needs of the present without compromising the ability of future generations to meet their own needs' (World Commission on Environment and Development, 1987).

Porter and Kramer (2006) argue that companies that pursue their economic objectives at the expense of the society in which they operate will find that their success will be illusory and temporary. Conversely a healthy society needs successful companies to create jobs, wealth and improved living standards.

In a later article Porter and Kramer (2011) argue that neither a business nor a society should pursue policies that benefit their interests at the expense of the other since a temporary gain for one will undermine the long-term prosperity of both. They recommend that companies should follow the principle of shared value, which they define as policies and operating practices that enhance the competitiveness of a company while simultaneously advancing economic and social conditions in the communities in which it operates. Porter and Kramer provide the following examples of how shared value thinking is transforming the value chain:

- *Energy use and logistics*: Some companies are redesigning their logistical systems to reduce transportation systems. Marks and Spencer has overhauled its supply chain by stopping the purchase of supplies from one hemisphere and transporting to another. This is expected to result in £175 million annual savings by 2016 while hugely reducing carbon emissions.

- *Resource usage*: Advances in technology are providing opportunities for companies to develop new approaches for reducing the usage of water, raw materials and packaging. Coca-Cola reduced its worldwide consumption of water by nearly 20 per cent between 2004 and 2012.

- *Procurement*: Nestlé required a reliable supply of specialized coffees and redesigned its procurement by working intensively with local growers, providing advice on farming practices, guaranteeing bank loans and helping to secure inputs such as pesticides and fertilizers. The company has succeeded over the years in improving the standard of living of local farmers while ensuring itself a stable supply of high quality commodities at a competitive cost.

- *Distribution*: Re-examining distribution practices provides opportunities for creating shared value. Kindle, iTunes and the publishing and newspaper industry have established alternative electronic distribution approaches that reduce paper and transportation usage.

Further examples of how some companies are using opportunities throughout the value chain to create shared value and sustainability by increasing revenues, controlling costs, building trust and managing risk are illustrated in a report by Accenture and the Chartered Institute of Management Accountants (2011) (see Exhibit 23.1).

Environmental cost management

Management accounting systems have given insufficient attention to creating shared value. Instead, the response has been reactive rather than proactive by focusing on managing escalating environmental

EXHIBIT 23.1 Business benefits from sustainability

Company value chain	Revenue generation	Cost control	Building trust	Risk management
Procurement and logistics • Supply chain • Warehousing • Equipment • Inbound logistics	The **Co-operative** switched its own-label chocolate to Fairtrade suppliers in 2002, resulting in a 50% sales volume uplift in the following 12 months.	**Walmart** substantially exceeded a target of 25% improvement in fleet efficiency against 2005 baseline within one year.	**Walmart's** ethical standards programme for sourcing merchandise is recognized as one of the 'gold standards' in the industry.	In July 2009, energy drink manufacturer **Red Bull** was ordered to pay over £270 000 in fines and costs for breaking recycling laws.
Operations • Products • Services • Operations • Buildings • Manufacturing	**Philips** earns 38% of total revenue from 'green product' sales (up from 31% in 2009). **M&S's** 'Plan A' generated £50m profit from new products – such as M&S Energy which provides insulation and solar panels for 300 000 customers – and reduced costs in only the third year of its operation in 2009–10.	**IKEA** saved £1m by removing plastic bags from checkouts in the UK in 30 months. Its stores are 9% more energy efficient compared to 2005. Japanese pharmaceutical firm **Tanabe Seiyaku** hit annual savings of ¥33m with new environmental accounting techniques.	**GE's** brand value increased by 17% after the launch of 'Ecomagination', a business initiative to meet customer demand for more energy-efficient products.	**Taylerson's Malmesbury Syrup** realized that sales of their products were linked to cold weather and would decline within the next 20 years as winters become milder. The product range was reviewed and they now provide syrups to be used with ice creams and cold frappes.
Marketing, sales and service • Marketing • Sales • CRM • Retail • Customer service • Outbound logistics	**Vodafone's** 'Carbon Connections' report demonstrates a potential for 113Mt reduction in CO_2e and €43bn in cost reductions through 1bn new mobile connections.	**M&S's** 'Marks and Start' programme (work experience for disadvantaged adults) has lower attrition rates than comparable schemes for new employees.	77% of consumers have, in the past year, refused to buy products/services from companies they do not trust. Trust must be built or sales are put at risk.	The **Co-operative Bank** showed the risk associated with a loss of trust, citing the 'flight to trust' after the banking crisis as one of the key drivers of a 38% increase in their own current account sales in 2009.
Support activities • Finance • Technology • R&D • HR • Legal • Firm infrastructure	**Novo Nordisk** bring products to market faster by including environmental, social and economic impacts in new drug applications.	**Fife Council** have identified additional cost avoidance opportunities of £75m that can be achieved by improving its carbon reductions by a further 3% per annum between 2007 and 2021.	Graduating MBAs from leading **North American and European business schools** are willing to forgo financial benefits to work for a more ethical employer.	**Ribena** noticed that local weather patterns have been changing, affecting their blackcurrant harvests. They have been developing new varieties of blackcurrants that will thrive in a changing climate.

costs arising from meeting regulatory requirements and seeking to avoid litigation and fines. Environmental costs are large in some industrial sectors. For example, Ranganathan and Ditz (1996) reported that Amoco's environmental costs at its Yorktown refinery were at least 22 per cent of operating costs. Henri *et al.* (2014) have also reported that industry's total environmental protection expenditure for the European Union is now more than 45 billion euros representing approximately 0.4 per cent of gross domestic product. Therefore, selecting the least costly method of compliance has become a major objective. These developments have resulted in some companies focusing on measuring, reporting and monitoring environmental costs. In 2005 the International Federation of Accountants (IFAC) issued a guidance document that provides a general framework and set of definitions for environmental management accounting (see www.ifac.org).

Nevertheless, there is evidence to suggest that many companies have not been able to identify their total environmental costs and do not recognize that they can be controlled and reduced (Epstein and Roy, 1997). A study by Bartolomeo *et al.* (2000) involving interviews with accountants and environmental managers in 84 companies in Germany, Italy, the Netherlands and the UK reported that only 50 per cent of the European companies were explicitly tracking any of a number of named environmental costs. They concluded that opportunities existed for many companies to become more active in environmental management accounting and that the pressures on them to do so will increase. A more recent study by Henri *et al.* (2014 and 2016) of 319 Canadian manufacturing firms concluded that many of the sampled firms did not track environmental costs extensively.

Henri *et al.* also reported that there was a statistical positive relationship between the tracking of environmental costs and the implementation of environmental initiatives. They attribute their findings to the fact that the tracking of environmental costs provides feedback that focuses organizational attention on the search for innovative ways to reduce environmental costs and their impacts. More specifically, the tracking of environmental costs facilitates the understanding of the links between costs and output, and provides insights into possible cost reductions through specific actions on cost drivers, such as the reduction in the material and energy intensity of goods or services, the reduction in the dispersion of toxic materials and improvement in recyclability by product and process redesign. They conclude that the tracking of environmental costs acts (i) as a catalyst for efficiency improvements *within the same cost structure*; and (ii) it acts as a catalyst for new initiatives which help to create a *different cost structure*.

In most cost accounting systems, environmental costs are hidden within general overheads and are either not allocated to cost objects or are allocated on an arbitrary basis within the allocation of general overheads. Thus, crucial relationships are not identified between environmental costs and the responsible products, processes and underlying activities. For example, Ranganathan and Ditz (1996) point out that the principal environmental issue facing Spectrum Glass, a major manufacturer of speciality sheet glass, is the use and release of cadmium. It discovered that only one product (ruby red glass) was responsible for all of its cadmium emissions but the cost accounting system allocated a portion of this cost to all products. This process resulted in ruby red glass being undercosted and other products being overcosted.

Environmental costs should be accumulated by separate cost pools, analysed by appropriate categories and traced to the products or processes that caused the costs using ABC concepts. Knowledge of the amount and categories of environmental costs, and their causes, provides the information that managers need to not only manage environmental costs more effectively by process redesign but to also reduce the pollutants emitted to the environment.

The United Nations Division for Sustainable Development (UNDSD) identified input/output analysis as a technique that could be used to reduce the usage of environmental resources and costs. Inflows of resources such as water, materials and energy are recorded and balanced with outflows on the basis that, what comes in, must go out. For example if 10 000kg/litres of a resource has been acquired but only 9000kg/litres have been used in the productive process then the 1000kg/litres difference must be accounted for. The balance may represent avoidable waste which actions should be taken to eliminate in the future. By accounting for inputs and outputs in this way, both in terms of physical quantities and, at the end of the process, in monetary terms too, businesses can seek to reduce environmental costs.

Hansen and Mendoza (1999) point out that environmental costs are incurred because of poor environmental quality controls and thus are similar in nature to quality costs discussed in Chapter 22. They advocate that an environmental cost report should be periodically produced, based on the principles of a cost of quality report (see Exhibit 22.2) to indicate the total environmental costs to the organization associated with the creation, detection, remedy and prevention of environmental degradation. Adopting a similar classification as that used for quality costs, the following four categories of environmental costs can be reported:

1 Environmental prevention costs are the costs of activities undertaken to prevent the production of waste that could cause damage to the environment. Examples include the costs associated with the design and operation of processes to reduce contaminants, training employees, recycling products and obtaining certification relating to meeting the requirements of international and national standards.

2 Environmental detection costs are the costs incurred to ensure that a firm's activities, products and processes conform to regulatory laws and voluntary standards. Examples include inspection of products and processes to ensure regulatory compliance, auditing environmental activities and performing contamination tests.

3 Environmental internal failure costs are the costs incurred from performing activities that have produced contaminants and waste that have not been discharged into the environment. Such costs are incurred to eliminate or reduce waste to levels that comply with regulatory requirements. Examples include the costs of disposing of toxic materials and recycling scrap.

4 Environmental external failure costs are the costs incurred on activities performed after discharging waste into the environment. Examples include the costs of cleaning up contaminated soil, restoring land to its natural state and cleaning up oil spills and waste discharges. Clearly this category of costs has the greatest impact on a company in terms of adverse publicity. For example, the cost to BP of the oil leak arising from the Deepwater Horizon oil disaster was estimated to be $40bn. The disaster has had a dramatic negative impact on BP's image (see Real World Views 23.1).

The environmental cost report should be similar in format to the cost of quality report (see Exhibit 22.2) with each category of costs expressed as a percentage of sales revenues (or operating costs) so that comparisons can be made with previous periods, other organizations and divisions within the same group. The environmental cost report should be used as an attention directing device to make top management aware of how much is being spent on environmental costs and the relative amount in each category. The report also draws management's attention to those areas that have the greatest potential for cost reduction. The same principles as those described for quality cost reporting also apply. That is, investing more in prevention and detection activities has the potential to significantly reduce environmental failure costs. A major limitation of environmental cost reports is that they only report those environmental costs for which the company is responsible. The report does not include externality costs that are caused by a firm but borne by society. Examples include losing land for recreational use and damaging ecosystems from solid waste disposal. Attempts should be made to develop non-financial and/or qualitative measures that draw attention to how an organization is contributing to becoming environmentally responsible and a good social citizen.

The role of management accounting in supporting the creation of shared value and sustainable development

In addition to managing and controlling environmental costs, management accounting systems should support the creation of shared value and sustainable development. A report titled 'Sustainability Performance Management' by Accenture and the Chartered Institute of Management Accountants (2011) identified that the two major sustainability roles for the finance function were assisting in providing information for making the business case for creating shared value by reconfiguring the value and developing new products and tracking sustainability related key performance indicators. The environmental consequences of products should be evaluated using the life cycle cost management approach described in Chapter 22. In other words, the environmental consequences and opportunities for creating shared value should be managed at the planning and design stage and not at the manufacturing stage when a substantial proportion of the environmental costs and outcomes will already have been determined.

Incorporating a society/environmental perspective within a balanced scorecard framework has been adopted by some companies to link their environmental strategy to concrete performance measures. The balanced scorecard framework requires that within the scorecard the environmental objectives are clearly specified. Typical objectives include minimizing the use of hazardous materials, minimizing energy requirements, minimizing the release of pollutants and other opportunities for creating shared value. These objectives should be translated into specific performance measures. In addition, within the scorecard, firms should describe the major initiatives for achieving each objective and also establish targets for each performance measure. For feedback reporting, actual performance measures should also be added.

FOCUS ON ETHICAL BEHAVIOUR

Management accounting practices have developed to provide information that assists managers to maximize future profits. It is too simplistic, however, to assume that the only objective of a business firm is to maximize profits. The profit maximization objective should be constrained by the need for firms to also give high priority to their social responsibilities and ensure that their employees adopt high standards of ethical behaviour. Managers have responsibility to avoid the narrow pursuit of profits at any cost.

Identification of what is acceptable ethical behaviour has attracted much attention in recent years with numerous examples of companies attracting negative coverage for ethical failings and their impact on reported profits. For example, Volkswagen (VW) Europe's biggest car maker has suffered a dramatic decline in its reputation after the revelation that it fitted software designed to cheat emission tests to 11 million cars worldwide. VW has set aside €18.4 billion to cover the costs of legal action, compensation and refits. Commentators predict that the scam could end up costing the company more than twice this amount. Public distrust and protests against corporate misdemeanours have resulted in calls for increased regulation and the need to focus on improving ethical behaviour.

A global survey of business ethics by the Chartered Global Management Accountant (CGMA, 2012) reported that approximately 80 percent of the responding organizations provided a code of ethics or similar document to guide staff about ethical standards in their work. One of the key messages to emerge from the survey was an 'ethics divide' whereby there was a stated strong commitment to ethical codes and behaviour, but in practice high pressure to act unethically. Approximately 30 percent of the respondents stated that they sometimes or always felt under pressure to compromise their organization's standards of ethical conduct. Pressures were most apparent in some emerging economies.

The survey concluded that based on their skills and roles, management accountants have a critical part to play in the management of ethical performance and an obligation to uphold ethical standards. Professional accounting organizations play an important role in promoting a high standard of ethical behaviour by their members. Both of the professional bodies representing management accountants, in the UK (Chartered Institute of Management Accountants), and in the USA (The American Institute of Certified Public Accountants), have issued codes of ethical guidelines for their members and established mechanisms for monitoring and enforcing professional ethics. The guidelines are concerned with ensuring that accountants follow fundamental principles relating to:

- integrity (being honest and not being a party to any falsification);
- objectivity (not being biased or prejudiced);
- confidentiality and professional competence and due care (maintaining the skills required to ensure a competent professional service);
- compliance with relevant laws and regulations.

You can view each organization's ethical standards at www.cimaglobal.com/ethics and www.aicpa.org /research/standards/codesofconduct/pages/default.aspx

The above discussion suggests that management accountants will be faced with increasingly ethical challenges in the future and are at risk of being pressurized to act unethically. You will remember from Chapter 20 that transfer pricing can be used to enable one division of a multinational to sell products and services to another division at an artificial price in order to make profits seem higher in a low-tax country and lower in a high-tax one. This process has attracted a considerable amount of negative publicity on the grounds that the behaviour is unethical and there is evidence to suggest that consumers are penalizing firms they perceive as engaging in unethical behaviour by migrating to their competitors. For example, many consumers at Starbucks in the UK migrated to its rival, Costa, because of their perception that Starbucks did not pay a fair amount of UK taxes.

We also noted in Chapter 16 that flaws in the performance measurement systems used by banks contributed to the financial crisis in the banking sector in 2008. Bonuses and performance measures were based on short-term, rather than long-term performance that did not take risk into account. Managers were paid large commissions for selling mortgage loans to customers that were a large risk to the banks due to their low credit worthiness. In many cases, the employees of the banks were paid commissions on the date that the loan agreements were signed, while the loans lasted for 25 years, but if the borrowers defaulted the employees were not required to repay the commission. This practice resulted in many banks having a high volume of questionable loans with a high probability of default. This raises the question as to whether the managers were engaging in unethical behaviour or did the system of performance evaluation encourage the behaviour? So where should the blame be assigned? Is the reward system at fault or the unethical behaviour? Or both?

It is apparent from the above illustrations debate about what is right or wrong or ethical or unethical can be subject to different views and all the management accountant can do is refer to a company's and professional accountancy bodies for guidance. However, where actions are proposed that are illegal or contrary to regulatory requirements the management accountant should present documentary evidence that such actions should not be undertaken.

INFORMATION TECHNOLOGY

During the past two decades advances in information technology (IT) have had a profound impact on business activities including management accounting practices and the role of the management accountant. Prior to the 1990s companies developed their own company specific stand alone information systems such as an accounting information system, a materials procurement system and a production system that were applicable only to specific parts of the organization. These systems were not integrated with each other.

During the late 1980s and the 1990s larger companies replaced these with commercially available software integrated packages called enterprise resource planning systems (ERPS). An ERPS is a single system comprising of a set of integrated sub-systems software modules specializing in particular business functions that aim to control all information flows within a company. Users can use their personal computers (PCs) to access the organization's single database and follow developments almost as they happen. Using real time data enables managers to analyse information quickly and thus continually improve the efficiencies of processes. A major feature of ERPS systems is that all data are entered only once, typically where they originate. There are ERPS packages on the market provided by companies such as SAP, Baan, Oracle and J.D. Edwards. ERPS have been implemented in most large companies and are also widely used in medium- and smaller-sized companies with SAP being the market leader.

Companies installed software such as ERPS on their own servers (a large powerful computer that responds to a request across a computer network to provide a network or data services). The emergence of cloud computing enables software to be located on servers outside the company owned by an external IT provider. The provider then makes the software available over the internet to the companies. With cloud computing, resources are provided in return for monthly subscriptions or on a pay-as-you

REAL WORLD VIEWS 23.2

Management accounting in the future

In the March 2012 edition of CIMA's *Financial Management* journal, Christian Doherty asks what will management accountants ten years on be grappling with? This question has been posed before (see, for example, Scapens *et al.*, 2003) and technology is a factor which is often cited as being something which will change management accounting. Doherty (2012) mentions a number of trends which are likely to affect how business is done and, thus, how management accountants do their work.

Technology is viewed by Doherty as a potential 'liberator', allowing management accountants to become more influential in decision-making. Technology developments such as Big Data have become a key tool in the provision of decision-making information (see CGMA, 2014). However, management accountants need to be cautious that increasing amounts of data do not overwhelm them. A second factor mentioned by Doherty (2012) is the need to provide insight, not information. Put simply, reporting may not be enough; rather, management accountants of the future must be able to provide professional insightful advice to other managers and directors. Third, while the BRICS (Brazil, Russia, India, China, South Africa) economies receive a lot of attention as some of the fastest growing, these are likely to be joined by others such as Columbia, Indonesia, Vietnam and Turkey. These new markets may present new opportunities for many firms, either in increasing sales or a manufacturing base, for example. Again, management accountants need to be centre stage to help take advantage of any opportunities. Finally, reporting is likely to become increasingly broad, with issues like sustainability, risk assessment and business valuation coming to the fore. More recently, in 2016 the IMA CEO reinforced the analytical skills needed of management accountants to provide 'predictive analytics (forecasting future events) and prescriptive analytics (actions and interventions, based on historical and future trends)'.

Questions

1 Do you think technological developments will always be an issue for management accountants?

2 Based on the brief summary above, what kinds of skills other than technical accounting training do management accountants need?

References

AccountingWeb (2016) Why the Future of Management Accounting Looks Bright, available at www.accountingweb.com/practice/growth/why-the-future-of-management-accounting-looks-bright

CGMA (2014) The Big Data Pathway, *CGMA*, November 2014. Available at www.cgma.org/Resources/Reports/Pages/big-data.aspx

Doherty, C. (2012) Management accounting in 2022, *Financial Management*, March, CIMA. Available at www.fm-magazine.com

Scapens, R., Ezzamel, M., Burns, J. and Baldvinsdottir, G. (2003) *The Future Direction of UK Management Accounting*, London, CIMA.

---

go basis. In the latter case this results in some IT costs becoming variable instead of fixed and in the former case capital expenditure relating to the acquisition of the software is replaced with monthly rental type payments. Therefore cost considerations can significantly influence the decision as to whether to adopt cloud computing. Other factors to be taken into account relate to the fact that software updates are implemented by the provider so there is no need for companies to update their own software. A potential disadvantage, however, of cloud computing is that security and data protection risks are beyond the company's control and determined by the external cloud provider.

Recently the term 'Big Data' has been widely publicized. **Big data** is a term that describes the large volume of raw data, both structured and unstructured, that inundates a business on a daily basis. It includes information such as email messages, social media postings, phone calls, purchase transactions, website traffic and video streams. Approximately 90 per cent of the data is estimated to be unstructured. The amount of data that is being created is so voluminous they cannot be reasonably analysed using database management systems or traditional software programs (Warren *et al.*, 2015).

The challenge is to explore and analyse this raw data to obtain meaningful information that is useful for decision-making.

It is important to understand the difference between data and information. Data are mere records of raw facts that are not organized to be meaningful whereas information is data that has been organized in a way so that it becomes understandable and useful for a particular purpose. For example, management accounting systems record data that is structured and aggregated into performance reports. Information, however, on its own only becomes valuable when it is transformed into knowledge which guides managers to make correct decisions.

The volume of information has exploded in recent years but it is not the volume of information that matters but what is done with the available information. Users of information must perceive it as being useful and helpful. An important role of management accounting is to ensure that users are not faced with information overload whereby users are provided with too much information to the extent that it becomes unmanageable and no longer useful.

The above IT developments have had a significant impact on the work of management accountants. In particular, it substantially reduces routine information gathering and the processing of information that was traditionally done by management accountants. Prior to the 1990s accountants were considered to be the information managers but this role relating to the design and implementation of IT systems has now been taken over by IT specialists. In addition, non-accounting managers often have a Masters degree in business administration and have a greater understanding of accounting information. Instead of managers asking management accountants for information, they can access the system to derive the information they require directly from personal computers, laptops and tablets from different locations anywhere in the world and do their own analyses.

These developments have freed up management accountants from undertaking the routine and mundane tasks and enabled them to adopt the role of advisers and internal consultants to the business. Management accountants are now becoming more involved in interpreting the information generated from the IT systems and providing business support for managers. In addition, management accountants will also need to be aware of the latest developments in IT in order to assess what can be achieved from these developments.

GLOBALIZATION AND MANAGEMENT ACCOUNTING INTERNATIONAL PRACTICES

Globalization and developments in information technology have had a significant impact on management accounting. The growth in multinational companies has resulted in management accountants being responsible for overseeing the operation of management accounting systems in many different countries. Do management accounting practices differ across national borders?

Granlund and Lukka (1998) argue that there is a strong current tendency towards global homogenization of management accounting practices within the industrialized parts of the world. They distinguish between management accounting practices at the macro and micro levels. The macro level relates to concepts and techniques; in other words, it relates mainly to the content of this book. In contrast, the micro level is concerned with the behavioural patterns relating to how management accounting information is actually used. At the macro level, Granlund and Lukka suggest that the convergence of management accounting practices in different countries has occurred because of intensified global competition, developments in information technology, the increasing tendency of transnational companies to standardize their practices, the global consultancy industry and the use of globally applied textbooks and teaching.

Firms throughout the world are adopting similar integrated enterprise resource planning systems or standardized software packages that have resulted in the standardization of data collection formats and reporting patterns of accounting information. In multinational companies, this process has resulted in the standardization of the global flow of information, but it has also limited the ability to generate locally relevant information. Besides the impact of integrated IT systems, it is common for the headquarters/parent company of a transnational enterprise to force foreign divisions to adopt similar accounting practices to those of the headquarters/parent company. Global consultancy companies tend to promote the same standard solutions globally. Finally, the same textbooks are used globally and university and professional accounting syllabuses tend to be similar in different countries.

At the micro level, Granlund and Lukka acknowledge that differences in national and corporate culture can result in management accounting information being *used* in different ways across countries. For example, there is evidence to suggest that accounting information is used in a more rigorous/rigid manner to evaluate managerial performance in cultures exhibiting certain national traits, and in a more flexible way in cultures exhibiting different national traits.

INTELLECTUAL CAPITAL AND THE KNOWLEDGE BASE ECONOMY

During the past two decades the world's economy has rapidly changed from an industrial to a knowledge base. In the new knowledge economy, wealth is created by developing and managing knowledge (Ricceri and Guthrie, 2009). These value creating knowledge resources are commonly referred to as intellectual capital.

The term intellectual capital has been defined as the intangible benefits accessible by a firm from its workforce, and more broadly, from its established relationships with groups such as customers, suppliers and competitors (Gowthorpe, 2009). It is often used interchangeably with other terms such as 'knowledge capital', 'knowledge economy' and 'intangible assets'. Examples of items that represent intellectual capital include resources such as the organization's reputation, the morale of its staff, customer satisfaction, knowledge and skills of employees, established relationships with suppliers etc.

REAL WORLD VIEWS 23.3

Seismic shift from tangible to intangible value

In the March 2016 edition of CIMA's *Financial Management* journal, Lawrie Homes interviewed Noel Togoe, CIMA'S director of Education. Togoe stated that value measurement has been an area of dramatic change affecting the financial management landscape. The shift from tangible to intangible value has been seismic. It's something that makes us think differently about management accounting. As recently as 30 years ago, the balance sheet represented about 80 per cent of the value of quoted firms on average. Today it's about 17 per cent. It's common knowledge that products will give your firm a competitive edge for only a limited time, because it's possible for your rivals to copy them. But you can often derive a sustainable competitive advantage from relationships. These cannot be reverse-engineered or replicated, because you need all the right cultural conditions.

It is intangible factors – culture, reputation, relationships, processes and the innovative potential of the workforce – that give an organization its long-term advantage. If part of the work of managers is to enhance the value of the organization, preserve the value of the organzation and ensure that stakeholders get value from the organization, they need to pay attention to the drivers of value. If the drivers of value are intangible, you need to pay attention to them, but we don't seem to have got to that.

Questions

1 Provide examples of companies where most of their value can be attributed to intellectual capital rather than physical assets.

2 What do you think are the key intellectual capital drivers of corporate value?

Reference

Holmes, L. (2016), Insight track, *Financial Management*, March, 32–4.

Recently, increased attention has been given to the importance of intellectual capital arising from the observed dramatic differences between the book and market values of many companies, particularly the dotcom companies in the late 1990s. Successful companies today tend to be those that continually innovate, relying on new technologies and the skills and knowledge of their employees rather than just their tangible physical assets.

Although it is problematic as to whether monetary values can be assigned to most internally generated intangible assets representing intellectual capital, it is important that they are considered in order to provide a greater understanding of the process of value creation. Otherwise there is a danger that a firm will be unable to assess the value of future business opportunities. This presents a challenge as to how to identify, measure and report on the value of intellectual capital.

One approach that has been suggested to calculate the value of an organization's intellectual capital is to take the difference between its market value (the number of shares in issue multiplied by the market value of the share) and the net book value of its assets. The gap between the two figures represents the market-to-book ratio and provides an indication of the value of intellectual capital assets that are not reflected in its financial statements. The problem with this approach is that it values intellectual capital as one asset and makes no attempt to separate the items that might comprise it. In addition, the market value of a company is subject to wide fluctuations due to factors unrelated to changes in intellectual capital. Another approach is to disclose information relating to intellectual capital, without attempting to assign any monetary value to it. For a review of some of the approaches that can be used to measure and value intellectual capital you should refer to Starovic and Marr (2010).

At present there is no consensus as to what represents a recommended approach to managing and reporting intellectual capital. Management accountants should be at the forefront of this process, using their skills and expertise in measurement and control to develop systems capable of accommodating intellectual capital. It may take some time to reach agreement on what constitutes the best approach and experimentation will be necessary in order to determine the best way forward.

INTEGRATED REPORTING

Recently, a new type of external corporate reporting called integrated reporting has been advocated. Integrated reporting has been rapidly gaining international recognition and is now being widely implemented in South Africa. Current corporate reports tend to focus on detailed historical financial information and critics have argued that there is a need for a report that provides a bigger picture of a company's short and long-term performance. The Integrated Reporting Committee (IRC) of South Africa (2011) defined integrated reporting as the bringing together of material information about an organization's strategy, governance, performance and prospects in a way that reflects the commercial, social and environmental context within which it operates.

Integrated reporting aims to provide information on financial and non-financial performance in a single document, showing the relationship between financial and non-financial performance and how these inter-related dimensions are creating or destroying value for shareholders and other stakeholders. The IRC discussion paper suggested that the following key elements should be included in an integrated report:

- a concise overview of the organization's structure, including governance and its main activities;
- a description of material risks and opportunities, based on a review of financial, social, environmental, economic, and governance issues;
- a description of the strategic objectives of the business as influenced by an assessment of the external environment and internal resource constraints; and
- an account of the organization's performance based on its strategic objectives in terms of key performance and risk indices.

Increasingly, businesses are expected to report not just on profit but on their impact on the wider perspectives relating to the economy, society and the environment. A study by Adams *et al.* (2016) examined the published accounts of Heineken, Unilever, GlaxoSmithKline and the National Australia Bank, and found that these companies were starting to think about their social investment activities in terms of value creation and are linking them to strategy. They concluded that integrated reporting offers significant potential for changing how organizations think about their social investments.

Integrated reporting aims to provide an overview of an organization's activities and performance in this broader context by communicating the mission and strategy of the organization and linking performance measurement to strategy. Integrated external corporate reporting therefore has many similarities with the balanced scorecard approach (see Chapter 21) that is used for internal performance management. Where integrated reporting is adopted it is likely that it will draw off internal management accounting information, performance management and non-financial measures. It is therefore likely that management accounting will have a greater input into external corporate reporting in those companies that adopt integrated reporting.

SUMMARY

The following items relate to the learning objectives listed at the beginning of the chapter.

- **Explain the principles of sustainable development and shared value.**

Sustainable development is an approach to progress which meets the needs of the present without compromising the ability of future generations to meet their own needs. Shared value relates to operating practices that enhance the competitiveness of a company while simultaneously advancing economic and social conditions in the communities in which it operates.

- **Describe environmental management accounting.**

Environmental management accounting has been reactive rather than proactive by focusing on managing escalating environmental costs arising from meeting regulatory requirements and seeking to avoid litigation and fines. It includes the tracking and reporting of environmental costs, input–output analysis and periodically producing an environmental cost report analysed by environmental prevention costs, detection costs, internal failure costs and external failure costs. Management accounting should also assist in making the business case for creating shared value by reconfiguring the value chain. Some companies have incorporated a society/environmental perspective within a balanced scorecard framework in order to link their environmental strategy to concrete performance measures.

- **Explain the role of the management accountant in avoiding unethical behaviour.**

The management accountant should ensure that any business practices that they are a party to conform with their organization's code of ethics and the guidelines established by their professional accountancy body. Where actions are proposed that are illegal or contrary to regulatory requirements the management accountant should present documentary evidence indicating that such actions should not be undertaken.

- **Explain how today's information technology is changing the role of the management accountant.**

IT developments have freed up management accountants' from undertaking the routine and mundane tasks and enabled them to adopt the role of advisers and internal consultants to the business. Management accountants are now becoming more involved in interpreting the information generated from the IT systems and providing business support for managers.

- **Discuss whether globalization causes management accounting practices to differ across national borders.**

  At the macro level there has been a convergence of management accounting practices across different countries arising from developments in information technology, the increasing tendency of transnational companies to standardize their practices, the global consultancy industry and the use of globally applied textbooks and teaching.

- **Explain the meaning of intellectual capital.**

  Intellectual capital has been defined as the intangible benefits accessible by a firm from its workforce, and more broadly, from its established relationships with groups such as customers, suppliers and competitors. It is often used interchangeably with other terms such as 'knowledge capital', 'knowledge economy' and 'intangible assets'.

- **Describe integrated reporting.**

  Integrated reporting aims to provide information on the financial and non-financial performance in a single document that reports on an organization's impact on the wider perspectives relating to the economy, society and the environment.

KEY TERMS AND CONCEPTS

Big data A term that describes the large volume of raw data, both structured and unstructured, that inundates a business on a daily basis. It includes information such as email messages, social media postings, phone calls, purchase transactions, website traffic and video streams.

Cloud computing Enables software to be located on servers outside the company owned by an external IT provider. The provider then makes the software available over the internet to the companies.

Data Mere records of raw facts that are not organized to be meaningful.

Enterprise resource planning system (ERPS) A set of integrated software application modules that aim to control all information flows within a company.

Environmental detection costs The costs incurred to ensure that a firm's activities, products and processes conform to regulatory laws and voluntary standards.

Environmental external failure costs The costs incurred on activities performed after discharging waste into the environment.

Environmental internal failure costs The costs incurred from performing activities that have produced contaminants and waste that have not been discharged into the environment.

Environmental prevention costs The costs of activities undertaken to prevent the production of waste that could cause damage to the environment.

Ethical behaviour Behaviour that is consistent with the standards of honesty, fairness and social responsibility that have been adopted by the organization.

Information Data that has been organized in a way so that it becomes understandable and useful for a particular purpose.

Information overload A situation that arises when users are provided with too much information to the extent that it becomes unmanageable and no longer useful.

Input/output analysis A technique that can be used to reduce the usage of environmental resources and costs. Inflows of resources such as water, materials and energy are recorded and balanced with outflows on the basis that, what comes in, must go out.

Integrated reporting An external report that aims to provide information on the financial and non-financial performance in a single document relating to the economy, society and the environment.

Intellectual capital The intangible benefits accessible by a firm from its workforce, and more broadly, from its established relationships with groups such as customers, suppliers and competitors. It is often used interchangeably with other terms such as 'knowledge capital', 'knowledge economy' and 'intangible assets.'

Shared value Policies and operating practices that enhance the competitiveness of a company while simultaneously advancing economic and social conditions in the communities in which it operates.

RECOMMENDED READING

The entire publication of the March 2016 issue of *Financial Management* is devoted to the future of management accounting. This publication can be accessed at www.fm-magazine.com. For a discussion of environmental and sustainability issues you should refer to special issues of *Management Accounting Research* (2013, volume 24, issue 4), *Accounting, Organizations and Society* (2014, volume 39, issue 6) and *British Accounting Review* (2014, volume 46, issue 4). A report by the

Chartered Global Management Accountants discusses how management accounting can contribute to shared value. The report is titled 'Sustainable business: shared value in practice' and can be accessed at www.cgma .org/resources/reports/pages/sustainablebusiness .aspx. Finally, you should note that the entire publication of the June 2017 issue of *Financial Management* (www .fm-magazine.com) is devoted to issues relating to ethical behaviour and management accounting.

REVIEW QUESTIONS

23.1 Why was there virtually no innovation in management accounting practices until the mid 1980s (p. 627).

23.2 Explain what is meant by the term shared value and provide examples of how shared value can be created (p. 629).

23.3 Describe input/output analysis (p. 631).

23.4 Discuss the value of an environmental cost report (p. 632).

23.5 Describe how management accounting can support shared value and sustainable development (pp. 632–633).

23.6 Provide examples of unethical behaviour in an organization (pp. 633–634).

23.7 Describe enterprise resource planning systems and their impact on management accountants. (p. 634).

23.8 What factors influence the decision as to whether to adopt cloud computing? (p. 635)

23.9 Describe the meaning of the term Big Data (p. 635).

23.10 Distinguish between data and information (p. 636).

23.11 Explain why management accounting practices tend not to differ across countries (pp. 636–637).

23.12 Explain the meaning of intellectual capital and its implications for management accounting (pp. 637–638)

REVIEW PROBLEMS

23.13 Advanced. Environmental management is considered to be one of the most important issues facing companies today. An effective environmental costing system will not only support a company's environmental management but may also improve the financial performance of the organization.

Required:
Explain THREE ways in which an environmental costing system can lead to improved financial performance. *(5 marks)*

CIMA P2 Performance Management

23.14 Advanced. P plc is a multinational conglomerate company with manufacturing divisions, trading in numerous countries across various continents. Trade takes place between a number of the divisions in different countries, with partly completed products being transferred between them. Where a transfer takes place between divisions trading in different countries, it is the policy of the board of P plc to determine centrally the appropriate transfer price without reference to the divisional managers concerned. The board of P plc justifies this policy to divisional managers on the grounds that its objective is to maximize the conglomerate's post-tax profits and that the global position can be monitored effectively only from the head office.

Required:

(a) Explain and critically appraise the possible reasoning behind P plc's policy of centrally determining transfer prices for goods traded between divisions operating in different countries. *(10 marks)*

(b) Discuss the ethical implications of P plc's policy of imposing transfer prices on its overseas divisions in order to maximize post-tax profits. *(10 marks)*

CIMA Stage 4 Strategic Management Accounting and Marketing

23.15 Advanced: Environmental reporting and life cycle costing. PLX Refinery Co is a large oil refinery business in

Kayland. Kayland is a developing country with a large and growing oil exploration and production business which supplies PLX with crude oil. Currently, the refinery has the capacity to process 200 000 barrels of crude oil per day and makes profits of $146m per year. It employs about 2000 staff and contractors. The staff are paid $60 000 each per year on average (about twice the national average pay in Kayland).

The government of Kayland has been focused on delivering rapid economic growth over the last 15 years, However, there are increasing signs that the environment is paying a large price for this growth with public health suffering. There is now a growing environmental pressure group, Green Kayland (GK), which is organizing protests against the companies that it sees as being the major polluters.

Kayland's government wishes to react to the concerns of the public and the pressure groups. It has requested that companies involved in heavy industry contribute to a general improvement in the treatment of the environment in Kayland.

As a major participant in the oil industry with ties to the nationalized oil exploration company (Kayex), PLX believes it will be strategically important to be at the forefront of environmental developments. It is working with other companies in the oil industry to improve environmental reporting since there is a belief that this will lead to improved public perception and economic efficiency of the industry. PLX has had a fairly good compliance record in Kayland, with only two major fines being levied in the last eight years for safety breaches and river pollution ($1m each).

The existing information systems within PLX focus on financial performance. They support financial reporting obligations and allow monitoring of key performance metrics such as earnings per share and operating margins. Recent publications on environmental accounting have suggested there are a number of techniques [such as input/output analysis, activity-based costing (ABC) and a life cycle view] that may be relevant in implementing improvements to these systems.

PLX is considering a major capital expenditure programme to enhance capacity, safety and efficiency at the refinery. This will involve demolishing certain older sections of the refinery and building on newly acquired land adjacent to the site. Overall, the refinery will increase its land area by 20 per cent.

Part of the refinery extension will also manufacture a new plastic, Kayplas. Kayplas is expected to have a limited market life of five years after which it will be replaced by Kayplas2. The refinery accounting team has forecast the following data associated with this product and calculated PLX's traditional performance measure of product profit for the new product:

All figures are $m

	2019	2020	2021	2022	2023
Revenue	25.0	27.5	30.1	33.2	33.6
Costs					
Production costs	13.8	15.1	16.6	18.3	18.5
Marketing costs	5.0	4.0	3.0	3.0	2.0
Development costs	5.6	3.0	0.0	0.0	0.0
Product profit	0.6	5.4	10.5	11.9	13.1

Subsequently, the following environmental costs have been identified from PLX's general overheads as associated with Kayplas production.

	2019	2020	2021	2022	2023
Waste filtration	1.2	1.4	1.5	1.9	2.1
Carbon dioxide exhaust extraction	0.8	0.9	0.9	1.2	1.5

Additionally, other costs associated with closing down and recycling the equipment in Kayplas production are estimated at $18m in 2023.

The board wishes to consider how it can contribute to the oil industry's performance in environmental accounting, how it can implement the changes that this might require and how these changes will benefit the company,

Required:

(a) Discuss different cost categories that would aid transparency in environmental reporting both internally and externally at PLX. *(4 marks)*
(b) Explain and evaluate how the three environmental accounting techniques mentioned can assist in managing the environmental and strategic performance of PLX. *(9 marks)*
(c) Evaluate the costing approach used for Kayplas's performance compared to a life cycle costing approach, performing appropriate calculations. *(7 marks)*

ACCA P5 Advanced Performance Management

23.16 Advanced: Environmental reporting. FGH Telecom (FGH) is one of the largest providers of mobile and fixed line telecommunications in Ostland. The company has recently been reviewing its corporate objectives in the light of its changed business environment. The major new addition to the strategic objectives is under the heading: 'Building a more environmentally friendly business for the future'. It has been recognized that the company needs to make a contribution to

ensuring sustainable development in Ostland and reducing its environmental footprint. Consequently, it adopted a goal that, by 2024, it would have reduced its environmental impact by 60 per cent (compared to year 2008).

The reasons for the board's concern are that the telecommunications sector is competitive and the economic environment is increasingly harsh, with the markets for debt and equities being particularly poor. On environmental issues, the government and public are calling for change from the business community. It appears that increased regulation and legislation will appear to encourage business towards better performance. The board has recognized that there are threats and opportunities from these trends. It wants to ensure that it is monitoring these factors and so it has asked for an analysis of the business environment with suggestions for performance measurement.

Additionally, the company has a large number of employees working across its network. Therefore, there are large demands for business travel. FGH runs a large fleet of commercial vehicles in order to service its network along with a company car scheme for its managers. The manager in charge of the company's travel budget is reviewing data on carbon dioxide emissions to assess FGH's recent performance.

Recent initiatives within the company to reduce emissions have included:

(a) the introduction in 2017 of a homeworking scheme for employees in order to reduce the amount of commuting to and from their offices; and
(b) a drive to increase the use of teleconferencing facilities by employees.

Data on FGH Telecom:

Carbon dioxide emissions

Measured in millions of kgs	2008 Base year	2016	2017
Commercial fleet diesel	105.4	77.7	70.1
Commercial fleet petrol	11.6	0.4	0.0
Company car diesel	15.1	14.5	12.0
Company car petrol	10.3	3.8	2.2
Other road travel (diesel)	0.5	1.6	1.1
Other road travel (petrol)	3.1	0.5	0.3
Rail travel	9.2	9.6	3.4
Air travel (short haul)	50	4.4	3.1
Air travel (long haul)	5.1	7.1	5.4
Hire cars (diesel)	0.6	1.8	2.9
Hire cars (petrol)	6.7	6.1	6.1
Total	172.6	127.5	106.6

Required:

(a) Evaluate the data given on carbon dioxide emissions using suitable indicators. Identify trends from within the data and comment on whether the company's behaviour is consistent with meeting its targets. *(9 marks)*
(b) Suggest further data that the company could collect in order to improve its analysis and explain how this data could be used to measure the effectiveness of the reduction initiatives mentioned. *(3 marks)*

ACCA P5 Advanced Performance Management

PART SIX

THE APPLICATION OF QUANTITATIVE METHODS TO MANAGEMENT ACCOUNTING

In this part, we examine the application of quantitative methods to various aspects of management accounting. Chapter 24 examines the contribution of mathematical and statistical techniques in determining cost behaviour patterns for cost–volume–profit analysis and the planning and control of costs and revenues. Chapter 25 concentrates on the application of quantitative models to determine the optimum investment in inventories and Chapter 26 looks at the application of linear programming to decision-making and planning and control activities. Rather than delaying the chapters on the application of quantitative techniques to management accounting until Part Six, you may prefer to read Chapter 24 immediately after reading Chapter 8 on cost–volume–profit analysis. Chapter 25 is self-contained and may be assigned to follow any of the chapters in Part Four. Chapter 26 should be read only after you have studied Chapter 9.

24
COST ESTIMATION AND COST BEHAVIOUR

LEARNING OBJECTIVES After studying this chapter, you should be able to:

- identify and describe the different methods of estimating costs;

- calculate regression equations using the high–low, scattergraph and least-squares techniques;

- explain, calculate and interpret the coefficient of determination test of reliability;

- explain the meaning of the term correlation coefficient;

- identify and explain the six steps required to estimate cost functions from past data;

- describe the learning curve and compute the average and incremental labour hours for different output levels.

Determining how cost will change with output or other measurable factors of activity is of vital importance for decision-making, planning and control. The preparation of budgets, the production of performance reports, the calculation of standard costs and the provision of relevant costs for pricing and other decisions all depend on reliable estimates of costs and distinguishing between fixed and variable costs, at different activity levels.

Unfortunately, costs are not easy to predict, since they behave differently under different circumstances. For example, direct labour can be classified as a variable cost where a company uses casual labour hired on a daily basis so that the employment of labour can be exactly matched to meet the production requirements. In contrast, direct labour may be classified as a step-fixed cost for activities where a fixed number of people are employed and this number is maintained even when there is a temporary reduction in the quantity of the activity used. Depreciation is often quoted as a non-variable cost (also known as a fixed cost), but it may well be variable if asset value declines in direct proportion to usage. Therefore we cannot generalize by categorizing direct labour as a variable cost and depreciation as a non-variable cost.

Many costs are fairly easy to classify as purely variable (e.g. direct materials), fixed (e.g. rental of equipment) or step fixed (e.g. labour costs) but others fall into a mixed-cost category (also known as semi-variable costs). In Chapter 2, it was pointed out that a semi-variable cost is a cost that has both a fixed and variable component. For example, the cost of maintenance is a semi-variable cost consisting of planned maintenance that is undertaken whatever the activity, and a variable element that is directly related to activity. Thus, it is the semi-variable costs that we need to separate into their fixed and variable categories.

Frequently the only information that is available for a semi-variable cost is the cost of the activity and a measure of activity usage. For example, records may only be available for the total cost of the maintenance activity for a given period and the number of maintenance hours used during that period. To separate the total cost into its fixed and variable elements it is necessary to use one of the techniques described in this chapter.

Whether a cost is fixed or variable with respect to a particular activity measure or cost driver is also affected by the length of the time span under consideration. The longer the time span the more likely the cost will be variable. For example, maintenance staff salaries are likely to be fixed in the short run and will thus remain unchanged when the volume of maintenance hours changes. However, in the long run, maintenance salaries are likely to vary with the maintenance time required. If maintenance activity expands, extra staff will be appointed but, if activity contracts, staff will be redeployed or made redundant. It is therefore important to specify the length of the time period under consideration when predicting costs for different activity levels.

The importance of accurately estimating costs and the complexity of cost behaviour means that accountants must use increasingly sophisticated techniques. Advances in information technology have enabled more sophisticated techniques to be used for estimating costs, even by small businesses. These developments have led to an increasing awareness of the important potential of mathematical and statistical techniques for estimating costs and it is the aim of this chapter to provide an understanding of these techniques.

Some non-mathematical techniques will also be explained so that you can assess the additional benefits that can be obtained from using the more sophisticated techniques. We shall then examine the effect of experience on cost, which is normally referred to as the learning curve. The emphasis in this chapter will be on manufacturing costs and we shall consider various techniques for estimating how these costs change with activity; similar techniques, however, can be applied to non-manufacturing costs that change with activity.

A major objective of this chapter is to ascertain the activity measure or cost driver that exerts the major influence of the cost of a particular activity. A cost driver can be defined as any factor whose change causes a change in the total cost of an activity. Examples of cost drivers include direct labour hours, machine hours, units of output and number of production run set-ups. Throughout this chapter, the terms 'cost driver' and 'activity measure' will be used synonymously.

GENERAL PRINCIPLES APPLYING TO ESTIMATING COST FUNCTIONS

Before we consider the various methods that are appropriate for estimating costs, we need to look at some of the terms that will be used. A regression equation identifies an estimated relationship between a dependent variable (cost) and one or more independent variables (i.e. an activity measure or cost driver) *based on past observations*. When the equation includes only one independent variable, it is referred to as simple regression and it is possible in this situation to plot the regression equation on a graph as a regression line. When the equation includes two or more independent variables, it is referred to as multiple regression. If there is only one independent variable and the relationship can be assumed to be linear, the regression line can be described by the equation for a straight line:

$$y = a + bx$$

Assuming that we wish to express the relationship between the dependent variable (cost) and the independent variable (activity), then:

$y = $ total cost for the period at an activity level of x
$a = $ total non-variable (fixed) cost for the period
$b = $ average variable cost per unit of activity
$x = $ volume of activity levels or cost driver for the period

If non-variable (fixed) costs for a particular period are £5000, the average unit variable cost is £1, and direct labour hours represent the cost driver, then:

$$\text{total cost} = £5000 + [£1 \times \text{direct labour hours} (x)]$$

or

$$y = a + bx$$

so that

$$y = £5000 + £1x$$

The term cost function is also used to refer to a regression equation that describes the relationship between a dependent variable and one or more independent variables. Cost functions are normally estimated from past cost data and activity levels. Cost estimation begins with measuring *past* relationships between total costs and the potential drivers of those costs. The objective is to use past cost behaviour patterns as an aid to predicting future costs. Any expected changes of circumstances in the future will require past data to be adjusted in line with future expectations.

There is a danger that cost functions derived from past data may be due to a spurious correlation in the data that can end at any time without warning. High correlation is only likely to continue if the relationship between the variables is economically plausible. Cost functions should not be derived solely on the basis of past observed statistical relationships. The nature of the observed statistical relationship should make sense and be economically plausible. If these conditions do not exist one cannot be confident that the estimated relationship will be repeated when the cost function is used to predict outcomes using a different set of data.

Economic plausibility exists when knowledge of operations or logic implies that a cause-and-effect relationship may exist. For example, the number of component parts is a potential cost driver for material handling costs since the greater the number of parts the higher the material handling costs. Logic suggests that a potential cause-and-effect relationship exists.

COST ESTIMATION METHODS

The following approaches to cost estimation will be examined:

1 engineering methods;

2 inspection of the accounts method;

3 graphical or scattergraph method;

4 high–low method;

5 least-squares method.

These approaches differ in terms of the costs of undertaking the analysis and the accuracy of the estimated cost functions. They are not mutually exclusive and different methods may be used for different cost categories.

Engineering methods

Engineering methods of analysing cost behaviour are based on the use of engineering analyses of technological relationships between inputs and outputs – for example, work sampling and time and motion studies. The approach is appropriate when there is a physical relationship between costs and the cost driver. The procedure when undertaking an engineering study is to make an analysis based on *direct* observations of the underlying physical quantities required for an activity and then to convert the final results into cost estimates. Engineers, who are familiar with the technical requirements, estimate the quantities of materials and the labour and machine hours required for various operations; prices and rates are then applied to the physical measures to obtain the cost estimates.

The engineering method is useful for estimating costs of repetitive processes where input–output relationships are clearly defined. For example, this method is usually satisfactory for estimating costs that are usually associated with direct materials, labour and machine time, because these items can be directly observed and measured. However, the engineering method is not a method that can be used for separating semi-variable costs into their fixed and variable elements.

The engineering method is not restricted to manufacturing activities. It can be applied to well-structured administrative and selling activities such as typing, invoicing and purchasing. It is not generally appropriate, however, for estimating costs that are difficult to associate directly with individual units of output, such as many types of overhead cost, since these items cannot easily be directly observed and measured.

Inspection of the accounts

The inspection of accounts method requires that the departmental manager and the accountant inspect each item of expenditure within the accounts for a particular period, and then classify each item of expense as a wholly fixed, wholly variable or a semi-variable cost. A single average *unit* cost figure is selected for the items that are categorized as variable, whereas a single *total* cost for the period is used for the items that are categorized as fixed. For semi-variable items the departmental manager and the accountant agree on a cost function that appears to best describe the cost behaviour. The process is illustrated in Example 24.1.

EXAMPLE 24.1

The following cost information has been obtained from the latest monthly accounts for an output level of 10 000 units for a cost centre:

	(£)
Direct materials	100 000
Direct labour	140 000
Indirect labour	30 000
Depreciation	15 000
Repairs and maintenance	10 000
	295 000

The departmental manager and the accountant examine each item of expense and analyse the expenses into their variable and non-variable elements. The analysis might be as follows:

	Unit variable cost (£)	Total non-variable cost (£)
Direct materials	10.00	
Direct labour	14.00	
Indirect labour		30 000
Depreciation		15 000
Repairs and maintenance	0.50	5 000
	24.50	50 000

Note that repairs and maintenance have been classified as a semi-variable cost consisting of a variable element of £0.50 per unit of output plus £5000 non-variable cost. A check on the *total* cost calculation indicates that the estimate of a unit variable cost of £24.50 will give a total variable cost of £245 000 at an output level of 10 000 units. The non-variable costs of £50 000 are added to this to produce an estimated total cost of £295 000. The cost function is therefore $y = 50\,000 + £24.50x$. This cost function is then used for estimating total cost centre costs at other output levels.

One problem with this method is that the analysis of costs into their variable and non-variable elements can be very subjective. Also, costs are normally based on the latest details that are available from the accounts and these figures may not be typical of either past or future cost behaviour. Whenever possible, cost estimates should be based on a series of observations.

Graphical or scattergraph method

This method involves plotting on a graph the total costs for each activity level. The total cost is represented on the vertical (Y axis) and the activity levels are recorded on the horizontal (X axis). A straight line is fitted to the scatter of plotted points by visual approximation. Figure 24.1 illustrates the procedure using the data presented in Example 24.2.

You will see by referring to Figure 24.1 that the maintenance costs are plotted for each activity level, and a straight line is drawn through the middle of the data points as closely as possible so that the distances of observations above the line are equal to the distances of observations below the line.

The point where the straight line in Figure 24.1 cuts the vertical axis (i.e. £240 000) represents the non-variable costs, item a in the regression formula $y = a + bx$. The unit variable cost b in the regression formula is found by observing the differences between any two points on the straight line (see the dashed line in Figure 24.1 for observations of 160 and 240 hours) and completing the following calculations:

$$\frac{\text{difference in cost}}{\text{difference in activity}} = \frac{£720\,000 - £560\,000}{240\text{ hours} - 160\text{ hours}} = £2000\text{ per hour}$$

This calculation is based on a comparison of the changes in costs that can be observed on the straight line between activity levels of 160 and 240 hours. This gives a regression formula:

$$y = £240\,000 + £2000x$$

If x is assigned a value of 100 hours then:

$$y = £240\,000 + (£2000 \times 100) = £440\,000$$

FIGURE 24.1

Graph of maintenance costs at different activity levels

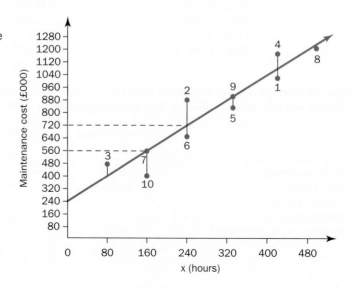

EXAMPLE 24.2

The total maintenance costs and the machine hours for the past ten four-weekly accounting periods were as follows:

Period	Machine hours x	Maintenance cost y (£000)
1	400	960
2	240	880
3	80	480
4	400	1200
5	320	800
6	240	640
7	160	560
8	480	1200
9	320	880
10	160	440

You are required to estimate the regression equation using the graphical method.

The graphical method is simple to use, and it provides a useful visual indication of any lack of correlation or erratic behaviour of costs. However, the method suffers from the disadvantage that the determination of exactly where the straight line should fall is subjective and different people will draw different lines with different slopes, giving different cost estimates. To overcome this difficulty, it is preferable to determine the line of best fit mathematically using the least-squares method, which we will describe later in this chapter.

High–low method

The high–low method consists of selecting the periods of highest and lowest activity levels and comparing the changes in costs that result from the two levels. This approach is illustrated in Example 24.3.

EXAMPLE 24.3

The monthly recordings for output and maintenance costs for the past 12 months have been examined and the following information has been extracted for the lowest and highest output levels:

	Volume of production (units)	Maintenance costs (£)
Lowest activity	5 000	22 000
Highest activity	10 000	32 000

The variable cost per unit is calculated as follows:

$$\frac{\text{difference in cost}}{\text{difference in activity}} = \frac{£10\,000}{5\,000} = £2 \text{ variable cost per unit of output}$$

FIGURE 24.2
High–low method

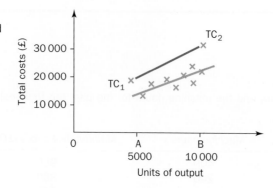

The non-variable (fixed) cost can be estimated at any level of activity (assuming a constant unit variable cost) by subtracting the variable cost portion from the total cost. At an activity level of 5000 units, the total cost is £22 000 and the total variable cost is £10 000 (5000 units, at £2 per unit). The balance of £12 000 is therefore assumed to represent the non-variable cost. The cost function is therefore:

$$y = £12\,000 + £2x$$

The method is illustrated in Figure 24.2, with points A and B representing the lowest and highest output levels, and TC_1 and TC_2 representing the total cost for each of these levels. The other crosses represent past cost observations for other output levels. The straight (blue) line joining the observations for the lowest and highest activity levels represent the costs that would be estimated for each activity level when the high–low method is used.

You will see from this illustration that the method ignores all cost observations other than the observations for the lowest and highest activity levels. Unfortunately, cost observations at the extreme ranges of activity level are not always typical of normal operating conditions, and therefore may reflect abnormal rather than normal cost relationships. If you compare the two straight lines you can see how the high–low method can give inaccurate cost estimates. The lower straight (green) line, using the graphical or scattergraph approach described in the previous section, incorporates all of the observations. It is likely to provide a better estimate of the cost function than a method that relies on only two observations. The high–low method cannot therefore be recommended.

The least-squares method

This is a mathematical method of determining the regression line of best fit. It is important for you to understand how this method works, although you are unlikely to be asked to compute these values without help. Spreadsheet packages have regression routines that will perform these calculations for you (see 'Guide to Excel' within the digital support resources accompanying this book). You should also note that examination questions generally provide you with formulae 24.1 and 24.2 and the associated values for the variables shown in Exhibit 24.1. It is most unlikely that you will be required to compute the values shown in Exhibit 24.1.

The least squares method is based on the principle that the sum of the squares of the vertical deviations from the line that is established using the method is less than the sum of the squares of the vertical deviations from any other line that might be drawn. The regression equation for a straight line ($y = a + bx$) that meets this requirement can be found from the following two equations by solving for a and b:

$$a = \frac{\sum y}{n} - \frac{b \sum x}{n} \tag{24.1}$$

$$b = \frac{n \sum xy - \sum x \sum y}{n \sum x^2 - \left(\sum x\right)^2} \tag{24.2}$$

EXHIBIT 24.1 Past observations of maintenance costs

Hours x	Maintenance cost y (£)	x^2	xy	y^2
90	1500	8100	135000	2250000
150	1950	22500	292500	3802500
60	900	3600	54000	810000
30	900	900	27000	810000
180	2700	32400	486000	7290000
150	2250	22500	337500	5062500
120	1950	14400	234000	3802500
180	2100	32400	378000	4410000
90	1350	8100	121500	1822500
30	1050	900	31500	1102500
120	1800	14400	216000	3240000
60	1350	3600	81000	1822500
$\Sigma x = 1260$	$\Sigma y = 19800$	$\Sigma x^2 = 163800$	$\Sigma xy = 2394000$	$\Sigma y^2 = 36225000$

where n is the number of observations and $\sum$ represents the sum of the variables specified in the above formulae.

Exhibit 24.1 is used to illustrate the least-squares method. It is assumed that past information is available for total maintenance cost and machine hours used. We can now insert the data derived from Exhibit 24.1 into the above formulae.

Applying the above formulae 24.1 and 24.2, we must first calculate the value of b using formula 24.2:

$$b = \frac{12(2394000) - (1260)(19800)}{12(163800) - (1260)^2} = 378020000/378000 = £10$$

$$a = \frac{19800}{12} - \frac{(10)(1260)}{12} = £600$$

We can now use the above cost function ($y = £600 + £10x$) to predict the cost incurred at different activity levels, including those for which we have no past observations. For example, at an activity level of 100 hours the cost prediction is £600 non-variable cost, plus £1000 variable cost (100 hours × £10). The regression line and the actual observations (represented by the dots) are recorded in Figure 24.3.

FIGURE 24.3
Regression line $y = 600 + 10x$ compared with actual observations

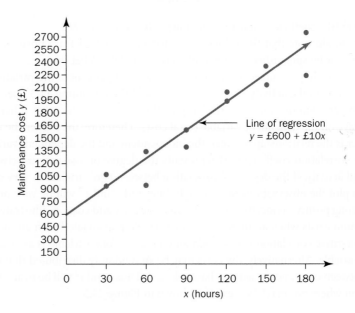

The closer the vertical distances of the plotted actual observations are to the straight line, the more reliable is the estimated cost function in predicting cost behaviour. In other words, the closer the observations are to the line, the stronger the relationship between the independent variable (machine hours in our example) and the dependent variable (i.e. total maintenance cost).

TESTS OF RELIABILITY

In Exhibit 24.1, the cost function was derived using machine hours as the activity measure/cost driver. However, a number of other potential cost drivers exist, such as direct labour hours, units of output and number of production runs. Various tests of reliability can be applied to see how reliable potential cost drivers are in predicting the dependent variable. The simplest approach is to plot the data for each potential cost driver and examine the distances from the straight line derived from a visual fit (using the graphical method) or the least-squares regression equation. A more sophisticated approach is to compute the coefficient of variation (known as r^2). The coeffeicient of variation is the square of the correlation coefficient (known as r). It is a goodness of fit measure that indicates how well the predicted values of the dependent variable (i.e. the estimated cost observations represented by y), based on the chosen independent variable (i.e. machine hours (x) in our example shown in Exhibit 24.1), matches the actual cost observations (Y). In particular, the coefficient of variation measures the percentage variation in the dependent variable that is explained by the independent variable.

When you are required to calculate the coefficient of determination most examination questions provide you with the following formula for the correlation coefficient (r):

$$r = \frac{n\sum xy - \sum x \sum y}{\sqrt{\left(n\sum x^2 - \left(\sum x\right)^2\right)\left(n\sum y^2 - \left(\sum y\right)^2\right)}} \tag{24.3}$$

Applying the data derived from Exhibit 24.1 to formula 24.3:

$$R \text{ (correlation coefficient)} = \frac{12(2\,394\,000) - (1260)(19\,800)}{\sqrt{[12(163\,800) - (1260)^2][(12 \times 36\,225\,000) - (19\,800)^2]}}$$

$$= \frac{3\,780\,000}{4\,015\,654} = 0.941$$

so that r^2 (the coefficient of determination) $= (0.941)^2 = 0.8861$.

You should note that the values computed in Exhibit 24.1 are normally provided in examination questions or by spreadsheet regression analysis models. What does a coefficient of determination of 0.8861 mean? In percentage terms, it means that 88.61 per cent of the variation in total cost is explained by variations in the activity base (cost driver) and the remaining 11.39 per cent is explained by either random variation or random variation plus the combined effect that other omitted explanatory variables have on the dependent variable (total cost). Therefore, the higher the coefficient of variation, the stronger is the relationship between the independent and the dependent variable.

The correlation coefficient (r) represents the degree of association between two variables, such as cost and activity. If the degree of association between two variables is very close, it will be almost possible to plot the observations on a straight line, and r and r^2 will be very near to 1. In this situation, a very strong positive association exists between activity and costs, as illustrated in Figure 24.4. A positive correlation exists when an increase in one variable is associated with an increase in the other variable and a negative correlation exists when an increase in one variable is associated with a decrease in the other variable. Alternatively, the costs may be so randomly distributed that there is little or no correlation between costs and the activity base selected. Thus r and r^2 will be near to zero. An illustration of the situation where no correlation exists is shown in Figure 24.5.

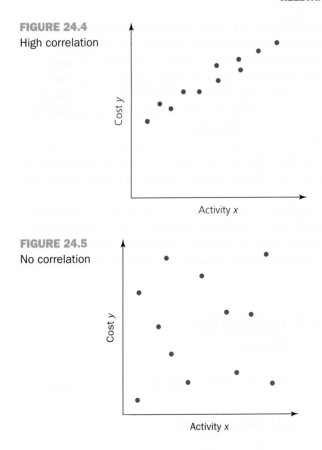

FIGURE 24.4
High correlation

FIGURE 24.5
No correlation

RELEVANT RANGE AND NON-LINEAR COST FUNCTIONS

It may be very misleading to use a cost estimation equation (cost function) to estimate the total costs for ranges of activities outside the range of observations that were used to establish the cost function. This is because a cost function is normally only valid within the range of the actual observations that were used to establish the equation.

You will see from Figure 24.6 that in the past the company has operated only between activity levels x_1 and x_2 (this represents the actual observations). A cost equation developed from this information may provide satisfactory cost estimates for activity levels between x_1 and x_2, but it may not do so for activity levels outside this range of observations. For example, the dashed line that meets the vertical axis at A might represent a cost equation that has been developed from these observations; the dashed line will represent a

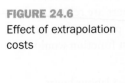

FIGURE 24.6
Effect of extrapolation costs

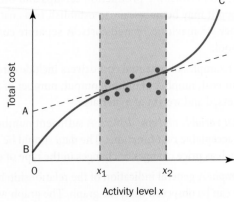

satisfactory estimate of total cost only between activity levels x_1 and x_2. However, any extrapolation of the dashed line outside the range of observations may result in an unsatisfactory estimate of total cost.

You will remember that in Chapter 8 it was stressed that linear cost functions may only apply over the relevant production range (i.e. between activity levels x_1, and x_2 in Figure 24.6), and that over a very wide range of activity a curvilinear (non-linear) relationship may exist, similar to the curved line BC in Figure 24.6. It therefore follows that the extrapolation of the dashed line represents an unsatisfactory estimate outside the relevant range if a curvilinear relationship exists.

In practice, the problem of extrapolation may not occur, since the majority of decisions are normally taken within the relevant operating range over which the firm has had experience of operating in the past. However, if decisions are to be based on cost information that is projected beyond the relevant range, the cost estimates must be used with care.

To determine whether a curvilinear relationship exists, the observations should be plotted on a graph, so that a simple examination of the graph may indicate whether or not such relationships exist. Indeed, it is a good idea always to prepare graphs and look carefully at the plotted data to ensure that some of the important requirements of cost estimation are not violated – blind reliance on mathematical techniques can be very dangerous.

A SUMMARY OF THE STEPS INVOLVED IN ESTIMATING COST FUNCTIONS

We can now summarize the stages involved in the estimation of a cost function based on the analysis of past data. They are:

1 select the dependent variable y (the cost variable) to be predicted;

2 select the potential cost drivers;

3 collect data on the dependent variable and cost drivers;

4 plot the observations on a graph;

5 estimate the cost function;

6 test the reliability of the cost function.

It may be necessary to undertake each of these stages several times for different potential cost drivers before an acceptable cost function can be identified:

1 *Select the dependent variable y*: The choice of the cost (or costs) to be predicted will depend on the purpose of the cost function. If the purpose is to estimate the indirect costs of a production or activity cost centre, then all indirect costs associated with the production (activity) centre that are considered to have the same cause-and-effect relationship with the potential costs drivers should be grouped together. For example, if some overheads are considered to be related to performing production set-ups and others are related to machine running hours then it may be necessary to establish two cost pools: one for set-up-related costs and another for machine-related costs. A separate cost function would be established for each cost pool.

2 *Select potential cost drivers*: Examples of potential cost drivers include direct labour hours, machine hours, direct labour cost, number of units of output, number of production run set-ups, number of orders processed and weight of materials.

3 *Collect data on the dependent variable and cost drivers*: A sufficient number of past observations must be obtained to derive acceptable cost functions. The data should be adjusted to reflect any changes of circumstance, such as price changes or changes in the type of equipment used.

4 *Plot the observations on a graph*: A general indication of the relationship between the dependent variable and the cost driver can be observed from the graph. The graph will provide a visual

Cost estimating in mining projects

South African energy and chemicals company Sasol, like many companies dealing with large-scale projects, needs to prepare cost estimates. Sasol specialize in high value liquid fuels, chemicals and low-carbon electricity. In 2014, the company decided to invest $8.9 billion in the Lake Charles Chemical Project in Louisiana, USA. The project would create a 'a world-scale 1.5 million ton per year ethane cracker, and six downstream chemical units' (Sasol, 2016).

By the third quarter of 2016, the total estimated cost of completing the plant had risen to $11 billion. An investor project fact sheet for the Lake Charles project (see Sasol 2016) revealed the reasons for the increased cost. First, costs of construction increased due to poor soil and sub-surface conditions, which was compounded by poor weather. Second, the cost of contract labour proved to be higher than expected due to higher wage rates, higher engineering hours and lower productivity than planned. Third, the total labour cost was higher than estimated due to the use of higher skilled labour, which in turn implied higher wages rates. Despite the higher costs, the company expects the project to be completed on time and the press release notes they still regard the Lake Charles project as a sound strategic investment.

Questions

1 Based on the information given, do you think it possible to develop a cost model to estimate costs of large scale projects such as the Lake Charles project?

2 When the plant is operational, do you think it is possible to develop a cost estimation model for production outputs?

References

'About Sasol', available at www.sasol.com/about -sasol/company-profile/overview, accessed 15 December 2016.

Sasol (2016), Lake Charles Project Fact Sheet, available at www.sasol.com/investor-centre /lake-charles-chemicals-project/lake-charles -chemicals-project-fact-sheet-23082016, accessed 15 December 2016.

indication as to whether a linear cost function can approximate the cost behaviour and also highlight extreme or abnormal observations. These observations should be investigated to ascertain whether they should be excluded from the analysis.

5 *Estimate the cost function*: The cost function should be estimated using the approaches described in this chapter.

6 *Test the reliability of the cost function*: The reliability of the cost function should be tested. The cost function should be plausible. Cost functions should not be derived solely on the basis of observed past statistical relationships. Instead, they should be used to confirm or reject beliefs that have been developed from a study of the underlying process. The nature of the statistical relationship should be understood and make economic sense.

COST ESTIMATION WHEN THE LEARNING EFFECT IS PRESENT

When employees perform new tasks they are likely to take less time as they become more familiar with performing the task so that less labour time is required for the production of each unit of output. This phenomenon has been observed in a number of manufacturing situations, and is known as the learning curve effect. From the experience of aircraft production during World War II, aircraft manufacturers found that the rate of improvement was so regular that it could be reduced to a formula, and the labour hours required could be predicted with a high degree of accuracy from a learning curve. Based on this information, experiments have been undertaken in other industries with learning curves, and these experiments also indicate some regularity in the pattern of a worker's ability to learn a new task.

ADVANCED READING

REAL WORLD VIEWS 24.2

New aircraft engines – a learning curve effect

Modern day aircraft are complex pieces of engineering, increasingly using more technology, composite materials and more efficient engines. Aircraft engines are in particular improving not only in fuel efficiency, but also in range, thus contributing to lower fares for us all.

Many modern aircraft, such as the Airbus A320neo, use geared turbo-fan engines (GTF). These relatively new engine design types use a gearing mechanism to achieve faster rotation speeds, and as a result are more fuel efficient and weigh less. They are however more expensive to purchase and more complex to manufacture. Pratt & Whitney are one manufacturer of GTF engines and their PW1000G engine entered service in early 2016. However, the *Air Transport World* website reported in September 2016 that Pratt & Whitney were taking twice as long to build the PW1000G engines, and were behind their budgeted output level. This of course has a knock-on effect for aircraft manufacturers, as their aircraft would in turn be delayed. As a result, Pratt and Whitney are reported to have made payments to airlines to compensate for lost earnings.

Questions

1 Do you think a learning curve effect is at play in the manufacture of the PW1000G engines?

2 Can you think of any reasons why any learning curve effect may have been slower than predicted?

References

Air Transport World (2016), 'Pratt & Whitney struggling with GTF fan blade learning curve', available at atwonline.com/engines/utc-ceo-pratt-whitney -struggling-gtf-fan-blade-learning-curve, accessed 16 December 2016.

The first time a new operation is performed, both workers and operating procedures are untried. As the operation is repeated, workers become more familiar with the work, labour efficiency increases and the labour cost per unit declines. This process continues for some time, and a regular rate of decline in cost per unit can be established at the outset. This rate of decline can then be used in predicting future labour costs. The learning process starts from the point when the first unit comes off the production line. From then on, each time cumulative production is doubled, the average time taken to produce each unit of cumulative production is estimated to be a certain percentage of the average time per unit of the previous cumulative production.

An application of the 80 per cent learning curve is presented in Exhibit 24.2, which shows the labour hours required on a sequence of six orders where the cumulative number of units is doubled for each order. The first unit was completed on the first order in 2000 hours; for each subsequent order, the *cumulative production* was doubled (see column 3), so that the average hours per unit were 80 per cent of the average hours per unit of the previous *cumulative production*. For example, the *cumulative average time* shown in column 4 for each unit of output is calculated as follows:

$$
\begin{aligned}
\text{order number } 1 &= 2000 \text{ hours} \\
2 &= 1600 \text{ hours } (80\% \times 2000) \\
3 &= 1280 \text{ hours } (80\% \times 1600) \\
4 &= 1024 \text{ hours } (80\% \times 1280) \\
5 &= 819 \text{ hours } (80\% \times 1024) \\
6 &= 655 \text{ hours } (80\% \times 819)
\end{aligned}
$$

Exhibit 24.2 provides information for specific quantities only. No information is available for other quantities such as ten, 20 or 30 units, although such information could be obtained either graphically or mathematically.

EXHIBIT 24.2 Labour hours for 80 per cent learning curve

Number of units			Cumulative hours		Hours for each order	
(1)	(2)	(3)	(4)	(5)	(6)	(7)
		Cumulative		Total		Per unit
Order no.	Per order	production	Per unit	(3) × (4)	Total	(6) ÷ (2)
1	1	1	2000	2000	2000	2000
2	1	2	1600	3200	1200	1200
3	2	4	1280	5120	1920	960
4	4	8	1024	8192	3072	768
5	8	16	819	13104	4912	614
6	16	32	655	20960	7856	491

Graphical method

The quantities for the average time per unit of cumulative production (column 4 of Exhibit 24.2) are presented in graphical form in Figure 24.7. The entries in column 4 are plotted on the graph for each level of cumulative production, and a line is drawn through these points. (You should note that more accurate graphs can be constructed if the observations are plotted on log–log graph paper.)

The graph shows that the average time per unit declines rapidly at first and then more slowly, until eventually the decline is so small that it can be ignored. When no further improvement is expected and the regular efficiency level is reached, the situation is referred to as the **steady-state production level**. The cumulative average hours per unit is 953 hours for ten units and 762 hours for 20 units. To obtain the total number of hours, we merely multiply the average number of hours by the cumulative quantity produced, which gives 9530 total hours for ten units and 15240 total hours for 20 units.

Mathematical method

The learning curve can be expressed in equation form as:

$$Y_x = aX^b \qquad (24.4)$$

where Y_x is defined as the average time per unit of cumulative production to produce X units, a is the time required to produce the first unit of output and X is the number of units of output under

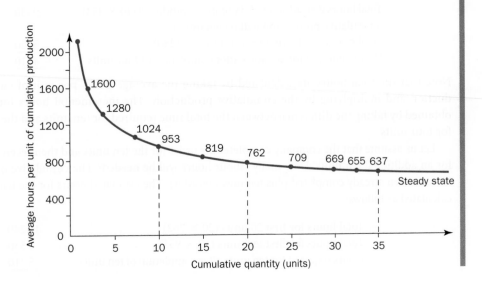

FIGURE 24.7
80 per cent
learning curve

consideration. The exponent *b* is defined as the ratio of the natural logarithm (denoted by *ln*) of the learning curve improvement rate (e.g. 0.8 for an 80 per cent learning curve) divided by the natural logarithm of 2. The improvement exponent can take on any value between -1 and zero. For example, for an 80 per cent learning curve:

$$b = \frac{ln\ 0.8}{ln\ 2} = \frac{-0.2231}{0.6931} = -0.322$$

The average time taken per unit of cumulative production to produce ten and 20 units can therefore be calculated as follows:

$$\begin{aligned} Y_{10} &= 2000 \times 10^{-0.322} \\ &= 2000 \times 0.476431 \\ &= \underline{953} \end{aligned}$$

and

$$\begin{aligned} Y_{20} &= 2000 \times 20^{-0.322} \\ &= 2000 \times 0.381126 \\ &= \underline{762} \end{aligned}$$

A computation of the exponent values may be made by using a calculator with exponent functions. For example, *ln* 0.8 and *ln* 2 is derived by simply inserting these figures into a calculator and pressing the natural log function denoted by the key marked 'ln'. The above calculation of 0.476431 (derived from $10^{-0.322}$) is obtained by entering 10 followed by the multiplication sign then pressing the Y^x and entering -0.322 followed by the equal sign.

ESTIMATING INCREMENTED HOURS AND INCREMENTAL COST

Incremental hours cannot be determined directly from the learning curve graph or formula, since the results are expressed in terms of average hours per unit of cumulative production. It is possible, however, to obtain incremental hours by examining the differences between total hours for various combinations of cumulative hours. For example, assume that for Exhibit 24.2 the company has completed orders such that cumulative production is four units and that an enquiry has been received for an order of six units. We can calculate the incremental hours for these six units as follows:

Total hours if an additional six units are produced (10 × 953) (cumulative production will be ten units)	9530
Total hours for the first four units (4 × 1280)	5120
Hours required for six units after completion of four units	= 4410

Note that the total hours are calculated by taking the average hours per unit of cumulative production and multiplying by the cumulative production. The incremental hours for six units are obtained by taking the difference between the total time required for ten units and the time required for four units.

Let us assume that the company completes the order for the ten units and then receives a new order for an additional ten units. How many labour hours will be needed? The cumulative quantity is now 20 units (ten already completed plus ten now on order). The estimated hours for the ten new units are calculated as follows:

Total hours for first 20 units (20 × 762)	15240
Total hours for first ten units (10 × 953)	9530
Hours required for ten units after completion of ten units	5710

The learning curve can be used to estimate labour costs and those other costs that vary in direct proportion to labour costs. Note that the learning effect only applies to direct labour costs and those variable overheads that are a direct function of labour hours of input. It does not apply to material costs, non-variable costs or items that vary with output rather than input.

SUMMARY

The following items relate to the learning objectives listed at the beginning of the chapter.

- **Identify and describe the different methods of estimating costs.**

The following approaches can be used to estimate costs: (a) engineering methods; (b) inspection of accounts method; (c) graphical or scattergraph method; (d) high–low method; (e) least-squares method; and (f) multiple regression analysis. With engineering studies a detailed study of each operation is undertaken under controlled conditions, based on high levels of efficiency, to ascertain the quantities of labour and materials required. Target prices are then applied based on efficient purchasing to ascertain the standard costs. The engineering method is most appropriate for estimating direct costs for repetitive processes where input–output relationships are clearly defined. The inspection of accounts method requires that a subjective estimate is made of the fixed and variable elements for each item of expenditure within the accounts for a particular period. The remaining methods are described below.

- **Calculate regression equations using high–low, scattergraph and least-squares techniques.**

The high–low method consists of selecting the periods of highest and lowest activity levels and comparing the changes in costs that result from these two levels. The variable cost per unit is derived by dividing the difference in cost between the two levels by the differences in activity. Fixed costs are computed by deducting the derived variable cost from total cost at either the lowest or highest output level (see Example 24.3 for an illustration of the calculations). The scattergraph method involves plotting on a graph the total cost for each observed activity level. A straight line is drawn through the middle of the scatter of points so that the distances of observations below the line are equal to the distances above the line. The variable cost per unit is derived from the straight line by dividing the difference in cost by the difference in activity. The intercept gives the estimated fixed cost (see Example 24.2 and Figure 24.1 for an illustration of the computations). The least-squares method determines mathematically the line of best fit. It is based on the principle that the sum of the squares of the vertical deviations from the line that is established using this method is less than the sum of the squares of the vertical deviations from any other line that might be drawn (see Exhibit 24.1 for an illustration of the computations). Because this method uses all of the observations and determines the line of best fit mathematically it is considered superior to the high–low or scattergraph methods.

- **Explain, calculate and interpret the coefficient of variation test of reliability.**

Various tests of reliability can be applied to ascertain how reliable potential independent variables (i.e. cost drivers) are in predicting the dependent variable (i.e. the actual cost observations). One such test is the coefficient of variation (r^2). It is a goodness of fit measure that indicates how well the predicted values of the dependent variable, based on the chosen independent variable, matches the actual cost observations. In particular, the coefficient of variation measures the percentage variation in the dependent variable that is explained by the independent variable. You should refer to Exhibit 24.1 and formula 24.3 for an illustration of the calculation of the coefficient of determination.

- **Explain the meaning of the term correlation coefficient.**

The correlation coefficient measures the degree of association between two variables. If the degree of association between the two variables is very close it will almost be possible to plot the relationship on a straight line and the correlation coefficient will be very close to 1. A positive correlation exists when an increase in one variable is associated with an increase in the other variable, whereas a negative correlation exists when an increase/decrease in one variable is associated with a decrease/increase in the other variable. Alternatively, zero correlation exists where there is little or no association between two variables.

● **Identify and explain the six steps required to estimate cost functions from past data.**

The following six steps are required: (a) select the cost (dependent) variable to be predicted; (b) select potential cost drivers (i.e. the causes of costs); (c) collect data on the dependent variable and the selected cost driver; (d) plot the observations on a graph; (e) estimate the cost function; and (f) test the reliability of the cost function.

● **Describe the learning curve and compute the average and incremental labour hours for different output levels.**

If the labour content per unit is expected to decline, as workers become more familiar with a process, learning curve principles can be applied. Previous experience in some industries has found that the rate of improvement was so regular that it could be reduced to a formula and that the labour hours required could be predicted with a high degree of accuracy from a learning curve. The learning curve is based on the principle that the learning process starts from the point when the first unit comes off the production line. From then on, each time cumulative production is doubled, the average time taken to produce each unit of cumulative production will be a certain percentage (often assumed to be 80 per cent) of the average time per unit of the previous cumulative production. See Exhibit 24.2 for an illustration of the application of the learning curve.

● **Additional learning objective presented in Appendix 24.1.**

Appendix 24.1 includes an additional learning objective: to describe multiple regression analysis and indicate the circumstances when it should be used. The least-squares regression method described in the main body of the chapter assumes that total costs are determined by one variable only (i.e. activity). Multiple regression can be used when it is considered that total costs are determined by more than one variable. Thus, if a single activity measure is found to be unreliable, and other variables are considered to significantly influence total costs, multiple regression analysis should be used.

APPENDIX 24.1: MULTIPLE REGRESSION ANALYSIS

ADVANCED READING

The least-squares regression equation was based on the assumption that total cost was determined by one activity-based variable only. However, other variables besides activity are likely to influence total cost. A certain cost may vary not only with changes in the hours of operation but also with the weight of the product being made, temperature changes or other factors. With simple least-squares regression, only one factor is taken into consideration; but with multiple regression, several factors are considered in combination. As far as possible, all the factors related to cost behaviour should be brought into the analysis so that costs can be predicted and controlled more effectively.

The equation for simple regression can be expanded to include more than one independent variable. If there are two independent variables and the relationship is assumed to be linear, the regression equation will be:

$$y = a + b_1 x_1 + b_2 x_2$$

Item a represents the non-variable cost item. Item b_1 represents the average change in y resulting from a unit change in x_1, assuming that x_2 and all the unidentified items remain constant. Similarly, b_2 represents the average change in y resulting from a unit change in x_2 assuming that x_1 remains constant. Multiple regression equations can be derived using Microsoft Excel.

Multiple regression analysis is based on the assumption that the independent variables are not correlated with each other. When the independent variables are highly correlated with each other, it is very difficult, and sometimes impossible, to separate the effects of each of these variables on the dependent variable. This occurs when there is a simultaneous movement of two or more independent variables in the same direction and at approximately the same rate. This condition is called multicollinearity. Multicollinearity can be found in a variety of ways. One way is to measure the correlation between the independent variables. Generally, a coefficient of correlation between independent variables greater than 0.70 indicates multicollinearity.

KEY TERMS AND CONCEPTS

Activity measure Any factor whose change causes a change in the total cost of an activity, also known as a cost driver.

Coefficient of determination A measure that shows how much of the variation in a dependent variable is caused by variations in an independent variable and how much by random variation and other independent variables.

Coefficient of variation The square of the correlation coefficient, measuring the percentage variation in the dependent variable that is explained by the independent variable.

Correlation coefficient The strength of the linear relationship between two variables.

Cost driver The basis used to allocate costs to cost objects in an ABC system.

Cost function A regression equation that describes the relationship between a dependent variable and one or more independent variables.

Dependent variable A variable, such as cost, that changes when an independent variable, such as volume, is varied.

Engineering methods Methods of analysing cost behaviour that are based on the use of engineering analyses of technological relationships between inputs and outputs.

Goodness of fit A measure that indicates how well the predicted values of the dependent variable, based on the chosen independent variable, match actual observations.

High–low method A method of analysing cost behaviour that consists of selecting the periods of highest and lowest activity levels and comparing the changes in costs that result from the two levels in order to separate fixed and variable costs.

Independent variable A variable such as volume, machine time or another cost driver, that affects the value of a dependent variable, such as cost.

Inspection of accounts method A method of analysing cost behaviour that requires the departmental manager and the accountant to inspect each item of expenditure within the accounts for a particular period, and then classify each item as a wholly fixed, wholly variable or a semi-variable cost.

Learning curve A graphical representation of the rate at which a worker learns a new task.

Learning curve effect Changes in the efficiency of the labour force as workers become more familiar with the tasks they perform that may render past information unsuitable for predicting future labour costs.

Least-squares method A mathematical method of analysing cost behaviour that involves determining the regression line of best fit.

Multicollinearity A condition that occurs when there is simultaneous movement of two or more independent variables in the same direction and at approximately the same rate, indicating that the independent variables are highly correlated with each other.

Multiple regression A regression equation that includes two or more independent variables.

Regression equation An equation that identifies an estimated relationship between a dependent variable (cost) and one or more independent variables based on past observations.

Simple regression A regression equation that only contains one independent variable.

Steady-state production level The level of production when no further improvement is expected and the regular efficiency level is reached.

Tests of reliability Statistical and graphical methods of testing the strength of the relationship between independent and dependent variables.

RECOMMENDED READING

This chapter has provided an introduction to the various cost estimation techniques. For a more detailed discussion of these techniques, you should refer to Chapter 6 of Groot and Selto (2013).

KEY EXAMINATION POINTS

In recent years emphasis has switched from calculation to interpretation. Do make sure you can interpret regression equations and explain the meaning of the various statistical tests of reliability. Different formulae can be used to calculate regression equations and r^2 but the formulae specified in the chapter should be given. The examiner will have set the question assuming you will use the formula. Do not worry if you are unfamiliar with the formula. All that is necessary is for you to enter the figures given in the question into it.

Remember with learning curves that only labour costs and variable overheads that vary with labour costs are subject to the learning effect. A common requirement is for you to calculate the incremental hours per order. Make sure that you understand columns 6 and 7 of Exhibit 24.2.

ASSESSMENT MATERIAL

The review questions are short questions that enable you to assess your understanding of the main topics included in the chapter. The numbers in parentheses provide you with the page numbers to refer to if you cannot answer a specific question.

The review problems are more complex and require you to relate and apply the content to various business problems. The problems are graded by their level of difficulty. Solutions to review problems that are not preceded by the term 'IM' are provided in a separate section at the end of the book. Solutions to problems preceded by the term 'IM' are provided in the Instructor's Manual accompanying this book that can be downloaded from the lecturer's digital support resources. Additional review problems with fully worked solutions are provided in the *Student Manual* that accompanies this book.

REVIEW QUESTIONS

24.1 Explain what is meant by the term 'cost function'. (p. 648)

24.2 Under what circumstances can the engineering method be used to estimate costs? (p. 648)

24.3 Describe the high–low method. (pp. 651–652)

24.4 What is the major limitation of the high–low method? (pp. 651–652)

24.5 Describe how the scattergraph method is used to analyse costs into their fixed and variable elements. (pp. 649–650)

24.6 Describe the least-squares method. Why is this method better than the high–low and scattergraph methods? (pp. 652–654)

24.7 When is multiple regression required to explain cost behaviour? (p. 662)

24.8 Describe the steps that should be followed in estimating cost functions. (pp. 656–657)

24.9 Why is a scattergraph a useful first step in estimating cost functions? (pp. 656–657)

24.10 Describe what is meant by the learning curve effect. (pp. 658–659)

24.11 Define the steady-state production level. (p. 659)

24.12 Describe what is meant by 'goodness of fit'. (p. 654)

24.13 Explain the meaning of coefficient of variation. (p. 654)

REVIEW PROBLEMS

24.14 Intermediate. The table below shows the output, total costs and the cost inflation index for a business in two periods. Cost behaviour patterns were the same in both periods.

Output level	Total cost	Inflation index
12 000 units	$21 000	1.05
16 000 units	$26 780	1.03

The variable cost per unit at an inflation index of 1.08 will be:

(a) $1.56
(b) $1.45
(c) $1.50
(d) $1.62

(2 marks)

CIMA P1 Performance Operations

24.15 Basic. A company is estimating its costs based on past information. The total costs incurred by the company at different levels of output were as follows:

Output (units)	Total costs $
160 000	2 420 000
185 000	2 775 000
190 000	2 840 000

The company uses the high–low method to separate total costs into their fixed and variable elements. Ignore inflation.

The estimated total costs for an output of 205 000 units is:

(a) $2 870 000
(b) $3 050 000
(c) $3 064 211
(d) $3 080 857   (2 marks)

The company has now established that there is a stepped increase in fixed costs of $30 000 when output reaches 180 000 units.

The estimate of total costs for an output of 175 000 units using the additional information is:

(a) $2 645 000
(b) $2 275 000
(c) $2 615 000
(d) $2 630 000   (2 marks)

CIMA P1 Performance Operations

24.16 Advanced: Cost estimation using linear regression. Albatross Plc, the Australian subsidiary of a British packaging company, is preparing its budget for the year to 30 June 2019. In respect of fuel oil consumption, it is desired to estimate an equation of the form $y = a + bx$, where y is the total expense at an activity level x, a is the fixed expense and b is the rate of variable cost.

The following data relates to the year ending 30 June 2018:

Month	Machine hours (£000)	Fuel oil expense (£000)	Month	Machine hours (£000)	Fuel oil expense (£000)
July	34	640	January	26	500
August	30	620	February	26	500
September	34	620	March	31	530
October	39	590	April	35	550
November	42	500	May	43	580
December	32	530	June	48	680

The annual total and monthly average figures for the year ending 30 June 2018 were as follows:

	Machine hours (000)	Fuel oil expense ($)
Annual total	420	6840
Monthly average	35	570

You are required to:

(a) estimate fixed and variable elements of fuel oil expense from the above data by both the following methods:

(i) high and low points   (4 marks)
(ii) least-squares regression analysis;   (8 marks)

(b) compare briefly the methods used in (a) above in relation to the task of estimating fixed and variable elements of a semi-variable cost;   (7 marks)

(c) accepting that the coefficient of determination arising from the data given in the question is approximately 0.25, interpret the significance of this fact.   (6 marks)

ICAEW Management Accounting

24.17 Advanced: Learning curve calculation and implications. Mic Co. produces microphones for mobile phones and operates a standard costing system. Before production commenced, the standard labour time per batch for its latest microphone was estimated to be 200 hours. The standard labour cost per hour is $12 and resource allocation and cost data were therefore initially prepared on this basis.

Production of the microphone started in July and the number of batches assembled and sold each month was as follows:

Month	No. of batches assembled and sold
July	1
August	1
September	2
October	4
November	8

The first batch took 200 hours to make, as anticipated, but, during the first four months of production, a learning effect of 88 per cent was observed, although this finished at the end of October. The learning formula is shown on the formula sheet and at the 88 per cent learning rate the value of b is -0.1844245.

Mic Co. uses 'cost plus' pricing to establish selling prices for all its products. Sales of its new microphone in the first five months have been disappointing. The sales manager has blamed the production department for getting the labour cost so wrong, as this, in turn, caused the price to be too high. The production manager has disclaimed all responsibility, saying that, 'As usual, the managing director prepared the budgets alone and didn't consult me and, had he bothered to do so, I would have told him that a learning curve was expected.'

Required:

(a) Calculate the actual total monthly labour costs for producing the microphones for each of the five months from July to November.   (9 marks)
(b) Discuss the implications of the learning effect coming to an end for Mic Co., with regard to costing, budgeting and production.   (4 marks)
(c) Discuss the potential advantages and disadvantages of involving senior staff at Mic Co. in the budget setting process, rather than the managing director simply imposing the budgets on them.   (7 marks)

ACCA F5 Performance Management

24.18 Advanced: Use of learning curve to determine life cycle/target cost. Cam Co. manufactures webcams, devices which can provide live video and audio streams via personal computers. It has recently been suffering from liquidity problems and hopes that these will be eased by the launch of its new webcam, which has revolutionary audio sound and visual quality. The webcam is expected to have a product life cycle of two years. Market research has already been carried out to establish a target selling price and projected lifetime sales volumes for the product. Cost estimates have also been prepared, based on the current proposed product specification. Cam Co. uses life cycle costing to work out the target costs for its products, believing it to be more accurate to use an average cost across the whole lifetime of a product, rather than potentially different costs for different years. You are provided with the following relevant information for the webcam:

Projected lifetime sales volume	50 000 units
Target selling price per unit	$200
Target profit margin (35% selling price)	$70
Target cost per unit	$130
Estimated lifetime cost per unit	$160
(see note below for detailed breakdown)	

Note: Estimated lifetime cost per unit:

	$	$
Manufacturing costs		
Direct material (bought in parts)	40	
Direct labour	26	
Machine costs	21	
Quality control costs	10	
Rework costs	3	
		100
Non-manufacturing costs		
Product development costs	25	
Marketing costs	35	
		60
Estimated lifetime cost per unit		160

The average market price for a webcam is currently $150.

The company needs to close the cost gap of $30 between the target cost and the estimated lifetime cost. The following information has been identified as relevant:

1 Direct material cost: all of the parts currently proposed for the webcam are bespoke parts. However, most of these can actually be replaced with standard parts costing 55 per cent less. However, three of the bespoke parts, which currently account for 20 per cent of the estimated direct material cost, cannot be replaced, although an alternative supplier charging 10 per cent less has been sourced for these parts.

2 Direct labour cost: the webcam uses 45 minutes of direct labour, which costs $34.67 per hour. The use of more standard parts, however, will mean that whilst the first unit would still be expected to take 45 minutes, there will now be an expected rate of learning of 90 per cent (where '*b*' = −0.152). This will end after the first 100 units have been completed.

3 Rework cost: this is the average rework cost per webcam and is based on an estimate of 15 per cent of webcams requiring rework at a cost of $20 per rework. With the use of more standard parts, the rate of reworks will fall to 10 per cent and the cost of each rework will fall to $18.

Required:

(a) Recalculate the estimated lifetime cost per unit for the webcam after taking into account points 1 to 3 above.
(12 marks)

(b) Explain the 'market skimming' (also known as 'price skimming') pricing strategy and discuss, as far as the information allows, whether this strategy may be more appropriate for Cam Co. than charging one price throughout the webcam's entire life. *(8 marks)*

ACCA F5 Performance Management

24.19 Advanced: Learning curve and planning and operating variances and consequences of not incorporating the learning effect. Bokco is a manufacturing company. It has a small permanent workforce but it is also reliant on temporary workers, whom it hires on three-month contracts whenever

production requirements increase. All buying of materials is the responsibility of the company's purchasing department and the company's policy is to hold low levels of raw materials in order to minimize inventory holding costs. Bokco uses cost plus pricing to set the selling prices for its products once an initial cost card has been drawn up. Prices are then reviewed on a quarterly basis. Detailed variance reports are produced each month for sales, material costs and labour costs. Departmental managers are then paid a monthly bonus depending on the performance of their department.

One month ago, Bokco began production of a new product. The standard cost card for one unit was drawn up to include a cost of $84 for labour, based on seven hours of labour at $12 per hour. Actual output of the product during the first month of production was 460 units and the actual time taken to manufacture the product totalled 1860 hours at a total cost of $26 040.

After being presented with some initial variance calculations, the production manager has realized that the standard time per unit of seven hours was the time taken to produce the first unit and that a learning rate of 90 per cent should have been anticipated for the first 1000 units of production. He has consequently been criticized by other departmental managers who have said that, 'He has no idea of all the problems this has caused.'

Required:

(a) Calculate the labour efficiency planning variance and the labour efficiency operational variance AFTER taking account of the learning effect.

Note: The learning index for a 90 per cent learning curve is −0.1520 *(5 marks)*

(b) Discuss the likely consequences arising from the production manager's failure to take into account the learning effect before production commenced. *(5 marks)*

ACCA F5 Performance Management

24.20 Advanced: Learning curve applied to target costing and calculation of learning rate. WTI is planning to launch a new component. Production volume will be limited, with only 128 components to be produced in total.

WTI expects the manufacture of the first component to take 25 direct labour hours. It is anticipated there will be a 90 per cent learning curve that will continue until all 128 components have been produced. Direct labour is paid at a rate of $15 per hour.

Non labour-related costs are expected to be $265 per component; this will apply to all 128 components produced. There are no product-specific fixed costs associated with this new component.

WTI is going to use a target costing approach for the new component. Based on the market research it has undertaken, WTI plans to sell the components for $530 each. WTI requires an average profit margin of 20 per cent of the selling price over the life of this new component.

Note: The learning index for a 90 per cent learning curve = −0.152.

Required:

(a) Calculate the time required to produce the 128th component. *(3 marks)*

(b) Calculate the value of any cost gap between the target cost of 128 components in total and the expected cost of 128 components in total. *(3 marks)*

(c) Calculate the rate of learning required to close the cost gap you calculated in part (b) in order to achieve the required profit margin of 20 per cent. *(4 marks)*

CIMA P2 Performance Management

24.21 Advanced: Calculation of learning rate and contract completion using the learning curve. Maxmarine plc builds boats. Earlier this year the company accepted an order for 15 specialized 'Crest' boats at a fixed price of £100000 each. The contract allows four months for building and delivery of all the boats and stipulates a penalty of £10000 for each boat delivery late.

The boats are built using purchased components and internally manufactured parts, all of which are readily available. However, there is only a small team of specialized technicians and boatyard space is limited, so that only one boat can be built at a time. Four boats have now been completed and as Maxmarine plc has no previous experience of this particular boat the building times have been carefully monitored as follows:

Boat number	Completion time (days)
1	10.0
2	8.1
3	7.4
4	7.1

Maxmarine plc has 23 normal working days in every month and the first four boats were completed with normal working.

Management is now concerned about completing the contract on time.

The management accountant's estimate of direct costs per boat, excluding labour costs, is as follows:

	(£000)
Purchased components	40
Manufactured parts	15
Other direct expenses	5
	60

Direct labour costs are £2500 per day for the normal 23 working days per month. Additional weekend working days at double the normal pay rates can be arranged up to a maximum of seven days per month (making 30 possible working days per month in total).

Overheads will be allocated to the contract at a rate of £3000 per normal working day and no overheads will be allocated for overtime working.

Requirements:

(a) Using the completion time information provided, calculate the learning rate showing full workings. *(6 marks)*

(b) Discuss the limitations of the learning curve in this type of application. *(6 marks)*

(c) Calculate whether it would be preferable for Maxmarine plc to continue normal working or to avoid penalties by working weekends. Support your calculations with any reservations or explanations you consider appropriate. *(13 marks)*

ICAEW Management Accounting

IM24.1 Intermediate. Discuss the conditions that should apply if linear regression analysis is to be used to analyse cost behaviour. *(6 marks)*

ACCA Level 2 Management Accounting

IM24.2 Intermediate.

(a) Briefly discuss the problems that occur in constructing cost estimation equations for estimating costs at different output levels. *(7 marks)*

(b) Describe four different cost estimation methods and for each method discuss the limitations and circumstances in which you would recommend their use. *(18 marks)*

IM24.3 Intermediate. Explain the 'learning curve' and discuss its relevance to setting standards. *(5 marks)*

ACCA Level 2 Management Accounting

IM24.4 Advanced.

(a) Comment on factors likely to affect the accuracy of the analysis of costs into fixed and variable components. *(8 marks)*

(b) Explain how the analysis of costs into fixed and variable components is of use in planning, control and decision-making techniques used by the management accountant. *(9 marks)*

ACCA Level 2 Management Accounting

IM24.5 Advanced: Comparison of independent variables for cost estimates. Abourne Ltd manufactures a microcomputer for the home use market. The management accountant is considering using regression analysis in the annual estimate of total costs. The following information has been produced for the 12 months ended 31 December:

Month	Total cost Y (£)	Output, X_1 (numbers)	Number of employees, X_2 (numbers)	Direct labour hours, X_3 (hours)
1	38200	300	28	4480
2	40480	320	30	4700
3	41400	350	30	4800
4	51000	500	32	5120
5	52980	530	32	5150
6	60380	640	35	5700
7	70440	790	41	7210
8	32720	250	41	3200
9	75800	820	41	7300
10	71920	780	39	7200
11	68380	750	38	6400
12	33500	270	33	3960
	$\sum Y =$ 637200	$\sum X_1 =$ 6300	$\sum X_2 =$ 420	$\sum X_3 =$ 65220

Additionally:

$$\sum Y^2 = 36614.05 \times 10^6$$
$$\sum X_1^2 = 3.8582 \times 10^6$$
$$\sum X_2^2 = 14954$$
$$\sum X_3^2 = 374.423 \times 10^6$$
$$\sum X_1 Y = 373.5374 \times 10^6$$
$$\sum X_2 Y = 22.81284 \times 10^6$$
$$\sum X_3 Y = 3692.2774 \times 10^6$$

The management accountant wants to select the best independent variable (X_1, X_2 or X_3) to help in future forecasts of total production costs using an ordinary least-squares regression equation. He is also considering the alternatives of using the high–low and multiple regression equations as the basis for future forecasts.

You are required to:

(a) Identify which one of the three independent variables (X_1, X_2 or X_3) given above is likely to be the least good estimator of total costs (Y). Give your reasons, but do not submit any calculations. *(3 marks)*

(b) Compute separately, for the remaining two independent variables, the values of the two parameters α and β for each regression line. Calculate the coefficient of determination (R^2) for each relationship. *(6 marks)*

(c) State, with reasons, which one of these independent variables should be used to estimate total costs in the future given the results of (b) above. *(3 marks)*

(d) Devise the two equations which could be used, using the high–low technique, instead of the two regression lines computed in (b) above and comment on the differences found between the two sets of equations. *(5 marks)*

(e) Comment critically on the use of high–low and ordinary least-squares regression as forecasting and estimating aids using the above results as a basis for discussion. In addition, comment on the advantages and problems of using multiple regression for forecasting and estimating; and state whether, in your opinion, the management accountant should consider using it in the present circumstances.

(8 marks)

Note: The following formulae can be used to answer the above question.

$$\beta = \frac{\sum xy - n\bar{x}\bar{y}}{\sum x^2 - n\bar{x}^2}$$

$$\alpha = \bar{y} - \beta\bar{x}$$

$$R^2 = \frac{\alpha\sum y + \beta\sum xy - n\bar{y}^2}{\sum y^2 - n\bar{y}^2}$$

$$Se = \sqrt{\frac{\sum y^2 - \alpha\sum y - \beta\sum xy}{n - 2}}$$

$$s\beta = \frac{Se}{\sqrt{\sum x^2 - nx^2}}$$

ICAEW P2 Management Accounting

IM24.6 Advanced: Calculation of coefficient of determination. A management accountant is analysing data relating to retail sales on behalf of marketing colleagues. The marketing staff believes that the most important influence on sales is local advertising undertaken by the retail store. The company also advertises by using regional television areas. The company owns more than 100 retail outlets, and the data below relate to a sample of ten representative outlets:

Outlet number	Monthly sales (£000)	Local advertising by the retail store (£000 per month)	Regional advertising by the company (£000 per month)
	y	x_1	x_2
1	220	6	4
2	230	8	6
3	240	12	10
4	340	12	16
5	420	2	18
6	460	8	20
7	520	16	26
8	600	15	30
9	720	14	36
10	800	20	46

The data have been partly analysed and the intermediate results are available below:

$$\sum y = 4550 \quad \sum y^2 = 2\,451\,300 \quad \sum x_1 y = 58\,040$$
$$\sum x_1 = 113 \quad \sum x_1^2 = 1533 \quad \sum x_2 y = 121\,100$$
$$\sum x_2 = 212 \quad \sum x_2^2 = 6120 \quad \sum x_1 x_2 = 2780$$

You are required to examine closely, using coefficients of determination, the assertion that the level of sales varies more with movements in the level of local advertising than with changes in the level of regional company advertising.

(8 marks)

Note that the coefficient of determination for y and x_1 may be calculated from

$$r^2 = \frac{n\sum x_1 y - \sum x_1 \sum y}{\left(n\sum x_1^2 - \left(\sum x_1\right)^2\right) \times \left(n\sum y^2 - \left(\sum y\right)^2\right)}$$

CIMA Stage 3 Management Accounting Techniques

IM24.7 Advanced: Estimates of sales volume and revenues using regression analysis and calculation of optimum price using differential calculus. The Crispy Biscuit Company (CBC) has developed a new variety of biscuit that it has successfully test marketed in different parts of the country. It has, therefore, decided to go ahead with full-scale production and is in the process of commissioning a production line located in a hitherto unutilized part of the main factory building. The new line will be capable of producing up to 50 000 packets of new biscuit each week.

The factory accountant has produced the following schedule of the expected unit costs of production at various levels of output:

	Production level (packets per week)				
	(10000)	(20000)	(30000)	(40000)	(50000)
Unit costs (pence)					
Labour (1)	20.0	15.0	13.3	12.5	12.0
Materials	8.0	8.0	8.0	8.0	8.0
Machine costs (2)	8.0	5.0	4.0	3.5	3.2
Total direct costs	36.0	28.0	25.3	24.0	23.2
Factory overhead (3)	9.0	7.0	6.3	6.0	5.8
Total costs	45.0	35.0	31.6	30.0	29.0

1. The labour costs represent the cost of the additional labour that would require to be taken on to operate the new line.
2. Machine costs include running costs, maintenance costs and depreciation.
3. Factory overhead costs are fixed for the factory overall but are allocated to cost centres at 25 per cent of total direct costs.

In addition to establishing product acceptability, the test marketing programme also examined the likely consumer response to various selling prices. It concluded that the weekly revenue likely to be generated at various prices was as follows:

Retail price	Revenue to CBC
£0.62	£15190
£0.68	£14960
£0.78	£11310
£0.84	£10500
£0.90	£10350
£0.98	£4900

The above prices represent the prices at which the product was test marketed, but any price between £0.60 and £0.99 is a possibility. The manufacturer receives 50 per cent of the retail revenue.

Requirements:

(a) Estimate the variable costs of producing the new biscuit, using any simple method (such as the high–low method).

(3 marks)

(b) Using linear regression, estimate the relationship between the price charged by CBC and the expected demand.

(6 marks)

(c) Using the above estimates, calculate the optimum price and evaluate how sensitive your solution is to changes in this price.

(8 marks)

(d) Outline the practical problems faced in attempting to derive a unit cost for a new product. *(8 marks)*

ICAEW P2 Management Accounting

The question provided the following formula for answering this question:

$$b = \frac{\sum(x - \bar{x})(y - y)}{\sum(x - \bar{x})^2} \text{ or } \frac{n\sum xy - \sum x \sum y}{n\sum x^2 - (\sum x)^2}$$

$$\text{and } a = \bar{y} - b\bar{x}$$

IM24.8 Advanced: Learning curves. Present a table of production times showing the following columns for E. Condon Ltd, which produces up to 16 units while experiencing a 90 per cent learning curve, the first unit requiring 1000 hours of production time:

1. units produced;
2. total production time (hours);
3. average production time per unit in each successive lot (hours);
4. cumulative average production time per unit (hours);
5. percentage decline in (4). *(10 marks)*

ICAEW Management Accounting

IM24.9 Advanced: The application of the learning curve to determine target cash flows. Leano plc is investigating the financial viability of a new product X. Product X is a short life product for which a market has been identified at an agreed design specification. It is not yet clear whether the market life of the product will be six months or 12 months.

The following estimated information is available in respect of product X:

(i) Sales should be 10 000 units per month in batches of 100 units on a just-in-time production basis. An average selling price of £1200 per batch of 100 units is expected for a six month life cycle and £1050 per batch of 100 units for a 12 month life cycle.
(ii) An 80 per cent learning curve will apply in months 1 to 7 (inclusive), after which a steady state production time requirement will apply, with labour time per batch stabilizing at that of the final batch in month 7. Reductions in the labour requirement will be achieved through natural labour turnover. The labour requirement for the first batch in month 1 will be 250 hours at £10 per hour.
(iii) Variable overhead is estimated at £4 per labour hour.
(iv) Direct material input will be £500 per batch of product X for the first 200 batches. The next 200 batches are expected to cost 90 per cent of the initial batch cost. All batches thereafter will cost 90 per cent of the batch cost for each of the second 200 batches.
(v) Product X will incur directly attributable fixed costs of £15 000 per month.
(vi) The initial investment for the new product will be £75 000 with no residual value irrespective of the life of the product.

A target cash inflow required over the life of the product must be sufficient to provide for:

(a) the initial investment plus 33⅓ per cent thereof for a six month life cycle or
(b) the initial investment plus 50 per cent thereof for a 12 month life cycle.

Note: learning curve formula:

$$y = ax^b$$

where

y = average cost per batch
a = cost of initial batch

x = total number of batches
b = learning factor ($= -0.3219$ for 80 per cent learning rate)

Required:

(a) Prepare detailed calculations to show whether product X will provide the target cash inflow over six months and/or 12 months. *(17 marks)*
(b) Calculate the initial batch labour hours at which the cash inflow achieved will be exactly equal to the target figure where a six-month life cycle applies. It has been determined that the maximum labour and variable overhead cost at which the target return will be achieved is £259 000. All other variables remain as in part (a). *(6 marks)*
(c) Prepare a report to management which:

(i) explains why the product X proposal is an example of a target costing/pricing situation; *(3 marks)*
(ii) suggests specific actions that may be considered to improve the return on investment where a six-month product cycle is forecast; *(6 marks)*
(iii) comments on possible factors that could reduce the rate of return and that must, therefore, be avoided. *(3 marks)*

ACCA Paper 9 Information for Control and Decision Making

IM24.10 Advanced: Application of learning curve to determine the incremental costs for different production batches. Limitation plc commenced the manufacture and sale of a new product in the fourth quarter of the previous year. In order to facilitate the budgeting process for quarters 1 and 2 of the next year, the following information has been collected:

(i) Forecast production/sales (batches of product):

quarter 4 of the previous year	30 batches
quarter 1 of the next year	45 batches
quarter 2 of the next year	45 batches

(ii) It is estimated that direct labour is subject to a learning curve effect of 90 per cent. The labour cost of batch 1 of quarter 4 of the previous year was £1440 (at £12 per hour). The labour output rates from the commencement of production of the product, after adjusting for learning effects, are as follows:

Total produced (batches)	Overall average time per batch (hours)
15	79.51
30	71.56
45	67.28
60	64.40
75	62.25
90	60.55
105	59.15
120	57.96

Labour hours worked and paid for will be adjusted to eliminate spare capacity during each quarter. All time will be paid for at £12 per hour.

(iii) Direct material is used at the rate of 200 units per batch of product for the first 20 batches of quarter 4 of the previous year. Units of material used per batch will fall by 2 per cent of the original level for each 20 batches thereafter as the learning curve effect improves the efficiency with which the material is used. All material will be bought at £1.80 per unit during the next year. Delivery of the total material requirement for a quarter will be made on day one of the quarter. Stock will be held in storage capacity hired at a cost of £0.30 per quarter per unit held in stock. Material will be used at an even rate throughout each quarter.

(iv) Variable overhead is estimated at 50 per cent of direct labour cost during the next year.

(v) All units produced will be sold in the quarter of production at £1600 per batch.

Required:

(a) Calculate the labour hours requirement for the second batch and the sum of the labour hours for the third and fourth batches produced in quarter 4 of the previous year.   (3 marks)

(b) Prepare a budget for each of quarters 1 and 2 for the next year showing the contribution earned from the product. Show all relevant workings.   (14 marks)

(c) The supplier of the raw material has offered to deliver on a 'just-in-time' basis in return for a price increase to £1.90 per unit in quarter 1 of the next year and £2 per unit thereafter.

(i) Use information for quarters 1 and 2 of the next year to determine whether the offer should be accepted on financial grounds.

(ii) Comment on other factors which should be considered before a final decision is reached.

(8 marks)

(d) Limitation plc wish to prepare a quotation for 12 batches of the product to be produced at the start of quarter 3 of the next year.

Explain how the learning curve formula $y = ax^b$ may be used in the calculation of the labour cost of the quotation. Your answer should identify each of the variables y, a, x and b. No calculations are required.

(5 marks)

ACCA Level 2 Cost and Management Accounting II

25

QUANTITATIVE MODELS FOR THE PLANNING AND CONTROL OF INVENTORIES

LEARNING OBJECTIVES After studying this chapter, you should be able to:

- justify which costs are relevant and should be included in the calculation of the economic order quantity (EOQ);

- calculate the EOQ using the formula and tabulation methods;

- determine whether or not a company should purchase larger quantities in order to take advantage of quantity discounts;

- calculate the optimal safety stock when demand is uncertain;

- describe the ABC classification method;

- explain just-in-time purchasing.

Management of inventories (stocks) is of vital importance in both manufacturing and merchandising organizations (note that the terms stocks and inventories are used interchangeably throughout this chapter). In manufacturing organizations, inventories consist of raw materials, work in progress and finished goods. Merchandising companies such as supermarkets, retail departmental stores and wholesalers sell tangible products that they have previously purchased in the same basic form from suppliers. Therefore they have only finished goods inventory. Inventory management is of little importance in service organizations since they have minimal inventories.

It is essential that inventories are managed efficiently so that such investments do not become unnecessarily large. A firm should determine its optimum level of investment in inventories – and, to do this, two conflicting requirements must be met. First, it must ensure that inventories are sufficient to meet the requirements of production and sales; and, second, it must avoid holding surplus inventories that are unnecessary because of the costs involved. The optimal inventory level lies somewhere between these two extremes. In Chapter 22, we examined just-in-time systems as a mechanism for managing inventories. Our objective in this chapter is to examine the application of quantitative models for determining the optimum investment in inventories.

WHY DO FIRMS HOLD INVENTORIES?

There are three general reasons for holding inventories: the transactions motive, the precautionary motive and the speculative motive. The transactions motive occurs whenever there is a need to hold inventories to meet production and sales requirements and it is not possible to meet these requirements instantaneously. A firm might also decide to hold additional amounts of inventories because of uncertainty relating to demand for future production and sales requirements, uncertainty in the supply of raw materials in manufacturing organizations or purchased goods in merchandising organizations. This represents a precautionary motive, which applies only when future supply and demand is uncertain.

When it is expected that future input prices may change, a firm might maintain higher or lower inventory levels to *speculate* on the expected increase or decrease in future prices. In general, quantitative models do not take into account the speculative motive. Nevertheless, management should be aware that optimum inventory levels do depend to a certain extent on expected price movements. For example, if prices of input factors are expected to rise significantly, a firm should consider increasing its inventories to take advantage of a lower purchase price. However, this decision should be based on a comparison of future cost savings with the increased costs due to holding additional inventories.

Where a firm is able to predict the demand for its inputs and outputs with perfect confidence and where it knows with certainty that the prices of inputs will remain constant for some reasonable length of time, it will have to consider only the transactions motive for holding inventories. To simplify the introduction to the use of models for determining the optimum investment in inventories, we shall begin by considering some quantitative models which incorporate only the transactions motive for holding inventories.

RELEVANT COSTS FOR QUANTITATIVE MODELS UNDER CONDITIONS OF CERTAINTY

The relevant costs that should be considered when determining optimal inventory levels consist of holding costs and ordering costs. Holding costs usually consist of the following:

1 opportunity cost of investment in inventories;
2 incremental insurance costs;
3 incremental warehouse and storage costs;
4 incremental material handling costs;
5 cost of obsolescence and deterioration of inventories.

The relevant holding costs for use in quantitative models should include only those items that will vary with the levels of inventories. Costs that will not be affected by changes in inventory levels are not relevant costs. For example, in the case of warehousing and storage only those costs should be included that will vary with changes in the number of units ordered. Salaries of storekeepers, depreciation of equipment and fixed rental of equipment and buildings are often irrelevant because they are unaffected by changes in inventory levels in the short term.

To the extent that funds are invested in inventories, there is an opportunity cost of holding them. This opportunity cost is reflected by the required return that is lost from investing in inventories rather than some alternative investment. The opportunity cost should be applied only to those costs that vary with the number of units purchased. The relevant holding costs for other items such as material handling, obsolescence and deterioration are difficult to estimate, but we shall see that these costs are unlikely to be critical to the investment decision. Normally, holding costs are expressed as a percentage rate per pound of average investment.

Ordering costs usually consist of the clerical costs of preparing a purchase order, receiving deliveries and paying invoices. Ordering costs that are common to all inventory decisions are not relevant and only the incremental costs of placing an order are used in formulating the quantitative models.

The costs of acquiring inventories through buying or manufacturing are not a relevant cost to be included in the quantitative models, since the models assume that the acquisition costs remain unchanged, irrespective of the order size or inventory levels. The acquisition cost is not therefore a relevant cost, but the ordering and holding costs will change in relation to the order size, and these will be relevant for decision-making models. In many situations, however, quantity discounts are available when a firm orders in larger batches so the acquisition costs are not constant per unit for all order quantities. We shall discuss the effect of quantity discounts later in this chapter.

DETERMINING THE ECONOMIC ORDER QUANTITY

If we assume certainty, the optimum order will be determined by those costs that are affected by either the quantity of inventories held or the number of orders placed. If more units are ordered at one time, fewer orders will be required per year. This will mean a reduction in the ordering costs. However, when fewer orders are placed, larger average inventories must be maintained, which leads to an increase in holding costs. The problem is therefore one of trading off the costs of carrying large inventories against the costs of placing more orders. The optimum order size is the order quantity that will result in the total amount of the ordering and holding costs being minimized. This optimum order size is known as the economic order quantity (EOQ); it can be determined by tabulating the total costs for various order quantities, by a graphical presentation or by using a formula. All three methods are illustrated using the information given in Example 25.1.

Tabulation method

It is apparent from Example 25.1 that a company can choose to purchase small batches (e.g. 100 units) at frequent intervals or large batches (e.g. 10000 units) at infrequent intervals. The annual relevant costs for various order quantities are set out in Exhibit 25.1.

You will see that the economic order quantity is 400 units. At this point, the total annual relevant costs are at a minimum.

EXAMPLE 25.1

A company purchases a raw material from an outside supplier at a cost of £9 per unit. The total annual demand for this product is 40000 units, and the following additional information is available:

	(£)	(£)
Required annual return on investment in inventories (10% × £9)	0.90	
Other holding costs per unit	0.10	
Holding costs per unit		1.00
Cost per purchase order:		
Clerical costs, stationery, postage, telephone, etc.		2.00
You are required to determine the optimal order quantity.		

EXHIBIT 25.1 Relevant costs for various order quantities

Order quantity	100	200	300	400	500	600	800	10000
Average inventory in units[a]	50	100	150	200	250	300	400	5000
Number of purchase orders[b]	400	200	133	100	80	67	50	4
Annual holding costs[c]	£50	£100	£150	£200	£250	£300	£400	£5000
Annual ordering cost	£800	£400	£266	£200	£160	£134	£100	£8
Total relevant cost	£850	£500	£416	£400	£410	£434	£500	£5008

[a]If there are no inventories when the order is received and the units received are used at a constant rate, the average inventory will be one-half of the quantity ordered. Even if a minimum safety stock (inventory) is held, the average inventory relevant to the decision will still be one-half of the quantity order, because the minimum inventory will remain unchanged for each alternative order quantity.
[b]The number of purchase orders is ascertained by dividing the total annual demand of 40000 units by the order quantity.
[c]The annual holding cost is ascertained by multiplying the average inventory by the holding cost of £1 per unit.

Graphical method

The information tabulated in Exhibit 25.1 is presented in graphical form in Figure 25.1 for every order size up to 800 units. The vertical axis represents the relevant annual costs for the investment in inventories and the horizontal axis can be used to represent either the various order quantities or the average inventory levels; two scales are actually shown on the horizontal axis so that both items can be incorporated. You will see from the graph that as the average inventory level or the order quantity increases, the holding cost also increases. Alternatively, the ordering costs decline as inventory levels and order quantities are increased. The total cost line represents the summation of both the holding and the ordering costs.

Note that the total cost line is at a minimum for an order quantity of 400 units and occurs at the point where the ordering cost and holding cost curves intersect. That is, the economic order quantity is found at the point where the holding costs equal the ordering costs. It is also interesting to note from the graph (see also Exhibit 25.1) that the total relevant costs are not particularly sensitive to changes in the order quantity. For example, if you refer to Exhibit 25.1 you will see that a 25 per cent change in the order quantity from 400 units to either 300 or 500 units leads to an increase in annual costs from

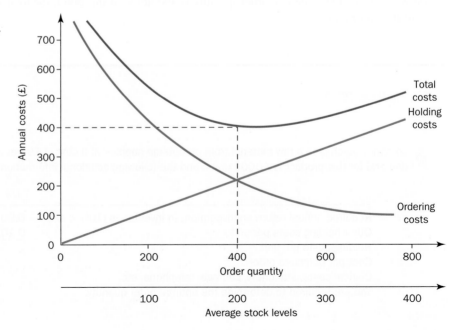

FIGURE 25.1
Economic order
quantity graph

£400 to £410 or £416, an increase of 2.5 per cent or 4 per cent. Alternatively, an increase of 50 per cent in the order quantity from 400 units to 600 units leads to an increase in annual costs from £400 to £434 or 8.5 per cent.

Formula method

The economic order quantity can be found by applying a formula that incorporates the basic relationships between holding and ordering costs and order quantities. These relationships can be stated as follows: the number of orders for a period is the total demand for that item of inventory for the period (denoted by D) divided by the quantity ordered in units (denoted by Q). The total ordering cost is obtained by multiplying the number of orders for a period by the ordering cost per order (denoted by O), and is given by the formula:

$$\frac{\text{total demand for period}}{\text{quantity ordered}} \times \text{ordering cost per order} = \frac{DO}{Q}$$

Assuming that holding costs are constant per unit, the total holding cost for a period will be equal to the average inventory for the period, which is represented by the quantity ordered divided by two ($Q/2$), multiplied by the holding cost per unit (denoted by H); it is therefore given by:

$$\frac{\text{quantity ordered}}{2} \times \text{holding cost per unit} = \frac{QH}{2}$$

The total relevant cost (TC) for any order quantity can now be expressed as:

$$\text{TC} = \frac{DO}{Q} + \frac{QH}{2}$$

We can determine a minimum for this total cost function by differentiating the above formula with respect to Q and setting the derivative equal to zero (see note 1 at the end of the chapter for an explanation of how the formula is derived). We then get the economic order quantity Q:

$$Q = \sqrt{\left(\frac{2DO}{H}\right)}$$

or

$$Q = \sqrt{\left(\frac{2 \times \text{total demand for period} \times \text{cost per order}}{\text{holding cost per unit}}\right)}$$

If we apply this formula to Example 25.1, we have:

$$Q = \sqrt{\left(\frac{2 \times 40\,000 \times 2}{1}\right)} = 400 \text{ units}$$

ASSUMPTIONS OF THE EOQ FORMULA

The calculations obtained by using the EOQ model should be interpreted with care, since the model is based on a number of important assumptions. One of these is that the holding cost per unit will be constant. While this assumption might be correct for items such as the funds invested in inventories, other costs might increase on a step basis as inventory levels increase. For example, additional storekeepers might be hired as inventory levels reach certain levels. Alternatively, if inventories decline, it may be that casual stores labour may be released once inventories fall to a certain critical level.

Another assumption that we made in calculating the total holding cost is that the average balance in inventory was equal to one-half of the order quantity. If a constant amount of inventory is not used per day, this assumption will be violated; there is a distinct possibility that seasonal and cyclical factors will produce an uneven usage over time. We shall examine how the analysis can be modified to incorporate uncertainty in inventory usage later in the chapter. Despite the fact that much of the data used in the model represent approximations, calculation of the EOQ is still likely to be useful. If you examine Figure 25.1, you will see that the total cost curve tends to flatten out, so that total cost may not be significantly affected if some of the underlying assumptions are violated or if there are minor variations in the cost predictions. For example, assume that the cost per order in Example 25.1 was predicted to be £4 instead of the correct cost of, say, £2. The cost of this error would be as follows:

$$\text{revised EOQ} = \sqrt{\left(\frac{2\,DO}{H}\right)} = \sqrt{\left(\frac{2 \times 40\,000 \times 4}{1}\right)} = 565$$

TC for revised EOQ but using the correct ordering cost $= \dfrac{DO}{Q} + \dfrac{QH}{2}$

$$= \frac{40\,000 \times 2}{565} + \frac{565 \times 1}{2} = £425$$

TC for original EOQ of 400 units based on actual ordering cost

$$= \frac{40\,000 \times 2}{400} + \frac{400 \times 1}{2} = £400$$

$$\therefore \text{cost of prediction error} = £25$$

The cost of the prediction error of £25 represents an error of 6 per cent from the optimal financial result. Similarly, if the holding cost was predicted to be £2 instead of the correct cost of £1, the calculations set out above could be repeated to show a cost of prediction error of approximately 6 per cent.

APPLICATION OF THE EOQ MODEL IN DETERMINING THE OPTIMUM BATCH SIZE FOR A PRODUCTION RUN

The economic order quantity formula can be adapted to determine the optimum batch size for production runs when a set-up cost is incurred only once for each batch produced. Set-up costs include incremental labour, material, machine down time and other ancillary costs of setting up facilities for production. The objective is to find the optimum number of units that should be manufactured in each production run, and this involves balancing set-up costs against inventory holding costs. To apply the EOQ formula to a production run problem, we merely substitute set-up costs for the production runs in place of the purchase ordering costs.

To illustrate the formula, let us assume that the annual sales demand D for a product is 9000 units. Labour and other expenditure in making adjustments in preparation for a production run require a set-up cost (S) of £90. The holding cost is £2 per unit per year. The EOQ model can be used for determining how many units should be scheduled for each production run to secure the lowest annual cost. The EOQ formula is modified to reflect the circumstances: the symbol O (ordering costs) is replaced by the symbol S (set-up cost). Using the formula:

$$Q = \sqrt{\left(\frac{2DS}{H}\right)} + \sqrt{\left(\frac{2 \times 9000 \times 90}{2}\right)} = 900$$

With an annual demand of 9000 units and an optimum batch size of a production run of 900 units, ten production runs will be required throughout the year.

QUANTITY DISCOUNTS

Circumstances frequently occur where firms are able to obtain quantity discounts for large purchase orders. Because the price paid per unit will not be the same for different order sizes, this must be taken into account when the economic order quantity is determined. However, the basic EOQ formula can still be used as a starting point for determining the optimum quantity to order. Buying in larger consignments to take advantage of quantity discounts will lead to the following savings:

1 A saving in purchase price, which consists of the total amount of discount for the period.

2 A reduction in the total ordering cost because fewer orders are placed to take advantage of the discounts.

These cost savings must, however, be balanced against the increased holding cost arising from higher inventory levels when larger quantities are purchased. To determine whether or not a discount is worthwhile, the benefits must be compared with the additional holding costs. Consider the information presented in Example 25.2.

The starting point is to calculate the economic order quantity and then to decide whether the benefits exceed the costs if the company moves from the EOQ point and purchases larger quantities to obtain the discounts. The procedure is as follows:

$$\text{EOQ} = \sqrt{\left(\frac{2 \times 9000 \times 5}{4}\right)} = 150 \text{ units}$$

The savings available to the firm if it purchases in batches of 1000 units instead of batches of 150 units are as follows:

	(£)
1 Saving in purchase price	1890
(3% of annual purchase cost of £63 000)	
2 Saving in ordering cost	
$\dfrac{DO}{Q_d} - \dfrac{DO}{Q} = \dfrac{9000 \times 5}{1000} - \dfrac{9000 \times 5}{150}$	255
(Q_d represents the quantity order to obtain the discount and Q represents EOQ)	
Total savings	2145

The additional holding cost if the larger quantity is purchased is calculated as:

$$\frac{(Q_d - Q)H}{2} = \frac{(1000 - 150) \times £4}{2} = £1700$$

The additional savings of £2145 exceed the additional costs, and the firm should adopt the order quantity of 1000 units. If larger discounts are available, for example by purchasing in batches of 2000 units,

---

EXAMPLE 25.2

A company purchases a raw material from an outside supplier at a cost of £7 per unit. The total annual demand for this product is 9000 units.

The holding cost is £4 per unit and the ordering cost is £5 per order. A quantity discount of 3 per cent of the purchase price is available for orders in excess of 999 units. Should the company order in batches of 1000 units and take advantage of quantity discounts?

a similar analysis should be applied that compares the savings from purchasing in batches of 2000 units against purchasing in batches of 1000 units. The amount of the savings should then be compared with the additional holding costs. Note that the EOQ formula serves as a starting point for comparing the savings against the costs of a change in order size.

DETERMINING WHEN TO PLACE THE ORDER

To determine the point at which the order should be placed to obtain additional inventories (i.e. the **re-order point**), we must ascertain the time that will elapse between placing the order and the actual delivery of the inventories. This time period is referred to as the **lead time**. In a world of certainty, the re-order point will be:

Lead time × the daily / weekly usage during the lead time period

If we assume that an annual usage of a raw material is 6000 units and the weekly usage is constant then if there are 50 working weeks in a year, the weekly usage will be 120 units. If the lead time is two weeks, the order should be placed when inventories fall to 240 units. The economic order quantity can indicate how frequently the inventories should be purchased. For example, if the EOQ is 600 then, with an annual demand of 6000 units, ten orders will be placed every five weeks. However, with a lead time of two weeks, the firm will place an order three weeks after the first delivery when the inventory will have fallen to 240 units (600 units EOQ less three weeks usage at 120 units per week). The order will then be repeated at five-weekly intervals. The EOQ model can therefore under certain circumstances be used to indicate when to replenish inventories and the amount to replenish. This process is illustrated in Figure 25.2.

UNCERTAINTY AND SAFETY STOCKS

In practice, demand or usage of stocks (inventories) is not known with certainty. In addition, there is usually a degree of uncertainty associated with the placement of an order and delivery of the stocks. To protect itself from conditions of uncertainty, a firm will maintain a level of **safety stocks** for raw materials, work in progress and finished goods inventories. Thus safety stocks are the amount of inventories that are carried in excess of the expected use during the lead time to provide a cushion against running out of inventories because of fluctuations in demand. The calculation of the re-order point of 240 units in the example shown in the previous section is:

Lead time (two weeks) × weekly usage during the lead time period (two weeks at 120 units per week)

FIGURE 25.2
Re-order points and the fluctuation of inventory levels under conditions of certainty

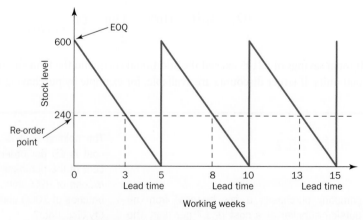

Assumptions:
EOQ = 600 units; lead time = two weeks; usage per week = 120 units;
Re-order point 240 units; order placed at end of weeks three, eight, 13, etc.

REAL WORLD
VIEWS 25.1

Buffer stocks due to natural events

Safety or buffer stocks are held for many reasons. For example, road authorities might want to hold sufficient stock of grit salt in case of bad weather, or firms might build stock of key materials if a price rise is impending.

In recent times climate change has brought more extreme weather conditions more frequently globally. This too has had an effect of the levels of stocks held by some businesses, and indeed even on supply. In the Philippines, rice has been traditionally grown, but an increasing population and less available has seen an increasing reliance on imported rice. During 2016, the government was considering the import of an additional 250 000 metric tonnes as a precaution against the impact of La Niña in early 2017. At the end of August 2016, the National Food Authority (NFA) awarded a contract for the supply of rice to the world's top rice exporters, Thailand and Vietnam. They were offered 100 000 and 150 000 metric tonnes respectively under a government-to-government (G2G) procurement scheme. The NFA also stated it would conduct more G2G procurement in the last quarter to ensure adequate rice inventory (22 days). At the end of August 2016, the NFA's rice inventory stood at 578 700 metric tons, sufficient for 18 days, which is more than the recommended buffer stock of 15 days at any given time.

Question

1 Can you think of the additional costs of holding increased rice stocks as suggested above?

References

'Rice imports may be needed as La Niña buffer', Business World Online, available at www .bworldonline.com/content.php?section =Economy&title=nfa-rice-imports-may-be -needed-as-la-ni&241a-buffer&id=133978, accessed December 11, 2016.
Information on rice growing in the Philippines available at ricepedia.org/philippines

---

The firm will run out of inventory if actual demand increases to 140 units per week or if the lead time is three weeks. A firm might respond to this possibility by setting a re-order point of 420 units based on a *maximum usage* of 140 units per week and a lead time of three weeks. This will consist of a re-order point based on *average usage* and lead time of 240 units (two weeks at 120 units) plus the balance of 180 units *safety stocks* to cover the possibility that lead time and expected usage will be greater than expected. Thus when demand and lead time are uncertain the re-order point is computed as follows:

$$(\text{Average rate of usage} \times \text{lead time}) + \text{safety stock}$$

THE USE OF PROBABILITY THEORY FOR DETERMINING SAFETY STOCKS

In the above illustration, the safety stock was calculated on the basis of maximum demand and delivery time. It may well be that the probability of both these events occurring at the same time is extremely low. Under such circumstances the managers of the company are adopting a very risk-averse approach and taking no chances of running out of inventory. Maintaining high safety stocks may not be in the company's best interests if the cost of holding the excessive inventories exceeds the costs that will be incurred if the company runs out of inventory. It is therefore desirable to establish a sound quantitative procedure for determining an acceptable level of safety stocks. The level should be set where the cost of a stock-out plus the cost of holding the safety stocks are minimized.

Stock-out costs are the opportunity cost of running out of stock. In the case of finished goods the opportunity cost will consist of a loss of contribution if customers take their business elsewhere because orders cannot be met when requested. In the case of regular customers who are permanently lost because of a failure to meet delivery, this will be the discounted value of the lost contribution on future sales. When a stock-out occurs for raw materials and work in progress inventories, the cost of being out of stock is the cost of the stoppage in production and the resulting inefficiencies that occur. This may be reflected by an estimate of the labour costs of idle time assuming that sales are *not* lost because of the stock-out. Clearly, stock-out costs are very difficult to estimate.

Once the stock-out costs have been estimated, the costs of holding safety inventories should be compared for various demand levels. However, it is preferable to attach probabilities to different potential demand levels and to decide on the appropriate quantity of safety inventories by comparing the expected cost values or probability distributions for various levels of safety inventories. Let us now illustrate this process.

By constructing probability distributions for future demand and lead time, it is possible to calculate the expected values for various safety stock levels. Suppose, for example, the total usage for an item for stock *over a two-week lead time* is expected to be as follows:

Usage (units)	60	120	180	240	300	360	420
Probability	0.07	0.08	0.20	0.30	0.20	0.08	0.07

The average usage during the two week lead time is 240 units, and it is assumed that the lead time is known with certainty. If the firm carries no safety stock, the re-order point will be set at 240 units (i.e. average usage during the lead time), and there will be no stock-outs if actual usage is 240 units or less. However, if usage during the lead time period proves to be 300 units instead of 240 there will be a stock-out of 60 units, and the probability of this occurring is 0.20. Alternatively, if usage is 360 or 420 units, there will be stock-outs of 120 units and 180 units respectively with associated probabilities of 0.08 and 0.07. By maintaining a safety stock of 180 units (420 units − 240 units), the firm ensures that a stock-out will *not* occur.

Assuming we estimate stock-out costs of £5 per unit and a holding cost of £1 per unit for the period, we can calculate the expected stock-out cost, holding cost and total cost for various levels of safety stock. This information is presented in Exhibit 25.2. Note that if the re-order point is set at 360 units a stock-out will only occur if usage is 420 units. Alternatively, if the re-order point is set at 300 units there will be a stock-out of 60 units if usage is 360 units (probability = 0.08) and 120 units if usage is 420 units (probability = 0.07).

You will see that a safety stock of 60 units represents the level at which total expected costs are at their lowest. Hence a re-order point of 300 units will be set, consisting of the average usage during the lead time of 240 units plus a safety stock of 60 units. If the probability distributions for each two-weekly period are expected to remain unchanged throughout the year, this safety stock (60 units) should be maintained.

EXHIBIT 25.2 Expected costs for various safety stocks

Average usage (units)	Safety stock (units)	Re-order point (units)	Stock-out (units)	Stock-out cost (£5 per unit)	Probability	Expected stock-out cost (£)	Holding cost[a] (£)	Total expected cost (£)
240	180	420	0	0	0	0	180	180
240	120	360	60	300	0.07	21	120	141
240	60	300	120	600	0.07	42		
			60	300	0.08	24		
						66	60	126
240	0	240	180	900	0.07	63		
			120	600	0.08	48		
			60	300	0.20	60		
						171	0	171

[a]To simplify the analysis, it is assumed that a safety stock is maintained throughout the period. The average safety stock will therefore be equal to the total of the safety stock.

However, if demand is expected to vary throughout the year, the calculations presented in Exhibit 25.2 must be repeated for the probability distributions for each period in which the probability distribution changes. The safety stock should then be adjusted prior to the commencement of each period.

Because of the difficulty in estimating the cost of a stock-out, some firms might prefer not to use quantitative methods to determine the level of safety inventories. Instead, they might specify a maximum probability of running out of inventory. If the firm in our illustration does not wish the probability of a stock-out to exceed 10 per cent, it will maintain a safety stock of 120 units and a re-order point of 360 units. A stock-out will then occur only if demand is in excess of 360 units; the probability of such an occurrence is 7 per cent.

CONTROL OF INVENTORY THROUGH CLASSIFICATION

In large firms, it is quite possible for tens of thousands of different items to be stored. It is clearly impossible to apply the techniques outlined in this chapter to all of these. It is therefore essential that inventories be classified into categories of importance so that a firm can apply the most elaborate procedures of controlling inventories only to the most important items. The commonest procedure is known as the ABC classification method. This is illustrated in Exhibit 25.3.

The ABC method requires that an estimate be made of the total purchase cost for each item of inventory for the period. The sales forecast is the basis used for estimating the quantities of each item of inventory to be purchased during the period. Each item is then grouped in decreasing order of annual purchase cost. The top 10 per cent of items in inventory in terms of annual purchase cost are categorized as A items, the next 20 per cent as B items and the final 70 per cent as C items. If we assume there are 10 000 inventory items then the top 1000 items in terms of annual purchase costs will be classified as A items and so on. In practice, it will be unnecessary to estimate the value of many of the 7000 C items, since their annual purchase cost will be so small it will be obvious that they will fall into the C category.

EXHIBIT 25.3 ABC Classification of inventories

Stage 1. For each item in inventory, multiply the estimated usage for a period by the estimated unit price to obtain the total purchase cost:

Item	Estimated usage	Unit price (£)	Total purchase cost (£)
1	60 000	1.00	60 000
2	20 000	0.05	1 000
3	1 000	0.10	100
4	10 000	0.02	200
5	100 000	0.01	1 000
6	80 000	2.00	160 000

(This list is continued until all items in inventory are included.)

Stage 2. Group all the above items in descending order of purchase price and then divide into class A (top 10 per cent), class B (next 20 per cent) and then class C (bottom 70 per cent). The analysis might be as follows:

	Number of items in inventory		Total cost	
	No	%	Amount (£)	%
Class A	1 000	10	730 000	73
Class B	2 000	20	190 000	19
Class C	7 000	70	80 000	8
	10 000	100	1 000 000	100

You will see from Exhibit 25.3 that 10 per cent of all inventory items (i.e. the A items) represents 73 per cent of the total cost; 20 per cent of the items (B items) represents 19 per cent of the total cost; and 70 per cent of the items (C items) represents 8 per cent of the total cost. It follows that the greatest degree of control should be exerted over the A items, which account for the high investment costs, and it is the A category items that are most appropriate for the application of the quantitative techniques discussed in this chapter. For these items, an attempt should be made to maintain low safety stocks consistent with avoiding high stock-out costs. Larger orders and safety stocks are likely to be a feature of the C-category items. Normally, re-order points for these items will be determined on a subjective basis rather than using quantitative methods, the objective being to minimize the expense in controlling these items. The control of B-category items is likely to be based on quantitative methods, but they are unlikely to be as sophisticated as for the A-category items.

The percentage value of total cost for the A, B and C categories in Exhibit 25.3 is typical of many manufacturing companies. In practice, it is normal for between 10 per cent and 15 per cent of the items in inventory to account for between 70 per cent and 80 per cent of the total value of purchases. At the other extreme, between 70 per cent and 80 per cent of the items in inventory account for approximately 10 per cent of the total value. The control of inventory levels is eased considerably if it is concentrated on that small proportion of inventory items that account for most of the total cost.

OTHER FACTORS INFLUENCING THE CHOICE OF ORDER QUANTITY

Shortage of future supplies

For various reasons, a firm may depart from quantitative models that provide estimates of the economic order quantity and the re-order point. A company may not always be able to rely on future supplies being available if the major suppliers are in danger of experiencing a strike. Alternatively, future supplies may be restricted because of import problems or transportation difficulties. In anticipation of such circumstances, a firm may over-order so that inventories on hand will be sufficient to meet production while future supplies are restricted.

Future price increases

When a supplier announces a price increase that will be effective at some future date, it may be in a firm's interest to buy in excess of its immediate requirements before the increase becomes effective. Indeed, in times of rapid inflation firms might have an incentive to maintain larger inventories than would otherwise be necessary.

Obsolescence

Certain types of inventory are subject to obsolescence. For example, a change in technology may make a particular component worthless. Alternatively, a change in fashion may cause a clothes retailer to sell inventories at considerably reduced prices. Where the probability of obsolescence is high or goods are of a perishable nature, frequent purchases of small quantities and the maintenance of low inventories may be appropriate, even when the EOQ formula may suggest purchasing larger quantities and maintaining higher inventory levels.

Steps to reduce safety stocks

When demand is uncertain, higher safety stocks are likely to be maintained. However, safety stocks may be reduced if the purchasing department can find new suppliers who will promise quicker and more reliable delivery. Alternatively, pressure may be placed on existing suppliers for faster delivery. The lower the average delivery time, the lower will be the safety stock that a firm needs to hold and the total investment in inventories will be reduced.

MATERIALS REQUIREMENT PLANNING

In this chapter, we have focused on the determination of re-order points and order quantities (i.e. the EOQ) in non-complex production environments. The approaches described can also be extended to more complex manufacturing environments using a system called materials requirement planning (MRP). This topic tends to be included in the curriculum of operational management courses rather than management accounting courses. If your curriculum requires an understanding of MRP you will find that this topic is covered in Learning Note 25.1 in the digital support resources accompanying this book (see Preface for details).

JUST-IN-TIME (JIT) PURCHASING ARRANGEMENTS

In Chapter 22, the JIT business philosophy was described as a mechanism for cost management. It was pointed out that JIT philosophy focuses on the elimination of waste by seeking to eliminate non-value added activities, reducing production batch sizes and minimizing inventories. The JIT philosophy views inventories as representing waste. Many firms have extended the JIT philosophy to the purchasing function and as an alternative approach to EOQ models for inventory management. You should therefore refer back to Chapter 22 and read the section on just-in-time systems at this point.

In recent years many companies have developed strategic supply partnerships involving JIT purchasing arrangements whereby materials and goods are delivered immediately before they are used.

REAL WORLD VIEWS 25.2

Holiday season inventories

Chinese computer manufacturer Lenovo had an annual turnover of $45 billion for the year-ended 31 March 2016, of which 66 per cent was in the personal computer market. This market includes desktops, tablets and notebooks.

A report on the internet in October 2016 noted the company was increasing its inventory levels to five months' worth. One site noted 'While it's not unusual for computer companies to begin increasing inventory to prepare for holiday sales, having this much inventory is a bit odd. If things don't turn out according to plan, it may leave Lenovo sitting on three months of inventory.' Techradar, a website which details and reviews all types of technology devices, listed one model of Lenovo laptop on sale for £149 in the weeks before Christmas. This price was considerably lower than some competitor prices. Such low prices may be achievable due to the location of Lenovo's manufacturing facilities in lower cost countries – namely China, India and Mexico.

Questions

1 Can you think of business reasons why increasing inventories in advance of a busy period is a good idea? What other busy periods might electronic/technology companies experience?

2 Can you think of any potential problems not mentioned which could/do arise when inventory is increased in this way?

References

'Lenovo stockpiling inventory', available at www.custompcreview.com/news/lenovo-stockpiling-notebook-inventory-signal-huge-promotions-holiday-season/33535, accessed 10 December 2016.

Lenovo Annual Report 2016, available at www.lenovo.com/ww/lenovo/pdf/report/E_099220160603a.pdf, accessed 12 December 2016.

Techradar – www.techradar.com/news/mobile-computing/laptops/laptop-deals-cheap-laptops-1296090, accessed 12 December 2016.

By arranging with suppliers for more frequent deliveries, inventories can be cut to a minimum. JIT purchasing also normally requires suppliers to inspect materials before their delivery and guarantee their quality so that the incoming goods do not have to be inspected. This can result in considerable savings in material handling expenses. This improved service is obtained by giving more business to fewer suppliers and placing long-term purchase orders. Therefore the supplier has an assurance of long-term sales, and can plan to meet this demand.

For JIT purchasing to be successful close cooperation with suppliers, including providing them with planned production schedules, is essential. Thus, a major feature of JIT purchasing is that suppliers are not selected on the basis of price alone. Performance in terms of the quality of the components and materials supplied, the ability to always deliver as needed and a commitment to JIT purchasing are also of vital importance. Dependability in terms of delivery and quality is essential since a JIT system is highly vulnerable to any disruption in supplies arising from late deliveries or poor quality. Stock-outs arising from the unavailability of a single item can disrupt the entire production process in manufacturing organizations, or in a merchandising company the failure to meet customer demand can have a dramatic impact on customer goodwill and future sales.

Companies that have implemented JIT purchasing techniques claim to have substantially reduced their investment in raw materials and work in progress inventories. Other advantages include significant quantity discounts, savings in time from negotiating with fewer suppliers and a reduction in administrative work from issuing long-term orders to a few suppliers rather than individual purchase orders to many suppliers.

REAL WORLD VIEWS 25.3

From JIT to Real Time

Just-in-Time (JIT) manufacturing and inventory systems have been operated by many companies to reduce manufacturing time, reduce waste and ultimately increase profitability. The JIT concept is based on close relationships with key suppliers, which means a high degree of information exchange. However, even in such highly organized operations, Murphy's Law – anything that can go wrong will go wrong – still applies and this gives rise to the expression Just in Case inventory control. For example, after the 2011 earthquake and tsunami that hit Japan, many electronic components were in short supply, causing problems for those using tight JIT production schedules (Reuters, 2011).

Technological developments in recent years have offered some help to tight JIT logistic scheduling. Scott Dulman (2016), writing for *Supply and Demand Chain Executive*, reports how the Internet of Things (IoT, which is essentially internet-enabled devices) provides in-transit visibility of goods as trucks and even shipping units can be tracked real-time via the Internet. This may be particularly relevant at busy times, when whole supply chains come under pressure. For example, with an IoT enabled delivery truck, a retailer can know a delivery is a short distance away from their premises – due to a traffic delay perhaps. This information allows them to plan accordingly.

Questions

1 As a management accountant, do you think you would have a role in evaluating use of technologies such as IoT devices?

2 Can you think how costs might be reduced by such technologies?

References

Dullman (2016), 'The Internet of Things, Machine Learning and In-Transit Visibility Revolutionizing Supply Chain', available at www.sdcexec.com /article/12257563/the-internet-of-things-machine -learning-and-in-transit-visibility-revolutionizing-supply -chain, accessed 15 December 2016.

'How Real-Time Data Boosts Just-in-Time Manufacturing Models', available at www.mbtmag.com/article /2016/08/how-real-time-data-boosts-just-time -manufacturing-models, accessed 15 December 2016.

Reuters (2011), 'Disasters show flaws in just-in-time production', available at www.reuters.com/article /us-japan-supplychain-sp-idUSTRE72K5AL20110321, accessed 15 December 2016.

The proponents of JIT claim that giving more business to a few high-quality suppliers and placing long-term purchasing orders results in a dramatic decline in ordering costs. They also claim that holding cost, in terms of maintaining inventory levels, has been seriously underestimated in the past. How will a reduction in the ordering cost and a revised estimated increase in the holding cost per unit affect the EOQ? If you refer back to the EOQ formula, you will see that a decrease in the ordering cost reduces the numerator and the increase in the holding cost increases the denominator so that the EOQ declines. Therefore under JIT purchasing, the EOQ model supports more frequent purchases of lower quantities.

Finally, you should note that the JIT philosophy can also be applied to reducing the optimum batch size for a production run that was discussed earlier in this chapter. In Chapter 22, it was pointed out that a JIT production system aims to reduce and eventually eliminate set-up times. Set-up time is the amount of time required to adjust equipment settings and to retool for a different product. JIT manufacturing firms have sought to reduce set-up times by investing in advanced manufacturing technologies that enable some machine settings to be adjusted automatically instead of manually. Alternatively, some set-up times can be eliminated entirely by redesigning products or the production process so that machines do not have to be reset each time a different product has to be made. You will see by referring back to the earlier section relating to the application of the EOQ formula for determining the optimum batch size for a production run, that a reduction in set-up cost (i.e. the symbol 'S' in the numerator of the formula) arising from reduced set-up times, reduces the optimum batch size for a production run. As with JIT purchasing the EOQ model supports more frequent production runs of smaller batch sizes when set-up times are reduced.

SUMMARY

The following items relate to the learning objectives listed at the beginning of the chapter.

- **Justify which costs are relevant and should be included in the calculation of the economic order quantity (EOQ).**

The relevant costs that should be considered when determining the EOQ consist of holding costs and ordering costs. The relevant holding costs should include only those items that will vary with the levels of stocks. Examples include the opportunity cost in terms of the return that is lost from the capital tied up in stocks and incremental insurance, material handling and warehousing and storage costs. Ordering costs usually consist of the incremental clerical costs of preparing a purchase order, receiving deliveries and paying invoices. The purchase price is not normally a relevant cost since the cost per unit will be the same, irrespective of the order size. Note that special techniques can be applied to incorporate quantity discounts.

- **Calculate the EOQ using the tabulation and formula methods.**

The tabulation method merely involves listing the ordering and holding costs for each potential order quantity over a selected period. The order costs are computed by multiplying the number of orders by the incremental cost per order. To compute the holding costs, the average inventory level is multiplied by the holding cost per unit. Assuming constant usage, average inventory levels are derived by dividing the potential order quantities by 2. The computation of the EOQ using both methods was illustrated using Example 25.1.

- **Determine whether or not a company should purchase larger quantities in order to take advantage of quantity discounts.**

To ascertain whether larger quantities should be purchased the sum of the savings in purchase price arising from the discounts and the reduced ordering costs arising from fewer purchases are compared with the additional holding costs resulting from the increased inventory levels associated with the larger order quantity. The computation was illustrated using Example 25.2.

● **Calculate the optimal safety stock when demand is uncertain.**

Potential alternative levels of safety stock are added to estimated average usage for a particular period to derive potential re-order points. The expected cost, based on probabilities of demand, is determined for each potential re-order point. The optimal safety stock is represented by the safety stock associated with the re-order point that has the lowest expected cost. The analysis should include stock-out costs (i.e. the opportunity cost of running out of inventory). The computation of the optimal safety stock was illustrated in Exhibit 25.2.

● **Describe the ABC classification method.**

The ABC method classifies inventories into categories of importance so that the most elaborate procedures of controlling inventories can be applied to the most important items. The ABC classification method requires that an estimate be made of the total purchase cost for each item in inventory for a period. Each item is then grouped in decreasing order in terms of their purchase cost for the period. The top 10 per cent of items in inventory in terms of the purchase cost for the period are classified as 'A' items, the next 20 per cent as 'B' items and the final 30 per cent as 'C' items. It is generally found that the 'A' items can account for over 70 per cent of the total purchase cost for a period. The most sophisticated procedures for planning and controlling inventories are applied to the 'A' items.

● **Explain just-in-time purchasing.**

The JIT philosophy also extends to adopting JIT purchasing techniques, whereby the delivery of materials immediately precedes their use. By arranging with suppliers for more frequent deliveries, inventories can be cut to a minimum. This improved service is obtained by giving more business to fewer suppliers and placing long-term purchase orders. For JIT purchasing to be successful, close cooperation with suppliers is essential.

NOTE

1 The steps are as follows;

$$TC = \frac{DO}{Q} + \frac{QH}{2}$$

$$\frac{dDC}{dQ} = \frac{-DO}{Q^2} + \frac{H}{2}$$

Set:

$$\frac{dTC}{dQ} = 0 : \frac{H}{2} - \frac{DO}{Q^2} = 0$$

$$HQ^2 = 2DO = 0$$

$$Q^2 = \frac{2DO}{H}$$

Therefore:

$$Q^2 = \sqrt{\left(\frac{2DO}{H}\right)}$$

KEY TERMS AND CONCEPTS

ABC classification method A method of classifying stock in categories of importance in terms of value of purchases.

Cost of the prediction error The cost of failing to predict accurately one or more variables in the EOQ formula.

Economic order quantity (EOQ) The optimum order size that will result in the total amount of the ordering and holding costs being minimized.

Holding costs The costs of holding stock, comprising opportunity costs of investment, incremental insurance, storage and handling costs and the cost of obsolescence and deterioration.

JIT purchasing arrangements Strategic partnerships with suppliers that involve the delivery of materials and goods immediately before they are required.

Lead time The time that elapses between placing an order and the actual delivery of stocks.

Ordering costs The incremental clerical costs involved in ordering, receiving and paying for stock.

Precautionary motive Holding stock because of uncertainty about future demand and supply.

Re-order point The point at which the order should be placed to obtain additional stocks.

Safety stocks The amount of raw materials, work in progress and finished goods that are held in excess of the expected use during the lead time to provide a cushion against running out of stocks because of fluctuations in demand.

Speculative motive Holding stock in order to speculate on the expected increase or decrease in future prices.

Stock-out costs The opportunity cost of running out of stock.

Transactions motive Holding stock in order to meet future production and sales requirements.

RECOMMENDED READING

For additional reading relating to inventory management, you should refer to an article titled 'Stock Control' that can be accessed at www.accaglobal.com/uk /en/student/exam-support-resources/fundamentals -exams-study-resources/f2/technical-articles.html

KEY EXAMINATION POINTS

A common mistake is to unitize fixed ordering and holding costs and include these costs in the EOQ formula. The EOQ should be calculated using variable unit costs. The EOQ formula does not include the cost of purchasing materials, since it is assumed that the cost per unit is the same for all order quantities. If the question includes quantity discounts, you should adopt the approach illustrated in this chapter.

The EOQ formula should not be used when the purchase cost per unit varies with the quantity ordered. Instead, you should prepare a schedule of the relevant costs for different order quantities. You should also ensure that you can cope with problems where future demand is uncertain. Compare your answers with review problems 25.19 and 25.20. Sometimes examination questions (see review problem 25.12) require you to calculate maximum, minimum and re-order stock levels. You should use the following formulae:

Re-order level = maximum usage × maximum lead time
Minimum stock level = Re-order level − average usage during average lead time
Maximum stock level = Re-order level + EOQ − minimum usage for the minimum lead time

ASSESSMENT MATERIAL

The review questions are short questions that enable you to assess your understanding of the main topics included in the chapter. The numbers in parentheses provide you with the page numbers to refer to if you cannot answer a specific question.

The review problems are more complex and require you to relate and apply the chapter content to various business problems. The problems are graded by their level of difficulty. Solutions to review problems that are not preceded by the term 'IM' are provided in the Instructor's Manual accompanying this book that can be downloaded from the lecturer's digital support resources. Additional review problems with fully worked solutions are provided in the *Student Manual* that accompanies this book.

REVIEW QUESTIONS

25.1 What are holding costs? Provide some examples. (p. 672)

25.2 What are ordering costs? Provide some examples. (p. 673)

25.3 What determines which holding and ordering costs should be included in the economic order quantity calculation? (pp. 672–673)

25.4 What are the assumptions underlying the economic order quantity? (pp. 675–676)

25.5 Define lead time. (p. 678)

25.6 Explain what is meant by the re-order point. (p. 678)

25.7 What are stock-out costs? Provide some examples. (pp. 679–680)

25.8 Explain how safety stocks are used to deal with demand uncertainty. (pp. 679–680)

25.9 Describe the ABC classification method. What purposes does it serve? (pp. 681–682)

25.10 Describe the other factors, besides the economic order quantity, that should be taken into account when choosing an order quantity. (pp. 682–683)

25.11 What are the essential features of just-in-time purchasing arrangements? (pp. 683–684)

REVIEW PROBLEMS

25.12 Basic. A domestic appliance retailer with multiple outlets stocks a popular toaster known as the Autocrisp 2000, for which the following information is available:

Average sales	75 per day
Maximum sales	95 per day
Minimum sales	50 per day
Lead time	12–18 days
Re-order quantity	1750

(i) Based on the data above, at what level of stocks would a replenishment order be issued?

(a) 1050
(b) 1330
(c) 1710
(d) 1750

(ii) Based on the data above, what is the maximum level of stocks possible?

(a) 1750
(b) 2860
(c) 3460
(d) 5210   *(2 marks)*

CIMA Stage 1 Cost Accounting

25.13 Basic. PR is a retailer of bicycles. The most popular children's bicycle has an annual demand of 30 000 units. Demand is predictable and spread evenly throughout the year.

The bicycles are purchased by PR for $200 each. Ordering costs are $150 per order and the annual cost of holding one bicycle in inventory is $25.

Required:

(i) Calculate the economic order quantity (EOQ) for the children's bicycle.   *(2 marks)*

(ii) Calculate the total annual ordering and holding costs for the bicycle assuming the company purchases the EOQ, does not hold any buffer inventory and the lead time is zero.   *(3 marks)*

CIMA P1 Performance Operations

25.14 Basic: Calculation of number of orders and holding costs. N Ltd's chief executive believes the company is holding excessive stocks and has asked for the management accountant to carry out an investigation.

Information on the two stock items is given below:

Stock item	Purchase price $ per unit	Administration cost $ per order	Demand units	Holding cost per year % of purchase price
G	200	80	15 000 per year	13.33
H	25	28	2 800 per year	8.00

The company's stock ordering policy is based on the economic order quantity (EOQ).

Required:

(a) Determine the number of orders per year that the company will place for item G.   *(3 marks)*

(b) Determine the annual holding cost of the stock of item H.   *(3 marks)*

CIMA Management Accounting Fundamentals

25.15 Intermediate: Relevant costs and cost of prediction error. The annual demand for an item of raw materials is 4000 units and the purchase price is expected to be £90 per unit. The incremental cost of processing an order is £135 and the cost of storage is estimated to be £12 per unit.

(a) What is the optimal order quantity and the total relevant cost of this order quantity?

(b) Suppose that the £135 estimate of the incremental cost of processing an order is incorrect and should have been £80. Assume that all other estimates are correct. What is the cost of this prediction error, assuming that the solution to part (a) is implemented for one year?

(c) Assume at the start of the period that a supplier offers 4000 units at a price of £86. The materials will be delivered immediately and placed in the stores. Assume that the incremental cost of placing this order is zero and that the original estimate of £135 for placing an order for the economic batch size is correct. Should the order be accepted?

(d) Present a performance report for the purchasing officer, assuming that the budget was based on the information presented in (a) and the purchasing officer accepted the special order outlined in (c).   *(10 marks)*

25.16 Intermediate: Calculation of annual stockholding costs and impact of quantity discounts. BB manufactures a range of electronic products. The supplier of component Y has informed BB that it will offer a quantity discount of 1.0 per cent if BB places an order of 10 000 components or more at any one time.

Details of component Y are as follows:

Cost per component before discount	$2.00
Annual purchases	150 000 components
Ordering costs	$360 per order
Holding costs	$3.00 per component per annum

Required:

(i) Calculate the total annual cost of holding and ordering inventory of component Y using the economic order quantity and ignoring the quantity discount. *(2 marks)*

(ii) Calculate whether there is a financial benefit to BB from increasing the order size to 10 000 components in order to quality for the 1.0 per cent quantity discount. *(3 marks)*

CIMA P1 Performance Operations

25.17 Advanced: Impact of JIT on inventory costs. CDE has recently won a contract to supply a component to a major car manufacturer that is about to launch a new range of vehicles. This is a great success for the design team of CDE as the component has many unique features and will be an important feature of some of the vehicles in the range.

CDE is currently building a specialized factory to produce the component. The factory will start production on 1 January. There is an expected demand for 140 000 units of the component.

Forecast sales and production costs are:

Quarter	1	2	3	4
Sales (units)	19 000	34 000	37 000	50 000
	$	$	$	$
Variable production cost per unit	60	60	65	70

Fixed production overheads for the factory are expected to be $2.8 million.

A decision has to be made about the production plan. The choices are:

Plan 1: Produce at a constant rate of 35 000 units per quarter

Inventory would be used to cover fluctuations in quarterly demand. Inventory holding costs will be $13 per unit and will be incurred quarterly based on the average inventory held in each of the four quarters.

Plan 2: Use a just-in-time (JIT) production system

The factory would be able to produce 36 000 units per quarter in 'normal' time and up to a further 20 000 units in 'overtime'. However, each unit produced in 'overtime' would incur additional costs equal to 40 per cent of the forecast variable production cost per unit for that quarter.

Required:

(a) Produce calculations using the above data to show which of the two plans would incur the lowest total cost.
(6 marks)

(b) Explain TWO reasons why the decision about the production plan should not be based on your answer to part (a) alone. *(4 marks)*

CIMA P2 Performance Management

25.18 Advanced: Relevant costs and calculation of optimum batch size. Pink Ltd is experiencing some slight problems concerning two stock items sold by the company.

The first of these items is product Exe, which is manufactured by Pink. The annual demand for Exe of 4000 units, which is evenly spread throughout the year, is usually met by production taking place four times per year in batches of 1000 units. One of the raw material inputs to product Exe is product Dee which is also manufactured by Pink. Product Dee is the firm's major product and is produced in large quantities throughout the year. Production capacity is sufficient to meet in full *all* demands for the production of Dees.

The standard costs of products Exe and Dee are:

Standard costs – per unit

	Product	
	Exe	Dee
	(£)	(£)
Raw materials – purchased from external suppliers	13	8
– Dee standard cost	22	—
Labour – unskilled	7	4
– skilled	9	5
Variable overheads	5	3
Fixed overheads	4	2
Standard cost	£60	£22

Included in the fixed overheads for Exe are the set-up costs for each production run. The costs of each set-up, which apply irrespective of the size of the production run, are:

Costs per set-up

		(£)
(i)	Labour costs – skilled labour	66
(ii)	Machine parts	70
	Total	£136

The 'machine parts' relate to the cost of parts required for modifications carried out to the machine on which Exe is produced. The parts can be used for only one run, irrespective of run length, and are destroyed by replacement on reinstatement of the machine. There are no set-up costs associated with Dee.

The cost of financing stocks of Exe is 15 per cent per annum. Each unit of Exe in stock requires 0.40 square metres of storage space and units *cannot* be stacked on top of each other to reduce costs. Warehouse rent is £20 per square metre per annum and Pink is only required to pay for storage space actually used.

Pink is not working to full capacity and idle time payments are being made to all grades of labour except unskilled workers. Unskilled labour is not guaranteed a minimum weekly wage and is paid only for work carried out.

The second stock item causing concern is product Wye. Product Wye is purchased by Pink for resale and the 10 000 unit annual demand is again spread evenly throughout the year. Incremental ordering costs are £100 per order and the normal unit cost is £20. However, the suppliers of Wye are now offering quantity discounts for large orders. The details of these are:

Quantity ordered	Unit price (£)
Up to 999	20.00
1 000 to 1 999	19.80
2 000 and over	19.60

The purchasing manager feels that full advantage should be taken of discounts and purchases should be made at £19.60 per unit using orders for 2000 units or more. Holding costs for Wye are calculated at £8.00 per unit per year and this figure will not be altered by any change in the purchase price per unit.

Required:

(a) Show the optimum batch size for the production of Exes. If this differs from the present policy, calculate the annual savings to be made by Pink Ltd from pursuing the optimal policy. Briefly explain the figures incorporated in your calculations. (The time taken to carry out a production run may be ignored.) *(10 marks)*

(b) Advise Pink Ltd on the correct size of order for the purchase of Wyes. *(6 marks)*

(c) Briefly describe two major limitations, or difficulties inherent in the practical application, of the model used in (a) to determine the optimum batch size. *(4 marks)*

ACCA P2 Management Accounting

25.19 Advanced: Safety stocks and probability theory.

A company has determined that the EOQ for its only raw material is 2000 units every 30 days. The company knows with certainty that a four-day lead time is required for ordering. The following is the probability distribution of estimated usage of the raw material for the month:

Usage (units)	1800	1900	2000	2100	2200	2300	2400	2500
Probability	0.06	0.14	0.30	0.16	0.13	0.10	0.07	0.04

Stock-outs will cost the company £10 per unit, and the average monthly holding cost is £1 per unit:

(a) Determine the optimal safety stock.

(b) What is the probability of being out of stock? *(10 marks)*

25.20 Advanced: Safety stocks, uncertain demand and quantity discounts.

Kattalist Ltd is a distributor of an industrial chemical in the northeast of England. The chemical is supplied in drums that have to be stored at a controlled temperature.

The company's objective is to maximize profits and it commenced business on 1 October:

The managing director's view

The company's managing director wishes to improve stock holding policy by applying the economic order quantity model. Each drum of the chemical costs £50 from a supplier and sells for £60. Annual demand is estimated to be for 10 000 drums, which the managing director assumes to be evenly distributed over 300 working days. The cost of delivery is estimated at £25 per order and the annual variable holding cost per drum at £45 plus 10 per cent of purchase cost. Using these data, the managing director calculates the economic order quantity and proposes that this should be the basis for purchasing decisions of the industrial chemical in future periods.

The purchasing manager's view

Written into the contract of the company's purchasing manager is a clause that he will receive a bonus (rounded to the nearest £1) of 10 per cent of the amount by which total annual inventory holding and order costs before such remuneration are below £10 000. Using the same assumptions as the managing director, the purchasing manager points out that in making his calculations the managing director has not only ignored his bonus but also the fact that suppliers offer quantity discounts on purchase orders. In fact, if the order size is 200 drums or above, the price per drum for an entire consignment is only £49.90, compared to £50 when an order is between 100 and 199 drums; and £50.10 when an order is between 50 and 99 drums.

The finance director's view

The company's finance director accepts the need to consider quantity discounts and pay a bonus, but he also feels the managing director's approach is too simplistic. He points out that there is a lead time for an order of three days and that demand has not been entirely even over the past year. Moreover, if the company has no drums in stock, it will lose specific orders as potential customers will go to rival competitors in the region to meet their immediate needs.

To support his argument, the finance director summarizes the evidence from salesmen's records over the past year, which show the number of drums demanded during the lead times were as follows:

Drums demanded during three-day lead time	Number of times each quantity of drums was demanded
106	4
104	10
102	16
100	40
98	14
96	14
94	2

In the circumstances, the managing director decides he should seek further advice on what course of action he should take.

Requirements:

(a) Calculate the economic order quantity as originally determined by the company's managing director. *(1 mark)*

(b) Calculate the optimum economic order quantity, applying the managing director's assumptions and after allowing for the purchasing manager's bonus and for supplier quantity discounts, but without using an expected value approach. *(3 marks)*

(c) Adopting the financial director's assumptions and an expected value approach, and assuming that it is a condition of the supplier's contract that the order quantity is to be constant for all orders in the year, determine the expected level of safety (i.e. buffer) stock the company should maintain. For this purpose, use the figures for the economic order quantity you have derived in answering (b). (Show all workings and state any assumptions you make.) *(5 marks)*

(d) As an outside consultant, write a report to the managing director on the company's stock ordering and stockholding policies, referring where necessary to your answers to (a)–(c). The report should refer, *inter alia,* to other factors he should consider when taking his final decisions on stock ordering and stock holding policies. *(9 marks)*

Note: Ignore taxation. *(Total 18 marks)*

ICAEW Management Accounting and Financial Management Part Two

IM25.1 Intermediate: Calculation of EOQ and frequency at ordering.

A company is planning to purchase 90 800 units of a particular item in the year ahead. The item is purchased in boxes, each containing ten units of the item, at a price of £200 per box. A safety stock of 250 boxes is kept.

The cost of holding an item in stock for a year (including insurance, interest and space costs) is 15 per cent of the purchase area. The cost of placing and receiving orders is to be estimated from cost data collected relating to similar orders, where costs of £5910 were incurred on 30 orders. It should be assumed that ordering costs change in proportion to the number of orders placed. Two per cent should be added to the above ordering costs to allow for inflation.

Required:

Calculate the order quantity that would minimize the cost of the above item and determine the required frequency of placing orders, assuming that usage of the item will be even over the year. *(8 marks)*

ACCA Foundation Stage Paper 3

IM25.2 Intermediate: Calculation of EOQ.

Sandy Lands Ltd carries an item of inventory in respect of which the following data apply:

fixed cost of ordering per batch	£10
expected steady quarterly volume of sales	3125 units
cost of holding one unit in stock for one year	£1

You are required to:

(i) calculate the minimum annual cost of ordering and stocking the item; *(4 marks)*

(ii) calculate to the nearest whole number of units the optimal batch size if the expected steady quarterly volume of sales:

first falls to 781 units and
second rises to 6250 units;

and to state the relationship between the rates of change of sales and the optimal batch size; *(4 marks)*

(iii) explain the basis of the derivation of the formula for the optimal batch size which is given in the table of formulae. *(4 marks)*

ICAEW Management Accounting

IM25.3 Intermediate: Calculation of EOQ and a make-or-buy decision. A company is considering the possibility of purchasing from a supplier a component it now makes. The supplier will provide the components in the necessary quantities at a unit price of £9. Transportation and storage costs would be negligible.

The company produces the component from a single raw material in economic lots of 2000 units at a cost of £2 per unit. Average annual demand is 20000 units. The annual holding cost is £0.25 per unit and the minimum stock level is set at 400 units. Direct labour costs for the component are £6 per unit, fixed manufacturing overhead is charged at a rate of £3 per unit based on a normal activity of 20000 units. The company also hires the machine on which the components are produced at a rate of £200 per month.

Should the company make the component? *(5 marks)*

IM25.4 Intermediate: Calculation of minimum purchase cost when cost per unit is not constant. A company is reviewing the purchasing policy for one of its raw materials as a result of a reduction in production requirement. The material, which is used evenly throughout the year, is used in only one of the company's products, the production of which is currently 12000 units per annum. Each finished unit of the product contains 0.4kg of the material; 20 per cent of the material is lost in the production process. Purchases can be made in multiples of 500kg, with a minimum purchase order quantity of 1000kg.

The cost of the raw material depends on the purchase order quantity as follows:

Order quantity (kg)	Cost per kg (£)
1000	1.00
1500	0.98
2000	0.965
2500	0.95
3000 and above	0.94

Costs of placing and handling each order are £90, of which £40 is an apportionment of costs that are not expected to be affected in the short term by the number of orders placed. Annual holding costs of stock are £0.90 per unit of average stock, of which only £0.40 is expected to be affected in the short term by the amount of stock held.

The lead time for the raw materials is one month, and a safety stock of 250kg is required.

Required:

(a) Explain, and illustrate from the situation described above, the meaning of the terms 'variable', 'semi-variable' and 'fixed' costs. *(8 marks)*

(b) Calculate the annual cost of pursuing alternative purchase order policies and thus advise the company regarding the purchase order quantity for the material that will minimize cost. *(14 marks)*

ACCA Level 1 Costing

IM25.5 Advanced: Evaluation of an increase in order size incorporating quantity discounts. Whirlygig plc manufactures and markets automatic dishwashing machines. Among the components that it purchases each year from external suppliers for assembly into the finished article are window units, of which it uses 20000 units per annum.

It is considering buying in larger amounts in order to claim quantity discounts. This will lower the number of orders placed but raise the administrative and other costs of placing and receiving orders. Details of actual and expected ordering and carrying costs are given in the table below:

	Actual	Proposed
O = Ordering cost per order	£31.25	£120
P = Purchase price per item	£6.25	£6.00
I = (annual) Inventory holding cost (as a percentage of the purchase price)	20%	20%

To implement the new arrangements will require reorganization costs estimated at £10000, which can be wholly claimed as a business expense for tax purposes in the tax year before the system comes into operation. The rate of corporate tax is 33 per cent, payable with a one-year delay.

Required:

(a) Determine the change in the economic order quantity (EOQ) caused by the new system. *(4 marks)*

(b) Calculate the payback period for the proposal and comment on your results. *(10 marks)*

(c) Briefly discuss the suitability of the payback method for evaluating investments of this nature. *(6 marks)*

ACCA Paper 8 Managerial Finance

IM25.6 Advanced: Quantity discounts and calculation of EOQ. Wagtail Ltd uses the 'optimal batch size' model (see below) to determine optimal levels of raw materials. Material B is consumed at a steady, known rate over the company's planning horizon of one year; the current usage is 4000 units per annum. The costs of ordering B are invariant with respect to order size; clerical costs of ordering have been calculated at £30 per order. Each order is checked by an employee engaged in using B in production who earns £8 per hour irrespective of his output. The employee generates a contribution of £1 per hour when not involved in materials checks and the stock check takes five hours. Holding costs amount to £15 per unit per annum.

The supplier of material B has very recently offered Wagtail a quantity discount of £0.24 a unit on the current price of £24, for all orders of 400 or more units of B.

You are required to:

(a) calculate the optimal order level of material B, ignoring the quantity discount; *(3 marks)*

(b) evaluate whether the quantity discount offered should be taken up by Wagtail; *(5 marks)*

(c) explain how uncertainties in materials usage and lead time may be incorporated into the analysis. *(8 marks)*

Note: Ignore taxation.

ICAEW P2 Financial Management

IM25.7 Advanced: Calculation of EOQ and a comparison of relevant purchasing costs of different suppliers. Mr Evans is a wholesaler who buys and sells a wide range of products, one of which is the Laker. Mr Evans sells 24000 units of the Laker each year at a unit price of £20. Sales of the Laker normally follow an even pattern throughout the year but to protect himself against possible deviations Mr Evans keeps a minimum stock of 1000 units. Further supplies of the Laker are ordered whenever the stock falls to this minimum level and the time lag between ordering and delivery is small enough to be ignored.

At present, Mr Evans buys all his supplies of Lakers from May Ltd and usually purchases them in batches of 5000 units. His most recent invoice from May Ltd was as follows:

	(£)
Basic price: 5000 Lakers at £15 per unit	75 000
Delivery charge: Transport at £0.50 per unit	2 500
Fixed shipment charge per order	1 000
	78 500

In addition, Mr Evans estimates that each order he places costs him £500, comprising administrative costs and the cost of sample checks. This cost does not vary with the size of the order.

Mr Evans stores Lakers in a warehouse that he rents on a long lease for £5 per square foot per annum. Warehouse space available exceeds current requirements and, as the lease cannot be cancelled, spare capacity is sublet on annual contracts at £4 per square foot per annum. Each unit of Laker in stock requires two square feet of space. Mr Evans estimates that other holding costs amount to £10 per Laker per annum.

Mr Evans has recently learnt that another supplier of Lakers, Richardson Ltd, is willing, unlike May Ltd, to offer discounts on large orders. Richardson Ltd sells Lakers at the following prices:

Order size	Price per unit (£)
1–2999	15.25
3000–4999	14.50
5000 and over	14.25

In other respects (i.e. delivery charges and the time between ordering and delivery), Richardson Ltd's terms are identical to those of May Ltd.

You are required to:

(a) calculate the optimal re-order quantity for Lakers and the associated annual profit Mr Evans can expect from their purchase and sale, assuming that he continues to buy from May Ltd;   (10 marks)

(b) prepare calculations to show whether Mr Evans should buy Lakers from Richardson Ltd rather than from May Ltd and, if so, in what batch sizes;   (8 marks)

(c) explain the limitations of the methods of analysis you have used.   (7 marks)

Note: Ignore taxation.

ICAEW Elements of Financial Decisions

IM25.8 Advanced: Calculation of EOQ and discussion of safety stocks. A company needs to hold a stock of item X for sale to customers.

Although the item is of relatively small value per unit, the customers' quality control requirements and the need to obtain competitive supply tenders at frequent intervals result in high procurement costs.

Basic data about item X are as follows:

Annual sales demand (D) over 52 weeks	4095 units
Cost of placing and processing a purchase order (procurement costs, C_s)	£48.46
Cost of holding one unit for one year (C_h)	£4.00
Normal delay between placing purchase order and receiving goods	3 weeks

You are required to:

(a) calculate:

(i) the economic order quantity for item X;

(ii) the frequency at which purchase orders would be placed, using that formula;

(iii) the total annual procurement costs and the total annual holding costs when the EOQ is used;   (6 marks)

(b) explain why it might be unsatisfactory to procure a fixed quantity of item X at regular intervals if it were company policy to satisfy all sales demands from stock and if:

(i) the rate of sales demand could vary between 250 and 350 units per four-week period

(ii) the delivery delay on purchases might vary between three and five weeks suggesting in each case what corrective actions might be taken;   (6 marks)

(c) describe in detail a fully developed stock control system for item X (or other fast moving items), designed to ensure that stock holdings at all times are adequate but not excessive. Illustrate your answer with a freehand graph, not to scale.   (8 marks)

CIMA Stage 4 Financial Management

IM25.9 Advanced: Calculation of EOQ, safety stocks and stockholding costs where demand is uncertain. The financial controller of Mexet plc is reviewing the company's stock management procedures. Stock has gradually increased to 25 per cent of the company's total assets and, with finance costs at 14 per cent per annum, currently costs the company £4.5 million per year, including all ordering and holding costs.

Demand for the company's major product is not subject to seasonal fluctuations. The product requires £6 million of standard semi-finished goods annually that are purchased in equal quantities from three separate suppliers at a cost of £20 per unit. Three suppliers are used to prevent problems that could result from industrial disputes in a single supplier.

Stock costs £2 per unit per year to hold, including insurance costs and financing costs and each order made costs £100 fixed cost and £0.10 per unit variable cost. There is a lead time of one month between the placing of an order and delivery of the goods. Demand fluctuation for the company's finished products results in the following probability distribution of monthly stock usage:

Usage per month	19 400	23 000	25 000	27 000	30 000
Probability	0.10	0.22	0.36	0.20	0.12

The cost per unit of running out of stock is estimated to be £0.4.

Required:

(a) Calculate the economic order quantity for the semi-finished goods.   (3 marks)

(b) Determine what level of safety stock should be kept for these goods.   (8 marks)

(c) Calculate the change in annual stock management costs that would result if the goods were bought from only one supplier. Assume that no quantity discounts are available.   (5 marks)

(d) The financial controller feels that JIT (just-in-time) stock management might be useful for the company, but the three suppliers will only agree to this in return for an increase in unit price.

Explain the possible advantages and disadvantages of JIT and briefly discuss whether or not Mexet should introduce it.   (9 marks)

ACCA Level 3 Financial Management

IM25.10 Advanced: Calculation of stockholding costs, costs of stock-outs when demand is uncertain and a discussion of JIT. Rainbow Ltd is a manufacturer that uses alkahest in many of its products. At present the company has an alkahest plant on a site close to the company's main factory. A summary of the alkahest plants budget for the next year is shown below:

Production	3 000 000 litres of alkahest
Variable manufacturing costs	£840 000
Fixed manufacturing costs	£330 000

The budget covers costs up to and including the cost of piping finished alkahest to the main factory. At the main factory, alkahest can be stored at a cost of £20 per annum per thousand litres, but additional costs arise in storage because alkahest evaporates at a rate of 5 per cent per annum. Production of alkahest is adjusted to meet the demands of the main factory; in addition, safety stocks of 60000 litres are maintained in case of disruption of supplies.

The alkahest plant has a limited remaining life and has been fully depreciated. The management of Rainbow Ltd is considering whether the plant should be retained for the time being or should be closed immediately. On closure, the equipment would be scrapped and the site sold for £400000. Employees would be redeployed within the company and supplies of alkahest would be bought from an outside supplier.

Rainbow Ltd has found that Alchemy plc can supply all its alkahest requirements at £370 per thousand litres. Transport costs of £30 per thousand litres would be borne by Rainbow Ltd. There would be administration costs of £15000 per year, in addition to order costs of £60 for each delivery. It has been decided that if purchases are made from Alchemy plc the safety stock will be increased to 100000 litres.

Rainbow Ltd has 250 working days in each year and a cost of capital of 15 per cent per annum. The company's current expectations for demand and costs apply for the foreseeable future.

Requirements:

(a) Calculate the total annual costs of the options available to Rainbow Ltd for its supply of alkahest and interpret the results for management. *(10 marks)*

(b) Calculate the expected annual stock-outs in litres implied by a safety stock of 100000 litres and calculate the stock-out cost per litre at which it would be worthwhile to increase safety stock from 100000 litres to 120000 litres, under the following assumptions:

(i) for any delivery there is a 0.8 probability that lead time will be five days and a 0.2 probability that lead time will be ten days

(ii) during the lead time for any delivery there is a 0.5 probability that Rainbow Ltd will use alkahest at the rate of 10000 litres per day and a 0.5 probability that the company will use alkahest at the rate of 14000 litres per day. *(6 marks)*

(c) Explain the requirements for the successful adoption of a just-in-time inventory policy and discuss the relative costs and benefits of just-in-time policies compared with economic order quantity policies. *(9 marks)*

ICAEW P2 Management Accounting

26

THE APPLICATION OF LINEAR PROGRAMMING TO MANAGEMENT ACCOUNTING

LEARNING OBJECTIVES After studying this chapter, you should be able to:

- describe the situations when it may be appropriate to use linear programming;
- explain the circumstances when the graphical method can be used;
- use graphical linear programming to find the optimum output levels;
- formulate the initial linear programming model using the simplex method;
- explain the meaning of the term shadow prices.

In Chapter 9, we considered how accounting information should be used to ensure the optimal allocation of scarce resources (also known as **bottleneck activities**). To refresh your memory, you should now refer back to Example 9.3 to ascertain how the optimum production programme can be determined. You will see that where a scarce resource exists that has alternative uses, the contribution per unit should be calculated for each of these uses. The available capacity of this resource is then allocated to the alternative uses on the basis of the contribution per scarce resource.

Where more than one scarce resource exists, the optimum production programme cannot easily be established by the process described in Chapter 9. In such circumstances, there is a need to resort to linear programming techniques to establish the optimum production programme. Our objective in this chapter is to examine how linear programming techniques can be applied to determine the optimum production programme in situations where more than one scarce resource exists. Initially, we shall assume that only two products are produced, so that the optimum output can be determined using a two-dimensional graph. Where more than two products are produced, the optimal output cannot easily be determined using the graphical method. Instead, the optimal output can be determined using a non-graphical approach that is known as the simplex method.

Linear programming is a topic that is sometimes included in operational management courses rather than management accounting courses. You should therefore check your course content to ascertain if you will need to read this chapter.

LINEAR PROGRAMMING

Linear programming is a powerful mathematical technique that can be applied to the problem of rationing limited facilities and resources among many alternative uses in such a way that the optimum benefits can be derived from their utilization. It seeks to find a feasible combination of output that will maximize or minimize the objective function. The objective function refers to the quantification of an objective, and usually takes the form of maximizing profits or minimizing costs. Linear programming may be used when relationships can be assumed to be linear and where an optimal solution does, in fact, exist.

To comply with the linearity assumption, it must be assumed that the contribution per unit for each product and the utilization of resources per unit are the same whatever quantity of output is produced and sold within the output range being considered. It must also be assumed that units produced and resources allocated are infinitely divisible. This means that an optimal plan that suggests we should produce 94.38 units is possible. However, it will be necessary to interpret the plan as a production of 94 units.

We shall now apply this technique to the problem outlined in Example 26.1, where there is a labour restriction plus a limitation on the availability of materials and machine hours. The contributions per scarce resource are as follows:

	Product Y (£)	Product Z (£)
Labour	2.33 (£14/6 hours)	2.00 (£16/8 hours)
Material	1.75 (£14/8 units)	4.00 (£16/4 units)
Machine capacity	3.50 (£14/4 hours)	2.67 (£16/6 hours)

EXAMPLE 26.1
Multiple resource constraint problem

The LP company currently makes two products. The standards per unit of product are as follows:

Product Y	(£)	(£)	Product Z	(£)	(£)
Product Y			Product Z		
Standard selling price		110	Standard selling price		118
Less standard costs:			Less standard costs:		
Materials (eight units at £4)	32		Materials (four units at £4)	16	
Labour (six hours at £10)	60		Labour (eight hours at £10)	80	
Variable overhead			Variable overhead		
(four machine hours at £1)	4		(six machine hours at £1)	6	
		96			102
Contribution		14	Contribution		16

During the next accounting period, the availability of resources are expected to be subject to the following limitations:

Labour	2880 hours
Materials	3440 units
Machine capacity	2760 hours

The marketing manager estimates that the maximum sales potential for product Y is limited to 420 units. There is no sales limitation for product Z. You are asked to advise how these limited facilities and resources can best be used so as to gain the optimum benefit from them.

This analysis shows that product Y yields the largest contribution per labour hour and product Z yields the largest contribution per unit of scarce materials, but there is no clear indication of how the quantity of scarce resources should be allocated to each product. Linear programming should be used in such circumstances.

The procedure is, first, to formulate the problem algebraically, with Y denoting the number of units of product Y and Z the number of units of product Z that are manufactured by the company. Second, we must specify the objective function, which in this example is to maximize contribution (denoted by C), followed by the input constraints. We can now formulate the linear programming model as follows:

$$\text{Maximize } C = 14Y + 16Z \text{ subject to}$$
$$8Y + 4Z \leq 3440 \text{ (material constraint)}$$
$$6Y + 8Z \leq 2880 \text{ (labour constraint)}$$
$$4Y + 6Z \leq 2760 \text{ (machine capacity constraint)}$$
$$0 \leq Y \leq 420 \text{ (maximum and minimum sales limitation)}$$
$$Z \geq 0 \text{ (minimum sales limitation)}$$

In this model, 'maximize C' indicates that we wish to maximize contribution with an unknown number of units of Y produced, each yielding a contribution of £14 per unit, and an unknown number of units of Z produced, each yielding a contribution of £16. The labour constraint indicates that six hours of labour are required for each unit of product Y that is made and eight hours for each unit of product Z. Thus (6 hours $\times$ Y) + (8 hours $\times$ Z) cannot exceed 2880 hours. Similar reasoning applies to the other inputs.

Because linear programming is nothing more than a mathematical tool for solving constrained optimization problems, nothing in the technique itself ensures that an answer will 'make sense'. For example, in a production problem, for some very unprofitable product, the optimal output level may be a negative quantity, which is clearly an impossible solution. To prevent such nonsensical results, we must include a non-negativity requirement, which is a statement that all variables in the problem must be equal to or greater than zero. We must therefore add to the model in our example the constraint that Y and Z must be greater than or equal to zero, i.e. $Z \geq 0$ and $0 \leq Y \leq 420$. The latter expression indicates that sales of Y cannot be less than zero or greater than 420 units. The model can be solved graphically or by the simplex method. When no more than two products are manufactured, the graphical method can be used, but this becomes impracticable where more than two products are involved and it is then necessary to resort to the simplex method.

GRAPHICAL METHOD

Taking the first *constraint for the materials* input $8Y + 4Z \leq 3440$ means that we can make a maximum of 860 units of product Z when production of product Y is zero. The 860 units is arrived at by dividing the 3440 units of materials by the four units of material required for each unit of product Z. Alternatively, a maximum of 430 units of product Y can be made (3440 units divided by eight units of materials) if no materials are allocated to product Z. We can therefore state that:

$$\text{when } Y = 0, Z = 860$$
$$\text{when } Z = 0, Y = 430$$

These items are plotted in Figure 26.1, with a straight line running from $Z = 0$, $Y = 430$ to $Y = 0$, $Z = 860$. Note that the vertical axis represents the number of units of Y produced and the horizontal axis the number of units of Z produced.

The area to the left of line $8Y + 4Z \leq 3440$ contains all possible solutions for Y and Z in this particular situation, and any point along the line connecting these two outputs represents the maximum combinations of Y and Z that can be produced with not more than 3440 units of materials. Every point to the right of the line violates the material constraint.

FIGURE 26.1

Constraint imposed by limitations of materials

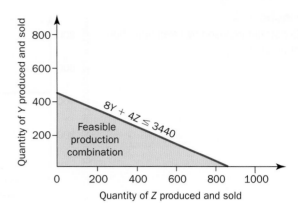

FIGURE 26.2

Constraint imposed by limitations of labour

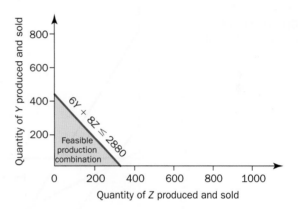

FIGURE 26.3

Constraint imposed by machine capacity

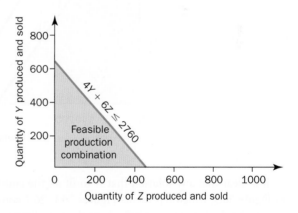

The *labour constraint* $6Y + 8Z \leq 2880$ indicates that if production of product Z is zero, then a maximum of 480 units of product Y can be produced (2880/6), and if the output of Y is zero then 360 units of Z (2880/8) can be produced. We can now draw a second line $Y = 480$, $Z = 0$ to $Y = 0$, $Z = 360$, and this is illustrated in Figure 26.2. The area to the left of line $6Y + 8Z \leq 2880$ in this figure represents all the possible solutions that will satisfy the labour constraint.

The *machine input constraint* is represented by $Z = 0$, $Y = 690$ and $Y = 0$, $Z = 460$, and the line indicating this constraint is illustrated in Figure 26.3. The area to the left of the line $4Y + 6Z \leq 2760$ in this figure represents all the possible solutions that will satisfy the machine capacity constraint.

The final constraint is that the *sales output* of product Y cannot exceed 420 units. This is represented by the line $Y \leq 420$ in Figure 26.4, and all the items below this line represent all the possible solutions that will satisfy this sales limitation.

FIGURE 26.4

Constraint imposed by sales limitation of product Y

FIGURE 26.5

Combination of Figures 26.1–26.4

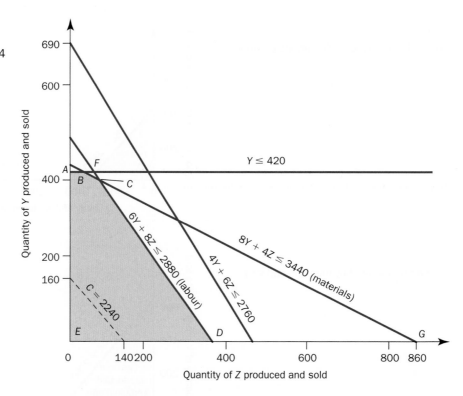

It is clear that any solution that is to fit *all* the constraints must occur in the shaded area *ABCDE* in Figure 26.5, which represents Figures 26.1–26.4 combined together. The point must now be found within the shaded area *ABCDE* where the contribution C is the greatest. The maximum will occur at one of the corner points *ABCDE*. The objective function is $C = 14Y + 16Z$, and a random contribution value is chosen that will result in a line for the objective function falling within the area *ABCDE*.

If we choose a random total contribution value equal to £2240, this could be obtained from producing 160 units (£2240/£14) of Y at £14 contribution per unit or 140 units of Z (£2240/£16) at a contribution of £16 per unit. We can therefore draw a line $Z = 0$, $Y = 160$ to $Y = 0$, $Z = 140$. This is represented by the dashed line in Figure 26.5. Each point on the dashed line represents all the output combinations of Z and Y that will yield a total contribution of £2240. The dashed line is extended to the right until it touches the last corner of the boundary *ABCDE*. This is the optimal solution and is at point C, which indicates an output of 400 units of Y (contribution £5600) and 60 units of Z (contribution £960), giving a total contribution of £6560.

The logic in the previous paragraph is illustrated in Figure 26.6. The shaded area represents the feasible production area *ABCDE* that is outlined in Figure 26.5, and parallel lines represent possible

FIGURE 26.6

Combination levels from different potential combinations of products Y and Z

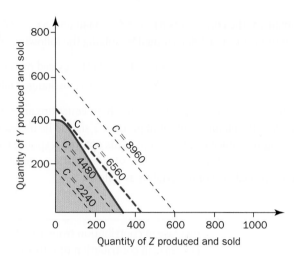

contributions, which take on higher values as we move to the right. If we assume that the firm's objective is to maximize total contribution, it should operate on the highest contribution curve obtainable. At the same time, it is necessary to satisfy the production constraints, which are indicated by the shaded area in Figure 26.6. You will see that point C indicates the solution to the problem, since no other point within the feasible area touches such a high contribution line.

It is difficult to ascertain from Figure 26.5 the exact output of each product at point C. The optimum output can be determined exactly by solving the simultaneous equations for the constraints that intersect at point C:

$$8Y + 4Z = 3440 \tag{26.1}$$

$$6Y + 8Z = 2880 \tag{26.2}$$

We can now multiply equation (26.1) by 2 and equation (26.2) by 1, giving:

$$16Y + 8Z = 6880 \tag{26.3}$$

$$6Y + 8Z = 2880 \tag{26.4}$$

Subtracting equation (26.4) from equation (26.3) gives:

$$10Y = 4000$$

and so:

$$Y = 400$$

We can now substitute this value for Y onto equation (26.3), giving:

$$(16 \times 400) + 8Z = 6880$$

and so:

$$Z = 60$$

You will see from Figure 26.5 that the constraints that are binding at point C are materials and labour. It might be possible to remove these constraints and acquire additional labour and materials resources by paying a premium over and above the existing acquisition cost. How much should the company be prepared to pay? To answer this question, it is necessary to determine the optimal use from an additional unit of a scarce resource.

We shall now consider how the optimum solution would change if an additional unit of materials were obtained. You can see that if we obtain additional materials, the line $8Y + 4Z \leq 3440$ in Figure 26.5 will shift upwards and the revised optimum point will fall on line CF. If one extra unit of materials is obtained, the constraints $8Y + 4Z \leq 3440$ and $6Y + 8Z \leq 2880$ will still be binding, and the new optimum plan can be determined by solving the following simultaneous equations:

$$8Y + 4Z = 3441 \text{ (revised materials constraint)}$$
$$6Y + 8Z = 2880 \text{ (unchanged labour constraint)}$$

The revised optimal output when the above equations are solved is 400.2 units of Y and 59.85 units of Z. Therefore the planned output of product Y should be increased by 0.2 units, and planned production of Z should be reduced by 0.15 units. This optimal response from an independent marginal increase in a resource is called the **marginal rate of substitution**. The change in contribution arising from obtaining one additional unit of materials is as follows:

	(£)
Increase in contribution from Y (0.2 × £14)	2.80
Decrease in contribution of Z (0.15 × £16)	(2.40)
Increase in contribution	0.40

Therefore the value of an additional unit of materials is £0.40. The value of an independent marginal increase of scarce resource is called the **opportunity cost** or **shadow price**. We shall be considering these terms in more detail later in the chapter. You should note at this stage that, for materials purchased in excess of 3440 units, the company can pay up to £0.40 over and above the present acquisition cost of materials of £4 and still obtain a contribution towards fixed costs from the additional output.

From a practical point of view, it is not possible to produce 400.2 units of Y and 59.85 units of Z. Output must be expressed in single whole units. Nevertheless, the output from the model can be used to calculate the revised optimal output if additional units of materials are obtained. Assume that 100 additional units of materials can be purchased at £4.20 per unit from an overseas supplier. Because the opportunity cost (£0.40) is in excess of the additional acquisition cost of £0.20 per unit (£4.20 − £4), the company should purchase the extra materials. The marginal rates of substitution can be used to calculate the revised optimum output. The calculation is:

Increase Y by 20 units (100 × 0.2 units)
Decrease Z by 15 units (100 × 0.15 units)

Therefore the revised optimal output is 420 outputs (400 + 20) of Y and 35 units (60 − 15) of Z. You will see later in this chapter that the substitution process outlined above is applicable only within a particular range of material usage.

We can apply the same approach to calculate the opportunity cost of labour. If an additional labour hour is obtained, the line $6Y + 8Z = 2880$ in Figure 26.5 will shift to the right and the revised optimal point will fall on line *CG*. The constraints $8Y + 4Z = 3440$ and $6Y + 8Z = 2880$ will still be binding, and the new optimum plan can be determined by solving the following simultaneous equations:

$$8Y + 4Z = 3440 \text{ (unchanged materials constraint)}$$
$$6Y + 8Z = 2881 \text{ (revised labour constraint)}$$

The revised optimal output when the above equations are solved is 399.9 units of Y and 60.2 units of Z. Therefore the planned output of product Y should be decreased by 0.1 units and planned production of Z should be increased by 0.2 units. The opportunity cost of a scarce labour hour is:

	(£)
Decrease in contribution from Y (0.1 × £14)	(1.40)
Increase in contribution from Z (0.2 × £16)	3.20
Increase in contribution (opportunity cost)	1.80

SIMPLEX METHOD

Where more than two products can be manufactured using the scarce resources available, the optimum solution cannot be established from the graphical method. In this situation, a mathematical programming technique known as the simplex method must be used. This method also provides additional information on opportunity costs and marginal rates of substitution that is particularly useful for decision-making and also for planning and control. Some courses only include the graphical method in their curriculum, so you should check your course curriculum to ascertain whether you need to read the following sections that relate to the simplex method.

The simplex method involves many tedious calculations, but there are standard spreadsheet packages that will complete the task within a few minutes. The aim of this chapter is not therefore to delve into these tedious calculations but to provide you with an understanding of how the simplex linear programming model should be formulated for an input into a spreadsheet package and also how to interpret the optimal solution from the output from the spreadsheet package. However, if you are interested in how the optimal solution is derived you should read this section and then refer to Learning Note 26.1 in the digital support resources accompanying this book (see Preface for details) but do note that examination questions do not require you to undertake the calculations. They merely require you to formulate the initial model and interpret the final matrix showing the optimum output derived from the model. Example 26.1 is now used to illustrate the simplex method.

To apply the simplex method, we must first formulate a model that does not include any *inequalities*. This is done by introducing what are called slack variables to the model. Slack variables are added to a linear programming problem to account for any constraint that is unused at the point of optimality and one slack variable is introduced for each constraint. In our example, the company is faced with constraints on materials, labour, machine capacity and maximum sales for product Y. Therefore S_1 is introduced to represent unused material resources, S_2 represents unused labour hours, S_3 represents unused machine capacity and S_4 represents unused potential sales output. We can now express the model for Example 26.1 in terms of equalities rather than inequalities:

$$\text{Maximize } C = 14Y + 16Z$$
$$8Y + 4Z + S_1 = 3440 \text{ (materials constraint)}$$
$$6Y + 8Z + S_2 = 2880 \text{ (labour constraint)}$$
$$4Y + 6Z + S_3 = 2760 \text{ (machine capacity constraint)}$$
$$1Y + S_4 = 420 \text{ (sales constraint for product Y)}$$

For labour (6 hours $\times$ Y) + (8 hours $\times$ Z) plus any unused labour hours (S_2) will equal 2880 hours when the optimum solution is reached. Similar reasoning applies to the other production constraints. The sales limitation indicates that the number of units of Y sold plus any shortfall on maximum demand will equal 420 units.

We shall now express all the above equations in matrix form (sometimes described as in tableau form), with the slack variables on the left-hand side:

Initial matrix

Quantity	Y	Z	
$S_1 = 3440$	−8	−4	(1) (material constraint)
$S_2 = 2880$	−6	−8	(2) (labour constraint)
$S_3 = 2760$	−4	−6	(3) (machine hours constraint)
$S_4 = 420$	−1	0	(4) (sales constraint)
$C = 0$	+14	+16	(5) contribution

Note that the quantity column in the matrix indicates the resources available or the slack that is not taken up when production is zero. For example, the S_1 row of the matrix indicates that 3440 units of materials are available when production is zero. Column Y indicates that eight units of materials, six labour hours and four machine hours are required to produce one unit of product Y and this will reduce the potential sales of Y by one. You will also see from column Y that the production of one unit of Y will yield £14 contribution. Similar reasoning applies to column Z. Note that the entry in the contribution row (i.e. the C row) for the quantity column is zero because this first matrix is based on nil production, which gives a contribution of zero.

The simplex method involves the application of matrix algebra to generate a series of matrices until a final matrix emerges that represents the optimal solution based on the initial model. Learning Note 26.1 explains how the final matrix is derived (see the digital resources). The final matrix containing the optimal solution is shown below:

Final matrix			
Quantity	S_1	S_2	
$Y = 400$	$-\frac{1}{5}$	$+\frac{1}{10}$	(1)
$Z = 60$	$+\frac{3}{20}$	$-\frac{1}{5}$	(2)
$S_3 = 800$	$-\frac{1}{10}$	$+\frac{4}{5}$	(3)
$S_4 = 20$	$+\frac{1}{5}$	$-\frac{1}{10}$	(4)
$C = 6560$	$-\frac{2}{5}$	$-1\frac{4}{5}$	(5)

Interpreting the final matrix

The final matrix can be interpreted using the same approach that was used for the initial matrix but the interpretation is more complex. The contribution row (equation 5) of the final matrix contains only negative items, which signifies that the optimal solution has been reached. The quantity column for any products listed on the left-hand side of the matrix indicates the number of units of the product that should be manufactured when the optimum solution is reached. 400 units of Y and 60 units of Z should therefore be produced, giving a total contribution of £6560. This agrees with the results we obtained using the graphical method. *When an equation appears for a slack variable, this indicates that unused resources exist.* The final matrix therefore indicates that the optimal plan will result in 800 unused machine hours (S_3) and an unused sales potential of 20 units for product Y (S_4). The fact that there is no equation for S_1 and S_2 means that these are the inputs that are fully utilized and that limit further increases in output and profit.

The S_1 column (materials) of the final matrix indicates that the materials are fully utilized. (*Whenever resources appear as column headings in the final matrix, this indicates that they are fully utilized.*) So, to obtain a unit of materials, the column for S_1 indicates that we must alter the optimum production programme by increasing production of product Z by $\frac{3}{20}$ of a unit and decreasing production of product Y by $\frac{1}{5}$ of a unit. The effect of removing one scarce unit of material from the production process is summarized in Exhibit 26.1.

EXHIBIT 26.1 The effect of removing one unit of material from the optimum production programme

	S_3	S_4	S_1	S_2	
	Machine capacity	Sales of Y	Materials	Labour	Contribution (£)
Increase product Z by $\frac{3}{20}$ of a unit	$-\frac{9}{10}(\frac{3}{20} \times 6)$	—	$-\frac{3}{5}(\frac{3}{20} \times 4)$	$-1\frac{1}{5}(\frac{3}{20} \times 8)$	$+2\frac{2}{5}(\frac{3}{20} \times 16)$
Decrease product Y by $\frac{1}{5}$ of a unit	$+\frac{4}{5}(\frac{1}{5} \times 4)$	$+\frac{1}{5}$	$+1\frac{3}{5}(\frac{1}{5} \times 8)$	$+1\frac{1}{5}(\frac{1}{5} \times 6)$	$-2\frac{4}{5}(\frac{1}{5} \times 14)$
Net effect	$-\frac{1}{10}$	$+\frac{1}{5}$	$+1$	Nil	$-\frac{2}{5}$

Look at the machine capacity column of Exhibit 26.1. If we increase production of product Z by $3/20$ of a unit then more machine hours will be required, leading to the available capacity being reduced by $9/10$ of an hour. Each unit of product Z requires six machine hours, so $3/20$ of a unit will require $9/10$ of an hour ($3/20 \times 6$). Decreasing production of product Y by $1/5$ unit will release $4/5$ of a machine hour, given that one unit of product Y requires four machine hours. The overall effect of this process is to reduce the available machine capacity by $1/10$ of a machine hour. Similar principles apply to the other calculations presented in Exhibit 26.1.

We shall now reconcile the information set out in Exhibit 26.1 with the materials column (S_1) of the final matrix. The S_1 column of the final matrix indicates that, to release one unit of materials from the optimum production programme, we should increase the output of product Z by $3/20$ and decrease product Y by $1/5$ of a unit. This substitution process will lead to the unused machine capacity being reduced by $1/10$ of a machine hour, an increase in the unfulfilled sales demand of product Y (S_4) by $1/5$ of a unit and a reduction in contribution of $£2/5$. All this information is obtained from column S_1 of the final matrix, and Exhibit 26.1 provides the proof. Note that Exhibit 26.1 also proves that the substitution process that is required to obtain an additional unit of materials releases exactly one unit. In addition, Exhibit 26.1 indicates that the substitution process for labour gives a net effect of zero, and so no entries appear in the S_1 column of the final matrix in respect of the labour row (i.e. S_2).

The contribution row of the final matrix contains some vital information for the accountant. The figures in this row represent opportunity costs (also known as shadow prices) for the scarce factors of materials and labour. For example, the reduction in contribution from the loss of one unit of materials is $£2/5$ (£0.40) and from the loss of one labour hour is $£1 4/5$ (£1.80). Our earlier studies have indicated that this information is vital for decision-making and we shall use this information again shortly to establish the relevant costs of the resources.

The proof of the opportunity costs can be found in Exhibit 26.1. From the contribution column we can see that the loss of one unit of materials leads to a loss of contribution of £0.40.

Substitution process when additional resources are obtained

Management may be able to act to remove a constraint that is imposed by the shortage of a scarce resource. For example, the company might obtain substitute materials or it may purchase the materials from an overseas supplier. A situation may therefore occur where resources additional to those included in the model used to derive the optimum solution are available. In such circumstances, the marginal rates of substitution specified in the final matrix can indicate the optimum use of the additional resources. However, when additional resources are available it is necessary to *reverse* the signs in the final matrix. The reason is that the removal of one unit of materials from the optimum production programme requires that product Z be increased by $3/20$ of a unit and product Y decreased by $1/5$ of a unit.

If we then decide to return released materials to the optimum production programme, we must reverse this process – that is, increase product Y by $1/5$ of a unit and reduce product Z by $3/20$ of a unit. The important point to remember is that *when considering the response to obtaining additional resources over and above those specified in the initial model, the signs of all the items in the final matrix must be reversed.*

We can now establish how we should best use an additional unit of scarce materials. Inspection of the final matrix indicates that product Y should be increased by $1/5$ of a unit and product Z reduced by $3/20$, giving an additional contribution of £0.40. Note that this is identical with the solution we obtained using the graphical method.

Note that this process will lead to an increase in machine hours of $1/10$ hour (S_3) and a decrease in potential sales of product Y by $1/5$ (S_4). Similarly, if we were to obtain an additional labour hour, we should increase production of Z by $1/5$ of a unit and decrease production of product Y by $1/10$ of a unit, which would yield an additional contribution of £1.80. These are the most efficient uses that can be obtained from additional labour and material resources. From a practical point of view, decisions will not involve the use of fractions; for example, the LP company considered here might be able to obtain 200 additional labour hours; the final matrix indicates that optimal production plan should be altered by increasing production of product Z by 40 units (200 × ⅕ of a unit) and decreasing production of product Y by 20 units. This process will lead to machine capacity being reduced by 160 hours and potential sales of product Y being increased by 20 units.

It is possible that examination questions may present the final matrix in a different format to the approach illustrated in this chapter. You should refer to the Key examination points section at the end of the chapter for an explanation of how you can reconcile the alternative approaches.

USES OF LINEAR PROGRAMMING

Calculation of relevant costs

The calculation of relevant costs is essential for decision-making. When a resource is scarce, alternative uses exist that provide a contribution. An opportunity cost is therefore incurred whenever the resource is used. The relevant cost for a scarce resource is calculated as:

$$\text{acquisition cost of resource} + \text{opportunity cost}$$

When more than one scarce resource exists, the opportunity cost should be established using linear programming techniques. Note that the opportunity costs of materials and labour are derived from the

---

REAL WORLD VIEWS 26.1

Uses of linear programming – linear programming in the supply chain

SAP, the global leader in enterprise resource planning (ERP) systems, offers several tools to help a business find an optimal solution to scheduling and planning problems. The advanced planner and optimizer (APO) offers solutions to help firms find the best and most cost-effective solution in areas like demand planning, production planning, transportation planning and supply network planning. The later module, supply network planning (SNP) allows planners to determine optimal production plans, distribution plans and purchasing plans. According to SAP's documentation, the SNP module offer an optimizer that will obtain the most cost-effective solution based on the following criteria:

- production, procurement, storage and transportation costs;
- costs for increasing the production capacity, storage capacity, transportation capacity and handling capacity;
- costs for violating (falling below) the safety stock level;

- costs for late delivery;
- stock-out costs.

The optimizer uses linear programming method to take account of all planning factors simultaneously. According to SAP's documentation, as more constraints are activated, the optimization problem becomes more complex and takes more time to complete. The SNP module offers several variants on linear programming to allow maximum applicability to varying problem scenarios.

Questions

1 Can you think of factors that might affect production, procurement, storage or transportation costs as referred to above?

2 Given the apparently large number of factors taken into account by the optimizer in SNP, do you think the business and/or the system can run the optimizer programme frequently?

Reference

help.sap.com/saphelp_scm41/helpdata/en/09/707b37 db6bcd66e10000009b38f889/content.htm

final row (monetary figures expressed in fractions) of the third and final matrix. Let us now calculate the relevant costs for the resources used by the LP company. The costs are as follows:

materials = £4.40 (£4 acquisition cost plus £0.40 opportunity cost)
labour = £11.80 (£10 acquisition cost plus £1.80 opportunity cost)
variable overheads = £1.00 (£1 acquisition cost plus zero opportunity cost)
fixed overheads = nil

Because variable overheads are assumed to vary in proportion to machine hours, and because machine hours are not scarce, no opportunity costs arise for variable overheads. Fixed overheads have not been included in the model, since they do not vary in the short term with changes in activity. The relevant cost for fixed overheads is therefore zero.

Selling different products

We shall now assume that the company is contemplating selling a modified version of product Y (called product L) in a new market. The market price is £160 and the product requires ten units input of each resource. Should this product L be manufactured? Conventional accounting information does not provide us with the information necessary to make this decision. Product L can be made only by restricting output of Y and Z, because of the input constraints, and we need to know the opportunity costs of releasing the scarce resources to this new product. Opportunity costs were incorporated in our calculation of the relevant costs for each of the resources, and so the relevant information for the decision is as follows:

	(£)	(£)
Selling price of product L		160
Less relevant costs:		
Materials (10 × 4.40)	44	
Labour (10 × 11.80)	118	
Variable overhead (10 × 1.00)	10	
Contribution		172
		(−12)

Total planned contribution will be reduced by £12 for each unit produced of product L.

Maximum payment for additional scarce resources

Opportunity costs provide important information in situations where a company can obtain additional scarce resources, but only at a premium. How much should the company be prepared to pay? For example, the company may be able to remove the labour constraint by paying overtime. The final matrix indicates that the company can pay up to an additional £1.80 over and above the standard wage rate for each hour worked in excess of 2880 hours and still obtain a contribution from the use of this labour hour. The total contribution will therefore be improved by any additional payment below £1.80 per hour. Similarly, LP will improve the total contribution by paying up to £0.40 in excess of the standard material cost for units obtained in excess of 3440 units. Hence the company will increase short-term profits by paying up to £11.80 for each additional labour hour in excess of 2880 hours and up to £4.40 for units of material that are acquired in excess of 3440 units.

Control

Opportunity costs are also important for cost control. For example, material wastage is reflected in an adverse material usage variance. The responsibility centre should therefore be identified not only with the acquisition cost of £4 per unit but also with the opportunity cost of £0.40 from the loss of one scarce unit of materials. This process highlights the true cost of the inefficient usage of scarce resources and encourages responsibility heads to pay special attention to the control of scarce factors of production. This approach is particularly appropriate where a firm has adopted an optimized production technology (OPT) strategy (see Chapter 9) because variance arising from bottleneck operations will be reported in terms of opportunity cost rather than acquisition cost.

Managing constraints

When scarce resources are fully utilized they are referred to as bottleneck operations/resources. It is important that managers seek to increase the efficiency and capacity of bottleneck operations. Capacity can be increased by working overtime on the bottleneck, subcontracting some of the work that is undertaken by bottleneck operations, investing in additional capacity at the bottleneck and implementing business process improvements such as business process engineering and total quality management processes described in Chapter 22.

Capital budgeting

Linear programming can be used to determine the optimal investment programme when capital rationing exists. This topic tends not to form part of the management accounting curriculum for most courses. You should refer to Learning Note 26.2 (see the digital resources) if you wish to study how linear programming can be used in capital investment appraisal.

Sensitivity analysis

Opportunity costs are of vital importance in making management decisions, but production constraints do not exist permanently, and therefore opportunity costs cannot be regarded as permanent. There is a need to ascertain the range over which the opportunity cost applies for each input. This information can be obtained from the final matrix. For materials, we merely examine the negative items for column S_1 in the final matrix and divide each item into the quantity column as follows:

$$Y = 400/(-\tfrac{1}{5}) = -2000$$
$$S_3 = 800/(-\tfrac{1}{10}) = -8000$$

The number closest to zero in this calculation (namely -2000) indicates by how much the availability of materials used in the model can be reduced. Given that the model was established using 3440 units of materials, the lower limit of the range is 1440 units (3440 − 2000). The upper limit is determined in a similar way. We divide the positive items in column S_4 into the quantity column as follows:

$$Z = 60/\tfrac{3}{20} = 400$$
$$S_4 = 20/\tfrac{1}{5} = 100$$

The lower number in the calculation (namely 100) indicates by how much the materials can be increased. Adding this to the 3440 units of materials indicates that the upper limit of the range is 3540 units. The opportunity cost and marginal rates of substitution for materials therefore apply over the range of 1440 to 3540 units.

We shall now consider the logic on which these calculations are based. The lower limit is determined by removing materials from the optimum production programme. We have previously established from the final matrix and Exhibit 26.1 that removing one unit of material from the optimum production programme means that product Y will be reduced by $\tfrac{1}{5}$ and machine capacity will be reduced by $\tfrac{1}{10}$ of an hour. Since the final matrix indicates an output of 400 units of product Y, this reduction can only be carried out 2000 times (400/$\frac{1}{5}$) before the process must stop. Similarly, 800 hours of machine capacity are still unused, and the reduction process can only be carried out 8000 times (800/$\frac{1}{10}$) before the process must stop. Given the two constraints on reducing materials, the first constraint that is reached is the reduction of product Y. The planned usage of materials can therefore be reduced by 2000 units before the substitution process must stop. The same reasoning applies (with the signs reversed) in understanding the principles for establishing the upper limit of the range.

Similar reasoning can be applied to establish that the opportunity cost and marginal rates of substitution apply for labour hours over a range of 2680 to 3880 hours. For any decisions based on scarce inputs outside the ranges specified a revised model must be formulated and a revised final matrix produced. From this matrix, revised opportunity costs and marginal rates of substitution can be established.

SUMMARY

The following items relate to the learning objectives listed at the beginning of the chapter.

● **Describe the situations when it may be appropriate to use linear programming.**

Conventional limiting factor analysis (see Chapter 9) should be used when there is only one scarce factor. Linear programming can be used to determine the production programme that maximizes total contribution when there is more than one scarce input factor.

● **Explain the circumstances when the graphical method can be used.**

The graphical method can be used with two products. Where more than two products are involved, the simplex method should be used.

● **Use graphical linear programming to find the optimum output levels.**

Production/sales quantities for one of the two products are labelled on the horizontal axis and the vertical axis is used for the other product. Combinations of the maximum output (based on the two products) from fully utilizing each resource, and any sales volume limitations, are plotted on the graph. A series of contribution lines are plotted based on the potential output levels for each product that will achieve a selected total contribution. The optimum output levels are derived at the point where the feasible production region touches the highest contribution line. The process is illustrated in Figure 26.5 using the data presented in Example 26.1.

● **Formulate the initial linear programming model using the simplex method.**

Assuming that the objective function is to maximize total contribution, the objective function should initially be specified expressed in terms of the contributions per unit for each product. Next, the constraints should be listed in equation form with slack variables introduced to ensure that model is specified in terms of equalities rather than inequalities. The initial matrix is prepared by converting the linear programming model into a matrix format. The process is illustrated using Example 26.1.

● **Explain the meaning of the term shadow prices.**

The simplex method of linear programming generates shadow prices (also known as opportunity costs) for each of those scarce resources that are fully utilized in the optimum production programme. The shadow prices represent the reduction in total contribution that will occur from the loss of one unit of a scarce resource. Conversely, they represent the increase in total contribution that will occur if an additional unit of the scarce resource can be obtained.

KEY TERMS AND CONCEPTS

Bottleneck activities Activities or operations where constraints apply arising from demand exceeding available capacity.

Bottleneck operations/resources Scarce resources that are fully utilized and therefore can present limiting factors.

Linear programming A mathematical technique used to determine how to employ limited resources to achieve optimum benefits.

Marginal rate of substitution The optimal response from an independent marginal increase in a resource.

Objective function In linear programming, the objective to be minimized or maximized.

Opportunity cost The value of an independent marginal increase of a scarce resource, also known as the shadow price.

Shadow price The value of an independent marginal increase of a scarce resource, also known as the opportunity cost.

Simplex method A mathematical technique used in linear programming to solve optimization problems.

Slack variable A variable that is added to a linear programming problem to account for any constraint that is unused at the point of optimality and so turn an inequality into an equality.

KEY EXAMINATION POINTS

A common error is to state the objective function in terms of profit per unit. This is incorrect, because the fixed cost per unit is not constant. The objective function should be expressed in terms of contribution per unit. You should note that there are several ways of formulating the matrices for a linear programming model. The approach adopted in this chapter was to formulate the first matrix with positive contribution signs and negative signs for the slack variable equations. The optimal solution occurs when the signs in the contribution row are all negative. Sometimes examination questions are set that adopt the opposite procedure. That is, the signs are the reverse of the approach presented in this chapter.

For an illustration of this approach, see review problem IM 26.7. A more recent approach is to present the output from the model as a computer printout. You should refer to the solution to review problem 26.15 to make sure you understand this approach.

Most examination questions include the final matrix and require you to interpret the figures. You may also be required to formulate the initial model. It is most unlikely that you will be required to complete the calculations and prepare the final matrix. However, you may be asked to construct a graph and calculate the marginal rates of substitution and opportunity costs.

ASSESSMENT MATERIAL

The review questions are short questions that enable you to assess your understanding of the main topics included in the chapter. The numbers in parentheses provide you with the page numbers to refer to if you cannot answer a specific question.

The review problems are more complex and require you to relate and apply the content to various business problems. The problems are graded by their level of difficulty. Solutions to review problems that are not preceded by the term 'IM' are provided in a separate section at the end of the book. Solutions to problems preceded by the term 'IM' are provided in the Instructor's Manual accompanying this book that can be downloaded from the lecturer's digital support resources. Additional review problems with fully worked solutions are provided in the *Student Manual* that accompanies this book.

REVIEW QUESTIONS

26.1 Describe the situations when it may be appropriate to use linear programming. (pp. 694–695)

26.2 Explain what is meant by the term 'objective function'. (p. 695)

26.3 What is the feasible production area? (p. 698)

26.4 What is the marginal rate of substitution? (p. 700)

26.5 Explain what is meant by the term 'shadow price'. (p. 700)

26.6 Explain the circumstances when it is appropriate to use the simplex method. (p. 701)

26.7 What are slack variables? (p. 701)

26.8 Provide illustrations of how the information derived from linear programming can be applied to a variety of management accounting problems. (pp. 704–706)

26.9 Explain how sensitivity analysis can be applied to the output of a linear programming model. (p. 706)

REVIEW PROBLEMS

26.10 Intermediate. Taree Limited uses linear programming to establish the optimal production plan for the production of its two products, A and U, given that it has the objective of minimizing costs. The following graph has been established bearing in mind the various constraints of the business. The clear area indicates the feasible region.

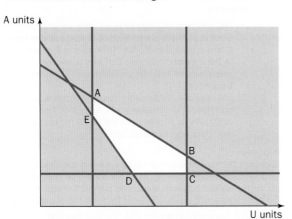

Which points are most likely to give the optimal solution?

(a) A and B only
(b) A, B and C only
(c) D and E only
(d) B, D and E only.   (2 marks)

ACCA – Financial Information for Management

26.11 Advanced: Optimal output and calculation of maximum amount to pay for a scarce resource using the graphical approach. THS produces two products from different combinations of the same resource. Details of the products are shown below:

	E per unit	R per unit
Selling price	$99	$159
Material A ($2 per kg)	3kgs	2kgs
Material B ($6 per kg)	4kgs	3kgs
Machining ($7 per hour)	2 hours	3 hours
Skilled labour ($10 per hour)	2 hours	5 hours
Maximum monthly demand (units)	unlimited	1500

THS is preparing the production plan for next month. The maximum resource availability for the month is:

Material A	5000kgs
Material B	5400kgs
Machining	3000 hours
Skilled labour	4500 hours

Required:

(a) *Identify*, using graphical linear programming, the optimal production plan for products E and R to maximize THS's profit in the month.   (13 marks)

The production manager has now been able to source extra resources:

- An employment agency would supply skilled labour for a monthly fee of $1000 and $14 per hour worked;
- A machine that has the same variable running costs per hour as the current machinery can be leased. The leased machine would be able to run for 2000 hours per month.

Required:

(b) *Calculate* the maximum amount that should be paid next month to lease the machine. (Note: you should assume that a contract has already been signed with the employment agency.)   (8 marks)

(c) *Explain* TWO major factors that should be considered before deciding to lease the machine. (Note: you should assume that the data supplied are totally accurate.)
                                                       (4 marks)

CIMA P2 Performance Management

26.12 Advanced: Optimal output and calculation of shadow prices using the graphical approach. The Cosmetic Co. is a company producing a variety of cosmetic creams and lotions. The creams and lotions are sold to a variety of retailers at a price of $23.20 for each jar of face cream and $16.80 for each bottle of body lotion. Each of the products has a variety of ingredients, with the key ones being silk powder, silk amino acids and aloe vera. Six months ago, silk worms were attacked by disease causing a huge reduction in the availability of silk powder and silk amino acids. The Cosmetic Co. had to dramatically reduce production and make part of its workforce, which it had trained over a number of years, redundant.

The company now wants to increase production again by ensuring that it uses the limited ingredients available to maximize profits by selling the optimum mix of creams and lotions. Due to the redundancies made earlier in the year, supply of skilled labour is now limited in the short term to 160 hours (9600 minutes) per week, although unskilled labour is unlimited. The purchasing manager is confident that they can obtain 5000 grams of silk powder and 1600 grams of silk amino acids per week. All other ingredients are unlimited. The following information is available for the two products:

	Cream	Lotion
Materials required: silk powder (at $2.20 per gram)	3 grams	2 grams
– silk amino acids (at $0.80 per gram)	1 gram	0.5 grams
– aloe vera (at $1.40 per gram)	4 grams	2 grams
Labour required: skilled ($12 per hour)	4 minutes	5 minutes
– unskilled (at $8 per hour)	3 minutes	1.5 minutes

Each jar of cream sold generates a contribution of $9 per unit, whilst each bottle of lotion generates a contribution of $8 per unit. The maximum demand for lotions is 2000 bottles per week, although demand for creams is unlimited. Fixed costs total $1800 per week. The company does not keep inventory although if a product is partially complete at the end of one week, its production will be completed in the following week.

Required:

(a) On the graph paper provided, use linear programming to calculate the optimum number of each product that the Cosmetic Co. should make per week, assuming that it wishes to maximize contribution. Calculate the total contribution per week for the new production plan. All workings MUST be rounded to two decimal places.
                                                       (14 marks)

(b) Calculate the shadow price for silk powder and the slack for silk amino acids. All workings MUST be rounded to two decimal places.   (6 marks)

ACCA F5 Performance Management

26.13 Advanced: Determination of optimum production plan using simultaneous equations (not using a graphical approach). PTP produces two products from different combinations of the same resources. Details of the selling price and costs per unit for each product are shown below:

	Product E	Product M
	$	$
Selling price	175	125
Material A ($12 per kg)	60	24
Material B ($5 per kg)	10	15
Labour ($20 per hour)	40	20
Variable overhead	14	28
($7 per machine hour)		

The fixed costs of the company are $50000 per month.

PTP aims to maximize profits from production and sales. The production plan for June is currently under consideration.

The following resources are available in June:

Material A	4800kg
Material B	3900kg
Labour	2500 hours
Machine hours	5000 hours

Required:

(a) (i) Identify the objective function and the constraints to be used in a linear programming model to determine the optimum production plan for June. *(3 marks)*
The solution to the linear programming model shows that the only binding constraints in June are those for Material A and Material B.

(ii) Produce, using simultaneous equations, the optimum production plan and resulting profit for June. (You are NOT required to draw or sketch a graph.) *(5 marks)*
Based on the optimal production plan for June, the management accountant at PTP has determined that the shadow price for Material A is $7 per kg.

(b) Explain the meaning of the shadow price for Material A.
(2 marks)

26.14 Advanced: Optimum production programme and interpretation of the solution of a linear programming model.
LM produces two products from different quantities of the same resources using a just-in-time (JIT) production system. The selling price and resource requirements of each of these two products are as follows:

Product	L	M
Unit selling price ($)	70	90
Variable costs per unit:		
Direct labour ($7 per hour)	28	14
Direct material ($5 per kg)	10	45
Machine hours ($10 per hour)	10	20
Fixed overheads absorbed	12	6
Profit per unit	10	5

Fixed overheads are absorbed at the rate of $3 per direct labour hour.

Market research shows that the maximum demand for products L and M during December will be 400 units and 700 units respectively.

At a recent meeting of the purchasing and production managers to discuss the company's production plans for December, the following resource availability for December was identified:

Direct labour	3500 hours
Direct material	6000kg
Machine hours	2000 hours

Required:

(a) Prepare calculations to show, from a financial perspective, the optimum production plan for December and the contribution that would result from adopting your plan. *(6 marks)*

(b) You have now presented your optimum plan to the purchasing and production managers of LM. During the presentation, the following additional information became available:

(i) The company has agreed to an order for 250 units of product M For a selling price of $90 per unit from a new overseas customer. This order is in addition to the maximum demand that was previously predicted and must be produced and delivered in December;

(ii) The originally predicted resource restrictions were optimistic. The managers now agree that the availability of all resources will be 20 per cent lower than their original predictions.

Required:
Construct the revised resource constraints and the objective function to be used to identify, given the additional information above, the revised optimum production plan for December.
(6 marks)

(c) The resource constraints and objective function requested in part *(b)* above have now been processed in a simplex linear programming model and the following solution has been printed:

Product L	400	Product L other value	0
Product M	194	Product M other value	506
Direct labour	312		
Direct material ($)	1.22		
Machine hours	312		
Contribution ($)	10934.00		

Required:
Analyse the meaning of each of the above eight values in the solution to the problem. Your answer should include a proof of the last five of the individual values listed. *(13 marks)*

CIMA P5 Performance Management

26.15 Advanced: Interpretation of the linear programming solution. Woodalt plc has two automated machine groups X and Y, through which timber is passed in order to produce two models of an item of sports equipment. The models are called 'Traditional' and 'Hightech'.

The following forecast information is available for the year to 31 December:

	'Traditional'	'Hightech'
(i) Maximum sales potential (units)	6000	10000
(ii) Equipment unit data:		
Selling price	£100	£90
Machine time: group X (hours)	0.5	0.3
group Y (hours)	0.4	0.45

(iii) Machine groups X and Y have maximum operating hours of 3400 and 3840, respectively. The sports equipment production is the sole use available for the production capacity.

(iv) The maximum quantity of timber available is 34000 metres. Each product unit requires four metres of timber. Timber may be purchased in lengths as required at £5 per metre.

(v) Variable machine overhead cost for machine groups X and Y is estimated at £25 and £30 per machine hour, respectively.

(vi) All units are sold in the year in which they are produced.

A linear programme of the situation has been prepared in order to determine the strategy which will maximize the contribution for the year to 31 December and to provide additional decision-making information. Appendix 3.1 below shows a print-out of the solution to the LP model.

Required:

(a) Formulate the mathematical model from which the input to the LP programme would be obtained. *(4 marks)*

(b) Using the linear programme solution in Appendix 3.1 where appropriate, answer the following in respect of the year to 31 December:

(i) State the maximum contribution and its distribution between the two models. *(3 marks)*

(ii) Explain the effect on contribution of the limits placed on the availability of timber and machine time. *(3 marks)*

(iii) In addition to the sports equipment models, Woodalt plc has identified additional products that could earn contribution at the rate of £20 and £30 per machine hour for machine groups X and Y, respectively. Such additional products would be taken up only to utilize any surplus hours not required for the sports equipment production.

Prepare figures that show the additional contribution which could be obtained in the year to 31 December from the additional sales outlets for each of machine groups X and Y. *(4 marks)*

(iv) Explain the sensitivity of the plan to changes in contribution per unit for each sports equipment product type. *(2 marks)*

(v) Woodalt plc expects to be able to overcome the timber availability constraint. All other parameters in the model remain unchanged. (*The additional products suggested in (iii) above do not apply.*)

Calculate the increase in contribution which this would provide. *(2 marks)*

(vi) You are told that the amended contribution maximizing solution arising from (v) will result in the production and sale of the 'Traditional' product being 3600 units.

Determine how many units of the 'Hightech' product will be produced and sold. *(2 marks)*

(c) Suggest ways in that Woodalt plc may overcome the capacity constraints that limit the opportunities available to it in the year to 31 December. Indicate the types of cost that may be incurred in overcoming each constraint. *(6 marks)*

(d) Explain why Woodalt plc should consider each of the following items before implementing the profit maximizing strategy indicated in Appendix 3.1:

(i) product specific costs;
(ii) customer specific costs;
(iii) life cycle costs.

Your answer should include relevant examples for each of (i) to (iii). *(9 marks)*

Appendix 3.1
Forecast strategy evaluation for the year to 31 December

Target cell (max) (£)

Cell	Name	Final value
C2	Contribution	444 125

Adjustable cells (units)

Cell	Name	Final value
A1	Traditional	4250
B1	Hightech	4250

Adjustable cells (units and £)

Cell	Name	Final value	Reduced cost	Objective coefficient	Allowable increase	Allowable decrease
A1	Traditional	4250	0	55.50	26.17	6.50
B1	Hightech	4250	0	49.00	6.50	15.70

Constraints (quantities and £)

Cell	Name	Final value	Shadow price	Constraint R.H. side	Allowable increase	Allowable decrease
C3	Timber	34 000	9.8125	34 000	1733.33	6800
C4	Machines X	3 400	32.5	3400	850	850
C5	Machines Y	3 612.5	0	3840	IE+30	227.5

ACCA Information for Control and Decision Making

IM26.1 Intermediate: Optimal output using the graphical approach. G Limited, manufacturers of superior garden ornaments, is preparing its production budget for the coming period. The company makes four types of ornament, the data for which are as follows:

Product	Pixie (£ per unit)	Elf (£ per unit)	Queen (£ per unit)	King (£ per unit)
Direct materials	25	35	22	25
Variable overhead	17	18	15	16
Selling price	111	98	122	326

Direct labour hours:	Hours per unit	Hours per unit	Hours per unit	Hours per unit
Type 1	8	6	—	—
Type 2	—	—	10	10
Type 3	—	—	5	25

Fixed overhead amounts to £15 000 per period.

Each type of labour is paid £5 per hour but because of the skills involved, an employee of one type cannot be used for work normally done by another type.

The maximum hours available in each type are:

Type 1	8 000 hours
Type 2	20 000 hours
Type 3	25 000 hours

The marketing department judges that, at the present selling prices, the demand for the products is likely to be:

Pixie	Unlimited demand
Elf	Unlimited demand
Queen	1500 units
King	1000 units

You are required:

(a) to calculate the product mix that will maximize profit, and the amount of the profit; *(14 marks)*

(b) to determine whether it would be worthwhile paying Type 1 Labour for overtime working at time and a half and, if so, to calculate the extra profit for each 1000 hours of overtime; *(2 marks)*

(c) to comment on the principles used to find the optimum product mix in part (a), pointing out any possible limitations; *(3 marks)*

(d) to explain how a computer could assist in providing a solution for the data shown above. *(3 marks)*

CIMA Stage 3 Management Accounting Techniques

IM26.2 Advanced: Optimal output using the graphical approach and the impact of an increase in capacity. A company makes two products, X and Y. Product X has a contribution of £124 per unit and product Y £80 per unit. Both products pass through two departments for processing and the times in minutes per unit are:

	Product X	Product Y
Department 1	150	90
Department 2	100	120

Currently there is a maximum of 225 hours per week available in department 1 and 200 hours in department 2. The company can sell all it can produce of X but EU quotas restrict the sale of Y to a maximum of 75 units per week.

The company, which wishes to maximize contribution, currently makes and sells 30 units of X and 75 units of Y per week.

The company is considering several possibilities including:

(i)   altering the production plan if it could be proved that there is a better plan than the current one;

(ii) increasing the availability of either department 1 or department 2 hours. The extra costs involved in increasing capacity are £0.5 per hour for each department;

(iii) transferring some of its allowed sales quota for Product Y to another company. Because of commitments, the company would always retain a minimum sales level of 30 units.

You are required to:

(a) calculate the optimum production plan using the existing capacities and state the extra contribution that would be achieved compared with the existing plan;   *(8 marks)*

(b) advise management whether it should increase the capacity of either department 1 or department 2 and, if so, by how many hours and what the resulting increase in contribution would be over that calculated in the improved production plan;   *(7 marks)*

(c) calculate the minimum price per unit for which it could sell the rights to its quota, down to the minimum level, given the plan in (a) as a starting point.   *(5 marks)*

CIMA Stage 3 Management Accounting Techniques

IM26.3 Advanced: Maximizing profit and sales revenue using the graphical approach. Goode, Billings and Prosper plc manufactures two products, Razzle and Dazzle. Unit selling prices and variable costs, and daily fixed costs are:

	Razzle (£)	Dazzle (£)
Selling price per unit	20	30
Variable costs per unit	8	20
Contribution margin per unit	12	10
Joint fixed costs per day	£60	

Production of the two products is restricted by limited supplies of three essential inputs: Raz, Ma and Taz. All other inputs are available at prevailing prices without any restriction. The quantities of Raz, Ma and Taz necessary to produce single units of Razzle and Dazzle, together with the total supplies available each day, are:

	kg per unit required		Total available
	Razzle	Dazzle	(kg per day)
Raz	5	12.5	75
Ma	8	10	80
Taz	2	0	15

William Billings, the sales director, advises that any combination of Razzle and/or Dazzle can be sold without affecting their market prices. He also argues very strongly that the company should seek to maximize its sales revenues subject to a minimum acceptable profit of £44 per day in total from these two products.

In contrast, the financial director, Silas Prosper, has told the managing director, Henry Goode, that he believes in a policy of profit maximization at all times.

You are required to:

(a) calculate:

(i)   the profit and total sales revenue per day, assuming a policy of profit maximization;   *(10 marks)*

(ii) the total sales revenue per day, assuming a policy of sales revenue maximization subject to a minimum acceptable profit of £44 per day;   *(10 marks)*

(b) suggest why businessmen might choose to follow an objective of maximizing sales revenue subject to a minimum profit constraint;   *(5 marks)*

ICAEW Management Accounting

IM26.4 Advanced: Optimal output and shadow prices using the graphical approach. Usine Ltd is a company whose objective is to maximize profits. It manufactures two speciality chemical powders, gamma and delta, using three processes: heating, refining and blending. The powders can be produced and sold in infinitely divisible quantities.

The following are the estimated production hours for each process per kilo of output for each of the two chemical powders during the period 1 June to 31 August:

	Gamma (hours)	Delta (hours)
Heating	400	120
Refining	100	90
Blending	100	250

During the same period, revenues and costs per kilo of output are budgeted as:

	Gamma (£ per kilo)	Delta (£ per kilo)
Selling price	16 000	25 000
Variable costs	12 000	17 000
Contribution	4 000	8 000

It is anticipated that the company will be able to sell all it can produce at the above prices and that at any level of output fixed costs for the three month period will total £36 000.

The company's management accountant is under the impression that there will only be one scarce factor during the budget period, namely blending hours, which cannot exceed a total of 1050 hours during the period 1 June to 31 August. He therefore correctly draws up an optimum production plan on this basis.

However, when the factory manager sees the figures he points out that over the three-month period there will not only be a restriction on blending hours, but in addition the heating and refining hours cannot exceed 1200 and 450 respectively during the three month period.

Requirements:

(a) Calculate the initial production plan for the period 1 June to 31 August as prepared by the management accountant, assuming blending hours are the only scarce factor. Indicate the budgeted profit or loss and explain why the solution is the optimum.   *(4 marks)*

(b) Calculate the optimum production plan for the period 1 June to 31 August, allowing for both the constraint on blending hours and the additional restrictions identified by the factory manager and indicate the budgeted profit or loss. *(8 marks)*

(c) State the implications of your answer in (b) in terms of the decisions that will have to be made by Usine Ltd with respect to production during the period 1 June to 31 August after taking into account all relevant costs. *(2 marks)*

(d) Under the restrictions identified by the management accountant and the factory manager, the shadow (or dual) price of one extra hour of blending time on the optimum production plan is £27.50. Calculate the shadow (or dual) price of one extra hour of refining time. Explain how such information might be used by management and, in so doing, indicate the limitations inherent in the figures. *(6 marks)*

Note: Ignore taxation.
Show all calculations clearly.

ICAEW Management Accounting and Financial Management I
Part Two

IM26.5 Advanced: Formulation of initial tableau and interpretation of final tableau. The Alphab Group has five divisions A, B, C, D and E. Group management wishes to increase overall group production capacity per year by up to 30 000 hours. Part of the strategy will be to require that the minimum increase at any one division must be equal to 5 per cent of its current capacity. The maximum funds available for the expansion programme are £3 000 000.

Additional information relating to each division is as follows:

Division	Existing capacity (hours)	Investment cost per hour (£)	Average contribution per hour (£)
A	20 000	90	12.50
B	40 000	75	9.50
C	24 000	100	11
D	50 000	120	8
E	12 000	200	14

A linear programme of the plan has been prepared in order to determine the strategy that will maximize additional contribution per annum and to provide additional decision-making information. The Appendix to this question shows a print-out of the LP model of the situation.

Required:

(a) Formulate the mathematical model from which the input to the LP programme would be obtained. *(6 marks)*

(b) Use the linear programme solution in the Appendix in order to answer the following:

 (i) State the maximum additional contribution from the expansion strategy and the distribution of the extra capacity between the divisions. *(3 marks)*

 (ii) Explain the cost to the company of providing the minimum 5 per cent increase in capacity at each division. *(3 marks)*

 (iii) Explain the effect on contribution of the limits placed on capacity and investment. *(2 marks)*

 (iv) Explain the sensitivity of the plan to changes in contribution per hour. *(4 marks)*

 (v) Group management decides to relax the 30 000 hours capacity constraint. All other parameters of the model remain unchanged. Determine the change in strategy that will then maximize the increase in group contribution. You should calculate the increase in contribution that this change in strategy will provide. *(6 marks)*

(vi) Group management wishes to decrease the level of investment while leaving all other parameters of the model (as per the Appendix) unchanged.

 Determine and quantify the change in strategy that is required indicating the fall in contribution that will occur. *(6 marks)*

(c) Explain the limitations of the use of linear programming for planning purposes. *(5 marks)*

Appendix
Divisional investment evaluation
Optimal solution – detailed report

Variable	Value
1 DIV A	22 090.91
2 DIV B	2 000.00
3 DIV C	1 200.00
4 DIV D	2 500.00
5 DIV E	2 209.09

	Constraint	Type	RHS	Slack	Shadow price
1	Max. hours	<=	30 000.00	0.00	11.2727
2	DIV A	>=	1 000.00	21 090.91	0.0000
3	DIV B	>=	2 000.00	0.00	−2.7955
4	DIV C	>=	1 200.00	0.00	−1.6364
5	DIV D	>=	2 500.00	0.00	−4.9091
6	DIV E	>=	600.00	1 609.09	0.0000
7	Max. funds	<=	3 000 000.00	0.00	0.0136

Objective function value = 359 263.6

Sensitivity analysis of objective function coefficients

Variable	Current coefficient	Allowable minimum	Allowable maximum
1 DIV A	12.50	10.7000	14.0000
2 DIV B	9.50	−Infinity	12.2955
3 DIV C	11.00	−Infinity	12.6364
4 DIV D	8.00	−Infinity	12.9091
5 DIV E	14.00	12.5000	27.7778

Sensitivity analysis of right-hand side values

	Constraint	Type	Current value	Allowable minimum	Allowable maximum
1	Max. hours	<=	30 000.00	18 400.00	31 966.67
2	DIV A	>=	1 000.00	−Infinity	22 090.91
3	DIV B	>=	2 000.00	0.00	20 560.00
4	DIV C	>=	1 200.00	0.00	18 900.00
5	DIV D	>=	2 500.00	0.00	8 400.00
6	DIV E	>=	600.00	−Infinity	2 209.09
7	Max. funds	<=	3 000 000.00	2 823 000.00	5 320 000.00

Note: RHS = Right-hand side

ACCA Paper 9 Information for Control and Decision Making

IM26.6 Formulation of initial tableau and interpretation of final tableau using the simplex method.

(a) The Argonaut Company makes three products, Xylos, Yo-yos and Zicons. These are assembled from two components, Agrons and Bovons, which can be produced internally at a variable cost of £5 and £8 each respectively. A limited quantity of each of these components may be available for purchase from an external supplier at a quoted price which varies from week to week.

The production of Agrons and Bovons is subject to several limitations. Both components require the same three production processes (L, M and N), the first two of which have limited availabilities of 9600 minutes per week and 7000 minutes per week respectively. The final process (N) has effectively unlimited availability but for technical reasons must produce at least one Agron for each Bovon produced. The processing times are as follows:

Process	L	M	N
Time (mins) required to produce			
1 Agron	6	5	7
1 Bovon	8	5	9

The component requirements of each of the three final products are:

Product	Xylo	Yo-yo	Zicon
Number of components required			
Agrons	1	1	3
Bovons	2	1	2

The ex-factory selling prices of the final products are given below, together with the standard direct labour hours involved in their assembly and details of other assembly costs incurred:

Product	Xylo	Yo-yo	Zicon
Selling price	£70	£60	£150
Direct labour hours used	3	3.5	8
Other assembly costs	£4	£5	£15

The standard direct labour rate is £10 per hour. Factory overhead costs amount to £4350 per week and are absorbed to products on the basis of the direct labour costs incurred in their assembly. The current production plan is to produce 100 units of each of the three products each week.

Requirements:

(i) Present a budgeted weekly profit and loss account, by product, for the factory.   (4 marks)
(ii) Formulate the production problem facing the factory manager as a linear program:

   1 assuming there is no external availability of Agrons and Bovons;   (5 marks)
   2 assuming that 200 Agrons and 300 Bovons are available at prices of £10 and £12 each, respectively.   (4 marks)

(b) In a week when no external availability of Agrons and Bovons was expected, the optimal solution to the linear program and the shadow prices associated with each constraint were as follows:

Production of Xylos	50 units
Production of Yo-yos	0 units; shadow price £2.75
Production of Zicons	250 units

Shadow price associated with:

Process L	£0.375 per minute
Process M	£0.450 per minute
Process N	£0.000 per minute
Agron availability	£9.50 each
Bovon availability	£13.25 each

If sufficient Bovons were to become available on the external market at a price of £12 each, a revised linear programming solution indicated that only Xylos should be made.

Requirement:

Interpret this output from the linear program in a report to the factory manager. Include calculations of revised shadow prices in your report and indicate the actions the manager should take and the benefits that would accrue if the various constraints could be overcome.   (12 marks)

ICAEW P2 Management Accounting

IM26.7 Advanced: Formulation of an initial tableau and interpretation of a final tableau using the simplex method.

Hint: Reverse the signs and ignore entries of 0 and 1.

The Kaolene Co. Ltd has six different products all made from fabricated steel. Each product passes through a combination of five production operations: cutting, forming, drilling, welding and coating.

Steel is cut to the length required, formed into the appropriate shapes, drilled if necessary, welded together if the product is made up of more than one part and then passed through the coating machine. Each operation is separate and independent, except for the cutting and forming operations, when, if needed, forming follows continuously after cutting. Some products do not require every production operation.

The output rates from each production operations, based on a standard measure for each product, are set out in the tableau below, along with the total hours of work available for each operation. The contribution per unit of each product is also given. It is estimated that three of the products have sales ceilings and these are also given below:

Products	X_1	X_2	X_3	X_4	X_5	X_6
Contribution per						
unit (£)	5.7	10.1	12.3	9.8	17.2	14.0
Output rate per hour:						
Cutting	650	700	370	450	300	420
Forming	450	450	—	520	180	380
Drilling	—	200	380	—	300	—
Welding	—	—	380	670	400	720
Coating	500	—	540	480	600	450
Maximum sales						
units (000)	—	—	150	—	20	70
	Cutting	Forming	Drilling	Welding	Coating	
Production hours						
available	12000	16000	4000	4000	16000	

The production and sales for the year were found using a linear programming algorithm. The final tableau is given below.

Variables X_7 to X_{11} are the slack variables relating to the production constraints, expressed in the order of production. Variables X_{12} to X_{14} are the slack variables relating to the sales ceilings of X_3, X_5 and X_6 respectively.

After analysis of the above results, the production manager believes that further mechanical work on the cutting and forming machines costing £200 can improve their hourly output rates as follows:

Products	X_1	X_2	X_3	X_4	X_5	X_6
Cutting	700	770	410	500	330	470
Forming	540	540	—	620	220	460

The optimal solution to the new situation indicates the shadow prices of the cutting, drilling and welding sections to be £59.3, £14.2 and £71.5 per hour respectively.

X_1	X_2	X_3	X_4	X_5	X_6	X_7	X_8	X_9	X_{10}	X_{11}	X_{12}	X_{13}	X_{14}	Variable in basic solution	Value of variable in basic solution
1	0	−1.6	−0.22	−0.99	0	10.8	0	−3.0	−18.5	0	0	0	0	X_1	43287.0 units
0	0	−0.15	−0.02	0.12	0	−1.4	1	−0.3	0.58	0	0	0	0	X_8	15747.81 hours
0	1	0.53	0	0.67	0	0	0	3.33	0	0	0	0	0	X_2	13333.3 units
0	0	1.9	1.08	1.64	1	0	0	0	12	0	0	0	0	X_6	48019.2 units
0	0	0.06	0.01	0	0	−1.3	0	0.37	0.63	1	0	0	0	X_{11}	150806.72 hours
0	0	1	0	0	0	0	0	0	0	0	1	0	0	X_{12}	150000.0 units
0	0	0	0	1	0	0	0	0	0	0	0	1	0	X_{13}	20000.0 units
0	0	−1.9	−1.0	−1.6	0	0	0	0	−12	0	0	0	1	X_{14}	21980.8 units
0	0	10.0	4	6.83	0	61.7	0	16.0	62.1	0	0	0	0	$(Z_j - C_j)$	£1053617.4

Requirements:

(a) Explain the meaning of the seven items ringed in the final tableau. *(9 marks)*

(b) Show the range of values within which the following variables or resources can change without changing the optimal mix indicated in the final tableau:

  (i) c_4: contribution of X4
  (ii) b_5: available coating time. *(4 marks)*

(c) Formulate the revised linear programming problem taking note of the revised output rates for cutting and forming. *(5 marks)*

(d) Determine whether the changes in the cutting and forming rates will increase profitability. *(3 marks)*

(e) Using the above information discuss the usefulness of linear programming to managers in solving this type of problem. *(4 marks)*

ICAEW P2 Management Accounting

BIBLIOGRAPHY

Abernethy, M.A., Lillis, A.M., Brownell, P. and Carter, P. (2001) Product diversity and costing system design: field study evidence, *Management Accounting Research*, 12(3), 261–80.

Abu-Serdaneh, J. (2004) Transfer pricing in UK manufacturing companies, PhD dissertation, University of Huddersfield.

Accenture and the Chartered Institute of Management Accountants (2011) *Sustainability performance management: How CFO'S can unlock value*, Chartered Institute of Management Accountants.

Accounting Standards Committee (1988) Accounting for Stocks and Work in Progress (SSAP 9).

Adams, C.A., Potter, B., Singh, P.A. and York, J. (2016) Exploring the implications of integrated reporting for social investment (disclosures), *British Accounting Review*, 48(3), 283–96.

Ahmed, M.N. and Scapens, R.W. (2000) Cost allocation in Britain: towards an institutional analysis, *European Accounting Review*, 9(2), 159–204.

Al-Omiri, M. and Drury, C. (2007) A survey of the factors influencing the choice of product costing systems in UK organizations, *Management Accounting Research*, 18(4), 399–424.

Al-Sayed, M. and Dugdale, D. (2016) Activity-based innovations in the UK manufacturing sector: Extent, adoption process patterns and contingency factors, *British Accounting Review*, 48, 38–58.

American Accounting Association (1957) *Accounting and Reporting Standards for Corporate Financial Statements and Preceding Statements and Supplements*, 4.

American Accounting Association (1966) *A Statement of Basic Accounting Theory*, American Accounting Association.

Amey, L.R. (1975) Tomkins on residual income, *Journal of Business Finance and Accounting*, 2(1), Spring, 55–68.

Ansari, S. (1979) Towards an open system approach to budgeting, *Accounting, Organisations and Society*, 4(3), 149–61.

Ansari, S.L., Bell, J.F. and Okano, H. (2008) A review of literature of target costing and cost management, in Chapman, C.S., Hopwood, A.G. and Shields, M.D. (eds) *Handbook of Management Accounting Research*, Vol. 2, Elsevier, pp. 507–30.

Armitage, H.M. and Nicholson, R. (1993) Activity based costing: a survey of Canadian practice, Issue Paper No. 3, Society of Management Accountants of Canada.

Arnold, G.C. and Hatzopoulos, P.D. (2000) The theory–practice gap in capital budgeting: evidence from the United Kingdom, *Journal of Business Finance and Accounting*, 27(5) and (6), June/July, 603–26.

Ask, U., Ax, C. and Jonsson, S. (1996) Cost management in Sweden: from modern to post-modern, in Bhimani, A. (ed.) *Management Accounting: European Perspectives*, Oxford University Press, pp. 199–217.

Atkinson, H. (2006) Strategy implementation: a role for the balanced scorecard? *Management Decision*, 44(10), 1441–60.

Atkinson, M. and Tyrrall, D. (1997) International transfer pricing: the taxman cometh, *Management Accounting (UK)*, December, 32–4.

Ax, C., Greve, J. and Nilsson, U. (2008) The impact of competition and uncertainty on the adoption of target costing, *International Journal of Production Economics*, 115(1), 92–103.

Ballas, A. and Venieris, G. (1996) A survey of management accounting practices in Greek firms, in Bhimani, A. (ed.) *Management Accounting: European Perspectives*, Oxford University Press, 123–39.

Barbato, M.B., Collini, P. and Quagli, C. (1996) Management accounting in Italy, in Bhimani, A. (ed.) *Management Accounting: European Perspectives*, Oxford University Press, 140–63.

Barrett, M.E. and Fraser, L.B. (1977) Conflicting roles in budget operations, *Harvard Business Review*, July–August, 137–46.

Bartelsman, E.J. and Beetsma, R.M. (2003) Why pay more? Corporate tax avoidance through transfer pricing in OECD countries, *Journal of Public Economics*, 87, 2225–52.

Bartolomeo, M., Bennett, M., Bouma, J., Heydkamp, P., James, P. and Wolters, T. (2000) Environmental management accounting in Europe: current practice and future potential, *European Accounting Review*, 9(1), 31–52.

Baxter, W.T. and Oxenfeldt, A.R. (1961) Costing and pricing: the cost accountant versus the economist, *Business Horizons*, Winter, 77–90; also in *Studies in Cost Analysis*, 2nd edn (ed. D. Solomons) Sweet and Maxwell (1968) pp. 293–312.

Bebbington, J. and Thomson, I. (2013) Sustainable development, management and accounting: Boundary crossing, *Management Accounting Research*, 24(4), 277–83.

Bhimani, A., Horngren, C.T., Datar, S.M. and Foster, G. (2008) *Management and Cost Accounting*, FT Prentice-Hall.

Bjornenak, T. (1997a) Diffusion and accounting: the case of ABC in Norway, *Management Accounting Research*, 8(1), 3–17.

Bjornenak, T. (1997b) Conventional wisdom and accounting practices, *Management Accounting Research*, 8(4), 367–82.

Boer, G. (1990) Contribution margin analysis: no longer relevant/strategic cost management: the new paradigm, *Journal of Management Accounting Research (USA)*, Fall, 24–7.

Borkowski, S.C. (1990) Environmental and organizational factors affecting transfer pricing: a survey, *Journal of Management Accounting Research*, 2, 78–99.

Bourmistrova, A. and Kaarbøeb, K. (2013) From comfort to stretch zones: A field study of two multinational companies applying beyond budgeting, *Management Accounting Research* 24(3), 196–211.

Boyns, T., Edwards, J.R. and Emmanuel, C. (1999) A longitudinal study of the determinants of transfer pricing change, *Management Accounting Research*, 10(2), 85–108.

Brealey, R.A., Myers, S.C. and Allen, F. (2016) *Principles of Corporate Finance*, McGraw-Hill.

Brierley, J.A., Cowton, C.J. and Drury, C. (2001) Research into product costing practice: a European perspective, *European Accounting Review*, 10(2), 215–56.

Bromwich, M. (1990) The case for strategic management accounting: the role of accounting information for strategy in competitive markets, *Accounting, Organisations and Society*, 1, 27–46.

Bromwich, M. and Bhimani, A. (1989) *Management Accounting: Evolution not Revolution*, Chartered Institute of Management Accountants.

Bromwich, M. and Bhimani, A. (1994) *Management Accounting: Pathways to Progress*, Chartered Institute of Management Accountants.

Bromwich, M. and Walker, M. (1998) Residual income past and future, *Management Accounting Research*, 9(4), 392–419.

Brounen, D., de Jong, A. and Koedijk, K. (2004) Corporate finance in Europe: confronting theory with practice, *Financial Management*, 33(4), 71–101.

Bruggeman, W., Slagmulder, R. and Waeytens, D. (1996) Management accounting changes: the Belgian experience, in Bhimani, A. (ed.) *Management Accounting: European Perspectives*, Oxford University Press, pp. 1–30.

Bukh, P.N. and Malmi, T. (2005) Re-examing the cause-and-effect principle of the balanced scorecard, in Jönsson, S. and Mouritsen, J. (eds) *Accounting in Scandinavia – The Northern Lights*, Malmö, Liber, 87–113.

Burchell, S., Clubb, C., Hopwood, A.G., Hughes, J. and Jahapier, J. (1980) The roles of accounting in organizations and society, *Accounting, Organisations and Society*, 1, 5–27.

Burrows, G. and Chenhall, R.H. (2012) Target costing: first and second comings, *Accounting History Review*, 22(2), 127–142.

Burrows, G.H. (1994) Allocations and common costs in long-run investment and pricing decisions: an historical perspective, *Abacus*, 30(1), 50–64.

Cats-Baril, W.L. *et al.* (1986) Joint product costing, *Management Accounting (USA)*, September, 41–5.

Chan, C.W. (1998) Transfer pricing negotiation outcomes and the impact of negotiator mixed-motives and culture: empirical evidence from the US and Australia, *Management Accounting Research*, 9(2), 139–61.

Charles, I. (1985a) The economics approach to transfer price, *Accountancy*, June, 110–12.

Charles, I. (1985b) Transfer-price solution where market exists, *Accountancy*, July, 96.

Chartered Global Management Accountant (CGMA) (2012) *Sustainable Business: Shared Value in Practice*, Chartered Institute of Management Accountants.

Chartered Institute of Management Accountants, Management accounting tools for today and tomorrow, www.cimaglobal.com/ma

Chartered Institute of Management Accountants (2005) *Management Accounting: Official Terminology*, CIMA Publishing.

Chartered Institute of Management Accountants (2014) *Rethinking the Value Chain – The Extended Value Chain*, Chartered Institute of Management Accountants.

Cheatham, C.B. and Cheatham, L.R. (1996) Redesigning cost systems: is standard costing obsolete? *Accounting Horizons*, December, 23–31.

Chenhall, R.H. (2003) Management control system design within its organizational context: findings from contingency-based research and directions for the future, *Accounting, Organizations and Society*, 28, 127–68.

Chenhall, R.H. and Langfield-Smith, K. (1998a) Adoption and benefits of management accounting practices: an Australian perspective, *Management Accounting Research*, 9(1), 120.

Chenhall, R.H. and Langfield-Smith, K. (1998b) The relationship between strategic priorities, management techniques and management accounting: an empirical investigation using a systems approach, *Accounting, Organisations and Society*, 23(3), 243–64.

Chenhall, R.H. and Morris, D. (1985) The impact of structure, environment and interdependence on the perceived usefulness of management accounting systems, *Accounting Review*, 1, 16–35.

Chow, C., Haddad, K. and Williamson, J. (1997) Applying the balanced scorecard to small companies, *Management Accounting*, August, 21–7.

Clarke, P.J. (1992) Management Accounting Practices and Techniques in Irish Manufacturing Firms. 15th Annual Congress of the European Accounting Association, Madrid, Spain.

Coad, A. (1996) Smart work and hard work: explicating a learning orientation in strategic management accounting, *Management Accounting Research*, 7(4), 387–408.

Cohen, M.D., March, J.G. and Olsen, J.P. (1972) A garbage can model of organizational change, *Administrative Science Quarterly*, March, 1–25.

Cools, M. and Emmanuel, C. (2007) Transfer pricing, the implications of fiscal compliance, in Chapman, C.S., Hopwood, A.G. and Shields, M.D. (eds) *Handbook of Management Accounting Research*, Vol. 2, Elsevier, pp. 573–85.

Cooper, R. (1990a) Cost classifications in unit-based and activity- based manufacturing cost systems, *Journal of Cost Management*, Fall, 4–14.

Cooper, R. (1990b) Explicating the logic of ABC, *Management Accounting*, November, 58–60.

Cooper, R. (1996) Costing techniques to support corporate strategy: evidence from Japan, *Management Accounting Research*, 7, 219–46.

Cooper, R. and Kaplan, R.S. (1988) Measure costs right: make the right decisions, *Harvard Business Review*, September/October, 96–103.

Cooper, R. and Kaplan, R.S. (1991) *The Design of Cost Management Systems: Text, Cases and Readings*, Prentice-Hall.

Cooper, R. and Kaplan, R.S. (1992) Activity based systems: measuring the costs of resource usage, *Accounting Horizons*, September, 1–13.

Cornick, M., Cooper, W. and Wilson, S. (1988) How do companies analyse overhead? *Management Accounting*, June, 41–3.

Coughlan, P. and Darlington, J. (1993) As fast as the slowest operations: the theory of constraints, *Management Accounting (UK)*, June, 14–17.

Cress, W. and Pettijohn, J. (1985) A survey of budget-related planning and control policies and procedures, *Journal of Accounting Education*, 3, Fall, 61–78.

Currie, W. (1990) Strategic management of advanced manufacturing technology, *Management Accounting*, October, 50–2.

Currie, W. (1991a) Managing technology: a crisis in management accounting, *Management Accounting*, February, 24–7.

Currie, W. (1991b) Managing production technology in Japanese industry, *Management Accounting*, June, 28–9, July/August, 36–8.

Cyert, R.M. and March, J.G. (1969) *A Behavioural Theory of the Firm*, Prentice-Hall.

Darlington, J., Innes, J., Mitchell, F. and Woodward, J. (1992) Throughput accounting: the Garrett Automative experience, *Management Accounting (UK)*, April, 32–5, 38.

De Bono, J. (1997) Divisional cost of equity capital, *Management Accounting (UK)*, November, 40–1.

Dekker, H. and Smidt, P. (2003) A survey of the adoption and use of target costing in Dutch firms, *International Journal of Production Economics*, 84(3), 293–306.

Dekker, H.C. (2003) Value chain analysis in interfirm relationships: a field study, *Management Accounting Research*, 14(1), 1–23.

Dirsmith, M.W. and Jablonsky, S.F. (1979) MBO, political rationality and information inductance, *Accounting, Organisations and Society*, 1, 39–52.

Drucker, P.F. (1964) Controls, control and management, in Bonini, C.P., Jaedicke, R. and Wagner, H. (eds) *Management Controls: New Directions in Basic Research*, McGraw-Hill.

Drury, C. and El-Shishini, H. (2005) *Divisional Performance Measurement*, Chartered Institute of Management Accountants.

Drury, C. and Tayles, M. (1994) Product costing in UK manufacturing organisations, *The European Accounting Review*, 3(3), 443–69.

Drury, C. and Tayles, M. (2000) *Cost System Design and Profitability Analysis in UK Companies*, Chartered Institute of Management Accountants.

Drury, C. and Tayles, M. (2005) Explicating the design of overhead absorption procedures in UK organizations, *British Accounting Review*, 37(1), 47–84.

Drury, C. and Tayles, M. (2006) Profitability analysis in UK organizations: an exploratory study, *British Accounting Review*, 38(4), 405–25.

Drury, C., Braund, S., Osborne, P. and Tayles, M. (1993) A survey of management accounting practices in UK manufacturing companies, ACCA Research Paper, Chartered Association of Certified Accountants.

Dugdale, D. (1989) Contract accounting and the SSAP, *Management Accounting*, June, 624.

Dugdale, D. and Jones, T.C. (1998) Throughput accounting: transformation practices? *British Accounting Review*, 30(3), 203–20.

Dugdale, D. and Lyne, S. (2006), Are budgets still needed? *Financial Management*, November, 32–5.

Dugdale, D., Jones, T.C. and Green, S. (2006) *Contemporary Management Accounting Practices in UK Manufacturing Companies*, Chartered Institute of Management Accountants.

Ekholm, B.-G. and Wallin, J. (2000) Is the annual budget really dead? *European Accounting Review*, 9(4), 519–39.

Elliott, J. (1998a) International transfer pricing: the consultative document, *Management Accounting (UK)*, March, 34–5.

Elliott, J. (1998b) International transfer pricing: a survey of UK and non-UK groups, *Management Accounting (UK)*, November, 48–50.

Emmanuel, C. and Mehafdi, M. (1994) *Transfer Pricing*, Academic Press.

Emmanuel, C., Otley, D. and Merchant, K. (1990) *Accounting for Management Control*, International Thomson Business Press.

Emmanuel, C.R. and Otley, D. (1976) The usefulness of residual income, *Journal of Business Finance and Accounting*, 13(4), Winter, 43–52.

Emsley, D. (2000) Variance analysis and performance: two empirical studies, *Accounting, Organisations and Society*, 25, 1–12.

Emsley, D. (2001) Redesigning variance analysis for problem solving, *Management Accounting Research*, 12(1), 21–40.

Epstein, M. and Manzoni, J.F. (1998) Implementing corporate strategy: from tableaux de bord to balanced scorecards, *European Management Journal*, 16(2), 190–203.

Epstein, M. and Roy, M.J. (1997) Environmental management to improve corporate profitability, *Journal of Cost Management*, Nov–Dec, 26–34.

Ernst & Young and The Institute of Management Accountants (2003) *The Ernst & Young and IMA Survey of Management Accounting*, Ernst & Young LLP, New York.

Ezzamel, M., Willmott, H. and Worthington, F. (2008) Manufacturing shareholder value: the role of accounting in organizational transformation, *Accounting, Organization and Society* 33, 107–40.

Fisher, I. (1930) *The Theory of Interest*, Macmillan.

Fisher, J. (1995) Contingency-based research on management control systems: categorization by level of complexity, *Journal of Accounting Literature*, 14, 24–53.

Fitzgerald, L. and Moon, P. (1996) *Performance Management in Service Industries*, Chartered Institute of Management Accountants.

Fitzgerald, L., Johnston, R., Brignall, T.J., Silvestro, R. and Voss, C. (1991) *Performance Measurement in Service Businesses*, Chartered Institute of Management Accountants.

Fitzgerald, L., Johnston, R., Silvestro, R. and Steele, A. (1989) Management control in service industries, *Management Accounting*, April, 44–6.

Flower, J. (1973) *Computer Models for Accountants*, Haymarket, Chs 4, 5.

Foster, G. and Horngren, C.T. (1988) Cost accounting and cost management in a JIT environment, *Journal of Cost Management for the Manufacturing Industry*, Winter, 4–14.

Franco-Santos, M. and Bourne, M. (2005) An examination of the literature relating to issues affecting how companies manage through measures, *Production Planning and Control*, 16(2), pp. 114–124.

Franklin, L. (1998) Taxation and the capital expenditure decision, *Management Accounting (UK)*, November, 44–6.

Fremgen, J.M. and Liao, S.S. (1981) *The Allocation of Corporate Indirect Costs*, National Association of Accountants, New York.

Friedman, A.L. and Lynne, S.R. (1995) *Activity-based Techniques: The Real Life Consequences*, Chartered Institute of Management Accountants.

Friedman, A.L. and Lynne, S.R. (1997) Activity-based techniques and the death of the beancounter, *European Accounting Review*, 6(1), 19–44.

Friedman, A.L. and Lynne, S.R. (1999) *Success and Failure of Activity-based Techniques: A Long-term Perspective*, Chartered Institute of Management Accountants.

Galloway, D. and Waldron, D. (1988) Throughput accounting – 1: the need for a new language for manufacturing, *Management Accounting*, November, 34–5.

Gardiner, S.C. (1993) Measures of product attractiveness and the theory of constraints, *International Journal of Retail and Distribution*, 21(7), 37–40.

Goldratt, E.M. and Cox, J. (1984) *The Goal*, London, Gower.

Goldratt, E.M. and Cox, J. (1992) *The Goal* (2nd edn), London, Gower.

Gordon, L.A. and Narayanan, V.K. (1984) Management accounting systems, perceived environmental uncertainty and organizational structure: an empirical investigation, *Accounting, Organizations and Society*, 9(1), 33–47.

Gould, J.R. (1964) Internal pricing on firms when there are costs of using an outside market, *Journal of Business*, 37(1), January, 61–7.

Govindarajan, V. (1984) Appropriateness of accounting data in performance evaluation: an empirical evaluation of environmental uncertainty as an intervening variable, *Accounting, Organisations and Society*, 9(2), 125–36.

Govindarajan, V. (1988) A contingency approach to strategy implementation at the business unit level: integrating administrative mechanisms with strategy, *Academy of Management Journal*, 33, 828–53.

Govindarajan, V. and Gupta, A.K. (1985) Linking control systems to business unit strategy: impact on performance, *Accounting, Organisations and Society*, 10(1), 51–66.

Gowthorpe, C. (2009) Wider still and wider? A critical discussion of intellectual capital recognition, measurement and control in a boundary theoretical context, *Critical Perspective on Accounting*, 20, 823–34.

Granlund, M. and Lukka, K. (1998) It's a small world of management accounting practices, *Journal of Management Accounting Research*, 10, 151–79.

Granlund, M. and Malmi, T. (2002) Moderate impact of ERPS on management accounting: a lag or permanent outcome? *Management Accounting Research*, 13(3), 299–321.

Green, F.B. and Amenkhienan, F.E. (1992) Accounting innovations: a cross sectional survey of manufacturing firms, *Journal of Cost Management for the Manufacturing Industry*, Spring, 58–64.

Groot, T. and Selto, F. (2013) *Advanced Management Accounting*, Pearson Education, Harlow.

Guilding, C., Craven, K.S. and Tayles, M. (2000) An international comparison of strategic management accounting practices, *Management Accounting Research*, 11(1), 113–35.

Guilding, C., Drury, C. and Tayles, M. (2005) An empirical investigation of the importance of cost-plus pricing, *Managerial Auditing Journal*, 20(2), 125–37.

Guilding, C., Lamminmaki, D. and Drury, C. (1998) Budgeting and standard costing practices in New Zealand and the United Kingdom, *International Journal of Accounting*, 33(5), 41–60.

Hansen, D.R. and Mendoza, R. (1999) Costos de impacto ambiental: su medicion, asignacion, y control, *INCAE Revista*, X(2), 1999.

Harris, D.G. (1993) The impact of US tax law revision on multinational corporations' capital location and income shifting decisions, *Journal of Accounting Research*, 31(Supplement), 111–39.

Hassan, Y. and Davood, D. (2012) A comparative study of the adoption and implementation of target costing in the UK, Australia and New Zealand, *International Journal of Production Economics*, 135(1), 382–92.

Henri, J.F., Boiral, O. and Roy, M.-J. (2014) The tracking of environmental costs: motivations and impacts, *European Accounting Review*, 23(4), 647–61.

Henri, J.F., Boiral, O. and Roy, M.-J. (2016) Strategic cost management and performance: The case of environmental costs, *British Accounting Review*, 48, 269–82.

Hergert, M. and Morris, D. (1989) Accounting data for value chain analysis, *Strategic Management Journal*, 10, 175–88.

Hiromoto, T. (1991) Restoring the relevance of management accounting, *Journal of Management Accounting Research*, 3, 1–15.

Hirshleifer, J. (1956) On the economies of transfer pricing, *Journal of Business*, July, 172–84.

Holzer, H.P. and Norreklit, H. (1991) Some thoughts on the cost accounting developments in the United States, *Management Accounting Research*, March, 3–13.

Hope, J. and Fraser, R. (1999a) Beyond budgeting: building a new management model for the information age, *Management Accounting*, January, 16–21.

Hope, J. and Fraser, R. (1999b) Take it away, *Accountancy*, May, 66–7.

Hope, J. and Fraser, R. (2001) Figures of hate, *Financial Management*, February, 22–5.

Hope, J. and Fraser, R. (2003b) New ways of setting rewards: the beyond budgeting model, *Californian Management Review*, 45(2), Winter, 104–119.

Hopper, T. and Bui, B. (2016) Has Management Accounting Research been critical? *Management Accounting Research*, 31(1), 10–30.

Hopper, T., Kirkham, L., Scapens, R.W. and Turley, S. (1992) Does financial accounting dominate management accounting – a research note, *Management Accounting Research*, 3(4), 307–11.

Hopwood, A.G. (1976) *Accountancy and Human Behaviour*, Prentice-Hall.

Hopwood, A.G. (1978) Towards an organisational perspective for the study of accounting and information systems, *Accounting, Organisations and Society*, 3(1), 3–14.

Imoisili, O.A. (1989) The role of budget data in the evaluation of managerial performance, *Accounting, Organizations and Society*, 14(4), 325–35.

Innes, J. (1998) Strategic management accounting, in Innes, J. (ed.) *Handbook of Management Accounting*, Gee, Ch. 2.

Innes, J. and Mitchell, F. (1995a) A survey of activity-based costing in the UK's largest companies, *Management Accounting Research*, June, 137–54.

Innes, J. and Mitchell, F. (1995b) Activity-based costing, in Ashton, D., Hopper, T. and Scapens, R.W. (eds) *Issues in Management Accounting*, Prentice-Hall, pp. 115–36.

Innes, J., Mitchell, F. and Sinclear, D. (2000) Activity-based costing in the UK's largest companies: a comparison of 1994 and 1999 survey results, *Management Accounting Research*, 11(3), 349–62.

Integrated Reporting Committee (IRC) of South Africa (2011) *Framework for Integrated Reporting and the Integrated Report*, SAICA.

ISO Survey (2014) International Accreditation Forum www .iaf.nu/articles/ISO_Survey_2014/449

Israelsen, P., Anderson, M., Rohde, C. and Sorensen, P.E. (1996) Management accounting in Denmark: theory and practice, in Bhimani, A. (ed.) *Management Accounting: European Perspectives*, Oxford University Press, 31–53.

Ittner, C.D., Larcker, D.F. and Rajan, M.V. (1997) The choice of performance measures in annual bonus contracts, *Accounting Review*, 72(2), 231–55.

Ittner, D and Larcker, D. (2003) Coming up short on non-financial performance measurement, *Harvard Business Review*, 70 (January–February), 71–9.

Jacob, J. (1996) Taxes and transfer pricing: income shifting and the volume of intrafirm transfers, *Journal of Accounting Research*, 34(2), 301–15.

Johnson, G., Scholes, K. and Whittington, R. (2017) *Exploring Strategy*, Pearson Education.

Johnson, H.T. and Kaplan, R.S. (1987) *Relevance Lost: The Rise and Fall of Management Accounting*, Harvard Business School Press.

Jones, M. and Pendlebury, M. (2010) *Public Sector Accounting*, FT Prentice-Hall.

Jones, T.C. and Dugdale, D. (1998) Theory of constraints: transforming ideas? *British Accounting Review*, 30(1), 73–92.

Jones, T.C. and Dugdale, D. (2002) The ABC bandwagon and the juggernaut of modernity, *Accounting, Organizations and Society*, 27, 121–63.

Joseph, N., Turley, S., Burns, J., Lewis, L., Scapens, R.W. and Southworth, A. (1996) External financial reporting and management information: a survey of UK management accountants, *Management Accounting Research*, 7(1), 73–94.

Joye, M.P. and Blayney, P.J. (1990) Cost and management accounting practice in Australian manufacturing companies: survey results, Monograph No. 7, University of Sydney.

Joye, M.P. and Blayney, P.J. (1991) Strategic management accounting survey, Monograph No. 8, University of Sydney.

Kald, M. and Nilsson, F. (2000) Performance measurement at Nordic companies, *European Management Journal*, 1, 113–27.

Kaplan, R. (2009) Conceptual foundations of the balanced scorecard, in Chapman, C., Hopwood, A. and Shields, M. (eds) *Handbook of Management Accounting Research*, Vol. 3, Elsevier, 1253–69.

Kaplan, R. and Anderson, S. (2004) Time-driven activity-based costing, *Harvard Business Review*, 82(11), 131–8.

Kaplan, R. and Anderson, S. (2007) The innovation of time-driven activity-based costing, *Journal of Cost Management*, 21(2), 5–15.

Kaplan, R.S. (1990) Contribution margin analysis: no longer relevant/strategic cost management: the new paradigm, *Journal of Management Accounting Research (USA)*, Fall, 2–15.

Kaplan, R.S. (1994a) Management accounting (1984–1994): development of new practice and theory, *Management Accounting Research*, September and December, 247–60.

Kaplan, R.S. (1994b) Flexible budgeting in an activity-based costing framework, *Accounting Horizons*, June, 104–109.

Kaplan, R.S. and Atkinson, A.A. (2013) *Advanced Management Accounting*, Pearson Education, Ch. 3.

Kaplan, R.S. and Cooper, R. (1998) *Cost and Effect: Using Integrated Systems to Drive Profitability and Performance*, Harvard Business School Press.

Kaplan, R.S. and Norton, D.P. (1992) The balanced scorecard: measures that drive performance, *Harvard Business Review*, Jan–Feb, 71–9.

Kaplan, R.S. and Norton, D.P. (1993) Putting the balanced scorecard to work, *Harvard Business Review*, Sep–Oct, 134–47.

Kaplan, R.S. and Norton, D.P. (1996a) Using the balanced scorecard as a strategic management system, *Harvard Business Review*, Jan–Feb, 75–85.

Kaplan, R.S. and Norton, D.P. (1996b) *Translating Strategy into Action: The Balanced Scorecard*, Harvard Business School Press.

Kaplan, R.S. and Norton, D.P. (2001a) *The Strategy-focused Organization*, Harvard Business School Press.

Kaplan, R.S. and Norton, D.P. (2001b) Balance without profit, *Financial Management*, January, 23–6.

Kaplan, R.S. and Norton, D.P. (2001c) Transforming the balanced scorecard from performance measurement to strategic management: Part 1, *Accounting Horizons*, March, 87–104.

Kaplan, R.S. and Norton, D.P. (2001d) Transforming the balanced scorecard from performance measurement to strategic management: Part 2, *Accounting Horizons*, June, 147–60.

Kaplan, R.S. and Norton, D.P. (2005) The office of strategy management, *Harvard Business Review* (February), 72–80.

Kaplan, R.S. and Norton, D.P. (2006a) *Alignment: Using the Balanced Scorecard to Create Corporate Synergies*, Harvard Business School Press.

Kaplan, R.S. and Norton, D.P. (2006b) How to implement a new strategy without disrupting your organization, *Harvard Business Review* (March), 100–109.

Kaplan, R.S., Weiss, D. and Deseh, E. (1997) Transfer pricing with ABC, *Management Accounting (USA)*, 20–8.

Kato, Y. (1993) Target costing support systems: lessons from leading Japanese companies, *Management Accounting Research*, March, 33–48.

Keef, S. and Roush, M. (2002) Does MVA measure up? *Financial Management*, January, 20–1.

Kennedy, A. and Dugdale, D. (1999) Getting the most from budgeting, *Management Accounting (UK)*, February, 22–4.

Klassan, K., Lang, M. and Wolfson, M. (1993) Geographic income shifting by multinational corporations in response to tax rate changes, *Journal of Accounting Research*, 31(Supplement), 141–73.

Kohli, C. and Suri, R. (2011) The price is right? Guidelines for pricing to enhance profitability, *Business Horizons*, 54(6), 563.

KPMG (2011) Transfer pricing issues and solutions for digital media, www.kpmg.com/global/en/issues and insights/articlespublications/pages/transfer-pricing-digital-media-2011.

Kraus, K. and Lind, J. (2010) The impact of the corporate balanced scorecard on corporate control – A research note, *Management Accounting Research*, 21(4), 265–77.

Langfield-Smith, K. (1997) Management control systems and strategy: a critical review, *Accounting, Organizations and Society*, 22, 207–32.

Langfield-Smith, K. (2008) Strategic management accounting; how far have we come in 25 years? *Accounting, Auditing and Accountability Journal*, 21, 204–28.

Lauderman, M. and Schaeberle, F.W. (1983) The cost accounting practices of firms using standard costs, *Cost and Management (Canada)*, July/August, 21–5.

Lee, T.A. (1996) *Income and Value Measurement*, Thomson Business Press.

Libby, T. and Lindsay, R.M. (2010) Beyond budgeting or budgeting reconsidered? A survey of North American budgeting practice, *Management Accounting Research*, 21(1), 56–75.

Lindblom, C.E. (1959) The science of 'Muddling Through', *Public Administration Review*, Summer, 79–88.

Lord, B.R. (1996) Strategic management accounting: the emperor's new clothes? *Management Accounting Research*, 7(3), 347–66.

Lovata, L.M. and Costigan, M.L. (2002) Empirical analysis of adopters of economic value added, *Management Accounting Research*, 13(2), 251–72.

Lucas, M.R. (2003) Pricing decisions and the neoclassical theory of the firm, *Management Accounting Research*, 14(3), 201–18.

Lukka, K. and Granlund, M. (1996) Cost accounting in Finland: Current practice and trends of development, *European Accounting Review*, 5(1), 1–28.

Lukka, K. and Granlund, M. (2002) The fragmented communication structure within the accounting academia: the case of activity-based costing genres, *Accounting, Organizations and Society*, 27, 165–90.

Lynch, R.L. and Cross, K.F. (1991a) *Measure Up! How to Measure Corporate Performance*, Blackwell.

Lynch, R.L. and Cross, K.F. (1991b) *Measure Up – The Essential Guide to Measuring Business Performance*, Mandarin, London.

Macintosh, N.B. (1985) *The Social Software of Accounting and Information Systems*, Wiley.

Macintosh, N.B. (1994) *Management Accounting and Control Systems: An Organisational and Behavioural Approach*, Wiley.

Mak, Y.T. and Roush, M.L. (1994) Flexible budgeting and variance analysis in an activity-based costing environment, *Accounting Horizons*, June, 93–104.

Mak, Y.T. and Roush, M.L. (1996) Managing activity costs with flexible budgets and variance analysis, *Accounting Horizons*, September, 141–6.

Malmi, T. (2001) Balanced scorecards in Finnish companies: a research note, *Management Accounting Research*, 12(2), 207–20.

Malmi, T. and Brown, D.A. (2008) Management control systems as a package – opportunities, challenges and research directions, *Management Accounting Research*, 19(4), 287–300.

Melnyk, S.A., Bititci, U., Platts, K, Tobias, J. and Andersene, B. (2014) Is performance measurement and management fit for the future? *Management Accounting Research*, 25(2), 173–86.

Merchant, K.A. and Shields, M.D. (1993) When and why to measure costs less accurately to improve decision making, *Accounting Horizons*, June, 76–81.

Merchant, K.A. and Van der Stede, W. (2017) *Modern Management Control Systems: Text and Cases*, Pearson Education.

Milani, K. (1975) The relationship of participation in budget setting to industrial supervisor performance and attitudes: a field study, *The Accounting Review*, April, 274–84.

Miles, R.E. and Snow, C.C. (1978) *Organizational Strategies, Structure and Process*, McGraw-Hill.

Mills, R.W. (1988) Pricing decisions in UK manufacturing and service companies, *Management Accounting*, November, 38–9.

Monden, Y. and Hamada, K. (1991) Target costing and Kaizen costing in Japanese automobile companies, *Journal of Management Accounting Research*, Autumn, 16–34.

Moon, P. and Fitzgerald, L. (1996) *Performance Measurement in Service Industries: Making it Work*, Chartered Institute of Management Accountants.

Moore, P.G. and Thomas, H. (1991) *The Anatomy of Decisions*, Penguin.

Narayanan, V.G. and Sarkar, R.G. (2002) The impact of activity-based costing on managerial decisions at Insteel industries: a field study, *Journal of Economics and Management Strategy*, 11(2), 257–88.

Neely, A., Adams, C. and Crowe, P. (2001) The performance prism in practice, *Measuring Business Excellence*, 5(2), 6–12.

Neely, A.D., Adams, C. and Kennerley, M. (2002) *The Performance Prism: The Scorecard for Measuring and Managing Business Success*, Pearson Education, London, UK.

Neely, A.D., Gregory, M.J. and Platts, K.W. (1995) Performance measurement system design – a literature review and research agenda, *International Journal of Operations & Production Management*, 15(4), 80–116.

Nicholls, B. (1992) ABC in the UK – a status report, *Management Accounting*, May, 22–3.

Norreklit, H. (2000) The balance on the balanced scorecard – a critical analysis of some of its assumptions, *Management Accounting Research*, 11(1), 65–88.

Norreklit, H. (2003) The balanced scorecard: what is the score? A rhetorical analysis of the balanced scorecard, *Accounting, Organizations and Society*, 28, 591–619.

O'Hanlon, J.O. and Peasnell, K. (1998) Wall's Street's contribution to management accounting: the Stern Stewart EVA® financial management system, *Management Accounting Research*, 9(4), 421–44.

Oliveras, E. and Amat, O. (2002) The balanced scorecard assumptions and the drivers of business growth. Paper presented at the 25th Annual Congress of the European Accounting Association, Copenhagan, Denmark.

Olve, N., Roy, J. and Wetter, M. (2000) *Performance Drivers: A Practical Guide to Using the Balanced Scorecard*, Wiley.

Osni, M. (1973) Factor analysis of behavioural variables affecting budgetary stock, *Accounting Review*, 535–48.

Ostergren, K. and Sensaker, I. (2011) Management control without budgets: A field study of 'beyond budgeting' in practice, *European Accounting Review*, 20(1), 149–81.

Ostrenga, M.R. (1991) Return on investment through costs of quality, *Journal of Cost Management*, Summer, 37–44.

Otley, D. (1999) Performance management: a framework for management control systems research, *Management Accounting Research*, 10(4), 363–82.

Otley, D.T. (1978) Budget use and managerial performance, *Journal of Accounting Research*, 16(1), Spring, 122–49.

Otley, D.T. (1980) The contingency theory of management accounting: achievement and prognosis, *Accounting, Organizations and Society*, 5(4), 413–28.

Otley, D.T. (1987) *Accounting Control and Organizational Behaviour*, Heinemann.

Ouchi, W.G. (1979) A conceptual framework for the design of organizational control mechanisms, *Management Science*, 833–48.

Oyelere, P.B. and Emmanuel, C.R. (1998) International transfer pricing and income shifting: evidence from the UK, *European Accounting Review*, 7(4), 623–35.

Pendlebury, M.E. (1994) Management accounting in local government, *Financial Accountability and Management*, May, 117–29.

Pere, T. (1999) How the execution of strategy is followed in large organisations located in Finland. Masters Thesis, Helsinki School of Economics and Business Administration.

Perera, S., McKinnon, J.L. and Harrison, G.L. (2003) Diffusion of transfer pricing innovation in the context of commercialization – a longitudinal study of government trading enterprises, *Management Accounting Research*, 14(2),140–64.

Perrin, J. (1987) The costs and joint products of English teaching hospitals, *Financial Accountability and Management*, 3(2), 209–30.

Pfeffer, J. and Salancik, G.R. (1974) Organisational decision making as a political process: the case of a university budget, *Administrative Science Quarterly*, June, 135–50.

Phyrr, P.A. (1976) Zero-based budgeting – where to use it and how to begin, *S.A.M. Advanced Management Journal*, Summer, 5.

Pike, R., Neale, B. and Linsley, P. (2015) *Corporate Finance and Investment*, Prentice-Hall Europe.

Pike, R.H. (1996) A longitudinal study of capital budgeting practices, *Journal of Business Finance and Accounting*, 23(1), 79–92.

Plunkett, J.J., Dale, B.G. and Tyrrell, R.W. (1985) *Quality Costs*, London, Department of Trade and Industry.

Pogue, M. (2009) The risks of uncertainty, *Student Accountant*, Association of Chartered Certified Accountants, October, 1–95 (see ACCA Student Accountant technical article archive at www.accaglobal.com/students /student_accountant/archive/).

Porter, M. (1980) *Competitive Strategy Techniques Analysing Industries and Competitors*, New York, Free Press.

Porter, M. (1985) *Competitive Advantage*, New York, Free Press.

Porter, M.E. and Kramer, M.R. (2006) Strategy and society: The link between competitive advantage and social responsibility, *Harvard Business Revue*, 84(12), 78–92.

Porter, M.E. and Kramer, M.R. (2011) Creating shared value, *Harvard Business Revue*, 89(1/2), 62–77.

Ramadan, S.S. (1989) The rationale for cost allocation: a study of UK companies, *Accounting and Business Research*, Winter, 31–7.

Ranganathan, J. and Ditz, D. (1996) Environmental accounting: a tool for better management, *Management Accounting*, February, 38–40.

Reece, J.S. and Cool, W.R. (1978) Measuring investment centre performance, *Harvard Business Review*, May/June, 29–49.

Ricceri, F. and Guthrie, J. (2009) Critical analysis of international guidelines for the management of knowledge resources, in Jemielniak, D. and Kociatkiewicz, J. (eds) *Handbook on Research on Knowledge Intensive Organisations*, Hershey, PA, Information Science Press.

Rigby, D. and Biolodeau, B. (2013) *Executive Guide – Management Tools 2007*, Bain & Company Publishing. www.bain.com/management_tools/Management_Tools_and_Trends_

Roslender, R. (1992) *Sociological Perspectives on Modern Accountancy*, Routledge.

Roslender, R. (1995) Accounting for strategic positioning: responding to the crisis in management accounting, *British Journal of Management*, 6, 45–57.

Roslender, R. (1996) Relevance lost and found: critical perspectives on the promise of management accounting, *Critical Perspectives on Accounting*, 7(5), 533–61.

Roslender, R. and Hart, S.J. (2002) Integrating management accounting and marketing in the pursuit of competitive advantage: the case for strategic management accounting, *Critical Perspectives on Accounting*, 13(2), 255–77.

Roslender, R. and Hart, S.J. (2003) In search of strategic management accounting: theoretical and field study perspectives, *Management Accounting Research*, 14(3), 255–80.

Ryan, N. (2011) Economic value added versus profit-based measures of Performance, *Student Accountant*, Association of Chartered Certified Accountants, July, 1–9 (see ACCA Student Accountant technical article archive at www.accaglobal.com/students/student_accountant/archive/).

Ryan, N. (2011) Economic value added versus profit-based measures of Performance – Part 2, *Student Accountant*, Association of Chartered Certified Accountants, August, 1–4 (see ACCA Student Accountant technical article archive at www.accaglobal.com/students/student_accountant/archive/).

Ryan, N. (2012) Benchmarking and use of targets in public sector organisations, *Student Accountant*, Association of Chartered Certified Accountants, September, 1–9 (see ACCA Student Accountant technical article archive at www.accaglobal.com/students/student_accountant/archive/).

Saez-Torrecilla, A., Fernandez-Fernandez, A., Texeira-Quiros, J. and Vaquera-Mosquero, M. (1996) Management accounting in Spain: trends in thought and practice, in Bhimani, A. (ed.) *Management Accounting: European Perspective*, Oxford University Press, pp. 180–90.

Samuels, J.M., Wilkes, F.M. and Brayshaw, R.E. (1999) *Management of Company Finance*, Chapman and Hall.

Scapens, R., Jazayeri, M. and Scapens, J. (1998) SAP: integrated information systems and the implications for management accountants, *Management Accounting (UK)*, September, 46–8.

Scapens, R.W. (1991) *Management Accounting: A Review of Recent Developments*, Macmillan.

Scarborough, P.A., Nanni, A. and Sakurai, M. (1991) Japanese management accounting practices and the effects of assembly and process automation, *Management Accounting Research*, 2, 27–46.

Scherrer, G. (1996) Management accounting: a German perspective, in Bhimani, A. (ed.) *Management Accounting: European Perspectives*, Oxford University Press, pp. 100–22.

Schwarzbach, H.R. (1985) The impact of automation on accounting for direct costs, *Management Accounting (USA)*, 67(6), 45–50.

Seal, W., Cullen, J., Dunlop, D., Berry, T. and Ahmed, M. (1999) Enacting a European supply chain: a case study on the role of management accounting, *Management Accounting Research*, 10(3), 303–22.

Sen, P.K. (1998) Another look at cost variance investigation, *Accounting Horizons*, February, 127–37.

Shank, J. and Govindarajan, V. (1992) Strategic cost management: the value chain perspective, *Journal of Management Accounting Research*, 4, 179–97.

Shank, J.K. (1989) Strategic cost management: new wine or just new bottles? *Journal of Management Accounting Research (USA)*, Fall, 47–65.

Sibbet, D. (1997) 75 years of management ideas and practice 1922–1997, *Harvard Business Review*, 75(5), 2–12.

Silk, S. (1998) Automating the balanced scorecard, *Management Accounting*, May, 38–44.

Simmonds, K. (1981) Strategic management accounting, *Management Accounting*, 59(4), 26–9.

Simmonds, K. (1982) Strategic management accounting for pricing: a case example, *Accounting and Business Research*, 12(47), 206–14.

Simmonds, K. (1986) The accounting assessment of competitive position, *European Journal of Marketing, Organisations and Society*, 12(4), 357–74.

Simon, H.A. (1959) Theories of decision making in economics and behavioural science, *The American Economic Review*, June, 233–83.

Simons, R. (1987) Accounting control systems and business strategy, *Accounting, Organizations and Society*, 12(4), 357–74.

Simons, R. (1998) *Performance Measurement and Control Systems for Implementing Strategy: Text and Cases*, Prentice-Hall.

Simons, R. (1999) *Performance Measurement and Control Systems for Implementing Strategy*, Prentice-Hall.

Sizer, J. (1989) *An Insight into Management Accounting*, Penguin, Chs 11, 12.

Sizer, J. and Mottram, G. (1996) Successfully evaluating and controlling investments in advanced manufacturing technology, in Drury, C. (ed.) *Management Accounting Handbook*, Butterworth-Heinemann.

Skinner, R.C. (1990) The role of profitability in divisional decision making and performance, *Accounting and Business Research*, Spring, 135–41.

Slater, K. and Wootton, C. (1984) *Joint and By-product Costing in the UK*, Institute of Cost and Management Accounting.

Soin, K., Seal, W. and Cullen, J. (2002) ABC and organizational change: an institutional perspective, *Management Accounting Research*, 13(2), 151–72.

Solomons, D. (1965) *Divisional Performance: Measurement and Control*, R.D. Irwin.

Soonawalla, K. (2006) Environmental management accounting, in Bhimani, A. (ed.) *Contemporary Issues in Management Accounting*, Oxford University Press, pp. 381–406.

Speckbacher, G., Bischof, J. and Pfeiffer, T. (2003) A descriptive analysis on the implementation of balanced scorecards in German-speaking countries, *Management Accounting Research*, 14(4), 361–88.

Starovic, D. and Marr, B. (2010) *Understanding Corporate Value, Managing and Reporting Intellectual Capital*, Chartered Institute of Management Accountants.

Stedry, A. and Kay, E. (1966) The effects of goal difficulty on performance: a field experiment, *Behavioural Science*, November, 459–70.

Stern, J., Stewart, G. and Chew, D. (1995) The EVA financial management system, *Journal of Applied Corporate Finance*, Summer, 32–46.

Stewart, G.B. (1991) *The Quest for Value: A Guide for Senior Managers*, Harper Collins.

Stewart, G.B. (1994) EVA$^{(TM)}$: fact and fantasy, *Journal of Applied Corporate Finance*, Summer, 71–84.

Stewart, G.B. (1995) EVA$^{(TM)}$ works but not if you make common mistakes, *Fortune*, 1, May, 81–2.

Tang, R. (1992) Canadian transfer pricing in the 1990s, *Management Accounting (USA)*, February.

Tani, T., Okano, H., Shimizu, N., Iwabuchi, Y., Fukuda, J. and Cooray, S. (1994) Target cost management in Japanese companies: current state of the art, *Management Accounting Research*, 5(1), 67–82.

Thompson, J.D. (1967) *Organisations in Action*, McGraw-Hill.

Thompson, J.D. and Tuden, A. (1959) Strategies, structures and processes of organizational decision, in Thompson, J.D. *et al.* (eds) *Comparative Studies in Administration*, University of Pittsburg Press.

Thompson, J.L. and Martin, F. (2014) *Strategic Management*, Cengage Learning EMEA.

Tomkins, C. (1973) *Financial Planning in Divisionalised Companies*, Haymarket, Chs 4 and 8.

Tomkins, C. (1975) Another look at residual income, *Journal of Business Finance and Accounting*, 2(1), Spring, 39–54.

Tomkins, C. and Carr, C. (1996) Editorial in Special Issue of Management Accounting Research: Strategic Management Accounting, *Management Accounting Research*, 7(2), 165–7.

Trenchard, P.M. and Dixon, R. (2003) The clinical allocation of joint blood product costs, *Management Accounting Research*, 14(2), 165–76.

Virtanen, K., Malmi, T., Vaivio, J. and Kasanen, E. (1996) Drivers of management accounting in Finland, in Bhimani, A. (ed.) *Management Accounting: European Perspectives*, Oxford University Press, pp. 218–41.

Warren, J.D, Moffitt, K.C. and Byrnes, P. (2015) Accounting horizons, *American Accounting Association*, 29(2), 397–407.

Wiersma, E. (2009) For which purposes do managers use balanced scorecards, an empirical study, *Management Accounting Research*, 20(4), 239–51.

World Commission on Environment and Development (1987) *Tokyo Declaration*, Tokyo, WCED.

Yazdifar, H. and Askarany, D. (2012) A comparative study of the adoption and implementation of target costing in the UK, Australia and New Zealand, *International Journal of Production Economics*, 135, 382–92.

Yoshikawa, T., Innes, J., Mitchell, F. and Tanaka, M. (1993) *Contemporary Cost Management*, Chapman and Hall.

Young, P.H. (1985) *Cost Allocation: Methods, Principles, Applications*, North-Holland.

Zuriekat, M. (2005) Performance measurement systems: an examination of the influence of contextual factors and their impact on performance with specific emphasis on the balanced scorecard approach. PhD dissertation, University of Huddersfield.

GLOSSARY

ABC classification method A method of classifying stock in categories of importance in terms of value of purchases.

Abnormal gain A gain that occurs when the level of a normal loss is less than expected.

Abnormal losses Losses that are not inherent to the production process and which are not expected to occur under efficient operating conditions, also known as controllable losses.

Absorption costing system A costing system that allocates all manufacturing costs, including fixed manufacturing costs, to products and values unsold stocks at their total cost of manufacture.

Accounting rate of return A method of appraising capital investments where the average annual profits from a project are divided into the average investment cost, also known as return on investment and return on capital employed.

Action controls Observing the actions of individuals as they go about their work, also known as behavioural controls.

Activities The aggregation of many different tasks, events or units of work that causes the consumption of resources.

Activity The aggregation of different tasks, events or units of work that causes the consumption of resources.

Activity cost centre A cost centre in which costs are accumulated by activities.

Activity cost drivers A cost driver used to assign the costs assigned to an activity cost centre to products.

Activity measure Any factor whose change causes a change in the total cost of an activity, also known as a cost driver.

Activity-based budgeting (ABB) An approach to budgeting that takes cost objects as the starting point, determines the necessary activities and then estimates the resources that are required for the budget period.

Activity-based cost management (ABCM) The cost management applications applied to activity-based costing, without the need to assign activity costs to products, also known as activity-based management.

Activity-based costing (ABC) A system of cost allocation that aims to use mainly cause-and-effect cost allocations by assigning costs to activities.

Activity-based management (ABM) The cost management applications applied to activity-based costing, without the need to assign activity costs to products, also known as activity-based cost management.

Allocation base The basis used to allocate costs to cost objects.

Annual percentage rate (APR) A discount or interest rate quoted as a rate per annum.

Annuity An asset that pays a fixed sum each period for a specific number of periods.

Appraisal costs The costs incurred to ensure that materials, products and services meet quality conformance standards.

Arbitrary allocation The allocation of costs using a cost base that is not a significant determinant of cost.

Aspiration level The level of performance that the person responsible for the budget hopes to attain.

Assignable causes Factors that can be assigned to a known cause, which may or may not be worth investigating further.

Average cost A method of valuing stock that has been purchased at different prices that values all items at the average cost.

Avoidable costs Costs that may be saved by not adopting a given alternative.

Backflush costing A simplified costing system that is applied when a just-in-time production philosophy is adopted and which focuses first on the output of the organization and then works backwards when allocating cost between cost of goods sold and inventories, with no separate accounting for work in progress.

Balanced scorecard A strategic management tool that integrates financial and non-financial measures of performance in a single concise report, with the aim of incorporating performance management within the strategic management process.

Balancing allowance An adjusting payment made by the tax authorities when the estimated realizable value of an asset is less than its written down value, reflecting insufficient allowances that have been claimed.

Balancing charge An adjusting payment made to the tax authorities when the estimated realizable value of an asset exceeds its written-down value, reflecting excess allowances that have been claimed.

Batch costing Costing that makes use of a combination of job costing and process costing techniques, also known as operation costing.

Batch production functional layout A plant layout in which products pass in batches through a number of specialist departments that normally contain a group of similar machines.

Batch-related activities Activities that are performed each time a batch of goods is produced.

Behavioural controls Controls that involve observing the actions of individuals as they go about their work, also known as action controls.

Benchmarking A mechanism for achieving continuous improvement by measuring products, services or activities against those of other best performing organizations.

Beta The relationship between the risk of a security and the risk of the market portfolio.

Beyond budgeting A term used to describe alternative approaches, such as rolling forecasts, that can be used instead of annual budgeting.

Big data A term that describes the large volume of raw data, both structured and unstructured, that inundates a business on a daily basis. It includes information such as e-mail messages, social media postings, phone calls, purchase transactions, website traffic and video streams.

Bill of materials A document stating the required quantity of materials for each operation to complete the product.

Blanket overhead rate An overhead rate that assigns indirect costs to cost objects using a single overhead rate for the whole organization, also known as plant-wide rate.

Bottleneck activities Activities or operations where constraints apply arising from demand exceeding available capacity.

Bottleneck operations/resources Scarce resources that are fully utilized and therefore can present limiting factors.

Bottom-up budget setting Allowing individuals to participate in the setting of budgets and targets.

Break-even chart A chart that plots total costs and total revenues against sales volume and indicates the break-even point.

Break-even point The level of output at which costs are balanced by sales revenue and neither a profit nor loss will occur.

Budget A financial plan for implementing management decisions.

Budgetary control process The process of comparing actual and planned outcomes, and responding to any deviations from the plan.

Budgeted activity The activity level based on the capacity utilization required for the next budget period.

Budgeted costs Expected costs for an entire activity or operation.

Budgeted overhead rate An overhead rate based on estimated annual expenditure on overheads and levels of activity.

Budgeting The implementation of the long-term plan for the year ahead through the development of detailed financial plans.

Business process reengineering Examining business processes and making substantial changes to how the organization operates and the redesign of how work is done through activities.

Business-sustaining activities Activities performed to support the organization as a whole, also known as facility sustaining activities.

By-products Products that are incidental to the production of joint products and have a low relative sales value.

Capacity usage ratio A measure of capacity calculated by dividing the actual hours utilized by the budgeted hours to be utilized.

Capital allowances Standardized depreciation allowances granted by the tax authorities with the aim of enabling the net cost of assets to be deducted as an allowable expense over a given time period, also known as writing-down allowances (WDAs) and depreciation tax shields.

Capital asset pricing model (CAPM) A model that shows the relationship between risk and expected rate of return on an investment.

Capital market line A graphical representation of the risk return relationship from combining lending or borrowing with the market portfolio.

Capital rationing The limiting of capital available for investment that occurs whenever there is a budget ceiling or a market constraint on the amount of funds that can be invested during a specific period of time.

Cash budget A budget that aims to ensure that sufficient cash is available at all times to meet the level of operations that are outlined in all other budgets.

Cause-and-effect allocation The use of an allocation base that is a significant determinant of cost, also known as driver tracing.

Cellular manufacturing A plant layout based on product flow lines, which are normally U shaped.

Cloud computing Enables software to be located on servers outside the company owned by an external IT provider. The provider then makes the software available over the internet to the companies.

Coefficient of determination A measure that shows how much of the variation in a dependent variable is caused by variations in an independent variable and how much by random variation and other independent variables.

Coefficient of variation A ratio measure of dispersion derived by dividing the standard deviation divided by the expected value.

Committed costs Costs that have not yet been incurred but that will be incurred in the future on the basis of decisions that have already been made, also known as locked-in costs.

Committed resources Resources that have to be acquired in discrete amounts in advance of usage, where the supply cannot be continually adjusted in the short run to match exactly the usage of resources.

Compounding interest The concept of adding the interest earned to the original capital invested so that further interest is generated.

Constant gross profit percentage method A method of allocating joint costs so that the overall gross profit percentage is the same for each product.

Consumption ratio The proportion of each activity consumed by a product.

Contingency theory An approach to management accounting that takes account of situational factors faced by organizations.

Continuous budgeting An approach to budgeting in which the annual budget is broken down into months for the first three months and into quarters for the rest of the year, with a new quarter being added as each quarter ends, also known as rolling budgeting.

Continuous improvement An ongoing search to reduce costs, eliminate waste and improve the quality and performance of activities that increase customer value or satisfaction.

Contract costing A job costing system that is applied to relatively large cost units that take a considerable amount of time to complete, such as construction and civil engineering work.

Contribution graph A graph that plots variable costs and total costs against sales volume, and fixed costs represent the difference between the total cost line and the variable cost line.

Contribution margin The margin calculated by deducting variable expenses from sales revenue.

Contribution margin ratio The proportion of sales available to cover fixed costs and provide for profit, calculated by dividing the contribution margin by the sales revenue, also known as profit–volume ratio.

Control The process of ensuring that a firm's activities conform to its plan and that its objectives are achieved.

Control account A summary account, where entries are made from totals of transactions for a period.

Control process The process of comparing actual and planned outcomes and responding to any deviations from the plan.

Controllability principle The principle that it is appropriate to charge to an area of responsibility only those costs that are significantly influenced by the manager of that responsibility centre.

Controllable investment The net asset base that is controllable or strongly influenced by divisional managers.

Controllable losses Losses that are not inherent to the production process and which are not expected to occur under efficient operating conditions, also known as normal losses.

Controllable profit A profit figure that is computed by deducting from divisional revenues all those costs that are controllable by a divisional manager.

Controls Measurement and information used to help determine what control action needs to be taken.

Conversion cost The sum of direct labour and manufacturing overhead costs; it is the cost of converting raw materials in to finished products.

Corporate objectives Specific, measurable statements, often expressed in financial terms, of what the organization as a whole wishes to achieve.

Correlation coefficient The strength of the linear relationship between two variables.

Cost accounting Accounting concerned with cost accumulation for inventory valuation to meet the requirements of external reporting and internal profit measurement.

Cost allocation The process of assigning costs to cost objects where a direct measure of the resources consumed by these cost objects does not exist.

Cost centre A location to which costs are assigned, also known as a cost pool.

Cost centres Responsibility centres whose managers are normally accountable for only those costs that are under their control, also known as expense centres.

Cost driver The basis used to allocate costs to cost objects in an ABC system.

Cost function A regression equation that describes the relationship between a dependent variable and one or more independent variables.

Cost leadership strategy A strategy adopted by an organization that aims to be the lowest cost producer within a market segment thus enabling it to compete on the basis of lower selling prices than its competitors.

Cost object Any activity for which a separate measurement of costs is desired.

Cost of capital The financial return that an organization could receive if, instead of investing cash in a capital project, it invested the same amount in securities on the financial markets, also known as the opportunity cost of an investment, the minimum required rate of return, the discount rate and the interest rate.

Cost of quality report A report indicating the total cost to the organization of producing products or services that do not conform with quality requirements.

Cost of resources supplied The cost of resources supplied for an activity, whether or not all these resources are actually required, which may include the cost of some unused capacity.

Cost of resources used The cost of resources actually used for an activity, which excludes the cost of any unused capacity.

Cost of the prediction error The cost of failing to predict accurately one or more variables in the EOQ formula.

Cost of unused capacity The difference between the cost of resources supplied and the cost of resources used.

Cost pool A location to which overhead costs are assigned, also known as a cost centre.

Cost–benefit analysis (CBA) An investment appraisal technique developed for use by non-profit making organizations that defines the costs and benefits of a project in much wider terms than those included in investment appraisals undertaken in the pursuit of profit maximization.

Cost-plus pricing An approach to pricing customized products and services that involves calculating product costs and adding the desired profit margin.

Costs of non-compliance Internal and external failure costs, also known as costs of non-conformance.

Costs of non-conformance Internal and external failure costs, also known as costs of non-compliance.

Costs of quality compliance Prevention and appraisal costs, also known as costs of quality conformance.

Costs of quality conformance Prevention and appraisal costs, also known as costs of quality compliance.

Cultural controls A set of values, social norms and beliefs that are shared by members of the organization and that influence their actions.

Customer perspective One of the perspectives considered on the balanced scorecard, focusing on how the organization appears to its customers.

Customer profitability analysis The analysis of profits by individual customers or customer categories.

Customer value propositions The attributes that drive core objectives and measures relating to the customer perspective of an organization.

Customer-sustaining activities Activities that are performed to support the relationship with customers.

Cycle time The length of time from start to completion of a product or service and is the sum of processing time, move time, wait time and inspection time.

Data Mere records of raw facts that are not organized to be meaningful.

Decision packages A decision package represents the incremental packages reflecting different levels of effort that may be expended to undertake a specific group of activities within an organization.

Decision tree A diagram showing several possible courses of action and possible events and the potential outcomes for each of them.

Decreasing returns to scale A situation that arises when unit costs rise as volume increases.

Defender strategy Firms pursuing a defender strategy perceive a great deal of stability in their external environment. They compete on product price, quality and customer service rather than innovation and product and market development.

Degree of operating leverage The contribution margin divided by the profit for a given level of sales.

Dependent variable A variable, such as cost, that changes when an independent variable, such as volume, is varied.

Depreciation tax shields Standardized depreciation allowances granted by the tax authorities with the aim of enabling the net cost of assets to be deducted as an allowable expense over a given time period, also known as capital allowances and writing-down allowances (WDAs).

Differential cash flows The cash flows that will be affected by a decision that is to be taken, also known as incremental cash flows.

Differential costs The difference between the costs of each alternative action under consideration, also known as incremental costs.

Differentiation strategy A strategy adopted by an organization that seeks to offer products or services that are considered by its customers to be superior or unique relative to its competitors.

Direct cost tracing The process of assigning a cost directly to a cost object.

Direct costing A costing system that assigns only direct costs to products or services and includes them in the inventory valuation.

Direct costing system A costing system that assigns only direct manufacturing costs, not fixed manufacturing costs, to products or services. Also known as variable costing system or marginal costing system.

Direct labour costs Labour costs that can be specifically and exclusively identified with a particular cost object.

Direct labour hour rate An hourly overhead rate calculated by dividing the cost centre overheads by the number of direct labour hours.

Direct material costs Material costs that can be specifically and exclusively identified with a particular cost object.

Discount rate The financial return that an organization could receive if, instead of investing cash in a capital project, it invested the same amount in securities on the financial markets, also known as the opportunity cost of an investment, the minimum required rate of return, the cost of capital and the interest rate.

Discounted cash flow (DCF) A technique used to compare returns on investments that takes account of the time value of money.

Discounted payback method A version of the payback method of appraising capital investments in which future cash flows are discounted to their present values.

Discounted present value The value today of cash to be received in the future, calculated by discounting.

Discounted rate of return A technique used to make capital investment decisions that takes into account the time value of money, representing the true interest rate earned on an investment over the course of its economic life, also known as internal rate of return (IRR).

Discounting The process of converting cash to be received in the future into a value at the present time by the use of an interest rate.

Discretionary costs Costs such as advertising and research where management has some discretion as to the amount it will budget.

Discretionary expense centres Cost centres where output cannot be measured in quantitative terms and there are no clearly observable relationships between inputs and outputs.

Diversification strategy A strategy of investing in a range of different projects in order to minimize risk.

Divisional net profit before taxes A profit figure obtained by allocating all general and administrative expenses to divisions.

Divisional profit contribution Controllable profit, less any non- controllable expenses that are attributable to a division and that would be avoidable if the division were closed.

Divisionalized organizational structure A decentralized organizational structure in which a firm is split into separate divisions.

Driver tracing The use of an allocation base that is a significant determinant of cost, also known as cause-and-effect allocation.

Dual-rate transfer pricing A method of transfer pricing that uses two separate transfer prices to price each interdivisional transaction.

Duration drivers A cost driver used to assign the costs assigned to an activity cost centre to products that is based on the amount of time required to perform an activity.

E-business The use of information and communication technologies to support any business activities, including buying and selling.

E-commerce The use of information and communication technologies to support the purchase, sale and exchange of goods.

Economic order quantity (EOQ) The optimum order size that will result in the total amount of the ordering and holding costs being minimized.

Economic value added (EVA$^{(TM)}$) A refinement of the residual income measure that incorporates adjustments to the divisional financial performance measure for distortions introduced by generally accepted accounting principles, trademarked by the Stern Stewart consulting organization.

Employee empowerment Providing employees with relevant information to allow them to make continuous improvements to the output of processes without the authorization by superiors.

Engineering methods Methods of analysing cost behaviour that are based on the use of engineering analyses of technological relationships between inputs and outputs.

Engineering studies Detailed studies of each operation, based on careful specifications of materials, labour and equipment and on controlled observations of operations.

Enterprise resource planning system (ERPS) A set of integrated software application modules that aim to control all information flows within a company.

Environmental detection costs The costs incurred to ensure that a firm's activities, products and processes conform to regulatory laws and voluntary standards.

Environmental external failure costs The costs incurred on activities performed after discharging waste into the environment.

Environmental internal failure costs The costs incurred from performing activities that have produced contaminants and waste that have not been discharged into the environment.

Environmental prevention costs The costs of activities undertaken to prevent the production of waste that could cause damage to the environment.

Equivalent production The term used when work in progress is converted into finished equivalents.

Ethical behaviour Behaviour that is consistent with the standards of honesty, fairness and social responsibility that have been adopted by the organization.

Events In the context of risk and uncertainty, factors that are outside the decision-maker's control, also known as states of nature.

***Ex post* budget adjustments** The adjustment of a budget to the environmental and economic conditions that the manager's actually faced during the period.

***Ex post* variance analysis approach** An approach to variance analysis in which actual results are compared with adjusted standards based on the conditions in which managers actually operated during the period.

Expected value A figure calculated by weighting each of the possible outcomes by its associated probability.

Expected value of perfect information The maximum amount it is worth paying for additional information in an uncertain situation, calculated by comparing the expected value of a decision if the information is acquired against the expected value in the absence of the information.

Expense centres Responsibility centres whose managers are normally accountable for only those costs that are under their control, also known as cost centres.

External failure costs The costs incurred when products or services fail to conform to requirements or satisfy customer needs after they have been delivered.

Facility sustaining costs Common costs that are incurred to support the organization as a whole and which are normally not affected by a decision that is to be taken.

Facility-sustaining activities Activities performed to support the organization as a whole, also known as business sustaining activities.

Feedback control Monitoring outputs achieved against desired outputs and taking whatever corrective action is necessary if a deviation exists.

Feedback loops Parts of a control system that allow for review and corrective action to ensure that actual outcomes conform with planned outcomes.

Feed-forward control Comparing predictions of expected outputs with the desired outputs and taking corrective action to minimize any differences.

Final products Products sold by a receiving division to the outside world.

Financial accounting Accounting concerned with the provision of information to parties that are external to the organization.

Financial perspective One of the perspectives considered on the balanced scorecard, focusing on how the organization looks to shareholders.

First in, first out (FIFO) A method of valuing stock that has been purchased at different prices that assumes that the first item received was the first to be issued.

First stage allocation bases The various bases, such as area, book value of machinery and number of employees, used to allocate indirect costs to production and service centres.

Fixed costs Costs that remain constant for a specified time period and which are not affected by the volume of activity.

Fixed overhead expenditure variance The difference between the budgeted fixed overheads and the actual fixed overhead spending.

Flexible budgets Budgets in which the uncontrollable volume effects on cost behaviour are removed from the manager's performance reports.

Flexible resources Types of resources whose supply can be continually adjusted to match exactly the usage of resources.

Focusing strategy A strategy that involves seeking competitive advantage by focusing on a narrow segment of the market that has special needs that are poorly served by other competitors in the industry. Competitive advantage is based on adopting either a cost leadership or product/service differentiation strategy within the chosen segment.

Full cost The estimated sum of all resources that are committed to a product or service in the long run, also known as long-run cost.

Full costing system A costing system that allocates all manufacturing costs, including fixed manufacturing costs, to products and values unsold stocks at their total cost of manufacture.

Functional analysis A process that involves decomposing a product into its many elements or attributes and determining a price or value for each element that reflects the amount the customer is prepared to pay.

Further processing costs Costs incurred by a joint product or by-product after the split-off point that can be traced to the product involved.

General rate of inflation The average rate of inflation for all goods and services traded in an economy.

Goal congruence The situation that exists when controls motivate employees to behave in a way that is in tune with the organization's goals.

Goodness of fit A measure that indicates how well the predicted values of the dependent variable, based on the chosen independent variable, match actual observations.

Hard capital rationing A term used to refer to situations where the amount of capital investment is restricted because of external constraints such as the inability to obtain funds from the financial markets.

High–low method A method of analysing cost behaviour that consists of selecting the periods of highest and lowest activity levels and comparing the changes in costs that result from the two levels in order to separate fixed and variable costs.

Holding costs The costs of holding stock, comprising opportunity costs of investment, incremental insurance, storage and handling costs, and the cost of obsolescence and deterioration.

Increasing returns to scale A situation that arises when unit costs fall as volume increases.

Incremental budgeting An approach to budgeting in which existing operations and the current budgeted allowance for existing activities are taken as the starting point for preparing the next annual budget and are then adjusted for anticipated changes.

Incremental budgets Budgets in which expenses for an item within the budget are based on the previous budgeted allowance plus an increase to cover higher prices caused by inflation.

Incremental cash flows The cash flows that will be affected by a decision that is to be taken, also known as differential cash flows.

Incremental costs The difference between the costs of each alternative action under consideration, also known as differential costs.

Independent variable A variable such as volume, machine time or another cost driver, that affects the value of a dependent variable, such as cost.

Indirect costs Costs that cannot be identified specifically and exclusively with a given cost object, also known as overheads.

Information Data that has been organized in a way so that it becomes understandable and useful for a particular purpose.

Information overload A situation that arises when users are provided with too much information to the extent that it becomes unmanageable and no longer useful.

Input/output analysis A technique that can be used to reduce the usage of environmental resources and costs. Inflows of resources such as water, materials and energy are recorded and balanced with outflows on the basis that, what comes in, must go out.

Inspection of accounts method A method of analysing cost behaviour that requires the departmental manager and the accountant to inspect each item of expenditure within the accounts for a particular period and then classify each item as a wholly fixed, wholly variable or a semi-variable cost.

Integrated cost accounting system An accounting system in which the cost and financial accounts are combined in one set of accounts.

Integrated reporting An external report that aims to provide information on the financial and non-financial performance in a single document relating to the economy, society and the environment.

Intellectual capital The intangible benefits accessible by a firm from its workforce, and more broadly, from its established relationships with groups such as customers, suppliers and competitors. It is often used interchangeably with other terms such as 'knowledge capital', 'knowledge economy' and 'intangible assets'.

Interest rate The financial return that an organization could receive if, instead of investing cash in a capital project, it invested the same amount in securities on the financial markets, also known as the opportunity cost of an investment the minimum required rate of return, the cost of capital and the discount rate.

Interlocking accounting system An accounting system in which the cost and financial accounts are maintained independently.

Interlocking cost accounting system An accounting system in which the cost and financial accounts are maintained independently.

Intermediate products Goods transferred from the supplying division to the receiving division.

Internal business perspective One of the perspectives considered on the balanced scorecard, focusing on what the organization needs to excel at.

Internal failure costs The internal costs incurred when products and services fail to meet quality standards or customer needs.

Internal rate of return (IRR) A technique used to make capital investment decisions that takes into account the time value of money, representing the true interest rate earned on an investment over the course of its economic life, also known as discounted rate of return.

Internet commerce The buying and selling of goods and services over the internet.

Investment centres Responsibility centres whose managers are responsible for both sales revenues and costs and also have responsibility and authority to make capital investment decisions.

Irrelevant costs and revenues Future costs and revenues that will not be affected by a decision.

JIT purchasing arrangements Strategic partnerships with suppliers that involve the delivery of materials and goods immediately before they are required.

Job cards A source document that records the amount of time spent on a particular job, together with the employee's hourly rate, so that direct labour costs can be assigned to the appropriate cost object.

Job-order costing system A system of assigning costs to products or services that is used in situations where many different products or services are produced.

Joint products Products that have a high relative sales value and are crucial to the commercial viability of the organization.

Just-in-time (JIT) production methods The design of the production process that involves producing the required items, at the required quality and in the required quantities, at the precise time they are required.

Just-in-time (JIT) purchasing arrangements Strategic partnerships with supplies that involve the delivery of materials and goods immediately before they are required.

Kaizen costing Making improvements to a process during the manufacturing phase of the product life cycle through small incremental amounts, rather than through large innovations.

Kanbans Visible signalling systems that authorize the production of parts and their movement to the location where they will be used.

Labour cost accounting The allocation of labour costs to jobs, overhead account and capital accounts.

Labour efficiency variance The difference between the standard labour hours for actual production and the actual labour hours worked during the period multiplied by the standard wage rate per hour.

Lag measures Outcome measures that mostly fall within the financial perspective and are the results of past actions.

Last in, first out (LIFO) A method of valuing stock that has been purchased at different prices that assumes that the last item received was the first to be issued.

Lead measures Non-financial measures that are the drivers of future financial performance.

Lead time The time that elapses between placing an order and the actual delivery of stocks.

Lean manufacturing systems Systems that seek to reduce waste in manufacturing by implementing just-in-time production systems, focusing on quality, simplifying processes and investing in advanced technologies.

Learning and growth perspective One of the perspectives considered on the balanced scorecard, focusing on how the organization can continue to improve and create value.

Learning curve A graphical representation of the rate at which a worker learns a new task.

Learning curve effect Changes in the efficiency of the labour force as workers become more familiar with the tasks they perform that may render past information unsuitable for predicting future labour costs.

Least-squares method A mathematical method of analysing cost behaviour that involves determining the regression line of best fit.

Life cycle costing The estimation of costs over a product's entire life cycle in order to determine whether profits made during the manufacturing phase will cover the costs incurred during the pre- and post-manufacturing stages.

Limiting factors Scarce resources that constrain the level of output.

Line item budgets The traditional format for budgets in non-profit organizations, in which expenditures are expressed in considerable detail, but the activities being undertaken are given little attention.

Linear programming A mathematical technique used to determine how to employ limited resources to achieve optimum benefits.

Locked-in costs Costs that have not yet been incurred but that will be incurred in the future on the basis of decisions that have already been made, also known as committed costs.

Long-run cost The estimated sum of all resources that are committed to a product or service in the long run, also known as full cost.

Long-term plan A top level plan that sets out the objectives that an organization's future activities will be directed towards, also known as a strategic plan.

Machine hour rate An hourly overhead rate calculated by dividing the cost centre overheads by the number of machine hours.

Management accounting Accounting concerned with the provision of information to people within the organization to aid decision- making and improve the efficiency and effectiveness of existing operations.

Management by exception A system in which a manager's attention and effort can be concentrated on significant deviations from the expected results.

Management control system The entire array of controls used by an organization.

Manufacturing cycle efficiency (MCE) A measure of cycle time that is calculated by dividing processing time by processing time plus the non-value added activities of inspection time, wait time and move time.

Margin of safety The amount by which sales may decrease before a loss occurs.

Marginal cost The additional cost of one extra unit of output.

Marginal costing system A costing system that assigns only variable manufacturing costs, not fixed manufacturing costs, to products and includes them in the inventory valuation, also known as variable costing system or direct costing system.

Marginal rate of substitution The optimal response from an independent marginal increase in a resource.

Marginal revenue The additional revenue from one extra unit of output.

Market portfolio A portfolio containing all shares, or a representative sample of shares, listed on a national stock exchange.

Master budget A document that brings together and summarizes all lower level budgets and which consists of a budgeted profit and loss account, a balance sheet and cash flow statement.

Material mix variance The difference between the mix of materials actually used and the predetermined mix included in the calculation of the standard cost of an operation.

Material price variance The difference between the standard price and the actual price per unit of materials multiplied by the quantity of materials purchased.

Material usage variance The difference between the standard quantity required for actual production and the actual quantity used multiplied by the standard material price.

Materials requisition A source document that records the cost of acquisition of the materials issued for manufacturing a product, or providing a specific service, so that the cost of the materials can be assigned to the appropriate cost object.

Materials yield variance The difference between the standard output for a given level of inputs and the actual output attained.

Maximax criterion A decision rule based on the assumption that the best possible outcome will always occur and the decision make should therefore select the largest payoff.

Maximin criterion A decision rule based on the assumption that the worst possible outcome will always occur and the decision-maker should therefore select the largest payoff under this assumption.

Minimum required rate of return The financial return that an organization could receive if, instead of investing cash in a capital project, it invested the same amount in securities of equal risk on the financial markets, also known as the opportunity cost of an investment, the cost of capital, the discount rate and the interest rate.

Mission statement A statement that provides in very general terms a summary of what the organization does to achieve its vision, its broad purpose and reason for its existence, the nature of the business(es) it is in and the customers it seeks to serve and satisfy.

Mixed costs Costs that contain both a fixed and a variable component, also known as semi-variable costs.

Model of resource consumption A model that focuses on the cost of using resources, as opposed to the cost of supplying resources.

Money cash flows Cash flows expressed in monetary units at the time when they are received.

Money rates of return The rates of return quoted on securities that reflect anticipated inflation, also known as nominal rates of return.

Multicollinearity A condition that occurs when there is simultaneous movement of two or more independent variables in the same direction and at approximately the same rate, indicating that the independent variables are highly correlated with each other.

Multiple regression A regression equation that includes two or more independent variables.

Mutually exclusive In the context of comparing capital investments, a term used to describe projects where the acceptance of one project excludes the acceptance of another.

Net marginal revenue The marginal (incremental) revenue from the sale of an extra unit (or a specified number of incremental units) of the final product less the marginal/incremental conversion costs (excluding the transfer price).

Net present value (NPV) The present value of the net cash inflows from a project less the initial investment outlay.

Net realizable value method A method of allocating joint costs on the basis of net realizable value at the split-off point, which is calculated by deducting further processing costs from sales revenues.

Nominal cash flows Cash flows expressed in monetary units at the time when they are received.

Nominal rates of return The rates of return quoted on securities that reflect anticipated inflation, also known as money rates of return.

Non-value added activity An activity where there is an opportunity for cost reduction without reducing the product's service potential to the customer.

Non-volume-based cost drivers A method of allocating indirect costs to cost objects that uses alternative measures instead of assuming that a product's consumption of overhead resources is directly related to the number of units produced.

Normal activity A measure of capacity required to satisfy average customer demand over a longer term period after taking into account seasonal and cyclical fluctuations.

Normal losses Unavoidable losses that are inherent to the production process and can be expected to occur in efficient operating conditions, also known as uncontrollable losses.

Objective function In linear programming, the objective to be minimized or maximized.

Objective probabilities Probabilities that can be established mathematically or compiled from historical data.

Operating leverage A measure of the sensitivity of profits to changes in sales.

Operation costing Costing that makes use of a combination of job costing and process costing techniques, also known as batch costing.

Opportunity cost The value of an independent marginal increase of a scarce resource, also known as the shadow price.

Opportunity cost of an investment The financial return that an organization could receive if, instead of investing cash in a capital project, it invested the same amount in securities of equal risk on the financial markets, also known as the minimum required rate of return, the cost of capital, the discount rate and the interest rate.

Opportunity costs Costs that measure the opportunity that is sacrificed when the choice of one course of action requires that an alternative is given up.

Optimized production technology (OPT) An approach to production management that is based on the principle that profits are expanded by increasing the throughput of the plant, which it aims to achieve by identifying and dealing with bottlenecks.

Ordering costs The incremental clerical costs involved in ordering, receiving and paying for stock.

Output controls Collecting and reporting information about the outcomes of work effort, also known as results controls.

Outsourcing The process of obtaining goods or services from outside suppliers instead of producing the same goods or providing the same services within the organization.

Overhead analysis sheet A document used to assign manufacturing overheads to production and service cost centres.

Overheads Another term for indirect costs, which are costs that cannot be specifically traced to a particular cost object.

Pareto analysis A type of analysis based on the observation that a very small proportion of items account for the majority of value.

Participation The extent that individuals are able to influence the figures that are incorporated in their budgets or targets.

Payback method A simple method to appraise capital investments, defined as the length of time that is required for a stream of cash proceeds from an investment to recover the original cash outlay.

Payroll accounting The computation of the gross pay for each employee and calculation of payments to be made to employees, government, pension funds, etc.

Penetration pricing policy An approach to pricing that involves charging low prices initially with the intention of gaining rapid acceptance of the product.

Perfectly competitive market A market where the product is homogeneous and no individual buyer or seller can affect the market prices.

Performance reports Performance reports show budget and actual performance (normally listed by items of expenses) at frequent intervals (normally monthly) for each responsibility centre.

Period cost adjustment The record of under- and over-recovery of fixed overheads at the end of a period.

Period costs Costs that are not included in the inventory valuation of goods and which are treated as expenses for the period in which they are incurred.

Personnel controls Helping employees to perform well through the use of selection and placement, training, job design and the provision of necessary resources.

Physical measures method A method of allocating joint costs in proportion to volume.

Plant-wide rate An overhead rate that assigns indirect costs to cost objects using a single overhead rate for the whole organization, also known as a blanket overhead rate.

Post-completion audits Audits that are undertaken when an investment is in operation, comparing actual results with the estimated results that were included in the investment proposal.

Practical capacity Theoretical capacity less activity lost arising from unavoidable interruptions.

Precautionary motive Holding stock because of uncertainty about future demand and supply.

Present value The value today of cash to be received in the future.

Prevention costs The costs incurred in preventing the production of products or services that do not conform to specification.

Previous process cost The cost that is transferred from the previous process and is always fully complete in respect of closing WIP.

Price setters Firms that have some discretion over setting the selling price of their products or services.

Price takers Firms that have little or no influence over setting the selling price of their products or services.

Price-skimming policy An approach to pricing that attempts to exploit sections of the market that are relatively insensitive to price changes.

Prime cost The sum of all direct manufacturing costs.

Priority-based budgeting An approach to budgeting in which projected expenditure for existing activities starts from base zero rather than last year's budget, forcing managers to justify all budget expenditure, also known as zero-based budgeting.

Priority-based incremental budgets Budgets in which managers specify what incremental activities or changes would occur if their budgets were increased or decreased by a specified percentage, leading to budget allocations being made by comparing the change in costs with the change in benefits.

Probability In the context of risk, the likelihood that an event or state of nature will occur, normally expressed in decimal form with a value between 0 and 1.

Probability distribution A list of all possible outcomes for an event and the probability that each will occur.

Product costs Costs that are identified with goods purchased or produced for resale and which are attached to products and included in the inventory valuation of goods.

Product flow line A plant layout in which groups of dissimilar machines are organized into product or component family flow lines so that individual items can move from process to process more easily.

Product life cycle The period of time from initial expenditure on research and development to the withdrawal of support to customers.

Product line-sustaining expenses Expenses relating to supporting a product line and not to any brand or product within that product line.

Production cell A self-contained area in which a team works on a product family.

Production efficiency ratio A process efficiency measure calculated by dividing the standard hours of output by the actual hours of input.

Product-sustaining activities Support activities that are performed to enable the production and sale of individual products and which are not related to the volume of each product.

Profit centre A division or part of an organization in which the manager does not control the investment and is responsible only for the profits obtained from operating the assets assigned by corporate headquarters.

Profitability index The present value of a project divided by its investment outlay.

Profit–volume graph A graph that plots profit/losses against volume.

Profit–volume ratio The proportion of sales available to cover fixed costs and provide for profit, calculated by dividing the contribution margin by the sales revenue, also known as contribution margin ratio.

Prospector strategy Firms pursuing a prospector strategy perceive high uncertainty in their environment and are continually searching for new market opportunities. They compete through new product innovations and market development.

Pull manufacturing system A system that pulls products through the manufacturing process so that each operation produces only what is necessary to meet the demand of the following operation.

Purchasing efficiency variance The general market price less the actual price paid, multiplied by the quantity purchased.

Purchasing planning variance The original target price less the general market price at the time of purchase, multiplied by the quantity purchased.

Push manufacturing system A system in which machines are grouped into work centres based on the similarity of their functional capabilities and one process supplies parts to the subsequent process without any consideration as to whether the next process is ready to work on the parts or not.

Qualitative or non-financial factors Non-monetary factors that may affect a decision.

Random or uncontrollable factors Factors that cannot be assigned to a known cause.

Real cash flows Cash flows expressed in terms of today's purchasing power assuming no future inflation.

Real rate of return The rate of return on an investment that would be required in the absence of inflation.

Regression equation An equation that identifies an estimated relationship between a dependent variable (cost) and one or more independent variables based on past observations.

Regret criterion A decision rule based on the fact that if a decision-maker selects an alternative that does not turn out to be the best, he or she will experience regret and therefore decisions should be made that will minimize the maximum possible regret.

Relative performance evaluation The evaluation of the performance of a responsibility centre relative to the performance of similar centres within the same company or of similar units outside the organization.

Relevant costs and revenues Future costs and revenues that will be changed by a particular decision, whereas irrelevant costs and revenues will not be affected by that decision.

Relevant range The output range at which an organization expects to be operating with a short-term planning horizon.

Re-order point The point at which the order should be placed to obtain additional stocks.

Residual income Controllable profit less a cost of capital charge on the investment controllable by the divisional manager.

Resource cost driver A cause-and-effect cost driver used to allocate shared resources to individual activities.

Responsibility accounting The creation of responsibility centres and the accumulation of costs and revenues so that the deviations from budget can be attributed to the individual who is accountable for the responsibility centre.

Responsibility centre A unit or department within an organization for whose performance a manager is held responsible.

Results controls Collecting and reporting information about the outcomes of work effort, also known as output controls.

Return on capital employed A method of appraising capital investments where the average annual profits from a project are divided into the average investment cost, also known as the accounting rate of return and return on investment.

Return on investment (ROI) A method of appraising capital investments where the average annual profits from a project are divided into the average investment cost, also known as the accounting rate of return and return on capital employed.

Revenue centres Responsibility centres where managers are mainly accountable for financial outputs in the form of generating sales revenues.

Reverse engineering The dismantling and examination of a competitor's product in order to identify opportunities for product improvement and/or cost reduction, also known as tear down analysis.

Risk A term applied to a situation where there are several possible outcomes and there is relevant past experience to enable statistical evidence to be produced for predicting the possible outcomes.

Risk averter An individual who, given a choice between more or less risky alternatives with identical expected values, prefers the less risky option.

Risk-free gilt-edged securities Bonds issued by the UK government for set periods of time with fixed interest rates.

Risk neutral An individual who, given a choice between more or less risky alternatives with identical expected values, would be indifferent to both alternatives because they have the same expected values.

Risk premium The extra average return from investing in the market portfolio compared with a risk free investment.

Risk seeker An individual who, given a choice between more or less risky alternatives with identical expected values, prefers the riskier option.

Rolling budgeting An approach to budgeting in which the annual budget is broken down into months for the first three months and into quarters for the rest of the year, with a new quarter being added as each quarter ends, also known as continuous budgeting.

Safety stocks The amount of raw materials, work in progress and finished goods that are held in excess of the expected use during the lead time to provide a cushion against running out of stocks because of fluctuations in demand.

Sales margin mix variance The actual sales quantity less the actual sales quantity in budgeted proportions, multiplied by the standard margin.

Sales margin price variance The difference between the actual contribution margin and the standard margin multiplied by the actual sales volume.

Sales margin volume variance The difference between the actual sales volume and the budgeted volume multiplied by the standard contribution margin.

Sales quantity variance The actual sales quantity in budgeted proportion less the budgeted sales quantity, multiplied by the standard margin.

Sales value at split-off point method A method of allocating joint costs in proportion to the estimated sales value of production.

Security market line A graphical representation of the relationship between risk (measured in terms of beta) and expected return for securities with different levels of risk.

Semi-fixed costs Costs that remain fixed within specified activity levels for a given amount of time but which eventually increase or decrease by a constant amount at critical activity levels; also known as step-fixed costs.

Semi-variable costs Costs that contain both a fixed and a variable component, also known as mixed costs.

Sensitivity analysis Analysis that shows how a result will be changed if the original estimates or underlying assumption changes.

Sequential allocation method A method of allocating service departments' overheads to production departments in a certain order, also known as the step allocation method.

Service departments Departments that exist to provide services to other units within the organization, also known as support departments.

Service-sustaining activities Support activities that are performed to enable the production and sale of individual services and which are not related to the volume of each service provided.

Shadow price The value of an independent marginal increase of a scarce resource, also known as the opportunity cost.

Shared value Policies and operating practices that enhance the competitiveness of a company while simultaneously advancing economic and social conditions in the communities in which it operates.

Simple regression A regression equation that only contains one independent variable.

Simplex method A mathematical technique used in linear programming to solve optimization problems.

Single most likely estimate The outcome with the highest probability attached to it.

Slack variable A variable that is added to a linear programming problem to account for any constraint that is unused at the point of optimality and so turn an inequality into an equality.

Social controls The selection of people who have already been socialized into adopting particular norms and patterns of behaviour to perform particular tasks.

Soft capital rationing A term used to refer to situations where an organization imposes an internal budget ceiling on the amount of capital expenditure.

Special studies A detailed non-routine study that is undertaken relating to choosing between alternative courses of action.

Speculative motive Holding stock in order to speculate on the expected increase or decrease in future prices.

Split-off point The point in a production process at which a joint product or by-product separates from the other products.

Stakeholders Various parties that have an interest in an organization. Examples include managers, shareholders and potential investors, employees, creditors and the government.

Standard cost centres Cost centres where output can be measured and the input required to produce each unit of output can be specified.

Standard costs Target costs that are predetermined and should be incurred under efficient operating conditions.

Standard deviation The square root of the mean of the squared deviations from the expected value.

Standard hours The number of hours a skilled worker should take working under efficient conditions to complete a given job.

Standard hours produced A calculation of the amount of time, working under efficient conditions, it should take to make each product.

States of nature In the context of risk and uncertainty, factors that are outside the decision-maker's control, also known as events.

Statistical quality control charts A graph of a series of successive observations of operations taken at regular intervals to test whether a batch of produced items is within preset tolerance limits.

Steady-state production level The level of production when no further improvement is expected and the regular efficiency level is reached.

Step allocation method A method of allocating service departments' overheads to production departments in a certain order, also known as the sequential allocation method.

Step-fixed costs Costs that remain fixed within specified activity levels for a given amount of time but which eventually increase or decrease by a constant amount at critical activity levels; also known as semi-fixed costs.

Stock-out costs The opportunity cost of running out of stock.

Stores ledger account A record of the quantity and value of each individual item of material stored by the organization.

Stores requisition A document giving formal authorization for the issue of materials, listing the type and quantity of materials issued and details of the job number, product code or overhead account for which they are required.

Strategic control Control that focuses outside the organization, looking at how a firm can compete with other firms in the same industry.

Strategic management accounting The provision of information to support the strategic decisions in organizations.

Strategic plan A top-level plan that sets out the objectives that an organization's future activities will be directed towards, also known as a long-term plan.

Strategic positioning The choice of strategies an organization uses to achieve sustainable competitive advantage.

Strategy The courses of action that must be taken to achieve an organization's overall objectives.

Subjective judgements Judgements made by senior managers of a responsibility head's performance based on the senior manager's own experience, knowledge and interpretation of the performance level achieved.

Subjective probabilities Probabilities that are based on an individual's expert knowledge, past experience and on observations of current variables that are likely to affect future events.

Sunk costs Costs that have been incurred by a decision made in the past and that cannot be changed by any decision that will be made in the future.

Supply chain management Managing linkages in the supply chain by examining supplier costs and modifying activities to reduce these costs.

Support departments Departments that exist to provide services to other units within the organization, also known as service departments.

Target costing A technique that focuses on managing costs during a product's planning and design phase by establishing the target cost for a product or service that is derived from starting with the target selling price and deducting a desired profit margin.

Tear-down analysis The dismantling and examination of a competitor's product in order to identify opportunities for product improvement and/or cost reduction, also known as reverse engineering.

Tests of reliability Statistical and graphical methods of testing the strength of the relationship between independent and dependent variables.

Theoretical maximum capacity A measure of maximum operating capacity based on 100 per cent efficiency with no interruptions for maintenance or other factors.

Theory of constraints (TOC) A five-step process of maximizing operating profit when faced with bottleneck and non-bottleneck operations.

Throughput accounting A management accounting methodology that gives priority to throughput over inventories and operational expenses.

Time driven ABC A simplified approach for operating ABC in large organizations where employees are surveyed to estimate the percentage of time they expect to spend on activities and expenses are assigned to the activities based on the average percentages derived from the survey. The quantities of work for activities are obtained in order to derive the cost driver rates, which are then used to assign to resources the customers or products that use the activities.

Time sheets Source documents that record the time spent by an employee on particular jobs that can be used to allocate direct labour costs to the appropriate cost object.

Time value of money The concept that a specific amount of cash is worth more now than it will be in the future.

Top-down budget setting Imposing budgets and targets from above, without the participation of the individuals involved.

Total fixed overhead variance The difference between the standard fixed overhead charged to production and the actual fixed overhead incurred.

Total labour variance The difference between the standard labour cost for the actual production and the actual labour cost.

Total material variance The difference between the standard material cost for the actual production and the actual cost.

Total quality management (TQM) A customer-oriented process of continuous improvement that focuses on delivering products or services of consistently high quality in a timely fashion.

Total sales margin variance The difference between actual sales revenue less the standard variable cost of sales and the budgeted contribution.

Total variable overhead variance The difference between the standard variable overheads charged to production and the actual variable overheads incurred.

Traditional costing systems Widely used costing systems that tend to use arbitrary allocations to assign indirect costs to cost objects.

Transaction drivers A cost driver used to assign the costs assigned to an activity cost centre to products that is based on the number of times an activity is performed.

Transactions motive Holding stock in order to meet future production and sales requirements.

Two-part transfer pricing system A method of transfer pricing where the receiving division acquires intermediate products at the variable cost of production and the supplying division also charges a fixed fee.

Unavoidable costs Costs that cannot be saved, whether or not an alternative is adopted.

Uncertainty A term applied to a situation where there are several possible outcomes and but there is little previous statistical evidence to enable probabilities to be attached to possible outcomes.

Uncontrollable losses Unavoidable losses that are inherent to the production process and can be expected to occur in efficient operating conditions, also known as normal losses.

Under- or over-recovery of overheads The difference between the overheads that are allocated to products or services during a period and the actual overheads that are incurred.

Unit objectives Specific, measurable statements, often expressed in financial terms, of what individual units within an organization wish to achieve.

Unit-level activities Activities that are performed each time a unit of the product or service is produced.

Value added activity An activity that customers perceive as adding usefulness to the product or service they purchase.

Value analysis A systematic interdisciplinary examination of factors affecting the cost of a product or service in order to devise means of achieving the specified purpose at the required standard of quality and reliability at the target cost, also known as value engineering.

Value-based management (VBM) A management principle that states that management should first and foremost consider the interests of shareholders in its business decisions.

Value chain The linked set of value creating activities all the way from basic raw material sources for component suppliers through to the ultimate end use product or service delivered to the customer.

Value chain analysis The analysis, coordination and optimization of the linked set of value creating activities all the way from basic raw material sources for component suppliers through to the ultimate end use product or service delivered to the customer.

Value engineering A systematic interdisciplinary examination of factors affecting the cost of a product or service in order to devise means of achieving the specified purpose at the required standard of quality and reliability at the target cost, also known as value analysis.

Variable costing system A costing system that assigns only variable manufacturing costs, not fixed manufacturing costs, to products and includes them in the inventory valuation, also known as marginal costing system or direct costing system.

Variable costs Costs that vary in direct proportion to the volume of activity.

Variable overhead efficiency variance The difference between the standard hours of output and the actual hours of input for the period multiplied by the standard variable overhead rate.

Variable overhead expenditure variance The difference between the budgeted flexed variable overheads for the actual direct labour hours of input and the actual variable overhead costs incurred.

Variance The difference between the actual cost and the standard cost.

Variance analysis The analysis of factors that cause the actual results to differ from predetermined budgeted targets.

Vision statement A statement that clarifies the beliefs and governing principles of an organization, what it wants to be in the future or how it wants the world in which it operates to be.

Volume capacity variance The difference between the actual hours of input and the budgeted hours of input for the period multiplied by the standard fixed overhead rate.

Volume efficiency variance The difference between the standard hours of output and the actual hours of input for the period multiplied by the standard fixed overhead rate.

Volume variance The difference between actual production and budgeted production for a period multiplied by the standard fixed overhead rate.

Volume-based cost drivers A method of allocating indirect costs to cost objects that correlates a product's consumption of overhead resources with the number of units produced.

Wage rate variance The difference between the standard wage rate per hour and the actual wage rate multiplied by the actual number of hours worked.

Weighted average cost of capital The overall cost of capital to an organization, taking into account the proportion of capital raised from debt and equity.

Writing-down allowances (WDAs) Standardized depreciation allowances granted by the tax authorities with the aim of enabling the net cost of assets to be deducted as an allowable expense over a given time period, also known as capital allowances and depreciation tax shields.

Written-down value The original cost of an asset minus depreciation.

Zero-based budgeting An approach to budgeting in which projected expenditure for existing activities starts from base zero rather than last year's budget, forcing managers to justify all budget expenditure, also known as priority-based budgeting.

Zero-defects policy A focus on continuous improvement with the ultimate aim of achieving zero defects and eliminating all internal and external failure costs.

APPENDICES

APPENDIX A

PRESENT VALUE OF £1 AFTER N YEARS = $£1/(1+k)^n$

Years hence	1%	2%	4%	6%	8%	10%	12%	14%	15%	16%
1	0.990	0.980	0.962	0.943	0.926	0.909	0.893	0.877	0.870	0.862
2	0.980	0.961	0.925	0.890	0.857	0.826	0.797	0.769	0.756	0.743
3	0.971	0.942	0.889	0.840	0.794	0.751	0.712	0.675	0.658	0.641
4	0.961	0.924	0.855	0.792	0.735	0.683	0.636	0.592	0.572	0.552
5	0.951	0.906	0.822	0.747	0.681	0.621	0.567	0.519	0.497	0.476
6	0.942	0.888	0.790	0.705	0.630	0.564	0.507	0.456	0.432	0.410
7	0.933	0.871	0.760	0.665	0.583	0.513	0.452	0.400	0.376	0.354
8	0.923	0.853	0.731	0.627	0.540	0.467	0.404	0.351	0.327	0.305
9	0.914	0.837	0.703	0.592	0.500	0.424	0.361	0.308	0.284	0.263
10	0.905	0.820	0.676	0.558	0.463	0.386	0.322	0.270	0.247	0.227
11	0.896	0.804	0.650	0.527	0.429	0.350	0.287	0.237	0.215	0.195
12	0.887	0.788	0.625	0.497	0.397	0.319	0.257	0.208	0.187	0.168
13	0.879	0.773	0.601	0.469	0.368	0.290	0.229	0.182	0.163	0.145
14	0.870	0.758	0.577	0.442	0.340	0.263	0.205	0.160	0.141	0.125
15	0.861	0.743	0.555	0.417	0.315	0.239	0.183	0.140	0.123	0.108
16	0.853	0.728	0.534	0.394	0.292	0.218	0.163	0.123	0.107	0.093
17	0.844	0.714	0.513	0.371	0.270	0.198	0.146	0.108	0.093	0.080
18	0.836	0.700	0.494	0.350	0.250	0.180	0.130	0.095	0.081	0.069
19	0.828	0.686	0.475	0.331	0.232	0.164	0.116	0.083	0.070	0.060
20	0.820	0.673	0.456	0.312	0.215	0.149	0.104	0.073	0.061	0.051

Years hence	18%	20%	22%	24%	25%	26%	28%	30%.	35%
1	0.847	0.833	0.820	0.806	0.800	0.794	0.781	0.769	0.741
2	0.718	0.694	0.672	0.650	0.640	0.630	0.610	0.592	0.549
3	0.609	0.579	0.551	0.524	0.512	0.500	0.477	0.455	0.406
4	0.516	0.482	0.451	0.423	0.410	0.397	0.373	0.350	0.301
5	0.437	0.402	0.370	0.341	0.328	0.315	0.291	0.269	0.223
6	0.370	0.335	0.303	0.275	0.262	0.250	0.227	0.207	0.165
7	0.314	0.279	0.249	0.222	0.210	0.198	0.178	0.159	0.122
8	0.266	0.233	0.204	0.179	0.168	0.157	0.139	0.123	0.091
9	0.225	0.194	0.167	0.144	0.134	0.125	0.108	0.094	0.067
10	0.191	0.162	0.137	0.116	0.107	0.099	0.085	0.073	0.050
11	0.162	0.135	0.112	0.094	0.086	0.079	0.066	0.056	0.037
12	0.137	0.112	0.092	0.076	0.069	0.062	0.052	0.043	0.027
13	0.116	0.093	0.075	0.061	0.055	0.050	0.040	0.033	0.020
14	0.099	0.078	0.062	0.049	0.044	0.039	0.032	0.025	0.015
15	0.084	0.065	0.051	0.040	0.035	0.031	0.025	0.020	0.011
16	0.071	0.054	0.042	0.032	0.028	0.025	0.019	0.015	0.008
17	0.060	0.045	0.034	0.026	0.023	0.020	0.015	0.012	0.006
18	0.051	0.038	0.028	0.021	0.018	0.016	0.012	0.009	0.005
19	0.043	0.031	0.023	0.017	0.014	0.012	0.009	0.007	0.003
20	0.037	0.026	0.019	0.014	0.012	0.010	0.007	0.005	0.002

APPENDIX B

PRESENT VALUE OF AN ANNUITY OF £1 RECEIVED ANNUALLY FOR

$$N \text{ YEARS} = \frac{£1}{k}\left(1 - \frac{1}{(1 + k)^n}\right)$$

Years hence	1%	2%	4%	6%	8%	10%	12%	14%	15%	16%	18%
1	0.990	0.980	0.962	0.943	0.926	0.909	0.893	0.877	0.870	0.862	0.847
2	1.970	1.942	1.886	1.833	1.783	1.736	1.690	1.647	1.626	1.605	1.566
3	2.941	2.884	2.775	2.673	2.577	2.487	2.402	2.322	2.283	2.246	2.174
4	3.902	3.808	3.630	3.465	3.312	3.170	3.037	2.914	2.855	2.798	2.690
5	4.853	4.713	4.452	4.212	3.993	3.791	3.605	3.433	3.352	3.274	3.127
6	5.795	5.601	5.242	4.917	4.623	4.355	4.111	3.889	3.784	3.685	3.498
7	6.728	6.472	6.002	5.582	5.206	4.868	4.564	4.288	4.160	4.039	3.812
8	7.652	7.325	6.733	6.210	5.747	5.335	4.968	4.639	4.487	4.344	4.078
9	8.566	8.162	7.435	6.802	6.247	5.759	5.328	4.946	4.772	4.607	4.303
10	9.471	8.983	8.111	7.360	6.710	6.145	5.650	5.216	5.019	4.833	4.494
11	10.368	9.787	8.760	7.887	7.139	6.495	5.937	5.453	5.234	5.029	4.656
12	11.255	10.575	9.385	8.384	7.536	6.814	6.194	5.660	5.421	5.197	4.793
13	12.134	11.343	9.986	8.853	7.904	7.103	6.424	5.842	5.583	5.342	4.910
14	13.004	12.106	10.563	9.295	8.244	7.367	6.628	6.002	5.724	5.468	5.008
15	13.865	12.849	11.118	9.712	8.559	7.606	6.811	6.142	5.847	5.575	5.092
16	14.718	13.578	11.652	10.106	8.851	7.824	6.974	6.265	5.954	5.669	5.162
17	15.562	14.292	12.166	10.477	9.122	8.022	7.120	6.373	6.047	5.749	5.222
18	16.398	14.992	12.659	10.828	9.372	8.201	7.250	6.467	6.128	5.818	5.273
19	17.226	15.678	13.134	11.815	9.604	8.365	7.366	6.550	6.198	5.877	5.316
20	18.046	16.351	13.590	11.470	9.818	8.514	7.469	6.623	6.259	5.929	5.353

Years hence	20%	22%	24%	25%	26%	28%	30%	35%	36%	37%
1	0.833	0.820	0.806	0.800	0.794	0.781	0.769	0.741	0.735	0.730
2	1.528	1.492	1.457	1.440	1.424	1.392	1.361	1.289	1.276	1.263
3	2.106	2.042	1.981	1.952	1.923	1.868	1.816	1.696	1.673	1.652
4	2.589	2.494	2.404	2.362	2.320	2.241	2.166	1.997	1.966	1.935
5	2.991	2.864	2.745	2.689	2.635	2.532	2.436	2.220	2.181	2.143
6	3.326	3.167	3.020	2.951	2.885	2.759	2.643	2.385	2.339	2.294
7	3.605	3.416	3.242	3.161	3.083	2.937	2.802	2.508	2.455	2.404
8	3.837	3.619	3.421	3.329	3.241	3.076	2.925	2.598	2.540	2.485
9	4.031	3.786	3.566	3.463	3.366	3.184	3.019	2.665	2.603	2.544
10	4.192	3.923	3.682	3.571	3.465	3.269	3.092	2.715	2.649	2.587
11	4.327	4.035	3.776	3.656	3.544	3.335	3.147	2.752	2.683	2.618
12	4.439	4.127	3.851	3.725	3.606	3.387	3.190	2.779	2.708	2.641
13	4.533	4.203	3.912	3.780	3.656	3.427	3.223	2.799	2.727	2.658
14	4.611	4.265	3.962	3.824	3.695	3.459	3.249	2.814	2.740	2.670
15	4.675	4.315	4.001	3.859	3.726	3.483	3.268	2.825	2.750	2.679
16	4.730	4.357	4.033	3.887	3.751	3.503	3.283	2.834	2.757	2.685
17	4.775	4.391	4.059	3.910	3.771	3.518	3.295	2.840	2.763	2.690
18	4.812	4.419	4.080	3.928	3.786	3.529	3.304	2.844	2.767	2.693
19	4.844	4.442	4.097	3.942	3.799	3.539	3.311	2.848	2.770	2.696
20	4.870	4.460	4.110	3.954	3.808	3.546	3.316	2.850	2.772	2.698

ANSWERS TO REVIEW PROBLEMS

CHAPTER 2

2.14 **(i)** SV (or variable if direct labour can be matched exactly to output)
(ii) F
(iii) F
(iv) V
(v) F (Advertising is a discretionary cost. See Chapter 15 (the budgeting process) for an explanation of this cost.)
(vi) SV
(vii) F
(viii) SF
(ix) V

2.15 Answer = **(d)**

2.16 Answer = **(d)**

2.17 Answer = **(d)**

2.18 Answer = **(b)**

2.19 Variable costs are constant per unit of output. The costs per unit of output are as follows:

	Cost per unit 125 units (£)	Cost per unit 180 units (£)
T1	8.00	8.00
T2	14.00	14.00
T3	19.80	15.70
T4	25.80	25.80

Answer = **(c)**

2.20 See the description of cost behaviour in Chapter 2 for the answer to these questions. In particular the answer should provide graphs for fixed costs, variable costs, semi-fixed costs and semi-variable costs.

2.21 See Chapter 2 for the answer to this question.

2.22 **(a)** See 'functions of management accounting' in Chapter 1 for the answer to this question. In particular your answer should stress that the cost accountant provides financial information for stock valuation purposes and also presents relevant information to management for decision-making and planning and cost control purposes. For example, the cost accountant provides information on the costs and revenues of alternative courses of action to assist management in selecting the course of action which will maximize future cash flows. By coordinating plans together in the form of budgets and comparing actual performance

with plans the accountant can pinpoint those activities which are not proceeding according to plan.
(b) **(i)** Direct costs are those costs which can be traced to a cost objective. If the cost objective is a sales territory then *fixed* salaries of salesmen will be a direct cost. Therefore the statement is incorrect.
(ii) Whether a cost is controllable depends on the level of authority and time span being considered. For example, a departmental foreman may have no control over the number of supervisors employed in his department but this decision may be made by his superior. In the long term such costs are controllable.
(iii) This statement is correct. See 'sunk costs' in Chapter 2 for an explanation of why this statement is correct.

2.23 See Chapter 2 for the answer to this question.

2.24 Cost information is required for the following purposes:
(a) costs for stock valuation and profit measurement;
(b) costs for decision-making;
(c) costs for planning and control.

For the alternative measures of cost that might be appropriate for each of the above purposes see Chapter 2.

2.25 **(i)** See Chapter 2 for a definition of opportunity cost and sunk cost.
(ii) *Opportunity cost:* If scarce resources such as machine hours are required for a special contract then the cost of the contract should include the lost profit that would have been earned on the next best alternative. This should be recovered in the contract price.
     Sunk cost: The original cost of equipment used for a contract is a sunk cost and should be ignored. The change in the resale value resulting from the use of the equipment represents the relevant cost of using the equipment.
(iii) The significance of opportunity cost is that relevant costs do not consist only of future cash outflows associated directly with a particular course of action. Imputed costs must also be included. The significance of sunk costs is that past costs are not relevant for decision-making.

2.26 See Chapter 2 for an explanation of the terms avoidable costs and unavoidable costs and Chapter 3 for an explanation of cost centres. A cost unit is a unit of product or service for which costs are ascertained. In a manufacturing organization a cost unit will be a unit of output produced within a cost centre. In a service organization, such as an educational establishment, a cost unit might be the cost per student.

2.27 (a) (i)   Schedule of annual mileage costs

	5000 miles (£)	10000 miles (£)	15000 miles (£)	30000 miles (£)
Variable costs:				
Spares	100	200	300	600
Petrol	380	760	1140	2280
Total variable cost	480	960	1440	2880
Variable cost per mile	0.096	0.096	0.096	0.096
Fixed costs				
Depreciation[a]	2000	2000	2000	2000
Maintenance	120	120	120	120
Vehicle licence	80	80	80	80
Insurance	150	150	150	150
Tyres[b]	–	–	75	150
	2350	2350	2425	2500
Fixed cost per mile	0.47	0.235	0.162	0.083
Total cost	2830	3310	3865	5380
Total cost per mile	0.566	0.331	0.258	0.179

Notes

[a]Annual depreciation = $\dfrac{£5500 \text{ (cost)} - £1500 \text{ (trade-in-price)}}{2 \text{ years}}$ = £2000

[b]At 15000 miles per annum tyres will be replaced once during the two-year period at a cost of £150. The average cost per year is £75. At 30000 miles per annum tyres will be replaced once each year.

Comments

Tyres are a semi-fixed cost. In the above calculations they have been regarded as a step fixed cost. An alternative approach would be to regard the semi-fixed cost as a variable cost by dividing £150 tyre replacement by 25000 miles. This results in a variable cost per mile of £0.006.

Depreciation and maintenance cost have been classified as fixed costs. They are likely to be semi-variable costs, but in the absence of any additional information they have been classified as fixed costs.

(ii) See Figure 2.27.

(iii) The respective costs can be obtained from the vertical dashed lines in the graph (Figure 2.27).

FIGURE 2.27

The step increase in fixed cost is assumed to occur at an annual mileage of 12500 and 25000 miles, because tyres are assumed to be replaced at this mileage

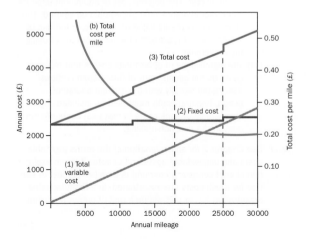

(b) The *cost per mile* declines as activity increases. This is because the majority of costs are fixed and do not increase when mileage increases. However, *total cost* will increase with increases in mileage.

2.28 (a) (i)   For an explanation of sunk and opportunity costs see Chapter 2. The down payment of £5000 represents a sunk cost. The lost profit from subletting the shop of £1600 p.a. ((£550 × £12) – £5000) is an example of an opportunity cost. Note that only the £5000 additional rental is included in the opportunity cost calculation. (The £5000 sunk cost is excluded from the calculation.)

(ii) The relevant information for running the shop is:

	(£)
Net sales	100000
Costs (£87000 – £5000 sunk cost)	82000
	18000
Less opportunity cost from subletting	1600
Profit	16400

The above indicates that £16400 additional profits will be obtained from using the shop for the sale of clothing. It is assumed that Mrs Johnson will not suffer any other loss of income if she devotes half her time to running the shop.

(b) The CIMA terminology defines a notional cost as 'A hypothetical cost taken into account in a particular situation to represent a benefit enjoyed by an entity in respect of which no actual expense is incurred.' Examples of notional cost include:

(i) Interest on capital to represent the notional cost of using an asset rather than investing the capital elsewhere.

(ii) Including rent as a cost for premises owned by the company so as to represent the lost rent income resulting from using the premises for business purposes.

CHAPTER 3

3.15 Overhead absorbed (£714000) = Actual hours (119000) × Pre-determined overhead rate.

Pre-determined overhead rate = £714000/119000 = £6.

Budgeted overheads (£720000) = Budgeted machine hours × Budgeted overhead rate (£6).

Budgeted machine hours = £720000/£6 = 120000 hours. Answer = **(c)**

3.16 Overhead absorbed (30000 × $3.50) = £105000

Overhead incurred = $108875

Under-absorbed = $3875

Answer = **(a)**

3.17

	£
Absorbed overheads (4500 units × £8)	36000
Over absorbed overheads	(6000)
Actual overheads incurred	30000

Answer = **(a)**

3.18 Answer = **(d)**

3.19 Because production is highly automated it is assumed that overheads will be most closely associated with machine hours. The pre-determined overhead rate will therefore be £18 derived from dividing budgeted overheads (£180 000) by the budgeted machine hours (10 000). Therefore the answer is **(b)**.

3.20

Direct materials	10 650
Direct labour	3 260
Prime cost	13 910
Production overhead (140 × $8.50)	1 190
Non-manufacturing overheads and profit (60% × $13 910)	8 346
Estimated price	23 446

Answer = **(c)**

3.21 Direct cost $95 000

Proportion of cost centre X (46 000 + (0.10 × 30 000)) × 0.50 = $24 500

Proportion of cost centre Y (30 000*0·3) = $9000

Total overhead cost for P $128 500

Answer = **(d)**

3.22 (a)

	Total (£)	A (£)	B (£)	C (£)	X (£)	Y (£)
			Departments			
Rent and rates[a]	12 800	6000	3600	1200	1200	800
Machine insurance[b]	6000	3000	1250	1000	500	250
Telephone charges[c]	3200	1500	900	300	300	200
Depreciation[b]	18 000	9000	3750	3000	1500	750
Supervisors' salaries[d]	24 000	12 800	7200	4000		
Heat and light[a]	6400	3000	1800	600	600	400
	70 400					
Allocated		2800	1700	1200	800	600
		38 100	20 200	11 300	4900	3000
Reapportionment of X		2450 (50%)	1225 (25%)	1225 (25%)	(4900)	
Reapportionment of Y		600 (20%)	900 (30%)	1500 (50%)		(3000)
		£41 150	£22 325	£14 025		
Budgeted D.L. hours[e]		3200	1800	1000		
Absorption rates		£12.86	£12.40	£14.02		

Notes

[a]Apportioned on the basis of floor area.

[b]Apportioned on the basis of machine value.

[c]Should be apportioned on the basis of the number of telephone points or estimated usage. This information is not given and an alternative arbitrary method of apportionment should be chosen. In the above analysis telephone charges have been apportioned on the basis of floor area.

[d]Apportioned on the basis of direct labour hours.

[e]Machine hours are not given but direct labour hours are. It is assumed that the examiner requires absorption to be on the basis of direct labour hours.

(b)

	Job 123 (£)	Job 124 (£)
Direct material	154.00	108.00
Direct labour:		
Department A	76.00	60.80
Department B	42.00	35.00
Department C	34.00	47.60
Total direct cost	306.00	251.40

Overhead:

Department A	257.20	205.76
Department B	148.80	124.00
Department C	140.20	196.28
Total cost	852.20	777.44
Profit	284.07	259.15

(c) Listed selling price　1136.27　1036.59

Note

Let SP represent selling price.

Cost + 0.25SP = SP

Job 123: £852.20 + 0.25SP = 1SP

$$0.75\ SP = £852.20$$

Hence SP = £1136.27

For Job 124:　　　0.75SP = £777.44

Hence SP = £1036.59

(d) For the answer to this question see sections on materials recording procedure and pricing the issues of materials in Chapter 4.

3.23 (a) The calculation of the overhead absorption rates are as follows: Forming department machine hour rate = £6.15 per machine hour (£602 700/98 000 hours)

Finishing department labour hour rate = £2.25 per labour hour (£346 500/154 000 hours)

The forming department is mechanized, and it is likely that a significant proportion of overheads will be incurred as a consequence of employing and running the machines. Therefore a machine hour rate has been used. In the finishing department several grades of labour are used. Consequently the direct wages percentage method is inappropriate, and the direct labour hour method should be used.

(b) The decision should be based on a comparison of the incremental costs with the purchase price of an outside supplier if spare capacity exists. If no spare capacity exists then the lost contribution on displaced work must be considered. The calculation of incremental costs requires that the variable element of the total overhead absorption rate must be calculated. The calculation is:

Forming department variable machine hour rate = £2.05 (£200 900/98 000 hours)

Finishing department variable direct labour hour rate = £0.75 (£115 500/154 000 hours)

The calculation of the variable costs per unit of each component is:

	A (£)	B (£)	C (£)
Prime cost	24.00	31.00	29.00
Variable overheads: Forming	8.20	6.15	4.10
Finishing	2.25	7.50	1.50
Variable unit manufacturing cost	34.45	44.65	34.60
Purchase price	£30	£65	£60

On the basis of the above information, component A should be purchased and components B and C manufactured. This decision is based on the following assumptions:

(i) Variable overheads vary in proportion to machine hours (forming department) and direct labour hours (finishing department).

(ii) Fixed overheads remain unaffected by any changes in activity.

(iii) Spare capacity exists.

For a discussion of make or buy decisions see Chapter 9.

(c) Production overhead absorption rates are calculated in order to ascertain costs per unit of output for stock valuation and profit measurement purposes. Such costs are inappropriate for decision-making and cost control. For an explanation of this see the section in Chapter 3 titled 'different costs for different purposes'.

3.24 (a) (i) Fixed production overheads = $15 400 000
Budgeted material cost = $22 000 000
Fixed production overhead absorption rate
= $15 400 000 / 22 000 000 = 70%

	Anti-ageing cream $000	Facial masks $000	Collagen fillers $000	Total $000
Fixed production overhead	8260	4340	2800	15 400

(ii) Calculation of cost driver quantities

	Anti-ageing cream	Facial masks	Collagen fillers
Budgeted production per annum (units)	1 000 000	1 200 000	600 000
Batch size (units)	1 000	2 000	1 500
Number of batches	1 000	600	400
Number of machine set-ups	3 000	1 800	1 600
Number of purchase orders	2 000	1 200	400
Processing time (minutes)	2 000 000	3 600 000	2 400 000

Calculation of cost driver rates

Activity	Activity cost $000	Cost driver	Cost driver rate
Machine set up	3600	Number of machine set ups	$3 600 000/6400 = $562.50 per set-up
Quality inspection	1200	Number of quality inspections	$1 200 000/2000 = $600 per inspection
Processing	6500	Processing time	$6 500 000/8 000 000 = $0.8125 per minute
Purchasing	1800	Number of purchase orders	$1 800 000/3600 = $500 per purchase order
Packaging	2300	Number of units	$2 300 000/2 800 000 = $0.821 per unit

Assignment of overheads to products

	Anti-ageing cream $000	Facial masks $000	Collagen fillers $000	Total $000
Sales	60 000	38 000	22 000	120 000
Direct material	11 800	6 200	4 000	22 000
Direct labour	3 700	2 400	1 900	8 000
Machine set ups	(3 000 × $562.50) 1688	(1 800 × $562.50) 1012	(1 600 × $562.50) 900	3 600
Quality inspections	(1 000 × $600) 600	(600 × $600) 360	(400 × $600) 240	1 200
Processing	(2 000 000 × $0.8125) 1625	(3 600 000 × $0.8125) 2925	(2 400 000 × $0.8125) 1950	6 500
Purchasing	(2 000 × $500) 1000	(1 200 × $500) 600	(400 × $500) 200	1 800
Packaging	(1 000 000 × $0.821) 821	(1 200 000 × $0.821) 986	(600 000 × $0.821) 493	2 300
Gross profit	38 766	23 517	12 317	74 600

3.25 (a) Annual activity per cost driver

	A	B	Total
No. of procedures	14 600	22 400	37 000
Admin time per procedure (hours)	14 600	33 600	48 200
Patient hours	350 400	1 075 200	1 425 600
Number of meals	14 600	89 600	104 200

Cost driver rates

Administrative costs	$1 870 160/48 200 = $38.80 per admin hour
Nursing costs	$6 215 616/1 425 600 = $4.36 per patient hour
Catering costs	$966 976/104 200 = $9.28 per meal
General facility costs	$8 553 600/1 425 600 = $6 per patient hour

Overhead allocation procedure

	A	B
Administrative costs	38.80	58.20
Nursing costs	104.64	209.28
Catering costs	9.28	37.12
General facility costs	144.00	288.00
	296.72	592.60
Add direct costs:		
Surgical	1 200.00	2 640.00
Anaesthesia	800.00	1 620.00
Total cost per procedure	2 296.72	4 852.60

(b) When activity-based costing (ABC) is used the cost for Procedure A is approximately $2297 compared with $2476 calculated by the current blanket overhead system. For Procedure B, the cost using ABC is approximately $4853 compared and $4736 with the current system resulting in the cost of Procedure A decreasing and the cost of Procedure B increasing with ABC. This is mainly due to the fact that the largest proportion of the overhead costs is the nursing and general facility costs. These costs are driven by the number of patient hours. Procedure B has double the number of patient hours compared with Procedure A and thus allocates double the amount of costs. This is not taken into account with the current system which assumes that all overheads are driven by the number of procedures and allocates approximately 40 per cent of the overheads to Procedure A (14 600/37 000 procedure) and the remaining 60 per cent to Procedure B. Therefore the ABC system assigns the costs based on the use of resources driving the overheads.

The major disadvantage of using ABC is that it is more costly to implement and operate. Given that the majority of the overhead costs consist of nursing costs and general facility costs, and both are driven by the number of patient hours, similar costs will be reported if all overhead costs are allocated on the basis of number of patient hours. Using this allocation base would result in an absorption rate of $12.35 per hour ($17 606 352/1 425 600 hours). Therefore the overhead costs allocated to Procedure

A would be $296 (24 × $12.35) and $592 (48 × $12.35) giving virtually identical results to the more expensive ABC system. It is recommended that this more accurate, but simplistic system, replace the existing system.

3.26 (a) (i)

	Machining (£)	Finishing (£)	Assembly (£)	Materials handling (£)	Inspection (£)
Initial cost	400 000	200 000	100 000	100 000	50 000
Reapportion:					
Materials handling	30 000	25 000	35 000	(100 000)	10 000
	430 000	225 000	135 000	—	60 000
Inspection	12 000 (20%)	18 000 (30%)	27 000 (45%)	3 000 (5%)	(60 000)
	442 000	243 000	162 000	3 000	—
Materials handling	900 (30%)	750 (25%)	1 050 (45%)	(3 000)	300 (10%)
	442 900	243 750	163 050	—	300
Inspection	60 (20%)	90 (30%)	135 (45%)	15 (5%)	(300)
	442 960	243 840	163 185	(15)	—
	5	4	6		
	442 965	243 844	163 191		

(ii) Let

x = material handling
y = inspection
$x = 100 000 + 0.05y$
$y = 50 000 + 0.1x$

Rearranging the above equations:

$$x - 0.05y = 100 000 \quad (1)$$
$$-0.1x - y = 50 000 \quad (2)$$

Multiply equation (1) by 1 and equation (2) by 10:

$$x - 0.05y = 100 000$$
$$-x + 10y = 500 000$$

Adding the above equations:

$$9.95y = 600 000$$
$$y = 60 301$$

Substituting for y in equation (1):

$$x - 0.05 × 60 301 = 100 000$$
$$x = 103 015$$

Apportioning the values of x and y to the production departments in the agreed percentages:

		Machining (£)	Finishing (£)	Assembly (£)
Initial cost		400 000	200 000	100 000
(x) Materials handling	(0.3)	30 905 (0.25)	25 754 (0.35)	36 055
(y) Inspection	(0.2)	12 060 (0.3)	18 090 (0.45)	27 136
		442 965	243 844	163 191

(b) Reapportioning production service department costs is necessary to compute product costs for stock valuation purposes in order to meet the financial accounting requirements. However, it is questionable whether arbitrary apportionments of fixed overhead costs provides useful information for decision-making. Such apportionments are made to meet stock valuation requirements, and they are inappropriate for decision-making, cost control and performance reporting.

An alternative treatment would be to adopt a variable costing system and treat fixed overheads as period costs. This would eliminate the need to reapportion service department fixed costs. A more recent suggestion is to trace support/service department costs to products using an activity-based costing system (ABCS). For a description of ABCS you should refer to Chapter 11.

(c) For the answer to this question see 'Under- and over-recovery of overheads'.

CHAPTER 4

4.10 Closing stock in units = 100 opening balance + 200 receipts − 150 issues = 150 units
LIFO valuation = (100 × £62) + (50 × £6700/100)
= £9550
FIFO valuation = 150 × £62 = £9300
Therefore the LIFO valuation is greater than FIFO valuation by £250

Answer = **(b)**

4.11 Average price per unit after the issue on the 5th
= [(100 units × £2900/200) = £1450
Average price after the receipt on the 7th = [(400 × £17.50) + £1450]/500 = £16.90
Value of issues = (100 × £2900/200) + (360 × £16.90) = £7534

Answer = **(b)**

4.12 Closing stock (units) = 300 + 400 + 500 − 600 − 300
= 300
The issue of 600kg on the 13th will consist of the 400kg on the 4th and 200kg of the opening stock and the issue of the 300kg on the 25th will be from the 500kg purchased on the 18th.
Therefore the closing stock will consist of 100kg of the opening stock and 200kg from the purchase on the 18th
Valuation = (100 × £11) + (200 × £13) = £3700

Answer = **(c)**

4.13 Answer = **(d)**

4.14 The debit to the profit or loss account implies that overheads were under absorbed. Overhead expenditure was in line with budget, so the cause of the under absorption was that the actual activity was less than budget. A shortfall of 800 direct labour hours would lead to an under absorption of 800 direct labour hours × $5 per hour = $4000.

Answer = **(a)**

4.15 In the financial accounts there is a total stock decrease of £2900 (£1000 materials and £1900 finished goods) and a decrease of £3200 in the costs accounts (£1200 materials and £2000 finished goods). Since a stock decrease represents an increase in cost of goods sold and a decrease in profits the cost accounting profit will be £300 less than the financial accounting profit. In other words, the financial accounting profit will be £300 greater than the cost accounting profit.

Answer = **(a)**

4.16 The cost of goods sold will be debited with £100 000 (1000 units at £100). Included within this figure will be £55 000 for conversion costs (1000 units at £55). Conversion costs actually incurred were £60 000. Assuming that an adjustment is made at the end of each month for conversion costs that have not been applied £5000 will be debited in April resulting in the cost of sales account having a debit balance of £105 000 (£100 000 + £5000). Therefore the answer is **(c)**.

4.17 (a) (i)

Stores ledger card – FIFO method

Date	Receipts Qty	Price (£)	Value (£)	Issues Qty	Price (£)	Value (£)	Balance Qty	Value (£)
1 April							40	400
4 April	140	11	1540				180	1940
10 April				40	10	400		
				50	11	550		
				90		950	90	990
12 April	60	12	720				150	1710
13 April				90	11	990		
				10	12	120		
				100		1110	50	600
16 April	200	10	2000				250	2600
21 April				50	12	600		
				20	10	200	180	1800
				70		800		
23 April				80	10	800	100	1000
26 April	50	12	600				150	1600
29 April				60	10	600	90	1000

(ii) ### Stores ledger card – LIFO method

Date	Receipts Qty	Price (£)	Value (£)	Issues Qty	Price (£)	Value (£)	Balance Qty	Value (£)
1 April							40	400
4 April	140	11	1540				180	1940
10 April				90	11	990	90	950
12 April	60	12	720				150	1670
13 April				60	12	720		
				40	11	440		
				100		1160	50	510
16 April	200	10	2000				250	2510
21 April				70	10	700	180	1810
23 April				80	10	800	100	1010
26 April	50	12	600				150	1610
				50	12	600		
29 April				10	10	100		
				60		700	90	910

(b) Cost of material used in April: LIFO – £4260; FIFO – £4350

(c) The weighted-average method determines the issue price by dividing the total value by the number of units in stock. This will tend to smooth out price fluctuations and the closing stock valuation will fall between that resulting from the FIFO and LIFO methods. In times of rising prices the cost of sales figure will be higher than FIFO but lower than LIFO.

4.18 (a)

Stores ledger control account

	(£)		(£)
Opening balances b/f	24175	Materials issued:	
Creditors – materials		Work in progress	
purchased		control	26350
		Production overhead	
	76150	control	3280
		Closing stock c/f	70695
	£100325		£100325

Wages control account

	(£)		(£)
Direct wages:		WIP	15236
Wages accrued a/c	17646	Capital equipment a/c	2670
Employees'		Factory overhead	
contributions a/c	4364	(idle time)	5230
Indirect wages:		Factory overhead	
Wages accrued a/c	3342	(indirect wages)	4232
Employees'			
contributions a/c	890		
Balances (Wages			
accrued a/c)	1126		
	27368		27368

Work in progress control account

	(£)		(£)
Opening balance b/f	19210	Finished goods	
Stores ledger –		control–cost of	
materials issued	26350	goods transferred	62130
Wages control direct			
wages	15236	Closing stock c/f	24360
Production overhead			
control: overhead			
absorbed (15236			
× 150%)	22854		
Profit and loss a/c:			
stock gain[a]	2840		
	£86490		£86490

Finished goods control account

	(£)		(£)
Opening balance b/f	34164	Profit and loss a/c:	
Working in progress:		cost of sales	59830
cost of goods sold	62130	Closing stock c/f	
	£96294	(difference)	36464
			£96294

Production overhead control account

	(£)		(£)
Prepayments b/f	2100	Work in progress:	
Stores ledger:		absorbed overheads	
materials issued		(15236 × 150%)	22854
for repairs	3280	Capital under	
		construction a/c:	
Wages control: idle		overheads	
time of direct		absorbed	
workers	5230	(2670 × 150%)	4005
Wages control: indirect		Profit and loss a/c:	
workers' wages		underabsorbed	
(3342 + 890)	4232	overhead balance	183
Cash/creditors: other			
overheads incurred	12200		
	£27042		£27042

Profit and loss account

	(£)		(£)
Cost of goods sold	59 830	Sales	75 400
Gross profit c/f	15 570		
	£75 400		75 400
Selling and distribution		Gross profit b/f	
overheads	5 240	Stock gain[a]:	15 570
Production overhead		WIP control	2 840
control: underabsorbed			
overhead	183		
Net profit c/f	12 987		
	£18 410		£18 410

Note

[a]The stock gain represents a balancing figure. It is assumed that the stock gain arises from the physical count of closing stocks at the end of the period.

Note that value of materials transferred between batches will be recorded in the subsidiary records, but will not affect the control (total) accounts.

(b) (i) Large increase in raw material stocks. Is this due to maintaining uneconomic stock levels or is it due to an anticipated increase in production to meet future demand?

(ii) WIP stock gain.

(iii) Idle time, which is nearly 25 per cent of the total direct wages cost.

(iv) The gross direct wages are £22 010 (£17 646 + £4 364), but the allocation amounts to £23 136 (£15 236 + £5 230 + £2670).

(c) Stocks are valued at the end of the period because they represent unexpired costs, which should not be matched against sales for the purpose of calculating profits. Stocks represent unexpired costs, which must be valued for inclusion in the balance sheet. Manufacturing expense items such as factory rent are included in the stock valuations because they represent resources incurred in transforming the materials into a more valuable finished product. The UK financial accounting regulations (SSAP 9) states that 'costs of stocks (and WIP) should comprise those costs which have been incurred in bringing the product to its present location and condition, including all related production overheads.'

4.19 (a) See 'Accounting entries for a JIT manufacturing system' in Chapter 4 for the answer to this question. The answer should point out that a backflush accounting system is a simplified and less accurate system that works backwards when allocating costs between the cost of goods sold and inventories. It is appropriate for a JIT system when the value of stocks and WIP are of insignificant value.

(b) (i) The journal entries and the ledger accounts are as follows:

	Dr £	Cr £
1. Raw materials inventory a/c	5 575 000	
Creditors		5 575 000
2. Conversion costs	4 883 000	
Bank		1 735 000
Creditors		3 148 000
3. Finished goods inventory	10 080 000	
Raw materials inventory a/c		5 460 000
Conversion costs: – labour		1 722 000
– overheads		2 898 000
4. Cost of sales (206 000 × £48)	9 888 000	
Finished goods inventory		9 888 000

Raw materials inventory

1. Creditors	£5 575 000	3. Finished goods	£5 460 000
		Balance c/fwd	£115 000
	£5 575 000		£5 575 000

Finished goods inventory

3. Raw materials	£5 460 000	4. Cost of sales	£9 888 000
Conversion		Balance	
costs	£4 620 000	c/fwd	£192 000
	£10 080 000		£10 080 000

Conversion costs

2. Bank	£1 735 000	3. Finished goods	£4 620 000
Creditors	£3 148 000	Balance c/fwd	£263 000
	£4 883 000		£4 883 000

Cost of sales

4. Finished goods		To Profit and	
	£9 888 000	Loss a/c	£9 888 000
	£9 888 000		£9 888 000

The inventory balances as at 30 November are:

	£
Raw materials account	115 000
Finished goods account	192 000
	307 000

Note that the balance of the conversion costs account will be transferred to the profit and loss account at the end of the period.

(ii) In a perfect JIT system stocks of raw materials and finished goods would be zero. In other words, completed units would be identical to sales (206 000 units) resulting in zero finished good stocks. In practice, the system approximately meets the requirements of a perfect JIT system since finished goods stock (4000 units) is approximately 2 per cent of the units sold.

CHAPTER 5

5.12 Cost per unit = $43 700/(0.95 × 20 000) = $2.30
Abnormal loss = (19 000 − 18 800) × $2.30 = $460
Answer = **(c)**

5.13 The input cost consists of materials of £9000 plus conversion costs of £13 340 giving a total of £22 340.
Cost per unit =

$$\frac{\text{Input cost (£22 340) lesss crap value of normal loss (100 × £3)}}{\text{Expected output (2000 × 0.95 = 1900 units)}}$$

= £11.60

Answer = **(b)**

5.14 Completed units (2000) less opening WIP equivalent production (180) = 1820 current total equivalent units for the period.
Cost of completed production = (1820 × $10) + opening WIP ($1710) = $19 910

Answer = **(a)**

5.15 Cost per equivalent unit (480 000/10 000) = $48

Degree of completion = ((144 000/48)/4000) = 75%

Answer = **(d)**

5.16 Input = Opening WIP (2000 units) + Material input (24 000) = 26 000

Output = Completed units (19 500) + Closing WIP (3000) + Normal Loss (2400) = 24 900

Abnormal Loss = 1100 units (Balance of 26 000 − 24 900)

Equivalent units (FIFO)

	Completed units less Opening WIP equiv. units	Closing WIP equiv. units	Abnormal loss equiv. units	Total equiv. units
Materials	17 500 (19 500 − 2000)	3000 (100%)	1100 (100%)	21 600
Conversion	18 700 (19 500 − 800)	1350 (45%)	1100 (100%)	21 150

It is assumed that losses are detected at the end of the process and that the answer should adopt the short-cut method and ignore the normal loss in the cost per unit calculations.

Answer = **(c)**

5.17 (a) The debit side (input) indicates that 4000 units were input into the process but the output recorded on the credit side is 3850 units thus indicating that the balance must represent an abnormal loss of 150 units. The accounting entries for abnormal losses are to debit the abnormal loss account and credit the process account. Therefore the answer is **A**.

(b) and **(c)**.

The calculation of the closing WIP value and the cost of finished goods is as follows:

Cost element	Total cost ($)	Completed units	Abnormal loss equivalent units	Closing WIP equivalent units	Total equivalent units	Cost per unit ($)	Closing WIP ($)
Materials[1]	15 300	2750	150	700	3600	4.25	2975.00
Labour	8125	2750	150	350	3250	2.50	875.00
Production overhead	3498	2750	150	280	3180	1.10	308.00
	27 923					7.85	4158.00

Finished goods (2750 × $7.85) 21 587.50
Abnormal loss (150 × $7.85) 1177.50
27 923.00

Note

[1]£16 000 materials less £700 scrap value of the normal loss. The above computation is based on the short-cut method described in the Appendix of Chapter 5.

Therefore the answer is **B** for both parts **(b)** and **(c)**.

5.18 (a) Input = 15 000 (14 000 + 3000 − 2000)

Answer = **C**

(b) Equivalent production for materials = 14 000 completed units − opening WIP (2000) + closing WIP (3000) = 15 000 units

Materials cost per unit = £3.40 (£51 000/15 000)

Equivalent production for conversion costs = 14 000 completed units − opening WIP (2000 × 0.6) + closing WIP (3000 × 0.3) = 13 700 units

Cost per unit = £14.10 (£193 170/13 700)

Closing stock = (3000 × £3.40) + (900 × £14.10) = £22 890

Answer = **D**

5.19 (a) Closing WIP = 160 units (200 + 1000 − 1040)

WIP value = £1280 (160 × 0.40 × £20)

Answer = **B**

(b) Completed production equivalent units = 960 [1040 − (0.4 × 200)]

Cost of completed production = (960 × £20) + £1530 opening WIP = £20 730

Answer = **C**

5.20 The normal loss is 180 units (10 per cent of 1800 units) and the actual loss is 180 units. Therefore there are no abnormal losses in process. It is assumed that the sale proceeds from the normal loss relates primarily to the materials input. Hence the sales proceeds are deducted from materials in the unit cost calculation. Assuming that losses occur prior to the WIP stage of completion it is appropriate to use the short cut method to compute the unit costs. The calculations are as follows:

Cost element	Total cost (£)	Completed units	WIP equiv. units	Total equiv. units	Cost per unit (£)
Materials	484 000[a]	1920	500	2420	200
Labour	322 320[b]	1920	450	2370	136
Overheads	156 880[b]	1920	200	2120	74
					410

Notes:

[a]Opening WIP plus current cost less sales value of normal loss
[b]Opening WIP plus current cost

Cost of completed production = 1920 units × £410 = £787 200

5.21

Process 1 account

	(kg)	(£)		(kg)	(£)
Material	3000	750	Normal loss (20%)	600	120
Labour		120	Transfer to process 2	2300	1150
Process plant time		240	Abnormal loss	100	50
General overhead (120/£204 × £357)		210			
	3000	1320		3000	1320

$$\text{cost per unit} = \frac{\text{cost of production less scrap value of normal loss}}{\text{expected output}}$$

$$= \frac{£1320 − £120}{2400\text{kg}} = £0.50$$

Process 2 account

	(kg)	(£)		(kg)	(£)
Previous process cost	2300	1150	Normal loss	430	129
Materials	2000	800	Transfer to finished stock	4000	2400
Labour		84			
General overhead (£84/£204 × £357)		147			
Process plant time		270			
		2451			
Abnormal gain (130kg at £0.60)	130	78			
	4430	2529		4430	2529

$$\text{cost per unit} = \frac{£2451 − £129}{3870\text{kg}} = £0.60$$

Finished stock account

(£)

Process 2	2400

Normal loss account (income due)

	(£)		(£)
Process 1 normal loss	120	Abnormal gain account	39
Process 2 normal loss	129	Balance or cash received	230
Abnormal loss account	20		
	269		269

Abnormal loss account

	(£)		(£)
Process 1	50	Normal loss account	
		(100 × £0.20)	20
		Profit and loss account	30
	50		50

Abnormal gain account

	(£)		(£)
Normal loss account		Process 2	78
(Loss of income			
130 × £0.30)	39		
Profit and loss account	39		
	78		78

5.22 (a)

Fully complete production = Input (36000) − Closing WIP (8000)
= 280000kg
Normal loss = 2800 (10% × 28000kg)
Abnormal loss = 800 (Actual loss (3600) − 2800)
Good output = 24400 − (28000 − 3600)

(b) The short-cut method described in Chapter 5 is used to compute the unit costs. This method allocates the normal loss between completed units, WIP and the abnormal loss. Because the units actually lost are fully complete it is likely that losses are detected on completion. Therefore the short-cut method is not theoretically correct. Nevertheless the computations suggest that it was the examiner's intention that the question should be answered using the short-cut method. The revised answer is as follows:

	(£)	Completed units	Abnormal loss	WIP	Total equiv. unit	Cost per units (£)	WIP (£)
Previous process cost	166000	24400	800	8000	33200	5.00	40000
Conversion cost	73000	24400	800	4000	29200	2.50	10000
	239000					7.50	50000
Completed units (24400 × £7.50)							183000
Abnormal loss (800 × £7.50)							6000
							239000

Distillation process account

	(kg)	(£)		(kg)	(£)
Input from mixing	36000	166000	Finished goods	24400	183000
Labour		43800	Abnormal loss	800	6000
Overheads		29200	Normal loss	2800	—
			Closing WIP	8000	50000
	36000	239000		36000	239000

(c) If the scrapped production had a resale value the resale value would be credited to the process account (thus reducing the cost of the process account). The accounting entries would be as follows:
Dr Cash
Cr Process Account (with sales value of normal loss)
Cr Abnormal Loss Account (with sales value of abnormal loss)

5.23 (a)

Process G Account

	Litres	£		Litres	£
Opening WIP	2000	24600	Output (W4): Ex		
Costs arising:			opening WIP	2000	
Direct			Started and		
materials	12500	99600	finished in month	8000	
Conversion		155250		10000	221520
			Normal loss (0.08 ×		
			12500)	1000	3000
			Abnormal loss (W2)	500	11100
			Closing WIP (W3)	3000	43830
	14500	279450		14500	279450

Workings
W1 Calculation of cost per equivalent unit

Cost element	Current period costs (£)	Completed units less opening WIP equiv. units	Closing WIP equiv. units	Abnormal loss equiv. units[2]	Current total equiv. units (£)	Cost per unit (£)
Materials	96600[1]	8000	3000	500	11500	8.40
Conversion cost	155250	9400	1350	500	11250	13.80

[1]£99600 current period cost − scrap value of normal loss (12500 × 0.08 × £3)
[2]Input = Opening WIP (2000 litres) + Material input (12500) = 14500

Output = Completed units (10000) + Closing WIP (3000) + Normal Loss (1000) = 14000
Abnormal Loss = 500 units (Balance of 14500 − 14000)
W2 Value of abnormal loss = 500 × (£8.40 + £13.80) = £11100
W3 Value of closing stock = (3000 × £8.40) + (1350 × £13.80) = £43830
W4 Value of completed production = (8000 × £8.40) + (9400 × £13.80) + Opening WIP (£24600) = £221520

(b) Organizations where it would be appropriate to use service costing include hospitals and hotels. Typical cost units include inpatient days and occupied rooms per night.

CHAPTER 6

6.10 Joint costs apportioned to H: ((330000/(420000 + 330000)) × $350000 = $154000
Closing inventory valuation (HH): (30000/330000) × (154000 + 66000) = $20000

Answer = **(c)**

6.11 Cost apportioned to product A ($12000 × 600/1000 = $7200)
Cost of sales for the period 480/600 × $720) = $5760
Sales for the period = $5760/0.6 = $9600
Gross profit earned = $9600 × 40% = $3840

Answer = **(c)**

6.12 Production = units sold + closing stock − opening stock
J = 6000 + 300 − 100 = 6200
K = 4000 + 200 − 400 = 3800
Apportioned to J = (6200/10 000) × £110 000 = £68 200

Answer = **(d)**

6.13 Sales value of production:
W = $120 000 (12 000 × $10)
X = $120 000 (10 000 × $12)
Joint costs will therefore be apportioned to each product in the ratio of 1:1 so the amount apportioned to product X will be $388 080 ($776 160/2)
Closing inventory of X = $77 616 (0.2 × $388 080)

Answer = **(d)**

6.14 (a)

Process G

	Litres	£		Litres	£
Raw material	60 000	381 000	Output (W3)		
Direct labour		180 000	P1 (W4)	36 250	507 500
Direct expenses		54 000	P2 (W4)	21 750	304 500
Production			Normal loss		
overheads (W1)		198 000	(W2)	3000	15 000
Abnormal gain					
(W4)	1000	14 000			
	61 000	827 000		61 000	827 000

Workings
W1 Production overheads = 110% × 180 000
= £198 000
W2 Normal loss = 5% × 60 000 = 3000 litres at £5
= £15 000
W3 Total output = 61 000 (input + abnormal gain) − 3000 normal loss = 58 000 litres
P1 and P2 is produced in the ratio 5:3
P1 = (5/8) × 58 000 = 36 250 litres
P2 = (3/8) × 58 000 = 21 750 litres

W4 Cost per litre:
Net total cost = Input cost (381 000 + 180 000 + 54 000 + 198 000) − value of normal loss 15 000 = £798 000
Expected output = 60 000 × 95% = 57 000 litres
Cost per litre = £798 000/57 000 = £14
Abnormal gain = 1000 × £14 = £14 000

Joint products:
P1 36 250 × £14 = £507 500
P2 21 750 × £14 = £304 500

(b) Each 100 litres of product P1 sold at point of split-off without further processing generates revenue of £2000 (100 × £20)
The revenue (from PP1) arising from further processing is £2340 (100 × 0.9) × £26 resulting in additional revenue of £340 but the additional cost of further processing is £400 (100 × £4).
Therefore product P1 should not be further processed into product PP1.

(c) (i) Direct expenses are costs, other than material and labour, which are specifically identifiable with process G. An example of such a cost would be the cost of hiring special equipment that is required only for process G.

(ii) Production overheads are general factory wide costs that cannot be specifically identified with individual processes.

6.15 (a)

Process K account

	Litres	£		Litres	£
Materials			Normal loss		
input	90 000	450 000	(4% × 90 000)	3600	1800
Conversion			Abnormal loss [W1]		
costs		216 000	(4800 − 3600)	1200	9000
			Output:		
			Product P1 [W2]	56 800	355 000
			Product P2 [W2]	28 400	284 000
	90 000	666 000		90 000	666 000

W1 The expected output is 86 400 litres (90 000 × 0.96) and the actual output is 85 200 litres resulting in an abnormal loss of 1200 litres.
Cost per unit of output = Input cost (£666 000 − value of normal loss of £18 000) divided by the expected output of 86 400 litres = £7.50
Abnormal loss valuation = £9000 (1200 × 7.50)
W2 The total output (85 200) is in the ratio 2:1 (P1:P2) giving 56 800 litres of P1 and 28 400 litres of P2
The combined total output of P1 and P2 is valued at £639 000 (85 200 × 7.50) and is allocated to P1 and P2 in the ratio of the sales value of production.
P1:P2 = (56 800 × £25):(28 400 × £40) = 1.25:1
Product P1 valuation = (1.25/2.25) × £639 000
= £355 000
Product P2 valuation = (1.00/2.25) × £639 000
= £284 000

(b) Each 100 litres of product P1 sold at point of split-off without further processing generates revenue of £2500 (100 × £25)
The revenue (from XP1) arising from further processing is £2760 (100 × 0.92) × £30 resulting in additional revenue of £260 but the additional cost of further processing is £300 (100 × £3).
Therefore product P1 should not be further processed into product XP1.

6.16 (a)

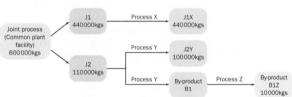

(b) (i) *Physical units allocation basis*

	Total (£000)	Product J1X Cost per unit[b]	Product J2Y Total (£000)	Cost per unit[b]
Joint costs[a]	440	1.100	110	1.100
Further processing costs	410	1.025	135	1.350
By-product net revenues		0.000	(5)	(0.050)
Total cost	850	2.125	240	2.400
Sales	970	2.425	450	4.500
Manufacturing profit	120	0.300	210	2.100

Notes
[a]Apportioned 440 000: 110 000kg
[b]Divided by 400 000kg for J1X and 100 000kg for J2Y

(ii) *Net realizable value allocation basis*

	Total (£000)	Product J1X Cost per unit[a]	Product J2Y Total (£000)	Cost per unit[b]
Joint costs	350	0.875	200	2.000
Further processing costs	410	1.025	135	1.350
By-product net revenues	___	0.000	(5)	(0.050)
Total cost	760	1.900	330	3.300
Sales	970	2.425	450	4.500
Manufacturing profit	210	0.525	120	1.200

Notes

[a]Divided by 400 000kg for J1X and 100 000kg for J2Y

[b]Net realizable values are calculated as follows:

Product J1X: Sales (£970 000) − Further processing costs (£410 000) = £560 000.

Product J2Y: Sales (£450 000) + By-product net revenue (£5 000) − Further processing costs (£135 000) = £320 000. Joint costs are therefore apportioned in the ratio of £560 000: £320 000.

For comments on the above two methods of joint cost allocations see 'methods of allocating joint costs' in Chapter 6.

(c) (i) The answer requires a comparison of the incremental revenues with the incremental costs of further processing. It is assumed that direct materials, direct labour and variable overheads are incremental costs. Note that the order represents 10 per cent of the current volume of J2Y. The extra costs of 10 000kg of J2Y are as follows:

10% of common facility variable costs		50 000
10% of finishing process (Y)		13 000
		63 000
Net revenue from J2Y:		
Sales (10 000kg at £4)	40 000	
Net revenue from sale of 1 000kg of by-product B1Z (£1500 − (10% × £7000))	800	40 800
Shortfall		22 200

It would appear that by itself the order is not justifiable because there is a £22 000 shortfall. By itself a minimum selling price of £6.22 (£4 + £22 200/10 000kg) is required to break-even. However, production of 10 000kg of J2Y will result in an extra output of 40 000kg of J1. To convert J1 into J1X, incremental further processing costs of £38 500 (10 per cent of J1X current incremental costs of £338 500) will be incurred. For the offer to be justifiable the extra output of J1X must generate sales revenue in excess of £60 700 (£38 500 incremental costs plus £22 200 shortfall from the order). This represents a minimum selling price of approximately £1.51 per kg (£60 700/40 000kg) compared with the current market price of £2.425.

(ii) The following should be included in the answer:

(i) Does the company have sufficient capacity to cope with the 10 per cent increase in output? If not the opportunity cost of the lost output should be incorporated in the above analysis.

(ii) Are any of the fixed overheads incremental costs?

(iii) Direct labour is assumed to be an incremental cost. Is this correct or can the existing labour force cope with the extra output from the order?

(iv) What are the long-run implications? At the present selling price the order should be viewed as a one time special short-term order. For a more detailed discussion of the issues involved here you should refer to 'special pricing decisions' in Chapter 9.

CHAPTER 7

7.13 There was no opening inventory and closing inventory was 1000 units. Therefore fixed overheads of $10 000 (1000 units × $10) will be included in the closing inventory valuation with an absorption costing system compared with fixed overheads being a period cost with a marginal costing system. Therefore profit will be $10 000 less with a marginal costing system.

Answer = **(c)**

7.14 Standard absorption costing will include $96 000 of the period's overhead (2000 units × 4 labour hours × $12 per hour) in the closing inventory valuation. Under standard marginal costing the $96 000 would be charged against the period's profit resulting in profit being reduced by $96 000 to $368 000.

Answer = **(a)**

7.15 In month 1 production exceeds sales so absorption costing profit will exceed marginal costing profit. In month 2 sales exceed so production marginal costing profit will exceed absorption costing profit
A and C satisfy month 1, C and D satisfy month 2.
Therefore **C** satisfies both

7.16 (i)

	January $000	February $000
Opening stock		15.4
Add production cost ($77 per unit)	770.0	885.5
Less closing stock ($77 per unit)	15.4	38.5
	754.6	862.4
Under-/(over-) recovery of fixed overheads (W1)	30.00	(28.0)
	784.6	834.4
Sales ($135/$140 per unit)	1323.0	1568.0
Profit	538.4	733.6

Workings:
W1 January under absorption of fixed overhead (10 000 units × $32) − $350 000 = $30 000
February over absorption of fixed overhead (11 500 units × $32) − $340 000 = $28 000

(ii) Profit using absorption costing $538.40k
Profit using marginal costing $532.00k
Difference $ 6.40k
Increase in inventory in January = 200 units
Absorbed fixed overheads included in inventory under absorption costing:
200 units × $32 = $6400

7.17 (a) Fixed overheads per unit = $15000/10000 units = $1.50
Production exceeds sales so that absorption costing
will be greater than the marginal costing profit by the
amount of fixed overheads included in the increase in
inventories. Therefore the absorption profit will exceed
the marginal costing profit by $750 (500 units × $1.50).

Answer = **(iii)**

(b)

	$	$
Sales (10 300 × $6.40)		65 920
Cost of sales:		
Variable costs (10 300 × $3.60)	37 080	
Fixed overheads (10 300 × $1.50)	15 450	
	52 530	
Under-absorbed fixed overheads		
($15 700 − $15 000)	700	53 230
Profit		12 690

Answer = **(ii)**

7.18

	(£)
Calculation of product cost	
Materials	10
Labour	2
Variable production cost	12
Variable distribution cost	1
Total variable cost	13
Fixed overhead (£10 000/1000 units)	10
Total costs	23

The product costs for stock valuation purposes are as follows:
Variable costing   £12 (variable production cost)
Absorption costing   £22 (variable production cost +
                        fixed manufacturing overhead)
It is assumed that all of the fixed overhead relates to
production. Note that the distribution cost is per unit *sold*
and not per unit *produced*.

(a) (i)   *Variable costing*

	t_1	t_2	t_3
Opening stock	1 200	1 200	1 200
Production	12 000	12 000	12 000
	13 200	13 200	13 200
Closing stock	1 200	1 200	1 200
Cost of sales	12 000	12 000	12 000
Sales at £25 per unit	25 000	25 000	25 000
Gross profit	13 000	13 000	13 000
Distribution costs	1 000	1 000	1 000
Fixed labour costs	5 000	5 000	5 000
Fixed overhead costs	5 000	5 000	5 000
Net profit	£2 000	£2 000	£2 000
Total profit £6 000			

Absorption costing

	t_1 (£)	t_2 (£)	t_3 (£)
Opening stock	2 200	2 200	2 200
Production	22 000	22 000	22 000
	24 200	24 200	24 200
Closing stock	2 200	2 200	2 200
Cost of sales	22 000	22 000	22 000
Sales at £25 per unit	25 000	25 000	25 000
Gross profit	3 000	3 000	3 000
Distribution cost	1 000	1 000	1 000
Net profit	£2 000	£2 000	£2 000
Total profit £6 000			

(ii)   *Variable costing*

	t_1 (£)	t_2 (£)	t_3 (£)
Opening stock	1 200	7 200	4 800
Production	18 000	9 600	8 400
	19 200	16 800	13 200
Closing stock	7 200	4 800	1 200
Cost of sales	12 000	12 000	12 000
Sales at £25 per unit	25 000	25 000	25 000
Gross profit	13 000	13 000	13 000
Distribution costs	1 000	1 000	1 000
Fixed labour costs	5 000	5 000	5 000
Fixed overhead costs	5 000	5 000	5 000
Net profit	£2 000	£2 000	£2 000
Total profit £6 000			

Absorption costing

	t_1 (£)	t_2 (£)	t_3 (£)
Opening stock	2 200	13 200	8 800
Production	33 000	17 600	15 400
	35 200	30 800	24 200
Under-/(over) recovery	(5 000)	2 000	3 000
	30 200	32 800	27 200
Closing stock	13 200	8 800	2 200
Cost of sales	17 000	24 000	25 000
Sales at £25 per unit	25 000	25 000	25 000
Gross profit	8 000	1 000	—
Distribution cost	1 000	1 000	1 000
Net profit	£7 000	—	£(1 000)
Total profit £6 000			

(iii)   *Variable costing*

	t_1 (£)	t_2 (£)	t_3 (£)
Opening stock	1 200	7 200	4 800
Production	12 000	12 000	12 000
	13 200	19 200	16 800
Closing stock	7 200	4 800	1 200
Cost of sales	6 000	14 400	15 600
Sales at £25 per unit	12 500	30 000	32 500
Gross profit	6 500	15 600	16 900
Distribution costs	500	1 200	1 300
Fixed labour costs	5 000	5 000	5 000
Fixed overhead costs	5 000	5 000	5 000
Net profit	£(4 000)	£4 400	£5 600
Total profit £6 000			

Absorption costing

	t_1 (£)	t_2 (£)	t_3 (£)
Opening stock	2 200	13 200	8 800
Production	22 000	22 000	22 000
	24 200	35 200	30 800
Closing stock	13 200	8 800	2 200
Cost of sales	11 000	26 400	28 600
Sales at £25 per unit	12 500	30 000	32 500
Gross profit	1 500	3 600	3 900
Distribution cost	500	1 200	1 300
Net profit	£1 000	£2 400	£2 600
Total profit £6 000			

(b) For the answer to this question see Chapter 7: Note that profits are identical for both systems in (i), since production equals sales. In (ii) and (iii) profits are higher with absorption costing when production exceeds sales, whereas profits are higher with variable costing when production is less than sales. Taking the three periods as a whole there is no change in the level of opening stock in t_1 compared with the closing stock in t_3, so that the disclosed profit for the three periods is the same under both systems. Also note that the differences in profits disclosed in (a) (ii) and (a) (iii) is accounted for in the fixed overheads included in the stock valuation changes.

CHAPTER 8

8.11 Contribution/sales (%) = (0.33 × 40% Aye) + (0.33 × 50% Bee) + (0.33 × ? Cee) = 48%
Cee = 54% (Balancing figure)
The total contribution/sales ratio for the revised sales mix is: (0.40 × 40% Aye) + (0.25 × 50% Bee) + (0.35 × 54% Cee) = 47.4%

Answer = **(c)**

8.12 At the break-even point, contribution is equal to fixed costs so the contribution to sales ratio is 40 per cent ($320 000/$800 000)
To earn a profit of $200 000 the required contribution is equal to the fixed costs plus the required profit ($320 000 + $200 000)/0.40 = $1 300 000

Answer = **(b)**

8.13 Weighted average contribution/sales ratio =

$$\frac{(30\% \times 2 + (20\% \times 5) + (25\% \times 3)}{10} = 23.5\%$$

Break-even sales = Fixed costs (£100 000)/contribution to sales ratio
= £425 532

Answer = **(c)**

8.14 (i) Contribution per unit = $24.00 − $8.60 − $1.20 = $14.20
Break-even point = $880 400/$14.20 = 62 000 units

(ii) Margin of safety = (90 000 − 62 000) / 90 000 = 31.1%

(iii) Revised contribution per unit = $25.00 − $8.60 − $2.00 = $14.40
Break-even point = $890 400/$14.40 = 61 833 units

8.15 (i) p = total sales revenue
q = total cost (fixed cost + variable cost)
r = total variable cost
s = fixed costs at the specific level of activity
t = total loss at the specific level of activity
u = total profit at that level of activity
v = total contribution at the specific level of activity
w = total contribution at a lower level of activity
x = level of activity of output sales
y = monetary value of cost and revenue function for level of activity

(ii) At event m the selling price per *unit* decreases, but it remains constant. Note that p is a straight line, but with a lower gradient above m compared with below m.

At event n there is an increase in fixed costs equal to the dotted line. This is probably due to an increase in capital expenditure in order to expand output beyond this point. Also note that at this point the variable cost per unit declines as reflected by the gradient of the variable cost line. This might be due to more efficient production methods associated with increased investment in capital equipment.

(iii) Break-even analysis is of limited use in a multi-product company, but the analysis can be a useful aid to the management of a small single product company. The following are some of the main benefits:

(a) Break-even analysis forces management to consider the functional relationship between costs, revenue and activity, and gives an insight into how costs and revenue change with changes in the level of activity.

(b) Break-even analysis forces management to consider the fixed costs at various levels of activity and the selling price that will be required to achieve various levels of output.

You should refer to Chapter 8 for a discussion of more specific issues of break-even analysis. Break-even analysis can be a useful tool, but it is subject to a number of assumptions that restrict its usefulness (see, especially, 'Cost–volume–profit analysis assumptions').

8.16 *Preliminary calculations:*

	Sales (units)	Profit/(loss)
November	30 000	£40 000
December	35 000	£60 000
Increase	5 000	£20 000

An increase in sales of 5 000 units increases contribution (profits) by £20 000. Therefore contribution is £4 per unit. Selling price is £10 per unit (given) and variable cost per unit will be £6.

At £30 000 unit sales:

Contribution	minus	Fixed costs	= Profit
£120 000	minus	?	= £40 000
∴ Fixed costs = £80 000			

The above information can now be plotted on a graph. A break-even chart or a profit–volume graph could be constructed.

A profit–volume graph avoids the need to calculate the profits since the information can be read directly from the graph. (See Figure 1 for a break-even chart and Figure 2 for a profit–volume graph.)

(a) (i) Fixed costs = £80000.

(ii) Variable cost per unit = £6.

(iii) Profit–volume =

$$\frac{\text{Contribution per unit (£4)}}{\text{Selling price per unit (£10)}} \times 100 = 40\%$$

(iv) Break-even point = 20000 units.

(v) The margin of safety represents the difference between actual or expected sales volume and the break-even point. Therefore the margin of safety will be different for each month's sales. For example, the margin of safety in November is 10000 units (30000 units – 20000 units). The margin of safety can be read from Figure 2 for various sales levels.

(b) and (c) See the sections on 'the accountants' cost–volume–profit model' and 'cost–volume–profit analysis assumptions' in Chapter 8 for the answers.

8.17 (a)

	August (£)	September (£)	Change (£)
Sales	80000	90000	10000
Cost of sales	50000	55000	5000
Selling and distribution	8000	9000	1000
Administration	15000	15000	Nil

The only activity measure that is given is sales revenue. An increase in sales of £10000 results in an increase in cost of sales of £5000 and an increase in selling and distribution costs of £1000. It is therefore assumed that the increase is attributable to variable costs and variable cost of sales is 50 per cent of sales and variable selling and distribution costs are 10 per cent of sales.

Fixed costs are derived by deducting variable costs from total costs for either month. The figures for August are used in the calculations below:

	Total cost (£)	Variable cost (£)	Fixed cost (Balance) (£)
Cost of sales	50000	40000	10000
Selling and distribution	8000	8000	Nil
Administration	15000	Nil	15000
			25000

Total cost = £25000 fixed costs + variable costs (60 per cent of sales)

(b) The following items are plotted on the graph (Figure 3):

	Variable cost	Total cost
Zero sales	Nil	£25000 fixed cost
£80000 sales	£48000 (60%)	£73000
£90000 sales	£54000 (60%)	£79000
£50000 sales	£30000 (60%)	£55000
£100000 sales	£60000	£85000

Break-even point

$$= \frac{\text{Fixed costs (£25000)}}{\text{Contribution to sales ratio (0.40)}} = £62500 \text{ sales}$$

Area of contribution = Area AOB

FIGURE 1
Break-even chart

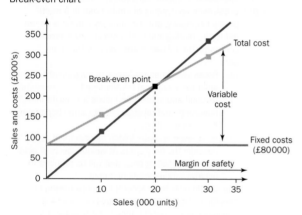

FIGURE 2
Profit–volume graph

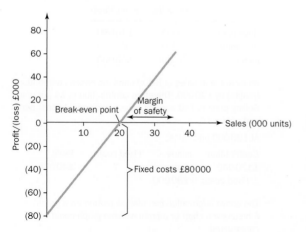

FIGURE 3
Contribution break-even graph

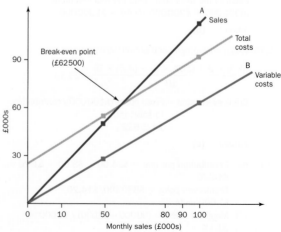

(c)

	(£)
Actual sales = 1.3 × Break-even sales (£62 500)	= 81 250
Contribution (40% of sales)	= 32 500
Fixed costs	= 25 000
Monthly profit	= 7 500
Annual profit	= 90 000

(d)

	(£)
Annual contribution from single outlet (£32 500 × 12)	= 390 000
Contribution to cover lost sales (10%)	= 39 000
Specific fixed costs	= 100 000
Total contribution required	529 000

Required sales = £529 000/0.4 = £1 322 500

(e) The answer should draw attention to the need for establishing a sound system of budgeting and performance reporting for each of the different outlets working in close conjunction with central office. The budgets should be merged together to establish a master budget for the whole company.

8.18 (a) Let x = number of units of output
Total cost for 30 000 units or less = £50 000 + 5x
(where 5 = variable cost per unit)
Total cost for more than 30 000 units = £100 000 + 5x

(b)

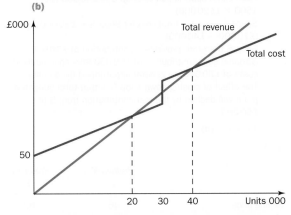

(c) There are two break-even points resulting in the production plan being profitable only between 20 000 and 30 000 units and above 40 000 units. The production plan should be set based on these considerations.

8.19 (a)

	T	C	R	Total
Unit selling price ($)	1 600	1 800	1 400	
Unit variable cost ($)	628	716	531	
Unit contribution ($)	972	1 084	869	
Sales volume	420	400	380	
Total contribution ($)	408 240	433 600	330 220	1 172 060
Total sales ($)	672 000	720 000	532 000	1 924 000

Note
The unit variable cost includes 40 per cent of the direct labour cost

Weighted average contribution/sales ratio =
$1 172 060/$1 924 000 = 60.92%.

(b) Fixed labour costs = [(420 × $220) + (400 × $240) + (380 × $190)] × 0.6 = $156 360
Total fixed costs = $156 360 + $55 000 = $211 360.

Breakeven sales revenue = fixed costs/weighted average contribution/sales ratio
= $211 360/60.92% = $346 947
Margin of safety = Budgeted sales revenue ($1 924 000) – breakeven sales revenue ($346 947)
= $1 577 053.

(c) Total variable cost = (420 × $628) + (400 × $716) + (380 × $531) = $751 940
Total cost = $751 940 variable cost + $211 360 fixed costs = $963 300
Total sales revenue $1 924 000
The above total figures are plotted on the graph below for a sales volume of 100 units

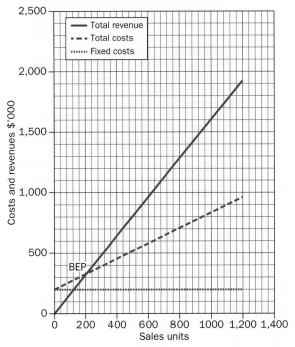

(d) If the more profitable products are sold first the company will cover its fixed costs more quickly resulting in the breakeven point being lower. This is because a lower sales volume will be required to cover fixed costs and break even.

8.20 (a) BEP = $\dfrac{400\,000 \text{ (fixed costs)} \times £1\,000\,000 \text{ (sales)}}{£420\,000 \text{ (contribution)}}$

= 952 380

(b) (i)

	(£)	(£)
Revised selling price		9.00
Less variable costs:		
Direct materials	1.00	
Direct labour	3.50	
Variable overhead	0.60	
Delivery expenses	0.50	
Sales commission (2% of selling price)	0.18	5.78
Contribution per unit		3.22
Number of units sold		140 000
Total contribution (140 000 × 3.22)		450 800
Fixed costs		400 000
Profit from proposal (i)		50 800

(ii)

Desired contribution	= 480 000
Contribution per unit for present proposal	= 3.22
Required units to earn large profit	= 149 068

(c) (i) The variable cost of selling to the mail order firm is:

	(£)
Direct material	1.00
Direct labour	3.50
Variable overhead	0.60
Delivery expenses	nil
Sales commission	nil
Additional package cost	0.50
	5.60

To break even, a contribution of £1.20 is required (60 000 fixed cost/50 000 units sold). Therefore selling price to break even is £6.80 (£5.60 + £1.20).

(ii) To earn £50 800 profit, a contribution of £110 800 (£60 000 + £50 800) is required. That is, a contribution of £2.22 per unit is required. Therefore required selling price is £7.82 (£5.60 + £2.22).

(iii) To earn the target profit of £80 000, a contribution of £140 000 is required. That is, £2.80 per unit. Therefore required selling price = £8.40 (£5.60 + £2.80).

(d) Contribution per unit is £3.22 per (B)

Unit sold	160 000
Total contribution	£515 200
Fixed costs	£430 000
Profit	£85 200

CHAPTER 9

9.15

Product	A	B	C	D
Selling price per unit	$160	$214	$100	$140
Raw material cost	$24	$56	$22	$40
Direct labour cost at $11 per hour	$66	$88	$33	$22
Variable overhead cost	$24	$18	$24	$18
Contribution per unit	$46	$52	$21	$60
Direct labour hours per unit	6	8	3	2
Contribution per labour hour	$7.67	$6.50	$7	$30
Rank	2	4	3	1
Normal monthly hours (total units × hours per unit)	1800	1000	720	800

If the strike goes ahead only 2160 labour hours will be available so the company should make all of D, then allocate the remaining 1360 hours to A (2160 − 800 hrs).

Answer = **A**

9.16 The 400 labour hours unused capacity has zero relevant cost. The remaining 100 hours can be obtained from diverting production from product X. The relevant cost of this alternative consists of the labour cost (100 hours × £12) plus the lost contribution from the use of these labour hours (100/2 × £4 = £200), giving a total of

£1 400 (see 'determining the relevant costs of direct labour' in Chapter 9 for an explanation of this point). In other words, the relevant cost is the lost contribution before deducting unavoidable labour costs. The other alternative is to work overtime resulting in an additional (relevant) cost of £1 800 (100 hours at £18 per hour). Therefore it is cheaper to divert labour hours from the production of product X.

Therefore answer = **(c)**

9.17 The original purchase price is a sunk cost and therefore not a relevant cost. The relevant cost of the materials in stock is $1 000 (100 reams at $10 net realizable value). An additional 150 reams must be purchased for $3 900 (150 × $26) resulting in a relevant cost of $4 900.

Answer = **(b)**

9.18 The relevant cost of the skilled labour is the hourly wage rate of £8 per hour plus the lost contribution of £10 per hour (£25/2.5 hours) giving £18 per hour. The labour hours required to produce one unit of output is derived from dividing the labour cost (£25) by the hourly wage rate. The total relevant cost of labour is £1 620 (90 hours × £18).

Answer = **(c)**

9.19 Apportioned fixed costs = £120 000 (0.6 × £200 000)
Fixed costs apportioned to Shop S = £40 000 (500/1500 × £120 000)
Specific avoidable fixed cost for Shop S = £30 000 (£70 000 − £40 000)
Shop S therefore provides a contribution of £30 000 (variable cost contribution of £60 000 less specific fixed costs of £30 000) to general apportioned fixed costs. The effect of closing down shop S is that total budgeted profit will decline by the lost contribution from S to £50 000.

Answer = **(a)**

9.20 (i)

	Product A $	Product B $
Selling price	46	62
Material cost	(18)	(16)
Throughput contribution	28	46
Machine hours per unit	0.5 hours	0.8 hours
Return per machine hour	56	57.50

(ii)

	Product A	Product B	Total
Return per machine hour	$56	$57.50	
Ranking	2	1	
Units produced	3200	8000	
Machine hours	1600	6400	8000
Contribution per machine hour	$56	$57.5	
Total contribution	$89 600	$368 000	$457 600
Factory costs			$248 000
Total profit			$209 600

9.21 (a) The relevant costs of the order are as follows:

	$
Lunch[1]	0
Engineers' costs[2]	500
Technical advisor[3]	480
Site visits[4]	0
Training costs[5]	125
Handsets[6]	2184
Control system[7]	7600
Cable[8]	1300
Total relevant cost	12189

Notes

[1] This is a sunk cost and is therefore not relevant to the decision.

[2] One of the engineers has spare capacity so there will be no additional cost in undertaking the contract. Undertaking the contract will result in Contract X being delayed by one week so that T's costs will increase by $500.

[3] The overtime costs represent the additional costs that will be incurred if the contract is undertaken ($60 × 8 hours).

[4] This cost will be paid by the customer so no additional site visit costs will be incurred by T Co.

[5] The monthly salary cost is irrelevant since it will be paid whether or not the contract is undertaken. However, the commission of $125 is an incremental cost associated with the contract.

[6] The handsets are in regular use and undertaking the contract will necessitate replacement of 80 handsets at $18.20 each. The remaining 40 handsets will be purchased at £18.20 so the relevant cost is $2184 (120 × $18.20).

[7] The original cost of the Swipe 1 is a sunk cost and not relevant. However, since the company could sell it for $3000 if it did not use it for this contact. It represents an opportunity cost. The current market price of Swipe 1 is not relevant since the company does not intend to replace it. In order to use Swipe 1 on the contract, it must be converted at a cost of $4600. The relevant cost is $7600 since this is less than the cost of a new Swipe 2 ($10800).

[8] The cost of the inventory represents a sunk cost and is not relevant. The replacement cost of $1.30 per metre is the relevant cost.

(b) You should refer to 'Identifying relevant costs and revenues', 'Determining the relevant costs of direct labour and materials' and 'Opportunity costs' in Chapter 9 for discussing the principles used in part (a). The explanation of the implications of the minimum price should point out that the relevant cost represents the minimum price and starting point for determining a price. It represents a price at which T Co. will be no better or worse off if it did not carry out the work. The answer should also point out that prices based on covering relevant costs represent short-run prices but that the final agreed price should be attractive enough to encourage repeat orders. For additional points you should refer to the four factors referred to in 'Special pricing decisions' in Chapter 9 and 'A price-setting firm facing short-run pricing decisions' in Chapter 10.

9.22 (a) The relevant costs are as follows:

	Keypads $	Display screens $
Direct materials[1]	164000	118320
Direct labour	40000	60000
Heat and power avoidable costs[2]	44000	58000
Machine avoidable fixed costs[3]	4000	6000
Machine variable batch set-up costs[3]	27500	30000
Avoidable depreciation and insurance costs[4]	33600	38400
Total relevant cost	313100	310720
Cost of buying in[5]	328000	344000

The above figures indicate it is cheaper to manufacture the components.

Notes

[1] Keypads = $80000 + ($80000 × 1.05) Display screens = $116000 × 1.02

[2] Keypads = $64000 – $20000 Display screens = $88000 – $30000

[3] Fixed costs are assumed to be avoidable:
Current number of batches: = 160 for both components (80000/500)
Current cost per batch: Keypads = $22000/160 = $137.50 Display screens = $24000/160 = $150
New number of batches = 200 for both components (80000/400)
New batch-related costs: Keypads = 200 × $137.50 Display screens = 200 × $150

[4] It is assumed that 40 percent of depreciation and insurance costs are avoidable that assets depreciate according to units of output.

[5] Keypads = 80000 × $4.10 Display screens = 80000 × $4.30

(b) Both products are cheaper to produce internally. Producing the maximum demand of either product will not utilize all of the available labour hours so both products will be produced internally. Therefore avoidable fixed costs will be incurred irrespective of the decision and only variable costs will be relevant for determining the allocation of the output.

	Keypads $	Display screens $
Buy	4.1	4.3
Variable cost of making ($231500/ 80000) ($208320/80000)	2.89	2.6
Saving from making per unit	1.21	1.7
Labour hour per unit	0.5	0.75
Saving from making per unit of limiting factor	2.42	2.27
Ranking	1	2

Since keypads produce the larger saving per scarce factor (labour hours), the maximum supply of keypads should be produced internally. The production of 100000 keypads requires 50000 labour hours resulting in the remaining 50000 hours being allocated to the production of 66666 display screens (50000 hours/0.75 hours per unit). Therefore 33334 display screens (100000 − 66666) should be purchased.

(c) The following non-financial factors should be considered:

- The reliability of the supplier. The supplier is a new company and may not be able to meet demand. Outsourcing is high risk since the failure rate of new companies is high. The company needs to ascertain if there is a competitive market with alternative suppliers to ensure that it is not totally reliant on the supplier.

- The contracted price is for 2 years and after this the supplier may significantly increase prices if the manufacturer no longer has the facilities to produce internally. Again it is necessary to ensure that there is a competitive market for the supply of the components.

- The quality of the components provided by the supplier. Poor quality of components may lead to a future loss of sales or increased warranty costs.

- Reliability in meeting promised delivery dates. Late deliveries may result in lost sales of the final products arising from customers migrating to competitors.

9.23 (a)

	S	T	B	Total	Available
Material m² per unit	5	0.5	1.5		
Labour hours per unit	3	1	2.25		
Demand – budget and order (units)	3000	7000	5000		
Material m² required	15000	3500	7500	26000	14500
Labour hours required	9000	7000	11250	27250	30000

Production is constrained by material availability

	S	T	B
	$	$	$
Selling price	250	40	100
Direct materials ($X per m²)	100	10	30
Direct labour ($X per hour)	36	12	27
Variable overhead ($3 per machine hour)	9	3	6.75
Contribution per unit	105	15	36.25
Material m² per unit	5	0.5	1.5
Contribution per material m²	21	30	24.17
Rank	3rd	1st	2nd

The following is the allocation of the scarce materials based on meeting the new customer's order:

	S	T	B	Total
New customer order (units)	1000	1000	1000	
Material required m²	5000	500	1500	7000
Production (units)	0	6000	3000	
Material required m²	0	3000	4500	7500
Production plan (units)	1000	7000	4000	

Note that after meeting the demand for the new customer 6000 units of T will be produced requiring 3000m² and the remaining 4500m² will be allocated to producing 3000 units of B. The profit calculations are derived from deducting total fixed costs from the total product contributions as follows:

S(1000 × $105) + T(7000 × $15) + B(4000 × $36.25) − Fixed cost of $300 000 = $55 000

(b) The optimal production plan will result in the demand for product S, apart from the new customer, not being met. If these customers also buy the other products they may go elsewhere if the company does not offer a full product range. Also the optimal plan is based on the assumptions that were budgeted at the start of the year. This may not consider the latest external demand as a result of the feature in the fashion magazine. The potential change in the market is not therefore considered.

(c) (i)

	S	T	B
	$	$	$
Production (units)	4000	5000	4000
Revenue	1000000	200000	400000
Contribution	420000	75000	145000
Total contribution			640000
Total revenue			1600000
Weighted average C/S ratio			40%
Fixed costs			300000
Breakeven revenue			750000

The break-even sales revenue is derived by dividing the fixed costs of $750000 by the contribution/sales ratio of 40%.

(c) (ii)

$$\text{Margin of safety} = \frac{\text{Budgeted sales revenue ($1600000) − break-even revenue ($750000)}}{\text{Budgeted sales revenue ($1600000)}} = 53\%$$

(iii) See 'cost–volume–profit assumptions' in Chapter 8 for the answer to this question. In particular, the constant sales mix assumption should be explained.

9.24 (a) *Resource requirements*

	Direct labour (hours)	Direct materials (kg)
P1 (500 units)	1250	100
P2 (400 units)	600	160
P3 (600 units)	1800	240
C1 (250 units)	250	25
C2 (150 units)	225	30
Total	4125	555
Available	4300	420

Direct materials are the scarce resource so the optimal output should be determined based on the contribution per kg of materials.

	P1 $ per unit	P2 $ per unit	P3 $ per unit	C1 $ per unit	C2 $ per unit
Selling price	155	125	175	50	80
Direct labour at $10 per hour	25	15	30	10	15
Direct materials at $50 per kg	10	20	20	5	10
Variable o'head at $40 per m/c hour	10	15	20	10	20
Contribution	110	75	105	25	35
Direct materials per unit (kg)	0.2	0.4	0.4	0.1	0.2
Contrib. per kg of direct materials	550	187.5	262.5	250	175
Ranking	1	4	2	3	5
Units sold	500	137	600	250	1
Direct materials usage	100	54.8	240	25	0.2

To satisfy the above optimal production (excluding C2) 419.8kg of materials are required and since P2 requires 0.4kg, it is not possible to produce the 138th unit. However, the unused materials (0.2kg) can be used to produce 1 unit of C2.

(b) The shadow price (see Chapter 26) represents the additional contribution gained from obtaining one more unit of a scarce resource or the contribution lost from the loss of one unit of the resource. If one additional kg in excess of current restriction of 420kg can be obtained it will be allocated to the production of P2 and yield a contribution of $187.5 (see schedule in (a) above).

Therefore the shadow price is $187.5 but when demand of P2 is increased to its maximum of 400 units an extra 105.2kg [(400 − 137) × 0.4] will be required. Once these additional materials have been acquired additional kg will be used to sell C2. Each additional kg of materials will yield a contribution of $175. This is the shadow price when more than 505.2kg of materials are available.

The question also refers to a shadow price of $200. This applies when only an additional 0.2kg of materials are available (i.e. material requirements can be increased from 420kg to 420.2kg). Instead of allocating the unused 0.2kg to C2 the unused materials plus the extra 0.2kg purchased would provide 0.4kg of materials to enable one unit of P2 to be produced yielding a contribution of $75 but this will be at the expense of reducing C2 by one unit resulting in a lost contribution of $35. This substitution process will increase contribution by $40 for 0.2kg of materials so the shadow price for 1kg of materials is $200 (1kg/0.2kg × $40) based on this substitution process.

(c) The contribution from one batch of the products in the ratio 9L:6M:5N is as follows:

	L	M	N	Total
Sales mix	9	6	5	
	$	$	$	$
Contribution	200	300	180	
Total contribution	1800	1800	900	4500

The number of batches to break even is $2700000/4500 = 600 batches
Therefore the break-even sales volume is 5400L (9 × 600), 3600M (600 × 6) and 3000N (600 × 5)

(d)

	L	M	N	Total
Sales budget (units)	6300	4200	3500	
	$	$	$	
Contribution per unit	200	300	180	
Total contribution	1260000	1260000	630000	3150000
Fixed costs				2700000
Profit				450000

Contribution from L can drop by $450000.

The contribution per unit, and therefore selling price per unit, can fall by $450000/6300 = $71.43 per unit.

The current selling price per unit is $300.

Therefore the sensitivity is $71.43/$300 = 23.8%

9.25 (a) *Throughput return per factory hour*

	Large panels	Small panels
Selling price ($)	12600	3800
Materials ($)	4300	1160
Throughput per unit	8300	2640
Hours per unit required on Machine M	1.4	0.6
Throughput return per factory hour ($)	5928.57	4400

Cost per factory hour

Total factory cost (i.e. other operational expenses = $12m)

Total time available on bottleneck resource
(12 hours × 5 days × 50 weeks × 90%)
= $4444.44

Throughput accounting ratio

Throughput return per factory hour/cost per factory hour

Large panels = $1.33 (5928.57/4444.44)
Small panels = $0.99 (4400/4444.44)

For an organization to generate a profit contribution the return per factory hour should exceed the cost per factory hour. In other words, the throughput accounting ratio should exceed 1. Given that the throughput accounting ratio is just under 1 for small panels, steps should be taken to increase the throughput return or reduce the cost per hour for small panels.

(b) The optimum production plan is calculated as follows:

Product	No. of units	Hours per unit	Total hours	T/P per hour	Total T/P
Small panels	1000	0.6	600	$4400	$2640000
Large panels	500 (W1)	1.4	2100	$5928.57	$12449997
Total			2700		$15089997
Less total factory costs					($12000000)
Profit					$3089997

W1
The minimum contractual output for small panels is 1000 units requiring 600 hours. The remaining 2100 hours (2700 hours less 600 hours allocated to small panels) should be allocated to producing 1500 large panels (2100 hours/1.4 hours).

(c) The company can increase production capacity and hence to increase throughput without making any additional capital expenditure by:

1. Training workers to operate all three machines so that if a worker was absent another worker could operate the machine in order to keep it running. This could also avoid lunch time hours being lost by staggering lunchtimes thus enabling Machine M to be kept running for the whole working day.
2. Machine M only operates at 90 per cent capacity because of productive hours being lost because of maintenance. Emphasis on preventive and essential maintenance being undertaken outside the usual working day may enable productive hours to be increased.

The working hours of the factory could be increased in order to increase the productive hours of Machine M.

9.26 (a) Within a production environment, the throughput accounting ratio (TAR) is defined as return per factory hour/cost per factory hour. Within a hospital environment, this ratio can be expressed as return per hospital hour/cost per hospital hour. Throughput accounting defines cost per hospital hour as all operational costs excluding direct materials (i.e. salaries plus general overheads) divided by the total hours of bottleneck resource (the surgeon's time). Therefore the cost per hospital hour is:

$$\frac{\$45000 + \$38000 + \$75000 + \$90000 + \$50000 + \$250000 = \$548000}{\text{Surgeon's time (40 hours × 47 weeks = 1880 hours)}} = \$291.49$$

The return per hospital hour is defined for throughput accounting as:

$$\frac{\text{Selling price per unit (\$4250) less material costs (\$1000 + \$45 + \$5.60)}}{\text{Time on bottleneck resource (surgeon's time = 1.25 hours)}} = \$2559.52$$

TAR = $2559.52/$291.49 = $8.78

(b) The procedures are ranked by TAR's for the bottleneck resource:

	A	B	C
	$	$	$
TAR	8.96	9.11	8.78
Ranking	2	1	3

The procedures are now allocated for the bottleneck resource in accordance with the above rankings:

Procedure	Number	Hours per unit	Total hours	Return per hour ($)	Total return
B	800	1	800	2654.40	2123520
A	600	0.75	450	2612.53	1175638.5
C	504	1.25	630	2559.52	1612497.6
			1880		4911656.1

Procedure A and B utilize 1250 hours leaving the remaining 630 hours of the bottleneck resource to be allocated to performing 504 units of procedure C (630 hours/1.25 hours).

Total profit = Total return ($4911656) less salaries plus general overheads ($548000) = $4363656

(c) The proposal is to meet the maximum demand of all three procedures by following the optimum production plan shown in (b) plus the unutilized demand of procedure C (696 procedures). An examination of the time required to meet the maximum demand for all of the members of staff (with the exception of the surgeon) indicates that sufficient time is available.

The additional return from undertaking the 696 procedures is $2226782 (696 × 1.25 hours × $2559.52 per hour). The additional costs are $750000 (equipment) plus $90000 (surgeon) resulting in an increase in total profit of $1386782 ($2226782 − $840000).

It is worthwhile equipping the second theatre provided that a suitably qualified surgeon can be employed.

CHAPTER 10

10.13 Profits will be increased up to the point where marginal cost equals marginal revenue (see Chapter 2 for a definition of marginal cost and marginal revenue). The following schedule shows the calculation of marginal cost and marginal revenues for different output levels.

Demand Units	Selling Price per unit £	Total Revenue £ units × unit selling price	Marginal Revenue £	Cost per unit £ units × cost per unit	Total Cost £	Marginal Cost £
1100	48	52800	52800	22	24200	24200
1200	46	55200	2400	21	25200	1000
1300	45	58500	3300	20	26000	800
1400	42	58800	300	19	26600	600

Marginal cost exceeds marginal revenue at output levels above 1300 units. Therefore profits are maximized at an output level of 1300 units and a selling price of £45 per unit.

10.14 (a) Variable cost plus 20% = £30 × 1.20 = £36

Total cost plus 20% = £37 × 1.20 = £44.40
Advantages of variable costs include that it avoids arbitrary allocations, identifies short-term relevant costs,

simplicity and mark-up can be increased to provide a contribution to fixed costs and profit. The disadvantages are that it represents only a partial cost, it is short-term oriented and ignores price/demand relationships.

Advantages of total cost include that it attempts to include all costs, reduces the possibility that fixed costs will not be covered and simplicity. The disadvantages are that total cost is likely to involve some arbitrary apportionments and the price/demand relationship is ignored.

(b) See 'pricing policies' in Chapter 10 for the answer to this question. The answer should point out that price skimming is likely to lead to a higher initial price whereas a pricing penetration policy is likely to lead to a lower initial price.

10.15 (a)

Activity	Cost driver rate
Sales visits	$250 per visit ($50000/200)
Order processing	$100 per order ($70000/700)
Normal deliveries	$50 per normal delivery ($120000/240)
Urgent deliveries	$2000 per urgent delivery ($60000/30)

	B $000	D $000
Costs		
Sales visits	6	3
Orders processing	7.5	2
Normal deliveries	22.5	7.5
Urgent deliveries	10	0
Total costs	46	12.5
Factory contribution	75	40.5
Profit	29	28

(b) ST could increase its profits by:

- changing the behaviour of its customers, particularly in relation to urgent deliveries;
- considering how it could change its operations to reduce the costs of these activities;
- Changing the selling prices to reflect the costs caused by customer consumption of the above resources.

10.16 (a)

	$	Note
Food and drink at meeting	–	1
Material Z	78000	2
Construction workers	–	3
Engineers	4485	4
Specialist machine	15250	5
Windows	1500	6
Other materials	6000	7
Fixed overhead	–	8
Profit margin	–	9
Total relevant cost	105235	

Notes

1. The food and drink costs are sunk and therefore do not represent relevant costs.
2. The 550kg currently in inventory will need to be replaced and therefore should be valued at replacement cost. The remaining 650kg will also need to be replaced so the relevant cost is $78000 (1200 × $65).
3. Spare capacity exists and no additional costs will be incurred so the relevant cost is zero.

4. Additional costs of $4680 ($52 × 90 hours) will be incurred if the engineers work overtime whereas a profit contribution of $4485 ($1495 × 3 units of product Y) will be lost if production of product Y is reduced. The relevant cost is the lower of the two options ($4485).

5. The incremental rental cost is $15 250 whereas the net cost of purchase is $20 000 so the additional relevant cost is the lower of the alternatives.

6. The cost of producing the windows is sunk and irrelevant. If the windows are not used for the conference the sales will not be lost since the chief executive will visit the client to secure the sale. The chief executive's time is not a relevant cost since he is paid a fixed salary. If the windows are used for the contract an additional conference non-attendance fee of $1500 will be incurred. Therefore the relevant cost is $1500.

7. The incremental/relevant cost is $6000.

8. The fixed cost will be incurred whether or not the contract is undertaken so it is not a relevant cost.

9. The profit mark-up is not relevant since the objective is to establish a minimum price to cover the relevant cost.

(b) See 'A price setting firm facing a short-run pricing decision' in Chapter 10 for the answer to this question. The answer should also point out that the quoted minimum price does not include a profit margin.

(c) A market skimming pricing strategy is likely to be appropriate to launch the houses in the new country. A market skimming pricing policy charges a high price for the product initially where the product is unique and there are significant barriers to entry for competitors. The price is reduced as new competitors enter the market with a similar product. The high-quality materials and unique energy saving technology used in the houses should enable high prices to be initially set as this provides a differential advantage for sales to customers who would like to have houses with this technology. This market skimming approach will allow DLW to recover the research and development costs incurred to develop the energy saving technology.

10.17 (a) The question states that the sales volume and prices of the pre-booked discount and standard tickets are fixed and only the price of the family ticket is subject to change. The price of $185 has been set to maximize profits but the question implies that the optimum price will change if the cost structure arising from the equipment hire changes. If the equipment is hired fixed costs will increase to $6 750 000 and unit variable cost will decline to $11.50 ($12.50 × 0.92).

The demand function given in the question is $P = a - bx$, where P = price and x = quantity, so it is necessary to find a value for a and b. Each increase or decrease in price of $5 results in a corresponding increase or decrease in demand of 25 tickets. Annual demand is expected to be 675 tickets at a price of £185. For demand to be zero the selling price would have to increase by 27 increments (675/25) of $5. Therefore if the selling price was increased to $320 demand would be zero. To increase demand by one unit, selling price must be reduced by $0.20 ($5/25). Thus the optimum price (P) for an output of x units is:

$P = 320 - 0.2x$.

Total revenue (TR) = $320x - 0.2x^2$

so MR (see Appendix 10.1 at the end of Chapter 10 or formula $MR = a - 2bx$ given in the question) =

$320 - 0.4x$

Marginal cost = $11.50 × 4 = $46

MC = MR where:

$46 = 320 - 0.4x$

$0.4x = 274$

$x = 685$

$P = 320 - (0.2 × 685)$

Optimum selling price (P) = $183 yielding a sales revenue of $3 760 650 (685 × 30 days × $183) Variable overheads = 685 × $46 × 30 days = $945 300

Contribution = $2 815 350

The financial benefit from hiring the equipment can be determined from comparing the difference in profits from hiring the equipment with the profits from not hiring the equipment. The revenues from the sale of the pre-booked discount and standard tickets will remain unchanged so are not relevant to the calculation. However, the variable costs relating to these tickets will change and must be taken into account. The calculation is as follows:

Original contribution from Premium Family Tickets ($185SP – $50 VC) × 675 × 30 days)	2 733 750
Revised contribution from Premium Family Tickets	2 815 350
Increased contribution from Premium Family Tickets	81 600
Reduced variable costs on other tickets (1500 + 8000 people × 30 days × (8% × $12.50)	285 000
Hire fee	(250 000)
Net benefit	116 600

(b)

Change in profit required	$116 600
Contribution per Standard ticket ($39 – $11.50)	$27.50
Number of Standard tickets ($116 600/$27.50)	4 240
Reduction in tickets per day (4240/30)	141.33
Sensitivity (141.33/8000)	1.8%

Sales of standard tickets would have to fall by 1.8% for each day of the month for the decision to hire the equipment to change. Besides the competitor's action unexpected changes in the weather could also cause a drop in sales of tickets.

(c) See 'Feedback and feed-forward controls' in Chapter 16 for the answer to this question. At PPP, the periodic comparison of actual results against the budget that has been set at the start of the year is an example of feedback control. Feed-forward control at PPP uses the revised forecast at the start of every month and uses the projection as the basis for taking future actions relating to pricing policies and promotional campaigns. The latest forecast is used for comparing the forecast position with the required position. The aim of feed-forward controls is to be proactive and anticipate future actions that are required.

10.18 (a) Material cost = $2 400 000/200 000 = $12 per unit. Labour cost = $1 200 000/200 000 = $6 per unit. Variable overhead cost using high-low method: ($1 850 000 – $1 400 000)/(350 000 – 200 000) = $3 per unit.

Total variable cost per unit = $21.

Fixed costs = $1 400 000 – (200 000 × $3) = $800 000

(b) The demand function given in the question is $P = a - bx$, where P = price and x = quantity, so it is necessary to find a value for a and b. Each increase or decrease in price of $2 results in a corresponding increase or decrease in demand of 2000 units. Annual demand is expected to be 250 000 units at a price of $60. For demand to be zero the selling price would have to increase by 125 increments (250 000/2000) of $2. Therefore if the selling price was increased to $310 demand would be zero. To increase demand by one unit, selling price must be reduced by $0.001 ($2/2000). Thus the maximum price (P) for an output of x units is:

$P = 310 - 0.001x$.

Total revenue (TR) $= 310x - 0.001x^2$

so MR (see Appendix 10.1 at the end of Chapter 10 or formula $MR = a - 2bx$ given in the question) $= 310 - 0.002x$

Marginal cost (MC) as calculated in (a) $= \$21$

MC $=$ MR where:

$21 = 310 - 0.002x$

$0.002x = 289$

$x = 144\,500$

$P = 310 - (0.001 \times 144\,500)$

Optimum selling price (P) $= \$165.50$ yielding a sales revenue of $23 914 750 (144 500 × $165.50)

Variable overheads $= 144\,500 \times \$21 = \$3\,034\,500$

Fixed overheads $= \$800\,000$

Therefore profit $= \$20\,080\,250$

(c) The conditions are as follows:

- Where a product is new and different and customers are prepared to pay high prices in order to obtain the product early. The company's product is 'innovative' so it may well meet this requirement.
- Where barriers to entry (e.g. high investment costs, patent protection costs) exist deterring other competitors motivated by the high prices being charged from entering the market. According to the information given high development costs apply.
- Where products have a short life resulting in the need to recover development costs and make a profit quickly. The company has a short three-year life cycle.

Because of the limited information available it is not possible to make a specific recommendation. It may be appropriate to launch the product initially at a higher price to establish demand at this price since it is preferable to lower a price after launch rather than to raise it. The optimum pricing approach in (b) above is based on pricing theory which does not exactly match the real world. Also, the data is derived from similar but not identical products that may not apply to this particular product.

10.19 (a) (i) The profit maximizing fee can be derived using either calculus or a tabulation approach. At a price of $400 per room demand is 1440 rooms (2400 rooms × 0.75 × 0.8). Each increase or decrease in price of $10 results in a corresponding decrease or increase in demand by 40 rooms. Therefore, if the selling price were increased to $760, demand would be zero. To increase demand by one unit, selling price must be reduced by $0.25 ($10/40 units). Thus the maximum selling price (P) for an output of x units is:

$P = \$760 - \$0.25X$

Therefore total revenue for a demand of X units is:

$TR = 760X - 0.25X^2$

$MR = 760 - 0.5X$

$MC = 200$ (2 persons × $100).

Maximum profit is achieved where MR = MC

Therefore $760 - 0.5X = 200$

So $X = (760 - 200)/0.5 = 1120$ units

Therefore the selling price per double room at the profit-maximizing level (P):

$= 760 - 0.25 \times 1120$

$= 760 - 280$

$= \$480$

Alternatively the following tabular approach can be used to find the profit maximizing combination of selling price per room and quantity of double rooms demanded.

Selling price per room per night ($)	Quantity demanded	Variable costs per room per night ($)	Contribution per night ($)
380	1520	200	273 600
390	1480	200	281 200
400	1440	200	288 000
410	1400	200	294 000
420	1360	200	299 200
430	1320	200	303 600
440	1280	200	307 200
450	1240	200	310 000
460	1200	200	312 000
470	1160	200	313 200
480	1120	200	313 600
490	1080	200	313 200

(ii) The profit attributable to the tournament is as follows:

Sales revenue		No of rooms	Fee/room	Nights	Total $000
Double		1120	480	5	2688
Single	15%	360	300	5	540
Family	10%	240	600	5	720
Total revenue					3948

Variable costs (W1):

Double	$2 \times 1120 \times 100 \times 5$	= 1120
Single	$1 \times 360 \times 100 \times 5$	= 180
Family	$4 \times 240 \times 100 \times 5$	= 480
Total variable costs:		1780
Incremental fixed costs:		
Double rooms		516 000
Single & family rooms		300 000
Profit		1 352 000

W1 Number of guests per room × number of rooms × variable cost per guest night × number of nights.

(b) Marginal cost will decline from $200 to $160 profit maximized where:

$760 - 0.5X = 160$

So $X = (760 - 160)/0.5 = 1200$ units (double rooms)

Therefore the selling price per double room at the profit-maximizing level (P):

$= 760 - 0.25 \times 1200$

$= 760 - 300$

$= \$460$

Alternatively the tabular approach illustrated in (a) above can be used to find the profit maximizing combination of selling price per room and quantity of double rooms demanded. The revised profit attributable to staging the Robyn Cup is as follows:

Sales revenue:		No of rooms	Fee	Nights	Total $000
Double		1200	460	5	2760
Single	15%	360	300	5	540
Family	10%	240	600	5	720
Total revenue					4020

Variable costs:

Double	$2 \times$	$1200 \times 80 \times 5$	$= 960$
Single	$1 \times$	$360 \times 80 \times 5$	$= 144$
Family	$4 \times$	$240 \times 80 \times 5$	$= 384$
Total variable costs:			1488

Incremental fixed costs:

Double rooms	516
Single & family rooms	300
Additional fixed costs	200
Profit	1516

Management would be advised to undertake changes in proposed operational activities on purely financial grounds as this would result in an increased profit of ($1 516 000 − $1 352 000) = $164 000.

(c) The following actions might be considered:

- Management could sell a range of souvenirs etc. to visitors to the golf tournament.
- Management could offer guests a price reduction for staying extra nights at the hotel either before or after the golf tournament

10.20 There are four stages to the product life cycle: the introduction, growth, maturity and decline stages. In the introduction stage, the product is unique and hence the company can charge a high price. The company has just launched an innovative new product using a market skimming pricing policy. This is a policy that is likely to be appropriate at the introductory stage of a product's life cycle where an initial high selling price is set to take advantage of the innovative aspects of the product when demand is not very sensitive to price changes.

As the end of the introduction stage sales may begin to decline as there are fewer new customers and competitors are attracted by the high initial selling price. The company will seek to avoid this competition by lowering its selling price to deter competitors from entering the market and also to make its product more affordable to the wider market.

In the growth stage, the company will maintain its lower selling price to continue to attract new customers. If the market becomes very competitive, the company may need to be further reductions in the selling price to maintain the growth unless the original product can be differentiated in other ways.

In the maturity stage, the selling price of the product is likely to be stable but may be further reduced so that the product continues to be profitable for as long as possible.

In the decline stage, the company will be less concerned with the future effect of the current selling price and should adopt a selling price that maximizes short-run profits. If the product is not profitable inventories should be minimized and any unsold stock may have to be sold at less than unit cost.

10.21 The question relates to the pricing of customized products in a price setting firm. Generally the marginal cost approach to pricing refers to using variable cost as the cost base to determine cost-plus selling prices. However, marginal cost can also be viewed as representing short-run incremental costs which are normally interpreted to represent direct labour and material costs. In contrast, absorption costs include a share of fixed overheads and are normally considered to represent an estimate of the resources that are committed to producing a product in the long-term. A full description of variable (marginal) and absorption costing is provided in Chapter 7. The discussion of the second part of the question should incorporate issues discussed in the sections relating to short-run and long-run pricing decisions faced by a price setting firm. In particular, the answer should draw attention to the fact that adopting a policy of accepting business at a price that exceeds variable cost is appropriate only for one time special orders and is only justifiable if certain conditions as specified in the text are met.

In the long-run firms can adjust the supply of virtually all of their resources. Therefore a product or service should be priced to cover all of the resources that committed to it. Thus absorption costing principles should be used for determining the cost base for long-run decisions when using cost-plus pricing for customized products.

CHAPTER 11

11.19 (a) Large-scale service organizations have a number of features that have been identified as being necessary to derive significant benefits from the introduction of ABC:

(i) They operate in a highly competitive environment;

(ii) They incur a large proportion of indirect costs that cannot be directly assigned to specific cost objects;

(iii) Products and customers differ significantly in terms of consuming overhead resources;

(iv) They market many different products and services. Furthermore, many of the constraints imposed on manufacturing organizations, such as also having to meet financial accounting stock valuation requirements, or a reluctance to change or scrap existing systems, do not apply. Many service organizations have only recently implemented cost systems for the first time. This has occurred at the same time as when the weaknesses of existing systems and the benefits of ABC systems were being widely publicized. These conditions have provided a strong incentive for introducing ABC systems.

(b) The following may create problems for the application of ABC:

(i) Facility sustaining costs (such as property rents etc.) represent a significant proportion of total costs and may only be avoidable if the organization ceases business. It may be impossible to establish appropriate cost drivers;

(ii) It is often difficult to define products where they are of an intangible nature. Cost objects can therefore be difficult to specify;

(iii) Many service organizations have not previously had a costing system and much of the information required to set up an ABC system will be nonexistent. Therefore introducing ABC is likely to be expensive.

(c) The uses for ABC information for service industries are similar to those for manufacturing organizations:

(i) It leads to more accurate product costs as a basis for pricing decisions when cost-plus pricing methods are used;

(ii) It results in more accurate product and customer profitability analysis statements that provide a more appropriate basis for decision-making;

(iii) ABC attaches costs to activities and identifies the cost drivers that cause the costs. Thus ABC provides a better understanding of what causes costs and highlights ways of performing activities more effectively by reducing cost driver transactions. Costs can therefore be managed more effectively in the long term. Activities can also be analysed into value-added and non-value added activities and by highlighting the costs of non-value added activities attention is drawn to areas where there is a potential for cost reduction without reducing the products' service potentials to customers.

(d) The following aspects would be of most interest to a regulator:

(i) The costing method used (e.g. marginal, traditional full cost or ABC). This is of particular importance to verify whether or not reasonable prices are being set and that the organization is not taking advantage of its monopolistic situation. Costing information is also necessary to ascertain whether joint costs are fairly allocated so that cross-subsidization from one service to another does not apply;

(ii) Consistency in costing methods from period to period so that changes in costing methods are not used to distort pricing and profitability analysis;

(iii) In many situations a regulator may be interested in the ROI of the different services in order to ensure that excessive returns are not being obtained. A regulator will therefore be interested in the methods and depreciation policy used to value assets and how the costs of assets that are common to several services (e.g. corporate headquarters) are allocated. The methods used will influence the ROI of the different services.

11.20 (a) *Absorption costing production cost per unit*

Product	X	Y	Z	Total
Budgeted annual production (units)	20000	16000	22000	
Labour hours per unit	2.5	3	2	
Total labour hours	50000	48000	44000	142000

Overhead absorption rate = $1377400/142000
= $9.70 per hour.

Product	X $ per unit	Y $ per unit	Z $ per unit
Direct materials	25	28	22
Direct labour	30	36	24
Overhead ($9.70 × 2.5/3/2)	24.25	29.10	19.40
Full cost per unit	79.25	93.10	65.40

(b) *ABC production cost per unit*

Product	X	Y	Z	Total
Budgeted annual production (units)	20000	16000	22000	
Batch size	500	800	400	
Number of batches	40	20	55	115
Number of purchase orders per batch	4	5	4	
Total number of orders	160	100	220	480
Machine hours per unit	1.5	1.25	1.4	
Total machine hours	30000	20000	30800	80800

Cost driver rates:
Cost per machine set up $280000/115 = $2434.78
Cost per order $316000/480 = $658.33
Cost per machine hour   ($420000 + $361400)/80800 = $9.67

Allocation of overheads to each product:

Product	X $	Y $	Z $	Total
Machine set up costs	97391	48696	133913	280000
Material ordering costs	105333	65833	144834	316000
Machine running and facility costs	290100	193400	297836	781336
Total	492824	307929	576583	1377336
Number of units produced	20000	16000	22000	
Overhead cost per unit	$24.64	$19.25	$26.21	
Total cost per unit:	*$ per unit*	*$ per unit*	*$ per unit*	
Direct materials	25	28	22	
Direct labour	30	36	24	
Overhead	24.64	19.25	26.21	
ABC cost per unit	79.64	83.25	72.21	

The failure to allocate $64 of the machine running and facility costs is due to rounding differences.

(c) The cost of product X is similar for both systems and the selling price will thus be unchanged. Product Y is overcosted by $10 and product Z is undercosted by approximately $7 with the traditional absorption costing system. This will result in a reduction in selling price of product Y and an increase in the price of product Z using cost-plus pricing. Given that demand for product Y is elastic the reduction in price should result in an increase in demand whereas the inelastic demand for product Z may result in demand remaining unchanged.

11.21 (a) *Calculation of cost driver quantities*

	Tablets	Convertible laptops	All-in-one PCs	Total
Budgeted production per annum (units)	10000	12000	6000	28000
Average number of units per order	10	6	4	
Number of orders	1000	2000	1500	4500
Parts per unit	20	35	25	
Total number of parts	200000	420000	150000	770000
Assembly time per unit (minutes)	20	40	30	
Total assembly time (minutes)	200000	480000	180000	860000
Software applications per unit	2	3	4	
Total number of software applications	20000	36000	24000	80000

Calculation of cost driver rates

Activity	Activity cost $000	Cost driver	Cost driver rate
Manufacturing scheduling	162	Number of orders	$162000/4500 = $36 per order
Parts handling	2464	Number of parts	$2464000/770000 = $3.20 per part
Assembly	4472	Assembly time	$4472000/860000 = $5.20 per minute
Software installation and testing	2000	Number of software applications	$2000000/80000 = $25.00 per application
Packaging	1302	Number of units	$1302000/28000 = $46.50 per unit

Assignment of overheads to products

	Tablets $000	Convertible Laptops $000	All-in-one PCs $000	Total $000
Manufacturing scheduling	(1000 × $36) 36	(2000 × $36) 72	(1500 × $36) 54	162
Parts handling	(200000 × $3.20) 640	(420000 × $3.20) 1344	(150000 × $3.20) 480	2464
Assembly	(200000 × $5.20) 1040	(480000 × $5.20) 2496	(180000 × $5.20) 936	4472
Software installation and testing	(20000 × $25) 500	(36000 × $25) 900	(24000 × $25) 600	2000
Packaging	(10000 × $46.50) 465	(12000 × $46.50) 558	(6000 × $46.50) 279	1302
Total production overhead costs	2681	5370	2349	10400

Activity-based costing gross profit analysis

	Tablets $000	Convertible laptops $000	All-in-one PCs $000	Total $000
Sales	3640	12480	9880	26000
Direct material	800	2800	2200	5800
Direct labour	300	1200	800	2300
Production overheads	2681	5370	2349	10400
Gross profit	(141)	3110	4531	7500

(b) Gross profits per unit

	Tablets	Convertible laptops	All-in-one PCs
Current absorption costing system	$108 ($1084k/10k)	$291	$488
ABC	($14) (−$141K/10k)	$259	$755

Under the traditional absorption costing system each of the products was making a profit whereas a loss is reported with ABC. Under the traditional absorption costing system production overheads were charged to products based on sales revenue resulting in Tablets, which have a relatively low proportion of the total sales revenue (14 per cent), being charged with a relatively low level of fixed production overheads. ABC assigns costs on the basis of the actual consumption of activities resulting in Tablets being charged significantly more production overheads than before.

(c) ABC provides information for decisions relating to product pricing and product mix. ABC also provides information about the various activities and the cost

drivers for each activity. This enables the company to focus on those activities with the highest costs in order to determine whether they can be eliminated or performed more efficiently. Activities can be classified as value-added and non-value added so that the focus can be on action to reduce or eliminate the non-value added activities.

11.22 (a) *Calculation of the cost-plus selling price using the traditional costing system*

The direct labour hour overhead absorption rate is calculated by dividing $14190000 total overheads by 71400 direct labour hours (23800 × 3) resulting in a direct labour hour rate of $198.74 per hour. The cost and selling price per unit for order 11784 consisting of 16 units is:

	$
Direct costs ($31360/16 units ordered)	1960.00
Overhead costs (3 hours at 198.74 per hour)	596.22
Total cost	2556.22
Profit margin (45%)	1150.30
Selling price	3706.52

Calculation of the cost-plus selling price using an ABC system

	Total of cost of activity $000s	No. of driver units	Cost per driver unit $
No. of minutes on calls to customer	7735	899600	8.60
No. of purchase orders raised	2451	21400	114.53
No. of components used in production	1467	618800	2.37
Administration of production (absorbed as general overhead)	2537	71400	35.53

	Driver units used on the order	Costs allocated to the order $	Cost per unit of the order $
No. of minutes on calls to customer	1104	9492	593.28
No. of purchase orders raised	64	7330	458.13
No. of components used in production	512	1214	75.86
Administration of production (absorbed as general overhead)	48	1706	106.60

The cost and selling price per unit based on the above information is:

	$
Direct costs	1960.00
Overheads allocated using ABC:	
Customer service	593.28
Purchasing and receiving	458.13
Stock management	75.86
Administration of production	106.60
Total cost	3193.87
Profit margin (45%)	1437.24
Selling price	4631.11

The above computations indicate that the two costing systems result in significant differences in the pricing of the order with the price using the ABC system being approximately 25 per cent higher than the price using the traditional costing system. The company currently uses a simplistic traditional absorption costing system using a blanket (plant wide) overhead rate based on a single cost centre and a single cost driver. The ABC system uses a greater number of cost centres/pools based on activities and several different cost drivers that cause activity resource consumption. Costs are assigned to products based on cost driver usage thus enabling ABC systems to more accurately measure the resources consumed by products. Traditional cost systems tend to report less accurate product costs because they use cost drivers where no cause-and-effect relationships are used to assign overhead costs to products.

Traditional costing systems tend to overcost high volume products and undercost low volume products (see 'Volume-based and non-volume based cost drivers' in Chapter 10 for a more detailed explanation). Given that the product cost generated by the costing system for order 11784 is significantly lower for the traditional costing system, it is likely to be a low volume product order (16 units) relative to other orders. Other high volume products produced by the company are likely to be overcosted by the traditional system thus resulting in lower cost-plus selling prices.

ABC systems are likely to be preferred to traditional costing systems where:

- There is intensive competition.
- Overhead costs are a high proportion of total costs.
- A diverse range of products are produced all consuming resources in significantly proportions.

Overhead costs at RL are 23 per cent of total costs and the different product costs generated for the order suggest that high product diversity exists so there are strong arguments for adopting ABC. With a better understanding of what is causing the costs from adopting the ABC system there is a greater potential for reducing costs of the activities and thus selling prices. The ABC costs should motivate the company to re-examine the cost-plus prices suggested by the new system. Cost-plus pricing should be used in a flexible manner and not rigorously applied based on the revised costs generated by the ABC system. You should refer to 'Limitations of cost-plus pricing' and 'Reasons for using cost-plus pricing' in Chapter 11 for a more detailed explanation.

(b) The traditional budgetary approach is criticized because it sets fixed targets that are not responsive to change during the budget period. Budgets can be perceived as an imposition of a top-down control approach that does not encourage employee empowerment. The beyond budgeting approach involves replacing the annual system of a centrally created budget with a more flexible system of targets. Instead of monitoring variances from the budget, the focus is on the achievement of strategic goals and comparing performance against suitable benchmarks. Rolling forecasts, produced on a monthly or quarterly basis that are revised by line managers are suggested as the main alternative to the annual budget. The targets are intended to guide rather than constrain budgetees in an attempt to improve their motivation. In other words, rolling forecasts have been advocated because they do not have the same

compulsory image or stifle creativity when compared with traditional budgeting.

Beyond budgeting is considered appropriate in industries where there are rapid changes in the business environment and innovation and flexibility needs to be encouraged. This appears to be the case for RL which operates in a sector dominated by technological change. The culture of encouraging employee empowerment associated with beyond budgeting also may help to combat the problems faced by RL of losses key staff.

Despite the criticisms of traditional budgeting various studies suggest that it is alive and well and that many companies are taking steps to overcome the criticisms (see 'Criticisms of budgeting' in Chapter 15 for an explanation).

11.23 (a) (i) Direct labour hour overhead rate = Total overheads (£12 000 000)/Total direct labour hours (500 000) = £24

	Sunshine (£)	Roadster (£)	Fireball (£)
Direct labour at £5 per hour	1 000 000	1 100 000	400 000
Materials	800 000	960 000	360 000
	(£400 per unit)	(£600 per unit)	(£900 per unit)
Overheads at £24 per hour	4 800 000	5 280 000	1 920 000
Total cost	6 600 000	7 340 000	2 680 000
Sales revenue	8 000 000	9 600 000	3 200 000
Profit	1 400 000	2 260 000	520 000
Total cost per unit	3 300	4 587.5	6 700
Selling price per unit	4 000	6 000	8 000
Profit per unit	700	1 412.5	1 300

Total profit = £4 180 000

(ii) The cost driver rates are as follows:
Deliveries to retailers £2 400 000/250 = £9 600
Set-ups £6 000 000/100 = £60 000
Deliveries inwards £3 600 000/800 = £4 500

	Sunshine (£)	Roadster (£)	Fireball (£)
Direct labour at £5 per hour	1 000 000	1 100 000	400 000
Materials	800 000 (£400 per unit)	960 000 (£600 per unit)	360 000 (£900 per unit)
Overheads:			
Deliveries	960 000 (100 × £9 600)	768 000 (80 × £9 600)	672 000 (70 × £9 600)
Set-ups	2 100 000 (35 × £60 000)	2 400 000 (40 × £60 000)	1 500 000 (25 × £60 000)
Purchasing	1 800 000 (400 × £4 500)	1 350 000 (300 × £4 500)	450 000 (100 × £4 500)
Total cost	6 660 000	6 578 000	3 382 000
Sales revenue	8 000 000	9 600 000	3 200 000
Profit/(loss)	1 340 000	3 022 000	(182 000)
Total cost per unit	3 330	4 111.25	8 455
Selling price per unit	4 000	6 000	8 000
Profit/(loss) per unit	670	1 888.75	(455)

Total profit = £4 180 000

(b) (i) The report should include the following points:

- The direct costs are identical for both costing methods.
- Direct labour is a relatively minor cost but the existing method that allocates overhead costs on the basis of direct labour hours overstates their importance.
- The existing method is based on the assumption that there is a cause-and-effect

relationship between overheads and labour hours. This assumption appears to be unlikely based on the information given in the question. If this assumption is incorrect then misleading results will be reported.

- ABC attempts to allocate overheads based on using several different cost drivers rather than the single base used with the existing method.
- ABC seeks to assign overheads based on cause-and-effect cost drivers. The accuracy of the reported ABC product costs depends on the extent to which the cause-and-effect assumption is correct.
- For additional comments see 'A comparison of traditional and ABC systems' and 'Volume-based and non-volume-based cost drivers' in Chapter 11.

(ii) The comment by the finance director is incorrect since Fireball is profitable with the existing system but unprofitable with the ABC system. The message from the two systems can have a significant impact on overall profits. The reason for the difference in product profits is that Fireball has the lowest volume but it makes the greatest relative demand on the three activities identified by the ABC system. Because Fireball uses a lower proportion of direct labour hours than the other products the existing system allocates a lower share of overheads to Fireball.

The marketing director argues that incremental costs are required for the pricing decision. It is important to distinguish between short-term and long-term incremental costs. ABC seeks to report long-term incremental costs. If decisions are based on short-term incremental cost opportunities will be lost to reduce capacity and the longer-term incremental costs will remain unchanged. ABC recognizes that longer-term incremental costs can be reduced by making decisions that ensure that activities should be undertaken only where incremental revenues exceed long-term incremental costs. It is important that facility-sustaining costs are omitted from the costs reported by the ABC system since they are neither short-term nor long-term incremental costs.

The managing director is correct that the cost per activity should not remain constant over the longer term. Attempts should be made to reduce the costs of activities and improve their efficiency. Thus ABC reported costs should be reviewed and revised at periodic intervals. Also some costs (i.e. facility sustaining costs) do not change with activity and are not variable with any activity measure. Such costs should be excluded from the reported costs or reported separately as facility sustaining costs.

The chairman is correct that the profitability analysis based on maintaining the same product mix will yield the same total profits. However, different profits/losses are reported by products and making future decisions on the basis of ABC information compared with the existing system should result in a different product mix and therefore have an impact on total future profits. For example, assuming that the costs reported by the ABC system are all based on

cause-and-effect relationships then a decision may be made to discontinue production of Fireball. This is not apparent with the existing system. However, it is important that decisions should not be based solely on financial factors and non-financial factors should also be taken into account.

11.24 (a) The following profitability statement is based on the hierarchical approach illustrated in Figure 11.2 in Chapter 11.

Product	W $	X $	Y $	Z $	Total $
Sales	1300000	2260000	2120000	1600000	7280000
Direct materials	300000	910000	940000	500000	2650000
Direct labour	400000	1040000	640000	600000	2680000
Overhead:					
Machine related	80000	78000	32000	120000	310000
Batch related	50000	65000	40000	75000	230000
Gross contribution	470000	167000	468000	305000	1410000
Overhead:					
Product specific	500000	50000	100000	50000	700000
Net contribution	(30000)	117000	368000	255000	710000
General overhead					310000
Profit					400000

Note

Machine-related costs are $0.40 per hour ($310000/775000) and are assigned to products on the basis of machine hours used. Production is in 100 usage batches. The cost per batch is $50 ($230000/4600) and costs are assigned on the basis of batch usage (e.g. 1000 batches of W, 1300 batches of X etc.).

(b) (i) The profit statement shown in the question is unsuitable for decision-making because it is based on the arbitrary allocation of fixed costs rather than cause-and-effect allocations. Also some of the allocated fixed overheads are facility sustaining costs that are common and unavoidable to all alternatives so dropping an individual product will not result in a decline in these costs. The profit statement in (a) overcomes these criticisms by using only cause-and-effect allocations and not allocating general fixed overheads to individual products.

(ii) The profit statement shows that W has a negative net contribution and unless there are important qualitative factors this product should be discontinued since this would increase the company's profits by $30000. This differs from the original profit statement, which showed that products W and Y were profitable and products X and Z were loss making. Products X, Y and Z should be continued because they all have a positive net contribution.

(c) The specific fixed cost of product W is $500000 and the contribution to sales ratio is 0.36154 ($470000/$1300000). Therefore, the breakeven sales value is $500000/0.36154 = $1382973 so the break-even sales volume is $1382973/$13 = 106383 units. Since production must be in batches of 100 units then to break even 1064 batches must be produced and sold.

(d) For the answer to this question, see 'Value analysis' in Chapter 22. The answer should point out that the company should compare its products with those provided by its competitors to ascertain if their products have superior features and whether these features are important to their customers. If they are, these features should be incorporated in WTL's products. The company should also review the design of its products to ascertain if redesign can reduce costs without reducing the value of the products to its customers.

11.25 (a)

Order Number 377
Summary total cost statement

	$000	$000
Unit-based costs:		
Direct material cost ($180 × 5000)	900	
Direct labour cost ($150 × 5000)	750	
Power cost ($120 × 5000)	600	2250
Batch-related costs:		
Design work ($30000 × 5)	150	
Machine set up ($34000 × 5)	170	
Production scheduling ($60000 × 5)	300	
Selling – batch expediting – ($60000 × 5)	300	
Admin. – invoicing & accounting		
($24000 × 5)	120	
Distribution ($12000 × 5)	60	1100
Product sustaining costs:		
Engineering design & support (per order)	350	
Production line maintenance (per order)	1100	
Marketing (per order)	200	1650
Total cost excluding business/facility sustaining costs		5000
Business/Facility sustaining costs:		
Relating to production, administration, selling & distribution based on overall business/facility time used.		
30% × $5000000		1500
Total cost of order		6500

Note: number of batches – 5000 units/1000 – 5 batches

(b) *Unit based costs*
Direct material and labour costs are driven by the quantity, quality and price of the resources required for each unit of output for the product.

Batch related costs
The cost of undertaking set-ups is the driver influencing the cost of setting up the machines. The cost of engineering design and support is influenced by the number of design hours required for each batch.

Product sustaining costs
Marketing costs are influenced by the number of marketing visits to a client per order. The production line maintenance cost is influenced by the number of hours of production line maintenance required per order.

Business sustaining costs
These costs are absorbed at an arbitrary rate of 30 per cent of total cost excluding business sustaining costs. Business sustaining costs are incurred for the business as a whole and are not identifiable with individual cost objects. Because there is no identifiable cause-and-effect cost driver an arbitrary

allocation method must be used if these costs are to be assigned to cost objects.

Investigation of the cause(s) of a cost driver occurring at its present level allows action to be considered that will lead to a reduction in the cost per unit of cost driver. The following causes may be identified:

Material price may be higher than necessary due to a failure to select the most cost efficient supplier. This may be remedied by reviewing the mechanisms that are used to select the most appropriate suppliers.

Set-up costs may be higher than necessary because larger than necessary batch sizes are being processed. If batch sizes were increased from 1000 to 1250 units only four batches would need to be processed and the costs assigned to the order would be reduced.

The amount of production line maintenance will be dependent on the level of skill of the maintenance staff. Maintenance costs may be reduced by retraining of the maintenance staff or outsourcing the maintenance.

(c) The following problems may be encountered:

- The difficulty in identifying activities (see 'Identifying activities' in Chapter 11;
- The difficulty in identifying appropriate cost drivers for each activity (see 'Selecting appropriate cost drivers for assigning the cost of activities to cost objects' in Chapter 11);
- Difficulty in obtaining and collecting cost driver data;
- Problems in determining appropriate denominator level when calculating the cost driver rates (see Learning note 11.1 in the digital resources accompanying this book);
- Lack of staff expertise.

CHAPTER 12

12.11 Expected income with advertising =
$(£200000 × 0.95) + (£70000 × 0.05) = £193500$
Expected income without advertising =
$(£200000 × 0.7) + (£70000 × 0.3) = £161000$
The maximum amount the company should pay for advertising is the increase in expected value of £32500. Therefore the answer is **(a)**.

12.12 Expected value of new building = $(0.8 × £2$ million) + $(0.2 × £1$ million) $- £1$ million = £0.8 million
Expected value of upgrade = $(0.7 × £2$ million) + $(0.3 × £1$ million $-$ upgrade (?) = £1.7 million $-$ upgrade
Cost of upgrade to make the company financially indifferent = £0.9 million $(1.7 - 0.8$ million)
Answer = **(b)**

12.13 Only the outcomes that yield a contribution of $40 or more are considered:

$60 – $20 = $40 Joint probability is 0.30 × 0.25 = 0.0750
$64 – $20 = $44 Joint probability is 0.25 × 0.25 = 0.0625
$64 – $24 = $40 Joint probability is 0.25 × 0.40 = 0.1000
$68 – $20 = $48 Joint probability is 0.45 × 0.25 = 0.1125
$68 – $24 = $44 Joint probability is 0.45 × 0.40 = 0.1800
$68 – $26 = $42 Joint probability is 0.45 × 0.35 = 0.1575
                                                          0.6875

12.14 (i)

The minimum profit at a selling price of $80 is $50 000
The minimum profit at a selling price of $90 is $60 000
The minimum profit at a selling price of $100 is $70 000
The minimum profit at a selling price of $110 is $75 000
Therefore if the manager wants to maximize the minimum profit a selling price of $110 would be chosen.

(ii) A regret matrix can be produced as follows:

Competitor reaction	Selling price			
	$80	$90	$100	$110
Strong	$10 000	$0	$10 000	$5 000
Medium	$30 000	$20 000	$10 000	$0
Weak	$10 000	$0	$10 000	$20 000
Maximum regret	$30 000	$20 000	$10 000	$20 000

Therefore if the manger wants to minimize the maximum regret a selling price of $100 would be chosen.

12.15 *Expected values ($000)*

Project A ($700 × 0.3) + ($400 × 0.2) + ($300 × 0.5)
= $440
Project B ($800 × 0.3) + ($500 × 0.2) + ($400 × 0.5)
= $540
Project C ($700 × 0.3) + ($600 × 0.2) + ($500 × 0.5)
= $580
On the basis of expected value Project C would be chosen.

Expected value with perfect information ($000)
If good select Project B = ($800 × 0.3) = $240
If fair select Project C = ($600 × 0.2) = $120
If poor select Project C = ($500 × 0.5) = $250
Expected value with perfect information is $240 + $120 + $250 = $610
The maximum amount that should be paid is = $30k ($610k − $580k)

12.16

Demand	Probability	Machine A $000	Machine B $000	Machine C $000
High	35%	100 × 0.35 = 35	140 × 0.35 = 49	180 × 0.35 = 63
Medium	40%	150 × 0.40 = 60	160 × 0.40 = 64	140 × 0.40 = 56
Low	25%	200 × 0.25 = 50	100 × 0.25 = 25	80 × 0.25 = 20
Expected value		145	138	139

Without the benefit of perfect information Machine A would be chosen since it has the highest expected value (EV) of $145k.
With perfect information:
If research suggests low demand: select Machine A and earn $200k
If research suggests medium demand: select Machine B and earn $160k
If research suggests high demand: select Machine C and earn $180k
EV (with perfect information) = ($180k × 0.35) + ($160k × 0.40) + ($200k × 0.25) = $177k
Therefore the value of perfect information is $177k − $145k = $32k

12.17 (i) A risk neutral decision maker will tend to ignore risk and choose the course of action that gives the highest expected value. The expected value of the probability distribution is $13. This is more than the

current delivery cost of $12.50 so the risk neutral decision maker will wish to remain with the third party delivery service.

(ii) A risk averse decision maker seeks to avoid a high levels of risk. A risk averse decision maker is likely to focus on the 51% chance that delivery costs per unit will be higher than the current cost of $12.50 and ignore the fact that there is also a 35 per cent probability that the delivery cost per unit will be lower than the current unit cost of $12.50. A risk averse decision maker therefore wish to remain with the third party delivery service.

(iii) A risk seeker is a decision maker that focuses on the best possible outcomes and is unlikely to be put off by the low probability of any of the potential adverse outcomes. A risk seeker is likely to focus on the 23 per cent probability that the delivery cost per unit will be $11 or lower and will want to establish the in-house delivery service and ignore the fact that there is a 35 per cent chance that delivery costs per unit will be $14.20 or higher.

12.18 *Decision Tree*

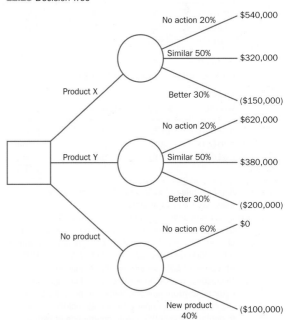

The expected values are:
Launch product X ($540 000 × 0.2) + ($320 000 × 0.5) − ($150 000 × 0.3) = $223 000
Launch Product Y ($620 000 × 0.2) + ($380 000 × 0.5) − ($200 000 × 0.3) = $254 000
Launch no product (0) − ($100 000 × 0.4) = −$40 000
Using expected values the company should launch Product Y

12.19 (a) *Unit contributions*

	$	$
Selling price	30	35
Up to 100 000 units	18	23
Above 100 000 units	19	24

Selling price of $30

Sales volume	Unit contribution $	Total contribution $'000	Fixed Costs $'000	Advertising Costs $'000	Profit $'000
120 000	19	2280	450	900	930
110 000	19	2090	450	900	740
140 000	19	2660	450	900	1310

Selling price of $35

Sales volume	Unit contribution $	Total contribution $'000	Fixed costs $'000	Advertising costs $'000	Profit $'000
108 000	24	2592	450	970	1172
100 000	23	2300	450	970	880
94 000	23	2162	450	970	742

(b) *Expected value at a selling price of $30*

Sales volume	Profit $'000	Probability	EV of profit $'000
120 000	930	0·4	372
110 000	740	0·5	370
140 000	1310	0·1	131
			873

Expected value at a selling price of $35

Sales volume	Profit $'000	Probability	EV of profit $'000
108 000	1172	0·3	351.6
100 000	880	0·3	264
94 000	742	0·4	296.8
			912.4

A selling price of $35 would be chosen using the expected value approach.

(c) Under this decision rule the alternative which offers the highest outcome for the worst outcome would be chosen. At the selling price of $35 the lowest profit is $742 000 compared with a lowest profit of $740 000 at a price of $30, so $35 would be chosen.

(d) Uncertainty mainly arises because of changes in the external environment and these are normally beyond the control of a company. Examples include changes in demand, competition (e.g. emergence of overseas competition), technological advances resulting in the firm's products becoming obsolete and global changes in input prices etc.

12.20 (i) The answer should describe the decision-maker's different attitudes to risk (risk averse, risk seeker and risk neutral) as outlined in 'Attitudes to risk by individuals' in Chapter 12. The expected value calculations (see W4) indicates that the expected profit is significant (around $5m) compared with the current operating profit of $20.4m and the project would have a significant impact on the company's future if it failed. The decision is likely to be made on the basis of maximizing shareholder value subject to taking risk into account. Studies suggest that shareholders are risk averse and the fact that the question also states that the shareholders are concerned about earning volatility also supports the view that they are risk averse.

The forecast price of steel is a major cost input and a major uncertainty but this has been eliminated by the negotiation of a fixed price contract. It should also be noted that winning the bid may lead to additional future contracts so to secure the bid it may be better to sacrifice increasing short-term profits in order to maximize longer term profits. In other words, the risk of not obtaining future contracts is a significant factor that should be taken into account. Another risk relates to the danger of actual costs escalating in excess of those budgeted for the bid resulting in a significant reduction in the actual profit.

(ii) *Workings*

(W1) Variable cost per unit:

	$
Steel	11 412
Engine/transmission	9500
Electronics	8450
Other	4810
Labour	13 800
	47 972

(W2) Fixed costs per design package for different demand levels:

Demand Design package type	500 $	750 $	1000 $
1	7 500 000	7 500 000	7 500 000
2	8 750 000	8 750 000	8 750 000
3	10 000 000	10 000 000	10 000 000

It is apparent from the above schedule that the highest fixed cost per unit is for design type 3 package at a demand level of 500 units giving a unit fixed cost of $20 000 ($10m/500). Therefore the highest total cost per unit is $67 972 ($47 972 + $20 000 unit fixed cost). Thus all potential outcomes conform with the government's requirement of a maximum per unit total cost of $70 000.

(W3) Profit per design package for different demand levels[1]:

Demand Design package type	500 $	750 $	1000 $
1	4 557 500	6 836 250	9 115 000
2	3 307 500	5 586 250	7 865 000
3	2 057 500	4 336 250	6 615 000

Note
[1]The profit for each design package is calculated by multiplying the unit contribution of $9115 (variable cost of $47 972 × 0.19) by the different demand levels, adding the government's fixed sum for development of $7.5m less fixed costs for each package type as per the above schedule (e.g. design package type 1 = (500 × $9115) + $7.5m government contribution – $7.5m fixed costs = $4 557 500)

(W4) Expected values of the profits for the different demand levels:

Package 1 = ($4 557 500 × 0.85) + ($6 836 250 × 0.10) + ($9 115 000 × 0.05) = $5 013 250
Package 2 = ($3 307 500 × 0.25) + ($5 586 250 × 0.50) + ($7 865 000 × 0.25) = $5 586 250
Package 3 = ($2 057 500 × 0.20) + ($4 336 250 × 0.50) + ($6 615 000 × 0.30) = $4 564 025

(W5) Maximum and minimum profits derived from W3:

Design package type	Maximum outcome ($)	Minimum outcome ($)
1	9115000	4557500
2	7865000	3307500
3	6615000	2057500
Maximum outcome (maximax)	9115000 (option 1)	
Maximum outcome (maximin)		4557500 (option 1)

(W6) The following schedule shows the maximum regret based on the profits shown in W3:

Demand Design package chosen	500 $	750 $	1000 $	Max. regret $
1	0	0	0	0
2	1250 000	1250 000	1250 000	1250 000
3	2500 000	2500 000	2500 000	2500 000

Minimum of maximum regret = Package 1

Evaluation of the contract

W1 indicates that the contract complies with the government requirement of a maximum cost of $70000 per unit. If we wish to assess risk without taking into account the probability estimates provided by the risk manager then it is appropriate to use maximin, maximax and regret criteria. Risk averse decision-makers will aim to maximize the minimum possible returns and adopt a maximin approach and choose design package 1 with a maximum profit of approximately $4.6m. Alternatively, if they are very pessimistic they may choose to focus on the lost profit (regret) compared with the best outcome shown in W6 and minimize the maximum level of regret that they could suffer under any of the scenarios. In this case, they will choose design package 1, which will lead to no regret. Risk seekers will focus on the best outcome and adopt a maximax method and choose demand option 1 which has a maximax profit of $9115000 (see W5).

A risk neutral manager will not focus on optimistic or pessimistic outcomes. Instead, he or she will focus on average outcomes using probabilities and choose the maximum expected values of the outcomes. W4 shows that the maximum expected value is $5586250 if design package option 2 is chosen.

(iii) The choice of method will depend on the attitude to risk by the decision-makers at Mackerel. Given that the shareholders appear to be risk averse, the profit from the contract is significant being approximately 25 per cent of existing profits for the company as a whole and the economic environment is difficult there are strong arguments for taking a low risk approach and choosing design package option 1. This option has the least risk. The use of expected values is dependent on accurate probability estimates and the question implies that the probabilities of each outcome have not been widely debated within the company. The expected value of option 2 exceeds that of option 1 by $573000 (approximately 10 per cent) and given the extra risk associated with option 2 it is recommended that option 1 is chosen.

12.21 (a) Budgeted income statement for year ended 31 May 2019

	$	$
Fee income from Equine College (W1) Student category:		
Surgery	4536000	
Dentistry	3150000	
Business management	3402000	11088000
Operating costs (W2)		(6760000)
		4328000
Riding school fee income (W3)		
Rider category:		
Beginner	1843200	
Competent	2027520	
Advanced	3379200	7249920
Operating costs (W4)		(6095000)
Budgeted profit (Riding School)		1154920
		5482920

Workings

(W1)

The surgery fee income is calculated as follows:

Number of students (30% × 1200) =	360
Fee per student 12000 × 1.05 ($)	12600
Budgeted fee income ($)	4536000

The fee income for dentistry and business management is calculated in a similar manner.

(W2)

Operating costs = $6500000 × 1.04

(W3)

Riding School fee income

	Number of lessons	Charge per lesson ($)	Fee income ($)
240 horses × 4 per day × 320 days × 80% =	245760		
Beginner (50%)	122880	15	1843200
Competent (25%)	61440	(30 × 1.1) = 33	2027520
Advanced (25%)	61440	(50 × 1.1) = 55	3379200
			7249920

(W4)

Operating costs = $5750000 × 1.06 = $6095000

(b) (i)

% change	p[1]	Capacity utiliz.	p[2]	Joint p[3]	Equine College Revenue[4] $	Riding School Revenue[5] $	Total costs $	Net profit $	EV of net profit[6] $
		90%	0.10	0.02	11088000	8156160	12855000	6389160	127783
No change 0.20		80%	0.60	0.12	11088000	7249920	12855000	5482920	657950
		70%	0.30	0.06	11088000	6343680	12855000	4576680	274601
Decrease by 10%		90%	0.10	0.06	9979200	8156160	12855000	5280360	316822
	0.60	80%	0.60	0.36	9979200	7249920	12855000	4374120	1574683
		70%	0.30	0.18	9979200	6343680	12855000	3467880	624218
Decrease by 20%		90%	0.10	0.02	8870400	8156160	12855000	4171560	83431
	0.20	80%	0.60	0.12	8870400	7249920	12855000	3265320	391838
		70%	0.30	0.06	8870400	6343680	12855000	2359080	141545
				1.00			Expected value of profit =		4192872

Notes

[1] Probability of changes in student fees at Equine College.
[2] Probability of capacity utilization of Riding School.
[3] Joint probability of change in student fees and capacity utilization.
[4] Fee income calculated in (a) reduced by 0, 10 per cent and 20 per cent.
[5] Fee income calculated in (a) for 80 per cent capacity adjusted for 90 per cent and 70 per cent capacity levels.
[6] Net profit × joint probability

(ii) The expected value is the weighted average of the possible outcomes listed in (b) (i) and does not represent any of the actual outcomes listed. The use of expected outcome assumes that the decision-makers adopt a risk neutral attitude that do not take into account the variability of the range of possible outcomes that are used to derive the expected value.

(iii) The government may have decided to open an academy because:

- EMA operated the only Equine College in Hartland at full capacity in the previous year thus implying that demand exceeds the available supply for the facilities provided by the college.
- The government is actively promoting environmental initiatives and may wish to encourage future use of horse transportation instead of petrol/diesel vehicles.
- Hartland is a developing county with a large agricultural sector and the government is wishing to ensure that the necessary infrastructure exists to support the agricultural sector.

12.22 (a) The net income for the various alternatives is shown in the decision tree accompanying this answer. For option 1 the net income is $640 ($720 – $80) per member. For option 2 the net income per member if costs are $120 is $600 ($720 – $120) and $540 ($720 – $180) if costs are $180. The joint probabilities for option 2 are calculated as follows:

Joint probability of 6000 members × $600 net income per member = (0.4 × 0.5) = 0.2
Joint probability of 6000 members × $540 net income per member = (0.4 × 0.5) = 0.2
Joint probability of 6500 members × $600 net income per member = (0.6 × 0.5) = 0.3
Joint probability of 6500 members × $540 net income per member = (0.6 × 0.5) = 0.3

The expected value of the annual net income is calculated by multiplying the above joint probabilities by the net income for each outcome as follows:

$0.2 \times \$3.6m = \$0.72m$
$0.2 \times \$3.24m = \$0.648m$
$0.3 \times \$3.9m = \$1.170m$
$0.3 \times \$3.51m = \underline{£1.053m}$
Expected value = $\underline{\$3.591m}$

For the three-year period the expected values are:

Option 1 $10.08m ($3.36m × 3)

Option 2 $10.413m [($3.591m × 3) – ($0.36m capital cost)]

Therefore option 2 should be chosen.

(b) To ascertain the value of perfect information we need to compare the expected value (EV) of the decision if the information is acquired against the expected value with the absence of the information.
With perfect information and assuming membership numbers were 6000 the annual net income EV would be:

$(£3.6m \times 0.5) + (£3.24m \times 0.5) = \$3.42m$
Over the three-year period the outcome would be ($3.42m × 3) – 0.36m capital cost = $9.9m
Therefore option 1 yielding an outcome of $10.08m would be chosen.

If membership numbers were 6500 the annual net income EV would be:

$(\$3.9m \times 0.5) + (\$3.51m \times 0.5) = \$3.705m$
Over the three-year period the outcome would be ($3.705 × 3) – $0.36m capital = $10.755m and option 2 would be chosen.
Therefore EV with perfect information = (0.4 × $10.08m) + (0.6 × $10.755) = $10.485m.
Without perfect information the EV is $10.413m. Therefore the value of perfect information, being the maximum price the company should be prepared to pay, is $72 000 ($10.485m – $10.413m).

(c) Expected values represent the long run average of an outcome that would be expected if a decision was to be repeated many times. There is no guarantee that the actual outcome will be equal to the expected value. Also the expected value does not appear in the probability distribution. Estimating accurate probabilities is also difficult because this situation has not arisen before. The expansion decision is a one-off decision, rather than a decision that will be repeated many times. It may be preferable to compare the outcome for option 1 with the probability distribution of the potential outcomes derived from the final column of the decision tree for option 2 shown below:

Outcome of 9.36m [($3.24 × 3) – $0.36m] with a probability of 0.2
Outcome of 10.17m [$3.51m × 3) – $0.36m] with a probability of 0.3
Outcome of 10.44m [($3.6m × 3) – $0.36m] with a probability of 0.2
Outcome of 11.34m [$3.9m × 3) – $0.36m] with a probability of 0.3

There is a probability of 0.8 that option 2 will yield the higher outcome.

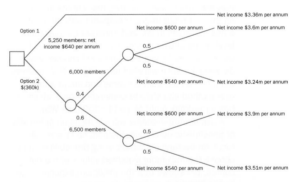

12.23 (a) (i)   See the decision tree shown in Figure Q12.23.

(ii) 1 The assumption underlying the maximin technique is that the worst outcome will occur. The decision-maker should select the outcome with the largest possible payoff assuming the worst possible outcome occurs. From the decision tree we can see that the payoffs for the worst possible outcomes are as follows:

	Payoff (£000)
Hire of machine 200	55
Hire of machine 300	45
Hire of machine 600	38.5
Do not franchise	90

The decision is not to franchise using the maximum criterion.

2 The expected values for each alternative (see Figure Q12.22) are as follows:

	(£000)
Hire of machine 200	87.0
Hire of machine 300	101.0
Hire of machine 600	99.0
Do not franchise	90.0

The company will maximize the expected value of the contributions if it hires the 300 batch machine.

3 The probability of a contribution of less than £100 000 for each alternative can be found by adding the joint probabilities from payoffs of less than £100 000. The probabilities are as follows:

Hire of machine 200	= 0.85
Hire of machine 300	= 0.55
Hire of machine 600	= 0.65
Do not franchise	= 1.00

The company should hire the 300 machine adopting this decision criterion.

(b) The approaches in part (a) enable uncertainty to be incorporated into the analysis and for decisions to be based on range of outcomes rather than a single outcome. This approach should produce better decisions in the long run. The main problem with this approach is that only a few selected outcomes with related probabilities are chosen as being representative of the entire distribution of possible outcomes. The approach also gives the impression of accuracy, which

is not justified. Comments on the specific methods used in (a) are as follows:

Maximin: Enables an approach to be adopted which minimizes risk. The main disadvantage is that such a risk-averse approach will not result in decisions that will maximize long-run profits.

Expected value: For the advantages of this approach see 'Expected value' in Chapter 12. The weaknesses of expected value are as follows:

(i) It ignores risk. Decisions should not be made on expected value alone. It should be used in conjunction with measures of dispersion.

(ii) It is a long-run average payoff. Therefore it is best suited to repetitive decisions.

(iii) Because it is an average, it is unlikely that the expected value will occur.

Probability of earning an annual contribution of less than £100 000: This method enables decision-makers to specify their attitude towards risk and return and choose the alternative that meets the decision-makers risk–return preference. It is unlikely that this approach will be profit-maximizing or result in expected value being maximized.

CHAPTER 13

13.13

Year		Cash flow $	Discount factor @ 8%	Present value $	Discount factor @ 20%	Present value $
0	Initial investment	(70 000)	1.000	(70 000)	1.000	(70 000)
1–3	Cash inflows per annum	30 000	2.577	77 310	2.106	63 180
3	Residual value	10 000	0.794	7 940	0.579	5 790
	Net present value			15 250		(1 030)

IRR by interpolation:

$8\% + (15\,250/(15\,250 + 1\,030)) \times (20\% - 8\%) = 19.2\%$

If the company's cost of capital increases to more than 19.2 per cent the investment will no longer be viable. The current cost of capital is 8 per cent so it can increase by 140 per cent before the investment is no longer viable.

13.14 (a) (i) This is a relevant incremental cost

(ii) Depreciation is reflected in the investment outlay and disposable value at the end of a project's life. Therefore depreciation is not a relevant cost.

(iii) The further training costs are incremental and relevant

(iv) This is a relevant and incremental cost

(v) This is a sunk and irrelevant cost

(vi) This is irrelevant because it is already reflected in the discounting process within the NPV calculation

(b) (i) Increase in sales = ($11m – $10m) = $1m
Increase due to the project = ($1m – $0.2m) = $800 000

(ii) Total sales in year 1 = $11m
Savings ($11m × 0.01) = $110 000

FIGURE Q12.23

(b) (iii) Present value ($75 000 × 3.791 annuity factor for 5 years) = $284 325

(c) The answer is **B** because the IRR of 14% is higher than the cost of capital of 10%.

13.15 Payment will be made 35 days early.
Number of compounding periods = 365/35= 10.429
$1+ r = (1.00/0.98)^{10.429}$
$1+ r = 1.2345$
so the effective annual interest rate of the early settlement discount is 23.45%
The correct answer is **(c)**.

13.16 Investment A = $(1.017)^4$ = 6.975%
Investment B = $(1.034)^2$ = 6.916%
Investment C = $(1.054)^{12/9}$ = 7.264%
Investment D = 7%

Answer = **(c)**

13.17 The yield on similar bonds is 10 per cent so this is used as the discount rate.

Year(s)	Description	Cash flow $	Discount factor (10%)	Present value $
1–4	Interest	8	3.170	25.36
4	Redemption	100	0.683	68.30
0	Purchase price			93.66

13.18

Year(s)	Description	Cash flow	Discount factor (3%)	Present value $	Discount factor (6%)	Present value $
0	Purchase	103	1.000	(103.00)	1.000	(103.00)
1-4	Interest	6	3.717	22.30	3.465	20.79
4	Redemption	100	0.888	88.80	0.792	79.20
NPV				8.10		(3.01)

By interpolation
3% + (($8.10/($8.10 + $3.01)) × 3) = 5.19%
The bond's yield to maturity is 5.19%

13.19 The PV of a perpetuity = Annual cash flow/cost of capital where the cash flows start at the *end* of the first year. Here the cash flows start at the beginning of the first year so:
PV = $300 + $300/0.12 = $2800

Answer = **(b)**

13.20 The annual percentage rate (APR) is 12.68%, which is based on annual payments.

Monthly interest rate = $^{12}\sqrt{1.1268} - 1 = 0.01$ so that $r = 1\%$

In other words a monthly interest rate compounded for 12 periods at 1 per cent is equivalent to an annual rate of 12.68 per cent. This is derived from using the compound interest formula used in the chapter = $(1 + 0.01)^{12} - 1 = 0.1268 = 12.68\%$

To determine the future value of an annuity where a constant amount is invested each period the future =

$A\left[\dfrac{(1 + r)^n - 1}{r}\right]$ where r is the rate of interest per period and A is the annuity amount.

Future value = $50 \times \left[\dfrac{1.01^{13\times12} - 1}{.01}\right] = £18610$

Answer = **(d)**

13.21 Because the investment is a constant amount each period we can use the annuity future value formula shown in the answer to question 13.19:

Future value = $A\left[\dfrac{(1 + r)^n - 1}{r}\right]$

where r is the rate of interest per period and A is the annuity amount.

$£7000 = A\left[\dfrac{1.005^{12 \times 5} - 1}{.005}\right]$

£7 000 = 69.77A
A = £100.33
Answer = **(c)**

13.22 The loan represents the present value of a series of repayments over a three year period. Since the payments are constant per period we can use the following annuity present value formula:

Present value = $\dfrac{A}{r}\left[1 - \dfrac{1}{(1 + r)^n}\right]$

where A is the annuity amount and r is the interest rate per period. The annual interest rate must be converted to a monthly rate since we are dealing with monthly repayments.
Monthly interest rate = $^{12}\sqrt{1.10} - 1 = .0079$ (i.e. 0.79%)

Present value (2 000) = $\dfrac{A}{0.0079}\left[1 - \dfrac{1}{1.0079^{36}}\right]$

$2000 = \dfrac{A}{0.0079}(0.2467)$

2 000 (0.0079) = 0.2467A
A =15.8/.2467 = £64.04
Answer = **(b)**

13.23 (a) Applying the formula shown in question 13.19:

Future value = $50 \times \left[\dfrac{1.01^{10\times12} - 1}{0.01}\right] = £11501.94$

We must now compound forward a further 5 years at an annual rate of 15 per cent:
£11 501.95 × $(1.15)^5$ = £23 134.53

(b) (i) *Loan 1*
APR of 9.38% results in a monthly rate of $^{12}\sqrt{1.0938} = 1.0075$ so that $r = .0075$ (i.e. .75%)
The loan represents the present value of a series of repayments over a three-year period. Since the payments are constant per period we can use the following annuity present value formula:

Present value = $\dfrac{A}{r}\left[1 - \dfrac{1}{(1 + r)^n}\right]$

where A is the annuity amount and r is the interest rate per period.

Present value (2 000) = $\dfrac{A}{0.0075}\left[1 - \dfrac{1}{1.0075^{36}}\right]$

$2000 = \dfrac{A}{0.0075}(0.23585)$

2 000 (0.0075) = 0.23585A
A = 15/.23585 = £63.60

Loan 2
APR of 12.68% results in a monthly rate of $^{12}\sqrt{1.1268} = 1.01$ so that $r = .01$ (i.e. 1%)

$$\text{Present value (2000)} = \frac{A}{0.01}\left[1 - \frac{1}{1.01^{24}}\right]$$

$$2000 = \frac{A}{.01}(0.2124)$$

$$2000\,(.01) = 0.2124A$$
$$A = 20/.2124 = £94.16$$

(ii) Loan 1 total amount repaid = £63.60 × 36 = £2289.60
Loan 2 total amount repaid = £94.16 × 24 = £2259.84
Loan 2 is the slightly cheaper loan

13.24 (a) *Project 1*

Internal failure cost savings
Current expected value of savings ($000s) = ($300 × 0.5) + ($500 × 0.3) + ($700 × 0.2) = $440
Expected savings ($000s) in year 1 = $440 × 1.04 × 80% = $366.08

External failure cost savings
Current expected value of savings ($000s) = ($1300 × 0.6) + ($1900 × 0.3) + ($3000 × 0.1) = $1650
Expected savings ($000s) in year 1 = ($1650 × 1.04 × 80%) = $1372.8

Raw material cost future savings
Expected savings ($000s) in year 1 = 50000 × $62 × 1.04 = $3224
Net cash flows in year1
$366080 + $1372800 + $3224000 = $4962880

(b) (i) *Project 2 NPV*
Expected savings in year 1 = $110 ($370 − $260) × 50000 × $110 × 1.04 = $5720000
Additional annual fixed costs = $5m − $15m/5 depreciation = $2m
Net Present Value

	Year 0 $000	Year 1 $000	Year 2 $000	Year 3 $000	Year 4 $000	Year 5 $000
Initial Investment	(15000)					
Working capital	(1000)					1000
Cost savings		5720	5949	6187	6434	6691
Fixed costs		(2000)	(2000)	(2000)	(2000)	(2000)
Net cash flows	(16000)	3720	3949	4187	4434	5691
Discount factor @ 8%	1000	0.926	0.857	0.794	0.735	0.681
Present value	(16000)	3445	3384	3324	3259	3876

NPV = 1288000
Note that the cost savings increase at 4% per annum because of the increased production.

(ii) *Project 2 IRR*
Using a higher discount rate of 12 per cent to apply the trial and error process the NPV is $503000 as shown in the following calculation:

	Year 0 $000	Year 1 $000	Year 2 $000	Year 3 $000	Year 4 $000	Year 5 $000
Net cash flows	(16000)	3720	3949	4187	4434	5691
Discount factor @ 12%	1.000	0.893	0.797	0.712	0.636	0.567
Present value	(16000)	3322	3147	2981	2820	3227

Based on discount rates of 8 per cent and 12 per cent and using interpolation IRR
8% + (1288/(1288 + 503)) × 4% = 10.9%

(c) The projects are mutually exclusive and it was pointed out in Chapter 13 that the NPV method should be

used to rank mutually exclusive projects. Using the NPV criterions project 1 should be chosen since it has the higher NPV. However, capital rationing applies (see Chapter 14). Project 1 requires $4m more investment funds than project 2. If the $4m could be invested to yield a NPV in excess of the NPV of $1338000 from project 1 less the NPV of $1288000 from project 2 then project 2 should be chosen.

(d) See 'Comparison of NPV and IRR' in Chapter 13 for the answer to this question.

13.25 (a) The expected value of Year 1 car parking charges is:
($60 × 40%) + ($50 × 25%) + ($70 × 35%) = $61 × 1.05 inflation factor = $64.05
Year 1 sales revenue = (600 × 0.75) × $64.05 × 52 weeks = $1499k
Year 1 contribution = $1499k × 0.8 = $1199k

Fixed Costs
Year 1 Staff costs = $350k × 1.04 inflation factor = $364k
Year 1 Security system costs = $100k × 1.04 inflation = $104k
The above cash flows are entered in year 1 of the following cash flow statement and the cash flows for the remaining years are adjusted by the appropriate inflation rate.

Cash flows	Year 1 $000	Year 2 $000	Year 3 $000	Year 4 $000	Year 5 $000
Contribution	1199	1259	1322	1388	1457
Leasing costs	(50)	(50)	(50)	(50)	(50)
Staff costs	(364)	(379)	(394)	(409)	(426)
Security system costs	(104)	(108)	(112)	(117)	(122)
Net cash flows	681	722	766	812	859

Taxation

	Year 1 $000	Year 2 $000	Year 3 $000	Year 4 $000	Year 5 $000
Net cash flows	681	722	766	812	859
Taxation @ 30%	(204)	(217)	(230)	(244)	(258)

Net present value

	Year 0 $000	Year 1 $000	Year 2 $000	Year 3 $000	Year 4 $000	Year 5 $000	Year 6 $000
Land purchase and development	(8000)					10000	
Net cash flows		681	722	766	812	859	
Tax payment		(102)	(108)	(115)	(122)	(129)	
Tax payment		0	(102)	(109)	(115)	(122)	(129)
Net cash flow after tax	(8000)	579	512	542	575	10608	(129)
Discount factors @ 8%	1.000	0.926	0.857	0.794	0.735	0.681	0.630
Present value	(8000)	536	439	430	423	7224	(81)

The project has a positive NPV of $971k and therefore should be accepted.

(b) NPV at 12%

	Year 0 $000	Year 1 $000	Year 2 $000	Year 3 $000	Year 4 $000	Year 5 $000	Year 6 $000
Net cash flow after tax	(8000)	579	512	542	575	10608	(129)
Discount factors @ 12%	1.000	0.893	0.797	0.712	0.636	0.567	0.507
Present value	(8000)	517	408	386	366	6015	(65)

Net present value = −$373k
IRR = 8% + (($971k/($971k + $373k)) × (12% − 8%))
= 8% + 2.9%
= 10.9%

(c) The three element of the time value of money are risk, the opportunity cost arising from the delay in inflows/outflows and inflation. You should refer to 'The opportunity cost of an investment' in Chapter 13 for an explanation of risk and 'Compounding and discounting' in Chapter 13 for the opportunity cost arising from the delay in inflows/outflows. The inflation element relates to the fact that if there is inflation then investors also need to be compensated for the loss in purchasing power.

13.26 (a) Project A = 3 years + $\left(\dfrac{350 - 314}{112}\right)$ = 3.32 years

Project B = 3.0 years
Project C = 2.00 years

(b) Accounting rate of return = average profit/average investment
Project A = 79/175 = 45%
Project B = 84/175 = 48%
Project C = 70/175 = 40%
Note that average profit = (sum of cash flows − investment cost)/project's life.

(c) The report should include:

(i) NPVs of each project (project A = £83 200 (W1), project B = £64 000 (W2), project C = £79 000 (W3). A simple description of NPV should also be provided. For example, the NPV is the amount over and above the cost of the project which could be borrowed, secure in the knowledge that the cash flows from the project will repay the loan.

(ii) The following rankings are based on the different evaluation procedures:

Project	IRR	Payback	ARR	NPV
A	2	3	2	1
B	3	2	1	3
C	1	1	3	2

(iii) A discussion of each of the above evaluation procedures.

(iv) IRR is subject to the following criticisms:

1 Multiple rates of return can occur when a project has unconventional cash flows.

2 It is assumed that the cash flows received from a project are re-invested at the IRR and not the cost of capital.

3 Inability to rank mutually exclusive projects.

4 It cannot deal with different sized projects. For example, it is better to earn a return of 35 per cent on £100 000 than 40 per cent on £10 000.

Note that the above points are explained in detail in Chapter 13.

(v) Payback ignores cash flows outside the payback period, and it also ignores the timing of cash flows within the payback period. For example, the large cash flows for project A are ignored after the payback period. This method may be appropriate for companies experiencing liquidity problems who wish to recover their initial investment quickly.

(vi) Accounting rate of return ignores the timing of cash flows, but it is considered an important

measure by those who believe reported profits have a significant impact on share prices.

(vii) NPV is generally believed to be the theoretically correct evaluation procedure. A positive NPV from an investment is supposed to indicate the increase in the market value of the shareholders' funds, but this claim depends upon the belief that the share price is the discounted present value of the future dividend stream. If the market uses some other method of valuing shares then a positive NPV may not represent the increase in market value of shareholders' funds. Note that the cash flows have been discounted at the company's cost of capital. It is only suitable to use the company's cost of capital as the discount rate if projects A, B and C are equivalent to the average risk of all the company's existing projects. If they are not of average risk then project risk-adjusted discount rates should be used.

(viii) The projects have unequal lives. It is assumed that the equipment will not be replaced. If the equipment is to be replaced, it will be necessary to consider the projects over a common time horizon using the techniques described for projects with unequal lives in Learning Note 14.1.

(ix) It is recommended that NPV method is used and project A should be selected.

(d) Stadler prefers project C because it produces the highest accounting profit in year 3. Stadler is assuming that share prices are influenced by short-run reported profits. This is in contrast with theory, which assumes that the share price is the discounted present value of the future dividend stream. Stadler is also assuming that the market only has access to reported historical profits and is not aware of the future benefits arising from the projects. The stock market also obtains company information on future prospects from sources other than reported profits. For example, press releases, chairman's report and signals of future prosperity via increased dividend payments.

Workings
(W1) Project A = (100 × 0.8333) + (110 × 0.6944) + (104 × 0.5787) + (112 × 0.4823) + (138 × 0.4019) + (160 × 0.3349) + (180 × 0.2791) − £350
(W2) Project B = (40 × 0.8333) + (100 × 0.6944) + (210 × 0.5787) + (260 × 0.4823) + (160 × 0.4019) − £350
(W3) Project C = (200 × 0.8333) + (150 × 0.6944) + (240 × 0.5787) + (40 × 0.4823) − £350

CHAPTER 14

14.13 (1 + nominal/money rate) = (1 + real rate) × (1 + expected rate of inflation)
(1 + nominal/money rate) = (1.06) × (1.03) = 1.0918
nominal/money rate = (1.0918 − 1) = 9.18%

Answer = **(d)**

14.14 Net cash flows per annum = $101 000 − $30 000 − $5000 = $66 000
PV of net cash flows = $66 000 × 3.605 = $237 930
NPV = $237 930 − $150 000 = $87 930
The PV of the sales revenue = $101 000 × 3.605
= $364 105

The percentage change in the selling price that will result in the project being rejected is:
$87 930/$364 105 = 24.15%

14.15 (i) The NPV of the project at 12% is $8675. If the present value of the fixed costs were to increase by more than $8675 then the project would no longer be viable so fixed costs can increase by 9.6% ($8675/$90 125).

    (ii) • Sensitivity analysis enables a company to identify how the impact of changes in variables affects the planned outcome.
        • Sensitivity analysis enables identification critical variables that are of vital importance.

14.16 NPV = $280 000
Present value of the annual cash inflow = $320 000 × 3.037 = $971 840
Present value of the annual cash inflow can decline to $691 840 ($971 840 − $280 000) before NPV becomes negative so annual cash flows can decline to $227 803 ($691 840/3.037).
Sensitivity = ($320 000 − $227 803)/$320 000 = 28.8%

Answer = **(d)**

14.17

Project	Investment $	Profitability index	Present value $	Ranking
A	12 000	1.20	14 400	3
B	8 000	1.05	8 400	4
C	20 000	1.60	32 000	1
D	16 000	1.40	22 400	n/a
E	14 000	1.30	18 200	2

The company should invest in projects C, E and half of A. This will yield a NPV of $17 400 ($57 400 − $40 000).

14.18 You should refer to Learning note 14.1 in the digital resources that accompany this book for an explanation of the annualized equivalent method.

		Replace after Year 1		Replace after Year 2		Replace after Year 3	
Year	Discount factor	Cash flows $	Present value $	Cash flows $	Present value $	Cash flows $	Present value $
0	1.00	(25 000)	(25 000)	(25 000)	(25 000)	(25 000)	(25 000)
1	0.943	13 000	12 259	(5 000)	(4 715)	(5 000)	(4 715)
2	0.890			7 000	6 230	(8 000)	(7 120)
3	0.840					(6 000)	(5 040)
Present value			(12 741)		(23 485)		(41 875)
Cumulative discount factor			0.943		1.833		2.673
Annualised equivalent cost			13 511		12 812		15 666

The lowest annualized equivalent cost occurs with the 2-year replacement period so the optimum replacement cycle is to replace every 2 years.

14.19 (a) It is assumed that the cost of capital is a nominal rate. The NPV can be calculated by discounting real cash flows at the real discount rate or nominal cash flows at the nominal discount rate. The real

discount rate (1 + real discount rate) is (1 + nominal rate)/(1 + anticipated inflation rate) = 0.0485 (1.08/1.03 − 1).
The annual cash flows in current prices are £20 000 (£5 × 4 000 units).
NPV based on real cash flows and the real discount rate:
(£20 000)/(1.0485) + (20 000)/(1.0485)² + (20 000)/(1.0485)³ − £50 000 = £4640
NPV based on discounting nominal cash flows at the nominal discount rate:
(£20 000 × 1.03)/1.08 + (£20 000 × 1.03²)/1.08² + (£20 000 × 1.03³)/1.08³ − £50 000 = £4640

Answer = **(a)**

(b) NPV will be zero where:
Annual cash flows (£20 000) × Annuity discount factor = Investment outlay (£50 000)
Annuity discount factor = 2.5 (£50 000/20 000)
For a three year life the annuity tables indicate a factor of 2.531 for 9 per cent and 2.487 for 10 per cent. Using interpolation a factor of 2.5 is equivalent to 9.7 per cent. Note that this is a real discount rate (based on using real cash flows). To convert to a nominal (monetary rate):
(1 + nominal rate) = (1 + real discount rate) × (1 + anticipated inflation rate) = (1 + .097) × (1.04) = 1.141
Nominal rate = 1.141 − 1 = 14.1%

Answer = **(c)**

14.20 (a) *Gross profits years 1–5*
Year 1: 100 000 customers × 52 weeks × $200 = $1040m × 20% = $208m
Year 2: 120 000 customers × 52 weeks × $200 = $1248m × 20% = $250m
Year 3: 150 000 customers × 52 weeks × $200 = $1560m × 20% = $312m
Year 4: 160 000 customers × 52 weeks × $200 = $1664m × 20% = $333m
Year 5: 170 000 customers × 52 weeks × $200 = $1768m × 20% = $354m

Calculation of taxation payable

	Year 1 $m	Year 2 $m	Year3 $m	Year 4 $m	Year 5 $m
Gross profit	208	250	312	333	354
Lost profit from existing sales	(62)	(75)	(94)	(100)	(106)
Other operating costs	(60)	(65)	(70)	(75)	(80)
Lease income	20	20	20	20	20
Fee to PQ	(30)	(30)	(30)	(30)	(30)
Fee to PQ	(2)	(3)	(3)	(3)	(4)
Net cash flows	74	97	135	145	154
Tax depreciation	(4)	(3)	(2)	(2)	(4)
Taxable profit	70	94	133	'43	150
Taxation @ 30%	21	28	40	43	45

Note that tax depreciation in year 5 represents a balancing allowance of $4m ($15m initial cost less cumulative writing down allowances of $11m.

Net present value calculation

	Year 0 $m	Year 1 $m	Year 2 $m	Year 3 $m	Year 4 $m	Year 5 $m	Year 6 $m
Investment/ residual value	(445)					350	
Net cash flows		74	97	135	145	154	
Tax payment		(11)	(14)	(20)	(22)	(23)	
Tax payment			(10)	(14)	(20)	(21)	(22)
Net cash flow after tax	(445)	63	73	101	103	460	(22)
Discount factors @ 12%	1.000	0.893	0.797	0.712	0.636	0.567	0.507
Present value	(445)	56	58	72	66	261	(11)

Note that the investment outlay = $340m purchase of warehouse + $90 m expansion + $15m for the delivery fleet.

NPV is + $57m (i.e. the sum of the final row) so the project should go ahead.

(b) The following factors need to be considered:

1 The reliability of PQ since LM is reliant on PQ to provide the IT technology and delivery service to its customers for the five year period of the contract.

2 The ability of the retailer to provide the quality and reliability of service that LM's customers will expect.

(c)

		Replace after Year 1		Replace after Year 2		Replace after Year 3	
Year	Discount Factor @12%	Cash flows $	Present value $	Cash flows $	Present value $	Cash flows $	Present value $
0	1.000	(25000)	(25000)	(25000)	(25000)	(25000)	(25000)
1	0.893	10000	8930	(6000)	(5358)	(6000)	(5358)
2	0.797			2000	1594	(8000)	(6376)
3	0.712					(8000)	(5696)
Net present value			(16070)		(28764)		(42430)
Cumulative discount factor			0.893		1.690		2.402
Annualized equivalent			(17996)		(17020)		(17664)

The lowest annualized equivalent cost occurs if the vehicles are replaced every two years.

14.21 (a) The NPV calculations can be adjusted in two basic ways to account for inflation. Real cash flows can be discounted at the real discount rate or inflation adjusted cash flows can be discounted at a discount rate which incorporates a premium for inflation. It is only appropriate to leave the cash flows in terms of present-day prices and discount these cash flows at the real cost of capital when all the cash flows are expected to increase at the general level of inflation. The cash flows in the question are subject to different levels of inflation. In particular, capital allowances are based on the original cost and do not change in line with changing prices. Therefore the cash flows should be adjusted for inflation and discounted at a cost of capital which incorporates a premium for inflation. The inflation adjusted revenues, expenses and taxation liabilities are:

Year	1	2	3	4	5
Sales at 5% inflation (W1)	3675	5402	6159	6977	6790
Materials at 10% inflation	(588)	(907)	(1198)	(1537)	(1449)
Labour at 10% inflation	(1177)	(1815)	(2396)	(3075)	(2899)
Overheads at 5% inflation	(52)	(110)	(116)	(122)	(128)
Capital allowances (W2)	(1125)	(844)	(633)	(475)	(1423)
Taxable profits	733	1726	1816	1768	891
Taxation at 35%	256	604	636	619	312

The interest payments are not included because they are taken into account when the cash flows are discounted.

Workings

(W1) Year 1 = £3500 (1.05), year 2 = £4900 $(1.05)^2$, year 3 = £5320 $(1.05)^3$, year 4 = £5740 $(1.05)^4$, year 5 = £5320 $(1.05)^5$. The same approach is used to calculate the inflation adjusted cash flows for the remaining items.

(W2) 25% writing down allowances on £4500 with a balancing allowance in year 5.

The cash flow estimates and NPV calculation are as follows:

Year	0	1	2	3	4	5	6
Inflows							
Sales	—	3675	5402	6159	6977	6790	—
Outflows							
Materials	—	588	907	1198	1537	1449	—
Labour	—	1177	1815	2396	3075	2899	—
Overheads	—	52	110	116	122	128	—
Fixed assets	4500						
Working capital (W1)	300	120	131	144	156	(851)	—
Taxation			256	604	636	619	312
Total outflows	4800	1937	3219	4458	5526	4244	312
Net cash flows	(4800)	1738	2183	1701	1451	2546	(312)
Discount factors at 15%		0.870	0.756	0.658	0.572	0.497	0.432
Present values	(4800)	1512	1650	1119	830	1265	(135)

The NPV is £1 441 000 and it is therefore recommended that the project should be undertaken. Note that the interest cost is already incorporated in the DCF calculation and should not be included in the cash flows when calculating present values.

Workings

(W1) It is assumed that the working capital is released at the end of the project. Year 1 = 400 (1.05) − 300, year 2 = 500 $(1.05)^2$ − 420, and so on.

(b) Calculating the IRR will produce an NPV of zero. NPV is £1 441 000 at a 15 per cent discount rate. In order to use the interpolation method to calculate the IRR, it is necessary to ascertain a negative NPV. At a discount rate of 30 per cent the NPV is

Year	Cash flow (£000)	Discount factor	PV (£000)
0	(4800)	1.0000	(4800)
1	1738	0.7692	1337
2	2183	0.5917	1292
3	1701	0.4552	774
4	1451	0.3501	508
5	2546	0.2693	686
6	(312)	0.2071	(65)
			(268)

Using the interpolation method, the IRR is

$$15\% + \frac{1441}{1441 - (-205)} = 15\% = 28\%$$

(c) See 'Sensitivity analysis' in Chapter 14 for a description and discussion of the weaknesses of sensitivity analysis. Other traditional techniques include the use of probability distributions to calculate expected net present value and standard deviation, simulation and certainty equivalents. More recent techniques include portfolio theory and the capital asset pricing model. Theorists would suggest that risk should be incorporated into the analysis by discounting the expected value of a project's cash flows at a risk-adjusted discount rate using the capital asset pricing model.

14.22 (a) *Contribution Years 1–5*

Year 1: 100 000 × $20 = $2000k
Year 2: 100 000 × 1.2 = 120 000 × $20
= $2400k × 1.04 = $2496k
Year 3: 120 000 × 1.2 = 144 000 × $20
= $2880k × 1.04^2 = $3115k
Year 4: 144 000 × 1.2 = 172 800 × $20
= $3456k × 1.04^3 = $3888k
Year 5: 172 800 × 1.2 = 207 360 × $20
= $4147k × 1.04^4 = $4852k

Fixed costs

Depreciation per annum $1.7m [($10m – $1.5m)/5]
Fixed costs (excluding depreciation) per annum =
$0.8m ($2.5m – $1.7m) increasing at 4 per cent per annum after year 1.

Taxation payable

	Year 1 $000	Year 2 $000	Year 3 $000	Year 4 $000	Year 5 $000
Contribution	2000	2496	3115	3888	4852
Fixed costs	(800)	(832)	(865)	(900)	(936)
Net cash flows	1200	1664	2250	2988	3916
Tax depreciation	(2500)	(1875)	(1406)	(1055)	(1664)
Taxable profit	(1300)	(211)	844	1933	2252
Taxation @ 30%	390	63	(253)	(580)	(676)

Note that the tax depreciation (WDAs) are calculated at 25 per cent on a reducing balance basis:

Year 1 = 0.25 × $10m, Year 2 = 0.25 × ($10m – $2.5m), Year 3 = 0.25 × ($10m – $4.375m), Year 4 = 0.25 × ($10m – $5.781m), Year 5 = Net cost of $10m – $1.5m sale proceeds – accumulated depreciation of $6.836m resulting in a balancing allowance of $1.664m.

Net present value

	Year 0 $000	Year 1 $000	Year 2 $000	Year 3 $000	Year 4 $000	Year 5 $000	Year 6 $000
Investment/ residual value	(10 000)					1500	
Working capital	(3000)	(120)	(125)	(130)	(135)	3510	
Net cash flows		1200	1664	2250	2988	3916	
Tax cash flow		195	32	(127)	(290)	(338)	
Tax cash flow			195	31	(126)	(290)	(338)
Net cash flow after tax	(13 000)	1275	1766	2024	2437	8298	(338)
Discount factors @ 12%	1.000	0.893	0.797	0.712	0.636	0.567	0.507
Present value	(13 000)	1139	1408	1441	1550	4705	(171)

The sum of the final row of the above schedule results in a negative NPV of $2 928 000 so the project should not go ahead.

(b) (i) In order to use interpolation it is necessary to use a discount rate that generates a positive NPV. Given that NPV is negative at 12 per cent it is necessary to try a lower rate, say 4 per cent. The following calculation of at a discount rate of 4 per cent gives a positive NPV of $298 000.

	Year 0 $000	Year 1 $000	Year 2 $000	Year 3 $000	Year 4 $000	Year 5 $000	Year 6 $000
Net cash flow after tax	(13 000)	1275	1766	2024	2437	8298	(338)
Discount factors @ 4%	1.000	0.962	0.925	0.889	0.855	0.822	0.790
Present value	(13 000)	1227	1634	1799	2084	6821	(267)

Using interpolation IRR = 4% + (($298k/ ($298k + $2928)) × 8) = 4.74%

(ii) The cost of capital is 12 per cent so it must fall to below 4.74 per cent for the project to be acceptable so the cost of capital would need to reduce by 4.6 per cent [(12 – 4.74)/12 = 61%]

14.23 (a) *Calculations of expected net present value and profitability indices*

Project A
NPV (£70 000 × 3.605) – £246 000 = £6350

Profitability index $= \dfrac{\text{present value of cash inflows}}{\text{initial outlay}}$

$$= \frac{252 350}{246 000} = 1.026$$

Project B
NPV (£75 000 × 0.893) + (£87 000 × 0.797) + (£64 000 × 0.712) – £180 000 = £1882

Profitability index $= \dfrac{181 882}{180 000} = 1.010$

Project C
NPV (£48 000 × 1.69) + (£63 000 × 0.712) + (£73 000 × 0.636) – £175 000 = (£2596)

Profitability index $= \dfrac{172 404}{175 000} = 0.985$

Project D
NPV (£62 000 × 3.037) – £180 000 = £8294

Profitability index $= \dfrac{188 294}{180 000} = 1.046$

Project E
NPV (£40 000 × 0.893) + (£50 000 × 0.797) + (£60 000 × 0.712) + (£70 000 × 0.636) + (£40 000 × 0.567) – £180 000 = £5490

Profitability index $= \dfrac{185 490}{180 000} = 1.031$

Project F
NPV 5 (£35 000 × 0.893) + (£82 000 × 1.509) – £150 000 = £4993

Profitability index $= \dfrac{154 993}{150 000} = 1.033$

Project rankings	NPV	PI
1	D	D
2	A	F
3	E	E
4	F	A
5	B	B
6	C	C

The rankings differ because NPV is an absolute measure whereas the profitability index is a relative measure that takes into account the different investment cost of each project.

(b) The objective is to select a combination of investments that will maximize NPV subject to a total capital outlay of £620000. Projects A and E are mutually exclusive and project C has a negative NPV. The following are potential combinations of projects:

Projects	Expected NPV (£)	Total expected NPV (£)	Total Outlay (£)
A, B, D	6350 + 1882 + 8294	16526	606000
A, B, F	6350 + 1882 + 4993	13225	576000
A, D, F	6350 + 8294 + 4993	19637	576000
B, D, E	1882 + 8294 + 5490	15666	540000
B, D, F	1882 + 8294 + 4993	15169	510000
D, E, F	8294 + 5490 + 4993	18777	510000

Note that it is not possible to combine four projects within the constraints outlined above and that expected NPV cannot be increased by combining two projects. Accepting projects A, D and F will maximize NPV. This combination will require a total capital outlay of £576000, and the unused funds will be invested to yield a return of 9 per cent. The risk-adjusted discount rate for the investment will also be 9 per cent. Therefore the NPV of funds invested in the money market will be zero.

(c) Where a company rejects projects with positive NPVs because of capital rationing, the IRR forgone on the most profitable project that has been rejected represents the opportunity cost of capital. For a more detailed explanation of this point see 'capital rationing' in Chapter 14. Therefore the director is correct in stating that the company's cost of capital might not be appropriate.

(d) *Advantages of mathematical programming:*

(i) Ability to solve complex problems incorporating the effects of complex interactions.
(ii) Speed in solving the problem using computer facilities.
(iii) The output from the model can highlight the key constraints to which attention should be directed.
(iv) Sensitivity analysis can be applied. The effects of changes in the variables can be speedily tested.

Disadvantages of mathematical programming:

(i) Divisibility of projects may not be realistic, and integer programming may have to be used.
(ii) Constraints are unlikely to be completely fixed and precise, as implied in the mathematical models.
(iii) Not all the relevant information can be quantified.
(iv) All the information for the model may not be available. For example, it may not be possible to specify the constraints of future periods.

(v) All the relationships contained within the formulation may not be linear.
(vi) All the potential investment opportunities may not be identified and included in the analysis.
(vii) The linear programming formulation assumes that all the project's cash flows are certain, and therefore it cannot incorporate uncertainty. The solution produced can only be considered optimal given this restrictive assumption.

14.24 (a) Because future cash flows are uncertain there is a need to express how NPV calculations might be affected by the level of uncertainty. NPV calculations are normally based on the most likely cash flows and if uncertainty is not taken into account there is a danger that managers might place too much confidence in the results of the investment appraisal. When the level of uncertainty is incorporated into the analysis managers may reject projects with positive high NPVs because the cash flows are subject to very high levels of uncertainty. Alternatively, other projects with lower NPVs, and lower uncertainty, may be deemed to be more attractive.

(b) Annual cash flows = $20000 \times (£3 - £1.65) - £10000$
$$= £17000$$
Payback period = £50000/£17000
$$= 2.94 \text{ years (assuming that the}$$
cash flows occur evenly throughout the year).

The company uses a payback period of two years and since the project has a payback of nearly three years it will be rejected using the payback method. The answer should also describe the deficiencies of the payback (see Chapter 13 for an outline of the disadvantages of the payback method).

(c) NPV = Annual cash flows (£17000) $\times$ 3.605 discount factor − investment outlay (£50000) = £11285.

Sales volume sensitivity analysis
Let SV = Sales volume

NPV will be zero when:
$(1.35SV - £10000)3.605 = £50000$
$4.86675 SV - £36050 = £50000$
$SV = 17681$ units
This represents a decrease of 2319 units (i.e. 11.6%)

Selling price sensitivity analysis
Let SP = Selling price
NPV will be zero when:
$((20000SP - (£1.65 \times 20000))3.605 - (£10000 \times 3.605) = £50000$
$72100SP - £118965 - £36050 = £50000$
$72100SP = £205015$
$SP = £2.843$ (A decrease of 15.7 pence or 5.2%)

Unit variable cost sensitivity analysis
Let VC = Variable cost
NPV will be zero when:
$((£20000 \times £3) - 20000VC))3.605 - (£10000 \times 3.605) = £50000$
$£216300 - 72100VC - £36050 = £50000$
$72100VC = £130250$
$VC = £1.8065$ (An increase of 15.7 pence or 9.5%).
For a discussion of the use of sensitivity analysis for investment appraisal see 'sensitivity analysis' in Chapter 14. In particular, the answer should describe the objectives and limitations of sensitivity analysis.

(d) Expected value of sales volume = $(17500 \times 0.3) + (20000 \times 0.6) + (22500 \times 0.1) = 19500$ units

Expected NPV = $(19\,500 \times £1.35 \times 3.605) -$
$(£10\,000 \times 3.605) - £50\,000 = £8852$

The project still has a positive expected NPV and should be adopted based on the expected value of the cash flows. However, the expected value is based on using the weighted average of the potential cash flows and is thus unlikely to occur in practice. An examination of the probability distribution indicates that positive NPVs will occur for the normal and good economic states. If the poor economic state occurs the NPV will be as follows:

$(17\,500 \times £1.35 \times 3.605) - (£10\,000 \times 3.605) -$
$£50\,000 = (£882)$

Thus there is a 30 per cent chance that the project will yield a negative NPV and a 70 per cent chance that the project will yield a positive NPV. It is possible that managers may consider a 30 per cent risk of a negative NPV to be unacceptable. The decision is likely to depend on the managers' attitude towards risk, the current profitability of the company and how the cash flows correlate with existing activities. Assigning probabilities to the potential outcomes has produced useful information that may help managers to make better investment decisions. The disadvantage of this approach is that the estimates of the probabilities of future economic states are likely to be subject to a high degree of uncertainty and subjectivity.

CHAPTER 15

15.19 This is an example of feedforward control because the manager is using a forecast to assist in making a future decision

Answer = **(a)**

15.20 (i)

Product	A1	A2
Sales (units)	32000	56000
Increase/(decrease) in inventory	1000	(2000)
Production budget (units)	33000	54000

(ii)

Material	B3			B4		
	A1	A2	Total	A1	A2	Total
Production budget (units)	33000	54000	87000	33000	54000	87000
Kg per unit	8	4		4	3	
Material usage (kg)	264000	216000	480000	132000	162000	294000

(iii)

Material	B3 Total	B4 Total
Material usage (kg)	480000	294000
Less: opening inventory	(30000)	(20000)
Plus: closing inventory	24000	14700
Material purchases (kg)	474000	288700
Price per kg	$1.25	$1.80
Material purchases $	$592500	$519660

15.21

Cash budget

	January $000	February $000	March $000
Cash sales	75	80	90
Receipts from credit sales (W1)	245	253	254
Total receipts	320	333	344
Payment for purchases (W2)	(180)	(195)	(200)
Expenses paid	(122)	(123)	(123)
Forklift trucks		(100)	
Total payments	(302)	(418)	(323)
Net cash	18	(85)	21
Opening balance	15	33	(52)
Closing balance	33	(52)	(31)

Workings

(W1) Credit sales − receipts

	Total sales $000	January $000	February $000	March $000
October	250	20		
November	250	25	20	
December	250	200	25	20
January	260		208	26
February	260			208
Total		245	253	254

(W2) Credit purchases − payments

	Total purchases $000	January $000	February $000	March $000
November	180	45		
December	180	135	45	
January	200		150	50
February	200			150
Total		180	195	200

15.22 (a) For the answer to this question, you should refer to 'Rolling budgets' in Chapter 15. The answer should point out that instead of a 12-month period remaining static it would be updated by one month on a monthly basis so that a 12-monthly budget is always available. When the budget is initially prepared for year ending 30 November the first month (December) is prepared in detail and the later months in less detail because of the greater uncertainty about the future. At the end of the first month, the budget for the next month (January) is prepared in detail and the remaining 11 months updated based on updated information.

(b) The major problem with rolling budgets is that they are very time consuming to administer. This is a major problem in this company that only employs one part-qualified accountant who is already overworked and may not have the time or experience to operate a system of monthly rolling budgets. Rolling budgets are more appropriate for businesses that face rapid change but the question indicates that the business is very stable from year to year. Rather than implementing monthly rolling budgets quarterly rolling budgets would be preferable but annual budgeting may be preferred because of the stable operating environment.

With the present system the sales managers have been set targets that are easy to achieve and so are likely to react badly to the new system that requires them to work hard all year round. A further problem is that the sales managers will not know the target for the whole year in advance and having met the target for the month may be encouraged to defer seeking extra work for the month until the next month thus obtaining easier targets.

(c) The major problem with the current scheme is that the reward system is stepped with the first $1.5m of fee income target being too easy to reach and the second $1.5m being too difficult. Therefore managers are not motivated to earn additional fees once the initial target has been reached. An alternative approach would be to replace the current system with a commission given to managers based on a percentage of fee income rather than a percentage of salary. Currently the company is paying each of the three sales managers a bonus of $30 000 (20% of $150 000) representing 2 per cent of the fee income target of $1 500 000. Therefore an alternative system would be to pay 2 per cent commission on all sales.

(d) The use of the accountant's own spreadsheets involve keying in a large amount of data from existing records so there is a high probability of errors if the data that are entered are not checked. Also the use of any formulae in the spreadsheets will result in the generation of incorrect data if the formulae are wrong. Rolling budgets are far more complex and this significantly increases the chance of errors in the spreadsheets. If spreadsheets are used data entry and any changes in the variables should be carefully checked.

15.23 (a) *Budgeted income*

Income from pupils registered on 1 June $724 500
Expected number of new joiners: $(0.2 \times 50) + (0.3 \times 20) + (0.5 \times 26) = 29$
Expected income from new joiners at $(29 \times \$900) = \$26 100$
Total expected income = $750 600.

Budgeted expenditure

Repairs and maintenance: $30 000 \times 1.03 = \$30 900.$
Salaries: $[(\$620 000 - \$26 000)/2] + [(\$620 000 - \$26 000) \times 1.02)/2]$
= $297 000 + \$302 940 = \$599 940.$
Expected capital expenditure = $(0.7 \times \$145 000) + (0.3 \times \$80 000) = \$125 500.$
Total expected expenditure = $756 340.
Budget deficit = $5740 ($750 600 - $756 340)

(b) The main advantages of incremental budgets are simplicity and speed of budget preparation. Incremental budgeting is more appropriate for organizations that have stable activities where changes in revenue and expenditure are mainly attributable to inflation. The major disadvantages of incremental budgeting are that they encourage inefficiency because incremental budgets use the preceding year's data (which may contain inefficiencies) as the base for determining the budget. Therefore errors from one year are carried forward to the next year. Managers may also be motivated to attempt to use their entire budget up for one year, even if they do not need to, just to ensure that the budget is maintained again the next year.

(c) See 'Zero-based budgeting' in Chapter 15 for the answer to this question.

(d) A simplistic form of ZBB may be appropriate for the school if it is applied to selective areas. For areas

where budgeting is straightforward such as staff salaries, which are likely to be fixed over the budget period, incremental budgeting should still be used. ZBB is more appropriate for discretionary expenses. For example, the extent to which sports education is provided involves discretionary activities and it would be appropriate to establish decision packages for various levels of packages of activities in order to prioritize which activities should be undertaken.

15.24 (a) At present incremental budgeting is used in all the divisions. Incremental budgeting is widely used because it is simple to apply, easy to understand by the budgetees and can be easily administered by the finance department. It is most suited to organizations that operate in a stable environment where historic information may provide a suitable basis for considering small incremental changes for setting annual budgets. The major weakness of incremental budgeting are that it consolidates existing practices into the targets and so tends to stifle innovation. As a result, past inefficiencies and waste inherent in the current ways of doing things are perpetuated. A further problem is that incremental budgeting can encourage budgetees to spend up to their budget limits in order to ensure that they get an increment from the highest possible base level figure in the next budget.

Incremental budgets may continue to be appropriate in divisions S and H that operate in a stable environment. Also any attempt to make major changes to the planning and control systems may result in a resistance to change by staff when any new system may only make marginal improvements. The disadvantage of not making any changes to the planning and control systems is that continuous improvement and cost reduction are not prioritized.

Division F is a rapidly growing business so incremental budgets are likely to represent out of date targets. The current problems of management dissatisfaction and poor quality control may be a direct result of a reliance on out-of-date targets that do not reflect the changing environment. Hence the budgets are not seen as relevant by the managers. At M, incremental budgeting does not result in past and proposed expenditure being questioned and this approach is inappropriate where budgeted costs are recharged to user divisions. The system does not encourage M to question existing base costs since it can pass the costs on to user divisions.

(b) For an explanation of how a system of rolling budgets operates see 'Rolling budgets' in Chapter 15. The rolling budget for Division F would be as follows:

	Current year Q1 $000	Q2 $000	Q3 $000	Q4 $000	Total $000	Next year Q1 $000
Revenue	17 932	18 470	19 024	19 595	75 021	20 183
Cost of sales	9863	10 159	10 464	10 778	41 264	11 101
Gross profit	8069	8311	8560	8817	33 757	9082
Distribution costs	1614	1662	1712	1764	6752	1817
Administration costs	4214	4214	4214	4214	16 856	4214
Operating profit	2241	2435	2634	2839	10 149	3051

The entries for Q1 represent the actual results and the entries for the remaining items (apart from administration costs) have been increased at a rate of 3 per cent per quarter. It is assumed that administration costs are fixed over the next four quarters. When the actual results for Q2 are available, the budgets for Q3 and Q4 will be updated and a new budget for Q5 added. The rolling budget can thus reflect the rapid growth of the division so managers are not faced with a lower budget that does not take into account current growth. It is therefore less likely that growth will be inhibited because of inadequate budgets. The major disadvantage of rolling budgets is that it is time consuming to administer.

(c) In part (a), it was pointed out that incremental budgeting may be inappropriate for M division. Zero-based budgeting has been proposed as an alternative for overcoming the deficiencies of incremental budgeting. You should refer to 'Zero-based budgeting' in Chapter 15 for a description of this budgeting method. Marketing mostly consist of discretionary expenses arising from different marketing campaigns that are not suited to incremental budgeting. If ZBB is operated at the M division managers should justify to senior management the budgets at the start for each of the marketing campaigns from a zero base. If a cost element within a campaign cannot be justified no resources are allocated. This approach may result in a more supportive attitude towards the budgeting process by the manufacturing divisional managers when they are aware that any recharges to them are based on greater fairness and control.

(d) DG currently adopts a top-down approach to budgeting but with some degree of participation by the divisional managers. Given the dissatisfaction that currently exists, senior management should consider greater participation by the divisional managers in the budget process. This would involve the divisional managers preparing divisional budgets. For a discussion of the benefits and limitations and the circumstances where it is most appropriate to adopt a more participatory approach you should refer to 'Participation in the budget and target setting process' in Chapter 16. The participatory budget process implemented at DG should be a two-way process of a top-down statement of objectives and strategies and a bottom-up budget preparation and top-down approval by senior management (see 'Negotiation of budgets' in Chapter 15).

15.25 (a) Activity based budget for six months ending 30 June

Production	Product A 9000 units Per unit (£)	Total (£000)	Product B 15000 units Per unit (£)	Total (£000)	Total £000
Product unit-based					
Materials[a]	60.000	540.0	45.000	675.0	1215.0
Labour, power etc.[b]	16.000	144.0	10.000	150.0	294.0
	76.000	684.0	55.000	825.0	1509.0
Batch based					
Production scheduling					29.6
WIP movement					36.4
Purchasing and receipt					49.5
Sub-total[c]		63.0		52.5	115.5
Machine set-up[d]		15.0		25.0	40.0
	8.667	78.0	5.167	77.5	155.5
Product sustaining					
Material scheduling[e]		9.0		9.0	18.0
Design/testing[f]		9.6		6.4	16.0
	2.067	18.6	1.027	15.4	34.0
Product line sustaining					
Product line development[g]		20.0		5.0	25.0
Product line maintenance[h]		6.0		3.0	9.0
	2.889	26.0	0.533	8.0	34.0
Factory sustaining					
General factory administration[i]					125.0
General factory occupancy[j]					67.0
	8.000	72.0	8.000	120.0	192.0
Totals	97.623	878.6	69.727	1045.9	1924.5

Notes

[a] Output × material cost per unit given in the question.

[b] Machine hours = (9000 × 0.8) + (15000 × 0.5) = 14700
Rate per hour = (£294000/14700) = £20
Product A = 0.8 hours × £20

[c] Product batches required = (9000/100) + (15000/200) = 165
Cost per batch = £115500/165 = £700
Assigned to product A = 90 batches at £700 = £63000

[d] Cost per set up = £40000/40 = £1000 per set up
Assigned to product A = 15 set ups × £1000

[e] Components purchased = 180000 for product A (9000 × 20) and 180000 for product B (15000 × 12) resulting in equal costs being allocated to each product.

[f] Design and testing allocated in the ratio 12 : 8 as given in the question.

[g] Allocated 80% and 20% as indicated in the question.

[h] Production line maintenance cost per maintenance hour = £9000/450 = £20
Allocated to product A = 300 hours at £20 per hour = £6000

[i] £768000 × 25% = £192000/number of units (24000) = £8 per unit
Allocated to A = £72000 (9000 units × £8)

(b) See 'Activity hierarchies' and 'Designing ABC systems' in Chapter 11 for the answer to this question. Note that cost pools are also known as cost centres. An explanation of cost pools can be found in Chapter 3.

(c) Steps include:

- Ascertaining what activities are being carried out and investigate whether they are necessary.
- Ascertaining how effectively the activities are carried out and investigate ways of performing activities more effectively.
- Identify value-added and non-value-added activities and give priority to reducing non-value-added activities.
- Benchmark (see Chapter 22) activities against best practice.

15.26 See 'Criticisms of budgeting' in Chapter 15 for the answer to this question.

15.27 (a) In the public sector, precise objectives are difficult to define in a quantifiable way, and the actual accomplishments are even more difficult to measure. In most situations, outputs cannot be measured in monetary terms. By 'outputs' we mean the quality and amount of the services rendered. Quality is difficult to define and measure in a quantifiable way. In profit-oriented organizations output can be measured in terms of sales revenues and profits. The effect of this is that budgets in the public sector tend to be mainly concerned with the input of resources (i.e. expenditure), whereas budgets in profit organizations focus on the relationships between inputs (expenditure) and outputs (sales revenue). In the public sector, there is unlikely to be the same emphasis on what was intended to be achieved for a given input of resources. The budgeting process tends to compare what is happening in cash input terms with the estimated cash inputs rather than the relationship between inputs and outputs. In other words, there is little emphasis on measures of managerial performance in terms of the results achieved. The reason for this is that there is no clear relationship between resource inputs and the benefits flowing from the use of these resources. Finally, the budget process tends to more difficult in the public sector because limited resources make it difficult to achieve the desired results. Any shortcomings in the results tend to be highly publicized and may often be subject to political scrutiny by different pressure groups.

(b) See 'Incremental budgeting' and 'Zero-based budgeting' in Chapter 15.

(c) See 'Zero-based budgeting' in Chapter 15 for the answer to this question.

(d) Incremental budgeting, as with all planning and control mechanisms, is subject to a number of limitations (see 'Incremental budgets' in Chapter 15) but the comment that there is no longer a place for incremental budgeting in most organizations represents an extreme view. Zero budgeting is subject to a number of limitations and these should be carefully considered before concluding that there is no place for incremental budgeting. The limitations of zero-base budgeting are:

- ZBB has never achieved the widespread adoption that the proponents envisaged since its introduction many years ago. It does not appear to have been widely accepted in practice.
- The major reason for the lack of adoption of ZBB is that it is considered to be too costly and time consuming to implement and operate.
- The process of identifying decision packages and determining their purpose, cost and benefits is extremely time consuming.
- There are often too many decision packages to evaluate and there is frequently insufficient information to enable them to be ranked.
- Managers may not have the skills to implement and operate ZBB unless they have had appropriate training.

ZBB is most appropriate for discretionary expenses. Such expenses tend to be the dominant ones in the public sector. Incremental budgeting is more appropriate in commercial organizations where well-defined input/output relationships exist that can easily be quantified. Incremental budgeting is simple to operate and easily understand where these circumstances apply. Rather than seeking to implement ZBB in the public sector it may be preferable to implement priority-based incremental budgeting (see Chapter 15 for an explanation).

CHAPTER 16

16.20 Fixed production overhead = 8000 × $5 = $40 000
Flexed budgeted contribution = 6000 × ($118 − $101)
= $102 000
Flexed budget profit = $102 000 − $40 000 = $62 000

Answer = **(a)**

16.21 *Task 1:*

Performance statement – month to 31 October

| Number of guest days = | Original budget | 9 600 |
| | Flexed budget | 11 160 |

	Flexed budget (£)	Actual (£)	Variance (£)
Controllable expenses			
Food (1)	23 436	20 500	2936F
Cleaning materials (2)	2 232	2 232	0
Heat, light and power (3)	2 790	2 050	740F
Catering staff wages (4)	8 370	8 400	30A
	36 828	33 182	3646F
Non-controllable expenses			
Rent, rates, insurance and depreciation (5)	1 860	1 860	0

Notes:
(1) £20 160/9600 × 11 160.
(2) £1920/9600 × 11 160.
(3) £2400/9600 × 11 160.
(4) £11 160/40 × £30.
(5) Original fixed budget based on 30 days but October is a 31-day month (£1 800/30 × 31).

Task 2:

(a) See the sections on 'Multiple functions of budgets (motivation)' in Chapter 15, and 'Setting financial performance targets' in Chapter 16 for the answers to this question.

(b) Motivating managers ought to result in improved performance. However, besides motivation, improved performance is also dependent on managerial ability, training, education and the existence of a favourable environment. Therefore motivating managers is not guaranteed to lead to improved performance.

(c) The use of a fixed budget is unlikely to encourage managers to become more efficient where budgeted expenses are variable with activity. In the original performance report actual expenditure for 11.160 guest days is compared with budgeted expenditure for 9600 days. It is misleading to compare actual costs at one level of activity with budgeted costs at another level of activity. Where the actual level of activity is above the budgeted level, adverse variances are likely to be reported for variable cost items. Managers will therefore be motivated to reduce activity so that favourable variances will be reported. Therefore it is not surprising that Susan Green has expressed concern that the performance statement does not reflect a valid reflection of her performance. In contrast, most of Brian Hilton's expenses are fixed and costs will not increase when volume increases. A failure to flex the budget will therefore not distort his performance.

To motivate, challenging budgets should be set and small adverse variances should normally be regarded as a healthy sign and not something to be avoided. If budgets are always achieved with no adverse variances this may indicate that undemanding budgets may have been set which are unlikely to motivate best possible performance. This situation could apply to Brian Hilton who always appears to report favourable variances.

16.22 (a) The current traditional budgeting method does not appear appropriate for a company that faces a rapidly changing external environment and has corporate objectives that focus on innovation and continuous product development. The budgeting system is subject to the following weaknesses:

- The budgets are only prepared annually which is inappropriate given the company's objectives and environment in which it operates. The company faces considerable uncertainty in costs (e.g. silver prices), exchange rates, selling prices and sales volume which makes it extremely difficult to forecast on an annual basis. Rolling budgets are likely to be more appropriate for a rapidly changing environment.

- A rigid budget constrained style of budget evaluation is used where deviations from planned targets are not tolerated. This approach is inappropriate for companies operating in an uncertain environment (see Chapter 16). Using only rigid, annual budgets has resulted in P Division being unable to cope with changes in demand or one-off events such as the factory fire. It has also resulted in short-term cost cutting to achieve the budgeted net profit (e.g. by closing one of the research and development (R&D) facilities even though R&D is a key competitive advantage of the company). G Division also did not take on additional staff to cope with increased demand following reopening of their customer's factory. This also may be due to the managers being constrained by the budget. This action has been to the long-term detriment of the company because it has resulted in the loss of the preferred supplier status with its main customer.

- The budget process appears to be very bureaucratic and time consuming. Approval of the budgets often occurs after the start of the budget period resulting in the budgets already being out of date. Managers therefore find the budgeting process demotivating. Also the fact that the directors revise the budgets after they have been prepared has a demotivational effect. There is a need for managers to have greater participation and be involved in negotiation process prior to the authorization of the annual budget.

- The controllability principle has not been applied and fixed budgets rather than flexible budgets appear to be used. Managers are discouraged from deviating from the original fixed budget and are evaluated on factors which are outside their control. No attempt is made to distinguish between planning and operating variances. For example, the manager of P Division did not make technical modifications to its components because of the extra costs. This resulted in a failure to supply components for use in the new model of smartphone and the company having to heavily discount the inventories of the old version in order to achieve planned sales volumes.

- The absence of information relating to the frequency of feedback reporting suggests

infrequent feedback resulting in a failure to respond to deviations from plan.

- Performance reporting is internally focused despite the rapidly changing environment. More emphasis should be given to relative performance evaluation (see Chapter 16) using information from external sources to enable performance to be assessed in a more meaningful way.

- The current system does not encourage goal congruence or coordination and communication between divisions. Divisional managers are evaluated on the financial performance of their own division and are therefore likely to prioritize the interests of their own division rather than the company as a whole. For example, P Division did not re-allocate its manufacturing facilities to G Division, even though G Division needed these facilities to cope with the extra demand following reopening of the customer's factory.

(b) The answer should describe the main features of beyond budgeting (see 'Beyond budgeting' in Chapter 15). The likely impact of the company moving to beyond budgeting will be as follows:

- The company operates in a rapidly changing environment resulting in the need to quickly respond and develop new products. The company will therefore be able to change its budget plans frequently by replacing annual incremental budgeting with regular rolling budgets. Short-term performance measures should be replaced with key performance measures that focus on the long-term success of the organization.

- Beyond budgeting places greater emphasis on longer-term non-financial targets using relative performance evaluation involving external benchmarks to analyse it to assess performance. The ability to be seen as the preferred supplier with key customers could be a key objective and performance measure of the divisional managers.

- Beyond budgeting places greater emphasis on empowering managers make decisions that are in the long-term interests of the business. It therefore allows managers to respond quickly to changes in the external environment by implementing innovative actions to external change.

- The company currently applies a top-down approach to budgeting. Adopting beyond budgeting will require a bottom-up budget setting process with a more devolved decision-making structure.

- Beyond budgeting requires that resources should be made available for managers to take advantage of opportunities in the market, such as the smartphone designed for playing games. This would enable managers to react to changes in material prices and foreign currency exchange rates by having the authority to purchase silver at times when the prices are low.

- Presently divisional managers compete for resources when setting budgets and this has resulted in a lack of goal congruence. Beyond budgeting encourages managers to work together for the good of the business and to share knowledge and resources. This is particularly important where product innovation is a key success factor. Each division has its own IT systems but effectively sharing knowledge and responding to the changing external environment requires shared IT facilities.

- Appropriate training and the implementation of appropriate information systems will be required to implement the above changes.

16.23 (a) Managers should be evaluated based on the circumstances which they faced during the period. The overall market fell by 12 per cent during the evaluation period but there was no change to the target for the performance evaluation. It is appropriate to analyse the difference between the original budget and the actual results by their planning and operational variances using the revised sales target of $266 000 less 12 per cent ($234 080) and adjusting the targets for the other items by 12 per cent:

	$
Revised budgeted sales given market fall	234 080
Budgeted gross margin	60%
Revised budgeted gross margin	140 448
Original budgeted gross margin	159 600
Planning variance	19 152 A
Actual sales	237 100
Revised budgeted sales	234 080
	3 020 F
Budgeted gross margin	60%
Operational variance	1 812 F

The revised analysis indicates that the adverse gross profit variance shown in the question of $17 340 consists of an adverse planning variance of $19 152 and a favourable operating variance of $1 812. Therefore given the change in the environment the manager's efforts have resulted in $1 812 greater profit than expected and not the $17 340 adverse impact suggested by the original analysis.

A revised report should analyse the individual cost variances (cost of sales, marketing, staff and property costs) into their controllable and non-controllable elements. Inventory purchasing is done centrally so the branch manager is unlikely to be accountable for the price variances relating to cost of sales but they are likely to be accountable for the usage variances. It is unlikely that the branch managers should be responsible price variances relating to heating or lighting, property management rentals or their own salary. They may be held accountable for the usage element of heating and lighting and part-time salaries. Finally, the budget for any items of expenses that vary with sales volume should be adjusted to reflect the 12 per cent sales decline to enable planning and operational variances to be reported.

(b) The answer should point out that a budget constrained style of performance evaluation and a top-down non-participative budgeting approach is being used. The answer should point out the deficiencies of a budget constrained style and compare this style of evaluation with a profit conscious and non-accounting styles of evaluation (see 'Side-effects from using accounting information for performance evaluation' in Chapter 16). The answer should also point out that the current unhappiness of the shop managers is likely to have arisen because of the current style of evaluation. Possible improvements include distinguishing between the controllable and non-controllable items as outlined in (a) in the performance report

and adding non-financial measures to the managerial performance evaluation.

16.24 (a) *Meeting only the lowest budget targets.* This implies that once the budget has been agreed the budget holder will be satisfied just with achieving only the budgeted level of performance and not exceeding it.

Using more resources than necessary. This may arise when a manager is aware that the budget could be achieved by using less resources but continues to use excess resources in order not to be seen to overachieve and thus preserve the budget allowance for future budgets.

Making the budget whatever it takes. Budgetees may view the maximization of bonuses as their main priority and focus on achieving the targets even if this leads to a lack of goal congruence (see 'Harmful side-effects of controls' in Chapter 16 for a more detailed answer).

Competing against other divisions, business units and departments. Managers may focus on maximizing their own performance even if this is at the expense of other departments or the company as a whole.

Ensuring that what is in the budget is spent. Managers may consider that they can only preserve their budget allowance for various items of expenses for the following year by ensuring that the budget is spent. This may be particularly applicable to discretionary expenses.

Providing inaccurate forecasts. Budget holders may seek to provide inaccurate forecasts to build in some slack into the budget targets in order to avoid what they perceive as difficult targets.

Meeting the target but not beating it. This relates to budgetees considering that the incentive is only to achieve the budget and not exceed it.

Avoiding risks. Managers may prefer to avoid uncertainty in setting or achieving targets because by avoiding risks they have greater control in achieving the budget.

(b) *Meeting only the lowest targets and using more resources than necessary.*

Variable costs of $200 per tonne have been agreed so there is no incentive to achieve a better level of performance. Also more resources than necessary may be used to achieve the variable cost because of the lack of incentive.

Making the bonus whatever it takes and meeting the budget target but not beating it. A bonus is paid for achieving an output of 100 000 units so managers may ignore waste, quality and on-time delivery as long as they achieve the targeted output.

Competing against other divisions etc. At present, the division obtains its materials from selected suppliers who have been used for some years but there is evidence that similar materials could be obtained from another division but this does not appear to have been considered, because there is no incentive to do so.

Ensuring that what is in the budget is spent. There is a fixed budget allowance of $50m so there will be a reluctance to under spend since this may result in a reduced budget allowance next year.

Providing inaccurate forecasts. There is no external reference point relating to the 15 per cent processing loss because of ageing machinery. The manager may have deliberately biased this information to reduce the pressure in meeting the budget requirements.

Avoiding risks. The fact that none of the items listed in note 5 of the question have been pursued may be due to risk avoidance.

(c) *Meeting only the lowest targets and meeting the target but not beating it.* The bonus system could be changed so that an extra bonus can be obtained arising from increments in meeting demand over 100 000 units, or base the bonus on the ability to always meet the demands of the receiving division. Alternatively, consider making the division a profit centre so that they are rewarded with extra profits for meeting demand in excess of 100 000 units.

Using more resources than necessary. There is no mention of the managers being evaluated on the basis of variances from standard. Using more resources than necessary would be reflected in unfavourable variances that should be incorporated into the performance evaluation process.

Making the bonus whatever it takes. Again it may be preferable to base the bonus on the ability to be able to meet the demand of the receiving divisions without any delivery delays.

Competing against other divisions etc. Implement a requirement within the group that divisions should give priority to internal sourcing where divisions are prepared to supply at the same price and quality as outside suppliers.

Ensuring that what is in the budget is spent and providing inaccurate forecasts. Providing assurance to managers that under spending will not automatically result in a reduced budget allowance next year and also allowing greater participation in the budget negotiation process. Ensuring that a profit-conscious style of budget evaluation is applied (see Chapter 16).

Avoiding risk. Providing a guarantee to management that any adverse effects from undertaking the initiatives listed in note 5 will be taken into account in the budget evaluation process and guaranteeing that managers will not suffer a reduction in bonus arising from adverse effects of new initiatives, provided they have had top management approval. In other words, ensuring that a profit conscious style of evaluation is applied.

16.25 See 'Feedback and feed-forward controls' in Chapter 16 for the answer to this question. In particular, the answer should point out that the company has to produce budgets (feed-forward controls) showing acceptable cost targets in order to receive the first payment of its subsidy. The first draft of the budget will be compared with target costs that have been established by the government's transport office to ensure that the company qualifies for the subsidy. The budget will be revised incorporating changes in providing the service if the first draft of the budget does not achieve the required cost target. Care must be taken to ensure that the proposed budget also meets the social objectives.

The transport company will compare actual monthly costs with the budgeted costs (feedback controls) significant variances will require investigation and appropriate remedial action. This is particularly important because failure to achieve the cost target will result in not receiving the balance of the subsidy payment.

16.26 See 'Participation in budget and target-setting process' in Chapter 16 for the answer to this question. In addition to the advantages and disadvantages listed in Chapter 16 the answer could draw attention to the positive motivational

impact arising from staff feeling that they are being respected because of their knowledge and experience relating to running the college. The following additional disadvantages could also be included in the answer:

- senior staff may spend a great deal of time arguing with each other and top management relating to the content and level of difficulty of the budget;
- the participative process can be very time-consuming;
- senior staff may be excellent in their chosen area but lack the knowledge and skills to engage in the management of the budget process.

16.27 (a) For the answer to this question see 'Controllability principle' in Chapter 16. The answer should describe the controllability principle and outline the difficulties in practice of distinguishing between controllable and non-controllable items.

(b) The answer should draw off the material in Chapter 16 relating to dealing with distorting effects before and after the measurement period. Within the latter category the answer should discuss variance analysis, flexible performance standards, relative performance evaluations and subjective performance evaluations. In addition, the answer should incorporate aspects of the section in Chapter 16 titled 'Guidelines for applying the controllability principle.'

(c) You should refer to 'Establishing cost targets' in Chapter 17 for the answers to the first two items and 'Negotiation of budgets' in Chapter 15 for the answer to the third item.

16.28 (a) Management accounting control systems are essentially concerned with encouraging individuals within an organization to alter their behaviour so that the overall aims of the organization are effectively attained. Aspects of accounting control systems that influence human behaviour include the setting of goals, encouraging individuals to accomplish these goals, motivating desirable performance, evaluating performance and suggesting when corrective action must be taken. If attention is not given to the behavioural aspects, and how individuals respond to accounting control systems, harmful side-effects can occur and individuals may be motivated to engage in behaviour that is not organizationally desirable (see 'Harmful side-effects of controls' in Chapter 16 for a more detailed explanation.

(b) For performance monitoring the answer should draw off the content presented in the sections on 'Results or output controls' and 'Harmful side-effects of controls' in Chapter 16. In particular, the answer should draw attention to the negative behavioural consequences arising from:

- The difficulties in measuring performance of responsibility centres;
- Distinguishing between controllable and non-controllable items;
- Difficulty in measuring key variables that are not easy to quantify (e.g. enhancing customer satisfaction);
- Problems in ensuring that the system encourages goal congruence (Figure 16.2 could be used as an illustration);
- Concentrating on achieving the performance measures rather than what needs to be achieved (e.g. rejecting activities that result in a decline in the existing ROI even when acceptance is in the best interests of the organization);

- Over-emphasis on short-term results at the expense of long-term results.

  Behavioural issues relating to budgeting include negative behavioural consequences arising from:

- negative effects from imposed budgets without any participation;
- inappropriate levels of budget difficulty (e.g. being either too difficult or easily attainable);
- inappropriate style of budget evaluation (e.g. adoption of a budget constrained style);
- at the budgetary control stage a failure to distinguish between controllable and non-controllable activities and to apply the principles of flexible budgeting and *ex-post* budget adjustments.

In terms of transfer pricing, behavioural issues relate to the fact that a transfer pricing system attempts to achieve a number of conflicting objectives – encouraging managers to make sound decisions, providing appropriate information for performance measurement and enhancing divisional autonomy. In the section titled 'purposes of transfer pricing' you will find an explanation of how behavioural issues can arise in relation to a failure to achieve each of these objectives.

16.29 (a) Although the senior managers appear to be involved in the budget process it is clear that they do not have any real impact in the process since the budgets they have been involved in are amended without any consultation. They are involved in what is called pseudo participation. This approach will probably have a worse impact than not involving the partners at all since staff will feel that they have wasted their time in preparing the budget which is then ignored. The benefit of participation leading to ownership of the budget and thus feeling personally responsible in achieving the budget is lost, and the partners will not be motivated to achieve the budgeted cost. There is also the additional possibility that the managers may be motivated to deliberately fail to achieve the budgeted costs in order to prove that their own budget was correct and that the changes implemented by the senior partner were wrong.

(b) The following non-financial indicators could be used:

- amount of staff time spent on developing new products and services and details of the number of new products and services developed;
- response time between an enquiry and the first meeting of the client in order to measure response time;
- number of staff training days which will provide an indication of the firm's investment in people.

CHAPTER 17

17.15 Idle time variance = unproductive hours (5500) × standard wage rate (£540000/60000 hours) = £49500 Adverse
Labour efficiency variance = (standard productive hours − actual productive hours) × standard wage rate
[(14650 × 60000 hours/15000 units) − 56000] × £9 = £23400 Favourable

17.16 Variances for the period = $2000 adverse. Note that overhead capacity and efficiency variances are sub-variances of the volume variance so only the volume variance should be taken into account.

Budgeted profit − adverse variances ($2000) = Actual profit ($27000)
Budgeted profit = $27000 + $2000 = $29000

Answer = **(d)**

17.17 (a) Sales price variance = (actual margin − budgeted margin) × actual sales volume
(£17 − £12) × 8200 = £41000 Favourable
(Answer = **(ii)**)
Note that fixed overhead rate per unit is £4 (£34800/8700)

(b) Sales volume = (actual sales volume − budgeted sales volume) × Standard margin
(8200 − 8700) × £12 = 6000 Adverse
(Answer = **(i)**)

(c) Fixed overhead volume = (actual production − budgeted production) × standard fixed overhead rate
(8200 − 8700) × £4 = £2000 Adverse
(Answer = **(i)**)

17.18 (a) (i) A fixed overhead volume variance only occurs with an absorption costing system. The question indicates that a volume variance has been reported. Therefore the company must operate an absorption costing system and report the sales volume variance in terms of profit margins, rather than contribution margins.
Budgeted profit margin = budgeted profit (£4250)/budgeted volume (1500 units) = £2.83
Adverse sales volume variance in units 5 £850/£2.83 = 300 units
Therefore actual sales volume was 300 units below budgeted sales volume
Actual sales volume = 1200 units (1500 units − 300 units)

(ii) Standard quantity of material used per units of output: budgeted usage (750kg)/budgeted production (1500 units) = 0.5kg
Standard price = budgeted material cost (£4500)/budgeted usage (750kg) = £6
Material usage variance = (standard quantity − actual quantity) standard price
£150A = (1550 × 0.5kg = 775kg − AQ)
£6 − £150 = 4650 − 6AQ
6AQ = 4800
Actual quantity used = 800kg

(iii) Material price variance = (standard price − actual price) × actual purchases
£1000F = (£6 − actual price) × 1000kg
£1000F = £6000 − 1000AP
1000AP = £5000
AP = £5 per kg
Actual material cost = 1000kg × £5 = £5000

(iv) Standard hours per unit of output
$$= \frac{\text{Budgeted hours (1125)}}{\text{Budgeted output (1500 units)}}$$
= 0.75 hours
Standard wage rate = budgeted labour cost (£4500)/budgeted hours (1125) = £4
Labour efficiency variance = (standard hours − actual hours) × standard rate
£150A = (1550 × 0.75 = 1162.5 − actual hours) × £4 − £150 = 4650 − 4AH
4AH = £4800
Actual hours = 1200

(v) Total labour variance = standard cost −
actual cost
(£200A + £150A) = (1550 × 0.75 hrs × £4) −
Actual cost
£350A = £4650 − actual cost
Actual cost = £5000

(vi) Standard variable overhead cost per unit
$$= \frac{\text{Budgeted variable overheads (2250)}}{\text{Budgeted output (1500 units)}}$$
= £1.50 hours

Total variable overhead variance = standard cost
− actual cost
(£600A + £75A) = (1550 × £1.50 = £2325) −
actual cost £675a = £2325 − actual cost
Actual cost = £3000

(vii) Fixed overhead expenditure variance = budgeted
cost − actual cost
£2500F = £4500 − actual cost
Actual cost = £2000

(b) See Chapter 17 for an explanation of the causes of
the direct material usage, direct labour rate and sales
volume variances.

17.19 (a) The favourable material price variance suggests that
the wood was cheaper than the standard saving
$5100 on the standard. The concern is that this may
be due to obtaining cheaper lower quality wood. The
material usage variance indicates that the waste levels
of wood are worse than standard. It is possible that
the lower grade labour could have also contributed to
the waste level. There is an overall adverse variance of
$2400 when both the price and usage variances are
taken together so it appears that it has been a poor
decision to outsource the wood from a different supplier. The production manager is responsible for both
decisions and is therefore accountable for the variances arising from the decision. When the new labour
is trained it may be that the wood usage improves but
this will only become apparent in the next few months.
The impact that the new wood might have had on
sales should also be taken into account. Variances
should not be viewed as impacting on one department
and no one department should be viewed in isolation
to another. Sales are down and returns are up and this
is likely to be due to the purchase of poor quality wood.
The company uses traditional manual techniques
that normally requires skilled labour. The labour was
paid less, saving the company $43600 in wages but
the adverse efficiency and idle time variances total
$54200. Thus the decision had a negative impact on
profits during the first month. The efficiency variance
indicates that it took longer to produce the bats than
expected. The new labour was being trained in April
and so it is possible that the situation may improve
next month because of the learning effects.

(b) Material price variance ($5 − $196000/40000) ×
40000 = $4000 F
Material usage variance ((19200 × 2) − 40000) ×
$5/kg = $8000 Adv
Wage rate variance ($12 − $694000/62000) ×
62000 hours = $50000 Fav
Labour efficiency variance (19000 × 3 = 57000 −
61500) × $12 = $46800 Adv
Labour idle time variance 500 × $12 = $6000 Adv
Sales price variance (65 − 68) × 18000 = $54000 Adv
Sales volume contribution variance
(18000 − 19000) × $22 = $22000 Adv

17.20 (a)

	$	$
Budgeted profit (W1)		466000
Sales volume contribution variance		
(9000 units − 10000 units) × $63.60	63600A	
Selling price variance		
9000 units × ($184 − $180)	36000F	27600A
Cost variances:		
Direct material price variance		
74000kg × ($10.80 − $11.20)	29600A	
Direct material usage variance		
((9000 × 8kg) − 74000kg) × $10.80	21600A	
Direct labour rate variance		
10800 × ($18.00 − $19.00)	10800A	
Direct labour efficiency variance		
((9000 × 1.25) − 10800) × $18.00	8100F	
Variable overhead expenditure variance		
(10800 hours × $6) − $70000	5200A	
Variable overhead efficiency variance		
((9000 × 1.25) − 10800) × $6.00	2700F	
Fixed overhead expenditure variance		
($170000 − $168000)	2000F	54400A
Actual profit (W2)		384000

Workings
W1 Budgeted profit = Budgeted contribution ($63.60 × 10000) −
Fixed overheads ($170000)
W2 Actual profit for the period

			$
Sales	9000 units × $184		1656000
Direct materials	74000kg @ $11.20	828800	
Direct labour	10800 hours @ $19	205200	
Variable production overheads		70000	(1104000)
Contribution			552000
Fixed production overheads			(168000)
Actual profit			384000

(b)(i) See 'Standard absorption costing' in Chapter 17
for the answer to this question.

(ii) Unit profit margin instead of unit contribution
margin is used to calculate the sales volume profit
variance:
(9000 units − 10000 units) × $46.60 unit profit
= $46600 A
It would also be necessary to include the following fixed production overhead volume variance:
Fixed production overhead volume variance
(9000 units − 10000 units) × $17 = $17000 A
Note that the fixed overhead rate is derived by
dividing budgeted fixed overheads ($17000) by
the budgeted production (10000 units).

(c) See 'Some argument in support of absorption costing'
in Chapter 7 for the answer to this question.

17.21 (a) The variances shown below have been calculated
using the formulae presented in Exhibit 17.8 shown at
the end of Chapter 17.

Budgeted profit (4000 × £28)	112000
Sales volume profit variance (3200 − 4000) £28	(22400)A
Standard profit on actual sales	89600
Sales margin price variance	
[(£225 − £192) − (£220 − £192)] × 3200	16000F
	105600

Cost variances		Fav	Adv	
Material usage	[(3600 × 25) − 80000] £3.2	32000		
Material price	(3.2 − 3.5) 80000		24000	
Labour efficiency	[(4 × 3600) − 16000)] £8		12800	
Labour rate	(8 − 7) 16000	16000		
Var O/H eff	[(4 × 3600) − 16000)] £4		6400	
Var O/H exp	(£4 × 16000) − 60000	4000		
Fixed O/H exp	(256000 − 196000)	60000		
Fixed O/H eff	[(4 × 3600) − 16000)] £16		25600	
Fixed O/H capacity	[16000 − (4 × 4000)] £16	nil		
		112000	68800	43200
Actual profit				148800

(b) It appears that in the past budgets have been set based on easily attainable standards but apart from output the standard costs have remained unchanged. It is possible that cost targets therefore reflect easily attainable standards that may not provide sufficient motivation to implement cost efficiencies. In terms of output a challenging target has been set that is significantly in excess of past output. Not surprisingly, this output has not been met and it is possible that such a difficult target may have a detrimental impact on the motivation of the sales staff that are responsible for achieving the extra output. In terms of the managers responsible for the cost variances they are not affected by the more challenging output levels because flexible budgeting principles are applied whereby cost variances are based on the actual output achieved.

The adverse sales volume variance reflects the fact that a very demanding budget has been set with the budget being increased from the previous average volume of 3400 benches to 4000 benches. The sales price and sales volume variance may be inter-related and the increase in price may explain why actual sales of 3200 benches were lower than the previous average of 3400 benches.

Better quality materials have been purchased and this has not been reflected in the standards. This may have contributed to the favourable material price variance. The use of lower skilled labour may account for the favourable wage rate variance but this may also explain the adverse labour efficiency variance. Because new labour has been introduced there may be an initial learning effect. The adverse labour efficiency also accounts for the overhead efficiency variances. The value of the fixed overhead efficiency variance is questionable for control purposes (i.e. it is a sunk cost) and variable overheads may not vary proportionately with labour hours. The fixed overhead expenditure variance is very large and requires further investigation because discretionary expenditure may have been extensively reduced and this may have a detrimental long-term impact.

(c) Adopting a marginal costing approach will result in the budgeted profit being identical (£112000) to the marginal costing profit since budgeted output equals budgeted sales. The only differences in the variances calculated in (a) relate to the sales volume margin variance and the fixed overhead volume variances. The sales volume variance will now be expressed in terms of unit contribution margin (800 units at £92 = £73600 adverse) compared with an adverse variance of £22400 with absorption costing. With the marginal costing system fixed overheads are not unitized and assigned to the products so volume capacity and

efficiency variances do not apply. The marginal costing reconciliation statement will be as follows:

	£
Budgeted profit	112000
Sales volume contribution margin variance	(73600)A
Standard contribution on sales	38400
Sales margin price variance (unchanged)	16000F
Cost variances excluding fixed overhead volume variances (£43200 + £25600)	68800F
Actual profit	123200

Note that the marginal costing profit is £25 600 lower than the absorption costing profit because closing stocks are now restated at variable cost (400 × £128 = £51 200) instead of absorption cost (£76800). Therefore, one of the reasons for the increase in profit achieved by the new managing director shown in part (a) relates to the increase in stock levels of 400 units that has enabled fixed overheads of £25600 to be included in the closing stock and deferred as an expense to the next period. Marginal costing advocates that such costs are period costs. The revised statement shows a truer picture of the impact of failing to achieve the budgeted sales volume with an adverse variance of £73600 being reported compared with a variance of £22400 with the absorption costing profit. Nevertheless, it should be noted that there has been a significant improvement on average past profits of £56800 (3400 units at a contribution of £92 per unit less fixed costs of £256000). However, £60000 of this has been due to a decrease in fixed costs. It can be concluded that the absorption costing profit statement tends to overstate the impact of the actions implemented on the profit for the period.

17.22 (a) The favourable material price variance suggests that the purchasing manager has bought a cheaper product, saving $48000. Given that the question states that the market for buying seeds is stable it is unlikely that the variance is due to the manager taking advantage or market conditions. There is a large adverse material usage variance ($52000) suggesting that more waste than normal has occurred. This suggests that inferior quality seed may have been purchased. The sales price ($85000) and sales volume variances are negative and the question states that the marker for the sales of brown rice is stable. The adverse price variance suggests that this may have resulted from a fall in the quality of output arising from the purchase of inferior quality seeds. This may have also led to a fall in the volume of sales. It is therefore possible that the purchasing manager may be responsible for $110000 adverse variances (i.e. ($85000 + $52000 + $21000 − $48000).

The production director has increased wage rates and this has resulted in an adverse variance of $15000 in month 1. The variances suggest that the wage increase has had a positive motivational effect on the labour force. The labour efficiency variance is $18000 favourable; and so it is possible that a wage rise has encouraged the labour force to work harder. The $12000 favourable idle time variance suggests that the amount of idle time has reduced considerably. The question indicates that the machines are running well. Also the buyer has bought enough rice seeds so the idle time variance may be attributable to the motivational impact of the wage increase. Therefore the decision of the production manager may have resulted in favourable variances of $15000 ($18000 + $12000 − $15000).

The maintenance manager has delayed the annual maintenance of the machines and this has saved $8000. This will increase profits in the short term but may have adverse consequences later and may be reflected in adverse future variances arising from lost production and sales. The spending on maintenance has only been delayed so the saving has not been made in the longer term.

(b) The standard contribution given in the question is calculated as follows:

	$	$
Sales price		240
Less:		
Rice seed (1.4 tonnes × $60 per tonne)	84	
Labour productive time (2 hours at $18 per hour)	36	
Unproductive time (0.2222 hours at $18 per hour)	4	
Variable overhead (2 hours at $30 per hour)	60	
Variable cost of production		184
Standard contribution		56

Note that the hours paid are 10/9 × 2 productive hours = 2.2222 hours so unproductive time is 0.2222 hours.

Budgeted profit = (8400 units × $56 contribution = 470400 less $210000 fixed costs = $260400

Actual profit

	$	$
Sales		1800000
Less:		
Rice seed	660000	
Labour	303360	
Variable overhead	480000	
Marginal costs of production		1443360
Contribution		356640
Less fixed costs		200000
Actual profit		156640

Reconciliation of budgeted and actual profit

	$	$	$
	Adverse	Favourable	
Budget contribution			470400
Variances:			
Sales price	120000		
Sales volume	22400		
			142400
			328000
Material price		60000	
Material usage	48000		
Labour rate	18960		
Labour efficiency		18000	
Idle time		17600	
Variable overhead efficiency		30000	
Variable overhead expenditure	30000		
	96960	125600	28640
Actual contribution			356640
Budget fixed cost		210000	

Less: Fixed cost		
expenditure variance	10000	
Actual fixed cost		200000
Actual profit		156640

Workings

Sales price: (225 − 240)8000 = 120000 *Adv*

Sales volume: (8000 − 8400)56 = 22400 *Adv*

Material price: $\left(\frac{660000}{12000} - 60\right)112000 = 60000$ *Fav*

Material usage: (12000 − 11200*)60 = 48000 *Adv*
*(8000 × 1.4 = 11200)

Labour rate: (19.20 − 18)15800 = 18960 *Adv*

Labour efficiency: (16000 − 15000)18 = 18000 *Adv*

Idle time: [(.2222 hours × 8000) − 800 actual idle hours] × $18 = $17600 *Fav*

Variable overhead expenditure: $\left(\frac{48000}{15000} - 30\right)$ 15000 = 30000 *Adv*

Variable overhead efficiency variance: (15000 − 16000)30 = 30000 *Fav*

17.23 (a) See 'Purposes of standard costing' in Chapter 17 for the answer to this question.

(b) See 'Types of cost standards' in Learning note 17.1 for the answer. Currently attainable standards are generally considered to be appropriate for meeting all of the purposes specified in (a).

(c) Standard costing is best suited to manufacturing organizations but it can be applied to activities within service organizations where output can be measured and there are clearly defined input/output relationships. For a discussion of how standard costing might be affected by modern initiatives see 'Criticisms of standard costing' and 'Future role of standard costing' in Learning notes 18.4 and 18.5 in the digital resources.

(d) The answer to this question could discuss the problem of the joint price/usage variance (see Chapter 17) and the limitations of fixed overhead variances for cost control purposes (see also Chapter 17). In addition, the answer could question the linking of direct labour hours to overhead variances since overheads may be caused by cost drivers other than direct labour.

CHAPTER 18

18.10 (a) Market size variance = (budgeted market share percentage) × (actual industry sales − budgeted industry sales) × budgeted contribution
= (15000/75000) × (10% × 75000) × £80
= £120000A
Answer = **(C)**

(b) The market share variance is calculated as follows:
(Actual market share − budgeted market share) × (actual industry volume × budgeted average contribution)
[(13000/67500) − 0.20] (67500 × £80) =
£40000A Answer = **(A)**

18.11 (a) Material price:

(standard price actual price) × actual
quantity (£3 − £4) × 22 000   = £22 000A

Material usage:
(standard quantity − actual quantity) ×
standard price ((1400 × 15
= 21 000) − 22 000) × £3   = 3000A

Wage rate:
(standard rate − actual rate) × actual
hours (£10 − £11) × 6800   = £6800A

Labour efficiency:
((1400 × 5 = 7000) − 6800) × £10   = £2000F

Fixed overhead expenditure:
(budgeted fixed overheads − actual
fixed overheads) (1000 × £5 =
£5000 − £6000)   = £1000A

Volume efficiency:
(standard hrs − actual hrs) × FOAR
(1400 × 5 = 7000 − 6800) × £1   = 200F

Volume capacity:
(actual hrs − budgeted hrs) ×
FOAR (6800 − 5000) × £1   = £1800F

Variable overhead efficiency:
(standard hrs − actual hrs) × VOAR
(7000 − 6800) × £2   = £400F

Variable overhead expenditure:
(flexed budgeted variable overheads
− actual variable overheads)
(6800 × £2 − £11 000)   = £2600F

Sales margin price:
(actual selling price − standard
selling price) × actual sales
volume (£132 − £130) × 1200   = £2400F

Sales margin volume:
(actual sales volume − budgeted
sales volume) × standard margin
(1200 − 1000) × £20   = 4000F

Reconciliation of budgeted and actual profit

		Adverse (£)	Favourable (£)	(£)
Budgeted profit				20 000
Sales margin price			2400	
Sales margin volume			4000	
Material price		22 000		
Material usage		3000		
Wage rate		6800		
Labour efficiency			2000	
Fixed overhead expenditure		1000		
Fixed overhead efficiency			200	
Fixed overhead capacity			1800	
Variable overhead expenditure			2600	
Variable overhead efficiency			400	
		32 800	13 400	
Net adverse variance				19 400
Actual profit (W1)				600

Workings (W1)
The actual profit is calculated as follows:

	£	£
Sales (1200 × £132)		158 400
Less: Materials (22 000 × £4)	88 000	
Direct wages (6800 × £11)	74 800	
Variable overheads	11 000	
Fixed overheads	6 000	
	179 800	
Less closing stocks (200 × £110)	22 000	
Cost of sales		167 800
Profit		600

(b)

Stores ledger control account

Creditors	66 000	WIP	63 000
		Material usage variance	3000
	66 000		66 000

Variance accounts

Creditors	22 000		
Stores ledger (material usage)	3000	Wages control (labour efficiency)	2000
Wages control (wage rate)	6800	Fixed overhead (volume)	2000
Fixed overhead (expenditure)	1000	Variable overhead (expenditure)	2600
		Variable overhead (efficiency)	400
		Costing P + L a/c (balance)	25 800
	32 800		32 800

Costing P + L account

Cost of sales	132 000	Sales	158 400
Variance account (net variances)	25 800		
Profit for the period	600		
	158 400		158 400

WIP control account

Stores ledger	63 000	Finished goods stock	154 000
Wages control	70 000		
Fixed factory overhead	7 000		
Variable factory overhead	14 000		
	154 000		154 000

Wages control account

Wages accrued account	74 800	WIP	70 000
Labour efficiency variance	2 000	Wage rate variance	6 800
	76 800		76 800

Fixed factory overhead account

Expense creditors	6000	WIP	7000
Volume variance	2000	Expenditure variance	1000
	8000		8000

Variable factory overhead account

Expense creditors	11000	WIP	14000
Expenditure variance	2600		
Efficiency variance	400		
	14000		14000

Finished goods stock

WIP	154000	Cost of sales	132000
		Closing stock c/fwd	22000
	154000		154000

Cost of sales account

Finished goods stock	132000	Costing P + L a/c	132000

18.12 *Sales mix variance*

(Actual sales quantity) – (actual sales quantity in budgeted proportions) × standard contribution margin

Standard contributions per valet:
Full = $50 × 44.6% = $22.30 per valet
Mini = $30 × 55% = $16.50 per valet

Actual sales quantity in budgeted proportions (ASQBP):
Full: 7980 × (3600/5600) = 5130
Mini: 7980 × (2000/5600) = 2850

	Actual sales quantity	Actual sales in budgeted proportions	Difference	Standard margin ($)	Sales margin mix variance ($)
Full	4000	5130	–1130	22.30	25199A
Mini	3980	2850	+1130	16.50	18645F
					6554A

(a) (ii) *Sales quantity variance*

(Actual sales quantity in budgeted proportions) – (budgeted sales quantity) × standard contribution margin

	Actual sales in budgeted proportions	Budgeted sales	Difference	Standard margin ($)	Sales margin quantity variance ($)
Full	5130	3600	+1530	22.30	34119F
Mini	2850	2000	+ 850	16.50	14025F
					48144F

(b) See 'Sales mix and sales quantity variance' in Chapter 18 for the answer to this question.

(c) Given that actual sales revenue significantly exceeds budgeted sales revenue and that the sales quantity variance of $48144 is favourable, the sales performance was very good. The number of mini valets is 99 per cent above budget (3980 compared with 2000) but the full valets are also 11 per cent above budget (4000 compared with 3600). The mini valets are much higher but at a lower contribution per unit resulting in an adverse sales mix variance of $6554. This is likely to be due to the external economic factors arising from the significant decline in disposable

incomes within the country where the company operates. It appears that customers opted for the cheaper mini valet rather than the more expensive full valet. Also, there is now one less competitor than a year ago so the company may have gained some customers from the competitor. The above factors may explain the higher number of total valets being performed, particularly the less expensive types.

18.13 (a) *Material mix variance*

Material	Actual quantity Standard mix kg	Actual quantity Actual mix kg	Variance kg	Standard cost per kg $	Variance $
Lye	181512 × 0.25/1.35 = 33613.33	34080	(466.67)	10	(4666.70)
Coconut oil	181512 × 0.6/1.35 = 80672	83232	(2560)	4	(10240)
Shea butter	181512 × 0.5/1.35 = 67226.67	64200	3026.67	3	9080.01
	181512	181512			(5826.69)A

Material yield variance

Material	Standard quantity Standard mix	Actual quantity Standard mix kgs	Variance kgs	Standard cost per kg $	Variance $
Lye	0.25 × 136000 = 34000	33613.33	386.67	10	3866.70
Coconut oil	0.6 × 136000 = 81600	80672	928	4	3712
Shea butter	0.5 × 136000 = 68000	67226.67	773.33	3	2319.99
	183600	181512			9.898.69F

The yield variance is calculated in a different way to the approach described in Chapter 18. For the actual output (136000 batches) the standard quantities in the standard input mix are determined. They are compared with the actual quantities of inputs used based on the standard mix and the differences are multiplied by the standard input prices. This approach neutralizes the impact of the mix variance. Alternatively the approach described in Chapter 18 can be used. For an actual input of 181512kg an output of 134453 batches should result (181512kg/1.35kg per unit of output). Therefore output was 1547 batches (136000 – 134453) more than it should have been for the input (assuming it was in the standard mix). This difference is multiplied by the standard cost ($6.40) of 1 batch of output [(0.25 × $10) + (0.6 × $4) + (0.5 × $3)] giving a favourable variance of $9900. Note that the slight difference with the above answer arises because of rounding differences.

(b) (i) The materials mix variance focuses on inputs and the adverse variance indicates that the actual mix in both months was more expensive than the standard mix. The material yield variance focuses on output and the favourable variance indicates in both months, that for inputs used, a higher level of output was achieved compared with what was expected. The variances ignore quality issues and the impact of quality on sales. The focus is on material cost inputs and outputs.

(ii) As indicated above, both variances ignore quality issues that arise because of a change in mix. It appears from the question that sales have fallen (as indicated by the reporting of an adverse sales volume variance) because of the quality issues arising from the change in material mix. There may also be other reasons for the adverse sales volume variance but given the customer complaints the sales manager's views should be investigated and appropriate remedial action be taken to ensure that in the long term a mix is adhered to that doesn't result in a decline in sales.

18.14 (a) (i) Usage variance

	Std usage for actual output kg	Actual usage kg	Variance	Std cost per kg $	Variance $
Honey	2020	2200	(180)	20	(3600)
Sugar	1515	1400	115	30	3450
Syrup	1010	1050	(40)	25	(1000)
					(1150)A

(ii) Mix variance

	Actual qnty std mix kg	Actual qnty actual mix kg	Variance kg	Std cost per kg $	Variance $
Honey	2066.67	2200	(133.33)	20	(2666.60)
Sugar	1550	1400	150	30	4500
Syrup	1033.33	1050	(16.67)	25	(416.75)
					(1416.65)F

(iii) Yield variance

	Std quantity std mix kg	Actual qnty std mix kg	Variance kg	Std cost per kg $	Variance $
Honey	2020	2066.67	(46.67)	20	(933.40)
Sugar	1515	1550	(35)	30	(1050)
Syrup	1010	1033.33	(23.33)	25	(583.25)
					(2566.65)

The above usage and mix variances have been calculated following the approach described in the section titled 'Direct materials mix and yield variances' in Chapter 18. For the actual output of 101000 units the standard usage for actual output is 2020 kg of sugar (101000 × 20/1000), 1515kg of sugar (101000 × 15/1000) and 1010kg of syrup (101000 × 10/1000). To calculate the mix variance, it is necessary to ascertain the standard mix for the actual total quantity of inputs used (4650kg). The standard mix for one unit of output is 20 grams of honey, 15 grams of sugar and 10 grams of syrup giving a standard mix of 20/45 honey, 15/45 sugar and 10/45 syrup. Therefore for an actual input of 4650kg the standard mix is 2066.67kg of honey (4650kg × 20/25), 1550kg of sugar (4650 × 15/45) and 1033kg of syrup (4650 × 10/45).

The yield variance is calculated in a different way to the approach described in Chapter 18. For the actual output (101 000 units), the standard quantities in the standard input mix are determined. They are compared with the actual quantities of inputs used based on the standard mix and the differences are multiplied by the standard input prices. This approach neutralizes the impact of the mix variance. Alternatively the approach described in Chapter 18 can be used. For an actual

input of 4650kg an output of 103333 units should result (4650kg/45 grams per unit of output). Therefore output was 2333 units fewer than it should have been for the input (assuming it was in the standard mix). This shortfall is multiplied by the standard cost of one unit of output ($1.10) giving an adverse variance of $2566.

(b) (i) Expenditure variance

Cost driver rate = $52800/330 = $160	
Expected cost = 360 × $160	$57600
Actual cost	$60000
Variance	$2400A

(ii) Efficiency variance

Expected no. of units per set-up 264000/330 = 800	
Expected no. of set-ups for 320000 = 320000/800 =	400
Actual number of set-ups	360
Difference	40F
x standard rate per set-up	$160
Variance	$6400F

(c) See 'Designing ABC systems' in Chapter 11 for the answer to this question.

18.15 (a) *Performance report for April*

	$000	
Budget profit	1730.00	
Sales volume contribution planning variance	(173.75)	Adverse
Sales volume contribution operational variance	(312.75)	Adverse
Sales price variance	(132.00)	Adverse
Variable costs variance	(99.00)	Adverse
Fixed costs variance	(50.00)	Adverse
Actual profit	962.50	

Workings

Budget market share: 2000000/40000000 = 5%
Revised budget sales volume (5% × 37.5m) = 1875000
Budget contribution per unit: $3.50 – $2.11 = $1.39
Sales volume contribution planning variance
(2000000 – 1875000) × $1.39 = $173750
Sales volume contribution operational variance
(1875000 – 1650000) × $1.39 = $312750
Sales price variance:
($3.50 × 1650000) – $5643000 = ($132000)
Variable cost variance:
(1650000 × $2.11) – $3580500 = ($99000)

(b) The revised statement provides additional information relating to planning and operating variances. See 'Distinguishing between planning and operating variances' in Chapter 18 for an explanation of the benefits of this. The adverse sales volume contribution planning variance was caused by the change in the market and the manager should not be held accountable for this. However, the sales volume contribution operational variance is likely to be under the control of the manager.

18.16 (a)

(i)	Material Price Planning Variance	(Standard price − revised price) × actual quantity
	Sheets	($5 − $6) × 248 000 = $248 000 adverse
	Pillow cases	($5 − $6) × 95 000 = $95 000 adverse
	Total	$343 000 adverse
(ii)	Material Price Operational Variance	(Revised price − actual price) × actual quantity
	Sheets	($6 − $5.80) × 248 000 = $49 600 favourable
	Pillow cases	($6 − $5.80) × 95 000 = $19 000 favourable
	Total	$68 600 favourable
(iii)	Material Usage Planning Variance	(Standard quantity for actual production − revised quantity for actual production) × standard price
		Required for each pillow case = 0.5 m × 1.1 = 0.55 m
	Sheets	(240 000 − 240 000) × $5 = 0
	Pillow cases	(90 000 − 99 000) × $5 = $45 000 adverse
	Total	$45 000 adverse
(iv)	Material Usage Operational Variance	(Actual quantity − revised quantity for actual production) × standard price
	Sheets	(248 000 − 240 000) × $5 = $40 000 adverse
	Pillow cases	(95 000 − 99 000) × $5 = $20 000 favourable
	Total	$20 000 adverse

(b) The original standard cost for the actual production of 120 000 bed sheets was $1.2m (120 000 × 2m^2 × $5) and $0.45m for 180 000 pillow cases (180 000 × 0.5m^2 × $5) giving a total standard cost of $1.65m. The actual cost was $1.9894 m (248 000 + 95 000 m^2 of cotton at $5.80) giving a total variance of $339 400. The production manager is responsible for both buying and production usage and the above analysis suggests that the performance has been poor.

The world market price for cotton increased by 20 per cent and this should be taken into account when reviewing the production manager's performance. The production manager cannot be held responsible for the planning variance since he does not set the standard costs. He can only be held responsible for any difference between the $6 market price and the $5.80 actual price paid. The manager has performed well, as indicated by the favourable material price operating variance of $68 600.

More cotton was used for actual production than budgeted giving a total adverse material usage variance of $65 000 ($45 000 + $20 000). However, $45 000 of this variance related to a material usage planning variance arising from a request to change in the design of the pillowcases by the customer. This variance was not within the control of the production manager and should not be incorporated in the evaluation of the manager's performance. However, an adverse material usage operational variance of $20 000 has also been reported and the manager should be accountable

for this variance. The company was also unable to produce 10 000 pillowcases ordered by its customer in November. The manager should not be held accountable for this if it arose because of the late design change.

18.17 (a) The revised standards are as follows:

Direct material price = £2.30 × 1.03 = £2.369 per kg.
Direct material usage = 3 × 0.95 = 2.85kg. per unit
Wage rate = £12 × 1.04 = £12.48 per hour
Labour usage = 1.25/0.9 = 1.3888 hours per unit

Price/rate variances
Planning variance = (original standard price − revised standard price) × actual quantity
Material price = (£2.30 − £2.369) × (122 000 × 2.80 = −341 600) = £23 570 (A)
Wage rate = (£12 − £12.48) × (1.30 × 122 000 = 158 600) = £76 128 (A)
Operational variance 5 (revised standard price − actual price) × actual quantity
Material price = (£2.369 − £2.46) × 341 600 = £31 086 (A)
Wage rate = (£12.48 − £12.60) × 158 600 = £19 032 (A)

Quantity variances
Planning variance = (original standard quantity − revised standard quantity) × standard price
Material usage = [(122 000 × 3 = 366 000) − (122 000 × 2.85 = 347 700)] × £2.30 = £42 090 (F)
Labour efficiency = [(122 000 × 1.25 = 152 500) − (122 000 × 1.3888 = 169 444)] × £12 = £203 333 (A)
Operational variance = (revised standard quantity − actual quantity) × standard price
Material usage = (122 000 × 2.85 = 347 700 − 341 600) × £2.30 = £14 030 (F)
Labour efficiency = (122 000 × 1.3888 = 169 444.44 − 158 600) × £12 = £130 133 (F)

(b) The direct labour and material variances based on the standard cost data applied through the period consists of the sum of the planning and operational variances:

Material price = £23 570 + £31 086 = £54 656 (A)
Wage rate = £76 128 + £19 032 = £95 160
Material usage = £42 090 + £14 030 = £56 120 (F)
Labour efficiency = £203 333 − £130 133 = £73 200 (A)

(c) The variances calculated in **(b)** are based on the circumstances envisaged when the standards were originally set. When the circumstances have changed actual performance should be compared with a standard that reflects the changed conditions. If the standards are not changed the reported variances will include uncontrollable planning variances. For example, in **(b)** an adverse labour efficiency variance of £73 200 is reported but the approach adopted in **(a)** highlights that it consists of an adverse planning variance of £203 333 and a favourable operational variance of £130 133. Thus a different picture emerges when the variances are separated into uncontrollable planning variances and controllable operational variances. Attention is also directed for the need to update the standards.

(d) See 'Investigation of variances' in Chapter 18 for the answer to this question.

18.18 (a) Standard cost of materials per kg of output (0.65kg
× £4) + (0.3kg × £6) + (0.2kg × £2.50) = £4.90
Standard overhead rate = £12000/budgeted
standard quantity of ingredient F (4000 × 0.65) =
£4.6154 per kg of ingredient F
Standard overhead rate per kg of output of FDN =
0.65kg × £4.6154 = £3

	(£)
Standard cost of actual output:	
Materials (4200 × £4.90)	20580
Overheads (4200 × £3)	12600
	34180
Actual cost of output	
Materials	20380
Overheads (£7800 + £4800)	12600
	32980

Variance calculations
Material price variance = (standard price − actual
price) actual quantity
= (Standard price × actual quantity) − actual cost
= (£4 × 2840) + (£6 × 1210) + (£2.50 × 860)
= £20770 − £20380   390A

Material yield variance = (actual yield − standard yield) ×
standard material cost per unit of output
= (4200 − 4910 materials used/1.15) × £4.90
                                                        341A

Material mix variance (actual quantity in actual mix at
standard prices) − (actual quantity in standard mix at
standard prices)

		(£)	
F	(4910 × 0.65/1.15 = 2775 − 2840) × £4	260A	
D	(4910 × 0.30/1.15 = 1281 − 1210) × £6	426F	
N	(4910 × 0.20/1.15 = 854 − 860) × 2.50	15A	151F

Overhead efficiency variance = (standard quantity of
ingredient F − actual quantity) × standard overhead
rate per kg of ingredient F
= (4200 × 0.65 = 2730 − 2840) × £4.6154   508A

Overhead capacity variance = (budgeted input of
ingredient F − actual input) × standard overhead
rate per kg of ingredient F
= (4000 × 0.65 = 2600 − 2840) × £4.6154
                                                        1108A

Overhead expenditure = budgeted cost
(£12000) − actual cost (£12600)   600A

Reconciliation of standard cost and actual cost of output

	(£)	(£)
Standard cost of actual production		33180
Material variances		
Material price variance	390F	
Material yield variance	341A	
Material mix variance	151F	200F
Overhead variances:		
Overhead efficiency	508A	
Overhead capacity	1108A	
Overhead expenditure	600A	Nil
Actual cost		32980

(b)

Standard number of deliveries (4000 × 1.15kg)/460kg	10
Standard cost per supplier delivery (£4000/10)	£400
Standard number of despatches to customers (4000/100)	40
Standard cost per customer despatch (£8000/40)	£200
Actual output exceeds budgeted output by 5 per cent (4200/4000)	

Activity-based costing reconciliation statement

		(£)
Standard cost for actual output		
Deliveries (1.05 × 10 deliveries = 10.5 × £400 per delivery)	4200	
Despatches (1.05 × 40 despatches = 42 × £200 per despatch)	8400	12600
Activity usage variance		
Deliveries (10.5 − 12) × £400	600A	
Despatches (42 − 38) × £200	800F	200F
Activity expenditure variances		
Deliveries (12 × £400 = £4800 − £4800)	Nil	
Despatches (38 × £200 = £7600 − £7800)	200A	200A
Actual overheads		12600

Note that the expenditure variance has been flexed.
An alternative presentation would be to work in whole
numbers only since 10.5 deliveries is not feasible.

(c) See 'Designing ABC systems' in Chapter 11 for the
answer to this question. In particular, the answer
should stress the need to interview the employees
engaged on the activities to ascertain what causes the
activities.

18.19 (a) (i)   *Decision tree if an investigation is carried out*

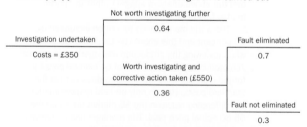

It is assumed that the £550 correction cost
applies to all variances that the initial investigation
indicates are worthy of further investigation. The
expected cost if the investigation is carried out is:

£350 + 0.36 × £550 (corrective action) +
0.36 × 0.3 × £2476[a] (continuing variance) =
£815

Note
[a]£2476 represents the PV of £525 for 5 months
at 2% (£525 × 4.7135) for variances that are
not eliminated.

(ii) *Decision tree if an investigation is not carried out*

Not worth investigating further

0.64

No investigation

Worth investigating but not done, so variance continues

(0.36)

The expected cost if no investigation is undertaken is: $0.36 \times £525 \times 4.7135 = £891$

(b) Applying the expected value decision rule, the company should follow a policy of investigating variances as a matter of routine. The expected cost of investigation is £815, compared with an expected cost if no investigation is undertaken of £891. On average, the benefits from investigation are £75 per variance.

(c) Examples of category 1 variances include:

(i) The variance is due to random uncontrollable factors and is under control. (See 'Random uncontrollable factors' in Chapter 18 for an explanation.)

(ii) Where the cause is obvious (e.g. a machine fault) and future action has been taken to remedy the situation.

Examples of category 2 variances include:

(i) Excessive usage of materials and labour due possibly to wrong working practices on a repetitive operation which is likely to continue if not corrected.

(ii) Where the variance is significant and exceeds a specified percentage of standard usage.

(d) The above analysis assumes that the average variance is £525 and additional costs of £525 in excess of standard continue for five months. Presumably, working practices are changed every five months. Costs of investigation and corrective action are £350 and £550 irrespective of the amount of the variance. It would therefore be appropriate to determine the value of variances which justify investigation. Let x = savings per month. The expected cost of investigation is equal to the expected cost of no investigation where:

$$£350 + (0.36 \times £550) + (0.36 \times 0.3 \times 4.7135x)$$
$$= 0.36 \times 4.7135x$$
$$x = £461$$

Only variances in excess of £461 should be investigated.

18.20 (a) See 'Criticisms of standard costing' and 'The future role of standard costing' in Learning notes 18.4 and 18.5 in the digital resources for the answer to this question.

(b) The creation of budget centres at the lowest defined management level would enable managers to participate in the budget setting process. Lower level managers would therefore be involved in the budget negotiation process, and this should improve communication with their superiors and create a greater awareness of the need for the activities of the budget centres to be in congruence with the goals of the organization. By participating in the process, it is claimed that managers will be more committed and strive to achieve their budgets. The creation of budget centres should also improve a manager's attitude towards the budget system. In particular, the potential for improved communication and the acceptance of budgets as relevant standards to achieve should lead to improved motivation.

Creating budget centres at lower levels will place greater administrative demands on operating the system and lengthen the budget preparation period.

In addition, the cost of reporting will be increased. Whether or not the additional benefits exceed the additional costs is likely to depend on the circumstances of the company. For example, in an environment where an organization faces considerable uncertainty or where an organization undertakes a diverse range of activities, decentralization and the creation of budget centres at lower levels might be preferable. However, where the activities of an organization can be programmed in detail and close coordination and swift reaction is necessary, it might be preferable not to create budget centres at lower levels. In particular, if the activities of budget centres are heavily dependent on the activities of other centres, there is a greater likelihood that the benefits from increased motivation will not outweigh the administrative and coordination difficulties.

18.21 For the answer to these questions see 'Criticisms of standard costing' and 'The future role of standard costing' in Learning notes 18.4 and 18.5 in the digital resources. In part **(c)** the answer should also include a discussion of the role of non-financial measures. See the section on operation processes in Chapter 21 for a discussion of non-financial measures in non-manufacturing organizations. The answer could also include a discussion of activity-based management. This topic is covered in Chapter 22.

18.22 (a) For the answer to this question see 'Investigation of variances' in Chapter 18. In particular the answer should explain that variances may be due to several causes, and not all are worthy of investigation. In addition the answer should stress the possible approaches to investigating variances:

(i) *Use of rule of thumb percentages:* For example, all variances in excess of 10 per cent of standard cost might be investigated. This approach ignores the costs and benefits of investigation.

(ii) *Use of statistical quality control charts:* Control limits are set using an analysis of historical results to indicate suitable confidence intervals. This method utilizes a statistical probability approach of not investigating a variance unless there is a high probability that the process is out of control.

(iii) *Use of a statistical decision theory approach:* This approach is described in Learning note 18.3 in the digital online resources.

It is unlikely that statistical decision theory can be applied in practice, because of the difficulty in estimating costs and benefits of investigation. Nevertheless, the approach provides a suitable model that gives a manager an insight into the important factors that should be considered when deciding whether or not to investigate a variance. Experience and an understanding of the model are likely to be the best way of establishing whether or not investigation is worthwhile.

(b) See Chapter 16 for the answer to this question.

(i) The level of budget difficulty is likely to have a motivational influence on a manager's actions to eliminate variances. If a manager believes a target to be unattainable, he or she is unlikely to strive to eliminate variances. (See 'The effect of budget difficulty on motivation and performance' in Chapter 16.)

(ii) Managers may manipulate information in order to avoid adverse variances. This is most likely to occur if a budget-constrained style of performance evaluation is used. Genuine performance improvements are most likely to occur if a profit- conscious style of evaluation is used. For a detailed discussion of styles of evaluation see 'Side effects from using accounting information in performance evaluation' in Chapter 16.

(iii) Managers are most likely to strive to eliminate variances if they accept the budget and this becomes a motivational target. Budget acceptance is more likely to be achieved by participation and not by imposed budgets. See 'Participation in the budgeting and target setting process' in Chapter 16 for a more detailed discussion of the influence of participation on acceptance of budgets.

(iv) The extent to which performance appraisal, future promotion and cash bonuses are tied to meeting the budget will provide a major motivation stimulus to meeting the budget. However, if too much stress is placed on meeting the budget, there is a danger that over-generous budgets will be sought or information will be distorted so as to avoid adverse variances.

(v) Performance reports comparing actual with budget should be provided soon after the end of the budget period (weekly or monthly). A manager is more likely to be motivated to eliminate variances if feedback reports are timely and understandable. A climate of failure and punishment should be avoided, and the emphasis should be on *helping* managers to eliminate adverse variances.

CHAPTER 19

19.14

	£m
Profit	89.20
Add back:	
Current depreciation (120 × 20%)	24.00
Development costs (£9.60 × 2/3)	6.40
Less: Replacement depreciation (£168 × 20%)	33.60
Adjusted profit	86.00
Less: Cost of capital charge (13% × £168)[a]	21.84
EVA	64.16

Note:
[a]13% × [Fixed assets (£168 − £33.6) + working capital (£27.2) + development costs (£6.4)]

Answer = **(a)**

19.15

	£m	£m
Net profit after tax		8.6
Add:		
Interest	2.3	
Development costs	6.3	
Advertising	1.6	10.2
Less development costs (1/3)		(2.1)
		16.7
Less cost of capital charge (£30m × 13%)		(3.9)
EVA		12.8

19.16 Divisional profit before depreciation = $2.7m × 15% = $405 000 per annum.
Less depreciation = $2.7m × 1/50 = $54 000 per annum.
Divisional profit after depreciation = $351 000
Imputed interest = $2.7m × 7% = $189 000
Residual income = $162 000.

Answer = **(c)**

19.17 (a) Return on investment = net profit/net assets
Division B = ($311 000 × 12)/$23 200 000 = 16.09%
Division C = ($292 000 × 12)/$22 600 000 = 15.5%

(b)

	B	C
	$	$
Net profit (monthly profit × 12)	3732	3504
Less: imputed interest charges:		
$23.2m × 10%	2320	
$22.6m × 10%		2260
Residual income	1412	1244

(c) Both divisions have ROIs below the target of 20 per cent suggesting that they have not performed well but this is because non-controllable head office costs are being allocated before calculating ROI. The ROIs using the old method before allocating head office expenses are:

B: ($311 000 + $155 000) × 12/$23.2m = 24.1%
C: ($292 000 + $180 000) × 12/$22.6m = 25.06%

From this it can be seen that both divisions have actually improved their performance.

The residual income figures indicate that both divisions have performed well by reporting positive figures, even when using net profit rather than controllable profit are used as the bases for the calculations. The cost of capital of the company is significantly lower than the target return on investment that the company is setting thus indicating that the divisions are adding value.

(d) Depreciation = ($2 120 000 − $200 000)/48 months = $40 000 per month.
Net profit for July = $311 000 + ($600 000 × 8.5%) − $40 000 = $322 000
Annualised net profit: $322 000 × 12 = $3 864 000
Net assets after investment = $23.2m + $2.12m = $25.32m.
ROI = $3.864m/25.32m = 15.26%
Therefore, Division B will not proceed with the investment, since it will cause a decrease in its ROI.

If RI is used the result is as follows:

	$000
Annualized net profit after investment	3864
Less imputed cost of capital (10% × $25.32m)	2532
Residual income	1332

Since the residual income is lower with the investment the divisional manager will be reluctant to invest if he or she focuses on the short term.

To ascertain whether the investment is in the best interests for the company as whole the NPV should be calculated:

	$000
PV of annual cash inflows ($600 000 × 8.5% × 12 months = $612 000) × annuity factor at 10% for 4 years (3.170)	1940
PV of sale proceeds in year 4 ($200 000 × 0.909)	182
	2112
Investment cost	2120
NPV	−8

The project has a negative NPV and should be rejected. Therefore both performance measures encourage goal congruence.

(e) The staff in both divisions have been used to achieving the targets and being rewarded for this. Suddenly, they find that even though divisional performance has improved, neither division is achieving its ROI target. This is a result of including the allocation of head office costs in the performance measure. Managerial evaluation should not be based on the allocation of uncontrollable costs but if senior management have reasons for doing so (see 'Surveys of practice' in Chapter 19 for possible reasons) the target ROI should be revised upwards. Staff are likely to become demotivated with the new system, which is clearly unfair. This is likely to result in the dysfunctional behavioural consequences described in Chapters 16 and 19.

19.18 (a) Value-based management (VBM) is based on the principle that the primary objective of companies whose shares are traded in the stock market is to maximize shareholder wealth. VBM seeks to maximize shareholder wealth by aligning performance measurement and evaluation with this objective. The principle measure used at the strategic level is economic value added (EVA™). This measure was developed with the aim of producing an overall financial measure that encourages senior managers to concentrate on the delivery of shareholder value. EVA™ is equivalent in the long term to the present value of future cash flows, which is the theoretical basis for share valuation. It is therefore important that the key financial measure that is used to measure divisional or company performance should be congruent with shareholder value. It is claimed that EVA™ is more likely to meet this requirement and also to reduce dysfunctional behaviour.

(b) *Calculation of EVA™*

	2017 $m	2018 $m
Profit after interest and tax	35.00	26.80
Add back interest after tax[2]		
[interest × (1 − tax rate)]	3.00	5.85
Adjusted profit	38.00	32.65
Cost of capital[1]	8.38	9.99
EVA™	29.62	22.66

Notes
[1]Cost of capital charge = (Capital employed at the start of the year) × (weighted average cost of capital)

WACC:
2017 (50% × 12.7%) + (50% × 4.2%) = 8.45%
2018 (50% × 15.3%) + (50% × 3.9%) = 9.60%
Capital employed at the start of the year:

2017 = $99.2m
2018 = $104.1m

Cost of capital charge:

2017 = 8.45% × $99.2m = $8.38m
2018 = 9.60% × $104.1m = $9.99m

[2]Net interest is added back to reported profit because the tax benefits of interest are allowed for as an expense in the computation of the tax liability.
[3]It is assumed that economic and accounting depreciation are the same, the taxation paid is the same as the tax included in the profits after tax calculation and that there are no non-cash expenses to adjust in the above calculation of adjusted profit.

Calculation of earning per share (profits after interest and tax/ average number of shares)

2017 21.875 cents ($35m/160m)
2018 16.75 cents ($26.8m/160m)

Comments
The above figures and the data in the question indicate that there has been a percentage decline in the following measures when 2018 is compared with 2017:

EVA™ = 23.5%
EPS = 23.4%
Main market index = 34.9%
Retailing sector index = 26.0%
Company share price = 12.3%

All of the company-based measures have declined but the company share price fall of 12% is lower than the sector decline (26%) and the market as a whole (35%). Market comparisons suggest that the market has a more favourable view of the company when compared with market/sector data. This view is consistent with the positive EVA™ for 2018. Although EVA™ has fallen from 2017 it has remained positive so the company continues to create value for its shareholders even in the poor economic environment. The positive EVA™ indicates that shareholder investment has been worthwhile even though the market has been falling.

(c) Value measures are considered to be superior to profit measures because they take into consideration the capital employed and cost of capital and also attempt to adjust profit measures to provide a better approximation of economic income. The major difficulty with using value-based measures like EVA™ compared to profit measures is that it is difficult to obtain a reasonable estimate for some of the EVA™ adjustments. For example, accurate calculations of the cost of capital and economic depreciation are difficult to determine (see Learning note 19.1 for how economic depreciation is calculated). EVA™ can also be subject to manipulation by choosing projects with high initial earnings but which are not justifiable on the basis of a long-term evaluation.

19.19 (a) The main advantage of using EVA™ is that it is linked to the overall corporate objective of increasing shareholder value. Using EVA™ encourages managers to make decisions that will increase EVA™, which in turn should result in an increase in shareholder value. Therefore divisional managers should also be motivated to work in the best interest of the company as a whole. Other advantages of EVA™ include:

- It incorporates the cost of capital in the calculation so that if EVA™ is positive the division will be generating a return above that required by the providers of finance.

- It provides an absolute profit measure showing the overall financial contribution to the company during the accounting period.
- The adjustments within the calculation of EVA^{TM} avoid the performance measurement distortions that can arise from following generally accepted accounting. This will result in a measure that provides a better approximation of the increase in present value during the year.
- EVA^{TM} encourages a greater focus on the longer-term by capitalizing discretionary costs and spreading the cost over the periods in which the benefits are received. This will reduce the dysfunctional behaviour by removing the temptation of managers to focus on short-term decision-making that increases short-term profits but generates lower profits in the longer term. This may be particularly appropriate in this company because of the importance of R&D.

EVA^{TM} has the following disadvantages:

- EVA^{TM} is complicated to calculate and for non-financial specialists to understand. The full version can require 160 accounting adjustments but a reasonable approximation of EVA^{TM} can be calculated using 10 accounting adjustments. Also ROI is widely used by outsiders so many companies prefer to use the same performance measure (ROI) for evaluating divisional performance as that used by outsiders to evaluate the company.
- EVA^{TM} should use a risk adjusted cost of capital, but this can be very difficult to estimate at the divisional level when divisions within the company face different level of risk. Many companies use a single weighted-average cost of capital for the company as a whole to compute divisional EVA^{TM} but this will be incorrect if it does not reflect the risk faced by an individual divisions.
- EVA^{TM} is an absolute financial measure and is inappropriate for comparing the performance of divisions which are not of similar size. Instead senior managers prefer to use a ratio measure, such as ROI, to compare divisional performance.

(b) The calculations of the ROI and RI are as follows:

	$m
Revenue	220
Divisional operating costs	121
Controllable profit	99
R&D costs recharged	11
Profit after R&D costs	88
Apportioned head office management fees	28
Divisional profit before tax	60

	ROI	RI $m
Based on controllable profit	23%	52.4
Based on profit after R&D	21%	41.4
Based on divisional profit	14%	13.4

Note that the RI calculations are after deducting a cost of capital charge of $46.6m (11% × $424m capital employed).

The question arises as to which profit figure to use for both ROI and RI. For a discussion of this issue you should refer to 'Alternative divisional performance measures' and 'Surveys of practice' in Chapter 19.

The RI and EVA^{TM} indicate that the division is performing well because both figures are positive but it is not possible to compare these two measures because of the accounting adjustments incorporated in the EVA^{TM} calculation. ROI should be compared with other divisions or similar companies to evaluate the division's performance.

(c) Appendix 2 presents Boston consultancy growth-market share matrix that classifies a company's business units into four categories based on market growth and market share relative to the largest competitor. Market growth is a proxy for industry attractiveness and relative market share serves as a proxy for competitive advantage. Stars have high growth in a fast growing industry and a high market share. They generate high profits and cash that is required for future investment. Cash cows have low growth in a mature slow growing industry and high market share with high profits and cash generation that can be used to invest in other business units. Investment needs to be low.

The Baby division is classified as a star thus suggesting that it should be an investment centre with the autonomy required to manage a division in a fast growing industry. However, it is unclear to what extent the division can make product investment decisions as the decision to commit to a new product appears to be determined by the R&D division which does the development work. If the Baby division does not have the autonomy to invest in new products it may be preferable to make it a profit centre.

A budget-constrained style of management (see Chapter 16) would be inappropriate since it would stifle the creativity necessary for such a division operating in a fast growing industry. A flexible profit-conscious or non-accounting style of management would be preferable that focuses on long-term success of the business giving emphasis to the non-financial measures that are critical to long-term success.

The Chocolate division is classified as a cash cow. Because future investment will be low there are strong arguments for making it a profit centre. However, the question indicates that performance has been limited because of having to wait for the approval of capital expenditure. To overcome such problems Chocolate could be classified as an investment centre so it does not have to wait for approval of limited capital. A budget-constrained management style would appear to be appropriate given the lack of uncertainty and growth in the industry in which the division operates. The question indicates that the Baby division managers see a R&D recharge cost in their performance reports but not the revenue which these new products are generating. Some attempt should be made to highlight the benefits received by the Baby division from R&D within the reporting system.

The R&D division has no source of external revenue other than internal recharges for its services. Therefore it should be a cost centre. Since the benefits arsing from investing in R&D are uncertain, the division should not be constrained by over-emphasizing accounting controls that may stifle creativity and the generation of product development ideas. Therefore a non-accounting style of leadership may be preferable.

19.20 (a) (i)

	Year 1 $m	Year 2 $m	Year 3 $m
	$m	$m	$m
Net cash inflow	12.5	18.5	27.0
Less: depreciation	15.0	15.0	15.0
Profit/(loss)	(2.5)	3.5	12.0
Less: cost of capital (at 10% of wdv)	(4.5)	(3.0)	(1.5)
RI	(7.0)	0.5	10.5

A positive NPV of $1.937m indicates that the investment should be undertaken. The residual income is also positive over the three-year life of the proposal but it has a negative value of $7m in year 1. This is likely to lead to its rejection by the management of Alpha Division because they participate in a bonus scheme that is based on short-term performance evaluation. The short-term focus on performance evaluation may lead to the rejection of investment opportunities such as the one under consideration and this would be detrimental to the Delta Group. Management of the Delta Group should seriously consider changing the focus of the bonus scheme.

(ii) The variable short-run contribution margin is inappropriate for performance evaluation, because it does not include fixed costs that are controllable by the divisional manager. For example, a manager may not be motivated to control non-variable labour costs or equipment rentals, since they fall below the variable short-run contribution line and are not included in the performance measure. For a discussion of controllable profit and divisional profit you should refer to 'Alternative divisional profit measures' in Chapter 19. The variable short-run contribution measure will include sales to external customers and also inter-divisional sales at adjusted market price. The fact that transfers are at adjusted market price should mean that none of the performance measures given in the question are distorted by the transfer prices that are used. Labour, equipment rental and depreciation costs are deducted from the variable short-run contribution to determine controllable profit. The inclusion of depreciation in the calculation of controllable profit is questionable if divisional managers do not have authority to determine divisional investment. In this situation it should be deducted from controllable profit to determine divisional profit. If head office finance and legal costs are allocated to divisions they should be regarded as non-controllable and deducted from controllable profit to calculate divisional profit. However, if they are charged to divisions according to usage it is appropriate to incorporate the actual quantity used by divisions at the budgeted price in the calculation of controllable profit.

(b) (i) The computation of EVA requires that adjustments are made to the financial accounting reported profits of $67m and $82m. Normally adjustments would be required to convert financial accounting depreciation to economic depreciation but no adjustments are required since financial accounting depreciation is equal to economic depreciation. EVA attempts to approximate economic profit/cash flow so non-cash expenses are added back. Net interest is also added back to the reported profit because the returns required by the providers of funds are reflected in the cost of capital adjustment in the EVA computation. Interest after tax that is added back to reported profit because interest will already have been allowed for as an expense in the computation of the taxation liability. The EVA calculation of capital employed attempts to approximate economic value at the commencement of each period. Because of insufficient information given in the question the book value of shareholders' funds plus long-term capital loans at the end of 2018 is used to determine economic capital employed at the commencement of 2019. Goodwill is added back to reported profit since it is part of the intangible asset value of the business and the write-off of $45 million is also added back to capital employed because it is an element of the total value of the business.

The calculation of EVA for each year is as follows:

Adjusted profit:	2019 $m	2020 $m
Profit after tax	67	82
Amortization of goodwill	5	5
Other non-cash expenses	12	12
Interest expense	4.2	4.2
Adjusted profit	88.2	103.2

Adjusted capital employed:	$m	$m
Year beginning	279	340
Non-capitalized leases	16	16
Goodwill	45	50
Adjusted capital employed	340	406

The EVA cost of capital should be based on the weighted cost of capital for the target capital structure (50% debt and 50% equity):

WACC 2019: $(16\% \times 50\%) + (10\% \times 0.7 \times 50\%) = 11.5\%$

WACC 2020: $(18\% \times 50\%) + (10\% \times 0.7 \times 50\%) = 12.5\%$

EVA is calculated as follows:

EVA 2019 $= 88.2 - (340 \times 11.5\%) = \$49.1$ million

EVA 2020 $= 103.2 - (406 \times 12.5\%) = \$52.45$ million

Therefore the Gamma Group has added significant value for both years.

(ii) The disadvantages of EVA include:

- EVA is an absolute measure rather than a ratio measure so it is difficult to undertake inter-divisional or inter-company comparisons;
- the calculation is complicated because of the number of adjustments required;
- approximations of economic depreciation are very difficult to determine.

19.21 (a) (i)   *Calculation of ROI*

ROI:	Operating profit	Total assets less current liabilities	Return on investment (%)
Ayetown	396	1720	23.02
Beetown	441	3160	13.96
Ceetown	703	3820	18.40

Calculation of RI

RI:	Operating profit ($000)	Required rate return	Total assets ($000)	Required return on investment ($000)	Residual income ($000)
Ayetown	396	12%	1800	216	180
Beetown	441	12%	3400	408	33
Ceetown	703	12%	4300	516	187

Note that the question states that total assets are used to calculate RI.

Calculation of EVA

	Pre-tax operating profit ($000)	After tax operating profit ($000)	($000) WACC	Total assets less curr. Liab. ($000)	Cost of capital charge ($000)	EVA ($000)
Ayetown	396	277.2	13.67%	1720	235.12	42.08
Beetown	441	308.7	13.67%	3160	431.97	−123.27
Ceetown	703	492.1	13.67%	3820	522.19	−30.09

Tax is payable at 30% so the after tax operating profit is 70% of the pre-tax operating profit. The cost of capital charge is 13.67% of total assets less current liabilities. WACC is calculwated as follows:

Market value ($000)

equity	9000	Ke	0.15	1350
debt	1800	Kd	0.07	126
	10800			1476
WACC = 1476/10800				13.67%

Note that the cost of equity is 15% and the after-tax cost of debt is $\frac{(100-30)}{100} \times 10\% = 7\%$

The following is a summary of the financial performance of the three centres:

Heath centre	Return on investment (%)	Residual income ($000)	Economic value added ($000)
Ayetown	23.02	180.00	42.08
Beetown	13.96	33.00	−123.27
Ceetown	18.40	187.00	−30.09

Ayetown is the most successful of the three centres based on ROI. A major weakness of ROI is that it is a relative rather than an absolute measure and thus does not focus on measuring value-added. RI is an absolute measure and indicates that Ceetown is the most successful centre but it is only slightly more successful than Ayetown. Beetown's RI and EVA is significantly lower than the other two centres. Ayetown has the highest EVA and it is the only centre which has a positive EVA. Value is added when the after tax operating profit exceeds the cost of investing the required capital. Therefore in order to

improve EVA, managers need to earn more operating profit using the same amount of capital, or invest capital in higher-earning projects. EVA is generally preferred to RI because it incorporates adjustments to convert the financial accounting profit to an approximation of economic profit and, by incorporating a cost of capital charge, provides a better measure the economic value-added. The above analysis suggests that Ayetown is the most successful centre.

(ii)   The ROI of Beetown is currently 13.96 per cent. In order to obtain an ROI of 20 per cent, operating profit would need to increase to (20% × $3160000) = $632000, based on the current level of net assets. The question identifies the following alternative ways (to be considered) by which a target ROI of 20 per cent could be achieved:

1   Increase revenues. The current contribution/sales ratio is 73 per cent ($1533/$2100). Operating profit needs to increase by $191000 ($632000 − $441000) to achieve a ROI of 20 per cent. Therefore revenue needs to increase by $191000/0.73 = $261644 (i.e 12.46 per cent) to achieve the target ROI.
2   Total operating costs would need to fall by $191000 in order to obtain an ROI of 20 per cent. This represents a percentage decrease in total costs (567 + 1092) of 191000/1659000 = 11.5%. If fixed costs remain unchanged then variable costs would need to fall from $567000 to $376000, which represents a decrease of 33.7 per cent.
3   The net asset base would need to fall to a level of $2205000($441000/0.20), which represents a percentage decrease of 30.2 per cent (i.e. $3160000 − $2205000 = 955000/3160000 = 30.2%).

(iii)   The marketing director is correct in recognizing that success is dependent on levels of service quality provided but this is only one element of success. If the number of complaints is incorporated into the performance measurement system the comparison of the three centres should be based on a relative measure such as the number of complaints per 1000 client days. The answer should draw attention to the fact that a balanced scorecard approach (see Chapter 21) should be used that incorporates a range of financial and non-financial performance measures that are linked to strategy. The answer should also draw attention to the fact that the number of complaints is a lagging measure of future profits and there is a need for a performance measurement system to incorporate both lagging and leading measures (see Chapter 21 for an explanation).

(b) It is assumed that HFG is unrelated to SFO so a major problem is why should SFO share information with a potential future competitor? Many organizations are reluctant to reveal confidential information to competitors. To ensure the full cooperation of SFO it will be necessary for HFG to provide sound arguments that this process will also be beneficial to SFO. A further problem is that benchmarking could have an adverse motivational impact on the staff of HFG since they may consider that top management are not confident that they have the ability to change existing business processes and activities. Also staff may consider that benchmarking will lead to changes that may result in their jobs being and working conditions under threat. Finally, benchmarking is costly so management must be assured that there is a high probability that the benefits will exceed the costs.

19.22 (a) The computation of EVA^{TM} shown below requires that adjustments are made to the financial accounting reported profits. EVA^{TM} attempts to approximate economic profit/cash flow so non-cash expenses (e.g. provision for doubtful debts and depreciation) are added back to the operating profit. Adjustments are also required to convert financial accounting depreciation to economic depreciation. Research and development expenditure is added back because it represents an investment that will yield future benefits. Therefore it should be capitalized and allocated to future periods based on the benefits received in the particular period. In this situation, all of the benefits from the current year expenditure of $12m are obtained in future years so the full amount is added back. To approximate cash flow cash taxes, rather than tax provisions, must be deducted from operating profit. Financing charges/net interest are not included in the adjusted profit because the returns required by the providers of funds are reflected in the cost of capital adjustment in the EVA^{TM} computation. Given that operating profit is before financing charges there is no need to add back this item to operating profit. The cost of capital deduction in the EVA^{TM} calculation incorporates the taxation benefits arising from debt financing so the tax payment should be adjusted to show what the tax payment would have been without any interest/financing charges. Therefore the tax saving of $5.75m ($23m financing charges × 25% tax rate) on interest paid is added back to the tax payment to indicate what the tax payment would have been without the interest/financing charges. The calculation of EVA^{TM} for each year is as follows:

	$m	$m
Operating profit		68.00
Add back:		
Accounting depreciation	59.00	
Provision for doubtful debts	2.00	
Research and development	12.00	
Other non-cash items	7.00	80.00
		148.00
Less:		
Economic depreciation	83.00	
Tax (cash paid)	9.00	
Lost tax relief on interest	5.75	97.75
Adjusted profit		50.25
Cost of capital charge (8.65% × $645.5)[1]		55.84
EVA^{TM}		−5.59

Note
[1] The cost of capital charge should be based on the approximate economic value of capital employed at the commencement of each period. The calculation is as follows:

	$m
Capital employed at the start of the period	637
Other non-cash items incurred in the previous year[2]	6
Provision for doubtful debts at the start of the year[3]	2.5
Adjusted start of the year figure	645.5

The after tax cost of debt is 3.75% [5% × (1 tax rate)] and the cost of equity finance is 16% so the weighted average cost of capital is:

$$(16\% \times 0.4) + (3.75\% \times 0.6) = 8.65\%$$

Notes
[2] No adjustment is made for depreciation to the capital employed at the start of the period because economic depreciation was identical to accounting depreciation in the previous year.
[3] The provision for doubtful debts in the statement of financial position (balance sheet) at the end of the year was $4.5m and the charge/increase during the year was $2.0m so the provision at the start of the year would have been $2.0m.

Comments

The company is currently reducing economic value since it is failing to cover the economic cost of capital and in the long term will have a negative impact on shareholder value. The company needs to increase its adjusted profit of $50.25m or reduce its cost of capital or reduce its capital base by identifying under utilized assets.

(b) The regulatory ROCE is 5.9% ($46m/$779m) and is therefore within the allowed return of 6% so there is little scope for increasing profitability since the maximum operating profit on a capital of $779m is $46.7m (6% of $779m). The company should therefore concentrate on increasing the activities of the non-regulated sector because the profit margins of this sector are 31.9% ($22m/$69m revenue) compared with 16.7% ($46m/$276m) in the regulated sector. The impact of the constraint on performance management is that with the regulated sector the focus should be o n controlling costs by seeking cost savings rather than increasing selling prices so as to avoid the regulator questioning the overcharging of customers. Within the non-regulated areas there is more scope for increasing profitability by increasing revenues by expanding market share and developing new businesses with high profit margins.

19.23 *Division A*

Both items represent discretionary expenditure. Management can choose to determine whatever is deemed necessary to spend on these activities but the amount of expenditure should seek to maximize long-term profitability. The proposed actions are likely to harm long-term profitability but they will have a beneficial short-term effect on the divisional performance measure. There are no financial accounting issues involved and, although the published accounts are likely to be slightly misleading, there would not be any problem in getting the accounts externally audited. Divisional management are, however, manipulating the budget for their own benefit at the expense of the long-term success of the organization. They are therefore engaging in unethical behaviour.

Division B

This action is an attempt to defer expenditure. The cost of consultancy services received to date should, however, be accrued and provided for in the current year's accounts for the division. This would prevent the divisional management from enhancing the profit for the current period and thus affect the bonuses. A failure to make a provision would be in breach of financial accounting regulations. If management does not make the provision it will be acting in an unethical manner and if the accountant becomes aware of the circumstances it is his, or her, professional duty to insist that the provision is made. Failure to do so would be classed as unethical behaviour. If no provision is made next year's budgeted expenses should be increased to reflect the deferred expenditure. As with division A the divisional managers are motivated to manipulate the results to achieve the budget.

Division C

Financial accounting regulations require that revenues are recognized at the point of delivery. Therefore the action does not contravene financial accounting regulations and there should be no problems with the audit of the accounts. However, future profitability may be impaired because stocks will be very low at the end of the year. This may result in a loss in future profits arising from lost sales from a failure to meet demand and also a loss of customer goodwill. The behaviour is therefore unethical and also requires that some existing customers become involved in the collusion. The motivational desire to obtain the bonus is causing the dysfunctional behaviour.

Comment on whether group management action is necessary

None of the actions are illegal but it is questionable whether managers should be able to earn bonuses arising from the actions. On the other hand divisions have been created to enhance managerial autonomy and any interference by corporate top management will undermine divisional autonomy. Some dysfunctional behaviour is likely to apply with all performance measurement systems and, as long as major dysfunctional consequences do not arise, it could be argued that the actions should be tolerated as part of the costs of decentralization. Non-interference also ensures that the motivational benefits arising from divisional autonomy are not eroded. If major dysfunctional consequences do arise from the current system then it will be necessary for central management to take appropriate action to reduce the harmful side effects. For a discussion of potential actions see 'Addressing the dysfunctional consequences of short-term financial measures' in Chapter 19.

CHAPTER 20

20.15 Division M generates a contribution to profit of $80 ($850 – $770) for the group as a whole for every motor sold externally. The incremental cost for every motor which Division S has to buy from outside of the group is $60 per unit ($800 – [$770 – $30]). Therefore, from the group's perspective as many external sales as possible should be made before any internal transfers are made. Division M's total capacity is 60 000 units so 30 000 units should be sold externally and the remaining 30 000 units transferred to Division S. From the group's perspective, the cost of supplying these internally is $60 per unit ($800 – $740) cheaper than buying externally. Division S's remaining demand of 5000 units should be bought form the external supplier at $800 per unit.

Therefore the group's current policy will need to be changed. In order to determine the transfer price which should be set for the internal sales of 30 000 motors, the perspective of both divisions should be considered. Division M can only sell the motors to Division S and the lowest price it would be prepared to charge is the marginal cost of $740 of making these units but it will also wish to make a profit on each unit transferred. From Division S's perspective it can buy as many external motors as it needs from outside the group at a price of $800 per unit so this will be the maximum price which it is prepared to pay. Therefore, the transfer price should be set somewhere

between $740 and $800. The total group profit will be the same irrespective of where in this range the transfer price is set.

20.16 (a) In this situation, head office only allows Division A will sell 80 000 baths and purchase its fittings from Division B. Division A will therefore purchase 80 000 units from Division B and Division B will use the balance of its production capacity to sell 120 000 units externally at $80.

Profit statement

	Division A $000	Division B $000	Company $000
Sales revenue:			
External (1)	36 000	9 600	45 600
Interdivisional transfers	0	6 000	
Total	36 000	15 600	45 600
Variable costs:			
External material costs (2)	(16 000)	(1 000)	(17 000)
Interdivisional transfers (3)	(6 000)	0	
Labour costs (4)	(3 600)	(3 000)	(6 600)
Total	(25 600)	(4 000)	(23 600)
Fixed costs	(7 440)	(4 400)	(11 840)
Profit	2 960	7 200	10 160

Workings ($000)
(1) External sales and interdivisional transfers
   Div A: 80 000 × $450 = $36 000
   Div B: 120 000 × $80 = $9 600
   Div B interdivisional transfers: 80 000 × $75 = $6 000
(2) External material costs
   Div A: 80 000 × $200 = $16 000
   Div B: 200 000 × $5 = $1 000
(3) Interdivisional transfers
   Div A: 80 000 × $75 = $6 000
(4) Labour costs
   Div A: 80 000 × $45 = $3 600
   Div B: 200 000 × $15 = $3 000

(b) and **(c)** The manager of Division A will maximize his/her profits by purchasing 80 000 bath fittings at the lowest price (the outside the company's price of $65 per unit). The manager of Division B will wish to sell the maximum demand (180 000 units) of bath fittings to the external market at $80 per unit and transfer the remaining capacity (20 000) units at a transfer price above variable cost. Since Division B can sell 180 000 bath fittings at $80 per the most profitable choice for the company as a whole is for Division B to sell 180 000 units externally at $80 and for Division A to buy similar type of fittings outside at $65 per unit. Division B will have unutilized capacity of 20 000 units and since its variable cost is $20 per unit it is best for the company as a whole if these 20 000 units are transferred internally rather than purchased outside for $65 per unit. Therefore the optimum output is for Division B to sell 180 000 units externally and transfer 20 000 units internally and for Division A to sell 80 000 units externally (buying 60 000 units externally and 20 000 units internally).

To encourage the divisional managers to make the above decisions, the transfer price should be set above Division B's variable cost of $20 and not higher than the outside price faced by Division A ($65). Therefore the optimum transfer price is within the range is from $20 to $65. Instead of head office imposing a transfer price within the above range divisional autonomy could be promoted by allowing the divisional managers to negotiate a transfer price, given the circumstances presented in the question. Provided that the managers are competent if would be rational for them to agree a transfer price within the above range. The following profit statements are based on a transfer price of $65 but statements could be prepared for any transfer price within the optimal range.

	Division A $000	Division B $000	Company $000
Sales revenue:			
External (1)	36000	14400	50400
Internal sales (2)		1300	
Total	36000	15700	50400
Variable costs:			
External material cost (3)	(19900)	(1000)	(20900)
Interdivisional transfers (2)	(1300)		
Labour costs	(3600)	(3000)	(6600)
Total	(24800)	(4000)	(27500)
Fixed costs	(7440)	(4400)	(11840)
Profit	3760	7300	11060

Workings ($000)
(1) External sales
 Div A: 80000 × $450 = $36000
 Div B: 180000 × $80 = $14400
(2) Internal sales/interdivisional transfers
 20000 × $65 = $1300
(3) Material costs
 Div A: 60000 × $65 for outside purchase of fittings + (80000 × $200) = $19900
 Div B: 200000 × $5 = $1000

20.17 (a) If Division B buys all of its components from division S (80000) then division S will sell its remaining capacity (95000) on the external market. This will result in unfulfilled demand of 55000 components (total demand of 150000 − 95000) in the external market. In terms of the transfer price 55000 of the components transferred will have an opportunity cost equal to the lost sales revenue of $50. This could be restated as variable cost ($44) + lost contribution ($6) giving a transfer price of $50. The remaining 25000 units transferred to division B do not have an opportunity cost so the relevant cost is the marginal cost of $44. The profit statements will be as follows:

	S $	B $	Working
Sales			
Internal	3850000		1
External	4750000	7200000	2
	8600000	7200000	
Variable costs			
Components			
Internal	0	3850000	3
External	7700000		4
Other variable	0	1888000	5
Fixed costs	560000	1460000	
Profit	340000	2000	

Workings:
1 (55000 × $50) + (25000 × $44) = $3850000
2 95000 × $50 = $4750000 Division S, 16000 × $450 = $7200000
3 Same as Division S internal sales revenue
4 175000 × $44 = $7700000
5 16000 × $118 = $1888000

(b) (i)

	S $	B $	SBA $	Working
Sales				
Internal	0	0	0	
External	7500000	7200000	14700000	1
	7500000	7200000	14700000	
Variable costs				
Components				
Internal	0	0	0	
External	6600000	3360000	9960000	2
Other variable	0	1888000	1888000	3
Fixed costs	560000	1460000	2020000	
Profit	340000	492000	832000	

Workings:
1 Division S = 150000 maximum external demand × $50; division B = 16000 × $450 = $7200000
2 Division S = 150000 × $44 variable cost = $6600000, division B = 80000 × $42 = $3360000
3 16000 × $118 = $1888000

(b) (ii)

Profit requirement $	450000
Remaining production capacity	25000 (175000 − 150000)
Additional contribution required $	110000 (450000 − 340000)
Contribution per component $	4.40 (110000/25000)
Variable cost $	44
Required selling price $	48.40 (44 + 4.40)

(c) The motivation for outsourcing is that the external supplier may be able provide the component at a lower cost than SBA is currently incurring internally. Specialist component manufacturers may be more efficient arising from utilizing the latest manufacturing technology. The major disadvantage of outsourcing is that there is a potential loss of control and a danger that SBA will be at the mercy of the supplier when negotiating a new contract. This danger will be minimized if there are many other suppliers that can provide the component at a competitive price. A close relationship will be required between the two organizations requiring a knowledge of lead times and the demand cycle at SBA. Outsourcing the manufacture of components may also result in spare capacity at SBA. Can this be utilized or can cost savings be achieved from reducing capacity?

20.18 (a) The variable costs per unit of output for sales *outside* the company are £11 for the intermediate product and £49 [£10(A) + £39(B)] for the final product. Note that selling and packing expenses are not incurred by the supplying division for the transfer of the intermediate product. It is assumed that the company has sufficient capacity to meet demand at the various selling prices.

Optimal output of intermediate product for sale on external market

Selling price (£)	20	30	40
Unit contribution (£)	9	19	29
Demand (units)	15000	10000	5000
Total contribution (£)	135000	190000	145000

Optimal output is 10000 units at a selling price of £30.

Optimal output for final product

Selling price (£)	80	90	100
Unit contribution (£)	31	41	51
Demand (units)	7200	5000	2800
Total contribution (£)	223200	205000	142800

Optimal output is 7200 units at a selling price of £80.
Optimal output of Division B based on a transfer price of £29

Division B will regard the transfer price as a variable cost. Therefore total variable cost per unit will be £68 (£29 + £39), and Division B will calculate the following contributions:

Selling price (£)	80	90	100
Unit contribution (£)	12	22	32
Demand (units)	7200	5000	2800
Total contribution (£)	86400	110000	89600

The manager of Division B will choose an output level of 5000 units at a selling price of £90. This is sub-optimal for the company as a whole. Profits for the *company as a whole* from the sale of the final product are reduced from £223200 (7200 units) to £205000 (5000 units). The £205000 profits would be allocated as follows:

> Division A £95000 [5000 units at (£29 – £10)]
> Division B £110000

(b) At a transfer price of £12, the variable cost per unit produced in Division B will be £51 (£12 + £39). Division B will calculate the following contributions:

Selling price (£)	80	90	100
Unit contribution (£)	29	39	49
Demand (units)	7200	5000	2800
Total contribution (£)	208800	195000	137200

The manager of Division B will choose an output level of 7200 units and a selling price of £80. This is the optimum output level for the company as a whole. Division A would obtain a contribution of £14400 [7200 × (£12 – £10)] from internal transfers of the intermediate product, whereas Division B would obtain a contribution of £208800 from converting the intermediate product and selling as a final product. Total contribution for the company as a whole would be £223200. Note that Division A would also earn a contribution of £190000 from the sale of the intermediate product to the external market.

20.19 (a) (i) With Quotation 1 the proposed internal transfer price is $10.50 ($15 less 30%) and the locally available price is $9. Division B would therefore purchase ankle supports from a local supplier in order to increase its profitability. Division A has spare production capacity of 10000 units (the maximum capacity is 160000 units and

total demand is 150000 units). Division A could, therefore, supply 10000 units of ankle supports at its variable cost of $7 per unit ($350000/50000) giving a total cost of $70000. The cost of purchasing 10000 units from the local supplier is $90000. In order to maximize group profits, Division A should quote its variable cost of $7 per unit for each of the 10000 units required by Division B and group profit will increase by $20000.

As regards Quotation 2 Division B would again wish to purchase from a local supplier in order to increase its reported profits Division A quotes a transfer price of $10.50. Division A could potentially supply 18000 ankle supports by using its spare capacity for 10000 units and switching production of 8000 units from sales of the type of support that earns the lowest contribution per unit. The 10000 units of spare capacity can be supplied at a variable cost of $7 per unit and the additional 8000 units would have to be diverted from the type of existing support that yields the lowest contribution per unit. The calculations are as follows:

Product	Knee support	Ankle support	Elbow support	Wrist support
Selling price per unit($)	24	15	18	9
Variable cost per unit ($)	10	7	8	4
Contribution per unit ($)	14	8	10	5

Division A should offer to transfer the additional 8000 ankle supports at $12 per unit [variable cost ($7) + contribution foregone ($5)]. Division B would reject the offer and buy externally at $9 per unit. This would ensure that the profit of the group is not adversely affected by any transfer decision.

(ii) The answer should draw attention to the general rule for transfer pricing, which is that the transfer price should be set at the variable cost per unit of the supplying division plus the opportunity cost per unit of the supplying division. You should refer to 'Marginal/variable cost plus opportunity cost transfer prices' in Chapter 20 for a more detailed explanation.

(b) Because the two divisions operate in different countries that are subject to different tax rates it is necessary to work out the impact on profits and taxes arising from the decision whether Division B buys from Division A or buys locally. If division B buys locally the implications for SSA group are as follows:

	$
Division A sales:	
60000 wrist supports at a contribution of $5 per unit	300000
Taxation at 40%	120000
After tax benefit of sales	180000
Division B purchases:	
18000 ankle supports at a cost of $9 per unit	162000
Taxation benefit at 20%	32400
After tax cost of purchases	129600
Net benefit to SSA Group – $180000 – $129600	50400

If Division B buys internally from Division A the financial implications for SSA group are as follows:

	$
Division A sales:	
External:	
52 000 wrist supports at a contribution of $5 per unit	260 000
18 000 ankle supports to Division B at a contribution of ($15 × 70%) − $7 = $3.5 per unit	63 000
	323 000
Taxation at 40%	129 200
After tax benefit of sales	193 800
Division B purchases:	
18 000 ankle supports at cost of $10.50 per unit	189 000
Taxation benefit at 20%	37 800
After tax cost of purchases	151 200
Net benefit to SSA Group	$42 600

Therefore SSA group will be $7 800 worse off ($50 400 − $42 600) if Division B purchases the ankle supports from Division A instead of the local supplier.

20.20 (a) (i)

	Division P $	Division R $
Internal transfers sales revenues[1]	4 812 500	
External sales[2]	4 125 000	10 000 000
	8 937 500	10 000 000
Internal transfers		4 812 500
Variable costs[3]	7 000 000	1 250 000
Fixed costs	1 500 000	1 000 000
Profit before tax	437 500	2 937 500
Tax	196 875	734 375
Profit after tax	240 625	2 203 125

Notes
[1] 625 tonnes × $7000 × 1.1
[2] P = 375 tonnes × $11 000, R = 625 tonnes/1.25 = 500 tonnes × $20 000
[3] P = 1000 × 7000, R = 625 tonnes × $20 000

(ii) The transfer price of $7700 per tonne for processed coffee beans is significantly below the market price of $11 000 per tonne. Setting the transfer price at $7700 compared to $11 000 reduces profit before tax by $2 062 500 (625 tonnes × $3300) for Division P and increases the profit of Division R by the same amount.

HPR is therefore moving $2 062 500 of taxable profit from country Y (where the tax rate is 45%) to country Z (where the tax rate is 25%). Country Y's tax authorities would view the transfer price of $7700 as not representing an arms' length transaction because it is below $11 000 per tonne market price and may require that an arms' length transfer price is introduced to ensure tax is not avoided.

(b) Division P has a capacity of 1000 tonnes and external demand for processed coffee beans is 800 tonnes at $11 000 per tonne. For an output above 800 tonnes, it is assumed that there is no demand so the opportunity cost is zero. Meeting the demand of 625 tonnes from Division R means that external sales by Division P are reduced from 800 tonnes to 375 tonnes so lost sales are 425 tonnes but the remaining internal transfers of 200 tonnes does not result in any lost sales by Division P. If transfers are made at opportunity cost 425 tonnes will be transferred at the market price of $11 000 and the remaining 200 tonnes will be transferred at the variable cost of $7000 per tonne. The contributions for each division are as follows:

	Division P $	Division R $
Internal transfers sales revenues[1]	6 075 000	
External sales[2]	4 125 000	10 000 000
	10 200 000	10 000 000
Internal transfers		6 075 000
Variable costs[3]	7 000 000	1 250 000
Contribution	3 200 000	2 675 000

Notes
[1] (425 tonnes × $11 000) + (200 tonnes × $7000)
[2] P = 375 tonnes × $11 000, R = 625 tonnes/1.25 = 500 tonnes × $20 000
[3] P = 1000 × 7000, R = 625 tonnes × $20 000

(c) One of the objectives of decentralization is to give managers greater autonomy. There is little point in giving autonomy by creating divisions and then imposing transfer prices. This results in the concept of divisional autonomy and decentralization being undermined. Imposed transfer prices can also lead to managers considering that the transfer price has an adverse impact on the divisional profit measure resulting in negative motivational consequences. See 'Evaluating divisional performance' in Chapter 20 for a more detailed explanation.

20.21 (a) In Chapter 20 it was pointed out that a sound transfer pricing system should motivate divisional managers to make good economic divisions (i.e. encourage goal congruence) and provide information that is useful for evaluating the managerial and economic performance of the divisions. Electrical components are transferred at market prices. There is a competitive external market for these generic components. Where there is a competitive external market price it is appropriate to use the market price as the transfer price since it meets the goal congruence and performance evaluation requirements of a sound transfer pricing system (see 'Market-based transfer prices' in Chapter 20 for an explanation). However, the assembly division could argue that the market price should be adjusted to reflect the fact that the internal transfer of components does not require the incurrence of costs of $269 000 relating to transport, marketing and bad debts. These should be deducted from the market price in order to determine an adjusted market price. If this is done, then the components division contribution to head office costs will be reduced from $383 000 (1557 − 804 − 370) to $114 000 ($383 000 − $269 000) and the contribution from the assembly will be increased by $269 000.

Housing components are transferred at actual production costs since there is no external market. This transfer price only covers the components actual production costs so the division will not obtain any contribution towards allocated fixed costs or profit from these transfers of housing components. Given that housing component transfers represents 84 per cent (8204/9761) of the division's revenue it is unlikely that the division will ever earn a significant profit. Transfers are also at actual cost rather than budgeted costs so the components division has no incentive to reduce the costs because any inefficiencies will be recovered by the transfer price. This lack of incentive could explain the adverse variance of $575000 reported by the components division. The use of actual production costs does not provide a useful measure of performance because it is unlikely that the components division will ever earn a suitable profit or provide a sound basis for motivating divisional managers to make good economic divisions (see 'Cost plus a mark-up transfer prices' and 'Full cost transfer prices without a mark-up' in Chapter 20 for an explanation). To meet these objectives it would be preferable to introduce a two-part transfer pricing system as described in Chapter 20.

(b) The change in transfer policy will reduce the revenue of the components division and the cost of sales of the assembly divisions by the fixed production costs of the housing components ($1.302m). The components division will therefore report a loss of $1.38m ($1.302 + 0.78) and the assembly division a profit of $4.021m (2.719 + 1.302). The price does not therefore provide a good measure of the economic performance of the components division since the competitive advantage of the business arises from the housing designs but the change increases the importance of the assembly division which does not represent the value-adding element of the business. However, using a variable cost transfer pricing has decision-making advantages (see Chapter 20). The conflict between the performance reporting/decision-making conflict can be resolved by introducing the two-part transfer pricing system described in (a) above. Note that the change in the transfer pricing does not result in a change to the overall company profit.

(c) Changing the housing components division from a profit centre to a cost centre would appear to be preferable to it remaining as part of the components division profit centre if the current or proposed transfer pricing system is maintained. With the current full cost transfer pricing system a loss of $78 000 is reported and with the proposed transfer pricing system a loss of 1.38m. The continuous reporting of losses is likely to be very de-motivating to the divisional manager if housing components and electrical components are combined as one profit centre. The problems arises from the fact that there is no external market for the housing components and treating it as a profit centre may not be justifiable when the majority of business (84 per cent) of the components division relates to housing components rather than electrical components. The solution would appear to be to introduce a two-part transfer pricing system that will generate a profit contribution from housing components or to establish housing components as a separate cost centre. The manager of the housing components should then be valuated on controlling costs and quality.

The question indicates that the electrical division would make a small profit if it is treated as a separate profit centre so it would appear to be appropriate to treat it as a separate profit centre. The profit reported would mean that it would continue to sell to the assembly division. Currently head office costs of $461 000

are allocated to the components division and it would be necessary to allocate these costs between the housing components cost centre and the electrical components division if the proposed change was implemented.

The assembly division is unaffected by the changes and the change has no impact on the reported profits of the company as a whole apart from the future benefits arising from the greater motivation arising from the proposed organizational changes.

20.22 (a) The report should include the following proposed measures of divisional performance:

	Manufacturing and sales	Service
Controllable ROI (operating profit/ capital employed)	30%	16%
Controllable RI (operating profit less notional interest charge)	$270m	$2.6m
Profits before tax/capital employed	23%	13%
EVA™ (see below for the calculation)	$158m	$1.1m

EVA™ is calculated as follows:

	Manufacturing and sales $m	Service $m
Operating profit	386	6.0
Add back non-cash expenses[1]	4	0.3
Less tax[2]	116	1.8
Adjusted profit	274	4.5
Cost of capital charge (notional interest × capital employed)	116	3.4
EVA™	158	1.1

Notes

[1] Depreciation is a non-cash expense that should be added back and be replaced by economic depreciation. Given that no information is given in the question relating to economic depreciation it is assumed that accounting and economic depreciation are identical. Financing charges/ net interest should not be included in the adjusted profit because the returns required by the providers of funds are reflected in the cost of capital adjustment in the EVA™ computation. No information is given in the question regarding interest payments so it is not possible to incorporate any adjustments in the EVA™ computation.

[2] It is assumed that the cash tax payment is identical to the tax on operating profits charge (30% × operating profit) and no adjustments are required to determine what the tax payment would have been without any interest/ financing charges.

Comments

For a discussion of the above divisional performance measures you should refer to each of these measures in Chapter 20. In addition, the answer should point out that all the measures indicate that both divisions are performing well with ROIs in excess of the 9% cost of capital. Ideally, ROI should be compared against a target return. Also, both divisions have a positive residual income and economic value added which suggests they are adding value. Unlike ROI, both EVA™ and RI are not useful in comparing the relative performance of divisions of dissimilar size because they are absolute measures.

(b) For a discussion of the criteria for designing a transfer pricing system, see 'Purposes of transfer pricing' in Chapter 20. You should also refer to Chapter 20 for a discussion of market-based and cost-plus transfer pricing.

Workings

Variable cost per repair = Labour (2 × $18) + variable overheads (2 × $12) + parts ($75) = $135

Total cost per repair = Variable cost ($135) + fixed divisional overhead (2 × $25) = $185

Warranty repairs each year = 39 600 (9% × 440 000 units)

The divisional annual profits (before head office costs) using the price quoted by the local engineering company ($200 per repair) for 39 600 repairs are:

	Current recharge agreement $000	Market price ($200) $000
Sales revenue	10 000	7920
Variable costs	5346	5346
Contribution	654	2574
Fixed costs (39 600 × $50)	1980	1980
Divisional profits (before head office costs)	2674	594

Variable cost per unit for a repair = $135 ($5346/39 600) Total cost per unit per repair $185 [($5346 + $1980)/39 600]

Comments

The external market price is likely to be appropriate since there is the opportunity to outsource at a charge $200 per repair. If the market price is used the above figures indicate that divisional profit declines from $2.67m to $0.59m but this would still provide the motivation for the service division to undertake the warranty work. There is a danger, however, if the company outsources the work that the company will lose control of a very important part of its business since the warranty is a key selling point for JHK. It may not be able to control the quality of the repair work if this is outsourced.

The proposed market price should motivate service division to make the correct decision on whether to continue to do the warranty work in-house or whether to outsource it and free capacity for other opportunities. If external work offers a better contribution than warranty work, the service division will choose external work. The transfer price should also produce a sound performance (profit) measure and enhance divisional autonomy since head office is not imposing a transfer price.

The question does not provide any information relating to the volume of the work outsourced or the potential demand for using the freed capacity to undertake other work. It should be noted that the proposed contract is for all of the warranty repairs so it is essential that JHK ensures that all of the freed capacity can be used on more profitable work. The length of the contract is important but the risk of losing the repair facilities in the long term does not apply since JHK will retain the production facilities so it can revert to undertaking the warranty work once the contract has been completed.

Cost-based methods are difficult to justify when a market price exists. The minimum price that could be charged is the variable cost of $135 per repair but this would not provide a contribution to the service division's fixed costs and profits and so there would not be any incentive for the service division to do this work. It would therefore prioritize external sales over internal ones. Alternatively, the price could be set at a full cost of $185 per repair but this would not generate profits on repairs. However, service division managers would still be motivated to perform the warranty work. M/S division managers would accept any cost below the alternative of $200 per repair for outsourcing the work. The cost-based approach could be based on the existing agreement. The service division would have to charge $253 per repair ($10m/39 600) in order to make the same divisional profit as it enjoys under the current agreement but this would not encourage the service division to outsource the work unless it could undertake other work in excess of $253 per repair.

(c) The new system should result in more and better quality information that will be easier for managers to access and perform their own analysis. It should also be possible for senior managers to make better decisions using more up-to-date real time information. The single database should avoid situations where the same data are held in different systems thus avoiding duplication. Care should be taken to ensure that managers are not faced with information overload so the system should be designed to give access to only those areas that it is appropriate for a manager to access. Prior to its introduction attempts should be made to ensure that the system meets cost/benefit criteria but it must be recognized that many of the benefits will be extremely difficult to measure.

20.23 (a) (i) At present the selling price is $375 and demand is 2000 units. Each increase or decrease in price of $25 results in a corresponding decrease or increase in demand of 500 units. Therefore if the selling price was increased to $475, demand would be zero. To increase demand by one unit the selling price must be reduced by $0.05 ($25/500) so the maximum selling price for an output of x units is: SP = $475 − 0.05x$
The total revenue for an output of x units is $475x − \$0.05x^2$
Therefore marginal revenue (MR) = $475 − 0.1x$
Marginal cost (MC) = $310
MR = MC where $475 − 0.1x = 310$
so $x = 1650$
Therefore SP at the optimal output level = $475 − 0.05 (1650) = \$392.50$

(ii) Monthly contribution for YD = 1650 × $82.50 ($392.50 − $310) = $136 125
Monthly contribution for GH = 1650 × [($250 transfer price) − (2 × $70 variable cost)] = $181 500
Monthly contribution from GHYD = 1650 × ($392.50 − $200 variable cost) = $317 625

(b) (i) Given that the question states that there is sufficient capacity within the company the optimal transfer price for the transferred component is the variable cost of $70 so the marginal cost for the company as a whole is $200 (two components at $70 from GH plus YD's own variable cost of $60).
MR = MC where $475 − 0.1x = 200$ so $x = 2750$
Therefore SP at the optimal output level = $475 − 0.05(2750) = \$337.50$

(ii) Monthly contribution for YD = 2750 × $137.50 ($337.50 − $200) = $136 125
GH will now transfer the component at variable cost so the monthly contribution from internal sales will be zero and therefore the GHYD group contribution will be $378 125

(c) The original company contribution from the sale of 4000 CX was $350 000 (GH 4000 × $55 contribution = $220 000 + $130 000). When the optimum price for the component was determined in part (a) the total company contribution decreased to $317 625 but in part (b) with an internal transfer price based on company variable cost the total company contribution increased to $378 125. The transfer price that is set clearly has an important impact on the profitability of the group.

Setting the transfer price of the intermediate product at variable cost where spare capacity exists maximizes group profit but results in all of the profits from interdivisional trading being allocated to the receiving division YD. Transfer prices at variable cost encourage the correct decisions but do not result in a satisfactory measure of divisional performance.

A possible solution is for the transfer price to be based on marginal (variable) costs plus a fixed lump sum fee as illustrated in Chapter 20. Alternatively, the external selling price could be used as the transfer price but with the output levels and selling price of CX being determined centrally as in part (b). The company contribution from product CX would still be $378 125 but it would be shared YD $75 625 and GH $302 500. This approach will also result in an imposed transfer price and a loss of divisional autonomy with the manager of YD being unhappy because of the reduced contribution.

CHAPTER 21

21.14 (i) The EVA^{TM} calculation is as follows:

	$m
Operating profit	551.4
Add back	
Non-cash expenses	15.1
Marketing capitalized	23.1
Operating lease expenses	40.0
Research and development	10.0
Less	
Depreciation on leased assets (115/4)	28.8
Tax	130.0
Lost tax relief on interest	24.5
NOPAT	456.3
Capital employed	
At the start of the year (unadjusted)	2282.0
Adjustment for marketing spend	
capitalized in previous year	23.1
Capitalized operating leases in previous year	115.0
Adjusted capital employed at the start	
of the year	2420.1

WACC = (1/2 × 16%) + (1/2 × 6.8% × (1 − 30%)) = 10.38%

EVA^{TM} = NOPAT ($456.3m) − [(WACC (10.38%) × Capital employed ($2420.1)] = $205.1m

Non-cash expenses of $15.1m are correctly added back since EVA^{TM} seeks to convert figures derived from accrual accounting to cash flows because cash flows provide a better measure of economic value.

Marketing activities of $23.1m per annum are for the long-term benefit and are correctly added back because they generate future value for the business. Also the prior year expenditure of $23.1m has been capitalized and is therefore correctly added to capital employed in order to derive an estimate of the adjusted capital employed at the start of the year. Operating lease expenses of $40m are also correctly added back to profit since they represent capital expenditure and the operating leases added back to capital employed of $115m presumably relates to the capitalized value of operating leases at the start of the year that have arisen from previous expenditure. An appropriate depreciation charge ($115m/4 year life) is included in the calculation of net operating profit after tax since the capitalized value of operating leases are now treated as assets of the business. Research and development (R&D) expenditure should be treated the same as long-term marketing spending. Note that there was no R&D expenditure in the previous year so no adjustment is required to the opening capital employed figure. The tax cost in the calculation should be the amount of tax cash payment in the current period (adjusted for lost tax on interest as explained in the EVATM calculation shown in Chapter 19) and not the adjusted amount of tax charged in the accounts. The WACC is incorrectly calculated because it should be based on the after-tax cost of debt. The capital employed figure should be based on the adjusted figure at the start of the year.

Because no information is given in the question it is assumed that the accounting depreciation which will have been used to calculate the operating profit is equivalent to economic depreciation that should be used to calculate EVA^{TM}. Also, none of the marketing spending in the previous year that is included in the opening adjusted capital employed has been written off since no indication is given of the periods when the benefits will be received.

(ii) Given that the products of IC range from complex to simple the current measure of units produced per labour hour does not represent homogenous output that reflects the skill and effort which is required for producing different units of output. Revenue per employee provides a better measure of productivity.

The weakness of the existing measure of the reduction in wastage is that it focuses only on power consumption. The costs assigned to the units wasted (or the revenues lost) should provide a better measure of wastage.

The greater innovation of products is measured by the number of products launched but this does not distinguish between successful and unsuccessful products. A better measure would be the percentage of revenue derived from products introduce this year.

(iii) *Just-in-time manufacturing (JIT)*
The answer should provide an explanation of the benefits of JIT (see Chapter 22). JIT should improve productivity as production lines will be made more flexible in order to meet changes in demand but it should be noted that there could be a negative impact as the JIT philosophy requires frequent changes in

production lines that require more time to be spent setting up new production runs. Adopting JIT should also result in a reduction in wastage and losses in inventory. The project may not immediately change any of the existing KPIs since the focus is on producing the right products at the right time rather than producing more products for any given input.

Kaizen costing

See Chapter 22 for an explanation of kaizen costing. In particular, the answer should point out that the kaizen costing aims to reduce current costs of production through continuous improvement. Each period, targets for lower costs are established and performance is monitored against these using variances. At the end of the period, a new lower cost goal is set for the next period. The aim is to focus on continuous improvement. Because kaizen costing aims to reduce waste and improve productivity it is linked to the first two CSFs so it should have an impact on the KPIs that relate to productivity and resource consumption. The focus is on improving the production process rather than developing new products so it may not have an impact on new product introductions.

Costs of quality and a 'zero defects' approach to manufacturing

See Chapter 22 for an explanation of quality cost management and the costs of quality. The TQM philosophy aims to focus on prevention and avoid failure costs. This project should affect the CSFs relating to improved productivity and waste by reducing defective products. This project is also unlikely to affect the number of new products launched since it focuses on the production process rather than product development.

(iv) Moving to a single database for the organization will integrate the subsystems from the different functions (manufacturing, marketing, finance and logistics). This integration is likely to be achieved by using an enterprise resource planning system (ERPS).

An ERPS supports JIT manufacturing as close links between production scheduling and demand forecasts will be required in order to link production runs with demand forecasts/orders. Also, the production schedules will need to be coordinated with inventory levels so that inventory is minimized before new production begins. The ERPS will also enable communication with suppliers and customers to be coordinated.

Kaizen costing requires cross-functional communication whereby the design team communicates with production so that changes in design can be quickly implemented by production. Quality improvements will be incorporated within revised finance targets within the integrated system and used as the new kaizen cost targets which will need to be continually monitored and updated. The new integrated database will enable quality improvements and changes to production processes to be communicated across IC's different sites.

21.15 (a)

Objectives	Performance measures	Justification
Financial perspective		
Improve operating profit margins (or asset utilization)	Percentage increase in profit/sales or economic value added (EVA).	The question indicates that the changes have been implemented partly in an attempt to increase profit so it is appropriate to incorporate this measure. If the investment base has changed significantly it may be preferable to use EVA.
Increase revenue	Percentage increase in total revenue	The question also indicates that the changes have been implemented partly in an attempt to increase revenues so it is also appropriate to incorporate this measure.
Customer perspective		
Increase customer acquisition	Total sales to new customers	The changes were made to attract new customers so the proposed measure provides feedback on the impact of the changes that were made.
Increase customer retention	Number of customers cancelling their contacts each period.	Measures were introduced in an attempt to retain customers. This proposed measure also provides feedback on the impact of the changes that were made.
Internal business perspective		
Improve after sales service quality	Number of complaints each period or percentage of total calls that are not resolved after one call.	The company transferred its call centre back to the home country in order to reduce the number of complaints and also reduce the number of calls to resolve an issue. Either of the proposed performance measures should provide feedback on the action that has been taken.
Reduce number of broadband contracts cancelled.	Number of broadband contracts cancelled each period.	This measure should provide feedback on the impact of the attempt to improve the broadband service quality.
Learning and growth perspective		
Increase employee satisfaction	Percentage of staff leaving per period	This measure should result in an improvement in customer service since it focuses on the retention of experienced staff. The end result should help to attract new customers and thus increase revenues.
Employee skill levels	Training hours per employee	This measure should also encourage an improvement in customer service thus helping to attract new customers and maintain existing customers.

(b) The company should consider increasing the minimum contract period from 3 months to 12 months. Significant set-up costs will be incurred for new customers and it is unlikely that profits will be earned from customers that leave soon after the three-month period has expired.

Pay-tv customers own the boxes so they can cancel their contract after the first three months and can use the set-top box with its free channels after cancellation. The company should consider renting the boxes rather than selling them and also provide an option to introduce a purchase charge for the boxes if they choose to cancel.

21.16 (a) See 'The balanced scorecard' in Chapter 21 for the answer to this question.

(b) The measures proposed for the financial perspective (share price and earnings per share) are identical to the existing performance measures that have been used. They represent historical short-term measures and it is claimed that economic value added provides a better measure of the economic value added to shareholder wealth. If earnings per share and share price are also retained it is preferable to show the growth in these measures over time.

The customer perspective focuses only on the patients but does not take into account other customers who pay for the products (e.g. government and insurers). Measures of cost comparisons and customer satisfaction with competitors would be appropriate.

The internal process perspective measure appear to directly address one of the objectives from the board's strategy (improve the efficiency of drug development) by incorporating appropriate measures of manufacturing excellence and efficiency in the testing process.

The learning and growth perspective focuses on the innovation objective. Appropriate measures include time to the market and the percentage of drugs that are finally improved. The trend in improvements in these measures and comparisons with industry competitors should also be reported for these measures.

(c) The key stakeholders are the government, the drug companies, the healthcare providers and their funders, and the patients. The government is an influential stakeholder because it has the power (by the appointment of trustees) over senior appointments and the funding of BDR. The drug companies have influence over BDR since they determine the testing environment for the products. Although BDR must be seen to be independent of the drug companies it is in BDR's interest to have a successful drug development industry in order to achieve its goal of encouraging new drug development. The healthcare providers will have an interest in the quality of the approval process so they can have confidence in the medication that they prescribe. The patients will have an interest in development in new innovative treatments being quickly and safely brought to market.

(d) The objectives at BDR are more qualitative and more of a non-financial nature when compared with PT. It will therefore be more difficult to set quantifiable measures. There is also the danger that any quantifiable measures that are established will be focused on to a greater extent than the qualitative objectives. BDR will have a more complex balanced scorecard compared with PT due to the diverse nature of its important stakeholders. The principal stakeholder is the government and this presents political dimensions that will influence performance measurement. The primary objective at PT is financial whereas BDR has are several key objectives that are difficult to prioritize. Stakeholders may also have conflicting objectives so it will be more difficult to prioritize the measures that are incorporated in the balanced scorecard.

21.17 (a) Success within areas focusing on the customer perspective will lead to improved customer satisfaction. This should improve the customer perception of services provided by the company and thus lead to an increase in market share and also the potential to increase selling prices if the company is perceived to offer a better service. This in turn should lead to an increase in sales revenues and the increase in selling prices should improve the profit margins. Increased volumes should improve capacity utilization

by increasing the loads delivered by the vehicles. The end result should be an increase in return on capital employed arising from an improvement in operating profit without additional capital expenditure.

(b) In order to meet customers' transport needs it is necessary to be able to meet all delivery requests. This can be measured as follows:

$$\frac{\text{Total number of packages transported } (548\,000)}{\text{Total number of customer transport requests } (610\,000)}$$
$$= 89.8\%$$

Ability to deliver packages quickly will depend on the distances travelled for the different packages so it is inevitable that long distance deliveries will take longer than short distance deliveries. Therefore, a measure based on time taken per kilometre which a package travels should be used:

$$\frac{\text{Total minutes spent in transit by each package}}{\text{Total package kilometres travelled } (65\,760\,000)}$$
$$= 2.0$$

Ability to deliver packages on time requires that the packages are delivered within the time window given to the customer. This can be measured as follows:

$$\frac{\text{Deliveries within window } (548\,000 - 21\,920)}{\text{Total number of packages transported } (548\,000)}$$
$$= 96\%$$

The ability to deliver packages safely can be measured by the number of undamaged packages delivered within the time window given to the customer:

$$\frac{\text{Deliveries of undamaged packages } (548\,000 - 8220)}{\text{Total number of packages transported } (548\,000)}$$
$$= 98.5\%$$

The obvious danger of measuring performance using the number of complaints is that some customers may not bother to complain when a package is not delivered safely or on time. Instead they may migrate to competitors resulting in the company losing repeat business. This could be avoided by introducing a system that monitors late deliveries and also providing some form of compensation for late deliveries for both customers that complain and do not complain. Some customers may also make unreasonable complaints or complaints may arise because of factors that are beyond the company's control. The measure records all complaints without distinguishing whether they are reasonable or not. This can be overcome by using the number or customers that have been compensated because of delivery problems rather the total number of complaints.

(c) It is assumed that senior management are members of the board resulting in them being involved in setting their own rewards. Therefore there is a danger that easily achievable targets will be set, resulting in potential large bonuses that will reduce profits that could be distributed to shareholders or reinvested in the business to increase shareholder value. The bonus scheme should be linked to the BSC to ensure that the objectives of the senior management are congruent with those of the shareholders. At present, return on capital represents a key performance measure within the financial perspective but a value based measure such as economic value added is preferable since this measure is more closely linked to shareholder value.

The current method of performance evaluation is too subjective and it is proposed that managers should be involved in setting their own bonus targets. Given that the targets are used to set the financial rewards, there is a danger that easily achievable standards will be set. Challenging targets should be set at a higher management level. Targets are set that are easily achievable or very difficult to achieve will not motivate the managers. At the operational level attempts should be made to ensure that the targets mainly include items that are controllable by the managers. Ideally measures applicable to the operation managers should cascade down from the strategic measures in the BSC. These measures will normally fall within the customer and process perspectives.

21.18 (a) The answer should provide a description of the four perspectives of the balanced scorecard (BSC) as described in Chapter 21. In particular, the description should emphasize that an organization's strategy is implemented by specifying the major objectives for each of the four objectives and translating them into specific targets, performance measures and initiatives.

Within the financial perspective Soup currently uses return on capital employed (ROCE) as its key financial performance measure, but as indicated in Chapter 19 (see 'Return on investment') this can encourage short-term decisions to be taken at the expense of long-term success. It is apparent that Soup has purchased old trains and not invested in new trains. The question indicates that the trains are becoming unreliable and their condition is deteriorating and in the long term this will reduce customer satisfaction and financial performance. This may account for soup's high ROCE (see 'Impact of depreciation' in Chapter 19). Maximizing ROCE may have encouraged Soup not to reinvest. Replacing ROCE with EVA provides a more suitable measure of increasing shareholder value (see Chapter 19 for an explanation).

Within the customer perspective Soup currently measures growth in passenger numbers which does provide some indication of customer satisfaction but in many situations passengers may have no alternative but to travel with Soup because of the lack of competition in some geographical areas. Soup could obtain more forward looking qualitative performance measures by using customer surveys to ascertain the importance and quality of the services provided by Soup (e.g. frequency and reliability of trains, overcrowding, comfort, wireless access etc.). The responses to the customer survey will enable Soup to focus on improving performance in the key areas identified by the survey.

Measures within the internal business perspective are likely to focus on reliability and overcrowding. The number of train journeys not arriving on time (analysed by the time length of the delay) and the number of train journeys cancelled could be used as measures of reliability. Overcrowding can be measured by the percentage of seats occupied, analysed by different routes and time periods. These measures also provide a measure of the utilization of services. High levels of utilization are necessary to support the measures within the financial perspective.

The innovation and learning perspective should focus on forward looking measures. Typical measures relate to the quality of online information systems available to customers and displayed on the trains, staff absenteeism, number of training hours, number of suggested improvements per employee, etc.

(b) Seat occupancy measured by the number of seats occupied expressed as a percentage of the total number of seats available can be used to measure the extent of overcrowding. Seats available per train is 490 (7 coaches × 70 seats) in Region A and 420 (7 coaches × 60 seats) in Region B.

	Region A	Region B
Seats available per train	490 (7 coaches × 70 seats)	420 (6 coaches × 70 seats)
Seats available per day:		
Peak times	1960 (490 × 4)	1680 (420 × 4)
Other times	2940 (490 × 6)	3360 (420 × 8)
Seat occupancy:		
Peak times	128% (2500/1960)	83% (1400/1680)
Other times	83% (2450/2940)	55% (1850/3360)

Total seat occupancy = Number of passengers (8200)/Total seats available (9940) = 82.5%

The total seat occupancy ratio of 82.5 per cent indicates that on average the number of seats are not fully utilized. However, this measure is misleading since overcrowding may exist during peak times. Indeed, the above ratios indicate that 22 per cent of the passengers (i.e. 540) travelling at peak times in Region A are unable to obtain a seat. This represents 7 per cent (540/8200) of all passengers. There are significant variations between regions and times travelled but overcrowding only occurs at peak times in Region A. The above analysis suggests that the claim that Soup's trains are overcrowded appears to be exaggerated.

(c) Care must be taken to avoid a proliferation of measures. It is important that the BSC does not become a long list of measures and objectives resulting in information overload. Another problem that Soup may encounter relates to the weighting that should be given to the performance measures in order to assess the relative importance that management assigns to each performance measure. Determining the weighting, however, is difficult but in the absence of weighting each measure will be viewed as being of equal importance.

Also some objectives are easier to measure than others. For example, it is apparent from the answer to part (b) that seat occupancy as a measure of overcrowding is easy to measure whereas measuring customer satisfaction is far more subjective and difficult to measure.

The measures chosen may also conflict. Passengers wish to avoid overcrowded trains but high levels of utilization of seat capacity and running fully occupied trains contributes to improved short-term financial measures.

For an explanation of other problems that are likely to be encountered you should refer to the answer to Problem 21.19 (part iv).

21.19 (i) In Learning note 21.1 (see the digital resources) the following unique characteristics were identified that distinguished service companies from manufacturing organizations.

1 Most services are intangible resulting in there being no physical product. For Kolmog it is a night's stay in a hotel. For example, the customer will be influenced by the comfort of the room, the meals served, the attitude of staff, the checking in and out

process, and so on. This makes managing and controlling the operation complex because it is difficult to establish exactly what an individual customer is buying.

2 It is difficult to standardize a service since outputs vary from day to day. Services tend to be provided by individuals whose performance is subject to variability that significantly affects the service quality the customer receives.

3 The production and consumption of many services are inseparable so they cannot be stored. In a hotel if a room is unoccupied, the sales opportunity is lost for ever and the resource is wasted.

(ii) The strategic performance report is entirely financial in nature and does not include measures relating to items identified in the organization's stated mission. It focuses on aspects of shareholder value using earning per share (EPS) growth, share price performance and return on capital employed (ROCE). The analysis of items as a percentage of revenue is a useful financial measure but external comparisons are required to interpret the competitive position. Also, the analysis of results is only meaningful if comparative figures are provided with previous periods and competitors operating within the same business environment. Year on year growth figures are given but no external comparative information or inflation rates are given to interpret the performance. Summary budget figures and variances are also not included in the report. Various traditional non-financial measures such as occupancy rates and revenue per available room would improve the report.

The major omission is that there is no attempt to measure the goal of being the No. 1 hotel chain by including measures relating to product innovation, customer or employee loyalty. No attempt is made to include external and competitive data in the report.

(iii) The proposed scorecard has the advantage of using only a small number of measures and thus avoids the danger of information overload. The financial perspective focuses on measures of strategic financial performance using share price and ROCE benchmarked to Kolmog's main competitors. This supports the objective of maximizing shareholder value. ROCE is a widely used measure of overall financial performance but this may now be less useful for Kolmog since it now rents the hotels rather than investing in the asset base thus reducing the capital dependence of the business. It may be more appropriate to introduce revenue growth as a measure since this contributes to the objective of being the leading hotel chain in Ostland.

The customer perspective is addressed by the customer survey scores. This partially supports the objective of strengthening the brand by consistently delighting customers. Growth in revenues from returning business could be added as a measure to support the objective of improving brand loyalty.

The internal process perspective is addressed using variance analysis based on a comparison of performance against budget for each hotel. Internal comparisons should be made with other hotels within the group but care should be made to compare hotels operating within a similar environment (e.g. city/business hotels may have different performance outcomes to country/holiday hotels). If suitable data is available, external comparisons of key operating performance metrics (e.g. occupancy levels) should also be made with competitors.

The learning and growth perspective is addressed by staff turnover as a measure of employee satisfaction. Satisfied and highly motivated staff are a key driver of customer satisfaction but surveys of staff attitudes may provide a better measure of employee loyalty/satisfaction. However, Kolmog's objective of delivering innovative products and services does not appear to have been addressed within the proposed scorecard. A possible metric would be percentage of revenue generated from new hotel services.

Kolmog should benchmark the scorecard measures against their competitors in order to assess whether it is achieving its primary objective of becoming the No. 1 hotel in Ostland.

(iv) The following difficulties are likely:

- Avoiding a proliferation of measures. It is important that the BSC does not become a long list of measures and objectives resulting in information overload.
- Determining metrics that measure qualitative/non-financial areas.
- Translating the strategic measures down to the organization to the operational level.
- Seeking to avoid the use of performance metrics that conflict with each other (e.g. increasing market share in unprofitable areas may conflict with the metrics within the financial perspective)
- Ensuring that the performance measures link to the strategic goals and that each performance measure is part of a cause-and-effect relationship involving a link from strategy formulation to financial outcomes and is well understood by the staff.
- Ensuring that performance evaluation is linked to measures derived from the balanced scorecard rather than using traditional measures used prior to the introduction of the scorecard.

(v) For a discussion relating to the purpose for setting targets that are challenging you should refer to 'Setting financial performance targets and determining how challenging they should be' in Chapter 16. In particular, the answer should stress that targets must be challenging enough to motivate employees to maximize performance but not so challenging that they demotivate because they are viewed as unlikely to be achievable. It appears that in the past, targets have been set that have been too difficult to achieve, resulting in few employees receiving a bonus and the remainder not expecting a bonus. There is a danger that employees make no effort other than the minimum required to keep their job. The new targets should be perceived as being difficult but achievable.

Standards represent the performance targets that have been set. Employees must accept the targets if they are to be committed to achieving them. Allowing employees to participate in setting the standards increases the probability that they will be committed to achieving them. The danger is that employees may seek to establish easily attainable targets if the reward system is based on the same target that the employee has been involved in setting. Ideally, relative performance targets should be used whereby employees performance can be evaluated relative to similar units inside or outside the organization. Targets should also be fair with different types of hotels being measured against similar standards.

The rewards should be clear, easily understandable and accepted by the managers. They should also be based on the controllability principle as described in Chapter 16. The system proposed at Kolmog has the following potential problems:

- It appears that the finance department at head office sets the budget. Hotel managers should be involved in budget setting.
- The use of company average customer satisfaction is a poor measure since it is company wide and is not based on responsibility centre performance. Customer satisfaction is within the control of each hotel manager and should be internally and externally compared with competitors operating within a similar hotel environment.
- The reward of up to 30 per cent of salary is based on the regional managers' assessment of managers of performance against the target. This is very subjective. Ideally, a more objective basis should be used but if the current system is maintained the regional managers' assessment should be clearly understood with detailed objective feedback being provided at the annual appraisal.

21.20 (a) The key areas of performance referred to in the question are listed in Learning note 21.1 – financial, competitiveness, quality of service, flexibility, resource utilization and innovation.

Financial
- There has been a continuous growth in sales turnover during the period – increasing by 50 per cent in 2015, 10 per cent in 2016 and 35 per cent in 2017.
- profits have increased at a higher rate than sales turnover – 84 per cent in 2015, 104 per cent in 2016 and 31 per cent in 2017.
- Profit margins (profit/sales) have increased from 14 per cent in 2015 to 31 per cent in 2017.

Competitiveness
Market share (total turnover/total turnover of all restaurants) has increased from 9.2 per cent in 2014 to 17.5 per cent in 2017. The proposals submitted to cater for special events has increased from 2 in 2014 to 38 in 2018. This has also been accompanied by an increase in the percentage of contracts won which has increased over the years (20 per cent in 2014, 29 per cent in 2015, 52 per cent in 2016 and 66 per cent in 2017). Although all of the above measures suggest good performance in terms of this dimension the average service delay at peak times increased significantly in 2017. This area requires investigating.

Quality of service
The increasing number of regular customers attending weekly suggests that they are satisfied with the quality of service. Other factors pointing to a high level quality of service are the increase in complimentary letters from satisfied customers. Conversely, the number of letters of complaints and reported cases of food poisoning have not diminished over the years. Therefore the performance measures do not enable a definitive assessment to be made on the level of quality of service.

Innovation/flexibility
Each year the restaurant has attempted to introduce a significant number of new meals. There has also an increase each year in the number of special theme evenings introduced and the turnover from special events has increased significantly over the years.

These measures suggest that the restaurant has been fairly successful in terms of this dimension.

Resource utilization
The total meals served have increased each year. Idle time and annual operating hours with no customers have also decreased significantly each year. There has also been an increase in the average number of customers at peak times. The value of food wasted has varied over the years but was at the lowest level in 2017. All of the measures suggest that the restaurant has been particularly successful in terms of this dimension.

(b) *Financial*
Details of the value of business assets are required to measure profitability (e.g. return on investment). This is important because the seating capacity has been increased. This may have resulted in an additional investment in assets and there is a need to ascertain whether an adequate return has been generated. Analysis of expenditure by different categories (e.g. food, drinks, wages, etc.) is required to compare the trend in financial ratios (e.g. expense categories as a percentage of sales) and with other restaurants.

Competitiveness
Comparison with other restaurants should be made in respect of the measures described in (**a**) such as percentage of seats occupied and average service delay at peak times.

Quality of service
Consider using mystery shoppers (i.e. employment of outsiders) to visit this and competitor restaurants to assess the quality of service relative to competitors and to also identify areas for improvement.

Innovation/flexibility
Information relating to the expertise of the staff and their ability to perform multi-skill activities is required to assess the ability of the restaurant to cope with future demands.

Resource utilization
Data on the number of employees per customer served, percentage of tables occupied at peak and non-peak times would draw attention to areas where there may be a need to improve resource utilization.

21.21 (a) The key features of performance measures are that:

- they should measure the extent to which the business is currently meeting its objectives that are necessary to implement its current strategy;
- objectives should be translated into performance measures, targets and initiatives and feedback and feed-forward controls should provide information about the extent to which a company is achieving its key strategic aims;
- feedback should include measures on the efficiency of resource utilisation within the organization;
- they should provide a mix of financial and non-financial measures of performance in respect of the key variables that are necessary to compete successfully in today's competitive environment;
- they should contain internal and external measures of performance;
- they should link to the targets set to the employee reward system;
- they should specify an appropriate time dimension for achieving the different targets.

The key performance indicators (KPIs) at Cod do not have many of the above features. They are focused purely on financial performance and do not address issues relating to quality, customer service and product innovation. These are all mentioned in the mission statement. The KPIs also give little attention to external features such as customer satisfaction or share price performance. It is also unclear how they link to employee motivation and the reward system.

(b) For an explanation of the performance pyramid, you should refer to Learning note 21.1 in the digital support resources accompanying this book (see Preface for details).

(c) Lynch and Cross state that the driving forces that are appropriate to achieve the organization's financial and marketing strategies are customer satisfaction, flexibility and productivity. At present Cod's KPIs do not incorporate customer satisfaction (quality/service standards), flexibility (innovation and the ability to adapt to change in the external business environment) and productivity (efficiency and waste).

The following additional measures could be added to address the above driving forces:

Customer satisfaction
Percentage of orders generating a complaint (5.4 per cent in the current year compared to 5.0 per cent in the previous year).
Preferred supplier status (58 per cent of market in the current year compared with 50 per cent in the previous year (this is based on the assumption that there is a market for only 24 possible appliance manufacturing customers that offer this status).

Flexibility represented by measures of innovation
One new product has been launched each year and 4 are in development in the current year compared with 3 in the previous year.

Productivity
The operational performance measures suggested by the pyramid are quality, delivery, cycle time and waste.

Quality:
Internal and external failure quality costs of $4.35m in the current year and $3.46m in the previous year provide measures of inefficient production. The number of customer complaints also provide a measure of quality but these measures should also be presented as a percentage of total number of customers. The number of complaints in 'other' category is high and should be analysed in more detail. The level of training days and long-term unfilled posts provides an indication of the employee environment in terms of their impact on quality and delivery but to interpret them they should be compared with industry benchmarks.

Delivery:
The number of complaints relating to late delivery should be reported but should be further analysed by the severity of the complaints.

Cycle time:
Currently no useful information being collected to allow measurement of the cycle times of processes.

Waste:
No figures are collected that indicate waste in production. Idle time for employees, materials wastage and usage variances should be reported.

21.22 (a) The answer should begin with a brief description of the performance pyramid and the performance

pyramid diagram (see Learning note 21.1 in the digital resources). The performance pyramid begins with the corporate vision. The company's objective is to maximize shareholder wealth by maintaining flexibility to adapt to that market demand through close control of all stages of the supply chain. The current performance measures shown in the report appear to broadly measure these factors in some way but may need to be improved.

Return on capital employed (ROCE) does not directly measure shareholder wealth and no indication is given that measures are reported that relate more directly to shareholder wealth (e.g. dividends per share and share price growth compared with competitors). This absence of reporting of and attention to shareholder wealth measures may explain why there has been some criticism from institutional investors that shareholder growth has not been strong.

Flexibility to adapt to the market is measured through the average time to market and the design awards won provide an indication of the innovative abilities of the employees. The ability of the manufacturing supply chain to restock fast selling products is not measured. There is no indication that there is close control of production process as there appears to have been some criticism from customers of the durability of Graviton's clothes.

The next level of the pyramid in translating the objectives derived from the corporate mission is to focus on market and financial performance measures at lower levels within the organization. Financial measures, such as profit margins, are not reported. Productivity measures relating to waste are important since designs may become obsolete. The problem of obsolescence is important in the clothing industry for fashionable products since it is important to be able to meet demand but avoid obsolescence so details of percentage of production that is written off as obsolete is required.

Market performance is determined by customer satisfaction and flexibility. The company measures flexibility through time to market and delivery since these are important in achieving the corporate mission. Customer satisfaction is measured through the revenue growth and the winning of design awards provides a broad indication of market reaction to new designs. There is no indication that quality measures feature in the reporting system and these may be important measures of customer satisfaction.

(b) Myopia relates to focusing excessively on short-term performance at the expense of longer term performance. At factory site 2, there has been an excellent return on a low capital employed figure but a significant adverse variance in the equipment repairs account. This could be due to a failure to invest in new machinery, resulting in excess repair work on old machinery. Using ROCE as a performance measure may encourage this behaviour since old machinery will have a low written down value, which can result in reporting a higher ROCE than would occur if the old assets were replaced. This problem can be avoided by using unconventional depreciation methods (See 'The impact of depreciation' in Chapter 19 for an explanation) or using longer term measures beyond one accounting period that captures the effect of such behaviour.

Gaming occurs when managers engage in dysfunctional behaviour by focusing on maximizing their own performance rather than maximizing the performance of the organization as a whole (see 'Harmful side-effects of controls' in Chapter 16 for a more detailed explanation). An example of this behaviour occurs in factory site 1 by delaying invoicing for completed orders in order to ensure that profit targets are met in both the current and the next accounting period. This behaviour can be reduced by ensuring that the manager is rewarded for average gains over long periods rather than focusing on a single period and not relying excessively on short-term financial measures. They should be supplemented with non-financial measures that are critical to the long-term success of the organization.

Ossification relates to an unwillingness to change from an existing system even when evidence suggests that the new system represents an improvement. This occurs with the board resisting change at Graviton. The CEO will need to persuade them that the current set of performance measures are leading to long-term difficulties in achieving their overall goal of enhancing shareholder wealth and that these difficulties can be reduced by changing the existing system.

21.23 (a) (i) Efficiency measures focus on the relationship between outputs and inputs. Optimum efficiency levels are achieved by maximizing the output from a given input or minimizing the resources used in order to achieve a particular output. Measures of effectiveness attempt to measure the extent to which the outputs of an organization achieve the latter's goals. An organization can be efficient but not effective. For example, it can use resources efficiently but fail to achieve its goals.

In organizations with a profit motive, effectiveness can be measured by return on investment. Inputs and outputs can be measured. Outputs represent the quality and amount of service offered. In profit-orientated organizations output can be measured in terms of sales revenues. This provides a useful proxy measure of the quality and amount of services offered. In non-profit-making organizations outputs cannot be easily measured in monetary terms. Consequently, it is difficult to state the objectives in quantitative terms and thus measure the extent to which objectives are being achieved.

If it is not possible to produce a statement of a particular objective in measurable terms, the objectives should be stated with sufficient clarity that there is some way of judging whether or not they have been achieved. However, the focus will tend to be on subjective judgements rather than quantitative measures of effectiveness. Because of the difficulty in measuring outputs, efficiency measures tend to focus entirely on input measures such as the amount of spending on services or the cost per unit of input.

(ii) Similar problems to those of measuring effectiveness and efficiency in non-profit-making organizations arise in measuring the performance of non-manufacturing activities in profit-orientated organizations. This is because it is extremely difficult to measure the output of non-manufacturing activities. For a discussion of the problems that arise when measuring the performance of non-manufacturing activities see Learning note 16.1, effectiveness and efficiency tests.

(b) (i) *Adherence to appointment times*
1 percentage meeting appointment times;
2 percentage within 15 minutes of appointment time;
3 percentage more than 15 minutes late;
4 average delay in meeting appointments.

Ability to contact and make appointments
It is not possible to obtain data on all those patients who have had difficulty in contacting the clinic to make appointments. However, an indication of the difficulties can be obtained by asking a sample of patients at periodic intervals to indicate on a scale (from no difficulty to considerable difficulty) the difficulty they experienced when making appointments. The number of complaints received and the average time taken to establish telephone contact with the clinic could also provide an indication of the difficulty patients experience when making appointments.

Monitoring programme

1 Comparisons with programmes of other clinics located in different regions.
2 Questionnaires asking respondents to indicate the extent to which they are aware of monitoring facilities currently offered.
3 Responses on level of satisfaction from patients registered on the programme.
4 Percentage of population undertaking the programme.

(ii) Combining the measures into a 'quality of care' measure requires that weights be attached to each selected performance measure. The sum of the performance measures multiplied by the weights would represent an overall performance measure. The problems with this approach are that the weights are set subjectively, and there is a danger that staff will focus on those performance measures with the higher weighting and pay little attention to those with the lower weighting.

CHAPTER 22

22.16 (a)

Life cycle cost per unit	$
R&D costs	160000
Product design costs	800000
Marketing costs	3950000
Fixed production costs	1940000
Fixed distribution costs	240000
Fixed selling costs	360000
Administration costs	2600000
Variable manufacturng costs	12400000
$(100000 \times \$40 + 200000 \times \$42)$	
Variable distribution costs	1300000
$(100000 \times \$4 + 200000 \times \$4.50)$	
Variable selling costs	940000
$(100000 \times \$3 + 200000 \times \$3.20)$	
Total costs	24690000

Cost per unit = $24690000/300000 = \$82.30$

(b) Total labour time for first 100 units:

$y = ax^b$

$b = -0.0740005$

If $x = 100$, then $y = 0.5 \times 100^{-0.0740005}$

= 0.3556 hours per unit.

Total hours for 100 units = 35.56 hours

Time for 99th unit

$y = 0.5 \times 99^{-.0740005}$

= 0.3559 hours per unit.

Total hours for 99 units = 35.23 hours.

Time for 100th unit = 35.56 hours – 35.23 hours

= 0.33 hours

The total labour cost over life of the product for year 2 is:

100 units at 0.3556 per unit	=	36 hours
99 900 at 0.33 hours per unit	=	32 967 hours
		33 003 hours

giving a total cost $792 072 (33 003 hours at $24 per hour)

The total labour cost over life of the product for year 3 is $1 716 000 (200 000 × 0.33 × $26).

Total revised lite cycle cost	$
Total labour cost	2 508 072
Other life cycle costs from (a)	24 690 000
Less labour cost included in (a)	(3 800 000)
(100 000 × 0.5 × $24) + (200 000 × 0.5 × $26)	
Total revised life cycle costs	23 398 072

Cost per unit = $23 398 072/300 000 = $77.99

(c) See 'Life cycle cost management' in Chapter 22 for the answer to this question.

22.17 (a)

	$
Sales price	25.00
25% profit margin	6.25
Target cost	18.75

	$	Working
Component A	2.15	
Component B	1.75	
Materials	2.50	1
Labour (0.4 hours at $15 per hour)	6.00	
Production overhead cost	1.89	
Distribution and sales cost	2.38	
Royalty fee	3.75	2
Forecast cost	20.42	
Cost gap	1.67	

Workings:

1 0.6kg × $4 per kg = $2.40/0.96 = $2.50

2 $25 × 0.15 = $3.75

(b) Inbound logistics includes purchasing, receipt and storage of components and materials from a number of suppliers. Adopting just-in-time (JIT) purchasing may significantly reduce storage costs. The JIT supplier takes the responsibility for the quality of products supplied and meeting the required delivery schedules (See 'JIT purchasing arrangements' in Chapter 22 for a more detailed answer).

Scheduled deliveries fall within the outbound logistics category. Following the same schedule each week irrespective of load appears to be inefficient because the delivery process does not take into account the toy requirements at retail stores. Therefore the company may be delivering to retail outlets that do not require toys and thus incurring excessive transportation costs. A data processing system needs implementing that ensures that deliveries are matched with demand and that avoids small inefficient deliveries.

The company sells toy Z through its network of retail outlets. It may be possible to reduce costs by offering the toy for sale via the PBB website.

22.18 (a) *Cost of quality report*

	Volume	Rate	Cost
		$	$
Prevention costs			
Supplier review			60 000
Appraisal costs			
Equipment testing	400	30	12 000
Internal failure costs			
Down time			375 000
Manufacturing rework	800	380	304 000
Total internal failure costs			679 000
External failure costs			
Customer support	500	58	29 000
Warranty repair	650	2600	1 690 000
Total external failure costs			1 719 000
Total quality costs			2 470 000

(b) See 'Cost of quality reports' in Chapter 22 for the answer to this question.

22.19 (a) The answer should point out that quality costs include costs of conformance (consisting of prevention and appraisal costs) and costs of non-conformance (consisting of internal and external failure costs). You should refer to Chapter 22 for a description of these costs. The costs of quality will probably be hidden in overheads and there is a need to extract the information and report quality costs within the above categories in a cost of quality report (see Chapter 22). The identification and collection of these costs will probably lead to greater management focus on the quality issue as 'what gets measured, gets done'.

The cost of quality report can be used as an atten-tion directing device to make the top management of a company aware of how much is being spent on quality-related costs and the areas where they should focus their attention. The report draws management's attention to the possibility of reducing total quality costs by a wiser allocation of costs among the four quality categories. For example, by spending more on the prevention costs, the amount of spending in the internal and external failure categories can be substantially reduced, and therefore total spending can be lowered. Also, by designing quality into the products and processes, appraisal costs can be reduced, since far less inspection is required.

(b) Kaizen costing involves making constant, small, incremental cost reductions throughout the production process during the product's life. With target costing the focus is on the product and cost reductions are achieved primarily through product design. In contrast, kaizen costing focuses on the production processes and cost reductions are derived primarily through the increased efficiency of the production process. Therefore the potential cost reductions are smaller with kaizen costing because the products are already in the manufacturing stage of their life cycles and a significant proportion of the costs will have become locked in. Kaizen costing applies functional analysis to create a target cost reduction ratio for each production function and this is then used to provide a target for further future reductions. Unlike standard costing, which focuses more on cost containment, kaizen costing focuses on cost reduction and continuous improvement.

Kaizen costing relies heavily on employee empowerment. They are assumed to have superior knowledge about how to improve processes because they are closest to the manufacturing processes and customers and are likely to have greater insights into how costs can be reduced. Thus, a major feature of kaizen costing is that workers are given the responsibility to improve processes and reduce costs. This should increase staff motivation but there may be initial difficulties in this company since employees may have been used to rigorous control procedures that have not enabled them to participate in making process improvements.

(c) The answer should describe just-in-time (JIT) production and purchasing and the resulting benefits (see 'Just-in-time systems' in Chapter 22). The answer should also point out some of the problems that need to be overcome when introducing JIT manufacturing and purchasing. They include increased reliance on suppliers in terms of adhering to strict delivery and quality requirements since failure to meet these requirements can have a major impact on the production process (e.g. production stoppages) and failing to meet customer delivery dates. It is therefore important that reliable local suppliers are available that can meet these requirements. It is also important that staff are trained to meet the JIT requirements (e.g. workers must be trained to multitask). New measures relating to spare capacity and bottlenecks must be established to ensure that JIT aims are achieved and changes to the management accounting system should be made to support JIT (see 'JIT and management accounting' in Chapter 22).

22.20 (a) Benchmarking involves the following:

1 Identify an activity that needs to be improved and identify organizations that are prepared to participate in the process. (GH has identified administration operations relating to teaching and research and the government has selected two large universities, rather than smaller universities, that are comparable for benchmarking. If possible it would be appropriate to include overseas universities in the exercise since they might adopt different approaches to practices that are uniform in Teeland.)

2 Identify key drivers of costs and revenues and appropriate performance indicators. (The key drivers have been identified and information extracted based on the activity per driver.)

3 Measure performance of the activities for all of the organisations participating in the benchmarking process. (The appropriate data have been gathered

as requested by the government education ministry. This stage will more difficult in the private sector where there is no regulatory body and information may be commercially sensitive.)

4 Compare performances. (This is the stage that is required in part (b) of the question.)

5 Identify and implement areas for improvement. (The procedures used at the benchmarked universities should be studied in detail and best practice should be implemented at GU.)

6 Monitor improvements. (After completion the benchmarking process should be subject to review to ascertain if the improvements have been achieved.)

(b) Below details of the performance comparison arising from the benchmarking exercise are presented:

	GU	AU	BU
	$	$	$
Research			
contract management	78	87	97
laboratory management	226	257	281
Teaching facilities management	951	1197	920
Student support services	71	89	73
Teachers support services	506	532	544
Accounting	204	204	197
Human resources	156	156	191
IT managenent	817	803	737
General services	2153	2088	2286

Note

It is assumed that the performance drivers are as follows:

Research categories – Research contract values supported

Teaching facilities and student support – Student numbers

Remaining categories – Staff numbers

Therefore the performance comparison for the research categories is per $000 of contract value supported, teaching facilities and student support services per student and the remaining items per staff member.

Comments

The performance comparison indicates that GU is the most successful university in controlling costs associated with research contracts. AU spends most per student on its teaching facilities and student support although it has the smallest number of students. Higher student pass rates and future success in gaining employment may reflect the more expensive teaching environment at AU but these quality measures are not incorporated in the benchmarking exercise. In accounting and general services, all the universities are similar and in human resources management, BU is 22% higher than the other universities. In IT management BU's costs are 10% lower than GU's. It should be noted, however, that comparing performance is difficult because of differences such as the mix of subjects taught and researched.

22.21 (a)

Prevention costs:	Quantity	Rate $	Total costs $000	% of sales
Design engineering	48000	96	4608	1.28
Process engineering	54000	70	3780	1.05
Training			180	0.05
Total prevention costs			8568	2.38
Appraisal costs:				
Inspection				
(manufacturing)	288000	50	14400	4.00
Product testing			72	0.02
Total appraisal costs			14472	4.02
Internal failure costs:				
Rework				
(Manufacturing)	2100	4800	10080	2.80
Total internal failure				
costs			10080	2.80
External failure costs:				
Customer support				
(Marketing)	2700	240	648	0.18
Transportation costs				
(Distribution)	2700	280	756	0.21
Warranty repair				
(Customer service)	2700	4600	12420	3.45
Total external failure				
costs			13824	3.84
Total costs for all 4				
categories			46944	13.04
Opportunity costs	1800	7200	12960	3.60
Total quality costs			59904	16.64

Quality cost statements frequently exclude opportunity costs such as the foregone contribution on lost sales arising from poor quality. This is because the lost sales are very difficult to estimate. Because of this many companies omit the opportunity costs arising from lost sales from their cost of quality reports. A compromise is to report opportunity costs separately (as in the above statement) and draw management's attention that estimates of such costs may be subject to a significant margin of error.

(b)

Option:		Rate	Option 1	Option 2
Cost of quality items:		$	$	$
Additional design				
engineering costs	2000	96		192000
Additional process				
engineering costs	5000	70		350000
Additional inspection				
and testing costs	10000	50	500000	
Savings in rework costs:				
Option 1	720	1920	−1382400	
Option 2	960	1920		−1843200
Savings in customer support costs:				
Option 1	600	96	−57600	
Option 2	840	96		−80640
Saving in transportation costs:				
Option 1	600	210	−126000	
Option 2	840	210		−176400
Savings in warranty repair costs:				
Option 1	600	1700	−1020000	
Option 2	840	1700		−1428000
Additional sales:				
Option 1	300	7200	−2160000	
Option 2	360	7200		−2592000
Incremental savings			−4246000	−5578240

Option 2 is preferable since it provides the greater incremental savings.

22.22 (a) The absorption cost per dish for the customer repair department is $8.03 ($707000/ (16000 × 5.5 dishes). This cost is added to other direct costs that are incurred to obtain a total cost per dish. In addition, the financial director (FD) adds an additional $100 per specialized dish in order to compensate for the extra work involved. This results in an over-absorption of total cost since $8.03 fully absorbs the costs so an extra $160 000 (1600 specialized dishes at $100) of costs will absorbed.

The ABC cost per dish is computed as follows:

	Standard dishes	Specialized dishes
Activity cost assignment	$537320	$169680
Number of orders	14400	1600
Average dish per order	6	1
Total number of dishes	86400	1600
ABC cost per dish	$6.22	$106.05

The company sells two different types of dish that utilize different quantities of resources resulting in the ABC system highlighting customer care costs of $106.05 per unit for specialized dishes and $6.22 for standard dishes. Therefore the current system overcosts the standard dishes and understates the profit contribution. The cost of specialized dishes of $106.05 using ABC is similar to the finance director's estimate of $108.03 but no attempt has been made to adjust the cost of standard dishes to reflect the over-absorption of overheads outlined above arising from the FD's adjustment.

The major activities that contribute to this higher cost of specialized dishes are handling sales enquiries/preparing quotes and handling complaints. The cost per dish for these activities for specialized dishes is significantly higher than the unit costs for standard dishes. This is not surprising, as the specialized dishes require a customized service which cannot be standardized.

ABC highlights the activities that are causing the higher product/service costs thus highlighting the potential for cost reduction or ensuring that customers pay for the resources consumed. It should, however be questioned whether the ABC analysis meets the cost/benefit criterion given that the FD's estimate of resource consumption is similar to the ABC analysis provided that a correction for the over-allocation of total costs is made.

(b) The ABC analysis indicates that handling enquiries and quotes and post-sale complaints handling are the high cost activities that in total consume 65 per cent of the resources of the customer care department. These activities therefore have the potential for significantly reducing total costs. Approximately 46 per cent (16000/35000) of enquiries are converted to orders. Ideally, this ratio should be benchmarked with competitors but this may be difficult given the commercially sensitive nature of this information.

Complaints handling is a non-value added activity which should be prioritized for further investigation in order to minimize these activities. The ABC analysis highlights the high costs of this activity, accounting for approximately 25 per cent of total costs of the customer care department. The number of complaints is high accounting for 20 per cent (3200/16 000) of orders. The high cost and level of complaints is of particular concern given that they have been identified by customers and thus represent external failure costs. The causes of the complaints should be investigated and eliminated.

22.23 (a) (i) *Performance report for period ending 30 November (traditional analysis)*

Expenses	Budget (£)	Actual (£)	Variance (£)
Salaries	600 000	667 800	67 800A
Supplies	60 000	53 000	7 000F
Travel cost	120 000	127 200	7 200A
Technology cost	100 000	74 200	25 800F
Occupancy cost	120 000	137 800	17 800A
Total	1 000 000	1 060 000	60 000A

Performance report for period ending 30 November (Activity-based analysis)

Activities	(£)	(£)	(£)
Routing/scheduling – new products	200 000	169 600	30 400F
Routing/scheduling – existing products	400 000	360 400	39 600F
Remedial re-routing/ scheduling	50 000	127 200	77 200A
Special studies – specific orders	100 000	84 800	15 200F
Training	100 000	159 000	59 000A
Management and administration	150 000	159 000	9 000A
Total	1 000 000	1 060 000	60 000A

(ii) See 'Activity-based budgeting' in Chapter 15 for the answer to this question. In particular, the answer should stress:

- **(i)** The enhanced visibility of activity-based budgeting (ABB) by focusing on outcomes (activities) rather than a listing by expense categories.
- **(ii)** The cost of activities are highlighted thus identifying high cost non-value added activities that need to be investigated.
- **(iii)** ABB identifies resource requirements to meet the demand for activities whereas traditional budgeting adopts an incremental approach.
- **(iv)** Excess resources are identified that can be eliminated or redeployed.
- **(v)** ABB enables more realistic budgets to be set.
- **(vi)** ABB avoids arbitrary cuts in specific budget areas in order to meet overall financial targets.
- **(vii)** It is claimed that ABB leads to increased management commitment to the budget process because it enables management to focus on the objectives of each activity and compare the outcomes with the costs that are allocated to the activity.

(iii) The ABB statement shows a comparison of actual with budget by activities. All of the primary value-adding activities (i.e. the first, second and fourth activities in the budget statement) have favourable variances. Remedial rerouting is a non-value added activity and has the highest adverse variance. Given the high cost, top priority should be given to investigating the activity with a view to eliminating it, or to substantially reducing the cost by adopting alternative working practices. Training and management and administration are secondary activities which support the primary activities. Actual training expenditure exceeds budget by 50 per cent and the reason for the over-spending should be investigated.

For each activity it would be helpful if the costs were analysed by expense items (such as salaries, supplies, etc.) to pinpoint the cost build up of the activities and to provide clues indicating why an overspending on some activities has occurred.

Cost driver usage details should also be presented in a manner similar to that illustrated in Exhibit 15.2 in Chapter 15. Many organizations that have adopted ABC have found it useful to report budgeted and actual cost driver rates. The trend in cost driver rates is monitored and compared with similar activities undertaken within other divisions where a divisionalized structure applies. As indicated in Chapter 15, care must be taken when interpreting cost driver rates.

For additional points to be included in the answer see 'activity-based management' in Chapter 22.

(b) The cost driver rates are as follows:
Product design = £250 per design hour (£2m/ 8000 hours)
Purchasing = £50 per purchase order (£200 000/ 4000 orders)
Production (excluding depreciation) = £100 per machine hour ((£1 500 000 – £300 000)/12 000 hours)
Packing = £20 per cubic metre (£400 000/20 000)
Distribution = £5 per kg (£600 000/120 000)
The activity-based overhead cost per unit is as follows:

		(£)
Product design	(400 design hours at £250 per hour = £100 000 divided by life-cycle output of 5 000 units)	20.00
Purchasing	(5 purchase orders at 50 units per order costing a total of £250 for an output of 250 units)	1.00
Production	(0.75 machine hours at £100 per machine hour)	75.00
Depreciation	(Asset cost over life cycle of 4 years = 16 quarters' depreciation at £8 000 per quarter divided by life-cycle output of 5 000 units)	25.60
Packing	(0.4 cubic metres at £20)	8.00
Distribution	(3kg at £5)	15.00
Total cost		144.60

22.24 (a) The factors influencing the preferred costing system are different for every firm. The benefits from implementing ABC are likely to be influenced by the level of competition, the number of products sold, the diversity of the product range and the proportion of overheads and direct costs in the cost structure. Companies operating in a more competitive environment have a greater need for more accurate cost information, since competitors are more likely to take advantage of any errors arising from the use of distorted cost information generated by a traditional costing system. Where a company markets a small number of products special studies can be undertaken using the decision-relevant approach. Problems do not arise in determining which product or product combinations should be selected for undertaking special studies. Increased product diversity arising from the manufacture and sale of low-volume and high-volume products favours the use of ABC systems. As the level of diversity increases so does the level of distortion reported by traditional costing systems. Finally, organizations with a large proportion of overheads and a low proportion of direct costs are likely to benefit from ABC, because traditional costing systems can be relied upon only to report accurately direct product costs. Distorted product costs are likely to be reported where a large proportion of overheads are related to product variety rather than volume.

(b) For a more detailed answer to this question you should refer to 'Activity-based management' in Chapter 22. In particular, the answer should draw attention to the fact that ABM attaches costs to activities and identifies the cost drivers that cause the costs. Thus ABM provides a better understanding of what causes costs, and highlights ways of performing activities more efficiently by reducing cost driver transactions.

Costs can therefore be managed more effectively in the long run. Activities can be analysed into value-added and non-value added activities and by highlighting the costs of non-value added activities attention is drawn to areas where there is an opportunity for cost reduction, without reducing the products' service potentials to customers.

Finally, the cost of unused activity capacity is reported for each activity, thus drawing attention to where capacity can be reduced or utilized more effectively to expand future profitability.

(c) See 'Target costing' in Chapter 22 for the answer to this question.

CHAPTER 23

23.13

1   Cost reductions arising from a reduction in wastage and disposal costs and any possible additional revenues as a result of recycling waste.

2   By meeting the environmental concerns of customers the company's image will be improved and this may generate increased sales.

3   A lack of awareness of environmental costs can result in environmental penalty and clean-up costs (e.g. the BP oil spill in the Gulf of Mexico has cost the company billions of dollars in penalties and fines).

23.14 (a) See 'International transfer pricing' in Chapter 20 for the answer to this question. Besides the ethical issues and legal considerations other criticisms relate to the distortions in the divisional profit reporting system. Also divisional autonomy will be undermined if the transfer prices are imposed on the divisional managers.

(b) The ethical limitations relate to multinational companies using the transfer pricing system to reduce the amount paid in custom duties, taxation and the manipulation of dividends remitted. Furthermore, using the transfer prices for these purposes is likely to be illegal, although there is still likely to be some scope for manipulation that is within the law. It is important that multinational companies are seen to be acting in a socially responsible manner. Any bad publicity relating to using the transfer pricing system purely to avoid taxes and custom duties will be very harmful to the image of the organization. Nevertheless tax management and the ability to minimize corporate taxes is an important task for management if it is to maximize shareholder value. Thus it is important that management distinguish between tax avoidance and tax evasion. Adopting illegal practices is not acceptable and management must ensure that their transfer pricing policies do not contravene the regulations and laws of the host counties in which they operate.

23.15 (a) Environmental costs can be categorized as environmental prevention, detection and internal and external failure costs. Periodically, an environmental cost report should be presented with costs reported by these four cost categories (see 'Environmental cost management' in Chapter 23 for an explanation of the report and the four cost categories).

(b) In an input/output analysis, all incoming and outgoing materials and energy flows are summarized over the entire production site and represented on a table. With this approach, an approximate evaluation of the environmental relevance of a company's operations can be made. One major difficulty is that the analysis does not support the allocation of the material flows to the products or specific processes resulting in the origins of the inputs and outputs cannot be identified.

ABC analyses cost by activities rather than departments and thus reports information on activities that cross departmental boundaries. ABC thus gives visibility to the cost of undertaking the environmental activities that make up the organization. With traditional costing systems environmental costs tend to be hidden in the overhead costs across many different departments. This will assist the company in identifying and controlling environmental costs.

A life cycle view estimates and accumulates costs and revenues over a product's entire life cycle rather than one accounting period in order to determine whether the profits earned during the manufacturing phase will cover the costs incurred during the pre- and post-manufacturing stages. Identifying the costs incurred during the different stages of a product's life cycle provides an insight into understanding and managing the total costs incurred throughout its life cycle. In particular, life cycle costing helps management to understand the cost consequences of developing and making a product and to identify areas in which cost reduction efforts are likely to be most effective.

(c) The costing approach used by the company ignores capital costs, environmental costs and the cost of decommissioning. A life cycle analysis aims to capture the costs over the entire life cycle of the product. The life cycle analysis is as follows:

	$m
Production costs	82.3
Marketing costs	17
Development costs	8.6
	107.9
Environmental costs	
Waste filtration	8.1
Carbon dioxide extrasust extractor	5.3
	13.4
Other costs	
Decommissioning costs	18
Total costs	139.3

Total revenues are $149.4m giving a lifetime profit of $10.1m. Life cycle costing provides visibility at the design stage of the costs that will be incurred at each stage of the production process and identifies in advance important costs that need to be focused on (e.g. the high costs of decommissioning). The traditional product profit analysis shows a surplus of $41.5m over the life of the product but it does not incorporate environmental and decommissioning costs.

23.16 (a) *Workings in millions of kg*

	2008 Base year	2016	2017	Change on base year
Commercial Fleet Diesel	105.4	77.7	70.1	−33%
Commercial Fleet Petrol	11.6	0.4	0.0	−100%
Company Car Diesel	15.1	14.5	12.0	−21%
Company Car Petrol	10.3	3.8	2.2	−79%
Other road travel (Diesel)	0.5	1.6	1.1	120%
Other road travel (Petrol)	3.1	0.5	0.3	−90%
Rail travel	9.2	9.6	3.4	−63%
Air Travel (short haul)	5.0	4.4	3.1	−38%
Air Travel (long haul)	5.1	7.1	5.4	6%
Hire Cars (Diesel)	0.6	1.8	2.9	383%
Hire Cars (Petrol)	6.7	6.1	6.1	−9%
Total	172.6	127.5	106.6	
Index	100%	74%	62%	

The following is an analysis by the three main categories (road, air and rail travel):

	2008 Base year	2016	2017	Changs on base year
Road travel	153.3	106.4	94.7	−38%
Air travel	10.1	11.5	8.5	−16%
Rail travel	9.2	9.6	3.4	−63%
Total	172.6	127.5	106.6	−38%

The company's goal is that by 2024, it will have reduced its environmental impact by 60% (compared to 2008). Overall, it has cut emissions by 38% in the first nine years (from 100% in the base year to 62% nine years later). There was a reduction of 16% in the last year of measurement. If this rate of improvement is maintained then the company will reduce its emissions by approximately 80%) by the end of the target period. The analysis by the three main categories indicates that the largest cut has been in rail-related emissions (63%). Road emissions are the dominant

category and they have fallen by 38% but it appears that they will meet the target reduction of 60% in nine years' time. Air travel is not falling at the same pace but this may be due to greater globalization of the industry requiring managers to visit overseas suppliers and clients. Rail travel has the largest percentage reduction. The major change shown in the above workings is the move from petrol to diesel-powered motor vehicles, which, in the commercial fleet, is almost complete.

(b) The analysis could be improved by collecting data on the total distances travelled so that the effect of switching away from physical meetings and using teleconferencing facilities can be measured. Data relating to overseas travel could be monitored since cutting air travel appears to be an area where improvements can be made. The collection of data relating to distance travelled will enable the average emission per km travelled to be measured.

CHAPTER 24

24.14 Removing inflation from the costs
$21000/1.05 = $20000
$26780/1.03 = $26000
The variable cost per unit = ($26000 − $20000)/ (16000 − 12000) = $1.50
At inflation of 8% = $1.50 × 1.08 = $1.62

Answer = **(d)**

24.15 (a) Variable cost per unit = ($2840000 − $2420000)/
(190000 − 160000
= $420000/30000
= $14 per unit

Fixed costs = $2840000 − (190000 × $14)
= $180000

Total costs at 205000 units = (205000 × $14) + $180000
= $3050000

Answer = **(b)**

(b) Cost before stepped increase = $2840000 − $30000
= $2810000

Variable cost per unit = ($2810000 − $2420000)/
(190000 − 160000)
= $390000/30000
= $13

Fixed costs at 190000 units = $2840000 − (190000 × $13)
= $370000

Total costs at 175000 units = (175000 × $13) + ($370000 − $30000)
= $2615000

Answer = **(c)**

24.16 (a) (i) *High- and low-point method*

	Machine hours 000s	Fuel oil expenses (£000's)
High point (June 2018)	48	680
Low point (January 2018)	26	500
Difference	22	180

Variable cost per machine hour £8.182 (£180/22) Substituting for January 2018

	(£000)
Variable cost (26 × £8.182) =	212.73
Fixed cost (difference)	287.27
Total cost	500.00

The total cost equation is $y = 287.27 + 8.182x$

(ii) *Least-squares regression method*

	Hours	Fuel oil		
	x	y	x^2	xy
July	34	640	1156	21760
August	30	620	900	18600
September	34	620	1156	21080
October	39	590	1521	23010
November	42	500	1764	21000
December	32	530	1024	16960
January	26	500	676	13000
February	26	500	676	13000
March	31	530	961	16430
April	35	550	1225	19250
May	43	580	1849	24940
June	48	680	2304	32640
	$\Sigma x = 420$	$\Sigma y = 6840$	$\Sigma x^2 = 15212$	$\Sigma xy = 241670$

Using the formula given in the chapter:

$$b = \frac{(12 \times 241670) - (420 \times 6840)}{(12 \times 15212) - (420)^2}$$

$$= 4.4336$$

$$a = (6840/12) - \frac{(4.4336)(420)}{12}$$

$$= 414.824$$

$$Y = 414.82 + 4.43x$$

(b) For the answer to this question see Chapter 24.

(c) An r^2 calculation of 0.25 means that 75 per cent of the total variation of y from its mean is not caused by variations in x (machine hours). This means that a large proportion of changes in fuel oil expenses do not result from changes in machine hours. The cost must depend on factors other than machine hours. Other measures of activity might be examined in order to test whether they are closely related to changes in costs. If other measures do not yield a close approximation then this might indicate that cost is dependent on several variables. In these circumstances multiple regression techniques should be used.

24.17 (a)

Month	Cumulative number of batches	Cumulative average hours per batch	Cumulative total hours	Incremental number of batches	Incremental total hours	Actual labour cost per month $
July	1	200	200	1	200	2400
August	2	176 (200 × 0.88)	352 (2 × 176)	1	152	1824
September	4	154.88	619.52	2	267.52	3210.24
October	8	136.294	1090.352	4	470.832	5649.984
November (W1)	16	124.4	1990.36	8	900.008	10800.096

W1
The learning rate benefits ceased after the production of the eighth batch.
Time for 7th batch:
$Y = ax^b = 200 \times 7^{-0.1844245}$
= 139.693 hours.
Total time for 7 batches = 139.693 × 7 = 977.851 hours.

Total time for 8 batches = 1090.352 hours.
Therefore the 8th batch required 112.501 hours (1090.352 − 977.851)
Time for batches 9–16 = 112.501 × 8 = 900.008 hours.
Cumulative average time for batches 1–16 = 1090.352 + 900.008 = 1990.36 hours.
Cumulative average time for 16 batches = 1990.36/16 = 124.4 hours per batch

(b) From November onwards the learning process ceased and the time taken to produce each batch is constant. Therefore future decisions in terms of costing (cost-plus pricing, profitability analysis etc.), budgeting (resource allocation) and production (production scheduling) should be based on the time taken to produce the 8th batch. The costing, resource allocation and production scheduling decisions for the past decisions will have been distorted since they were based on a standard time of 200 hours per batch. The company should investigate whether additional staff training might extend the learning process and focus on a continuous improvement philosophy as a mechanism for further reducing the standard time taken to produce the 8th batch.

(c) See 'Participation in the budget and target setting process' in Chapter 16 for the answer to this question.

24.18 (a) Revised target cost

	$	$
Manufacturing costs:		
Direct material (W1)	21.60	
Direct labour (W2)	10.96	
Machine costs	21.00	
Quality control costs	10.00	
Rework costs (W3)	1.80	65.36
Non-manufacturing costs:		
Product development cost	25.00	
Marketing cost	35.00	60.00
		125.36

Workings:
W1
Parts to be replaced by standard parts = $40 × 0.8 = $32.
Revised cost at 45% reduction = $14.40.
Bespoke parts original cost = $40 × 20% = $8.
Revised cost (90%) $7.20
Revised direct material cost = $14.40 + $7.20 = $21.60
Working 2: Direct labour

W2
Direct labour cost per unit for first one hundred units:
Applying the learning curve formula $Y = ax^b$ (see Chapter 24)
$45 \times 100^{-0.152} = 22.346654$ minutes
Total time for 100 units = 234.6654 minutes.
Time for the 100th unit:
Time for 99 units = $45 \times 99^{-0.152} = 22.380818$ minutes.
Total time for 99 units = 2215.701 minutes.
Therefore the time taken for the 100th unit = 2234.6654 − 2215.701 = 18.9644 minutes.
Time for remaining 49900 units = 946323.56 minutes (49900 × 18.9644 minutes)
Total labour time for 50000 units = 948558.23 minutes (2234.67 minutes + 946323.56 minutes)

Therefore total labour cost = 948 558.23/60 minutes × $34.67 = $548 108.56.
Therefore average labour cost per unit = $548 108.56/50 000 units = $10.96.

W3:
Rework total cost = 50 000 × 10% × $18 = $90 000.
Cost per average unit = $90 000/50 000 = $1.80.

(b) See Pricing policy' in Chapter 10 for an explanation of a price skimming policy. Although the question provides limited information it would appear that a price skimming policy may be appropriate for the company. The product is new and different (having, superior audio sound and visual quality) so customers may be prepared to pay high prices in order to obtain what is perceived to be a superior product. The product also has a short life cycle resulting in a need to recover development costs and make a profit quickly so high initial prices when demand is likely to be inelastic may be appropriate. The company is also experiencing liquidity problems so a short-term focus adopting a price skimming policy may assist in solving current liquidity problems.

24.19 (a) Revised hours for actual production:
Cumulative time per hour for 460 units is calculated by using the learning curve formula: $Y = ax^b$
$a = 7$
$x = 460$
$b = -0.1520$
$y = 7 \times 460^{-0.1520} = 2.7565054$
Revised time for 460 units = 1268 hours.
Labour efficiency planning variance
(Original standard hours for actual production − revised hours for actual production) × std rate
$([460 \times 7] - 1268) \times \$12 = \$23 424F$
Labour efficiency operational variance
(Revised hours for actual production − actual hours for actual production) × std rate
$(1268 - 1860) \times \$12 = \$7104A$

(b) The likely consequences are:

- The company uses cost plus pricing for its products so the price of the product will be overstated and this may result in the sales volume being lower than expected, together with a reduction in sales revenue.
- The sales manager will be held responsible for sales being less than expected and the resulting adverse variance may result in a loss in bonus even though the adverse variance was beyond the manager's control. Besides having an adverse demotivational effect there will be a loss of confidence in the performance measurement system.
- The company will have hired too many temporary staff due to the new product being produced more quickly than originally thought. They have been hired on three-month contracts resulting in the company having to pay the staff for the full three months even though all of them are unlikely to be needed. This will result in unnecessary costs being incurred.
- Production will be higher than anticipated and there is a danger that the company may have run out of raw materials, leading to a stop in production. This may have required emergency purchases at additional costs resulting in the purchasing manager loosing his or her bonus because of an adverse purchase price variance.

24.20 (a) $Y = ax^b = 25 \times 128^{-0.152} = 11.96$ hours cumulative average time for first 128 components
Total time for first 128 components = 11.96 hours × 128 = 1530.88 hours
Cumulative average time for first 127 components = $= 25 \times 127^{-0.152} = 11.97$ hours
Total time for first 127 components = 11.97 hours × 127 = 1520.19 hours
Time for component 128 = 1530.88 − 1520.19 = 10.69 hours

(b)

	Average for 128 components $	Total 128 components $
Sales price	530	
Required margin	20%	
Target cost	424	54 272
Labour 11.96 hours*$15	179.40	22 963.20
Other costs	265	33 920
Expected cost	444.40	56 883.20
Cost gap	20.40	2 611.20

(c) Cost gap = $2611.20
Target labour cost: $22 963.20 − $2611.20 = $20 352
Target labour hours: $20 352 / $15 = 1356.8
Target cumulative average time per component: 1356.8/128 components = 10.6 hours

If you refer to Exhibit 24.2 in Chapter 24 you will see that the cumulative average time per unit can be calculated as follows:

Time required by the first unit (2000 hours) × (Learning rate)^n
Where n represents the number of times cumulative production is doubled so that:
Cumulative production of 2 units gives a cumulative average time per unit of 1600 hours (2000 × 0.8)
Cumulative production of 4 units gives a cumulative average time per unit of 1280 hours (2000 × $(0.8)^2$)
Cumulative production of 8 units gives a cumulative average time per unit of 1024 hours (2000 × $(0.8)^3$)
and so on

Using the data given in the question $n = 7$ and the cumulative average time required for 128 units is 10.6 hours so:

Cumulative production of 128 units = 25 hours time required for the first unit × (Learning rate)^7 = 10.6 hours cumulative average time per unit
(Learning rate)^7 = 0.424 (10.6/25)
$7\sqrt{0.424} = 0.88$ giving a learning rate of 88%

24.21 (a)

Cumulative production (boats)	Completion time (days)	Cumulative time (days)	Average time (days)
1	10.0	10.0	10.0
2	8.1	18.1	9.05 (18.1/2)
3	7.4	25.5	8.50 (25.5/3)
4	7.1	32.6	8.15 (32.6/4)

As production doubles from one to two boats, average time falls to 90.5 per cent of the time for producing the first boat. As production doubles from two to four boats, average time falls to 90.06 per cent (8.15/9.05) of the previous average. The objective is to calculate the average learning rate. You should now refer to Exhibit 24.2 in Chapter 24. You can see that the average time for producing four units is 0.64 of the time for producing the first unit (1280/2000). The average learning rate is $\sqrt{0.64}$ = 0.8 or 80 per cent. The average time for producing eight units is 0.512 of the time for producing the first unit (1024/2000). The average learning rate is $_3\sqrt{0.512}$ = 0.8. Similarly, the average time for producing 16 units is 0.4095 of the time for producing the first unit (819/2000). The average learning rate is $_4\sqrt{0.4095}$ = 0.80. In Exhibit 24.2 the learning rate remained constant at 80 per cent throughout, and it was therefore unnecessary to calculate the average learning rate.

Applying the approach outlined above, the average time for four boats is 0.815 of the time for the first boat, thus indicating an average learning rate of $\sqrt{0.815}$ = 0.903 or 90.3 per cent.

An alternative approach is to use the learning curve equation:

$$y_x = ax^b$$

where y_x is defined as the cumulative average time required to produce x units, a is the time required to produce the first unit of output and x is the number of units of output under consideration. The exponent b is defined as the ratio of the logarithm of the learning curve improvement rate to the logarithm of 2.

Therefore:

$$y^4 = 10 \times 4^b$$
$$8.15 = 10 \times 4^b$$
$$4^b = 0.815$$

Our objective is to calculate the exponent function that, when multiplied by 4, equals 0.815. A trial-and-error approach is now adopted:

exponent function for 80% learning curve = -0.322 (see Chapter 24)
exponent function for 90% learning curve = -0.152 (log 0.9/log 2) exponent function for 91% learning curve = -0.136 (log 0.91=log 2)

$$4^{-0.322} = 0.64$$
$$4^{-0.152} = 0.810$$
$$4^{-0.136} = 0.828$$

The average learning rate is between 90 per cent and 91 per cent.

(b) The following points should be discussed:

(i) Only four observations have been used, and this might be insufficient to establish an average learning rate for the production of 15 boats.

(ii) It is assumed that working methods, equipment and staff will remain constant. Improvements in working procedures, staff changes or absenteeism might affect the learning rate.

(iii) Uncertainty as to when the learning process will stop. If the learning process stops before the steady-state phase is reached then the assumption that the learning rate will continue might result in inaccurate estimates.

(iv) The learning rate may not be constant throughout the process, and the use of an average learning rate might result in inaccurate estimates for different output levels.

(c) Materials, other direct expenses and overheads will remain unchanged irrespective of whether the boats

are completed in normal time (possibly involving penalties) or working weekends. Overheads appear to be fixed since they are allocated on the basis of *normal* working days. The total times required, assuming a 90 per cent learning rate, are as follows:

Average time for 15 boats = y_{15} = $10 \times 15^{-0.152}$
= 6.6257 days
Total time for 15 boats = 15×6.6257
= 99.4 days
Total time for 14 boats = $14 \times 10 \times 14^{-0.152}$
= 93.7 days
Total time for 13 boats = $13 \times 10 \times 13^{-0.152}$
= 88.0 days

The contract is for 4 months (therefore 92 working days are available without overtime or 120 days with overtime) and penalties are charged at £10000 per boat late. Thirteen boats can be delivered within the contract period. To complete 15 boats within the contract period, it will be necessary to work 7.4 days (99.4 days – 92 days) overtime. If overtime is not worked, two boats will incur a penalty. Without overtime, the total labour cost plus penalties will be:

(99.4 days × £2500 = £248500) + (2 × £10000) = £268500

With overtime, the total labour cost will be:

(92 days × £2500 = £230000) + (7.4 days × 5000) = £267000

It is assumed that payments can be made for part days only. It is slightly cheaper to work overtime and avoid the penalty cost. Another possibility is to complete 14 boats using overtime and deliver 1 boat late:

Cost for 14 boats = (92 days × £2500)
+ (1.7 days × £5000)   = £238500
Cost for 15th boat = (5.7 days × £2500)
+ (1 × £10000)   = £24250
                                  £262750

The most profitable alternative is to deliver one boat late. Other factors to be considered include:

(i) the four factors outlined in part (b);

(ii) the possibility of bad weather affecting production times;

(iii) the effect on customer goodwill and the possibility of not obtaining future orders if the contract is not completed on time;

(iv) the promise of overtime work might induce the workforce to slow down in order to obtain overtime work.

CHAPTER 25

25.12 (i) Re-order level = Maximum usage × maximum lead time
= 95 × 18 = 1710

Answer = **(c)**

(ii) Maximum stock = Re-order level + Re-order quantity − minimum usage during minimum lead time
= 1710 + 1750 − (50 × 12)
= 2860

Answer = **(b)**

25.13 (i) $EOQ = \sqrt{\dfrac{2 \times 150 \times 30000}{25}} = 600$ units

(ii) Number of orders $= 30000/600 = 50$ per year
Ordering costs $= 50 \times \$150 = \$7500$
Holding costs $= 600 \times 0.5 \times \$25 = \$7500$
Total ordering and holding costs $= \$15000$

25.14 (a) $EOQ = \sqrt{(2 \times 15000 \times 80)/(0.1333 \times 200)} = 300$ units
Number of orders per year $= 15000/300 = 50$ orders

(b) $EOQ = \sqrt{(2 \times 2800 \times 28)/(25 \times 0.08)} = 280$ units
Holding cost $= 280/2 \times £2 = \$280$

25.15 (a)

$EOQ = \sqrt{\left(\dfrac{2\,DO}{H}\right)} = \sqrt{\dfrac{2 \times 4000 \times 135}{12}} = 300$

The relevant cost is

holding cost $+$ ordering cost $= \dfrac{300 \times 12}{2} + \dfrac{4000 \times 135}{300} = 3600$

(b)

Revised $EOQ = \sqrt{\left(\dfrac{2 \times 4000 \times 80}{12}\right)} = 231$

The relevant cost is

holding cost $+$ ordering cost $= \dfrac{231 \times 12}{2} + \dfrac{4000 \times 80}{231} = 2772$

The relevant cost using the original EOQ of 300 units but with an incremental ordering cost of £80 is

$\dfrac{300 \times 12}{2} + \dfrac{4000 \times 80}{300} = 2867$

Cost of prediction error $= £95$ $(£2867 - £2772)$

(c) The annual costs of purchasing, ordering and holding the materials consist of:
Special offer at £86:
holding cost $+$ ordering cost $+$ purchase cost

$\dfrac{4000 \times 12}{2} + 0 = 4000 \times 86 = £368000$

Normal price of £90:

$\dfrac{300 \times 12}{2} + \dfrac{4000 \times 135}{300} + 4000 \times 90 = £363600$

Additional cost of specific offer £4400
Therefore the purchase of 4000 units at £86 is not recommended.

(d)

	Budget (£)	Actual (£)	Variance (£)
Material cost	360000	344000	16000F
	(4000 × £90)	(4000 × £86)	
Ordering cost	1800	0	1800F
$\left(\dfrac{D}{Q} \times O\right)$			17800F

It can be seen that favourable variances would appear on the performance report, and goal congruence would not exist. The performance evaluation system conflicts with the EOQ decision model. This is because the purchasing officer is not charged for the use of capital but the EOQ model includes a charge for the use of capital. Therefore if an imputed capital

charge is not included in the performance report, there is a danger that goal congruence will not exist. The revised performance report including a capital charge is shown below:

	Budget (£)	Actual (£)	Variance (£)
Material cost	360000	344000	16000F
Ordering cost	1800	0	1800F
Holding cost	1800	24000	22200A
			4400A

25.16 (i) EOQ

$\sqrt{\dfrac{2 \times 150000 \times 360}{3.00}} = 6000$ units

Total cost of inventory management using EOQ is:
Cost of ordering inventory $+$ cost of holding inventory

$\dfrac{DO}{Q} + \dfrac{QH}{2} = \dfrac{15000 \times 360}{6000} + \dfrac{3.00 \times 6000}{2}$

$= \$9000 + \$9000$
$= \$18000$

(ii) Total cost of inventory management using 10000 units is:

$\dfrac{DO}{Q} + \dfrac{QH}{2} = \dfrac{150000 \times 360}{10000} + \dfrac{3.00 \times 10000}{2}$

$= \$5400 + \$15000$
$= \$20400$

Additional inventory management cost if 10000 components are purchased $= \$2400$. Value of the discount is $(150000 \times \$2.00) \times 1$ per cent $= \$3000$
It is therefore worthwhile to purchase 10000 components and take the quantity discount

25.17 (a)

Quarter	1	2	3	4
JIT production level	19000	34000	37000	50000
Difference in production with constant level of production	(16000)	(1000)	2000	15000
Standard unit variable cost ($)	$60	$60	$65	$70
Incremental production cost without overtime ($)	(960000)	(60000)	130000	1050000
Overtime production (units)			1000	14000
Overtime premium per unit ($)			26.00	28.00
Overtime production cost ($)			26000	392000
Total incremental production cost	(960000)	(60000)	156000	1442000

Incremental production costs (Quarters 1 – Quarters 4) = $578000

Inventory costs saved by JIT system:

Unit	1	2	3	4
Opening inventory	0	16000	17000	15000
Production	35000	35000	35000	35000
Sales	19000	34000	37000	50000
Closing inventory	16000	17000	15000	0
average inventory	8000	16500	16000	7500
Holding cost $	104000	214500	208000	97500

Total holding cost = $624000
Therefore overall there is a saving of $46000 by changing to a JIT system.

(b) With the JIT system, there are no inventories and therefore sales may be lost if there are any production bottlenecks or inferior quality production. CDE may need to invest in quality control systems to ensure that the units produced are of satisfactory quality.

Accurate demand estimates are essential since if actual demand is different from estimated demand either surplus stocks or the inability to meet demand may arise resulting in a loss of customer goodwill. To overcome uncertainty, safety stocks may be required. It is important that the degree of uncertainty relating to the demand estimates should be considered prior to making a final decision relating to adopting the JIT system.

25.18 (a) The question requires the calculation of the optimum number of units to be manufactured in each production run in order to secure the lowest annual cost. In Chapter 25 we noted that the formula for the optimum number of units to be manufactured (Q) is as follows:

$$Q = \sqrt{\left(\frac{2DS}{H}\right)}$$

where D = total demand for period, S = set-up costs and H = holding cost per unit. The set-up costs and holding cost per unit to be used in the formula are relevant or incremental costs. Those costs that will not change as a result of changes in the number of units manufactured in each batch should not be included in the analysis. These costs include:

(i) Skilled labour costs. (Skilled labour is being paid idle time. Its total cost will not alter as a result of the current decision.)

(ii) Fixed overheads. (These costs are independent of the batch size.)

Therefore the relevant cost of producing product Exe is as follows:

			(£)
Raw materials – external suppliers			13
Dee standard cost: Raw materials	8		
Unskilled labour	4		
Variable overheads	3	15	
Unskilled labour			7
Variable overheads			5
Incremental cost of production			40

The relevant decision variables for the formula are as follows:

Annual demand of Exe (D) = 4000 units

Set-up costs (S) = £70 (skilled labour of £66 is not an incremental cost)

Annual holding costs = £14 [cost of storage (£8) plus cost of capital tied up in stocks (£6)]

Storage cost per unit (0.40 m^2 × £20) = £8

Incremental interest tied up in each unit of Exe stock (15% × £40 incremental cost of Exe) = £6

Applying the above figures to the formula, we have:

$$Q = \sqrt{\left(\frac{2 \times 4000 \times £70}{£14}\right)}$$
$$= 200 \text{ units}$$

	(£)
Cost of current policy	
Set-up costs (4 production runs at £70)	280
Holding costs (average stocks × unit holding cost)	
$\dfrac{1000}{2} \times £14$	7000
Total cost	7280
Cost of optimum policy	
Set-up costs [(4 000/200) production runs at £70]	1400
Holding costs (average stocks × unit holding cost)	
$\dfrac{200}{2} \times £14$	1400
Total cost	2800
Annual savings (£7280 – £2800)	£4480

(b) $Q = \sqrt{\left(\dfrac{DO}{H}\right)}$

where D = annual demand, O = incremental ordering cost per order, H = holding cost per unit. For producing Wye:

$$Q = \sqrt{\left(\frac{2 \times 10\,000 \times £100}{£8}\right)} = 500 \text{ units}$$

Buying in larger quantities in order to take advantage of bulk discounts results in the following savings:

(i) a saving in purchase price for the period consisting of the total amount of the discount for the period;

(ii) a reduction in total ordering cost because of fewer orders being placed to take advantage of bulk discounts.

The above cost savings must be compared with the increased holding costs resulting from higher stock levels.

We now compare the cost savings with the increased holding costs from increasing the quantity purchased from the EOQ of 500 units to the lowest purchase quantity at which Wye can be purchased at £19.80 per unit (i.e. 1000 units):

	(£)
Savings in purchase price (10 000 annual purchases at £0.20)	2000
Saving in ordering cost[a]	
$\dfrac{DO}{Q_d} = \dfrac{DO}{Q} = \dfrac{10\,000 \times 100}{1000} - \dfrac{10\,000 \times 100}{500}$	1000
Total savings	3000

Note

[a]Q_d represents quantity ordered to obtain discount and Q represents EOQ.

The additional holding cost if the larger quantity is purchased is calculated as follows:

$$\frac{(Q_d - Q)H}{2} = \frac{(1000 - 500) \times £8}{2} = £2000$$

Therefore a saving of £1000 is made if the firm purchases in quantities of 1000 units at a price of £19.80 per unit.

We now follow the same procedure in order to determine whether it would be better to purchase in quantities of 2000 units:

	(£)
Savings in purchase price (10 000 annual purchases at £0.40)	4000
Saving in ordering cost[a]	

$$\frac{DO}{Q_d} - \frac{DO}{Q} = \frac{10\,000 \times 100}{2000} - \frac{10\,000 \times 100}{500} = \underline{1500}$$

Total savings 5500

The additional holding cost if we purchase in 2000-unit quantities instead of 500-unit quantities is as follows:

$$\frac{(Q_d - Q)H}{[2]} = \frac{(2000 - 500) \times £8}{2} = £6000$$

Therefore an additional £500 will be incurred if the firm purchases in 2000-unit batches compared with purchasing in 500-unit batches.

The above analysis indicates that Pink should purchase in batches of 1000 units at a price of £19.80 per unit.

(c) Limitations include the following:

(i) It is very difficult to obtain relevant data. Incremental holding, ordering and set-up costs are very difficult to estimate in practice. In addition, many of the fixed costs that were excluded in the analysis may not be fixed over the whole range of output. Some fixed costs may increase in steps as the quantity purchased is increased.

(ii) Model assumes certainty. A more sophisticated approach is required where the demand and the cost structure are uncertain.

(iii) Model assumes that demand is constant throughout the year. In practice, there may be seasonal variations in demand throughout the year.

25.19 (a)

Safety stock	Stockout	Stockout cost at £10 (£)	Probability	Expected cost (£)	Total (£)
500	0	0	0	0	0
400	100	1000	0.04	40	40
300	200	2000	0.04	80	
	100	1000	0.07	70	150
200	300	3000	0.04	120	
	200	2000	0.07	140	
	100	1000	0.10	100	360
100	400	4000	0.04	160	
	300	3000	0.07	210	
	200	2000	0.10	200	
	100	1000	0.13	130	700
0	500	5000	0.04	200	
	400	4000	0.07	280	
	300	3000	0.10	300	
	200	2000	0.13	260	
	100	1000	0.16	160	1200

Safety stock	Stockout cost (£)	Holding cost (£)	Total cost (£)
0	1200	0	1200
100	700	100	800
200	360	200	560
300	150	300	450
400	40	400	440
500	0	500	500

The optimal safety stock is 400 units.

(b) The probability of being out of stock at an optimal safety stock of 400 units is 0.04.

25.20 (a)

$$EOQ = \sqrt{\left(\frac{2DO}{H}\right)} = \sqrt{\frac{2 \times 10\,000 \times 25}{(45 + 5)}} = 100 \text{ units}$$

(b) Without any discount prices the EOQ =

$$\sqrt{\frac{2 \times 10\,000 \times 25}{(45 + 5.01)}} = 99.99 \text{ units}$$

Thus it is preferable to purchase 100 units at £50 rather than pay £50.10 for purchasing 99 units. To ascertain whether it is worthwhile increasing the purchase quantity from 100 to 200 units we must compare the total costs at each of these quantities:

	(£)
Total costs with a reorder quantity of 100 units	
Annual holding cost (100/2 × £50)	2500
Annual ordering costs (10 000/100 × £25)	2500
	5000
Purchasing manager's bonus (10% × £5000)	500
Annual purchase cost (10 000 × £50)	500 000
Total annual costs	505 500
Total costs with a reorder quantity of 200 units	
Annual holding costs (200/2 × £49.99)	4999
Annual ordering costs (10 000/200 × £25)	1250
	6249
Purchasing manager's bonus (10% × (£10 000 − £6249))	375
Annual purchase cost (10 000 × £49.90)	499 000
Total annual costs	505 624

The optimal order quantity is still 100 units.

(c) The probability distribution of demand over the three day lead time is as follows:

Demand lead time	Frequency	Probability	Expected value
106	4	0.04	4.24
104	10	0.10	10.40
102	16	0.16	16.32
100	40	0.40	40.00
98	14	0.14	13.72
96	14	0.14	13.44
94	2	0.02	1.88
	100	1.00	100.00

It is assumed that the reorder point will be set at 100 units (expected value). The expected costs for various levels of safety stock are as follows:

Safety stock (units)	Reorder point (units)	Stockout per order (units)	Stockout per year[a] (units)	Probability of stockout	Expected stockout cost[b] (£)	Holding cost[c] (£)	Total expected cost[d] (£)
6	106	0	0	0	0	270	270
4	104	2	200	0.04	80	180	260
2	102	2	200	0.10	200		
		4	400	0.04	160	90	450
0	100	2	200	0.16	320		
		4	400	0.10	400		
		6	600	0.04	240	0	960

Notes
[a]During the year 100 orders will be made (10 000 units annual demand/EOQ of 100 units). Stockout per year in units is calculated by multiplying the stockouts per order by 100 orders.
[b]Expected stockout costs = annual stockout in units × probability of stockout × £10 lost contribution.
[c]Holding cost = safety stock × (holding cost of £50 saving of 10% on purchasing manager's bonus).
[d]It is assumed that stockout costs are equal to the lost contribution on the lost sales.

Conclusion
Costs are minimized if a safety stock of 4 units is maintained.

(d) The following items should be included in the report:

  (i) The disadvantages of ordering from only one supplier (e.g. vulnerability of disruption of supplies due to strikes/production difficulties or bankruptcy);

  (ii) Failure to seek out cheap or alternative sources of supply;

  (iii) It is assumed no large price increases are anticipated that will justify holding additional stocks or that the stocks are not subject to deterioration or obsolescence;

  (iv) It is assumed that lead time will remain unchanged. However, investigations should be made as to whether this, or other suppliers, can guarantee a shorter lead time;

  (v) The need to ascertain the impact on customer goodwill if a stockout occurs. The answer to **(c)** assumes that the company will merely lose the contribution on the sales and long-term sales will not be affected if a stockout occurs.

CHAPTER 26

26.10 Where the objective function is to minimize total costs the potential optimal solutions will be at the points closest to the origin that fall within the feasible region. Therefore the optimal solution will be at either points E or D. Note that total costs are lower for E compared with A since E and A entail the same output of U units but E has a lower output of A units.

Answer = **(c)**

26.11 (a) Contribution line: 35E + 66R
Constraints:

  Direct material A: 3E + 2R ≤ 5000
  Direct material B: 4E + 3R ≤ 5400
  Machine hours: 2E + 3R ≤ 3000
  Skilled labour: 2E + 5R ≤ 4500
  Demand: 0 ≤ R ≤ 1500
From the graph, it can be seen that the two binding constraints are those relating to machine hours and skilled labour. The optimum output can be determined exactly by solving the simultaneous equations for the binding constraints:

  2E + 5R = 4500
  2E + 3R = 3000

So that 2R = 1500 and R = 750
Substituting for R gives a value of 375 for E

(b) By inspecting the graph, it can be seen that the removal of the labour constraint and the extension of the dashed contribution line will result in an optimal solution when production of E is zero and R is 1000. This will yield a contribution of $66 000 based on an assumed hourly rate of $10 but this rate only

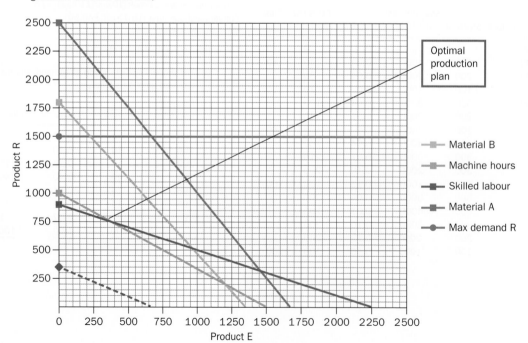

applies to the existing capacity of 4500 hours. To produce 1000 units of R 5000 labour hours are required so an additional 500 hours must be purchased at an extra cost of $4 per hour plus a fixed fee of $1000. Therefore the revised contribution will be $63 000.

   If the machine is hired there will be no labour and materials constraints and extending the contribution line outwards results in the maximum demand for R and material B being the binding constraints.

   Solving the simultaneous equations:

R = 1500
4E + 3R = 5400
so R = 1500 and E = 225.

This output gives a contribution of $106 875 based on a labour rate of $10 per hour but 7950 hours [(1500 × 5) + (225 × 2)] are required. Therefore an extra labour cost of $14 800 [(3450 × $4) + $1000] will be incurred resulting in a revised contribution of $92 075.

   The maximum that should be paid to lease the machine is $29 075 ($92 075 − $63 000).

(c) Hiring the machine will result in a considerable increase in the supply of labour and this may result in additional supervisory and overhead costs. The new machinery will increase the capacity to 5000 machine hours but the production plan requires 4950 hours so breakdowns could have a significant impact on proposed plans.

26.12 (a) Let x = no. of jars of face cream to be produced and y = no. of bottles of body lotion to be produced. The objective is to maximize contribution (C):

$C = 9x + 8y$

The constraints are:

Silk powder $3x + 2y \leqslant 5000$
Silk amino acids $1x + 0.5y \leqslant 1600$
Skilled labour $4x + 5y \leqslant 9600$
Non-negativity constraints $x, y \geq 0$
Sales constraint $y \leqslant 2000$

The above items are drawn on the graph accompanying this answer:

Silk powder $3x + 2y = 5000$
If $x = 0$, then $2y = 5000$, therefore $y = 2500$
If $y = 0$, then $3x = 5000$, therefore $x = 1666.7$

Silk amino acids $1x + 0.5y = 1600$
If $x = 0$, then $0.5y = 1600$, therefore $y = 3200$
If $y = 0$, then $x = 1600$

Skilled labour $4x + 5y = 9600$
If $x = 0$, then $5y = 9600$, therefore $y = 1920$
If $y = 0$, then $4x = 9600$, therefore $x = 2400$
and $y = 2000$ (sales constraint)

The contribution equation ($C = 9x + 8y$) line is established following the approach described in Chapter 26 and the contribution line is extended outwards until it reaches the furthest point within the shaded feasible region. This is at the point marked 'c' in the graph. Solving the simultaneous equations for the two constraints that intersect at point 'c':

$4x + 5y = 9600$
$3x + 2y = 5000$

Multiplying the first equation by 3 and the second by 4:
$12x + 15y = 28800$
$12x + 8y = 20000$

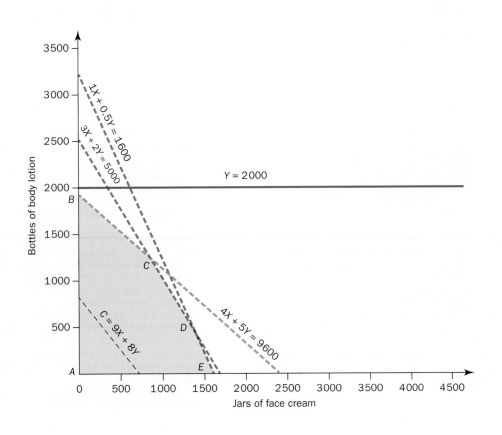

Subtract the second equation from the first one:

$7y = 8800$, so $y = 1257.14$.
If $y = 1257.14$ and:
$4x + 5y = 9600$
then $5 \times 1257.14 + 4x = 9600$
so $x = 828.58$
If $C = 9x + 8y$
$C = \$7457.22 + \$10\,057.12 = \$17\,514.34$

(b) The shadow price for silk powder can be found by solving the two simultaneous equations intersecting at point c, and adding one more hour to the equation for silk powder.

$4x + 5y = 9600$
$3x + 2y = 5001$

Multiplying the first equation by 3 and the second one by 4:

$12x + 15y = 28\,800$
$12x + 8y = 20\,004$

Subtract the second one from the first one
$7y = 8796$, therefore $y = 1256.57$
$3x + (2 \times 1256.57) = 5001$
Therefore $x = 829.29$

$C = (9 \times 829.29) + (8 \times 1256.57) = \$17\,516.17$
Original contribution = $\$17\,514.34$
Therefore shadow price for silk powder is $\$1.83$ per gram.
The slack for amino acids is calculated as follows:
$(828.58 \times 1) + (0.5 \times 1257.14) = 1457.15$ grams used. Available = 1600 grams resulting in a slack of 142.85 grams

26.13 (a) (i)   Let E = the number of units of Product E produced and sold in June.
Let M = the number of units of Product M produced and sold in June.
Maximize $51E + 38M$ subject to:
$5E + 2M \leq 4800$ (Material A)
$2E + 3M \leq 3900$ (Material B)
$2E + M \leq 2500$ (Labour)
$2E + 4M \leq 5000$ (Machine hours)
$E, M \geq 0$ (Non-negativity)

(ii) The optimum output can be determined by solving the simultaneous equations for the binding constraints:
$5E + 2M = 4800$ (1)
$2E + 3M = 3900$ (2)
Multiply equation (1) by 2 and equation (2) by 5
$10E + 4M = 9600$ (3)
$10E + 15M = 19\,500$ (4)
$11M = 9900$ (equation 4 − equation 3)
$M = 900$
Substitute into equation (1)
$E = 600$

Substitute values into the objective function:
Contribution: $(51 \times 600) + (38 \times 900) =$
$\$64\,800$
Less fixed costs $\$50\,000$
Profit = $\$14\,800$

(b) If one more kg of material A were available at the normal cost of $\$12$, this would generate an additional $\$7$ of contribution. Therefore, the shadow price of $\$7$ for material A represents the maximum premium that the company should pay to acquire one more kg of material A.

26.14 (a) The resources required to meet the demand are as follows:

	L	M	Total
Maximum demand (units)	400	700	
Direct labour (hours)	1600	1400	3000
Direct material (kg)	800	6300	7100
Machine hours	400	1400	1800

Direct material is the limiting factor.

Product	L	M
	$	$
Unit selling price	70	90
Variable costs per unit:		
Direct labour ($7 per hour)	28	14
Direct material ($5 per kg)	10	45
Machine hours ($10 per hour)	10	20
Contribution per unit	22	11
Contribution per kg	11	1.22
Ranking	1	2
Output (units)	400	577
Materials used (kg)	800	5193
Contribution	8800	6347

Total contribution = $\$15\,147$

(b) Maximize $C = 22L + 11M$
Subject to:
Direct labour $4L + 2M \leq 2300$
Direct material $2L + 9M \leq 2550$
Machine hours $1L + 2M \leq 1100$

(c) The value of 400 represents the optimum number of units produced for product L and the other value of zero for product L is the unsatisfied demand of zero because maximum demand is also 400. The entry of 194 for product M and the other value of 506 refers to an optimum production of 194 units of M and the 506 to the unsatisfied sales demand of L (700 maximum demand less 194 units optimum production). The value of 312 for direct labour and machine hours indicates that there are 312 unused machine hours and 312 unused labour hours. This can be proved by, for machine hours, comparing the outputs to the machine hours available:

400 units of L use 1 hour each =	400 hours
194 units of M use 2 hours each =	388 hours
Total hours used	788 hours
Hours available	1100 hours
Hours unused	312 hours

A similar proof could have been provided for labour hours.
   The value of $\$1.22$ is the shadow price of the direct materials. This is the maximum additional price that should be paid for an extra kg of direct material above the current cost of $\$5$ per kg. The fact that there is a shadow price for this resource indicates that it is a binding constraint. This shadow price can be proved because 1 extra kg of direct material would be used to increase the output of product M. Each unit of M requires 9kg so 0.11 additional units of M could be produced from 1 extra kg of material. Each unit of M yields a contribution of $\$11$ so 0.11 units yields $\$1.22$ contribution.
   The entry of 312 for direct labour hours represents the number of unused labour hours and the value of

$10 934 is the contribution earned from the optimum production plan consisting of 400 units of L at $22 each = $8800 plus 194 units of M at $11 each = $2134

26.15 (a) Traditional (T) contribution per unit = £55.50 (£100 − (0.5 × £25 + 0.4 × £30 overheads + £20 timber))
Hightech (H) contribution per unit = £49
The linear programming model is as follows:
Maximize 55.5T + 49H (contribution) Where

$$0.5T + 0.3H = 3400 \text{ (capacity } X)$$
$$0.4T + 0.45H = 3840 \text{ (capacity } Y)$$
$$4T + 4H = 3000 \text{ (timber available)}$$

subject to $0 < T \le 6000$ and $0 \le H \le 10 000$

(b) (i) The maximum contribution is shown as £444 125 and is derived as follows:
Traditional = 4250 units × £55.50 = £235 875
Hightech = 4250 units × £49.00 = £208 250

(ii) The shadow prices indicate the extra contribution that can be obtained for each extra metre of timber (£9.81 25) or additional machine group X hour (£32.50). Machine group Y has a zero shadow price because there is still some available capacity (slack) which has not been utilized (3840 hours available − 3612.5 hours allocated = 227.5 unused hours).

(iii) There is no surplus capacity for machine group X and 227.5 hours surplus capacity for machine group Y giving an additional contribution of £6825 (227.5 hours × £30 = £6825).

(iv) The adjustable cells table show the sensitivity of the plan to changes in the contribution per unit of each product. For the 'Traditional' product the contribution would have to be greater than £81.67 (i.e. an increase of £26.17) or less than £49 (i.e. a decrease of £6.50) for a change in the planned sales mix to occur. For the 'Hightech' product the contribution would have to exceed £55.50 (i.e. an increase of £6.50) or be less than £33.30 (i.e. a decrease of £15.70) for a change in the planned sales mix to occur.

(v) For each additional metre an extra contribution of £9.8125 can be obtained but the parameters of the existing model indicate that this applies only for an extra 1733.33 metres of timber. The additional contribution from an extra 1733.33 metres of timber is £17 008 (1 733.33 × £9.8125).

(vi) A total of 35 733.33 metres (34 000 + 1733.33) will be allocated to production. The timber requirements for producing 'Hightech' are 14 400 metres resulting in 21 333.33 metres (35 733.33 − 14 400) being available for 'Traditional'. This will result in the production of 5 333.33 units of 'Traditional'.

(c) The following should be considered as a means of overcoming the capacity constraints:

- Investigate alternative sources of supply for the timber. Such supplies may only be obtainable at additional costs (e.g. purchasing from overseas suppliers).
- Increase the operating hours of the machinery. This may result in additional overtime payments to operators or require the appointment of extra staff.
- Increase the output per machine hour. This may result in additional labour payments and an increase in maintenance costs.
- Acquire additional machinery. To ascertain whether this is worthwhile, a capital investment appraisal should be undertaken that incorporates the cash flow consequences over the whole life of the machinery.
- Sub-contract some of the production to outside companies. This is likely to be more expensive than the internal incremental production costs and may also create quality control problems.

(d) Only variable costs are included in the model. Therefore product specific (avoidable) fixed costs are not taken into account. Such costs may be relevant if they are avoidable or involve step functions. Examples include staff dedicated to a single product such as marketing costs attributable to only one of the products.

Customer specific costs may differ between customers. For example distribution costs may vary according to the location of customers or some customers may rely on many small volume frequent orders whereas others may rely on large volume infrequent orders. The costs of servicing the latter category of customers are likely to be less than the former.

Life cycle costs represent the costs incurred over a product's life cycle from the introduction, growth, maturity and decline stages. Costs may vary at the different stages. If one of the products is at the introductory stage it may incur additional marketing costs in order to promote it. Thus costs may differ between the two products if they are subject to different stages within their life cycles.

CREDITS

Chapter 11

Page 263: © monkeybusinessimages/Thinkstock – Real World Views 11.2

Page 266: © Thomas Northcut/Thinkstock – Real World Views 11.3

Chapter 12

Page 291: © satori13/Thinkstock – Real World Views 12.2

Chapter 13

Page 309: © HHakim/Thinkstock – Real World Views 13.1

Page 323: © gbphotostock/Thinkstock – Real World Views 13.3

Page 324: © mouse_sonya/Thinkstock – Real World Views 13.4

Chapter 14

Page 346: © turk_stock_photographer/Thinkstock – Real World Views 14.2

Page 350: © MariusLtu/Thinkstock – Real World Views 14.3

Chapter 15

Page 385: © AndreyPopov/Thinkstock – Real World Views 15.2

Chapter 16

Page 409: © Serge_Bertasius/Thinkstock – Real World Views 16.2

Chapter 17

Page 448: © monkeybusinessimages/Thinkstock – Real World Views 17.2

Chapter 18

Page 476: © Viperfzk/Thinkstock – Real World Views 18.1

Chapter 19

Page 512: © Digital Vision./Thinkstock – Real World Views 19.5

Chapter 20

Page 537: © artisteer/Thinkstock – Real World Views 20.1

Page 540: © violinconcertono3/Thinkstock – Real World Views 20.2

Chapter 22

Page 592: © Ingram Publishing/Thinkstock – Real World Views 22.1

Page 604: © RyanFletcher/Thinkstock – Real World Views 22.3

Page 605: © Elenathewise/Thinkstock – Real World Views 22.4

Page 614: © monkeybusinessimages/Thinkstock – Real World Views 22.6

Chapter 23

Page 635: © Mckyartstudio/Thinkstock – Real World Views 23.2

Chapter 24

Page 658: © Sparky2000/Thinkstock – Real World Views 24.2

Chapter 25

Page 679: © Queensbury/Thinkstock – Real World Views 25.1

INDEX